PREMIER 2017

New York

ACKNOWLEDGMENTS

Special thanks to the team that made this book possible:

Arthur Ahn, Mikhail Alexeef, Gina Allison, Matthew Belinkie, Kim Bowers, Brian Carlidge, Lauren Challman, Gerard Cortinez, Elisa Davis, Boris Dvorkin, Steve Ferges, Paula Fleming, Dan Frey, Joanna Graham, Adam Grey, Allison Harm, Craig Harman, Jack Hayes, Adam Hinz, Gar Hong, Rebecca Houck, Xandi Kagstrom, Sarah Krentz, Jennifer Land, Edwina Lui, Jenny Lynch, Keith Lubeley, Heather Maigur, Rachel Mason, Jennifer Moore, Jason Moss, Walt Niedner, Robert Reiss, Shmuel Ross, Glen Stohr, Sascha Strelka, Gene Suhir, Ethan Weber, Lee A. Weiss, and many others who have contributed materials and advice over the years.

Published by Kaplan Publishing, a division of Kaplan, Inc.
750 Third Avenue
New York, NY 10017

Printed in the United States of America

10 9 8 7 6 5 4 3 2 1

ISBN: 978-1-5062-0557-1

Kaplan Publishing books are available at special quantity discounts to use for sales promotions, employee premiums, or educational purposes. For more information or to order books, please call the Simon & Schuster special sales department at 866-506-1949.

Table of Contents

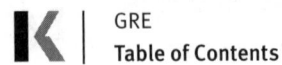

http://kaptest.com/publishing

The material in this book is up-to-date at the time of publication. However, the Educational Testing Service may have instituted changes in the test or test registration process after this book was published. Be sure to read carefully the materials you receive when you register for the test.

If there are any important late-breaking developments—or changes or corrections to the Kaplan test preparation materials in this book—we will post that information online at **kaptest.com/publishing**. Check to see if any information is posted there regarding this book.

How to Use This Book

WELCOME TO KAPLAN GRE PREMIER 2017

Congratulations on your decision to pursue a graduate degree, and thank you for choosing Kaplan for your GRE preparation. You've made the right choice in acquiring this book—you're now armed with a comprehensive GRE program that is the result of decades of researching the GRE and teaching many thousands of students the skills they need to succeed. You have everything you need to score higher—let's start by walking through what you need to know to take advantage of this book and the Online Center.

YOUR BOOK

There are two main components to your *Kaplan GRE Premier* study package: your book and your Online Center. This book contains the following:

- Detailed instruction covering the essential Verbal Reasoning, Quantitative Reasoning, and Analytical Writing concepts
- Time-tested and effective Kaplan Methods and strategies for every question type
- One full-length practice test and chapter-end practice questions with detailed answer explanations
- A DVD containing instruction and graduate school admission guidance from elite Kaplan faculty

YOUR ONLINE CENTER

Your Online Center lets you access additional instruction and practice materials to reinforce key concepts and sharpen your GRE skills. Resources include the following:

- Five full-length practice tests
- Exclusive to GRE Complete customers: 1,000 question Quiz Bank you can use to create customized quizzes

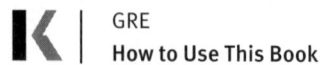

- Ten 20-question Quantitative practice sets
- Ten 20-question Verbal practice sets
- Five Analytical Writing practice sets of two prompts each
- Detailed answer explanations and sample essay responses
- Online answer grid for the practice test found in this book
- Academic support from Kaplan faculty via our Facebook page: **www.facebook.com/kaplangradprep**

GETTING STARTED

1. Register your Online Center.
2. Take a GRE practice test to identify your strengths and weaknesses.
3. Create a study plan.
4. Learn and practice using this book and your Online Center.

Step 1: Register Your Online Center

Register your Online Center using these simple steps:

1. Go to **kaptest.com/GREComplete2017**.
2. Follow the onscreen instructions. Please have a copy of your book available.

Access to the Online Center is limited to the original owner of this book and is nontransferable. Kaplan is not responsible for providing access to the Online Center to customers who purchase or borrow used copies of this book. Access to the Online Center expires one year after you register.

Step 2: Take a GRE Practice Test

It's essential to take a practice test early on. Doing so will give you the initial feedback and diagnostic information that you need to achieve your maximum score.

Your diagnostic test is Multi-Stage Test (MST) 1, which is found in your Online Center. MST 1, like all of Kaplan's online full-length tests, is a multi-stage test, which is the same format as the actual GRE. The multi-stage test format feels different from a paper-based test and is scored differently, so the more you practice with MSTs, the better off you'll be. However, for your convenience, we've also included a practice test in this book. This practice test, which includes full-length Analytical Writing, Verbal, and Quantitative sections, will give you a chance to familiarize yourself with the various question types. It also allows you to accurately gauge the content you know and identify areas for practice and review. (Use the online answer grid available in your Online Center to enter your responses from the practice test in this book to see a detailed breakdown of your performance by question type and topic.)

Review the detailed answer explanations to better understand your performance. Look for patterns in the questions you answered correctly and incorrectly. Were you stronger in some areas than others? This analysis will help you target your practice time to specific concepts.

Step 3: Create a Study Plan

Use what you've learned from your diagnostic test to identify areas for closer study and practice. Take time to familiarize yourself with the key components of your book and Online Center. Think about how many hours you can consistently devote to GRE study. We have found that most students have success with about three months of committed preparation before Test Day.

Schedule time for study, practice, and review. One of the most frequent mistakes in approaching study is to take practice tests and not review them thoroughly—review time is your best chance to gain points. It works best for many people to block out short, frequent periods of study time throughout the week. Check in with yourself frequently to make sure you're not falling behind your plan or forgetting about any of your resources.

Step 4: Learn and Practice

Your book and Online Center come with many opportunities to develop and practice the skills you'll need on Test Day. Read each chapter of this book and complete the practice questions. Depending on how much time you have to study, you can do this work methodically, covering every chapter, or you can focus your study on those question types and content areas that are most challenging for you. You will inevitably need more work in some areas than in others, but know that the more thoroughly you prepare, the better your score will be.

Remember also to take and review the practice sets in your Online Center. These quizzes give you additional test-like questions so you can put into practice the skills you are learning. As always, review the explanations closely.

Initially, your practice should focus on mastering the needed skills and not on timing. Add timing to your practice as you improve fundamental proficiency. As soon as you are comfortable with the question types and Kaplan Methods, take and review the additional full-length practice tests in your Online Center.

If you find that you would like access to more of Kaplan's practice tests and quizzes, as well as in-depth instruction on the question types and strategies, look into the variety of course options available at **kaptest.com/GRE**.

Thanks for choosing Kaplan. We wish you the best of luck on your journey to graduate school.

PART ONE

Getting Started

CHAPTER 1

Introduction to the GRE

This book will explain more than just a few basic strategies. It will prepare you for practically everything that you are likely to encounter on the GRE. This may sound too good to be true, but we mean it. We are able to do this because we don't explain test questions in isolation or focus on particular test problems. Instead, we explain the underlying principles behind *all* of the questions on the GRE. We give you the big picture.

UNDERSTANDING THE GRE

Let's take a look at how the GRE is constructed. The GRE, or Graduate Record Examination, is a computer-based exam required by many graduate schools for admission to a wide variety of programs at the graduate level. You need to know firsthand the way this test is put together if you want to take it apart. In this section, you will learn about the purposes of the GRE and ways you can learn to be successful on it.

The Purposes of the GRE

The GRE is designed to assess readiness for a wide variety of graduate programs. The ways in which graduate schools use GRE scores vary. Scores are often required as part of the application for entrance into a program, but they also can be used to grant fellowships or financial aid. Each section of the GRE is designed to assess general skills necessary for graduate school. Some of these skills include the ability to read complex informational text and understand high-level vocabulary words in the Verbal Reasoning section, respond to an issue in written form in the Analytical Writing section, and apply general mathematical concepts to a variety of problem types in the Quantitative Reasoning section. Graduate school admissions officers often view the GRE score as an important indicator of readiness for graduate-level studies. In addition, graduate school admissions officers are comparing hundreds or even thousands of applications, and having a quantitative factor, such as a GRE score, makes the job of comparing so many applicants much easier. Just by having this book and making a commitment to yourself to be as well prepared as possible for this exam, you've already taken the crucial first step toward making your graduate school application as competitive as possible. For free events geared at improving other aspects of your applications, visit **www.kaptest.com/GRE**.

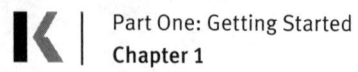

The Secret Code

Doing well on the GRE requires breaking down the "secret code" upon which each and every test is constructed. Like all of the tests created by the Educational Testing Service (ETS), the GRE is based on psychometrics, the science of creating "standardized" tests. For a test to be standardized, it must successfully do three things. First, the test must be reliable. In other words, a test taker who takes the GRE should get approximately the same score if she takes a second GRE (assuming, of course, that she doesn't study with Kaplan materials during the intervening period). Second—and this is closely related to our first point—it must test the same concepts on each test. Third, it must create a "bell curve" when a pool of test takers' scores are plotted; in other words, some people will do very well on the test and some will do very poorly, but the great majority will score somewhere in the middle.

What all this boils down to is that to be a standardized test, the GRE has to be predictable. And this is what makes the GRE and other standardized tests coachable. Because ETS has to test the same concepts in each and every test, certain Reading Comprehension question types appear over and over again, as do certain math patterns. Moreover, the GRE has to create some questions that most test takers will get wrong—otherwise, it wouldn't be able to create its bell curve. This means that hard questions will usually contain "traps"—wrong answer choices that will be more appealing than the correct answer to a large percentage of test takers. Fortunately, these traps are predictable (this is what we mean by the "secret code"), and we can teach you how to recognize and avoid them. The goal of this comprehensive program is to help you break the code.

Acquire the Skills

It has been argued that the GRE isn't a fair or effective predictor of the skills a person needs for graduate-level study. And you may be concerned that your scores on the GRE will not be a fair or accurate representation of the strong work you will do in your advanced degree program. Take heart: none of the GRE experts who work at Kaplan were *born* knowing how to ace the GRE. No one is. That's because these tests do not measure innate skills; they measure *acquired* skills. People who are good at standardized tests are simply people who've already acquired these skills, whether in math class, or by reading a lot, or by studying logic in college, or—perhaps most efficiently—in one of Kaplan's GRE courses. But they have, perhaps without realizing it, acquired the skills that spell success on tests like the GRE. And if *you* haven't, you have nothing whatsoever to feel bad about. It's time to acquire them now.

Same Problems—But Different

As we noted, the testmakers use some of the same problems on every GRE. We know it sounds incredible, but it's true—only the words and numbers change. They test the same principles over and over. Here's an example.

$$2x^2 = 32$$

Quantity A	Quantity B
x	4

This is a type of math problem known as a Quantitative Comparison. Your job is to examine the relationship and pick **(A)** if Quantity A is bigger, **(B)** if Quantity B is bigger, **(C)** if they're equal, or **(D)** if not enough information is given to solve the problem.

Most people answer **(C)**, that the quantities are equal. They divide both sides of the centered equation by 2 and then take the square root of both sides to get $x = 4$. However, this is incorrect. x doesn't have to be 4. It could be 4 *or* −4; that is, the quantities could be equal *or* Quantity B could be bigger. Both work, so the answer is **(D)** because the answer cannot be determined from the information given. If you just solve for 4, you'll get this problem—and every one like it—wrong. ETS figures that if you get burned here, you'll get burned again next time. Only next time, it won't be $2x^2 = 32$; it will be $y^2 = 36$ or $s^4 = 81$.

The concepts tested on any particular GRE—right triangles, simple logic, word relationships, and so forth—are the underlying concepts at the heart of *every* GRE. ETS makes changes only after testing them exhaustively. This process is called *norming*, which means taking a normal test and a changed test and administering them to a random group of students. As long as the group is large enough for the purposes of statistical validity and the students get consistent scores from one test to the next, then the revised test is just as valid and consistent as any other GRE.

That may sound technical, but norming is actually a straightforward process. We do it at Kaplan all the time—for the tests that we write for our students. The tests in this book and your online Study Plan, for instance, are normed exams. While the interactive, computer-based test experience of the GRE is impossible to reproduce on paper, the paper-based test in our book is a normed exam that will produce a roughly equivalent score.

HOW THE GRE IS ORGANIZED

The Graduate Record Examination (GRE) is administered on computer and is approximately four hours long, including breaks. The exam consists of six sections, with different amounts of time allotted for you to complete each section.

Basics of the GRE	
Exam Length	4 hours, including breaks
Scoring Scale	130–170 (1-point increments) for Verbal and Quantitative; 0–6 for Analytical Writing
Format	Multi-stage test (MST), a computer-based format that allows students to navigate forward and backward within each section of the test
Number of Test Sections	6 sections, including an experimental or research section
Breaks	One 10-minute break after your third section; 1-minute breaks between all other sections
Analytical Writing	One section with two 30-minute tasks: analyze an issue and analyze an argument
Verbal Reasoning	Two 30-minute sections with approximately 20 questions each
Quantitative Reasoning	Two 35-minute sections with approximately 20 questions each; onscreen calculator available

Your test will also contain an experimental section—an additional Verbal Reasoning or Quantitative Reasoning section that ETS puts on the test so that ETS can norm the new questions it creates for use on future GREs. That means that if you could identify the experimental section, you could doodle for half an hour, guess in a random pattern, or daydream and still get exactly the same score on the GRE. However, the experimental section is disguised to look like a real section—there is no way to identify it. All you will really know on the day of the test is that one of the subject areas will have three sections instead of two. Naturally, many people try to figure out which section is experimental. But because ETS really wants you to try hard on it, it does its best to keep you guessing. If you guess wrong, you could blow the whole test, so we urge you to treat all sections as scored unless you are told otherwise.

Lastly, instead of an experimental section, your test could contain a research section. This section is unscored and will be indicated as such. If you have a research section on the test, it will be the last section. Pay careful attention to the directions at the beginning of the section.

SCORING

The Analytical Writing section is scored on a scale of 0–6 in half-point increments. (See Chapter 15, "Introduction to Analytical Writing," for details on this scoring rubric.) The Verbal Reasoning and Quantitative Reasoning sections each yield a scaled score within a range of 130 to 170 in one-point increments. You cannot score higher than 170 for either the Verbal Reasoning or the Quantitative Reasoning sections, no matter how hard you try. Similarly, it's impossible to score lower than 130 for Verbal Reasoning or Quantitative Reasoning.

But you don't receive *only* scaled scores; you also receive a percentile rank, which rates your performance relative to that of a large sample population of other GRE takers. Percentile scores tell graduate schools just what your scaled scores are worth. For instance, even if everyone got very high scaled scores, universities would still be able to differentiate candidates by their percentile scores. The following tables give a cross section of the percentile ranks* that correspond with certain scaled scores on each section of the GRE, based on test takers between August 1, 2011, and April 30, 2014. For the full percentile-to-score conversion tables, see **https://www.ets.org/s/gre/pdf/gre_guide_table1a.pdf.**

Verbal Reasoning	
Percentile Ranking	**Scaled Score**
99	169–170
95	165
87	161
78	158
63	154
50	151
36	148
22	144
10	140

Quantitative Reasoning	
Percentile Ranking	**Scaled Score**
98	170
95	168
86	163
78	160
64	156
52	153
37	149
21	145
10	141

Analytical Writing	
Percentile Ranking	**Score**
99	6.0
98	5.5
93	5.0
80	4.5
56	4.0
38	3.5
15	3.0
7	2.5
2	2.0

Universities pay great attention to percentile rank. It's important that you do some research into the programs you're thinking about. Admissions officers from many top graduate school programs consider the GRE the most important factor in graduate school admissions. Some schools have cutoff scores below which they don't even consider applicants. But be careful! If a school tells you it looks for applicants scoring an average of 150 per section, that doesn't mean those scores are good enough for immediate acceptance. Some students will be accepted with scores below that average, and some students may be denied admission even with scores that are higher. Consider the score of 150 per section as an initial target score, but also be sure the rest of your application is strong. You owe it to yourself to find out what kinds of scores *impress* the schools you're interested in and to work hard until you get those scores. Every day we see students work hard and achieve their target scores. Work hard, and you can be among them.

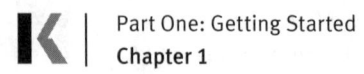

A final note about percentile rank: the sample population to which you are compared to determine your percentile is not the group of people who take the test on the same day as you do. ETS doesn't want to penalize an unlucky candidate who takes the GRE on a date when everyone else happens to be a rocket scientist. Instead, it compares your performance with that of test takers from the past three years. Don't worry about how other people do—strive for your best score. We often tell our students, "Your only competition in this classroom is yourself."

CANCELLATION AND MULTIPLE-SCORES POLICY

Unlike many things in life, the GRE allows you a second chance. If at the end of the test, you feel that you've definitely not done as well as you could have, you have the option to cancel your score. Although score cancellation is available, the option to use *ScoreSelect* means there's rarely a good reason to cancel scores. If you cancel, your scores will be disregarded. (You also won't get to see them.) Canceling a score means that it won't count; however, you will not receive any refund for your test fee.

Two legitimate reasons to cancel your score are illness and personal circumstances that may have caused you to perform unusually poorly on that particular day.

But keep in mind that test takers historically underestimate their performance, especially immediately following the test. They tend to forget about all of the things that went right and focus on everything that went wrong. So unless your performance has been terribly marred by unforeseen circumstances, don't cancel your score. Even if you do cancel your score, it is possible to reinstate it within 60 days for a fee. (See **www.ets.org/gre/revised_general/test_day/policies/** for details.)

Also, ETS now offers test takers more choices in determining which scores to report to schools. The *ScoreSelect* option allows GRE test takers to choose—*after* viewing their scores on Test Day—to report their scores from only the most recent test they took or from all of the GRE tests they have taken in the past five years. Additionally, if a student sends score reports after Test Day, the student can have full freedom to report scores from any testing administration(s), not just the most recent. However, test takers cannot report only Quantitative Reasoning scores or only Verbal Reasoning scores from a given test—results from any testing administration must be reported in full. For more on the *ScoreSelect* option, go to **www.ets.org/gre/revised_general/about/scoreselect**.

Requested score reports are sent to schools 10–15 days after the exam. All GRE testing administrations will remain valid (and usable) in your ETS record for five years. If you choose to report multiple scores, most grad schools will consider the highest score you have for each section, although there are a few exceptions. Check with individual schools for their policies on multiple scores.

Lastly, know that schools receiving your scores will have access to photos taken of you at the test center, plus your Analytical Writing essays from each test administration whose scores you choose to report.

TEST REGISTRATION

You should obtain a copy of the *GRE Information and Registration Bulletin*. This booklet contains information on scheduling, pricing, repeat testing, cancellation policies, and more. You can receive the booklet by calling the Educational Testing Service at (609) 771-7670 or (866) 473-4373 or by downloading it from **www.ets.org/gre**.

The computer-based GRE General Test is offered year-round. To register for and schedule your GRE, use one of the following options. (If you live outside the United States, Canada, Guam, the U.S. Virgin Islands, or Puerto Rico, visit **www.ets.org/gre** for instructions on how to register.)

Registering earlier is strongly recommended because spaces often fill quickly.

Register Online

You can register online (if you are paying with a credit or debit card) at **www.ets.org/gre**. Once the registration process is complete, you can print out your voucher immediately (and can reprint it if it is lost). If you register online, you can confirm test center availability in real time.

Register by Phone

Call 1-800-GRE-CALL or 1-800-473-2255. Your confirmation number, reporting time, and test center location will be given to you when you call. Payments can be made with an American Express, Discover, JCB, MasterCard, or Visa credit or debit card.

Register by Mail

Complete the Authorization Voucher Request Form available for download at **www.ets.org/gre/pdf/cbt_authorization_voucher_form.pdf**. Mail the fee and signed voucher request form in the envelope provided to the address printed on the voucher.

ETS advises that you allow up to three weeks for processing before you receive your voucher in the mail. When you receive your voucher, call to schedule an appointment. Vouchers are valid for one year from the date of issue. When you register, make sure you list a first- and second-choice test center.

GRE CHECKLIST

Before the Test

- Choose a test date.
- Register online at **www.ets.org/gre**, by phone at 1-800-GRE-CALL, or by mail.
- Receive your admission voucher in the mail or online.
- Check out your test center.
    - Know the directions to the building and room where you'll be tested.
- Create a test prep calendar to ensure that you're ready by the day of the test.
    - On a calendar, block out the weeks you have to prepare for the test.
    - Based on your strengths and weaknesses, establish a detailed plan of study and select appropriate lessons and practice. (Don't forget to include some days off!)
- Stick to the plan; as with any practice, little is gained if it isn't methodical. Skills can't be "crammed" at the last minute.
- Reevaluate your strengths and weaknesses from time to time and revise your plan accordingly.

The Day of the Test

- Make sure you have your GRE admission voucher and acceptable ID.
- Leave yourself plenty of time to arrive at the test site stress-free.
- Arrive at the test site at least 30 minutes early for the check-in procedures.
- Don't worry—you're going to do great!

GRE SUBJECT TESTS

Subject Tests are designed to test the fundamental knowledge that is most important for successful graduate study in a particular subject area. To do well on a GRE Subject Test, you must have an extensive background in the particular subject area—the sort of background you would be expected to have if you had majored in the subject. Subject Tests enable admissions officers to compare students from different colleges with different standards and curricula. Not every graduate school or program requires Subject Tests, so check admissions requirements at those schools in which you're interested.

ORGANIZATION, SCORING, AND TEST DATES

All Subject Tests are administered in paper-based format and consist exclusively of multiple-choice questions that are designed to assess knowledge of the areas of the subject that are included in the typical undergraduate curriculum.

On Subject Tests, you'll earn one point for each multiple-choice question that you answer correctly, but you'll lose one-quarter of a point for each incorrectly answered question. Unanswered questions aren't counted in the scoring. Your raw score is then converted into a scaled score, which can range from 200 to 990. The range varies from test to test.

Some Subject Tests also contain subtests, which provide more specific information about your strengths and weaknesses. The same questions that contribute to your subtest scores also contribute to your overall score. Subtest scores, which range from 20 to 99, are reported along with the overall score. For further information on scoring, you should consult the relevant Subject Test Descriptive Booklet, available from ETS. Subject Tests are offered three times a year: in October, November, and April. Note that not all of the Subject Tests are offered on every test date; consult **www.ets.org/gre** for upcoming test dates and registration deadlines.

Subjects

Currently, seven Subject Tests are offered.

Biochemistry, Cell, and Molecular Biology

This test consists of about 175 questions and is divided among three subscore areas: biochemistry, cell biology, and molecular biology and genetics.

Biology

This test consists of about 200 questions divided among three subscore areas: cellular and molecular biology, organismal biology, and ecology and evolution.

Chemistry

This test consists of about 130 questions. There are no subscores, and the questions cover the following topics: analytical chemistry, inorganic chemistry, organic chemistry, and physical chemistry.

Literature in English

This test consists of about 230 questions on literature in the English language. There are two basic types of questions: factual questions that test your knowledge of writers and literary or critical movements typically covered in the undergraduate curriculum, and interpretive questions that test your ability to read various types of literature critically.

Mathematics

This test consists of about 66 questions on the content of various undergraduate courses in mathematics. Most of the test assesses your knowledge of calculus, linear algebra, abstract algebra, and number theory.

Physics

This test consists of approximately 100 questions covering mostly material from the first three years of undergraduate physics. Topics include classical mechanics, electromagnetism, atomic physics, optics and wave phenomena, quantum mechanics, thermodynamics and statistical mechanics, special relativity, and laboratory methods. About 9 percent of the test covers advanced topics, such as nuclear and particle physics, condensed matter physics, and astrophysics.

Psychology

This test consists of approximately 205 questions drawn from courses most commonly included in the undergraduate curriculum. Questions fall into three categories. The experimental or natural science–oriented category includes questions on learning, language, memory, thinking, sensation and perception, and physiological psychology/behavioral neuroscience. The social or social science–oriented category includes questions on clinical and abnormal psychology, lifetime development, social psychology, and personality. Together, these make up about 83 percent of the test, and each of the two categories provides its own subscore. The other 17 percent or so of the questions fall under the "general" category, which includes the history of psychology, tests and measurements, research design and statistics, and applied psychology.

For more information, consult ETS's Subject Test section at **www.ets.org/gre**.

Multi-Stage Test Mechanics

HOW THE MST WORKS

The multi-stage test, or MST, differs in some critical ways from the typical standardized test. An MST is a computer-based test that you take at a special test center at a time you schedule. Below is a chart that highlights some of the key features of the GRE MST:

MST Features
The test adapts one section at a time, altering the difficulty level of your second Quantitative and Verbal sections based on your performance on the first of each.
You may answer questions in any order within a section and change your answers to previously answered questions within a section.
An onscreen calculator is provided for the Quantitative Reasoning sections.
Mark & Review buttons are available to help you keep track of questions you want to revisit.
The MST lasts about 4 hours, including breaks.

Now that you have a sense of the overall format and structure of the GRE MST, let's look more closely at what the term *multi-stage test* means, how the MST adapts to your performance, and how these factors determine your score.

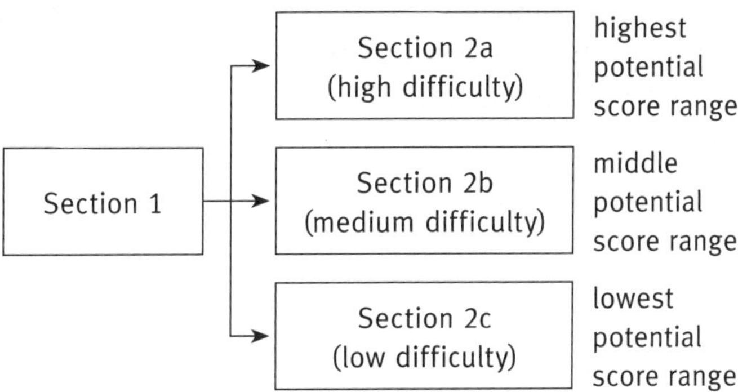

The chart above depicts a simplified version of how adaptivity works on the MST. Depending on your performance on the first Quantitative or Verbal section, you may get channeled into a harder or easier second Quantitative or Verbal section. The difficulty of the second section determines your score range—roughly speaking, the "ceiling" and "floor" of your potential Quantitative or Verbal score. Ultimately, your score will be determined by two factors: (1) the difficulty of the questions you receive and (2) the number of questions you answer correctly.

Therefore, it is important to do as well as possible on the first section since that will put you in the best position to achieve a great score. That said, your performance on the second section is still a crucial determinant of your ultimate score. (Note that the test only adapts within a given subject. In other words, your performance on the Verbal section will not affect the difficulty of a subsequent Quantitative section.)

Understanding the adaptive nature of the MST is interesting and somewhat useful in your prep, but it is actually counterproductive to think too much about it on Test Day. Many test takers try to gauge how they are doing on the exam by assessing the difficulty of the second section they receive. Doing this on Test Day is, at best, a waste of brainpower. At worst, it can cause you to become distracted by counterproductive thoughts ("These questions are too easy! What am I doing wrong?"). Just focus on solving the questions in front of you and do your best.

Simply put, the more questions you get right on the first section, the better off you'll be. The same goes for the second section. Therefore, your goal will be to get as many questions right as possible—not terribly mind-blowing! But how do you do that? Specifically, how can you use the structure of the MST to your advantage as you try to achieve this goal?

Let's now discuss the best ways to navigate the MST and how you can use these functionalities on Test Day to get as many correct answers as possible.

NAVIGATING THE GRE MST INTERFACE

Let's preview the primary computer functions that you will use to move around on the MST. ETS calls them "testing tools." They're basically tabs that you can click with your mouse to navigate through the section. The following screen is typical for a multi-stage test.

Directions: Choose the word or set of words for each blank that best fits the meaning of the sentence as a whole.

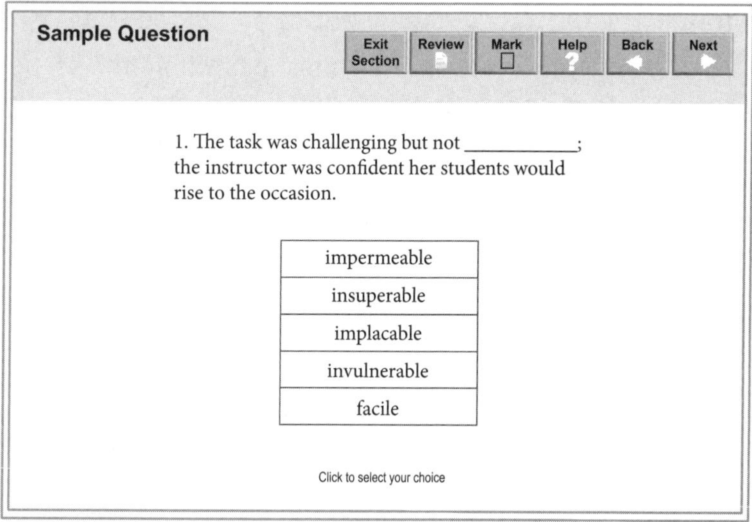

Here's what the various buttons do:

The Time Button (not pictured)

Clicking on this button turns the time display at the top of the screen on or off. When you have five minutes left in a section, the clock will automatically turn on, and the display will change from hours and minutes to hours, minutes, and seconds.

The Quit Test Button (not pictured)

Hitting this button ends the test prematurely. *Do not* use this button unless you want all of your scores canceled and your test invalidated.

The Exit Section Button

This allows you to exit the section before the time is up. Try not to end the section early—use any extra time to review any problems you flagged or felt concerned about.

The Review Button

This button will allow you to view your progress on all the questions you have looked at so far within the section you're working on. The items you have marked for review will have a check mark next to them. The chart on the screen will also have a column indicating whether or not you have answered a question.

The Mark Button

This button allows you to mark a question for review later. The question will have a check mark next to it in the review section.

The Help Button

This button leads to directions and assistance on how to use the test interface. *But beware:* the test clock won't pause just because you click on Help.

The Back Button

This button allows you to return to previous questions within the section. Note that you may only go back to questions in the section you're currently working on.

The Next Button

Hit this when you want to move on to the next question. You cannot proceed until you have hit this button.

Calculator (not pictured; Quantitative Reasoning section only)

This button opens the onscreen calculator on Quantitative Reasoning sections. It's a pretty basic calculator, and the questions tend to be conceptual in nature, but the calculator still can help you to avoid simple computational errors. Note that you can click on the "Transfer Display" button on the calculator to transfer your answer into a numeric entry box.

MST SECTION MANAGEMENT TECHNIQUES

Section management is an especially important skill to develop for the GRE. The MST allows you to move around within the section you're working on. This can be a great help if you know how to use this functionality to your advantage, but it can also be a source of uncertainty—with the ability to approach each section in whatever order you wish, where should you start? How can you best use the allotted time to rack up as many points as possible? Here are some principles to follow:

Approach the exam as you would a paper-based one. Since it's impossible (and certainly not a good use of your mental effort) to judge the difficulty level of questions while you're working on them, just focus on doing the best you can on each question—as far as you are concerned, they are all of equal importance to your score. Pace yourself so that you can capitalize on all the questions that you are capable of getting correct.

Don't get bogged down on any one question. If you feel that you are getting stuck, mark the question and go to the next one. Use the Mark and Review buttons to tag questions that you wish to return to later in the section. Sometimes when you take a second look at a question, you'll immediately see how to approach those aspects you previously found challenging.

You can also use the Mark button to indicate that you should come back and review the question if you have time at the end of that section. You can do this whether or not you've answered the question. This way, you can better organize your time by keeping track of which questions you are done with and which ones need a second look. Even if you are marking a question to come back to later, you may want to enter an answer the first time through. If you run out of time, you'll be glad that you at least put in a guess.

Use extra time at the end of a section to check your work. This is a major advantage of the MST. Always check the review screen before you finish a section to ensure you haven't forgotten to answer a question.

You may find that it is beneficial to start with some of the question types that take less time to answer. For example, you may find that you score highest on the Verbal section when you answer the Sentence Equivalence questions first. Use the practice sets in this book and your online MSTs to find the approach that works best for you.

There is no penalty for guessing on the GRE. As far as the MST is concerned, leaving an answer blank is the same as selecting an incorrect answer. Therefore, you should guess on every question so you at least have a chance of getting it right. But you should always guess strategically. This book will provide many tools, such as elimination strategies and estimation, that will make you an excellent strategic guesser.

Finally, the onscreen timer can work to your advantage, but if you find yourself looking at it so frequently that it becomes a distraction, you should turn it off for 10 or 15 minutes and try to refocus your attention on the test. You may be concerned about your pacing, but being distracted by the timer can be just as damaging to your score as running out of time. As with a traditional paper-and-pencil test, you don't want to get hung up on clock management.

MST: THE UPSIDE

To sum up, there are many good things about the MST, including the following:

- There will be only a few other test takers in the room with you—it won't be like taking a test in one of those massive lecture halls with distractions everywhere.
- You get a 10-minute break after the third section and a 1-minute break between each of the other sections. The breaks are optional, but you should use them to relax, stretch, and clear your head before the next section.
- You can sign up for the GRE just two days before the test (though we recommend signing up much earlier!), and registration is very easy.
- The MST is convenient to schedule. It's offered at more than 175 centers, three to five days a week (depending on the center), all year long.
- Perhaps the MST's best feature is that it gives you your unofficial Verbal Reasoning and Quantitative Reasoning scores immediately.

MST: THE DOWNSIDE

There are also some less attractive features of the MST:

- The MST is a long test requiring lots of endurance.
- As with any computer-based test, you can't cross off an answer choice to use the process of elimination. Use your scratch paper to avoid reconsidering choices you've already eliminated.
- You have to scroll through Reading Comprehension passages and read them onscreen.
- You'll be given scratch paper to make notes or perform calculations, but if you need more, you'll have to turn in the scratch paper that you've already used before obtaining new paper.
- Many people find that spending considerable time (especially four hours!) in front of a computer screen tires them out and causes eyestrain.
- Having a calculator provided for you on the Quantitative Reasoning sections may seem like a gift, but it comes with a price. The questions on the Quantitative Reasoning section are now more conceptual and less calculation based. Basically, you won't have to worry about doing long division, but the problems will be less straightforward.
- Being able to go back and change your answers may be a plus, but it can lead to pacing issues for some test takers, who will leave questions blank and then either forget to come back to them or run out of time.
- If you wish to take the GRE again, there is a mandatory waiting period: you can only test every 21 calendar days. So if you don't get the scores you need the first time, you'll need to wait three weeks until you can test again. This can be a problem if you're on a tight deadline.

PAPER-BASED GRE STRATEGIES

If you are located outside of the United States, Canada, Guam, the U.S. Virgin Islands, and Puerto Rico, you may take the paper-based version of the GRE (check **www.ets.org/gre** for test dates). It consists of six sections: two Analytical Writing sections, two Verbal Reasoning sections, and two Quantitative Reasoning sections. There is no experimental or research section on the paper-based GRE.

Note that registration for the paper-based test fills up much more quickly than for the MST. You will need to plan ahead to register for the test.

You have approximately 3 hours and 30 minutes to complete the entire test. The test-taking strategies for the paper-based test are different from those for the MST. One strategy we recommend is to keep track of answers you've eliminated by crossing out wrong answer choices in your test booklet. Here are some targeted strategies for each section of the paper-based GRE.

Analytical Writing

For the Analytical Writing section, if you are not using a transcriber, you will have to handwrite your essay, so we suggest you write clearly and legibly. For more tips and strategies for conquering the Analytical Writing section, refer to Chapter 15.

Verbal Reasoning Section

Before you start a Verbal Reasoning section, glance over it completely but quickly to familiarize yourself with it. With Reading Comprehension, you can preview the question stems to help guide your reading, but don't try to memorize them or answer the questions without reading the passages. We recommend that you answer the questions you're most comfortable with first. Make sure you set aside at least 15 minutes in each Verbal Reasoning section for Reading Comprehension.

Always try to be aware of how long you're spending on each question; this might require more effort than it does on the MST, since you won't have an onscreen timer. If you find yourself getting hung up on a hard question, move on and come back to it later if you have time. You want to give yourself every opportunity to answer as many questions as you are capable of answering correctly.

The Verbal Reasoning sections on the paper-based test have 25 questions—5 more than each section on the MST. The question types and formats on the paper-based Verbal sections are the same as those on the MST, with one exception: the question format that requires you to highlight a sentence, Select-in-Passage, is not available.

Quantitative Reasoning Section

As on the Verbal Reasoning sections, it will behoove you to stay aware of your pacing on the Quantitative Reasoning sections. Calculators are now permitted on the GRE and will be provided at the testing center. Still, don't forget to use your scratch paper for any calculations that are more quickly or accurately performed by hand. Feel free to skip around within this section as well and do all the problems you can do; then come back to the harder ones.

The Quantitative Reasoning sections of the paper-based test have 25 questions—5 more than each section on the MST. The question types and formats on the paper-based Quantitative sections are the same as those on the MST. You will also mark all of your answers directly in the test book, which means you don't have to worry about filling in a separate answer grid!

This chapter has given you an understanding of the GRE MST and paper-based test formats. Let's now turn to the test sections and get you ready for each one.

PART TWO

Verbal Reasoning

CHAPTER 3

Introduction to Verbal Reasoning

OVERVIEW

The Verbal Reasoning section of the GRE tests complex reasoning skills and your ability to analyze the relationships between words and sentences. Vocabulary will be tested contextually, and the reading passages are both dense and written with a sophisticated level of diction. The goal of the test's content, with its emphasis on analytical skills, is to make the test an accurate indicator of your ability to understand what you're reading and apply reasoning skills to the various question types. These skills will translate directly to study at the graduate level.

In this section of the book, we'll take you through all the types of Verbal Reasoning questions you'll see on the GRE and give you the strategies you'll need to answer them quickly and correctly. Also, the vocabulary words you'll most frequently encounter on the test are included in Appendices A–C in the "GRE Resources" section at the back of this book. Think of the glossary and word lists there as building blocks for the questions you will see on the test.

VERBAL REASONING QUESTION TYPES

The GRE contains two Verbal Reasoning sections with approximately 20 questions each. Each section will last 30 minutes and be composed of a consistent, predictable selection of the following question types:

- Text Completion
- Reading Comprehension
- Sentence Equivalence

The Verbal Reasoning portion of the GRE draws heavily upon your vocabulary and assesses your comprehension of written material. Specifically, it evaluates your ability to do the following:

- Analyze sentences and paragraphs
- Derive a word's meaning based upon its context
- Detect relationships among words
- Understand the logic of sentences and paragraphs
- Draw inferences
- Recognize major, minor, and irrelevant points
- Summarize ideas
- Understand passage structure
- Recognize an author's tone, purpose, and perspective

Within each section of Verbal Reasoning questions on the GRE, you will see an assortment of question types.

PACING STRATEGY

The GRE allows you to move freely backward and forward within each section, which can be a big advantage on Test Day. If you get stuck on a particular question, you can flag it and come back to it later when you have time. You only score points for correct answers, so you don't want to get bogged down on one problem and lose time you could have used to answer several other questions correctly. You also are not penalized for incorrect answers, so never leave a question blank.

You will have 30 minutes to work on each Verbal Reasoning section. The approximately 20 questions in each section will be an assortment of Text Completion, Sentence Equivalence, and Reading Comprehension items. However, these types of questions are not distributed equally. The chart below shows how many questions you can expect of each type, as well as the average amount of time you should spend per question type.

	Text Completion	Sentence Equivalence	Reading Comprehension
Number of Questions	approx. 6	approx. 4	approx. 10
Time per Question	1–1.5 minutes, depending on the number of blanks	1 minute	1–3 minutes, depending on the length, to read the passage and 1 minute to answer each question

Use these timing estimates as you work on practice questions and exams. With repetition, you will become comfortable keeping to the same amounts of time on Test Day. Additionally, you will be prepared to use the Mark and Review buttons to your advantage while taking the actual test.

NAVIGATING THE VERBAL REASONING SECTION OF THIS BOOK

The next chapter, Verbal Foundations and Content Review, will review the classic verbal concepts and topics that you will encounter on the GRE. This section of the book also includes individual chapters on Text Completion, Sentence Equivalence, and Reading Comprehension questions. Each of those chapters includes an introduction and definition of the relevant question types, followed by a review and examples of the strategies to follow to answer those questions quickly and correctly. In addition, you'll find a practice set with answers and explanations for each of the question types you'll encounter on the GRE.

Finally, at the end of this section, you'll find the Verbal Reasoning Practice Sets, which include not only practice questions but also answers and explanations. Use the Verbal Reasoning Practice Sets to test your skills and pinpoint areas for more focused study. When you are finished with this section of the book, you will have prepared for every question type you might encounter on the Verbal Reasoning section of the GRE.

CHAPTER 4

Verbal Foundations and Content Review

INTRODUCTION TO VERBAL FOUNDATIONS AND CONTENT REVIEW

The GRE Verbal section tests critical thinking skills that are essential to handling graduate-level work. To do well on this section, you will need to grasp how ideas relate to one another in sentences and passages. To measure this skill, the GRE evaluates your mastery of college-level vocabulary and your ability to read dense academic text for meaning. There are many strategies you can use to improve your vocabulary and reading comprehension.

- To improve your vocabulary:
    - Learn words in context
    - Tell stories about words
    - Use flashcards
    - Keep a vocabulary journal
    - Think like a thesaurus—word groups and word roots
    - Use all your senses
    - Use other people
    - Use other languages
    - Use online resources
    - Learn very common GRE words
- To improve your reading comprehension:
    - Attack the passage
    - Change your reading habits

This chapter will cover all of these strategies to improve your GRE vocabulary and reading comprehension, boosting your performance on Text Completion, Sentence Equivalence, and Reading Comprehension questions. In addition, you'll find short practice sets that will introduce you to each of these question types.

THE KAPLAN GUIDE TO IMPROVING YOUR VOCABULARY

According to the Global Language Monitor, there are over 1,000,000 words in the English language. According to the *Oxford English Dictionary,* there are "only" about 170,000 words in current use. Either way, that's a lot of words. Estimates put the vocabulary of most American college graduates at around 20,000 words. If you've taken a practice test and thought, "There are so many words I don't know!" you're not alone.

Fortunately, you can efficiently build your GRE vocabulary and see a significant increase in your Verbal score. You can do this by choosing a few strategies from the following pages that appeal to you and working with them every day over a number of weeks or months.

Be warned: You won't feel as though you're making progress at first. You'll learn a bunch of new words, then do some practice questions and see a plethora of words you still don't know. That's because there are an awful lot of words. You may feel discouraged. But don't give up! By spending at least 10 minutes a day on vocabulary, using the effective strategies given here, you will reach critical mass so that you can eliminate incorrect answers on Text Completion and Sentence Equivalence questions and choose the answers that match your predictions. Here are some facts that should help you feel confident about this task.

- The testmaker prefers certain types of words. On the test, you can expect to see the kind of vocabulary that commonly appears in literature and in academic journal articles. Also, you can expect to see a preponderance of words with Latin and Greek roots and prefixes. Thus, it is virtually unthinkable that you would need to know what *gabelle* means (a gabelle was a tax on salt in France before the French Revolution, and the word was derived from Arabic). However, a word like *incontrovertible* (from Latin, with *in-* meaning "not" and *controvertible* relating to "controversial," so "not controversial" or "undoubtedly true") is a word that the testmaker would expect you to be familiar with or to be able to figure out. After all, in graduate school you may well need to discuss whether an idea is incontrovertible or not.
- You often don't need to know the exact definition of a word to get a question correct. In fact, often just knowing whether a word has a positive or negative connotation is enough. Consider the word *ignominy.* That's not a word most of us use every day. But think about words you know that start with *igno...,* like

ignore and *ignorant*. It's not nice to ignore someone, and no one wants to look ignorant in front of other people. If the sentence is "It took her years to overcome the ________ of giving such an important speech when she was completely unprepared," you can predict "something bad" for the blank and make a good guess that *ignominy* fits. (In fact, *ignominy* means "shame" or "humiliation"—it's very negative, and it fits the sentence perfectly.)

The following strategies will help you learn the general meaning of the words you're most likely to see on the GRE.

Learn Words in Context

When you're not studying for the GRE, where do you see words and need to know what they mean? In things you read. Therefore, a good way to expand your vocabulary is through reading. When you read, you see words in a context that will help you remember them.

Your neighborhood or campus library has hard-copy books, magazines, and newspapers that you can read for free, and increasingly libraries can loan out ebooks as well. Check with a library near you to see what's available. If you don't want to worry about getting the book back on time, classic literature is generally available for purchase in bookstores or online for low prices. Moreover, a lot of excellent, vocabulary-rich material is available online at no charge. You can have reading material with you, whether in your bag or on your mobile device, all the time, so you can improve your GRE Verbal score throughout the day whenever you have a few minutes!

When you're reading, make sure to have handy (a) a notebook or notes app so you can jot down the words you don't know (see "Keep a Vocabulary Journal" below) and (b) a good dictionary or dictionary app so you can look up the words. (In a lot of e-readers, you can highlight or double-click a word to bring up its definition.) When you look up a word's meaning, also see what the dictionary says about its etymology and synonyms/antonyms and check whether the dictionary shows the word used in a sentence. If it does, compare how the word is used in the sentence you just read with how it's used in the dictionary's example sentence. If it doesn't, then make up your own sentence, using the word in a way that's relevant to you. You might also make flashcards (see "Use Flashcards" below) with your new words so you can easily keep practicing them.

Oh, and if you come across any words in this chapter that you're unfamiliar with, write them down and look them up! There's no time like the present to start improving your GRE score.

Here are some ideas for reading where you will encounter a myriad of GRE-type words. As you consider these resources, think about what you like to read. If you try to force yourself to read material you find tedious, you're unlikely to keep up the regular routine your GRE vocabulary growth depends on, so read things you find interesting. Ask yourself these questions:

- Are you a more avid reader of fiction or nonfiction?
- Do you prefer to immerse yourself in books, or does short work better fit your available time or attention span?
- Are there particular topics that interest you?

The lists of resources below are far from exhaustive; feel free to explore the library, bookstores, your own bookshelves and those of friends and family, and the Internet for more ideas. And, of course, the Internet is a dynamic entity, so while all URLs provided here work as this book goes to press, we can't guarantee they will work forever.

Magazines

All of the publications listed here are available at newsstands and bookstores and by subscription, and they offer extensive content online at no charge.

- *The Atlantic* (**theatlantic.com**) publishes a selection of nonfiction articles and short stories written at a high level. A visit to this publication's website quickly turned up words such as *affluent*, *ensue*, and *notorious*.
- *The Economist* (**economist.com**) covers current world events with an international focus. On a visit to this website, we soon encountered *putative*, *sectarian*, and *opulently*.
- *National Geographic* (**nationalgeographic.com**) is known in part for the amazing photography that illustrates its stories about the natural environment and human societies. Words found there included *riposte*, *harried*, and *mesmerizing*.
- *The New Yorker* (**newyorker.com**) publishes in-depth feature articles on a wide variety of topics as well as short fiction. A visit to the magazine's website quickly turned up words including *candid*, *endemic*, and *neophyte*.
- *Scientific American* (**scientificamerican.com**) covers science for a lay audience with topics ranging from dinosaurs to DNA to dreams. This is an excellent resource for readers with a background in the humanities or social sciences to get more comfortable with science reading. A few cool words found here: *herbivorous*, *ravaged*, *malady*.

Again, have you seen any words you don't know? Jot them down and start expanding your GRE vocabulary right now!

Newspapers

By reading newspapers, you will improve not only your vocabulary but also your knowledge of current events, which are often excellent examples to draw from when writing your essays for the Analytical Writing Assessment. You will find the following publications a rich source of GRE words.

- *The New York Times* (**nytimes.com**) is a daily newspaper of national and international scope. On the website, you can access section front pages and read up to 10 articles a month at no charge. The *New York Times* is also available in print and digital subscriptions, and single issues are available at many newsstands and bookstores.
- *The Wall Street Journal* (**wsj.com**) is published Monday through Friday and focuses on national and international news with implications for the economy and business.
- *The Washington Post* (**washingtonpost.com**) is a daily newspaper with substantial reporting on national politics and international news coverage.

Literature

If you enjoy fiction, try acquainting yourself with GRE words by reading novels and short stories from the canon of English literature. No matter whether your tastes run more toward Jane Austen or Alice Walker, Ray Bradbury or Charlotte Brontë, Willa Cather or Arthur Conan Doyle, Charles Dickens or Junot Díaz, Ralph Ellison or Ernest Hemingway, Daphne du Maurier or Toni Morrison, Amy Tan or J.R.R. Tolkien, John Updike or Herman Melville . . .

Alternatively, grab yourself a smorgasbord of authors in the form of a short-story anthology; collections with titles containing phrases such as "Best Short Stories," "Great Short Stories," or "Classic Short Stories" are good bets.

There are over 50,000 titles available online for free through Project Gutenberg via the website at **projectgutenberg.org**. Alternatively, the website at **americanliterature.com** features thousands of classic short stories and novels. The website—which is not actually confined to American literature—has a Short Story of the Day feature; bookmark it and read something different every day.

Nonfiction

Literary nonfiction is a great source of GRE vocabulary as well. Look for collections of classic essays on a range of topics by searching for anthologies with phrases like "Great Essays" or "Best Essays" in the title. Enjoy a particular topic? Search for books with phrases like "Best Science Writing" or "Best Political Writing."

Another good choice for high-level vocabulary is long-form journalism. You'll find these in-depth pieces in the magazines and newspapers listed above. Online, check out **longform.org** for current and historical articles covering just about any topic you can think of and easily searched by subject. (**Longform.org** also features a selection of literary short stories.)

Tell Stories About Words

The previous section explained how seeing words in context can help you remember their meaning. As we mentioned earlier, Appendix C: Common GRE Words in Context actually provides context for you. In addition, when you study words using flashcards or lists of words, such as Appendix A: Kaplan's Word Groups and Appendix B: Kaplan's Root List at the back of this book (see below for more on flashcards, word groups, and word roots), you can make up a meaningful context that will help you remember each word.

Take the word *gregarious* as an example. Do you know someone named Greg who is gregarious? (It means "sociable.") Or maybe your friend Greg isn't gregarious at all. Either way, you've got a little story to tell about that word.

Sometimes words look like they mean one thing but actually mean something completely different, and while this may be confusing at first, it can actually be an opportunity to learn the word. Here's how this works. Take the word *noisome* as an example. You might reasonably deduce it means something like "noisy"—but it doesn't. It actually means "offensive" in some way and is especially used to mean "really bad smelling." Now, if you were given a choice of roommates, whom would you prefer: the noisy one or the noisome one? Have you ever had a noisome roommate? When you make up a sentence that contrasts the word with its non-meaning, you won't forget what the word really means.

Here's another example. Most people instinctively think the word *pulchritudinous* must have a negative connotation; it just looks and sounds unpleasant. However, it actually means "very beautiful." Are you surprised when a pulchritudinous movie star dates someone who isn't very attractive? The etymology of a word, or how the word has come to mean what it means, can be a great starting point for storytelling about the word. Take the word *decadence*. It turns out that the root *cadere* is from the Latin for "to fall." Thus, you might fall hard for that *decadent* chocolate cake and fall right off your diet. Someone with a *cadaverous* appearance looks very ill, as though she might fall right over dead any minute and become a corpse (a *cadaver*). The past participle of *cadere* in Latin is *cas*, so a *cascade* is a waterfall. You might have heard the expression "a cascade effect," meaning a series of events that come one after another in a manner similar to a waterfall. Can you imagine going over a *cascade* with your *decadent* chocolate cake in hand and becoming a *cadaver*? Or, less dramatically, eating *decadent* chocolate cake during a picnic by a beautiful *cascade* and not becoming a *cadaver*? Again, by telling these little stories and forming vivid mental images, you'll lock in the meanings of words and won't forget them.

Stories don't have to be based on personal experience or made up. They can come from current events, popular culture, or history. Here's a history lesson with a GRE vocabulary lesson inside it: During World War II, the Germans used the *Enigma* machine to *encrypt* messages. However, the Allies figured out how to *decrypt* these messages, and knowing what the Germans were planning was a great benefit to the Allied side. *Enigma* means "mystery," so it was a good name for an *encryption* machine since *encrypt* means "to put a message into code." As you might imagine, *decrypt* means the opposite—"to decode." The adjectives *enigmatic* and *cryptic* mean "mysterious" and "secret," respectively. You can see that by connecting the words you learn in a story, you can commit their meanings to memory.

Bottom line: Memorizing lists of hundreds of words and their definitions would be very boring. Plus, it can be a futile strategy since you may forget the words soon after you learn them, well before Test Day. Instead, think up a sentence or story that uses the word. If it's funny or weird, or has special personal significance, it will be extra memorable—and the word will stick with you, too.

Use Flashcards

Flashcards are one of the most popular ways of preparing for the GRE Verbal section. You have several options, depending on whether you prefer cards you can hold in your hand or the convenience of a phone app. The purchase of a boxed set of flashcards may include access to a phone app as well, so you may be able to kill two birds with one stone.

If you choose to work with printed cards, you can buy a set of flashcards, such as *Kaplan GRE Vocabulary Flashcards*. Look for cards that include each word's part of speech. A lot of words mean different things depending on whether they're being used as, for example, a noun or a verb. For instance, a malevolent person seeking vengeance might *desert* ("abandon") his foe in the *desert* ("arid area") without leaving her any water. Also, look for cards that include not only the definition of the word but also a sentence using the word. As we said above, learning the word in context is the best way to remember it. Finally, cards that include synonyms for the word are extra helpful because the associations with other words will help you learn this word and you'll learn groups of words at a time (see "Think Like a Thesaurus" below).

Another option is to make your own cards. This is certainly more work, but by the time you look up the word and then write out its part of speech, its definition, any synonyms, and a sentence using it, you may know the word pretty well.

If you are a visual learner, consider color-coding your flashcards. Here's one way to do this: If a word has a positive connotation, write it in green or put a green dot next to it; if it has a neutral connotation, write it in black or use a black dot; if it has a negative connotation, write it in red or use a red dot. Then on the test, if you see the word *penury* and can't quite remember the definition, you might still remember seeing it on the flashcard with a big red dot next to it and know it's negative (*penury* means "extreme poverty"). As we said at the beginning of this chapter, often just knowing the charge of a word is enough to choose it as a correct answer or eliminate it as incorrect on the GRE.

It's hard to beat the convenience of flashcards on your phone. Waiting in line at the store? Waiting for someone to text you back? Waiting for the bus? Hey, how much of our lives do we spend waiting anyway? Well wait no more. Instead, whip out your phone and add a few more words to your GRE vocabulary. Look for the same things in a phone app as in hard-copy cards: part of speech, definition, synonyms, and an example sentence.

Keep a Vocabulary Journal

Keeping a vocabulary journal may sound like a lot of work, but it's actually an efficient way to capture words so their meanings stick with you. Especially if you are a kinesthetic or visual learner, a vocabulary journal can be the key to unlocking your GRE Verbal score. A number of studies have shown that writing out words by hand helps some people learn better. So get a notebook and start keeping that vocabulary journal.

What do you write in a word journal? Pretty much the same things you would put on homemade flashcards: unfamiliar words, their definitions, synonyms and antonyms, and sentences using the words. However, you have more room in a notebook, so you can write more. For example, you could make notes about the etymology of a word, or you could write a couple of different sentences using the word. Use different colors of ink to help you remember the positive, negative, or neutral tone of words or to make the word stand out in the example sentences you write. Some students like to illustrate the word by drawing a picture or affixing a picture from a magazine or that they print out from a website. Every couple of pages, you could write a brief story (a few sentences) that uses all the words on those pages, and maybe some of their synonyms and antonyms as well.

Fill up a Notebook? Start Another One!

When you encounter a word you don't know, you may not have time to look it up just then. No problem. Write it down anyway and give it half a page. Later when you're studying, you can fill in some of the information about the word. Then when you review it again in a few days, you can add more information. By Test Day, you will be completely sanguine about your recall of every word in your journal. (Don't know the word "sanguine"? Make it the first word in your notebook!)

Think Like a Thesaurus—Word Groups and Word Roots

Learning words one at a time is all well and good, but wouldn't it be better to learn them in bunches? That's where word groups and word roots really help. We've already alluded to these in previous sections of this chapter. For example, if you're using flashcards or a vocabulary journal to study, use them to associate a word with its synonyms—a group of words with similar meanings. That's what we mean by a "word group." And in "Tell Stories About Words," we discussed using a word's root (like *cadere* in *decadent* and *cadaver)* to associate that word with related words.

Word Groups

Remember that to get a Text Completion or Sentence Equivalence question correct, you often only need to know a word's approximate meaning. Here's how you can use word groups to know exactly that. In Kaplan's word groups (the complete list is in Appendix A), you'll find this list:

Investigate

appraise
ascertain
assay
descry
peruse

A good point of entry to this list is the relatively common word *appraise*, which means "to determine the value of something." You may have performance *appraisals* at work (and if your boss thinks you're doing a good job, then he will *praise* you). You may also have had or heard of having a home or a piece of art *appraised* in order to *ascertain* its worth. *Ascertain* is another word in this list that, if you don't already know it, is easy to learn because it means "to make *certain* of."

The other words in this group are less commonly used, but you can quickly master them by associating them with the words you do know. *Assay* can mean "to evaluate, analyze, or test." For example, by assaying your strengths and weaknesses on the GRE, you can ascertain what topics you most need to study. Or perhaps you will *assay* your vocabulary knowledge by asking a friend to test you on the words in this book, because such an *appraisal* will help you determine which words to study. Then after *assaying* your current GRE skill by taking a practice test, you will raise your score by *perusing* ("reading thoroughly") this book. These words are by no means synonyms, but they all relate to a careful study or evaluation of something. By making up a story that associates these words in a personally meaningful way, you can efficiently pick up their general sense.

Now let's say that in the middle of the GRE, you see the word *descry* and you can't remember that it means "to detect by looking carefully." Uh-oh. But you do remember seeing it in that list with *appraise* and *ascertain*, so you know it must relate to a thorough examination. Is it a good fit for the blank in this sentence?

> Although the sailor climbed the mast every morning to carefully scan the misty horizon with the ship's telescope, he was unable to ____ even a hint of land.

The word "Although" sets up a contrast between the great effort the sailor is putting forth to search for land and his inability to find it. *Descry* it is!

Word Roots

Word roots work much the same way. By studying words grouped by their roots, you can learn the meanings of handfuls of words at a time. This is an efficient way to study. As we saw above, you can also use word roots as the basis for making up sentences about words that help you remember them.

Remember the words *desert* (verb) and *desert* (noun) from the section on flashcards? These words are what are known as *homographs*, because they are spelled or written (the root *graph*) the same (*hom*) way. *Homophones* are words that are pronounced (*phon*) the same way, like *air* and *heir* or *bore* and *boar*. In Appendix B, you'll find Kaplan's list of word roots. Here's what it says about these three roots:

(H)OM: same	**GRAM/GRAPH: to write, to draw**	**PHON: sound**
anomaly: deviation from the common rule	**diagram:** a figure made by drawing lines; an illustration	**euphony:** the quality of sounding good
homeostasis: a relatively stable state of equilibrium	**epigram:** a short poem; a pointed statement	**megaphone:** a device for magnifying the sound of one's voice
homogeneous: of the same or a similar kind of nature; of uniform structure of composition throughout	**grammar:** a system of language and its rules	phonetics: the study of the sounds used in speech
homonym: one of two or more words spelled and pronounced alike but different in meaning	**graph:** a diagram used to convey mathematical information	**polyphony:** the use of simultaneous melodic lines to produce harmonies in musical compositions
homosexual: of, relating to, or exhibiting sexual desire toward a member of one's own sex	**graphite:** mineral used for writing, as the "lead" in pencils	**telephone:** a device for transmitting sound at a distance
	photograph: a picture, originally made by exposing chemically treated film to light	

Just as with word groups, you can find a point of entry to a word root by starting with a word you know. You certainly know what *grammar* is because you've studied it in school, and you know what a *photograph* and a *diagram* are, but the word *epigram* is less common. If you don't know what *epigram* means, you can learn it now: Was her terse *epigram* written with good *grammar*? In his presentation, what worked best to get his point across: his *diagram*, his *photograph*, or his *epigram*? An *epigram* is something short written to make a point.

The history of words' meanings provides stories that help with learning them, too. For example, starting with the Ancient Greeks and continuing into early modern times, physicians believed that four humors based on bodily fluids determined health. Today we still have the words *sanguine* ("optimistic, confident," from old words for "blood"), *choleric* and *bilious* ("irritable," from words for "yellow bile"), *phlegmatic* ("calm, lacking energy," from "phlegm"), and *melancholic* ("sad, gloomy" from words for "black bile"). So the same medical beliefs that led to draining blood from sick people to make them "better" live on in our language.

Do be careful when studying word roots. Watch out for these potential pitfalls:

- **Just because two words look similar does not mean they share the same root.** Here's an example. The words *aver* and *avert* differ by only one letter. However, *aver* ("to state or prove as true") comes from the Latin *vērus* ("truth") and shares a root with *verity, verify, verdict, veracity,* and *verisimilitude*, while *avert* ("to turn away, prevent") comes from the Latin *vertere* ("to turn") and is related to *convert, subvert, introvert, extrovert, incontrovertible* (from the top of the chapter), and *vertigo*. The two words have no relationship.
- **The same root or prefix can have different meanings.** Take for example *embellish* and *belligerent*. Both have *bell* as a root, but *embellish* means "to make prettier" and comes from the Latin *bellus* for "pretty," while *belligerent* means "at war or eager to fight" and comes from the Latin *bellum* for "war." Confusing? Yes. However, this is yet another opportunity to learn these similar-looking words, because you can tell a story that associates them but makes their different meanings clear. For example, if you accused someone of *embellishing* his war stories, he might become angry and *belligerent*. Have you ever pointed out that someone was stretching the truth and seen them get angry? If so, then you've got *embellish* and *belligerent*. Next!
- **Smaller words inside larger words aren't necessarily a Greek or Latin root.** Consider the word *adumbrate*. It would be easy to see the word *dumb* ("not intelligent" or "not able to speak") in the middle and think that was the root. In fact, the root is *umbr* ("shadow"), the same root as in *umbrella*, which shades you from the sun or rain. The prefix *ad-* means "toward," and *adumbrate* means "to foreshadow," or to give a hint of what's coming, as in "The ticking clock in the first paragraph adumbrates the fact that the protagonist runs out of time at the end of the story."

In addition to Appendix B in the back of this book, there are many print and online resources you can use to learn more about word roots. Most dictionaries provide a short summary of words' origins. In addition, some students have found *Word Power Made Easy,* by Norman Lewis, entertaining as well as chock-full of engaging descriptions of what words mean. A popular website for finding out about the history of words is **etymonline.com**. The site has search functionality and a bibliography.

Use All Your Senses

We've emphasized the importance of reading words in the context of other words, but reading isn't the only way to learn words. Plus, learning words in other ways can be fun—it can feel like playing charades or Pictionary. Here are some ideas that engage different parts of your brain in learning.

- Say the word aloud. Speaking engages Broca's area of the brain, just above the left ear in most people. Plus, you hear yourself say the word, engaging still more of the brain. While you're at it, say the word's definition and a sentence using the word out loud, too. Want to make the word even more memorable? If you're comfortable doing so, say the word in a funny voice that matches the meaning or "charge" of the word. You'd say *insouciant* ("carefree") in a very different voice than you'd say *moribund* ("near death").
- Make up a song with the words you are learning in it. Singing engages even more of the brain than speaking. If you learned the English alphabet song as a kid, you could probably still sing it, along with a lot of other children's songs. This can be a great way to learn a group of related words.
- Not going to sing, not even in the shower? Write a poem with the word in it. No pressure—you're not trying to win the Nobel Prize in Literature, just learn vocabulary words. Everyone can write haiku (traditionally, a three-line poem with five syllables on the first line, seven on the second, and five on the third). Or maybe you could write silly rhymes like Dr. Seuss.
- Draw a picture representing the word. For instance, you might draw someone wagging her finger and looking disapproving to illustrate *discountenance* ("to disapprove"). Work the word into the picture if you can. Or you can write words in your journal or on flashcards in a font that you design to match their meaning or charge.
- If you're having someone quiz you on GRE words and you find yourself answering with a hand gesture—"Oh, *attenuate* . . . that means, you know [move your hand while bringing your thumb and fingers together]"—go with it! *Attenuate* means "to become thinner or weaker," and if you can associate a hand gesture with that definition, then you know the word.
- You don't need to stop with hand gestures. Feel free to move your whole body to act out the meaning or charge of a word. For *exalt* ("to praise"), maybe you jump up and give an invisible friend a high-five; for *commiserate* ("to sympathize"), maybe you give your invisible friend a hug.

Use Other People

You don't need to learn GRE vocabulary on your own. Your friends, family members, and coworkers may be excited to get in on the action. If you carry flashcards around with you, whip out a few and ask someone to quiz you. As they learn the words too, they may think of sentences or little stories that will help you remember them. This can definitely be a group project.

You can also incorporate the words you are learning into your everyday conversation. Did you make a mistake at work? You can tell your coworkers, "I hope our boss merely *reproves* [gently criticizes] me instead of *castigating* [harshly scolding] me." They may be impressed. More likely they'll be amused, or possibly *bemused* ("confused"). Maybe they'll even want to get in on the fun. Feel tired after a long day? Tell your friends you are *flagging* and *enervated*. They'll say that if you've been using words like that all day, it's no wonder. Then you could say that a promise of ice cream afterward would *indubitably galvanize* you into wanting to go out to a movie.

Use Other Languages

If you've ever studied (or grew up speaking) a Romance language such as Spanish, French, or Italian, it will help you on the GRE. If you've ever studied Latin, even just for a year a long time ago, it will help a lot. The only language tested on the GRE is English, but if you've learned a Romance language, you've probably noticed that quite a few words were spelled similarly and had similar meanings in that language and in English. Here are just a few examples:

English	French	Spanish
affable (friendly)	affable	afable
apprehend (to learn)	apprendre	aprender
extraordinary (exceptional)	extraordinaire	extraordinario
indubitable (undoubted)	indubitable	indudable
liberty (freedom)	liberté	libertad
salutary (healthful)	salutaire	saludable

Overlaps between words in these languages usually indicate a common Latin root, so when you noticed the similarities, you were learning the roots of words. This knowledge will help you recognize other related words in English.

Use Online Resources

Several publishers of dictionaries host websites with not only the ability to search for words' meanings but also a thesaurus feature, quizzes and games, and a word-of-the-day feature. Sign up to get the word of the day and wake up every morning to a new word on your phone. Then make sure to use the word at least three times during the day! Most online dictionaries are also available via mobile apps. Here are some sites to check out:

- **dictionary.com** (largely based on the *Random House Dictionary*)
- **macmillandictionary.com** (based on the *Macmillan English Dictionary*)
- **merriam-webster.com** (based on *Merriam-Webster's Collegiate Dictionary*)
- **oxforddictionaries.com/us/** (produced by the publishers of the *Oxford English Dictionary*)

Another site that many GRE students enjoy is **freerice.com**, which will quiz you on one word after another. The words start out very easy, but as you answer correctly, your level goes up and the words get tougher. For every question you get right, this nonprofit website donates 10 grains of rice to the United Nations' World Food Programme. You'll see bowls filling up with rice as you answer questions correctly. So build your vocabulary and feed hungry people—truly a win-win.

These resources aren't targeted at the kinds of words that show up frequently on the GRE, the way the words in Appendixes A, B, and C of this book are. Nonetheless, these are fun, convenient ways to help you sharpen your vocabulary consciousness every day. By looking at a "word of the day" every morning as you wait for your bread to toast, you're preparing your brain to learn words all day. The same thing happens when you take a break from whatever else you're doing and play a few rounds of a vocabulary game. And did we mention these are *fun*? There's no rule against having fun while you expand your word knowledge. In fact, approaching your prep in a spirit of play will make it even more effective!

Learn Very Common GRE-Level Words

Maybe you're ready to use some of these strategies to improve your vocabulary and your GRE score, but you're not sure where to start. After all, there are a lot of words. Rest assured, no one knows all the words in the English language, nor will the GRE test them all. Your best bet is to memorize common college-level vocabulary words, such as the ones on this list, because words like these are the most likely to appear on the GRE.

ABSTAIN	ADULTERATE	ANOMALY
APATHY	ASSUAGE	AUDACIOUS
CAPRICIOUS	CORROBORATE	DESICCATE
ENGENDER	ENIGMA	EPHEMERAL
EQUIVOCAL	ERUDITE	FERVID
GULLIBLE	HOMOGENEOUS	LACONIC
LAUDABLE	LOQUACIOUS	LUCID
MITIGATE	OPAQUE	PEDANT
PLACATE	PRAGMATIC	PRECIPITATE
PRODIGAL	PROPRIETY	VACILLATE
VOLATILE	ZEAL	

Start with these, which are listed in Appendix C: Common GRE-Level Words in Context at the end of this book. Then move on to the 150 other very common GRE words in that section. It is very likely that at least a few of these words will appear on your GRE test, and they're an excellent starting point for learning even more words.

Some Final Thoughts

You've been in school a long time, and you've read a lot of words. You may feel as though a lot of GRE vocabulary is new to you, but it almost certainly isn't. At some point, you've seen almost every word you'll see on Test Day, and you understood it well enough in context to understand what you were reading. Those words have left some trace in your brain's neural pathways. Your job in studying words is to activate those connections and strengthen them so the words' meanings are readily available to you during the test.

Not only have you seen most of these words before (even if you don't remember them), but once you start to learn them, you'll begin to see and hear them everywhere—on your favorite television shows, in news stories, even in social media memes. This will be more reinforcement of your learning!

Choose a couple of strategies from this chapter to use every day. When you take the practice test toward the end of this book, make sure to review the explanations for each question thoroughly and use your vocabulary-learning strategies to study every word you weren't sure of. This definitely applies to words in the Text Completion and Sentence Equivalence questions, but if you encounter words in Reading Comprehension passages that are unfamiliar, make sure to learn those words, too.

To acquaint you with the types of GRE questions that test critical thinking skills along with vocabulary knowledge, here is a short practice set of Text Completion and Sentence Equivalence questions. See how many words you know and don't know and then, as you read the explanations, think about how you are going to learn the obscure words so they'll be familiar the next time you see them.

TEXT COMPLETION AND SENTENCE EQUIVALENCE PRACTICE SET

Directions: For each blank select one entry from the corresponding column of choices. Fill all blanks in the way that best completes the text.

1. All Jon cared about was getting an A, so because the team project did not count toward his grade in the course, he felt ________ the work and did not do his share.

   A apathy toward
   B zeal for
   C loathing for
   D cheerful about
   E antagonism toward

2. To her friends' (i) ________, because she had never expressed an interest in travel, Lovia decided to teach English in Thailand, (ii) ________ in that country for a year.

Blank (i)	Blank (ii)
A delight	D sojourning
B astonishment	E retiring
C dismay	F persevering

3. The citizens met with their senator to express (i) _______, arguing that if tax rates (ii) _______ any further, taxes would become (iii) ________, allowing hard-working individuals to keep little of their well-earned income.

Blank (i)	Blank (ii)	Blank (iii)
A euphoria	D economized	G congruent
B composure	E escalated	H confiscatory
C apprehension	F elaborated	I consummate

Directions: Select the two answer choices that, when used to complete the sentence, fit the meaning of the sentence as a whole and produce completed sentences that are alike in meaning.

4. Our manager holds as a ________ that an employee with a messy desk is irredeemably lazy, and she therefore demands that all members of her staff keep their work areas meticulously organized.

   [A] whim
   [B] dogma
   [C] hypothesis
   [D] fancy
   [E] tenet
   [F] polity

5. Elena liked Joe a great deal, but she soon tired of his friends, pseudointellectuals who propounded inane theories based on ________ interpretations of neo-Marxism and existentialism.

   [A] spurious
   [B] terse
   [C] fallacious
   [D] succinct
   [E] bellicose
   [F] blithe

6. Despite the many pleasures of staying in a hotel, such as a hot shower and clean sheets, many people ________ such comforts in favor of cold water from a nearby stream and a sleeping bag in order to savor a revitalizing proximity to nature.

   [A] extol
   [B] deprecate
   [C] renounce
   [D] spurn
   [E] discountenance
   [F] eulogize

TEXT COMPLETION AND SENTENCE EQUIVALENCE PRACTICE SET ANSWERS AND EXPLANATIONS

1. A

The sentence begins by telling you that Jon only cares about getting an A, and then it says that the team project did not impact his grade. The blank needs a term for how Jon "felt" about the project, and the keywords "so because" indicate that the blank will be consistent with the information given. Furthermore, the keyword "and" in the last part of the sentence means the blank will be consistent with Jon not doing his share of the work. Predict that Jon will not care about the team project or will feel "indifference" toward it. Answer choice (A) *apathy* is a match for your prediction and the correct answer. *Apathy* is composed of a- ("not") and *path* ("emotion") and is related to words like *empathy*, *sympathy*, and *antipathy*. Learn these words as a group with the same root.

The word *zeal* ("strong interest"), choice **(B)**, is the opposite of what is needed. Note that *zealous* means "very enthusiastic" and a *zealot* is "a fanatic" for some cause. Another word beginning with *z*, *zest*, also means "great enthusiasm." Learn these words as a group with related meanings. Choice **(D)** *cheerful* is incorrect for the same reason; it is positive, but you need a neutral or mildly negative word. Choice **(C)** *loathing* means "extreme dislike" and choice **(E)** *antagonism* means "dislike" or "conflict"; both words are too negative. While Jon does not care about the project, he has no reason to hate it. When you studied literature, you may have learned that the *protagonist* is the main character of the story and the *antagonist* is the person with whom the main character experiences conflict.

2. B, D

The sentence says that Lovia had never been interested in travel but she is going to Thailand. Her decision would come as a "surprise" to her friends, and choice **(B)** *astonishment* is correct for blank (i). There is no evidence to support the idea that her friends are feeling either *delight* **(A)** or *dismay* **(C)** about her decision. You need a neutral word for this blank.

Lovia will be abroad for a year, so the choice that fits blank (ii) is **(D)** *sojourning* ("staying temporarily"). This word is related to *journey*, which also relates to travel, and to *journal*. You might think of a personal journey as a record of one's "trip" through life. She is not **(E)** *retiring* because she will be working as a teacher. **(F)** *persevering* means "being persistent" or "overcoming obstacles," and nothing in the sentence indicates that she will encounter adversity.

3. C, E, H

People can "express" a wide range of thoughts and feelings (blank (i)), and tax rates can go up, go down, or stay the same (blank (ii)). Start with the third blank, which has the most context clues.

The word for blank (iii) must be consistent with the last part of the sentence, which is about not letting people keep their money—or taking their money away from them. The match is choice **(H)** *confiscatory* ("seizing property"). This word's root is the same as in the word *fiscal*, meaning "financial": Your *fiscal* condition is reduced if the authorities *confiscate* your property. Choice **(G)** *congruent* means "in agreement"; when you study geometry for the Quantitative section, you will study *congruent* shapes, which are identical to or in complete agreement with each other. Choice **(I)** *consummate* when used as an adjective means "perfect." This has the same root as *summit*, or "highest point," and if someone describes you as the *consummate* professional, she is saying that you bring together (*con-*) the highest or best qualities of a professional.

Given that the tax rates might become *confiscatory*, the citizens must be concerned that taxes will "rise," so this is your prediction for blank (ii). Choice **(E)** *escalated* is correct. Think of riding up an *escalator* in a building. Or think of *scaling*, or climbing, a wall—*escalate* and *scale* share the same root. Choice **(D)** *economized* would relate to "spending less money," and choice **(F)** *elaborated* would mean "to develop." Neither of these choices describes rising taxes.

Now for blank (i): Because the citizens believe taxes will go up and take most of their money, and they are meeting with their senator about this prospect, they are undoubtedly worried. Choice **(C)** *apprehension* conveys worry or fear and is correct. *Apprehension* is an interesting word because it can mean "capture," "understanding," or "fear." Here's a sentence to think about: If the criminal had *apprehended* that the police would soon *apprehend* him, he would have felt *apprehension*. Choice **(A)** *euphoria* means "bliss" and is the opposite of what these folks are feeling. Choice **(B)** *composure* means "calm" and also does not reflect what the citizens feel.

4. B, E

When this manager sees a messy desk, she forms a harshly negative opinion of the employee, and as a result ("therefore"), she "demands" that her staff keep their desks clean. Based on the sentence, you can conclude that the manager holds a "strong belief" on this subject. Answer choices **(B)** *dogma* and **(E)** *tenet* both mean an "idea held to be true" and are the correct answers. If someone is *dogmatic*, that person is very opinionated. Imagine someone refusing to let go of an idea like a dog refusing to let go of a bone! *Tenet* comes from the Latin word meaning "to hold" and shares its root with *tenable* ("can be held, defensible") and *tenacity* ("holding on persistently").

Choices **(A)** *whim* and **(D)** *fancy* both relate to a "passing thought." While these words can have similar meanings, they do not fit the context of this sentence. Choice **(C)** *hypothesis* is a "guess" or a starting point for exploring a problem, not a strongly held belief. Choice **(F)** *polity* means a "government" (think "politics") and does not fit the sentence.

5. A, C

Elena liked Joe, but the keyword "but" indicates she has a negative view of his friends. Why? They are "pseudointellectuals" and their theories are "inane." The prefix *pseudo-* means "fake," and *inane* means "silly." Either one of these clues tells you that they don't understand the complex philosophies mentioned in the sentence. Predict that the word in the blank means their "interpretations" are actually misinterpretations; that is, they are "false." Choices **(A)** *spurious* and **(C)** *fallacious* both relate to "falseness" and fit the sentence. The word *spurious* is derived from the Latin word for "illegitimate child." It is not etymologically related to the word *spur*, but you can think of a railroad spur, which looks like any other track but is not the main line and doesn't go very far. *Fallacious*, like *fallacy* and *false*, comes from a Latin word for "deceive."

Choices **(B)** terse and **(D)** succinct both relate to "not using many words," and the sentence gives no reason to believe Joe's friends do not talk much (one rather imagines the opposite). Choice **(E)** bellicose means "looking for a fight" (the root is bell meaning "war"), and while this is a negatively charged word, it does not fit the clues in the sentence; his friends are wrong but not necessarily argumentative. Choice **(F)** blithe means "cheerful" or "without worries" (it shares a root in Old English with bliss, which is "extreme happiness"); this is a positively charged word.

6. C, D

The keyword "Despite" signals a contrast, so people who camp instead of staying indoors "reject" the comforts of a hotel. Choice **(C)** *renounce* means "to put aside," and choice **(D)** *spurn* means "to reject scornfully." You may have heard or read the expression "to *spurn* someone's advances," meaning to let someone know that you are absolutely not interested in a romantic relationship. These words both give the sentence the same sense and are correct.

Choices **(A)** *extol* and **(F)** *eulogize* both mean "to praise highly." People who opt for camping would praise being close to nature highly, according to the sentence, but this blank relates to the hotel experience. Thus, these are the opposite of what is needed. By the way, don't confuse a *eulogy* with an *elegy*: Both are often written about someone who has died, but a eulogy is prose while an elegy is a poem and the focus of a eulogy is on praising the subject while an elegy's focus is on expressing grief. Choices **(B)** *deprecate* and **(E)** *discountenance* are negatively charged, which might have made them tempting. However, both mean "to express disapproval," and while the sentence indicates that nature lovers reject staying in a hotel for themselves, there is no evidence that they disapprove of other people staying in hotels.

THE KAPLAN GUIDE TO IMPROVING YOUR READING COMPREHENSION SKILLS

Many people preparing to take the GRE give Reading Comprehension little attention. There are a few reasons for this. One is that they've been reading since they started school as children, so the idea that they need to practice reading now seems ridiculous. "I know how to read!" they think. "So why put limited study time into reading?"

Another reason is that the correct answers to Reading Comprehension questions can seem subjective. A test prepper might take a practice test or try some practice questions and think, "I'm never going to understand why this answer is better than that one. I'm just never going to grasp how the testmaker thinks. Better to invest my study time elsewhere."

Yet another rationale is that learning all the words that might appear on the Verbal section seems like such a daunting task (see the previous section of this chapter for tips to make it less intimidating) that test takers allocate all their Verbal study time to vocabulary, with none left over for reading.

Let's rebut these one at a time:

- GRE Reading Comp requires a particular kind of reading. You are probably skilled at reading for school and work, and you may enjoy reading for fun. But to do well on the GRE Verbal section, you need to read to answer very specific kinds of questions, and this is a skill that takes practice.
- The answers to Reading Comp questions are *not* subjective. The test will not make you guess among correct answers, one of which is "better" than the others. Instead, there are *right* answers and *wrong* answers, and every wrong answer is incorrect for a reason. You can objectively evaluate answer choices based on information in the passage.
- Only half the Verbal section consists of Text Completion and Sentence Equivalence questions. The other half is Reading Comp. Thus, it is important to your Verbal score that you master the reading passages and questions.

If you have taken a practice test and answered almost all the Reading Comprehension questions correctly, then by all means, invest your preparation efforts elsewhere. If that is not the case, read on.

ATTACK THE PASSAGE

The GRE will present you with academic passages, most of one paragraph but some of several paragraphs, and it will ask you predictable types of questions about certain features of the text. The GRE is primarily concerned with your ability to grasp the main idea of what you read, differentiate fact from opinion and one person's opinion from another's, make supported inferences based on the text, and understand how the author has developed her ideas or the structure of the passage. The GRE will also ask you to analyze the logic of arguments. While some questions will test your ability to accurately identify a fact or idea in the passage, the test is always open-book. That is, as questions come up on the right side of the screen, the passage will always be available on the left side of the screen for you to research.

Note that the GRE is *not* interested in testing your ability to learn facts about philosophy or physics or physiology. Thus, you are *not* studying to learn something about a topic, as you are accustomed to do in school. Passages are often full of details that you will not see a question about, so time spent learning them is time wasted.

In fact, if the word *reading* triggers you to begin *studying*, as you would if you needed to take a test or write a paper for class, then don't think of this task as "reading." Instead, think of it as *attacking the passage*.

Attacking the passage means interrogating the passage, actively asking the same questions the test is likely to ask you. What's the author's point? Why is the author comparing X to Y? What is the author's attitude toward Z? By asking these questions as you read, you will be ready for the questions the test asks you. Watch a GRE expert take apart a science passage:

> There is no doubt that dogs have been domesticated for thousands of years, since the last Ice Age. What is less certain is the process of domestication that brought wolves, a predator of livestock and a danger to humans themselves, into the family as helper and companion.
>
> GRE expert's mental paraphrase: *What is the author's topic? Domestication of dogs. What is the author's position? Apparently, that we don't know exactly how Spot got to sleep on the bed.*

Attacking the passage means focusing on keywords that signal important ideas and changes in a passage's direction, which are often the targets of questions. Focus on these sentences, making sure you understand what the author is saying. Keywords also indicate when the author is using an example to illustrate a main point or breaking an overall process into a sequence of events or steps. You can read these sentences more lightly, simply noting where the information is if you need it.

> There is no doubt that dogs have been domesticated for thousands of years, beginning during the last Ice Age. What is less certain is the process of domestication that brought wolves, a predator of livestock and a danger to humans themselves, into the family as helper and companion. One widely accepted theory is that Paleolithic humans captured wolf cubs and raised them to serve as alarms when other large predators, such as cats in the *Smilodon* genus, approached. However, . . .
>
> GRE expert's mental paraphrase: *Sure enough, "One . . . theory" indicates that there is more than one idea about this. Then "However" signals a contrasting theory. It will be interesting to see whether the author takes a side.*

Attacking the passage means mentally paraphrasing as you read. GRE passages are often written in dense academic language, which makes answering questions about them harder. You can make answering questions easier by recasting the concepts in the same language you would use to explain them to a friend.

> There is no doubt that dogs have been domesticated for thousands of years, beginning during the last Ice Age. What is less certain is the process of domestication that brought wolves, a predator of livestock and a danger to humans themselves, into the family as helper and companion. One widely accepted theory is that Paleolithic humans captured wolf cubs and raised them to serve as alarms when other large predators, such as cats in the *Smilodon* genus, approached. However, some paleoanthropologists are skeptical that humans would have befriended members of a species they viewed as inimical and sought to decimate. These scientists posit that some wolves—those best at reading human body language indicating hostile or tolerant intent and at adopting submissive, ingratiating behaviors such as tail wagging—approached early human settlements, first to scavenge and then to solicit handouts.
>
> GRE expert's mental paraphrase: *So some scientists think taming wolves was our idea. But others think buddying up to us was actually their idea.*

Attacking the passage means taking notes, or making a **passage map**. Writing down the passage's broad **topic**, its narrower **scope** (the aspect of the topic the author's interested in), and the author's **purpose**, as well as the key ideas from each paragraph, will accomplish three goals. First, by digesting these important elements of the passage so you can briefly jot them down in a few words, you will ensure you really understand them. Second, if you capture the essential elements of the passage in your map, you can answer many questions just from your notes, saving time. Third, just as a road map tells you how to get to your friend's house, your passage map will tell you where to find that detail the GRE is asking about, again saving time.

> There is no doubt that dogs have been domesticated for thousands of years, beginning during the last Ice Age. What is less certain is the process of domestication that brought wolves, a predator of livestock and a danger to humans themselves, into the family as helper and companion. One widely accepted theory is that Paleolithic humans captured wolf cubs and raised them to serve as alarms when other large predators, such as cats in the *Smilodon* genus, approached. However, some paleoanthropologists are skeptical that humans would have befriended members of a species they viewed as inimical and indeed sought to decimate. These scientists posit that some wolves—those best at reading human body language indicating hostile or tolerant intent and at adopting submissive, ingratiating behaviors such as tail wagging—approached early human settlements, first to scavenge and then to solicit handouts. Natural selection then favored those wolves most pleasing to humans, specifically those most friendly and trainable, as these animals would elicit the most food and shelter; their descendants are today's dogs, from Chihuahuas to Great Danes. Thus, if we accept that wolves took the initiative to join their lives with ours,

it is not a much greater leap to believe that our species have coevolved such that those humans with traits that best satisfied wolves benefitted most from wolves' protection and passed on those canid-friendly characteristics to their offspring. It is no wonder that so many people love dogs.

GRE expert's passage map:

Topic: Domestication of wolves/dogs

Scope: Theories of how it happened

Purpose: To argue for idea that wolves approached humans

Theory #1: Humans caught wolf cubs, used them for protection

Theory #2: Wolves chose to hang out near human settlements, get fed. If true, then we "coevolved"—people selected for wolf-pleasing traits. People ♥ dogs → theory #2.

Attacking the passage does not mean reading faster. It means reading at a speed that allows you to do all of the above: interrogate the text, spot keywords and focus on the important ideas they highlight, mentally paraphrase, and map the passage. At first, this may mean reading more slowly than you will read on Test Day, given the Verbal section's timing. However, as you practice, you will get faster. Even better, when you are thoroughly prepared to answer the questions, they will take much less time, thereby saving you time overall.

Bottom line: If you read the passage but then can't answer the GRE's questions about it, then reading it didn't do you much good. Instead, *attack the passage* using the strategies briefly introduced here and discussed in much greater depth in Chapter 7. Then also use the approaches in Chapter 7 for analyzing the questions, researching and predicting the answers, and avoiding common types of wrong answers to master Reading Comprehension.

Change Your Reading Habits

It can be hard to put away old reading habits in favor of *attacking the passage*. Fortunately, you don't need to practice this skill only when you're studying for the GRE.

In fact, you can practice anytime you are reading for school, for work, to keep up with current events, or any other reason. Approach the textbook chapter, memo, article, or whatever it may be as though you were taking the GRE. By practicing this type of reading whenever you have a chance, you will soon work past the initial awkwardness, and reading this way will become second nature. Plus, you are adding to the total time you are investing in your GRE score.

Then when you practice with GRE-type passages and questions, like the ones you'll find next in this chapter and throughout this book (Chapter 7: Reading Comprehension, Chapter 8: Verbal Reasoning Practice Sets, Chapter 20: Practice Test), as well as in your online practice tests (MSTs), you will see significant improvement!

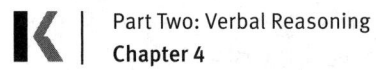

READING COMPREHENSION PRACTICE SET

Questions 1 – 3 are based on the passage below.

Among the earliest published literature by African Americans were slave narratives—autobiographical accounts of the lives of slaves who lived primarily in the American South in the early to mid-1800s. These accounts—which included letters, notes, and diaries—often discussed escapes, slave auctions, interactions with plantation owners and abolitionists, and the forced separation of family members, often parents and children. Some of the best-known slave narratives were written by Josiah Henson and Frederick Douglass. In the last three decades, a renewed awareness of the lives of enslaved African Americans has prompted a wave of novels and biographies, sometimes called "neo-slave narratives," in which modern writers such as Toni Morrison and Octavia Butler offer a historical or fictional representation of the lives of slaves.

1. The author would likely consider each of the following a slave narrative EXCEPT:

   (A) an autobiography by a freeborn African American man who lived in New Orleans in the 1830s.
   (B) personal papers of African American field hands who were enslaved in Alabama.
   (C) correspondence between two sisters who were auctioned to different plantation owners in rural Georgia.
   (D) a letter smuggled to an escaped slave from her brother, a slave in South Carolina.
   (E) the diary of a Mississippi slave who was captured while attempting to escape.

2. Consider each of the following choices separately and select all that apply. With which of the following statements would the author be likely to agree?

   [A] No neo-slave narratives were published later than the early to mid-1800s.
   [B] Neo-slave narratives are written primarily by women, while most slave narratives were written by men.
   [C] Some neo-slave narratives are fictional, but all slave narratives are first-hand accounts.

3. The passage provides the most support for which one of the following conclusions?

   Ⓐ The work of abolitionists in the Northern states helped bring about the publication of slave narratives.
   Ⓑ All of the narratives published in the early to mid-1800s were written by slaves living in Southern states.
   Ⓒ Most slave narratives were not published until over a century after they were written.
   Ⓓ In the mid-1900s, fewer people knew about slave narratives than have people in the last ten years.
   Ⓔ Neo-slave narratives such as those by Butler and Morrison have helped to bring attention to slave narratives by earlier writers.

Questions 4 – 6 are based on the passage below.

The problematic relationship between Heidegger's political views and his seminal status as a philosopher is a continuing point of contention in the historical assessment of his achievements. His contributions to Continental philosophy in works such as *Sein und Zeit* have been read, in some circles, through the critical lens of his affiliation with National Socialism in Nazi Germany during the Second World War. His writing during that time covered a broad range of subjects, including philosophy, politics, and aesthetics. His work on ontology directly influenced his contemporary philosophical thinkers, such as Jean-Paul Sartre. Though he is widely regarded within philosophical circles as one of the preeminent luminaries, along with Husserl, in the modern development of ontology, certain scholars and thinkers militate against the value of his thought in its entirety. To regard Heidegger's work highly would be, in their eyes, to absolve him of his support of the politics of Nazism, even though he is being evaluated solely on the basis of his contributions to the study of philosophy and not in any political context.

4. Select the sentence in the passage in which the author summarizes the competing attitudes toward Heidegger within the academic community.

5. Consider each of the following choices separately and select all that apply. The author asserts which of the following about Heidegger?

   [A] Some academics view him positively for both his political and philosophical work.
   [B] His legacy has been affected by opinions he expressed during World War II.
   [C] Some academics view him positively, while others cannot countenance him at all.

6. Which conclusion is implied by the author in his description of the status of Heidegger's legacy?

   (A) Heidegger's work should not be given serious recognition due to his political views.
   (B) The Second World War fostered a climate of intellectual innovation in Europe.
   (C) It is possible to critically evaluate Heidegger's contributions to philosophy while not absolving him of responsibility for his political views.
   (D) Scholars should consider the entire body of work of a thinker, in every field to which he or she contributed, when assessing that thinker's legacy in any one field.
   (E) It is impossible to divorce the study of politics from the study of philosophy.

Questions 7–10 are based on the passage below.

A common misconception is that color refers only to a wavelength of light in the visual spectrum, from about 400 nanometers (violet) to about 700 nanometers (red). When an object reflects light of a given wavelength, we see that object as the corresponding color. So, for example, we might see a Braeburn apple as red and a Granny Smith apple as green because they reflect light of different wavelengths. However, color is not merely a property of an external physical object but rather the result of an interaction among that object, the light that shines on it, and, finally but most significantly, the manner in which the human eye and brain make sense of the reflected light stimulus. Thus, the study of color can properly fall as much within the realm of psychology as that of physics.

Experience is one psychological factor that informs our perception of color. For example, a child eating by a campfire that emits a great deal of yellow light may believe that the melted Cheddar cheese served on white bread on a white paper plate is actually a white cheese like Swiss or Monterey Jack. This occurs because the yellow light reflects off both the plate and the bread, which the child knows are white, and off the cheese, which the child isn't sure about. All the objects therefore appear to be the same color, and the child assumes that color is white. On the other hand, an adult with experience viewing things in firelight would intuitively adjust her perception to account for the yellow light and would not make the same mistake.

Color is also perceived differently depending on its context. The noted abstract painter Josef Albers produced an influential body of work based on this phenomenon, including his series *Homage to the Square* featuring nested squares of different colors. In one psychological experiment testing perception, the letter

X is presented against two colored backgrounds. Although the letter is identical each time it is presented, it appears olive green in one context and lavender in the other context. This effect is achieved when the *X* is given a low-saturation blue color, or gray-blue, and the backgrounds are also low-saturation colors with hues on either side of blue on the color wheel. Because blue falls between purple and green on the color wheel, a gray-blue *X* against a gray-purple background will look gray-green, or olive, and the same *X* against an olive background will look gray-purple, or lavender. In a similar manner, an intermediate color will look different against different primary color backdrops; teal, for instance, will look green against a blue background and blue against a green background.

Other subjective factors also influence the experience of color. These include cultural norms (Westerners most often name blue as their favorite color, whereas in China red is preferred) and simply what we learn about color. Consider that if a child learns that stop signs are "red," the child will call them "red." Another person in that society will also have learned to call stop signs "red." However, whether the two people are experiencing the same color is unknown since that experience exists only in the mind. Therefore, if one were to tell an interior designer that color is an immutable physical property of objects, one would meet with skepticism. Before placing the electric blue sofa in a client's living room, the designer considers the color of light the various light fixtures will emanate, the colors of the carpet and walls, and her client's feelings about electric blue, which after all may not even be the same color in the client's mind as it is in the designer's.

7. Which of the following statements best expresses the main idea of the passage?

   (A) Color is primarily a psychological construct, and therefore the study of physics is not relevant to an understanding of how color is perceived.

   (B) The phenomenon of color is a combined effect of the wavelength of light that shines on an object, the wavelength of light reflected by the object, and the human mind's perception of the light stimulus that comes to the eye.

   (C) Scientists have determined that although people may perceive color differently in different situations, color is an immutable characteristic of objects.

   (D) Creative professionals, such as artists and interior designers, view color significantly differently than do scientists.

   (E) To say that an object is a particular color is meaningless because color is a subjective perception influenced by experience, culture, and context and cannot therefore be ascertained to be a specific physical characteristic.

8. The author would be most likely to agree with which of the following ideas?

   Ⓐ When attempting to achieve a particular aesthetic effect, a graphic designer should consider how the color used for the border of an advertisement will appear next to the color of the text.

   Ⓑ A decorator working for a client in China would not purchase an electric blue sofa for that individual's living room, because blue is not a preferred color in China.

   Ⓒ Companies designing packaging for their products should avoid using gray tones because these would cause different customers to see the colors differently, thereby rendering the brand message inconsistent.

   Ⓓ Because red is a primary color, a wall should not be painted red if a sofa of an intermediate color will be placed against it, as the sofa's color may be distorted by its proximity to the wall.

   Ⓔ Artists often explore the interaction of adjacent colors when juxtaposing different forms in the composition of their paintings.

9. Consider each of the following choices separately and select all that apply. According to the passage, which of the following accurately describes human perception of color?

   Ⓐ A low-saturation color against a low-saturation background of an adjacent hue on the color wheel will appear a similar shade as the other adjacent hue.

   Ⓑ An intermediate color against a background that is one of the intermediate color's component primary colors will be difficult to distinguish from that background.

   Ⓒ Letters written in an intermediate color or in a low-saturation color are more likely to be misread by children than by adults.

10. The author mentions Josef Albers in paragraph 3 in order to

    (A) argue that artists are aware of how humans perceive color and use this phenomenon to enhance the impact of their work.
    (B) illustrate the idea that color is fundamentally a subjective, aesthetic phenomenon rather than a scientific one.
    (C) demonstrate that a child would probably see a painting in the *Homage to the Square* series differently than would an adult.
    (D) explain that humans perceive the color of regular shapes, such as squares, differently than they perceive the color of less regular shapes, such as food on a plate or a letter of the alphabet.
    (E) provide an example that reinforces the importance of the concept that color is a subjective experience manufactured in part within the human mind.

READING COMPREHENSION PRACTICE SET ANSWERS AND EXPLANATIONS

1. A

The first two sentences outline defining characteristics of slave narratives and provide examples of the kind of content they might include. Of the answer choices, the only one that falls outside the scope of the question is **(A)**; slave narratives were written by enslaved people, not by free people. Choices **(B)**, **(C)**, **(D)**, and **(E)** all fit the passage's criteria in terms of subject matter, authorship, and geography; choice **(A)** is the only one that deviates.

2. C

The passage's last sentence tells us that neo-slave narratives have been published in the last three decades, so clearly they have been published more recently than the mid-1800s. Choice **(A)** is incorrect. Although the authors of the slave narratives mentioned are both men and the authors of the neo-slave narratives mentioned are both women, there's no basis for us to conclude that this distinction holds true on a broader scale, **(B)**. Only choice **(C)** addresses a distinction the author draws between slave and neo-slave narratives. The passage supports the statement that all slave narratives were autobiographical, whereas neo-slave narratives may be biographical or fictional.

3. D

This question asks us to evaluate which conclusions follow logically from what the author says. The mention of "renewed awareness" implies a previous lapse or reduction in interest, so **(D)** is a reasonable conclusion. The passage doesn't mention abolitionists or the process that led to the narratives' publication, so **(A)** is out of scope. The language of **(B)** is too extreme; you're told that the narratives were primarily, not completely, authored by slaves from the South. Choice **(C)** directly contradicts the first sentence of the passage. Choice **(E)** reverses the order of events presented in the passage; renewed interest in the narratives led to Butler and Morrison's writing, not the other way around.

4. Though he is widely regarded within philosophical circles as one of the preeminent luminaries, along with Husserl, in the modern development of ontology, certain scholars and thinkers militate against the value of his thought in its entirety.

The sentence you're looking for is one that sums up how the intellectual community, as a whole, views Heidegger. This means the sentence should encompass all parties, both those that are receptive to him and those that view him negatively. The second sentence, "His contributions to Continental philosophy in works such as *Sein und Zeit* have been read, in some circles, through the critical lens of his affiliation with National Socialism in Nazi Germany during the Second World War," may be tempting, but this is telling you the way in which his work has been interpreted, not the reactions or attitudes of the academic community. It also doesn't mention any "competing" feelings toward his work. The last sentence provides justification for *why* certain scholars view him as they do, but it does not account for the other schools of thought. The next-to-last sentence, "Though he is widely regarded within philosophical circles as one of the preeminent luminaries, along with Husserl, in the modern development of ontology, certain scholars and thinkers militate against the value of his thought in its entirety," sums up the complete range of reaction to Heidegger across the academic community.

5. B, C

Choice **(A)** is incorrect. The author nowhere explicitly states or implies that anyone has a positive reaction to Heidegger's political views. She only intimates that scholars working in the study of philosophy have been influenced by his work in that field. Choice **(B)** is correct because the author states that Heidegger's work, even in philosophy, has been viewed through this "critical lens." Answer choice **(C)** is also correct. The author cites philosophers, such as Sartre, who have reacted positively to Heidegger's philosophy and asserts that those who view him negatively do so because they cannot abide absolving him of guilt for his support of the Nazis.

6. C

This question asks you to engage the text at a deep level and to infer what the author is suggesting. It is important to pay close attention to the author's tone. The passage's main idea is the evaluation of a thinker's body of work by academic scholars in different fields. The author points out both Heidegger's tremendous accomplishments in the field of philosophy and his less-than-admirable involvement with the Nazi party. Choice **(B)** is dealt with nowhere in the passage. Choice **(E)** goes beyond the scope of the passage. Choice **(A)** is incorrect, because the author emphasizes Heidegger's influence on philosophers like Sartre and makes certain to point out that it is in "their eyes" that Heidegger is so viewed, not the author's own. Choice **(D)** is incorrect because it is the opposite of what the author implies. Choice **(C)** is the correct answer because, in the last sentence of the passage, the author stresses that it is only Heidegger's contributions to philosophy that are being considered, not his political views. The author seems to be suggesting that the two can be judged apart from one another.Part Two

7. B

In the first paragraph, the author states that color is not only a function of wavelength, and then the keyword "However" signals what color actually is: "not merely" a physical property "but rather" the product of an interaction among the object's properties (specifically, how it reflects light), the light itself, and the human observer. The rest of the passage elaborates on this interaction of the physical properties of light and the perception of light. Answer choice **(B)** states this idea and is correct.

Choice **(A)** is extreme because of the words "primarily" in the first part and "not relevant" in the second part; in the last sentence of paragraph 1, the author says the study of color is appropriate for both psychology and physics. The word "immutable" in choice **(C)** means "unchanging" and thus directly contradicts the main idea of the passage, which is that color is a construct of multiple factors and these factors can vary for any given object. Choice **(D)** might be inferred from the passage, but this is not the main point of the passage, which is about the nature of color and not about people's reactions to color. Choice **(E)** is extreme due to the word "meaningless." Although objects may appear different colors to different people under different conditions, and one can never be sure what another person means by the word *red*, the author never says it is without meaning to, for example, describe an apple as red.

8. A

To prepare to answer this Inference question, review the points the author has made in the passage. The correct answer must be true given what the author has said. In paragraph 3, the author states that the color of an object changes depending on nearby colors. Therefore, answer choice **(A)** is supported.

Choice **(B)** misuses the detail that blue is not the favorite color of most Chinese. This does not mean that no Chinese person would like an electric blue sofa—after all, most people own objects of many colors, including colors that are not their favorite—and some Chinese people may prefer blue. Choice **(C)** is not supported. Using low-saturation or grayish tones next to each other can result in colors looking different than they would in isolation or next to other colors, but it does not result in different people perceiving the colors differently. Choice **(D)** is a distortion. The passage states that an item of an intermediate color that is placed near a color-wheel-adjacent primary color, such as orange placed near red, will look more like the primary color on the other side of it (orange next to red will look more yellow). Nothing suggests this effect is undesirable, so choice **(D)**'s "should not" is unsupported. Also, the passage only discusses the interaction of intermediate and primary colors that are next to each other on the color wheel, but this answer choice refers to any intermediate color being placed next to red. Finally, although one artist, Josef Albers, worked with color in this way, the passage does not suggest that artists in general "often" do this, and choice **(E)** is incorrect.

9. A

"According to the passage" signals a Detail question. Research each answer choice to determine whether it matches an idea stated in the passage. Choice **(A)** is stated in paragraph 3, as shown by the example of gray-blue looking either gray-blue or gray-green when placed against a background of the other color. Answer choice **(B)** is a 180, or the opposite of what is true. An intermediate color placed next a component primary color will look more like the other component primary color, thus contrasting more sharply. Choice **(C)** is incorrect. According to paragraph 2, children may interpret colors differently than do adults because children lack experience interpreting color under different lighting conditions, but this has nothing to do with intermediate or low-saturation colors.

10. E

"In order to" signals a Logic question. It is asking why the author included Albers in the passage. Review your passage map. It should note that the author's overall purpose is to explain why color is as much psychological construct as physical property. Then the main idea of paragraph 3, where Albers is mentioned, is that people see color differently depending on context. Thus, paragraph 3 is about a particular aspect of how color is a psychological construct. The author must mention Albers to support this idea, and answer choice **(E)** correctly states this.

The author is not making an argument about artists, so **(A)** is out. Choice **(B)** is incorrect because the author says in paragraph 1 that color does result in part from the physical properties of light and can properly be studied by physicists; the author does not mention Albers to say that color is solely a nonscientific phenomenon. **(C)** uses an idea from paragraph 2; this is not the point being made in paragraph 3. **(D)** states a comparison between different types of shapes that the passage never makes.

CHAPTER 5

Text Completion

INTRODUCTION TO TEXT COMPLETION

In the Text Completion question type, you will be asked to select one entry for each blank from the corresponding column of choices. Each question may include as many as three blanks.

You will find about six Text Completion questions in each Verbal Reasoning section. In each of these questions, one or more words from the sentence will be missing. This question type tests your ability to read critically—to recognize the point of the sentence and find the best word(s) to fit this meaning.

The directions for Text Completion will look like this:

> Each sentence below has one or more blanks, each blank indicating that something has been omitted. Beneath the sentence are five words for one-blank questions and sets of three words for each blank for two- and three-blank questions. Choose the word or set of words for each blank that best fits the meaning of the sentence as a whole.

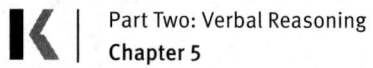

A Text Completion question with one blank will look like this:

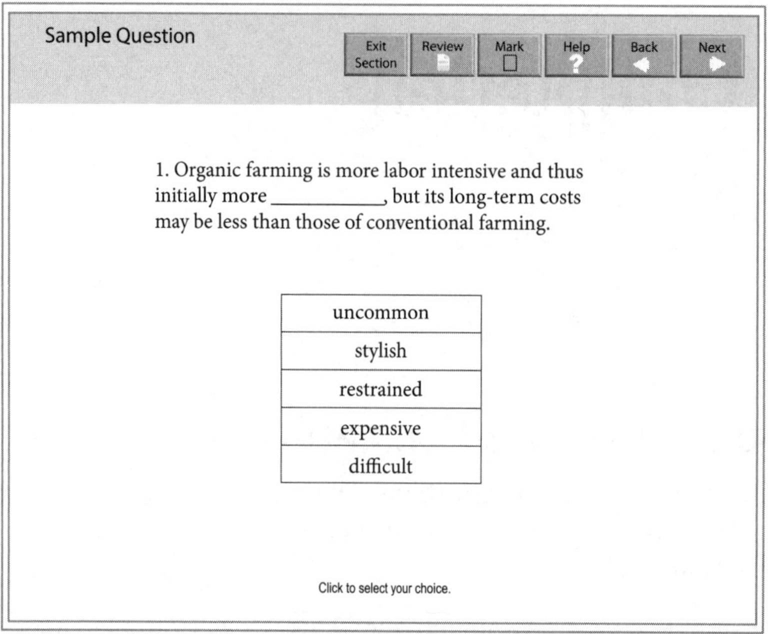

A Text Completion question with two blanks will look like this:

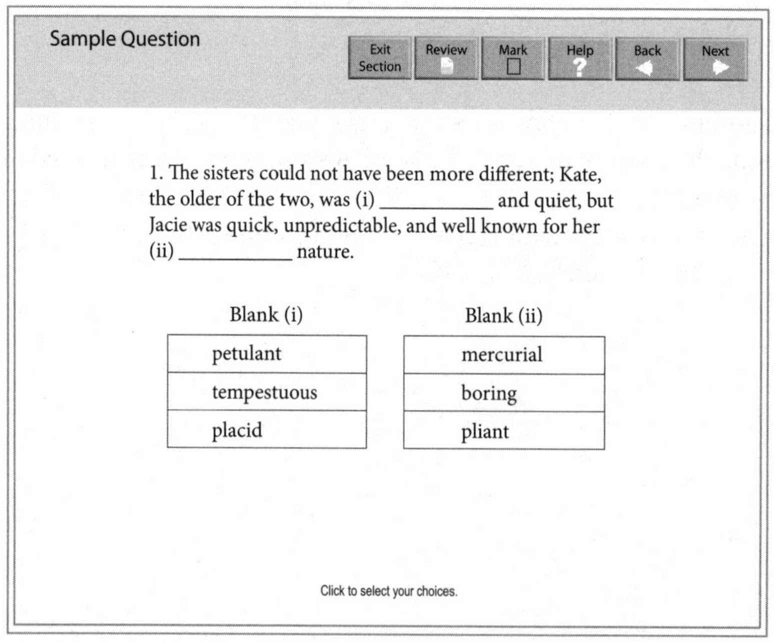

A Text Completion question with three blanks will look like this:

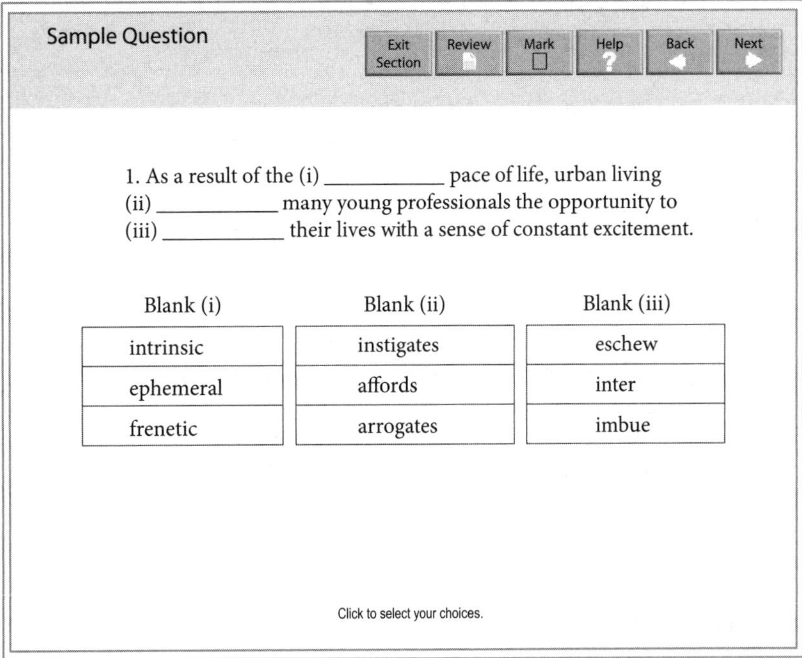

THE KAPLAN METHOD FOR TEXT COMPLETION (ONE-BLANK)

STEP 1 **Read the sentence, looking for clues.**

STEP 2 **Predict an answer.**

STEP 3 **Select the choice that most closely matches your prediction.**

STEP 4 **Check your answer.**

HOW THE KAPLAN METHOD FOR TEXT COMPLETION (ONE-BLANK) WORKS

Now let's discuss how the Kaplan Method will help you answer these questions correctly.

STEP 1

Read the sentence, looking for clues.

There are always clues in the sentence that will point you to the right answer. The missing words in Text Completion questions will usually have a relationship with key words in the sentence. Key words and key phrases are descriptors that lead to the meaning of the missing words.

A road sign is a structural key word that signals a connection between ideas; it also determines the direction of the relationship. There are road signs in the GRE that tell you to go straight ahead and those that tell you to take a detour. A semicolon also functions as a road sign, indicating a close connection between two clauses.

"Straight-ahead" road signs are used to make one part of the sentence support or elaborate upon another part. They continue the sentence in the same direction. The positive or negative connotation of what follows is not changed by these clues.

"Detour" road signs change the direction of the sentence. They make one part of the sentence contradict or qualify another part. The positive or negative connotation of an answer is changed by these clues.

Review the following examples of road signs. Interpreting the road sign will help you to determine which way the sentence is going and predict what words will best complete the blanks.

Straight-ahead road signs:	Detour road signs:
And	*But*
Since	*Despite*
Also	*Yet*
Thus	*However*
Because	*Unless*
; (semicolon)	*Rather*
Likewise	*Although*
Moreover	*While*
Similarly	*On the other hand*
In addition	*Unfortunately*
Consequently	*Nonetheless*
	Conversely

STEP 2

Predict an answer.

Once you've found the road sign and the key word(s) relevant to the blank, predict an answer for the blank. Your prediction does not have to be a sophisticated or complex word or phrase; it just needs to be a paraphrase that logically fits into the sentence. By predicting, you avoid the temptation of trying every answer choice on its own, which can take up valuable time on Test Day.

STEP 3

Select the choice that most closely matches your prediction.

Quickly go through the choices, see which one most closely matches, and eliminate whichever choices do not fit your prediction. If none of the choices match your prediction, reread the question and revisit Steps 1 and 2.

STEP 4

Check your answer.

This step is simply double-checking that you did your work correctly and that your answer choice is correct in context. If your answer makes sense when you read your choice back into the sentence, you can confirm and move on. If your choice does not make sense when you read it back into the sentence, you should reread the question and revisit Steps 1–3.

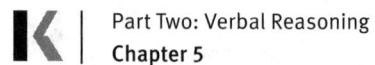

How to Apply the Kaplan Method for Text Completion (One-Blank)

Now let's apply the Kaplan Method to a Text Completion (One-Blank) question:

> The yearly financial statement of a large corporation may seem ________ at first, but the persistent reader soon finds its pages of facts and figures easy to decipher.
>
> (A) bewildering
> (B) surprising
> (C) inviting
> (D) misguided
> (E) uncoordinated

STEP 1

Read the sentence, looking for clues.

The sentence contains the detour road sign *but*, which indicates that the correct answer will mean the opposite of another key word or key phrase in the sentence. The key phrase to note in this example is "easy to decipher."

STEP 2

Predict an answer.

Knowing that the blank must contrast with the phrase "easy to decipher," you can predict that the missing word will be similar to "difficult to understand."

STEP 3

Select the choice that most closely matches your prediction.

Quickly go through the choices and see which one most closely matches "difficult to understand," which in this case is choice **(A)** *bewildering*.

STEP 4

Check your answer.

Plugging the word *bewildering* into the sentence fits the context: "The yearly financial statement of a large corporation may seem *bewildering* at first, but the persistent reader soon finds its pages of facts and figures easy to decipher."

Now let's apply the Kaplan Method to a second Text Completion (One-Blank) question:

Although the initial cost of installing solar panels to produce electricity can be ________, the financial benefits are realized for years to come in the form of reduced electric bills.

Ⓐ encouraging
Ⓑ minimal
Ⓒ exciting
Ⓓ misleading
Ⓔ exorbitant

STEP 1

Read the sentence, looking for clues.

The sentence contains the detour road sign *although*, which indicates that the correct answer will mean the opposite of a key word or key phrase in the sentence. The key phrase to note in this example is "reduced electric bills."

STEP 2

Predict an answer.

Knowing that the blank must contrast with the phrase "reduced electric bills," you can predict that the correct answer will be similar to "increased or high payments or costs."

STEP 3

Select the choice that most closely matches your prediction.

Quickly go through the five choices and see which one most closely matches "increased or high payments or costs," which in this case is choice **(E)** *exorbitant*.

STEP 4

Check your answer.

Plugging the word *exorbitant* into the sentence fits the context: "Although the initial cost of installing solar panels to produce electricity can be *exorbitant*, the financial benefits are realized for years to come in the form of reduced electric bills."

THE KAPLAN METHOD FOR TEXT COMPLETION (TWO-BLANK AND THREE-BLANK)

STEP 1 **Read the sentence, looking for clues.**

STEP 2 **Predict an answer for the easier/easiest blank.**

STEP 3 **Select the choice that most closely matches your prediction.**

STEP 4 **Predict and select for the remaining blanks.**

STEP 5 **Check your answers.**

HOW THE KAPLAN METHOD FOR TEXT COMPLETION (TWO-BLANK AND THREE-BLANK) WORKS

Now let's discuss how the Kaplan Method for Text Completion changes when there are multiple blanks.

STEP 1

Read the sentence, looking for clues.

This step is the same.

STEP 2

Predict an answer for the easier/easiest blank.

Instead of immediately making a prediction for the first blank, take a moment to identify the easier/easiest blank to work with. Once you've found the road sign and the key word(s) relevant to the easier/easiest blank, predict an answer for that blank.

STEP 3

Select the choice that most closely matches your prediction.

This step is the same.

STEP 4

Predict and select for the remaining blanks.

Once you have completed the easier/easiest blank, you have more context in which to interpret the remaining blanks.

For two-blank Text Completions, use the context to help you choose the answer for the remaining blank. If the answers for the second blank are not working out, you know you need to go back to Step 2.

For three-blank Text Completions, repeat Steps 2 and 3 for the next easiest blank. You now have two completed blanks to provide context for the last, most difficult blank. This way, your approach to two- and three-blank questions is just a logical extension of your approach to one-blank questions.

STEP 5

Check your answers.

This step is the same.

How to Apply the Kaplan Method for Text Completion (Two-Blank and Three-Blank)

Now let's apply the Kaplan Method to a Text Completion (Two-Blank) question:

> Everyone believed the team was favored with athletic talent and a seasoned, successful coaching staff; consequently, it was difficult to (i) ________ why the team was (ii) ________ so badly against one of the worst teams in the division.

Blank (i)	Blank (ii)
A fathom	D elevating
B interpolate	E dominating
C explore	F floundering

STEP 1

Read the sentence, looking for clues.

In this sentence, the straight-ahead road sign "consequently" indicates that the correct answer will support or elaborate on another word or phrase in the text. The key word to note in this example is "badly."

STEP 2

Predict an answer for the easier/easiest blank.

Knowing that the second blank must support or elaborate on the phrase "so badly," you can predict that the correct answer will be similar to "not doing very well."

STEP 3

Select the answer choice that most closely matches your prediction.

Quickly go through the three choices and see which one most closely matches "not doing very well," which, in this case, is choice **(F)** *floundering*.

STEP 4

Predict and select for the remaining blanks.

Once you have completed the easier blank, you have a context in which to interpret the remaining missing word.

For the remaining blank, select the choice that will most logically complete the sentence. The first clause in the sentence indicates that the team should be good. However, the team is doing poorly, and this is "difficult" for everyone because it does not make sense. In other words, it is hard to understand. The answer choice most like "understand" is **(A)** *fathom.*

STEP 5

Check your answers.

Plugging the selected words into the sentence fits the context: "Everyone believed the team was favored with athletic talent and a seasoned, successful coaching staff; consequently, it was difficult to *fathom* why the team was *floundering* so badly against one of the worst teams in the division."

Now let's apply the Kaplan Method to a Text Completion (Three-Blank) question:

> It seemed there would be no resolving the matter since both sides felt they had reached an (i) _______; neither side would (ii) _______, and the resulting (iii) _______ would keep their relationship strained and fragile for years to come.

Blank (i)	
A	apogee
B	epiphany
C	impasse

Blank (ii)	
D	capitulate
E	regress
F	impugn

Blank (iii)	
G	acrimony
H	cacophony
I	sinecure

STEP 1

Read the sentence, looking for clues.

In this sentence, there are clues in the phrases "no resolving the matter" and "strained and fragile," which, along with the straight-ahead road signs "since" and "and," suggest that the correct answers are going to describe or support a conflict between disagreeing parties. In this example, you may already sense the words that complete at least one of the blanks just from the construction of the sentence.

STEP 2

Predict an answer for the easier/easiest blank.

Determine that the answer for the first blank must support or elaborate on the phrase "no resolving the matter."

STEP 3

Select the answer choice that most closely matches your prediction.

Quickly go through the choices and see which one most closely matches "no resolving the matter." You can predict the answer will be **(C)** *impasse.*

STEP 4

Predict and select for the remaining blanks.

For the remaining blanks, select the choice that will most logically complete the sentence. The sentence tells us the sides are at an *impasse*, or blocked path. Predict the answers for the second and third blanks by thinking how groups at an impasse would feel and act. Determine that they are not willing to **(D)** *capitulate*, or give in on their demands, and that the result would be **(G)** *acrimony*, or bitter feelings, between the two sides.

STEP 5

Check your answers.

Plugging the words *impasse*, *capitulate*, and *acrimony* into the sentence fits the context: "It seemed there would be no resolving the matter since both sides felt they had reached an *impasse*; neither side would *capitulate*, and the resulting *acrimony* would keep their relationship strained and fragile for years to come."

KAPLAN'S ADDITIONAL TIPS FOR TEXT COMPLETION QUESTIONS

Look for what's directly implied and not an ambiguous interpretation

The questions you'll encounter are written in sophisticated but still logical and straightforward prose. Therefore, the correct answer is the one most directly implied by the meanings of the words in the sentence. These sentences are constructed to allow you to identify the answer using the inferential strategies you just practiced.

Don't be too creative

Read the sentence literally, not imaginatively. Pay attention to the meaning of the words instead of to any associations or feelings that might come up for you.

Paraphrase long or complex sentences

You may encounter a sentence that, because of its length or structure, is hard to get a handle on. When faced with a complex sentence, slow down and put it in your own words. You could break it into pieces as well and tackle one phrase at a time.

Use word roots

In the GRE Resources section at the back of this book, you can learn the Latin and Greek roots of many common GRE words. If you can't figure out the meaning of a word, take a look at its root to try to get close to its meaning. Etymology can often provide clues to meaning, especially when you couple a root definition with the word in context.

TEXT COMPLETION PRACTICE SET

Try the following Text Completion questions using the Kaplan Method for Text Completion. If you're up to the challenge, time yourself; on Test Day, you'll want to spend only 1 to 1.5 minutes on each question, depending on the number of blanks.

1. The young man always had to have the last word; he would rather be disliked than ________.

   (A) gainsaid
   (B) selfish
   (C) remembered
   (D) praised
   (E) different

2. The giant squid's massive body, adapted for deep-sea life, breaks apart in the reduced pressures of shallower ocean depths, making the search for an intact specimen one of the most ________ quests in all of marine biology.

   (A) meaningful
   (B) elusive
   (C) popular
   (D) expensive
   (E) profitable

3. Although well built and well kept, the little brick house seemed (i) ________ compared to the ornate, almost (ii)________ new house beside it.

Blank (i)		Blank (ii)	
A	impressive	D	translucent
B	dilapidated	E	diminutive
C	desirable	F	ostentatious

4. The (i) ________ gave such an impassioned speech that even the most forlorn members of the crowd were briefly moved to (ii) ________.

Blank (i)		Blank (ii)	
A	orator	D	despair
B	miscreant	E	duress
C	interloper	F	ebullience

5. His explosive, rude remarks convinced many that he was (i) ________ and of (ii) ________ character, suddenly making his future as a politician seem (iii) ________.

Blank (i)		Blank (ii)		Blank (iii)	
A	indifferent	D	courageous	G	guaranteed
B	charming	E	virtuous	H	precarious
C	volatile	F	ignoble	I	facetious

TEXT COMPLETION PRACTICE SET ANSWERS AND EXPLANATIONS

1. A

The semicolon between these clauses is a straight-ahead road sign; these two ideas are closely related or elaborate upon each other. Since the blank is in the second clause, look to the first for direction. There you discover that this person always has to be right or have the last word in an argument. The second clause will be consistent with this notion; it explains just how much he needs to have the last word. He would rather be disliked than have what happen? A good prediction would be: "He'd rather be disliked than contradicted."

Choice **(A)** *gainsaid* matches the prediction, but look at the others just to be sure. Scanning the other choices quickly, you see that all of the remaining options do not support the first part of the sentence. None of these other choices reinforces the idea that he always has to be right, so even if you aren't familiar with the word *gainsaid*, you can still get the right answer.

2. B

The key word here is "intact," which means that although specimens have been collected, they have rarely (if ever) been in one piece when recovered. You can fairly assume that recovering an intact specimen is difficult. When you look for a synonym for "difficult" in the answer choices, you recognize *elusive* **(B)** as your answer.

3. B, F

In this case, the second blank is easier to predict than the first, so start with that one. The word "almost" before the second blank tells you the correct choice will be a word that means nearly the same as "ornate." Something *ostentatious* is considered showy, excessive, or ornate, so the correct choice is **(F)**.

There are several road signs, key words, and phrases in this sentence that give clues. "Although" with "compared" tells you there is something different about the two houses. The detour road sign "although" allows us to predict that the choice in the first blank will have a meaning opposite to "ornate" and will be close in meaning to "plain." Such a condition is not considered *impressive* **(A)** or *desirable* **(C)**, so the correct choice is **(B)** *dilapidated*.

4. A, F

The key phrase for the first blank is "impassioned speech." You can tell the correct answer for the first blank is someone who can speak expressively. *Miscreants* **(B)** and *interlopers* **(C)** are not necessarily excellent speakers, but *orators* are. The correct choice is **(A)**.

For the second blank, the key phrase here is "even the most forlorn"; "even" works as a detour road sign, and "forlorn" is negative, so you want a positive term. Since *despair* **(D)** and *duress* **(E)** are not positive, the answer is **(F)** *ebullience.*

5. C, F, H

For the first blank, the key phrase is "explosive, rude remarks." Choice **(A)** *indifferent* suggests neutrality, but being explosive and rude is far from being neutral. The second choice, *charming* **(B)**, does not make sense because someone who is "explosive" and "rude" is not seen as being charming. Choice **(C)** *volatile* means "unstable," the same as "explosive."

Since we know the subject of the sentence is explosive, rude, and volatile, we can predict his character will be seen in negative ways. Because *courageous* and *virtuous* have positive connotations, choice **(F)** *ignoble* is the correct choice.

With the information that he is explosive, rude, volatile, and ignoble, predict what kind of "future as a politician" he will have. This is the key phrase for identifying the third blank. His character suggests he is not popular, so we can conclude his future is not **(G)** *guaranteed.* Choice **(I)** *facetious* means "flippant," which does not make sense as a description of the politician's future. Choice **(H)** *precarious* means "uncertain," which fits the context of the sentence and is the correct choice.

CHAPTER 6

Sentence Equivalence

INTRODUCTION TO SENTENCE EQUIVALENCE

Each Verbal Reasoning section features approximately four Sentence Equivalence questions. In each sentence, one word will be missing, and you must identify two correct words to complete the sentence. The correct answer choices, when used in the sentence, will result in the same meaning for *both* sentences. This question type tests your ability to figure out how a sentence should be completed by using the meaning of the entire sentence.

The directions for Sentence Equivalence will look like this:

> Select the **two** answer choices that, when inserted into the sentence, fit the meaning of the sentence as a whole **and** yield complete sentences that are similar in meaning.

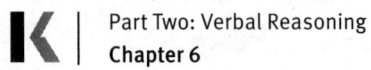

A Sentence Equivalence question will look like this:

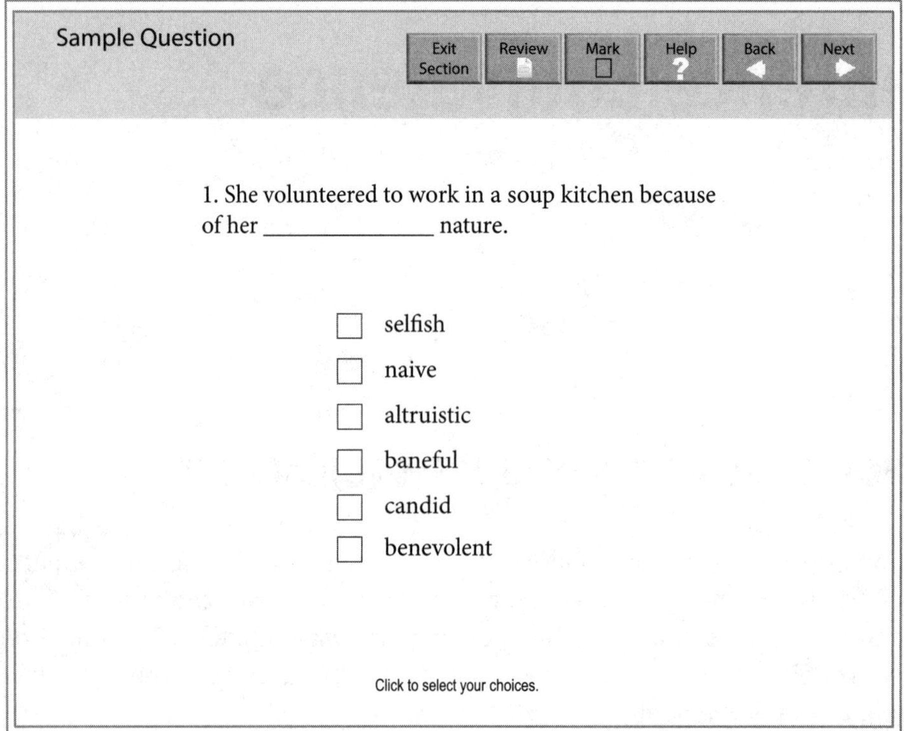

THE KAPLAN METHOD FOR SENTENCE EQUIVALENCE

STEP 1 **Read the sentence, looking for clues.**

STEP 2 **Predict an answer.**

STEP 3 **Select the two choices that most closely match your prediction.**

STEP 4 **Check your answers to see if the sentence retains the same meaning.**

How the Kaplan Method for Sentence Equivalence Works

Now let's discuss how the Kaplan Method will help you answer these questions correctly.

STEP 1

Read the sentence, looking for clues.

As you read the sentence, pay attention to the part of speech that the answer choice will be and compare it with the answer choices. Also look for specific words in the sentence that will help you to understand its meaning. These are called "key words" or "road signs"—descriptive phrases or contextual clues that suggest the meaning of the missing word.

Words that connect one part of a sentence to another ("straight-ahead" road signs) include the following:

And
Since
Also
Thus
Because
; (semicolon)
Likewise
Moreover
Similarly
In addition
Consequently

Words that indicate one part of the sentence contradicts another part of the sentence ("detour" road signs) include these:

But
Despite
Yet
However
Unless
Rather
Although
While
On the other hand
Unfortunately
Nonetheless
Conversely

Being aware of these road signs will help you to figure out the meaning of the sentence and the relationship of the missing word to other ideas in the sentence.

STEP 2

Predict an answer.

Once you have read the sentence and identified clues to words that will complete the sentence, predict an answer. Your prediction should be a word that you choose on your own *before* you look at the answer choices. The prediction word should also be a simple word that logically completes the sentence.

STEP 3

Select the two choices that most closely match your prediction.

Quickly review the six answer choices and choose the two words that, when plugged into the sentence, most closely make the intended meaning of the sentence match your prediction. Eliminate the answer choices that do not fit your prediction. Sometimes you will need to adjust your prediction in order to find two answer choices that match each other.

STEP 4

Check your answers to see if the sentence retains the same meaning.

Read the sentence with each answer choice plugged in to check that you have selected the correct answers. Make sure that both answer choices make sense in the context of the sentence. Pay close attention to the charge of a word's meaning. For example, "dislike" and "despise" both mean the same thing, but "despise" has a much *stronger* degree of charge to that meaning. Each sentence should have the same meaning. If one or both of your answers do not make sense when you reread the sentence, revisit the question and repeat Steps 1, 2, and 3.

How to Apply the Kaplan Method for Sentence Equivalence

Now let's apply the Kaplan Method to a Sentence Equivalence question.

1. She volunteered to work in a soup kitchen because of her ____________ nature.

   [A] selfish
   [B] naive
   [C] altruistic
   [D] baneful
   [E] candid
   [F] benevolent

STEP 1

Read the sentence, looking for clues.

One way to determine the correct answer in this sentence is to figure out the part of speech of the missing word. The missing word in this sentence is an adjective because it modifies the noun "nature." Another clue in this sentence is the key word "volunteer." A volunteer is someone who offers her time or skills without pay. The blank will be an adjective with a positive connotation that describes the type of person who volunteers.

STEP 2

Predict an answer.

Knowing that the blank must describe someone who offers her time or skills without pay, you can predict that the correct answer will be similar to "helpful."

STEP 3

Select the two choices that most closely match your prediction.

Quickly review the six answer choices to see which two words most closely match "helpful," which in this case are choice **(C)** *altruistic* and choice **(F)** *benevolent.*

STEP 4

Check your answers to see if the sentence retains the same meaning.

Plug each answer choice into the sentence to see if it matches the context. Make sure that each sentence has the same meaning:

> "She volunteered to work in a soup kitchen because of her altruistic nature."
>
> "She volunteered to work in a soup kitchen because of her benevolent nature."

Now let's apply the Kaplan Method to a second Sentence Equivalence question.

2. While the first speaker at the conference was confusing and unclear, the second speaker was ________.

   A articulate
   B experienced
   C melancholy
   D ambiguous
   E eloquent
   F vociferous

STEP 1

Read the sentence, looking for clues.

In this sentence, the clue word "while" is a detour road sign. "While" indicates that the second part of the sentence will mean the opposite of the first part of the sentence. The first speaker was described as "confusing" and "unclear," which are the key words in this question. The correct answer means the opposite.

STEP 2

Predict an answer.

Knowing that the blank will mean the opposite of "confusing" and "unclear," you can predict that correct answers will be similar to "clear."

STEP 3

Select the two choices that most closely match your prediction.

Quickly go through the six answer choices and see which two words most closely match "clear" in the context of speaking. In this case, these are choice **(A)** *articulate* and choice **(E)** *eloquent*.

STEP 4

Check your answers to see if the sentence retains the same meaning.

Plug each answer choice into the sentence to see if it matches the context. Make sure that each sentence has the same meaning:

> "While the first speaker at the conference was confusing and unclear, the second speaker was <u>articulate</u>."

> "While the first speaker at the conference was confusing and unclear, the second speaker was <u>eloquent</u>."

KAPLAN'S ADDITIONAL TIPS FOR SENTENCE EQUIVALENCE

Consider all answer choices.

Make sure to read and check all answer choices in the sentence before making your final choice. An answer may fit well in the sentence and closely match your prediction, but if there is no other answer choice that also completes the sentence with the same meaning, it isn't correct.

Paraphrase the question.

If you rephrase a difficult or longer sentence into your own words, it will be easier to make a prediction for the answer. Paraphrasing will also make sure that you understand the meaning of the sentence.

Look beyond synonyms.

Simply finding a synonym pair in the answer choices will not always lead you to the correct answer. Answer choices may include a pair of words that are synonyms but do not fit in the context of the sentence. Both of those two choices will be incorrect. The meaning of each sentence must be the same *and* correct. Be sure to try both words in the sentence, checking that each sentence has the same meaning, before making your final choice.

Use prefixes, suffixes, and roots.

Think about the meaning of the prefixes, suffixes, and roots in words that you know if you are struggling to figure out the definition of a word.

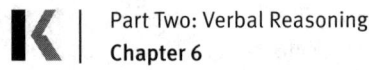

SENTENCE EQUIVALENCE PRACTICE SET

Try the following Sentence Equivalence questions using the Kaplan Method for Sentence Equivalence. If you're up to the challenge, time yourself; on Test Day, you'll want to spend only about one minute on each question.

1. He was unable to move his arm after the stroke; in addition, the stroke ____________ his ability to speak.

   [A] appeased
   [B] satisfied
   [C] impeded
   [D] helped
   [E] hindered
   [F] assisted

2. Although the lab assistant openly apologized for allowing the samples to spoil, her ____________ did not appease the research head, and she was let go.

   [A] insincerity
   [B] frankness
   [C] falsehoods
   [D] candor
   [E] inexperience
   [F] hesitation

3. Afterward the deceased man's wife could not stop crying; his daughter was similarly ____________.

   [A] overjoyed
   [B] morose
   [C] abashed
   [D] lucid
   [E] nonplussed
   [F] dolorous

4. Her last-minute vacation was ____________ compared to her usual trips, which are planned down to the last detail.

   [A] expensive
   [B] spontaneous
   [C] predictable
   [D] satisfying
   [E] impulsive
   [F] atrocious

5. After staying up all night, she felt extremely ____________; however, she still ran three miles with her friends.

   [A] apprehensive
   [B] lethargic
   [C] controversial
   [D] sluggish
   [E] vigorous
   [F] energetic

SENTENCE EQUIVALENCE PRACTICE SET ANSWERS AND EXPLANATIONS

1. C, E

The straight-ahead road sign "in addition" in this sentence is a clue that both parts of the sentence are related. Since the missing word is in the second part of the sentence, the first part gives a clue to what your prediction should be. The person had a stroke and was unable to move his arm.

Use this to make a prediction such as "He was unable to move his arm after the stroke; in addition, it prevented his ability to speak."

Quickly review the answer choices, looking for two words that closely match your prediction. Choices **(C)** *impeded* and **(E)** *hindered* both have the meaning "to interfere with" and produce sentences with equivalent meaning. The other four choices do not have meanings anywhere close to "prevented." Choices **(A)** *appeased*, **(B)** *satisfied*, **(D)** *helped*, and **(F)** *assisted* all have too positive a connotation to be correct. *Appeased* has the same meaning as *satisfied*, and *helped* and *assisted* both mean "to aid."

2. B, D

The clue in this sentence is the detour road sign "although," which indicates contrast. Her "open" apology would be expected to "appease" her boss, but she was fired anyway; paraphrasing further, she did something good but suffered bad consequences. The word in the blank will express the good thing she did, so you can predict that the correct answers will be similar to "honesty." Choices **(A)**, **(C)**, **(E)**, and **(F)** are not synonyms for "honesty," leaving choices **(B)** and **(D)**. **(B)** *frankness* and **(D)** *candor* both carry the meaning of "forthright." They're your answers.

3. B, F

The word "similarly" in this sentence is a straight-ahead road sign that you can use to figure out the blank. It indicates that the sentence will continue to move in the same direction. In the sentence, the wife was crying, and her daughter felt the same way.

Use this to make a prediction such as "Afterward, the late man's wife could not stop crying; his daughter was similarly sad."

Quickly review the answer choices, looking for a match. Both **(B)** *morose* and **(F)** *dolorous* fit the sentence and mean the same thing. Choice **(A)** *overjoyed* is the opposite of "sad," so it does not make sense. Someone who feels *abashed*, choice **(C)**, is embarrassed. A *lucid* person, choice **(D)**, is very clearheaded, and *nonplussed* **(E)** means perplexed.

4. B, E

The phrase "compared to her usual trips" is a clue that the first half of the sentence will have an opposite meaning to the second half; that is, her "last-minute" vacation was apparently *not planned in detail.*

You can use this phrase to make a prediction such as: "Her last-minute vacation was unplanned compared to her usual trips, which are planned down to the last detail."

Something that is unplanned is done without much preparation or careful thought. Both choice **(B)** and choice **(E)** match this prediction. Choice **(B)** *spontaneous* means something that happens without planning, and choice **(E)** *impulsive* means doing something without careful thought. Choice **(A)** *expensive* doesn't fit with "unplanned," nor does **(C)** *predictable* (the opposite), **(D)** *satisfying*, or **(F)** *atrocious*.

5. B, D

When someone stays up all night, she is usually very tired. The detour road sign in this sentence is "however" in the second clause. It indicates that the person in the sentence went running, which takes a lot of energy, even though she was up all night.

You can use this clue to make a prediction such as "After staying up all night, she felt extremely tired; however, she still ran three miles with her friends."

Scan the answer choices, looking for a match. You will find it in **(B)** *lethargic* and **(D)** *sluggish*, both of which mean "tired." Choices **(E)** *vigorous* and **(F)** *energetic* are the opposite of "tired." Choice **(A)** *apprehensive* can be used to describe someone who is anxious but not someone who is tired. Choice **(C)** *controversial* can be used to describe something that is open to debate.

CHAPTER 7

Reading Comprehension

INTRODUCTION TO READING COMPREHENSION

Reading Comprehension is the only question type that appears on all major standardized tests, and with good reason. No matter what academic discipline you pursue, making sense of densely written material is a core skill necessary for success in graduate school. That's why Reading Comprehension passages are on the GRE—to test this skill. Fittingly, ETS adapts its content from actual, graduate-level documents. The GRE traditionally takes its topics from four disciplines: social sciences, biological sciences, physical sciences, and the arts and humanities.

There are roughly 10 reading passages and 20 questions spread between the two Verbal Reasoning sections of the GRE. Some passages are only one paragraph in length, while others are longer. Each passage is then followed by one to six questions that will require you to perform one or more of the following skills: ascertain a passage's scope and purpose, consider what inferences can properly be drawn from the statements in a passage, research details in the text, understand the meaning of words and the function of sentences in context, and analyze the assumptions inherent in an argument.

Because the number of questions for each passage varies, there will always be a sentence introducing the passage that tells you exactly how many questions are associated with the passage. Here is an example of an introductory sentence and the passage that follows; these appear on the left of your screen. The first question about the passage also appears, on the right.

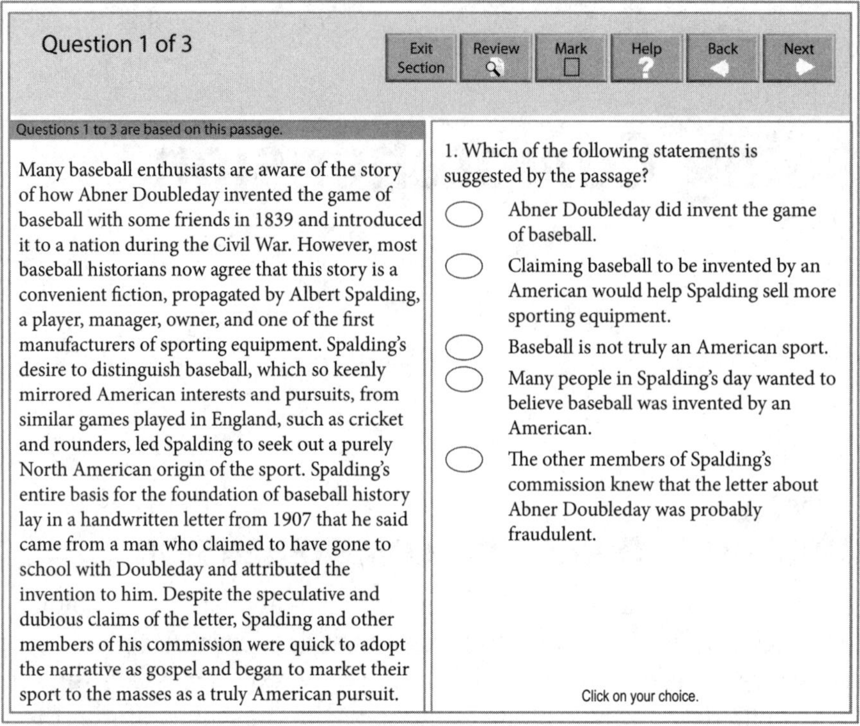
Question 1 of 3

Exit Section | Review | Mark | Help | Back | Next

Questions 1 to 3 are based on this passage.

Many baseball enthusiasts are aware of the story of how Abner Doubleday invented the game of baseball with some friends in 1839 and introduced it to a nation during the Civil War. However, most baseball historians now agree that this story is a convenient fiction, propagated by Albert Spalding, a player, manager, owner, and one of the first manufacturers of sporting equipment. Spalding's desire to distinguish baseball, which so keenly mirrored American interests and pursuits, from similar games played in England, such as cricket and rounders, led Spalding to seek out a purely North American origin of the sport. Spalding's entire basis for the foundation of baseball history lay in a handwritten letter from 1907 that he said came from a man who claimed to have gone to school with Doubleday and attributed the invention to him. Despite the speculative and dubious claims of the letter, Spalding and other members of his commission were quick to adopt the narrative as gospel and began to market their sport to the masses as a truly American pursuit.

1. Which of the following statements is suggested by the passage?

- Abner Doubleday did invent the game of baseball.
- Claiming baseball to be invented by an American would help Spalding sell more sporting equipment.
- Baseball is not truly an American sport.
- Many people in Spalding's day wanted to believe baseball was invented by an American.
- The other members of Spalding's commission knew that the letter about Abner Doubleday was probably fraudulent.

Click on your choice.

Reading Comprehension questions take one of three forms. The first, and most familiar, is the standard multiple-choice question. A question of this type will ask you to select the best answer from a set of five possible answers. The question shown above is a multiple-choice question.

The second type of question will present you with three answer choices, of which one or more are correct. Note the language in the box above the question stem: "Consider each of the choices separately and select all that apply." In these **all-that-apply** questions, you will not receive partial credit for selecting only *some* of the right answers—you must select *all* of the correct choices, and no incorrect ones, to receive full credit for the question. Here's an example:

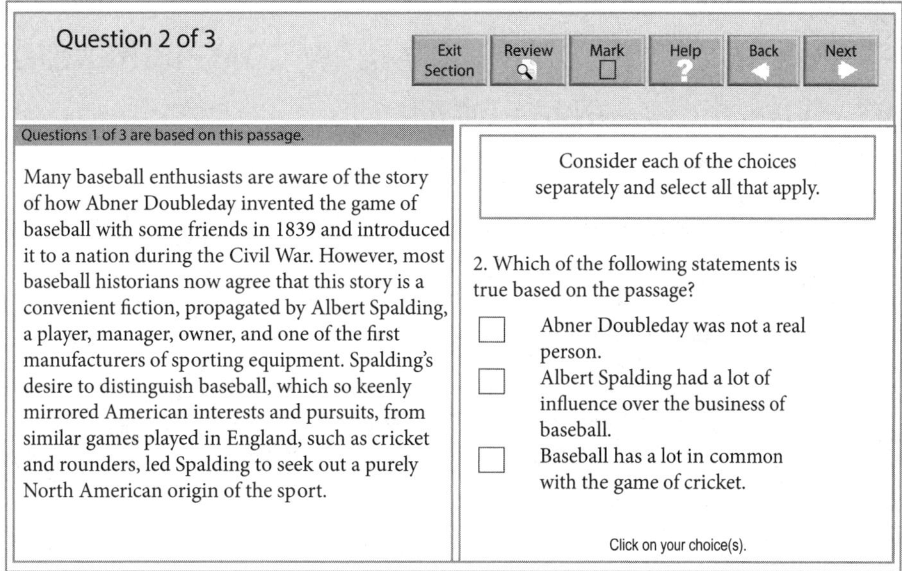

Finally, a third type of question asks you to find and then select within the passage a sentence that includes an important detail or that performs a certain function. In these **select-in-passage** questions, you will use your mouse to click on the sentence that specifically fulfills the task set out in the question stem. Here is an example of a select-in-passage question:

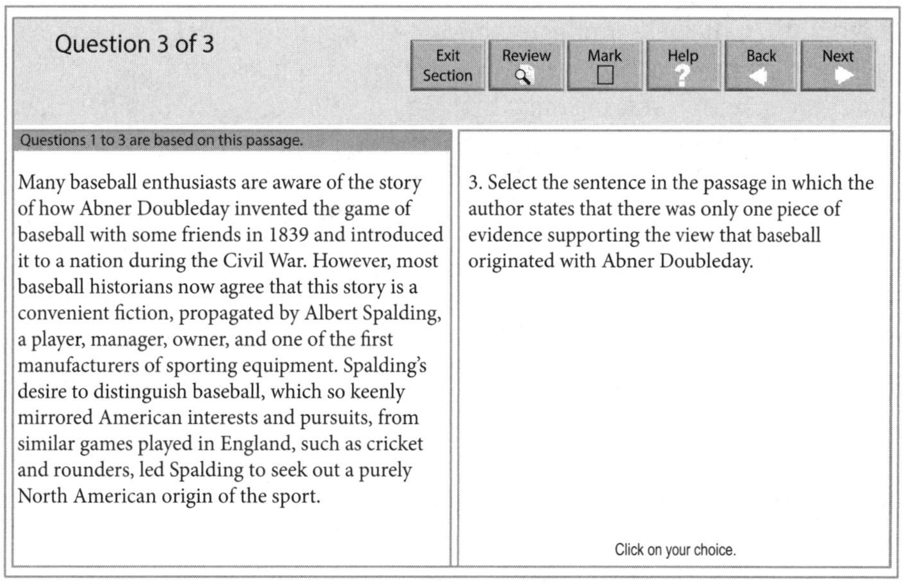

THE KAPLAN METHOD FOR READING COMPREHENSION

STEP 1 Read the passage strategically.

STEP 2 Analyze the question stem.

STEP 3 Research the relevant text in the passage.

STEP 4 Make a prediction.

STEP 5 Evaluate the answer choices.

Note: When a passage has just one question associated with it, Steps 1 and 2 are switched; read the question stem first, then read the passage.

As noted in Chapter 4: Verbal Foundations, many students think that because they have read a large number of academic texts for college classes, they can apply the same skills to achieve success on the GRE. However, answering Reading Comprehension questions correctly requires a different approach.

In school, you read to learn things about a subject. However, if a GRE passage is about the behavior of enzymes, you are not taking a biology test, and if it is about the influence of Appalachian music on composer Aaron Copland's work, you are not taking a music theory test. The makers of the GRE are not testing your subject knowledge; rather, they are interested in your critical thinking skills. Moreover, GRE Reading Comprehension questions are open-book—the passage stays on the screen throughout the question set, meaning that if a question asks about a detail, you can research it in the passage. Thus, memorizing details as you read is wasted effort. In fact, answering Detail questions from memory often leads to the wrong answer because the GRE supplies incorrect answer choices that are subtle distortions of passage content. The GRE wants to know whether you can grasp the overall structure of a passage so you can efficiently look up information you need to answer a question—a skill you'll use when completing papers and projects in graduate school—and *it rewards test takers who use this approach.*

Instead of reading to learn the material, focus on the big picture: *Why* did the author write the passage, and what are the passage's topic and scope? Sifting out these big-picture concepts from the surrounding details—reading *strategically*—is the key to success.

But reading strategically is only part of the battle. After all, you don't get any points for reading well. Instead, your goal is to answer questions correctly. And to answer Reading Comprehension questions correctly, you need to know the specific task a question asks you to perform, how to accomplish that task effectively, and how to avoid the GRE's common and predictable wrong-answer traps.

If learning a new way to read passages and answer questions seems daunting, don't worry. The GRE is a standardized test, and that means that the passages and questions in every Reading Comprehension section follow the same predictable patterns, over and over again. Success in the Reading Comprehension section, then, is simply a result of mastering a small handful of skills, including the ability to read the passage strategically, research the passage or your notes on the passage to answer specific questions, make clear predictions, and know what differentiates right answers from wrong answers. Those skills are intimately tied to the Kaplan Method for Reading Comprehension, a step-by-step approach that will help you maximize your performance in this section.

How the Kaplan Method for Reading Comprehension Works

STEP 1

READ THE PASSAGE STRATEGICALLY.

Note that this step is not simply "Read the passage." Step 1 is to read *strategically.* Reading strategically means giving more weight to some parts of the passage than to others.

That means that as you read, you will make sure to fully understand certain parts of the passage (things like the author's opinion, each paragraph's main idea, new theories, interesting discoveries) and read lightly through parts of the passage that are not as important (background information, supporting examples, rhetorical asides). Doing this will help you read efficiently while still capturing the important big-picture information that you'll need to answer questions. Noting the big-picture information means identifying the **topic, scope,** and **purpose** of a passage. The topic is what the passage is about, very broadly stated. The scope is that specific aspect of the topic that interests the author. The purpose is the author's reason for writing the passage.

On the GRE, authors write passages for the following reasons:

- To **explain** an aspect of a topic
- To **describe** the features of a thing or event
- To **analyze** how something works
- To **compare and contrast** two or more things—the author may simply describe how they are similar and/or different, or the author may also express an opinion about which is better
- To critique or **evaluate** how well or poorly something achieves a purpose—the author may only present other people's critiques or may offer her own opinion
- To **argue** for a position—the author has an opinion
- To **rebut** someone's position—the author disagrees with someone else's opinion

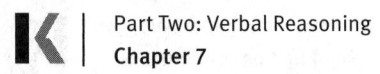

Here are some examples of big-picture summaries. Try to imagine the passage that each of these reflects.

Topic: World War II **Scope:** Impact of London blitz on children **Purpose:** To describe negative effects	**Topic:** Genetic diversity **Scope:** Hypothesis about role viruses may play in causing genetic mutations **Purpose:** To evaluate evidence for/against	**Topic:** Ethical systems **Scope:** Use of utilitarianism and Kantian ethics in business **Purpose:** To compare/contrast effects on profits

Just from knowing the topic, scope, and purpose, you probably find that you have a pretty good grasp of the gist of these passages, without even having read them. When you capture this information from a passage you read, you will have a solid foundation to answer GRE Reading Comprehension questions.

In addition, part of strategic reading is taking notes on the passage, or making a passage map. This means writing down the topic, scope, and purpose, as in the examples above, as well as the following information:

- Main idea of each paragraph
- Any opinion(s) offered—whose opinion and what it is
- Definition of any specialized term(s) central to the main idea
- Key examples—a few words identifying the example and what idea it illustrates

Your goal is not to rewrite the passage. After all, the passage is always going to be there on the screen, and writing down too much information would take too much time. Instead, in addition to mentally paraphrasing as you read, summarize important concepts and opinions, as well as terms and examples that are central to the author's main idea, by jotting down a few words on your scratch paper. You can and should use abbreviations and symbols, and sometimes a quick sketch will capture a concept more quickly and succinctly than words. Finally, no one will ever read this except you, so it doesn't need to be neat; as long as you understand what you've written, your passage map is doing its job.

One question that many students have initially is: How do I know what's important in a passage? Fortunately, GRE passages will tell you what's important with *keywords*—including the same kind of keywords you are already familiar with from Text Completion and Sentence Equivalence questions. Particularly important are keywords of *emphasis* and of *contrast*. Emphasis keywords (such as *very, important,* and *clearly)* are strong adjectives or adverbs that highlight the author's opinion or an idea the author views as significant or noteworthy. Contrast keywords (such as *but, yet,* and *however*) often indicate a significant conflict, disagreement, or change in thinking.

STRATEGIC READING: HOW TO USE KEYWORDS

When you strategically read a Reading Comprehension passage, you determine the passage's big picture: the passage's topic, scope, and purpose. The GRE provides savvy readers with keywords as clues to when to slow down and digest important parts of a passage and when to move quickly past unimportant details. Take a look at the following sentences:

> The students attended Dr. Robinson's lecture on international financial markets.
>
> The students have a solid understanding of global currency exchange rates.

Based on these two sentences, can you infer the contents of Dr. Robinson's lecture or its value to the students? Without keywords indicating the relationship between the sentences, you simply cannot determine what Dr. Robinson spoke about or whether the students learned anything. But add just one little phrase to the beginning of the second sentence, and a deduction can be made:

> The students attended Dr. Robinson's lecture on international financial markets.
>
> **As a result**, the students have a solid understanding of global currency exchange rates.

Now it's clear: the students gained their understanding of global currency exchange rates *because* they attended Dr. Robinson's lecture. But what if you saw this phrasing instead?

> The students attended Dr. Robinson's lecture on international financial markets.
>
> Nevertheless, the students have a solid understanding of global currency exchange rates.

In this instance, either Dr. Robinson didn't cover the topic of global currency exchange rates, or he did so inadequately. Either way, it's apparent that the students gained their knowledge of global currency exchange rates from some other source.

Here are the different types of keywords that will help you locate central ideas and opinions and grasp the structure of the passage:

- **Emphasis** and **opinion** keywords are used when the author wants to call attention to a specific point. These come in two varieties. Emphasis keywords, such as *very* and *critical*, point to ideas that are important to the author. Opinion keywords, such as *beneficial* or *dead end*, emphasize a positive or negative charge and point to attitudes toward or judgments about ideas. These opinions are frequently the focus of GRE questions. Be sure to distinguish between the author's opinions and those of others.

- **Contrast** keywords such as *but*, *however*, *nevertheless*, and *on the other hand* tell you that a change or disagreement is coming.
- **Continuation** keywords such as *moreover*, *furthermore*, *also*, and *in addition* tell you to expect more of the same line of reasoning.
- **Logic** keywords, which play an important role in answering Reasoning questions, alert you to an argument. **Conclusion** keywords such as *therefore* and *thus* indicate a supported claim or main point. **Evidence** keywords like *because*, *since*, and *for* announce the reasons used to support that conclusion. Again, be careful to distinguish between an argument the author is making and someone else's argument, which the author may be explaining without taking a position, agreeing with, or rebutting.
- **Illustration** keywords let you know that what follows is an example of a broader point. One example, of course, is *example. For instance* is another favorite in GRE passages.
- **Sequence/Grouping** keywords delineate how events or characteristics are related. *First, second,* and *third* are examples, as is a sequence like *17th century, 18th century,* and *today.* Science passages may group complicated phenomena using simpler keywords (*at a higher temperature* and *at a lower temperature*, for example). Look for these keywords especially in passages explaining steps in a scientific, social, or artistic process.

Of course, you don't get any points on the GRE for classifying a keyword or for writing down a note on your scratch paper. Instead, the purpose of focusing on keywords is to identify those parts of the passage that help you understand its big picture while at the same time ignoring less important details. Keywords also help you take control over your reading by helping you predict the function of the text that follows. Imagine that you saw a passage with the following structure on Test Day. Can you anticipate the kinds of details that would fill each of the blanks?

> The northern rabbit is exceptionally suited to cold climates because _____ ______________________________. Moreover, ___________________________ _______. However, one danger to this species' survival is _______________ __________________. Furthermore, __________________________________.

The emphasis keyword "exceptionally" tells you that the author believes the northern rabbit's adaptation to cold climates is significant, and you can expect the following text to focus on this idea. The evidence keyword "because" indicates the author will provide a reason the rabbit survives the cold so well. "Moreover," a continuation keyword, signals another reason. Then the contrast keyword "[h]owever" indicates a change in direction, so the next two blanks will include text describing potential threats to the northern rabbit's survival. While you can't predict the exact features that aid the rabbit (a special type of insulating fur? hibernation strategies?) or the specific dangers it faces (cold-climate predators? lack of food in the winter?), you do understand the overall structure of the passage. The details might change, but as long as the keywords remain the same, the overall gist of the passage does not. You actually know a lot about this passage just from the outline above, without any details!

Are keywords just as helpful when the passage begins discussing ideas and terms that you're unfamiliar with?

> Many biologists attribute Tasmanian devils' susceptibility to certain types of facial cancers to a lack of genetic diversity in the devils' overall population. These scientists base their conclusions on evidence showing that ______________________________. However, new research ______________________________. In fact, ______________________________.

This passage, like the one before it, is a scientific passage with a species of animal as the topic. However, the text is denser, and the terms the author uses—"certain types of facial cancers" and "lack of genetic diversity"—might throw off some untrained test takers who focus too much on details about the topic and not on the passage's overall structure. A well-trained test taker knows that "these scientists" will base their conclusions on data that show a connection between the concepts in the first sentence. As the expert reads, she knows that what follows "[h]owever" will introduce ideas that differ from those of "many biologists." By focusing on keywords, the expert knows to expect that the "new research" will present an alternative cause of the facial cancer. Furthermore, by starting a sentence with "In fact," the author may be signaling his own opinion on the matter—stating something he believes to be the truth. Again, simply on the basis of the outline above, you already know the gist of the passage.

With each GRE Reading Comprehension passage, focus on keywords to help you separate unimportant background information from the author's topic, scope, and purpose in writing, and to help you grasp the structure of the passage. Again, because the passage remains on screen as you answer the questions, you will be able to research details as necessary. In this way, you will read efficiently and be well prepared to answer questions correctly.

Note: When a passage has just one question associated with it, Steps 1 and 2 are switched; read the question stem first, then read the passage.

STEP 2

Analyze the question stem.

Once you have strategically read a passage to determine its topic, scope, and purpose and make a passage map, it is time to start answering the questions. Luckily, because the GRE is a standardized test, the questions that accompany a passage almost always fall into one of just a handful of categories:

- **Global**. These ask about the passage as a whole. Look for language in the question stem that asks you to determine a passage's main idea, primary purpose, or overall structure. Here are some examples of Global question stems:

  Which of the following most accurately describes the primary purpose of the passage?

  The author's tone could best be described as

- **Detail**. These ask you to research the text and identify a specific detail mentioned in the passage. Look for language in the question stem such as "according to the author" or "is mentioned in the passage." Here are some examples of Detail question stems:

  According the passage, the primary cause of unemployment in micronations is a lack of

  Which of the following was mentioned in the passage as a result of high employment?

- **Inference**. These questions ask for something that, though not stated explicitly in the text, must be true based on the information that is provide in the passage. Look for language in the question stem like "suggests," "implies," or "most likely agrees." Here are some examples of Inference question stems:

  The passage most strongly suggests that which of the following is true?

  With which of the following characterizations of medieval comedies would the author most likely agree?

- **Logic**. This type of question asks you to describe why the author included a certain word, phrase, or statement. Look for language like "in order to" or "primarily serves to." Here are some examples of Logic question stems:

  The author mentions Tussey's theory of copyright systems primarily in order to

  Which of the following most accurately describes the reason the author included the results of the experiments in lines 9–12?

- **Vocab-in-Context**. These relatively straightforward questions ask you to identify the specific way a word is used in the passage. Here are some examples of Vocab-in-Context questions:

  As it is used in line 16, "brilliant" most nearly means

  Which of the following most closely corresponds to the meaning of the word "effect" as it is used in line 26?

- **Reasoning**. These questions ask you to analyze an author's reasoning in an argument. They may ask you to identify an argument's assumption, point out a flaw in the author's reasoning, or strengthen or weaken the reasoning. Here are some examples of Reasoning questions:

  The ethicist's argument requires the assumption that

  Which of the following would cast the most doubt on the conclusion drawn by the scholar?

Now be honest: Did you just skim through that list of question types without taking the time to catalog and understand how the tasks are different? If you did, you're not alone. But take another look. The fact is, knowing the type of question you're dealing with is incredibly helpful. For one thing, different question types require different research and prediction steps. For another, different question types have different types of flawed answer choices, which you can learn to avoid. Knowing how to research a question effectively and how to avoid wrong answer traps will allow you to choose correct answers confidently and improve your performance.

ANALYZE THE QUESTION STEM: EXERCISE

In the following exercise, identify each question as one of the following types: Global, Detail, Inference, Logic, Vocab-in-Context, or Reasoning. In addition, for each example question, ask yourself:

- Are there any clues in this stem that will help me research a specific part of the passage?
- Would I be able to formulate a strong prediction for this question?

The pages following this drill will provide answers and explanations to these questions.

1. The passage implies which of the following about [xxxxx]?

   (A) Global
   (B) Detail
   (C) Inference
   (D) Logic
   (E) Other

2. According to the passage, each of the following is true about [xxxxx] EXCEPT

   (A) Global
   (B) Detail
   (C) Inference
   (D) Logic
   (E) Other

3. The author mentions [xxxxx] in order to

   (A) Global
   (B) Detail
   (C) Inference
   (D) Logic
   (E) Other

4. The main point of the passage is

   (A) Global
   (B) Detail
   (C) Inference
   (D) Logic
   (E) Other

5. Which of the following most accurately describes a flaw in the argument above?

   (A) Global
   (B) Detail
   (C) Inference
   (D) Logic
   (E) Other

6. As it is used in context, the word "[xxxxx]" in line 17 most nearly means

   (A) Global
   (B) Detail
   (C) Inference
   (D) Logic
   (E) Other

7. An appropriate title for the passage would be

   Ⓐ Global
   Ⓑ Detail
   Ⓒ Inference
   Ⓓ Logic
   Ⓔ Other

8. The author makes which of the following statements concerning [xxxxx]?

   Ⓐ Global
   Ⓑ Detail
   Ⓒ Inference
   Ⓓ Logic
   Ⓔ Other

9. The passage provides support for which of the following assertions about [xxxxx]?

   Ⓐ Global
   Ⓑ Detail
   Ⓒ Inference
   Ⓓ Logic
   Ⓔ Other

10. Which of the following best supports the author's conclusion that [xxxxx]?

   Ⓐ Global
   Ⓑ Detail
   Ⓒ Inference
   Ⓓ Logic
   Ⓔ Other

11. The function of the example in line xx is to

   Ⓐ Global
   Ⓑ Detail
   Ⓒ Inference
   Ⓓ Logic
   Ⓔ Other

12. The author indicates explicitly that which of the following has been [xxxxx]?

   Ⓐ Global
   Ⓑ Detail
   Ⓒ Inference
   Ⓓ Logic
   Ⓔ Other

Answers and Explanations

1. C

When you see "implies" or "suggests" in a question stem, you're dealing with an Inference question.

2. B

Language that points you to find something directly stated in the passage (here, the phrase "according to the passage") indicates a Detail question.

3. D

The phrase "in order to" means that this is a Logic question. Your task is to determine why the author has included the specific phrase or statement.

4. A

This is a Global question that asks for the entire passage's main point.

5. E

To answer this Reasoning question, separate the argument's conclusion from its evidence and then describe the way in which the evidence fails to fully support the conclusion.

6. E

This is clearly a Vocab-In-Context question.

7. A

Since the title of a passage reflects the content of the passage as a whole, this is a Global question.

8. B

Since the question asks for a specific statement made by the author, this is a Detail question.

9. C

The correct answer will be something that can be directly inferred from information in the passage.

10. E

This is a Reasoning question because the answer will support the conclusion. Notice that the word "support" is used differently than in the previous question. In this question, the answer strengthens (supports) the conclusion in the passage; in the prior question, the passage supported the answer.

11. D

This is a Logic question. It is asking what role the example plays in the passage, not for information or an inference about the example.

12. B

The word "explicitly" means that the question deals with something that is contained in the passage, not something that needs to be inferred.

How did you do? Were you able to correctly identify each question's type? How would you have proceeded differently to answer each of the different types of questions? It is easy to overlook the value of identifying question types in the Reading Comprehension section. However, knowing the type of question you're dealing with will help you research the passage more effectively. That, in turn, will help you more quickly formulate a prediction and more quickly find the correct answer.

STEP 3

Research the relevant text in the passage.

Once you have analyzed and fully understood the question stem, use your passage map for guidance. Global questions and some Inference and Logic questions are so general that you can simply use your understanding of the passage's topic, scope, and purpose as well as the structure of the passage to answer them. You can answer questions such as "What is the purpose of this passage?" or "Which of these statements expresses the author's conclusion?" directly from your notes.

Sometimes, however, the question stem will ask you to find a specific detail in the passage, draw an inference about a specific situation mentioned by the author, or identify the function of a specific phrase or sentence. Pay close attention to the research clues in the question stem, noting which part of the passage will help you answer the question. Then consult your passage map to refresh your memory of the main idea in that part of the passage. Finally, return to the passage and research the text of interest.

Take a look at the following two question stems. What would you say is the biggest difference between them?

1. The author of the passage would be most likely to agree with which of the following?
2. The author of the passage would be most likely to agree with which of the following statements regarding the nocturnal habits of newly discovered species in the Himalayan range?

Both are Inference questions. Both ask you to determine what the author of the passage would be likely to agree with. But where the questions differ is in your ability to research a specific part of the passage. In the first question stem, there are no clues pointing you to a specific portion of the passage. Instead, you'll have to consult your big-picture summary (topic, scope, purpose) and evaluate *each answer choice,* checking it against the passage.

For the second question stem, though, notice the numerous clues it provides. It asks you to determine the author's opinion of something explicitly stated in the passage—the nocturnal habits of newly discovered species in the Himalayan range. Untrained test takers might look at such a question stem and assume that their task is to answer the question based on their memory of the passage. But that's often a losing strategy. Your memory of the details of the passage will likely be fuzzy, plus wrong answers will often present subtle distortions of ideas in the text, even using words and phrases from the passage. Instead, check your passage map for key information you may have noted about these animals and to confirm where in the text the author discusses them. Then go to the passage itself and reread just the section with the author's comments on the nocturnal habits of these animals.

Researching the passage to determine the correct answer to a question is a skill that you can develop, just like every other step of the Kaplan Method. Each question type requires a slightly different research strategy.

- **Global.** Attack Global questions by using the topic, scope, and purpose you noted as you read the passage. *Eliminate* answers that reflect only a part of the passage or supporting ideas rather than the main idea.
- **Detail.** Because Detail questions ask you to find a specific detail in the passage, these questions will almost never include line references. Instead, you will have to use your knowledge of the passage or your passage map to research the relevant part of the passage. Correct answers to Detail questions will always be close paraphrases of the text, so make it a habit to research the passage and find direct support for your answer. *Eliminate* answer choices that distort what the author actually said about the matter at issue or that provide a correct detail about something else.
- **Inference.** Attack open-ended Inference questions that do not point you back to a specific part of the passage (like question number 1 above) as you would a Global question. Consult your big-picture summary and consider the author's main ideas and purpose. Because your predictions for these questions will of necessity be very general, you may need to check each answer choice against the information in the passage.

  For Inference questions that give specific research clues, consult the specific part of the passage referenced in the question. Take note of the particular language in the question stem: Are you being asked to infer something that the author believes, or are you inferring someone else's opinion? Focus on keywords that surround the relevant text in the passage.

  When evaluating answer choices for Inference questions, *eliminate* choices that reflect the author's (or someone else's) opinion but are worded too strongly (are Extreme) and those that are reasonable statements but wander beyond the scope of the passage (Out of Scope).

- **Logic.** Logic questions often contain line references or quote specific text from the passage. Consult your passage map for the author's overall purpose and for notes you've made about the specific part of the passage the referenced quote or phrase is from. Then go to the passage and read before and after the referenced text. Your task for these questions is to understand why the author included something in the passage, so consider how the passage would be affected if the reference text were not there. What function does it serve in the larger context of the passage? *Eliminate* choices that do not align with the author's purpose in writing.
- **Vocab-in-Context.** These questions are relatively straightforward, and researching is often simply a matter of finding the word in question in the passage, then considering how that word is used in context. The words asked about will have more than one meaning, usually a common one, and one or more uncommon

ones, and often the author has used the word for a less common meaning. Ask: What word could one use to replace the word referenced in the question? Use that prediction as you evaluate the answer choices.

- **Reasoning.** In Reasoning questions, you will most often be asked to analyze an argument, so your first task should be to identify the argument's conclusion and its evidence. The conclusion of an argument is simply the claim that the author is trying to convince you of; the evidence, then, is the information used to support that conclusion. Once you've separated an author's claim from her evidence for that claim, your task is to identify the author's assumption. The assumption in an argument is any unstated fact that must be true in order for the argument to make sense.

  Reasoning questions come in a variety of forms. A question might ask you to simply find an assumption of an argument, while another might ask you to identify a reasoning flaw. Some Reasoning questions will have you strengthen or weaken an argument, while others test your ability to resolve a paradox. See the section "How to Approach Reasoning Questions" toward the end of this chapter for examples of different types of Reasoning questions and predictable patterns to look for.

STEP 4

Make a prediction.

Making predictions is one of the hallmarks of expert GRE readers. Unprepared test takers fall into the testmaker's trap of using the *answer choices* to guide their thinking, but the testmaker does not write answers to help you clarify your thinking. If you approach the answer choices in this way, you may find yourself attempting to justify each choice as correct, and more than one answer choice will often appear reasonable.

Instead, use the information in the *passage* to arrive at a correct answer. After you have read the passage, identified the type of question you're dealing with, and researched as appropriate, take a few seconds to imagine what the correct answer should look like. This is your prediction. Then, when you begin to read the answers, you will be able to rule out those that do not match your prediction—that do not match information in the passage—even if they seem like reasonable or relevant statements. It is, after all, much easier to find the answer choice you are looking for if you already have an idea what it looks like.

Of course, it is unusual that an answer choice will exactly match your prediction, word for word. Often, for example, your prediction will be general and the correct answer will be a specific instantiation of your general idea. However, the *concept* in the correct answer will match, and this is what's important, not the exact language that is used. Note that if you mentally paraphrase the passage as you read, casting it into your own words, you will be prepared to recognize ideas in and inferences based on the passage when they are expressed in different terms.

Some question types, like open-ended Inference questions, might not lend themselves to a precise prediction. Other question types, like Detail questions, will nearly always lend themselves to a strong prediction. In your practice, you'll start to figure out which question types take general and more specific predictions.

It might help to think of GRE Reading Comprehension questions as short-answer instead of multiple-choice. If you imagine that the questions require you to write a short-answer response, you will formulate a short sentence as an answer—and this is your prediction! You will then use that prediction as you evaluate the choices, eliminating those that don't match and homing in on the choice or choices (for all-that-apply questions) that do.

If this step seems daunting, or if you find that no matter how hard you try to pause and predict an answer before evaluating the choices, you always rush through to the answers, try this exercise. Get some sticky notes and, during your next practice set of Reading Comprehension questions, cover up the answer choices with a sticky note. In your notebook, jot down what you think would be an appropriate response to the question.

With a strong prediction, you'll be much less likely to be tempted by wrong answer choices. Indeed, if you see an answer choice that matches your prediction, confidently select it and move on to the next question.

STEP 5

Evaluate the answer choices.

The first four steps of the Kaplan Method are all preparation for the final step: correctly answering the question. This step can be frustrating. How often have you found yourself in this position: you've read the passage and understand it; you've read the question stem and know your task; you've researched the passage and have an idea what the right answer choice looks like; but when you get to the answers, you find that two choices appear acceptable?

The testmaker is adept at writing deceptively appealing incorrect answer choices: that is, wrong answers that appear at first glance to be just as good as the correct answer. To recognize wrong answer choices on the GRE, it is valuable to know the ways in which the testmaker consistently creates wrong answers. In fact, just as there are predictable types of questions that the GRE recycles over and over again, there are also predictable and repeatable types of wrong answers.

- **Outside the Scope.** These answer choices misrepresent the scope of a particular part of the passage, often by drawing an irrelevant comparison to something not mentioned in the passage.
- **Extreme.** Be careful when you see answer choices that include extreme language like *always, never, mostly, rarely,* and so on. The passage must support such strong/extreme language for the choice to be correct.

- **Distortion.** These incorrect answer choices use specific language from the passage, but then distort the context or meaning of the details in the passage.
- **180.** These answer choices contradict (either subtly or explicitly) the statements made in the passage.
- **Half-Right/Half-Wrong.** These are especially common in longer answer choices, where the first clause of a long sentence is correct but then the second half goes awry.

Certain types of wrong answers will appear more frequently in certain types of questions and less frequently in others. For example, Outside the Scope and Extreme answer choices tend to show up in Inference questions, while Distortion answer choices are common in Detail and Function questions.

As you practice, pause and reflect not only on why *right* answers are *right* but also on what makes *wrong* answers *wrong*. Having a strong grasp what kinds of flawed answer choices to expect is nearly as powerful as researching accurately and making strong predictions. In time, you'll be able to quickly and effectively eliminate incorrect choices and zero in on the correct one.

By practicing the five steps of the Kaplan Method, you'll build your ability to attack Reading Comprehension passages with a consistent, methodical approach and reliably answer questions correctly. Now that you know what each step of the method entails, and why each step is so beneficial to your GRE score, let's take an even deeper look at each step using examples.

How to Apply the Kaplan Method for Reading Comprehension

STEP 1

Read the passage strategically.

Apply your strategic reading skills to the passage below. Focus on how the author's use of emphasis and contrast keywords telegraphs not just the author's intent but also the passage's overall structure. For each sentence, focus less on what is being said and more on why the author has included it. Is it simply background information? Is it the author's main idea? Is it someone else's opinion or belief? *By asking and answering these questions as you read, you will be well prepared for the questions the test asks.* Also, instead of trying to hold key ideas in your head, jot them down on scratch paper—make a passage map.

Questions 1 to 3 are based on this passage.

Many baseball enthusiasts are aware of the story of how Abner Doubleday invented the game of baseball with some friends in 1839 and introduced it to a nation during the Civil War. However, most baseball historians now agree that this story is a convenient fiction, propagated by Albert Spalding, a player, manager, owner, and one of the first manufacturers of sporting equipment. Spalding's desire to distinguish baseball, which so keenly mirrored American interests and pursuits, from similar games played in England, such as cricket and rounders, led Spalding to seek out a purely North American origin of the sport. Spalding's entire basis for the foundation of baseball history lay in a handwritten letter from 1907 that he said came from a man who claimed to have gone to school with Doubleday and attributed the invention to him. Despite the speculative and dubious claims of the letter, Spalding and other members of his commission were quick to adopt the narrative as gospel and began to market their sport to the masses as a truly American pursuit.

Below, check out how a GRE expert thinks as she reads the passage strategically, differentiating important information from background information.

Many baseball enthusiasts are aware of the story of how Abner Doubleday invented the game of baseball with some friends in 1839 and introduced it to a nation during the Civil War.

This is background information describing what "[m]any baseball enthusiasts" (not the author) believe. What follows might be new information that shows this understanding to be incorrect.

However, most baseball historians now agree that this story is a convenient fiction, propagated by Albert Spalding, a player, manager, owner, and one of the first manufacturers of sporting equipment.

The contrast keyword "[h]owever" indicates that what is commonly known is incorrect. Instead, the story of Doubleday was probably made up by a person named Spalding.

Spalding's desire to distinguish baseball, which so keenly mirrored American interests and pursuits, from similar games played in England, such as cricket and rounders, led Spalding to seek out a purely North American origin of the sport.

Here, the author tells us why why Spalding created this fictional story: Spalding wanted to create an "American" backstory, not an English one.

Spalding's entire basis for the foundation of baseball history lay in a handwritten letter from 1907 that he said came from a man who claimed to have gone to school with Doubleday and attributed the invention to him.

This is a detail that explains why Spalding credited baseball's invention to Doubleday—it concerns a letter (the details about the letter are not important—I can return later to research them if necessary).

Despite the speculative and dubious claims of the letter, Spalding and other members of his commission were quick to adopt the narrative as gospel and began to market their sport to the masses as a truly American pursuit.

The keyword "[d]espite" shows a contrast: while the letter didn't seem authentic, Spalding pushed the theory anyway. Why? To market the sport as uniquely "American."

Notice what a proficient GRE reader does. As she reads strategically, she "sums up" each sentence by mentally putting it into her own words. By paraphrasing, she separates key insights from nonessential background information. By the end, she understands the gist of the passage and has an excellent understanding of the passage's topic, scope, and purpose. Here is this reader's passage map.

Topic: Origin of baseball

Scope: Did Abner Doubleday invent baseball?

Purpose: To explain why Albert Spalding spread the story that Doubleday invented baseball

¶1 Wanted to market the sport as American

Claimed to have found a letter, but very sketchy

Your passage map probably doesn't use exactly the same words—everyone will map a passage a little differently—but your map should have captured the same ideas. Now apply Steps 2–5 to answer some questions about this passage.

1. Which of the following statements is suggested by the passage?

   (A) Abner Doubleday did invent the game of baseball.
   (B) Claiming baseball to be invented by an American would help Spalding sell more sporting equipment.
   (C) Baseball is not truly an American sport.
   (D) Many people in Spalding's day wanted to believe baseball was invented by an American.
   (E) The other members of Spalding's commission knew that the letter about Abner Doubleday was probably fraudulent.

STEP 2

Analyze the question stem.

The key phrase is "suggested by," which indicates this is an Inference question. The correct answer is not explicitly stated in the text but can be discerned by an accurate reading of the text.

STEP 3

Research the relevant section in the text.

This Inference question does not point to a particular statement in the passage, so you cannot research a particular sentence or section of the passage before approaching the answer choices. However, you can review your passage map so you have a firm grasp of the big picture of the passage; answer choices that contradict this or lie outside the scope of the passage can be eliminated. If any choices remain, you'll need to check each one against the information provided in the text until you find one that is fully supported.

STEP 4

Make a prediction.

Because of the open-ended nature of the question, you cannot formulate a precise prediction. However, your review of the passage map shows that because Spalding wanted to market baseball to Americans, he spread the story about an American, Doubleday, inventing it, even though Spalding had little evidence of this. Look for an answer choice that aligns with this main thrust of the passage, and look to eliminate choices that do not align.

STEP 5

Evaluate the answer choices.

Eliminate choice **(A)** because it contradicts the main thrust of the passage, which is that "most baseball historians," and the author, agree that Doubleday did not invent baseball. This was just a story that Spalding made up. Choice **(B)** might require some research. Spalding did make sporting equipment, and he was an avid promoter of baseball. However, he had a number of connections to baseball, and nowhere is it implied that he wanted to expand the fan base for the sport to increase sales of equipment. Choice **(C)** is Outside the Scope; the passage says that evidence for Doubleday's inventing baseball is very weak, but it never discusses who did invent the sport. Choice **(E)** can be researched in the last sentence, which mentions that "other members of [Spalding's] commission" promoted the story about Doubleday. However, the passage never says whether they believed the story or were skeptical of it. The correct answer is choice **(D)**, which is supported by evidence in the passage. Spalding and his commission were eager to spread a story about an American inventor because they knew it would help market the sport to Americans.

Now try an all-that-apply question on the same passage.

Consider each of the choices separately and select all that apply.

2. Which of the following statements is true based on the passage?

   [A] Abner Doubleday was not a real person.

   [B] Albert Spalding had a lot of influence over the business of baseball.

   [C] Baseball has a lot in common with the game of cricket.

STEP 2

Analyze the question stem.

The phrase is "based on the passage" means this is an Inference question. As with all GRE Inference questions, while the correct answer(s) won't be directly stated in the passage, it or they must be true given what is stated in the passage.

STEP 3

Research the relevant text in the passage.

This is another open-ended Inference question. Again, use your passage map to refresh your memory of the key ideas of the passage—any choice that contradicts these or is a 180°, wanders Outside of Scope, or is too Extreme can be eliminated immediately. Be prepared to research any remaining choices in the appropriate place in the text.

STEP 4

Make a prediction.

While a precise prediction is not possible, having read the passage strategically and already answered one open-ended Inference question about it, you have a strong sense of what kinds of statements would and would not be supported by the text.

STEP 5

Evaluate the answer choices.

Choice **(A)** is Outside of Scope of the passage, which only concerns whether Doubleday invented baseball; it does not discuss whether he existed at all. Choice **(B)** can reasonably be inferred. According to the second sentence, Spalding was a baseball player, manager, and owner, and according to the last sentence, he was a member of a commission that promoted the sport. In addition, he is believed responsible for perpetuating a widely believed myth about the origins of baseball. Thus, he was certainly influential in the game, and **(B)** is correct. Choice **(C)** is supported by the third sentence, in the middle of the passage, which describes cricket as a game "similar" to baseball. The similarity of the games was a reason Spalding was so eager to differentiate baseball by inventing an American origin story.

Now try a select-in-passage question. There is no need to approach this type of question any differently. Indeed, you can think of it as a multiple-choice question. There are five sentences in this passage, so they are your five answer choices.

3. Select the sentence in the passage in which the author states that there was only one piece of evidence supporting the view that baseball originated with Abner Doubleday.

STEP 2

Analyze the question stem.

A key to choosing the correct answer to select-in-passage questions is to read the question very carefully. A rushed reading might focus on words like "Abner Doubleday" and "baseball," and the test taker might think, "The whole passage is about that. How do I figure out which sentence to pick?" The words pointing you to the one and only sentence that fits the bill are "there was only one piece of evidence" for the Doubleday story. Only one sentence discusses the evidence for this origin myth.

STEP 3

Research the relevant text in the passage.

From your passage map, you know that the evidence was a letter.

STEP 4

Make a prediction.

You will look for the sentence that mentions the letter and says it was the only basis for the story.

STEP 5

Evaluate the answer choices.

You might recall that the passage begins by presenting background information and introducing the topic, that the story about Doubleday was largely the creation of Spalding. Only later does the passage discuss how Spalding came up with the story. So begin your scan for the correct sentence at the end of the passage. You'll quickly find the fourth sentence: **Spalding's entire basis for the foundation of baseball history lay in a handwritten letter from 1907 that he said came from a man who claimed to have gone to school with Doubleday and attributed the invention to him.** That fits the criteria of the question perfectly.

Some test takers feel less comfortable with passages about certain topics. Readers with a strong background in science may feel nervous about humanities passages, and readers well versed in the social sciences may approach physical science passages with some anxiety. However, the Kaplan Method and your strategic reading skills work equally well for all passages, no matter what your personal familiarity with the subject matter.

The last passage concerned history. Now try a passage with science content.

STEP 1

Read the passage strategically.

Practice each step of the Kaplan Method with this passage and its associated questions. Read this passage strategically, using keywords, mentally paraphrasing, and making a passage map. Then use your knowledge of the Reading Comprehension question types to analyze the question stem, research the necessary information, form a prediction, and evaluate the choices.

- For Step 1, map the passage on your scratch paper.
- For Steps 2–4, jot down your thinking to help yourself become conscious of each step. This type of practice will help you analyze what you are doing right and where you go wrong when you miss questions.
- For Step 5, eliminate incorrect answer(s) that do not address the question or are not supported by the passage. Choose the correct answer(s) that matches your prediction.

Questions 4 and 5 are based on this passage.

Many tea drinkers believe that different teas—black, green, oolong, and so forth—come from different plants. In fact, however, all tea leaves come from *Camellia sinensis*, a large evergreen shrub. Native to China, the plant is now cultivated throughout Asia and in Africa, Europe, and North and South America. The character of various teas depends in some measure on the climate and soil where the plant is grown but mostly on how the leaf is processed after it is harvested. An interesting case is black pu-erh tea, a specialty of China's Yunnan province. Unlike green or oolong tea, black pu-erh tea undergoes an oxidation process with the help of naturally occurring enzymes or, in the world of tea, is said to be "fermented." It then undergoes an additional step that differentiates it from other black teas: after oxidation, the leaves are aged in humid conditions, sometimes for several decades. Like all other teas, pu-erh contains antioxidants, which may help protect regular consumers from some cancers. It also contains caffeine, though not as much as most other black teas. What really sets it apart from all other teas is the fact that it naturally contains small quantities of lovastatin, a medication that physicians prescribe to lower cholesterol. It is possible that certain fungi that colonize the tea leaves produce lovastatin as a metabolic by-product. Most pu-erh connoisseurs, while appreciative of the tea's potential health benefits, are more intrigued by its taste, which they describe with words such as *woody*, *earthy*, and *leathery*. Clearly, an adventurous palate is necessary to enjoy this unusual beverage. Fortunately, those seeking a more conventional tea flavor have many options.

How did that go? Did you notice emphasis keywords that pointed to the author's opinion or significant details? Did you identify contrast keywords indicating a change in direction or an unexpected discovery? Were you able to capture the passage's topic, scope, and purpose and the main ideas in your passage map?

Here is a visual representation of how a GRE expert reads. This reader has trained himself to focus on key words and phrases, and these seem to leap out of the passage at him as though in bold print. These highlight the structure of the passage and point to the main ideas. He reads the less important details with less attention.

Many tea drinkers believe that different teas—black, green, oolong, and so forth—come from different plants. **In fact, however,** all tea leaves come from *Camellia sinensis,* a large evergreen shrub. Native to China, the plant is now cultivated throughout Asia and in Africa, Europe, and North and South America. The character of various teas depends in some measure on the climate and soil where the plant is grown **but mostly** on how the leaf is processed after it is harvested. An **interesting case** is black pu-erh tea, a specialty of China's Yunnan province. **Unlike** green or oolong tea, black pu-erh tea undergoes an oxidation process with the help of naturally occurring enzymes or, in the world of tea, is said to be "fermented." It then undergoes an **additional step** that **differentiates** it from other black teas: after oxidation, the leaves are aged in humid conditions, sometimes for several decades. **Like all other teas**, pu-erh contains antioxidants, which may help protect regular consumers from some cancers. It **also** contains caffeine, though not as much as most other black teas. **What really sets it apart** from all other teas is the fact that it naturally contains small quantities of lovastatin, a medication that physicians prescribe to lower cholesterol. It is **possible** that certain fungi that colonize the tea leaves produce lovastatin as a metabolic by-product. **Most** pu-erh connoisseurs, while appreciative of the tea's potential health benefits, are more **intrigued** by its taste, which they describe with words such as *woody*, *earthy*, and *leathery*. **Clearly,** an **adventurous** palate is necessary to enjoy this **unusual** beverage. **Fortunately,** those seeking a more conventional tea flavor have many options.

Take a look at the following passage map and see how yours compares. Again, there are many "right" ways to map a passage—just make sure you noted the important ideas.

Topic: Tea

Scope: Pu-erh tea—how it's made, characteristics

Purpose: Compare/contrast with other teas

¶1 Tea—same plant, grown widely, differences come from processing

All teas—antioxidants

Black teas—oxidized, caffeine

Black pu-erh tea—also aged, lovastatin, unusual taste

Now that you have read the passage strategically and made your map, try answering this question.

> Consider each of the choices separately and select all that apply.

4. The passage suggests that which of the following would be a correct statement about tea subjected to an aging process?

   [A] The aging process removes caffeine and antioxidants from tea leaves.

   [B] The aging process may be responsible for the presence of a medically significant agent.

   [C] Aged tea leaves produce a brew with a flavor distinct from that of unaged leaves.

Step 2—What kind of question is this?

Step 3—Where do you research?

Step 4—What is your prediction?

Step 5—What is your answer?

STEP 2

Analyze the question stem.

The keyword "suggests" means this is an Inference question. This question asks about a specific idea in the passage, "tea subjected to an aging process." The correct answer(s) must be true given the information that is provided in the passage.

STEP 3

Research the relevant section in the text.

The "tea subjected to an aging process" discussed in the passage is black pu-erh tea. According to the passage map, black pu-erh tea is different from other teas in two ways: it contains lovastatin, and it has an unusual flavor. If these details are not captured in your passage map, you can find them in the latter half of the passage, where black pu-erh tea is compared and contrasted with other teas.

STEP 4

Make a prediction.

You can infer that the ways in which pu-erh tea differs from other teas are due to the aging process it undergoes. The correct answer(s) will concern the cholesterol-lowering agent lovastatin and/or the tea's distinctive taste.

STEP 5

Evaluate the answers.

Answer choices **(B)** and **(C)** match this prediction. Choice **(A)** is Half-Right, Half-Wrong: the passage states that pu-erh contains "not as much" caffeine as other black teas, so the aging process can be inferred to remove some caffeine. However, the passage says that pu-erh tea (and all teas) contains antioxidants and does not indicate that the tea has fewer antioxidants than do other teas.

Now try another question about this passage.

5. Based on the passage, which of the following can be inferred about black teas?

   (A) Black teas taste more like green or oolong tea than like pu-erh tea.
   (B) People seeking health benefits from tea can experience exactly the same effects from black teas as from all other teas except pu-erh tea.
   (C) People who enjoy new and unusual foods will prefer pu-erh tea to black teas.
   (D) Black teas are oxidized but not subsequently stored in humid conditions to be aged.
   (E) Although black teas contain caffeine, they do not contain any substances that may protect against cancer.

Step 2—What kind of question is this?

Step 3—Where do you research?

Step 4—What is your prediction?

Step 5—What is your answer?

STEP 2

Analyze the question stem.

The word "inferred" leaves little doubt this is an Inference question. Again, this question is directed at specific information in the passage—this time what the passage says about black teas.

STEP 3

Research the relevant section in the text.

Review what the passage says about black teas. In discussing the processing steps that differentiate types of tea, the passage says that pu-erh tea is oxidized but that what makes it different from black tea is that it is also aged. Therefore, black teas are also oxidized, but they are not aged. The passage also says that most black teas contain more caffeine than black pu-erh. Moreover, the passage says that pu-erh is like "all other teas" in containing antioxidants, so black teas must contain antioxidants.

STEP 4

Make a prediction.

The correct answer will correspond to one or more of the ideas in Step 3.

STEP 5

Evaluate the answers.

Choice **(D)** says black teas are oxidized but not aged and is correct. Choices **(A)** and **(B)** both use comparisons between black teas and other teas that the passage does not support. Although the author says it is necessary to have an "adventurous palate" to enjoy pu-erh tea, this does not mean that people with adventurous tastes will prefer pu-erh tea to others; perhaps they will enjoy all kinds of tea equally. Therefore, choice **(C)** is incorrect. Because all teas contain antioxidants, which may protect against cancer, **(E)** is incorrect.

Now apply your Reading Comprehension skills to a longer passage, this one with a topic in the social sciences. Again, remember that neither the length of the passage nor the subject matter changes your approach. Use the Kaplan Method and your strategic reading skills to identify the important information and answer GRE questions.

- For Step 1, map the passage on your scratch paper.
- For Steps 2–4, jot down your thinking to help yourself become conscious of each step. This type of practice will help you analyze what you are doing right and where you go wrong when you miss questions.
- For Step 5, eliminate incorrect answer(s) that do not address the question or are not supported by the passage. Choose the correct answer(s) that matches your prediction.

STEP 1

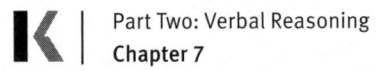

Read the passage strategically.

Questions 6 to 9 are based on this passage.

As the business world becomes ever more globalized and dynamic, freelance knowledge workers have come into their own. Technology drives rapid change in products and markets, and to keep up, companies find value in an on-demand workforce, one that they can adjust at will as new skills are needed. At the same time, the Internet means that a worker across the country or on the other side of the world can be as connected to a project's workflow as someone seated in the company's headquarters. Reflecting this reality, the U.S. Census Bureau's count of "nonemployer businesses" rose 29 percent from 2002 to 2012, and according to one study, 53 million Americans—more than one-third of the workforce—engage in freelance work. The growth of so-called contingent labor is forecast to continue unabated. Clearly, not all labor is equally empowered in the new paradigm. The barista placing the artistically styled froth on a customer's latte must be in the coffee shop. However, the systems analyst upgrading the shop's financial system that tracks the sales of lattes can be anywhere. Thus, workers with intellectual capital are in prime position to choose where they work and for whom.

The transition to a labor market of independent professionals has social and cultural implications. In much of the world, work is a major source of identity, so when work changes, identity changes. Instead of identifying as Widgets Incorporated employees who, whether they are an executive or a janitor, will someday earn a gold watch with the Widgets logo engraved on the back, workers identify as designers or social media gurus or software engineers. Rather than forging a common bond with coworkers in a mix of jobs around the proverbial water cooler, freelancers build geographically dispersed networks with other self-employed professionals with similar skill sets. Furthermore, in the twenty-first century the workplace has become a primary site of social connections and thus an important thread in the fabric of social cohesion, but instead of going to an office for a large portion of the day where they assume their workday persona, the new entrepreneurs work at home—even in bed, where they tap out messages to clients on their smartphone while wearing pajamas. And instead of relying on company benefits packages when working or government-administered unemployment payments when not working, these workers attempt to provide for themselves in defiance of the vicissitudes of life. Not partaking in any communal safety net, they argue that in an era when layoffs are commonplace, being self-employed is little more precarious than working for an employer. The cumulative result of these changes may be, on the one hand, an integration of personal and work life not seen since the Industrial Revolution moved people from farms into factories and, on the other hand, the atomization of society as individual contributors of labor rent themselves out impermanently to companies around the globe without meeting their coworkers face-to-face. Contributing further to social disruption is the bifurcation of the labor market into the independent self-employed and those still dependent on traditional jobs. It remains to be seen whether this new generation of professionals will appreciate the degree of vulnerability that accompanies their freedom and reach out to find common cause with employees who still draw a steady paycheck, working together to address issues of security and dignity in the workplace.

STEP 2–5

6. The author is primarily concerned with

   (A) how working conditions differ for freelancers and traditionally employed individuals.
   (B) the growth of freelance employment and its ramifications for workers and society.
   (C) the economic implications of a shift in the labor market toward freelance workers.
   (D) why some professional knowledge workers choose to freelance.
   (E) recent and forecast statistical trends in freelance employment.

Step 2—What kind of question is this?

Step 3—Where do you research?

Step 4—What is your prediction?

Step 5—What is your answer?

7. Select the sentence that best summarizes the author's conclusion about the historic impact of the growth of the independent workforce.

Step 2—What kind of question is this?

Step 3—Where do you research?

Step 4—What is your prediction?

Step 5—What is your answer?

8. Consider the choices and select all that apply. Based on the passage, one can infer that the author would likely agree with all of the following statements about self-employed freelancers EXCEPT

Ⓐ Unlike traditional employees, who are dependent on the local economy, freelancers can contract with companies anywhere in the world and so do not experience sudden changes in workload and income.
Ⓑ Freelancers who can use the globalized, technology-enhanced business environment to their advantage generally perform mental rather than physical labor.
Ⓒ Compared to workers in the traditional workforce, freelancers are likely to use the Internet to build relationships with people of different socio-economic status from themselves.

Step 2—What kind of question is this?

Step 3—Where do you research?

Step 4—What is your prediction?

Step 5—What is your answer?

9. The author mentions "government-administered unemployment payments" in paragraph 2 in order to

   (A) support the conclusion that freelance knowledge workers are financially insecure.
   (B) argue that the increase in the percentage of freelancers in the workforce is of benefit to society.
   (C) illustrate a way in which self-employed individuals impose a burden on the social safety net.
   (D) reject the notion that freelance professionals should be required to pay unemployment taxes.
   (E) provide evidence for the idea that freelancers are less integrated with society at large than are traditional employees.

Step 2—What kind of question is this?

Step 3—Where do you research?

Step 4—What is your prediction?

Step 5—What is your answer?

Answers and Explanations

Examine the following passage map. How does yours differ from the example? Below the map, you'll see each step of the Kaplan Method fully explained for each question. Did you correctly identify each question type? Did you research the relevant information? Did you craft an appropriate prediction?

Topic: Freelance workers

Scope: Trend and social implications

Purpose: To argue that society is less cohesive due to ↑ FWs

¶ 1: Rapid growth of freelance workforce, expected to continue
FWs mostly knowledge workers

¶ 2: Social/cultural consequences

Identity—with skills, not employer	}	*Loss of social cohesion*
Work at home alone, not in office		
Self-reliant, don't depend on employer, government		

Both FWs & traditional employees face economic uncertainty. Will they work together?

6. The author is primarily concerned with

Step 2: The phrase "primarily concerned with" indicates this is a Global question.

Step 3: Consult your passage map—the author is interested in the social implications of a growing freelance workforce.

Step 4: "How the growth of the contingent workforce will impact society"

Step 5: B

The first paragraph discusses the fact that freelance employment is becoming more common for knowledge workers, and the second paragraph argues that this trend will have "social and cultural implications," resulting in shifts in personal identity and "social disruption." Choice **(B)** is the correct answer to this Global question.

Although paragraph 2 mentions a number of ways in which freelancers' lifestyles differ from those of employees, the author mentions these details to support the larger point that an increase in freelancing is changing society. Therefore, choice **(A)** is incorrect. The author mentions the economic vulnerability of freelancers but only to support the discussion of their different approach to security from traditional employees, so choice **(C)** is incorrect. One can infer that freelancers enjoy the freedom of this mode of work and this may be why they choose self-employment, but explaining this is not the author's primary goal. Choice **(D)** is not correct. Choice **(E)** only reflects the ideas in the first paragraph; the author is concerned with more than statistical trends.

7. Select the sentence that best summarizes the author's conclusion about the historic impact of the growth of the independent workforce.

Step 2: This is a Detail question asking for the sentence containing a specific idea that the author states.

Step 3: According to the passage map, the impact of freelance workers is discussed in paragraph 2, so you will look there for the answer. A number of sentences describe changes brought about by growing numbers of these workers, but only one—toward the end of the paragraph—sums up the author's conclusion and puts the trend into historical perspective.

Step 4: The correct answer will be the sentence that mentions a historical fact and includes a key word or phrase suggesting a wrap-up of the author's ideas.

Step 5: The cumulative result of these changes may be, on the one hand, an integration of personal and work life not seen since the Industrial Revolution moved people from farms into factories and, on the other hand, a simultaneous atomization of society as individual contributors of labor rent themselves out impermanently to companies around the globe while staying at home.

The author discusses the effects of the increase in freelancing in paragraph 2, and she sets it in historical context in this sentence, where she compares it to the Industrial Revolution.

8. Based on the passage, one can infer that the author would likely agree with all of the following statements about self-employed freelancers EXCEPT

Step 2: The word "infer" signals an Inference question. Even if the word "infer" were not present, you could still tell that this is an Inference question from the phrase "the author would likely agree," which implies that you are being asked to make an inference rather than find a detail explicitly stated in the passage. Careful! This is an EXCEPT question, so you will need to rule out those choices the author would agree with. And because this is an all-that-apply question, there may be more than one correct answer—that is, more than one answer choice the author would NOT agree with.

Step 3: Use your passage map to refresh your memory of ideas the author has stated and therefore would agree with. The question hasn't given you any guidance about where in the passage to research, so save that effort until you have answer choices to evaluate.

Step 4: You can't formulate a specific prediction for a question like this one. After all, there are an infinite number of ideas the author would not agree with. However, in Step 5 you can compare the answer choices to ideas you know the author *would* agree with and eliminate them. On the cross-out list are these (from the passage map): freelance workforce is growing; knowledge workers are in the best position to freelance; freelance workers identify with their job title, not a company, and they work at home alone and are self-reliant; growth of freelance workforce means society is becoming less cohesive; both freelance and traditional workers face insecurity. Having a list like this in mind and using it to eliminate incorrect answer choices—a kind of "reverse prediction"—sets you up for success.

Step 5: A, C

In the first paragraph, the author says the demand for freelancers is increasing in part because companies want a workforce they can "adjust at will." In the last sentence, the author concludes by saying that freelancers have a "degree of vulnerability" that gives them common ground with other workers. Therefore, freelancers are not always financially secure, and the author would disagree with choice **(A)**, making it a correct answer to this EXCEPT question.

In the second paragraph, the author states that freelancers integrate different aspects of their own lives but are less connected to coworkers, resulting in an "atomization of society." They do build networks, the author says, but mostly with people similar to themselves. Therefore, the author would disagree with choice **(C)**, making this choice another correct answer. In paragraph 1, the author contrasts knowledge workers with a coffee shop barista and indicates that professionals with "intellectual capital are in prime position" to succeed as freelancers. Therefore, the author would agree with choice **(B)**, and this choice is incorrect.

9. The author mentions "government-administered unemployment payments" in paragraph 2 in order to

Step 2: The phrase "in order to" tells you this is a Logic question. You are being asked *why* the author mentions this detail, not for further information about it.

Step 3: According to your passage map, paragraph 2 is about the social consequences of the growth in the freelance workforce, specifically how this trend is causing society to become less cohesive. Reading the target sentence, you find the contrast keywords "instead of": "company benefits" and "unemployment benefits" are being contrasted with freelance workers' "attempt[s] to provide for themselves." The next sentence continues the contrast, starting with the word "[n]ot" and saying freelance workers reject "communal benefits."

Step 4: Predict that the author mentions this detail to support the idea that in contrast to traditional employees, freelance workers depend on themselves rather than on society.

Step 5: E

Read the lines around the quoted text in the passage and consult your passage map to answer this Logic question: the purpose of paragraph 2 is to argue that the increase in freelancers has profound social implications, namely that freelancers' work and personal lives are more integrated but these workers are less integrated with society. "Government-administered unemployment payments" are mentioned in a sentence that contrasts programs organized to protect the well-being of a group with the self-reliance of freelancers. Therefore, this detail is mentioned to support the idea that self-employed people are less connected to the social safety net, and answer choice **(E)** is correct.

Although the author implies elsewhere that freelancers are vulnerable to financial insecurity, the detail in this question is mentioned to support the idea that freelancers provide for themselves, not that sometimes they cannot do so; choice **(A)** is incorrect. If anything, the author seems troubled by the effect of a larger contingent labor force on society, so choice **(B)** does not work. Freelancers are self-reliant, according to the author, so **(C)** does not make sense. Finally, although it might logically follow that people who do not receive unemployment benefits should not pay unemployment taxes, the passage never discusses taxes of any kind, and choice **(D)** is out of scope.

HOW TO APPROACH REASONING QUESTIONS

Reasoning questions ask you to analyze and deconstruct an author's argument. The test might then ask you to do a number of things: identify one of the assumptions in the argument, point out the flawed reasoning in the argument, strengthen the argument by affirming the relationship between the evidence and the conclusion, or weaken the argument by introducing a previously overlooked alternative explanation. Just like every other question on the GRE, these questions follow predictable patterns and are beatable.

ANATOMY OF AN ARGUMENT

Before we get into those common patterns, let's briefly discuss how arguments are constructed. You might think of an argument as a disagreement between two parties. On the GRE, however, the word *argument* means that an author is advocating for a position or claim. When one person makes an argument, she does so by providing **evidence** that is used in support of a **conclusion**. A conclusion is often an opinion, a bold claim, a recommendation, a prediction, or the rebuttal of someone else's viewpoint. Evidence is the facts and/or opinions presented in support of the author's claim. To demonstrate, take a look at this argument. Can you tell which piece is the evidence and which is the conclusion?

> Michael refuses to eat things he is allergic to. Therefore, he definitely won't be ordering the salmon.

The second sentence is the conclusion, and the first is the evidence. How do you know? Well, the clearest giveaway is the conclusion keyword "[t]herefore." On the GRE, authors will often telegraph their conclusions by using clear keywords. Additionally, though, notice that the second sentence is a prediction. It's what the author believes will happen, based on the information provided in the first sentence. Using this kind of logic, you can separate evidence from conclusion, even in arguments without clear conclusion keywords.

Now that you've pulled apart that argument into evidence and conclusion, can you spot the assumption—that is, the fact that the author believes must be true but hasn't explicitly stated? If you're having trouble spotting it, ask yourself this: Is there any new term or idea that appears in the conclusion but was nowhere to be found in the evidence? The conclusion discusses "Michael," but so does the evidence. But aha! Check out that term "salmon" in the conclusion. The evidence never mentions salmon. Instead, the evidence discusses things that Michael "is allergic to." Connect the two: the author assumes that Michael is allergic to salmon.

Common Types of Arguments

To perform well on Reasoning questions, it helps tremendously to be able to identify common argument patterns.

Scope Shift Arguments

Arguments like the one about Michael and salmon—one in which the author moves from discussing one thing in the evidence to a different thing in the conclusion—are called scope shift arguments. Try analyzing another, more complex one. First pull apart the evidence and the conclusion. Then look for different terms that the author assumes must be related.

> Scientists who have devoted their lives to curing cancer work long hours away from their friends and family. Such social isolation can lead to emotional distress, even in researchers with the most stable of personalities. Therefore, scientists who devote their lives to curing cancer are at a greater risk than other people of suffering from symptoms of depression and anxiety.

How did that go? Did you correctly identify the last sentence as being the argument's conclusion? Once you identified the conclusion, did you notice a new term or idea that had not been explicitly mentioned before? Take a look at the argument again. This time, the different terms in the evidence and the conclusion are bolded.

> Scientists who have devoted their lives to curing cancer work long hours away from their friends and family. Such social isolation can lead to emotional distress, even in researchers with the most stable of personalities. Therefore, scientists who devote their lives to curing cancer are at a greater risk of **suffering from the symptoms of depression and anxiety**.

The author's assumption must be that emotional distress tends to lead to depression and anxiety. Now, imagine if that weren't true. What if it were established that a higher level of emotional distress does *not* correlate with higher levels of depression and anxiety? If that were true, the author's argument would no longer make sense. Therefore, the author must be assuming that emotional distress impacts whether one develops depression and anxiety.

If you were asked to weaken this argument, you would look for an answer choice that indicates emotional distress and risk for depression and anxiety are unrelated. If asked to strengthen the argument, you would choose an answer that supports such a relationship.

Representativeness Arguments

Another common argument pattern is one in which the conclusion is about a different population than the evidence. Take a look at this argument and see if you can determine the author's assumption. What logical leap does the author make as he moves from evidence to conclusion?

> Recently, Big Tech Corporation conducted a survey that asked workers to rate their direct managers. Of the workers who responded, over 70% rated their direct manager as "good" or "excellent." Clearly, the responses indicate that a majority of workers at Big Tech Corporation have a positive relationship with their direct manager.

This argument makes a number of assumptions. For one thing, the author assumes that people were being truthful in their responses. But if the survey was not anonymous, then respondents might reply in a manner that flatters their direct manager. Additionally, did you notice the scope shift between workers rating the managers as good or excellent and the claim that workers have a positive relationship with those managers? Perhaps a worker finds that a manager is good at his job, but the relationship between the two is chilly.

But there is still another assumption in this argument. Note the language "[o]f the workers who responded . . ." What if only 8 workers out of 100 responded? That would be too small a sample to draw a valid conclusion about Big Tech employees in general. Maybe only people who have good relationship with their managers responded to the survey; the others were too afraid or too unmotivated. The problem here, then, is one of representativeness. The author assumes that the respondents (however few) must represent the company as a whole.

On the GRE, be on the lookout for any argument in which information about one group is used to draw a conclusion about a larger group or a different group. If you are asked to weaken the argument, look for an answer that indicates the group in the evidence differs on a key characteristic from the group in the conclusion. If you are asked to strengthen the argument, look for a statement that says the two groups are similar in an important way.

Causal Arguments

There is yet another type of argument that you might encounter on the GRE. See if you can spot the logical jump that the dean of student security makes in this argument.

> Last month, Big University instituted a new security system that allows only those with official identification to enter academic buildings. Since that time, there have been fewer reports of unauthorized access in academic buildings at Big University. The dean of student security has concluded that the new security system is working.

Did you notice that the evidence presents two things that occurred at the same time (or in the same relative time frame) and, from that data, the dean drew the conclusion that one of those things must have caused the other thing to happen? This is a classic argumentative flaw in which correlation is confused with causation.

Causal arguments are easy to spot because their conclusions nearly always fit the pattern of "therefore, one thing is making another thing happen." In the argument above, we see that pattern by paraphrasing the conclusion as "The security system is causing the decrease in unauthorized entries." The dean is jumping too quickly to a claim of causation, without taking into account other factors. Couldn't something else be causing the reduction in unauthorized access? What if summer break began last month—then there would be fewer students on campus, which might explain the reduction in unauthorized entrances.

Note that there is also a scope shift in this argument. The dean assumes that "fewer reports" of improper access indicates fewer actual such incidents ("the new security system is working"). However, maybe unauthorized individuals are gaining entrance to the building just as much as before, but for some reason people are less likely to call security.

Scope shift, representativeness, and causal arguments make up the bulk of argument patterns you'll see on Test Day. Recognizing these patterns will help you spot the implicit assumptions in an argument. And once you recognize an argument's assumption(s)—that logical leap the author makes from the evidence to the conclusion—you'll be able to choose the answer that strengthens or weakens an argument, points out its reasoning flaw, or simply describes the assumption.

READING COMPREHENSION PRACTICE SET

Now it's your turn. In the passage and question set below, apply the Kaplan Method for Reading Comprehension, being cognizant of each step. If you're up to the challenge, time yourself. If you set a timer, give yourself 9 minutes. On Test Day, you'll want to invest about 1 to 1.5 minutes in reading each passage paragraph and 1 minute in answering each question.

Questions 1 and 2 are based on the passage below.

The idea of medical nanotechnology often conjures up the potentially troubling image of tiny machines and devices that both exist and operate far outside the scope of unmagnified human vision. Yet much of what constitutes nanotechnology is purely biological in form and function. For example, strands of DNA and the proteins that make up its structure are mere nanometers thick. Many of the basic functions of life occur on the nanoscale level. Efforts to understand or affect these functions are among the primary fields of nanotechnology. Gene study and gene therapy, two byproducts of medical nanotechnology, have already proven useful for identifying and treating a number of different diseases, sometimes even before symptoms of those diseases present themselves. Even so, genetic nanotechnology and treatments can give as much cause for concern as the idea of microscopic machines at work in the body. The possibility of altering an organism's genetic structure has been a subject of much debate as to what extent such an alteration would be both safe and ethical.

1. In the passage above, what roles do the highlighted sentences serve?

   (A) The first sentence is the main idea, and the second sentence restates the main idea.
   (B) The first sentence makes the central argument of the passage, and the second sentence supports the argument.
   (C) The first sentence provides the primary argument, and the second sentence is the secondary argument.
   (D) The first sentence is a secondary argument, and the second sentence is evidence against that argument.
   (E) The first sentence introduces the topic, and the second sentence is the conclusion.

2. According to the passage, all of the following statements are true EXCEPT:

   (A) Medical nanotechnology is a field of nanotechnology that is entirely biological in practice.
   (B) Nanotechnology has already led to medical practices that are currently in use.
   (C) There are valid concerns regarding the use of nanotechnology.
   (D) Some of what happens on the nanoscale is naturally occurring.
   (E) Gene therapy is a result of medical nanotechnology.

Questions 3–5 are based on the passage below.

Although it is an imperfect model for describing a complex market, the theory of supply and demand is a reasonably accurate method of explaining, describing, and predicting how the quantity and price of goods fluctuate within a market. Economists define supply as the amount of a particular good that producers are willing to sell at a certain price. For example, a manufacturer might be willing to sell 7,000 sprockets if each one sells for $0.45 but would be willing to sell substantially more sprockets, perhaps 12,000, for a higher price of $0.82. Conversely, demand represents the quantity of a given item that consumers will purchase at a set price; in the most efficient market, all buyers pay the lowest price available, and all sellers charge the highest price they are able. The intersection of these occurrences is graphically represented in supply and demand curves that show the prices at which a product becomes too expensive or too readily available.

3. Which one of the following best expresses the main idea of the passage?

   (A) explaining why buyers in a given market tend to seek the lowest price on available goods
   (B) offering a dissenting perspective on an obsolete economic model
   (C) persuading readers that the model of supply and demand is the best method for understanding market forces
   (D) providing an explanation of the two primary elements of an economic model and how they intersect
   (E) analyzing the fluctuation of supply and demand within a market

Consider each of the following choices separately and select all that apply.

4. If the producer of sprockets nearly doubles its prices as described in the passage, it follows that

   [A] buyers in the market will be likely to purchase more of the sprockets being sold.
   [B] the price of sprockets will continue to increase.
   [C] buyers in the market will be likely to purchase fewer of the sprockets being sold.

5. Select the sentence in the passage that illustrates an abstract concept presented by the author.

READING COMPREHENSION PRACTICE SET ANSWERS AND EXPLANATIONS

1. E

This Logic question asks for the role of the two highlighted sentences. The first highlighted sentence introduces an idea about medical nanotechnology—that it involves "tiny machines"—and the author spends the rest of the passage addressing this idea. The contrast keyword "Yet" at the beginning of the next sentence indicates that the author at least partially disagrees with this characterization of nanotechnology. Therefore, the first highlighted sentence is not an argument of the author's. Eliminate choices **(B)**, **(C)**, and **(D)**, all of which state that the first sentence is an "argument."

Now determine whether choice **(A)** or **(E)** correctly identifies the role of the second highlighted sentence. Beginning with the second sentence, "Yet . . . ," the author disagrees with the "potentially troubling image" in the first sentence, explaining that much of medical nanotechnology is biological, not mechanical. But the second highlighted sentence begins with the contrast keywords "Even so," indicating that the author does not entirely disagree with the first sentence. Indeed, the author opines that even when medical nanotechnology is biological in nature, it can still be "cause for concern." This authorial opinion is the author's conclusion about the subject, and choice **(E)** is correct. The second highlighted sentence does not restate anything, as in **(A)**, because its idea—that nanotechnology can have biological components but at the same time be troubling—has not yet been stated.

2. A

"According to the passage" signals a Detail question. The "EXCEPT" means the correct answer is a fact or idea that is *not* stated in the passage; the four incorrect answers present material that is in the passage. There are an infinite number of details that aren't in this passage, so forming a precise prediction of the correct answer is not possible. However, you can consult your passage map and review what you know the author says about medical nanotechnology in order to eliminate choices that reflect that information. Then research the remaining choices in the passage, eliminating those that are mentioned.

In your strategic reading of the passage, you should have noted that some people think of medical nanotechnology as involving small machines, but according to the author, a lot of it is actually biological. Key examples given involve genetics. The author concludes that genetic manipulation poses concerns about safety and ethics. Choice **(A)** uses word "entirely," making it Extreme and a likely correct answer to this EXCEPT question. In sentence 2, the author says that "much" (not all) of nanotechnology is biological, and choice **(A)** is correct.

Choice **(B)** is confirmed by the sentence "Gene study and gene therapy . . . have already proven useful . . ." Choice **(C)** is given in the passage's last sentence. Choice

(D) is present in the sentences "Yet much of what constitutes nanotechnology is purely biological . . ." and "Many of the basic functions of life occur on the nanoscale level," as well as the example of DNA. Choice **(E)** is stated in the sentence "Gene study and gene therapy, two byproducts of medical nanotechnology . . ."

3. D

The passage as a whole discusses the basic elements of the model of supply and demand, defining the two terms and describing how they work. That's choice **(D)**. Choice **(A)** is too narrow, focusing on only one of the two forces described. Choice **(B)** is out of scope because there's no mention of the model being obsolete; also, the author simply describes the model—she doesn't dissent from its contentions. Although the passage asserts that the supply and demand model is "reasonably accurate," the passage is primarily concerned with explaining the model, not with persuading readers that it is the "best" model. Therefore, you can rule out **(C)**. Although the theory of supply and demand does allow for the analysis of market forces, **(E)**, the passage itself provides only description, not analysis.

4. C

You are told that producers want to charge as much as possible and buyers want to pay as little as possible, so it makes sense that as prices rise, demand falls, choice **(C)**. Choice **(A)** is the opposite of what the passage implies, which is that demand decreases as prices rise. There's no evidence presented that this change in price will lead to further price increases, so you can rule out **(B)**.

5. For example, a manufacturer might be willing to sell 7,000 sprockets if each one sells for $0.45 but would be willing to sell substantially more sprockets, perhaps 12,000, for a higher price of $0.82.

The abstract concepts addressed in the passage are those of supply and demand, and the only example that illustrates supply and demand occurs in sentence 3. Sentence 1 introduces the supply and demand model. Sentence 2 defines the term *supply*. Sentence 4 explains demand, and sentence 5 describes a graphical representation of the two forces.

CHAPTER 8

Verbal Reasoning Practice Sets

In this section, you will take three practice sections consisting of 20 questions each. This section has been divided into two parts to allow you to check your answers at the halfway mark. You will use a diagnostic tool at that point to help you learn from your mistakes and continue on to the second set with more awareness of the traps you may encounter.

REVIEW OF THE KAPLAN METHODS FOR VERBAL REASONING QUESTION TYPES

Review the steps and strategies you have studied for answering each type of question quickly, efficiently, and correctly before starting your Practice Sets.

THE KAPLAN METHOD FOR TEXT COMPLETION (ONE-BLANK)

STEP 1 Read the sentence, looking for clues.

STEP 2 Predict an answer.

STEP 3 Select the choice that most closely matches your prediction.

STEP 4 Check your answer.

THE KAPLAN METHOD FOR TEXT COMPLETION (TWO-BLANK AND THREE-BLANK)

STEP 1 Read the sentence, looking for clues.

STEP 2 Predict an answer for the easier/easiest blank.

STEP 3 Select the choice that most closely matches your prediction.

STEP 4 Predict and select for the remaining blanks.

STEP 5 Check your answers.

THE KAPLAN METHOD FOR SENTENCE EQUIVALENCE

STEP 1 Read the sentence, looking for clues.

STEP 2 Predict an answer.

STEP 3 Select the two choices that most closely match your prediction.

STEP 4 Check your answers to see if the sentence retains the same meaning.

THE KAPLAN METHOD FOR READING COMPREHENSION

STEP 1 Read the passage strategically.

STEP 2 Analyze the question stem.

STEP 3 Research the relevant text in the passage.

STEP 4 Make a prediction.

STEP 5 Evaluate the answer choices.

VERBAL REASONING PRACTICE SET 1

Directions: Each sentence below has one or more blanks, each blank indicating that something has been omitted. Beneath the sentence are five words for one-blank questions and sets of three words for each blank for two- and three-blank questions. Choose the word or set of words for each blank that best fits the meaning of the sentence as a whole.

1. The patterns of the stock market seem ________ to many beginners, but they can be decoded with dedication and patience.

   (A) unwelcoming
   (B) arcane
   (C) harmonious
   (D) shocking
   (E) lucid

2. In spite of its popularity, *The Merchant of Venice* remains a (i) ________ play, with many critics (ii) ________ the extent of Shakespeare's anti-Semitism.

Blank (i)		Blank (ii)	
A	controversial	D	assuaging
B	celebrated	E	augmenting
C	histrionic	F	debating

3. Considered one of his most (i) ________ works, Mozart's *Requiem in D Minor* has a certain (ii) ________ in Western culture because of its incomplete status at the time of his death, and many (iii) ________ stories have arisen surrounding it; unfortunately, the truth is lost to us.

Blank (i)		Blank (ii)		Blank (iii)	
A	ignominious	D	obscurity	G	fraudulent
B	inconspicuous	E	indifference	H	apocryphal
C	famous	F	mystique	I	verified

4. Although Thomas Paine was most (i) __________ his political pamphlets, he was in fact (ii) __________ writer on many different subjects.

Blank (i)		Blank (ii)	
A	inimical to	D	an abstruse
B	condemned for	E	a prolific
C	famous for	F	a terrible

5. Because he was convinced of his own __________, Adam never acknowledged his mistakes.

Ⓐ genius
Ⓑ acclamation
Ⓒ shrewdness
Ⓓ infallibility
Ⓔ popularity

6. St. Elmo's fire is a weather phenomenon that, (i) __________ it has been documented since ancient times, was not (ii) __________ until recently.

Blank (i)		Blank (ii)	
A	because	D	incinerated
B	since	E	reported
C	although	F	understood

Questions 7–10 are based on the passage below.

It has been commonly accepted for some time now that certain scenes in Shakespeare's *Macbeth* are interpolations from the writing of another author; act III, scene 5, and parts of act IV, scene 1, have been determined to be the writing of one of his contemporaries, Thomas Middleton. This can be regarded as both illuminating and problematic, depending upon how the play is being studied. It allows us to infer a great deal about the conventions and practices of writing for the stage at the time. For example, playwriting may have been more collaborative than previously thought, or perhaps Elizabethan notions of plagiarism were different from ours. While historically significant, this does complicate our interpretation of the characters in the play. It is more difficult to assess authorial intention with regard to a character's motives if the text has been redacted by multiple authors.

7. Select the statement or statements that are correct according to the passage.

   - [A] The author feels that Shakespeare is guilty of plagiarism.
   - [B] The interpolations found in plays such as *Macbeth* make the assessment of authorial intention more straightforward.
   - [C] Our current understanding of plagiarism may have arisen after Shakespeare's time.

8. Consider the following choices and select all that apply. Which of the following could aid in the further study of the interpolations discussed in the above passage?

   - [A] an investigation into the existence and prevalence of collaborative writing partnerships during Shakespeare's time
   - [B] an examination of the themes and techniques of other writers contemporary with Shakespeare
   - [C] a search through legal documents of Shakespeare's time for references to plagiarism or intellectual property rights

9. Consider the following choices and select all that apply. Which CANNOT be inferred from the passage?

   [A] The example of interpolation discussed in the passage would be illegal today.
   [B] Authors and playwrights in Shakespeare's time might have recruited assistance when composing their works.
   [C] Shakespeare used Middleton's writing without his consent.

10. In the passage, the two highlighted statements play which of the following roles?

    (A) The first explains a concept, and the second presents an example of that concept.
    (B) The first presents an example of the main subject of the passage, and the second is a conclusion based on that example.
    (C) The first states the conclusion of the argument as a whole, and the second provides support for that conclusion.
    (D) The first provides evidence for a conclusion that the passage as a whole opposes, and the second presents the objection to that conclusion.
    (E) The first states the primary conclusion of the passage, and the second states the secondary conclusion.

Directions: For the following questions, select the **two** answer choices that, when inserted into the sentence, fit the meaning of the sentence as a whole **and** yield complete sentences that are similar in meaning.

11. Known to all as having a silver tongue, the orator easily distracts audiences from the meaning of his words with his ________ speech.

    A mellifluous
    B concise
    C stumbling
    D laconic
    E euphonic
    F strident

12. When the underdogs so soundly beat the team favored to win, their victory ________ the entire sports world.

    A horrified
    B estranged
    C shook
    D bored
    E alienated
    F stunned

13. Despite the efforts made by the municipal government to increase public transportation usage, many people of the city continued to drive their own vehicles, complaining that the bus schedules were too ________ to be relied upon.

    A irregular
    B exacting
    C circuitous
    D rigid
    E isolated
    F erratic

14. Word painting is a musical technique in which the progression of the notes __________ the meaning of the lyrics; a famous example of this can be found in Handel's *Messiah*, in which the notes rise with the mention of "mountains" and fall with the mention of "low."

- [A] affects
- [B] mimics
- [C] contrasts
- [D] reflects
- [E] opposes
- [F] renounces

Directions: Each passage in this group is followed by questions based on its content. After reading a passage, choose the best answer to each question. Answer all questions following a passage on the basis of what is stated or implied in that passage.

Questions 15 and 16 are based on the passage below.

In the decades leading up to the 1970s, the primarily French-speaking Canadian province of Québec saw its proportion of native French speakers diminish from year to year. The attrition of French was attributed to the preeminence of English in the workplace, particularly in affluent, "white-collar" jobs. The French-speaking majority was economically marginalized within its own province, as it was left with the choice of either working in lower-paying jobs or teaching its children English as a first language. The latter option would further erase Québec's cultural autonomy and singularity within a country that primarily spoke English. Facing the risk of linguistic extinction, the province passed *Loi 101* (Law 101): The Charter of the French Language. It established French as the only official language of the province, established the primacy of French in the workplace, and led to more economic equity. Since its passage in 1977, the percentage of people in Québec who speak French as a first language has begun to rise.

15. Which of the following is suggested in the passage as a reason for the decline of French in Québec?

Ⓐ the disparity of economic opportunities available to French and English speakers
Ⓑ an influx of English-speaking immigrants
Ⓒ efforts of French Canadians to further integrate themselves with Canadian culture
Ⓓ the emigration of French Canadians
Ⓔ the outlawing of French in the other provinces

16. According to the passage, *Loi 101* was significant in that it

Ⓐ was a final, unsuccessful attempt at enforcing the usage of French in Québec
Ⓑ curtailed the economic supremacy of English
Ⓒ restricted the teaching of English in schools
Ⓓ highlighted the distinctiveness of the cultural identity of Québec from that of the rest of Canada
Ⓔ provided for bilingual education

Questions 17–19 are based on the paragraph below.

The advent of online education in the first decade of the 21st century was the result of and a response to a number of factors that were both internal and external to the field of higher education. Traditional tertiary institutions, especially those that were privately endowed, raised tuition rates far in excess of the rate of inflation. This, in concert with a larger demand for postsecondary education for working adults, helped facilitate the introduction of online learning. However, it should be acknowledged that the relative simplicity of using the Internet as a platform, as well as its cost-effectiveness, was seized upon by entrepreneurs in the private sector. Online education is largely in the hands of for-profit companies. The question now becomes whether the democratization of higher education is worth the price of removing it from nonprofit, research-based universities.

17. The passage is concerned primarily with

Ⓐ the advent of online education
Ⓑ adult-oriented educational systems
Ⓒ the usefulness of the Internet in postsecondary education
Ⓓ economic and technological factors that influenced the development and current state of online education
Ⓔ the advantages and disadvantages of online education

18. The author's use of the term "seized upon" evokes an image of __________ on the part of the entrepreneurs.

Ⓐ accidental realization
Ⓑ opportunistic tactics
Ⓒ violent appropriation
Ⓓ collusive behavior
Ⓔ market manipulation

19. The highlighted section refers to

Ⓐ the cost of online education
Ⓑ the popularity of online courses
Ⓒ making education available to a wider range of students
Ⓓ the role of voting in class selection
Ⓔ whether or not a democratic society should have online education

Question 20 is based on the passage below.

Thermodynamics is concerned with changes in the properties of matter when we alter the external conditions. An example of this is a gas being compressed by the motion of a piston. The final outcome depends on how the change is made—if the piston is moved in slowly, we say that the compression is "reversible." This means that if we pull the piston back out, we retrace the same sequence of properties but in the reverse order; hence, the temperature of the gas will be the same when the piston has been pulled out as it was before the piston was pushed in. However, if the piston is moved in and out quickly, then the initial state (and temperature) will not be recovered—the gas will always be hotter than it was at the beginning. This is a manifestation, although not a statement, of the second law of thermodynamics. It also makes a difference whether there is a transfer of heat between the cylinder of gas and the external surroundings. If the cylinder is insulated, then the gas will heat on compression and cool on expansion (refrigeration uses this principle). On the other hand, if the cylinder can exchange heat with the surroundings, it will remain at the same temperature if the compression is slow enough.

20. This passage is primarily concerned with

- (A) describing the motion of a piston to demonstrate the laws of thermodynamics
- (B) explaining the conservation of heat during the motion of a piston
- (C) demonstrating how the second law of thermodynamics applies to pistons
- (D) explaining how thermodynamics function
- (E) discussing reversible compression

VERBAL REASONING PRACTICE SET 1 ANSWER KEY

1. B
2. A, F
3. C, F, H
4. C, E
5. D
6. C, F
7. C
8. A, B, C
9. A, C
10. B
11. A, E
12. C, F
13. A, F
14. B, D
15. A
16. B
17. D
18. B
19. C
20. A

DIAGNOSE YOUR RESULTS

Diagnostic Tool

Tally up your score and write your results below.

Total

Total Correct: __________ out of 20 correct

By Question Type

Text Completions (questions 1–6) __________ out of 6 correct
Sentence Equivalence (questions 11–14) __________ out of 4 correct
Reading Comprehension (questions 7–10, 15–20) __________ out of 10 correct

Look back at the questions you got wrong and think about your experience answering them.

STEP 1

Find the roadblocks.

If you struggled to answer some questions, then to improve your score, you need to pinpoint exactly what "roadblocks" tripped you up. To do that, ask yourself the following two questions.

Am I weak in the skills being tested?

The easiest way to determine this is to think in terms of what skills are required for each question type. If you're having trouble with Sentence Equivalence or Text Completion, you probably need to review your vocabulary word lists. Maybe you need to brush up on using word etymology to your advantage. If Reading Comprehension questions are bothersome, you need to work on your critical reading skills. If you know you need to brush up on your verbal skills, try the *Kaplan GRE Verbal Workbook*, which contains a focused review of all the verbal reasoning concepts tested on the GRE, as well as practice exercises to build speed and accuracy.

Did the question types throw me off?

Then you need to become more comfortable with them! Sentence Equivalence questions have a unique format, and Reading Comprehension can be daunting with its dense, complex passages. If you struggled, go back to the beginning of this chapter and review the Kaplan principles and methods for the question types you found challenging. Make sure you understand the principles and how to apply the methods. These strategies will help you improve your speed and efficiency on Test Day. Remember, it's not a reading or vocabulary test; it's a critical-reasoning test (even though your reading habits and command of vocabulary are indispensable tools that will help you earn a high score).

Also, get as much practice as you can so that you grow more at ease with the question type formats. For even more practice, try the *Kaplan GRE Verbal Workbook*, which includes practice sets for each question type.

STEP 2

Find the blind spots.

Did you answer some questions quickly and confidently but get them wrong anyway?

When you come across wrong answers like these, you need to figure out what you thought you were doing right, what it turns out you were doing wrong, and why that happened. The best way to do that is to **read the answer explanations!**

The explanations give you a detailed breakdown of why the correct answer is correct and why all the other answer choices are incorrect. This helps to reinforce the Kaplan principles and methods for each question type and helps you figure out what blindsided you so it doesn't happen again. Also, just as with your "roadblocks," try to get in as much practice as you can.

STEP 3

Reinforce your strengths.

Now read through all the answer explanations for the ones you got right. You should check every answer because if you guessed correctly without actually knowing how to get the right answer, reading the explanations will make sure that whatever needs fixing gets fixed. Work through them one more time. Again, this helps to reinforce the Kaplan principles and methods for each question type, which in turn helps you work more efficiently so you can get the score you want. Keep your skills sharp with more practice.

As soon as you are comfortable with all the GRE question types and Kaplan methods, complete a full-length practice test under timed conditions. In this way, practice tests serve as milestones; they help you to chart your progress. So don't save them all for the final weeks! For even more practice, you can also try the Kaplan GRE Quiz Bank. You get more than 2,500 questions that you can access 24/7 from any Internet browser, each with comprehensive explanations. You can even customize your quizzes based on question type, content, and difficulty level. Take quizzes in Timed Mode to test your stamina or in Tutor Mode to see explanations as you work. Best of all, you also get detailed reports to track your progress.

Visit **http://kaptest.com/GRE** for more details on our Quiz Bank and for more information on our other online and classroom-based options.

VERBAL REASONING PRACTICE SET 1 ANSWERS AND EXPLANATIONS

1. B

The road sign here is "but," which is a detour. The key words "can be decoded" indicate that the contrasting word in the blank means something like "mysterious" or "hard to understand." With that prediction in mind, look for an answer that suggests something incomprehensible, which rules out choices **(C)** *harmonious*, **(D)** *shocking*, and **(E)** *lucid*. Choice **(A)** *unwelcoming* is a possibility, but it refers more to a sense of unpleasantness than to perplexity. Answer choice **(B)** *arcane* is a perfect fit for the sense of something that cannot be easily understood.

2. A, F

Begin by taking note of the phrase "in spite of," which suggests that there will be an opposing idea in the sentence. The sentence describes the play as popular, so you can rule out choices **(B)** *celebrated* and **(C)** *histrionic* for the first blank because you are looking for a word contrasting with popularity. Based on the remaining option, **(A)** *controversial*, you are looking for a solution to the second blank that connotes uncertainty. Choices **(D)** *assuaging* and **(E)** *augmenting* are not possible, since neither means uncertainty. It is therefore answer choice **(F)** *debating* for the second blank. Read the sentence with the blanks filled in: if the play is controversial, it is not universally popular, and it makes sense that critics would debate some aspect of it.

3. C, F, H

When there are so many missing parts, it is often best to begin with whatever complete clause you can find; in this case, the final one. This will allow you to fill in the third blank. You are told that we do not know the truth, which allows you to eliminate both choices **(G)** *fraudulent* and **(I)** *verified*, because both indicate that concrete knowledge exists on the matter. Answer choice **(H)** *apocryphal* is the only possible answer. If you know that many apocryphal stories arose surrounding the work, you can make headway into both of the other blanks.

For the first blank, assume that if many stories are made up about something, it is widely talked about—this eliminates choice **(B)** *inconspicuous* without a doubt, and between choices **(A)** *ignominious* and **(C)** *famous*, the choice is fairly straightforward. When you know something is much talked about because it is "incomplete," you can suppose that a neutral synonym of "well-known" is going to be much more likely than a negative synonym of "shameful."

Finally, for the second blank, you can reject choices **(D)** *obscurity* and **(E)** *indifference* because you know the composition is well-known, so answer choice **(F)** *mystique* is the only logical choice (and is supported by the mention of *apocryphal* stories). Let's check our answer: "Considered one of his most *famous* works, Mozart's *Requiem in D Minor* has a certain *mystique* in Western culture, and many *apocryphal* stories have arisen surrounding it; unfortunately, the truth is lost to us." Everything fits in perfectly when you read back the sentence with the correct words filled in.

4. C, E

"Although", a detour road sign, starts off the sentence, indicating that the ideas of the first and second clause will be opposites. While external knowledge might tell you that Paine was, in fact, a famous writer, it is important to remember that the correct answer will be derived from clues in the sentence alone. Also, the key words "political pamphlets" and "many different subjects" tell us what is being contrasted here: one subject (politics) versus many subjects. You might predict that Paine was well-known for his political writing but was actually a good writer on many subjects.

For the first blank, **(C)** *famous for* is a perfect match for your prediction. Choices **(A)** *inimical to* and **(B)** *condemned for* are both negative and, therefore, incorrect. Then for the second blank, neither **(D)** *abstruse* nor **(F)** *terrible* indicate that Paine wrote well. However, **(E)** *prolific* author writes a lot, and it can be presumed that writing comes easily to him. Therefore, **(E)** is the correct answer for the second blank.

Choices **(D)** *abstruse* and **(E)** *terrible* could work in a different sentence, but there is no choice for the first blank that will allow the resulting sentence to make sense. The answer will always be clear and definite—choices **(C)** *famous for* and **(E)** *prolific* create a sentence that makes sense without requiring any other knowledge or qualifications.

5. D

Since Adam "never acknowledged his mistakes," you can assume that Adam does not want to admit to being wrong. Choices **(B)** *acclamation* and **(E)** *popularity* can be immediately discounted because they have nothing to do with being right or wrong. Choices **(A)** *genius* and **(C)** *shrewdness* might work in this sentence (they are both related to mental quickness, and someone convinced of his own intelligence might not want to admit to being wrong). However, answer choice **(D)** *infallibility* directly opposes the notion of being wrong and is, therefore, the correct answer.

6. C, F

Based on the choices, you know that there will be a conjunction between the clauses of the first and second blanks. The contrast of "ancient times" and "recently" tells you to predict a word for the first blank that suggests contrast, which eliminates choices **(A)** *because* and **(B)** *since*, leaving you with answer choice **(C)** *although*.

You know St. Elmo's fire has been documented for a long time, so discount choice **(E)** *reported* for the second blank. Choice **(D)** may be tempting, because *incineration* is related to fire, but it does not make sense in this sentence. That leaves **(F)** *understood*, which does make sense as a contrast with the phenomenon's having been documented.

7. C

This type of question gives you three statements and asks you to select which ones are true. Break it down statement by statement. Statement **(A)** is untrue because the term "plagiarism" is used in the passage in the phrase "perhaps Elizabethan notions of plagiarism were different from ours"—which indicates that one cannot be certain of what might have constituted plagiarism at the time. Statement **(B)** is a 180: the passage does refer to the assessment of authorial intention if the text has been redacted by several authors, but the passage states the exact opposite of statement **(B)**. Statement **(C)** is correct because you are told that our current notion of plagiarism might be different from the notion of plagiarism in Shakespeare's time.

8. A, B, C

This Inference question asks you to consider possibilities *based on* what is in the text but not necessarily *stated within* it. **(A)** The passage raises the question of how collaborative writing for the stage may have been during Shakespeare's time. Conducting an investigation into the existence of collaborative writing partnerships would be a good way to determine an answer for this question. **(B)** Familiarizing yourself with the style of other writers who might have helped write or had their work used in the writing of Shakespeare's plays would help in the determination of the actual authorship of passages in *Macbeth* (and other plays), as well as provide insight into authorial intention. Finally, **(C)** is an interesting alternative to a strictly literary study and would help to solve the question posed in the text of what constituted plagiarism in the Elizabethan era. All three are good choices for further study.

9. A, C

This is an Inference EXCEPT question: you must select the statements that you *cannot* infer from the passage. **(A)**, that this example of interpolation would be illegal today, is impossible to tell as the passage does not address issues of legality and we do not even know whether Middleton was a willing collaborator. **(B)** is suggested within the passage in the supposition that writing such as *Macbeth* might have, in fact, been collaborative—this allows you to eliminate choice **(B)**. **(C)** you know to be also a correct response for the same reason you specified for **(A)**—you do not know precisely Middleton's role in the composition. Answer choices **(A)** and **(C)** are both correct.

10. B

In this question, you are asked to determine the rhetorical roles of the two highlighted statements. The first highlighted statement is used as an example of the interpolations that the first clause in the sentence mentions. The highlighted portion states that parts of Shakespeare's work were in fact written by his peer Middleton. So the first highlighted portion appears to be an example.

The second highlighted statement presents an opinion regarding the impact of interpolations on literary analysis. According to this statement, because others wrote certain parts of Shakespeare's work, it is more difficult to determine a character's motives. Your prediction should be that the first statement is an example, and the second is an opinion or conclusion (remember that in arguments, the words "opinion" and "conclusion" will often be used interchangeably). Answer choice **(B)** matches this prediction perfectly.

The other choices miss the mark completely. For instance, choice **(A)** incorrectly states that the second highlighted portion is the example. Similarly, choice **(C)** indicates that the first statement is the opinion and the second is the evidence, the exact opposite of our prediction. **(D)** states that the passage opposes an argument, but there is no conflict addressed in the passage. Finally, choice **(E)** identifies both statements as conclusions, which is not correct.

11. A, E

The key here is that the sentence tells us that his "silver tongue" makes it hard to concentrate on the meaning of his words. To have a silver tongue is to be noted for the pleasantness of one's speech, so you are looking for a pair of answers that mean "pleasing." **(C)** *stumbling*, **(D)** *laconic*, and **(F)** *strident* all are unrelated to the pleasantness of his tone, and while **(B)** *concise* language may be an attribute of a skilled orator, it will not create a similar sentence to one created by either of the other two possible answers. **(A)** *mellifluous* and **(E)** *euphonic* both mean "to be sweet or pleasing," and both are often used in reference to speech.

12. C, F

For the favorite to lose is a surprise, so you are looking for choices that are synonyms of "surprised." Choice **(A)** *horrified* has a negative connotation not implied in the sentence. Likewise, the emotions conveyed in choices **(B)** *estranged* and **(E)** *alienated* would require more information than you are given to be considered as possible answers. **(D)** *bored* is the opposite of what you are looking for; something surprising is not boring. Answer choice **(C)** *shook* is often used in a metaphorical sense when a surprising event occurs, as is answer choice **(F)** *stunned*, and the two are synonyms of each another and of "surprised."

13. A, F

This is a good example of a sentence in which you are given more information than you need. In fact, the only clue you need lies in the final phrase "to be relied upon." Your answers will be antonyms of "reliable," which eliminates choices **(B)** *exacting*, **(C)** *circuitous* (a tempting choice because of the relationship between bus routes and the root word "circuit," but the meaning is not related to the sentence), **(D)** *rigid*, and **(E)** *isolated*. **(A)** *irregular* and **(F)** *erratic* both suggest that the buses are unreliable and, as is often (but not necessarily) the case with these questions, they are synonyms of each other.

14. B, D

While you might have no background in musical techniques, you never need information from outside the sentence to deduce the correct answer. The example given tells you that the progression of notes in the music seems to imitate the words of the lyrics. So, you need a word that gives the meaning "the progression of the notes mirrors the meaning of the lyrics." Choices **(C)** *contrasts*, **(E)** *opposes*, and **(F)** *renounces* are antonyms of the desired answer. While **(A)** *affects* could work in the sentence, it lacks a synonym and does not properly refer to the desired meaning of "mirrors." Answer choices **(B)** *mimics* and **(D)** *reflects* do, however, and thus you know that they are your desired choices.

15. A

You are asked why the use of the French language declined in Québec. Researching the passage, you see this mentioned in the first few lines. Specifically, you are told that the "preeminence" of the English language in the best jobs forced people to switch. This indicates that in order to take advantage of the best economic opportunities, one had to speak English. The passage suggests that French became an economically unviable language, stating that "the French-speaking majority was economically marginalized." Thus, the two groups had access to significantly different economic and professional opportunities. This is reflected in answer choice **(A)**.

Choices **(B)** and **(D)** are out of scope, as immigrant and emigrant populations are not mentioned. Furthermore, choice **(E)** is also beyond the scope of the passage, which does not mention the outlawing of French in other provinces. Finally, choice **(C)** is a 180, as the passage states the French sought to maintain their autonomy, not integrate themselves into other cultures.

16. B

This question asks you to summarize the significance of the law mentioned in the latter part of the passage. Based on the final sentence of the passage (which mentions the rise in French as the primary language), **(A)** is untrue—it was not an unsuccessful attempt. **(B)** is true because the passage specifies that the law "established the primacy of French in the workplace." No mention is made of language in schools, so you can dismiss options **(C)** and **(E)**. Finally, while the cultural identity of Québec is mentioned in the passage, the only results of *Loi 101* specified are the economic equity of the languages and the rise in the usage of French, so you can also reject **(D)** as a possible answer. Answer choice **(B)** is the only option that is based on the information in the passage.

17. D

You must be careful here. Just because **(A)** is a direct quotation of the opening of the passage does not make it the correct answer, and, indeed, the passage moves away from the origins of online education and into other facets of its expansion. **(B)** is not discussed in the passage, even though the author makes note that the demand for adult-oriented education was one of the contributing factors to the rise of online learning. Neither **(C)** nor **(E)** properly describes the entire scope of the passage. Only answer choice **(D)** can be said to encompass the entirety of the passage.

18. B

Here you are called to define a phrase based on its context. What you are looking for is an answer that accurately reflects what is described in the passage: the entrepreneurs saw an untapped potential for profit in the unanswered demand for online learning and "seized upon" it. **(A)** is a poor choice because it implies that their success in capitalizing on the demand was unintentional. **(B)** is a much better solution because it evokes the image of the entrepreneurs taking the opportunity available. **(C)** is highly unlikely because no mention of violence is made in the passage (and, indeed, in reference to online education this would be an unlikely choice to begin with). **(D)** can be eliminated as there is no mention of collusion on the part of for-profit education companies; similarly, **(E)** can be eliminated because those companies are never said to have manipulated the market in order to gain control of the online education market. Answer choice **(B)** is the only possible answer.

19. C

This type of question asks you to define the highlighted phrase based on the context. The key word here is "democratization." While the cost-effectiveness of online education is mentioned earlier in the passage, it is unlikely that **(A)** *the cost of online education* is the correct answer because the sense of the final sentence is that "it remains to be seen whether *making higher education more widely available through online institutions* is worth the price of removing it from nonprofit, research-based universities." Based on this, you can also discount **(B)** *the popularity of online courses* and **(D)** *the role of voting in class selection* because while they may be linked conceptually to the term "democracy," the context tells us this is not what the phrase here concerns. Answer choice **(C)** *making education available to a wider range of students* matches our prediction and properly clarifies the usage of the highlighted phrase in the passage. You can discount **(E)** because it goes well beyond the scope of the passage.

20. A

In a Global question such as this one, the correct answer will reflect the scope and purpose you noted while reading the passage. While the broad topic of the passage is thermodynamics, the bulk of the passage describes the motion of a piston and how the effects of that motion demonstrate the laws of thermodynamics. **(A)** expresses this idea exactly. **(D)** may be tempting since "thermodynamics" is the first word of the passage, but **(D)** is too broad and leaves out any mention of the piston, which plays a key role in the passage as a whole. Choices **(B)**, **(C)**, and **(E)** refer to specific subjects mentioned in the passage but do not refer to the passage as a whole.

VERBAL REASONING PRACTICE SET 2

1. Because she was so ________, Mary was uncomfortable speaking to large groups of people.

   (A) reticent
   (B) congenial
   (C) brusque
   (D) gregarious
   (E) scurrilous

2. The band's new album was universally panned by critics, with many ________ their change to a simpler sound.

   (A) lauding
   (B) ignorant of
   (C) tolerating
   (D) deriding
   (E) apathetic to

3. The cotton gin played a (i) ________ role in advancing the textile industry, (ii) ________ its negative effects can be seen in the rapid development of slavery as the economic base of the American South.

Blank (i)		Blank (ii)	
A	negligible	D	although
B	crucial	E	so
C	trivial	F	plus

4. Although he ________ an image of anti-authoritarianism, Johnny Cash was a frequent visitor to the White House and friends with several presidents during his life.

   (A) advocated
   (B) cultivated
   (C) patronized
   (D) supported
   (E) snubbed

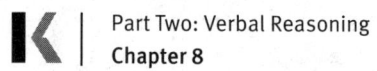

5. (i) ______ mushrooms are popular in many cuisines, it is (ii) ______ to eat those found in the wild, as many frequently found mushrooms resemble edible mushrooms but are, in fact, (iii) ______.

Blank (i)		Blank (ii)		Blank (iii)	
A	Considering	D	imprudent	G	poisonous
B	While	E	cheaper	H	bland
C	Because	F	ingenuous	I	toothsome

6. Though the poet's work was praised highly by critics, sales of his anthologies were (i) ______; it is possible the poor sales were due to his language being too (ii) ______ to be readily understood.

Blank (i)		Blank (ii)	
A	scanty	D	lucid
B	robust	E	prosaic
C	singular	F	abstruse

Question 7 is based on the passage below.

Criticisms of the automaticity model of reading acquisition include a lack of focus on comprehension as the ultimate goal of reading. Too much focus on fluency to the neglect of comprehension is a correlative criticism. Miscue analysis, tracking students' errors or "miscues," has demonstrated that even early readers use prediction as well as translation into dialect as they read, thereby using tools outside of those described in the automaticity model. A third criticism is that dyslexic readers, because of the inherent decoding problems they face, necessarily have trouble following the model and sustaining the reading rates recommended for fluency.

7. The passage suggests that all the following are flaws in the automaticity model of reading acquisition EXCEPT

   Ⓐ failure to consider all the methods commonly used by developing readers
   Ⓑ measuring reading ability by fluency
   Ⓒ prioritizing efficiency in reading over understanding
   Ⓓ insufficient research
   Ⓔ its application in groups of readers who have difficulties decoding reading material

Questions 8–10 are based on the passage below.

Toward the end of the 19th century, many scientists thought that all the great scientific discoveries had already been made and that there was not much left to do beyond some "tidying up." Max Planck, born in 1858, turned this notion upside down with his study of black-body radiation. Even in a vacuum, a hot body will tend to come to thermal equilibrium with a colder body by radiative heat transfer. This is the principle by which we derive energy from the sun. However, measurement of black-body radiation frequencies across a range of temperatures resulted in a parabolic curve, which theory in Planck's time could not explain. After many years of work devoted to this problem, Planck succeeded in quantitatively explaining the experimental data; his key insight was that energy comes in small, discrete packets, called quanta. His theory was the birth of what is called quantum mechanics, the revolutionary theory of matter that is fundamental to the modern understanding of physics, chemistry, and molecular biology.

8. Select the sentence that best describes the importance of Max Planck's work to modern science, as described in the passage.

9. Which of the following would best paraphrase the opening sentence?

   Ⓐ By the late 1800s, much of the scientific community felt it had completed the majority of its work and minor revisions were its only remaining task.
   Ⓑ By 1900, few scientists were still making significant discoveries, and most projects were revising current theories.
   Ⓒ At the end of the 19th century, scientists were concerned that they had run out of discoveries to make and could only perfect already proven theories.
   Ⓓ By 1900, the scientific community had declared that it had come to understand the natural laws of the universe.
   Ⓔ At the end of the 19th century, scientists ceased trying to formulate new theories.

10. Which of the following best describes the relationship between the highlighted portions of the passage?

   Ⓐ topic and scope
   Ⓑ theory and debunking
   Ⓒ problem and solution
   Ⓓ hypothesis and analysis
   Ⓔ thesis and synthesis

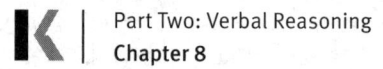

11. After naturally occurring smallpox was eradicated, the World Health Organization chose to ________ the remaining samples of the virus in hopes that they might be later used in developing the means to combat other viruses.

[A] eliminate
[B] duplicate
[C] preserve
[D] retain
[E] extirpate
[F] cultivate

12. The *Magna Carta* was one of the most ________ political declarations of the Middle Ages because it declared the monarch's powers to be limited by the law; although its practical effects were not immediate, it is commonly seen as the genesis of constitutional law in England.

[A] remarkable
[B] immense
[C] pivotal
[D] recondite
[E] ancient
[F] momentous

13. Though ________ filled the streets, people seemed unconcerned with the appearance of their city.

[A] detritus
[B] refuge
[C] gaudiness
[D] bedlam
[E] refuse
[F] barrenness

14. G. K. Chesterton's sense of humor is exemplified in his often ________ responses to his friend and rival George Bernard Shaw.

[A] punctilious
[B] vociferous
[C] waggish
[D] vicious
[E] scathing
[F] witty

Directions: Each passage in this group is followed by questions based on its content. After reading a passage, choose the best answer(s) to each question. Answer all questions following a passage on the basis of what is stated or implied in that passage.

Questions 15–18 are based on the passage below.

There is an anthropological theory that states that societies may be divided into one of two broad categories by their cultural motivators: shame or guilt. In a shame-based society, the ethical motivations are primarily external; one's behavior is governed based on potential effects on the social group (such as dishonoring one's family). By contrast, guilt-based societies rely more heavily on internal motivations; one's behavior is governed based on a set of internal guidelines. There is no society where one or the other is entirely absent, but the distinction lies in that, based on the accepted values of the society, one will come to be dominant over the other. It would seem that early Medieval Europe was primarily a shame-based society; indeed, the forms of shame-based motivators in courtly society were extremely highly developed, with express social laws governing various behaviors. This sort of shame may be seen to be divided into many forms, such as positive and negative shame; that is, prospective and retrospective (knowledge of the honor one will accrue or the shame one will avoid through future actions, and humiliation or other punishment after something harmful has been done, respectively), ethical and nonethical (dealing with higher, such as theological and abstract, concepts, and quotidian matters, respectively), and so on. These social structures may also be found in the contemporary tales of the chivalric world. An example of such may be seen in the frequent plot device of the knight committing adultery with the wife of his lord. Adultery with the wife of one's lord is a matter of treason and an explicit moral wrong, and yet the condemnation in these stories seems to focus on the perpetrator's violation of social norms (treason) rather than moral standards (adultery).

15. Read the following statements and select all that apply. Which of the following CANNOT be inferred from the passage?

    [A] Early Medieval Europe was unconcerned with moral codes.
    [B] Some cultures are neither shame-based nor guilt-based.
    [C] Guilt-based societies have few laws.

16. Select the sentence that describes the scope of the passage.

17. Consider the following choices and select all that apply. What can we infer about a society that focuses primarily upon a moral code of right and wrong?

    [A] It would be guilt-based.
    [B] It would tolerate adultery.
    [C] It would not have laws governing behavior.

18. Based on the passage, a society that prizes the harmony of the social group would most likely be

    (A) guilt-based
    (B) shame-based
    (C) extremely permissive
    (D) governed by a chivalric order
    (E) bereft of citizens with an internal code of moral right and wrong

Questions 19 and 20 are based on the passage below.

At the atomic scale, all matter exhibits properties commonly associated with both waves and particles. The classic experiment that demonstrates wavelike properties is the double-slit experiment, first performed by Thomas Young at the beginning of the 19th century. If a beam of light passes through two narrow slits and is projected onto a screen behind the slits, a pattern of light and dark fringes can be observed. The explanation for this is based on an analogy with ripples in water. If we drop two stones some distance apart, the ripples start to interfere with each other, sometimes amplifying when two crests or troughs meet, sometimes canceling when a crest meets a trough. A similar explanation holds for interference effects with visible light; the two slits act as independent sources in the same way as do the stones in water. This experiment provided convincing evidence in support of Christian Huygen's wave theory of light, which eventually supplanted the older particle theory of Isaac Newton. However, in the 20th century, Einstein showed that Newton was not entirely wrong. His analysis of the photoelectric effect showed that light could behave as a particle as well as a wave. Surprisingly, electrons, which we tend to think of as particles, also demonstrate interference effects, showing that they too are waves as well as particles.

19. Which of the following best summarizes the findings of Young's experiment, as described in the passage?

    Ⓐ The waves from independent light sources interact with one another in predictable patterns.
    Ⓑ Two light sources can cancel each other out, creating the observed dark fringes.
    Ⓒ Light exhibits properties of both particles and waves.
    Ⓓ Newton's theory was permanently debunked.
    Ⓔ Newton's theory was correct all along.

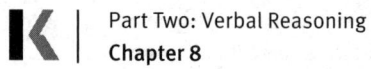

20. Based on the passage, what would we expect the light fringes in Young's experiment to represent?

   (A) the light particles from both slits landing on the screen
   (B) the amplification created by the combination of both sets of waves of light
   (C) the projection onto the screen where the light is not blocked out by the object with the slits
   (D) the amplification created by light particles
   (E) the projection onto the screen where the light is blocked by the object with the slits

VERBAL REASONING PRACTICE SET 2 ANSWER KEY

1. A
2. D
3. B, D
4. B
5. B, D, G
6. A, F
7. D
8. His theory was the birth of what is called...
9. A
10. C
11. C, D
12. C, F
13. A, E
14. C, F
15. A, B, C
16. It would seem that early Medieval Europe was primarily a shame-based society...
17. A
18. B
19. A
20. B

DIAGNOSE YOUR RESULTS

Diagnostic Tool

Tally up your score and write your results below.

Total

Total Correct: ________ out of 20 correct

By Question Type

Text Completions (questions 1–6) ________ out of 6 correct
Sentence Equivalence (questions 11–14) ________ out of 4 correct
Reading Comprehension (questions 7–10, 15–20) ________ out of 10 correct

Repeat the steps outlined on the Diagnose Your Results page that follows the Verbal Reasoning Practice Set 1 answer key.

VERBAL REASONING PRACTICE SET 2 ANSWERS AND EXPLANATIONS

1. A

Mary is quiet when in groups, so you should look to find a related word. You can thus quickly rule out choices **(B)** *congenial* and **(D)** *gregarious*. Answer choice **(A)** *reticent* properly matches the sense of the second clause, whereas choices **(C)** *brusque* and **(E)** *scurrilous* would require information beyond her being quiet in groups to be good choices.

2. D

The critics do not approve of the band's change, and the word "with" is a straight-ahead road sign here, so look for something that suggests criticism or rejection. This eliminates choices **(A)** *lauding* and **(C)** *tolerating*; furthermore, you know that the reception was strongly negative based on the phrase "universally panned," so you can eliminate choices **(B)** *ignorant of* and **(E)** *apathetic to* because both of these indicate a general lack of interest. This leaves answer choice **(D)** *deriding*, which provides the sense of a strong, negative reaction.

3. B, D

Looking at the sentence and choices, you know that the second word will be some kind of conjunction that connects the two parts of the sentence. You can see from the second part that there were negative effects, while in the first part of the sentence you see mention of industrial advances, suggesting that a contrasting conjunction is likely.

Thus, for the second blank, answer choice **(D)** *although* is an appropriate contrasting conjunction. Choices **(E)** and **(F)** are poor choices because they are contingent on the second clause either being a result of the first or building on the first, rather than contrasting with the first clause.

For the first blank, you can safely rule out choices **(A)** *negligible* and **(C)** *trivial* because we know from the second part of the sentence that the cotton gin had some notable effects. Choice **(B)** *crucial* is the only positive option for the first blank.

4. B

With the road sign "Although," you are given a contrast in this sentence about the way Johnny Cash presented himself—"an image of anti-authoritarianism" versus being closely connected with various U.S. presidents. Judging by the sentence, you would expect a term akin to "promoted," so you can remove **(E)** *snubbed* from the list; furthermore, you know it refers to his own image, not the image of others. Choices **(A)** *advocated*, **(C)** *patronized*, and **(D)** *supported* all imply outward action—to encourage an image of someone or something else. Answer choice **(B)** *cultivated* is the correct choice because it most clearly refers to developing his own image.

5. B, D, G

Three-blank sentences take a little longer to work out. Looking at the choices for the first blank, you can see that it is a conjunction, but you cannot be sure of which until you solve the rest of the sentence. The best place to begin in this sentence is actually at the end—you are given a very useful hint with the detour road sign "but," telling you that blank three will be an antonym to "edible." Looking through the choices, you can see that the correct answer is answer choice **(G)** *poisonous*. While you might not want to eat something **(H)** *bland*, this is not a direct antonym to "edible." Choice **(I)** *toothsome* means "palatable" or "desirable" and is the opposite of what the blank needs.

From here, work backwards to the second blank. Since you now know that you are talking about eating possibly poisonous mushrooms, you can predict that blank two will say that it is "unwise" to do so. Choice **(E)** *cheaper* is irrelevant to the context (and no mention of money is made elsewhere), and choice **(F)** *ingenuous*, meaning "innocent" or "sincere," is unrelated to the sentence. Answer choice **(D)** *imprudent* is a synonym of "unwise" and is therefore the answer you need.

Return to the first blank in the sentence. You are told that mushrooms are popular in many cuisines, and you are looking for an answer that connects the two ideas. Predict roughly "*although* mushrooms are popular in many cuisines, it is imprudent..."; what you are looking for is a conjunction marking this contradicting idea. Answer choice **(B)** *While* is the correct choice. For sentences with three blanks, especially, it is important to reread the sentence with all the blanks filled in: "*While* mushrooms are popular in many cuisines, it is *imprudent* to eat those found in the wild, as many frequently found mushrooms resemble edible mushrooms but are, in fact, *poisonous*." The sentence makes perfect sense.

6. A, F

Within the first half of the sentence, you are given the detour road sign "though" to contrast the high praise with the sales. Thus, choices **(B)** *robust* and **(C)** *singular* cannot be correct because they are too positive. Answer choice **(A)** *scanty*, on the other hand, contrasts appropriately with high praise, and it fits perfectly with "poor sales" later in the sentence.

The second half of the sentence offers a possible explanation for why the sales were poor, suggesting that it was too hard to understand the poet's language, which immediately removes choice **(D)** *lucid*. Choice **(E)** *prosaic* might trip you up; however, answer choice **(F)** *abstruse* is clearly the better choice for the second blank—it is an adjective indicating that the prose is difficult to understand.

7. D

Reading through the passage, you can determine answer choice **(D)** to be the correct answer, because there is no mention of the amount of research done or needed concerning the automaticity model. Research is out of scope. Choices **(A)**, **(B)**, and **(C)** are explicitly stated in the passage: **(A)** may be found in the description of early readers, and **(B)** and **(C)** may be found in the criticism of focusing on fluency over understanding. Choice **(E)** can be derived from the third criticism about dyslexia, which is that the automaticity model does not account for differences in decoding ability.

8. His theory was the birth of what is called...

This sentence provides a summary of the importance of his work.

9. A

While reading the paragraph, paraphrase the text in your head to make sure you understand it. The key aspect of this sentence is that, at the time, there were a number of scientists who believed that the major discoveries had been made and the remaining scientific work was to tweak and perfect current theories. With that in mind, you can look through the options to see which best fits this idea. Answer choice **(A)** is an excellent paraphrase of the sentence. **(B)** is problematic because there is a fundamental difference between scientists believing all the great discoveries to have been made and scientists making few new significant discoveries. You can also reject choices **(C)**, **(D)**, and **(E)** because their description of "scientists" and the "scientific community" as a whole is too broad. The original sentence only states "many scientists," suggesting that there were dissenters, such as Planck.

10. C

What you must keep in mind here is that you are asked for the relationship between the two highlighted phrases, not their relationship to the passage as a whole. A good way to attack this sort of question is to paraphrase each of the phrases and identify what it is saying on its own. The first phrase states an issue: that the current theory could not explain the parabolic curve scientists observed. The second phrase tells us of Planck's breakthrough discovery of quanta. Thus, you can predict that the answer will tell us the relationship is between the limitations of the current theory and Planck's solution. **(A)** is a trap because it uses words you frequently see elsewhere and are admonished to remember when considering any Reading Comprehension passage. However, *topic and scope* are irrelevant to this question, and choice **(A)** can be dismissed. **(B)** may be tempting because the first highlighted portion does contain the word "theory." However, based on the wording of the first phrase, it is clear that the issue with the current theory was recognized by the scientific community; thus, Planck's solution was not a challenge to a widely accepted belief, and "debunking" is not appropriate. In answer choice **(C)**, you are given *problem and solution*, which matches your prediction and is the correct answer. **(D)** is out of scope; a *hypothesis* is not brought up here, nor is that hypothesis being explained further. **(E)** is incorrect since the first highlighted sentence is not a *thesis*, or summary, of the paragraph, but rather an issue that needs to be addressed.

11. C, D

While you might be tempted to stray toward the answers meaning "destroy" due to the previous mention of eradication and due to the danger of the material (smallpox), you must carefully read through the sentence. It informs us that there is hope that the samples may have further uses, so you know they must be preserved. You can thus reject **(A)** *eliminate* and **(E)** *extirpate*. You are left with two pairs of synonyms, choices **(B)** *duplicate* and **(F)** *cultivate* as well as **(C)** *preserve* and **(D)** *retain*, so you must choose one of the sets. You are able to do this by focusing on what is in the sentence alone—the word "later" suggests saving the samples, not working with them immediately, so answer choices **(C)** and **(D)** are correct.

12. C, F

With strong words like "most," "declarations," and "genesis," the answer will be likewise a word of emphatic meaning. Furthermore, the sentence tells us of the importance of the *Magna Carta*, so you can predict synonyms of "significant" or "revolutionary." Choices **(D)** *recondite* and **(E)** *ancient* are both meaningless in the sentence, and you can eliminate them. Choice **(B)** *immense* can likewise be dismissed because nowhere is the size of the *Magna Carta* described, nor are there any synonyms among the other options. While choice **(A)** *remarkable* may be tempting, both answer choices **(C)** *pivotal* and **(F)** *momentous* connote a significant turning point, which **(A)** does not.

13. A, E

The key here is that the appearance of the city seems to be lacking, so you are looking for words that imply a deficiency in charm or physical beauty. Choice **(D)** *bedlam* could only make sense without the second clause, and choice **(F)** *barrenness* is a lack of something, so it could not fill the streets; furthermore, both are lacking synonyms in the other options. Choice **(C)** *gaudiness* does imply a lack of taste, but it is without a synonym as well. **(A)** *detritus* means "waste" or "debris," which is an excellent option for the blank, and with further investigation you can see it has a synonym in **(E)** *refuse*. **(B)** *refuge* is a trap for the careless, resembling *refuse* and being right below a synonym of *refuse*—be careful when you read the answers!

14. C, F

The words in the blank will describe Chesterton's particular style of humor. You are given a further clue to the answer in the description of Shaw as his "friend and rival." With this description in mind, you can dismiss choices **(B)** *vociferous*, **(D)** *vicious*, and **(E)** *scathing* as behavior unlikely to be shown toward a friend—remember, if the solution would demand further qualification such as "Chesterton was known to be as harsh to his friends as to his critics," then it is highly unlikely to be the correct answer. **(A)** *punctilious* is not a synonym of the remaining two answer choices, **(C)** *waggish* and **(F)** *witty*.

15. A, B, C

You are looking for statements that go beyond what can reasonably be inferred in the passage. **(A)** is a good choice, because while the passage mentions that it was "primarily a shame-based society," there is no mention of a lack of concern with moral codes; further, the passage notes that neither classification of societies is without some influence of the other. **(B)** also cannot be inferred; in fact, it is contradicted in the fourth sentence. As for **(C)**, while the passage mentions the complexity of the social guidelines of shame-based societies, there is no way you can infer that guilt-based societies have few laws. All three of the answers are correct.

16. It would seem that early Medieval Europe was primarily a shame-based society...

This sentence provides us with the particular focus of the passage on Medieval Europe, narrowed down from the topic of shame- and guilt-based societies in general.

17. A

The difference between the two kinds of societies, according to the author, is a matter of internal (guilt) and external (shame) motivators. What you must consider, then, is where a moral code might be placed. You are given one particularly useful clue in the phrase "internal guidelines" in sentence 3, which, even if it lacks the strength of a sense of moral right and wrong, still allows us to classify the society in the question as guilt based. Furthermore, in the example at the end of the passage, it is suggested that "moral standards" are an example of a trait of a guilt based society. The answer is **(A)**. Choice **(B)** is incorrect; don't be distracted by the description at the end of the passage that describes how medieval Europe, a shame-based society, dealt with adultery. Choice **(C)** is beyond the scope of the passage.

18. B

For this question, you must consider the description of the society in the question compared to what you are given in the passage. Early in the passage, you see mention of dishonoring one's family as an example of a damaging effect on the social group. This indicates that the society in the question would be a shame-based society as in the example, and the correct answer is **(B)**. Choice **(C)** is incorrect because there are certainly rules in a shame-based society. Similarly, you can reject **(E)**; it goes beyond the scope of the passage, which does not offer any evidence to suggest that individuals within a society that emphasizes social cohesion do not have an internally regulated morality. **(D)** is incorrect because there is insufficient information to support such an assertion.

19. A

The key to this question lies in the analogy of the ripples in the water, where two troughs or crests amplify each other but one trough and one crest negate each other. Likewise, with the light waves, the two separate light sources produce waves that interact with one another and, like the crests and troughs of the water, have predictable results: the light and dark fringes. Choice **(B)** describes a part of Young's findings, but you must reject it because it does not adequately describe the whole of his findings. Choice **(C)** cannot be the correct answer either, because the passage notes that it was not until Einstein that particle theory was returned to the theory of light. And likewise for choice **(D)**; you are told Einstein proved that Newton's theory was not entirely accurate and so it was not permanently debunked. Similarly, you cannot claim he was entirely correct, so **(E)** is out as well. This leaves choice **(A)**, which matches your prediction.

20. B

The answer, again, comes from the ripple analogy, where two meeting crests are amplified. Thus, choice **(B)** is likely to be the correct answer. You can dismiss **(A)** since Young's experiment is concerned solely with light as a wave, not as a particle, and answer choice **(C)** fails to take into account the purpose of his experiment: separating a single light source into two streams and recombining them on the screen. As for choice **(D)**, amplification of light particles is mentioned as a possibility, but this is out of the scope of the question. Choice **(E)** refers to Huygen's wave theory of light but not Young's experiment. You have a clear answer in choice **(B)**.

VERBAL REASONING PRACTICE SET 3

1. Veteran technical support staff members feel that their services are _______ by the use of computer programs to do the same work; they claim that technical support can't be provided procedurally but rather is a case-by-case effort that requires a skill set built upon training and experience.

   Ⓐ devalued
   Ⓑ tarnished
   Ⓒ ridiculed
   Ⓓ vituperated
   Ⓔ impaired

2. The spice saffron is made from the stigma of the *Crocus sativus* plant; the (i) _______ number of blossoms required to produce saffron and the (ii) _______ of the flower makes the spice the most expensive in the world.

Blank (i)	Blank (ii)
A vast	D color
B meager	E hardiness
C unique	F delicacy

3. The field of cryptozoology is the search for animals unknown to science and those for which we have no scientific attestation; (i) _______ physical evidence, it relies upon (ii) _______ sightings for proof of creatures such as the Loch Ness Monster.

Blank (i)	Blank (ii)
A ignoring	D anecdotal
B lacking	E imagined
C needing	F nominal

4. The humor of Oscar Wilde remains a classic example of _______ wit; his terse remarks and deadpan delivery belied an acerbic sarcasm and brilliant insight into the world around him.

   Ⓐ ostentatious
   Ⓑ pointed
   Ⓒ brazen
   Ⓓ orotund
   Ⓔ laconic

5. The neglect of the old theater was (i) _______ in the extreme (ii) _______ of the building, which was no longer safe to enter.

Blank (i)		Blank (ii)	
A	hinted at	D	dilapidation
B	suggested	E	depilation
C	manifest	F	radiance

6. The countless (i) _______ days left everyone (ii) _______ for the sudden downpour; the deluge brought traffic to a halt as it (iii) _______ the roads.

Blank (i)		Blank (ii)		Blank (iii)	
A	arid	D	waiting	G	inundated
B	calm	E	unprepared	H	soaked
C	humid	F	anxious	I	sprayed

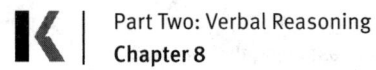

Questions 7–10 are based on the passage below.

The origins of the English language can be traced back to the Saxon and other Germanic settlers in Britain beginning in the 5th century CE. The English language's unusual nature can be attributed to the diverse linguistic origins of the groups that contributed to its development and their role in English society. Although English belongs to the Germanic language family and its grammatical and syntactical rules reflect this, English vocabulary can be seen to be from multiple origins. In fact, a large part of the vocabulary was not derived from the Germanic languages at all but is rather of Latin origin. This can be explained by the influence on Old English of Old French and Latin during the Norman Invasion in the 11th century. By the time of the Norman Invasion, Old English was already a language, with both its grammar and vocabulary based in the Germanic language family. However, the establishment of a ruling class who spoke a Romance language caused significant changes in the indigenous tongue. It is also interesting to note that there is a distinct correlation between the length of a word and its origin—most of the shorter words in the English language are derived from the Germanic languages, whereas the longer words are from a Latin background. One theory to explain this is that these more elaborate and complex words were primarily used by the elite after the Norman Invasion—who would have favored a Latin-based (or Romance) vocabulary—whereas words with the same meaning in the Old English were used primarily by the lower classes and thus fell into disuse. Modern English words, then, concerning more complex and theoretical rather than utilitarian ideas (astronomy, poetry, and epistemology), can generally be found to be of Romance origin, whereas more mundane words, such as pronouns and auxiliary verbs, can be traced back to a Germanic origin.

7. Which of the following is implied by the passage?

   Ⓐ English was more heavily influenced by Germanic languages than by Romance languages.

   Ⓑ In the 11th century, English speakers of the lower classes did not discuss abstract, theoretical topics.

   Ⓒ No auxiliary verbs in English can be traced back to a Latin-based origin.

   Ⓓ English owes some of its abnormality to the Norman Invasion.

   Ⓔ Fewer words in English are derived from Latin than from the Germanic languages.

8. Read the following answer choices and select all that apply. The passage suggests that the word "they," a pronoun, would most likely have which of the following origins?

   [A] Germanic
   [B] Romance
   [C] Norse

9. Based on the passage, what is a likely reason why English has not been reclassified as a Romance language?

   (A) It developed as a Germanic language in its first incarnation, Old English.
   (B) The core of the language, its grammar and syntax, is still Germanic.
   (C) A larger portion of the English vocabulary is Germanic rather than Romance.
   (D) The Normans felt an affinity for the local tongue, which was Germanic.
   (E) Neither linguistic heritage has a claim to preeminence.

10. Read the following choices and select all that apply. Which of the following can be inferred from the passage?

    [A] Searching for meaning based on the Latin root of a word is less likely to be useful in shorter words.
    [B] The language spoken by the Saxon and Germanic settlers entirely supplanted the indigenous tongue of 5th-century Britain.
    [C] The discussion of complex ideas during the Norman era in England was primarily the domain of the ruling class.

11. As modern scholarship continues to dim the possibility that Homer was a single historic figure, the question of authorship of his works has been raised; although we might never know who wrote them, scholars still need some way to refer to the author or authors of the *Iliad* and *Odyssey*, so the term "Homeric tradition" has been ________ as a possible new terminology.

    [A] selected
    [B] established
    [C] appropriated
    [D] bestowed
    [E] suggested
    [F] proposed

12. _______ commercial arsenic usage has diminished, its ongoing presence in water and soil continues to be a major public health concern, given the extremely high toxicity of the substance.

    A After
    B Although
    C Inasmuch as
    D Considering
    E While
    F Because

13. Early sewing machines were poorly received by textile workers, who feared the technology would _______ the demand for their skills; despite their protests, the sewing machine became popular both in the factory and in the home.

    A overwhelm
    B diminish
    C obviate
    D mitigate
    E eliminate
    F belittle

14. The protest march quickly turned into a riot, and in the response by police, several people on either side were killed and dozens more wounded; it would later be _______ remembered by both sides as a tragic accident, and no blame would be assigned.

    A indignantly
    B mournfully
    C spitefully
    D bitterly
    E soberly
    F melancholically

Questions 15–17 are based on the passage below.

The term *teleology* refers to the doctrine that things in nature have a final purpose. Thus, an eye is for seeing, a walk for health, a house for shelter, and a book for reading. Little *t* teleology so conceived, though, mustn't be confused with big *t* Teleology, according to which the whole of nature is either progressing, by virtue of some world-historical or cosmic force, toward some overarching purpose or is already the embodiment of some divine plan.

That teleology needn't entail Teleology is a cornerstone of evolutionary theory. From thc moment that organic life first appeared on Earth some 4.5 billion years ago, natural selection has been an inexorable, unceasing, and entirely mindless process of winnowing and sifting through a set of design plans. The geological record is littered with plant and animal species falling extinct under the pressures of climatic and geographical changes. Only those designs that natural selection has blindly hit upon and that have worked, designs that are well adapted to the specific environment and that therefore confer upon certain organisms or certain species some ostensible advantage, will be inheritable by their progeny. This implies that there is no Higher End, no Higher Purpose that governs the actions of intelligent and unintelligent life, only local purposes fitting into the materialist picture of "selfish genes" seeking to pass on genetic information to their descendants *ad infinitum*. There is therefore no Teleology from on high, only teleology all the way down.

15. According to the passage, the principal difference between teleology and Teleology could be understood in terms of the difference between

    Ⓐ quality and quantity
    Ⓑ example and concept
    Ⓒ property and object
    Ⓓ cause and effect
    Ⓔ part and whole

16. The primary purpose of the passage is to show how

Ⓐ new species come into being through a process called natural selection
Ⓑ evolution represents a change in our comprehension of all forms of life
Ⓒ evolution through a set of randomly generated, rather than intentional, procedures is possible
Ⓓ intelligent and sentient creatures are the inevitable results of natural selection
Ⓔ absolute ignorance works to create living beings much in the same way that absolute wisdom does

17. Read the following choices and select all that apply. Which of the following does the passage cite as a component of evolutionary theory?

[A] the fact that Teleology is not necessary for teleology
[B] the extinctions of many species
[C] the lack of a Higher Purpose for living organisms' behavior

Questions 18–20 are based on the passage below.

John Finnis developed his theory of natural law based on the structure that Thomas Aquinas provided, filling in areas where he felt that Aquinas's theory was lacking; he also amended other aspects of the theory to respond to a world much more culturally diverse than the one in which Aquinas lived. Unlike Aquinas, who gives only a vague account of the first precepts of the natural law, Finnis locates a specific number of basic human goods. Finnis avoids the charge that his theory falls into the "naturalistic fallacy" by asserting that these goods are not moral in themselves but become moral through human participation in them. In addition, these goods are not hierarchical, which allows a much greater range of freedom in choosing actions. Finally, Finnis's theory does not require the presence of God. Though curiosity about the nature of the universe is one of his basic human goods, the actual existence of God is not required by his theory.

Finnis's theory raises as many questions as it answers. While formulating an interesting answer to the "is/ought" problem and giving a much more robust definition of human volition than Aquinas, his solutions create their own problems. His account of the goods is stripped of any method for evaluation. The boundaries of each good are difficult to discern. Further, by asserting that each good is self-evident and equal to all the others, Finnis makes any action taken in furtherance of any of them equivalent morally. Finally, by removing the precepts of natural law from our natural habits and inclinations, placing them instead in self-evident goods, Finnis seems not to be describing our nature at all.

18. Based on the passage, what is the most likely meaning of "good" according to Finnis?

Ⓐ a physical object, such as foodstuffs or textiles
Ⓑ morally correct action as determined by God
Ⓒ an action that helps us achieve a desirable, material end
Ⓓ something self-evident that we ought to strive to embrace
Ⓔ something that is naturally occurring

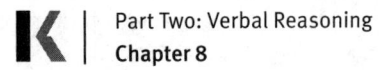

19. Based on the passage, the existence of which of the following would most likely undermine Finnis's definition of "goods"?

    Ⓐ proof of the existence of God
    Ⓑ goods that demand opposing actions
    Ⓒ the demands of our natural desires
    Ⓓ the definition of additional goods
    Ⓔ a method for evaluating goods

20. Read the following answer choices carefully and select all that apply. According to the passage, which of the following is NOT an improvement of Finnis's theory of natural law over Aquinas's?

    [A] avoiding the "naturalistic fallacy"
    [B] removing the necessity of God in his definition of "good"
    [C] curtailing freedom in human actions

VERBAL REASONING PRACTICE SET 3 ANSWER KEY

1. A
2. A, F
3. B, D
4. E
5. C, D
6. A, E, G
7. D
8. A
9. B
10. A
11. E, F
12. B, E
13. C, E
14. B, F
15. C
16. C
17. A, B, C
18. D
19. B
20. C

Diagnose Your Results

Diagnostic Tool

Tally up your score and write your results below.

Total

Total Correct: ________ out of 20 correct

By Question Type

Text Completions (questions 1–6) ________ out of 6 correct
Sentence Equivalence (questions 11–14) ________ out of 4 correct
Reading Comprehension (questions 7–10, 15–20) ________ out of 10 correct

Repeat the steps outlined on the Diagnose Your Results page that follows the Verbal Reasoning Practice Set 1 answer key.

VERBAL REASONING PRACTICE SET 3 ANSWERS AND EXPLANATIONS

1. A

The increase in automated support suggests a decline in demand for technical support workers, and the second half of the sentence tells you that you are looking for an answer that indicates that their services are being undervalued. **(B)** *tarnished*, **(C)** *ridiculed*, and **(D)** *vituperated* all suggest, beyond a negative image, a directly hostile one, which is not indicated by the sentence. **(E)** *impaired* might be acceptable from the first part of the sentence alone, but the value of their services implied by the second half can only support **(A)** *devalued.*

2. A, F

The first half of the sentence is just background, so it is from the second half that you must take your clues. It tells us that producing saffron is very costly, so you can anticipate that the number of blossoms required is a large rather than small number. Based on this, you can reject **(C)** *unique* and **(B)** *meager* for the first blank, leaving **(A)** *vast.*

The second blank implies a quality of the flower that makes it rare. The correct choice for the second blank is **(F)** *delicacy.* **(D)** *color* is irrelevant, and **(E)** *hardiness* is the opposite of your prediction.

3. B, D

The hint you are given is that cryptozoology lacks "scientific attestation"; that is, it has no scientific reason to be supported. So for the first blank, you are looking for a word that means "without." **(A)** *ignoring* would mean an intentional rejection of scientific evidence, rather than an absence thereof. **(C)** *needing* would work, but there is no choice for blank (ii) that has to do with physical evidence. Furthermore, "relies upon" points us to a limitation of their evidence. Therefore, **(B)** *lacking* makes the most sense for the first blank.

With regard, again, to scientific attestation, you can infer that the second blank implies that the sightings are not backed by scientific data, so you are looking for a solution that means "unscientific" or "unreliable." **(E)** *imagined* makes little sense, because it implies the sightings are not just inadequate but fictitious. **(D)** *anecdotal* provides us with the sense of unverifiable sightings and completes the first blank with "lacking" for the sense of being without. **(F)** *nominal* does not fit at all, as it means negligible, or in name only.

4. E

Based on the semicolon, you know that the second half of the sentence directly supports the statement made in the first, so you are looking for a word that implies the usage of few words and a dry delivery of his wit. **(A)** *ostentatious* and **(D)** *orotund* can be rejected on the grounds of the terseness and "deadpan delivery" of Wilde's remarks, and the fact that the biting nature of his wit is not readily apparent can allow us to discount **(B)** *pointed* and **(C)** *brusque*. Checking the remaining option, **(E)** *laconic*, you find that it fits the meaning of the sentence.

5. C, D

The key word here is "extreme," which indicates that you are looking for a word with very strong meaning for the first blank. Furthermore, you know that the building is "no longer safe to enter," so the second blank must refer to some sense of structural decay. Thus, you can expect the full sentence to be something like "The neglect of the old theater was apparent in the extreme deterioration of the building." For the first blank, **(A)** *hinted at* and **(B)** *suggested* can both be eliminated because they are too weak in meaning for "extreme." Furthermore, both words mean the same thing, so neither could be the single correct answer for the first blank. **(C)** *manifest* makes the most sense.

Out of the options for the second blank, **(D)** and **(E)** are very similar-looking words, but only **(D)** *dilapidation* refers to buildings—**(E)** *depilation* refers to hair removal. Always study the words carefully! **(F)** *radiance* is the opposite of what you need.

6. A, E, G

While you expect the final clause, which is preceded by a semicolon, to be related thematically to the rest of the sentence, grammatically it stands on its own. You can therefore figure out the third blank first without needing the other two. The key here is the word "deluge"—you know this is a major rainstorm. Hence, for the third blank, you can reject both **(H)** *soaked* and **(I)** *sprayed* because both are much weaker words than **(G)** *inundated*.

For the second blank, the key clue is "sudden." If it was sudden, then you can assume people were not expecting it—you can thus predict a word synonymous with "not expecting." **(D)** *waiting* and **(F)** *anxious* would both imply people were expecting the downpour; thus, **(E)** *unprepared* is clearly the correct choice.

Finally, for the first blank, this word will be the reason that people were not expecting a sudden storm. **(C)** *humid* doesn't work here, but between **(A)** *arid* and **(B)** *calm*, you may need to pause for a moment. **(B)** *calm* might work—it certainly contrasts with the eventfulness of the weather that followed—but **(A)** *arid* is a better answer because it implies that the weather was specifically very dry—the antithesis of the wetness of the storm. Plugging it all in, "The countless *arid* days left everyone *unprepared* for the sudden downpour; the deluge brought traffic to a halt as it *inundated* the roads." You can see that everything agrees.

7. D

This question is an Inference question. Therefore, we must eliminate the answer choices that don't necessarily follow from the passage. **(A)** is incorrect because we can't say with certainty that Germanic languages had a greater influence than Romance languages did. Yes, the Germanic influence came first and had a greater influence on grammar, but that does not mean its influence on English as a whole is greater. **(B)** is out of scope and extreme. Nothing suggests that the lower classes could *never* discuss abstract theoretical topics. For **(C)**, although we are told most mundane words, like auxiliary verbs, are of Germanic origin, that doesn't mean that *all* auxiliary words must be of Germanic origin. **(E)** is also incorrect because we aren't given any clues as to how many words are derived from each language family. **(D)** is correct because it's directly implied in the passage. The second sentence says that English has an "unusual nature," and the passage goes on to state that this is due to its vocabulary stemming from multiple origins, such as what was brought over by the Norman Invasion.

8. A

The question states that 'they' is a pronoun, so look in the passage for clues as to where pronouns are likely to be derived. The final sentence explicitly states that English pronouns are of Germanic origin, so you can safely select **(A)** as your answer. Although Old English and Norse are related, this is not mentioned in the passage, and choice **(C)** is meant as a distracter.

9. B

To answer this question, you are required to make a small inference from the text. The third sentence begins with a detour road sign, "Although," which indicates that the immediately following clause is a fact—in this case that English is a part of the Germanic language family and that the rules governing its structure reflect this. From this you can infer that the structural rules of a language are significant in its classification, which tells you that answer choice **(B)** is correct. **(A)** is factually correct, but there is no indication that the language's first incarnation is related to its current classification, so you cannot accept that as an explanation based on the passage. **(C)** concerns the balance of vocabulary origins between Germanic and Romance, but while the passage does speak of this at length, no mention of number of words as related to the classification of the language is made. **(D)** is not an option, as the Normans regarded English as lower class. **(E)** is incorrect, as the core of the language is noted to be Germanic. **(B)** is the correct choice.

10. A

As always, you must be careful about what you infer from a passage. For answer choice **(A)**, you would need to find something in the text that would suggest that the shorter the word, the less likely it may be derived from Latin—which you can find in the third-to-last sentence. There is no mention of the indigenous language before the arrival of the Germanic peoples, so you can dismiss **(B)**. **(C)** might seem tempting because the author notes that the words used for complex ideas today are primarily those that were used by the ruling class. However, while discussing complex ideas might seem more likely to be the habit of those with leisure time and education, the passage does not specify anything that would allow us to draw this conclusion, and **(C)** must be rejected.

11. E, F

From the sentence, you learn that scholars are in need of a new "way to refer to the author or authors"; furthermore, judging by the tone and topic of the sentence, you can safely assume that the answers you need will have a neutral tone. While it may seem possible for the solutions to render the phrase "the term *Homeric tradition* has been *rejected*," the straight-ahead road sign "so" renders this unlikely. You can predict that the answers will mean "the term has been put forward." The key to this question is the word "possible" near the end of the sentence. **(A)** *selected* and **(B)** *established* cannot be correct because that would mean the term has been decided upon. **(C)** *appropriated* and **(D)** *bestowed* likewise fail to match our prediction, leaving **(E)** *suggested* and **(F)** *proposed* as the choices that suggest that the term has been offered as an option but no decision has been made. That fits nicely with "possible."

12. B, E

From the meaning of the sentence, you can see that the correct answer choices will render the meaning "commercial arsenic usage has diminished, but its ongoing presence is a major health concern." Because the blank is placed at the start of the first clause, you need a sense of contradiction that gives the meaning "even though." **(A)** *After*, **(C)** *Inasmuch as*, **(D)** *Considering*, and **(F)** *Because* all lack the contradiction you need, leaving only **(B)** *Although* and **(E)** *While*, which are synonyms of each other and match the prediction.

13. C, E

The key to this sentence is to note that the textile workers feared a negative effect on the demand for their skills as a result of the sewing machine. The answer, then, must be indicative of their displeasure with the technology; furthermore, words like "poorly" and "protests" suggest that they felt very strongly about their fear of a decline in their trade, so you must also find words that reflect the strength of their views. **(A)** *overwhelm* is the opposite of what you need and can be rejected. **(B)** *diminish*, **(D)** *mitigate*, and **(F)** *belittle* are all possible choices, but none of these words are strong enough to convey the meaning you are looking for. **(C)** *obviate* and **(E)** *eliminate* suggest an absolute removal of demand for the workers' skills and match both the meaning and the strength of the prediction.

14. B, F

You are told in the final clause that it would be remembered as a "tragic accident" and that no blame was assigned. You are looking for adverbs that reflect this and can expect to find synonyms of "sadly," but you must be careful not to choose answers that suggest vitriol or blame. Based on this, you can see that **(A)** *indignantly*, **(C)** *spitefully*, and **(D)** *bitterly* can all be eliminated. **(B)** *mournfully* is an excellent choice because you often hear about mourning of a tragic accident. **(E)** *soberly*, meaning in this context "clearly," does not have any synonyms among the remaining answers. **(F)** *melancholically* is a direct synonym of **(B)** and matches your predicted answer.

15. C

The difference between teleology and Teleology is mentioned in the first paragraph. To paraphrase, Teleology is the idea that nature is progressing *toward* something, and teleology is the idea that nature progresses *by means of* something. From here you can begin to look at the options for answers. **(A)** *quality and quantity* do not make sense based on your predicted answer—there is no sense of amount in either concept. **(B)** *example and concept* and **(E)** *part and whole* are both inadequate—it may be tempting based on the phrase "teleology so conceived, though, mustn't be confused with." However, this does not suggest that teleology is a type of Teleology. **(C)** *property and object* is a good choice—teleology is something possessed within nature, and Teleology is its goal. **(D)** *cause and effect* also fails to properly describe the relation between the two, suggesting that teleology is a part of a larger Teleology. The passage describes the two as separate ideas, not one as a type of the other.

16. C

As always, begin by examining the passage's topic and scope, the latter of which is the subject of this question. The passage discusses how evolutionary theory rejects the notion of Teleology, instead demonstrating the development of species through the process of natural selection. **(A)** and **(B)** both are part of the description of how evolutionary theory describes the biological history of the world, but neither is the overall scope of the passage. **(C)** states that natural selection, a key part of evolutionary theory, obviates the need for Teleology—which is the focus (that is, the scope) of the passage. **(D)** is an end result but not the overall main argument and thus is incorrect. **(E)** suggests that teleology and Teleology are nearly equivalent, which, according to the passage, is incorrect.

17. A, B, C

This is a Detail question, so each correct answer must be cited somewhere in the passage. Choices **(A)**, **(B)**, and **(C)** are mentioned in the first, fifth, and tenth lines of the second paragraph, respectively, so all three choices are correct.

18. D

Remember, even in weighty passages like these, all the information that you need is in the text. **(A)** *a physical object* is not the right answer because the passage is talking about natural law and human behavior. You can also eliminate **(B)** *morally correct action as determined by God* because the passage specifies that "Finnis's theory does not require the presence of God." **(C)** *action that helps us achieve a desirable, material end* can be rejected for the same reason as **(A)**. Furthermore, you are given an example of one basic human good, according to Finnis: curiosity about the nature of the universe. **(D)** *something self-evident that we ought to strive to embrace* is supported by the text both in the phrase "each good is self-evident" and Finnis's example of how something is made good by human participation. **(E)** *what is naturally occurring* could only be a reasonable possibility based on the repeated usage of the term "natural"; however, "natural law" is a metaphysical concept, and **(E)** is also incorrect.

19. B

The key to answering this question is to bear in mind Finnis's definition of "goods" that you considered in the previous question. You can learn from the passage that they are self-evident and all equal, which points us towards **(B)** *goods that demand opposing actions*—if they are all equally important, then how can we choose between actions that would each further one good while distancing ourselves from the other? **(A)** *proof of the existence of God* is a poor choice, because while his argument does not rely on the existence of God as Aquinas's did, nowhere does the author imply that Finnis's theory hinged on the nonexistence of God. **(C)** *the demands of our natural desires* is likewise incorrect because of the emphasis on human volition and the notion that some actions are inherently "good" and others are not—to give in to your desires would not undermine his definition but simply fail to follow his admonition. **(D)** *the definition of additional goods* would not necessarily weaken his definition so long as the new goods were not in opposition to his already established goods. Similarly, **(E)** *a method for evaluating goods* could help fix a weakness in Finnis's theory rather than undermine it.

20. C

This is a fairly straightforward Reading Comprehension question. It does not require us to make any inferences from the text, just give the text a careful reading to determine whether each answer choice is referred to (and they all are). **(A)** and **(B)** are both listed explicitly under the adaptations Finnis made to strengthen Aquinas's argument, so you can dismiss them. **(C)**, our only remaining option, is correct, as its opposite is one of the adaptations.

PART THREE

Quantitative Reasoning

CHAPTER 9

Introduction to Quantitative Reasoning

OVERVIEW

The Quantitative Reasoning section of the GRE is designed to place most of its emphasis on your ability to reason quantitatively—to read a math problem, understand what it's asking, and solve it. The mathematical concepts tested on the GRE are similar to those tested on the SAT. You will see questions related to arithmetic, algebra, geometry, and data interpretation. There is no trigonometry or calculus on the GRE. The emphasis in the Quantitative Reasoning section is on your ability to reason, using your knowledge of the various topics. The goal is to make the test an accurate indicator of your ability to apply given information, think logically, and draw conclusions. These are skills you will need at the graduate level of study.

In this section of the book, we'll take you through all the types of Quantitative Reasoning questions you'll see on the GRE and give you the strategies you need to answer them quickly and correctly. Also, all of the mathematical concepts you'll encounter on the test are included in the "Math Reference" Appendix at the back of this book. Think of the examples there as building blocks for the questions you will see on the test.

QUANTITATIVE REASONING QUESTION TYPES

The GRE contains two Quantitative Reasoning sections with 20 questions each. Each section will last 35 minutes and be composed of a selection of the following question types:

- Quantitative Comparison
- Problem Solving
- Data Interpretation

The Quantitative Reasoning portion of the GRE draws heavily upon your ability to combine your knowledge of mathematical concepts with your reasoning powers. Specifically, it evaluates your ability to do the following:

- Compare quantities using reasoning
- Solve word problems
- Interpret data presented in charts and graphs

Within each Quantitative Reasoning section on the GRE, you will see an assortment of question types.

PACING STRATEGY

As a multi-stage test, the GRE allows you to move freely backward and forward within each section, which can be a big advantage on Test Day. If you get stuck on a particular question, you can mark it and come back to it later when you have time. You only score points for correct answers, so you don't want to get bogged down on one problem and lose time you could have used to answer several other questions correctly.

You will have 35 minutes to work on each Quantitative Reasoning section. The 20 questions in each section will be an assortment of Quantitative Comparison, Problem Solving, and Data Interpretation items. However, these types are not distributed equally. The chart below shows how many questions you can expect of each question type, as well as the average amount of time you should spend per question type.

	Quantitative Comparison	Problem Solving	Data Interpretation
Number of Questions	approx. 7–8	approx. 9–10	approx. 3
Time per Question	1.5 minutes	1.5–2 minutes	2 minutes

Try to keep these time estimates in mind as you prepare for the test. If you use them as you practice, you will be comfortable keeping to the same amounts of time on Test Day. Additionally, you will be prepared to use the Mark and Review buttons to your advantage while taking the actual test.

To Calculate or Not

An onscreen calculator will be available during the GRE. Numbers can be entered either by clicking on the numbers on the calculator with your mouse or by entering numbers from the keyboard. There are several points to consider about using the calculator on Test Day. A calculator can be a time-saver, and time is immensely important on a standardized test. But while calculators can speed up computations, they can also foster dependence, making it hard for you to spot the shortcuts in GRE questions. Using the calculator for a long, involved computation to answer a question will gobble up your allotted time for that question—and perhaps for several more. You may even make a mistake in your computation, leading to an incorrect answer. Remember, this is a *reasoning* test. The quantitative questions on the GRE are not designed to require lengthy computations.

If that is the case, why is a calculator provided? A calculator can be an asset for the occasional computation that a few questions require. It may prevent an error caused by a freehand calculation. The onscreen calculator provided is a simple four-function calculator. An image of the calculator is provided below, showing the function keys, including the square root key and change-of-sign key.

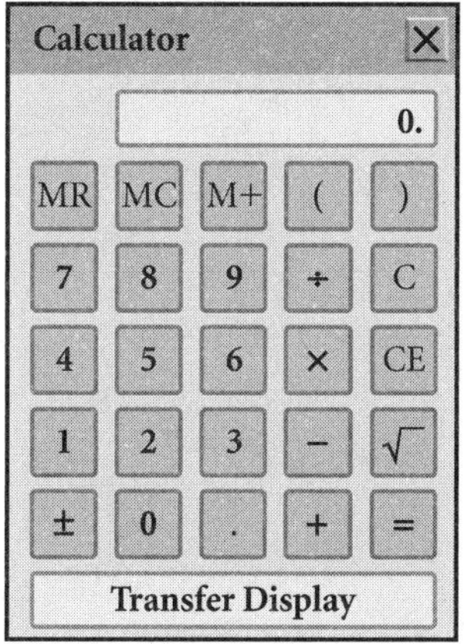

By not relying on the calculator, you will be free to focus on interpreting numbers and data and using your critical thinking skills. This is the intention of the writers of the test. For example, Problem Solving questions will likely involve more algebra than calculating, and Quantitative Comparison questions will require more reasoning than calculating.

NAVIGATING THE QUANTITATIVE REASONING SECTION OF THIS BOOK

The chapter immediately following this one concerns Math Foundations and Content Review and will review the classic math concepts and topics that you may encounter on the GRE. This section of the book also includes individual chapters on Quantitative Comparison, Problem Solving, and Data Interpretation questions. Each chapter includes an introduction to the relevant question types and then a review with strategies you can follow to answer those questions quickly and correctly. In addition, you'll find a practice set of questions with answers and explanations for each of the question types you'll encounter on the GRE.

Finally, at the end of this section, you'll find the Quantitative Reasoning Practice Sets, three sets of 20 Quantitative Reasoning questions with answers and explanations. Use the Practice Sets to test your skills and pinpoint areas for more focused study. When you are finished with this section of the book, you should be thoroughly prepared for any question you might encounter on the Quantitative Reasoning section of the GRE.

CHAPTER 10

Math Foundations and Content Review

ARITHMETIC

TERMS

Consecutive numbers: Numbers of a certain type, following one another without interruption. Numbers may be consecutive in ascending or descending order. The GRE prefers to test consecutive integers (e.g., $-2, -1, 0, 1, 2, 3, \ldots$), but you may encounter other types of consecutive numbers. For example:

$-4, -2, 0, 2, 4, 6, \ldots$ is a series of consecutive even numbers.

$-3, 0, 3, 6, 9, \ldots$ is a series of consecutive multiples of 3.

$2, 3, 5, 7, 11, \ldots$ is a series of consecutive prime numbers.

Cube: A number raised to the 3rd power. For example $4^3 = (4)(4)(4) = 64$, showing that 64 is the cube of 4.

Decimal: A fraction written in decimal system format. For example, 0.6 is a decimal. To convert a fraction to a decimal, divide the numerator by the denominator. For instance, $\frac{5}{8} = 5 \div 8 = 0.625$.

Decimal system: A numbering system based on the powers of 10. The decimal system is the only numbering system used on the GRE. Each figure, or digit, in a decimal number occupies a particular position, from which it derives its place value.

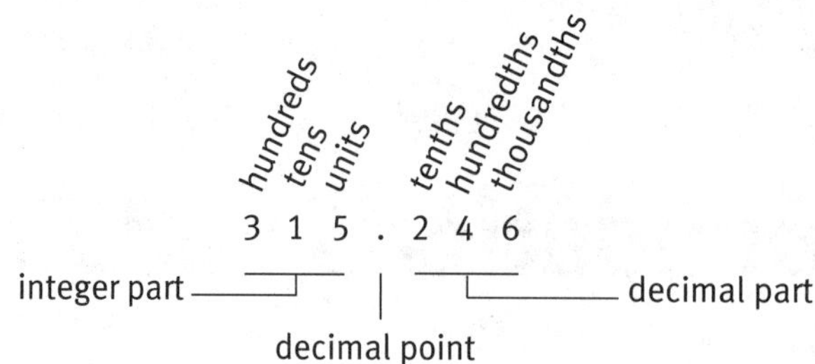

Denominator: The quantity in the bottom of a fraction, representing the whole.

Difference: The result of subtraction.

Digit: One of the numerals 0, 1, 2, 3, 4, 5, 6, 7, 8, or 9. A number can have several digits. For example, the number 542 has three digits: a 5, a 4, and a 2. The number 321,321,000 has nine digits but only four distinct (different) digits: 3, 2, 1, and 0.

Distinct: Different from each other. For example, 12 has three prime factors (2, 2, and 3) but only 2 distinct factors (2 and 3).

Element: One of the members of a set.

Exponent: The number that denotes the power to which another number or variable is raised. The exponent is typically written as a superscript to a number. For example, 5^3 equals (5)(5)(5). The exponent is also occasionally referred to as a "power." For example, 5^3 can be described as "5 to the 3rd power." The product, 125, is "the 3rd power of 5." Exponents may be positive or negative integers or fractions, and they may include variables.

Fraction: The division of a part by a whole. $\frac{\text{Part}}{\text{Whole}}$ = Fraction. For example, $\frac{3}{5}$ is a fraction.

Integer: A number without fractional or decimal parts, including positive and negative whole numbers and zero. All integers are multiples of 1. The following are examples of integers: −5, −4, −3, −2, −1, 0, 1, 2, 3, 4, 5.

Number Line: A straight line, extending infinitely in either direction, on which numbers are represented as points. The number line below shows the integers from −3 to 4. Decimals and fractions can also be depicted on a number line, as can irrational numbers, such as $\sqrt{2}$.

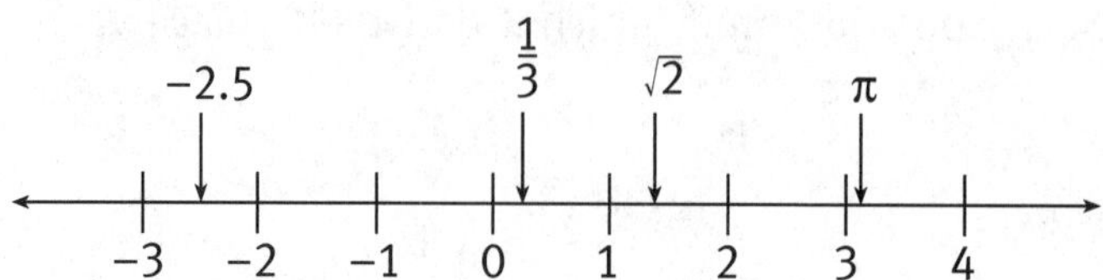

The values of numbers get larger as you move to the right along the number line. Numbers to the right of zero are *positive*; numbers to the left of zero are *negative*. **Zero is neither positive nor negative.** Any positive number is larger than any negative number. For example, $-300 < 4$.

Numerator: The quantity in the top of a fraction, representing the part.

Operation: A function or process performed on one or more numbers. The four basic arithmetic operations are addition, subtraction, multiplication, and division.

Part: A specified number of the equal sections that compose a whole.

Product: The result of multiplication.

Sequence: Lists that have an infinite number of terms, in order. The terms of a sequence are often indicated by a letter with a subscript indicating the position of the number in the sequence. For instance, a_3 denotes the third number in a sequence, while a_n indicates the *n*th term in a sequence.

Set: A well-defined collection of items, typically numbers, objects, or events. The bracket symbols { } are normally used to define sets of numbers. For example, {2, 4, 6, 8} is a set of numbers.

Square: The product of a number multiplied by itself. A squared number has been raised to the 2nd power. For example, $4^2 = (4)(4) = 16$, and 16 is the square of 4.

Sum: The result of addition.

Whole: A quantity that is regarded as a complete unit.

Symbols

$=$	is equal to
$\neq$	is not equal to
$<$	is less than
$>$	is greater than
$\leq$	is less than or equal to
$\geq$	is greater than or equal to
$\div$	divided by
π	pi (the ratio of the circumference of a circle to the diameter)
$\pm$	plus or minus
$\sqrt{\ }$	square root
$\angle$	angle

Rules of Operation

There are certain mathematical laws governing the results of the four basic operations: addition, subtraction, multiplication, and division. Although you won't need to know the names of these laws for the GRE, you'll benefit from understanding them.

PEMDAS

A string of operations must be performed in proper order. The acronym PEMDAS stands for the correct order of operations:

Parentheses

Exponents

Multiplication
Division
} simultaneously from left to right

Addition
Subtraction
} simultaneously from left to right

If you have trouble remembering PEMDAS, you can think of the mnemonic "Please Excuse My Dear Aunt Sally."

Example:

$66\,(3 - 2) \div 11$

If you were to perform all the operations sequentially from left to right, without using PEMDAS, you would arrive at an answer of $\frac{196}{11}$. But if you perform the operation within the parentheses first, you get $66(1) \div 11 = 66 \div 11 = 6$, which is the correct answer.

Example:

$$30 - 5(4) + \frac{(7-3)^2}{8}$$
$$= 30 - 5(4) + \frac{4^2}{8}$$
$$= 30 - 5(4) + \frac{16}{8}$$
$$= 30 - 20 + 2$$
$$= 10 + 2$$
$$= 12$$

Commutative Laws of Addition and Multiplication

Addition and multiplication are both commutative, which means that switching the order of any two numbers being added or multiplied together does not affect the result.

Example:

$$\begin{aligned} 5 + 8 &= 8 + 5 \\ (2)(3)(6) &= (6)(3)(2) \\ a + b &= b + a \\ ab &= ba \end{aligned}$$

Division and subtraction are not commutative; switching the order of the numbers changes the result. For instance, $3 - 2 \neq 2 - 3$; the left side yields a difference of 1, while the right side yields a difference of -1. Similarly, $\frac{6}{2} \neq \frac{2}{6}$; the left side equals 3, while the right side equals $\frac{1}{3}$.

Associative Laws of Addition and Multiplication

Addition and multiplication are also associative; regrouping the numbers does not affect the result.

Example:

$$\begin{aligned} (3 + 5) + 8 &= 3 + (5 + 8) \\ 8 + 8 &= 3 + 13 \\ 16 &= 16 \end{aligned}$$

$$\begin{aligned} (a + b) + c &= a + (b + c) \\ (ab)c &= a(bc) \end{aligned}$$

The Distributive Law

The distributive law of multiplication allows you to "distribute" a factor over numbers that are added or subtracted. You do this by multiplying that factor by each number in the group.

Example:

$$\begin{aligned} 4(3 + 7) &= (4)(3) + (4)(7) \\ 4(10) &= 12 + 28 \\ 40 &= 40 \end{aligned}$$

$$a(b + c) = ab + ac$$

The law works for the numerator in division as well.

$$\frac{a + b}{c} = \frac{a}{c} + \frac{b}{c}$$

However, when the sum or difference is in the denominator—that is, when you're dividing by a sum or difference—no distribution is possible.

$\frac{9}{4+5}$ is *not* equal to $\frac{9}{4} + \frac{9}{5}$.

NUMBER PROPERTIES

ADDING AND SUBTRACTING

Numbers can be treated as though they have two parts: a positive or negative sign and a number. Numbers without any sign are understood to be positive.

To add two numbers that have the same sign, add the number parts and keep the sign. For example, to add $(-6) + (-3)$, add 6 and 3 and then attach the negative sign from the original numbers to the sum: $(-6) + (-3) = -9$.

To add two numbers that have different signs, find the difference between the number parts and keep the sign of the number whose number part is larger. For example, to add $(-7) + (+4)$, subtract 4 from 7 to get 3. Because $7 > 4$ (the number part of -7 is greater than the number part of 4), the final sum will be negative: $(-7) + (+4) = -3$.

Subtraction is the opposite of addition. You can rephrase any subtraction problem as an addition problem by changing the operation sign from a minus to a plus and switching the sign on the second number. For instance, $8 - 5 = 8 + (-5)$. There's no real advantage to rephrasing if you are subtracting a smaller positive number from a larger positive number. But the concept comes in very handy when you are subtracting a negative number from any other number, a positive number from a negative number or a larger positive number from a smaller positive number.

To subtract a negative number, rephrase as an addition problem and follow the rules for addition of signed numbers. For instance, $9 - (-10) = 9 + 10 = 19$.

To subtract a positive number from a negative number or from a smaller positive number, change the sign of the number that you are subtracting from positive to negative and follow the rules for addition of signed numbers. For example, $(-4) - 1 = (-4) + (-1) = -5$.

MULTIPLICATION AND DIVISION OF POSITIVE AND NEGATIVE NUMBERS

Multiplying or dividing two numbers with the same sign gives a positive result.

Examples:

$$(-4)(-7) = +28$$
$$(-50) \div (-5) = +10$$

Multiplying or dividing two numbers with different signs gives a negative result.

Examples:

$$(-2)(+3) = -6$$
$$8 \div (-4) = -2$$

Absolute Value

The absolute value of a number is the value of a number without its sign. It is written as two vertical lines, one on either side of the number and its sign.

Example:

$$|-3| = |+3| = 3$$

The absolute value of a number can be thought of as the number's distance from zero on the number line. Since both 3 and -3 are 3 units from 0, each has an absolute value of 3. If you are told that $|x| = 5$, x could equal 5 or -5.

Properties of Zero

Adding zero to or subtracting zero from a number does not change the number.

$$x + 0 = x$$
$$0 + x = x$$
$$x - 0 = x$$

Examples:

$$5 + 0 = 5$$
$$0 + (-3) = -3$$
$$4 - 0 = 4$$

Notice, however, that subtracting a number from zero changes the number's sign. It's easy to see why if you rephrase the problem as an addition problem.

Example:

Subtract 5 from 0.

$0 - 5 = -5$. That's because $0 - 5 = 0 + (-5)$, and according to the rules for addition with signed numbers, $0 + (-5) = -5$.

The product of zero and any number is zero.

Examples:

$$(0)(z) = 0$$
$$(z)(0) = 0$$
$$(0)(12) = 0$$

Division by zero is undefined. For GRE purposes, that translates to "It can't be done." Since fractions are essentially division (that is, $\frac{1}{4}$ means $1 \div 4$), any fraction with zero in the denominator is also undefined. So when you are given a fraction that has an algebraic expression in the denominator, be sure that the expression cannot equal zero.

Properties of 1 and –1

Multiplying or dividing a number by 1 does not change the number.

$$\begin{aligned}(a)(1) &= a\\(1)(a) &= a\\a \div 1 &= a\end{aligned}$$

Examples:

$$\begin{aligned}(4)(1) &= 4\\(1)(-5) &= -5\\(-7) \div 1 &= -7\end{aligned}$$

Multiplying or dividing a nonzero number by -1 changes the sign of the number.

$$\begin{aligned}(a)(-1) &= -a\\(-1)(a) &= -a\\a \div (-1) &= -a\end{aligned}$$

Examples:

$$\begin{aligned}(6)(-1) &= -6\\(-3)(-1) &= 3\\(-8) \div (-1) &= 8\end{aligned}$$

Factors, Multiples, and Remainders

Multiples and Divisibility

A *multiple* is the product of a specified number and an integer. For example, 3, 12, and 90 are all multiples of 3: $3 = (3)(1)$; $12 = (3)(4)$; and $90 = (3)(30)$. The number 4 is not a multiple of 3, because there is no integer that can be multiplied by 3 and yield 4.

Multiples do not have to be of integers, but all multiples must be the product of a specific number and an integer. For instance, 2.4, 12, and 132 are all multiples of 1.2: $2.4 = (1.2)(2)$; $12 = (1.2)(10)$; and $132 = (1.2)(110)$.

The concepts of multiples and factors are tied together by the idea of *divisibility.* A number is said to be evenly divisible by another number if the result of the division is an integer with no remainder. A number that is evenly divisible by a second number is also a multiple of the second number.

For example, $52 \div 4 = 13$, which is an integer. So 52 is evenly divisible by 4, and it's also a multiple of 4.

On some GRE math problems, you will find yourself trying to assess whether one number is evenly divisible by another. You can use several simple rules to save time.

- An integer is divisible by 2 if its last digit is divisible by 2.
- An integer is divisible by 3 if its digits add up to a multiple of 3.
- An integer is divisible by 4 if its last two digits are a multiple of 4.
- An integer is divisible by 5 if its last digit is 0 or 5.
- An integer is divisible by 6 if it is divisible by both 2 and 3.
- An integer is divisible by 9 if its digits add up to a multiple of 9.

Example:

6,930 is a multiple of 2, since 0 is even.

. . . a multiple of 3, since $6 + 9 + 3 + 0 = 18$, which is a multiple of 3.

. . . not a multiple of 4, since 30 is not a multiple of 4.

. . . a multiple of 5, since it ends in zero.

. . . a multiple of 6, since it is a multiple of both 2 and 3.

. . . a multiple of 9, since $6 + 9 + 3 + 0 = 18$, which is a multiple of 9.

Properties of Odd/Even Numbers

Even numbers are integers that are evenly divisible by 2; *odd* numbers are integers that are not evenly divisible by 2. Integers whose last digit is 0, 2, 4, 6, or 8 are even; integers whose last digit is 1, 3, 5, 7, or 9 are odd. The terms *odd* and *even* apply only to integers, but they may be used for either positive or negative integers. 0 is considered even.

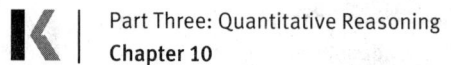

Rules for Odds and Evens

Odd + Odd	=	Even
Even + Even	=	Even
Odd + Even	=	Odd
Odd × Odd	=	Odd
Even × Even	=	Even
Odd × Even	=	Even

Note that multiplying any even number by *any* integer always produces another even number.

It may be easier to use the Picking Numbers strategy in problems that ask you to decide whether some unknown will be odd or even.

> **Example:**
>
> Is the sum of two odd numbers odd or even?
>
> Pick any two odd numbers, for example, 3 and 5: $3 + 5 = 8$. Since the sum of the two odd numbers that you picked is an even number, 8, it's safe to say that the sum of any two odd numbers is even.

Picking Numbers will work in any odds/evens problem, no matter how complicated. The only time you have to be careful is when division is involved, especially if the problem is in Quantitative Comparison format; different numbers may yield different results.

> **Example:**
>
> Integer x is evenly divisible by 2. Is $\frac{x}{2}$ even?
>
> By definition, any multiple of 2 is even, so integer x is even. And $\frac{x}{2}$ must be an integer. But is $\frac{x}{2}$ even or odd? In this case, picking two different even numbers for x can yield two different results. If you let $x = 4$, then $\frac{x}{2} = \frac{4}{2} = 2$, which is even. But if you let $x = 6$, then $\frac{x}{2} = \frac{6}{2} = 3$, which is odd. So $\frac{x}{2}$ could be even or odd—and you wouldn't know that if you picked only one number.

Factors and Primes

The *factors*, or *divisors*, of an integer are the positive integers by which it is evenly divisible (leaving no remainder).

Example:

What are the factors of 36?

36 has nine factors: 1, 2, 3, 4, 6, 9, 12, 18, and 36. We can group these factors in pairs: $(1)(36) = (2)(18) = (3)(12) = (4)(9) = (6)(6)$.

The *greatest common factor,* or greatest common divisor, of a pair of integers is the largest factor that they share.

Example:

What is the greatest common factor of 36 and 48?

To find the greatest common factor (GCF), break down both integers into their prime factorizations and multiply all the prime factors they have in common: $36 = (2)(2)(3)(3)$, and $48 = (2)(2)(2)(2)(3)$. What they have in common is two 2s and one 3, so the GCF is $(2)(2)(3) = 12$.

A *prime number* is an integer greater than 1 that has only two factors: itself and 1. The number 1 is not considered a prime, because it is divisible only by itself. The number 2 is the smallest prime number and the only even prime. (Any other even number must have 2 as a factor and therefore cannot be prime.)

Prime Factors

The *prime factorization* of a number is the expression of the number as the product of its prime factors (the factors that are prime numbers).

There are two common ways to determine a number's prime factorization. The rules given above for determining divisibility by certain numbers come in handy in both methods.

Method #1: Work your way up through the prime numbers, starting with 2. (You'll save time in this process, especially when you're starting with a large number, by knowing the first ten prime numbers by heart: 2, 3, 5, 7, 11, 13, 17, 19, 23, and 29.)

Example:

What is the prime factorization of 210?

$$210 = (2)(105)$$

Since 105 is odd, it can't contain another factor of 2. The next smallest prime number is 3. The digits of 105 add up to 6, which is a multiple of 3, so 3 is a factor of 105.

$$210 = (2)(3)(35)$$

The digits of 35 add up to 8, which is not a multiple of 3. But 35 ends in 5, so it is a multiple of the next largest prime number, 5.

$$210 = (2)(3)(5)(7)$$

Since 7 is a prime number, this equation expresses the complete prime factorization of 210.

Method #2: Figure out one pair of factors and then determine their factors, continuing the process until you're left with only prime numbers. Those primes will be the prime factorization.

Example:

What is the prime factorization of 1,050?

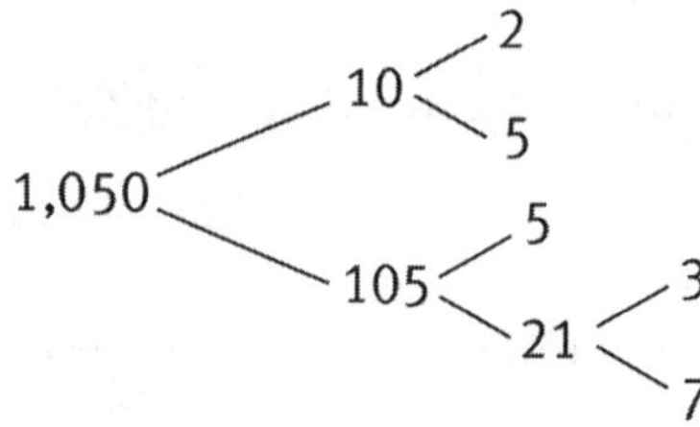

The distinct prime factors of 1,050 are therefore 2, 5, 3, and 7, with the prime number 5 occurring twice in the prime factorization. We usually write out the prime factorization by putting the prime numbers in increasing order. Here, that would be (2)(3)(5)(5)(7). The prime factorization can also be expressed in exponential form: $(2)(3)(5^2)(7)$.

The Least Common Multiple

The *least common multiple* of two or more integers is the smallest number that is a multiple of each of the integers. Here's one quick way to find it:

(1) Determine the prime factorization of each integer.

(2) Write out each prime number the maximum number of times that it appears in any one of the prime factorizations.

(3) Multiply those prime numbers together to get the least common multiple of the original integers.

Example:

What is the least common multiple of 6 and 8?

Start by finding the prime factors of 6 and 8.

$$6 = (2)(3)$$
$$8 = (2)(2)(2)$$

The factor 2 appears three times in the prime factorization of 8, while 3 appears as only a single factor of 6. So the least common multiple of 6 and 8 will be (2)(2)(2)(3), or 24.

Note that the least common multiple of two integers is smaller than their product if they have any factors in common. For instance, the product of 6 and 8 is 48, but their least common multiple is only 24.

In addition to answering questions using the term *least common multiple*, you'll find the concept useful whenever you're adding or subtracting fractions with different denominators.

Remainders

The *remainder* is what is "left over" in a division problem. A remainder is always smaller than the number you are dividing by. For instance, 17 divided by 3 is 5, with a remainder of 2. Likewise, 12 divided by 6 is 2, with a remainder of 0 (since 12 is evenly divisible by 6).

GRE writers often disguise remainder problems. For instance, a problem might state that the slats of a fence are painted in three colors, which appear in a fixed order, such as red, yellow, blue, red, yellow, blue.... You would then be asked something like, "If the first slat is red, what color is the 301st slat?" Since 3 goes into 300 evenly, the whole pattern must finish on the 300th slat and start all over again on the 301st. Therefore, the 301st would be red.

Exponents and Roots

Rules of Operations with Exponents

To multiply two powers with the same base, keep the base and add the exponents together.

Example:

$$2^2 \times 2^3 = (2 \times 2)(2 \times 2 \times 2) = 2^5$$

or

$$2^2 \times 2^3 = 2^{2+3} = 2^5$$

To divide two powers with the same base, keep the base and subtract the exponent of the denominator from the exponent of the numerator.

Example:

$$4^5 \div 4^2 = \frac{(4)(4)(4)(4)(4)}{(4)(4)} = 4^3$$

or

$$4^5 \div 4^2 = 4^{5-2} = 4^3$$

To raise a power to another power, multiply the exponents.

Example:

$(3^2)^4 = (3 \times 3)^4$

or

$(3^2)^4 = (3 \times 3)(3 \times 3)(3 \times 3)(3 \times 3)$

or

$(3^2)^4 = 3^{2 \times 4} = 3^8$

To multiply two powers with different bases but the same power, multiply the bases together and raise to the power.

Example:

$(3^2)\ (5^2) = (3 \times 3)(5 \times 5) = (3 \times 5)(3 \times 5) = (3 \times 5)^2 = 15^2$

A base with a negative exponent indicates the reciprocal of that base to the positive value of the exponent.

Example:

$$5^{-3} = \frac{1}{5^3} = \frac{1}{125}$$

Raising any non-zero number to an exponent of zero equals 1.

Examples:

$5^0 = 1$

$161^0 = 1$

$(-6)^0 = 1$

Commonly Tested Properties of Powers

Many Quantitative Comparison problems test your understanding of what happens when negative numbers and fractions are raised to a power.

Raising a fraction between zero and one to a power produces a smaller result.

Example:

$$\left(\frac{1}{2}\right)^2 = \left(\frac{1}{2}\right)\left(\frac{1}{2}\right) = \frac{1}{4}$$

Raising a negative number to an even power produces a positive result.

Example:

$(-2)^2 = 4$

Raising a negative number to an odd power gives a negative result.

Example:

$(-2)^3 = -8$

Raising an even number to any exponent gives an even number. Raising an odd number to any exponent gives an odd number.

Examples:

$8^5 = 32{,}768$, an even number

$5^8 = 390{,}625$, an odd number

Powers of 10

When 10 is raised to an exponent that is a positive integer, that exponent tells how many zeros the number would contain if it were written out.

Example:

Write 10^6 in ordinary notation.

The exponent 6 indicates that you will need six zeros after the 1: 1,000,000. That's because 10^6 means six factors of 10, that is, (10)(10)(10)(10)(10)(10).

To multiply a number by a power of 10, move the decimal point the same number of places to the right as the value of the exponent (or as the number of zeros in that power of 10).

Example:

Multiply 0.029 by 10^3

The exponent is 3, so move the decimal point three places to the right.

$$(0.029)10^3 = 0029. = 29$$

If you had been told to multiply 0.029 by 1,000, you could have counted the number of zeros in 1,000 and done exactly the same thing.

Sometimes you'll have to add zeros as placeholders.

Example:

Multiply 0.029 by 10^6.

Add zeros until you can move the decimal point six places to the right:

$$0.029 \times 10^6 = 0029000. = 29{,}000$$

To divide by a power of 10, move the decimal point the corresponding number of places to the left, inserting zeros as placeholders if necessary.

Example:

Divide 416.03 by 10,000

There are four zeros in 10,000, but only three places to the left of the decimal point. You'll have to insert another zero:

$$416.03 \div 10{,}000 = .041603 = 0.041603$$

By convention, one zero is usually written to the left of the decimal point on the GRE. It's a placeholder and doesn't change the value of the number.

Scientific Notation

Very large numbers (and very small decimals) take up a lot of space and are difficult to work with. So, in some scientific texts, they are expressed in a shorter, more convenient form called *scientific notation*.

For example, 123,000,000,000 would be written in scientific notation as 1.23×10^{11}, and 0.000000003 would be written as 3×10^{-9}. (If you're already familiar with the concept of negative exponents, you'll know that multiplying by 10^{-9} is equivalent to dividing by 10^9.)

To express a number in scientific notation, rewrite it as a product of two factors. The first factor must be greater than or equal to 1 but less than 10. The second factor must be a power of 10.

To translate a number from scientific notation to ordinary notation, use the rules for multiplying and dividing by powers of 10.

Example:

$5.6 \times 10^6 = 5{,}600{,}000$, or 5.6 million

Rules of Operations with Roots and Radicals

A *square root* of any non-negative number x is a number that, when multiplied by itself, yields x. Every positive number has two square roots, one positive and one negative. For instance, the positive square root of 25 is 5, because $5^2 = 25$. The negative square root of 25 is -5, because $(-5)^2$ also equals 25.

By convention, the radical symbol $\sqrt{}$ stands for the positive square root only. Therefore, $\sqrt{9} = 3$ only, even though both 3^2 and $(-3)^2$ equal 9.

When applying the four basic arithmetic operations, radicals (roots written with the radical symbol) are treated in much the same way as variables.

Addition and Subtraction of Radicals

Only like radicals can be added to or subtracted from one another.

Example:

$$2\sqrt{3} + 4\sqrt{2} - \sqrt{2} - 3\sqrt{3} =$$
$$(4\sqrt{2} - \sqrt{2}) + (2\sqrt{3} - 3\sqrt{3}) =$$
$$3\sqrt{2} + (-\sqrt{3}) =$$
$$3\sqrt{2} - \sqrt{3}$$

This expression cannot be simplified any further.

Multiplication and Division of Radicals

To multiply or divide one radical by another, multiply or divide the numbers outside the radical signs, then the numbers inside the radical signs.

Example:

$$(6\sqrt{3})2\sqrt{5} = (6)(2)(\sqrt{3})(\sqrt{5}) = 12\sqrt{15}$$

Example:

$$12\sqrt{15} \div 2\sqrt{5} = \left(\frac{12}{2}\right)\left(\frac{\sqrt{15}}{\sqrt{5}}\right) = 6\sqrt{\frac{15}{5}} = 6\sqrt{3}$$

Simplifying Radicals

If the number inside the radical is a multiple of a perfect square, the expression can be simplified by factoring out the perfect square.

Example:

$$\sqrt{72} = (\sqrt{36})\sqrt{2} = 6\sqrt{2}$$

PROPORTIONS AND MATH FORMULAS

Fractions

The simplest way to understand the meaning of a fraction is to picture the denominator as the number of equal parts into which a whole unit is divided. The numerator represents a certain number of those equal parts.

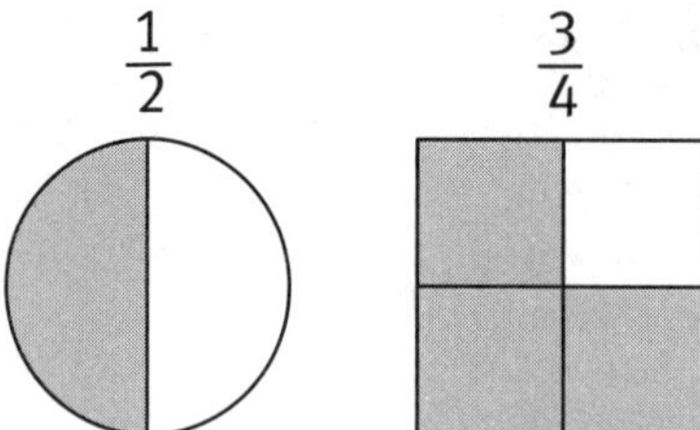

On the left, the shaded portion is one of two equal parts that make up the whole. On the right, the shaded portion is three of four equal parts that make up the whole.

The fraction bar is interchangeable with a division sign. You can divide the numerator of a fraction by the denominator to get an equivalent decimal. However, the numerator and denominator must each be treated as a single quantity.

Example:

Evaluate $\frac{5+2}{7-3}$

You can't just rewrite the fraction as $5 + 2 \div 7 - 3$, because the numerator and the denominator are each considered distinct quantities. Instead, you would rewrite the fraction as $(5 + 2) \div (7 - 3)$. The order of operations (remember PEMDAS?) tells us that operations in parentheses must be performed first. That gives you $7 \div 4$. Your final answer would be $\frac{7}{4}$, $1\frac{3}{4}$, or 1.75, depending on the form of the answer choices.

Equivalent Fractions

Since multiplying or dividing a number by 1 does not change the number, multiplying the numerator and denominator of a fraction by the same nonzero number doesn't change the value of the fraction—it's the same as multiplying the entire fraction by 1.

Example:

Change $\frac{1}{2}$ into an equivalent fraction with a denominator of 4.

To change the denominator from 2 to 4, you'll have to multiply it by 2. But to keep the value of the fraction the same, you'll also have to multiply the numerator by 2.

$$\frac{1}{2} = \frac{1}{2}\left(\frac{2}{2}\right) = \frac{2}{4}$$

Similarly, dividing the numerator and denominator by the same nonzero number leaves the value of the fraction unchanged.

Example:

Change $\frac{16}{20}$ into an equivalent fraction with a denominator of 10.

To change the denominator from 20 to 10, you'll have to divide it by 2. But to keep the value of the fraction the same, you'll have to divide the numerator by the same number.

$$\frac{16}{20} = \frac{16 \div 2}{20 \div 2} = \frac{8}{10}$$

Reducing (Canceling)

Most fractions on the GRE are in lowest terms. That means that the numerator and denominator have no common factor greater than 1.

For example, the final answer of $\frac{8}{10}$ that we obtained in the previous example was not in lowest terms, because both 8 and 10 are divisible by 2. In contrast, the fraction $\frac{7}{10}$ is in lowest terms, because there is no factor greater than 1 that 7 and 10 have in common. To convert a fraction to its lowest terms, we use a method called *reducing*, or *canceling*. To reduce, simply divide any common factors out of both the numerator and the denominator.

Example:

Reduce $\frac{15}{35}$ to lowest terms.

$\frac{15}{35} = \frac{15 \div 5}{35 \div 5} = \frac{3}{7}$ (because a 5 cancels out, top and bottom)

Sometimes it may be necessary to repeat the process and keep dividing out common factors until no common factor greater than 1 remains for the numerator and denominator.

Example:

Reduce $\frac{1{,}040}{1{,}080}$ to lowest terms.

$$\frac{1{,}040}{1{,}080} = \frac{104}{108} = \frac{52}{54} = \frac{26}{27}$$

Adding and Subtracting Fractions

You cannot add or subtract fractions unless they have the same denominator. If they don't, you'll have to convert each fraction to an equivalent fraction with the least common denominator. Then add or subtract the numerators (not the denominators!) and, if necessary, reduce the resulting fraction to its lowest terms.

Given two fractions with different denominators, the least common denominator is the least common multiple of the two denominators, that is, the smallest number that is evenly divisible by both denominators.

Example:

What is the least common denominator of $\frac{2}{15}$ and $\frac{3}{10}$?

The least common denominator of the two fractions will be the least common multiple of 15 and 10.

Because $15 = (5)(3)$ and $10 = (5)(2)$, the least common multiple of the two numbers is $(5)(3)(2)$, or 30. That makes 30 the least common denominator of $\frac{2}{15}$ and $\frac{3}{10}$.

Example:

$\frac{2}{15} + \frac{3}{10} = ?$

As we saw in the previous example, the least common denominator of the two fractions is 30. Change each fraction to an equivalent fraction with a denominator of 30.

$$\frac{2}{15}\left(\frac{2}{2}\right) = \frac{4}{30}$$

$$\frac{3}{10}\left(\frac{3}{3}\right) = \frac{9}{30}$$

Then add:

$$\frac{4}{30} + \frac{9}{30} = \frac{13}{30}$$

Since 13 and 30 have no common factor greater than 1, $\frac{13}{30}$ is in lowest terms. You can't reduce it further.

Multiplying Fractions

To multiply fractions, multiply the numerators and multiply the denominators.

$$\frac{5}{7}\left(\frac{3}{4}\right) = \frac{15}{28}$$

Multiplying numerator by numerator and denominator by denominator is simple. But it's easy to make careless errors if you have to multiply a string of fractions or work with large numbers. You can minimize those errors by reducing before you multiply.

Example:

Multiply $\left(\frac{10}{9}\right)\left(\frac{3}{4}\right)\left(\frac{8}{15}\right)$.

First, cancel a 5 out of the 10 and the 15, a 3 out of the 3 and the 9, and a 4 out of the 8 and the 4:

$$\left(\frac{\cancel{10}^{2}}{\cancel{9}_{3}}\right)\left(\frac{\cancel{3}^{1}}{\cancel{4}_{1}}\right)\left(\frac{\cancel{8}^{2}}{\cancel{15}_{3}}\right)$$

Then multiply numerators together and denominators together:

$$\left(\frac{2}{3}\right)\left(\frac{1}{1}\right)\left(\frac{2}{3}\right) = \frac{4}{9}$$

Reciprocals

To get the reciprocal of a common fraction, turn the fraction upside-down so that the numerator becomes the denominator, and vice versa. If a fraction has a numerator of 1, the fraction's reciprocal will be equivalent to an integer.

Example:

What is the reciprocal of $\frac{1}{25}$?

Inverting the fraction gives you the reciprocal, $\frac{25}{1}$. But dividing a number by 1 doesn't change the value of the number.

Since $\frac{25}{1}$ equals 25, the reciprocal of $\frac{1}{25}$ equals 25.

Dividing Common Fractions

To divide fractions, multiply by the reciprocal of the number or fraction that follows the division sign.

$$\frac{1}{2} \div \frac{3}{5} = \frac{1}{2}\left(\frac{5}{3}\right) = \frac{5}{6}$$

(The operation of division produces the same result as multiplication by the inverse.)

Example:

$$\frac{4}{3} \div \frac{4}{9} = \frac{4}{3}\left(\frac{9}{4}\right) = \frac{36}{12} = 3$$

Comparing Positive Fractions

Given two positive fractions with the same denominator, the fraction with the larger numerator will have the larger value.

Example:

Which is greater, $\frac{3}{8}$ or $\frac{5}{8}$?

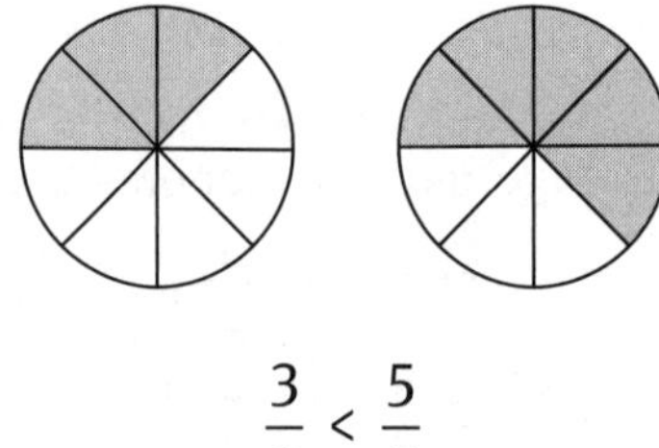

$$\frac{3}{8} < \frac{5}{8}$$

But if you're given two positive fractions with the same numerator but different denominators, the fraction with the smaller denominator will have the larger value.

Example:

Which is greater, $\frac{3}{4}$ or $\frac{3}{8}$?

The diagrams below show two wholes of equal size. The one on the left is divided into 4 equal parts, 3 of which are shaded. The one on the right is divided into 8 equal parts, 3 of which are shaded.

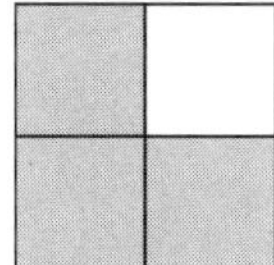

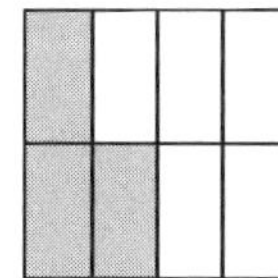

$\frac{3}{4}$ is clearly greater than $\frac{3}{8}$

If neither the numerators nor the denominators are the same, you have three options. You can turn both fractions into their decimal equivalents. Or you can express both fractions in terms of some common denominator and then see which new equivalent fraction has the largest numerator. Or you can cross multiply the numerator of each fraction by the denominator of the other. The greater result will wind up next to the greater fraction.

Example:

Which is greater, $\frac{5}{6}$ or $\frac{7}{9}$?

$$45 \; \frac{5}{6} \times \frac{7}{9} \; 42$$

Since $45 > 42$, $\frac{5}{6} > \frac{7}{9}$.

Mixed Numbers and Improper Fractions

A *mixed number* consists of an integer and a fraction.

An *improper fraction* is a fraction whose numerator is greater than its denominator. To convert an improper fraction to a mixed number, divide the numerator by the denominator. The number of "whole" times that the denominator goes into the numerator will be the integer portion of the improper fraction; the remainder will be the numerator of the fractional portion.

Example:

Convert $\frac{23}{4}$ to a mixed number.

Dividing 23 by 4 gives you 5 with a remainder of 3, so $\frac{23}{4} = 5\frac{3}{4}$.

To change a mixed number to a fraction, multiply the integer portion of the mixed number by the denominator and add the numerator. This new number is your numerator. The denominator will not change.

Example:

Convert $2\frac{3}{7}$ to a fraction.

$$2\frac{3}{7} = \frac{7(2) + 3}{7} = \frac{17}{7}$$

Properties of Fractions Between –1 and +1

The reciprocal of a fraction between 0 and 1 is greater than both the original fraction and 1.

Example:

The reciprocal of $\frac{2}{3}$ is $\frac{3}{2}$, which is greater than both 1 and $\frac{2}{3}$.

The reciprocal of a fraction between -1 and 0 is less than both the original fraction and -1.

Example:

The reciprocal of $-\frac{2}{3}$ is $-\frac{3}{2}$, or $-1\frac{1}{2}$, which is less than both -1 and $-\frac{2}{3}$.

The square of a fraction between 0 and 1 is less than the original fraction.

Example:

$$\left(\frac{1}{2}\right)^2 = \left(\frac{1}{2}\right)\left(\frac{1}{2}\right) = \frac{1}{4}$$

But the square of any fraction between 0 and -1 is greater than the original fraction, because multiplying two negative numbers gives you a positive product and any positive number is greater than any negative number.

Example:

$$\left(-\frac{1}{2}\right)^2 = \left(-\frac{1}{2}\right)\left(-\frac{1}{2}\right) = \frac{1}{4}$$

Multiplying any positive number by a fraction between 0 and 1 gives a product smaller than the original number.

Example:

$$6\left(\frac{1}{4}\right) = \frac{6}{4} = \frac{3}{2}$$

Multiplying any negative number by a fraction between 0 and 1 gives a product greater than the original number.

Example:

$$(-3)\left(\frac{1}{2}\right) = -\frac{3}{2}$$

DECIMALS

Converting Decimals

It's easy to convert decimals to common fractions, and vice versa. Any decimal fraction is equivalent to some common fraction with a power of 10 in the denominator.

To convert a decimal between 0 and 1 to a fraction, determine the place value of the last nonzero digit and set that value as the denominator. Then use all the digits of the decimal number as the numerator, ignoring the decimal point. Finally, if necessary, reduce the fraction to its lowest terms.

Example:

Convert 0.875 to a fraction in lowest terms.

The last nonzero digit is the 5, which is in the thousandths place. So the denominator of the common fraction will be 1,000. The numerator will be 875: $\frac{875}{1{,}000}$.

(You can ignore the zero to the left of the decimal point, since there are no nonzero digits to its left; it's just a "placeholder.")

Both 875 and 1,000 contain a factor of 25. Canceling it out leaves you with $\frac{35}{40}$.

Reducing that further by a factor of 5 gives you $\frac{7}{8}$, which is in lowest terms.

To convert a fraction to a decimal, simply divide the numerator by the denominator.

Example:

What is the decimal equivalent of $\frac{4}{5}$?

$$4 \div 5 = 0.8$$

Comparing Decimals

Knowing place values allows you to assess the relative values of decimals.

Example:

Which is greater, 0.254 or 0.3?

Of course, 254 is greater than 3. But $0.3 = \frac{3}{10}$, which is equivalent to $\frac{300}{1,000}$, while 0.254 is equivalent to only $\frac{254}{1,000}$. Since $\frac{300}{1,000} > \frac{254}{1,000}$, 0.3 is greater than 0.254.

Here's the simplest way to compare decimals: add zeros after the last digit to the right of the decimal point in each decimal fraction until all the decimals you're comparing have the same number of digits. Essentially, what you're doing is giving all the fractions the same denominator so that you can just compare their numerators.

Example:

Arrange in order from smallest to largest: 0.7, 0.77, 0.07, 0.707, and 0.077.

The numbers 0.707 and 0.077 end at the third place to the right of the decimal point—the thousandths place. Add zeros after the last digit to the right of the decimal point in each of the other fractions until you reach the thousandths place:

$$0.7 = 0.700 = \frac{700}{1,000}$$

$$0.77 = 0.770 = \frac{770}{1,000}$$

$$0.07 = 0.070 = \frac{70}{1,000}$$

$$0.707 = \frac{707}{1,000}$$

$$0.077 = \frac{77}{1,000}$$

$$\frac{70}{1,000} < \frac{77}{1,000} < \frac{700}{1,000} < \frac{707}{1,000} < \frac{770}{1,000}$$

Therefore, $0.07 < 0.077 < 0.7 < 0.707 < 0.77$.

Estimation and Rounding on the GRE

You should be familiar and comfortable with the practice of "rounding off" numbers. To round off a number to a particular place, look at the digit immediately to the right of that place. If the digit is 0, 1, 2, 3, or 4, don't change the digit that is in the place to which you are rounding. If it is 5, 6, 7, 8, or 9, change the digit in the place to which you are rounding to the next higher digit. Replace all digits to the right of the place to which you are rounding with zeros.

For example, to round off 235 to the tens place, look at the units place. Since it is occupied by a 5, you'll round the 3 in the tens place up to a 4, giving you 240. If you had been rounding off 234, you would have rounded down to the existing 3 in the tens place; that would have given you 230.

Example:

Round off 675,978 to the hundreds place.

The 7 in the tens place means that you will have to round the hundreds place up. Since there is a 9 in the hundreds place, you'll have to change the thousands place as well. Rounding 675,978 to the hundreds place gives you 676,000.

Rounding off large numbers before calculation will allow you to quickly estimate the correct answer.

Estimating can save you valuable time on many GRE problems. But before you estimate, check the answer choices to see how close they are. If they are relatively close together, you'll have to be more accurate than if they are farther apart.

Percents

The word *percent* means "hundredths," and the percent sign, %, means $\frac{1}{100}$. For example, 25% means $25\left(\frac{1}{100}\right) = \frac{25}{100}$. (Like the division sign, the percent sign evolved from the fractional relationship; the slanted bar in a percent sign represents a fraction bar.)

Percents measure a part-to-whole relationship with an assumed whole equal to 100. The percent relationship can be expressed as $\frac{\text{Part}}{\text{Whole}}(100\%)$. For example, if $\frac{1}{4}$ of a rectangle is shaded, the percent of the rectangle that is shaded is $\frac{1}{4}(100\%) = 25\%$.

Like fractions, percents express the relationship between a specified part and a whole; more specifically, percents express a relationship of a part out of 100. Thus, 25%, $\frac{25}{100}$, and 0.25 are simply different names for the same part-whole relationship.

Translating English to Math in Part-Whole Problems

On the GRE, many fractions and percents appear in word problems. You'll solve the problems by plugging the numbers you're given into some variation of one of the three basic formulas:

$$\frac{\text{Part}}{\text{Whole}} = \textit{Fraction}$$
$$\frac{\text{Part}}{\text{Whole}} = \textit{Decimal}$$
$$\frac{\text{Part}}{\text{Whole}}(100) = \textit{Percent}$$

To avoid careless errors, look for the key words *is* and *of*. *Is* (or *are*) often introduces the part, while *of* almost invariably introduces the whole.

Properties of 100%

Since the percent sign means $\frac{1}{100}$, 100% means $\frac{100}{100}$, or one whole. The key to solving some GRE percent problems is to recognize that all the parts add up to one whole: 100%.

Example:

All 1,000 registered voters in Smithtown are Democrats, Republicans, or independents. If 75% of the registered voters are Democrats and 5% are independents, how many are Republicans?

We calculate that 75% + 5%, or 80% of the 1,000 registered voters, are either Democrats or independents. The three political affiliations together must account for 100% of the voters; thus, the percentage of Republicans must be 100% − 80%, or 20%. Therefore, the number of Republicans must be 20% of 1,000, which is 20% (1,000), or 200.

Multiplying or dividing a number by 100% is just like multiplying or dividing by 1; it doesn't change the value of the original number.

Converting Percents

To change a fraction to its percent equivalent, multiply by 100%.

Example:

What is the percent equivalent of $\frac{5}{8}$?

$$\frac{5}{8}(100\%) = \frac{500}{8}\% = 62\frac{1}{2}\%$$

To change a decimal fraction to a percent, you can use the rules for multiplying by powers of 10. Move the decimal point two places to the right and insert a percent sign.

Example:

What is the percent equivalent of 0.17?

$$0.17 = 0.17\,(100\%) = 17\%$$

To change a percent to its fractional equivalent, divide by 100%.

Example:

What is the common fraction equivalent of 32%?

$$32\% = \frac{32\%}{100\%} = \frac{8}{25}$$

To convert a percent to its decimal equivalent, use the rules for dividing by powers of 10—just move the decimal point two places to the left.

Example:

What is the decimal equivalent of 32%?

$$32\% = \frac{32\%}{100\%} = \frac{32}{100} = 0.32$$

When you divide a percent by another percent, the percent sign "drops out," just as you would cancel out a common factor.

Example:

$$\frac{100\%}{5\%} = \frac{100}{5} = 20$$

Translation: There are 20 groups of 5% in 100%.

But when you divide a percent by a regular number (not by another percent), the percent sign remains.

Example:

$$\frac{100\%}{5} = 20\%$$

Translation: One-fifth of 100% is 20%.

Common Percent Equivalents

As you can see, changing percents to fractions, or vice versa, is pretty straightforward. But it does take a second or two that you might spend more profitably doing other computations or setting up another GRE math problem. Familiarity with the following common equivalents will save you time.

$\frac{1}{20} = 5\%$

$\frac{1}{12} = 8\frac{1}{3}\%$

$\frac{1}{10} = 10\%$

$\frac{1}{8} = 12\frac{1}{2}\%$

$\frac{1}{6} = 16\frac{2}{3}\%$

$\frac{1}{5} = 20\%$

$\frac{1}{4} = 25\%$

$\frac{3}{10} = 30\%$

$\frac{1}{3} = 33\frac{1}{3}\%$

$\frac{3}{8} = 37\frac{1}{2}\%$

$\frac{2}{5} = 40\%$

$\frac{1}{2} = 50\%$

$\frac{3}{5} = 60\%$

$\frac{5}{8} = 62\frac{1}{2}\%$

$\frac{2}{3} = 66\frac{2}{3}\%$

$\frac{7}{10} = 70\%$

$\frac{3}{4} = 75\%$

$\frac{4}{5} = 80\%$

$\frac{5}{6} = 83\frac{1}{3}\%$

$\frac{7}{8} = 87\frac{1}{2}\%$

$\frac{9}{10} = 90\%$

$\frac{11}{12} = 91\frac{2}{3}\%$

Using the Percent Formula to Solve Percent Problems

You can solve most percent problems by plugging the given data into the percent formula:

$$\frac{\text{Part}}{\text{Whole}}(100\%) = \text{Percent}$$

Most percent problems give you two of the three variables and ask for the third.

Example:

Ben spends $30 of his annual gardening budget on seed. If his total annual gardening budget is $150, what percentage of his budget does he spend on seed?

This problem specifies the whole ($150) and the part ($30) and asks for the percentage. Plugging those numbers into the percent formula gives you this:

$$\text{Percent} = \frac{30}{150}(100\%) = \frac{1}{5}(100\%) = 20\%$$

Ben spends 20% of his annual gardening budget on seed.

Percent Increase and Decrease

When the GRE tests percent increase or decrease, use the formula:

$$\text{Percent increase} = \frac{\text{Increase }(100\%)}{\text{Original}}$$

or

$$\text{Percent decrease} = \frac{\text{Decrease }(100\%)}{\text{Original}}$$

To find the increase or decrease, just take the difference between the original and the new. Note that the "original" is the base from which change occurs. It may or may not be the first number mentioned in the problem.

Example:

Two years ago, 450 seniors graduated from Inman High School. Last year, 600 seniors graduated. By what percent did the number of graduating seniors increase?

The original is the figure from the earlier time (two years ago): 450. The increase is $600 - 450$, or 150. So the percent increase is $\frac{150}{450}(100\%) = 33\frac{1}{3}\%$.

Example:

If the price of a $120 dress is increased by 25%, what is the new selling price?

To find the new whole, you'll first have to find the amount of increase. The original whole is $120, and the percent increase is 25%. Plugging in, we find that:

$$\begin{aligned} \frac{\text{Increase}}{120}(100\%) &= 25\% \\ \frac{\text{Increase}}{120} &= \frac{25}{100} \\ \frac{\text{Increase}}{120} &= \frac{1}{4} \\ \text{Increase} &= \frac{120}{4} \\ \text{Increase} &= 30 \end{aligned}$$

The amount of increase is $30, so the new selling price is $120 + $30, or $150.

Multi-Step Percent Problems

On some difficult problems, you'll be asked to find more than one percent or to find a percent of a percent. Be careful: You can't add percents of different wholes.

Example:

The price of an antique is reduced by 20 percent, and then this price is reduced by 10 percent. If the antique originally cost $200, what is its final price?

The most common mistake in this kind of problem is to reduce the original price by a total of 20% + 10%, or 30%. That would make the final price 70 percent of the original, or 70% ($200) = $140. This is not the correct answer. In this example, the second (10%) price reduction is taken off of the first sale price—the new whole, not the original whole.

To get the correct answer, first find the new whole. You can find it by calculating either $200 – (20% of $200) or 80% ($200). Either way, you will find that the first sale price is $160. That price then has to be reduced by 10%. Either calculate $160 – (10% ($160)) or 90% ($160). In either case, the final price of the antique is $144.

Picking Numbers with Percents

Certain types of percent problems lend themselves readily to the alternative technique of Picking Numbers. These include problems in which no actual values are mentioned, just percents. If you assign values to the percents you are working with, you'll find the problem less abstract.

You should almost always pick 100 in percent problems, because it's relatively easy to find percentages of 100.

Example:

The price of a share of company A's stock fell by 20 percent two weeks ago and by another 25 percent last week to its current price. By what percent of the current price does the share price need to rise in order to return to its original price?

(A) 45%
(B) 55%
(C) $66\frac{2}{3}\%$
(D) 75%
(E) 82%

Pick a value for the original price of the stock. Since this is a percent question, picking \$100 will make the math easy. The first change in the price of the stock was by 20% of \$100, or \$20, making the new price \$100 − \$20 = \$80.

The price then fell by another 25%. You know that 25% is the same as $\frac{1}{4}$, and $\frac{1}{4}$ of \$80 is \$20. Therefore, the current price is \$80 − \$20 = \$60. To return to its original price, the stock needs to rise from \$60 to \$100, that is, by \$100 − \$60 = \$40. Then \$40 is what percent of the current price, \$60?

$$\frac{40}{60}(100\%) = \frac{2}{3}(100\%) = 66\frac{2}{3}\%$$

Percent Word Problems

Percent problems are often presented as word problems. We have already seen how to identify the percent, the part, and the whole in simple percent word problems. Here are some other terms that you are likely to encounter in more complicated percent word problems:

Profit made on an item is the seller's price minus the cost to the seller. If a seller buys an item for \$10 and sells it for \$12, he has made \$2 profit. The percent of the selling price that is profit is as follows:

$$\frac{\text{Profit}}{\text{Original selling price}}(100\%) = \frac{\$2}{\$12}(100\%) = 16\frac{2}{3}\%$$

A *discount* on an item is the original price minus the reduced price. If an item that usually sells for $20 is sold for $15, the discount is $5. A discount is often represented as a percentage of the original price. In this case, the

$$\text{Percent discount} = \frac{\text{Discount}}{\text{Original price}}(100\%) = \frac{\$5}{\$20} = 25\%$$

The *sale price* is the final price after discount or decrease.

Occasionally, percent problems will involve *interest*. Interest is given as a percent per unit of time, such as 5% per month. The sum of money invested is the *principal*. The most common type of interest you will see is *simple interest*. In simple interest, the interest payments received are kept separate from the principal.

Example:

If an investor invests $100 at 20% simple annual interest, how much does she have at the end of three years?

The principal of $100 yields 20% interest every year. Because 20% of $100 is $20, after three years the investor will have three years of interest, or $60, plus the principal, for a total of $160.

In *compound interest*, the money earned as interest is reinvested. The principal grows after every interest payment received.

Example:

If an investor invests $100 at 20% compounded annually, how much does he have at the end of 3 years?

The first year the investor earns 20% of $100 = $20. So, after one year, he has $100 + $20 = $120.

The second year the investor earns 20% of $120 = $24. So, after two years, he has $120 + $24 = $144.

The third year the investor earns 20% of $144 = $28.80. So, after three years, he has $144 + $28.80 = $172.80.

Ratios

A *ratio* is the proportional relationship between two quantities. The ratio, or relationship, between two numbers (for example, 2 and 3) may be expressed with a colon between the two numbers (2:3), in words ("the ratio of 2 to 3"), or as a fraction $\frac{2}{3}$.

To translate a ratio in words to numbers separated by a colon, replace *to* with a colon.

To translate a ratio in words to a fractional ratio, use whatever follows the word *of* as the numerator and whatever follows the word *to* as the denominator. For example, if we had to express the ratio *of* glazed doughnuts *to* chocolate doughnuts in a box of doughnuts that contained 5 glazed and 7 chocolate doughnuts, we would do so as $\frac{5}{7}$.

Note that the fraction $\frac{5}{7}$ does not mean that $\frac{5}{7}$ of all the doughnuts are glazed doughnuts. There are $5 + 7$, or 12 doughnuts altogether, so of the doughnuts, $\frac{5}{12}$ are glazed. The $\frac{5}{7}$ ratio merely indicates the proportion of glazed to chocolate doughnuts. For every five glazed doughnuts, there are seven chocolate doughnuts.

Treating ratios as fractions can make computation easier. Like fractions, ratios often require division. And, like fractions, ratios ultimately should be reduced to lowest terms.

Example:

Joe is 16 years old, and Mary is 12 years old. Express the ratio of Joe's age to Mary's age in lowest terms.

The ratio of Joe's age to Mary's age is $\frac{16}{12} = \frac{4}{3}$, or 4:3.

Part:Whole Ratios

In a part:whole ratio, the "whole" is the entire set (for instance, all the workers in a factory), while the "part" is a certain subset of the whole (for instance, all the female workers in the factory).

In GRE ratio question stems, the word *fraction* generally indicates a part:whole ratio. "What fraction of the workers are female?" means "What is the ratio of the number of female workers to the total number of workers?"

Example:

The sophomore class at Milford Academy consists of 15 boys and 20 girls. What fraction of the sophomore class is female?

The following three statements are equivalent:

1. $\frac{4}{7}$ of the sophomores are female.
2. Four out of every seven sophomores are female.
3. The ratio of female sophomores to total sophomores is 4:7.

Ratio vs. Actual Number

Ratios are usually reduced to their simplest form (that is, to lowest terms). If the ratio of men to women in a room is 5:3, you cannot necessarily infer that there are exactly five men and three women.

If you knew the total number of people in the room, in addition to the male-to-female ratio, you could determine the number of men and the number of women in the room. For example, suppose you know that there are 32 people in the room. If the male-to-female ratio is 5 to 3, then the ratio of males to the total is 5:(5 + 3), which is 5:8. You can set up an equation as $\frac{5}{8} = \frac{\text{\# of males in room}}{32}$. Solving, you will find that the number of males in the room is 20.

Example:

The ratio of domestic sales revenues to foreign sales revenues of a certain product is 3:5. What fraction of the total sales revenues comes from domestic sales?

At first, this question may look more complicated than the previous example. You have to convert from a part:part ratio to a part:whole ratio (the ratio of domestic sales revenues to total sales revenues). And you're not given actual dollar figures for domestic or foreign sales. But since all sales are either foreign or domestic, "total sales revenues" must be the sum of the revenues from domestic and foreign sales. You can convert the given ratio to a part:whole ratio because the sum of the parts equals the whole.

Although it's impossible to determine dollar amounts for the domestic, foreign, or total sales revenues from the given information, the 3:5 ratio tells you that of every \$8 in sales revenues, \$3 comes from domestic sales and \$5 from foreign sales. Therefore, the ratio of domestic sales revenues to total sales revenues is 3:8, or $\frac{3}{8}$.

You can convert a part:part ratio to a part:whole ratio (or vice versa) only if there are no missing parts and no overlap among the parts—that is, if the whole is equal to the sum of the parts.

Example:

In a certain bag, the ratio of the number of red marbles to the number of blue marbles is 3:5. If there are only red and blue marbles in the bag, what is the ratio of the number of red marbles to the total number of marbles?

In this case, you can convert a part-to-part ratio (red marbles to blue marbles) to a part-to-whole ratio (red marbles to all marbles) because you know there are only red and blue marbles in the bag. The ratio of red marbles to the total number of marbles is 3:8.

Example:

Of the 25 people in Fran's apartment building, there are 9 residents who use the roof only for tanning and 8 residents who use the roof only for gardening. The roof is only used by tanners and gardeners.

Quantity A	Quantity B
The ratio of people who use the roof to total residents	17:25

In this question, we do not know if there is any overlap between tanners and gardeners. How many, if any, residents do both activities? Since we don't know, the relationship cannot be determined from the information given.

Ratios of More Than Two Terms

Most of the ratios that you'll see on the GRE have two terms. But it is possible to set up ratios with more than two terms. These ratios express more relationships, and therefore convey more information, than do two-term ratios. However, most of the principles discussed so far with respect to two-term ratios are just as applicable to ratios of more than two terms.

Example:

The ratio of x to y is 5:4. The ratio of y to z is 1:2. What is the ratio of x to z?

We want the y's in the two ratios to equal each other, because then we can combine the x:y ratio and the y:z ratio to form the x:y:z ratio that we need to answer this question. To make the y's equal, we can multiply the second ratio by 4. When we do so, we must perform the multiplication on both components of the ratio. Since a ratio is a constant proportion, it can be multiplied or divided by any number without losing its meaning, as long as the multiplication and division are applied to all the components of the ratio. In this case, we find that the new ratio for y to z is 4:8. We can combine this with the first ratio to find a new x to y to z ratio of 5:4:8. Therefore, the ratio of x to z is 5:8.

RATES

A *rate* is a special type of ratio. Instead of relating a part to the whole or to another part, a rate relates one kind of quantity to a completely different kind. When we talk about rates, we usually use the word *per*, as in "miles per hour," "cost per item," etc. Since *per* means "for one" or "for each," we express the rates as ratios reduced to a denominator of 1.

Speed

The most commonly tested rate on the GRE is speed. This is usually expressed in miles or kilometers per hour. The relationship between speed, distance, and time is given by the formula $\text{Speed} = \frac{\text{Distance}}{\text{Time}}$, which can be rewritten two ways: $\text{Time} = \frac{\text{Distance}}{\text{Speed}}$ and $\text{Distance} = (\text{Speed})(\text{Time})$.

Anytime you can find two out of the three elements in this equation, you can find the third.

For example, if a car travels 300 miles in 5 hours, it has averaged $\frac{300 \text{ miles}}{5 \text{ hours}} = 60$ miles per hour. (Note that speeds are usually expressed as averages because they are not necessarily constant. In this example, the car moved at an "average speed" of 60 miles per hour, but probably not at a constant speed of 60 miles per hour.)

Likewise, a rearranged version of the formula can be used to solve for missing speed or time.

Example:

How far do you drive if you travel for 5 hours at 60 miles per hour?

$$\begin{aligned} \text{Distance} &= (\text{Speed})(\text{Time}) \\ \text{Distance} &= (60 \text{ mph})(5 \text{ hours}) \\ \text{Distance} &= 300 \text{ miles} \end{aligned}$$

Example:

How much time does it take to drive 300 miles at 60 miles per hour?

$$\begin{aligned} \text{Time} &= \frac{\text{Distance}}{\text{Speed}} \\ \text{Time} &= \frac{300 \text{ miles}}{60 \text{ mph}} \\ \text{Time} &= 5 \text{ hours} \end{aligned}$$

Other Rates

Speed is not the only rate that appears on the GRE. For instance, you might get a word problem involving liters per minute or cost per unit. All rate problems, however, can be solved using the speed formula and its variants by conceiving of "speed" as "rate" and "distance" as "quantity."

Example:

How many hours will it take to fill a 500-liter tank at a rate of 2 liters per minute?

Plug the numbers into our rate formula:

$$\text{Time} = \frac{\text{Quantity}}{\text{Rate}}$$
$$\text{Time} = \frac{500\text{ liters}}{2\text{ liters per minute}}$$
$$\text{Time} = 250\text{ minutes}$$

Now convert 250 minutes to hours: 250 minutes $\div$ 60 minutes per hour $= 4\frac{1}{6}$ hours to fill the tank. (As you can see from this problem, GRE Problem Solving questions test your ability to convert minutes into hours and vice versa. Pay close attention to what units the answer choice must use.)

In some cases, you should use proportions to answer rate questions.

Example:

If 350 widgets cost $20, how much will 1,400 widgets cost at the same rate?

Set up a proportion:

$$\frac{\text{Number of widgets}}{\text{Cost}} = \frac{350\text{ widgets}}{\$20} = \frac{1{,}400\text{ widgets}}{\$x}$$

Solving, you will find that $x = 80$.

So, 1,400 widgets will cost $80 at that rate.

Combined Rate Problems

Rates can be added.

Example:

Nelson can mow 200 square meters of lawn per hour. John can mow 100 square meters of lawn per hour. Working simultaneously but independently, how many hours will it take Nelson and John to mow 1,800 square meters of lawn?

Add Nelson's rate to John's rate to find the combined rate.

200 meters per hour $+$ 100 meters per hour $=$ 300 meters per hour.

Divide the total lawn area, 1,800 square meters, by the combined rate, 300 square meters per hour, to find the number of required hours, 6.

Work Problems (Given Hours per Unit of Work)

The work formula can be used to find out how long it takes a number of people working together to complete a task. Let's say we have three people. The first takes a units of time to complete the job, the second b units of time to complete the job, and the third c units of time. If the time it takes all three working together to complete the job is T, then $\frac{1}{a} + \frac{1}{b} + \frac{1}{c} = \frac{1}{T}$.

Example:

John can weed the garden in 3 hours. If Mary can weed the garden in 2 hours, how long will it take them to weed the garden at this rate, working independently?

Set John's time per unit of work as a and Mary's time per unit of work as b. (There is no need for the variable c, since there are only two people.) Plugging in, you find that

$$\begin{aligned} \frac{1}{3} + \frac{1}{2} &= \frac{1}{T} \\ \frac{2}{6} + \frac{3}{6} &= \frac{1}{T} \\ \frac{5}{6} &= \frac{1}{T} \\ T &= \frac{6}{5} \text{ hours} \end{aligned}$$

Work Formula for Two

When there are only two people or machines in a combined work problem, we can use a simplified work formula.

$$\begin{aligned} \frac{1}{a} + \frac{1}{b} &= \frac{1}{T} \\ (ab)\left(\frac{1}{a} + \frac{1}{b}\right) &= \left(\frac{1}{T}\right)(ab) \\ \frac{ab}{a} + \frac{ab}{b} &= \frac{ab}{T} \\ b + a &= \frac{ab}{T} \\ T(b + a) &= \left(\frac{ab}{T}\right)T \\ T(b + a) &= ab \\ T &= \frac{ab}{a + b} \end{aligned}$$

Here, a = the amount of time it takes person a to complete the job, and b = the amount of time it takes person b to complete the job.

Example:

Let's use the same example from above: John takes 3 hours to weed the garden, and Mary takes 2 hours to weed the same garden. How long will it take them to weed the garden together?

$$\text{Work formula} = \frac{a \times b}{a + b} = \frac{3 \times 2}{3 + 2} = \frac{6}{5}\text{ hours}$$

AVERAGES

The *average* of a group of numbers is defined as the sum of the terms divided by the number of terms.

$$\text{Average} = \frac{\text{Sum of terms}}{\text{Number of terms}}$$

This equation can be rewritten two ways:

$$\text{Number of terms} = \frac{\text{Sum of terms}}{\text{Average}}$$

$$\text{Sum of terms} = (\text{Number of terms})(\text{Average})$$

Thus, any time you have two out of the three values (average, sum of terms, number of terms), you can find the third.

Example:

Henry buys three items costing \$2.00, \$1.75, and \$1.05. What is the average price (arithmetic mean) of the three items? (Don't let the phrase *arithmetic mean* throw you; it's just another term for *average*.)

$$\text{Average} = \frac{\text{Sum of terms}}{\text{Number of terms}}$$

$$\text{Average} = \frac{\$2.0 + \$1.75 + \$1.05}{3}$$

$$\text{Average} = \frac{\$4.80}{3}$$

$$\text{Average} = \$1.60$$

Example:

June pays an average price of $14.50 for 6 articles of clothing. What is the total price of all 6 articles?

$$\begin{aligned} \text{Sum of terms} &= (\text{Average})\ (\text{Number of terms}) \\ \text{Sum of terms} &= (\$14.50)\ (6) \\ \text{Sum of terms} &= \$87.00 \end{aligned}$$

Example:

The total weight of the licorice sticks in a jar is 30 ounces. If the average weight of each licorice stick is 2 ounces, how many licorice sticks are there in the jar?

$$\begin{aligned} \text{Number of terms} &= \frac{\text{Sum of terms}}{\text{Average}} \\ \text{Number of terms} &= \frac{30 \text{ ounces}}{2 \text{ ounces}} \\ \text{Number of terms} &= 15 \end{aligned}$$

Using the Average to Find a Missing Number

If you're given the average, the total number of terms, and all but one of the actual numbers, you can find the missing number.

Example:

The average annual rainfall in Boynton for 1976–1979 was 26 inches per year. Boynton received 24 inches of rain in 1976, 30 inches in 1977, and 19 inches in 1978. How many inches of rainfall did Boynton receive in 1979?

You know that total rainfall equals 24 + 30 + 19 + (number of inches of rain in 1979).

You know that the average rainfall was 26 inches per year.

You know that there were 4 years.

So, plug these numbers into any of the three expressions of the average formula to find that Sum of terms = (Average)(Number of terms):

$$
\begin{aligned}
24 + 30 + 19 + \text{inches in 1979} &= (26)(4) \\
73 + \text{inches in 1979} &= (26)(4) \\
73 + \text{inches in 1979} &= 104 \\
\text{inches in 1979} &= 31
\end{aligned}
$$

Another Way to Find a Missing Number: The Concept of "Balanced Value"

Another way to find a missing number is to understand that the *sum of the differences between each term and the mean of the set must equal zero.* Plugging in the numbers from the previous problem, for example, we find that:

$$
\begin{aligned}
(24 - 26) + (30 - 26) + (19 - 26) + (\text{inches in 1979} - 26) &= 0 \\
(-2) + (4) + (-7) + (\text{inches in 1979} - 26) &= 0 \\
-5 + (\text{inches in 1979} - 26) &= 0 \\
\text{inches in 1979} &= 31
\end{aligned}
$$

It may be easier to comprehend why this is true by visualizing a balancing, or weighting, process. The combined distance of the numbers above the average from the mean must be balanced with the combined distance of the numbers below the average from the mean.

Example:

The average of 63, 64, 85, and x is 80. What is the value of x?

Think of each value in terms of its position relative to the average, 80.

63 is 17 less than 80.

64 is 16 less than 80.

85 is 5 greater than 80.

So these three terms are a total of $17 + 16 - 5$, or 28, less than the average. Therefore, x must be 28 greater than the average to restore the balance at 80. So $x = 28 + 80 = 108$.

Average of Consecutive, Evenly Spaced Numbers

When consecutive numbers are evenly spaced, the average is the middle value. For example, the average of consecutive integers 6, 7, and 8 is 7.

If there is an even number of evenly spaced numbers, there is no single middle value. In that case, the average is midway between (that is, the average of) the middle two values. For example, the average of 5, 10, 15, and 20 is 12.5, midway between the middle values 10 and 15.

Note that not all consecutive numbers are evenly spaced. For instance, consecutive prime numbers arranged in increasing order are not evenly spaced. But you can use the handy technique of finding the middle value whenever you have consecutive integers, consecutive odd or even numbers, consecutive multiples of an integer, or any other consecutive numbers that are evenly spaced.

Combining Averages

When there is an equal number of terms in each set, and *only when there is an equal number of terms in each set*, you can average averages.

For example, suppose there are two bowlers and you must find their average score per game. One has an average score per game of 100, and the other has an average score per game of 200. If both bowlers bowled the same number of games, you can average their averages to find their combined average. Suppose they both bowled 4 games. Their combined average will be equally influenced by both bowlers. Hence, their combined average will be the average of 100 and 200. You can find this quickly by remembering that the quantity above the average and the quantity below the average must be equal. Therefore, the average will be halfway between 100 and 200, which is 150. Or, we could solve using our average formula:

$$\text{Average} = \frac{\text{Sum of terms}}{\text{Number of terms}} = \frac{4(100)+4(200)}{8} = 150$$

However, if the bowler with the average score of 100 had bowled 4 games and the bowler with the 200 average had bowled 16 games, the combined average would be weighted further toward 200 than toward 100 to reflect the greater influence of the 200 bowler than the 100 bowler upon the total. This is known as a *weighted average*.

Again, you can solve this by using the concept of a balanced average or by using the average formula.

Since the bowler bowling an average score of 200 bowled $\frac{4}{5}$ of the games, the combined average will be $\frac{4}{5}$ of the distance along the number line between 100 and 200, which is 180. Or, you can plug numbers into an average formula to find the following:

$$\begin{aligned}
\text{Average} &= \frac{\text{Sum of terms}}{\text{Number of terms}} \\
\text{Average} &= \frac{4(100) + 16(200)}{20} \\
\text{Average} &= \frac{400 + 3{,}200}{20} \\
\text{Average} &= 180
\end{aligned}$$

Example:

A teacher surprised her students with a 5 question pop quiz. 10% of the students answered no questions correctly, 20% had 2 right answers, 30% answered 3 questions correctly, 30% had 4 right answers and 10% had a perfect score. What was the weighted average of the number of correct answers?

$$\textit{Weighted Avg} = \frac{.1(0)+.2(2)+.3(3)+.3(4)+.1(5)}{0.1+0.2+0.3+0.1} = \frac{0.0+0.4+0.9+1.2+0.5}{1} = 3.0$$

ALGEBRA

Algebraic Terms

Variable: A letter or symbol representing an unknown quantity.

Constant (term): A number not multiplied by any variable(s).

Term: A numerical constant; also, the product of a numerical constant and one or more variables.

Coefficient: The numerical constant by which one or more variables are multiplied. The coefficient of $3x^2$ is 3. A variable (or product of variables) without a numerical coefficient, such as z or xy^3, is understood to have a coefficient of 1.

Algebraic expression: An expression containing one or more variables, one or more constants, and possibly one or more operation symbols. In the case of the expression x, there is an implied coefficient of 1. An expression does not contain an equal sign. x, $3x^2 + 2x$, and $\frac{7x+1}{3x^2-14}$ are all algebraic expressions.

Monomial: An algebraic expression with only one term. To *multiply monomials*, multiply the coefficients and the variables separately: $2a \times 3a = (2 \times 3)(a \times a) = 6a^2$.

Polynomial: The general name for an algebraic expression with more than one term. An algebraic expression with two terms is called a *binomial*.

Algebraic equation: Two algebraic expressions separated by an equal sign or one algebraic expression separated from a number by an equal sign.

Basic Operations

Combining Like Terms

The process of simplifying an expression by adding together or subtracting terms that have the same variable factors is called *combining like terms*.

Example:

Simplify the expression $2x - 5y - x + 7y$.

$2x - 5y - x + 7y = (2x - x) + (7y - 5y) = x + 2y$

Notice that the commutative, associative, and distributive laws that govern arithmetic operations with ordinary numbers also apply to algebraic terms and polynomials.

Adding and Subtracting Polynomials

To *add or subtract polynomials*, combine like terms.

$$(3x^2 + 5x + 7) - (x^2 + 12) = (3x^2 - x^2) + 5x + (7 - 12) = 2x^2 + 5x - 5$$

Factoring Algebraic Expressions

Factoring a polynomial means expressing it as a product of two or more simpler expressions. Common factors can be factored out by using the distributive law.

Example:

Factor the expression $2a + 6ac$.

The greatest common factor of $2a + 6ac$ is $2a$. Using the distributive law, you can factor out $2a$ so that the expression becomes $2a(1 + 3c)$.

Example:

All three terms in the polynomial $3x^3 + 12x^2 - 6x$ contain a factor of $3x$. Pulling out the common factor yields $3x(x^2 + 4x - 2)$.

Advanced Operations

Substitution

Substitution, a process of plugging values into equations, is used to evaluate an algebraic expression or to express it in terms of other variables.

Replace every variable in the expression with the number or quantity you are told is its equivalent. Then carry out the designated operations, remembering to follow the order of operations (PEMDAS).

Example:

Express $\frac{a - b^2}{b - a}$ in terms of x if $a = 2x$ and $b = 3$.

Replace every a with $2x$ and every b with 3:

$$\frac{a - b^2}{b - a} = \frac{2x - 9}{3 - 2x}$$

Without more information, you can't simplify or evaluate this expression further.

Solving Equations

When you manipulate any equation, *always do the same thing on both sides of the equal sign*. Otherwise, the two sides of the equation will no longer be equal.

To solve an algebraic equation without exponents for a particular variable, you have to manipulate the equation until that variable is on one side of the equal sign with all numbers or other variables on the other side. You can perform addition, subtraction, or multiplication; you can also perform division, as long as the quantity by which you are dividing does not equal zero.

Typically, at each step of the process, you'll try to isolate the variable by using the reverse of whatever operation has been applied to the variable. For example, in solving the equation $n + 6 = 10$ for n, you have to get rid of the 6 that has been added to the n. You do that by subtracting 6 from both sides of the equation: $n + 6 - 6 = 10 - 6$, so $n = 4$.

Example:

If $4x - 7 = 2x + 5$, what is the value of x?

Start by adding 7 to both sides. This gives us $4x = 2x + 12$. Now subtract $2x$ from both sides. This gives us $2x = 12$. Finally, let's divide both sides by 2. This gives us $x = 6$.

Inequalities

There are two differences between solving an *inequality* (such as $2x < 5$) and solving an *equation* (such as $2x - 5 = 0$).

First, the solution to an inequality is almost always a range of possible values, rather than a single value. You can see the range most clearly by expressing it visually on a number line.

The shaded portion of the number line above shows the set of all numbers between −4 and 0 excluding the endpoints −4 and 0; this range would be expressed algebraically by the inequality $-4 < x < 0$.

The shaded portion of the number line above shows the set of all numbers greater than −1, up to and including 3; this range would be expressed algebraically by the inequality $-1 < x \leq 3$.

The other difference when solving an inequality—and the only thing you really have to remember—is that **if you multiply or divide the inequality by a negative number, you have to reverse the direction of the inequality**. For example, when you multiply both sides of the inequality $-3x < 2$ by −1, you get $3x > -2$.

Example:

Solve for x: $3 - \frac{x}{4} \geq 2$

Multiply both sides of the inequality by 4: $12 - x \geq 8$

Subtract 12 from both sides: $-x \geq -4$

Multiply (or divide) both sides by −1 and change the direction of the inequality sign: $x \leq 4$.

As you can see from the number line, the range of values that satisfies this inequality includes 4 and all numbers less than 4.

Solving for One Unknown in Terms of Another

In general, in order to solve for the value of an unknown, you need as many distinct equations as you have variables. If there are two variables, for instance, you need two distinct equations.

However, some GRE problems do not require you to solve for the numerical value of an unknown. Instead, you are asked to solve for one variable in terms of the other(s). To do so, isolate the desired variable on one side of the equation and move all the constants and other variables to the other side.

Example:

In the formula $z = \frac{xy}{a + yb}$, solve for y in terms of x, z, a, and b.

Clear the denominator by multiplying both sides by $a + yb$: $(a + yb)z = xy$

Remove parentheses by distributing: $az + ybz = xy$

Put all terms containing y on one side and all other terms on the other side: $az = xy - ybz$

Factor out the common factor, y: $az = y(x - bz)$

Divide by the coefficient of y to get y alone: $\frac{az}{x - bz} = y$

Simultaneous Equations

We've already discovered that you need as many different equations as you have variables to solve for the actual value of a variable. When a single equation contains more than one variable, you can only solve for one variable in terms of the others.

This has important implications for Quantitative Comparisons. To have enough information to compare the two quantities, you usually must have at least as many equations as you have variables.

On the GRE, you will often have to solve two simultaneous equations, that is, equations that give you different information about the same two variables. There are two methods for solving simultaneous equations.

Method 1—Substitution

Step 1: Solve one equation for one variable in terms of the second.

Step 2: Substitute the result back into the other equation and solve.

Example:

If $x - 15 = 2y$ and $6y + 2x = -10$, what is the value of y ?

Solve the first equation for x by adding 15 to both sides.

$$x = 2y + 15$$

Substitute $2y + 15$ for x in the second equation:

$$\begin{aligned} 6y + 2(2y + 15) &= -10 \\ 6y + 4y + 30 &= -10 \\ 10y &= -40 \\ y &= -4 \end{aligned}$$

Method 2—Adding to Cancel

Combine the equations in such a way that one of the variables cancels out. To solve the two equations $4x + 3y = 8$ and $x + y = 3$, multiply both sides of the second equation by -3 to get $-3x - 3y = -9$. Now add the two equations; the $3y$ and the $-3y$ cancel out, leaving: $x = -1$.

Before you use either method, make sure you really do have two distinct equations. For example, $2x + 3y = 8$ and $4x + 6y = 16$ are really the same equation in different forms; multiply the first equation by 2, and you'll get the second.

Whichever method you use, you can check the result by plugging both values back into both equations and making sure they fit.

Example:

If $m = 4n - 10$ and $3m + 2n = 26$, find the values of m and n.

Since the first equation already expresses m in terms of n, this problem is best approached by substitution.

Substitute $4n - 10$ for m into $3m + 2n = 26$, and solve for n.

$$\begin{aligned} 3(4n - 10) + 2n &= 26 \\ 12n - 30 + 2n &= 26 \\ 14n &= 56 \\ n &= 4 \end{aligned}$$

Now solve either equation for m by plugging in 4 for n.

$m = 4n - 10$

$m = 4(4) - 10$

$m = 16 - 10$

$m = 6$

So $m = 6$ and $n = 4$.

Example:

If $3x + 3y = 18$ and $x - y = 10$, find the values of x and y.

You could solve this problem by the substitution method. But look what happens if you multiply the second equation by 3 and add it to the first:

$$\begin{array}{rcl} 3x + 3y & = & 18 \\ +(3x - 3y & = & 30) \\ \hline 6x & = & 48 \end{array}$$

If $6x = 48$, then $x = 8$. Now you can just plug 8 into either equation in place of x and solve for y. Your calculations will be simpler if you use the second equation: $8 - y = 10$; $-y = 2$; $y = -2$.

Example:

The GRE will sometimes reward you with a shortcut to finding combined value using multiple variables.

If $5x + 5y = 20$, what is the value of $x + y$?

We don't need the value of either variable by itself, but their sum. If we divided both sides by 5, we could find the value of $x + y$.

$$5x + 5y = 20$$
$$5\,(x + y) = 20$$
$$x + y = 4$$

Example:

If $3x - 5y = 10$ and $6y - 2x = 20$, what is the value of $x + y$?

By aligning the two equations with the same-variable order, you can see a shortcut to adding the two together to find the solution.

$$3x - 5y = 10$$
$$-2x + 6y = 20$$
$$x + y = 30$$

While we don't know the individual values for x or y, we don't need to know them.

Symbolism

Don't panic if you see strange symbols like ★, ✧, and ◆ in a GRE problem.

Problems of this type usually require nothing more than substitution. Read the question stem carefully for a definition of the symbols and for any examples of how to use them. Then, just follow the given model, substituting the numbers that are in the question stem.

Example:

An operation symbolized by ✯ is defined by the equation x ✯ $y = x - \frac{1}{y}$. What is the value of 2 ✯ 7?

The ✯ symbol is defined as a two-stage operation performed on two quantities, which are symbolized in the equation as x and y. The two steps are (1) find the reciprocal of the second quantity and (2) subtract the reciprocal from the first quantity. To find the value of 2 ✯ 7, substitute the numbers 2 and 7 into the equation, replacing the x (the first quantity given in the equation) with the 2 (the first number given) and the y (the second quantity given in the equation) with the 7 (the second number given). The reciprocal of 7 is $\frac{1}{7}$, and subtracting $\frac{1}{7}$ from 2 gives you the following:

$$2-\frac{1}{7}=\frac{14}{7}-\frac{1}{7}=\frac{13}{7}$$

When a symbolism problem involves only one quantity, the operations are usually a little more complicated. Nonetheless, you can follow the same steps to find the correct answer.

Example:

Let $x^\star$ be defined by the equation: $x^\star=\frac{x^2}{1-x^2}$. Evaluate $\left(\frac{1}{2}\right)^\star$.

$$\left(\frac{1}{2}\right)^\star=\frac{\left(\frac{1}{2}\right)^2}{1-\left(\frac{1}{2}\right)^2}=\frac{\frac{1}{4}}{1-\frac{1}{4}}=\frac{\frac{1}{4}}{\frac{3}{4}}=\frac{1}{4}\times\frac{4}{3}=\frac{1}{3}$$

Every once in a while, you'll see a symbolism problem that doesn't even include an equation. The definitions in this type of problem usually test your understanding of number properties.

Example:

✽x is defined as the largest even number that is less than the negative square root of x. What is the value of ✽81?

Ⓐ −82
Ⓑ −80
Ⓒ −10
Ⓓ −8
Ⓔ 8

Plug in 81 for x and work backward logically. The negative square root of 81 is −9 because $(-9)(-9) = 81$. The largest even number that is less than −9 is −10. (The number part of −8 is smaller than the number part of −9; however, you're dealing with negative numbers, so you have to look for the even number that would be just to the *left* of −9 along the number line.) Thus, the correct answer choice is **(C)** −10.

Sequences

Sequences are lists of numbers. The value of a number in a sequence is related to its position in the list. Sequences are often represented on the GRE as follows:

$$s_1, s_2, s_3, \ldots s_n, \ldots$$

The subscript part of each number gives you the position of each element in the series. s_1 is the first number in the list, s_2 is the second number in the list, and so on.

You will be given a formula that defines each element. For example, if you are told that $s_n = 2n + 1$, then the sequence would be $(2 \times 1) + 1$, $(2 \times 2) + 1$, $(2 \times 3) + 1, \ldots,$ or $3, 5, 7, \ldots$

Polynomials and Quadratics

The FOIL Method

When two binomials are multiplied, each term is multiplied by each term in the other binomial. This process is often called the *FOIL method*, because it involves adding the products of the First, Outer, Inner, and Last terms. Using the FOIL method to multiply out $(x + 5)(x - 2)$, the product of the first terms is x^2, the product of the outer terms is $-2x$, the product of the inner terms is $5x$, and the product of the last terms is -10. Adding, the answer is $x^2 + 3x - 10$.

Factoring the Product of Binomials

Many of the polynomials that you'll see on the GRE can be factored into a product of two binomials by using the FOIL method backward.

Example:

Factor the polynomial $x^2 - 3x + 2$.

You can factor this into two binomials, each containing an x term. Start by writing down what you know:

$$x^2 - 3x + 2 = (x \quad\;)(x \quad\;)$$

You'll need to fill in the missing term in each binomial factor. The product of the two missing terms will be the last term in the original polynomial: 2. The sum of the two missing terms will be the coefficient of the second term of the polynomial: -3. Find the factors of 2 that add up to -3. Since $(-1) + (-2) = -3$, you can fill the empty spaces with -1 and -2.

Thus, $x^2 - 3x + 2 = (x - 1)(x - 2)$.

Note: Whenever you factor a polynomial, you can check your answer by using FOIL to multiply the factors and obtain the original polynomial.

Factoring the Difference of Two Squares

A common factorable expression on the GRE is the difference of two squares (for example, $a^2 - b^2$). Once you recognize a polynomial as the difference of two squares, you'll be able to factor it automatically, since any polynomial of the form $a^2 - b^2$ can be factored into a product of the form $(a + b)(a - b)$.

Example:

Factor the expression $9x^2 - 1$.

$9x^2 = (3x)^2$ and $1 = 1^2$, so $9x^2 - 1$ is the difference of two squares.

Therefore, $9x^2 - 1 = (3x + 1)(3x - 1)$.

Factoring Polynomials of the Form $a^2 + 2ab + b^2$ or $a^2 - 2ab + b^2$

Any polynomial of this form is the square of a binomial expression, as you can see by using the FOIL method to multiply $(a + b)(a + b)$ or $(a - b)(a - b)$.

To factor a polynomial of this form, check the sign in front of the $2ab$ term. If it's a *plus* sign, the polynomial is equal to $(a + b)^2$. If it's a *minus* sign, the polynomial is equal to $(a - b)^2$.

Example:

Factor the polynomial $x^2 + 6x + 9$.

x^2 and 9 are both perfect squares, and $6x$ is $2(3x)$, which is twice the product of x and 3, so this polynomial is of the form $a^2 + 2ab + b^2$ with $a = x$ and $b = 3$. Since there is a plus sign in front of the $6x$, $x^2 + 6x + 9 = (a + 3)^2$.

Quadratic Equations

A *quadratic equation* is an equation of the form $ax^2 + bx + c = 0$. Many quadratic equations have two solutions. In other words, the equation will be true for two different values of x.

When you see a quadratic equation on the GRE, you'll generally be able to solve it by factoring the algebraic expression, setting each of the factors equal to zero, and solving the resulting equations.

Example:

$x^2 - 3x + 2 = 0$. Solve for x.

To find the solutions, or roots, start by factoring $x^2 - 3x + 2 = 0$ into $(x - 2)(x - 1) = 0$.

The product of two quantities equals zero only if one (or both) of the quantities equals zero. So if you set each of the factors equal to zero, you will be able to solve the resulting equations for the solutions of the original quadratic equation. Setting the two binomials equal to zero gives you this:

$$x - 2 = 0 \text{ or } x - 1 = 0$$

That means that x can equal 2 or 1. As a check, you can plug each of those values in turn into $x^2 - 3x + 2 = 0$, and you'll see that either value makes the equation work.

Alternative Strategies for Multiple-Choice Algebra

Backsolving

On GRE Problem Solving questions, you may find it easier to attack algebra problems by Backsolving. To Backsolve, substitute each answer choice into the equation until you find the one that satisfies the equation.

Example:

If $x^2 + 10x + 25 = 0$, what is the value of x?

(A) 25
(B) 10
(C) 5
(D) −5
(E) −10

The textbook approach to solving this problem would be to recognize the polynomial expression as the square of the binomial $(x + 5)$ and set $x + 5 = 0$. That's the fastest way to arrive at the correct answer of −5.

But you could also plug each answer choice into the equation until you found the one that makes the equation true. Backsolving can be pretty quick if the correct answer is the first choice you plug in, but here, you have to get all the way down to choice **(D)** before you find that $(-5)^2 + 10(-5) + 25 = 0$.

Example:

If $\frac{5x}{3} + 9 = \frac{x}{6} + 18$, $x =$

(A) 12
(B) 8
(C) 6
(D) 5
(E) 4

To avoid having to try all five answer choices, look at the equation and decide which choice(s), if plugged in for x, would make your calculations easiest. Since x is in the numerators of the two fractions in this equation and the denominators are 3 and 6, try plugging in a choice that is divisible by both 3 and 6. Choices **(A)** and **(C)** are divisible by both numbers, so start with one of them.

Choice **(A)**:

$$20 + 9 = 2 + 18$$
$$29 \neq 20$$

This is not true, so x cannot equal 12.

Choice **(C)**:

$$10 + 9 = 1 + 18$$
$$19 = 19$$

This is correct, so x must equal 6. Therefore, choice **(C)** is correct.

Backsolving may not be the fastest method for a multiple-choice algebra problem, but it's useful if you don't think you'll be able to solve the problem in the conventional way.

Picking Numbers

On other types of multiple-choice algebra problems, especially where the answer choices consist of variables or algebraic expressions, you may want to Pick Numbers to make the problem less abstract. Evaluate the answer choices and the information in the question stem by picking a number and substituting it for the variable wherever the variable appears.

Example:

If $a > 1$, the ratio of $2a + 6$ to $a^2 + 2a - 3$ is

(A) $2a$

(B) $a + 3$

(C) $\frac{2}{a - 1}$

(D) $\frac{2a}{3(3 - a)}$

(E) $\frac{a - 1}{2}$

You can simplify the process by replacing the variable a with a number in each algebraic expression. Since a has to be greater than 1, why not pick 2? Then the expression $2a + 6$ becomes $2(2) + 6$, or 10. The expression $a^2 + 2a - 3$ becomes $2^2 + 2(2) - 3 = 4 + 4 - 3 = 5$.

So now the question reads, "The ratio of 10 to 5 is what?" That's easy enough to answer: 10:5 is the same as $\frac{10}{5}$, or 2. Now you can just eliminate any answer choice that doesn't give a result of 2 when you substitute 2 for a. Choice **(A)** gives you 2(2), or 4, so discard it. Choice **(B)** results in 5—also not what you want. Choice **(C)** yields $\frac{2}{1}$ or 2. That looks good, but you can't stop here.

If another answer choice gives you a result of 2, you will have to pick another number for a and reevaluate the expressions in the question stem and the choices that worked when you let $a = 2$.

Choice **(D)** gives you $\frac{2(2)}{3(3-2)}$ or $\frac{4}{3}$, so eliminate choice **(D)**.

Choice **(E)** gives you $\frac{2-1}{2}$ or $\frac{1}{2}$, so discard choice **(E)**.

Fortunately, in this case, only choice **(C)** works out equal to 2, so it is the correct answer. But remember: When Picking Numbers, always check every answer choice to make sure you haven't chosen a number that works for more than one answer choice.

Using Picking Numbers to Solve for One Unknown in Terms of Another

It is also possible to solve for one unknown in terms of another by Picking Numbers. If the first number you pick doesn't lead to a single correct answer, be prepared to either pick a new number (and spend more time on the problem) or settle for guessing strategically among the answers that you haven't eliminated.

Example:

If $\frac{x^2 - 16}{x^2 + 6x + 8} = y$ and $x > -2$, which of the following is an expression for x in terms of y?

(A) $\frac{1 + y}{2 - y}$

(B) $\frac{2y + 4}{1 - y}$

(C) $\frac{4y - 4}{y + 1}$

(D) $\frac{2y - 4}{2 + y}$

(E) $\frac{y + 4}{y + 1}$

Pick a value for x that will simplify your calculations. If you let x equal 4, then $x^2 - 16 = 4^2 - 16 = 0$, and so the entire fraction on the left side of the equation is equal to zero.

Now, substitute 0 for y in each answer choice in turn. Each choice is an expression for x in terms of y, and since $y = 0$ when $x = 4$, the correct answer will have to give a value of 4 when $y = 0$. Just remember to evaluate all the answer choices, because you might find more than one that gives a result of 4.

Substituting 0 for y in choices **(A)**, **(C)**, and **(D)** yields $\frac{1}{2}$, $-\frac{4}{1}$, and $-\frac{4}{2}$, respectively, so none of those choices can be right. But both **(B)** and **(E)** give results of 4 when you make the substitution; choosing between them will require picking another number.

Again, pick a number that will make calculations easy. If $x = 0$, then $y =$

$$\frac{x^2 - 16}{x^2 + 6x + 8} = \frac{0 - 16}{0 + 0 + 8} = \frac{-16}{8} = -2$$

Therefore, $y = -2$ when $x = 0$. You don't have to try the new value of y in all the answer choices, just in **(B)** and **(E)**. When you substitute –2 for y in choice **(B)**, you get 0. That's what you're looking for, but again, you have to make sure it doesn't work in choice **(E)**. Plugging –2 in for y in **(E)** yields –2 for x, so **(B)** is correct.

TABLES, GRAPHS, AND CHARTS

Some questions, especially in Data Interpretation, combine numbers and text with visual formats. Different formats are suitable for organizing different types of information. The formats that appear most frequently on GRE math questions are tables, bar graphs, line graphs, and pie charts.

Questions involving tables, graphs, and charts may *look* different from other GRE math questions, but the ideas and principles are the same. The problems are unusual only in the way that they present information, not in what they ask you to do with that information.

Tables

The most basic way to organize information is to create a table. Tables are in some ways the most accurate graphic presentation format—the only way you can misunderstand a number is to read it from the wrong row or column—but they don't allow the reader to spot trends or extremes very readily.

Here's an example of a very simple table.

JOHN'S INCOME: 2007–2011	
Year	Income
2007	$20,000
2008	$22,000
2009	$18,000
2010	$15,000
2011	$28,000

An easy question might ask for John's income in a particular year or for the difference in his income between two years. To find the difference, you would simply look up the amount for both years and subtract the smaller income from the larger income. A harder question might ask for John's average annual income over the five-year period shown; to determine the average, you would have to find the sum of the five annual incomes and divide it by 5.

Bar Graphs

Here's the same information that you saw previously in a table. This time, it's presented as a bar graph.

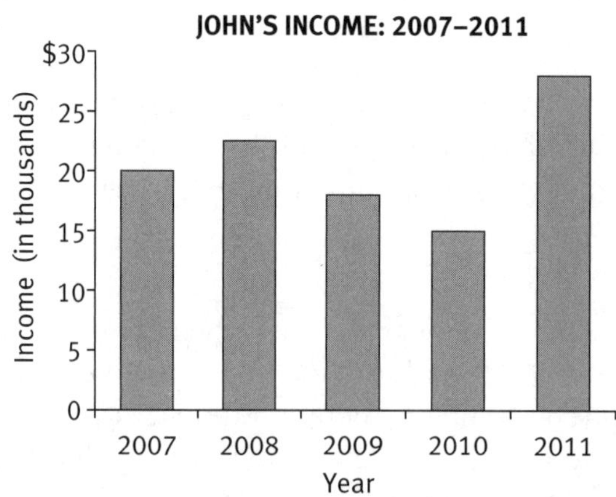

Bar graphs are somewhat less accurate than tables, but that's not necessarily a bad attribute, especially on the GRE, where estimating often saves time on calculations.

What's handy about a bar graph is that you can see which values are larger or smaller without reading actual numbers. Just a glance at this graph shows that John's 2011 income was almost double his 2010 income. Numbers are represented on a bar graph by the heights or lengths of the bars. For example, in the first of the two bar graphs below, the taller bar represents a value of 7.

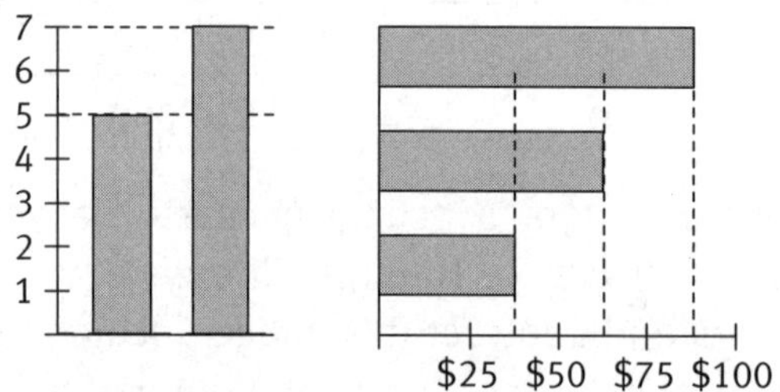

If the height or length of the bar falls between two numbers on the axis, you will have to estimate. For instance, in the second of the two bar graphs above, the shortest bar represents a value about halfway between $25 and $50, or about $37.50.

Histograms

Bar graphs that show relative frequencies or numbers of occurrences are called *histograms*. The *y*-axis on a histogram shows the frequency, while the *x*-axis might show category definitions, values, or ranges, depending on what is being graphed. These graphs can be useful in visualizing patterns and trends in the data.

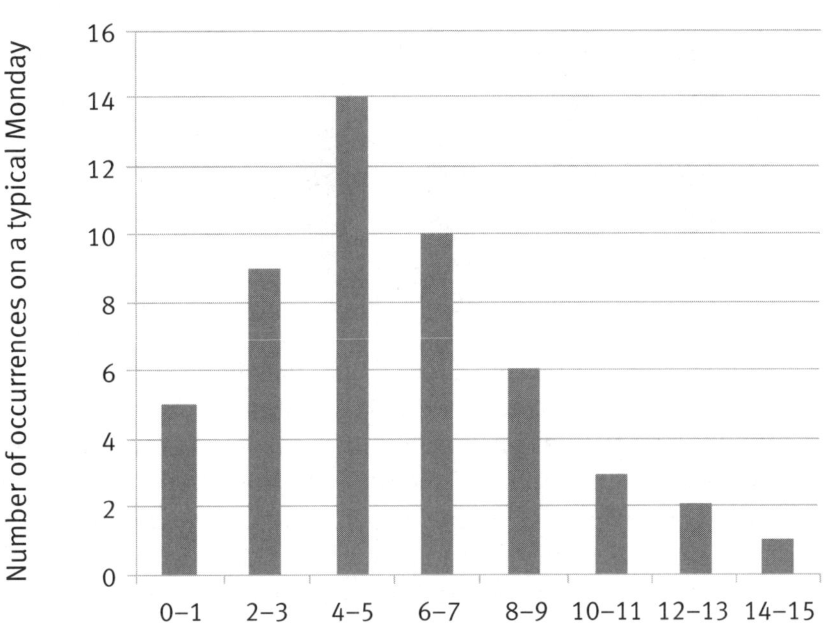

A quick inspection of this graph shows that the mode is 4–5 calls per minute and that the frequency distribution has a long right "tail" of occasional bursts of very high call volume. One drawback of histograms is that estimating the mean of the data can be very difficult.

Segmented Bar Graphs

"Regular" bar graphs only display one value for each bar. Segmented bar graphs, also called *stacked bar graphs*, display multiple quantities on each bar. These quantities represent different subgroups that sum to the amount at the top of each bar.

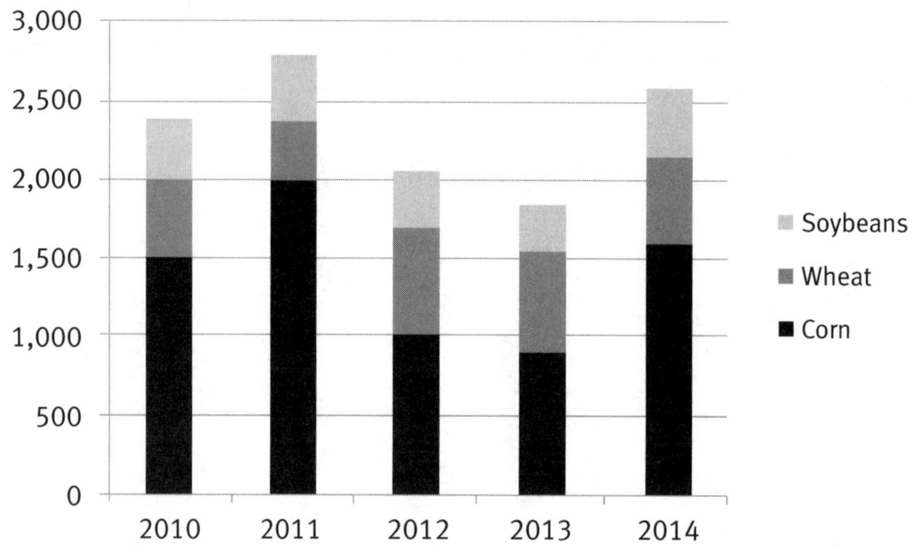

Values for the first category (in this case, corn) and the total can be read directly on stacked bar charts. For instance, in 2010, the farm produced 1,500 bushels of corn and 2,400 bushels in total. Values for other categories must be calculated by subtracting the value at the bottom of the portion of the bar for that category from the value at the top of that portion of the bar. Here, wheat production is represented by the middle portion, or medium gray area, of each bar. To determine the wheat crop for 2012, find the value at the bottom of the medium gray area of the 2012 bar, 1,000, and subtract that from the value at the top of the medium gray area, 1,700. Since 1,700 – 1,000 = 700, the wheat production in 2012 was 700 bushels.

Scatterplots

If two measured variables are related to each other, the data are called *bivariate* data. A scatterplot is often the best way to graphically display such data. One variable is plotted on the *x*-axis, and the other is plotted on the *y*-axis. Thus, each ordered pair of measured values represents one data point that is plotted on the graph.

Scatterplots are useful for visualizing the relationships between the two variables. A trend line shows the nature of that relationship and clearly highlights data points that deviate significantly from the general trend. The trend line can either be straight or curved, and it will frequently be drawn on the scatterplot in the question.

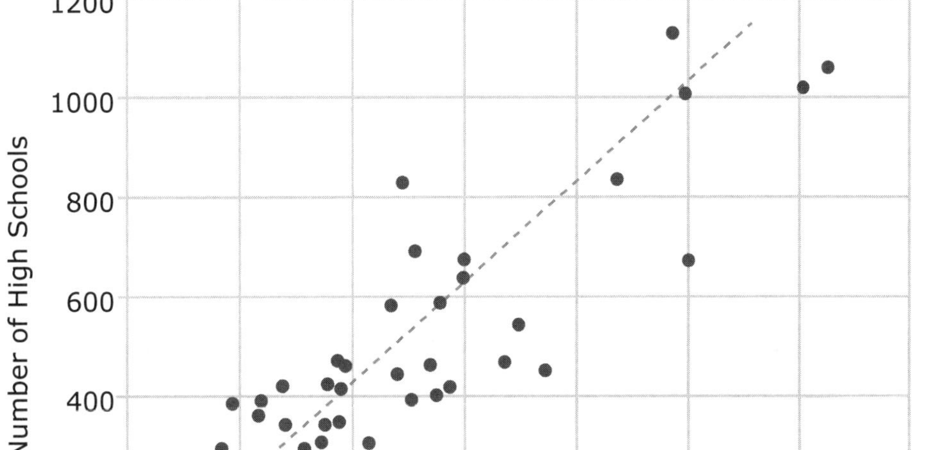

The trend line on this scatterplot slopes upward, meaning that as the number of elementary schools in a state increases, so do the number of high schools. Notice that the scales on the axes are different; even though the apparent slope of the trend line is about 1, the number of high schools increases at a lesser rate than the number of elementary schools. Trend lines can be used to make predictions by interpolating along the trend line or extrapolating beyond the trend line. For instance, to predict the expected number of high schools for a state with 2,000 elementary schools, follow the line for 2,000 up from the *x*-axis until it intersects the trend line at approximately 825 to 850 high schools.

Scatterplots are also useful to spot *outliers*, individual data points that deviate from the trend. For instance, in the scatterplot above, the data point for the state with 2,500 elementary schools and approximately 670 high schools is an outlier.

Line Graphs

Line graphs follow the same general principle as bar graphs, except that instead of using the lengths of bars to represent numbers, they use points connected by lines. The lines further emphasize the relative values of the numbers.

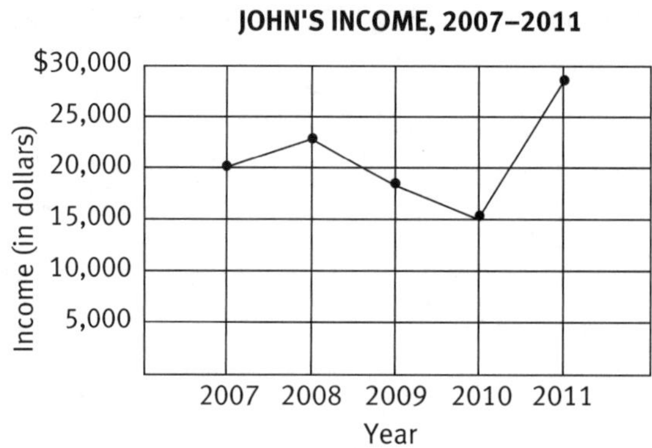

To read John's income for any particular year from this line graph, determine where a line drawn from the appropriate point would intersect the vertical axis.

Pie Charts

Pie charts show how things are distributed. The fraction of a circle occupied by each piece of the "pie" indicates what fraction of the whole that piece represents. In most pie charts, the percentage of the pie occupied by each "slice" will be shown on the slice itself or, for very narrow slices, outside the circle with an arrow or a line pointing to the appropriate slice.

The total size of the whole pie is usually given at the top or bottom of the graph, either as "TOTAL = xxx" or as "100% = xxx." To find the approximate amount represented by a particular piece of the pie, just multiply the whole by the appropriate percent.

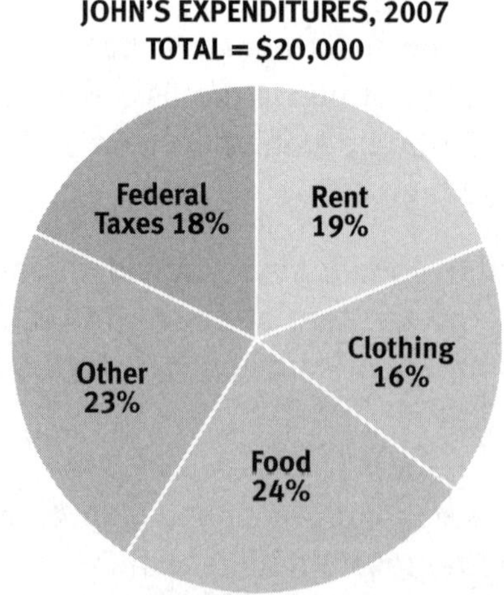

For instance, to find the total tax that John paid to the federal government in 2007, look at the slice of this chart labeled "Federal Taxes." It represents 18% of John's 2007 expenditures. Since his total 2007 expenditures were \$20,000, he paid 0.18(\$20,000) = \$3,600 in federal taxes in 2007.

One important note about pie charts: If you're not given the whole and you don't know both the percentage and the actual number that at least one slice represents, you won't be able to find the whole. Pie charts are ideal for presenting the kind of information that ratio problems present in words.

STATISTICS

Median, Mode, and Range

Median: The middle term in a group of terms that are arranged in numerical order. To find the median of a group of terms, first arrange the terms in numerical order. If there is an odd number of terms in the group, then the median is the middle term.

Example:

Bob's test scores in Spanish are 84, 81, 88, 70, and 87. What is his median score?

In increasing order, his scores are 70, 81, 84, 87, and 88. The median test score is the middle one: 84.

If there is an even number of terms in the group, the median is the average of the two middle terms.

Example:

John's test scores in biology are 92, 98, 82, 94, 85, and 97. What is his median score?

In numerical order, his scores are 82, 85, 92, 94, 97, and 98. The median test score is the average of the two middle terms, or $\frac{92 + 94}{2} = 93$.

The median of a group of numbers is often different from its average.

Example:

Caitlin's test scores in math are 92, 96, 90, 85, and 82. Find the difference between Caitlin's median score and the average (arithmetic mean) of her scores.

In ascending order, Caitlin's scores are 82, 85, 90, 92, and 96. The median score is the middle one: 90. Her average score is

$$\frac{82 + 85 + 90 + 92 + 96}{5} = \frac{445}{5} = 89$$

As you can see, Caitlin's median score and her average score are not the same. The difference between them is $90 - 89$, or 1.

Mode: The term that appears most frequently in a set.

Example:

The daily temperatures in city Q for one week were 25°, 33°, 26°, 25°, 27°, 31°, and 22°. What was the mode of the daily temperatures in city Q for that week?

Each of the temperatures occurs once on the list, except for 25°, which occurs twice. Since 25° appears more frequently than any other temperature, it is the mode.

A set may have more than one mode if two or more terms appear an equal number of times within the set and each appears more times than any other term.

Example:

The table below represents the score distribution for a class of 20 students on a recent chemistry test. Which score, or scores, are the mode?

Score	# of Students Receiving That Score
100	2
91	1
87	5
86	2
85	1
84	5
80	1
78	2
56	1

The largest number in the second column is 5, which occurs twice. Therefore, there were two mode scores on this test: 87 and 84. Equal numbers of students received those scores, and more students received those scores than any other score. Note that the modes are the scores that appeared most often, 84 and 87, not the number of times they appeared (5).

If every element in the set occurs an equal number of times, then the set has no mode.

Range: The distance between the greatest and least values in a group of data points.

Find the range of a set of numbers by subtracting the smallest number in the set from the largest. Note that sets with the same mean or median may have very different ranges. For instance, while the median of both the sets {−11, −6, −1, 4, 9} and {−3, −2, −1, 0, 1} is the same (that is, −1), the numbers in the first set are much more spread out. The range of the first set is 9 − (−11) = 20, while the range of the second set is 1 − (−3) = 4.

QUARTILES

Not many GRE questions ask about quartiles or the interquartile range, but if you are striving for a very high score, read on. The first step in determining quartiles is to arrange the terms in your data set in numerical order. Next, subdivide the set of terms into four quarters, each containing an equal number of terms. The largest number in the first (lowest) group will represent the first quartile, which is often written as Q_1. The largest number in the second group is Q_2. Similarly, Q_3 is the top of the third quartile, and Q_4 is the maximum value in the set.

Example:

List the values of the first, second, third, and fourth quartiles for the following group of numbers:

{0, 0, 0, 1, 1, 3, 7, 7, 8, 8, 9, 10, 11, 12, 13, 14}

Since there are 16 terms in the list, each quartile will contain 4 numbers. The terms are in numerical order, so they do not need to be rearranged. The largest number in the first quartile is 1, so $Q_1 = 1$. Every fourth number will be a quartile, so $Q_2 = 7$, $Q_3 = 10$, and $Q_4 = 14$.

The rules for determining quartiles if the number of terms is not evenly divisible by 4 can vary, so it is not likely that a GRE problem requiring you to determine quartiles will present a set for which the number of terms is not a multiple of 4.

Interquartile Range

The difference between the values of the third and first quartile values, $Q_3 - Q_1$, is the interquartile range. Because outliers fall into the bottom and top quartiles, they do not affect the interquartile range. For instance, set *A*: {0, 10, 10, 10, 10, 10, 10, 11, 11, 11, 11, 11} and set *B*: {0, 1, 2, 3, 4, 5, 6, 7, 8, 9, 10, 11} both have 12 elements and a range of 11, but the data distributions within that range are very different. The first data point (the zero) in the first set is an outlier that skews the value of the range. The interquartile range of set *A* is 11 – 10 = 1 and that of set *B* is 8 – 2 = 6. This comparison shows that, with the exception of the outlier, the data in set *A* are more closely spaced than the data in set *B*.

A straightforward way to visually display data dispersion by quartiles is a *boxplot*, also called a *box-and-whisker plot*. This visual depiction uses five values: *L*, the least number in the data; *G*, the greatest number; *M*, the median; Q_1, the first quartile; and Q_3, the third quartile. The interquartile range (which includes *M*) is drawn as a rectangular box, and straight lines extend from the sides of the box to the least and greatest values (*L* and *G*). A number line is drawn below the boxplot to show the numerical values of these points.

Example:

Draw a box-and-whisker plot for the set {7, 0, 3, 8, 1, 2, 7, 4, 8, 4, 5, 6, –3, 7, 3, 0}

The first step is to arrange the data in ascending order: {–3, 0, 0, 1, 2, 3, 3, 4, 4, 5, 6, 7, 7, 7, 8, 8}.

Next, identify the values needed for the box-and-whisker plot. $L = -3$ and $G = 8$. Since there are 16 elements in the set, $Q_1 = 1$, $Q_3 = 7$, and $M = 4$.

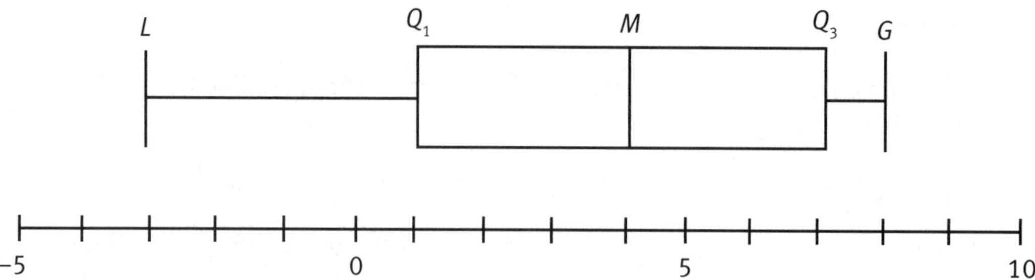

Percentiles

For large groups of numbers, the position of given data points is sometimes stated in percentiles rather than quartiles. The principle is the same as for quartiles, but there are 100 subdivisions instead of 4. Converting quartiles to percentiles is easy: Q_1 is the same value as the 25th percentile, Q_2 is the same value as the 50th percentile, Q_3 is the same value as the 75th percentile, and Q_4 is the same as the 100th percentile.

Standard Deviation

Like the range and the interquartile range, standard deviation is a way to measure how spread out the values in a given data set are. You probably won't have to calculate the standard deviation on Test Day, but you will need to understand how it behaves, so it's worthwhile to calculate it for a couple of lists of numbers to get a feel for it. Here's how standard deviation is calculated:

- Find the average of the data points.
- Find the difference between the average and each data point.
- Square each of the differences.
- Find the average of the squared differences.
- Take the square root of that average.

Example:

Calculate the standard deviation of 1, 3, 8, 11, and 12.

First, find the average: $\frac{1+3+8+11+12}{5}=\frac{35}{5}=7$

Next, determine the differences between each term and 7:

$(1 - 7) = -6$, $(3 - 7) = -4$, $(8 - 7) = 1$, $(11 - 7) = 4$, and $(12 - 7) = 5$.

Square each difference and find the average of the squared differences:

$$\frac{(-6)^2+(-4)^2+1^2+4^2+5^2}{5}=\frac{36+16+1+16+25}{5}=\frac{94}{5}$$

The standard deviation is the square root of that average:

$$\sqrt{\frac{94}{5}}=\sqrt{18.8}\approx 4.34$$

Note that the farther the data points are away from the mean, the greater the standard deviation will be. Also note that two sets whose data points are the same distance from the mean will have the same standard deviation. For example, the sets {2, 4, 6} and {8, 10, 12} will have the same standard deviation.

FREQUENCY DISTRIBUTIONS

A frequency distribution is a description of how often certain data values occur in a set and is typically shown in a table or histogram. As an example, take a look at the table below, which displays the frequency distribution of singing voices in a choir in two ways. The first delineates the *count* of singers for each vocal range; the second shows the *percentage* of the total choir for the different voices. Counts can be converted to percents by adding all the counts to get the total and then dividing the individual count for each category by that total to obtain the percentages.

For instance, in this chart, there are 75 total singers. If 15 of them are tenors, then tenors make up $\frac{15}{75}$ = 0.20 = 20% of the singers.

Soprano	12	16%
Alto	18	24%
Tenor	15	20%
Baritone	12	16%
Bass	18	24%

In a *relative frequency distribution*, also known as a *probability distribution*, the frequency with which given values occur is given in decimal form rather than as percentages. The value of a randomly chosen value from a known distribution of data is called a *random variable X*. The table below is an example of a probability distribution of such a variable. 5% of the values in the distribution are 0, 10% are 1, 20% are 2, and so on. Or, stated differently, the probability that a randomly selected value will be a zero is 0.05, the probability that a randomly selected value will be 1 is 0.10, the probability that a randomly selected value will be 2 is 0.20, etc.

X	*P(X)*
0	0.05
1	0.10
2	0.20
3	0.30
4	0.25
5	0.10

Note that you can calculate the mean by using a weighted average approach (discussed earlier in this chapter): 0.05(0) + 0.10(1) + 0.20(2) + 0.30(3) + 0.25(4) + 0.10(5) = 0 + 0.10 + 0.40 + 0.90 + 1.00 + 0.50 = 2.90.

We mentioned above that frequency distributions can be shown as histograms. If the sample set of an experiment is large enough, as in the example below, the histogram begins to closely resemble a continuous curve.

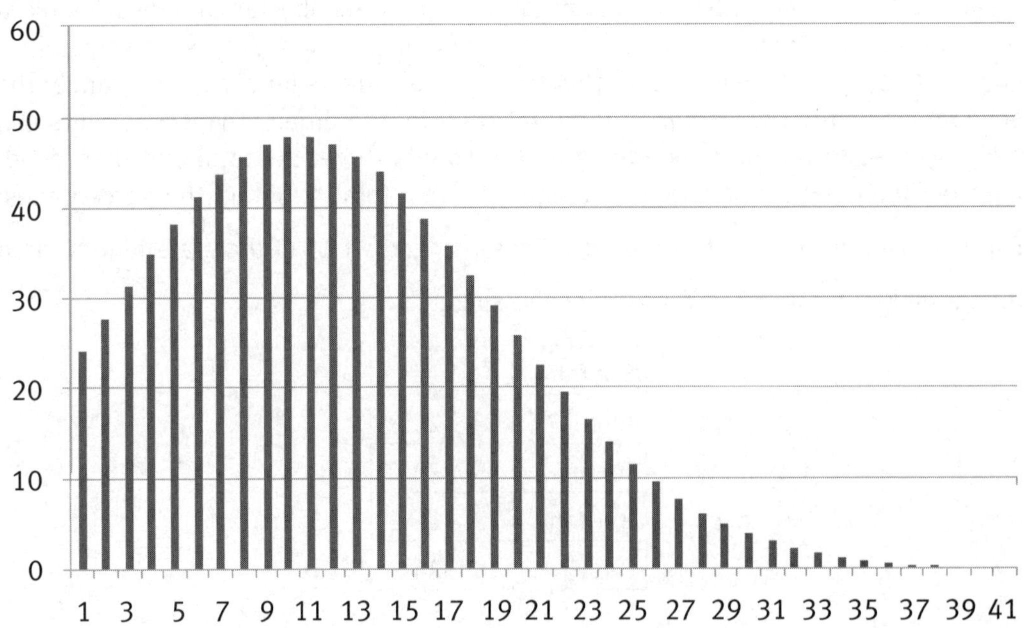

Normal Distribution

There is a special kind of frequency distribution, called the *normal distribution*, that is closely tied to the concept of standard deviation. Many natural data sets, such as the distribution of the heights of adult males in the United States, very closely approximate the normal distribution. This distribution is commonly referred to as a *bell curve* because of its shape. Only two parameters are needed to define any normal distribution: the mean and the standard deviation. In a normal distribution, the mean equals the median, and the data are symmetrically distributed around the mean, so the curve to the left of the mean is a mirror image of the curve to the right.

Normal Distributions

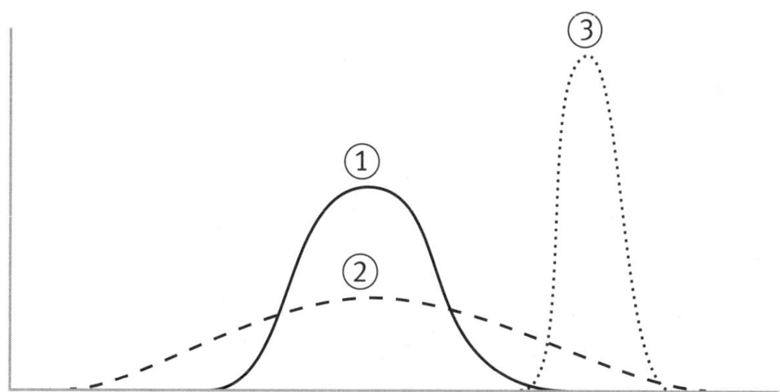

Normal curves 1 and 2 have the same mean, but curve 2 has a greater standard deviation—that is, curve 2 is much more spread out. Curve 3 has a greater mean value than either curve 1 or curve 2 but has a smaller standard deviation, so it is less spread out.

The graph below shows some important probability values that hold true for *all* normal distributions. The percentage of the area under any portion of a distribution curve equals the probability that a randomly selected event will fall within that area's range.

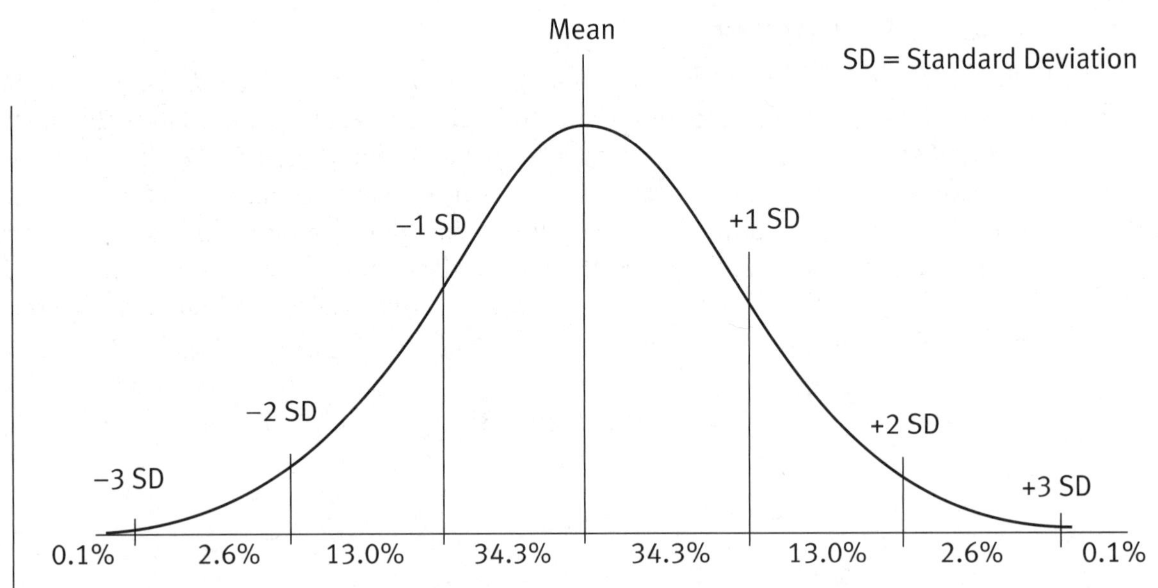

Areas of the Normal Distribution

Example

The lengths of boards cut at a sawmill are normally distributed with a mean of 96.00 inches and a standard deviation of 0.05 inch. What is the approximate probability that a randomly selected board will be longer than 96.10 inches?

A board longer than 96.10 inches would be 0.10 inches longer than the mean value. The standard deviation of the board lengths is 0.05 inches, so a 96.10 inch long board would be 2 standard deviations above the mean. Because these board lengths are normally distributed, 50% are at or below the mean, 34% are within the area between the mean and 1 standard deviation above the mean, and 13% are between 1 and 2 standard deviations above the mean. The probability that a random board would be less than or equal to 96.10 inches is approximately 50% + 34% + 13% = 97%, so the probability that a board would be longer is about 100% − 97% = 3%.

COUNTING METHODS AND PROBABILITY

SETS

Sets are groups of values that have some common property, such as the negative odd integers greater than −10 or all positive integers that are evenly divisible by 3. The items in sets are called *elements* or *members*. If all the elements in a set can be counted, such as "the number of species of birds in North America," that set is *finite*. If the elements in a set are limitless (e.g., "all positive numbers that are evenly divisible by 3"), that set is *infinite*. The set with no elements is called the *empty set*, which is represented by the symbol Ø. Logically, a set with any members is defined as *nonempty*. If all the elements of set *A* are among the elements of set *B*, then *A* is a *subset* of *B*. By definition, the empty set is a subset of all sets.

An important characteristic of sets is that elements are unique—that is, they are not repeated. For instance, the set of the numbers 1, 1, 2, 2, and 3 is {1, 2, 3}. Additionally, since order does not matter in sets, {1, 2, 3} is the same set as {3, 2, 1}.

Lists

A list is like a finite set except that the order of the elements matters and that duplicate members can be included. So 1, 2, 3 and 3, 2, 1 are different lists and 1, 2, 3, 2 is a valid list. Because order *does* matter in lists, elements can be uniquely identified by their position, such as "first element" or "fifth element." Notice that sets are usually enclosed within the curly brackets, { and }, but lists are not.

Set Operations

The *intersection* of two sets is a set that consists of all the elements that are contained in *both* sets. (You can think of it as the overlap between the sets.) The intersection of sets *A* and *B* is written as $A \cap B$. The *union* of two sets is the set of all the elements that are elements of *either* or *both* sets and is written as $A \cup B$. If sets have no common elements, they are referred to as *mutually exclusive*, and their intersection is the empty set.

Drawing *Venn diagrams* is a helpful way to analyze the relationship among sets.

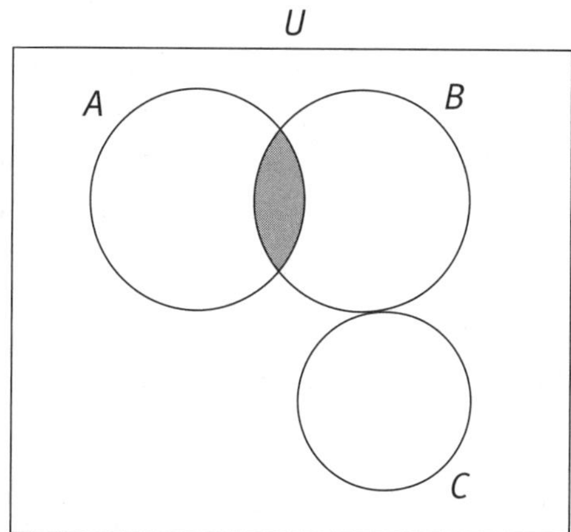

The set of all possible elements that have the characteristics of the sets represented by the circles in a Venn diagram is called a *universal set* and is represented by *U*. For instance, *U* could be the set of all species of birds in the world, *A* the set of species native to Europe, *B* those native to Asia, and *C* those native to Australia. In the diagram above, species from other continents are included within *U* but are not in any specific subset.

The *inclusion-exclusion principle* is a basic counting principle for sets. In the Venn diagram above, the shaded area represents $A \cap B$ (species native to both Europe and Asia), the elements that are within the intersection of A and B. Determining the number of elements in $A \cup B$ is a bit trickier. Merely adding the number of elements in A plus those in B is not correct because that would count the elements that show up in both sets twice. To find the number of elements in the union of two sets, use this formula:

$$|A \cup B| = |A| + |B| - |A \cap B|$$

This formula adjusts for the double-counting of elements that are in both sets. Notice that sets A and C are mutually exclusive, so $|A \cap C| = \emptyset$. For the diagram above, $|A \cup C| = |A| + |C|$.

Multiplication Principle

When choices or events occur one after the other and the choices or events are independent of one another, the total number of possibilities is the *product* of the number of options for each. For example, if a ballot offers 3 candidate choices for Office A, 4 for Office B, and 2 for Office C, the total number of different ways that a voter could fill out the ballot is $3 \times 4 \times 2 = 24$.

Occasionally, a GRE question may require a careful analysis of the number of options for each choice. If a website calls for a 3-letter password but no two letters can be the same, the total possibilities would be $26 \times 25 \times 24 = 15{,}600$ because the stipulation that no two letters be the same reduces the number of choices for the second and third letters.

In situations where choices are "or" rather than "and," as long as the two groups are mutually exclusive, *add* instead of multiplying. A menu has 3 choices for soup and 4 salad options; diners are permitted to select a soup *or* salad with their dinners. In this situation, the total number of choices available is $3 + 4 = 7$.

Combination

A combination question asks you how many unordered subgroups can be formed from a larger group.

Some combination questions on the GRE can be solved without any computation just by counting or listing possible combinations.

Example:

Allen, Betty, and Claire must wash the dishes. They decide to work in shifts of two people. How many shifts will it take before all possible combinations have been used?

It is possible, and not time-consuming, to solve this problem by writing a list. Call Allen "*A*," Betty "*B*," and Claire "*C*." There are three (*AB*, *AC*, *BC*) possible combinations.

The Combination Formula

Some combination questions use numbers that make quick, noncomputational solving difficult. In these cases, use the combination formula $\frac{n!}{k!(n-k)!}$, where n is the number of items in the group as a whole and k is the number of items in each subgroup formed. The ! symbol means factorial (for example, $5! = (5)(4)(3)(2)(1) = 120$).

Example:

The 4 finalists in a spelling contest win commemorative plaques. If there are 7 entrants in the spelling contest, how many possible groups of finalists are there?

Plug the numbers into the combination formula, such that n is 7 (the number in the large group) and k is 4 (the number of people in each subgroup formed).

$$\frac{7!}{4!(7-4)!}$$

$$\frac{7!}{4!3!}$$

At this stage, it is helpful to reduce these terms. Since 7 factorial contains all the factors of 4 factorial, we can write 7! as (7)(6)(5)(4!) and then cancel the 4! in the numerator and denominator.

$$\frac{(7)(6)(5)}{(3)(2)(1)}$$

We can reduce further by crossing off the 6 in the numerator and the (3)(2) in the denominator.

$$\frac{(7)(5)}{1} = 35$$

There are 35 potential groups of spelling contest finalists.

When you are asked to find potential combinations from multiple groups, multiply the potential combinations from each group.

Example:

How many groups can be formed consisting of 2 people from room A and 3 people from room B if there are 5 people in room A and 6 people in room B?

Insert the appropriate numbers into the combination formula for each room and then multiply the results. For room A, the number of combinations of 2 in a set of 5 is as follows:

$$\frac{n!}{k!(n-k)!} = \frac{5!}{2!3!} = \frac{(5)(4)(3)(2)(1)}{(2)(1)(3)(2)(1)}$$

Reducing this, you get $\frac{(5)(4)}{(2)} = 10$. For room B, the number of combinations of 3 in a set of 6 is as follows:

$$\frac{n!}{k!(n-k)!} = \frac{6!}{3!3!} = \frac{(6)(5)(4)(3)(2)(1)}{(3)(2)(1)(3)(2)(1)}$$

Reducing this, you get $\frac{(6)(5)(4)}{(3)(2)} = 20$.

Multiply these to find that there are $(10)(20) = 200$ possible groups consisting of 2 people from room A and 3 people from room B.

Sometimes the GRE will ask you to find the number of possible subgroups when choosing one item from a set. In this case, the number of possible subgroups will always equal the number of items in the set.

Example:

Restaurant A has 5 appetizers, 20 main courses, and 4 desserts. If a meal consists of 1 appetizer, 1 main course, and 1 dessert, how many different meals can be ordered at restaurant A?

The number of possible outcomes from each set is the number of items in the set. So there are 5 possible appetizers, 20 possible main courses, and 4 possible desserts. The number of different meals that can be ordered is $(5)(20)(4) = 400$.

Permutation

Within any group of items or people, there are multiple arrangements, or permutations, possible. For instance, within a group of three items (for example: *A*, *B*, *C*), there are six permutations (*ABC*, *ACB*, *BAC*, *BCA*, *CAB*, and *CBA*).

Permutations differ from combinations in that permutations are ordered. By definition, each combination larger than 1 has multiple permutations. On the GRE, a question asking "How many ways/arrangements/orders/schedules are possible?" generally indicates a permutation problem.

To find permutations, think of each place that needs to be filled in a particular arrangement as a blank space. The first place can be filled with any of the items in the larger group. The second place can be filled with any of the items in the larger group except for the one used to fill the first place. The third place can be filled with any of the items in the group except for the two used to fill the first two places, etc.

Example:

In a spelling contest, the winner will receive a gold medal, the second-place finisher will receive a silver medal, the third-place finisher will receive a bronze medal, and the fourth-place finisher will receive a blue ribbon. If there are 7 entrants in the contest, how many different arrangements of award winners are there?

The gold medal can be won by any of 7 people. The silver medal can be won by any of the remaining 6 people. The bronze medal can be won by any of the remaining 5 people. And the blue ribbon can be won by any of the remaining 4 people. Thus, the number of possible arrangements is $(7)(6)(5)(4) = 840$.

Probability

Probability measures the likelihood that an event will occur. Probability can be represented as a fraction, decimal, or percent. For example, if rain today is just as likely as not, then the probability of rain today can be expressed as $\frac{1}{2}$, 0.5, or 50%. You may also see a probability expressed in everyday language: "one chance in a hundred" means the probability is $\frac{1}{100}$. Every probability is expressed as a number between 0 and 1 inclusive, with a probability of 0 meaning "no chance" and a probability of 1 meaning "guaranteed to happen." The higher the probability, the greater the chance that an event will occur.

An *event* may include more than one *outcome*. For example, rolling an even number on a 6-sided die is the event that includes only the outcomes 2, 4, and 6. Many GRE probability questions are based on *random experiments* with a defined number of possible outcomes, such as drawing a random card from a full deck. If all the possible outcomes of the experiment are equally likely to occur, you can use this formula to calculate probability:

$$Probability = \frac{Number\ of\ Desired\ Outcomes}{Number\ of\ Possible\ Outcomes}$$

Example:

What is the probability of tossing a fair coin four consecutive times and having the coin land heads up exactly once?

Since a coin is tossed four times and each toss has two possible outcomes, the total number of outcomes, using the multiplication principle, is $2 \times 2 \times 2 \times 2 = 2^4 = 16$. The total number of desired outcomes can be easily counted: HTTT, THTT, TTHT, or TTTH. So there are 4 desired outcomes, and the probability of rolling exactly one head is $\frac{4}{16}=\frac{1}{4}=0.25$.

The total of the probabilities of all possible outcomes in an experiment must equal 1. For instance, the probability of a tossed coin landing heads up is $\frac{1}{2}$. The probability of the coin landing tails up is also $\frac{1}{2}$. There are no other possible outcomes, and $\frac{1}{2}+\frac{1}{2}=1$. By this same logic, if $P(E)$ is the probability that an event *will* occur, then $1 - P(E)$ is the probability that the event *will not* occur. This is a useful fact in many probability questions.

Example:

What is the probability of tossing a fair coin four consecutive times and having the coin land heads up 0, 2, 3, or 4 times?

In the last example, we found that the probability of the coin landing heads up exactly once is 0.25. To find the probability of the coin landing heads up *not* exactly once, subtract that probability from 1: $1 - 0.25 = 0.75$.

In many probability questions involving more than one event, the events are *independent*; one event does not affect the other. If the first toss of a fair coin results in a tail, the probability of the result of the second toss being a tail is still 0.5. In other cases the results are *not* independent. If there are 4 red disks and 4 green disks in a bag and 2 disks are withdrawn at random without replacement, the probability for the result of the second draw is *dependent* on the result of the first draw. If the first disk drawn is red, then only 3 red disks remain out of a total of 7, and the probability of drawing another red disk on the second draw is $\frac{3}{7}$. If, however, the first draw is green, then 4 of the remaining 7 disks are red, and the probability of drawing red on the second draw is $\frac{4}{7}$.

PROBABILITY OF MULTIPLE EVENTS

To calculate the probability of two or more independent events occurring, multiply the probabilities of the individual events. For example, the probability of rolling a 3 four consecutive times on a six-sided die would be $\left(\frac{1}{6}\right)\left(\frac{1}{6}\right)\left(\frac{1}{6}\right)\left(\frac{1}{6}\right)=\frac{1}{1{,}296}$.

You can also calculate the probability of two or more dependent events occurring by multiplying their individual probabilities, but you must calculate the probability of each dependent event as if the preceding event had resulted in the desired outcome or outcomes.

Example:

A bag contains 10 marbles, 4 of which are blue and 6 of which are red. If 2 marbles are removed without replacement, what is the probability that both marbles removed are red?

The probability that the first marble removed will be red is $\frac{6}{10}=\frac{3}{5}$. The probability that the second marble removed will be red will not be the same, however. There will be fewer marbles overall, so the denominator will be one less. There will also be one fewer red marble. (Note that since we are asking about the odds of picking two red marbles, we are only interested in choosing a second marble if the first was red. Don't concern yourself with situations in which a blue marble is chosen first.) If the first marble removed is red, the probability that the second marble removed will also be red is $\frac{5}{9}$. So the probability that both marbles removed will be red is $\left(\frac{3}{\cancel{5}}\right)\left(\frac{\cancel{5}}{9}\right)=\frac{3}{9}=\frac{1}{3}$.

What about the probability of one or another event occurring? On the GRE, you can interpret "the probability of *A* or *B*" to mean "the probability of *A* or *B* or both," and the formula for calculating this is similar to the inclusion-exclusion principle for sets described earlier in this chapter:

$$P(A \text{ or } B) = P(A) + P(B) - P(A \text{ and } B)$$

Example:

Events *A* and *B* are independent. *P*(*A*) is 0.60 and *P*(*A* or *B*) is 0.94. What is the probability that event *B* occurs?

Use the formula above: $P(A \text{ or } B) = P(A) + P(B) - P(A \text{ and } B)$. Since the events are independent, $P(A \text{ and } B) = P(A) \times P(B)$. Plug in the values given in the problem: $0.60 + P(B) - (0.60 \times P(B)) = 0.94$, then simplify:

$$0.60 + P(B) - 0.60P(B) = 0.94$$

$$0.60 + 0.40P(B) = 0.94$$

$$0.40P(B) = 0.34$$

$$P(B) = 0.85$$

GEOMETRY

LINES AND ANGLES

A *line* is a one-dimensional geometrical abstraction—infinitely long, with no width. A straight line is the shortest distance between any two points. There is exactly one straight line that passes through any two points.

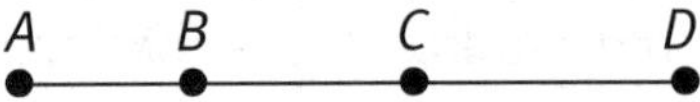

Example:

In the figure above, $AC = 9$, $BD = 11$, and $AD = 15$. What is the length of BC?

When points are in a line and the order is known, you can add or subtract lengths. Since $AC = 9$ and $AD = 15$, $CD = AD - AC = 15 - 9 = 6$. Now, since $BD = 11$ and $CD = 6$, $BC = BD - CD = 11 - 6 = 5$.

A *line segment* is a section of a straight line of finite length, with two endpoints. A line segment is named for its endpoints, as in segment AB.

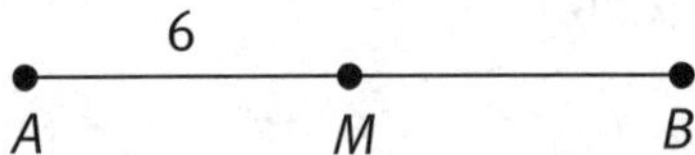

Example:

In the figure above, A and B are the endpoints of the line segment AB, and M is the midpoint ($AM = MB$). What is the length of AB?

Since AM is 6, MB is also 6, and so AB is $6 + 6$, or 12.

Two lines are *parallel* if they lie in the same plane and never intersect regardless of how far they are extended. If line ℓ_1 is parallel to line ℓ_2, we write $\ell_1 \parallel \ell_2$. If two lines are both parallel to a third line, then they are parallel to each other as well.

A *vertex* is the point at which two lines or line segments intersect to form an *angle*. Angles are measured in *degrees* (°).

Angles may be named according to their vertices. Sometimes, especially when two or more angles share a common vertex, an angle is named according to three points: a point along one of the lines or line segments that form the angle, the vertex point, and another point along the other line or line segment. A diagram will sometimes show a letter inside the angle; this letter may also be used to name the angle.

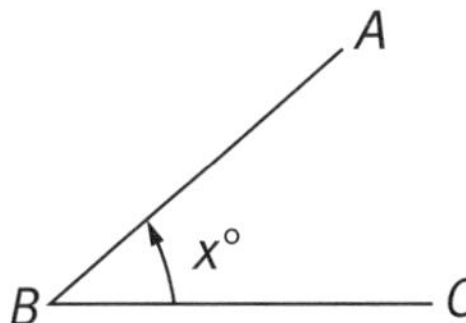

The angle shown in the diagram above could be called $\angle x$, $\angle ABC$, or $\angle B$. (We use a lowercase x because x is not a point.)

Sum of Angles Around a Point

The sum of the measures of the angles around a point is 360°.

$$a + b + c + d + e = 360$$

Sum of Angles Along a Straight Line

The sum of the measures of the angles on one side of a straight line is 180°. Two angles are *supplementary* to each other if their measures sum to 180°.

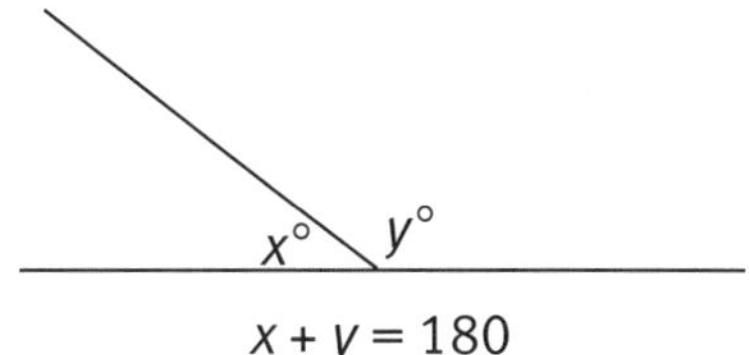

$$x + y = 180$$

Perpendicularity and Right Angles

Two lines are *perpendicular* if they intersect at a 90° angle (a right angle). If line ℓ_1 is perpendicular to line ℓ_2, we write $\ell_1 \perp \ell_2$. If lines ℓ_1, ℓ_2, and ℓ_3 all lie in the same plane, and if $\ell_1 \perp \ell_2$ and $\ell_2 \perp \ell_3$, then $\ell_1 \parallel \ell_3$, as shown in the diagram below.

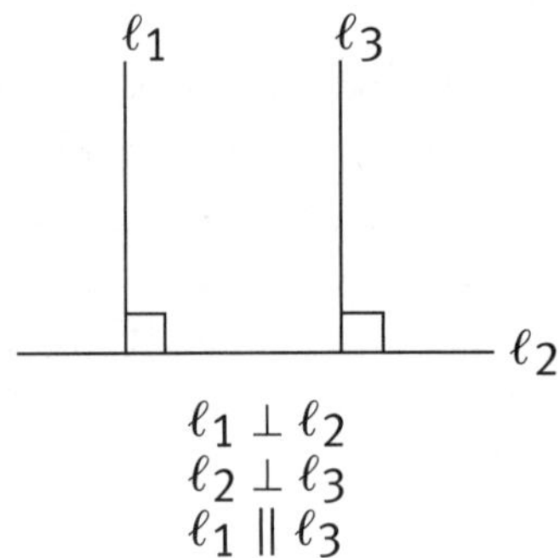

To find the shortest distance from a point to a line, draw a line segment from the point to the line such that the line segment is perpendicular to the line. Then, measure the length of that segment.

Example:

$\angle A$ of triangle *ABC* is a right angle. Is side *BC* longer or shorter than side *AB*?

This question seems very abstract, until you draw a diagram of a right triangle, labeling the vertex with the 90° angle as point *A*.

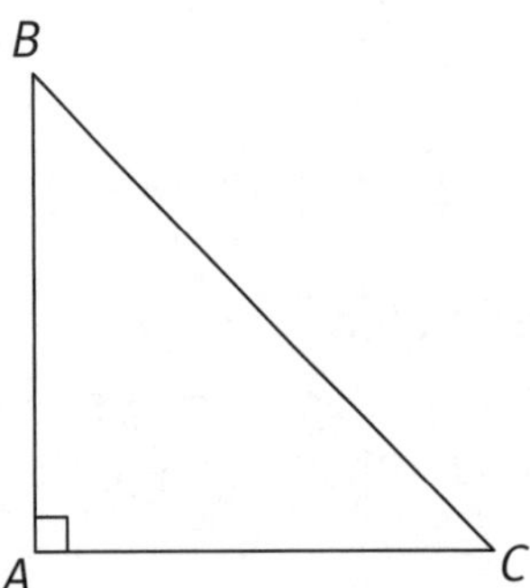

Line segment *AB* has to be the shortest route between point *B* and side *AC*, since side *AB* is perpendicular to side *AC*. If *AB* is the shortest line segment that can join point *B* to side *AC*, *BC* must be longer than *AB*. **Note:** the side opposite the 90° angle, called the *hypotenuse*, is always the longest side of a right triangle.

Two angles are *complementary* to each other if their measures sum to 90°. An *acute angle* measures less than 90°, and an *obtuse angle* measures between 90° and 180°. Two angles are *supplementary* if their measures sum to 180°.

Angle Bisectors

A line or line segment *bisects* an angle if it splits the angle into two smaller, equal angles. Line segment *BD* below bisects ∠*ABC*, and ∠*ABD* has the same measure as ∠*DBC*. The two smaller angles are each half the size of ∠*ABC*.

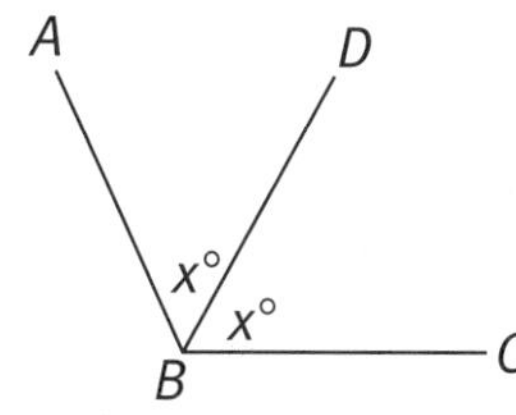

BD bisects ∠*ABC*
∠*ABD* + ∠*DBC* = ∠*ABC*

Adjacent and Vertical Angles

Two intersecting lines form four angles. The angles that are adjacent (next) to each other are *supplementary* because they lie along a straight line. The two angles that are not adjacent to each other are *opposite*, or *vertical*. Opposite angles are equal in measure because each of them is supplementary to the same adjacent angle.

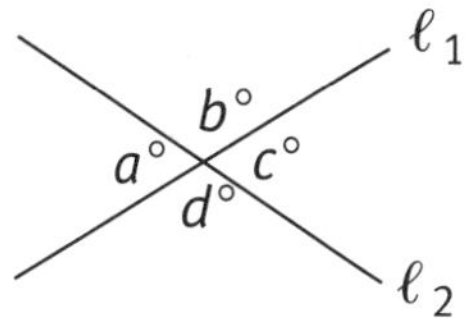

In the diagram above, ℓ_1 intersects ℓ_2 to form angles *a*, *b*, *c*, and *d*. Angles *a* and *c* are opposite, as are angles *b* and *d*. So the measures of angles *a* and *c* are equal to each other, and the measures of angles *b* and *d* are equal to each other. And each angle is supplementary to each of its two adjacent angles.

Angles Around Parallel Lines Intersected by a Transversal

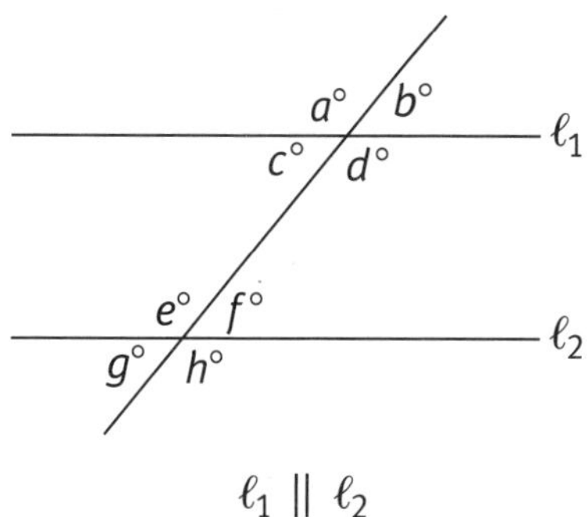

$\ell_1 \parallel \ell_2$

A line that intersects two parallel lines is called a *transversal*. Each of the parallel lines intersects the third line at the same angle. In the figure above, $a = e$.

Since a and e are equal, and since $a = d$ and $e = h$ (because they are opposite angles), $a = d = e = h$. By similar reasoning, $b = c = f = g$.

In short, when two (or more) parallel lines are cut by a transversal, all acute angles formed are equal, all obtuse angles formed are equal, and any acute angle formed is supplementary to any obtuse angle formed.

Example:

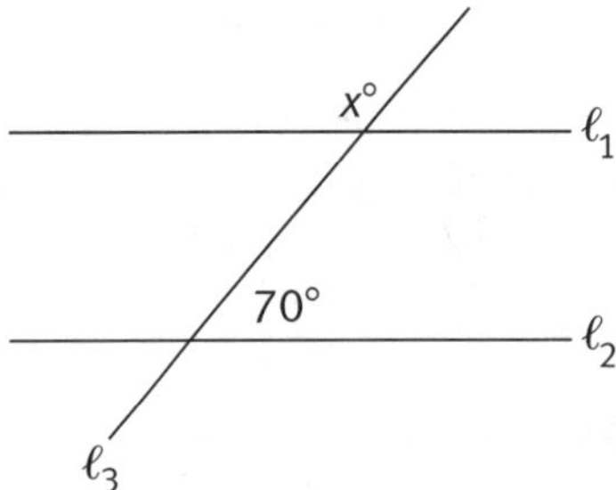

In the diagram above, line ℓ_1 is parallel to line ℓ_2. What is the value of x?

The angle marked $x°$ and the angle adjacent and to the left of the 70° angle on line ℓ_2 are corresponding angles. Therefore, the angle marked $x°$ must be supplementary to the 70° angle. If $70° + x° = 180°$, x must equal 110.

POLYGONS

Important Terms

Polygon: A closed figure whose sides are straight line segments. Families or classes of polygons are named according to their number of sides. A triangle has three sides, a quadrilateral has four sides, a pentagon has five sides, and a hexagon has six sides. Triangles and quadrilaterals are by far the most important polygons on the GRE; other polygons appear only occasionally.

Perimeter: The distance around a polygon; the sum of the lengths of its sides.

Vertex of a polygon: A point where two sides intersect (plural: *vertices*). Polygons are named by assigning each vertex a letter and listing them in order, as in pentagon *ABCDE* below.

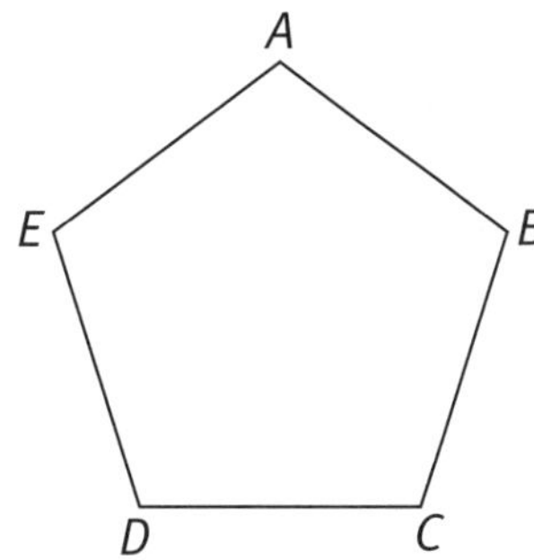

Diagonal of a polygon: A line segment connecting any two nonadjacent vertices.

Regular polygon: A polygon with sides of equal length and interior angles of equal measure.

Small slash marks can provide important information in diagrams of polygons. Sides with the same number of slash marks are equal in length, while angles with the same number of slash marks through circular arcs have the same measure. In the triangle below, for example, $a = b$, and angles X and Z are equal in measure.

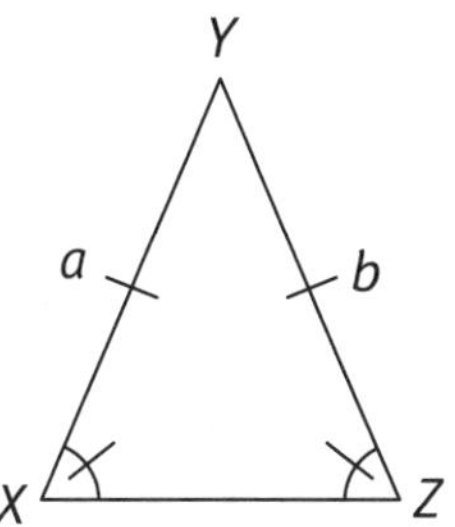

You can figure out the sum of the interior angles of a polygon by dividing the polygon into triangles. Draw diagonals from any vertex to all the nonadjacent vertices. Then, multiply the number of triangles by 180° to get the sum of the interior angles of the polygon. This works because the sum of the interior angles of any triangle is always 180°.

Example:

What is the sum of the interior angles of a pentagon ?

Draw a pentagon (a five-sided polygon) and divide it into triangles, as discussed above.

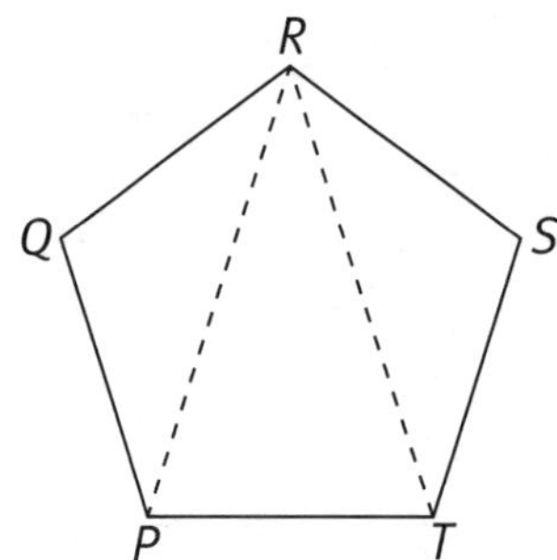

No matter how you've drawn the pentagon, you'll be able to form three triangles. Therefore, the sum of the interior angles of a pentagon is $3 \times 180° = 540°$.

Triangles

Important Terms

Triangle: A polygon with three straight sides and three interior angles.

Right triangle: A triangle with one interior angle of 90° (a right angle).

Hypotenuse: The longest side of a right triangle. The hypotenuse is always opposite the right angle.

Isosceles triangle: A triangle with two equal sides, which are opposite two equal angles. In the figure below, the sides opposite the two 70° angles are equal, so $x = 7$.

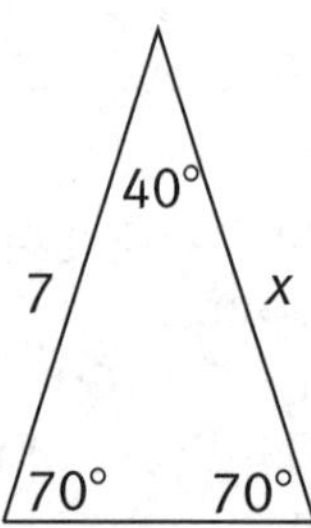

Legs: The two equal sides of an isosceles triangle or the two shorter sides of a right triangle (the ones forming the right angle). **Note:** the third, unequal side of an isosceles triangle is called the *base*.

Equilateral triangle: A triangle whose three sides are all equal in length and whose three interior angles each measure 60°.

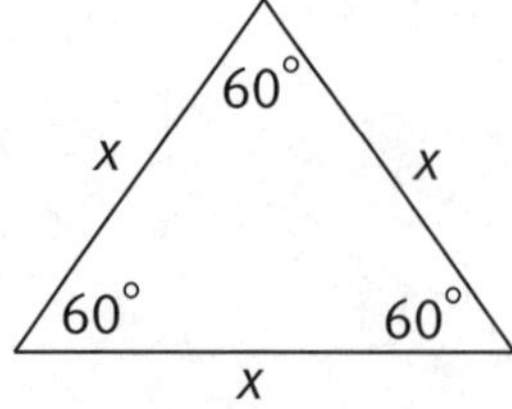

The *altitude*, or *height*, of a triangle is the perpendicular distance from a vertex to the side opposite the vertex. The altitude may fall inside or outside the triangle, or it may coincide with one of the sides.

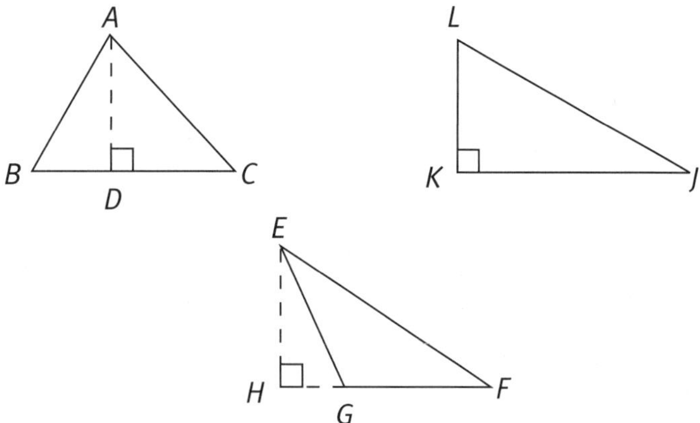

In the diagrams above, AD, EH, *and* LK *are altitudes.*

Interior and Exterior Angles of a Triangle

The sum of the interior angles of any triangle is 180°. Therefore, in the figure below, $a + b + c = 180$.

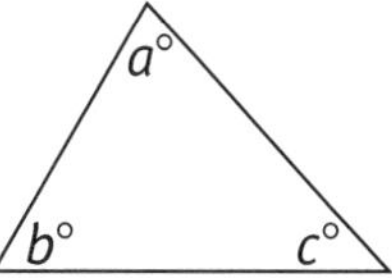

An *exterior angle of a triangle* is equal to the sum of the remote interior angles. The exterior angle labeled $x°$ is equal to the sum of the remote angles: $x = 50 + 100 = 150$.

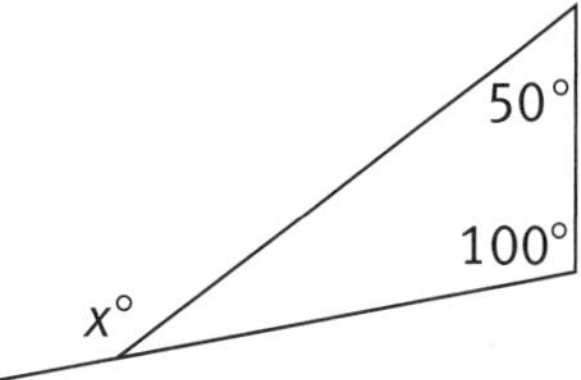

The three exterior angles of any triangle add up to 360°.

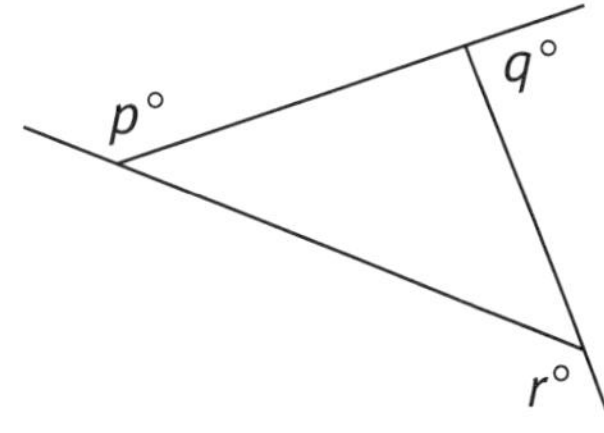

In the figure above, $p + q + r = 360$.

Sides and Angles

The sum of the lengths of any two sides of a triangle is greater than the length of the third side. In the triangle below, $b + c > a$, $a + b > c$, and $a + c > b$.

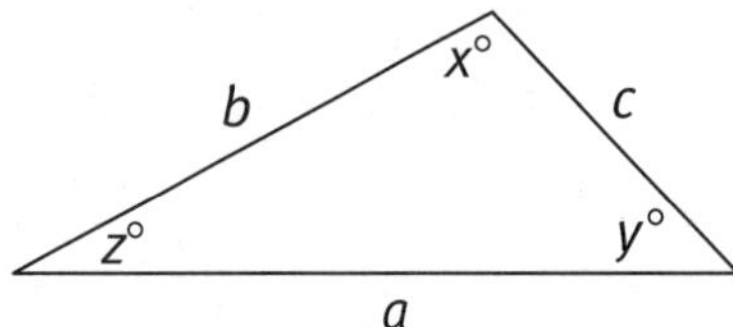

If the lengths of two sides of a triangle are unequal, the greater angle lies opposite the longer side, and vice versa. In the figure above, if $x > y > z$, then $a > b > c$.

Since the two legs of an isosceles triangle have the same length, the two angles opposite the legs must have the same measure. In the figure below, $PQ = PR$, and $\angle Q = \angle R$.

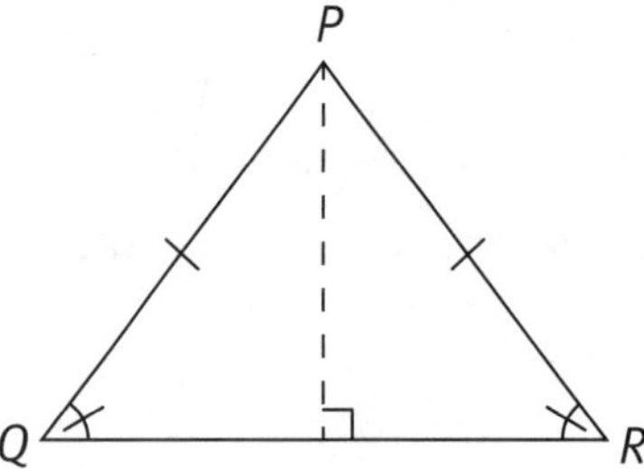

Perimeter and Area of Triangles

There is no special formula for the perimeter of a triangle; it is just the sum of the lengths of the sides.

Example:

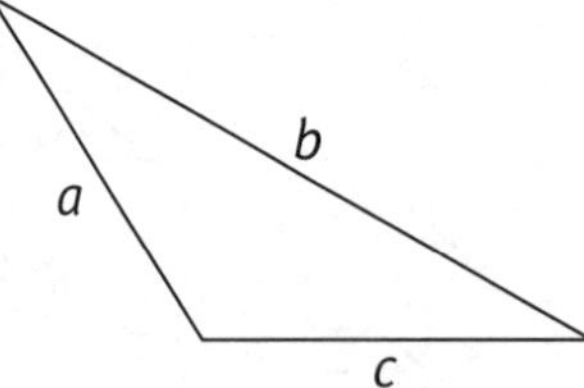

If $b = 2a$ and $c = \frac{b}{2}$, find the perimeter of the triangle above in terms of a.

Perimeter $= a + b + c = a + 2a + \frac{2a}{2} = 3a + \frac{2a}{2} = 3a + a = 4a$.

Incidentally, this is really an isosceles triangle, since $c = \frac{b}{2} = \frac{2a}{2} = a$.

The area of a triangle is $\left(\frac{1}{2}\right)$(Base)(Height).

Example:

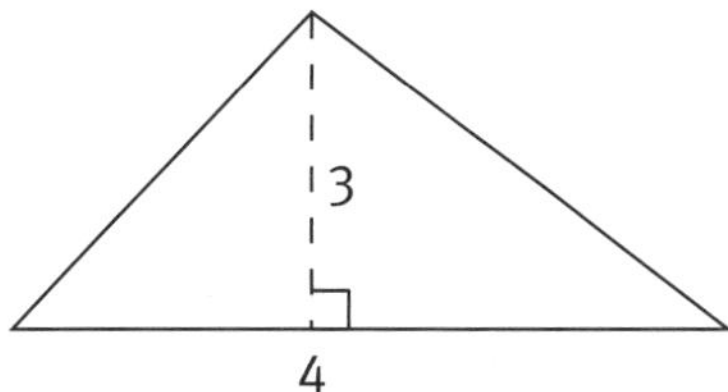

In the diagram above, the base has length 4, and the altitude has length 3. What is the area of the triangle?

$$\begin{aligned}\text{Area} &= \frac{1}{2}bh \\ &= \frac{bh}{2} \\ &= \frac{4 \times 3}{2} \\ &= 6\end{aligned}$$

Since the lengths of the base and altitude were not given in specific units, such as centimeters or feet, the area of the triangle is simply said to be 6 square units.

The area of a right triangle is easy to find. Think of one leg as the base and the other as the height. Then the area is one-half the product of the legs, or $\frac{1}{2} \times \text{Leg}_1 \times \text{Leg}_2$.

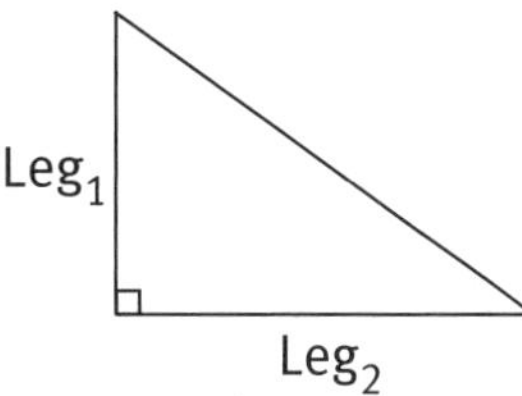

Right Triangles

The right angle is always the largest angle in a right triangle; therefore, the hypotenuse, which lies opposite the right angle, is always the longest side.

Pythagorean Theorem

The *Pythagorean theorem*, which holds for all right triangles and for no other triangles, states that the square of the hypotenuse is equal to the sum of the squares of the legs.

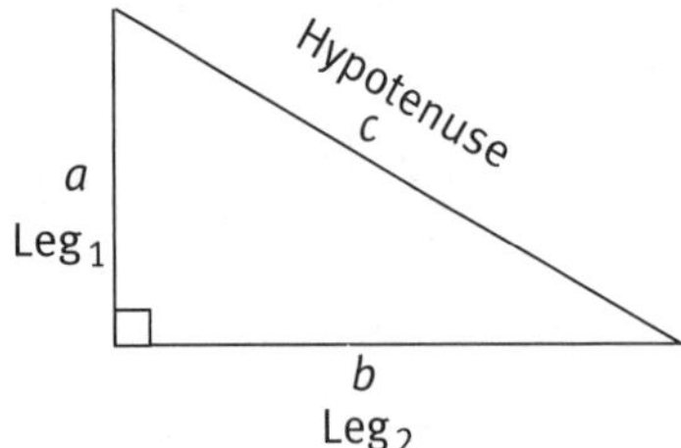

$(\text{Leg}_1)^2 + (\text{Leg}_2)^2 = (\text{Hypotenuse})^2$
or $a^2 + b^2 = c^2$

The Pythagorean theorem is very useful whenever you're given the lengths of any two sides of a right triangle; as long as you know whether the remaining side is a leg or the hypotenuse, you can find its length by using the Pythagorean theorem.

Example:

What is the length of the hypotenuse of a right triangle with legs of lengths 9 and 10?

$$\begin{aligned}(\text{Hypotenuse})^2 &= (\text{Leg}_1)^2 + (\text{Leg}_2)^2 \\ &= 9^2 + 10^2 \\ &= 81 + 100 \\ &= 181\end{aligned}$$

If the square of the hypotenuse equals 181, then the hypotenuse itself must be the square root of 181, or $\sqrt{181}$.

Pythagorean Triples

Certain ratios of integers always satisfy the Pythagorean theorem. You might like to think of them as "Pythagorean triples." One such ratio is 3, 4, and 5. A right triangle with legs of lengths 3 and 4 and a hypotenuse of length 5 is probably the most common kind of right triangle on the GRE. Whenever you see a right triangle with legs of 3 and 4, with a leg of 3 and a hypotenuse of 5, or with a leg of 4 and a hypotenuse of 5, you immediately know the length of the remaining side. In addition, any multiple of these lengths makes another Pythagorean triple; for instance, $6^2 + 8^2 = 10^2$, so a triangle with sides of lengths 6, 8, and 10 is also a right triangle.

The other triple that commonly appears on the GRE is 5, 12, and 13.

Special Right Triangles

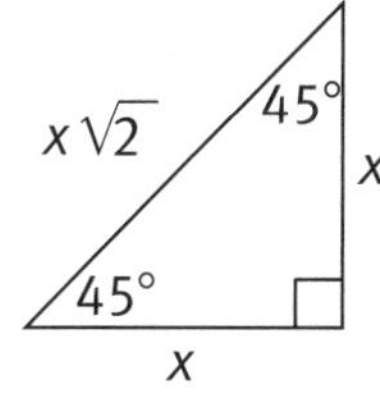

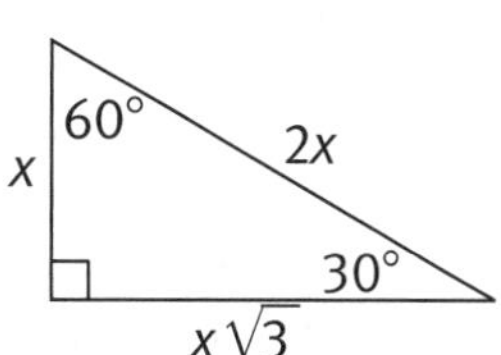

There are two more special kinds of right triangles for which you won't have to use the Pythagorean theorem to find the lengths of the sides. There are special ratios between the lengths of the sides in isosceles right triangles (45°/45°/90° right triangles) and 30°/60°/90° right triangles (right triangles with acute angles of 30° and 60°). As you can see in the first drawing above, the sides of an isosceles right triangle are in a ratio of $x:x:x\sqrt{2}$, with the $x\sqrt{2}$ in the ratio representing the hypotenuse. The sides of a 30°/60°/90° right triangle are in a ratio of $x:x\sqrt{3}:2x$, where $2x$ represents the hypotenuse and x represents the side opposite the 30° angle. (Remember: the longest side has to be opposite the greatest angle.)

Example:

What is the length of the hypotenuse of an isosceles right triangle with legs of length 4?

You can use the Pythagorean theorem to find the hypotenuse, but it's quicker to use the special right triangle ratios. In an isosceles right triangle, the ratio of a leg to the hypotenuse is $x:x\sqrt{2}$. Since the length of a leg is 4, the length of the hypotenuse must be $4\sqrt{2}$.

Triangles and Quantitative Comparison

All Quantitative Comparison questions require you to judge whether enough information has been given to make a comparison. In geometry, making this judgment is often a matter of knowing the correct definition or formula. For triangles, keep in mind the following:

- If you know two angles, you know the third.
- To find the area, you need the base and the height.
- In a right triangle, if you have two sides, you can find the third. And if you have two sides, you can find the area.
- In isosceles right triangles and 30°/60°/90° triangles, if you know one side, you can find everything.

Be careful, though! Be sure you know as much as you think you do.

Example:

Quantity A	Quantity B
Area of right triangle *ABC*, where $\overline{AB} = 5$ and $\overline{BC} = 4$	6

You may think at first that *ABC* must be a 3:4:5 right triangle. Not so fast! We're given two sides, but we don't know which sides they are. If *AB* is the hypotenuse, then it is a 3:4:5 triangle and the area is $\frac{1}{2}(3 \times 4) = 6$, but it's also possible that *AC*, the missing side, is the hypotenuse. In that case, the area would be $\frac{1}{2}(4 \times 5) = 10$. Because Quantity A can either be equal to Quantity B or can be larger than Quantity B, their relationship cannot be determined from the information given.

QUADRILATERALS

A *quadrilateral* is a four-sided polygon. Regardless of a quadrilateral's shape, the four interior angles sum to 360°.

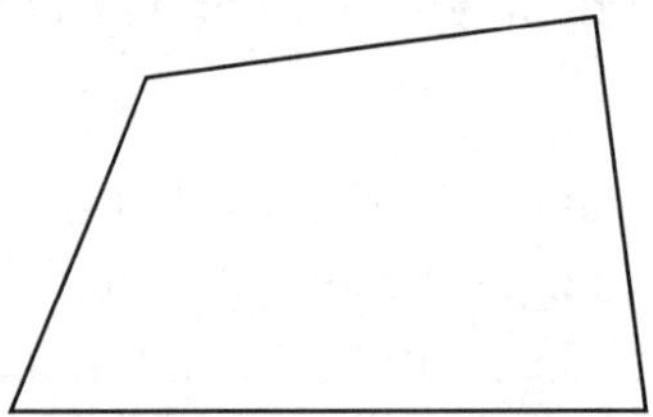

A *parallelogram* is a quadrilateral with two pairs of parallel sides. Opposite sides are equal in length; opposite angles are equal in measure; angles that are not opposite are supplementary to each other (measure of $\angle A$ + measure of $\angle D = 180°$ in the figure below).

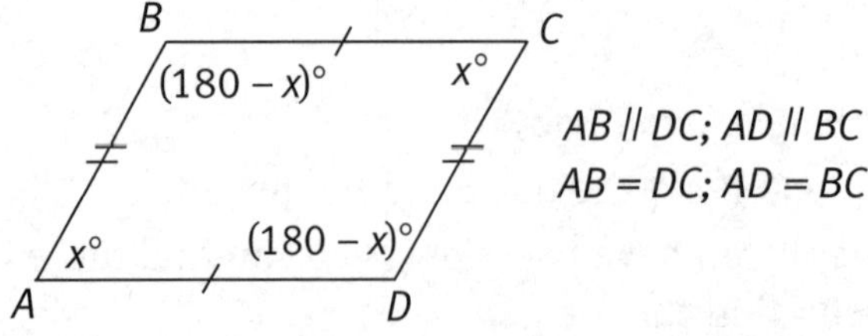

measure of $\angle A$ = measure of $\angle C$;
measure of $\angle B$ = measure of $\angle D$

A *rectangle* is a parallelogram with four right angles. Opposite sides are equal; diagonals are equal.

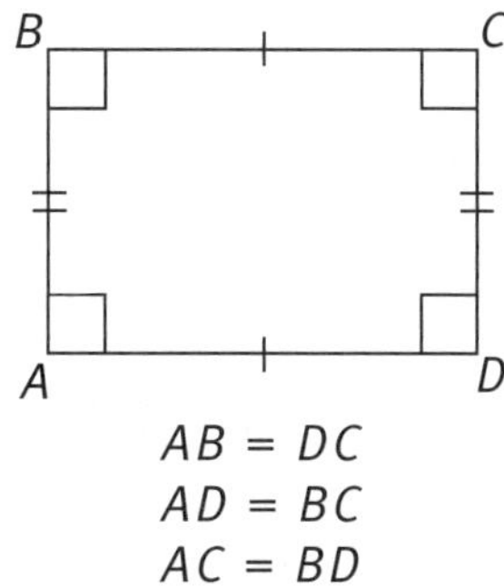

$AB = DC$
$AD = BC$
$AC = BD$

A *square* is a rectangle with equal sides.

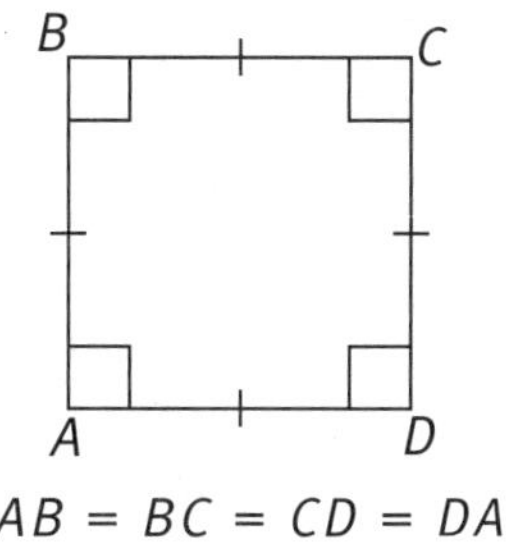

$AB = BC = CD = DA$

Perimeters of Quadrilaterals

To find the perimeter of any polygon, you can simply add the lengths of its sides. However, the properties of rectangles and squares lead to simple formulas that may speed up your calculations.

Because the opposite sides are equal, the *perimeter of a rectangle* is twice the sum of the length and the width: Perimeter = 2(Length + Width)

The perimeter of a 5 by 2 rectangle is $2(5 + 2) = 14$.

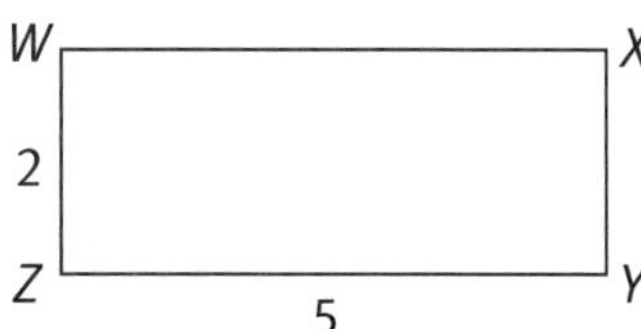

The *perimeter of a square* is equal to the sum of the lengths of the 4 sides. Because all 4 sides are the same length, Perimeter = 4 (Side). If the length of one side of a square is 3, the perimeter is $4 \times 3 = 12$.

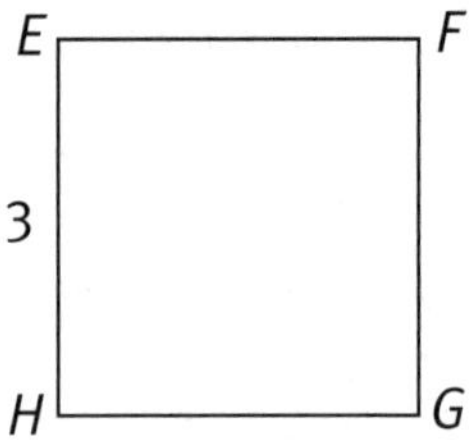

Areas of Quadrilaterals

Area formulas always involve multiplication, and the results are always stated in "square" units. You can see why if you look at the drawing below:

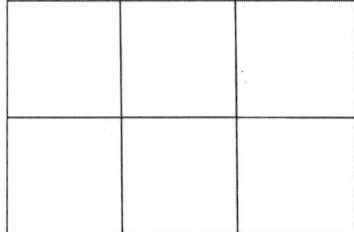

The rectangle is composed of six squares, all equal in size. Let's say that the side of a single small square is 1 unit. Then, we would say that a single square measures "1 by 1." That translates into math as 1×1, or 1^2—in other words, "one square unit."

As you can see from the drawing, there are 6 such square units in the rectangle. That's its area: 6 square units. But you could also find the area by multiplying the number of squares in a row by the number of squares in a column: 3×2, or 6. And since we've defined the length of the side of a square as 1 unit, that's also equivalent to multiplying the length of a horizontal side by the length of a vertical side: again, $3 \times 2 = 6$.

Formulas for Area

To find the area of a rectangle, multiply the *length* by the *width*.

$$\text{Area of rectangle} = \ell w$$

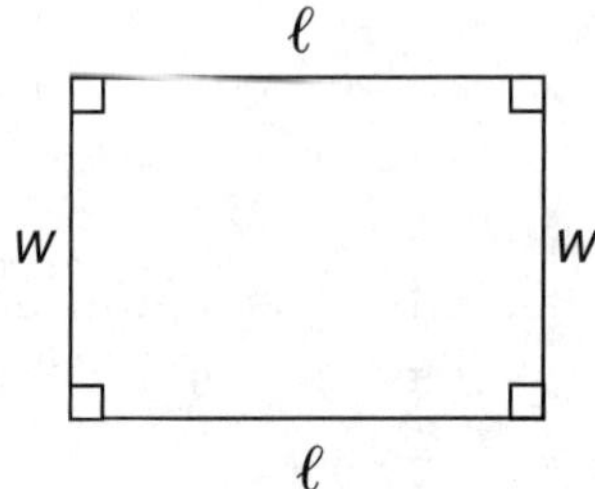

Since the length and width of a square are equal, the area formula for a square just uses the length of a *side*:

$$\text{Area of square} = (\text{Side})^2 = s^2$$

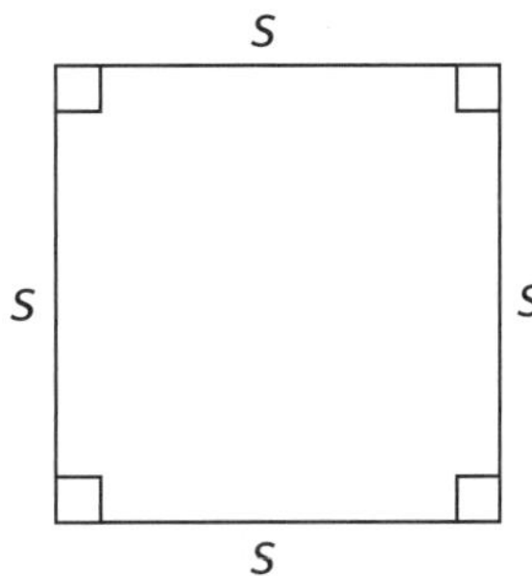

If you're working with a parallelogram, designate one side as the *base*. Then, draw a line segment from one of the vertices opposite the base down to the base so that it intersects the base at a right angle. That line segment will be called the *height*. To find the area of the parallelogram, multiply the length of the base by the length of the height:

$$\text{Area of parallelogram} = (\text{Base})(\text{Height}), \text{ or } A = bh$$

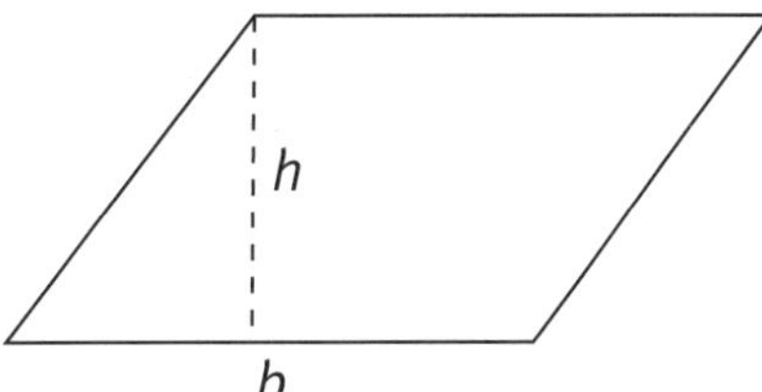

Remember the following:

- In a parallelogram, if you know two adjacent sides, you know all of them; and if you know two adjacent angles, you know all of them.
- In a rectangle, if you know two adjacent sides, you know the area.
- In a square, if you're given virtually any measurement (area, length of a side, length of a diagonal), you can figure out the other measurements.

Circles

Important Terms

Circle: The set of all points in a plane at the same distance from a certain point. This point is called the center of the circle. A circle is labeled by its center point; circle *O* means the circle with center point *O*.

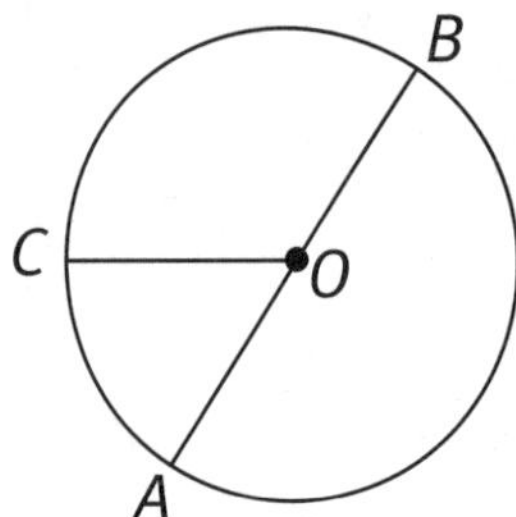

Diameter: A line segment that connects two points on the circle and passes through the center of the circle. *AB* is a diameter of circle *O* above.

Radius: A line segment that connects the center of the circle with any point on the circle (plural: *radii*). The radius of a circle is one-half the length of the diameter. In circle *O* above, *OA*, *OB*, and *OC* are radii.

Central angle: An angle formed by two radii. In circle *O* above, *AOC* is a central angle. *COB* and *BOA* are also central angles. (The measure of *BOA* happens to be 180°.) The total degree measure of a circle is 360°.

Chord: A line segment that joins two points on the circle. The longest chord of a circle is its diameter. *AT* is a chord of circle *P* below.

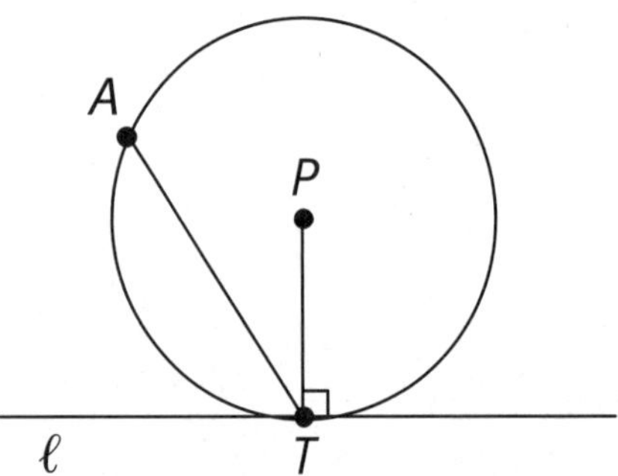

Tangent: A line that touches only one point on the circumference of a circle. A line drawn tangent to a circle is perpendicular to the radius at the point of tangency. In the diagram above, line ℓ is tangent to circle *P* at point *T*.

Circumference and Arc Length

The distance around a polygon is called its *perimeter*; the distance around a circle is called its *circumference*.

The ratio of the circumference of any circle to its diameter is a constant, called *pi* (π). For GRE purposes, the value of π is usually approximated as 3.14.

Since π equals the ratio of the circumference, C, to the diameter, d, we can say that $\pi = \frac{\text{Circumference}}{\text{Diameter}} = \frac{C}{d}$.

The formula for the circumference of a circle is $C = \pi d$.

The circumference formula can also be stated in terms of the radius, r. Since the diameter is twice the length of the radius, that is, $d = 2r$, then $C = 2\pi r$.

An *arc* is a section of the circumference of a circle. Any arc can be thought of as the portion of a circle cut off by a particular central angle. For example, in circle Q, arc ABC is the portion of the circle that is cut off by central angle AQC. Since arcs are associated with central angles, they can be measured in degrees. The degree measure of an arc is equal to that of the central angle that cuts it off. So in circle Q, arc ABC and central angle AQC would have the same degree measure.

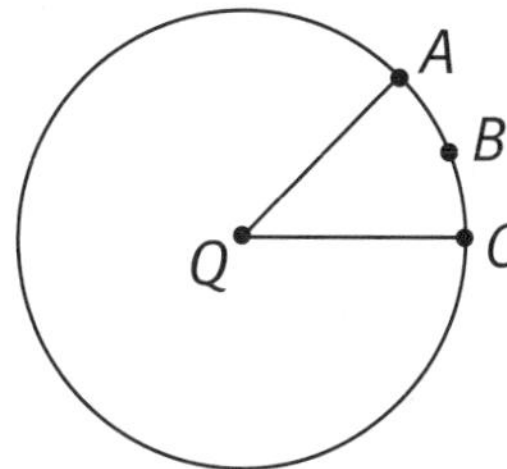

An arc that is exactly half the circumference of its circle is called a *semicircle*.

The length of an arc is the same fraction of a circle's circumference as its degree measure is of 360° (the degree measure of a whole circle). For an arc with a central angle measuring $n°$:

$$\begin{aligned}\text{Arc length} &= \frac{n}{360}(\text{Circumference}) \\ &= \frac{n}{360} \times 2\pi r\end{aligned}$$

Example:

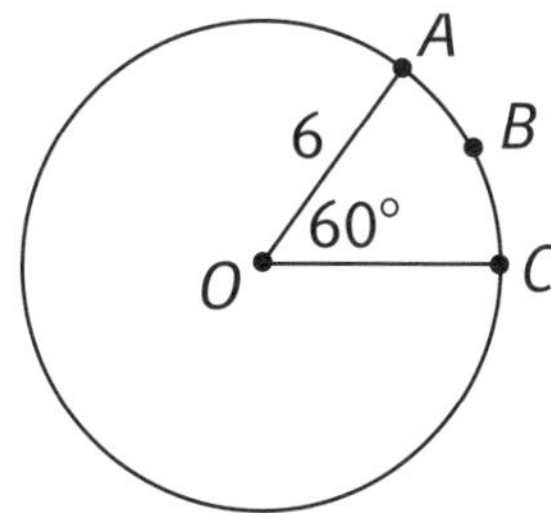

What is the length of arc ABC of circle O above?

$C = 2\pi r$; therefore, if $r = 6$, $C = 2 \times \pi \times 6 = 12\pi$. Since *AOC* measures 60°, arc *ABC* is $\frac{60}{360}$, or $\frac{1}{6}$ of the circumference. Thus, the length of arc *ABC* is $\frac{1}{6} \times 12\pi$, or 2π.

Area and Sector Area Formulas

The area of a circle is πr^2.

A *sector* is a portion of a circle's area that is bounded by two radii and an arc. The shaded area of circle *X* is sector *AXB*.

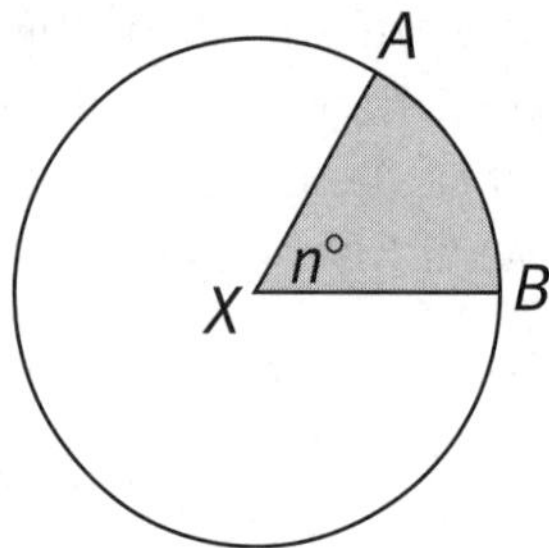

Like arcs, sectors are associated with central angles. And the process and formula used to find the area of a sector are similar to those used to determine arc length. First, find the degree measure of the sector's central angle and figure out what fraction that degree measure is of 360°. Then, multiply the area of the whole circle by that fraction. In a sector whose central angle measures n°:

$$\begin{aligned}\text{Area of sector} &= \frac{n}{360}(\text{Area of circle}) \\ &= \frac{n}{360}\pi r^2\end{aligned}$$

Example:

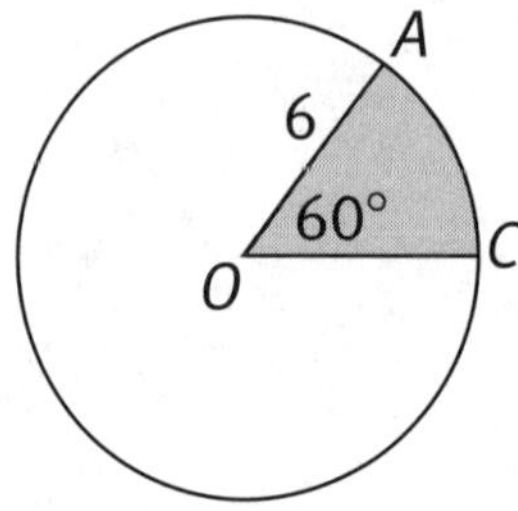

In circle *O* above, what is the area of sector *AOC*?

Since $\angle AOC$ measures 60°, a 60° "slice" of the circle is $\frac{60^\circ}{360^\circ}$, or $\frac{1}{6}$ of the total area of the circle. Therefore, the area of the sector is $\frac{1}{6}\pi r^2 = \frac{1}{6}(36\pi) = 6\pi$.

COORDINATE GEOMETRY

In coordinate geometry, the locations of points in a plane are indicated by ordered pairs of real numbers.

Important Terms and Concepts

Plane: A flat surface that extends indefinitely in any direction.

***x*-axis and *y*-axis:** The horizontal (x) and vertical (y) lines that intersect perpendicularly to indicate location on a coordinate plane. Each axis is a number line.

Ordered pair: Two numbers or quantities separated by a comma and enclosed in parentheses. An example would be (8,7). All the ordered pairs that you'll see in GRE coordinate geometry problems will be in the form (x,y), where the first quantity, x, tells you how far the point is to the left or right of the y-axis, and the second quantity, y, tells you how far the point is above or below the x-axis.

Coordinates: The numbers that designate distance from an axis in coordinate geometry. The first number is the x-coordinate; the second is the y-coordinate. In the ordered pair (8,7), 8 is the x-coordinate and 7 is the y-coordinate.

Origin: The point where the x- and y-axes intersect; its coordinates are (0,0).

Plotting Points

Here's what a coordinate plane looks like:

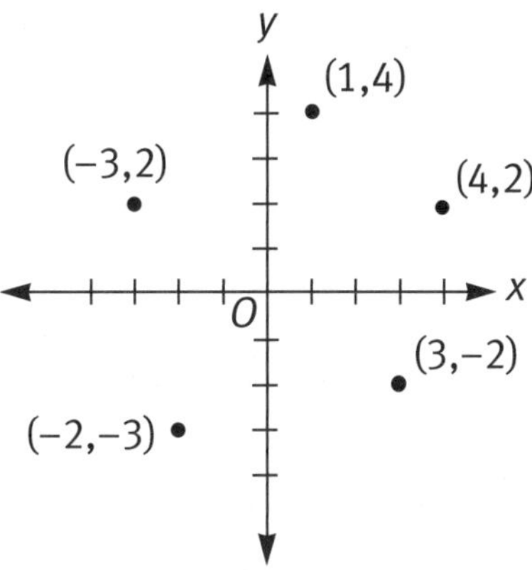

Any point in a coordinate plane can be identified by an ordered pair consisting of its x-coordinate and its y-coordinate. Every point that lies on the x-axis has a y-coordinate of 0, and every point that lies on the y-axis has an x-coordinate of 0.

When you start at the origin and move:

to the right	....	x is positive
to the left	....	x is negative
up	....	y is positive
down	....	y is negative

Therefore, the coordinate plane can be divided into four quadrants, as shown below.

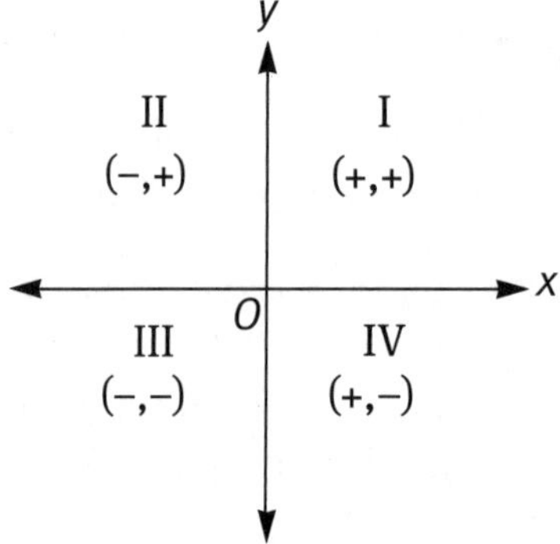

Distances on the Coordinate Plane

The distance between two points is equal to the length of the straight-line segment that has those two points as endpoints.

If a line segment is parallel to the *x*-axis, the *y*-coordinate of every point on the line segment will be the same. Similarly, if a line segment is parallel to the *y*-axis, the *x*-coordinate of every point on the line segment will be the same.

Therefore, to find the length of a line segment parallel to one of the axes, all you have to do is find the difference between the endpoint coordinates that do change. In the diagram below, the length of *AB* equals $x_2 - x_1$.

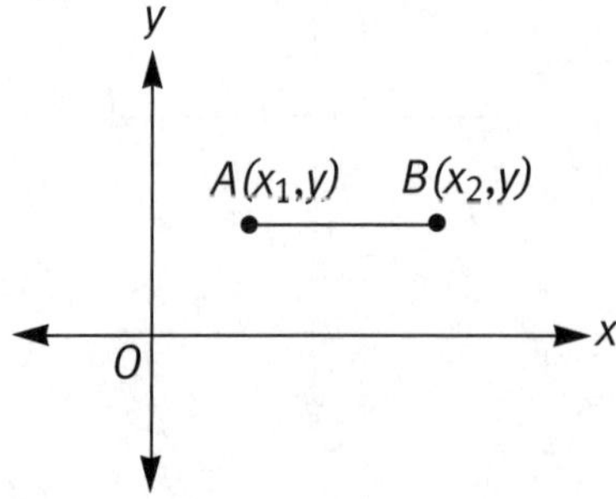

You can find the length of a line segment that is not parallel to one of the axes by treating the line segment as the hypotenuse of a right triangle. Simply draw in the legs of the triangle parallel to the two axes. The length of each leg will be the difference between the *x*- or *y*-coordinates of its endpoints. Once you've found the lengths of the legs, you can use the Pythagorean theorem to find the length of the hypotenuse (the original line segment).

In the diagram below, $(DE)^2 = (EF)^2 + (DF)^2$.

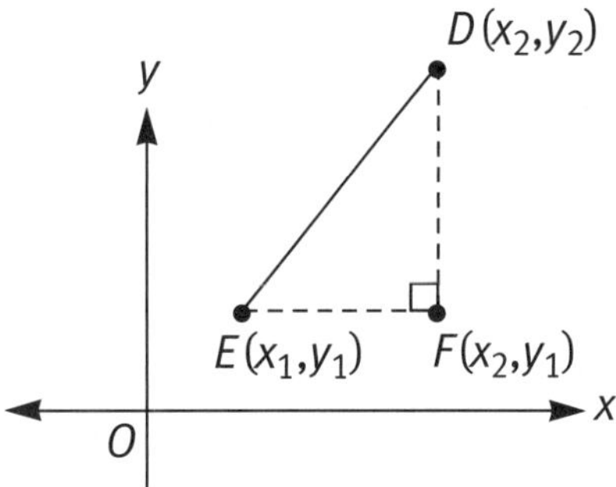

Example:

If the coordinates of point *A* are (3,4) and the coordinates of point *B* are (6,8), what is the distance between points *A* and *B*?

You don't have to draw a diagram to use the method just described, but drawing one may help you to visualize the problem. Plot points *A* and *B* and draw in line segment *AB*. The length of *AB* is the distance between the two points. Now draw a right triangle, with *AB* as its hypotenuse. The missing vertex will be the intersection of a line segment drawn through point *A* parallel to the *x*-axis and a line segment drawn through point *B* parallel to the *y*-axis. Label the point of intersection *C*. Since the *x*- and *y*-axes are perpendicular to each other, *AC* and *BC* will also be perpendicular to each other.

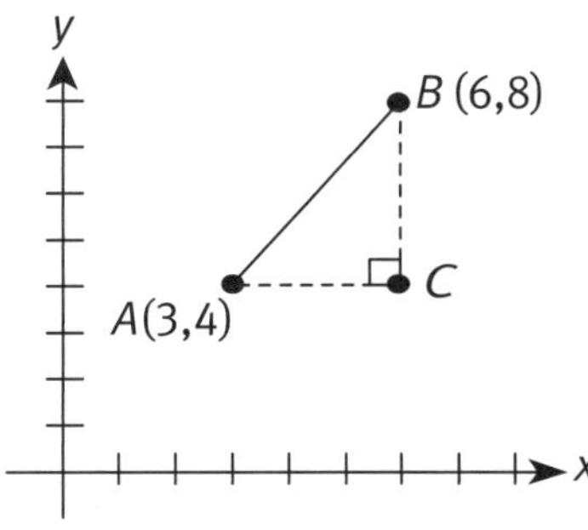

Point *C* will also have the same *x*-coordinate as point *B* and the same *y*-coordinate as point *A*. That means that point *C* has coordinates (6,4).

To use the Pythagorean theorem, you'll need the lengths of *AC* and *BC*. The distance between points *A* and *C* is simply the difference between their *x*-coordinates, while the distance between points *B* and *C* is the difference between their *y*-coordinates. So $AC = 6 - 3 = 3$, and $BC = 8 - 4 = 4$. If you recognize these as the legs of a 3:4:5 right triangle, you'll know immediately that the distance between points *A* and *B* must be 5. Otherwise, you'll have to use the Pythagorean theorem to come to the same conclusion.

Equations of Lines

Straight lines can be described by linear equations.

Commonly:

$$y = mx + b,$$

where *m* is the slope $\left(\dfrac{\Delta y}{\Delta x}\right)$ and *b* is the point where the line intercepts the *y*-axis, that is, the value of *y* where $x = 0$.

Lines that are parallel to the *x*-axis have a slope of zero and therefore have the equation $y = b$. Lines that are parallel to the *y*-axis have the equation $x = a$, where *a* is the *x*-intercept of that line.

If you're comfortable with linear equations, you'll sometimes want to use them to find the slope of a line or the coordinates of a point on a line. However, many such questions can be answered without determining or manipulating equations. Check the answer choices to see if you can eliminate any by common sense.

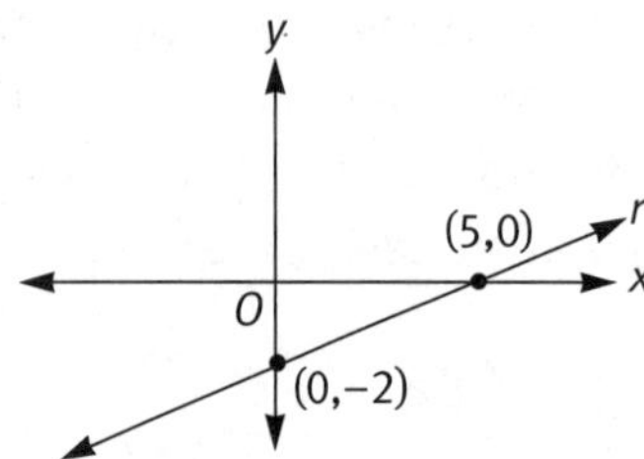

Example:

Line *r* is a straight line as shown above. Which of the following points lies on line *r*?

Ⓐ (6,6)
Ⓑ (7,3)
Ⓒ (8,2)
Ⓓ (9,3)
Ⓔ (10,2)

Line r intercepts the y-axis at (0,–2), so you can plug –2 in for b in the slope-intercept form of a linear equation. Line r has a rise (Δy) of 2 and a run (Δx) of 5, so its slope is $\frac{2}{5}$. That makes the slope-intercept form $y = \frac{2}{5}x - 2$.

The easiest way to proceed from here is to substitute the coordinates of each answer choice into the equation in place of x and y; only the coordinates that satisfy the equation can lie on the line. Choice **(E)** is the best answer to start with, because 10 is the only x-coordinate that will not create a fraction on the right side of the equal sign. Plugging in (10,2) for x and y in the slope-intercept equation gives you $2 = \frac{2}{5}(10) - 2$, which simplifies to $2 = 4 - 2$.

That's true, so the correct answer choice is **(E)**.

Solids

Important Terms

Solid: A three-dimensional figure. The dimensions are usually called length, width, and height (ℓ, w, and h) or height, width, and depth (h, w, and d). There are only two types of solids that appear with any frequency on the GRE: rectangular solids (including cubes) and cylinders.

Uniform solid: A solid that could be cut into congruent cross sections (parallel "slices" of equal size and shape) along a given axis. Solids you see on the GRE will almost certainly be uniform solids.

Face: The surface of a solid that lies in a particular plane. Hexagon *ABCDEF* is one face of the solid pictured below.

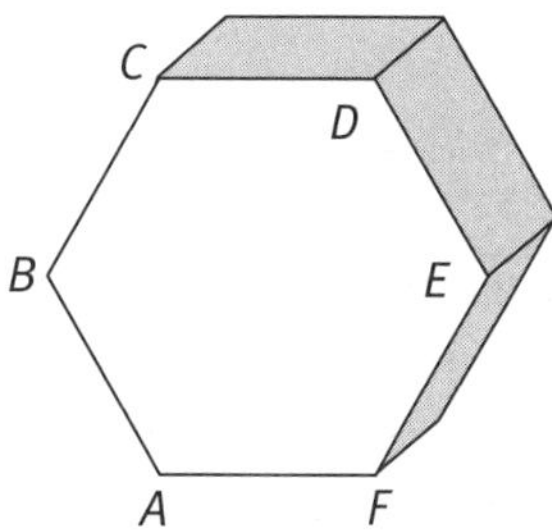

Edge: A line segment that connects adjacent faces of a solid. The sides of hexagon *ABCDEF* are also edges of the solid pictured above.

Base: The "bottom" face of a solid as oriented in any given diagram.

Rectangular solid: A solid with six rectangular faces. All edges meet at right angles. Examples of rectangular solids are cereal boxes, bricks, etc.

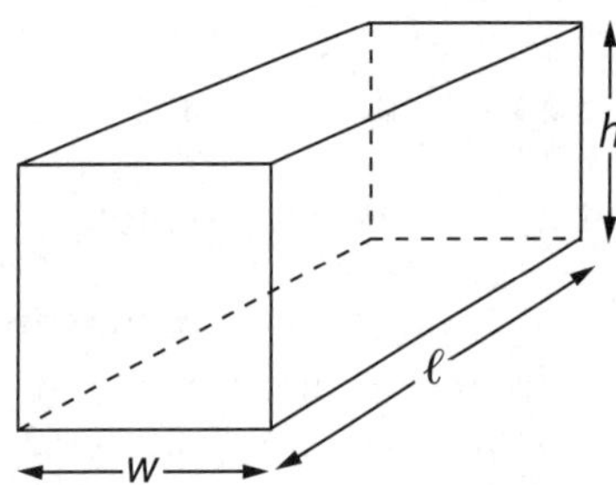

Cube: A special rectangular solid in which all edges are of equal length, *e*, and therefore all faces are squares. Sugar cubes and dice without rounded corners are examples of cubes.

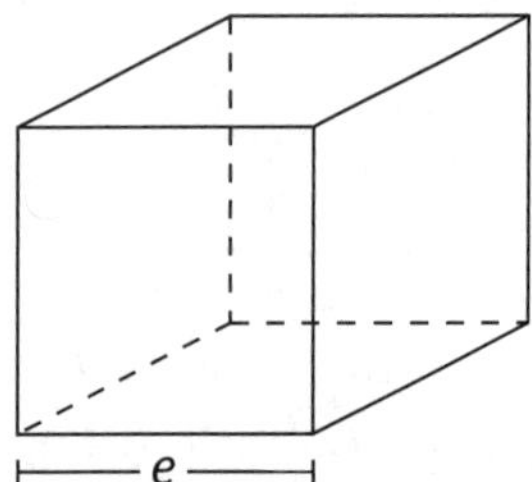

Cylinder: A uniform solid whose horizontal cross section is a circle—for example, a soup can or a pipe that is closed at both ends. A cylinder's measurements are generally given in terms of its radius, *r*, and its height, *h*.

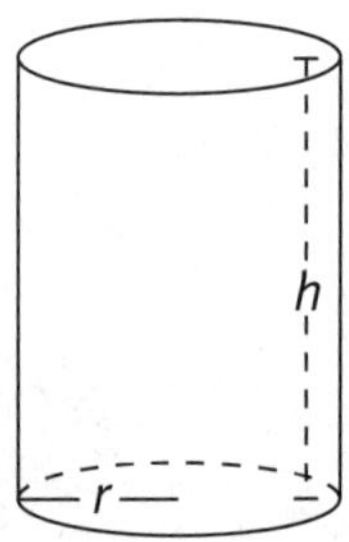

Lateral surface of a cylinder: The "pipe" surface, as opposed to the circular "ends." The lateral surface of a cylinder is unlike most other surfaces of solids that you'll see on the GRE, first because it does not lie in a plane and second because it forms a closed loop. Think of it as the label around a soup can. If you could remove it from the can in one piece, you would have an open tube. If you then cut the label and unrolled it, it would form a rectangle with a length equal to the circumference of the circular base of the can and a height equal to that of the can.

Formulas for Volume and Surface Area

Volume of a rectangular solid = (Area of base) (Height) = (Length × Width) (Height) = lwh

Surface area of a rectangular solid = Sum of areas of faces = $2lw + 2lh + 2hw$

Since a cube is a rectangular solid for which $l = w = h$, the formula for its volume can be stated in terms of any edge:

- Volume of a cube = lwh = (Edge)(Edge)(Edge) = e^3
- Surface area of a cube = Sum of areas of faces = $6e^2$

To find the volume or surface area of a cylinder, you'll need two pieces of information: the height of the cylinder and the radius of the base.

- Volume of a cylinder = (Area of base)(Height) = $\pi r^2 h$
- Lateral surface area of a cylinder = (Circumference of base)(Height) = $2\pi rh$
- Total surface area of a cylinder = Areas of circular ends + Lateral surface area = $2\pi r^2 + 2\pi rh$

MULTIPLE FIGURES

Some GRE geometry problems involve combinations of different types of figures. Besides the basic rules and formulas that you would use on normal geometry problems, you'll need an intuitive understanding of how various geometrical concepts relate to each other to answer these "multiple figures" questions correctly. For example, you may have to revisualize the side of a rectangle as the hypotenuse of a neighboring right triangle or as the diameter of a circumscribed circle. Keep looking for the relationships between the different figures until you find one that leads you to the answer.

Area of Shaded Regions

A common multiple-figures question involves a diagram of a geometrical figure that has been broken up into different, irregularly shaped areas, often with one region shaded. You'll usually be asked to find the area of the shaded (or unshaded) portion of the diagram. Your best bet will be to take one of the following two approaches:

- Break the area into smaller pieces whose separate areas you can find; add those areas together.
- Find the area of the whole figure; find the area of the region(s) that you're *not* looking for; subtract the latter from the former.

Example:

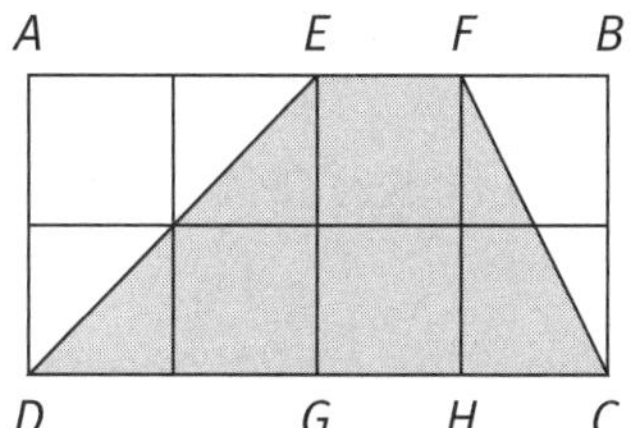

Rectangle *ABCD* above has an area of 72 and is composed of 8 equal squares. What is the area of the shaded region?

The first thing you have to realize is that, for the 8 equal squares to form a total area of 72, each square must have an area of 72 ÷ 8, or 9. Since the area of a square equals the square of the length of a side, each side of a square in the diagram must have a length of $\sqrt{9}$ or 3.

At this point, you choose your approach. Either one will work:

Approach 1:

Break up the shaded area into right triangle *DEG*, rectangle *EFHG*, and right triangle *FHC*. The area of triangle *DEG* is $\frac{1}{2}(6)(6) = 18$. The area of rectangle *EFHG* is (3)(6), or 18. The area of triangle *FHC* is $\frac{1}{2}(3)(6)$, or 9. The total shaded area is 18 + 18 + 9, or 45.

Approach 2:

The area of unshaded right triangle *AED* is $\frac{1}{2}(6)(6)$, or 18. The area of unshaded right triangle *FBC* is $\frac{1}{2}(3)(6)$, or 9. Therefore, the total unshaded area is 18 + 9 = 27. Subtract the total unshaded area from the total area of rectangle *ABCD*: 72 – 27 = 45.

Inscribed/Circumscribed Figures

A polygon is inscribed in a circle if all the vertices of the polygon lie on the circle. A polygon is circumscribed about a circle if all the sides of the polygon are tangent to the circle.

Square *ABCD* is inscribed in circle *O*. We can also say that circle *O* is circumscribed about square *ABCD*.

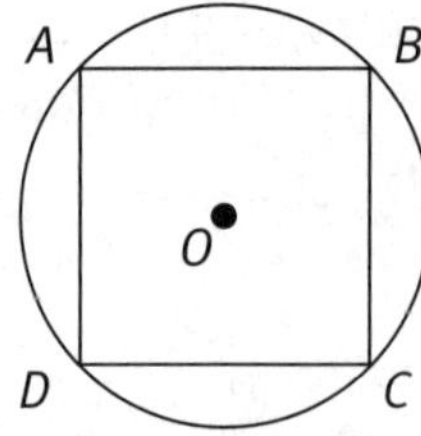

Square *PQRS* is circumscribed about circle *O*. We can also say that circle *O* is inscribed in square *PQRS*.

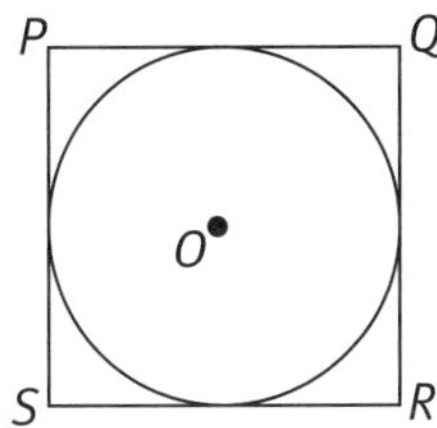

When a triangle is inscribed in a semicircle in such a way that one side of the triangle coincides with the diameter of the semicircle, the triangle is a right triangle.

Example:

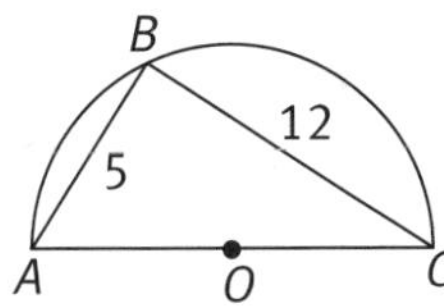

What is the diameter of semicircle *O* above?

AC is a diameter of semicircle *O* because it passes through center point *O*. So triangle *ABC* fits the description given above of a right triangle. Moreover, triangle *ABC* is a special 5:12:13 right triangle with a hypotenuse of 13. Therefore, the length of diameter *AC* is 13.

Example:

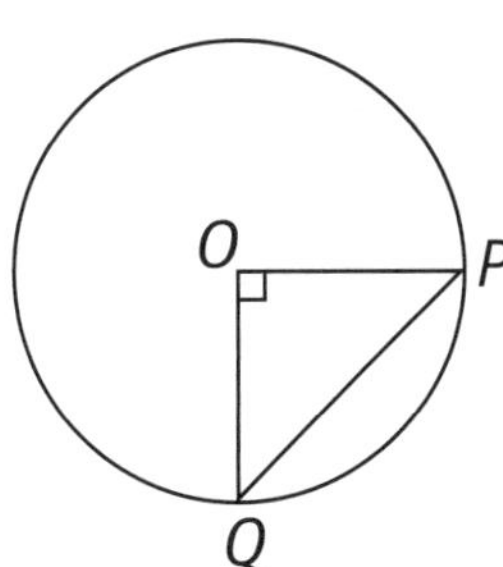

If the length of chord $PQ = 4\sqrt{2}$, what is the circumference of the circle with center *O*?

- (A) 4
- (B) 8
- (C) 4π
- (D) 8π
- (E) $8\pi\sqrt{2}$

To find the circumference, we need the radius, which is either *OP* or *OQ* in this circle. We are given the length of *PQ*. *PQ* is a chord of the circle (it connects two points on the circle), but it's also the hypotenuse of right triangle *OPQ*. Do we know anything else about that triangle? Since *OP* and *OQ* are both radii of the circle, they must have the same length, so the triangle is an isosceles right triangle. Using the ratio of the lengths of sides of a 45:45:90 right triangle, with *PQ* as the hypotenuse, the length of each radius is 4, making the circumference $2\pi r$ or 8π, answer choice (**D**).

OTHER TOPICS

DEALING WITH WORD PROBLEMS

The key to solving word problems is translation: turning English into math. Rather than having an equation set up for you, *you* have to decide what arithmetic or algebraic operations to perform on which numbers.

For example, suppose the core of a problem involves working with the equation $3j = s - 4$.

In a word problem, this might be presented as "If John had three times as many macaroons as he has now, he would have four fewer macaroons than Susan would."

Your job is to translate the problem from English into math. A phrase like "three times as many as John has" can be translated as $3j$; the phrase "four fewer than Susan" can be translated as "$s - 4$."

Many people dislike word problems. But on the GRE, the math involved is often easier than in other math problems. Once you've translated the language, most word problems boil down to rather simple mathematical concepts and processes—probably because the testmakers figure that the extra step of translation makes the problem difficult enough.

Here's a general approach to any word problem:

1. Read through the whole question once, without lingering over details, to get a sense of the overall problem.
2. Identify and label the variables or unknowns in a way that makes it easy to remember what they stand for.
3. Translate the problem into one or more equations, sentence by sentence. Be careful of the order in which you translate the terms. For example, consider the phrase "5 less than $4x$ equals 9." The *correct* way to translate it is "$4x - 5 = 9$." But many students make the mistake of writing the terms in the order in which they appear in words: "$5 - 4x = 9$."
4. Solve the equation(s).
5. Check your work, if time permits.

Translation Table

This table contains common phrases used in GRE math problems. The left column lists words and phrases that occur frequently; the right column lists the corresponding algebraic symbols.

Words and phrases	Symbol
equals, is, was, will be, has, costs, adds up to, is the same as	$=$
times, of, multiplied by, product of, twice, double, half, triple	$\times$
divided by, per, out of, each, ratio of _ to _	$\div$
plus, added to, sum, combined, and, total	$+$
minus, subtracted from, less than, decreased by, difference between	$-$
what, how much, how many, a number	variable (x, n, etc.)

Example:

Beatrice has three dollars more than twice the number of dollars Allan has.

Translate into $B = 3 + 2A$.

For Word Problems:

Add...

- when you are given the amounts of individual quantities and asked to find the total.

Example:

If the sales tax on a \$12.00 lunch is \$1.20, what is the total amount of the check?

$$\$12.00 + \$1.20 = \$13.20$$

- when you are given an original amount and an increase and are then asked to find the new amount.

Example:

The bus fare used to be 55 cents. If the fare increased by 35 cents, what is the new fare?

$$55 \text{ cents} + 35 \text{ cents} = 90 \text{ cents}$$

Subtract...

- when you are given the total and one part of the total and you want to find the remaining part or parts.

Example:

If 32 out of 50 children are girls, what is the number of boys?

$$50 \text{ children} - 32 \text{ girls} = 18 \text{ boys}$$

- when you are given two numbers and asked *how much more* or *how much less* one number is than the other. The amount is called the *difference*.

Example:

How much larger than 30 is 38?

$$38 \text{ (larger)} - 30 \text{ (smaller)} = 8$$

Multiply...

- when you are given an amount for one item and asked for the total amount of *many* of these items.

Example:

If 1 book costs $6.50, what is the cost of 12 copies of the same book?

$$12(\$6.50) = \$78.00$$

Divide...

- when you are given a total amount for *many* items and asked for the amount for *one* item.

Example:

If 5 pounds of apples cost $6.75, what is the price of 1 pound of apples?

$$\$6.75 \div 5 = \$1.35$$

- when you are given the size of one group and the total size for many such identical groups and are asked how many of the small groups fit into the larger one.

Example:

How many groups of 30 students can be formed from a total of 240 students?

$$240 \div 30 = 8 \text{ groups of } 30 \text{ students}$$

SPECIAL WORD PROBLEMS TIP #1
Don't try to combine several sentences into one equation; each sentence usually translates into a separate equation.

SPECIAL WORD PROBLEMS TIP #2
Pay attention to what the question asks for and make a note to yourself if it is not one of the unknowns in the equation(s). Otherwise, you may stop working on the problem too early.

Logic Problems

You won't always have to set up an equation to solve a word problem. Some of the word problems you'll encounter on the GRE won't fall into recognizable textbook categories. Many of these problems are designed to test your analytical and deductive logic. You can solve them with common sense and a little basic arithmetic. Ask yourself how it would be helpful to arrange the information, such as by drawing a diagram or making a table.

In these problems, the issue is not so much translating English into math as simply using your head. The problem may call for nonmath skills, including the ability to organize and keep track of different possibilities, the ability to visualize something (for instance, the reverse side of a symmetrical shape), the ability to think of the exception that changes the answer to a problem, or the ability to deal with overlapping groups.

Example:

If ! and $\int$ are digits and $(!!)(\int\int) = 60\int$, what is the value of $\int$?

Since each of the symbols represents a digit from 0–9, we know that the product of the multiplication equals a value from 600 to 609. We know that the two quantities multiplied each consist of a two-digit integer in which both digits are the same. So list the relevant two-digit integers (00, 11, 22, 33, 44, 55, 66, 77, 88, and 99) and see which two of them can be multiplied evenly into the 600 to 609 range. Only (11)(55) satisfies this requirement. The $\int$ symbol equals 5.

CHAPTER 11

Quantitative Comparison

INTRODUCTION TO QUANTITATIVE COMPARISON

In each Quantitative Comparison question, you'll see two mathematical expressions. One is Quantity A, and the other is Quantity B. You will be asked to compare them. Some questions include additional centered information. This centered information applies to both quantities and is essential to making the comparison. Since this type of question is about the relationship between the two quantities, you usually won't need to calculate a specific value for either quantity. Therefore, you do not want to rely on the onscreen calculator to answer these questions.

The directions for a Quantitative Comparison question will look like this:

Directions: Select the correct answer.

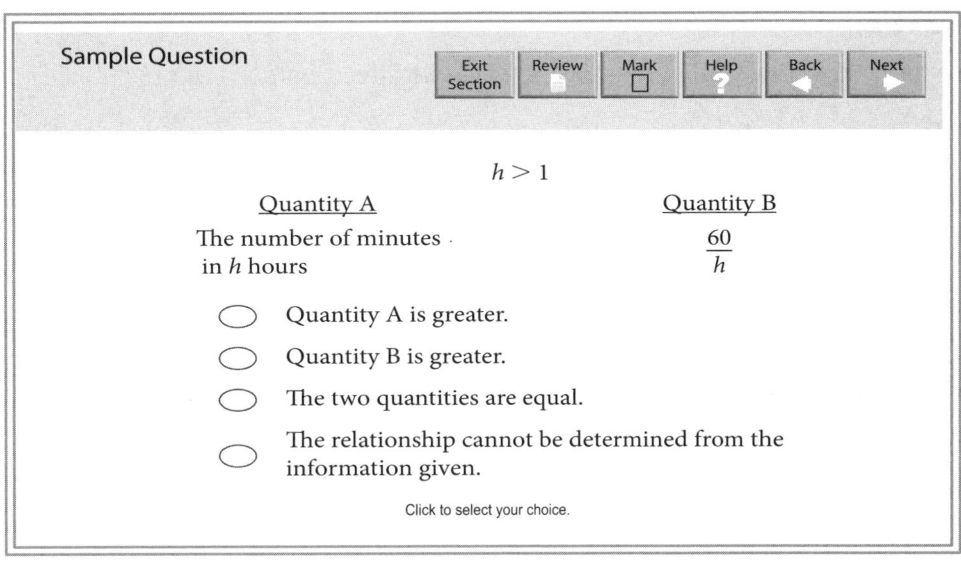

THE KAPLAN METHOD FOR QUANTITATIVE COMPARISON

STEP 1 Analyze the centered information and quantities.

STEP 2 Approach strategically.

How the Kaplan Method for Quantitative Comparison Works

Now let's discuss how the Kaplan Method for Quantitative Comparison works.

STEP 1

Analyze the centered information and the quantities.

Notice whether the quantities contain numbers, variables, or both. If there is centered information, decide how it affects the information given in the quantities. Note that a variable has the same value each time it appears within a question.

STEP 2

Approach strategically.

Think about a strategy you could use to compare the quantities now that you've determined the information you have and the information you need. There are a variety of approaches to solving a Quantitative Comparison question, and the practice examples will take you through several of these.

How to Apply the Kaplan Method for Quantitative Comparison

Now let's apply the Kaplan Method to a Quantitative Comparison question:

Quantity A	Quantity B
$\frac{1}{4}+\frac{1}{5}+\frac{1}{6}+\frac{1}{7}$	$\dfrac{1}{\frac{1}{4}+\frac{1}{5}+\frac{1}{6}+\frac{1}{7}}$

(A) Quantity A is greater.
(B) Quantity B is greater.
(C) The two quantities are equal.
(D) The relationship cannot be determined from the information given.

STEP 1

Analyze the centered information and the columns.

This problem would be a nightmare to calculate under timed conditions. But the only thing you need to figure out is whether one quantity is greater than the other. One thing you might notice is that choice **(D)** is not an option here. Because both quantities contain only numbers, there is a definite value for each quantity, and a relationship can be determined. Answer choice **(D)** is never correct when the quantities contain only numbers.

Note that the quantity on the left is the same as the quantity in the denominator of the fraction on the right. You can think about this problem as a comparison of x and $\frac{1}{x}$ (or the reciprocal of x), where x has a definite value. Your job now is to figure out just how to compare them.

STEP 2

Approach strategically.

Before you start to do a long calculation, think about what you already know. While you may not know the sum of the four fractions, you do know two things: $\frac{1}{4}+\frac{1}{4}+\frac{1}{4}+\frac{1}{4}=1$, and $\frac{1}{5}$, $\frac{1}{6}$, and $\frac{1}{7}$ are each less than $\frac{1}{4}$. Because the reciprocal of any number between 0 and 1 is greater than 1, and Quantity A is a positive number less than 1, its reciprocal in Quantity B is greater than 1. So choice **(B)** is correct. Quantitative Comparisons rarely, if ever, ask for exact values, so don't waste time calculating them.

Now let's apply the Kaplan Method to a second Quantitative Comparison question:

$$w > x > 0 > y > z$$

Quantity A	Quantity B
$w + y$	$x + z$

(A) Quantity A is greater.
(B) Quantity B is greater.
(C) The two quantities are equal.
(D) The relationship cannot be determined from the information given.

STEP 1

Analyze the centered information and the quantities.

In this problem, there are four variables: *w*, *x*, *y*, and *z*. You are asked to compare the values of the sums of pairs of variables. You know the relative values of the different variables, but you don't know the actual amounts. You do know that two of the variables (*w* and *x*) must be positive and two of the variables (*y* and *z*) must be negative numbers.

STEP 2

Approach strategically.

In this case, think about the different sums as pieces of the whole. If every "piece" in one quantity is greater than a corresponding "piece" in the other quantity, and if the only operation involved is addition, then the quantity with the greater individual values will have the greater total value. From the given information, we know the following:

- $w > x$
- $y > z$

The first term, *w*, in Quantity A is greater than the first term, *x*, in Quantity B. Similarly, the second term, *y*, in Quantity A is greater than the second term, *z*, in Quantity B. Because each piece in Quantity A is greater than the corresponding piece in Quantity B, Quantity A must be greater; the answer is **(A)**.

Now let's apply the Kaplan Method to a third Quantitative Comparison question:

The diameter of circle O is d, and the area is a.

Quantity A	Quantity B
$\frac{\pi d^2}{2}$	a

(A) Quantity A is greater.
(B) Quantity B is greater.
(C) The two quantities are equal.
(D) The relationship cannot be determined from the information given.

STEP 1

Analyze the centered information and the quantities.

In this problem, you are given additional information: the sentence that tells you the diameter of circle *O* is *d* and the area is *a*. This is important information because it gives you a key to unlocking this question. Given that information, you can tell that you are comparing the area, *a*, of circle *O* and a quantity that includes the diameter of the same circle. If you're thinking about the formula for calculating area given the diameter, you're thinking right!

STEP 2

Approach strategically.

Make Quantity B look more like Quantity A by rewriting a, the area of the circle, in terms of the diameter, d. The area of any circle equals πr^2, where r is the radius. Because the radius is half the diameter, you can substitute $\frac{d}{2}$ for r in the area formula to get $a = \pi r^2 = \pi\left(\frac{d}{2}\right)^2$ in Quantity B. Simplifying, you get $\frac{\pi d^2}{4}$.

Because both quantities contain π, we could compare $\frac{d^2}{2}$ to $\frac{d^2}{4}$. But let's take it one step further. You know that d is a distance and must be a positive number. That makes it possible to divide both quantities, $\frac{d^2}{2}$ and $\frac{d^2}{4}$, by d^2 and then just compare $\frac{1}{2}$ to $\frac{1}{4}$. This makes it easy to see that Quantity A is always greater because $\frac{1}{2} > \frac{1}{4}$. Choice **(A)** is correct.

KAPLAN'S ADDITIONAL TIPS FOR QUANTITATIVE COMPARISON QUESTIONS

Memorize the answer choices

It is a good idea to memorize what the Quantitative Comparison answer choices mean. This is not as difficult as it sounds. The choices are always the same. The wording and the order never vary. As you work through the practice problems, the choices will become second nature to you, and you will get used to reacting to the questions without reading the four answer choices, thus saving you lots of time on Test Day.

When there is at least one variable in a problem, try to demonstrate two different relationships between quantities

Here's why demonstrating two different relationships between the quantities is an important strategy: if you can demonstrate two different relationships, then choice **(D)** is correct. There is no need to examine the question further.

But how can this demonstration be done efficiently? A good suggestion is to look at the expression(s) containing a variable and notice the possible values of the variable given the mathematical operation involved. For example, if x can be any real number and you need to compare $(x + 1)^2$ to $(x + 1)$, pick a value for x that will make $(x + 1)$ a fraction between 0 and 1 and then pick a value for x that will make $(x + 1)$ greater than 1. By choosing values for x in this way, you are basing your number choices on mathematical properties you already know: a positive fraction less than 1 becomes smaller when squared, but a number greater than 1 grows larger when squared.

Compare quantities piece by piece

Compare the value of each "piece" in each quantity. If every "piece" in one quantity is greater than a corresponding "piece" in the other quantity, and the operation involved is either addition or multiplication, then the quantity with the greater individual values will have the greater total value.

Make one quantity look like the other

When the Quantities A and B are expressed differently, you can often make the comparison easier by changing the format of one quantity so that it looks like the other. This is a great approach when the quantities look so different that you can't compare them directly.

Do the same thing to both quantities

If the quantities you are given seem too complex to compare immediately, look closely to see if there is an addition, subtraction, multiplication, or division operation you can perform on both quantities to make them simpler—provided you do not multiply or divide by zero or a negative number. For example, suppose you have the task of comparing $1 + \frac{w}{1 + w}$ to $1 + \frac{1}{1 + w}$, where w is greater than 0. To get to the heart of the comparison, subtract 1 from both quantities and you have $\frac{w}{1 + w}$ compared to $\frac{1}{1 + w}$. To simplify even further, multiply both quantities by $(1 + w)$, and then you can compare w to 1.

Don't be tricked by misleading information

To avoid Quantitative Comparison traps, stay alert and don't assume anything. If you are using a diagram to answer a question, use only information that is given or information that you know must be true based on properties or theorems. For instance, don't assume angles are equal or lines are parallel unless it is stated or can be deduced from other information given.

A common mistake is to assume that variables represent only positive integers. As you saw when using the Picking Numbers strategy, fractions or negative numbers often show a different relationship between the quantities.

Don't forget to consider other possibilities

If an answer looks obvious, it may very well be a trap. Consider this situation: a question requires you to think of two integers whose product is 6. If you jump to the conclusion that 2 and 3 are the integers, you will miss several other possibilities.

Not only are 1 and 6 possibilities, but there are also pairs of negative integers to consider: -2 and -3, -1 and -6.

Don't fall for look-alikes

Even if two expressions look similar, they may be mathematically different. Be especially careful with expressions involving parentheses or radicals. If you were asked to compare $\sqrt{5x} + \sqrt{5x}$ to $\sqrt{10x}$, you would not want to fall into the trap of saying the two expressions were equal. Although time is an important factor in taking the GRE, don't rush to the extent that you do not apply your skills correctly. In this case, $\sqrt{5x} + \sqrt{5x} = 2\sqrt{5x}$, which is not the same as $\sqrt{10x}$ unless $x = 0$.

QUANTITATIVE COMPARISON PRACTICE SET

Try the following Quantitative Comparison questions using the Kaplan Method for Quantitative Comparison. If you're up to the challenge, time yourself: on Test Day, you'll want to spend only 1.5 minutes on each question.

1.

Quantity A	Quantity B
$x^2 + 2x - 2$	$x^2 + 2x - 1$

(A) Quantity A is greater.
(B) Quantity B is greater.
(C) The two quantities are equal.
(D) The relationship cannot be determined from the information given.

2. $x = 2y$; y is a positive integer.

Quantity A	Quantity B
4^{2y}	2^x

(A) Quantity A is greater.
(B) Quantity B is greater.
(C) The two quantities are equal.
(D) The relationship cannot be determined from the information given.

3. q, r, and s are positive numbers; $qrs > 12$.

Quantity A	Quantity B
$\frac{qr}{5}$	$\frac{3}{s}$

(A) Quantity A is greater.
(B) Quantity B is greater.
(C) The two quantities are equal.
(D) The relationship cannot be determined from the information given.

4. In triangle XYZ not given, the measure of angle X equals the measure of angle Y.

Quantity A	Quantity B
The degree measure of angle Z	The degree measure of angle X plus the degree measure of angle Y

Ⓐ Quantity A is greater.
Ⓑ Quantity B is greater.
Ⓒ The two quantities are equal.
Ⓓ The relationship cannot be determined from the information given.

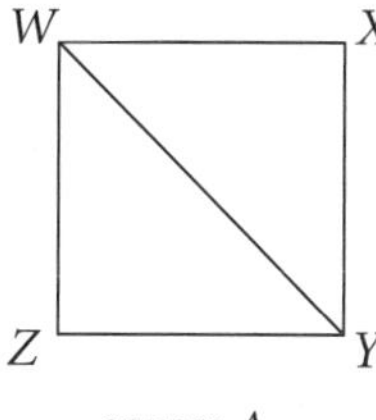

square A

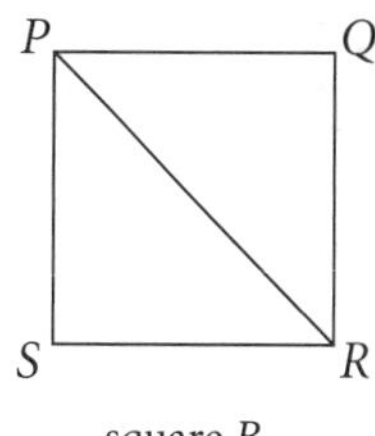

square B

5.

Quantity A	Quantity B
$\dfrac{\text{Perimeter of square } A}{\text{Perimeter of square } B}$	$\dfrac{\text{Length of } WY}{\text{Length of } PR}$

Ⓐ Quantity A is greater.
Ⓑ Quantity B is greater.
Ⓒ The two quantities are equal.
Ⓓ The relationship cannot be determined from the information given.

QUANTITATIVE COMPARISON PRACTICE SET ANSWERS AND EXPLANATIONS

1. B

Comparing the two quantities piece by piece, you find that the only difference is the third piece: −2 in Quantity A and −1 in Quantity B. You don't know the value of x, but whatever it is, x^2 in Quantity A must have the same value as x^2 in Quantity B, and $2x$ in Quantity A must have the same value as $2x$ in Quantity B. Because any quantity minus 2 must be less than that quantity minus 1, Quantity B is greater than Quantity A. The correct choice is **(B)**.

2. A

Replacing the exponent x in Quantity B with the equivalent value given in the centered information, you're comparing 4^{2y} with 2^{2y}. Because y is a positive integer, raising 4 to the exponent $2y$ will result in a greater value than raising 2 to the exponent $2y$. The correct choice is **(A)**.

3. D

Do the same thing to both quantities to make them look like the centered information. When you multiply both quantities by $5s$, you get qrs in Quantity A and 15 in Quantity B. Because qrs could be any integer greater than 12, qrs could be greater than, equal to, or less than 15. Choice **(D)** is correct.

4. D

Because angle $X =$ angle Y, at least two sides of the triangle are equal. You can draw two diagrams with X and Y as the base angles of a triangle. In one diagram, make the triangle tall and narrow so that angle X and angle Y are very large and angle Z is very small. In this case, Quantity B is greater. In the second diagram, make the triangle short and wide so that angle Z is much larger than angle X and angle Y. In this case, Quantity A is greater. Because more than one relationship between the quantities is possible, the correct answer is **(D)**.

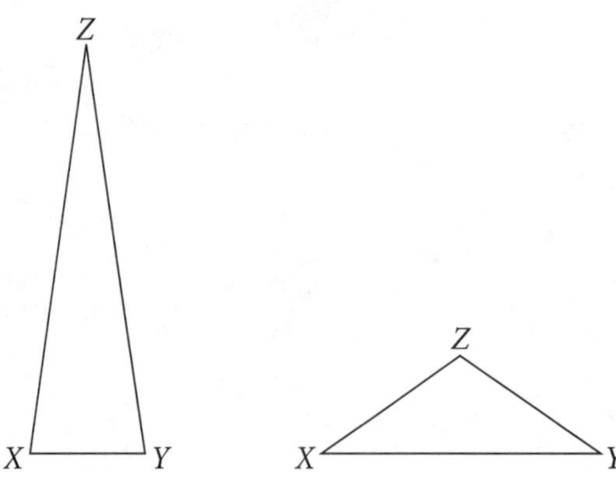

5. C

You don't know the exact relationship between square *A* and square *B*, but it doesn't matter. The problem is actually just comparing the ratios of corresponding parts of two squares. The relationship between the specific side lengths of both squares will also exist between them for any other corresponding length. If a side of one square is twice the length of a side of the second square, the diagonal will also be twice as long. The ratio of the perimeters of the two squares is the same as the ratio of the diagonals.

You can make this abstract relationship concrete by Picking Numbers for the sides of the two squares. Say, for example, that each side of square *A* is 2 and each side of square *B* is 3. Then the ratio of the perimeters is 8:12 or 2:3, and the ratio of the diagonals is $2\sqrt{2} : 3\sqrt{2}$ or $2:3$. Therefore, the quantities are equal. Choice **(C)** is correct.

CHAPTER 12

Problem Solving

INTRODUCTION TO PROBLEM SOLVING

Problem Solving can be broken up into several general mathematics categories: algebra, arithmetic, number properties, and geometry.

In a Problem Solving question, you may be asked to solve a pure math problem or a word problem involving a real-world situation. You will be asked to enter your answer into an onscreen box, select one answer, or select one or more options that correctly answer the problem.

The directions for a Problem Solving question requiring a single answer will look like this:

> **Directions:** Click to select your choice.

A Problem Solving question requiring you to select a single answer will look like this, with ovals next to each answer choice:

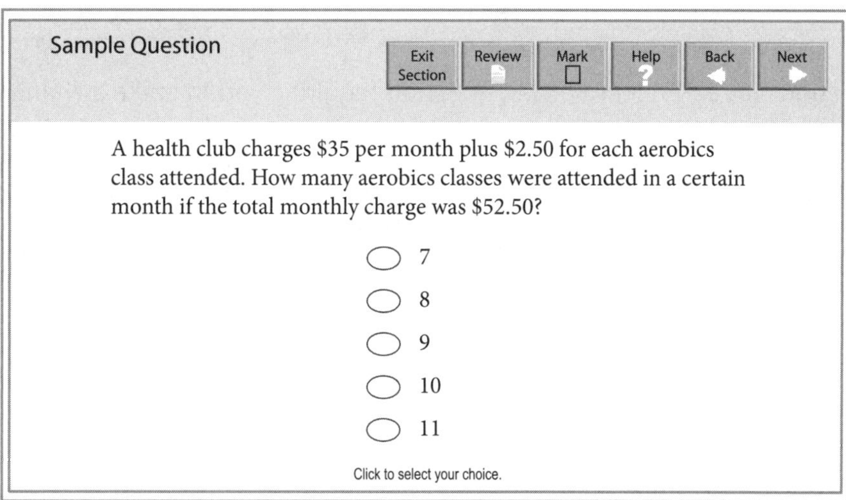

The directions for a Problem Solving question requiring you to select one or more answers will look like this:

> **Directions:** Click to select your choice(s).

If a Problem Solving question asks you to select your choice(s), at least one answer is correct, but as many as all the choices may be correct. You must select all of the correct choices (and none of the incorrect ones) for the question to be counted as correct.

A Problem Solving question requiring you to select one or more answers will look like this, with rectangles next to each answer choice:

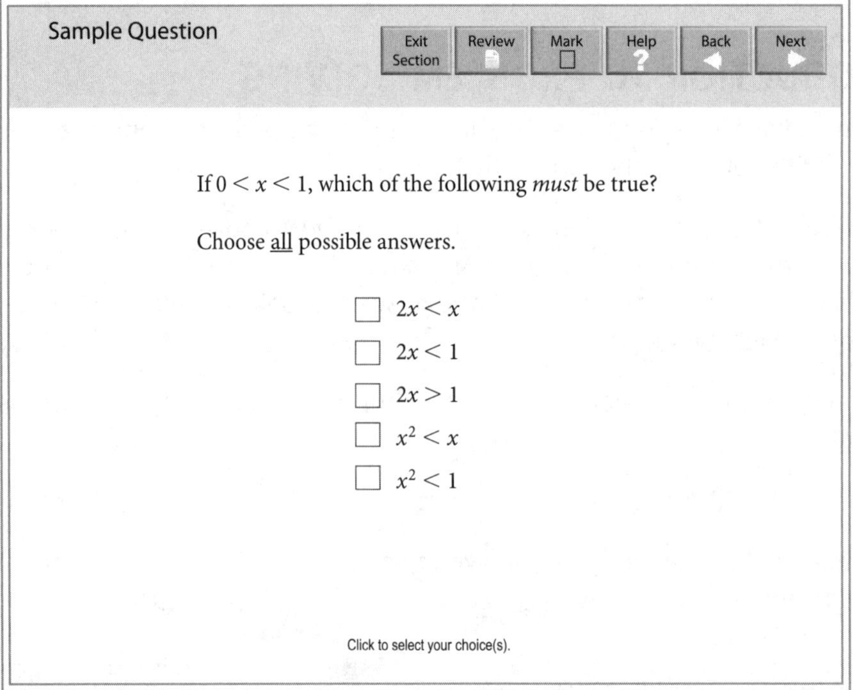

The directions for a Problem Solving question requiring you to make a Numeric Entry will look like this:

> **Directions:** Click in the box and type your numeric answer. Backspace to erase.

Enter your answer as an integer or decimal if there is one box or as a fraction if there are two boxes.

To enter an integer or decimal, type directly in the box or use the Transfer Display button on the calculator.

- Use the backspace key to erase.
- Use a hyphen to enter a negative sign; type a hyphen a second time to remove it. The digits will remain.
- Use a period for a decimal point.
- The Transfer Display button will enter your answer directly from the calculator.
- Equivalent forms of decimals are all correct. (*Example:* 0.14 = 0.140)
- Enter the exact answer unless the question asks you to round your answer.

To enter a fraction, type the numerator and denominator in the appropriate boxes.

- Use a hyphen to enter a negative sign.
- The Transfer Display button does not work for fractions.
- Equivalent forms of fractions are all correct. (*Example:* $\frac{25}{15} = \frac{5}{3}$.) If numbers are large, reduce fractions to fit in boxes.

A Problem Solving question with Numeric Entry will look like this:

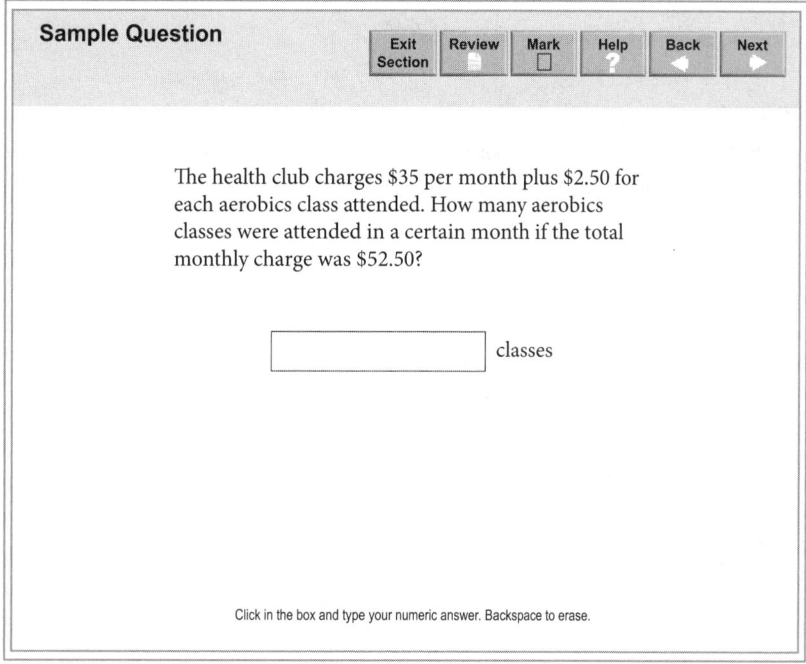

THE KAPLAN METHOD FOR PROBLEM SOLVING

STEP 1 Analyze the question.

STEP 2 Identify the task.

STEP 3 Approach strategically.

STEP 4 Confirm your answer.

HOW THE KAPLAN METHOD FOR PROBLEM SOLVING WORKS

Now let's discuss how the Kaplan Method for Problem Solving works:

STEP 1

Analyze the question.

Look at what the question is asking and what area of math is being tested. Also note any particular trends in the answer choices (e.g., numbers/variables, integers/non-integers) and what information is being given. Unpack as much information as possible.

STEP 2

Identify the task.

Determine what question is being asked before solving the problem. Ask yourself, "What does the correct answer represent?" The GRE intentionally provides wrong answers for test takers who get the right answer to the wrong question.

STEP 3

Approach strategically.

Depending on the type of problem, you may use straightforward math—the textbook approach—to calculate your answer, or you may choose one of the following strategies: Picking Numbers, Backsolving, or Strategic Guessing.

When Picking Numbers to substitute for variables, choose numbers that are manageable and fit the description given in the problem. Backsolving is another form of Picking Numbers; you'll start with one of the answer choices and plug that choice back into the question. Lastly, Strategic Guessing can be a great time-saver on the GRE—being able to make a smart guess on a question is preferable to taking too much time and thus compromising your ability to answer other questions correctly.

STEP 4

Confirm your answer.

Check that your answer makes sense. Also check that you answered the question that was asked.

How to Apply the Kaplan Method for Problem Solving

Now let's apply the Kaplan Method to a Problem Solving question:

> In a bag of candy, 7 of the candies are cherry flavored, 8 are lemon, and 5 are grape. If a candy is chosen randomly from the bag, what is the probability that the candy is *not* lemon?

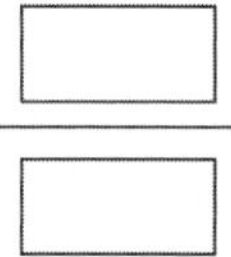

STEP 1

Analyze the question.

You are given the number of candies in a bag and asked to identify the probability that a randomly selected candy is not lemon flavored. You will have to type your answer into the box.

STEP 2

Identify the task.

The probability of an event is defined as $\frac{\text{Number of desired outcomes}}{\text{Number of possible outcomes}}$. You will need to find the number of desired outcomes (those in which you don't choose a lemon candy) and the total number of possible outcomes.

STEP 3

Approach strategically.

There are 20 candies in the bag, so there are 20 possible outcomes. Of all the candies, 12 are not lemon, so there are 12 desired outcomes. So, the probability of *not* lemon is $\frac{12}{20}$. You should avoid reducing fractions for Numeric Entry questions, since all equivalent forms will be counted as correct. Save your time for other questions and limit your risk of committing an error in calculation.

STEP 4

Confirm your answer.

Although it might be fun to get a bag of candies and check your answer in a real-world way, it's not practical, especially on Test Day. A more practical check would be to find the probability of choosing a lemon candy at random to be certain that $P(\text{lemon}) = 1 - P(\text{not lemon})$. There are 8 lemon candies out of 20, so this check can be done easily.

$$P(\text{lemon}) \stackrel{?}{=} 1 - P\,(\text{not lemon})$$
$$\frac{8}{20} \stackrel{?}{=} 1 - \frac{12}{20}$$
$$\frac{8}{20} \stackrel{?}{=} \frac{20}{20} - \frac{12}{20}$$
$$\frac{8}{20} = \frac{8}{20}$$

This check is a way to confirm that the correct numbers have been used in the problem and the correct answer has been found.

Now let's apply the Kaplan Method to a second Problem Solving question:

When n is divided by 14, the remainder is 10. What is the remainder when n is divided by 7?

Ⓐ 2
Ⓑ 3
Ⓒ 4
Ⓓ 5
Ⓔ 6

STEP 1

Analyze the question.

In this question, you are asked to compare the relationship between the numbers 14 and 7 used as divisors.

STEP 2

Identify the task.

The task is to use the fact that division of a number, n, by 14 yields a remainder of 10 to identify the remainder when the same number is divided by 7.

STEP 3

Approach strategically.

A good strategy for this question is to pick a number for n that satisfies the condition for division by 14 and then see what happens when it is divided by 7.

Any number divided by itself will give a remainder of zero. So if we need a remainder of 10, we want a number that is 10 more than the number we are dividing by. Be careful; you may be thinking of choosing $14 \div 7 = 2$ or $10 \div 2 = 5$. But these are both trap answer choices because the question also involves using a remainder. Therefore, 24 is a great number to pick here, because when we try 24:

$24 \div 14 = 1$ Remainder 10

Now that we've confirmed that 24 works, we answer the question that's being asked. Divide 24 by 7:

$24 \div 7 = 3$ Remainder 3

Answer choice **(B)** is the correct answer.

STEP 4

Confirm your answer.

You can quickly double-check your work, or you can try another number for *n* that results in a remainder of 10 when divided by 14:

$38 \div 14 = 2$ Remainder 10, and $38 \div 7 = 5$ Remainder 3

So the remainder is 3 in each case. The correct answer is **(B)**.

Now let's apply the Kaplan Method to a third Problem Solving question:

The line $4x + 6y = 24$ passes through which of the following points?

Indicate all possible answers.

- [A] (0,4)
- [B] (2,3)
- [C] (3,2)
- [D] (5,4)
- [E] (9,–1)

STEP 1

Analyze the question.

This question is about a line on the coordinate plane. The equation is a function that represents a line. The numbers in the parentheses in the answer choices represent points (x,y) that are mentioned in the equation.

STEP 2

Identify the task.

Your job is to identify which of the given points lie on the line. A line passes through a point if the coordinates of the point make the equation of the line true, so this is the same as saying that you need to find out which point(s), when plugged into the equation, make the equation true.

STEP 3

Approach strategically.

You need to find all correct answers, so test all of them. Substitute the first coordinate for x and the second coordinate for y.

(A) Test (0,4): $4x + 6y = 24 \rightarrow 4(0) + 6(4) = 0 + 24 = 24$. This works.
(B) Test (2,3): $4x + 6y = 24 \rightarrow 4(2) + 6(3) = 8 + 18 \neq 24$. Eliminate.
(C) Test (3,2): $4x + 6y = 24 \rightarrow 4(3) + 6(2) = 12 + 12 = 24$. This works.
(D) Test (5,4): $4x + 6y = 24 \rightarrow 4(5) + 6(4) = 20 + 24 \neq 24$. Eliminate.
(E) Test (9,–1): $4x + 6y = 24 \rightarrow 4(9) + 6(-1) = 36 - 6 \neq 24$. Eliminate.

So choices **(A)** and **(C)** are correct.

STEP 4

Confirm your answer.

Double-check your work to make sure you haven't made any careless errors, such as mistakenly plugging in a value for x when dealing with the variable y.

KAPLAN'S ADDITIONAL TIPS FOR PROBLEM SOLVING

Choose an efficient strategy

The GRE is not a traditional math test that requires that you show your work in order to get credit, testing the process as well as the answer. The GRE tests only the answer—not how you found it. Because time is often your biggest concern on the GRE, the best way to each solution is often the quickest way, and the quickest way is often not straightforward math. Through practice, you'll become familiar with approaching each question in a more strategic way.

Rely on Kaplan math strategies

Using Kaplan strategies is a way to use reasoning in conjunction with mathematics to answer a question quickly. There may also be cases in which you can combine approaches: for example, using straightforward math to simplify an equation, then picking manageable numbers for the variables to solve that equation.

Picking numbers

Problems that seem difficult can be good candidates for the Picking Numbers strategy. They include problems where either the question or the answer choices have variables, the problem tests a number property you don't recall, or the problem and the answer choices deal with percents or fractions without using actual values.

Backsolving

Backsolving is a similar strategy to Picking Numbers, except that you'll use one of the five answer choices as the number to pick. After all, the testmaker gives you the correct answer; it's just mixed in with the wrong answers. Remember, numerical answer choices are always in ascending or descending order. Use that information to your advantage when using Backsolving. Start with either **(B)** or **(D)** first, because you'll have a 40 percent chance of finding the correct answer based on your first round of calculations. If you don't happen to pick the correct answer the first time, reason whether the number you started with was too large or too small. If you test choice **(B)** when the answer choices are in ascending order and **(B)** turns out to be too large, then **(A)** is the correct answer. If **(B)** is too small, then test choice **(D)**. If **(D)** is too large, then **(C)** is the correct answer. If **(D)** is too small, then **(E)** is correct. The opposite would be true if the choices were in descending order. Backsolving allows you to find the correct answer without ever needing to test more than two of the answer choices.

Use strategic guessing

This is a good strategy if you can eliminate choices by applying number property rules or by estimating because gaps between answer choices are wide.

If some of the choices are out of the realm of possibility, eliminate them and move on.

PROBLEM SOLVING PRACTICE SET

Try the following Problem Solving questions using the Kaplan Method for Problem Solving. If you're up to the challenge, time yourself; on Test Day, you'll want to spend only about 2 minutes on each question.

1. If $r = 3s$, $s = 5t$, $t = 2u$, and $u \neq 0$, what is the value of $\frac{rst}{u^3}$?

Ⓐ 30
Ⓑ 60
Ⓒ 150
Ⓓ 300
Ⓔ 600

2. In the diagram, l_1 is parallel to l_2. The measure of angle q is 40 degrees. What is the sum of the measures of the acute angles shown in the diagram?

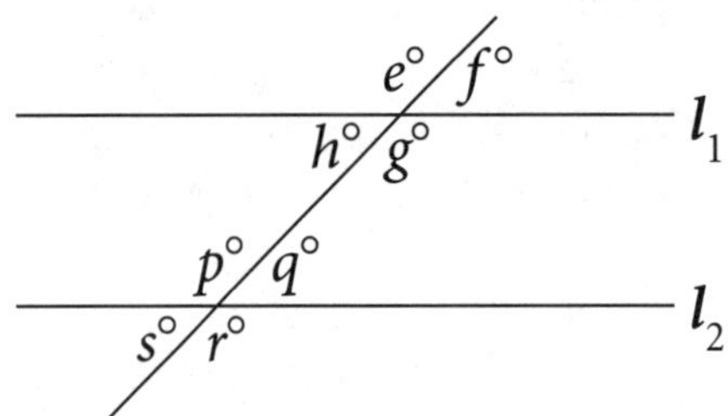

Note: Figure not drawn to scale.

[   ] degrees

3. At Central Park Zoo, the ratio of sea lions to penguins is 4:11. If there are 84 more penguins than sea lions, how many sea lions are there?

Ⓐ 24
Ⓑ 36
Ⓒ 48
Ⓓ 72
Ⓔ 121

4. Which of the following are prime numbers between $\frac{5}{2}$ and $\frac{43}{5}$? Indicate <u>all</u> possible answers.

   [A] 3
   [B] 4
   [C] 5
   [D] 7
   [E] 9

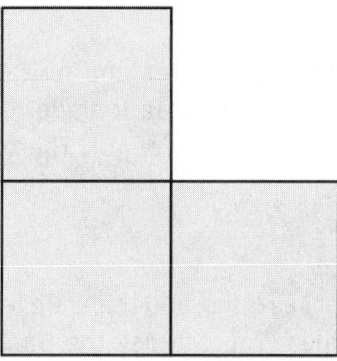

5. The figure above is made up of 3 squares. If the perimeter of the figure is 40 units, what is the area of the figure in square units?

   (A) 50
   (B) 75
   (C) 120
   (D) 150
   (E) 200

PROBLEM SOLVING PRACTICE SET ANSWERS AND EXPLANATIONS

1. E

The other variables all build upon u, so use the Picking Numbers strategy: pick a small number for u and find the values for r, s, and t. For instance, if $u = 1$, then $t = 2u$, so $t = 2$; $s = 5t$, so $s = 10$; and $r = 3s$, so $r = 30$.

So, $\frac{rst}{u^3} = \frac{30 \times 10 \times 2}{1 \times 1 \times 1} = 600$. The correct answer is (E).

2. 160

In the diagram, there are four acute angles and four obtuse angles created when the parallel lines are cut by the transversal. If angle q has a measure of 40°, then angles s, h, and f each also has a measure of 40°. Therefore, the sum of their degree measures is **160**.

3. C

You need to find the number of sea lions, and there are fewer sea lions than penguins, so starting small is a good idea. You can use the Backsolving strategy; start with choice **(B)**, 36. If there are 36 sea lions, then there are $36 + 84 = 120$ penguins, and the ratio of sea lions to penguins is $\frac{36}{120} = \frac{3}{10}$. This ratio is less than $\frac{4}{11}$, so your answer must be larger. If you try **(D)**, there are 72 sea lions and there are $72 + 84 = 156$ penguins, and the ratio of sea lions to penguins is $\frac{72}{156} = \frac{6}{13}$. Since this ratio is too large, the correct answer must be **(C)**.

4. A, C, D

You need to find a range of values between two improper fractions. First, change the improper fractions to mixed numbers: $\frac{5}{2} = 2\frac{1}{2}$ and $\frac{43}{5} = 8\frac{3}{5}$. Now, a prime number is a positive integer with only two distinct factors, 1 and itself. The prime numbers in the answer choices are 3, 5, and 7, and they are all between $2\frac{1}{2}$ and $8\frac{3}{5}$. So the correct answers are **(A)**, **(C)**, and **(D)**.

5. B

There are 8 side lengths of the squares that make up the perimeter, which you are told is 40. So, each side of each square must be 5 units. The area of each square can be found by squaring one side, so each square has an area of 25 square units. Since there are three squares, the total area of the figure is 75 square units. The correct answer is **(B)**.

CHAPTER 13

Data Interpretation

INTRODUCTION TO DATA INTERPRETATION QUESTIONS

Data Interpretation questions are based on information located in tables or graphs, and they are often statistics oriented. The data may be located in one table or graph, but you might also need to extract data from two or more tables or graphs. There will be a set of questions for you to answer based on each data presentation.

You may be asked to choose one or more answers from a set of answer choices or to enter your answer in a Numeric Entry field.

The directions for Data Interpretation questions will look like this:

Questions 15–17 are based on the following table.

PERCENT OF SALES PER CLIENT FOR CURTAIN FABRIC OVER THREE MONTHS

	May	June	July
The Home Touch	45%	25%	48%
Curtains Unlimited	30%	23%	23%
Max's Curtain Supply	9%	23%	17%
Valances by Val	13%	20%	8%
Wendy's Windows	3%	9%	4%

A Data Interpretation question that requires you to choose exactly one correct answer will look like this:

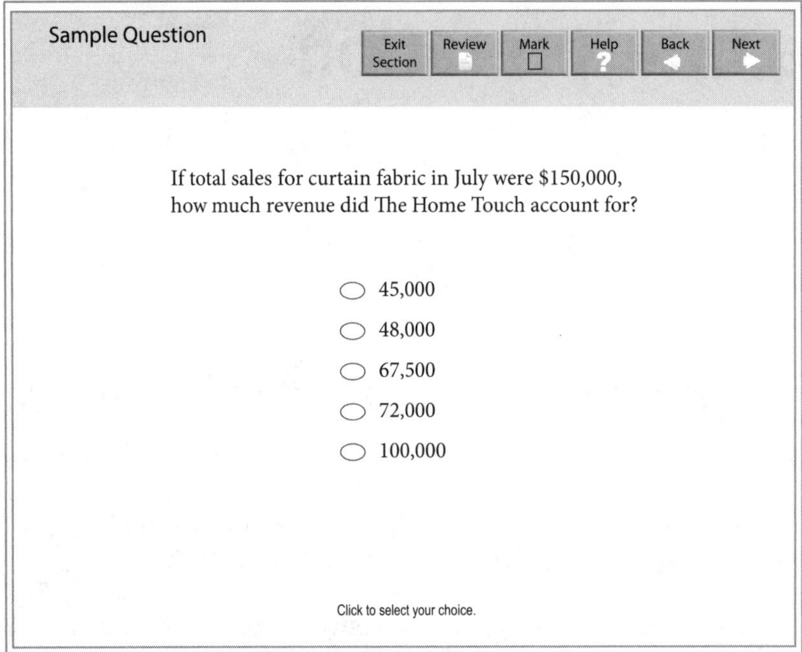

A Data Interpretation question that requires you to select all the answer choices that apply will look like this:

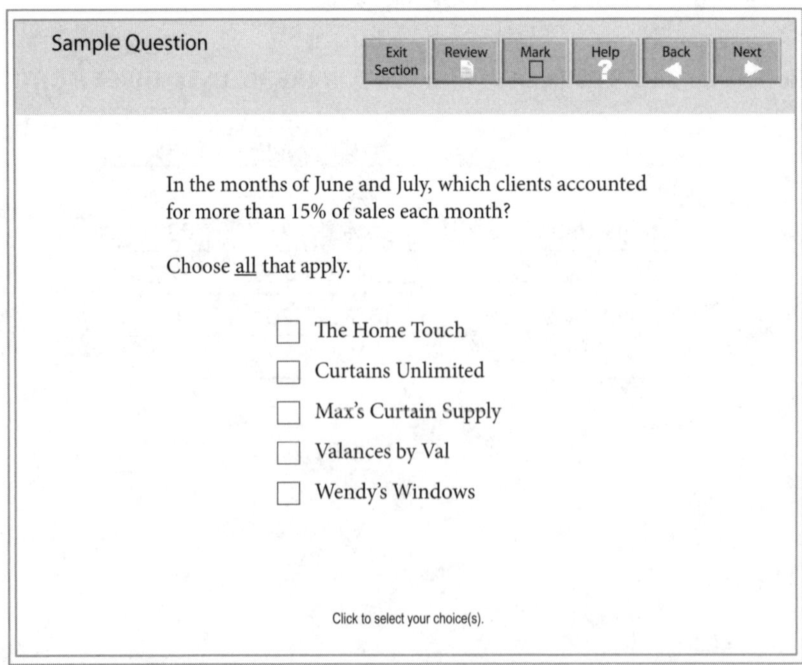

A Data Interpretation question that requires you to enter your numeric answer in a box will look like this:

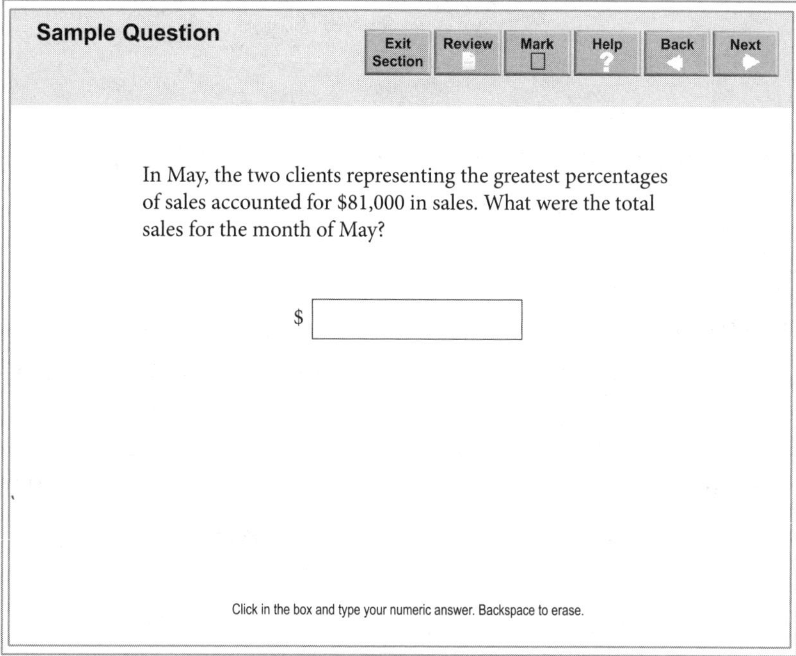

THE KAPLAN METHOD FOR DATA INTERPRETATION

STEP 1 Analyze the tables and graphs.

STEP 2 Approach strategically.

How the Kaplan Method for Data Interpretation Works

Now let's discuss how the Kaplan Method for Data Interpretation works.

STEP 1

Analyze the tables and graphs.

Tables, graphs, and charts often come in pairs that are linked in some way (for example, a manufacturer's total revenue and its revenue by product line). Familiarize yourself with the information in both graphs (or tables) and with how the two are related before attacking the questions. Scan the figures for these components:

- **Title**. Read the charts' titles to ensure you can get to the right chart or graph quickly.
- **Scale**. Check the units of measurement. Does the graph measure miles per minute or hour? Missing the units can drastically change your answer.
- **Notes**. Read any accompanying notes—the GRE will typically give you information only if it is helpful or even critical to getting the correct answer.
- **Key**. If there are multiple bars or lines on a graph, make sure you understand the key so you can match up the correct quantities with the correct items.

STEP 2

Approach strategically.

Data Interpretation questions are designed to test your understanding of fractions and percents and your attention to detail. Taking a split second to make sure you answered the right question can make the difference between a correct answer and the "right" answer to the wrong question.

Questions tend to become more complex as you move through a set. For instance, if a question set contains two graphs, the first question likely refers to just one graph. A later question will most often combine data from both graphs. If you don't use both graphs for this later question, the chances are good you have missed something.

No matter how difficult graph questions appear at first glance, you can usually simplify single-answer multiple-choice questions by taking advantage of their answer-choice format. By approximating the answer rather than calculating it wherever possible, you can quickly identify the right one. As we saw with Problem Solving, estimation can be one of the fastest ways to identify the correct answer in math problems. Data Interpretation questions benefit from this strategy, as they tend to be the most time-consuming questions to answer.

HOW TO APPLY THE KAPLAN METHOD FOR DATA INTERPRETATION

Now let's apply the Kaplan Method to a Data Interpretation question:

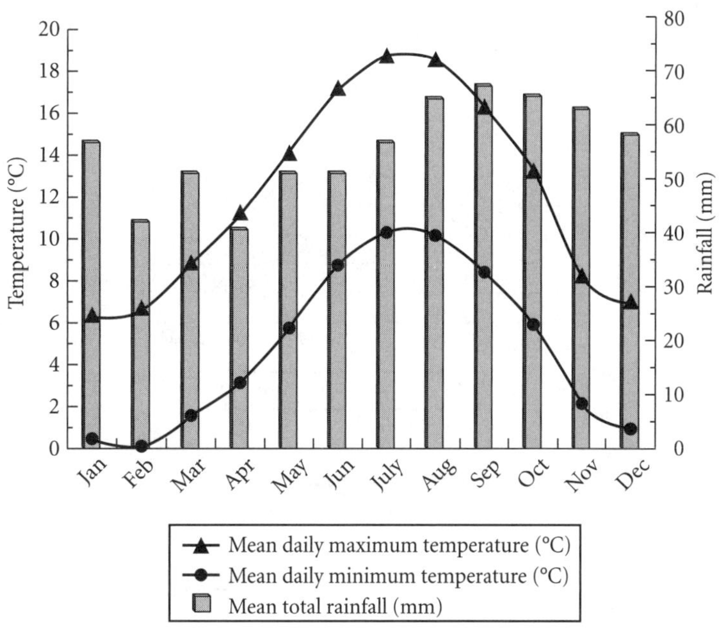

The Tourism Board of City S uses the information provided in the climograph to market the city as a tourist destination. One criterion is that the average monthly rainfall be less than 60 millimeters. What fraction of the months meet this criterion?

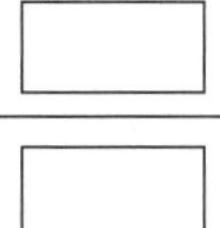

STEP 1

Analyze the tables and graphs.

Take the analysis of the graph step-by-step. Start with the title of the graph to verify that the data given are for City S. Then take note of the scale for each type of information—degrees Celsius for temperature and millimeters for rainfall. There are data for each month of the year, which means you will not have to convert the units to answer the question that's being asked.

STEP 2

Approach strategically.

The question asks only about rainfall; those data are given by the bars on the graph. According to the bars, rainfall is greater than 60 mm in August, September, October, and November. That's 4 of 12 months that *do not* meet the criteria, so 8 of 12 months *do* meet it. You may enter the fraction $\frac{8}{12}$ directly into the boxes, and your answer will be accepted. It is *not* required that you reduce it.

Now let's apply the Kaplan Method to a second Data Interpretation question:

CUSTOMERS WHO SWITCHED SERVICE PROVIDERS (IN MILLIONS OF CUSTOMERS)

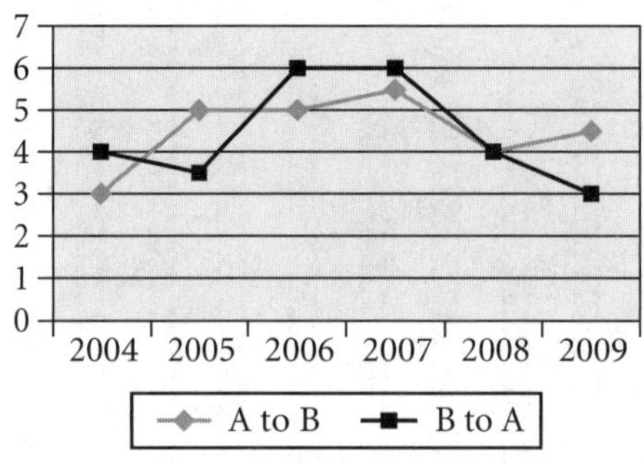

COMPANY A PROFIT 2008

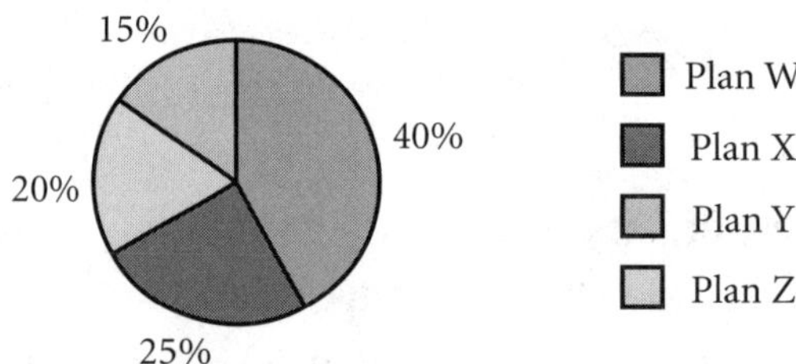

In 2008, Company A had a total profit of \$220 million. If half of the customers who switched to Company A were responsible for half of the profit for Plan X, how much did these customers contribute per person toward Company A's profit for the year?

- [A] \$1.10
- [B] \$13.75
- [C] \$20.25
- [D] \$27.50
- [E] \$55.00

STEP 1

Analyze the tables and graphs.

This question has information about numbers of customers switching service providers for various years. It also has information about one company's profit for the year 2008, so the data in the two graphs will be linked by the year 2008.

STEP 2

Approach strategically.

Approach the question methodically, starting with identifying the number of customers who switched to Company A. The line chart indicates that 4 million customers switched to Company A. This is the only information needed from the top graph.

The pie chart shows the breakdown of profit from the various plans offered and indicates that 25 percent of the profit came from Plan X.

The other information you need to get to the correct answer is given in the question stem:

- Profit of $220 million.
- Half of the customers who switched were responsible for half of Plan X's profits.

Now that your information is organized, all you need to do is the calculation. Plan X accounts for 25 percent of $220 million = $55 million. Half of $55 million is $27.5 million.

If 4 million people switched, then half of the people who switched would be 2 million.

The last step is to divide $27.5 by 2 (you can drop the zeroes in the millions because they will cancel out): $27.5 ÷ 2 = $13.75. The correct choice is **(B)**.

Now let's apply the Kaplan Method to a third Data Interpretation question:

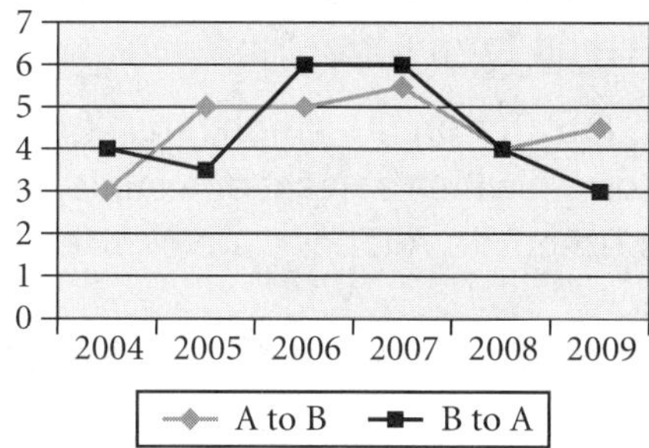

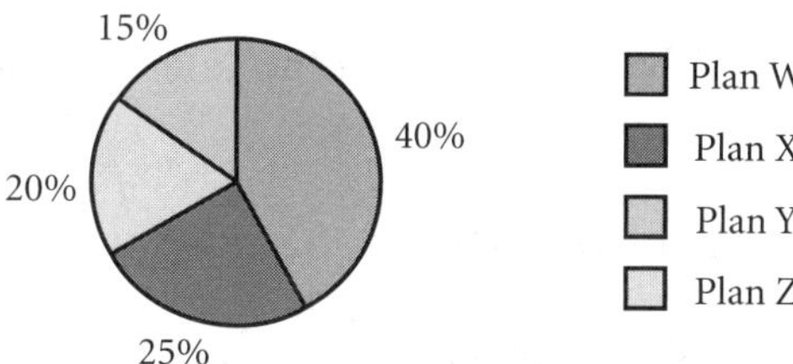

The management of Company B is most interested in the data for the years in which there were at least one million *more* customers who switched from

Company A to Company B than switched from Company B to Company A. In which years did this happen?

Choose all that apply.

A 2005
B 2006
C 2007
D 2008
E 2009

STEP 1

Analyze the tables and graphs.

This question asks for a comparison of facts between Company A and Company B. Take time to verify which line in the top graph represents customers switching to Company A and which line represents customers switching to Company B. Confirm that the title states that the data are given in millions and then look at the scale on the line graph.

STEP 2

Approach strategically.

After examining the line graph carefully, you are ready to gather the information needed to answer the question. The years that satisfy the requirement are those years for which the line representing A to B is at least one full horizontal row above the line representing B to A. Read the graph carefully because you must identify all the correct choices to get credit for a correct answer.

When you are clear what to look for on the graph, start from the left and identify the years 2005 and 2009 as those in which at least one million more customers switched from A to B than switched from B to A. These are choices **(A)** and **(E)**.

KAPLAN'S ADDITIONAL TIPS FOR DATA INTERPRETATION QUESTIONS

Slow Down

There's always a lot going on in Data Interpretation problems—both in the charts and in the questions themselves. If you slow down the first time through, you can avoid calculation errors and having to reread the questions and charts.

Pace Yourself Wisely

To ensure that you score as many points on the exam as possible, use the allotted time for a section wisely. Remember that each question type has the same value. If you must miss a few questions in a section, make them the ones that would take you the longest to answer, not the ones at the end of the section that you could have answered correctly but simply didn't get to. Data Interpretation questions are generally some of the more time-consuming ones to answer, and if answering them isn't one of your strong suits, save them for the end.

DATA INTERPRETATION PRACTICE SET

Try the following Data Interpretation questions using the Kaplan Method for Data Interpretation. If you're up to the challenge, time yourself; on Test Day, you'll want to spend only about 2 minutes on each question.

Questions 1–5 are based on the following graphs.

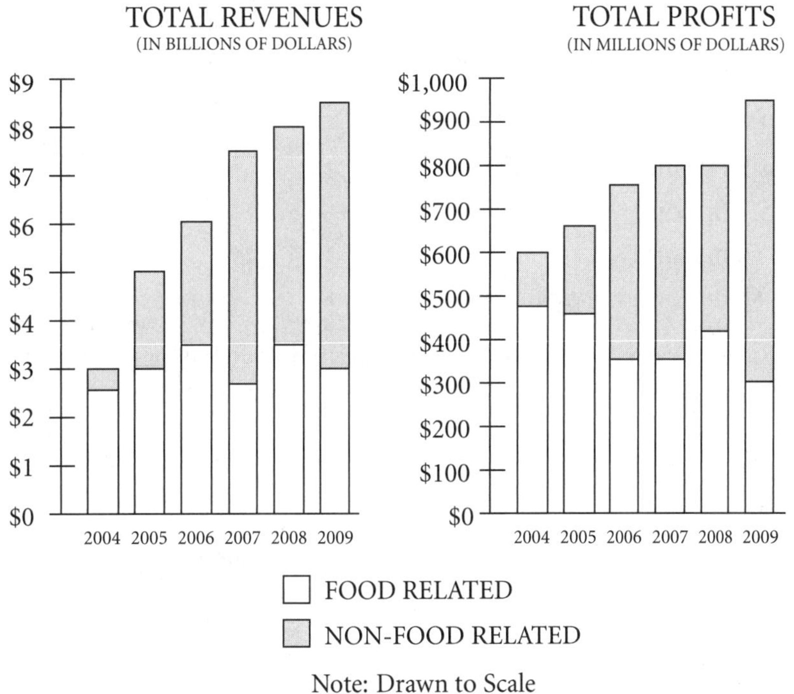

Note: Drawn to Scale

PERCENT OF REVENUES FROM FOOD-RELATED OPERATIONS IN 2009 BY CATEGORY

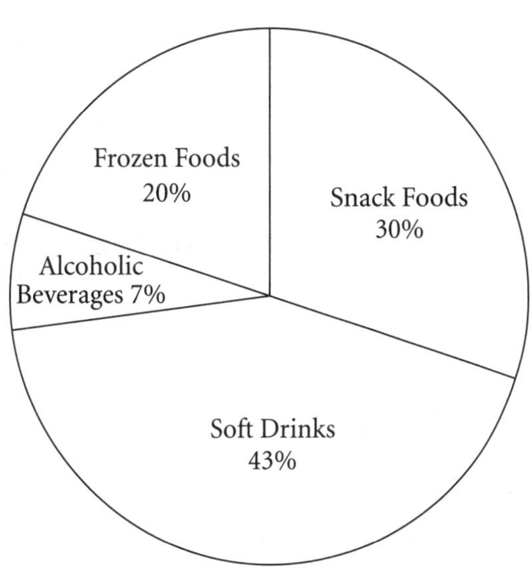

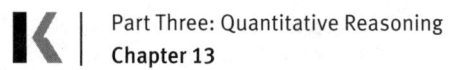

1. Approximately how much did total revenues increase from 2004 to 2007?

   (A) $0.5 billion
   (B) $1.5 billion
   (C) $4 billion
   (D) $4.5 billion
   (E) $5 billion

2. For the year in which profits from food-related operations increased over the previous year, total revenues were approximately:

   (A) $3.5 billion
   (B) $4.5 billion
   (C) $5.7 billion
   (D) $6 billion
   (E) $8 billion

3. In 2008, total profits represented approximately what percent of total revenues?

   (A) 50%
   (B) 20%
   (C) 10%
   (D) 5%
   (E) 1%

4. For the first year in which revenues from non-food-related operations surpassed $4.5 billion, total profits were approximately:

   (A) $250 million
   (B) $450 million
   (C) $550 million
   (D) $650 million
   (E) $800 million

5. In 2009, how many millions of dollars were revenues from frozen food operations?

   [ ] millions of dollars

DATA INTERPRETATION PRACTICE SET ANSWERS AND EXPLANATIONS

1. D

This question asks about total revenues, so you should refer to the left bar graph. Each bar in the graph has two components, but you want to look at the total height of the bars for 2004 and 2007 because the question asks about total revenues. Total revenues for 2004 appear to be \$3 billion, and for 2007 they appear to be about \$7.5 billion. So the increase is roughly \$7.5 billion – \$3 billion = \$4.5 billion. Answer choice **(D)** is correct.

2. E

You have to refer to both bar graphs to answer this question. First, refer to the right bar graph to find the lone year in which food-related profits increased over the previous year—the only year in which the unshaded portion of the bar increases in size is 2008. Now that you've zeroed in on the year, refer to the left bar graph to determine the total revenues for that year, which appear to be about \$8 billion. Answer choice **(E)** is correct.

3. C

This is a percent question, so start with the bar graphs. You need the figures from both food-related and non-food-related sources, so look at the total height of the bars. From the right bar graph, the total profits for 2008 appear to be \$800 million; from the left bar graph, total revenues for that year appear to be \$8 billion (i.e., \$8,000 million). Now, convert the part/whole into a percent:

$$\frac{800\text{ million}}{8\text{ billion}} = \frac{800\text{ million}}{8{,}000\text{ million}} = \frac{1}{10} = 10\%$$

4. E

First, find the year for which revenues from non-food-related operations surpassed \$4.5 billion on the left bar graph. Finding the correct bar is made more difficult by the fact that you have to deal with the shaded portion, which is at the top of the bar, not at the bottom. Looking carefully, you should then see that 2007 is the year in question. The question asks for total *profits*, so once again refer to the right bar graph, and you'll see the profits for that year are around \$800 million. This matches answer choice **(E)**.

5. 600

Finally, you have a question that refers to the pie chart. You are asked about revenues from frozen food operations, and the pie chart tells you that frozen foods represent 20 percent of all food-related revenues for 2009. To convert this into an amount, you need to locate the amount of food-related revenues for 2009. Once again, refer to the left bar graph, where you'll find that food-related revenues in 2009 were \$3 billion, or \$3,000 million. Then calculate that 20 percent of \$3,000 million is **\$600** million.

CHAPTER 14

Quantitative Reasoning Practice Sets

In this chapter, you will take three practice sections, composed of 20 questions each. A diagnostic tool is provided after each section to help you learn from your mistakes. Then you can continue to the next set with more awareness of the traps you may encounter.

REVIEW OF THE KAPLAN METHODS FOR QUANTITATIVE REASONING QUESTION TYPES

Before starting your practice sets, review the steps and strategies you have studied for answering each type of Quantitative Reasoning question quickly, efficiently, and correctly before starting your Practice Sets.

THE KAPLAN METHOD FOR QUANTITATIVE COMPARISON

STEP 1 Analyze the centered information and quantities.

STEP 2 Approach strategically.

THE KAPLAN METHOD FOR PROBLEM SOLVING

STEP 1 **Analyze the question.**

STEP 2 **Identify the task.**

STEP 3 **Approach strategically.**

STEP 4 **Confirm your answer.**

THE KAPLAN METHOD FOR DATA INTERPRETATION

STEP 1 **Analyze the tables and graphs.**

STEP 2 **Approach strategically.**

QUANTITATIVE REASONING PRACTICE SET 1

NUMBERS

All numbers are real numbers.

FIGURES

The position of points, lines, angles, and so on may be assumed to be in the order shown; all lengths and angle measures may be assumed to be positive.

Lines shown as straight may be assumed to be straight.

Figures lie in the plane of the paper unless otherwise stated.

Figures that accompany questions are intended to provide useful information. However, unless a note states that a figure has been drawn to scale, you should solve the problems by using your knowledge of mathematics, not by estimation or measurement.

DIRECTIONS

Each of the following questions, 1–8, consists of two quantities, Quantity A and Quantity B. You are to compare the two quantities and choose

Ⓐ if Quantity A is greater
Ⓑ if Quantity B is greater
Ⓒ if the two quantities are equal
Ⓓ if the relationship cannot be determined from the information given

Common Information

In a question, information concerning one or both of the quantities to be compared is centered above the two quantities. A symbol that appears in both quantities represents the same thing in Quantity A as it does in Quantity B.

1.

Quantity A	Quantity B
The number of distinct ways to form an ordered line of 3 people by choosing from 6 people	The number of distinct ways to form an unordered group of 3 people by choosing from 10 people

Ⓐ Quantity A is greater.
Ⓑ Quantity B is greater.
Ⓒ The two quantities are equal.
Ⓓ The relationship cannot be determined from the information given.

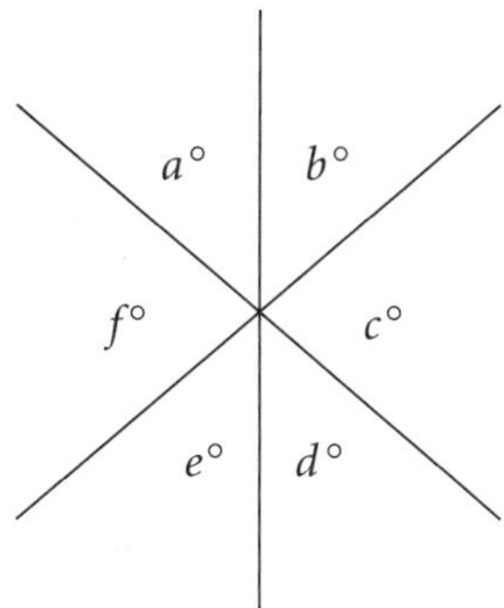

2.

Quantity A	Quantity B
$a + c + e$	$b + d + f$

Ⓐ Quantity A is greater.
Ⓑ Quantity B is greater.
Ⓒ The two quantities are equal.
Ⓓ The relationship cannot be determined from the information given.

$$7p + 3 = r$$
$$3p + 7 = s$$

3.

Quantity A	Quantity B
r	s

Ⓐ Quantity A is greater.
Ⓑ Quantity B is greater.
Ⓒ The two quantities are equal.
Ⓓ The relationship cannot be determined from the information given.

The original cost of a shirt is x dollars.

4.

Quantity A	Quantity B
x	The cost of the shirt if the original cost is first increased by 10% and then decreased by 10%

Ⓐ Quantity A is greater.
Ⓑ Quantity B is greater.
Ⓒ The two quantities are equal.
Ⓓ The relationship cannot be determined from the information given.

There were x dictionaries in a bookstore. After $\frac{1}{8}$ of them were purchased, 10 more dictionaries were shipped in, bringing the total number of dictionaries to 52.

5. Quantity A: x Quantity B: 50

Ⓐ Quantity A is greater.
Ⓑ Quantity B is greater.
Ⓒ The two quantities are equal.
Ⓓ The relationship cannot be determined from the information given.

There are n people in a room. One-third of them leave the room. Four people enter the room. There are now $\frac{5}{6}$ of the original number of people in the room.

6. Quantity A: n Quantity B: 20

Ⓐ Quantity A is greater.
Ⓑ Quantity B is greater.
Ⓒ The two quantities are equal.
Ⓓ The relationship cannot be determined from the information given.

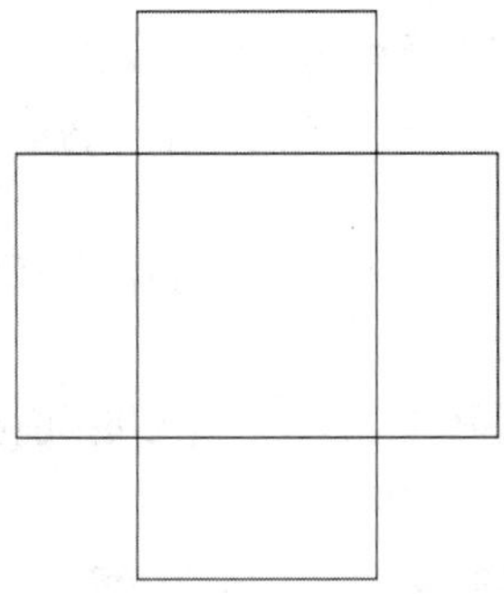

Note: Figure not drawn to scale.

Two rectangles with dimensions 2 meters by 4 meters overlap to form the figure above. All the angles shown measure 90°.

7. Quantity A: The perimeter of the figure, in meters Quantity B: 16

Ⓐ Quantity A is greater.
Ⓑ Quantity B is greater.
Ⓒ The two quantities are equal.
Ⓓ The relationship cannot be determined from the information given.

x is an integer.
$1 < x < 9$

8. Quantity A: $(\sqrt{x} + \sqrt{x})^2$ Quantity B: $x + x\sqrt{x}$

Ⓐ Quantity A is greater.
Ⓑ Quantity B is greater.
Ⓒ The two quantities are equal.
Ⓓ The relationship cannot be determined from the information given.

9. If $\frac{x}{y} = \frac{2}{3}$ and $x + y = 15$, which of the following is greater than y?

Indicate all possible choices.

[A] $\sqrt{65}$
[B] $\sqrt{82}$
[C] $\sqrt{99}$
[D] $\sqrt{101}$
[E] $\sqrt{122}$

10. The product of two integers is 10. Which of the following could be the average (arithmetic mean) of the two numbers?

Indicate all possible choices.

[A] -5.5
[B] -3.5
[C] -1.5
[D] 1.5
[E] 3.5

11. Which of the following is greater than the sum of the distinct prime factors of 210?

Indicate all possible choices.

[A] 12
[B] 17
[C] 19
[D] 21
[E] 24

12. The average (arithmetic mean) bowling score of n bowlers is 160. The average of these n scores together with a score of 170 is 161. What is the number of bowlers, n?

[ ] bowlers

13. Set T consists of five integers: the first five odd prime numbers when counting upward from zero. This gives set T a standard deviation of approximately 3.71. Which of the following values, if added to the set T, would increase the standard deviation of set T?

(A) 11
(B) 9
(C) 7.8
(D) 4.15
(E) 3.7

14.

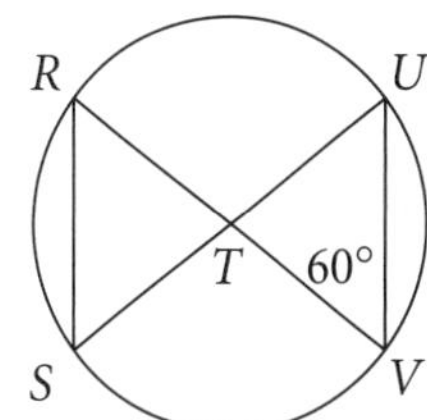

The circle shown has center T. The measure of angle TVU is 60°. If the circle has a radius of 3, what is the length of segment RS?

(A) 2
(B) $2\sqrt{2}$
(C) 3
(D) $3\sqrt{3}$
(E) $6\sqrt{2}$

15. What is the probability of rolling a total of 7 with a single roll of two fair six-sided dice, each with the distinct numbers 1–6 on each side?

(A) $\frac{1}{12}$

(B) $\frac{1}{6}$

(C) $\frac{2}{7}$

(D) $\frac{1}{3}$

(E) $\frac{1}{2}$

16. If it takes three days for 10 workers to finish building one house, how many days will it take 15 workers to finish four houses?

[ ] days

Questions 17–20 are based on the following graph and table.

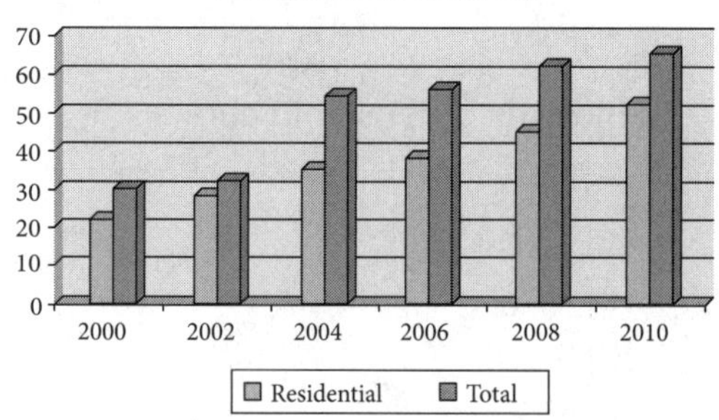

DAILY WATER USAGE STATISTICS

(with efficient appliances and good maintenance)

Use	Gallons per Capita
Showers	9
Clothes washers	10
Toilets	8
Leaks	4
Faucets	11
Other	4

17. Which best describes the range (in billions of gallons) for residential water consumption from 2000 to 2010, inclusive?

(A) 10
(B) 20
(C) 30
(D) 40
(E) 50

18. In the year in which total usage exceeded residential usage by the least number of gallons, approximately what percent of total usage was residential usage?

(A) 68%
(B) 75%
(C) 88%
(D) 95%
(E) 98%

19. In 2004, only 10,000 residents of town W lived in homes with efficient appliances and good maintenance. How many gallons per day were used by these residents for the three daily household purposes requiring the most water?

(A) 110,000
(B) 160,000
(C) 270,000
(D) 300,000
(E) 460,000

20. Households with efficient appliances and good maintenance can reduce water consumption by about 35%. If half of the residential consumption in town W in 2010 was by households with efficient appliances and good maintenance, how many gallons of water (in billions) were saved that year?

(A) 5
(B) 14
(C) 40
(D) 52
(E) 65

QUANTITATIVE REASONING PRACTICE SET 1 ANSWER KEY

1. C
2. C
3. D
4. A
5. B
6. A
7. C
8. A
9. B, C, D, E
10. A, B, E
11. C, D, E
12. 9
13. E
14. C
15. B
16. 8
17. C
18. C
19. D
20. B

DIAGNOSE YOUR RESULTS

Diagnostic Tool

Tally up your score and write your results below.

Total

Total Correct: ________ out of 20 correct

By Question Type

Quantitative Comparison (questions 1–8) ________ out of 8 correct

Problem Solving (questions 9–16) ________ out of 8 correct

Data Interpretation (questions 17–20) ________ out of 4 correct

Look back at the questions you got wrong and think about your experience answering them.

STEP 1

Find the roadblocks.

If you struggled to answer some questions, then to improve your score, you need to pinpoint exactly what "roadblocks" tripped you up. To do that, ask yourself the following two questions:

Am I weak in the skills being tested?

This will be very easy for you to judge. Maybe you've forgotten how to calculate an average or what PEMDAS stands for. If you know you need to brush up on your math skills, try the *Kaplan GRE Math Workbook*, which contains a focused review of all the fundamental math concepts tested on the GRE, as well as practice exercises to build speed and accuracy.

Did the question types throw me off?

Then you need to become more comfortable with them! Quantitative Comparisons have a unique format, and Data Interpretation can be daunting with its charts, graphs, and tables. If you struggled, go back to the beginning of the Quantitative Reasoning section of this book and review the Kaplan principles and methods for the question types you found challenging. Make sure you understand the principles and how to apply the methods. These strategies will help you improve your speed and efficiency on Test Day. Remember, it's not a math test; it's a critical reasoning test.

Also, get as much practice as you can so that you grow more at ease with the question formats. For even more practice, try the *Kaplan GRE Math Workbook,* which includes practice sets for each question type.

STEP 2

Find the blind spots.

Did you answer some questions quickly and confidently but get them wrong anyway?

When you come across wrong answers like these, you need to figure out what you thought you were doing right, what it turns out you were doing wrong, and why that happened. The best way to do that is to **read the answer explanations!**

The explanations give you a detailed breakdown of why the correct answer is correct and why all the other answers choices are incorrect. This helps to reinforce the Kaplan principles and methods for each question type and helps you figure out what blindsided you so it doesn't happen again. Also, just as with your "roadblocks," try to get in as much practice as you can.

STEP 3

Reinforce your strengths.

Now read through all the answer explanations for the ones you got right. You should check every explanation because, if you guessed correctly without actually knowing how to get the right answer, reading the explanations helps you make sure that you learn what you need to. Equally importantly, on a problem you knew how to do, there may be a faster way to get to the answer than the way you chose, or even just a different way. Understanding more than one approach to a given problem will deepen your critical thinking skills. Reading the explanation for a question you got right also helps to reinforce the Kaplan principles and methods for each question type, which in turn helps you work more efficiently so you can get the score you want. Keep your skills sharp with more practice.

As soon as you are comfortable with all the GRE question types and Kaplan methods, complete a full-length practice test under timed conditions. Practice tests serve as milestones; they help you to chart your progress! So don't save them all for the final weeks before your Test Day. For even more practice, you can also try the Kaplan GRE Quiz Bank. You get more than 2,500 questions that you can access 24/7 from any Internet browser, and each question comes with a comprehensive explanation. You can even customize your quizzes based on question type, content, and difficulty level. Take quizzes in Timed Mode to test your stamina or in Tutor Mode to see explanations as you work. Best of all, you also get detailed reports to track your progress.

Visit **kaptest.com/GRE** for more details on our Quiz Bank and for more information on our other online and classroom-based options.

QUANTITATIVE REASONING PRACTICE SET 1 ANSWERS AND EXPLANATIONS

1. C

Quantity A is a permutation because order matters. The number of ways 3 people chosen from a group of 6 can be arranged in a line, where order matters, is $6 \times 5 \times 4 = 120$. Quantity B is a combination because order does not matter. The number of ways 3 people can be selected from a group of 10, where order does not matter, is

$$_{10}C_3 = \frac{10!}{3!(10-3)!} = \frac{10 \times 9 \times 8}{3 \times 2 \times 1} = \frac{720}{6} = 120$$

The two quantities are equal.

2. C

There are three sets of vertical angles in this diagram: (a, d), (b, e), and (c, f). In Quantity A, you can substitute b for e because they are vertical angles and therefore equal; this leaves the sum $a + b + c$ in Quantity A. Because these are the three angles on one side of a straight line, they sum to 180°. Similarly, after substituting e for b in Quantity B, $b + d + f$ is the same thing as $d + e + f$, or also 180°. The two quantities are equal.

3. D

Pick a value for p and see what effect it has on r and s. If $p = 1$, $r = (7 \times 1) + 3 = 10$, and $s = (3 \times 1) + 7 = 10$, and the two quantities are equal. But if $p = 0$, $r = (7 \times 0) + 3 = 3$, and $s = (3 \times 0) + 7 = 7$, and Quantity A is less than Quantity B. Because there are at least two different possible relationships, the answer is **(D).**

4. A

Use the Picking Numbers strategy to answer this question. Suppose the original selling price of the shirt, x, is \$100. After a 10% increase in price, the shirt would sell for 110% of \$100, which is \$110. If there is a 10% decrease next, the shirt would sell for 90% of the current price. That would be 90% of \$110: $0.9 \times \$110 = \$99$. This price is less than the original amount, x, so Quantity A is greater.

5. B

Try to set the quantities equal. If x is 50, then the bookstore started out with 50 dictionaries. Then $\frac{1}{8}$ of them were purchased. You can see already that the quantities can't be equal, because $\frac{1}{8}$ of 50 won't yield an integer. But go ahead and see whether the answer is **(A)** or **(B)**. Because $\frac{1}{8}$ of 50 is close to 6, after these dictionaries were purchased, the store would have been left with about $50 - 6$ or

44 dictionaries. Then it received 10 more, giving a total of about 54 dictionaries. But this is more than the store actually ended up with; it only had 52. Therefore, it must have started with *fewer* than 50 dictionaries, and Quantity B is greater. (The last thing you care about is how many dictionaries it really had.)

6. A

There are n people in a room. One-third of them leave the room. So, there are $n - \frac{1}{3}n$ people in the room. Four people enter the room, so you have $n - \frac{1}{3}n + 4$ people. There are now $\frac{5}{6}$ of the original number of people in the room, therefore $n - \frac{1}{3}n + 4 = \frac{5}{6}n$. Now solve for n.

$$\begin{aligned} n - \frac{1}{3}n + 4 &= \frac{5}{6}n \\ \frac{2}{3}n + 4 &= \frac{5}{6}n \\ 4 &= \frac{5}{6}n - \frac{2}{3}n \\ 4 &= \frac{5}{6}n - \frac{4}{6}n \\ 4 &= \frac{1}{6}n \\ 24 &= n \end{aligned}$$

So, $n = 24$ and Quantity A is larger.

7. C

You may have thought this was a choice **(D)** question; after all, you don't know exactly where the boards overlap, whether in the middle of each board, as pictured, or near the end of one of the boards. But that doesn't matter; all you need to know is that they overlap and that all the angles are right angles. If the boards did not overlap, it would be easy to find the perimeter: $2 + 2 + 4 + 4 = 12$ for each board, or 24 for both boards. Now, because the boards do overlap, the perimeter of the figure will be smaller than that, but how much smaller? It will be smaller by the amount of that "lost perimeter" in the middle; the perimeter of the square where the boards overlap. (You know it's a square since all the angles are right angles.) The length of a side of that square is the shorter dimension of each of the boards: 2. Therefore, the perimeter of the square is 4×2 or 8. The perimeter of the figure, then, is $24 - 8$ or 16. The two quantities are equal.

8. A

Start by simplifying the quantity in Quantity A: $\left(\sqrt{x}+\sqrt{x}\right)^2$ is the same as $\left(2\sqrt{x}\right)^2$, which is $4x$. Subtract x from both quantities, and you're left with $3x$ in Quantity A and $x\sqrt{x}$ in Quantity B. Now divide both sides by x, and you're left with 3 in Quantity A and $\sqrt{x}$ in Quantity B. Square both quantities, and you get 9 in Quantity A and x in Quantity B. Since x is an integer between 1 and 9, exclusive, Quantity A is larger. If the algebra seems too abstract, go ahead and use the Picking Numbers strategy. If x equals 4, then Quantity A equals $(2 + 2)^2 = 16$, and Quantity B equals $4 + 8 = 12$.

9. B, C, D, E

If $\frac{x}{y} = \frac{2}{3}$, then $3x = 2y$ and $y = \frac{3x}{2}$. Substitute $y = \frac{3x}{2}$ into the equation $x + y = 15$: $x + \frac{3x}{2} = 15$, $2x + 3x = 30$, $5x = 30$, $x = 6$. Then, $y = \frac{3x}{2} = \frac{3(6)}{2} = 9$ and $y^2 = 81$. So any answer with greater than 81 under the radical will be greater than y. Therefore, the correct choices are **(B)**, **(C)**, **(D)**, and **(E)**.

10. A, B, E

The best place to start here is with pairs of positive integers that have a product of 10. The numbers 5 and 2 have a product of 10, as do 10 and 1. But remember that integers may be negative, so –1 and –10 are possible, as well as –2 and –5. The mean of –1 and –10 is –5.5; the mean of –2 and –5 is –3.5. The mean of 2 and 5 is 3.5. The correct answers are **(A)**, **(B)**, and **(E)**.

11. C, D, E

The prime factorization of 210 is $2 \times 3 \times 5 \times 7$. The sum of the prime factors is $2 + 3 + 5 + 7 = 17$. So, the correct choices are **(C)**, **(D)**, and **(E)**.

12. 9

Use the definition of *average* to write the sum of the first n bowlers' scores: $\frac{\text{sum of scores}}{n} = \text{average}$; therefore, $n \times \text{average} = \text{sum of scores}$. Substitute the values given in the question, and you have $160n = \text{sum of scores}$ for the initial set of bowlers. Now write the formula for the average again, using the additional score of 170. Now there are $n + 1$ bowlers.

$$\frac{\text{sum of scores}}{n} = \text{average}$$

$$\frac{160n + 170}{n + 1} = 161$$

Cross multiply and use algebra to solve for n.

$$\begin{aligned} 160n + 170 &= 161(n + 1) \\ 160n + 170 &= 161n + 161 \\ 170 - 161 &= 161n - 160n \\ 9 &= n \end{aligned}$$

There were **9** bowlers in the original group.

13. E

First, identify the numbers in set T: 3, 5, 7, 11, 13. The average of the numbers in set T is $\frac{3 + 5 + 7 + 11 + 13}{5} = \frac{39}{5} = 7.8$. Its standard deviation is given in the question stem as 3.71. In order to increase the standard deviation of a set of numbers, you must add a value that is more than one standard deviation away from the mean. One standard deviation below the mean for set T would be $7.8 - 3.71 = 4.09$, and one standard deviation *above* the mean would be $7.8 + 3.71 = 11.51$. Any value outside this range $4.09 \leq x \leq 11.51$ would increase set T's standard deviation, since it would make the set more "spread out" from the mean than it currently is. The only choice that does that is choice **(E)**.

14. C

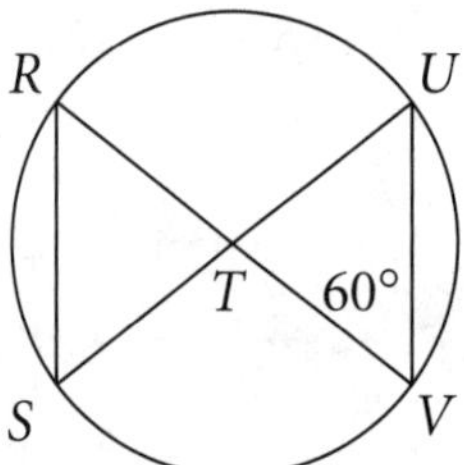

Solving this problem involves several steps, but none is too complicated. The circle has its center at point T. Start with the triangle on the right whose vertices are at T and two points on the circumference of the circle. This makes two of its sides radii of the circle, which we're told each have a length of 3. Because all radii must have equal length, this makes the triangle an isosceles triangle. In addition, you're told one of the base angles of this triangle has measure 60°. Thus, the other base angle must also have measure 60° (since the base angles in an isosceles triangle have equal measure). The sum of the two base angles is 120°, leaving 180° − 120° or 60° for the other angle, the one at point T (making ΔTUV an equilateral triangle with sides of 3).

Now, angle *RTS* is opposite this 60° angle, so its measure must also be 60°. Therefore, ΔRST is another equilateral triangle, and its sides are 3. Therefore, the length of *RS* is 3, choice **(C)**.

15. B

The probability formula is

$$\text{Probability} = \frac{\text{Number of desired outcomes}}{\text{Number of possible outcomes}}$$

When one die is rolled, there are six possible outcomes. When two dice are rolled, the number of possible outcomes is 6×6, or 36. Getting a total value of 7 can be achieved in the following ways: (1, 6), (2, 5), (3, 4), (4, 3), (5, 2), and (6, 1). There are six possible ways.

So the probability of rolling a total of 7 is $\frac{6}{36}$, which can be reduced to $\frac{1}{6}$, choice **(B)**.

16. 8

In the first scenario, each day $\frac{1 \text{ house}}{3 \text{ days}} = \frac{1}{3}$ of the house will be built. Because there are 10 workers, each person can build $\frac{1}{30}$ of a house each day. In the second scenario, there are 15 workers, so that means $15 \times \frac{1}{30} = \frac{1}{2}$ a house can be built each day. Four houses could, therefore, be built in 8 days:

$$\frac{4 \text{ houses}}{\frac{1}{2} \text{ house/day}} = 4 \times 2 = 8 \text{ days}$$

17. C

The residential usage (in billions) in 2000 was about 22; the usage was about 52 in 2010. The range is the difference because the residential usage increased over the time period. Therefore, $52 - 22 = 30$, and the range is about 30 billion gallons. The correct answer is **(C)**.

18. C

The two amounts were closest to each other in 2002. The residential amount appears to be about 28; the total appears to be about 32: $28 \div 32 = 0.875$. Choice **(C)** is the closest.

19. D

The three usages with the greatest amounts per person are faucets, washers, and showers, totaling 30 gallons per day. Multiply by 10,000 to get 300,000, choice **(D)**.

20. B

The residential consumption (in billions) in 2010 was approximately 52. Take half of that amount, 26, to represent the amount of water used by households with efficient appliances and plumbing. Let *W* represent the amount of water these households would have used otherwise.

Set up a percent equation to solve for *W*. Remember, the savings were 35%, so subtract 35 from 100 to find the percent that would have been used.

$$\begin{aligned} 26 &= (100\% - 35\%) \times W \\ 26 &= 65\% \times W \\ 26 &= 0.65 \times W \\ \frac{26}{0.65} &= W \end{aligned}$$

The savings in billions of gallons was $40 - 26 = 14$. The correct answer is **(B)**.

QUANTITATIVE REASONING PRACTICE SET 2

Numbers

All numbers are real numbers.

Figures

The position of points, lines, angles, and so on may be assumed to be in the order shown; all lengths and angle measures may be assumed to be positive.

Lines shown as straight may be assumed to be straight.

Figures lie in the plane of the paper unless otherwise stated.

Figures that accompany questions are intended to provide useful information. However, unless a note states that a figure has been drawn to scale, you should solve the problems by using your knowledge of mathematics, not by estimation or measurement.

Directions

Each of the following questions, 1–10, consists of two quantities, Quantity A and Quantity B. You are to compare the two quantities and choose

- (A) if Quantity A is greater
- (B) if Quantity B is greater
- (C) if the two quantities are equal
- (D) if the relationship cannot be determined from the information given

Common Information

In a question, information concerning one or both of the quantities to be compared is centered above the two quantities. A symbol that appears in both quantities represents the same thing in Quantity A as it does in Quantity B.

1. Quantity A: The average (arithmetic mean) of 100, 101, and 103

   Quantity B: The median of 100, 101, and 103

   Ⓐ Quantity A is greater.
   Ⓑ Quantity B is greater.
   Ⓒ The two quantities are equal.
   Ⓓ The relationship cannot be determined from the information given.

A and *B* are points on the circumference of the circle with center *O* (not shown). The length of chord *AB* is 15.

2. Quantity A: Circumference of circle *O*

   Quantity B: 12π

   Ⓐ Quantity A is greater.
   Ⓑ Quantity B is greater.
   Ⓒ The two quantities are equal.
   Ⓓ The relationship cannot be determined from the information given.

$$x = \frac{4}{3}r^2h^2$$

$$x = 1$$

r and *h* are positive.

3. Quantity A: h

   Quantity B: $\frac{\sqrt{3}}{2r}$

   Ⓐ Quantity A is greater.
   Ⓑ Quantity B is greater.
   Ⓒ The two quantities are equal.
   Ⓓ The relationship cannot be determined from the information given.

ΔABC lies in the xy-plane with C at (0,0), B at (6,0), and A at (x,y), where x and y are positive. The area of ΔABC is 18 square units.

4. Quantity A: y

   Quantity B: 6

   Ⓐ Quantity A is greater.
   Ⓑ Quantity B is greater.
   Ⓒ The two quantities are equal.
   Ⓓ The relationship cannot be determined from the information given.

For $x \neq y$, $x \Phi y = \frac{x + y}{x - y}$

$$p > 0 > q$$

5. Quantity A: $p \Phi q$

   Quantity B: $q \Phi p$

   Ⓐ Quantity A is greater.
   Ⓑ Quantity B is greater.
   Ⓒ The two quantities are equal.
   Ⓓ The relationship cannot be determined from the information given.

$x \neq 0$

6. Quantity A: $\frac{1}{x} + \frac{1}{x}$ Quantity B: $\frac{1}{x} \times \frac{1}{x}$

(A) Quantity A is greater.
(B) Quantity B is greater.
(C) The two quantities are equal.
(D) The relationship cannot be determined from the information given.

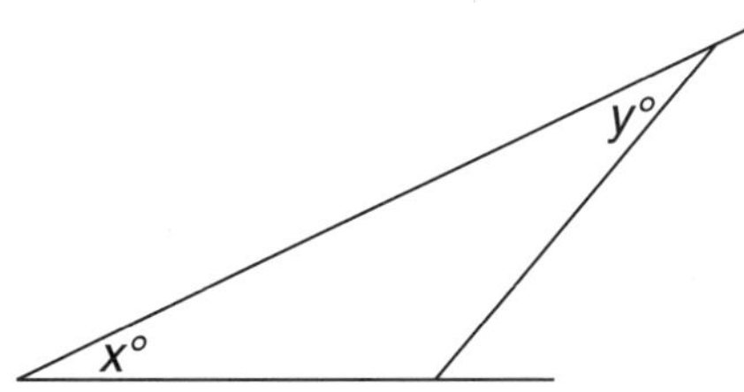

7. Quantity A: $x + y$ Quantity B: $180°$

(A) Quantity A is greater.
(B) Quantity B is greater.
(C) The two quantities are equal.
(D) The relationship cannot be determined from the information given.

$$\begin{aligned} 4x - 5y &= 10 \\ -3x + 6y &= 22 \end{aligned}$$

8. Quantity A: 33 Quantity B: $x + y$

(A) Quantity A is greater.
(B) Quantity B is greater.
(C) The two quantities are equal.
(D) The relationship cannot be determined from the information given.

$6(10)^n > 60{,}006$

9. Quantity A: n Quantity B: 6

(A) Quantity A is greater.
(B) Quantity B is greater.
(C) The two quantities are equal.
(D) The relationship cannot be determined from the information given.

In a four-digit positive integer y, the thousands digit is 2.5 times the tens digit.

10. Quantity A: The tens digits of y Quantity B: 4

(A) Quantity A is greater.
(B) Quantity B is greater.
(C) The two quantities are equal.
(D) The relationship cannot be determined from the information given.

11. What is the average (arithmetic mean) of $2x + 3$, $5x - 4$, $6x - 6$, and $3x - 1$?

(A) $2x + 4$
(B) $3x - 2$
(C) $3x + 2$
(D) $4x - 2$
(E) $4x + 2$

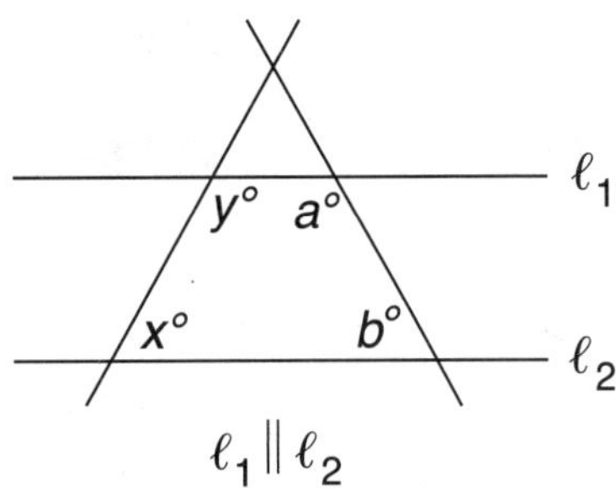

12. Which of the following statements must be true about the figure shown above?

(A) $x = a$
(B) $x = b$
(C) $a = b$
(D) $y = b$
(E) $x + y = a + b$

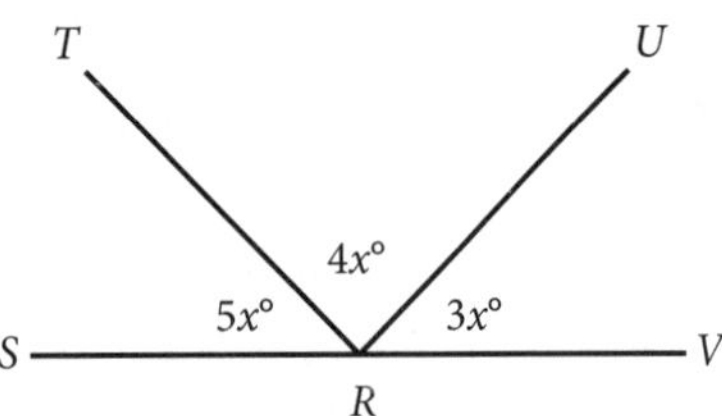

13. What is the degree measure of angle *SRU*?

(A) 15
(B) 45
(C) 105
(D) 135
(E) 180

14. There are at least 200 apples in a grocery store. The ratio of the number of oranges to the number of apples is 9 to 10. How many oranges could there be in the store?

Indicate all possible choices.

[A] 171
[B] 180
[C] 216
[D] 252
[E] 315

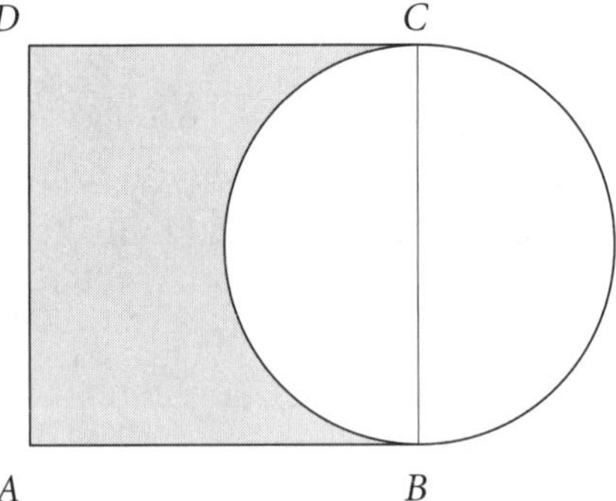

15. Square *ABCD* has a side length of 4. *BC* is the diameter of the circle. Which of the following is greater than or equal to the area of the shaded region, in square units?

Indicate all possible choices.

[A] $16 - 16\pi$
[B] $16 - 4\pi$
[C] $16 - 2\pi$
[D] $16 + \pi$
[E] $16 + 4\pi$

Questions 16–20 are based on the following graphs.

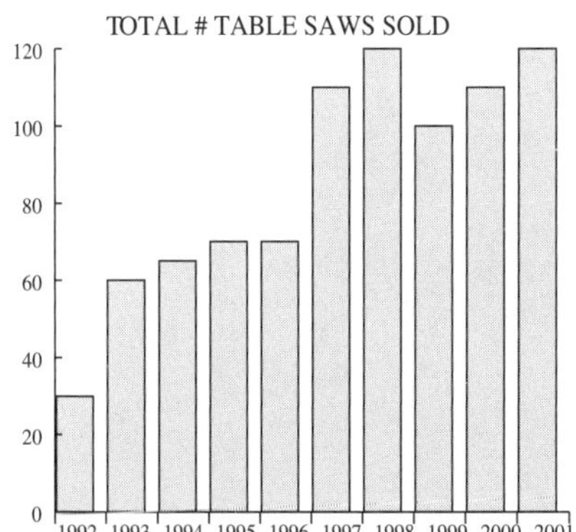

TOTAL PROFIT FROM TABLE SAW SALES (IN DOLLARS)

$100,000
$80,000
$60,000
$40,000
$20,000
0
1992 1993 1994 1995 1996 1997 1998 1999 2000 2001

BREAKDOWN OF PROFITS IN 1998

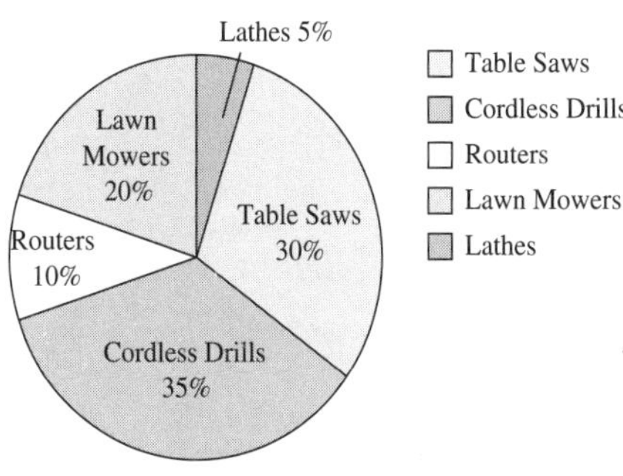

16. In 1998, what were the total profits from all hardware tool sales?

17. Which year had the greatest percentage increase in number of table saws sold from the previous year?

Ⓐ 1993
Ⓑ 1995
Ⓒ 1997
Ⓓ 2000
Ⓔ 2001

18. Of the following, what is the closest to the percentage change in profits from table saws between 1998 and 1999?

Ⓐ A 50% increase
Ⓑ A 33% increase
Ⓒ A 17% decrease
Ⓓ A 33% decrease
Ⓔ A 50% decrease

19. If the total manufacturing cost of table saws in 1993 was $22,000, what was the price per saw?

$ ☐

20. In 1998, what were the approximate profits from sales of cordless drills?

Ⓐ $50,000
Ⓑ $70,000
Ⓒ $80,000
Ⓓ $90,000
Ⓔ $100,000

QUANTITATIVE REASONING PRACTICE SET 2 ANSWER KEY

1. A
2. A
3. C
4. C
5. D
6. D
7. B
8. A
9. D
10. B
11. D
12. E
13. D
14. B, C, D, E
15. C, D, E
16. 200,000
17. A
18. D
19. 700
20. B

Diagnose Your Results

Diagnostic Tool

Tally up your score and write your results below.

Total

Total Correct: ________ out of 20 correct

By Question Type

Quantitative Comparison (questions 1–10) ________ out of 10 correct

Problem Solving (questions 11–15) ________ out of 5 correct

Data Interpretation (questions 16–20) ________ out of 5 correct

Repeat the steps outlined in the Diagnose Your Results page that follows the Quantitative Reasoning Practice Set 1 answer key.

QUANTITATIVE REASONING PRACTICE SET 2 ANSWERS AND EXPLANATIONS

1. A

This question requires no computation but only a general understanding of how averages work and what the word "median" means. The *median* of a group of numbers is the "middle number"; it is the value above which half of the numbers in the group fall and below which the other half fall. If you have an even number of values, the median is the average of the two "middle" numbers; if you have an odd number of values, the median is one of the values. Here, in Quantity B, the median is 101. In Quantity A, if the numbers were 100, 101, and 102, then the average would also be 101, but because the third number, 103, is greater than 102, then the average must be greater than 101. Quantity A is greater than 101, and Quantity B equals 101; Quantity A is larger.

2. A

Start with the information you are given. You know that the length of the chord is 15. What does that mean? Well, because you don't know exactly where *A* and *B* are, it doesn't mean too much, but it does tell you that the distance between two points on the circle is 15. That tells you that the diameter must be at least 15. If the diameter were less than 15, then you couldn't have a chord that was equal to 15, because the diameter is always the longest chord in a circle. The diameter of the circle is 15 or greater, so the circumference must be at least 15π. That means that Quantity A must be larger than Quantity B.

3. C

The equation in the centered information looks complicated, but we'll take it one step at a time. Because Quantity A has only *h* in it, solve the equation for *h*, leaving *h* on one side of the equal sign and *r* on the other side. First, substitute the value for *x* into the equation; then solve for *h* in terms of *r*.

$x = \frac{4}{3}r^2h^2$	Substitute 1 for *x*.
$1 = \frac{4}{3}r^2h^2$	Divide both sides by $\frac{4}{3}$.
$\frac{3}{4} = r^2h^2$	Take the positive square root of both sides, using the information that *r* and *h* are positive.
$\frac{\sqrt{3}}{2} = rh$	Divide both sides by *r* to get *h* alone.
$h = \frac{\sqrt{3}}{2r}$	The two quantities are equal.

4. C

Draw an *xy*-plane and label the points given to help solve this problem. You know where points *B* and *C* are; they're on the *x*-axis. You don't know where *A* is, however, which may make you think that the answer is choice **(D)**. But you're given more information: you know that the triangle has an area of 18. The area of any triangle is one-half the product of the base and the height. Make side *BC* the base of the triangle; you know the coordinates of both points, so you can find their distance apart, which is the length of that side. *C* is at the origin, the point (0, 0); *B* is at the point (6, 0). The distance between them is the distance from 0 to 6 along the *x*-axis, or just 6. So that's the base. What about the height? Because you know that the area is 18, you can plug what you know into the area formula.

$$\begin{aligned} \text{Area} &= \frac{1}{2} \times \text{base} \times \text{height} \\ 18 &= \frac{1}{2} \times 6 \times \text{height} \\ \text{height} &= \frac{18}{3} \\ \text{height} &= 6 \end{aligned}$$

That's the other dimension of the triangle. The height is the distance between the *x*-axis and point *A*. Now you know that *A* must be somewhere in the first quadrant, since both the *x*- and *y*-coordinates are positive. Don't worry about the *x*-coordinate of the point, because that's not what's being compared; you care only about the value of *y*. You know that the distance from the *x*-axis to the point is 6, because that's the height of the triangle, and that *y* must be positive. Therefore, the *y*-coordinate of the point must be 6. That's what the *y*-coordinate is: a measure of the point's vertical distance from the *x*-axis. (Note that if you hadn't been told that *y* was positive, there would be two possible values for *y*: 6 and −6. A point that's 6 units below the *x*-axis would also give a triangle with height 6.) You still don't know the *x*-coordinate of the point, and in fact you can't figure that out, but you don't care. You know that *y* is 6; therefore, the two quantities are equal.

5. D

With symbolism problems like this, it sometimes helps to put the definition of the symbol into words. For this symbol, you can say something like "$x \Phi y$ means take the sum of the two numbers and divide that by the difference of the two numbers." One good way to do this problem is to Pick Numbers. You know that *p* is positive and *q* is negative. So suppose *p* is 1 and *q* is −1. Figure out what $p \Phi q$ is first. You start by taking the sum of the numbers, or $1 + (-1) = 0$. That's the numerator of the fraction, and you don't really need to go any further than that. Whatever their difference is, because the numerator is 0, the whole fraction must equal 0. (The difference can't be 0 also, since $p \neq q$.) So that's $p \Phi q$. Now what about $q \Phi p$? Well, that's going to have the same numerator as $p \ \Phi \ q$: 0. The only thing that changes when you reverse the order of the numbers is the denominator of the fraction. So $q \ \Phi \ p$ has a numerator of 0, and that fraction must equal 0 as well.

So you've found a case where the quantities are equal. Try another set of values and see whether the quantities are always equal. If $p = 1$ and $q = -2$, then the sum of the numbers is $1 + (-2)$ or -1. So that's the numerator of the fraction in each quantity. Now for the denominator of $p \ \Phi \ q$, you need $p - q = 1 - (-2) = 1 + 2 = 3$. Then the value of $p \ \Phi \ q$ is $\frac{-1}{3}$. The denominator of $q \ \Phi \ p$ is $q - p = -2 - 1 = -3$. In that case, the value of $q \ \Phi \ p$ is $\frac{-1}{-3}$ or $\frac{1}{3}$. The quantities are different; therefore, the answer is **(D)**.

6. D

Picking Numbers will help you solve this problem. For $x = 1$, $\frac{1}{x} + \frac{1}{x} = \frac{1}{1} + \frac{1}{1} = 2$ and $\frac{1}{x} \times \frac{1}{x} = \frac{1}{1} \times \frac{1}{1} = 1$, so Quantity A is larger. For $x = -1$, $\frac{1}{x} + \frac{1}{x} = \frac{1}{-1} + \frac{1}{-1} = -2$ and $\frac{1}{x} \times \frac{1}{x} = \frac{1}{-1} \times \frac{1}{-1} = 1$, so Quantity B is larger. The quantities are different; therefore, the answer is **(D)**.

7. B

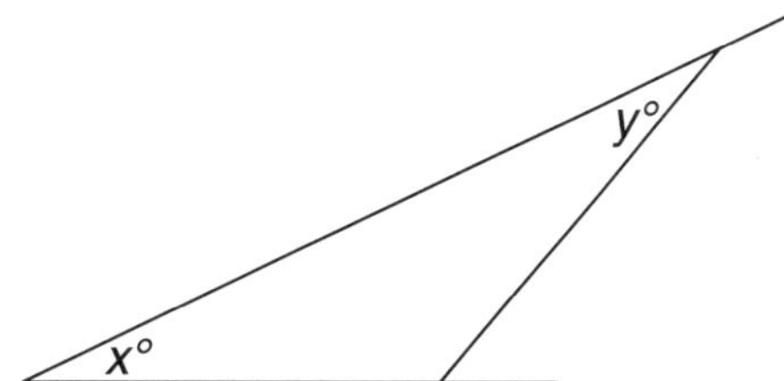

The sum of the three interior angles of a triangle is 180°. Because x and y are only two of the angles, their sum must be less than 180°. Quantity B is greater.

8. A

For the system of equations $4x - 5y = 10$ and $-3x + 6y = 22$, it is not necessary to solve for the values of x and y. Rather, you want to know about the sum of x and y. Notice what happens when you add the two equations.

$$\begin{array}{rcl} 4x - 5y & = & 10 \\ -3x + 6y & = & 22 \\ \hline x + y & = & 32 \end{array}$$

Because $x + y = 32$ and $33 > 32$, Quantity A is larger.

9. D

Divide both sides of the inequality by 6. You're left with $(10)^n > 10{,}001$. The number 10,001 can also be written as $10^4 + 1$, so you know that $(10)^n > 10^4 + 1$. Therefore, Quantity A, n, must be 5 or greater. Quantity B is 6. Because n could be less than, equal to, or greater than 6, you need more information.

10. B

Try to set the quantities equal. Could the tens digit of y be 4? If it is, and the thousands digit is 2.5 times the units digit, then the tens digit must be ... 10? That can't be right. A digit must be one of the integers 0–9; 10 isn't a digit. Therefore, 4 is too big to be the tens digit of y. You don't know what the tens digit of y is, but you know that it must be less than 4. Quantity B is greater than Quantity A.

11. D

To find the average, add the quantities together and divide by 4: $(2x + 3) + (5x - 4) + (6x - 6) + (3x - 1) = 16x - 8$ and $\frac{16x - 8}{4} = 4x - 2$. The correct choice is **(D).**

12. E

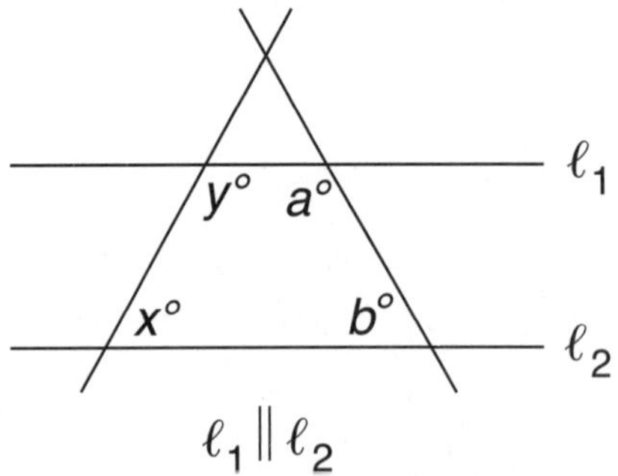

When a transversal cuts a pair of parallel lines, in this case ℓ_1 and ℓ_2, the angles are always supplementary and their sum is 180. So, the sum $(x + y)$ is equal to the sum $(a + b)$. The exact values of the individual angle measures cannot be determined from the figure. The answer is **(E).**

13. D

First, find the value of x, using the fact that there are 180° in a straight line. Set the sum of the angle measures equal to 180: $5x + 4x + 3x = 180$, $12x = 180$, and $x = 15$. Angle *SRU* equals $4x + 5x = 9x$, which is 135°. Choice **(D)** is correct.

14. B, C, D, E

You know that the ratio of oranges to apples is 9 to 10 and that there are at least 200 apples. The ratio tells you that there are more apples than oranges. At the minimum, there must be 180 oranges to satisfy the proportion $\frac{9}{10} = \frac{180}{200}$. There could be more than 200 apples, so any number of oranges greater than 180 for which the ratio 9:10 applies is also correct. All of the choices are multiples of 9, so the correct choices are **(B)**, **(C)**, **(D)**, and **(E)**.

15. C, D, E

The area of the shaded region is the area of the square minus the area of the portion of the circle that is inside the square. The area of a square is its side squared. The area of square *ABCD* is $4^2 = 4 \times 4$, which is 16. Now find the area of the portion of the circle that is inside the square. Because the diameter of the circle is a side of the square, you know that exactly one-half of the circle's area is inside the square. Also, because the diameter of the circle is twice the radius, the radius of the circle is $\frac{4}{2}$ or 2. The area of a circle with a radius r is πr^2. The area of the complete circle in this question is $\pi(2)^2$, which is 4π. So half the area of this circle is 2π. Thus, the area of the shaded region is $16 - 2\pi$.

That means that $16 - 4\pi$ and $16 - 16\pi$ are less than $16 - 2\pi$, so they cannot be correct choices. However, the sum of 16 and any positive number is greater than 16 and also greater than $16 - 2\pi$. So, the correct choices are **(C)**, **(D)**, and **(E)**.

16. 200,000

From the second bar graph, the profits from table saws in 1998 were $60,000. From the pie chart, table saws were 30% of the total profits. Let's call the total profits T dollars. Then 30% of T dollars is $60,000. So $0.3T = 60{,}000$, and

$$T = \frac{60{,}000}{0.3} = \frac{60{,}000}{\frac{3}{10}} = \frac{10 \times 60{,}000}{3} = \frac{600{,}000}{3} = 200{,}000.$$

17. A

Use the first bar graph to analyze number of table saws sold. The year with the biggest percent increase over the previous year will be the year in which the increase is the biggest fraction of the amount from the previous year. Notice that in 1993, the increase from 1992 was approximately 60 - 30, or 30. This is approximately a 100% increase, and it is the greatest percent increase over the previous year among all the years from 1993 to 2001. There was a greater increase in *number* of table saws from 1996 to 1997 than from 1992 to 1993, about $110 - 70 = 40$. However, the *percent* increase from 1996 to 1997 is approximately $\frac{40}{70} \times 100\%$, which is less than 100%, so choice **(A)** is correct.

18. D

In 1998, the profits from table saws were approximately \$60,000. In 1999, the profits from table saws were approximately \$40,000. From 1998 to 1999, there was a decrease in the profits from table saws. In general,

$$\text{Percent decrease} = \frac{\text{Original value} - \text{New value}}{\text{Original value}} \times 100\%$$

Here, the percent decrease is approximately

$$\frac{\$60{,}000 - \$40{,}000}{\$60{,}000} \times 100\% = \frac{\$20{,}000}{60{,}000} \times 100\% = \frac{1}{3} \times 100\% = 33\frac{1}{3}\%$$

A percent decrease of $33\frac{1}{3}\%$ is closest to **(D)**.

19. 700

In 1993, the profits were \$20,000. Using the formula Profit = Revenue − Cost, you can write Revenue = Cost + Profit. The cost was \$22,000. So the revenue was \$22,000 + \$20,000 = \$42,000. Because in 1993, 60 table saws were sold, each table saw was sold for $\frac{\$42{,}000}{60}$, which is **\$700**.

20. B

In 1998, the profits from table saws were about \$60,000, and this profit was 30% of the total profits. Let's call the total profits T dollars. Then 30% of T dollars is \$60,000. So $0.3T = 60{,}000$, and $T = \frac{60{,}000}{0.3} = 60{,}000 \times \frac{10}{3} = \frac{10 \times 60{,}000}{3} = \frac{600{,}00}{3} = 200{,}000.$

The total profits in 1998 were approximately \$200,000 (you may also have remembered this calculation from question 16). The profits from cordless drills were 35% of the total. So the profits from cordless drills were approximately 0.35(\$200,000), which is \$70,000 or answer choice **(B)**.

QUANTITATIVE REASONING PRACTICE SET 3

NUMBERS

All numbers are real numbers.

FIGURES

The position of points, lines, angles, and so on may be assumed to be in the order shown; all lengths and angle measures may be assumed to be positive.

Lines shown as straight may be assumed to be straight.

Figures lie in the plane of the paper unless otherwise stated.

Figures that accompany questions are intended to provide useful information. However, unless a note states that a figure has been drawn to scale, you should solve the problems by using your knowledge of mathematics, not by estimation or measurement.

DIRECTIONS

Each of the following questions, 1–8, consists of two quantities, Quantity A and Quantity B. You are to compare the two quantities and choose

- (A) if Quantity A is greater
- (B) if Quantity B is greater
- (C) if the two quantities are equal
- (D) if the relationship cannot be determined from the information given

COMMON INFORMATION

In a question, information concerning one or both of the quantities to be compared is centered above the two quantities. A symbol that appears in both quantities represents the same thing in Quantity A as it does in Quantity B.

The diameter of a circle equals the diagonal of a square whose side length is 4.

1. | Quantity A | Quantity B |
|---|---|
| The circumference of the circle | $20\sqrt{2}$ |

Ⓐ Quantity A is greater.
Ⓑ Quantity B is greater.
Ⓒ The two quantities are equal.
Ⓓ The relationship cannot be determined from the information given.

$$x < y < z$$
$$0 < z$$

2. | Quantity A | Quantity B |
|---|---|
| x | 0 |

Ⓐ Quantity A is greater.
Ⓑ Quantity B is greater.
Ⓒ The two quantities are equal.
Ⓓ The relationship cannot be determined from the information given.

3. | Quantity A | Quantity B |
|---|---|
| The number of distinct positive integer factors of 96 | The number of distinct positive integer factors of 72 |

Ⓐ Quantity A is greater.
Ⓑ Quantity B is greater.
Ⓒ The two quantities are equal.
Ⓓ The relationship cannot be determined from the information given.

$$x > 0$$

4. | Quantity A | Quantity B |
|---|---|
| $\frac{x + 1}{x}$ | $\frac{x}{x + 1}$ |

Ⓐ Quantity A is greater.
Ⓑ Quantity B is greater.
Ⓒ The two quantities are equal.
Ⓓ The relationship cannot be determined from the information given.

$$2^p = 4^q$$

5. | Quantity A | Quantity B |
|---|---|
| p | $2q$ |

Ⓐ Quantity A is greater.
Ⓑ Quantity B is greater.
Ⓒ The two quantities are equal.
Ⓓ The relationship cannot be determined from the information given.

6. | Quantity A | Quantity B |
|---|---|
| The number of seconds in 7 hours | The number of hours in 52 weeks |

Ⓐ Quantity A is greater.
Ⓑ Quantity B is greater.
Ⓒ The two quantities are equal.
Ⓓ The relationship cannot be determined from the information given.

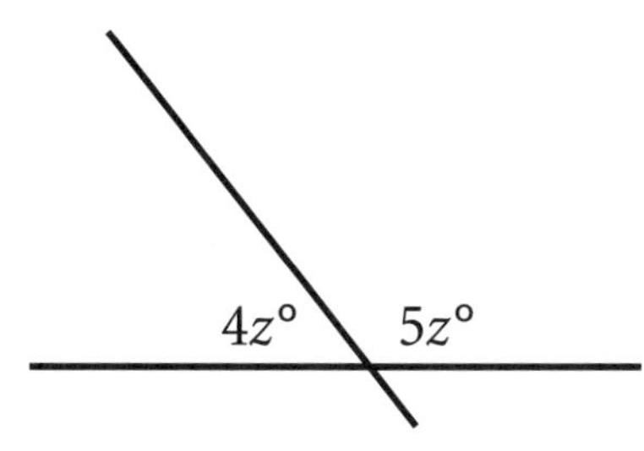

7. Quantity A: z — Quantity B: 20

(A) Quantity A is greater.
(B) Quantity B is greater.
(C) The two quantities are equal.
(D) The relationship cannot be determined from the information given.

$x > 2$

8. Quantity A: x^3 — Quantity B: $4x$

(A) Quantity A is greater.
(B) Quantity B is greater.
(C) The two quantities are equal.
(D) The relationship cannot be determined from the information given.

9. If $A \blacklozenge B = \dfrac{A + B}{B}$, and $C\clubsuit = C + 3$, what is the value of $(9\clubsuit) \blacklozenge 3$?

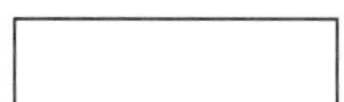

10. Rectangle A has a length of 12 inches and a width of 5 inches. Rectangle B has a length of 9 inches and a width of 10 inches. By what number must the area of rectangle A be multiplied in order to get the area of rectangle B?

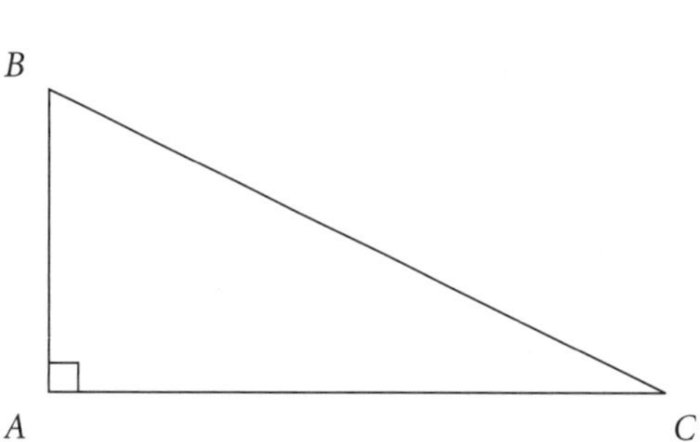

11. In right triangle ABC above, side AB has a length of 5 units, while side BC has a length of 13 units. What is the area of ABC, in square units?

[ ] square units

12. If the average test score of four students is 85, which of the following scores could a fifth student receive such that the average of all five scores is greater than 84 and less than 86?

Indicate all such scores.

[A] 88
[B] 86
[C] 85
[D] 83
[E] 80

13. Meg is twice as old as Rolf, but three years ago, she was two years older than Rolf is now. How old is Rolf now?

[ ] years old

14. The cost, in cents, of manufacturing x crayons is $570 + 0.5x$. The crayons sell for 10 cents each. What is the minimum number of crayons that need to be sold so that the revenue received recoups the manufacturing cost?

(A) 50
(B) 57
(C) 60
(D) 61
(E) 95

15. If $xy \neq 0$, $\frac{1 - x}{xy} =$

(A) $\frac{1}{xy} - \frac{1}{y}$
(B) $\frac{x}{y} - \frac{1}{x}$
(C) $\frac{1}{xy} - 1$
(D) $\frac{1}{xy} - \frac{x^2}{y}$
(E) $\frac{1}{x} - \frac{1}{y}$

Questions 16–20 refer to the following graphs:

TEAM REVENUES FOR 1997

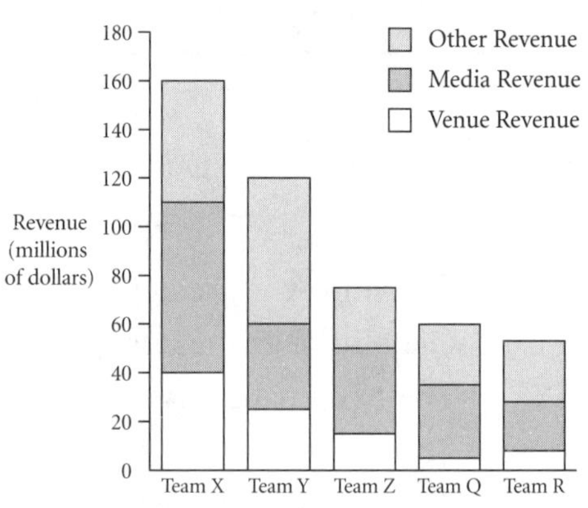

PERCENTAGES OF VENUE REVENUES FOR TEAM X, 1997

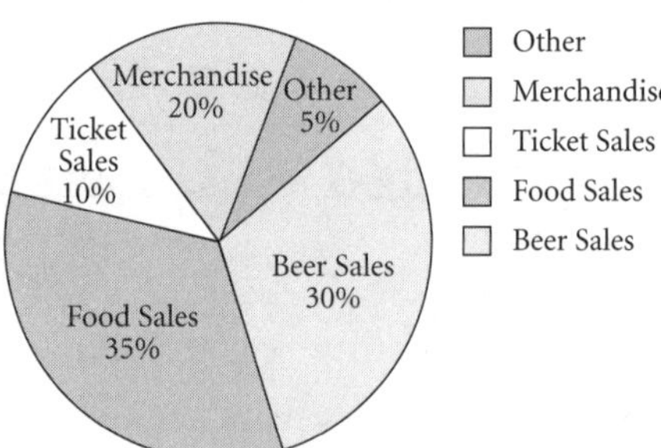

16. For the team with the median venue revenue in 1997, media revenue represented approximately what percent of that team's total revenue?

(A) 25%
(B) 30%
(C) 45%
(D) 70%
(E) 85%

17. Of the following, which is greater than the amount of revenue, in millions of dollars, earned by Team X through food sales in 1997?

    Indicate all such amounts.

    [A] 7
    [B] 10
    [C] 14
    [D] 18
    [E] 22

18. In 1997, which teams had media revenues of less than $25 million?

    Indicate all such teams.

    [A] Team X
    [B] Team Y
    [C] Team Z
    [D] Team Q
    [E] Team R

19. If Team Y earned total revenues of at least $150 million in 1998, then Team Y's total revenue could have increased by what percent from 1997 to 1998?

    Indicate all such percents.

    [A] 20%
    [B] 25%
    [C] 30%
    [D] 35%
    [E] 40%

20. The venue revenues for Team X from merchandise sales and ticket sales were approximately what percent of the venue revenues for Team X from food sales?

    (A) 43%
    (B) 53%
    (C) 67%
    (D) 71%
    (E) 86%

QUANTITATIVE REASONING PRACTICE SET 3 ANSWER KEY

1. B
2. D
3. C
4. A
5. C
6. A
7. C
8. A
9. 5
10. 1.5
11. 30
12. A, B, C, D
13. 5
14. C
15. A
16. C
17. D, E
18. E
19. B, C, D, E
20. E

DIAGNOSE YOUR RESULTS

Diagnostic Tool

Tally up your score and write your results below.

Total

Total Correct: ________ out of 20 correct

By Question Type

Quantitative Comparison (questions 1–8) ________ out of 8 correct

Problem Solving (questions 9–15) ________ out of 7 correct

Data Interpretation (questions 16–20) ________ out of 5 correct

Repeat the steps outlined in the Diagnose Your Results page that follows the Quantitative Reasoning Practice Set 1 answer key.

QUANTITATIVE REASONING PRACTICE SET 3 ANSWERS AND EXPLANATIONS

1. B

The diagonal of a square of side 4 is $4\sqrt{2}$. The circumference of a circle is π times the diameter. So, the circumference of this circle is $4\sqrt{2}\pi$. Now write Quantity B, $20\sqrt{2}$, as $4(5)\sqrt{2}$ and you can compare the quantities piece by piece. The factors of 4 and $\sqrt{2}$ are the same in both quantities, but π is less than 5. So, Quantity B is larger.

2. D

You could Pick Numbers here or else just use logic. You know that *z* is positive and that *x* and *y* are less than *z*. But does that mean that *x* or *y* must be negative? Not at all—they could be, but they could also be positive. For instance, suppose $x = 1$, $y = 2$, and $z = 3$. Then Quantity A would be larger. However, if $x = -1$, $y = 0$, and $z = 1$, then Quantity B would be larger. You need more information to determine the relationship between the quantities. The answer is **(D)**.

3. C

There are 12 positive integer factors of 96: 1, 2, 3, 4, 6, 8, 12, 16, 24, 32, 48, and 96. There are 12 positive integer factors of 72: 1, 2, 3, 4, 6, 8, 9, 12, 18, 24, 36, and 72. The two quantities are equal.

4. A

If $x > 0$, then $\frac{x+1}{x}$, which also equals $1 + \frac{1}{x}$, must be greater than 1. On the other hand, $\frac{x}{x+1}$ must be less than 1. This is because when $x > 0$, the numerator *x* is smaller than the denominator, so the ratio $\frac{x}{x+1} < 1$. Therefore, $\frac{x+1}{x} > \frac{x}{x+1}$ when $x > 0$, and Quantity A is greater.

5. C

For this question, notice the relationship between the bases, 2 and 4. When comparing exponents, it's easiest to work with equal bases.

You know that $4 = 2^2$. Therefore, $4^q = (2^2)^q = 2^{2q}$. Now you have $2^p = 2^{2q}$, so $p = 2q$. The quantities are equal, choice **(C)**.

6. A

Before you go to the trouble of multiplying the terms, let's see if there's a shortcut. For the GRE, make sure you know the common unit conversions for time. There are 60 seconds in a minute and 60 minutes in an hour, so there are $7 \times 60 \times 60$ seconds in 7 hours. There are 24 hours in a day and 7 days in a week, so there are $7 \times 24 \times 52$ hours in 52 weeks. Let's rewrite the quantities:

Quantity A	Quantity B
$7 \times 60 \times 60$	$7 \times 24 \times 52$

Taking away the common values gives you:

Quantity A	Quantity B
60×60	24×52

You still shouldn't do the math, however. The best strategy is to compare piece by piece, which shows that Quantity A is larger than Quantity B.

7. C

The sum of the measures of the angles on one side of a straight line is 180°. Therefore, $4z + 5z = 180$, so $9z = 180$. Divide both sides by 9 to find $z = 20$. **(C)** is the answer.

8. A

Since $x > 2$, you know $x > 0$ and you can divide both quantities by x without changing their relationship. Quantity A is then x^2 and Quantity B is 4. Since $x > 2$, the least value for x^2 is greater than $2^2 = 4$. Therefore, **(A)** is correct.

9. 5

Let's first find the value of 9♣. Then we'll find the value of (9♣)♦3.

Since C♣ $= C + 3$, 9♣ $= 9 + 3 = 12$.

Therefore, (9♣)♦3 = 12♦3.

Since $A \blacklozenge B = \dfrac{A + B}{B}$, $12 \blacklozenge 3 = \dfrac{12 + 3}{3} = \dfrac{15}{3}$.

Therefore, (9♣)♦3 = 5.

10. 1.5

The area of a rectangle is its length times its width.

The area of rectangle A is $12 \times 5 = 60$.

The area of rectangle B is $9 \times 10 = 90$.

So the area 60 of rectangle A must be multiplied by a number, which you can call x, to obtain the area 90 of rectangle B.

Then $60x = 90$. So $x = \frac{90}{60} = \frac{3}{2} = 1.5$.

11. 30

Here's a problem where it really pays to have learned the special right triangles. Because one leg of the right triangle is 5 and the hypotenuse is 13, you have a special right triangle, the 5:12:13 right triangle. So the length of AC is 12.

The area of a triangle is $\frac{1}{2}$ of the base times the height. The area of a right triangle is $\frac{1}{2} \times (\text{leg})_1 \times (\text{leg})_2$, because one leg can be considered to be the base and the other leg can be considered to be the height. So the area of triangle ABC is

$$\frac{1}{2} \times (AC) \times (AB) = \frac{1}{2} \times 12 \times 5 = 6 \times 5 = 30$$

The answer is **30**.

12. A, B, C, D

The average formula is as follows:

$$\text{Average} = \frac{\text{Sum of the terms}}{\text{Number of terms}}$$

Therefore,

$$\text{Sum of the terms} = \text{Average} \times \text{Number of terms}$$

The sum of the scores of the four students whose average was 85 is $85(4) = 340$. Let's call the fifth student's score x. If the new average is to be greater than 84 and less than 86 and the sum of the scores of all five students is $340 + x$, then $84 < \frac{340 + x}{5} < 86$. If you multiply all parts of the inequality by 5, you get $420 < 340 + x < 430$. Subtracting 340 from all parts of the inequality, you get $80 < x < 90$, making **(A)**, **(B)**, **(C)**, and **(D)** the correct choices.

13. 5

This question can be broken into two equations with two unknowns, Meg's age now (M) and Rolf 's age now (R). Equation (i) shows the relationship now; equation (ii) shows the relationship three years ago.

$$\text{(i) } M = 2 \times R \qquad \text{(ii) } M - 3 = R + 2$$

Substitute $2R$ for M in equation (ii) and solve for R:

$$\begin{aligned} M - 3 &= R + 2 \\ 2R - 3 &= R + 2 \\ 2R - R &= 2 + 3 \\ R &= 5 \end{aligned}$$

Rolf is **5** years old now.

14. C

The cost of manufacturing x crayons is $(570 + 0.5x)$ cents. Because each crayon sells for 10 cents, x crayons will sell for $10x$ cents. You want the smallest value of x such that $10x$ cents is at least $570 + 0.5x$ cents. So you must solve the equation $10x = 570 + 0.5x$ for the value of x that will recoup the investment.

$$\begin{aligned} 10x &= 570 + 0.5x \\ 9.5x &= 570 \\ x &= 60 \end{aligned}$$

The minimum number of crayons is 60, choice **(C)**.

Alternatively, you could have avoided setting up an algebraic equation by Backsolving, starting with either **(B)** or **(D)**.

15. A

You can write that $\frac{1-x}{xy} = \frac{1}{xy} - \frac{x}{xy}$. Canceling a factor of x from the numerator and denominator of $\frac{x}{xy}$, you have $\frac{x}{xy} = \frac{1}{y}$.

So, $\frac{1-x}{xy} = \frac{1}{xy} - \frac{x}{xy} = \frac{1}{xy} - \frac{1}{y}$. The answer is **(A)**.

16. C

Before you answer any graph question, begin by examining the graphs. Here you have two graphs, a segmented bar graph representing team revenue breakdowns for five teams and a pie chart showing the distribution of venue revenues for Team X.

You're now ready to attack the question, which asks you to find the team with the median venue revenue for 1997 and to determine what percent of that team's total revenue is media revenue. This question must refer to the first graph, and the first part of the question—finding the team with the median venue revenue—is straightforward. *Median* refers to the number in the middle. Looking at the white portions of the bars in the top graph, you see that Team Z has the median venue revenue. The fastest approach to the answer here (and throughout graph questions generally) is to approximate. The downside to bar graphs is that it's often very hard to get a read on the values. The upside is that if you approximate, often you don't have to read the values. Here you need to determine what percent of Team Z's bar is represented by media revenue (the segment in the middle—always be especially careful to isolate the correct piece of data). By approximating, you can see that the middle segment is about half of the entire bar. Thus the correct answer has to be close to 50%. The only answer choice that works is **(C)**, 45%.

17. D, E

The key to this question is that it involves both graphs. The question asks for the amount Team X earned through food sales, which takes you first to the pie chart, where you see that food sales accounted for 35% of the venue revenues for Team X. But to convert that to a dollar amount, you need a figure for the amount earned in venue revenues by Team X in 1997. According to the bar graph, this is \$40 million. Now, take 35% of \$40 million: $0.35 \times 40 = 14$, so the answer is any amount greater than 14. The answers are **(D)** and **(E)**.

18. E

Look at the bar graph: Team Q had media revenues of $35 - 5 = 30$ million, and Teams X, Y, and Z had media revenues greater than those of team Q. Team R had media revenue of $30 - 10 = 20$ million. The only correct choice is **(E)**.

19. B, C, D, E

Percent change problems are extremely popular graph questions, and as long as you set them up correctly, they are a great opportunity. This question asks for the approximate percent increase in Team Y's total revenue from 1997 to 1998, so you need to figure out (roughly) the amount of increase, place that over the original (or smaller) amount, and then convert the fraction into a percent. You are given the total revenue for 1998 as at least \$150 million, so you need to locate the total revenue for 1997 from the bar graph. It looks to be approximately \$120 million, so the amount of increase is \$30 million (or more), and the original amount is \$120 million. Now let's apply the formula:

$$\begin{aligned}\text{Percent increase} &= \frac{\$30 \text{ million}}{\$120 \text{ million}} \times 100\% \\ &= \frac{1}{4} \times 100\% \\ &= 25\%\end{aligned}$$

So, any percent greater than or equal to 25% is the answer. The answers are **(B)**, **(C)**, **(D)**, and **(E)**.

20. E

Looking at the bar graph, you see from the lowest portion of the bar for Team X that venue revenues of Team X were approximately 40 million dollars (call it 40m, for short). From the pie chart, the venue revenues of Team X from merchandise sales were approximately 20% of 40 million dollars, the venue revenues from ticket sales were approximately 10%, and the venue revenues from food sales were approximately 35%. The venue revenues of Team X from merchandise, in dollars, were approximately $0.2(40\text{m}) = 8\text{m}$. The venue revenues of Team X from ticket sales, in dollars, were approximately $0.1(40\text{m}) = 4\text{m}$. So the venue revenues of Team X from merchandise sales and ticket sales, in dollars, were approximately $8\text{m} + 4\text{m} = 12\text{m}$. The venue revenues of Team X from food sales, in dollars, were approximately $0.35(40\text{m}) = 14\text{m}$. The percent that the venue revenues of Team X that were from merchandise sales and ticket sales, out of the venue revenues of Team X that were from food sales, is approximately $\frac{12m}{14m} \times 100\% = \frac{6}{7} \times 100\% \approx 85.7\%$

To the nearest percent, 85.7% is 86%. Choice **(E)** is correct.

PART FOUR

Analytical Writing

CHAPTER 15

Introduction to Analytical Writing

OVERVIEW

The Analytical Writing section assesses not only how well you write but also the thought processes you employ to formulate and articulate a position. Your analytical and critical thinking skills will be tested by questions that ask you to evaluate complex arguments and form an argument of your own. The goal of the Analytical Writing section is to make the test an accurate indicator of your ability to understand and formulate an argument and to assess your analytical reasoning skills. These skills are exactly those you will need to perform well as a student at the graduate level.

In this section of the book, we'll take you through all the Analytical Writing Essay types you'll see on the GRE and give you the strategies you need to compose a well-written essay quickly and correctly. Also, all of the writing skills you'll need to perform well on the test are reviewed in the Writing Foundations and Content Review chapter.

ANALYTICAL WRITING ESSAY TYPES

The Analytical Writing Section of the GRE contains two different essay types. You'll be given 30 minutes for each essay. You'll be writing essays to address two different tasks:

- The Issue Task will provide a brief quotation on an issue of general interest and instructions on how to respond to the issue. You can discuss the issue from any perspective, making use of your own educational and personal background, examples from current or historical events, things you've read, or even relevant hypothetical situations. In this task, you will be developing your own argument.
- The Argument Task will contain a short argument that may or may not be complete and specific instructions on how to respond to the argument. You will assess the cogency of the argument, analyzing the author's chain of reasoning and evaluating his use of evidence. In this task, you do not develop your own argument but instead critique the argument presented in the prompt.

For each task, you'll be given one topic rather than a choice of several topics.

The Analytical Writing section will allow the graders to evaluate your ability to plan and compose a logical, well-reasoned essay under timed conditions. The essays are written on the computer, using a simple word-processing program. Only a score report is sent to the schools to which you apply.

The Analytical Writing portion of the GRE draws heavily upon your critical thinking abilities and your facility for understanding and analyzing written material. Specifically, it evaluates your ability to do the following:

- articulate and defend a position
- deconstruct and evaluate a complex argument
- develop a cogent argument
- assess the fundamental soundness of an argument
- recognize major, minor, and irrelevant points
- provide evidence and support for an argument
- detect the flaws in an unsound argument
- write articulately and effectively at a high level

How the Computer-Based Essays Are Administered

You can (and should) outline your essays on scratch paper, but your final answer must be typed into the computer before the end of the timed segment for you to receive a score for your work. At the start of the first Analytical Writing section, you will be given a brief tutorial on how to use the word-processing program. Don't worry. The GRE's word processor is simple and easy to use; the only functions you'll be able to use are *insert text*, *delete text*, *cut text*, *paste text*, and *undo*. You'll be well acquainted with these commands by the time you start writing. When practicing writing essays, turn off any auto-edit functions your word processor has. The GRE's word processor doesn't have these functions, so do your practice essays without them.

PACING STRATEGY

You'll have a limited amount of time to show the essay graders that you can think logically, analyze critically, and express yourself in clearly written English. Consequently, you'll need to know ahead of time how you're going to approach each essay. The Kaplan Method for Analytical Writing will help you plan and execute a clear, organized essay in the amount of time allotted. Note that the timing guidelines below are suggestions for how you should most effectively divide the 30 minutes you'll have for each of the essays. Different writers go through the different steps at their own pace, so don't feel chained to the breakdown below. As you practice, you will get a better sense of the amount of time you need to spend on each step to produce the best essay possible.

	Analyze an Issue	Analyze an Argument
Number of Questions	1	1
Time per Question	30 minutes	30 minutes

STEP 1
Take the Issue/Argument Apart: 2 minutes

STEP 2
Select the Points You'll Make: 4 minutes

STEP 3
Organize Your Thoughts: 2 minutes

STEP 4
Write Your Essay: 20 minutes

STEP 5
Proofread: 2 minutes

Try to keep these estimates in mind as you prepare for the test. If you use them as you work through the practice items, you will be comfortable keeping to the same amounts of time on Test Day.

SCORING

The essay scoring for the Analytical Writing sections is *holistic*, which means that the graders base your score on their overall impression of your essay, rather than deducting specific point values for errors. A holistic score emphasizes the interrelationship of content, organization, and syntax and denotes the unified effect of these combined elements.

The scoring scale is from 0 to 6, with 6 being the highest score. One human grader and one computer program will score each essay. If their scores differ by a certain margin, a second human grader will also score the essay, and the two human scores will be averaged.

Although the Analytical Writing section comprises two separate essays, ETS reports a single score that represents the average of your scores for the two essays, rounded to the nearest half-point.

You will receive your essay score, along with your official score report, within 10 to 15 days of your test date.

THE SCORING RUBRIC

Each of the two essays requires different reasoning and presentation, so each has slightly different grading criteria. However, the following rubric will give you a general idea of the guidelines graders have in mind when they score Analytical Writing essays.

6: "Outstanding" Essay

- Insightfully presents and convincingly supports an opinion on the issue or a critique of the argument
- Communicates ideas clearly and is generally well organized; connections are logical
- Demonstrates superior control of language: grammar, stylistic variety, and accepted conventions of writing; minor flaws may occur

5: "Strong" Essay

- Presents well-chosen examples and strongly supports an opinion on the issue or a critique of the argument
- Communicates ideas clearly and is generally well organized; connections are logical
- Demonstrates solid control of language: grammar, stylistic variety, and accepted conventions of writing; minor flaws may occur

4: "Adequate" Essay

- Presents and adequately supports an opinion on the issue or a critique of the argument
- Communicates ideas fairly clearly and is adequately organized; logical connections are satisfactory
- Demonstrates satisfactory control of language: grammar, stylistic variety, and accepted conventions of writing; some flaws may occur

3: "Limited" Essay

- Succeeds only partially in presenting and supporting an opinion on the issue or a critique of the argument
- Communicates ideas unclearly and is poorly organized
- Demonstrates less than satisfactory control of language: contains significant mistakes in grammar, usage, and sentence structure

2: "Weak" Essay

- Shows little success in presenting and supporting an opinion on the issue or a critique of the argument
- Struggles to communicate ideas; essay shows a lack of clarity and organization
- Meaning is impeded by many serious mistakes in grammar, usage, and sentence structure

1: "Fundamentally Deficient" Essay

- Fails to present a coherent opinion and/or evidence on the issue or a critique of the argument
- Fails to communicate ideas; essay is seriously unclear and disorganized
- Lacks meaning due to widespread and severe mistakes in grammar, usage, and sentence structure

0: "Unscorable" Essay

- Completely ignores topic
- Attempts to copy the task
- Written in a language other than English or contains undecipherable text

NAVIGATING THE ANALYTICAL WRITING SECTION OF THIS BOOK

The chapter immediately following this one is on Writing Foundations and Content and will review the classic writing techniques, concepts, and topics that you may encounter on the GRE. This section of the book also includes individual chapters on the Issue essay and the Argument essay questions. Each chapter includes an introduction and definition of the different tasks and a review and examples of the strategies to follow to answer those questions quickly and correctly.

Finally, at the end of this section, you'll find the Analytical Writing Practice. This will consist of two Issue essay prompts and two Argument essay prompts. At the end will be sample essays for each of the prompts. Use the Practice Prompts to test your writing skills and pinpoint areas for more focused study. When you are finished with this section of the book, you should be thoroughly prepared for any task you might encounter on the Analytical Writing section of the GRE.

CHAPTER 16

Analytical Writing Foundations and Content Review

INTRODUCTION TO ANALYTICAL WRITING FOUNDATIONS AND CONTENT REVIEW

The GRE tests your ability to construct a coherent, logical, and well-developed response to a writing prompt. This requires a mastery of grammatical, syntactical, and language concepts, as well as an awareness of audience and command of the writing process. These concepts include:

- Streamlining Wordy Phrases
- Eliminating Redundancy
- Avoiding Excessive Qualification
- Removing Unnecessary Sentences
- Avoiding Needless Self-Reference
- Using Active Voice rather than Passive Voice
- Including Strong Openings
- Avoiding Needlessly Vague Language
- Rewording Clichés
- Avoiding Jargon
- Ensuring Subject-Verb Agreement
- Avoiding Faulty Modification
- Avoiding Unclear Pronoun Reference
- Correctly Using Parallelism
- Using a Consistent Narrative Voice
- Avoiding Slang and Colloquialisms
- Avoiding Sentence Fragments and Run-Ons
- Correctly Using Commas
- Correctly Using Semicolons
- Correctly Using Colons
- Correctly Using Hyphens and Dashes
- Correctly Using Apostrophes

This chapter will cover all these grammatical and writing concepts and provide practice sets to help you conquer the writing task using the clearest, strongest language possible.

STREAMLINING WORDY PHRASES

Why use several words when one will do? Many people make the mistake of writing phrases such as *at the present time* or *at this point in time* instead of the simpler *now*, or *take into consideration* instead of simply *consider*, in an attempt to make their prose seem more scholarly or more formal. It doesn't work. Instead, their prose ends up seeming inflated and pretentious. Don't waste your words or your time.

WORDY: I am of the opinion that the aforementioned managers should be advised that they will be evaluated with regard to the utilization of responsive organizational software for the purpose of devising a responsive network of customers.

CONCISE: We should tell the managers that we will evaluate their use of flexible computerized databases to develop a customer network.

Streamlining Wordy Phrases Practice Set

Read the following sentences and revise the wordy phrases.

1. Government funding cripples the natural relationship of arts enthusiasts and artists by subsidizing work and makes artists less creative and forces the taxpayer to take on the burden of paying for art they don't like.

   ____

   ____

2. There are many reasons why some may believe that the services of one real estate agent are superior in quality to the services of another competing real estate agent or group of agents, including the personal service they provide, the care and quality of the work they do, and the communication lines they set up and keep open.

   ____

   ____

Streamlining Wordy Phrases Practice Set Answers and Explanations

Examples of the revised sentences with explanations:

1. The government should not subsidize artists, because it makes them less creative and forces taxpayers to pay for art they don't like.

The original sentence contained unnecessary repetition. The original sentence does not need to include both "funding" and "subsidizing," as both words refer to the same thing. The clause about "crippling the natural relationship" is also redundant, as that is implied by listing the negative effects government funding will have on both artists and the taxpayers.

2. **Reasons for choosing one real estate agent over another include personal service, care, communication, and quality of work.**

The revised sentence condenses the two main clauses, i.e. the main idea (choosing one real estate agent over another) and the subsequent list. It also pares down the unnecessary repetition. There is no need to explain that communication lines are set up and kept open, for example.

ELIMINATING REDUNDANCY

Redundancy means that the writer needlessly repeats an idea. For example, it's redundant to speak of *a beginner lacking experience*. The word *beginner* implies lack of experience by itself. You can eliminate redundant words or phrases without changing the meaning of the sentence.

Here are some common redundancies:

REDUNDANT	CONCISE
refer back	refer
few in number	few
small-sized	small
grouped together	grouped
in my own personal opinion	in my opinion
end result	result
serious crisis	crisis
new initiatives	initiatives

REDUNDANT: It is wise to plan ahead for unexpected problems.
CONCISE: It is wise to plan for unexpected problems.

In this example, "plan ahead" is redundant. In what situation would you "plan behind"? "Unexpected problems" is acceptable because, while some problems are unexpected, others are readily anticipated.

ELIMINATING REDUNDANCY PRACTICE SET

Read the following sentences and revise to eliminate redundancy.

1. All of these problems have combined together to create a serious crisis.

____

____

2. That monument continues to remain a significant tourist attraction.

____

____

ELIMINATING REDUNDANCY PRACTICE SET ANSWERS AND EXPLANATIONS

Examples of the revised sentences with explanations:

1. All of these problems have combined to create a crisis.

Crises are inherently serious, and things cannot combine apart. The adverb and adjective are redundant.

2. That monument remains a significant tourist attraction.

There is no need to reinforce "remain" with "continues." The verb "remain" implies that.

AVOIDING EXCESSIVE QUALIFICATION

Because the object of your essay is to convince your reader of your point of view, you will want to adopt a reasonable tone. There will likely be no single, clear-cut "answer" to the essay topic, so don't overstate your case. Occasional use of such qualifiers as *fairly*, *rather*, *somewhat*, and *relatively* and of such expressions as *seems to be*, *a little*, and a *certain amount of* will let the reader know you are reasonable, but overusing such modifiers weakens your argument. Excessive qualification makes you sound hesitant. Like wordy phrases, qualifiers can add bulk without adding substance.

WORDY: This rather serious breach of etiquette may possibly shake the very foundations of the corporate world.
CONCISE: This serious breach of etiquette may shake the foundations of the corporate world.

Just as bad is the overuse of the word *very*. Some writers use this intensifying adverb before almost every adjective in an attempt to be more forceful. If you need to add emphasis, look for a stronger adjective or adverb.

WEAK: Adelaide is a very good flautist.

STRONG: Adelaide is a virtuoso flautist.

STRONG: Adelaide plays beautifully.

And don't try to qualify words that are already absolute.

WRONG	CORRECT
more unique	unique
the very worst	the worst
completely full	full

Avoiding Excessive Qualification Practice Set

Read the following sentences and revise the excessive qualification(s).

1. She is a fairly excellent teacher.

____

____

2. It's possible that we might overcome these obstacles.

____

____

Avoiding Excessive Qualification Practice Set Answers and Explanations

Examples of the revised sentences with explanations:

1. She is an excellent teacher.

The use of the adverb "fairly" unnecessarily weakens the point of the sentence.

2. We might overcome these obstacles.

The word "might" implies that it's possible but not certain, so saying "it's possible" is unnecessary.

REMOVING UNNECESSARY SENTENCES

Brevity is crucial for success on a timed test that emphasizes content over form. Remember, the essays on this test will force you to economize your expression. This principle suggests several things:

- Don't write a sentence that strays from the thesis.
- Don't ask a question only to answer it; rhetorical questions are a no-no.
- Don't merely copy the essay's prompt.
- Don't write a whole sentence only to announce that you're changing the subject.

If you have something to say, say it without preamble. If you need to smooth over a change of subject, do so with a transitional word or phrase rather than with a meaningless sentence.

WORDY: Which idea of the author's is more in line with what I believe? This is a very interesting question.
CONCISE: The author's beliefs are similar to mine.

The author of the wordy example above is just wasting words and time. Get to the point quickly and stay there.

Removing Unnecessary Sentences Practice Set

Read the sentences and rewrite each pair as one concise statement.

1. What's the purpose of getting rid of the chemical pollutants in water? People cannot safely consume water that contains chemical pollutants.

   ____

   ____

2. I do not believe it is necessary to include the telemetry data. The telemetry data adds little of value to the study of stellar drift.

   ____

   ____

Removing Unnecessary Sentences Practice Set Answers and Explanations

Examples of the revised sentences with explanations:

1. People cannot safely consume water that contains chemical pollutants.

The first sentence is an unnecessary rhetorical question.

2. It is not necessary to include the telemetry data, as it adds little of value to the study of stellar drift.

In this situation, there are two different but related thoughts: the merits of the data, and whether or not to include it. It is therefore best to combine the sentences, which can be done elegantly without destroying the flow of the passage.

AVOIDING NEEDLESS SELF-REFERENCE

Avoid such unnecessary phrases as *I believe*, *I feel*, and *in my opinion*. There is no need to remind your reader that what you are writing is your opinion. Self-reference is another—very obvious—form of qualifying what you say.

WEAK: I am of the opinion that air pollution is a more serious problem than most people realize.
FORCEFUL: Air pollution is a more serious problem than most people realize.

Avoiding Needless Self-Reference Practice Set

Eliminate needless self-references in these sentences.

1. It seems to me that nuclear energy is safer and cleaner than burning fossil fuels. I think we should build more nuclear power plants.

____

____

2. The author, in my personal opinion, is stuck in the past.

____

____

Avoiding Needless Self-Reference Practice Set Answers and Explanations

Examples of the revised sentences with explanations:

1. **Nuclear energy is safer and cleaner than burning fossil fuels, so we should build more nuclear power plants.**

"It seems to me" and "I think" hedge unnecessarily and intrude on the argument. (Also note how combining these statements makes the argument flow better.)

2. **The author is stuck in the past.**

Unless specified otherwise, your writing will always express your opinion.

USING ACTIVE VOICE RATHER THAN PASSIVE VOICE

Using the passive voice is a way to avoid accountability (it's often referred to as the "politician's voice"). Put verbs in the active voice whenever possible. In the active voice, the subject performs the action (e.g., "we write essays"). In the passive voice, the subject is the receiver of the action and is often only implied (e.g., "essays are written by us").

PASSIVE: The estimate of this year's tax revenues was prepared by the General Accounting Office.
ACTIVE: The General Accounting Office prepared the estimate of this year's tax revenues.

The passive voice creates weak sentences and is usually the product of writing before you think. Avoid this by organizing your thoughts before you begin writing. Take a few minutes to find out what you want to say before you say it. To change from the passive to the active voice, ask yourself *who* or *what* is performing the action. In the sentence above, the General Accounting Office is performing the action; therefore, the General Accounting Office should be the subject of the sentence.

You should avoid the passive voice EXCEPT in the following cases:

- When you do not know who performed the action: *The letter was opened before I received it.*
- When you prefer not to refer directly to the person who performs the action: *An error has been made in computing these data.*

It is rare to have a good reason to use passive voice in either of the Analytical Writing essays on the GRE.

Using Active Voice Practice Set

Read the sentences and replace all instances of passive voice with active voice wherever possible.

1. The faulty wiring in the walls went unnoticed by the safety inspectors until it was too late.

   ____

   ____

2. The Spanish-American War was fought by brave but misguided men.

   ____

   ____

Using Active Voice Practice Set Answers and Explanations

Examples of the revised sentences with explanations:

1. The safety inspectors did not notice the faulty wiring in the walls until it was too late.

The safety inspectors are the ones doing (or not doing) the action, so they should be the subject of the sentence.

2. Brave but misguided men fought the Spanish-American War.

There is no need for the passive in this situation, as it is absolutely clear who did the fighting.

INCLUDING STRONG OPENINGS

Try not to begin a sentence with *there is, there are*, or *it is*. These roundabout expressions usually indicate that you are trying to distance yourself from the position you are taking. Again, weak openings often result from writing before you think.

Including Strong Openings Practice Set

Read the following sentences and revise to improve the openings.

1. There isn't much wilderness left, so we should protect what we have.

____

____

2. There are several reasons why this plane is obsolete.

____

____

Including Strong Openings Practice Set Answers and Explanations

Examples of the revised sentences with explanations:

1. We should protect what little wilderness we have left.

Notice how this statement takes a forceful position right away.

2. This plane is obsolete for several reasons.

The revised sentence is less timid and states its purpose in a stronger tone.

AVOIDING NEEDLESSLY VAGUE LANGUAGE

Don't just ramble on when writing your GRE essays. Choose specific, descriptive words. Vague language weakens your writing because it forces the reader to guess what you mean instead of concentrating fully on your ideas and style. The essay topics you'll be given aren't going to be obscure. You will be able to come up with specific examples and concrete information about the topics. Your argument will be more forceful if you stick to this approach.

WEAK: Ms. Brown is highly educated.
FORCEFUL: Ms. Brown has a master's degree in business administration.

WEAK: She is a great communicator.
FORCEFUL: She speaks persuasively.

Notice that sometimes, to be more specific and concrete, you will have to use more words than you might with vague language. This principle is not in conflict with the general objective of concision. Being concise may mean eliminating unnecessary words. Avoiding vagueness may mean adding necessary words.

AVOIDING NEEDLESSLY VAGUE LANGUAGE PRACTICE SET

Rewrite these sentences to replace vague language with specific, concrete language. You may need to invent details.

1. There are no boundaries to the age of library patrons, and the installation of vending machines is a scheme that potentially has ill effects where young readers are concerned.

   ____

   ____

2. Living upstairs from the band has been challenging.

   ____

   ____

AVOIDING NEEDLESSLY VAGUE LANGUAGE PRACTICE SET ANSWERS AND EXPLANATIONS

Examples of the revised sentences with explanations:

1. **Because the library is open to readers of all ages, including young readers who may overindulge in unhealthy treats, it would be unwise to install vending machines.**

The original sentence contains several overwrought phrases and never explains what the "ill effects" of vending machines would be. The rewritten version makes the argument directly.

2. **I can never get enough sleep because the band downstairs holds loud practice sessions every night.**

You could have rewritten this sentence in many different ways, but the important thing is to change the vague "has been challenging" to a more specific grievance.

REWORDING CLICHÉS

Clichés are overused expressions that may once have seemed colorful and powerful but are now dull and worn out. Time, pressure, and anxiety may make you lose focus; that's when clichés may slip into your writing. A reliance on clichés will suggest you are a lazy thinker. Keep them out of your essay.

WEAK: It began to rain cats and dogs when we arrived at the station.
FORCEFUL: A heavy rain began to fall when we arrived at the station.

Putting a cliché in quotation marks to indicate your distance from the cliché does not strengthen the sentence. If anything, it just makes weak writing more noticeable. If you notice any clichés in your writing, ask yourself if you could replace them with more specific language.

Rewording Clichés Practice Set

Read the following sentences and remove any clichés.

1. Be positive is my motto!

   ____

   ____

2. Beyond a shadow of a doubt, Jefferson was a great leader.

   ____

   ____

Rewording Clichés Practice Set Answers and Explanations

Examples of the revised sentences with explanations:

1. I prefer to praise positive actions than to dwell on negative ones.

The unrevised sentence crams two clichés into five words. The revised sentence is both more specific and more original, which will serve you better in writing an analytical essay.

2. Jefferson was a great leader.

The revised sentence makes an equally strong assertion, but has a less histrionic tone.

AVOIDING JARGON

Jargon includes two categories of words that you should avoid. First is the specialized vocabulary of a group, such as that used by doctors, lawyers, or baseball coaches. Second is the overly inflated and complex language that burdens many students' essays. You will not impress anyone with big words that do not fit the tone or context of your essay, especially if you misuse them. If you are not certain of a word's meaning or appropriateness, leave it out. An appropriate word, even a simple one, will add clarity to your argument. As you come across words you are unsure of, ask yourself, "Would a reader in a different field be able to understand exactly what I mean from the words I've chosen? Is there any way I can say the same thing more simply?"

WEAK: The company is not able to bankroll the project.
FORCEFUL: The company is not able to pay for the project.

The following are commonly used jargon words:

assistance	downside	optimize
ballpark	face time	originate
bandwidth	facilitate	parameter
blindside	finalize	prioritize
bottom line	input/output	target
conceptualize	maximize	time frame
cookie-cutter	mutually beneficial	user-friendly
designate	ongoing	utilize

Avoiding Jargon Practice Set

Revise the following sentences to remove the jargon.

1. When a parent attempts to correct the bad behavior of a child by positively reinforcing good behavior, this classical conditioning can become ineffective due to extinction.

____

____

2. Foreign diplomats should always interface with local leaders.

____

____

Avoiding Jargon Practice Set Answers and Explanations

Examples of the revised sentences with explanations:

1. **Attempting to correct a child's bad behavior by rewarding good behavior can become ineffective when the reward is withdrawn.**

The first sentence was loaded with jargon not readily understood by the average reader. The revised sentence expresses the exact same thought, but in less technically opaque language.

2. **Foreign diplomats should always talk to local leaders.**

The verb "interface" is most appropriately used in a technical context. It sounds jarring and pretentious in the unrevised sentence.

ENSURING SUBJECT-VERB AGREEMENT

A verb must agree with its subject regardless of intervening phrases. Do not let the words that come between the subject and the verb confuse you as to the number (singular or plural) of the subject. Usually, one word can be pinpointed as the grammatical subject of the sentence. Find the verb, no matter how far removed, and make sure that it agrees with that subject in number.

INCORRECT: The joys of climbing mountains, especially if one is a novice climber without the proper equipment, escapes me.

CORRECT: The *joys* of climbing mountains, especially if one is a novice climber without the proper equipment, *escape* me.

Watch out for collective nouns like *group*, *audience*, *committee*, or *majority*. These take a singular verb unless you are emphasizing the individuals forming the group.

CORRECT: A *majority* of the jury *thinks* that the defendant is guilty. (The collective is being emphasized.)

CORRECT: A *majority* of the committee *have signed* their names to the report. (The individual members of the committee are being emphasized.)

A subject that consists of two or more nouns connected by the conjunction *and* takes the plural form of the verb.

CORRECT: *Karl*, an expert in cooking Hunan chicken, *and George*, an expert in preparing Hunan spicy duck, *have combined* their expertise to start a new restaurant.

However, when the subject consists of two or more nouns connected by *or* or *nor*, the verb agrees with the CLOSEST noun.

CORRECT: Either the senators or the *president is* misinformed.

CORRECT: Either the president or the *senators are* misinformed.

Some connecting phrases look as though they should make a group of words into a plural but actually do not. The only connecting word that can make a series of singular nouns into a plural subject is *and*. In particular, the following connecting words and phrases do NOT result in a plural subject:

along with, as well as, besides, in addition to, together with

INCORRECT: The president, along with the secretary of state and the director of the CIA, are misinformed.

CORRECT: The *president*, along with the secretary of state and the director of the CIA, *is* misinformed.

You can usually trust your ear to give you the correct verb form. However, subject-verb agreement can be tricky in the following instances:

- when the subject and verb are separated
- when the subject is an indefinite pronoun
- when the subject consists of more than one noun

If a sentence that is grammatically correct still sounds awkward, you should probably rephrase your thought.

Ensuring Subject-Verb Agreement Practice Set

Read the sentences below and revise to ensure subject-verb agreement.

1. The arts is a very important topic to discuss at this point in our history.

    ____

    ____

2. The majority of the organization's members is over 60 years old.

    ____

    ____

Ensuring Subject-Verb Agreement Practice Set Answers and Explanations

Examples of the revised sentences with explanations:

1. The arts are a very important topic to discuss at this point in our history.

The verb is plural because the sentence is referring to more than one type of art, even though they collectively form a single topic of discussion.

2. The majority of the organization's members are over 60 years old.

The verb must be pluralized because the subject is more than one member.

AVOIDING FAULTY MODIFICATION

Modifiers should be placed as close as possible to what they modify. In English, the position of the word within a sentence often establishes the word's relationship to other words in the sentence. If a modifier is placed too far from the word it modifies, the meaning may be lost or obscured. Notice, in the following sentences, the ambiguity that results when the modifying phrases are misplaced:

UNCLEAR: Gary and Martha sat talking about the problem in the office.
CLEAR: Gary and Martha sat in the office talking about the problem.

UNCLEAR: He only threw the ball eight yards.
CLEAR: He threw the ball only eight yards.

In addition to misplaced modifiers, watch for dangling modifiers: modifiers whose intended referents are not even present.

INCORRECT: Coming out of context, Peter was startled by Julia's perceptiveness.
CORRECT: Julia's remark, coming out of context, startled Peter with its perceptiveness.

Avoiding Faulty Modification Practice Set

Read the following sentences and revise the faulty modification.

1. Inspired by the new love in his life, it took Sam three months only to finish his novel.

 ____

 ____

2. Having been an avid lifelong reader, a bookstore with a café seems like heaven on earth to me.

 ____

 ____

Avoiding Faulty Modification Practice Set Answers and Explanations

Examples of the revised sentences with explanations:

1. Inspired by the new love in his life, Sam finished his novel in only three months.

The original sentence contains two faulty modifiers. First, it is Sam, not "it," who is "inspired," so Sam should appear right after the comma. Second, the point of the sentence is that Sam finished the novel in only three months, not that finishing the novel was the only thing he got done in that time.

2. A bookstore with a café seems like heaven on earth to an avid life-long reader like me.

In the unrevised sentence it is unclear whether it is the author or the bookstore that has been a life-long avid reader.

AVOIDING UNCLEAR PRONOUN REFERENCE

A pronoun is a word that replaces a noun in a sentence. Every time you write a pronoun—such as *he, him, his, she, her, hers, it, its, they, their, that*, or *which*—be sure there can be absolutely no doubt what its antecedent is. (An antecedent is the particular noun to which a pronoun refers.) Careless use of pronouns can obscure your intended meaning.

UNCLEAR: The teacher told the student he was talented. (Does *he* refer to *teacher* or *student*?)

CLEAR: The student was talented, and the teacher told him so.

CLEAR: The teacher considered himself talented and told the student so.

UNCLEAR: Sara knows more about history than Irina because she learned it from her father.

(Does *she* refer to *Sara* or *Irina*?) You can usually rearrange a sentence to avoid ambiguous pronoun references.

CLEAR: Because Sara learned history from her father, she knows more than Irina does.

CLEAR: Because Irina learned history from her father, she knows less about it than Sara does.

If you are worried that a pronoun reference will be ambiguous, rewrite the sentence so that there is no doubt. Don't be afraid to repeat the antecedent if necessary.

UNCLEAR: I would rather settle in Phoenix than in Albuquerque, although it lacks wonderful restaurants.

CLEAR: I would rather settle in Phoenix than in Albuquerque, although Phoenix lacks wonderful restaurants.

A reader must be able to pinpoint the pronoun's antecedent. Even if you think the reader will know what you mean, do not use a pronoun without a clear and appropriate antecedent.

INCORRECT: When you are painting, be sure not to get it on the floor.
(*It* could only refer to the noun *paint*. But do you see the noun *paint* anywhere in the sentence? Pronouns cannot refer to implied nouns.)
CORRECT: When you are painting, be sure not to get any paint on the floor.

Avoiding Unclear Pronoun Reference Practice Set

Revise the following sentences to correct unclear pronoun references.

1. Sports enthusiasts' desires should not trump the needs of the river and the quiet enjoyment of the people who live near the river. Their opinions should be taken into account.

 ____

 ____

2. Caroline telephoned her friends in California before going home for the night, which she had not done for weeks.

 ____

 ____

Avoiding Unclear Pronoun Reference Practice Set Answers and Explanations

Examples of the revised sentences with explanations:

1. **Sports enthusiasts' desires should not trump the needs of the river and the quiet enjoyment of the people who live near the river, whose opinions should be taken into account.**

In the original sentences, it is unclear if the pronoun "their" refers the people who live near the river, or the sports enthusiasts. Replacing "their" with "whose" clarifies matters.

2. **Caroline telephoned her California friends for the first time in weeks before she went home for the night.**

In the unrevised sentence, we do not know whether Caroline had not spent the night at home in weeks or whether she had not telephoned her friends in weeks.

CORRECTLY USING PARALLELISM

It can be rhetorically effective to use a particular construction several times in succession to provide emphasis. The technique is called *parallel construction*, and it is effective only when used sparingly.

Example: *As a* leader, Lincoln inspired a nation to throw off the chains of slavery; *as a* philosopher, he proclaimed the greatness of the little man; *as a* human being, he served as a timeless example of humility.

The repetition of the italicized construction provides the sentence with a strong sense of rhythm and organization and alerts the reader to the multiple aspects of Lincoln's character. Matching constructions must be expressed in parallel form. Writers often use parallel structure incorrectly for dissimilar items.

INCORRECT: They are sturdy, attractive, and cost only a dollar each. (The phrase *They are* makes sense preceding the adjectives *sturdy* and *attractive*, but it cannot be understood before *cost only a dollar each*.)
CORRECT: They are sturdy and attractive, and they cost only a dollar each.

Parallel constructions must be expressed in parallel grammatical form: all nouns, all infinitives, all gerunds, all prepositional phrases, or all clauses.

INCORRECT: All business students should learn word processing, accounting, and how to program computers.
CORRECT: All business students should learn word processing, accounting, and computer programming.

This principle applies to any words that might precede items in a series: either repeat the word before every element in a series or include it only before the first item. (In effect, your treatment of the second element of the series determines the form of all subsequent elements.)

INCORRECT: He invested his money in stocks, in real estate, and a home for retired performers.
CORRECT: He invested his money in stocks, in real estate, and in a home for retired performers.
CORRECT: He invested his money in stocks, real estate, and a home for retired performers.

A number of constructions always call for you to express ideas in parallel form. These constructions include the following:

X is as ________ as Y.
X is more ________ than Y.
X is less ________ than Y.
Both X and Y . . .
Either X or Y . . .
Neither X nor Y . . .
Not only X but also Y . . .

X and Y can stand for as little as one word or as much as a whole clause, but in any case, the grammatical structure of X and Y must be identical.

INCORRECT: The view from this apartment is as spectacular as from that mountain lodge.

CORRECT: The view from this apartment is as spectacular as the view from that mountain lodge.

Including Parallelism Practice Set

Read these sentences and revise to correct parallelism.

1. Homes sell faster or slowly for a wide variety of reasons.

____

____

2. The grocery baggers were ready, able, and were quite determined to do a great job.

____

____

Including Parallelism Practice Set Answers and Explanations

Examples of the revised sentences with explanations:

1. Homes sell faster or slower for all types of reasons.

In order for the parallel construction to work in this sentence, the two thoughts must have identical grammatical form. Therefore, "slower" is correct because it is grammatically similar to "faster."

2. The grocery baggers were ready, able, and quite determined to do a great job.

In this example, there is no need to repeat the verb; the phrase "quite determined to do a great job" can be treated as the final object in the series of terms.

USING A CONSISTENT NARRATIVE VOICE

True, we have advised you to avoid needless self-reference. But an occasional self-reference may be appropriate in your GRE essays. You may even call yourself *I* if you want, as long as you keep the number of first-person pronouns to a minimum. Less egocentric ways of referring to the narrator include *we* and *one*. If these more formal ways of writing seem stilted, stay with *I*.

"In my lifetime, I have seen many challenges to the principle of free speech."

"You can see how a free society can get too complacent when free speech is taken for granted."

"One must admit that one should not overgeneralize."

The method of self-reference you select is called the *narrative voice* of your essay. Any of the three previous narrative voices is acceptable. Nevertheless, whichever you choose, you must be careful not to shift narrative voice in your essay. If you use *I* in the first sentence, for example, do not use *you* in a later sentence. You can shift narrative voice when presenting someone else's point of view or when speaking hypothetically, but your authorial voice should always be consistent.

INCORRECT: In my lifetime, *I* have seen many challenges to the principle of free speech. *You* can see how a free society can get too complacent when free speech is taken for granted.

It is likewise wrong to shift from *you* to *one*:

INCORRECT: Just by following the news, *you* can readily see how politicians have a vested interest in pleasing powerful interest groups. But *one* should not generalize about this tendency.

USING A CONSISTENT NARRATIVE VOICE PRACTICE SET

Read the sentences below and revise the narrative voice to make it consistent.

1. Not all wilderness areas are similar to the glorious Ansel Adams landscapes that we all imagine. If you've seen pictures of the Arctic National Wildlife Refuge, one would be unimpressed by the "natural beauty" of that massive swamp.

___

___

2. I am disgusted by the waste we tolerate in this country. One cannot simply stand by without adding to such waste: living here makes you wasteful.

____

____

Using a Consistent Narrative Voice Practice Set Answers and Explanations

Examples of the revised sentences with explanations:

1. **Not all wilderness areas are similar to the glorious Ansel Adams landscapes that you might imagine. If you were to see pictures of ANWAR, you would be unimpressed by the "natural beauty" of that massive swamp.**

The narrative tone of most of the passage is personal and does not justify a switch to the more formal third-person "one" in the second sentence.

2. **I am disgusted with the waste we tolerate in this country. We cannot simply stand by without adding to such waste: living here makes us wasteful.**

In this passage, the tone and narrative are impassioned and emphatically first person. The reader is directly addressed and exhorted to join in a common cause. Therefore, the passage should retain both the singular and plural forms of the first-person pronoun.

AVOIDING SLANG AND COLLOQUIALISMS

Conversational speech is filled with slang and colloquial expressions. However, you should avoid slang on the GRE. Slang terms and colloquialisms, or overly casual sayings, can be confusing to the reader, since these expressions are not universally understood. Even worse, such informal writing may give readers the impression that you are poorly educated or arrogant. Always bear in mind the audience for whom your writing is intended. Finally, remember that contractions are not commonly used in formal writing, so try to avoid them altogether in your essays. You should be fine if you keep in mind the differences between *written* and *spoken* English.

INAPPROPRIATE: He is really into gardening.
CORRECT: He is an avid gardener.

INAPPROPRIATE: She plays a wicked game of tennis.
CORRECT: She excels at tennis.

INAPPROPRIATE: Myra has got to go to Memphis for a week.
CORRECT: Myra must go to Memphis for a week.

INAPPROPRIATE: Joan's been doing science for eight years now.
CORRECT: Joan has been a scientist for eight years now.

Avoiding Slang and Colloquialism Practice Set

Read the sentences below and revise the tone to eliminate slang and colloquialisms.

1. Gertrude has been rockin' the sales floor for almost thirty years now.

   ____

   ____

2. Normal human beings can't cope with repeated humiliation.

   ____

   ____

Avoiding Slang and Colloquialism Practice Set Answers and Explanations

Examples of the revised sentences with explanations:

1. Gertrude has excelled as a salesperson for almost thirty years.

The tone in the unrevised sentence is too informal. Do not try to make your writing sound like spoken language; the spoken and formal written registers are very different. Always spell out words in their entirety.

2. Normal human beings cannot tolerate repeated humiliation.

Avoid contractions wherever possible.

AVOIDING SENTENCE FRAGMENTS AND RUN-ONS

Every sentence in formal expository writing must have an independent clause: a clause that contains a subject and a predicate. A sentence fragment has no independent clause; a run-on sentence has two or more independent clauses that are improperly connected. As you edit your practice essays, check your sentence constructions, noting any tendency toward fragments or run-on sentences.

FRAGMENT: Global warming. That is what the scientists and journalists are worried about this month.
CORRECT: Global warming is the cause of concern for scientists and journalists this month.

FRAGMENT: Seattle is a wonderful place to live. Mountains, ocean, and forests, all within easy driving distance. If you can ignore the rain.
CORRECT: Seattle is a wonderful place to live, with mountains, ocean, and forests all within easy driving distance. However, it certainly does rain often.

FRAGMENT: Why is the author's position preposterous? Because he makes generalizations that are untrue.
CORRECT: The author's position is preposterous because he makes generalizations that are untrue.

Beginning single-clause sentences with coordinating conjunctions—*for, and, nor, but, or, yet*, and *so*—is acceptable in moderation.

CORRECT: Most people would agree that indigent patients should receive wonderful health care. But every treatment has its price.

Time pressure may also cause you to write two or more sentences as one. When you proofread your essays, watch out for independent clauses that are not joined with any punctuation at all or are only joined with a comma.

RUN-ON: Current insurance practices are unfair they discriminate against the people who need insurance most.

You can repair run-on sentences in any one of three ways. First, you could use a period to make separate sentences of the independent clauses.

CORRECT: Current insurance practices are unfair. They discriminate against the people who need insurance most.

You could also use a semicolon. A semicolon is a weak period. It separates independent clauses but signals to the reader that the ideas in the clauses are related.

CORRECT: Current insurance practices are unfair; they discriminate against the people who need insurance most.

The third method of repairing a run-on sentence is usually the most effective. Use a conjunction to turn an independent clause into a dependent one and to make explicit how the clauses are related. A comma is also called for when using one of the FANBOYS (**F**or, **A**nd, **N**or, **B**ut, **O**r, **Y**et, **S**o) coordinating conjunctions. You should insert a comma before one of these conjunctions when it separates two independent clauses.

CORRECT: Current insurance practices are unfair because they discriminate against the people who need insurance most.

CORRECT: Current insurance practices are unfair, for they discriminate against the people who need insurance most.

A common cause of run-on sentences is the misuse of adverbs like *however, nevertheless, furthermore, likewise*, and *therefore*.

RUN-ON: Current insurance practices are discriminatory, furthermore they make insurance too expensive for the poor.

CORRECT: Current insurance practices are discriminatory. Furthermore, they make insurance too expensive for the poor.

AVOIDING SENTENCE FRAGMENTS AND RUN-ONS PRACTICE SET

Read the sentences below and make revisions to correct fragments and run-on sentences.

1. The writer of this letter lays out a cogent argument about why Adams Realty is superior it is organized, has strong points with clear examples, and is convincing.

 ____

 ____

2. Leadership ability. That is the elusive quality that our current government employees have yet to capture.

 ____

 ____

AVOIDING SENTENCE FRAGMENTS AND RUN-ONS PRACTICE SET ANSWERS AND EXPLANATIONS

Examples of the revised sentences with explanations:

1. **The writer of this letter lays out a cogent, organized, and convincing argument with strong points and clear examples to illustrate the superiority of Adams Realty.**

The unrevised sentence is turgid and unruly. We have two choices: condense the series of nouns and adjectives, or break it into two different sentences. We've gone with concision for this example. By deleting the "it is," which really should indicate the start of a new sentence, we have put the adjectives describing the argument in a series with commas, and put the nouns into a prepositional phrase at the end of the sentence.

2. **Leadership ability is the elusive quality that our current government employees have yet to capture.**

This pair of sentences is fairly easy to revise. The first is a fragment that can easily be incorporated into the second, as the pronoun "that" refers to "Leadership ability."

CORRECTLY USING COMMAS

The proper use of commas constitutes one of the trickier points of style and usage. Different editors have different preferences and conventions for how and when to use commas. The guidelines below are ideally suited for use in terse, analytical essays, such as those asked for in the GRE Analytical Writing sections.

Use commas to separate items in a series. If more than two items are listed in a series, they should be separated by commas. The final comma—the one that precedes the word *and*—is optional (but be consistent throughout your essays).

CORRECT: My recipe for buttermilk biscuits contains flour, baking soda, salt, shortening and buttermilk.
CORRECT: My recipe for buttermilk biscuits contains flour, baking soda, salt, shortening, and buttermilk.

Don't place commas before the first element of a series or after the last element.

INCORRECT: My investment adviser recommended that I construct a portfolio of, stocks, bonds, commodities futures, and precious metals.
INCORRECT: The elephants, tigers, and dancing bears, were the highlights of the circus.

Use commas to separate two or more adjectives before a noun, but don't use a comma after the last adjective in the series.

INCORRECT: The manatee is a round, blubbery, bewhiskered, creature whose continued presence in American waters is endangered by careless boaters.
CORRECT: The manatee is a round, blubbery, bewhiskered creature whose continued presence in American waters is endangered by careless boaters.

Use commas to set off parenthetical clauses and phrases. (A parenthetical expression is one that is not necessary to the main idea of the sentence.)

CORRECT: Gordon, who is a writer by profession, bakes an excellent cheesecake.

The main idea is that Gordon bakes an excellent cheesecake. The intervening clause merely serves to identify Gordon; thus, it should be set off with commas.

Use commas after introductory, participial, or prepositional phrases.

CORRECT: Having watered his petunias every day during the drought, Harold was very disappointed when his garden was destroyed by insects.
CORRECT: After the banquet, Harold and Martha went dancing.

Use commas to separate independent clauses (clauses that could stand alone as complete sentences) connected by coordinating conjunctions such as *and, but, yet*, and so on.

INCORRECT: Susan's old car has been belching blue smoke from the tailpipe for two weeks, but has not broken down yet.
CORRECT: Susan's old car has been belching blue smoke from the tailpipe for two weeks, but it has not broken down yet.

INCORRECT: Zachariah's pet frog eats 50 flies a day, and never gets indigestion.

CORRECT: Zachariah's pet frog eats 50 flies a day, and it never gets indigestion.
CORRECT: Zachariah's pet frog eats 50 flies a day and never gets indigestion.

Using Commas Practice Set

Correct the punctuation errors in the following sentences.

1. Teaching, is not a popularity contest!

2. Pushing through the panicked crowd the security guards frantically searched for the suspect.

Using Commas Practice Set Answers and Explanations

Examples of the revised sentences with explanations:

1. Teaching is not a popularity contest!

The gerund "Teaching" functions as the subject of the main clause, and therefore cannot be set off by a comma.

2. Pushing through the panicked crowd, the security guards frantically searched for the suspect.

The participial phrase "Pushing through the panicked crowd" is not necessary to the main idea of the sentence, and should therefore be set off with a comma.

CORRECTLY USING SEMICOLONS

Use a semicolon without a coordinating conjunction (such as *and*, *or*, or *but*) to link two closely related independent clauses. Additionally, use semicolons to separate items in a series in which the items contain commas. Be certain that there are complete sentences on both sides of a semicolon unless you are using it to separate items in a series.

INCORRECT: Whooping cranes are an endangered species; and they are unlikely to survive if we continue to pollute.
CORRECT: Whooping cranes are an endangered species; there are only 50 whooping cranes in New Jersey today.
CORRECT: Three important dates in the history of the company are December 16, 1999; April 4, 2003; and June 30, 2007.

Use a semicolon between independent clauses connected by words like *therefore, nevertheless*, and *moreover.*

CORRECT: The staff meeting has been postponed until next Thursday; therefore, I will be unable to get approval for my project until then.
CORRECT: Farm prices have been falling rapidly for two years; nevertheless, the traditional American farm is not in danger of disappearing.

Using Semicolons Practice Set

Correct the punctuation errors in the following sentences.

1. Very few students wanted to take the class in physics, it was only the professor's kindness that kept it from being canceled.

____

____

2. Marcus has five years' experience in karate; but Tyler has even more.

____

____

Using Semicolons Practice Set Answers and Explanations

Examples of the revised sentences with explanations:

1. **Very few students wanted to take the class in physics; it was only the professor's kindness that kept it from being canceled.**

The two independent clauses in the sentence have to be separated by a semicolon or a conjunction. Since "only" does not function as a conjunction in this context, a semicolon is required for the sentence to be grammatically correct.

2. **Marcus has five years' experience in karate, but Tyler has even more.**

When using the coordinating conjunction "but" to separate the two clauses, it should be preceded by a comma, not a semicolon.

CORRECTLY USING COLONS

In formal writing, the colon is used only as a means of signaling that what follows is a list, definition, explanation, or concise summary of what has gone before. The colon usually follows an independent clause, and it will frequently be accompanied by a reinforcing expression like *the following, as follows*, or *namely* or by an explicit demonstrative pronoun like *this*.

CORRECT: Your instructions are as follows: read the passage carefully, answer the questions on the last page, and turn over your answer sheet.
CORRECT: This is what I found in the refrigerator: a moldy lime, half a bottle of stale soda, and a jar of peanut butter.

Be careful not to put a colon between a verb and its direct object.

INCORRECT: I want: a slice of pizza and a small green salad.
CORRECT: This is what I want: a slice of pizza and a small green salad. (The colon serves to announce that a list is forthcoming.)
CORRECT: I don't want much for lunch: just a slice of pizza and a small green salad. (Here what follows the colon defines what *don't want much* means.)

Context will occasionally make clear that a second independent clause is closely linked to its predecessor, developing the previous clause further, even without an explicit expression like those used above. Here, too, a colon is appropriate, although a period will always be correct too.

CORRECT: We were aghast: the "charming country inn" that had been advertised in such glowing terms proved to be a leaking cabin full of mosquitoes.

Using Colons Practice Set

Correct the punctuation errors in the following sentences.

1. The residents of Mason City do not just enjoy: swimming, boating, and fishing.

____

____

2. The chef has created a masterpiece, the pasta is delicate yet firm, the mustard greens are fresh, and the medallions of veal are melting in my mouth.

____

____

Using Colons Practice Set Answers and Explanations

Examples of the revised sentences with explanations:

1. The residents of Mason City do not just enjoy swimming, boating, and fishing.

The use of a colon is inappropriate in this situation because colons should not separate a verb and its direct object, such as "enjoy" and "swimming."

2. The chef has created a masterpiece: the pasta is delicate yet firm, the mustard greens are fresh, and the medallions of veal are melting in my mouth.

A colon should follow the word "masterpiece" to signal that a list is coming. Note that the list does not have to be single words; it can be composed of independent clauses.

CORRECTLY USING HYPHENS AND DASHES

Use a hyphen with the compound numbers twenty-one through ninety-nine and with fractions used as adjectives.

CORRECT: Sixty-five students constituted a majority.
CORRECT: A two-thirds vote was necessary to carry the measure.

Use a hyphen with the prefixes *ex-*, *all-*, and *self-* and with the suffix *-elect*.

CORRECT: The constitution protects against self-incrimination.
CORRECT: The president-elect was invited to chair the meeting.

Use a hyphen with a compound adjective when it comes before the word it modifies but not when it comes after the word it modifies.

CORRECT: The no-holds-barred argument continued into the night.
CORRECT: The argument continued with no holds barred.

Use a hyphen with any prefix used before a proper noun or adjective.

CORRECT: His pro-African sentiments were heartily applauded.
CORRECT: They believed that his accent was un-Australian.

Use a hyphen to separate component parts of a word to avoid confusion with other words or to avoid the use of a double vowel.

CORRECT: The sculptor was able to re-form the clay after the dog knocked over the bust.
CORRECT: The family re-entered their house after the fire marshal departed.

Use a dash to indicate an abrupt change of thought. (Two hyphens right next to each other will suffice to indicate a dash when you're typing your GRE essays.)

CORRECT: The inheritance must cover the entire cost of the proposal—Gail has no other money to invest.
CORRECT: To get a high score—and who doesn't want to get a high score?— you need to devote yourself to prolonged and concentrated study.

USING HYPHENS AND DASHES PRACTICE SET

Correct the punctuation errors in the following sentences.

1. Harry had every physical advantage—over his opponent—size, speed, strength, but luck was not on his side.

____

____

2. John and his ex wife remained on friendly terms.

____

____

USING HYPHENS AND DASHES PRACTICE SET ANSWERS AND EXPLANATIONS

Examples of the revised sentences with explanations:

1. **Harry had every physical advantage over his opponent—size, speed, strength—but luck was not on his side.**

The original sentence uses dashes to separate "over his opponent" from the rest of the sentence, which is wrong because that phrase is an essential part of the sentence. The list of advantages is a break in thought, so that's what the dashes need to set apart.

2. **John and his ex-wife remained on friendly terms.**

The prefix "ex" modifies the word "wife," and thus requires a hyphen.

CORRECTLY USING APOSTROPHES

Use an apostrophe in a contraction to indicate that one or more letters have been eliminated. But try to avoid using contractions altogether on the GRE: using the full form of a verb is more appropriate in formal writing.

CONTRACTED: We'd intended to address the question of equal rights, but it's too late to begin the discussion now.
FULL FORM: We had intended to address the question of equal rights, but it is too late to begin the discussion now.

One of the most common errors involving the apostrophe is using it in the contraction *you're* or *it's* to indicate the possessive form of *you* or *it*. When you write *you're*, ask yourself whether you mean *you are*. If not, the correct word is *your*. Similarly, are you sure you mean *it is*? If not, use the possessive form *its*.

INCORRECT: You're chest of drawers is ugly.
CORRECT: *Your* chest of drawers is ugly.

INCORRECT: The dog hurt it's paw.
CORRECT: The dog hurt *its* paw.

Use the apostrophe to indicate the possessive form of a noun.

NOUN	POSSESSIVE
the boy	the boy's
Harry	Harry's
the children	the children's
the boys	the boys'
the bass	the bass's

NOTE: Possessive forms can sometimes look like contractions. The word *boy's*, for example, could have one of three meanings:

- The boy's an expert at chess. (contraction: the boy is ...)
- The boy's left for the day. (contraction: the boy has ...)
- The boy's face was covered with pie. (possessive: the face of the boy)

The word *boys'* can have only one meaning: a plural possessive (the ____ of the boys).

CORRECT: Ms. Fox's office is on the first floor. (One person possesses the office.)
CORRECT: The Foxes' apartment has a wonderful view. (There are several people named Fox living in the same apartment. First you must form the plural; then add the apostrophe to indicate possession.)

Possessive pronouns do not use an apostrophe (with the exception of the neutral *one*, which forms its possessive by adding *'s*).

INCORRECT: The tiny cabin had been our's for many years.
CORRECT: The tiny cabin had been *ours* for many years.

Using Apostrophes Practice Set

Read the sentences below and revise for appropriate apostrophe use.

1. People should be allowed to keep their money and use it for the thing's they want.

____

____

2. The young men were students at the Boy's Latin School.

____

____

Using Apostrophes Practice Set Answers and Explanations

Examples of the revised sentences with explanations:

1. People should be allowed to keep their money and use it for the things they want.

The word "things" in this sentence is used as a direct object and not as a possessive. There is no need for an apostrophe, as the "s" is simply pluralizing it.

2. The young men were students at the Boys' Latin School.

The apostrophe should follow the "s" in "Boys," as the term refers to more than one boy.

In the chapters that follow, you will learn how to approach the two basic types of Analytical Writing tasks on the GRE. The Argument task will ask you to analyze an incomplete argument, while the Issue task will oblige you to come up with one of your own. Although each type of task requires you to approach an argument in distinctly different ways, both are built on the foundations you studied in this chapter.

CHAPTER 17

The Issue Essay

INTRODUCTION TO THE ISSUE ESSAY

The first of the Analytical Writing essay tasks is the Issue essay. On the Issue essay, you will be given a point of view about which you'll have to form an opinion, and then you'll need to provide a well-supported and justifiable case for that opinion.

The Issue essay requires you to construct your own argument by making claims and providing evidence to support your position on a given issue. The directions will ask you to take a position on the issue, and they'll instruct you to explain your position convincingly, using reasons and/or examples to back up your assertions.

For the assignment topic, expect about one to two sentences that discuss a broad, general issue, sometimes presenting only one point of view and sometimes presenting two conflicting points. Either way, the test will present a statement that could reasonably be either supported or argued against. Your job is to form an opinion on the topic and make a case for that opinion.

The directions for Issue essays will look like this:

> You have 30 minutes to plan and compose a response in which you evaluate the argument passage that appears below. A response to any other argument will receive a score of zero. Make sure that you respond according to the specific instructions and support your evaluation with relevant reasons and/or examples.

An Issue essay will always begin with a statement. It will look something like this:

> "The drawbacks to the use of nuclear power mean that it is not a long-term solution to the problem of meeting ever-increasing energy needs."

The second part of the directions, the prompt, will give specific directions for how to approach the essay. An Issue essay prompt will look something like this:

> Write a response in which you examine your own position on the statement. Explore the extent to which you either agree or disagree with it and support your reasoning with evidence and/or examples. Be sure to reflect on ways in which the statement might or might not be true and how this informs your thinking on the subject.

The Issue essay prompt may vary. Other prompts you may see for the Issue essay look like this:

- Write your own response to the recommendation in which you discuss why you either agree or disagree with it. Support your response with evidence and/or examples. Use a hypothetical set of circumstances to illustrate the consequences of accepting or rejecting the recommendation and explain how this informs your thinking.
- Develop a response to the claim in which you discuss whether or not you agree with it. Focus specifically on the most powerful or compelling examples that could be used to refute your position.
- Write a response in which you determine which view bears the closest resemblance to your own. In justifying your reasoning and supporting your position, be sure to include your reaction to both of the views presented.
- Develop a response to the claim in which you discuss whether or not you agree with it. Focus specifically on whether or not you agree with the reason upon which the claim is based.
- Write a response discussing your reaction to the policy stated above. Justify your reasoning for the position you take. Explain the potential consequences or implications for implementing such a policy and how this informs your position.

THE KAPLAN METHOD FOR ANALYTICAL WRITING

STEP 1 **Take the issue/argument apart.**

STEP 2 **Select the points you will make.**

STEP 3 **Organize, using Kaplan's essay templates.**

STEP 4 **Type your essay.**

STEP 5 **Proofread your work.**

HOW THE KAPLAN METHOD FOR ANALYTICAL WRITING WORKS

Now let's discuss how the Kaplan Method for Analytical Writing works for the Issue essay:

STEP 1

Take the issue apart.

Read the assignment and consider both sides of the issue. Use your scratch paper throughout Steps 1–3. Restate the issue in your own words. Consider the other side of the issue and put that into your own words as well.

STEP 2

Select the points you will make.

After you consider what both sides of the issue mean, think of reasons and examples for both sides and make a decision as to which side you will support or the extent to which you agree with the stated position.

STEP 3

Organize, using Kaplan's Issue essay template.

Organize your thoughts by outlining what you want to say so that you will be able to approach the actual writing process confidently and focus on expressing your ideas clearly. In the introduction, restate the prompt in your own words, state whether you agree or disagree, and give a preview of the supporting points you plan to make. In the middle paragraphs, give your points of agreement (or disagreement) and provide support. Determine what evidence you will use to support each point. Be sure to lead with your best argument. Think about how the essay as a whole will flow. Conclude by summing up your position on the issue.

- **Paragraph 1:** Paraphrase the issue (the statement, claim, recommendation, or policy); state your position. Summarize the goal of your essay, according to the specific instructions.

- **Paragraph 2:** State and elaborate upon the strongest point in support of your position, within the scope of the specific instructions.
- **Paragraph 3:** State and elaborate upon another point in support of your position, within the scope of the specific instructions.
- **Additional paragraphs, as time permits:** State and elaborate upon other points in support of your position, within the scope of the specific instructions. (Time valve #1: skip if need be.)
- **Next-to-last paragraph:** Address an opposition to your position and refute it with relevant detailed support. (Time valve #2: combine with conclusion if need be.)
- **Last paragraph:** Conclude by summarizing your position in a way that addresses the specific instructions.

STEP 4

Type your essay.

You shouldn't proceed with this step until you've completed the three preceding ones. Graders have a limited amount of time in which to read your essay, so start out and conclude with strong statements. Be emphatic and concise with your prose and link related ideas with transitions. This will help your writing flow and make things easier on the grader. Furthermore, you'll save time and energy by preparing your essay before you start typing it.

STEP 5

Proofread your work.

Save enough time to read quickly through the entire essay. Look for errors you can address quickly: capitalization, paragraph divisions, double-typed words, general typos, and small grammatical errors.

How to Apply the Kaplan Method for Analytical Writing to the Issue Essay

Now let's apply the Kaplan Method for Analytical Writing to an Issue prompt:

> "The drawbacks to the use of nuclear power mean that it is not a long-term solution to the problem of meeting ever-increasing energy needs."
>
> > Write a response in which you examine your own position on the statement. Explore the extent to which you either agree or disagree with it and support your reasoning with evidence and/or examples. Be sure to reflect on ways in which the statement might or might not be true and how this informs your thinking on the subject.

STEP 1

Take the issue apart.

Your first step is to dissect the issue. Take notes on your scratch paper. Start by restating the issue in your own words: "Although we have a need for alternate sources of energy, we cannot count on nuclear energy as a solution because of its major drawbacks."

Now, consider the other side of the issue—in your own words, this might be "Nuclear power is safe and effective and does not have such serious drawbacks as this statement would suggest."

STEP 2

Select the points you will make.

Your job, as stated in the directions, is to decide whether or not you agree with the statement and then to explain your decision. Some would argue that the use of nuclear power is too dangerous, while others would say that we can't afford not to use it. Which side do you take?

Remember, this isn't about showing the graders what your deep-seated beliefs about energy policy are—it's about showing that you can formulate an argument and communicate it clearly. The position you choose to take for the Issue essay does not have to be one you actually believe in.

Quickly jot down on your scratch paper the pros and cons of each side and choose the side for which you have the most relevant things to say. For this topic, that process might go something like this:

Arguments *for* the use of nuclear power:

- It is inexpensive compared to other forms of energy.
- Fossil fuels will eventually be depleted.
- Solar power is still too problematic and expensive.

Arguments *against* the use of nuclear power:

- It is harmful to the environment.
- It is dangerous to mankind.
- Safer alternatives already exist.
- Better alternatives may lie undiscovered.

Again, it doesn't matter which side you take. There is no *right* answer as far as the testmaker is concerned. Let's say that in this case, you decide that you have more relevant disadvantages than advantages on your list. In that case, you would choose to argue against nuclear power, irrespective of what your genuine beliefs might be.

STEP 3

Organize, using Kaplan's Issue essay template.

You should have already begun to think out your arguments—that's how you picked the side you did in the first place. Now's the time to write your arguments out, including those that weaken the opposing side. This step involves your own note taking, so feel free to use abbreviations.

Paragraph 1: Nuclear power is not a viable alternative to other energy sources.

Paragraph 2: Nuclear power creates radioactive waste.

Paragraph 3: Nuclear energy is an industry with related costs to consumers.

Paragraph 4: There are other, more environmentally friendly energy sources.

Paragraph 5: Further investment in nuclear power would be a waste of time and money.

STEP 4

Type your essay.

Remember, open up with a general statement indicating that you understand the issue and then assert your position. From there, make your main points. Note: As a basis for comparison, we've included an outstanding essay that deserves a score of 6. The second prompt will include an adequate essay that deserves a score of 4.

Sample Issue Essay 1

Proponents of nuclear energy as "the power source for the future" have long touted its relative economy, "clean-burning" technology, and virtually inexhaustible fuel supply. However, a close examination of the issue reveals that nuclear energy proves more problematic and dangerous than other forms of energy production and thus is not an acceptable solution to the problem of meeting ever-increasing energy needs.

First and foremost, nuclear power production presents the problem of radioactive waste storage. Fuel byproducts from nuclear fission remain toxic for thousands of years, and the spills and leaks from existing storage sites have been hazardous and costly to clean up. This remains true despite careful regulation and even under the best of circumstances. Even more appalling is the looming threat of accidents at the reactor itself: Incidents at the Three Mile Island and Chernobyl power plants and at other production sites have warned us that the consequences of a nuclear meltdown can be catastrophic and felt worldwide.

But beyond the enormous long-term environmental problems and short-term health risks, the bottom-line issue for the production of energy is one of economics. Power production in our society is a business just like any other, and the large companies that produce this country's electricity and gas claim they are unable to make alternatives such as solar power affordable. Yet—largely due to incentives from the federal government—there already exist homes heated by solar power and cars fueled by the sun. If the limited resources devoted to date to such energy alternatives have already produced working models, a more intensive, broadly based and supported effort is likely to make those alternatives less expensive and problematic.

Besides the benefits in terms of both cost and safety, renewable resources such as solar and hydroelectric power represent far better options in the long run for development: these options require money only for the materials needed to harvest the renewable resources. While sunlight and water are free, the innovative technologies and industrial strategies devised to harness them have created a geometric progression of spin-offs affecting fields as diverse as agriculture, real estate, space exploration, and social policy. These options also repeatedly produced secondary economic and social benefits, such as the large recreational and irrigation reservoirs created in the American Southwest behind large hydroelectric dams like the Hoover and Grand Coulee.

While it may now be clear that the drawbacks to the use of nuclear power are too great, it should also be apparent that the long-term benefits of renewable resources would reward investment. If these alternatives are explored more seriously than they have been in the past, safer and less expensive sources of power will undoubtedly live up to their promise. With limited resources at our disposal and a burgeoning global population to consider, further investment in nuclear power would mark an unconscionable and unnecessary waste of time and money.

STEP 5

Proofread your work.

Be sure to allot a few minutes after you have finished writing to review your essay. Though you do not have to write a grammatically flawless essay to score well, you will want to review so that you can catch some of the standout mistakes. You can practice your writing skills in Chapter 16: Analytical Writing Foundations and Content Review.

Assessment of Sample Issue Essay 1: "Outstanding," Score of 6

Now we'll look at how this essay would have been scored on the actual GRE Analytical Writing section:

This essay is carefully constructed throughout, enabling the reader to move effortlessly from point to point as the writer examines the multifaceted implications of the issue. The writer begins by acknowledging arguments for the opposing side and then uses his thesis statement ("a close examination of the issue reveals that nuclear energy proves more problematic and dangerous than other forms of energy production") to explain his own position on the issue. He proceeds to provide compelling reasons and examples to support the premise, and he then takes the argument to an effective conclusion. The writing is clean, concise, and almost error-free. Sentence structure is varied, and diction and vocabulary are strong and expressive.

How to Apply the Kaplan Method for Analytical Writing to Another Issue Essay

Now let's apply the Kaplan Method for Analytical Writing to a second Issue prompt:

> "People who hold high expectations for others are rewarded with high performance and respect."
>
> > Develop a response to the claim in which you provide specific reasons why you do or do not you agree with it. Focus specifically on the most powerful or compelling examples that could be used to support your position.

STEP 1

Take the issue apart.

Begin by putting the issue in your own words, "If you expect people to do well, they will, and they will respect you for it." Next, consider the other side of the issue, and do the same: "If you expect too much of people, they may get frustrated and perform at a lower level, or you may lose their respect."

STEP 2

Select the points you will make.

Your job, as stated in the directions, is to decide whether or not you agree with the statement and then to explain your decision. Some would argue that high expectations yield high results, while others may think that unrealistic high expectations may destroy confidence. Which side do you take?

Quickly think through the pros and cons of each side and choose the side for which you have the most relevant things to say. For this topic, that process might go something like this:

Arguments *for* holding people to high expectations:

- Without expectations, people don't know how they will be measured or to what level they should perform.
- High expectations convey confidence and trust.
- Striving to meet high expectations improves people's skills, and when these individuals succeed, their success leads to increased confidence and higher performance.

Arguments *against* holding people to high expectations:

- People could give up or lose confidence if they are unable to meet the expectations.
- You may be thought of as someone who is unyielding or only concerned with performance.

Remember, it doesn't matter which side you take. Strictly speaking, there is no *right* answer.

STEP 3

Organize, using Kaplan's Issue essay template.

Now's the time to write those arguments out, including counterarguments that weaken the opposing side.

Paragraph 1:
High expectations yield high performance and respect in every case, whether the expectations are met or unmet.

Paragraph 2:
Without expectations, people don't know how they will be measured or to what level they should perform. 2nd graders design skyscrapers; retirees train for Olympics.

Paragraph 3:
Challenges from teachers: high expectations convey confidence and trust.

Paragraph 4:
Higher performance improves people's skills and confidence once they meet the expectations. (Challenge office interns example)

Paragraph 5: (opposition)
People fail because others do not value them enough and believe they are capable of less than they actually are.

Paragraph 6: In all cases, high expectations are worth the risk.

STEP 4

Type your essay.

Sample Issue Essay 2

High expectations yield high performance and respect in every case, whether the expectations are met or unmet. Setting expectations allows people to know how they will be measured and to what level they should perform. They also convey confidence and a sense of trust. Once the expectations are met, people feel bolstered by their achievement and have a much stronger sense of self-confidence, leading to even higher performance. These results hold up in a variety of contexts, including in educational, business, and political realms.

The purpose of expectations is often lost in the assignment of a task. The expectations themselves may take the form of the actual tasks to be done, but really, the expectation is the ownership, resourcefulness, and skill of the person assigned the task. Expecting someone to do something overly challenging, such as asking second-graders to design a skyscraper or challenging a retiree to train for the Olympics, may seem egregious, but the stories that intrigue us most are usually about people rising to the challenge. Our own expectations are recalibrated when we learn of people exceeding the expectations we set ourselves to. We look to where the bar is set to see how we measure up. Given a bar, people will usually do what it takes to measure up.

Good teachers are often described as "hard, but fair." This is a good description of someone who holds high expectations for his or her students, and is rewarded by that assessment. A hard but fair teacher is one who challenges the students to exceed their own expectations of themselves, and often others' expectations of them. These are the teachers who assign fourth grade students research papers or ask eighth graders to take a 100-question math test in 100 minutes. Students take up the challenge because it feels good to succeed. They gain confidence and look at tasks unrelated to the classroom in new ways.

High performance breeds higher performance. Once someone has been resourceful or learned a new skill to achieve a task, the person feels empowered to be similarly resourceful achieving different tasks. In fact, a high performer may take on more challenges without prompting. This bears out in business: the neophyte office intern who pulls together a critical report through resourcefulness, skill, and a little luck is a familiar story, but for good reason. This intern with his or her fresh ideas stands out among the drones and is challenged further, rocketing to the proverbial top of the company. If the same expectations were put on the rest of the workforce, would other employees be as resourceful to achieve the expectations? Most likely, as long as the employee is motivated enough by the challenge.

Some people may be frustrated by high expectations, and some may simply ignore those expectations, but being presented with a challenge ultimately builds a person's confidence. No one ever failed because he or she was fairly challenged by a daunting task and supported while tackling it. People fail because others do not value them enough and believe they are capable of less than they actually are. In fact, just being challenged is often enough to shake up people's self-expectations and make them reconsider what they are actually capable of.

In all cases, high expectations are worth the risk. The challenge bolsters self-esteem and self-confidence, and yields high performance. It improves performance in classrooms, on the job, and in other areas where challenges present themselves.

STEP 5

Proofread your work.

Take the last couple of minutes to catch any glaring errors.

Assessment of Sample Issue Essay 2: "Adequate," Score of 4

Now we'll look at how this essay would have been scored on the actual GRE Analytical Writing section:

This essay is, on the whole, well constructed and laid out. The reader can systematically move from point to point as the writer examines the implications of the issue. The writer begins by agreeing with the statement and presenting specific reasons for agreeing. She gives examples to illustrate her point and organizes her essay well. The author's analysis is generally cogent. She asks the reader to take a bit of a leap with some of her claims. For example, claiming that "people will usually do what it takes to measure up" when given a bar is a conclusion not really supported by the paragraph leading us to that conclusion. She asserts that people are inherently encouraged, rather than discouraged, by daunting challenges, but never really justifies that assertion. However, the writing is clean and concise and includes only a few errors. Sentence structure is varied, and the author's diction is strong and expressive. For all these reasons, this essay receives a score of 4.

KAPLAN'S ADDITIONAL TIPS FOR THE ISSUE ESSAY

Don't Overcomplicate Your Prose

The types of issues that the essays use as their subject aren't supposed to be too abstruse or esoteric. Don't worry if you're not extremely familiar with a subject. Similarly, your responses shouldn't be too convoluted. Try to be as clear and linear in your writing as possible when supporting an argument. Bombastic flourishes of rhetoric may seem impressive when you first write them, but the point here is to assert and defend a position, not impress the graders with your vocabulary or wit. Substance will easily outweigh style.

Don't Worry about Whether or Not Your Position Is "Correct"

The purpose of the Issue essay is to develop an argument and defend it. You're going to be scored on how well supported your position is, not on whether it is the "right answer." Indeed, by design most of the topics chosen for this task are not black-and-white issues; they can be argued successfully from very different points of view.

Think about the Issue from Different Perspectives

An important skill you'll need in graduate school (as in life) is the ability to understand an issue or problem from someone else's point of view. Removing your own personal biases from the equation can be a great help, as it will force you to think about an issue logically and not just go with your gut reaction.

ISSUE ESSAY PRACTICE SET

Issue Essay 1

30 Minutes
Length: 1 essay

Directions: You will be given a statement that presents an issue you need to respond to, along with detailed instructions on how to respond to the statement. You have 30 minutes to plan and compose a response in which you develop an argument according to the instructions. A response to any other issue results in a score of zero.

> "The perceived greatness of any political leader has more to do with the challenges faced by that leader than with any of his or her inherent skills and abilities."

Write a response in which you examine your own position on the statement. Explore the extent to which you either agree or disagree with it and support your reasoning with evidence and/or examples. Be sure to reflect on ways in which the statement might or might not be true and how this informs your thinking on the subject.

Issue Essay 2

30 Minutes
Length: 1 essay

Directions:

You will be given a statement that presents an issue you need to respond to, along with detailed instructions on how to respond to the statement. You have 30 minutes to plan and compose a response in which you develop an argument according to the instructions. A response to any other issue results in a score of zero.

> "Progress should be the aim of any great society. People too often cling unnecessarily to obsolete ways of thinking and acting because of both a high comfort level and a fear of the unknown."

Write a response in which you examine your own position on the statement. Explore the extent to which you either agree or disagree with it and support your reasoning with evidence or examples. Be sure to reflect on ways in which the statement might or might not be true and how this informs your thinking on the subject.

ISSUE ESSAY PRACTICE SET ANSWERS AND EXPLANATIONS

Issue Essay Sample Essays and Assessments

What follows are top-scoring sample essays for each of the practice prompts. Note how the authors adhere to the Kaplan Method for Analytical Writing.

Issue Essay 1: "Outstanding," Score of 6

Perceptions of greatness in national and political leaders are largely determined by the seriousness of the problems that they face during their terms in office. Most national histories principally highlight individuals in the context of significant events in which the leaders played important roles. Most political leaders need to have large stores of inherent skill and ability just in order to become a political leader. However, history remembers those who lived in great times more fondly than those who did not. Examples of this are numerous and include the histories of Abraham Lincoln, Woodrow Wilson, and Winston Churchill—all men who are perceived as great leaders largely because of the times in which they lived.

Abraham Lincoln is often considered the greatest of all the American Presidents. He graces two units of the currency and has one of the largest monuments built in his honor in Washington D.C. However, Lincoln is considered great largely because he faced a great challenge—the civil war between the North and the South in the 1860s. Lincoln led the United States to victory over the rebels and reunited the country and is therefore considered great. This is not to say that Lincoln was not skilled. Many know that he was born in a log cabin and progressed to law school and eventually to the presidency. He was also a skilled orator. However another man, James Buchanan, also was born in a log cabin, went to law school, gave good speeches and ascended to the presidency. However there are no monuments to Buchanan in the capital or pictures of his face on the five-dollar bill.

Woodrow Wilson was another talented man who ascended to the presidency of the United States. However his talents are not what make his perceived greatness. In this age, few remember if Wilson was particularly smart, a very good speechmaker, or a good arbitrator. Most remember that he led the United States to victory in the first World War and therefore perceive him as great. At the time, however, Wilson was rather unpopular. In fact, he had so little sway with Congress that he was unable to get the United States to join the League of Nations—a fact that many claim helped lead to the second World War.

Winston Churchill was another man that history views favorably because of the incredible challenges that he faced. However, Churchill was not very popular before the war. When Franklin Roosevelt first met Churchill before either was the leader of his respective country, Roosevelt wrote in his diary that Churchill was full of himself and far too talkative. Early in his term as Prime Minister, Churchill even faced a no-confidence vote in Parliament. However, the events of World War II accorded him the perception of greatness in the eyes of history.

Many might argue that these men and other men and women were already great before history gave them great challenges. While it is impossible to definitely disprove this assertion and it may be true that they had great skill and ability, otherwise they would not have been political leaders, most examples point to the fact that the times make the man or woman. If the presidencies of Buchanan and Lincoln were switched, we would very likely have the Buchanan memorial instead. In summary, it is true that the perceived greatness of a political leader is more due to great challenges than great inherent ability. The historical examples of Lincoln, Wilson, and Churchill bear this out. All were talented, but so too are all political leaders. Only the leaders that live in eventful times are remembered as great.

Assessment of Essay 1

This essay is particularly well constructed; the author begins by acknowledging the arguments for how famous historical leaders should be judged. He asserts his position, "men are perceived as great leaders largely because of the times in which they lived" clearly and effectively. He proceeds to support his position with compelling evidence, drawing on his knowledge of three historical figures who are, by consensus, regarded as great. He contrasts the example of Lincoln with that of Buchanan, who had a similar background but lived under less trying circumstances. The writing is largely clear and direct, with skillful use of diction and few errors. For all these reasons, this essay receives a score of 6.

Issue Essay 2: "Outstanding," Score of 6

Keeping up with global progress is, doubtless, a desirable attribute of any society. However, to purport that the reasons certain societies may not progress at the same rate as "great" societies are their reluctance to break from their comfort zones and a fear of the unknown is to present an overly simplistic view. Such a view does not take into consideration the set of economic, political, and cultural constraints that affect every society's ability to progress on a global scale.

Before exploring these constraints, it would be useful to examine the use of the word "great" in the above context. The concept of what makes a society great is highly subjective; some may equate greatness with military might or economic dominance, while others would emphasize cultural achievement or progress in care for less privileged citizens. Whatever one's definition of greatness, however, it is ludicrous to suggest that any society actively rejects the desire to be great. Many societies face the seemingly insurmountable struggle to maintain societal structure in the face of economic need and/or political upheaval; the desire for greatness can only come when a society's basic structure is intact.

Societies facing severe economic challenges are virtually unable to progress in areas like medicine, militia, and agriculture even if they want to do so. Countries like Bolivia use a majority of their limited resources to maintain an agricultural status quo. Bolivian farmers are not afraid of the unknown or passively content with their current situation, but are using all of their resources to maintain a functional economic climate and structure. Given this situation, the luxury of advancements in medicine, economics and military power is simply not possible.

Also, societies embroiled in political upheaval, such as Bangladesh, are unable to send its young and talented members to university where they can spearhead progress; the most viable sectors of the population are required to serve in the military and/or to care for their families through difficult economic and political times. Maintaining a societal structure amid chaotic conditions engenders a lack of globally accepted progress, but as we have seen throughout time, episodes of great drama in any given society can yield important works of art, one such example being Albert Camus' *The Stranger*, written during the French Resistance.

Another point to consider is that, in some cases, an entire society's cultural history, including its artistic contributions, is preserved only through its living members' rich oral tradition and their active rejecting of progress in the worlds of technology, medicine, and science. This is evident when considering such so-called "primitive" societies as the African Masai or certain Native American tribes. The introduction of technology into the world of the Masai would inarguably lead to the demise of the entire society.

In conclusion, to devalue a society that isn't among the most progressive in the world is to discount the contributions a so-called "unprogressive" society can provide, such as artistic and cultural phenomena unique to a given society. Progress is a valuable tool for the advancement of a society, but blindly reaching for greatness can lead to a society's downfall just as much as ignoring it altogether can. The balance between accepting a society's constraints and highlighting its strengths is what will ultimately lead to a society's greatness.

Assessment of Essay 2

This is a particularly insightful essay. The author goes deeper with her argument than you might expect based on the prompt. The argument developed in this essay asks the reader to question his presuppositions and preconceived notions about what constitutes "greatness" as the term is applied to a society. Instead of merely answering the question of whether or not the progress of society is hindered by clinging to traditional views and obsolete ways of thinking, the reader is forced to reconsider what progress actually entails. This elicits the cultural bias of the reader and forces him to confront it. The author challenges the received notions of "great" and "progress" as "an overly simplistic view." From there, she proceeds to defend her position. She examines different cultural contexts and how we might understand "greatness" within those contexts. The essay is well constructed; the author begins by providing examples of how greatness must be understood contextually. She then adds several examples, such as the publication of Camus' *The Stranger*, to illustrate greatness produced under conditions we might think of as making progress impossible. The writing is clear and direct, contains few errors, and reveals skillful use of diction. For all these reasons, this essay receives a score of 6.

CHAPTER 18

The Argument Essay

INTRODUCTION TO THE ARGUMENT ESSAY

The second Analytical Writing task is the Argument essay. In the Argument essay passage, the author will try to persuade you of something—her conclusion—by citing some evidence. On the GRE, always read the argument with a critical eye. Look carefully for *assumptions* in the way the writer moves from evidence to conclusion. You aren't being asked to agree or disagree with the author's *position* or *conclusion*; instead, you must analyze the *chain of reasoning* used in the argument.

The screen directions ask you to decide how convincing you find the argument. Know that every argument presented for this essay on the GRE will be flawed. To make your case, first analyze the argument itself and evaluate its use of evidence; second, explain how a different approach or more information would make the argument better (or possibly worse).

The directions for an Argument essay will look like this:

> You have 30 minutes to plan and compose a response in which you evaluate the argument passage that appears below. A response to any other argument will receive a score of zero. Make sure that you respond according to the specific instructions and support your evaluation with relevant reasons and/or examples.

An Argument task will always begin with a passage containing an author's argument. It will look like this:

> The following is a memorandum from the business manager of a television station:
>
> "Over the past year, our late-night news program has devoted increased time to national news and less time to weather and local news. During this time period, most of the complaints received from viewers were concerned with our station's coverage of weather and local news. In addition, local businesses that used to advertise during our late-night news program have just canceled their advertising contracts with us. Therefore, in order to attract more viewers to the program and to avoid losing any further advertising revenues, we should restore the time devoted to weather and local news to its former level."

The second part of the directions, the prompt, will give specific directions for how to approach the essay. An Argument essay prompt will look like this:

Write a response in which you describe what specific examples or evidence are needed to evaluate the argument and how those examples or evidence would weaken or strengthen the argument.

The Argument essay prompt may vary. Other Argument essay prompts will look like this:

- Write a response in which you explore the assumptions, both implicit and explicit, in the author's argument. Explain how the argument hinges on these assumptions and what the implications are if the assumptions prove unfounded.
- Write a response in which you explain what information would be necessary in order to decide whether the recommendation and the argument on which it is based are reasonable. Be sure to explain how the answers to these questions or pieces of information would help to evaluate the recommendation.
- Write a response in which you discuss what questions would need to be answered to decide how likely the stated recommendation is to yield the predicted result. Be sure to explain how the answers to these questions would help to evaluate the recommendation.
- Write a response in which you discuss what questions would need to be answered in order to assess the reasonableness of both the prediction and the argument upon which it is based. Be sure to explain how the answers to these questions would help to evaluate the prediction.
- Write a response in which you discuss one or more viable alternatives to the proposed explanation. Justify, with support, why your explanation could rival the proposed explanation and explain how your explanation(s) can plausibly account for the facts presented in the argument.

THE KAPLAN METHOD FOR ANALYTICAL WRITING

STEP 1 **Take the issue/argument apart.**

STEP 2 **Select the points you will make.**

STEP 3 **Organize, using Kaplan's essay templates.**

STEP 4 **Type your essay.**

STEP 5 **Proofread your work.**

HOW THE KAPLAN METHOD FOR ANALYTICAL WRITING WORKS

Now let's discuss how the Kaplan Method for Analytical Writing works for the Argument essay:

STEP 1

Take the argument apart.

The first step to deconstructing an argument is to identify the conclusion, that is, the author's main point. After you've nailed down the conclusion, your next step is to locate the evidence used to support it. Lastly, identify the unstated assumptions (pieces of evidence that are not explicitly stated but that must be true in order for the argument to be convincing). Note any terms that are ambiguous and need defining.

STEP 2

Select the points you will make.

Identify all the important assumptions between the evidence and the conclusion. Think of additional evidence that might be found that could strengthen or weaken those assumptions.

STEP 3

Organize, using Kaplan's Argument essay template.

Organize your thoughts by outlining what you want to say. Think about how the essay as a whole will flow. In the introduction, show that you understand the argument by putting it into your own words. Point out the author's conclusion and the evidence used to support that conclusion. In each of the middle paragraphs, what you'll do will vary from essay to essay. You might need to reveal the argument's assumptions or flaws, discuss possible ways to strengthen or weaken the argument, identify important questions that would need to be addressed to evaluate the argument, or perform other tasks in accordance with that Argument essay's specific instructions. Regardless of the variation, however, the argument will always be weak, and you should conclude by saying that without additional evidence, you are not persuaded.

- **Paragraph 1:** Paraphrase the argument (the author's conclusion and evidence). Summarize the goal of your essay, according to the specific instructions.
- **Paragraph 2:** State and evaluate the most important assumption the author makes, question to be answered, or possible alternative explanation (depending on the specific instructions).
- **Paragraph 3:** State and evaluate another assumption the author makes, question to be answered, or possible alternative explanation (depending on the specific instructions).
- **Additional paragraphs, as time permits:** State and evaluate additional assumptions the author makes, questions to be answered, or possible alternative explanations (depending on the specific instructions). (Time valve: skip if need be.)
- **Last paragraph:** Conclude by summarizing your main points. Directly answer the task given in the specific instructions.

STEP 4

Type your essay.

You shouldn't proceed with this step until you've completed the three preceding ones. Graders have a limited amount of time to work with, so start out and conclude with strong statements. Be emphatic and concise with your prose, and use transitions to link related ideas. This will help your writing flow and make things easier on the grader.

STEP 5

Proofread your work.

Save enough time to read through your response in its entirety. As you do so, have a sense of the errors you are likely to make.

Now let's see how these steps work with an Argument assignment by applying the Kaplan Method to the example prompt question provided.

How to Apply the Kaplan Method for Analytical Writing to the Argument Essay

Now let's apply the Kaplan Method for Analytical Writing to a sample Argument prompt:

> "The problem of poor teacher performance that has plagued the state public school system is bound to become a good deal less serious in the future. The state has initiated comprehensive guidelines that oblige state teachers to complete a number of required credits in education and educational psychology at the graduate level before being certified."

Write a response that examines this argument's unstated assumptions. Make sure you explain how this argument depends on those assumptions and what the implications are if the assumptions are wrong.

STEP 1

Take the argument apart.

Conclusion (the point the argument is trying to make): The problem of poorly trained teachers that has plagued the state public school system is bound to become a good deal less serious in the future.

Evidence (facts offered to support the conclusion): The state has initiated comprehensive guidelines that oblige state teachers to complete a number of required credits in education and educational psychology at the graduate level before being certified.

Assumptions (unspoken conditions or beliefs necessary for the conclusion to make sense in light of the evidence):

- Credits in education will improve teachers' classroom performance.
- Current bad teachers haven't already met this standard of training.
- Current bad teachers will not still be teaching in the future or will have to be trained, too.

STEP 2

Select the points you will make.

Analyze the use of evidence in the argument. Determine whether there's anything relevant that's not discussed, such as the following:

- whether the training will actually address the cause of the problems
- what "poorly performing" means
- how to either improve or remove the bad teachers now teaching

Also determine what types of evidence would make the argument stronger or more logically sound. In this case, we need some new evidence to support the assumptions, such as the following:

- evidence verifying that this training will make better teachers
- evidence making it clear that current bad teachers haven't already had this training
- evidence suggesting why all or many bad teachers won't still be teaching in the future (or why they'll be better trained)

STEP 3

Organize, using Kaplan's Argument essay template.

For an essay on this topic, your opening sentence might look like this:

The argument that improved academic training, ensured by requiring credits in education and psychology, will substantially alleviate the current problem of poorly performing teachers may seem logical at first glance.

Paragraph 1: The argument is that improved academic training, ensured by requiring credits in education and psychology, will substantially alleviate the current problem of poorly performing teachers.

Paragraph 2: Will training address the cause of the problem?

Paragraph 3: "Poorly performing" is not precisely defined.

Paragraph 4: Has a similar state instituted similar guidelines and seen results?

Paragraph 5: The author has not presented well-defined terms and relies upon unproven assumptions; for these reasons the argument is not convincing.

Then use your notes as a working outline. In Argument essays, you'll primarily address the ways in which the assumptions seem unsupported. You might also recommend new evidence you'd like to see and explain why. Remember to lead with your best arguments.

STEP 4

Type your essay.

Begin writing your essay now. Your essay for this assignment might look like one of the following sample essays. Note: As bases for comparison, we've included one outstanding essay that deserves a score of 6 and—later in this chapter—one adequate essay that deserves a score of 4.

Sample Argument Essay 1

The argument that improved academic training, ensured by requiring credits in education and psychology, will substantially alleviate the current problem of poorly performing teachers may seem logical at first glance. However, her conclusion relies on assumptions for which there is no clear evidence, and it uses terms that lack definition.

First, the writer assumes that the required courses will produce better teachers. In fact, the courses might be entirely irrelevant to the teachers' failings. Suppose, for example, that the main problem lies in cultural and linguistic gaps between teachers and students; graduate level courses that do not address these issues would be of little use in bridging these gaps and improving educational outcomes. Furthermore, the writer assumes that poorly performing teachers lack this standard of training. In fact, the writer makes no useful correlation between classroom performance and level of training.

Additionally, the writer provides no evidence that poorly performing teachers who are already certified will either stop teaching in the near future or will undergo additional training. In its current form, the argument implies that only teachers seeking certification will receive the specified training. If this is the case, the bright future the writer envisions may be decades away. The argument's conclusion requires the support of evidence demonstrating that all teachers in the system who are identified as having "poor performance" will receive the remedial training and will then change their teaching methods accordingly.

The notion that the coursework will provide better teachers would be strengthened by a clear definition of "poor performance" in the classroom and by additional evidence that the training will address the relevant issues. The author's argument would be strengthened considerably if she provided evidence of a direct relationship between teachers' effectiveness in the classroom and their educational backgrounds.

In conclusion, the writer would not necessarily be wrong to assert that the state's comprehensive guidelines will potentially lead to some improvement in the educational environment in public schools. After all, the additional training will certainly not adversely affect classroom performance. But to support the current conclusion that the guidelines will effectively solve the state's problem, the writer must first define the scope of the problem more clearly and submit more conclusive evidence that the new requirements will, in fact, improve overall teaching performance.

STEP 5

Proofread your work.

Be sure to allot some time after you have finished writing to review your essay. While a few grammatical errors here and there won't harm your score, having enough of them will affect the overall clarity of your essay, and that certainly won't look good. You want to make sure the graders are as favorably disposed to you as possible, and a well-written essay makes their job less tedious.

Assessment of Sample Argument Essay 1: "Outstanding," Score of 6

Now we'll look at how this essay would have been scored on the actual GRE Analytical Writing Section:

This outstanding response demonstrates the writer's insightful analytical skills. The introduction notes the prompt's specious reasoning occasioned by unsupported assumptions and a lack of definition and evidence. The writer follows this up with a one-paragraph examination of each of the root flaws in the argument. Specifically, the author exposes these points undermining the argument:

- the assumption that the required courses will produce better teachers
- the assumption that poorly performing teachers currently in the schools have not already had the proposed training
- the complete lack of evidence that ineffective teachers currently working will either stop teaching in the future or will successfully adapt the required training to their classroom work

Each point receives thorough and cogent development (given the time constraints) in a smooth and logically organized discourse. This essay is succinct, economical, and error-free, with sentences that vary in length and complexity, while the diction and vocabulary stand out as both precise and expressive.

How to Apply the Kaplan Method for Analytical Writing to Another Argument Essay

Now let's apply the Kaplan Method for Analytical Writing to a second Argument prompt:

> "The commercial airline industry in the country of Freedonia has experienced impressive growth in the past three years. This trend will surely continue in the years to come, since the airline industry will benefit from recent changes in Freedonian society: incomes are rising; most employees now receive more vacation time; and interest in travel is rising, as shown by an increase in media attention devoted to foreign cultures and tourist attractions."
>
> > Write a response that examines this argument's unstated assumptions. Make sure you explain how this argument depends on those assumptions and what the implications are if the assumptions are wrong.

STEP 1

Take the argument apart.

Conclusion (the point the argument's trying to make): The upward trend of growth in Freedonia's airline industry will continue.

Evidence (basis offered to support the conclusion): Incomes are rising. Employees have more vacation time. Interest in travel is rising, as shown by increased media attention devoted to foreign cultures and tourist attractions.

Assumptions (unspoken conditions or beliefs necessary for the conclusion to make sense in light of the evidence):

- Incomes will continue to rise in the future.
- Employees will want to spend their vacation time abroad and not at home.
- Those who do wish to travel will want to go somewhere requiring air travel.
- The increased media attention on foreign cultures and tourist attractions is due to public interest in travel.
- The airline industry will directly benefit from these changes.

STEP 2

Select the points you will make.

Analyze the use of evidence in the argument. Determine whether there's anything relevant that's not discussed, such as the following:

- What actually caused the growth in the airline industry?
- The fact that employees may want to spend their increased disposable income and vacation time doing other things
- Whether the increased media attention on foreign cultures is due to other factors besides increased public interest in travel

Also determine what types of evidence would make the argument stronger or more logically sound. In this case, we need some new evidence to support the assumptions, such as the following:

- Evidence verifying that the positive economic changes in Freedonian society will continue
- Evidence suggesting the cause of the increased media coverage of foreign cultures is in fact due to an interest in travel

STEP 3

Organize, using Kaplan's Argument essay template.

For an essay on this topic, your opening sentence might look like this:

> The author believes that the recent growth in Freedonia's commercial airline industry will continue for years to come.

Paragraph 1: The conclusion is that the positive growth in Freedonia's commercial airline industry will continue. The evidence is that income, vacation time, and interest in travel are all on the rise.

Paragraph 2: The author assumes that the favorable economic conditions will continue. However, the cause of these conditions is not explained, and neither is the economy's relation to the airline industry.

Paragraph 3: The argument would be strengthened if we knew what caused the media attention and growth in the commercial airline industry.

Paragraph 4: What is the source of the economic conditions, and how do they relate to the airline industry?

Paragraph 5: If the author's assumptions are wrong, Freedonia's airline industry might experience trouble in the future.

Then use your notes as a working outline. In Argument essays, you'll primarily address the ways in which the assumptions seem unsupported. You might also recommend new evidence you'd like to see and explain why. Remember to lead with your best arguments.

STEP 4
Type your essay.

Sample Argument Essay 2

The author concludes that the positive growth in Freedonia's commercial airline industry will continue for years to come. The evidence is that incomes, vacation time, and interest in travel are all on the rise. While this argument may seem tenable at first glance, the conclusion relies on assumptions for which there is no clear evidence and on undefined terms.

First, the writer assumes that the favorable economic conditions in Freedonia will continue. It is entirely possible that they will not, and that employees will have neither the money nor the vacation time necessary to pay for expensive foreign vacations. Suppose, for example, that incomes do not continue to rise. People would not have the money to spend on expensive vacations. Secondly, do we really know that the citizens of Freedonia will *want* to spend their money on vacations? Also, how do we know they will want to visit places that necessitate air travel?

The argument would be strengthened considerably if the author provided evidence of a direct relationship between the increased media attention on foreign cultures and tourist attractions and the genuine desire to spend disposable income and vacation time traveling. The author does not explain where this interest comes from. Also, even if people are interested, it does not necessarily follow that they will be either willing or able to indulge that interest with extravagant holidays.

Furthermore, the writer does not explain the source of these economic conditions, nor what relation, if any, they have to the airline industry. What if the changes in Freedonian society that have led to higher incomes and more vacation time do not help the airline industry? Perhaps the economic changes are the result of protective tariffs and trade policies that make it harder for Freedonians to conduct business internationally. Perhaps the government is limiting imports and exports. These possibilities could shrink the growth of the airline industry.

If the writer is wrong about the assumptions he has made regarding Freedonian society, the implications for the commercial airline industry in Freedonia are less rosy. It would mean that there will be less income and no less interest in foreign travel.

STEP 5

Proofread your work.

Take the last couple of minutes to catch any glaring errors.

Assessment of Sample Argument Essay 2: "Adequate," Score of 4

Now we'll look at how this essay would have been scored on the actual GRE Analytical Writing section:

This essay is reasonably well constructed throughout, enabling the reader to move from point to point as the writer examines the multifaceted implications of the issue. The writer correctly identifies and articulates several assumptions that the argument makes but does not justify. The author does an adequate job of pointing out how the argument depends upon those assumptions for its cogency. The essay suffers because the writer jumps around a little bit. The paragraph explaining how the argument could be strengthened should be the second-to-last paragraph, not mixed into the body of the essay. Also, the explication of the economic climate of Freedonia, and its implications for foreign travel, is slight. Finally, the author's conclusion does not do a particularly good job of restating the author's position effectively. The writing itself is direct and includes relatively few errors. Sentence structure is not particularly varied, and the word choice and vocabulary are adequate. For these reasons, the essay earns an "Adequate" score of 4.

KAPLAN'S ADDITIONAL TIPS FOR THE ARGUMENT ESSAY

Try to Keep Things Simple

These essays aren't supposed to be so opaque in their logic that they can't be unpacked on Test Day. Similarly, your responses don't have to be abstruse or convoluted (and shouldn't be!). Try to be as clear and linear in your writing as possible when dissecting an argument.

Don't Worry about Agreeing or Disagreeing with the Argument

This is important. You don't have to agree or disagree with the argument itself. What you (and the graders) are interested in is your ability to *reason*. That means you have to understand the argument and grasp it well enough to be able to point out its assumptions (i.e., where the author takes a leap in logic by assuming, rather than proving, a point). You should not dispute the conclusion or the evidence, only the assumptions. Do not spend any time at all on your personal opinion about the conclusion.

Paraphrase Long or Complex Sentences

You may encounter a sentence that, because of its length or structure, is hard to get a handle on. When faced with a complex sentence, put it into your own words; this will make the argument itself much easier to decipher and wrestle with.

ARGUMENT ESSAY PRACTICE SET

ARGUMENT ESSAY 1

30 Minutes
Length: 1 essay

Directions

You will be given a brief passage that presents an argument, or an argument you need to complete, along with detailed instructions on how to respond to the passage. You have 30 minutes to plan and compose a response in which you analyze the passage according to the instructions. A response to any other argument results in a score of zero.

Note

You are not being asked to present your opinions on the subject. Make sure you respond to the instructions and support your analysis with pertinent reasons and/or examples.

Feel free to take a few minutes to consider the argument and instructions, and to plan your response, before you begin to write. Be certain your analysis is fully developed and logically organized, and make sure you leave enough time to review and revise what you've written.

The following appeared in the City Council Proceedings section of the local newspaper in Smithville:

> "The city council of Smithville has instituted changes to police procedures to improve the visibility of the police force. These changes require that the town hire more police officers, budget more funds for police overtime, and direct officers to patrol significantly more often on foot rather than from their patrol cars. These improvements in visibility will significantly lower the crime rate in Smithville and make its citizens feel safer."

Write a response in which you discuss what questions would need to be answered to decide how likely the stated recommendation is to yield the predicted result. Be sure to explain how the answers to these questions would help to evaluate the recommendation.

ARGUMENT ESSAY 2

30 Minutes
Length: 1 essay

Directions

You will be given a brief passage that presents an argument, or an argument you need to complete, along with detailed instructions on how to respond to the passage. You have 30 minutes to plan and compose a response in which you analyze the passage according to the instructions. A response to any other argument results in a score of zero.

Note

You are not being asked to present your opinions on the subject. Make sure you respond to the instructions and support your analysis with pertinent reasons and/or examples.

Feel free to take a few minutes to consider the argument and instructions, and to plan your response, before you begin to write. Be certain your analysis is fully developed and logically organized, and make sure you leave enough time to review and revise what you've written.

> "Tusk University should build a new recreational facility, both to attract new students and to better serve the needs of our current student body. Tusk projects that enrollment will double over the next 10 years, based on current trends. The new student body is expected to reflect a much higher percentage of commuter students than we currently enroll. This will make the existing facilities inadequate. Moreover, the cost of health and recreation club membership in our community has increased rapidly in recent years. Thus, students will find it much more advantageous to make use of the facilities on campus. Finally, an attractive new recreation center would make prospective students, especially athletically gifted ones, more likely to enroll at Tusk."

Write a response that examines this argument's unstated assumptions. Make sure you explain how this argument depends on those assumptions and what the implications are if the assumptions are wrong.

ARGUMENT ESSAY PRACTICE SET ANSWERS AND EXPLANATIONS

ARGUMENT ESSAY SAMPLE ESSAYS AND ASSESSMENTS

What follows are top-scoring sample essays for each of the practice prompts. Note how the authors adhere to the Kaplan Method for Analytical Writing.

Argument Essay 1 : "Outstanding," Score of 6

The city council of Smithville believes that increasing the visibility of its police force will reduce crime and increase the safety of its citizens. However, the memo provides no evidence to support this argument, and the city council may not be taking other variables, alternative solutions, or the citizens' desires into consideration.

The Smithville city council assumes that crime persists because the city's police force has too low a profile, but the memo never cites evidence to support this position. The council could do something as simple yet effective as asking the town librarian to review published studies to see if a parallel exists between a high police presence and reduced crime rates. It could also hire an independent research firm to see if a correlation exists between Smithville crime scenes and a lack of police activity.

The council should consider other factors that might account for the current crime rate. The police force may be under-trained or poorly managed. If so, adding more officers or encouraging officers to work longer hours could actually compound the problem. Here again, research could be a vital ally in the council's case: What have other towns with similar problems identified as causal factors? What training do their police forces receive? How are they deployed, on foot or in patrol cars? Answering questions like these might help clarify a solution to the town's problem. The council should also research historic solutions to the problem: How have towns like theirs reduced a growing crime rate? This research could bolster the council's position or provide alternative, less costly solutions that have successfully fought crime.

The council also assumes that a higher police presence automatically reduces citizen concerns over crime, but it doesn't take into consideration the relationship between the residents and the police. Some communities regard police officers with a great deal of distrust, and that attitude may be pronounced in a community where the police force is perceived as unable to cope with crime. Has the community itself, through its elected leaders, the police chief, op-ed pieces in the newspaper, or community groups, expressed a need for a stronger police force? The memo never says.

As it currently stands, the Smithville city council's memo announces a decision that appears to have been made in a vacuum. To convince citizens that bolstering the police force and changing patrol procedures is the way to fight crime, the memo needs to state how the council arrived at this decision. Only then can citizens feel that the council is taking the right course of action.

Assessment of Essay 1

The author successfully identifies and analyzes this argument's recommendation: that the way for Smithville to lower its crime rate and improve citizen safety is to increase police visibility.

In the opening paragraph, the essay restates the argument and then cites its unsupported assumptions. In the following four paragraphs, the author insightfully identifies flaws in the assumptions and perceptively suggests what would need to be known to make such a recommendation and how knowing this information would help in evaluating this recommendation.

Specifically, the author cites these points undermining the argument:

- The assumption that a higher police profile will lower the crime rate
- The assumption that no other cause exists for the high crime rate but low police visibility
- The lack of research into historically successful alternative solutions
- The assumption that the town's citizens will agree that the council's solution is the right one

Throughout the essay, the author uses well-organized paragraphs—each starts with a broad statement followed by supporting statements—and her ideas logically flow from one sentence to the next. She uses succinct, economical diction and rotates complex and simple sentences.

The essay concludes strongly by summarizing the evidence necessary for the council to recommend that higher police visibility will reduce crime and increase citizen safety. The essay remains focused and clear throughout, earning a score of 6.

Argument Essay 2 : "Strong," Score of 5

The author contends that Tusk University should build a new recreational facility to attract new students, and to better serve the needs of its current students. The argument also asserts that this will lead to greater enrollment over the next ten years. While it may prove to be a worthy project, the argument appears to rely on assumptions that lack conclusive supporting evidence. The writer would be well advised to address these issues to make the point of the argument more cogent and convincing.

First and foremost, the writer assumes, without providing any evidence, that recreational facilities will be a significant factor in attracting and serving students interested in Tusk.

This begs the question of the role of recreation and/or athletic facilities in the matriculation and retention of students in institutions of higher learning. In the absence of any reference to the academic mission of the University, or even of the role that the facility might have in attracting, retaining, or helping to fund areas more central to that mission, the writer's conclusion appears unsupported.

Secondly, the writer assumes, again without citing specific evidence, that the projected doubling of enrollment will by itself lead to an increase in demand for the new recreational facilities proposed. Even if the facilities would indeed be attractive relative to those available off campus, the author has provided no proof that a substantial part of the increased or even current enrollment would be inclined to consider the new facilities an asset to their education. Suppose for a moment that this enlarged commuter-based enrollment turns out to be largely made up of part-time students with jobs and family demands away from the campus. Would such a student body see the new facility as a priority? Would the schedules of such students allow them to take advantage of the improvement?

Finally, the author fails to describe what specific services, programs, and amenities the proposed new facility will provide, how and at what cost relative to facilities available elsewhere these will be made available to the university community, and how the financial burden of both building and operating the new center will be offset. Beyond these issues endemic to the campus setting, the writer presents no overview of the environmental, social, and public relations aspects of the project in a larger context, either intra- or extra-collegiate.

The issues raised here could easily be addressed by providing evidence that backs up the author's claim. By assembling sufficient and specific demographic and economic evidence to support the argument's questionable assumptions, the writer may not only be able to overcome the limitations of the current argument, but provide a rationale for the proposal beyond the terms offered here.

Assessment of Essay 2

This essay adequately targets the argument's unstated assumptions and inadequate evidence. The essay identifies and critiques the gaps in the author's chain of logic and reasoning that results from assuming the following:

- that recreational facilities will be a significant factor in attracting and serving students interested in Tusk
- that doubling of enrollment will by itself lead to an increase in demand and presumably in use for the new recreational facilities

The writer clearly grasps the argument's central weaknesses. But although the ideas are clear, the essay lacks transitional phrases and is not well organized. The writing feels rushed and lacks proofreading. While the writer demonstrates a better-than-adequate control of language and ably conforms to the conventions of written English, this 5 essay suffers from turgid prose and a lack of the more thorough development of a typical 6 response.

CHAPTER 19

Analytical Writing Practice Set

In this chapter, you will find four Analytical Writing prompts to practice on: two Analyze an Issue tasks and two Analyze an Argument tasks. When you complete the essays, read the sample essays and analysis to gauge whether your essays are similarly strong and whether they would earn a high score.

REVIEW OF THE KAPLAN METHOD FOR ANALYTICAL WRITING

Before starting your practice essays, review the steps and strategies you have studied for answering each type of Analytical Writing task quickly, thoughtfully, and cohesively.

STEP 1 Take the issue/argument apart.

STEP 2 Select the points you will make.

STEP 3 Organize, using Kaplan's essay templates.

STEP 4 Type your essay.

STEP 5 Proofread your work.

ANALYTICAL WRITING PRACTICE PROMPTS

Analyze an Issue Practice

You will be given a brief quotation that states or implies an issue of general interest, along with explicit instructions on how to respond to that topic. You have 30 minutes to plan and write an essay that communicates your perspective on the issue according to the instructions.

Respond to the instructions and support your position with relevant reasoning drawn from your academic studies, reading, observation, and/or experience.

Feel free to consider the issue for a few minutes before you begin to write. Be certain your ideas are fully developed and logically organized, and make sure you leave enough time to review and revise what you've written.

Issue Essay 1 Prompt

"Because people increasingly eat at restaurants, all restaurants should be required to display nutritional information about the meals they serve. This knowledge makes it easier for diners to make healthy choices and reduces the risk of diet-related health problems."

Write an essay in which you take a position on the statement above. In developing and supporting your viewpoint, consider ways in which the statement might or might not hold true. (Use a separate sheet of paper or a computer to write your essay.)

Issue Essay 2 Prompt

"All results of publicly funded scientific studies should be made available to the general public free of charge. Scientific journals that charge a subscription or newsstand price are profiting unfairly."

Write an essay in which you take a position on the statement above. In developing and supporting your viewpoint, consider ways in which the statement might or might not hold true. (Use a separate sheet of paper or a computer to write your essay.)

Analyze an Argument Practice

You will be given a brief passage that presents an argument or an argument you need to complete, along with detailed instructions on how to respond to the passage. You have 30 minutes to plan and compose a response in which you analyze the passage according to the instructions. A response to any other argument results in a score of zero.

Note: You are not being asked to present your opinions on the subject. Make sure you respond to the instructions and support your analysis with pertinent reasons and/or examples.

Feel free to take a few minutes to consider the argument and instructions and to plan your response, before you begin to write. Be certain your analysis is fully developed and logically organized, and make sure you leave enough time to review and revise what you've written.

Argument Essay 1 Prompt

The following appeared as part of a promotional campaign to sell advertising on channels provided by the local cable television company:

> "Advertising with Cable Communications Corp. is a great way to increase your profits. Recently, the Adams Car Dealership began advertising with Cable Communications, and over the last 30 days, sales are up 15% over the previous month. Let us increase your profits, just as we did for Adams Cars!"

Write a response that examines this argument's unstated assumptions. Make sure you explain how this argument depends on those assumptions and what the implications are if the assumptions are wrong. (Use a separate sheet of paper or a computer to write your essay.)

Argument Essay 2 Prompt

The following appeared in the *Ram*, the Altamonte High School student newspaper:

> "Of Altamonte students polled, 65 percent say they participate in either an intramural, varsity, or community sports team. Being a member of a sports team keeps one fit and healthy and promotes an active lifestyle. Since the majority of students are taking care of their physical fitness after or outside of school, Altamonte High should eliminate all physical education classes and put more resources into the development of the intramural and varsity sports teams."

Write a response in which you explain specific evidence needed to evaluate the argument and discuss how the evidence might weaken or strengthen the argument. (Use a separate sheet of paper or computer to write your essay.)

ANALYTICAL WRITING PRACTICE PROMPTS ANSWERS AND EXPLANATIONS

ANALYTICAL WRITING SAMPLE ESSAYS AND ASSESSMENTS

ISSUE ESSAY 1

"Outstanding" Essay (score of 6)

Requiring restaurants to publish the fat and calorie content of their meals has its detractors; they say that disclosing the makeup of meals will alarm diners, driving them away and reducing the restaurants' income. They also balk at the cost of determining these figures in the first place. But the benefits of such a program far outweigh its drawbacks. Disclosure lets people make informed eating choices, an important consideration given what we know about unhealthy diets. In addition, disclosure may end up benefiting the restaurants, both in terms of revenue and public relations.

People are eating in restaurants with increasing frequency, and we know that a healthy diet contributes to better overall health; studies show, for example, that a healthy diet lowers cholesterol and reduces the risk of heart disease. By contrast, a poor diet, one rich in fat and calories, contributes to obesity and diabetes, both of which are on the rise in the United States.

For these reasons, we should require that restaurants post nutritional information on the meals they serve. That way, people can choose the meals they want to eat, whether their desire is to eat healthily or not.

Restaurant owners are understandably concerned that disclosing information perceived as negative could scare people off, but if all restaurants have to comply, no single business should suffer. In addition, disclosure may encourage restaurants to find healthier ways to prepare their meals, which would benefit everyone.

Determining the fat and calorie content of meals will cost restaurants money initially, but such disclosure can benefit them overall; people will appreciate the openness of the disclosure and feel confident that they're in charge of their fat and calorie intake, instilling in them a sense of comfort and control, and making them more likely, rather than less so, to eat at a restaurant that lists fat and calorie contents.

Requiring restaurants to post nutrition information can benefit both owners and patrons. It can have immediate and lasting positive effects on diners who choose to eat healthily, and it can instill a sense of control and confidence in diners who appreciate knowing what they're eating, making them more likely to continue the trend of dining out.

Analyze an Issue Essay 1 Assessment

This essay is well constructed; the author begins by recognizing arguments against restaurant disclosure and then states his opinion ("Disclosure lets people make informed eating choices, an important consideration given what we know about unhealthy diets"). He proceeds to support his position with compelling evidence about health studies, medical trends, business operations, and public relations. The writing is clear and direct, and it reveals skillful use of diction. For all these reasons, this essay receives a score of 6.

Issue Essay 2

"Outstanding" Essay (score of 6)

Scientific journals that charge a subscription or newsstand price should amend this practice to avail the public of results of publicly funded research. The reasoning here is twofold: first, the public's taxes have paid for all or a part of the research, and second, scientific results should always be readily accessible to all interested parties.

A publicly funded project means, in effect, that the taxpayers own the research and have a right to the results free of charge. Granted, many research projects are funded by a combination of private contributions, institutional grants, and public funding. Even when this is the case, the public should not be punished for being one part of a coalition that may include profit-making groups. Perhaps the research committee will need to include in its duties finding venues to make research results readily available at no charge. The mere fact of public financial support of research, in whole or in part, entitles taxpayers to have access to the fruits of that research.

Another reason to let the public see results at no charge (besides being totally or partially financially responsible for such research) is that from a larger philosophical standpoint, people should be allowed access to scientific information. Innovation in the private sector and the market necessitate access to the latest research and developments. The result of making such research widely available is that the process becomes self-sustaining. New discoveries feed new developments in the private or industrial sector, which in turn fuel further research. Publishers of scientific journals may respond to such an argument by saying that they need to make a profit in order to cover their expenses of reporting, printing, handling, and mailing research results. With that said, shouldn't the government and private sponsors of a project cover these expenses and include them in their overhead, in the same proportion as their support of the research? Additionally, popular science magazines, using their revenues from advertisers and subscribers, might pay journals to reprint research in their magazines. This practice could also provide funds for making the information available for free to parties not interested in an entire slick magazine with multiple subjects.

It is supposed that some scientists and government officials will refuse to allow sensitive or secret scientific information to be available to the public for free. Governments should not disseminate sensitive or secret research publicly, but the scope of research we are talking about is what is already published in scientific journals and available for public consumption. It's also probably true that more transparency will promote more international research and more freedom to experiment. Soviet scientists in the former Soviet Union were not allowed to read about scientific endeavors outside of the USSR. This led to decades of wasted money, effort, and time; errors made that shouldn't have been; and a lot of reinventing of the wheel. Furthermore, other scientists, pharmacists, and pharmaceutical companies need access to professional journals to keep up on the cutting-edge information released post-research. Ethically speaking, they are charged with nurturing scientific debate and keeping the public safe and informed.

In conclusion, scientific journals that charge a subscription or newsstand price are profiting unfairly when they publish wholly or partially publicly funded research results. These journals need to adjust this practice for the benefit of the public and other professionals. The public's taxes have paid for all or a part of the research, and for ethical reasons, research results must always be readily accessible to all interested parties.

Analyze an Issue Essay 2 Assessment

From the very beginning, the author takes a specific position on the issue and supports it, using strong examples and reasons. The author includes counterarguments, such as the potential cost of publication that the scientific journals must foot, but she provides clear rebuttals with powerful supporting evidence. Her inclusion of the Soviet example gives a vivid illustration of the consequences of not freely sharing information, and it appeals to the reader's sense of public justice and safety. The writing is solid, well developed, and error-free, and the writer demonstrates a mastery of rhetorical language. For all these reasons, this essay receives a score of 6.

Argument Essay 1

"Outstanding" Essay (score of 6)

The promotional campaign by Cable Communications Corporation argues that all businesses would benefit from advertising with the cable television company in the form of increased profitability. As evidence to back up this assertion, the promotional campaign notes the experience of the Adams Car Dealership, a recent advertiser with Cable Communications Corporation. Over the last 30 days, Adams Cars has seen a 15% increase in sales over the previous month. The argument as it now stands is unconvincing because it is missing evidence that would make the argument more well reasoned. It also suffers from poorly defined vocabulary, which makes the argument less easy to understand.

The argument presupposes that the example of the Adams Car Dealership is relevant for other businesses. It could be that there is a particular advantage from advertising for car dealerships because car buyers are willing to travel around to buy a car. The same may not be said, for example, of a dry cleaner. In general, people will take their dry cleaning business to the closest dry cleaner because it is a commodity service and a relatively small expenditure. Thus, advertising would be much more effective for a car dealership than a dry cleaner. The statement also presupposes that business owners do not have a better option for advertising. A company may get a higher increase in profits by advertising in print media or online. For business owners to make an informed decision regarding their advertising expenditures, they need to see a comparison between Cable Communication's offering and the offerings of other advertising outlets.

The argument suffers from poorly defined vocabulary. The first piece of such vocabulary is the word "recently." From just this word, it is impossible to tell when the advertising began. If Adams' advertising began three months ago, it would not be very impressive that sales increased 15% between month two and month three of the advertising campaign. Why would there not have been a boost before the most recent month? If the promotional campaign told business owners exactly when Adams began advertising, the owners would have a better ability to evaluate the argument's conclusion. The author should also clarify the phrase "increase your profits." The promotional campaign's argument gives no details on the fees associated with advertising with Cable Communications. If Adams Cars had to develop an ad and pay large sums to Cable Communications to run the ad, the total cost of advertising with the cable company very well may have exceeded the additional profits derived from increased sales. Without additional information in this regard, business owners cannot possibly evaluate the argument's conclusion.

To convince business owners that they should advertise with Cable Communications, the promotional campaign should show additional evidence from a wide variety of businesses that have benefited by advertising with the company. The argument presupposes that the 15% increase in sales at Adams Car Dealership is a direct result of the recent advertising campaign with Cable Communications Corporation. It could be that the dealership had announced a sale for this month or that the previous month's sales were seasonably low—for example sales in March might always be better than sales in February due to some exogenous factor. In order to better believe that Adams benefited from the advertising campaign with Cable Communications, business owners need evidence that there was not some other factor causing the 15% increase. Perhaps evidence could be shown comparing the last 30 days of sales with the same period in the previous year, or the last time the dealership was running the same promotions.

To conclude, the promotional campaign by Cable Communications suffers from poorly defined vocabulary and lack of strong evidence. It turns upon unstated presuppositions, such as assuming that business owners do not have a better alternative for advertising. To better convince business owners of the benefits of advertising with Cable Communications, the company should provide additional details regarding the relevance of cable advertising to multiple business types, the exact nature of Adams' increase in sales, the ability of cable advertising to outperform other forms of advertising, and the true costs of advertising with Cable Communications. With this additional information, the promotional campaign would be much more convincing when it concludes that advertising with Cable Communications is a great way to increase a business's profits.

Analyze an Argument Essay 1 Assessment

The author successfully identifies and analyzes this argument's main contention: that advertising with Cable Communications will increase the profits of every business.

In the opening paragraph, the essay restates the argument and then cites its unsupported assumptions. In the following four paragraphs, the author insightfully identifies flaws in the assumptions and perceptively suggests ways to clarify them.

Specifically, the author cites these points undermining the argument:

1. The one-size-fits-all fallacy of the argument that all businesses would benefit from the exposure
2. The example of 15% profit increase is misleading—not all potential profits would be similar
3. The argument that cable advertising is the best possible option for businesses
4. Vague and misleading language, and not defining key terms

Throughout the essay, the author uses well-organized paragraphs—each starts with a broad statement followed by supporting statements—and his ideas logically flow from one sentence to the next. He uses succinct, economical diction and rotates complex and simple sentences.

The essay concludes strongly by making specific suggestions that would improve the essay's arguments. The essay remains focused and clear throughout, earning it a score of 6.

ARGUMENT ESSAY 2

"Outstanding" Essay (score of 6)

The Ram article falls short of presenting a convincing and logical argument for eliminating all physical education classes at Altamonte High School and putting more resources into the development of intramural and varsity sports. First, the article's statistics are unclear and poorly labeled; they lead to a faulty conclusion. Second, among other things, the article draws conclusions that go beyond what is supported by the evidence, concluding in the drastic recommendation that "Altamonte High should eliminate all physical education classes."

The statistics in the article are not properly labeled and, therefore, have the potential to be misleading: "...65 percent of Altamonte students polled." However, maybe only 100 out of 2,400 students were polled, which is not a legitimate sampling. Maybe only athletes were polled. Maybe only seniors, who tend to have more intramural and varsity members than freshmen, were polled.

The author also overlooks the extent to which the 65 percent of polled students participate in the intramural, varsity, and community teams—some students might be on multiple teams, but others might barely be involved. In any case, this part of the argument is an appeal-to-the-majority fallacy: "A majority of people do such-and-such, so it must automatically be the best way to go." Even if 65% is a completely legitimate statistic, this may not be enough of a majority when one is making decisions about the health and future of all our youth.

In addition, the Ram article draws conclusions beyond what the data supports: "Being a member of a sports team keeps one fit and healthy and promotes an active lifestyle." Just because some members of sports teams are fit and healthy does not logically mean that all are. Or maybe not all sports participants are sufficiently active. For example, perhaps some outfielders of the community sports team rarely get to run, catch, or throw and are never selected by their competitive coach for more challenging positions such as pitcher or catcher. Additionally, the author fails to note if any of these out-of-school activities teach nutrition, how to make healthy choices, how to avoid drug abuse and eating disorders, and other physical education goals beyond competition and teamwork.

In conclusion, the Ram article would be more convincing if the statistics were properly identified and labeled. In addition to data that is properly contextualized and understood, more precise and specific details would bolster the conclusion, such as how active the members of the intramural, varsity, and community teams are ("They stretch for 15 minutes and run for 30 minutes during warm-up"). With such details, the author could support all of the generalizations the article puts forth. Finally, the author of the article needs to justify why 65 percent, if indeed a legitimate sampling, is a sufficient majority for such a major change in school curriculum.

Analyze an Argument Essay 2 Assessment

The author successfully addresses several flaws of the argument in this response, including the potentially faulty or misunderstood statistics and classical reasoning errors, such as the appeal-to-the-majority fallacy and the hasty-generalization fallacy.

The author cites this evidence as potentially flawed:

- The polled students may reflect a sample size or makeup that is skewed, and the inclusion of better labeled or explained statistics would help support the argument.
- The illogical conclusion that what is good for a majority of students would be good for all the students.
- The hasty generalization that students who participate in sports teams are healthier and fitter than those who don't.

Throughout the essay, the paragraphs are well constructed and follow the blueprint of the thesis statement. Every claim is supported by evidence.

The essay concludes by suggesting ways to improve the article, which is what the prompt asks the writer to do. The suggestions are good ones that would definitely strengthen the article writer's argument. The essay remains focused and clear throughout, earning it a score of 6.

PART FIVE

Practice Test

CHAPTER 20

Practice Test

Before taking this practice test, find a quiet place where you can work without interruption for 3 hours and 45 minutes. Make sure you have a comfortable desk, several pencils, and scratch paper. Time yourself according to the time limits shown at the beginning of each section. For the most accurate results, you should go through all five sections in one sitting. Use the online answer grid available in your Online Center to enter your answers to the multiple-choice sections of this test to see a detailed breakdown of your performance by question type and topic. You'll find the answer key and explanations in the next chapter. Good luck!

Note that the time limits and section lengths for this paper-based practice GRE are the same as those for the computer-based GRE. On the actual test, you will have the capability to mark questions within a section to return to them later if time allows. It would be a good idea to use that same approach as you take the practice test. Also, write your essay if you're going to take the paper-based GRE, and type it if you plan to take the computer-based GRE, to better simulate the Test Day experience. You should type it with spell-check and grammar-check off.

ANALYTICAL WRITING 1: ANALYZE AN ISSUE

30 Minutes — 1 Question

Directions: You will be given a brief quotation that states or implies a topic of general interest, along with explicit instructions on how to respond to that topic. Your response will be evaluated according to how well you do the following:

- Respond to the specific directions the task gives you.
- Reflect on the complexities of the issue.
- Organize and develop your thoughts.
- Support your reasoning with relevant examples.
- Express yourself in standard written English.

> "Scientific theories, which most people consider as 'fact,' almost invariably prove to be inaccurate. Thus, one should look upon any information described as 'factual' with skepticism since it may well be proven false in the future."

Write an essay in which you take a position on the statement above. In developing and supporting your viewpoint, consider ways in which the statement might or might not hold true.

ANALYTICAL WRITING 2: ANALYZE AN ARGUMENT

30 Minutes — 1 Question

Directions: You will be presented with a short passage that asserts an argument or position, along with explicit instructions on how to respond to the passage. Your response will be evaluated according to how well you do the following:

- Respond to the specific directions the task gives you.
- Analyze and interpret important elements of the passage.
- Organize and develop your analysis.
- Support your reasoning with relevant examples.
- Express yourself in standard written English.

The following appeared in a memorandum from the owner of the Juniper Café, a small, local coffee shop in the downtown area of a small American city:

> "We must reduce overhead here at the café. Instead of opening at 6 a.m. weekdays, we will now open at 8 a.m. On weekends, we will only be open from 9 a.m. until 4 p.m. The decrease in hours of operations will help save money because we won't be paying for utilities, employee wages, or other operating costs during the hours we are closed. This is the best strategy for us to save money and remain in business without having to eliminate jobs."

Write a response in which you discuss what questions would need to be answered in order to assess the reasonableness of both the prediction and the argument upon which it is based. Be sure to explain how the answers to these questions would help to evaluate the prediction.

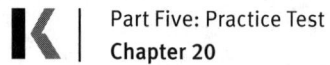

You have finished this section and now will begin the next section.

VERBAL REASONING 1

30 Minutes — 20 Questions

Directions: For each item, select the best answer choice using the directions given.

If a question has answer choices with **ovals**, then the correct answer will be a single choice. If a question's answer choices have **squares**, the correct answer may have more than one choice. Be sure to read all directions carefully.

Select one answer choice for the blank. Fill in the blank in such a way that it best completes the text.

1. Known for their devotion to their masters, dogs were often used as symbols of ______ in Medieval and Renaissance paintings.

   Ⓐ treachery
   Ⓑ opulence
   Ⓒ fidelity
   Ⓓ antiquity
   Ⓔ valor

2. By nature ______, the poet Philip Larkin nonetheless maintained a spirited correspondence with a wide circle of friends.

   Ⓐ voluble
   Ⓑ reclusive
   Ⓒ prolific
   Ⓓ gregarious
   Ⓔ pensive

For each blank, select an answer choice from the corresponding column of choices. Fill all blanks in such a way that they best complete the text.

3. Because the decision-making process was entirely (i) ______, there was no way to predict its outcome. The process was (ii) ______ rolling dice, where there is a finite number of possibilities but no way to accurately predict which two numbers will come up.

Blank (i)	Blank (ii)
A arbitrary	D likened to
B regimented	E belittled by
C unilateral	F dissimilar to

For the following questions, select the **two** answer choices that, when inserted into the sentence, fit the meaning of the sentence as a whole **and** yield complete sentences that are similar in meaning.

4. Although the heralded "variance in taxation bill" at first received much (i) ______, it has had a (ii) ______ impact on the majority of the middle-class population, who are burdened mainly by the relatively unvarying property tax.

Blank (i)		Blank (ii)	
A	commotion	D	negligible
B	acclaim	E	necessary
C	hullabaloo	F	detrimental

5. Critics' practice of making allusions to earlier work when reviewing a new piece is detrimental to the person reading the review prior to seeing the piece, as any (i) ______ viewpoint the reader already holds toward the referenced earlier piece will inevitably (ii) ______ the opinion of the unseen piece, potentially not allowing for (iii) ______ viewing of the new piece.

Blank (i)		Blank (ii)		Blank (iii)	
A	established	D	rebuke	G	biased
B	culpable	E	skew	H	impartial
C	thermic	F	complete	I	enjoyable

6. The shift away from fossil fuels as the world's primary energy source will not be sufficient to stabilize or reduce carbon emissions, and therefore carbon (i) ______ technologies should be implemented to (ii) ______ and store carbon waste.

Blank (i)		Blank (ii)	
A	sequestration	D	incarcerate
B	reduction	E	capture
C	diminution	F	liberate

7. W.C. Handy's self-conferred sobriquet, "The Father of the Blues," is widely _______; although he composed and published the first written blues song, other musicians had been playing the blues for several years.

   A professed
   B deconstructed
   C disputed
   D proven
   E contested
   F demonstrated

8. The expectation of instant gratification engendered by the ease and speed of modern communication can set one up for _______ in personal relationships if one's digital messages are not promptly returned.

   A chagrin
   B endearment
   C recompense
   D vexation
   E elation
   F pacifism

9. Anticipating the arrival of the baby panda, zookeepers _______ the panda exhibit to handle the influx of visitors, scientists, and veterinarians.

   A abridged
   B augmented
   C meliorated
   D maintained
   E truncated
   F neglected

10. Some scientists _______ that by sensing a change in barometric pressure or electricity, certain species of fish may be able to portend seismic events; just before a recent earthquake, several fish were observed leaping into the air from the ocean.

   A repudiate
   B authorize
   C foresee
   D hypothesize
   E question
   F contend

Questions 11 and 12 are based on the passage below.

Modern entomologists are primarily engaged in the research of insects that provide a direct benefit, or cause direct harm, to human interests. The benefits of researching and protecting insect life may be immediate, such as using an insect presence to control pests or diseases, or long-term, such as protecting benign native insect species from unnecessary human extirpation in order to maintain a balanced ecosystem. Research on harmful insect life endeavors to produce methods of insect control that are reliable and effective, while minimizing the effect of the control on other species. Although most insect orders include both pests and beneficial species, a few orders, such as lice and fleas, provide no benefits to humans and are said to be entirely parasitic.

Consider each of the following choices separately and select all that apply.

11. Which of the following statements is supported by the passage?

    [A] The majority of insect orders are capable of both advancing and inhibiting human interests.
    [B] An effective insect control method will never cause side effects to insect or animal life outside the targeted order.
    [C] Entomological research has facilitated the development of insect species that are considered parasitic.

12. In the context in which it appears, "extirpation" most nearly means

    (A) intrusion
    (B) excision
    (C) uprooting
    (D) obliteration
    (E) ablation

Question 13 is based on the passage below.

Instigated primarily by the Irish Republican Brotherhood, the Easter Rising of 1916 was a landmark event in the battle against English rule. Armed members of the Brotherhood, in concert with the Irish Volunteers, seized control of several government buildings in the capital city of Dublin and issued the Easter Proclamation, a proclamation of Irish independence.

However, the rebels were outnumbered by British forces, which had greater access to weapons and ammunition.

The siege ended with the unconditional surrender of the militant forces, and sixteen of their leaders were subsequently executed for their roles in the uprising. Those who survived, however, went on with renewed fervor to lobby for Ireland's independence, and the public nature of the uprising changed popular sentiment about British rule. While the Easter Rising was a failure by military and tactical standards, it is viewed as an important milestone in the 1919 establishment of the Republic of Ireland.

13. The two highlighted sentences play which of the following roles in the passage above?

- (A) The first provides support for the passage's conclusion; the second is that conclusion.
- (B) The first is a fact that would seem to contradict the passage's conclusion; the second is that conclusion.
- (C) The first states the main point of the passage; the second is a fact that seems at odds with that point.
- (D) The first provides support for an intermediate conclusion that supports a further conclusion stated in the passage; the second states that intermediate conclusion.
- (E) The first states an outside position that the passage as a whole supports; the second states the main point of the passage.

Questions 14–16 are based on the passage below.

Many Iranian Americans, whether they are immigrants or American born, identify themselves as being of Persian heritage. This descriptor is a frequent cause of confusion among non-Persians who know the country as Iran and understand Persia to be an antiquated name for the empire that encompassed part of Iran as well as parts of modern-day Pakistan and Afghanistan. Opponents of the term argue that because some Afghani and Pakistani groups refer to themselves as being of Persian heritage, the term loses meaning as a signifier of nationality. However, others argue that just as the English language recognizes *Spain* rather than *España*, English speakers should refer to the country as *Persia*, and not as *Iran*, which is the Persian translation of the country's name.

14. The author is primarily concerned with

(A) arguing that English usage of descriptors of nationality should reflect usage within the native languages of the countries in question
(B) clarifying how the fall of the Persian Empire has influenced the terminology that modern citizens of Iran use to define their nationality
(C) distinguishing among three groups that use the same term to describe their national identities
(D) explaining two opposing positions in an argument about the use of a descriptor of national identity
(E) persuading readers that in order for the term *Persian* to have a clear relationship to nationality, only Iranians, not Afghanis or Pakistanis, should use the term

Consider each of the following choices separately and select all that apply.

15. Based on the information in the passage, which of the following individuals might describe themselves as Persian?

[A] an Afghani-born woman who is a naturalized citizen of Iran
[B] an American man born in the United States to Iranian immigrant parents
[C] an American woman of English descent who has worked in Pakistan for 15 years

16. The passage cites which one of the following as a source of confusion for some non-Persians?

(A) the fact that some Afghani and Pakistani groups both refer to themselves as Persian
(B) the use in English of *Spain* rather than *España*
(C) the scope of the Persian Empire
(D) the loss of meaning in a signifier of nationality
(E) Iranian Americans' decision to self-identify as Persian

Questions 17–19 are based on the passage below.

In Greco-Roman societies, women applied white lead and chalk to their faces to attract attention. Ancient Egyptians wore light foundation to gild their skin, while their kohl eyeliner was only slightly heavier than the eye makeup popular in the mid-1960s. Persians believed that henna dyes, used to stain hair and faces dark, enabled them to summon the majesty of the earth. The European Middle Ages followed the Greco-Roman trend of pale faces. Those rich enough not to work outdoors and acquire a suntan wanted to flaunt their affluence by being pale. To look feminine, fashionable sixth-century women would achieve the same ideal by bleeding themselves. While pale of skin, regal 13th-century Italian women wore bright pink lipstick to show that they could afford makeup.

17. Which of the following statements presents a situation most analogous to that described in the highlighted sentence?

   Ⓐ Contrary to common opinion, zebras are dark animals, with white stripes where the pigmentation is inhibited.
   Ⓑ The frog's brown and yellow coloring, as well as its rough texture, allows it to blend in with tree trunks.
   Ⓒ The short-tailed cricket is known to eat its own wings to survive.
   Ⓓ To look masculine, birds called budgerigars display naturally occurring yellow fluorescent plumage on their crowns.
   Ⓔ The male blue-tailed iguana will chew down some of its spines to appear more masculine.

Consider each of the following choices separately and select all that apply.

18. Which of the following statements is supported by this passage?

   [A] The lightening of women's skin has often, but not always, been preferred.
   [B] A woman's social position could be revealed by her makeup.
   [C] The practice of lightening the skin originated in Greco-Roman societies.

19. The passage cites each of the following reasons for some cultures' preferring artificially pale skin EXCEPT

(A) to flaunt affluence
(B) to look golden
(C) to call forth the splendor of the earth
(D) to attract attention
(E) to look feminine

Question 20 is based on the passage below.

Solipsism is the belief that only oneself and one's own experiences are real, while anything else—a physical object or another person—is nothing more than an object of one's consciousness. Thus, in a sense, solipsism is the concept that nothing "exists" outside of one's own mind. As a philosophical position, solipsism is usually the unintended consequence of an overemphasis on the reliability of internal mental states, which provide no evidence for the existence of external referents.

20. In this passage, the author is primarily concerned with

(A) discussing the importance of a phenomenon
(B) refuting a hypothesis advanced by philosophers
(C) contrasting two schools of thought
(D) presenting the definition of a concept
(E) comparing a physical object to a person

You have finished this section and now will begin the next section.

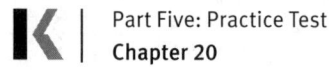

QUANTITATIVE REASONING 1

35 Minutes — 20 Questions

Directions: For each question, indicate the best answer, using the directions given.

You may use a calculator for all the questions in this section.

If a question has answer choices with **ovals**, then the correct answer is a single choice. If a question has answer choices with **squares**, then the correct answer consists of one or more answer choices. Read each question carefully.

Important Facts:

All numbers used are real numbers.

All figures lie in a plane unless otherwise noted.

Geometric figures, such as lines, circles, triangles, and quadrilaterals, **may or may not be** drawn to scale. That is, you should not assume that quantities such as lengths and angle measures are as they appear in a drawing. But you can assume that lines shown as straight are indeed straight, points on a line are in the order shown, and all geometric objects are in the relative positions shown. For questions involving drawn figures, base your answers on geometric reasoning rather than on estimation, measurement, or comparison by sight.

Coordinate systems, such as *xy*-planes and number lines, **are** drawn to scale. Therefore, you may read, estimate, and compare quantities in these figures by sight or by measurement.

Graphical data presentations, such as bar graphs, line graphs, and pie charts, **are** drawn to scale. Therefore, you may read, estimate, and compare data values by sight or by measurement.

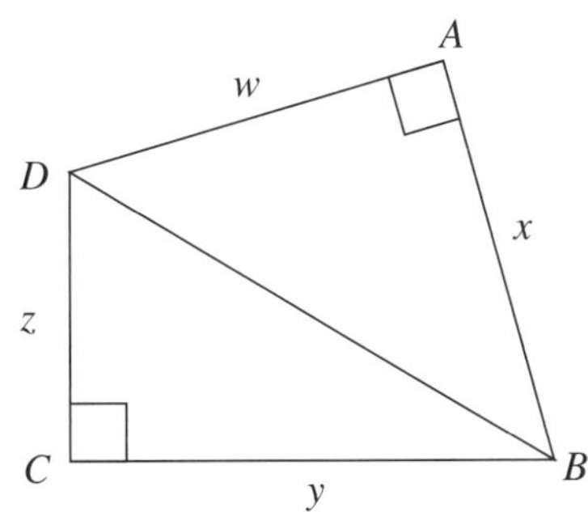

ΔABD and ΔCDB are right triangles.

1. | Quantity A | Quantity B |
|---|---|
| $w^2 + x^2$ | $y^2 + z^2$ |

Ⓐ Quantity A is greater.
Ⓑ Quantity B is greater.
Ⓒ The two quantities are equal.
Ⓓ The relationship cannot be determined from the information given.

2.

$$x + 4y = 6$$
$$x = 2y$$

Quantity A	Quantity B
x	y

Ⓐ Quantity A is greater.
Ⓑ Quantity B is greater.
Ⓒ The two quantities are equal.
Ⓓ The relationship cannot be determined from the information given.

3. In a certain accounting firm, each employee is either a manager, a technician, or an assistant. Twenty-five percent of all employees are managers. Of the remaining employees, one-third are assistants.

Quantity A	Quantity B
The number of managers	Half of the number of technicians

Ⓐ Quantity A is greater.
Ⓑ Quantity B is greater.
Ⓒ The two quantities are equal.
Ⓓ The relationship cannot be determined from the information given.

4. | Quantity A | Quantity B |
|---|---|
| $(a + 1)(b + 1)$ | $ab + 1$ |

Ⓐ Quantity A is greater.
Ⓑ Quantity B is greater.
Ⓒ The two quantities are equal.
Ⓓ The relationship cannot be determined from the information given.

5. In the two-digit number jk, the value of the digit j is twice the value of the digit k.

Quantity A	Quantity B
k	6

Ⓐ Quantity A is greater.
Ⓑ Quantity B is greater.
Ⓒ The two quantities are equal.
Ⓓ The relationship cannot be determined from the information given.

6. Henry purchased x apples, and Jack purchased 10 apples less than one-third of the number of apples Henry purchased.

Quantity A	Quantity B
The number of apples Jack purchased	$\frac{x-30}{3}$

Ⓐ Quantity A is greater.
Ⓑ Quantity B is greater.
Ⓒ The two quantities are equal.
Ⓓ The relationship cannot be determined from the information given.

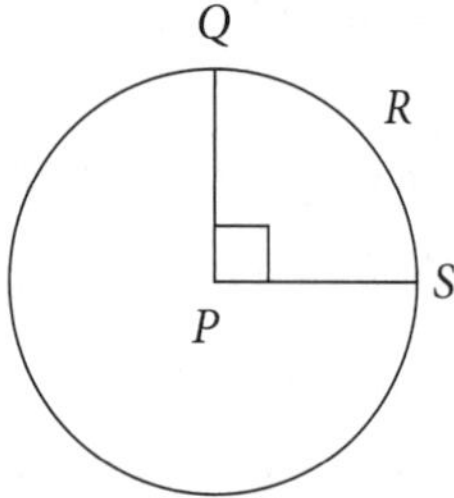

P is the center of a circle with diameter of 8.

7.

Quantity A	Quantity B
The length of arc QRS	2

Ⓐ Quantity A is greater.
Ⓑ Quantity B is greater.
Ⓒ The two quantities are equal.
Ⓓ The relationship cannot be determined from the information given.

8. $4 < x < 6$
$1 < y < 2$

Quantity A	Quantity B
The volume of a rectangular solid with a length of 5 feet, a width of 4 feet, and a height of x feet	The volume of a rectangular solid with a length of 10 feet, a width of 8 feet, and a height of y feet

Ⓐ Quantity A is greater.
Ⓑ Quantity B is greater.
Ⓒ The two quantities are equal.
Ⓓ The relationship cannot be determined from the information given.

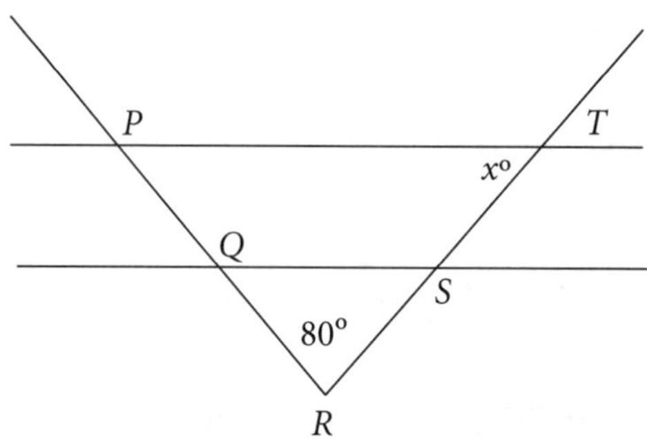

$PQ = ST \quad QR = RS$

9. In the figure shown above, what is x?

Ⓐ 40
Ⓑ 50
Ⓒ 60
Ⓓ 70
Ⓔ 80

10. A producer must select a duo, consisting of one lead actor and one supporting actor, from six candidates. What is the number of possible duos the producer could select?

[ ] possible duos

11. Jane must select three different items for each dinner she will serve. The items are to be chosen from among five different vegetarian and four different meat selections. If at least one of the selections must be vegetarian, how many different dinners could Jane create?

Ⓐ 30
Ⓑ 40
Ⓒ 60
Ⓓ 70
Ⓔ 80

12. A computer can perform 30 identical tasks in six hours. At that rate, what is the minimum number of computers that should be assigned to complete 80 tasks within three hours?

[ ] computers

13. Given a positive integer c, how many integers are greater than c and less than $2c$?

Ⓐ $\frac{c}{2}$
Ⓑ c
Ⓒ $c - 1$
Ⓓ $c - 2$
Ⓔ $c + 1$

14. If the ratio of $2a$ to b is 8 times the ratio of b to a, then $\frac{b}{a}$ could be which of the following?

Indicate <u>all</u> possible choices.

[A] -2
[B] $-\frac{1}{2}$
[C] $\frac{1}{4}$
[D] $\frac{1}{2}$
[E] 2

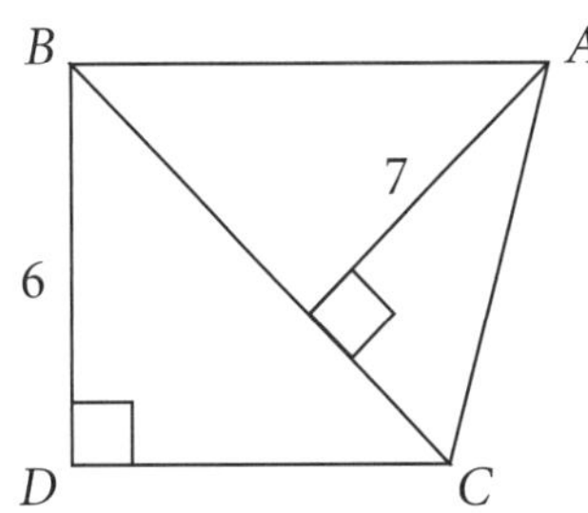

15. In the figure above, the area of ΔABC is 35. What is the length of DC?

[ ]

16. If $3^m = 81$, then $m^3 =$

Ⓐ 4
Ⓑ 9
Ⓒ 16
Ⓓ 64
Ⓔ 81

17. If $0 < x < 1$, which of the following must be true?

Indicate <u>all</u> possible choices.

[A] $2x < x$
[B] $2x < 1$
[C] $2x > 1$
[D] $x^2 < x$
[E] $x^2 < 1$

Questions 18–20 are based on the following graphs.

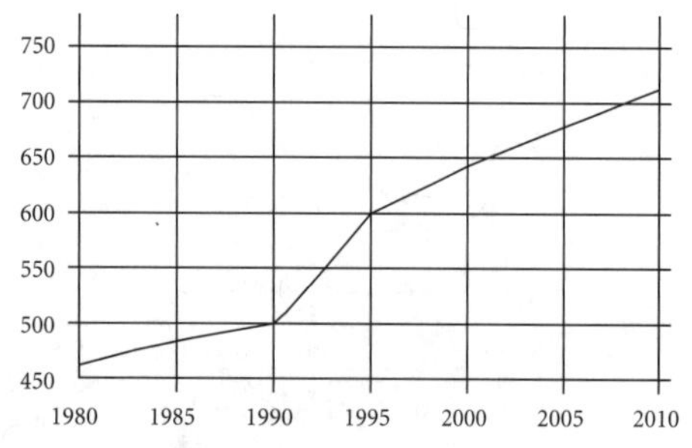

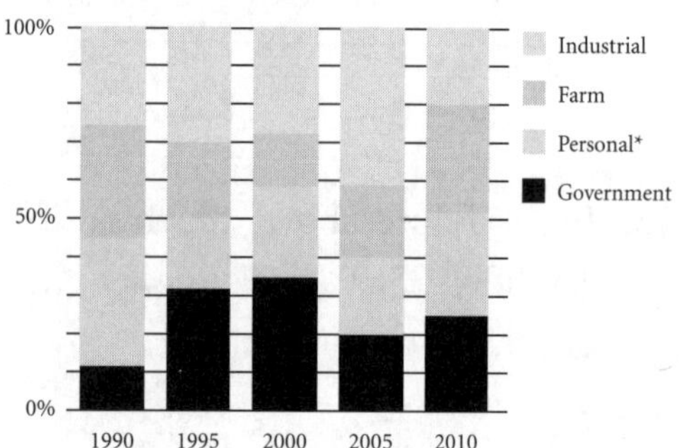

18. In 1995, how many of the categories shown had energy use greater than 150 million kilowatt-hours?

Ⓐ None
Ⓑ One
Ⓒ Two
Ⓓ Three
Ⓔ Four

19. If the population of Country Y in 2005 was 500 million, what was the per capita personal energy use in 2005? (in millions of kilowatt-hours)

Ⓐ 0.04
Ⓑ 0.14
Ⓒ 0.27
Ⓓ 0.37
Ⓔ 0.50

20. According to the graphs, total kilowatt-hours of energy for farm use increased between which of the following years?

Choose <u>all</u> that apply.

[A] 1990 and 1995
[B] 1995 and 2000
[C] 2000 and 2005
[D] 2005 and 2010

You have finished this section and now will begin the next section.

VERBAL REASONING 2

30 Minutes — 20 Questions

Directions: For each item, select the best answer choice using the directions given.

If a question has answer choices with **ovals,** then the correct answer will be a single choice. If a question's answer choices have **squares**, the correct answer may be more than one choice. Be sure to read all directions carefully.

Select one answer choice for the blank. Fill in the blank in such a way that it best completes the text.

1. The current need for diversification does not mean the organization should be diverted from its earlier and historical purpose; instead, this diversification should be construed as a means of _______ that purpose.

Ⓐ undermining
Ⓑ furthering
Ⓒ retracting
Ⓓ classifying
Ⓔ deterring

For each blank, select an answer choice from the corresponding column of choices. Fill all blanks in such a way that they best complete the text.

2. Animals rely on a combination of internal traits and external behaviors to survive. Bees, for example, have a keen sense of smell that enables them to (i) _______ kin from foe. Their ability to resist (ii) _______, by contrast, is deficient, making them vulnerable to disease. Scientists speculate that the observed extensive grooming among hive mates (iii) _______ various diseases, thus protecting the colony.

Blank (i)	Blank (ii)	Blank (iii)
A promulgate	D pathogens	G minimizes incursions by
B discern	E cold	H implicates replication of
C arbitrate	F poison	I simulates action by

3. A United Nations working group issued a report describing (i) _______ need to draw up valid plans for dealing with the global water crisis. The report emphasizes the critical necessity of galvanizing political efforts to (ii) _______ resources and (iii) _______ international attention on both water and sanitation.

Blank (i)	Blank (ii)	Blank (iii)
A an exigent	D produce ineffable	G foment
B a cretaceous	E retain abundant	H focus
C a specious	F mobilize limited	I ferment

Select one answer choice for the blank. Fill in the blank in such a way that it best completes the text.

4. Although the French general Henri Philippe Pétain was greatly honored for his role as military leader of France during World War I, he incurred _______ for his collaboration during the German occupation of France during World War II.

   Ⓐ status
   Ⓑ reputation
   Ⓒ kudos
   Ⓓ recompense
   Ⓔ obloquy

For each blank, select an answer choice from the corresponding column of choices. Fill all blanks in such a way that they best complete the text.

5. Cellophane—the transparent, plasticky film used everywhere to wrap food—is actually a paper product. Implausibly, this (i) _______ material is made from the same components as the opaque brown paper bag. Its inventor, Jacques E. Brandenberger, originally conceived of cellophane as a means to prevent stains, but after the wider utility of the product became (ii) _______ to him, he patented cellophane and it became (iii) _______.

Blank (i)	Blank (ii)	Blank (iii)
A diaphanous	D marketable	G amorphous
B standardized	E apparent	H ingenuous
C opaque	F fashionable	I ubiquitous

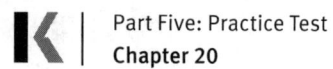

Select one answer choice for the blank. Fill in the blank in such a way that it best completes the text.

6. Unlike most other philosophers, who try to determine whether an objective reality exists, David Hume felt that the issue was _______.

   (A) pragmatic
   (B) challenging
   (C) theoretical
   (D) insoluble
   (E) esoteric

For the following questions, select the two answer choices that, when inserted into the sentence, fit the meaning of the sentence as a whole and yield complete sentences that are similar in meaning.

7. A portion of the population still disregards warnings about the _______ effects of nicotine and continues to smoke, believing no harm is done to its health, even though a plethora of evidence exists to the contrary.

   [A] deleterious
   [B] addictive
   [C] anemic
   [D] antagonistic
   [E] benign
   [F] pernicious

8. To the public's great shock, the group recently voted into power on a platform of peaceable reform conducted _______ acts against existing branches of government as soon as the election was over.

   [A] contumacious
   [B] endemic
   [C] erratic
   [D] estimable
   [E] irresolute
   [F] seditious

9. Photo retouching and inflated claims are so well concealed in most advertising campaigns that consumers are unaware of the _______ being employed.

   A cabal
   B artifice
   C hegemony
   D chicanery
   E dominance
   F imprecation

10. The performers agreed that the topic of marriage was an excellent theme for their upcoming performance at a conservative organization's charity event; however, the audience was unreceptive to the _______ jokes made during the show.

   A plucky
   B ribald
   C coarse
   D traitorous
   E politic
   F treacherous

Question 11 is based on the passage below.

Although sharks are classified as fish, they differ significantly in several respects from other freshwater and saltwater fish. Most significantly, a shark's skeleton is composed of lightweight, flexible cartilage, providing an advantage in hunting other marine life; other superclasses of fish have stable calcified skeletons. Additionally, sharks possess no swim bladder, the small organ that allows most fish to control their buoyancy; instead, a substantial liver filled with oil works to keep the sharks afloat.

11. In the argument given, the two highlighted sentences play which of the following roles?

   (A) The first supports the conclusion of the argument; the second summarizes a position that is in opposition to that conclusion.
   (B) The first provides support for the conclusion of the argument; the second provides that conclusion.
   (C) The first states the main point of the argument; the second states an opposing point.
   (D) The first serves as an intermediate conclusion; the second states the ultimate conclusion.
   (E) The first states the conclusion of the argument; the second provides support for that conclusion.

Question 12 is based on the passage below.

The Dewey decimal system provided the first standardized, easily understood method of classifying the items in a library's collection. Classification, in combination with the process of cataloging, meant that patrons could easily identify and locate for themselves items that had a certain title, were written by a certain author, or related to a given subject. Because the system was adopted at most libraries, patrons who learned the system could use it at any library.

12. Based on the information in the passage, it can be inferred that, prior to the implementation of the Dewey decimal system,

    (A) libraries were generally small enough that no classification system was needed.
    (B) libraries refused to make public the systems they used to classify books.
    (C) patrons may have relied heavily on library staff to identify and locate the materials they sought.
    (D) more people worked as librarians than after its use became widespread.
    (E) library patrons were never able to understand the order in which books were shelved.

Questions 13 and 14 are based on the passage below.

The first smallpox prevention methods were inoculations, intentional infections with active diseased matter that typically caused a mild illness and would later result in immunity. Modern epidemiologists believe that inoculated patients were less likely to contract a fatal case of smallpox because they contracted the disease through skin contact, not inhalation. However, due to extreme disparities in the type and amount of virus used, health practitioners could offer no real prediction of how severe a case a given patient might contract after being inoculated. Inoculation differs from vaccination, which uses a standard dose of dead or weakened virus culture and therefore poses a much lower risk of fatal infection. After a smallpox vaccine was developed in the 1790s, inoculation gradually fell from favor and was eventually banned in numerous jurisdictions.

Consider each of the following choices separately and select all that apply.

13. Which of the following statements is supported by the passage?

[A] Vaccination replaced inoculation because it was a safer method of protecting against disease.
[B] Two random doses of a vaccine are likely to be more similar than two random doses of an inoculum.
[C] Prior to the 1790s, live virus cultures were often used in tuberculosis inoculations.

14. In the context in which it appears, "contracted" most nearly means which of the following?

(A) agreed
(B) shrunk
(C) acquired
(D) shortened
(E) hired

Questions 15–20 are based on the passage below.

Surveying paradigmatic works of tragic literature from antiquity to the present alongside the immense and ever-growing body of secondary literature on the subject, the literary critic Terry Eagleton arrived at the pat judgment that not only had no satisfactory definition of tragedy been offered to date, but also that none besides the admittedly vacuous "very sad" could ever be offered. Overly broad definitions, which for all intents and purposes equate the tragic with seriousness, lead invariably to Scylla; overly narrow ones, such as the Renaissance-inspired struggle theory, to Charybdis. Notwithstanding this definitional dilemma, Eagleton's conclusion, as clear a case of defeatism as any heretofore advanced, leaves much to be desired.

In *A Definition of Tragedy*, Oscar Mandel, who is decidedly more sanguine than Eagleton on this score, discerns in Aristotle's *De Poetica* the rudiments of a substantive definition of the tragic. Following the spirit, albeit not the letter, of Aristotle's text, Mandel sets forth three requirements for any work to be counted as tragic, the third weighing most heavily in his account. First, it must have a protagonist whom we highly (or at least moderately) esteem. Second, it must show how the protagonist comes to suffer greatly. And, third, it must reveal how the protagonist's downfall was inevitably but unwittingly brought about by his or her own action. It is plain to see that, of the three requirements, the third (call this the *inevitability requirement*) is beyond question the most contentious as well as the most dubious. The truth is that the inevitability requirement is entirely too stringent. While it may be a sufficient condition, it is not, Mandel's assertions notwithstanding, the *sine qua non* of tragic literature.

One need look no further than Anton Chekhov's *Three Sisters*, a quintessential work of modern tragedy, to see why this is so. In a provincial capital quite remote from cosmopolitan Moscow, the well-educated, tireless, but spiritually drained sisters are ground down by the inexorable forces of time and fortune. Their failure to leave for Moscow, the childhood home they yearn for, can be understood as their failure to extricate themselves from the tedious and insufferable life brought on by their workaday habits. This suggests a certain acknowledgment on their part of their powerlessness to defy the hands of fate. In the final analysis, the question of whether the protagonist's fate is sealed in consequence of tragic action, as in Greek and Renaissance tragic dramas, or of inaction, as with modern tragedies, has very little to do with one of the absolutely essential ingredients of tragic literature. That ingredient, of course, is the profound sense of insurmountable powerlessness that yields an unnameable, implacable feeling expressing alienation from life itself.

15. While discussing Terry Eagleton's work, the author alludes to Scylla and Charybdis in order to

(A) point out the principal faults with Eagleton's ideas about tragedy
(B) argue for the importance of understanding myths in our investigation into the nature of tragedy
(C) establish that a dilemma pertaining to the essence of tragedy has its origin in myth
(D) illustrate how a dilemma common to other intellectual inquiries also applies to our understanding of tragedy
(E) delineate the potential problems that lie in wait for anyone who wishes to define tragedy

16. The primary purpose of the passage is to

Ⓐ criticize Eagleton's view that the most adequate definition of tragedy is "very sad"
Ⓑ cast doubt on Eagleton's and Mandel's views of tragic literature for failing to enumerate all the necessary conditions for tragedy
Ⓒ conclude, after analyzing the views of two literary theorists, that tragedy cannot be defined adequately
Ⓓ criticize Eagleton's view that tragedy cannot be adequately defined and Mandel's view that tragedy requires tragic action and to offer up another condition indispensable for tragedy
Ⓔ find fault with Eagleton's view that tragedy amounts to what is "very sad" and Mandel's view that tragedy requires great suffering in order to advance a new definition of tragedy in their place

17. The author's attitude toward *Three Sisters* can best be characterized as

Ⓐ laudatory
Ⓑ conciliatory
Ⓒ despondent
Ⓓ myopic
Ⓔ diffident

18. It can reasonably be inferred from the author's assessments of Eagleton's and Mandel's views of tragedy that

Ⓐ Mandel's and Eagleton's conceptions of tragedy can ultimately be dismissed
Ⓑ both theorists fall short of the mark of what constitutes tragedy, but for different reasons
Ⓒ the tragic has as much to do with what is very sad as it has to do with the inevitability requirement
Ⓓ the fact that tragic heroes undergo great suffering is at the center of both accounts
Ⓔ tragic literature is most fully understood when it combines the insights of many different thinkers

19. The author voices dissatisfaction with Mandel's conception of tragedy by

- (A) describing in some detail how a particular genre influences the way we think about tragic literature more generally
- (B) analyzing a work of literature in order to help us appreciate its supreme aesthetic value
- (C) raising a pointed objection and supporting the objection with a counterexample
- (D) quibbling with the main criteria, none of which are applicable to a particular work of literature
- (E) cogently defending conclusions about works of tragedy that, on pain of contradiction, Mandel cannot accept

20. Regarding the passage as a whole, the author's opinion of the first and second requirements spelled out in Mandel's definition of tragedy is most likely that

- (A) neither the first nor the second requirement fits very easily with the condition of powerlessness that the author defends in the final paragraph
- (B) the first, but not the second, requirement is essentially at odds with the author's claim that Chekhov's *Three Sisters* is a work that exemplifies the condition of powerlessness
- (C) the second, but not the first, requirement would have to be rejected on the grounds that it is ostensibly the case that the sisters in *Three Sisters* do not undergo great suffering
- (D) in light of the condition of powerlessness that the author endorses, it can be concluded that both requirements should not figure prominently in any account of tragedy
- (E) neither the first nor the second requirement should be necessarily ruled out in our attempt to grasp the essence of tragedy, provided that neither is antithetical to the condition of powerlessness

You have finished this section and now will begin the next section.

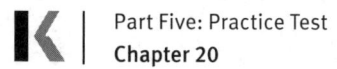

QUANTITATIVE REASONING 2

35 Minutes — 20 Questions

Directions: For each question, indicate the best answer, using the directions given.

You may use a calculator for all the questions in this section.

If a question has answer choices with **ovals**, then the correct answer is a single choice. If a question has answer choices with **squares**, then the correct answer consists of one or more answer choices. Read each question carefully.

Important Facts:

All numbers used are real numbers.

All figures lie in a plane unless otherwise noted.

Geometric figures, such as lines, circles, triangles, and quadrilaterals, **may or may not be** drawn to scale. That is, you should not assume that quantities such as lengths and angle measures are as they appear in a drawing. But you can assume that lines shown as straight are indeed straight, points on a line are in the order shown, and all geometric objects are in the relative positions shown. For questions involving drawn figures, base your answers on geometric reasoning, rather than on estimation, measurement, or comparison by sight.

Coordinate systems, such as *xy*-planes and number lines, **are** drawn to scale. Therefore, you may read, estimate, and compare quantities in these figures by sight or by measurement.

Graphical data presentations, such as bar graphs, line graphs, and pie charts, **are** drawn to scale. Therefore, you may read, estimate, and compare data values by sight or by measurement.

1. The perimeter of isosceles ΔABC is 40, and the length of side BC is 12.

Quantity A	Quantity B
The length of side AB	14

Ⓐ Quantity A is greater.
Ⓑ Quantity B is greater.
Ⓒ The two quantities are equal.
Ⓓ The relationship cannot be determined from the information given.

2. $$f(x) = (x + 3)^2$$

Quantity A	Quantity B
$f(0.5)$	9

Ⓐ Quantity A is greater.
Ⓑ Quantity B is greater.
Ⓒ The two quantities are equal.
Ⓓ The relationship cannot be determined from the information given.

3. 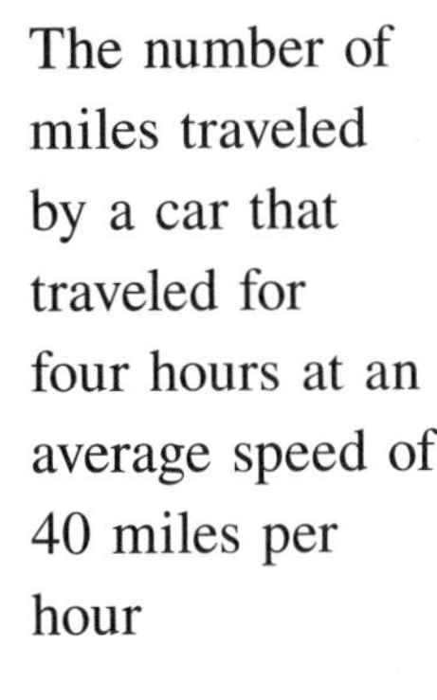

Quantity A	Quantity B
The number of miles traveled by a car that traveled for four hours at an average speed of 40 miles per hour	The number of miles traveled by a train that traveled for two and a half hours at an average speed of 70 miles per hour

Ⓐ Quantity A is greater.
Ⓑ Quantity B is greater.
Ⓒ The two quantities are equal.
Ⓓ The relationship cannot be determined from the information given.

4. A single cookie weighs between 5 and 15 grams. A single grape weighs exactly 1 gram.

Quantity A	Quantity B
The number of cookies in a bag that weighs 300 grams and contains only cookies	The number of grapes in a bag that weighs 50 grams and contains only grapes

Ⓐ Quantity A is greater.
Ⓑ Quantity B is greater.
Ⓒ The two quantities are equal.
Ⓓ The relationship cannot be determined from the information given.

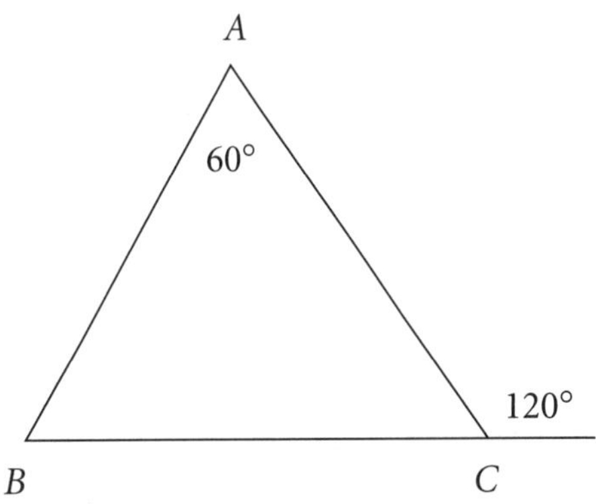

5.

Quantity A	Quantity B
The length of side AB	The length of side BC

Ⓐ Quantity A is greater.
Ⓑ Quantity B is greater.
Ⓒ The two quantities are equal.
Ⓓ The relationship cannot be determined from the information given

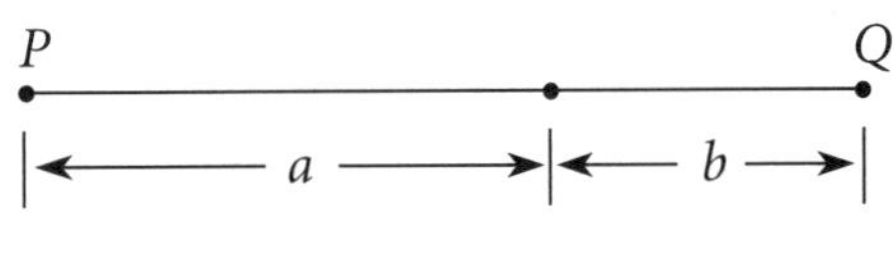

$$8a + 8b = 24$$

6.

Quantity A	Quantity B
The length of segment PQ	2

Ⓐ Quantity A is greater.
Ⓑ Quantity B is greater.
Ⓒ The two quantities are equal.
Ⓓ The relationship cannot be determined from the information given.

7. $x < y$

Quantity A	Quantity B
$y - x$	$x - y$

Ⓐ Quantity A is greater.
Ⓑ Quantity B is greater.
Ⓒ The two quantities are equal.
Ⓓ The relationship cannot be determined from the information given.

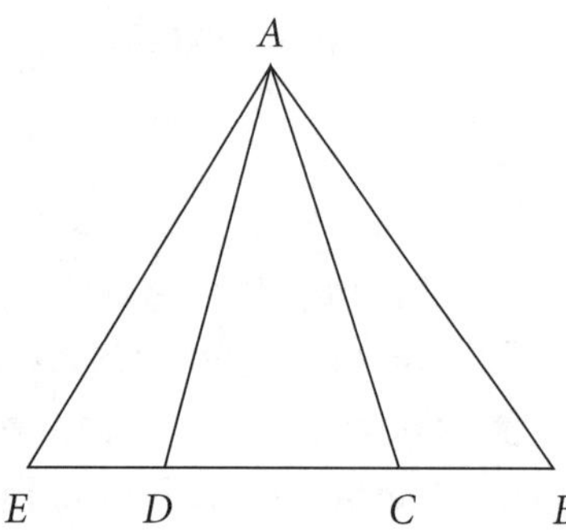

ΔABE is an equilateral triangle
The area of ΔACE = the area of ΔABD

8.

Quantity A	Quantity B
The length of side *AD*	The length of side *AC*

Ⓐ Quantity A is greater.
Ⓑ Quantity B is greater.
Ⓒ The two quantities are equal.
Ⓓ The relationship cannot be determined from the information given.

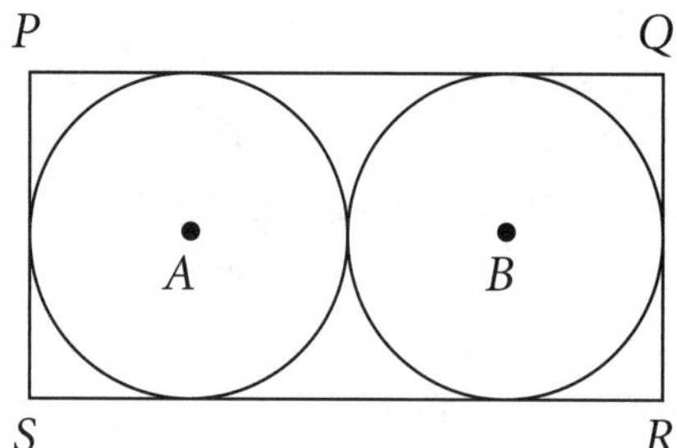

9. The two circles with centers *A* and *B* have the same radius, *r*. If $r = 3$, what is the perimeter of rectangle *PQRS*?

Ⓐ 12
Ⓑ 18
Ⓒ 24
Ⓓ 36
Ⓔ 48

10. What is the least integer value of x for which $1-\left(\frac{1}{4}\right)^x$ is greater than 0?

Ⓐ −2
Ⓑ −1
Ⓒ 0
Ⓓ 1
Ⓔ 2

11. If $\frac{p-q}{p}=\frac{2}{7}$, then $\frac{q}{p}=$

Ⓐ $\frac{2}{5}$
Ⓑ $\frac{5}{7}$
Ⓒ 1
Ⓓ $\frac{7}{5}$
Ⓔ $\frac{7}{2}$

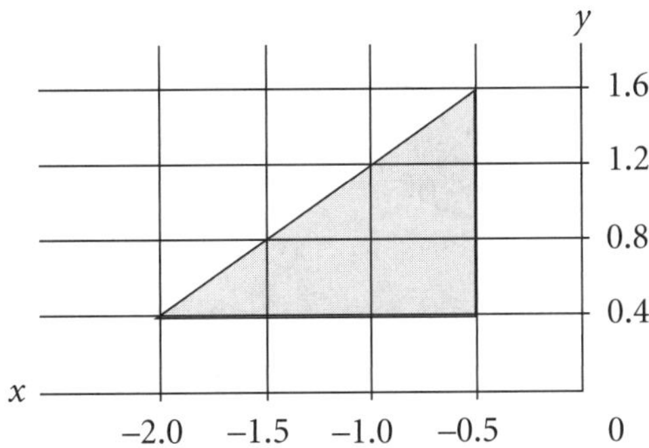

12. What is the area of the shaded region in the figure above?

[ ] square units

13. Which of the following is 850% greater than 8×10^3?

Ⓐ 8.5×10^3
Ⓑ 6.4×10^4
Ⓒ 6.8×10^4
Ⓓ 7.6×10^4
Ⓔ 1.6×10^5

14. Which of the following are divisible by exactly 4 distinct, positive integers?

Indicate all possible numbers.

[A] 4
[B] 6
[C] 8
[C] 12
[D] 14

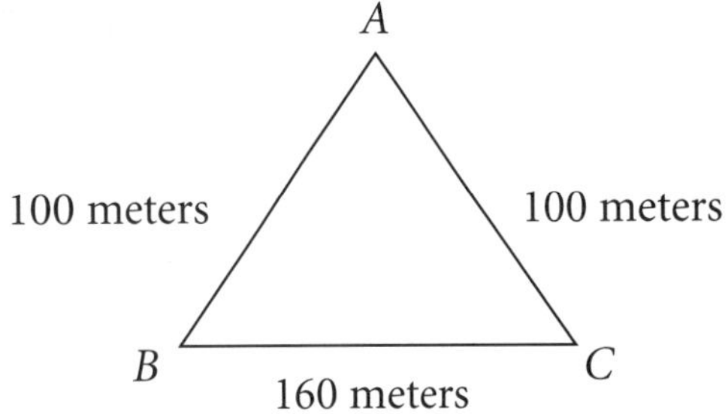

15 The figure above represents a triangular field. What is the minimum distance, in meters, that a person would have to walk to go from point A to a point on side BC?

[ ] meters

16. If the average of two numbers is $3y$ and one of the numbers is $y - z$, what is the other number, in terms of y and z?

Ⓐ $y + z$
Ⓑ $3y + z$
Ⓒ $4y - z$
Ⓓ $5y - z$
Ⓔ $5y + z$

17. Which points lie on the graph of $y = \dfrac{x^2}{x+1}$?

Indicate all possible choices.

[A] $(-3, -5)$
[B] $(-2, -4)$
[C] $(-1, -3)$
[D] $\left(1, \dfrac{1}{2}\right)$
[E] $\left(3, 2\dfrac{1}{2}\right)$

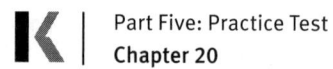

Questions 18–20 refer to the charts below.

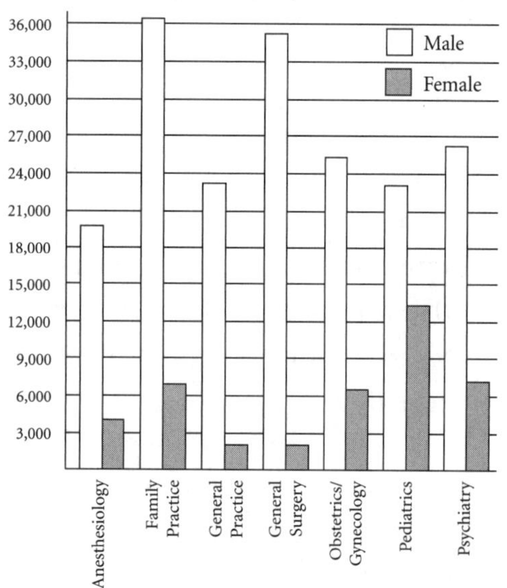

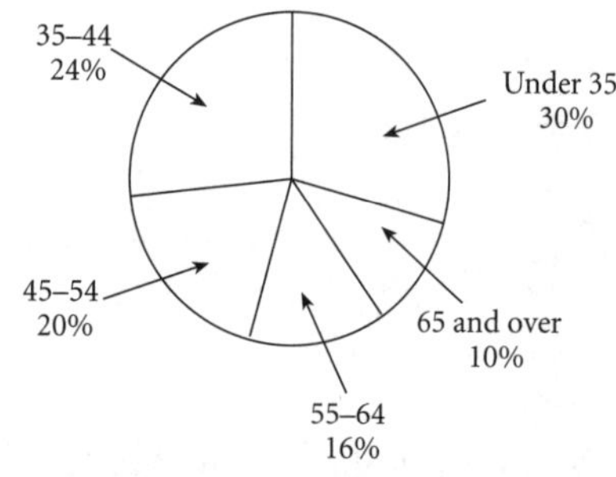

18. Which of the following physician specialties had the lowest ratio of males to females in 1986?

    (A) family practice
    (B) general surgery
    (C) obstetrics/gynecology
    (D) pediatrics
    (E) psychiatry

19. If the number of female general surgery physicians in the under-35 category represented 3.5 percent of all the general surgery physicians, approximately how many male general surgery physicians were under 35 years?

    (A) 9,200
    (B) 9,800
    (C) 10,750
    (D) 11,260
    (E) 11,980

20. Approximately what percent of all general practice physicians in 1986 were male?

    (A) 23%
    (B) 50%
    (C) 75%
    (D) 82%
    (E) 90%

Your Practice Test is now complete.

CHAPTER 21

Practice Test Answers

VERBAL REASONING 1 ANSWER KEY

1. C
2. B
3. A, D
4. B, D
5. A, E, H
6. A, E
7. C, E
8. A, D
9. B, C
10. D, F
11. A
12. D
13. C
14. D
15. A, B
16. E
17. E
18. A, B
19. C
20. D

QUANTITATIVE REASONING 1 ANSWER KEY

1. C
2. A
3. C
4. D
5. B
6. C
7. A
8. D
9. B
10. 30
11. E
12. 6
13. C
14. B, D
15. 8
16. D
17. D, E
18. C
19. C
20. C, D

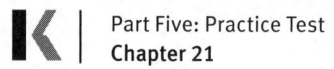

VERBAL REASONING 2 ANSWER KEY

1. B
2. B, D, G
3. A, F, H
4. E
5. A, E, I
6. D
7. A, F
8. A, F
9. B, D
10. B, C
11. E
12. C
13. A, B
14. C
15. E
16. D
17. A
18. B
19. C
20. E

QUANTITATIVE REASONING 2 ANSWER KEY

1. D
2. A
3. B
4. D
5. C
6. A
7. A
8. C
9. D
10. D
11. B
12. 0.9
13. D
14. B, C, E
15. 60
16. E
17. B, D
18. D
19. B
20. E

Diagnostic Tool

Tally up your score and write the results below.

You can also use the online answer grid available in your Online Center to enter your answers to the multiple-choice sections of this test. If you do so, you will receive a score estimate and a detailed breakdown of your performance by question type and topic. (The score you will receive is only an estimate, however, since a paper-based test, by definition, cannot mimic the adaptive nature and scoring algorithm of the GRE multi-stage test. For practice taking real MSTs, use the tests in your Online Center.)

Total

Total Correct: ________ out of 80

By Section

Verbal Reasoning ________ out of 40
Quantitative Reasoning ________ out of 40

VERBAL REASONING 1 ANSWERS AND EXPLANATIONS

1. C

This particular sentence has no detour road signs. Here the key phrase is "known for their devotion to their masters," so you might predict that the missing word means something like "loyalty" or "devotedness." The correct answer, **(C)** *fidelity,* is a close match for this prediction.

2. B

This sentence contains a detour road sign, "nonetheless," so you can expect the first part of the sentence to contrast with the fact that Larkin "maintained a spirited correspondence with a wide circle of friends." So you might predict that the missing word means something like "withdrawn" or "shy." Choice **(B)** matches this prediction: "By nature *reclusive*, Philip Larkin nonetheless maintained a spirited correspondence with a wide circle of friends." That makes perfect sense.

3. A, D

The road sign "because" in the first half of this sentence tells you that the second half will continue the thought of the first. The second half indicates that there was "no way to predict" the decision-making process's outcome, so a description of the process as "random" makes sense. The prediction matches **(A)** *arbitrary,* meaning "determined by chance, whim, or impulse." Choice **(B)** *regimented*, meaning "rigidly organized," means the opposite of what the sentence requires. Choice **(C)** *unilateral*, meaning "relating to only one side," is also incorrect—the fact that the decision-making process may have been entirely in the hands of one person does not logically lead to there being "no way to predict its outcome." The sentence compares the decision-making process to throwing dice, so a good prediction would be, "making decisions was *similar to* throwing dice." The best match is **(D)** *likened to.* Choice **(E)** *belittled by* doesn't make sense in context, and **(F)** *dissimilar to* means the opposite of what the sentence requires.

4. B, D

Look at blank (ii) first. The tax burden of most of the citizens comes from an "unvarying" tax, so the legislation mentioned earlier in the sentence must have had a *minor* effect on the middle class. **(D)** *negligible* matches perfectly. The road sign "although" indicates contrast, so the bill that produced "negligible" results must have been expected not only to have a significant effect, but a positive one. A prediction is "optimism" or "praise." **(B)** *acclaim* works best. **(C)** *hullabaloo* and **(A)** *commotion* are tempting choices, but they do not have sufficiently strong positive connotations, particularly as the bill is described as having been "heralded."

5. A, E, H

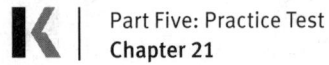

The three blanks are related in this sentence: blank (i) causes blank (ii) and prevents blank (iii). In the first blank, only an **(A)** *established* viewpoint could potentially **(E)** *skew* the reader's opinion, and an **(A)** *established* viewpoint would logically exclude an **(H)** *impartial* viewing. With the information given, only *established, skew,* and *impartial* logically follow each other.

6. A, E

This is a high-difficulty sentence, but elimination and prediction will help you out a great deal. The first clause and then the road sign "therefore" suggest that the clause with the blanks will provide an alternative to the fact that moving away from fossil fuels is insufficient to stabilize carbon emissions. Blank (ii) has a meaning similar to "store," so eliminate **(F)** *liberate.* **(D)** *incarcerate* means to put in prison and refers to people, not substances, so it cannot be correct. **(E)** *capture* matches. For blank (i), notice that the technologies must also be for "storing" carbon waste. Choices **(B)** *reduction* and **(C)** *diminution* can be eliminated. Choice **(A)** *sequestration* matches the prediction of "storing" and is correct.

7. C, E

To figure out what fits in the blank, note the detour road sign "although" between the first and second halves of the sentence. This tells you that what came before will be contradicted by what comes after. The first clause tells you that Handy's nickname is "self-conferred," so you can speculate that not everyone shares Handy's self-assessment. You could paraphrase the sentence this way to predict the blank: "Handy feels he's the father of the blues, but other musicians 'disagree.'" You're looking for a synonym for "disagree." You can eliminate choices **(A)**, **(D)**, and **(F)**, which say that Handy's moniker was *professed, proven,* or *demonstrated*—they mean the opposite of what you want. Choice **(B)**, which states that Handy's nickname was widely *deconstructed*, or "examined," *could* be right since other musicians came up with a different opinion, so keep it as a possibility. Choice **(C)**, *disputed,* has exactly the meaning you need, so keep this, too. That leaves choice **(E)** *contested*, which produces a sentence with the same meaning as choice **(C)**, so **(C)** and **(E)** are the correct answers.

8. A, D

In this sentence, which has no road signs, read for key words and what's implied (i.e., for logic). When an "expectation of instant gratification" isn't fulfilled, a feeling of disappointment would ensue. So the answer choices have to mean "disappointment." You can eliminate choices **(B)** and **(E)**, *endearment* and *elation*, right away since they have the opposite meaning. Choice **(F)** *pacifism*, "an opposition to war of any kind," isn't right for this sentence—an unreturned message would cause *conflict* in a relationship, rather than promote peace. Choice **(C)** *recompense* means "compensation" and can also be eliminated. That leaves **(A)** and **(D)**, *chagrin* and *vexation*, both of which match the prediction and have the right meaning for the sentence.

9. B, C

This is an intriguing sentence since the answer choices include two arcane words, *augmented* and *meliorated*. A good strategy for questions like this is to use the process of elimination on the answer choices. First, look at what the sentence implies, paraphrase it, and predict the answer: "The zookeepers are 'changing' the exhibit to handle more visitors." All the answer choices except **(D)** and **(F)**, *maintained* and *neglected*, express change, so eliminate those two. Of the remaining choices, **(A)** and **(E)**, *abridged* and *truncated*, mean "to make shorter," which, when applied to the sentence, wouldn't help the exhibit accommodate more traffic. The final choices are **(B)** and **(C)**, which are two high-level vocabulary words (meaning "added to" and "improved," respectively) and the correct answers.

10. D, F

Without structural road signs, you need to see if paraphrasing or key words can help you find synonyms. Scientists have observed odd fish behavior that precedes seismic events—the fish jump out of the water. Your paraphrase and prediction might look something like this: "Scientists 'theorize' that fish respond to physical precursors of seismic events." Both choices **(D)** and **(F)**, *hypothesize* and *contend*, fit this definition, and are therefore the correct answers. Choice **(A)** *repudiate* means to reject an idea, not present one. Scientists don't *authorize* information, so choice **(B)** is also incorrect. Choice **(C)** *foresee* does imply prediction, but one based on intuition, not on observed behavior. Finally, it wouldn't make sense for scientists to **(E)** *question* their own prediction in this context.

11. A

You're asked to find the statement or statements that have direct support in the passage. The last sentence in the passage states that most orders are not exclusively beneficial or exclusively parasitic, but include species with both characteristics. That's choice **(A)**. Choice **(B)** is too extreme, since the author speaks of minimizing harm to other species, not eliminating it. Choice **(C)** presents a scenario that's the opposite of what the passage expresses: facilitating the development of parasitic insects isn't in line with the goal of controlling pest species.

12. D

The word "extirpation" means "destruction" or "cutting out" or "uprooting." The phrase "protecting benign native insect species" implies that entomologists are trying to prevent these ecosystem-balancing species from destruction. *Obliteration*, choice **(D)**, is a good description of what they're trying to avoid. **(A)** *intrusion* might be tempting because ecosystems are sometimes protected from human activity altogether, but it is the species that is being protected from extirpation, not the ecosystem. Choices **(B)** *excision* and **(E)** *ablation* both refer to the surgical removal of tissue, another meaning of "extirpation" but not in accord with the context here. Choice **(E)** *uprooting* means pulling up a plant by the roots. This is yet another meaning of "extirpation" but again does not fit the context.

13. C

In this Function question, you have to characterize the relationship between the two highlighted phrases. The conclusion of this passage is that the Easter Rising was a key turning point in the battle against English rule. Thus, the first phrase, which calls the Easter Rising a "landmark event," is a paraphrase of the author's main conclusion. The second highlighted phrase, which calls the battle a "failure," would seem to contradict the conclusion that the battle was a positive turning point. The contrast key word "while," which precedes the second highlighted phrase, emphasizes the contradictory nature of the Easter Rising. Choice **(C)** matches both halves of the prediction perfectly. Choice **(A)** calls the first phrase evidence, which is incorrect. Choice **(B)** flips the two phrases' roles. Choice **(D)** refers to intermediate conclusions, which neither of the phrases is. Finally, choice **(E)** refers to an "outside position," which the passage does not have.

14. D

This Global question asks you to sum up the passage's purpose. The author's tone is one of explanation rather than argument, so you can rule out **(A)** *arguing that . . .* and **(E)** *persuading readers . . .* right away. The passage explains how the terms *Persian* and *Iranian* intersect and provides two perspectives on why one term might be preferable to the other. That's choice **(D)**. The author does not mention the fall of the Persian Empire, so choice **(B)** is incorrect. Although three groups are mentioned, the author doesn't focus on differentiating among them, so **(C)** isn't the best summary of the passage, either.

15. A, B

To select the correct choices, you must identify the groups to whom the term *Persian* applies according to the passage. Since both Iranian and Afghani people may use the descriptor, the woman in **(A)** could be described as Persian. The first sentence says that both Iranian immigrants and U.S.-born Iranian Americans identify as Persian, so the man in **(B)** also fits the criteria. However, it is clear that the term refers to heritage or citizenship or both, so it would not be accurate to describe someone of English descent who is an American citizen, choice **(C)**, as Persian.

16. E

The verb "cites" indicates that this is a Detail question, so look directly in the passage for the answer. The first two lines of the passage state that Iranian Americans call themselves Persian, and "this descriptor is a frequent cause of confusion among non-Persians." Bingo. Choice **(E)** is a perfect match. Choice **(A)** is a misused detail. It's a reason why some people oppose the use of the term *Persian*, not a reason why non-Persians are confused by the term. Similarly, choices **(B)**, **(C)**, and **(D)** all relate to arguments about whether the term *Persian* should be used; none of them have anything to do with the cause of some non-Persians' confusion, which is what the question asks for.

17. E

The question asks which choice is most analogous in meaning to the highlighted sentence, "To look feminine, fashionable sixth-century women would achieve the same ideal by bleeding themselves." All the choices are about animals, not people, but only **(E)** contains an analogous situation: self-destructive physical harm to (allegedly) produce an image befitting one's gender. Choice **(A)** mentions light and dark coloring, which the passage does discuss, but it's not analogous to the highlighted sentence in meaning. The second choice, **(B)**, concerns camouflage only. While **(C)** includes self-destructive physical harm, that harm is inflicted for survival purposes, not for the sake of appearing more masculine or feminine. The opening phrase of **(D)** sounds like the highlighted sentence, but the remainder of this answer choice discusses a naturally occurring trait, not a self-inflicted one.

18. A, B

The author describes several societies in which women lightened their skin as dictated by the fashion of the time, but she also cites a culture in which darker colors were preferred (Persians with henna dye). Hence, choice **(A)** is correct. The passage states that in 13th-century Italy, the use of makeup was a sign of social status, so choice **(B)** is correct. The passage begins with the Greco-Roman societies, but it doesn't say whether the practice of lightening skin originated there, so **(C)** is incorrect.

19. C

For varied reasons—*to flaunt affluence* **(A)**, *to attract attention* **(D)**, and *to look feminine* **(E)**—most of the societies described in the passage preferred white color or paleness on women's faces. These three choices are thus incorrect. The Egyptians preferred a light foundation also, but of a *golden* hue, so **(B)** is incorrect. In this passage, only the Persians went for a darker look with henna dye in their hair and on their skin to "summon the majesty" of the earth. Choice **(C)** is therefore a reason for preferring artificially darker rather than lighter skin, and it is the correct answer.

20. D

The passage discusses a particular "ism" (a theory or concept) called solipsism, which is the view that oneself is the only object of real knowledge or that nothing but the self exists. The best answer to the question, then, is **(D)**, *presenting the definition of a concept.* Choice **(A)** is close, except that solipsism is a belief, not a *phenomenon*, which is an observable fact or event that can be scientifically described. The author doesn't "refute" anything, so **(B)** is incorrect. Also, there are no key words, such as "conversely" or "on the other hand," to indicate "contrasting" schools of thought, so **(C)** is incorrect. The phrase "a physical object to a person" describes what the author means by "anything else" and is not the basis of any comparison, so **(E)** is incorrect.

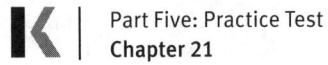

QUANTITATIVE REASONING 1 ANSWERS AND EXPLANATIONS

1. C

Right triangles *ABD* and *CDB* share a hypotenuse, segment *DB*. The shared hypotenuse should clue you to use the Pythagorean theorem. See that w and x are lengths of the legs of right triangle *ABD*; side *AD* has length w, side *AB* has length x. Also, y and z are lengths of the legs of right triangle *CDB*; side *CD* has length z, side *CB* has length y. Where a and b are lengths of the legs of a right triangle, and c is the length of the hypotenuse, $a^2 + b^2 = c^2$. So here $w^2 + x^2 =$ length BD^2; $y^2 + z^2$ also equals length BD^2. The quantities are equal, and the answer is **(C)**.

2. A

You have $x + 4y = 6$ and $x = 2y$, and you want to compare x and y. Let's start by finding y. Substitute $2y$ for x in the first equation and get $2y + 4y = 6$ or $6y = 6$. Divide both sides by 6 and get $y = 1$. If $y = 1$ and $x = 2y$, as the second equation states, x must equal 2. Because 2 is greater than 1, Quantity A is greater.

3. C

The problem doesn't say how many employees work at the firm, so let's pick a number. Since the problem involves percents, let's pick 100 as the total number of employees.

If there are 100 employees working at the firm, then one quarter of them, or 25, are managers. That leaves 75 employees, one-third of which, or 25, are assistants. Consequently, $100 - 25 - 25 = 50$ employees are left to be technicians. Now check the quantities. Quantity A, the number of managers, is 25. Quantity B, half the number of technicians, is half of 50, which is also 25. Pick **(C)** *the two quantities are equal.*

4. D

To make the quantities look as much alike as you can, use FOIL to multiply out Quantity A. You'll multiply $a \times b$, $1 \times b$, $1 \times a$, and 1×1 and get $ab + a + b + 1$. Quantity B also has $ab + 1$. Quantity A has the additional terms a and b. There is no information given about possible values for a or b. Because $a + b$ could be positive, negative, or zero, a relationship cannot be determined, and the answer is **(D)**.

You can also use Picking Numbers; let $a = 1$ and $b = 2$. Then Quantity A is $(1 + 1)(2 + 1) = 6$ and Quantity B is $(1 \times 2) + 1 = 3$. In this case, Quantity A is greater. But if you let $a = -1$ and $b = -2$, you have Quantity A $= (-1 + 1)(-2 + 1) = 0$ and Quantity B $= (-1 \times -2) + 1 = 3$. In this case, Quantity B is greater. You have demonstrated that a definite relationship cannot be determined, leading to answer choice **(D)**.

5. B

In the two-digit number *jk*, the value of digit *j* is twice the value of digit *k*. You have to compare the value of *k* in Quantity A with 6 in Quantity B. If you plug in 6 for *k*, it is not possible to enter "twice the value of the digit *k*" for the digit *j*. That is because *j* can only be a single digit; it cannot be 12. In other words, *k* has to be something less than 6, so the answer must be **(B)**. The value in Quantity B is greater.

6. C

Henry purchased *x* apples, and Jack purchased 10 apples less than one-third the number of apples Henry purchased. *One-third of* means the same as *one-third times*, and the number of apples Henry purchased is *x*. Thus, this boils down to $J=\frac{1}{3}x-10$. You can plug this in for Quantity A. We have $\frac{1}{3}x-10$ in Quantity A and $\frac{x-30}{3}$ in Quantity B. Now you can clear the fraction in Quantity B. Let's split Quantity B into two fractions: $\frac{x}{3}-\frac{30}{3}$. Leave the $\frac{x}{3}$ alone and cancel the factor of 3 from the numerator and denominator of $\frac{30}{3}$ and you're left with $\frac{x}{3}-10$. What's $\frac{x}{3}$? It's one-third of *x*. So Quantity A equals $\frac{1}{3}x-10$, while Quantity B also equals $\frac{1}{3}x-10$, and the answer is **(C)**.

7. A

The figure shows a circle with diameter 8. The circumference of the circle is therefore 8π. Since the 90° central angle cuts a quarter of the circle, the length of arc *QRS* must likewise be a quarter of the circumference. Quantity A is therefore one-quarter of 8π, or 2π. Because π is a positive number, 2π must be greater than 2. Pick **(A)** *Quantity A is greater.*

8. D

You can suspect **(D)** because there is a range of possible values for the variables. In Quantity A, you have the volume of a rectangular solid with length 5 feet, width 4 feet, and height *x* feet. The formula is length times width times height, so the volume is 5 times 4 times *x*, or 20*x*. The volume of Quantity B is therefore 10 times 8 times *y*, or 80*y*. If $4 < x < 6$, then the range of values for Quantity A is $80 < V < 120$. If $1 < y < 2$, then the range of values for Quantity B is $80 < V < 160$. Since the two ranges overlap, it's possible that the two quantities are equal or that one is greater than the other. So, the correct answer is **(D)**.

9. B

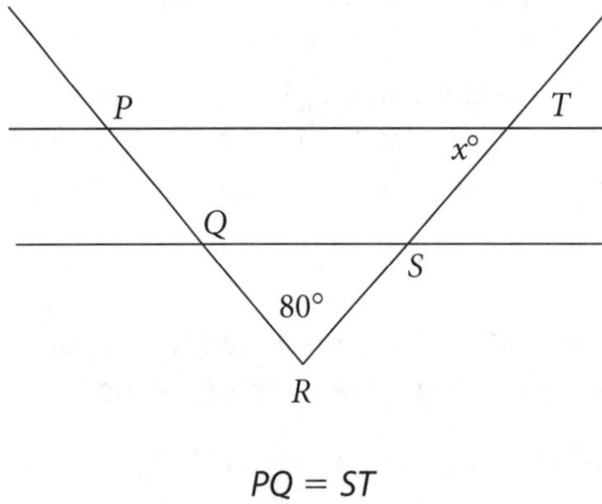

$$PQ = ST$$
$$QR = RS$$

The goal is to find x, the measure of one of the angles formed by the intersection of ST and PT. Now angle QRS is labeled 80°. You also know PQ and ST have the same length and QR and RS have the same length. If you add PQ and QR, you get PR. If you add ST and RS, you get RT. If you add equals to equals, you get equals, so $PQ + QR$ must be the same as $ST + RS$, which means that PR and RT are the same. Thus, you have isosceles triangle PRT, and you're given one angle that has measure 80 and a second angle that has measure x. The angle measuring x is opposite equal side PR. That means the other angle must have the same measure. The sum of the interior angles in a triangle always equals 180°. Thus, $x + x + 80$ must equal 180, $2x = 100$, and $x = 50$. The answer is **(B).**

10. 30

This is a permutation problem because the order in which the duo is chosen matters. The producer has two slots to fill. For the lead role, there are 6 people to choose from. For the supporting role, there will be 5 people to choose from. So the number of possible duos is $6 \times 5 =$ **30**.

11. E

The question asks for the number of different dinners Jane could make. Since the order of the selections in the dinner doesn't matter, this is a combination problem. But it involves three possible combination types: Veg, Meat, Meat; Veg, Veg, Meat; or Veg, Veg, Veg. We must calculate the possibilities for each type of combination and then add the results to find the total number of different combinations possible.

Let V represent vegetarian and M represent meat.

Then with V, M, M, she has 5 choices for the vegetarian
(she must choose 1) $\times$ 4 choices for meat (she must choose 2).

For V, V, M, she will choose 2 from among 5 for the vegetarian and 1 among 4 for the meat.

If she goes with V, V, V, the all-vegetarian menu, she will choose a subgroup of 3 from among 5 vegetarian choices.

If n and k are positive integers where $n = k$, then the number of different subgroups consisting of k objects that can be selected from a group consisting of n different objects, denoted by ${}_nC_k$, is given by the formula

$$ {}_nC_k = \frac{n!}{k!(n-k)!} $$

Here the total number of different possible servings for a plate is $({}_5C_1)({}_4C_2) + ({}_5C_2)({}_4C_1) + ({}_5C_3)$.

Now ${}_5C_1$ represents choosing 1 type of vegetable selection from 5 different types, so ${}_5C_1 = 5$. (The formula also gives this result.) Now we use the formula to find the next two combinations:

$$
\begin{aligned}
{}_4C_2 &= \frac{4!}{2!(4-2)!} = \frac{4!}{2!\times 2!} = \frac{4\times 3\times 2\times 1}{2\times 1\times 2\times 1} = 6 \\
{}_5C_2 &= \frac{5!}{2!(5-2)!} = \frac{5!}{2!\times 3!} = \\
&\quad \frac{5\times \cancel{4}^2\times \cancel{3}\times \cancel{2}\times \cancel{1}}{\cancel{2}\times 1\times \cancel{3}\times \cancel{2}\times \cancel{1}} = \\
&\quad \frac{5\times 4\times 3\times 2\times 1}{2\times 1\times 3\times 2\times 1} = 10
\end{aligned}
$$

Here ${}_4C_1$ corresponds to choosing 1 type of meat selection from 4 different types, so ${}_4C_1 = 4$. Then we use the formula again:

$$
\begin{aligned}
{}_5C_3 &= \frac{5!}{3!(5-3)!} = \frac{5!}{3!\times 2!} = \\
&\quad \frac{5\times 4\times 3\times 2\times 1}{3\times 2\times 1\times 2\times 1} = 10
\end{aligned}
$$

So the number of different possible dinners of these three items is $5 \times 6 + 10 \times 4 + 10 = 80$, choice **(E)**.

12. 6

You could find the number of tasks per hour from one computer, but that would add extra steps, because you want to find out how many computers you need to do a certain number of tasks in three hours. Well, if the computer can do 30 tasks in six hours, it can do 15 tasks in three hours. So, two computers could complete 30 tasks in that time. Three computers could do 45; four could do 60; five could do 75; six could do 90. You can't get by with five computers because you have to get 80 tasks done, so you'll need **6** computers.

13. C

Picking Numbers is the best strategy, since there are variables in the question and the answer choices. If $c = 3$, then $2c = 6$. There are two integers between 3 and 6, so plug $c = 3$ into the answer choices to see which one is equal to 2.

(A) $\frac{3}{2} \neq 2$

(B) $3 \neq 2$

(C) $3 - 1 = 2$

(D) $3 - 2 \neq 2$

(E) $3 + 1 \neq 2$

The only answer choice that equals 2 when $c = 3$ is **(C)**, so **(C)** is correct.

14. B, D

You're asked to find what $\frac{b}{a}$ *could* be; that tells you there may be more than one possible value for $\frac{b}{a}$. You're told the ratio of $2a$ to b is 8 times the ratio of b to a. That's awkward to keep track of in English—it's a little easier to write fractions. The ratio of $2a{:}b$ equals $8\left(\frac{b}{a}\right)$. So, $2\left(\frac{a}{b}\right) = 8\left(\frac{b}{a}\right)$, or $\frac{2a}{b} = \frac{8b}{a}$. Cross multiply to get $2a^2 = 8b^2$, or $a^2 = 4b^2$. Multiply each side of the equation by $\frac{1}{4a^2}$: $\frac{a^2}{4a^2} = \frac{4b^2}{4a^2}$. This is the same as $\frac{1}{4} = \frac{b^2}{a^2}$. Take the square root of both sides of the equation: $\pm\frac{1}{2} = \frac{b}{a}$. The ratio of b to a is $\frac{1}{2}$ or $-\frac{1}{2}$. So, **(B)** and **(D)** are the answers. This problem is also a great candidate for Backsolving, although since this question could have more than one correct answer, you would need to test all answer choices to see which ones work out.

15. 8

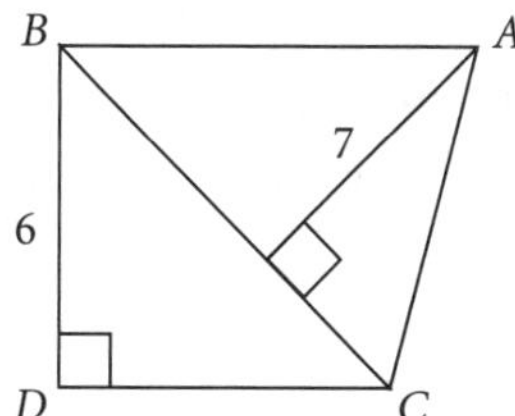

It is given that the area of triangle ABC is 35, and in the diagram, you're given a height for triangle ABC. If you use BC as the base of the triangle, the triangle's height is 7, so you can find the length of BC. The length BC, which is the base of triangle ABC, is also the hypotenuse of right triangle BDC. Given the hypotenuse and the length of leg BD, which is given in the diagram as 6, you'll be able to find the third leg of the triangle, side DC, which is what you're looking for.

Going back to triangle ABC, the area is 35 and the height is 7. The area of a triangle is $\frac{1}{2} \times \text{base} \times \text{height}$, so $\frac{1}{2} \times \text{base} \times \text{height}$ is 35. Therefore, $\frac{1}{2} \times 7 \times \text{length } BC$ is 35. That means $7 \times$ length BC is 70, so BC must have length 10. Now look at right triangle BDC. Here is a right triangle with one leg of length 6, the hypotenuse of length 10, and the third side unknown. That's one of the famous Pythagorean ratios—it's a 3:4:5 triangle. So DC must have length 2×4, or **8**.

16. D

First, find the value of m. You are told that 3^m is 81. Well, 81 is 9×9 and 9 is 3^2. So you have $3^2 \times 3^2 = 81$ or $3 \times 3 \times 3 \times 3 = 81$. There are four factors of 3 in 81, so m has the value 4. Now 4^3 is $4 \times 4 \times 4$ is 64. So **(D)** is correct. Note that **(A)** is a trap—that's the value of m, not m^3.

17. D, E

The problem states that x is between 0 and 1, so x must be a positive fraction (or decimal) less than 1. We can pick a number to get to the correct answer(s) here because both the question and the answer choices have variables. The decimal 0.5 is in the middle of the given range, so it's a good starting point.

(A) Incorrect. Doubling any positive value always produces a greater value, not a lesser value.

(B) Incorrect. $2 \times 0.5 = 1$; a smaller fraction could make this statement true, but our correct answer(s) must always be true.

(C) Incorrect. $2 \times 0.5 = 1$; a larger fraction could make this statement true, but our correct answer(s) must always be true.

(D) Correct. $0.5^2 = 0.25$; the square of any number between 0 and 1 (exclusive) will be less than the original number. This example illustrates that property.

(E) Correct. $0.25 < 1$; the square of any number between 0 and 1 (exclusive) will be less than 1. This is an example of that property. So, the correct answers are **(D)** and **(E)**.

18. C

To find how many categories had energy use greater than 150 million kilowatt-hours, you have to find out how many total kilowatt-hours were used in that year using the line graph. You see that 600 million kilowatt-hours were used in 1995. What is the relationship of 150 million kilowatt-hours to 600 million kilowatt-hours? It's 25% of 600 million kilowatt-hours, so you're looking for categories with more than 25% of the energy use for 1995. How many categories exceeded 25%? Just two, government and industrial. So your answer is **(C)**.

19. C

To find the per capita, or per person, personal energy use in Country Y in 2005, divide the personal energy use by the number of people. Since the question gives you the population—500 million people—you only need to find the personal energy use.

According to the top graph, total energy use in 2005 was about 675 million kilowatt-hours. According to the bottom graph, personal energy use was about 20% of the total, or $675 \times 0.20 = 135$ million kilowatt-hours. Divide this number by the population of Country Y in 2005: 135 million kilowatt-hours divided by 500 million people $= 0.27$ kilowatt-hours per person, or choice **(C)**.

20. C, D

Since this is an all-that-apply question, check each choice systematically.

Choice **(A)**: According to the bottom graph, energy for farm use decreased from 30% to 20% of the total between 1990 and 1995. Since 30 is 50% greater than 20, total energy use would have had to increase by at least 50% to compensate. The top graph shows that it did not, so choice **(A)** is incorrect.

Choice **(B)**: According to the bottom graph, energy for farm use decreased from 20% to a little more than 10% of the total between 1995 and 2000. Since 20 is double 10, total energy use would have had to nearly double in order to compensate—that definitely did not happen! Choice **(B)** is out.

The bottom graph shows that energy for farm use, as a percentage of the total, increased from 2000 onward. Since total energy use increased every year, total farm energy use must have increased also. Thus, without any calculation, you know that choices **(C)** and **(D)** must be correct.

VERBAL REASONING 2 ANSWERS AND EXPLANATIONS

1. B

"Instead" is a detour road sign that tells you that the second half of the sentence will say the opposite of the first half. That means diversification shouldn't "divert" the organization, so you're looking for a word that means the opposite of "divert". The answer is **(B)** *furthering*, which means "advancing or promoting." **(A)** *undermining*, **(C)** *retracting*, and **(E)** *deterring* are all the opposite of what you need—they say that diversification will negatively affect the historical purpose. Choice **(D)** *classifying* doesn't make sense in context.

2. B, D, G

The best way to approach the first blank is to consider the logic of this sentence and predict an answer. A "keen" sense of smell is a positive attribute. What should a bee with a keen sense of smell be able to do with regard to kin and foe? To **(A)** *promulgate* is to make known, in the sense of "to announce." **(B)** *discern* means "to perceive or recognize." And **(C)** *arbitrate* means "to decide between disputants." A bee would want to "recognize" friend from foe, whether or not it did either of the other two things, so **(B)** *discern* is the correct choice.

The road sign "by contrast" tells you that some other ability is not as good. Indeed, the bees have a "deficiency" of some kind, specifically one that makes them unable to protect themselves from disease. Which phrase most closely describes the desired response? Any of the three answer choices could work, but, as we said in the strategies section, the question gives you clues. Read the third sentence to see if the answer becomes clear. When you do, you'll note the key words "various diseases" matches one of the second blank's answer choices, *pathogens*. Let's hold on to **(D)** for now.

The third sentence is a bit convoluted, and some of the answer choices are uncommon words, so paraphrase it to put it into simpler terms and predict the answer: "Bees 'protect' their colony through grooming behavior." Only one of the answer choices, **(G)** *minimizes incursions by*, fits our prediction. If you substitute the other terms into the blank and reread the sentence, you can confirm **(G)** as the correct choice; neither **(H)** *implicates replication of* or **(I)** *simulates action by* makes sense in context.

Now that we have two of the blanks filled, we can return to blank (ii). When we read **(D)** *pathogens* into the sentence, the three sentences make sense together, and **(D)** is correct.

3. A, F, H

The key word in this sentence is "crisis." You need adjectives and verbs that play well off of it. If you don't know the meaning of *exigent*, you can use the process of elimination to identify the right answer. **(B)** *cretaceous* means "chalky," and one wouldn't describe a need as chalky.

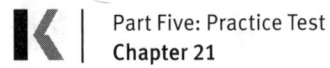

You can eliminate **(C)** *specious*—it means "false" and is the opposite of what you're looking for. That leaves **(A)** *exigent*, which means "immediate." It is the correct answer.

Which of the actions would be required in a situation of "critical necessity"? Recall that there is a water crisis, so the resource involved is water. The word *ineffable* means "unable to be expressed," so it makes no sense in this context. However, if you didn't know that word, you could use the process of elimination to narrow your choices. If there were a water crisis, water would not be *abundant*, so you can eliminate **(E)**. That leaves **(F)** *mobilize limited* resources. "Limited" makes sense in the context of a crisis, so it is the correct choice and a solid guess if you weren't certain of the meaning of choice **(D)**.

If you're galvanizing political efforts to stave off a crisis, it's likely you would want to **(H)** *focus*, or concentrate, international attention on water use. **(G)** *foment*, "to incite," and **(I)** *ferment*, "to brew," both have connotations about creating; neither makes sense in context, so both are incorrect.

4. E

The detour road sign "although" contrasts the honor Pétain received for World War I with what he "incurred" during World War II. The sentence's structure implies that the word in the blank will have a negative charge, so you can rule out the positive answer choices **(A)** *status* ("relative rank in a hierarchy") and **(C)** *kudos* ("congratulations"). Choice **(B)** *reputation* doesn't make sense—one earns a reputation; it is not "incurred". Choice **(D)** *recompense* doesn't make sense either, since the French wouldn't compensate someone for a dishonorable action. That leaves you with the correct answer, **(E)** *obloquy*, "disgrace or public censure." One would heap *obloquy* on a person who's done something hateful, like collaborating with the enemy.

5. A, E, I

This is a long set of sentences, so you should paraphrase them to make the topic easier to get a handle on: "Although people don't think of cellophane as paper, this ____________ material is made from the same stuff as paper bags. It was invented to prevent stains, but its usefulness became ____________ and resulted in a ____________ product."

For the first blank, you're looking for a term that describes cellophane. Even if you don't know what cellophane is, the key words "transparent, plasticky film" provide a great prediction for the blank. The correct answer is **(A)** *diaphanous*, which means "see-through." Choice **(B)** *standardized* has nothing to do with transparency. Choice **(C)** *opaque* means the opposite of what you need.

After Jacques saw how useful cellophane was, he decided to patent it. For the second blank, therefore, predict a word like "visible" or "evident." Choice **(E)** *apparent* is a great match. Choices **(D)** *marketable* and **(F)** *fashionable* may be true of cellophane, but the second blank describes the utility of cellophane, not cellophane itself. It wouldn't make sense to say that cellophane's utility became "marketable to" or "fashionable to" the very person who invented it.

Having filled in the first and second blanks, you quickly test the third. Nothing in the sentences describes cellophane as **(G)** *amorphous*, "shapeless," so eliminate it. Choice **(H)** is a trap—don't confuse *ingenuous*, or "innocent," with "ingenious," or "brilliant." You would expect a product with "overwhelming usefulness" to be **(I)** *ubiquitous*, "available everywhere," and that's the correct answer.

6. D

From the detour road sign "unlike," you can tell that Hume isn't trying to determine whether an objective reality exists. Why wouldn't he do so? Following this logic reveals the right word for the sentence. Hume disregarded objective reality not because he thought the issue was **(A)** *pragmatic*, "practical," or **(B)** *challenging*. That would have made him want to investigate it. He probably didn't try because he felt that the issue was either unverifiable or uninteresting. Choice **(D)** *insoluble*, "not capable of being solved," fits the blank best. It's unclear that Hume would be "unlike most other philosophers" if he thought the issue was **(C)** *theoretical* or **(E)** *esoteric* ("understood only by a select few"), so both are incorrect.

7. A, F

This is a long sentence and the blank occurs in the middle, so paraphrase it. As you do so note that the phrase "even though" is a detour road sign that indicates a contrast. A good paraphrase is, "People smoke, even though nicotine has a ________ effect on their health." You are looking for a pair of synonyms that have a negative tone and mean something like "bad" or "harmful." Choices **(A)** *deleterious* and **(F)** *pernicious* both mean "harmful," so that's the correct pair. Choice **(B)** *addictive* is a property of nicotine, but the sentence deals with nicotine's harmfulness, not its addictiveness. Choices **(C)** *anemic*, meaning "weak," and **(E)** *benign*, meaning "harmless," are contrary to the prediction. Finally, choice **(D)** *antagonistic*, meaning "hostile," is a tempting trap. While "hostile" is a negatively charged word, being hostile is not the same as causing harm.

8. A, F

The phrase "to the public's great shock" is a key phrase—it tells you there's a contrast between what was expected ("peaceable reform") and what really happened. The correct answers must mean something like "violent rebellion." *Contumacious* is a difficult vocabulary word, so we'll use the process of elimination to go through all the answer choices. Choice **(B)** *endemic* means "inherent," which doesn't fit the context of the sentence. Choices **(C)** and **(E)**, *erratic* and *irresolute*, both mean "unpredictable" or "uncertain." If you weren't sure of *irresolute*, consider its root, *resolute*, and think of a similar word, *resolution* in this case. A resolution is something you commit to doing, and irresolute is its opposite, "unsure" or "unable to make a decision." These two words are plausible choices because they imply that the group didn't fulfill its promises, but they don't work in context. You need a contrast with "peaceable reform," something that would result in people's shock—unpredictability and uncertainty aren't shocking.

Choice **(D)** *estimable*, "worthy," means the opposite of what you want. If you didn't know the meaning of this word, you could consider its root, *esti*. Think of words with a similar root that you *can* define, such as *esteem*. Knowing that esteem has a positive tone, you could deduce that *estimable* does as well, making it incorrect. That leaves you with choices **(A)** and **(F)**—*contumacious* and *seditious*—both of which mean "rebellious" and are the correct choices.

9. B, D

Some of the answer choices are fairly difficult words, but you can tell from the key word "concealed" that you want a word negative in tone. Based on that, two words pop out from the answer choices, **(B)** *artifice* and **(D)** *chicanery*, both of which are negative and both of which mean "deception." But you should go through the answer choices one at a time to confirm your selections.

Choice **(A)** *cabal* means "a secret group," and it doesn't work in context.

Choice **(B)** *artifice* sounds a lot like a word you're probably familiar with—"artificial," which means looking like one thing while actually being another. *Artifice* means "trickery." "Photo retouching and inflated claims" are forms of trickery, so this is one of the correct answers.

If you don't know the meaning of the word *hegemony* **(C)**, put it aside until you go through the other answer choices. Choice **(E)** *dominance* means "supremacy" or "domination," and it doesn't make sense in context. Eliminate it. Choice **(D)** *chicanery* also means "deception and trickery," so it's also correct. To determine the meaning of *imprecation*, choice **(F)**, think of a word with a similar root. One is "precarious," which means "dangerous." Are advertising ploys dangerous? No. This word is too extreme to work in context. That leaves you with only *hegemony* outstanding. Even if its meaning is unclear, you have, through the process of elimination, two synonymous answer choices that fit well in context, and you should go with them. *Hegemony* means "influence" or "dominance." If you knew this definition, you'd know that *hegemony* is a synonym for another answer choice, *dominance*, and this is another example of a question with two sets of synonyms in the answer choices.

10. B, C

While this sentence includes a classic detour road sign, "however," its structure is such that you can't identify what "however" is contradicting. As you've learned from

Kaplan's strategies, key words can help you figure out the missing word in a sentence. The key words in this sentence are "conservative" and "unreceptive." You need to predict the kind of joke a conservative audience at a charity event would receive poorly. Choice **(A)** *plucky* means "brave," so eliminate it. Choices **(B)** and **(C)**—*ribald* and *coarse*—both mean "vulgar." These are likely correct, but continue to test the other choices before answering definitively. Choices **(D)** and **(F)**—*traitorous* and *treacherous*—are synonyms that mean "disloyal." Although the performers betrayed the spirit of the event, this is not the meaning of the words needed to describe the jokes. Choice **(E)** *politic* means "diplomatic." This has the opposite meaning of the word you're looking for, so eliminate it. The correct answers are *ribald* and *coarse*.

11. E

The first highlighted sentence expresses the passage's main idea (sharks are different from other fish), and the second highlighted sentence explains one of the ways in which this is true (they have livers, not swim bladders). That's choice **(E)**. Since no opposing perspective is included, you can rule out **(A)**. Choice **(B)** reverses the roles of the two sentences; the second sentence supports the first, not vice versa. No opposing argument is addressed, and the author forms no intermediate conclusion, so **(C)** and **(D)** are incorrect.

12. C

This Inference question asks you to consider the information in the passage and speculate about the events that may have preceded those described. The phrase "for themselves" implies the patrons' ability to locate their own books, so it follows that they would previously have needed assistance from librarians, choice **(C)**. The passage says that Dewey was the first standardized method, but you have no basis to assume that no classification method existed before, **(A)**. Similarly, nothing suggests that libraries kept their methods confidential, **(B)**. Although Dewey helped patrons find materials themselves, no information in the passage implies that this change affected librarians' jobs directly, so you can eliminate **(D)**. As for choice **(E)**, the passage implies that patrons may have had difficulty locating items, but to say that they were never able to understand any given library's system is too extreme.

13. A, B

A lower risk of fatal disease meant that vaccination was safer than inoculation, so **(A)** is correct. Since the passage mentions "enormous variations" between batches of inoculum, the "standard dose" used in vaccines would be more likely to be consistent, so **(B)** is also correct. Choice **(C)** is incorrect because it deals with tuberculosis inoculations, which are beyond the scope of the passage.

14. C

This question refers to the second half of the second sentence, which begins, "Modern epidemiologists believe . . ." This sentence uses both the word "contract" and "contracted," and the meaning in context is the same for both. The passage discusses the process of inoculation: patients are given a mild case of the illness against which they wish to develop immunity. The sentence referred to by the question describes the effectiveness of the procedure in further detail: because the patients got the disease through their skin instead of through inhalation, it was less likely to be fatal. To form a prediction for the answer, you could read the sentence, substituting the simple words "got," "received," or "caught" for the word "contracted." The answer choices all represent possible meanings of the word "contracted," but only choice **(C)** *acquired* matches your prediction for a word that could substitute logically into the sentence as written.

15. E

The passage as a whole is concerned with how to come up with a good definition of tragedy. The author leads into Scylla and Charybdis by mentioning "overly broad definitions" and "overly narrow ones," respectively. Just afterward, she calls this situation a "definitional dilemma." From these clues, you're thus led to infer that Scylla and Charybdis are names for the dangers that may befall anyone who tries to come up with a good definition of tragedy. **(E)** is in line with this inference and is correct. **(A)** cannot be correct because Terry Eagleton begs off providing a good definition in the first place. He seems to think that the task is simply impossible. So broad and narrow definitions, represented by Scylla and Charybdis, respectively, are not signs of Eagleton's principal faults. **(B)** is outside the scope of the passage. The author is making no larger claim about the significance of myth. Similarly, **(C)** is outside the scope. While Scylla and Charybdis are drawn from myth, they in no way establish that Eagleton's dilemma has its origins in myth. Like **(B)** and **(C)**, **(D)** is also outside the scope. Because the author makes no reference to other intellectual inquiries, you have no reason for believing that they are applicable to the case at hand.

16. D

What is the main point of the passage? It is to criticize two authors' views of tragedy (paragraphs 1–2) and to generate a new necessary condition for tragedy (paragraph 3). The choice that most closely matches this understanding is **(D)**. Consider that **(A)** is too narrow: Mandel isn't even mentioned by this choice, despite the fact that he is the "main character" in the passage. The problem with **(B)** is that it includes Eagleton in the author's criticism of Mandel. In other words, the author *does* criticize Mandel for not providing all the necessary conditions for tragedy. But she *does not* have anything explicit to say about whether Eagleton falls prey to the same problem. Consequently, **(B)** is a distortion. Moreover, it is incomplete as it leaves out the author's own criterion, set forth in the final paragraph, for what constitutes tragedy. Choice **(C)** is the opposite of what the author says. The author implies throughout the passage that tragedy is definable. Though she pokes holes in both theorists' accounts, the author seems, if anything, more sympathetic to Mandel, who thinks that tragedy is definable, than she is to Eagleton, who does not. **(E)**, finally, is a distortion: the author takes issue with Mandel's view that tragedy requires the "inevitability requirement." She does not find fault with his view that tragedy requires great suffering.

17. A

This question tests your ability to identify GRE vocabulary words within the Reading Comprehension portion of the exam. At the very least, you should be thinking that the author *liked*, *esteemed*, and *pitied* these characters. She says as much when she describes them as being "well-educated, tireless, but spiritually drained" (lines 44–45). The only answer that comes close is **(A)** *laudatory*, meaning "worthy of praise." Choice **(B)**, *conciliatory*, means "intending to placate," so this does not work. Choice **(C)**, *despondent*, means "very sad." You could infer that the characters themselves are despondent, but "the author's attitude" is surely not despondent. Therefore, **(C)** is incorrect. Choice **(D)** *myopic* means "shortsighted," and that has nothing to do with the passage before you, let alone the author's attitude toward the protagonists in this work, so it can be eliminated. And **(E)** *diffident* means "modest" or "timid," and that's not on target. In sum, none but **(A)** rings true.

18. B

This Inference question is essentially asking you to consider not only what Eagleton and Mandel have in common, but also what they do not. What do they have in common? According to the author, they don't give us an adequate conception of tragedy. And now what are the main differences between them? They take different approaches to the task, with Eagleton throwing his hands up and saying, in effect, that tragedy can't be defined and Mandel digging his heels in and saying that it can. **(B)** captures what they share (that is, failure) and what they differ on (that is, the reasons for their respective failures). Regarding **(A)**, the author does not think that their ideas should be dismissed. Why would she have bothered methodically working through their ideas in the first place if this was her attitude toward their ideas? No, clearly she thinks that much can be learned from them. Thus, **(A)** is the opposite of what the passage says. As for choice **(C)**, the author's ultimate assessment is that neither Eagleton's nor Mandel's view will do. What's more, the passage never states whether the first thing about sadness should be weighed as *heavily* as the second thing about inevitability. For both of these reasons, **(C)** can't be inferred. **(D)** is incorrect because you can't validly infer from the fact that a work is very sad that the heroes have necessarily suffered greatly. In Eagleton's view, the fact of great suffering is, at best, probable and not certain. The key word in **(E)** is *combines*. The author does examine different thinkers' ideas, but her strategy is not to combine those ideas; her strategy is to criticize these ideas. Consequently, **(E)** can't be inferred.

19. C

In this question, you should *only* look at paragraph 3. Make sure that "present conception of tragedy" refers to Mandel's view. Think about what the opening sentence is doing: it's making clear to you the author's chief complaint with Mandel. And then consider that the rest of the paragraph is trying to provide evidence for the complaint already mentioned.

Thus, **(C)** is correct. No such luck with **(A)**. Don't be fooled: all talk of genre and influence goes beyond the bounds of the passage. You run into a similar problem with **(B)**. The author has nothing to say about aesthetic value, supreme or otherwise. In sum, **(A)** and **(B)** are outside the scope. On the face of it, **(D)** looks pretty good. True, the author is worrying about something in Mandel's definition. However, she is not taking issue with all three criteria—only with one criterion (the inevitability requirement). Consequently, **(D)** is incorrect. Turning to **(E)**, we don't see much to recommend it. For one thing, the author is not defending conclusions (she is, as the question tells you, simply voicing dissatisfaction). For another, she is not pointing out a trap that Mandel is falling into.

20. E

To begin with, understand the scope of the question squarely before you. The question has to do with the whole passage, not with one of its parts. Now think about the first two requirements. The first is that the protagonist is worthy of esteem; the second that he or she suffers greatly. Ask yourself: What do you think the author's opinion about these two requirements is? Does she like them? Dislike them? It's the first: she most likely thinks that they are good things. Evidence for the first part of this conclusion can be found in paragraph 3 where the author seems to look favorably on the characters in the modern tragedy *Three Sisters*. **(E)** puts this point even more delicately by making us see that both requirements are OK so long as they don't contradict the condition of powerlessness. Therefore, **(E)** is the correct answer.

(A) is the opposite of the correct answer. The author provides no reason to believe that these requirements would not fit with the condition of powerlessness. With respect to **(B)**, the first condition isn't at all at odds with the condition of powerlessness. The author implies as much in paragraph 3 when she shows that good characters in works of tragedy necessarily feel powerless. **(C)** is also incorrect. From all that you read in paragraph 3, you can reasonably conclude that the sisters do suffer a good deal. That leaves you with **(D)** to consider. **(D)** is without question quite tempting. Yet it goes outside the scope of the passage to say that both requirements should not figure prominently. You have reason to believe that they should figure *in some way*, but we can't know for sure *how* prominently they should figure. The answer is **(E)**.

QUANTITATIVE REASONING 2 ANSWERS AND EXPLANATIONS

1. D

The perimeter of *ABC* is 40 and the length of *BC* is 12, and you want to compare the length of *AB* with 14. In an isosceles triangle, there are two sides with equal length, but you don't know whether side *BC* is one of those sides or not. If side *BC* is the unequal side, there are two unknown sides plus 12, and they have a sum of 40, the perimeter. The two remaining sides have a sum of 28, so each is 14. That would mean that *AB* and *AC* would have length 14. Then the answer would be **(C)**. If *BC* is one of the equal sides, however, there are two sides with length 12 and a third unknown side, and the sum is 40. Because $12 + 12$ is 24, the third side has length 16. *AB* could be one of the sides of length 12 or the side of length 16. There are three possible lengths for side *AB*—16, 14, and 12—so the answer is **(D)**.

2. A

Plug 0.5 in for x and solve. $f(0.5) = (0.5+3)^2 = 3.5^2 = 12.25$. This is greater than 9, so the answer is **(A)**.

3. B

In both quantities, use the basic formula: rate $\times$ time $=$ distance. In Quantity A, 40 mph $\times$ 4 hours traveled gives you 160 miles. In Quantity B, 70 mph $\times$ $2\frac{1}{2}$ hours $=$ 175 miles. As 175 is greater than 160, the answer is **(B)**.

4. D

Quantity A cannot be precisely defined, but Quantity B can. The grape bag weighs 50 grams, and each grape weighs exactly 1 gram, so there must be 50 grapes in the bag. Quantity B is 50.

Now consider Quantity A. If every cookie in the bag is on the lighter end, weighing only 5 grams, then the number of cookies in the bag is 300 divided by 5, or 60. If, contrarily, the bag is full of the heaviest cookies in town, each weighing 15 grams, then there are 300 divided by 15, or 20, cookies in the bag. Thus, Quantity A is somewhere between 20 and 60, which means it could be less than, equal to, or greater than Quantity B. You have no idea which is the case, so pick **(D)**.

5. C

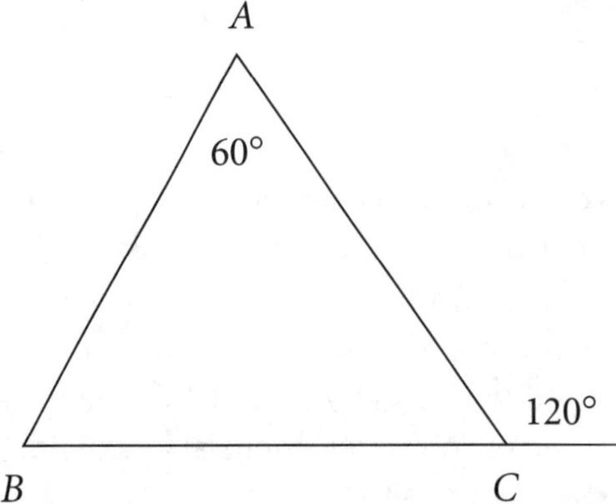

Here you have triangle *ABC*—base *BC* has been extended on one side and there is an exterior angle drawn in and labeled 120°. You want to compare side lengths *AB* and *BC*. In any triangle, the largest side will be opposite the largest angle, so you want to see which of these sides is opposite a larger angle. Angle *A* is labeled 60°, but is angle *C* less than, equal to, or greater than 60? Notice that the adjacent angle is 120°—the two together form a straight line, so their sum is 180°. And $180 - 120 = 60$, so angle *C* is a 60° angle. Since the angles are equal, the sides are equal, and the answer is **(C)**.

6. A

Notice the way the diagram is set up: $a + b$ is the same as *PQ*. The equation is $8a + 8b = 24$. Divide both sides by 8. You end up with $a + b = 3$. *PQ* is 3 and because 3 is greater than 2, the answer is **(A)**. Note that you did not have to solve for *a* or *b* individually.

7. A

All you know is that *x* is less than *y*, but even though you don't know their values, you know enough to determine a relationship. In Quantity A, you have $y - x$, the larger number minus the smaller number, so you must get a positive difference, even if both numbers are negative. In Quantity B, you have the smaller number minus the larger number—this time the difference is negative. So you can determine a relationship—you know the answer is **(A)**, Quantity A is always greater than Quantity B.

8. C

The area of a triangle equals $\frac{1}{2} \times \text{base} \times \text{height}$. Triangles *ACE* and *ABD* have the same height, because they have the same apex point *A*. The problem states that their areas are equal, so they must have the same base, too. Thus, $EC = DB$ and $ED = CB$. Since triangle *ABE* is equilateral, you also know that $AE = AB$. This means that sides *AD* and *AC* are equal as well. If they weren't, one of *ED* or *CB* would have to be longer than the other, and you already know they're equal. The answer is **(C)**.

9. D

If the radius of each circle is 3, then the diameter of each circle is 6. Then *PS* and *QR* each equal 6, and *PQ* and *SR* each equal 12. The perimeter of rectangle $PQRS = 6 + 12 + 6 + 12 = 36$. The answer is **(D)**.

10. D

In this question, you have a fraction as a base and must consider various values for *x*, the exponent. Consider what happens when $x = -1$. We know that $\left(\frac{1}{4}\right)^{-1} = \frac{1}{\left(\frac{1}{4}\right)^{1}} = 4.$

Putting that into the full equation, we get $1-\left(\frac{1}{4}\right)^{x} = 1-4 = -3.$ This is not greater than zero, and if $x = -2$, the result will be even lower, so choices **(A)** and **(B)** are out. Next, consider what happens when $x = 0$. Any base to the zero power equals 1; then $1-\left(\frac{1}{4}\right)^{x} = 1-1 = 0.$ You want the value of *x* that makes the expression greater than 0, so try $x = 1$: $1-\left(\frac{1}{4}\right)^{x} = 1-\left(\frac{1}{4}\right) = \frac{3}{4}$. The answer is **(D)**.

11. B

Begin with cross multiplication and use algebra to isolate $\frac{q}{p}$:

$\frac{p-q}{p} = \frac{2}{7}$	
$7(p - q) = 2p$	Cross multiply.
$7p - 7q = 2p$	Remove parentheses.
$5p = 7q$	Add $7q$; subtract $2p$ on both sides.
$\frac{5}{7} = \frac{q}{p}$	Divide both sides by $7p$.

Choice **(B)** is correct.

12. 0.9

The shaded region is a right triangle. So, use the numbers on the grid to calculate the base and height of the triangle. The length horizontally is $(-2.0) - (-0.5) = -2.0 + 0.5 = -1.5$. Distances are always positive, so use 1.5 as the base of the triangle. The height of the triangle is $1.6 - 0.4 = 1.2$. Use the equation for the area of a triangle:

$$A = \frac{1}{2}bh = \frac{1}{2} \times 1.5 \times 1.2 = 0.9$$

The area is **0.9**.

13. D

The question asks for the number that is 850% greater than 8×10^3. First, determine the value of 8×10^3. That number is 8,000. To 8,000, you need to add 850% of 8,000. Here's what the math looks like:

$8{,}000 + (850\% \times 8{,}000) = 8{,}000 + (8.5 \times 8{,}000) = 8{,}000 + 68{,}000 = 76{,}000$

In scientific notation, this is 7.6×10^4, choice **(D)**.

14. B, C, E

List the factors for each number to check for all correct choices.

Number	Factors	Number of Factors
4	1, 2, 4	3
6	1, 2, 3, 6	4
8	1, 2, 4, 8	4
12	1, 2, 3, 4, 6, 12	6
14	1, 2, 7, 14	4

So the correct choices are **(B)**, **(C)**, and **(E)**.

15. 60

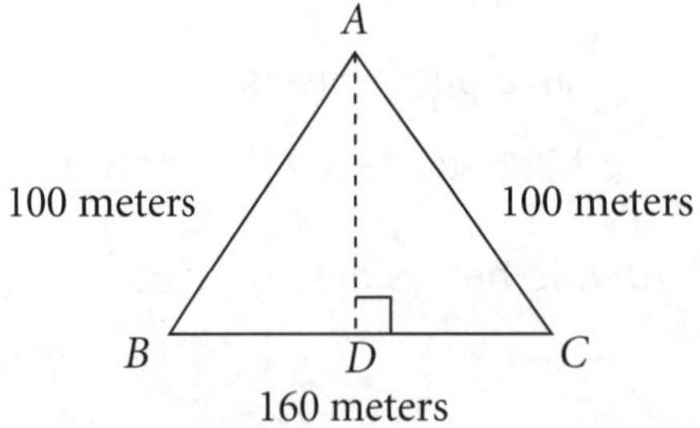

You're trying to find the shortest distance in meters a person would walk to go from point *A* to a point on side *BC* of the triangular field represented in the diagram. To get the shortest distance from point *A* to side *BC*, draw a perpendicular line from point *A* to side *BC*. Call the new vertex point *D*. Now two smaller right triangles, *ADC* and *ADB* have been created.

From the diagram, length *BC* is 160 meters, *AB* is 100 meters, and *AC* is 100 meters. Each of the two right triangles formed has 100 meters as the length of its hypotenuse.

What does that tell you about triangle *ABC*? *AB* and *AC* have the same length, so this is an isosceles triangle. That means that when you drew in the perpendicular distance from *A* down to *D*, you split the isosceles triangle *ABC* into two identical right triangles. Length *BD* is the same as length *CD*. So each of them is half of 160 meters, or 80 meters. Each right triangle has an hypotenuse of 100 meters and one leg of 80 meters. This is a 3:4:5 right triangle, with each member of the ratio multiplied by 20. So *AD* must have length **60**, and the minimum distance is 60 meters.

16. E

The average is $\frac{\text{The sum of terms}}{\text{The number of terms}}$. Here you have $y - z$ and the other number, which you can call x. The average of x and $y - z$ is $3y$, so $3y = \frac{x + y - z}{2}$. Multiplying both sides by 2 gives $6y = x + y - z$. Subtracting $y - z$ from both sides gives $5y + z = x$. So the other number, x, is $5y + z$, answer choice **(E)**.

17. B, D

Test each point. Substitute a value for x and compare the result to the given value for y in the ordered pair.

Let $x = -3$.

$$y = \frac{x^2}{x+1} = \frac{(-3)^2}{-3+1} = \frac{9}{-2} \neq -5$$

Let $x = -2$.

$$y = \frac{x^2}{x+1} = \frac{(-2)^2}{-2+1} = \frac{4}{-1} = -4$$

Let $x = -1$.

$$y = \frac{x^2}{x+1} = \frac{(-1)^2}{-1+1} = \frac{1}{0} \neq -3$$

Let $x = 1$.

$$y = \frac{x^2}{x+1} = \frac{1^2}{1+1} = \frac{1}{2}$$

Let $x = 3$.

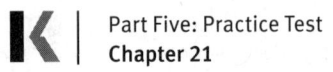

$$y = \frac{x^2}{x+1} = \frac{3^2}{3+1} = \frac{9}{4} \neq 2\frac{1}{2}$$

So, the correct answers are **(B)** and **(D)**.

18. D

You're looking for the lowest ratio of males to females. In the double bar graph, the males outnumber females in each double bar, so you want the specialty in which the numbers of males and females are closest. Skimming the bar graphs, you can see that in pediatrics, the female graph and the male graph are closer than any of the others. **(D)** *pediatrics* is the correct answer.

19. B

How many male general surgery physicians were under 35 years old? The pie chart breaks down general surgery physicians by age, so work with that. And because you're looking for a number of general surgery physicians, you know that you're going to have to find the total number of general surgery physicians and then break it down according to the percentages on the pie chart.

The number of female general surgery physicians in the under-35 category represented 3.5% of all the general surgery physicians. What this does is break that slice of the pie for under-35 into two smaller slices, one for men under 35 and one for women under 35. Now the whole slice for under-35-year-olds is 30% of the total, and the question states that the number of females under 35 is 3.5% of the total. So the difference between 30% and 3.5% (26.5%) must be the men in the under-35 category.

From the top graph, estimate the total number of general surgery physicians as 37,000 (35,000 male plus 2,000 female). Multiply 37,000 by 26.5%: $0.265 \times 37{,}000 = 9{,}805$, which is very close to **(B)**, the correct answer.

20. E

The bar graph doesn't give the total number of general practice physicians, but if you add the number of males to the number of females, you get the total number of GP physicians. To find the percent who are male, take the number of males and put it over the total number. There are about 2,000 women and about 23,000 men, making the total about 25,000. Well, if there are around 25,000 GP physicians altogether and 2,000 of them are female, that's around 8%. About 92% are male, which is closest to 90%, **(E)**.

ANALYTICAL WRITING 1 ANALYZE AN ISSUE ANSWERS AND EXPLANATIONS

SAMPLE ESSAY RESPONSES

Issue Essay Sample Response: Score of 6

Note that your essay need not be perfect to receive a very high score. It just needs to be a very strong rough draft.

At face value, the belief that "one should look upon any information described as 'factual' with skepticism since it may well be proven false in the future," seems ludicrous almost to the point of threatening anarchy. Yet not only does this belief prove well justified, it is also the linchpin around which our complex, highly technical society creates and consolidates its advances.

Science itself provides the best evidence and examples in support of this statement. One need look no further than contemporary medicine to see how far we have come from the days when illness was perceived as a sign of moral weakness or as a punishment from on high. In fact, the most outstanding characteristic of what we call "the scientific method" amounts to endless questioning of received theory in search of a more comprehensive explanation of what we perceive to be true. This iterative style of inquiry (and re-inquiry) perpetuates an ongoing scientific dialogue that catalyzes further breakthroughs in the developed world.

Furthermore, advances made through constant questioning are not limited to the scientific arena: the skeptical attitudes of ancient Greek philosophers, as well as those of Renaissance mariners, 19th century suffragists, and 20th century civil rights activists, have left the world a richer and more hopeful place. By refusing to accept the world as explained by contemporary "fact," these doubters helped give birth to societies and cultures in which human potential and accomplishment have been enabled to an unprecedented degree.

In contrast, those societies that cultivate adherence to received belief and a traditional non-skeptical approach have advanced very little over the centuries. In Tibet, for instance, the prayer wheels spin endlessly around a belief system as secure and unquestioning as the Himalayas themselves. While there may very well be things worth learning from such a society, Tibet has proven to lack adaptability and expansiveness and prefers to turn inward, away from the modern world. Such introspection has given Tibet neither immunity nor an array of defenses in the face of contemporary medical, social, and political problems. Thus, cultural inflexibility regarding received wisdom and convention comes with a price.

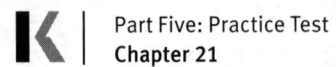

To conclude, it seems clear from the above discussion that a healthy skepticism remains the hallmark of Western epistemology as we face the future. A close look at the statement reveals that it is not advocating the wholesale rejection of orthodox thinking, but rather that we be open to redefining our assumptions. As the basis of our resiliency and creativity, this attitude offers the most positive prognosis for a society that revels in the solution of conundrums that its own constant questioning brings continually into view.

ANALYTICAL WRITING 2 ANALYZE AN ARGUMENT ANSWERS AND EXPLANATIONS

Argument Essay Sample Response: Score of 6

Again, note that an essay need not be perfect (this one contains quite a few typos) in order to achieve a very high score.

In this memo, the owner of the Juniper Café; concludes that cutting hours is the "best strategy for us to save money and remain in business without having to eliminate jobs." While the café 's employees are undoubtedly grateful for the intent of the memo, they may see that its logic is flawed. First, the memo does not provide enough supporting evidence to prove that the money saved by cutting hours would exceed the money lost by losing early-morning and weekend clients. Second, the owner does not seem to evaluate other options that would either cut back on overhead or change the café 's operation to bring in more revenue.

First, the owner relies on an unproven assumption about the cause of the overhead. He concludes, without justifying, that being open too many hours is causing too much overhead expense. There may be other causes, however, such as waste in other areas of management. While it is true that reducing café hours would save money spent on utilities, employee wages, and other operating costs, there is no evidence that those savings would outweigh the café's loss of business. The owner's message fails to give details of operating costs, wages, and utilities saved if the café is closed for the hours suggested by the memo. Perhaps the highest utility expenses are actually incurred between noon and 3 p.m., when the sun is the hottest and the café's air conditioning and refrigeration are most in use. The owner needs to do more research, including the habits and demography of the town. For example, since the café is located in the downtown area, perhaps *increasing* the number of hours the café is open would be a better solution.

Yes, it would cost more in overhead, but doing so might, in fact, make much more money for the café. Say, for instance, the Juniper becomes the only restaurant open on Friday and Saturday date nights, after the football games and movies let out. Second, the owner of the Juniper Caféis not considering that the café serves a small American city. Cutting early-morning hours at a café, in a downtown area, where businesspeople and city workers most likely stop for coffee or breakfast on their way to work, seems very short-sighted and ill-informed. Are there one or more other cafés that will gladly steal business from 6 a.m. to 8 a.m. weekdays and that will perhaps win the permanent loyalty of those customers for lunch and dinner?

Furthermore, the owner does not seem to have evaluated other options to save the café. There are other places where overhead costs could potentially be cut. Certainly the owner would benefit from a brainstorming session with all employees, to get other ideas on the table. Maybe a new, lower-rent freezer storage facility is nearby. Maybe employees can suggest cutting waste in the purchasing department or dropping services the café doesn't need. It stands to reason that there is a plurality of ways to decrease overhead, aside from simply cutting hours.

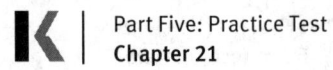

In conclusion, the memo as it stands now does not logically prove that reduction in those particular hours will result in financial and future success for the café. There are several unstated assumptions upon which the argument turns, principally the assertion that simply being open for a certain number of hours is causing crippling overhead expenses. The owner's argument would profit enormously from further research, which may affect the hours he chooses to cut. Customer polling could show that few people eat or want coffee in that part of town between 2 p.m. and 5 p.m., and the café could be closed between lunch and dinner, adding flex hours or overlapping shifts for the staff. The memo lacks outlining what other restaurant services are available in the area and how or if they affect the 6 a.m. to 8 a.m. block and weekend hours. Once the marketing research and brainstorming is complete, the owner of the Juniper Café will make a better informed choice for his café's operating hours.

ANALYTICAL WRITING SCORING RUBRIC

6: "Outstanding" Essay

- Insightfully presents and convincingly supports an opinion on the issue or a critique of the argument
- Communicates ideas clearly and is generally well organized; connections are logical
- Demonstrates superior control of language: grammar, stylistic variety, and accepted conventions of writing; minor flaws may occur

5: "Strong" Essay

- Presents well-chosen examples and strongly supports an opinion on the issue or a critique of the argument
- Communicates ideas clearly and is generally well organized; connections are logical
- Demonstrates solid control of language: grammar, stylistic variety, and accepted conventions of writing; minor flaws may occur

4: "Adequate" Essay

- Presents and adequately supports an opinion on the issue or a critique of the argument
- Communicates ideas fairly clearly and is adequately organized; logical connections are satisfactory
- Demonstrates satisfactory control of language: grammar, stylistic variety, and accepted conventions of writing; some flaws may occur

3: "Limited" Essay

- Succeeds only partially in presenting and supporting an opinion on the issue or a critique of the argument
- Communicates ideas unclearly and is poorly organized
- Demonstrates less than satisfactory control of language: contains significant mistakes in grammar, usage, and sentence structure

2: "Weak" Essay

- Shows little success in presenting and supporting an opinion on the issue or a critique of the argument
- Struggles to communicate ideas; essay shows a lack of clarity and organization
- Meaning is impeded by many serious mistakes in grammar, usage, and sentence structure

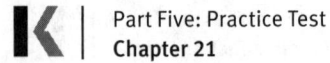

1: "Fundamentally Deficient" Essay

- Fails to present a coherent opinion and/or evidence on the issue or a critique of the argument
- Fails to communicate ideas; essay is seriously unclear and disorganized
- Lacks meaning due to widespread and severe mistakes in grammar, usage, and sentence structure

0: "Unscorable" Essay

- Completely ignores topic
- Attempts to copy the assignments
- Written in a foreign language or contains undecipherable text

PART SIX

Test Day and Beyond

CHAPTER 22

Take Control of the Test

Now that you're familiar with the content that makes up each section of the GRE, and are armed with the strategies and techniques you'll need to tackle all of the question types, you're ready to turn your attention to building the right mentality and attitude that will help you succeed on Test Day. Let's first go over the basic principles of good test mentality.

KAPLAN'S FOUR BASIC PRINCIPLES OF GOOD TEST MENTALITY

You are already armed with the weapons that you need to do well on the GRE. But you must wield those weapons with the right frame of mind and in the right spirit. This involves taking a certain stance toward the entire test and bolstering your stamina, confidence, and attitude.

Test Awareness

To do your best on the GRE, keep in mind that the test is different from other tests you've taken before, both in terms of its content and in terms of its scoring system. If you took a test in high school or college and got a quarter of the questions wrong, you probably received a mediocre grade. But this is not necessarily true with the GRE. The test is geared so that even the very best test takers don't necessarily get every question right.

What does this mean for you? Well, just as you shouldn't let one tough Reading Comprehension passage ruin an entire section, you shouldn't let what you consider to be a subpar performance on one section ruin your performance on the entire test. If you allow that subpar section to rattle you, it sets in motion a downward spiral that could do serious damage to your score. Losing a few extra points won't do you in, but losing your head will. Keeping your composure is an important test-taking skill.

Also, you should remember that if you feel you've done poorly on a section, it could very well be the experimental section. You'll have the opportunity immediately after you've taken the test to think about whether you want to cancel your score. You might underestimate your performance, since you're more likely to remember the questions you thought were more difficult. The major takeaway is to stay confident throughout the test.

Stamina

Overall, the GRE is a grueling experience. Remember, you'll be completing six full-length sections on Test Day (one Analytical Writing, two Verbal Reasoning, two Quantitative Reasoning, and one Experimental or Research). It is a true test of endurance, and some test takers run out of gas on the final few sections.

To avoid this, you must build up your test-taking stamina by taking as many full-length practice tests as possible several weeks before the test. If you do this, by Test Day, completing this test won't seem like such a daunting task.

You can download a free copy of the POWERPREP II software, including two multi-stage practice tests, directly from **gre.org**.

Another option, if you haven't already done so, would be to take a Kaplan course, either classroom-based or online. You could also set up special one-on-one tutoring sessions with Kaplan faculty. If you decide to go this route, visit **kaptest.com/GRE** or call 1-800-KAP-TEST for information on a Kaplan classroom or tutoring program.

Confidence

Confidence is self-sustaining, and unfortunately, so is its opposite—self-doubt. Confidence in your ability leads to quick, sure answers and an ease of concentration that translates into more points. If you lack confidence, you might lose concentration and end up reading sentences and answer choices two, three, or four times. This leads to timing difficulties, which only continue the downward spiral, causing anxiety and a tendency to rush. If you subscribe to the test-prep mindset that we've described, however, you'll be ready and able to take control of the test. Learn our techniques and then practice them over and over again. That's the way to score your best on the test.

Attitude

Those who fear the test or consider it an extra hurdle in the long race toward graduate school usually don't fare as well as those who see the GRE as an opportunity to show off the reading and reasoning skills that graduate schools are looking for. In fact, consider this: the test is designed to reward you. Those who look forward to the GRE as a challenge—or, at least, who enjoy the opportunity to distinguish themselves from the rest of the applicant pack—tend to score better than do those who resent it.

It may sound a little dubious, but take our word for it: altering your approach is proven to raise scores. Here are a few steps you can take to make sure you develop the right GRE attitude:

- Look at the GRE as a challenge, but try not to obsess over it; you certainly don't want to psych yourself out of the game.
- Remember that, yes, the GRE is obviously important, but contrary to what some people think, this one test will not single-handedly determine the outcome of your life. In many cases, it's not even the most important piece of your graduate application.
- Since the test is predictable, think of the GRE as a reward for understanding the same core skills that show up all the time.
- Remember that you're more prepared than most people. You've trained with Kaplan. You have the tools you need, plus the know-how to use those tools.

Kaplan's basic principles of good test mentality are as follows:

- Be aware of the test and keep your composure even when you are struggling with a difficult question; missing one question won't ruin your score for a section.
- Build your stamina by taking as many practice tests as you can.
- Be confident; you are already well on your way to a great score!
- Stay positive; consider the GRE an opportunity rather than an obstacle.

THE KAPLAN STRESS-MANAGEMENT SYSTEM

Is it starting to feel as if your whole life is a buildup to the GRE? You've known about it for years, worried about it for months, and now spent at least a few weeks in solid preparation for it. As the test gets closer, you may find that your anxiety is on the rise. You shouldn't worry. Armed with the preparation strategies that you've learned from this book, you're in good shape for Test Day. To calm any pre-test jitters that you may have, however, let's go over a few strategies for the couple of days before the test.

Tips for the Days Just Before the Exam

- The best test takers do less and less as the test approaches. Taper off your study schedule and take it easy on yourself. Give yourself time off, especially the evening before the exam. By that time, if you've studied well, everything you need to know is firmly stored in your memory bank. In fact, it's in your best interest to marshal your physical and psychological resources for the last 24 hours or so before the test. Keep the test out of your consciousness; go to a movie, take a pleasant walk, or just relax. Eat healthy meals and steer clear of sugar and caffeine. And, of course, get plenty of rest that night, and also the night before. It's hard to fall asleep earlier than you're used to, and you don't want to lie there worrying about the test.

- Most importantly, make sure you know where the test will be held and the easiest, quickest way to get there. You'll have great peace of mind by knowing that all the little details are set before Test Day.
- Visit the test site a few days in advance, particularly if you are especially anxious.

Handling Stress During the Test

The biggest source of stress will be the test itself. Fear not! The following are methods to relieve your stress during the test:

- Keep moving forward instead of getting bogged down in a difficult question. You don't have to get everything right to achieve a solid score. So don't linger out of desperation on a question that is going nowhere even after you've spent considerable time on it.
- Breathe! Weak test takers tend to share one major trait: they don't breathe properly as the test proceeds. They might hold their breath without realizing it or breathe irregularly. Improper breathing hurts confidence and accuracy. Just as importantly, it interferes with clear thinking.

TEST DAY

The night before Test Day, gather the following things together:

- ID
- admission ticket
- a watch
- a bottle of water
- aspirin or other painkiller, in case you get a headache
- a snack, such as fruit or an energy bar, to keep your energy up for the later sections of the test
- names of schools you'd like to receive your scores

Test Day should start with a moderate, high-energy breakfast. Cereal, fruit, bagels, or eggs are good. Avoid doughnuts, pastries, or anything else with a lot of sugar. Also, unless you are utterly catatonic without it, it's a good idea to stay away from coffee.

Yes, perhaps you drink two cups every morning and don't even notice it. But it's different during the test. Coffee won't make you alert (your adrenaline will do that much more effectively); it will just give you the jitters. Kaplan has done experiments in which test takers go into one exam having drunk various amounts of coffee and another exam without having drunk coffee. The results indicate that even the most caffeine-addicted test takers will lose their focus midway through the second section if they've had coffee, but they report no alertness problems without it.

When you get to the test center, you will be seated at a computer station. Some administrative questions will be asked before the test begins and, once you're done with those, you're set to go. While you're taking the test, a small clock will count down the time you have left in each section. The computer will tell you when you're done with each section and when you've completed the test.

Here are some last-minute reminders to help guide your work on the test:

- Take a few minutes now to look back over your preparation and give yourself credit for all the work you put into it. Confidence is far more useful than distress.
- Don't bother trying to figure out which section is the experimental section. It can't help you, and you might make a tragic mistake if you guess wrong. Instead, just do your best on every section.
- Dress in layers for maximum comfort. This way, you can adjust to the room's temperature accordingly.
- During the exam, try not to fixate on what your score is or how you're doing so far. It's counterproductive to continue to think about questions you've already answered or ones you haven't gotten to yet. If you worry about the next section, or the one you've just completed, you'll just feel overwhelmed. Instead, focus on the question-by-question task of picking the correct answer choice. Try to take things one step at a time. Concentrate on each question, each passage, and each essay prompt—on the mechanics, in other words—and you'll avoid cognitive confusion.

After all the hard work that you've put in preparing for and taking the GRE, make sure you take time to celebrate afterward. Plan to get together with friends the evening after the test. You prepared for the test ahead of time. You did your best. You're going to get a great score.

CHAPTER 23

Where and When to Apply

You probably know what you want to study as a graduate student, but where should you apply? The answer to this question is dependent on two main factors: which programs would be best for you, and which of these programs you can actually get into. This chapter will help you answer these questions—and many more you may have about the process of choosing a school for postgraduate study.

WHAT PROGRAMS YOU SHOULD CONSIDER

Once you have made the decision to pursue graduate studies, you should take the decision about where to go to school seriously—it will have a major influence on your daily life for the next several years and will influence your academic and career paths for years to come. Many students allow themselves to be influenced by a professor, a mentor, or school rankings and then find they're unhappy in a certain program because of its location, its workload, its cost, or some other unforeseen factor. If you complete your own research, even if it takes time and hard work, you will be happier with your own choice. Let's take a look at some of the factors you'll need to consider when choosing a school.

Your Goals

Keep your goals in mind when evaluating graduate programs. Before you take the leap, it's important that you have a pretty clear idea where your interests lie, what grad school life is like, and whether you're compatible with a particular program and its professors. Armed with this information, you should be able to successfully apply to the right programs, get accepted, and use your time in graduate school to help you get a head start on the post-graduation job search.

Students decide to enter master's and doctoral degree programs for a variety of reasons. Some want to pursue a career in academia. To teach at two-year colleges, you'll need at least a master's degree; to teach and do research at four-year colleges, universities, and graduate programs, you'll need a doctorate. Other people need graduate education to meet national and state licensing requirements in fields such as social work, engineering, and architecture. Some students want to change careers, while others expect an advanced degree to open up new opportunities in their current field.

Most master's programs are two years long, and master's students are generally one of two types: those on an academic track, where the degree program focuses on classical research and scholarship, and those on a practical track, where the degree program is actually a professional training course that qualifies people to enter or advance in a field such as social work or education.

Other options to consider if you're pursuing a master's degree are cooperative, joint, and interdisciplinary programs. In cooperative programs, you apply to, answer to, and graduate from one school, but you have access to classes, professors, and facilities at one or more cooperating schools. In joint- or dual-degree programs, you work toward two degrees simultaneously, either within the same school or at two neighboring schools. Interdisciplinary programs are generally run by a committee consisting of faculty from a number of different departments. You apply to, register with, and are graduated by only one of the departments; you and your faculty committee design your curriculum.

Doctoral programs are designed to create scholars capable of independent research that will add new and significant knowledge to their fields. At first, you'll be regarded as an apprentice in your field. Your first year or two in the program will be spent on coursework, followed by "field" or "qualifying" exams. Once you have passed those exams, demonstrating that you have the basic factual and theoretical knowledge of your field down cold, you'll be permitted to move on to independent research in the form of your doctoral dissertation. During most of this time, you can get financial aid in the form of stipends through teaching or research.

If you want to get a doctoral degree, you can get a master's and then apply to PhD programs, or you may enter directly into the doctoral program. The first method gives you flexibility but generally takes longer, costs more in the long run, and means reliving the application process. However, some doctoral programs in certain fields of study require a full master's degree for acceptance.

Program Reputation

Although you should not place too much stock in school and program rankings, you should consider a program's overall reputation. When you assess a program's reputation, don't just consider its national ranking but think about whether it fits your goals and interests. You can get information from a variety of sources, formal and informal.

Each year, various groups publish rankings of graduate programs: *U.S. News and World Report* on American graduate programs, *Maclean's* on Canadian programs, and many others. These rankings can give you a general sense of the programs in your field and may include profiles of distinguished professors, but they tell you nothing about departmental politics, job placement records, or financial aid possibilities.

You should find out which programs are highly regarded in the areas that interest you. You can learn these details through professional associations (such as the American Psychological Association for programs in psychology fields), comprehensive commercial directories of graduate programs (available through school or local libraries), and the Internet.

Don't forget to contact schools and departments directly. Most departments have a chairperson who is also the admissions contact; she can put you in touch with current students and alumni who are willing to discuss the program with you. The chair is usually willing to answer questions as well.

Try to speak to at least one current student and one alum from each program you're seriously considering. You'll find that many graduate students are quite outspoken about the strengths and weaknesses of professors, programs, and the state of the job market in their field.

If you're an undergraduate, or still have contacts from your undergraduate experience, ask your professors for their take on the various graduate programs. You'll often find that they have a great deal of inside information on academic and research trends, impending retirements, intellectual rivalries, and rising stars.

Remember, a program's reputation isn't everything, but the higher your school is regarded in the marketplace, the better your job prospects are likely to be upon graduation.

Location

Two key questions you should consider regarding a school's location are: How will it affect the overall quality of your graduate school experience, and how will it affect your ability to be employed once you are done with your studies? Some students prefer an urban setting. Others prefer a more rustic environment. Cost of living can also be a factor.

Geography may be an important criterion for you. Perhaps your geographical choices are limited by a spouse's job or other family obligations. Perhaps you already know where you want to live after graduation. If you're planning on a career in academia, you'll probably want to choose a nationally known program, regardless of where it's located. If, on the other hand, your program involves a practice component (physician's assistant, social work, education, or some interdisciplinary programs), you may want to concentrate your school search on the area in which you hope to live and work, at least initially.

Curriculum

To maximize the value of your graduate school experience, be sure that a department's areas of concentration match up with your own interests. Knowing a program's particular theoretical bent and practical selling points can help ensure that you choose a school that reflects your own needs and academic leanings. Does one school of thought or one style of research predominate? If so, is there anyone else working in the department with a different theoretical framework? Will you have opportunities to work within a variety of theories and orientations? What special opportunities are available? How well are research programs funded? Do the professors have good records at rounding up grants? In field or clinical work, what are the options? Are programs available in your area of interest?

Find the environment that works best for you. Don't put yourself in a situation in which you don't have access to the courses or training you're seeking. It's your education. Your time. Your energy. Your investment in your future. By being proactive, you can help guarantee that you maximize your graduate school experience.

Faculty

One of the most important decisions you make in your graduate school career will be your choice of adviser. This one person will help you with course selection as well as clinical, research, or field education opportunities; he can make or break the thesis/dissertation process. So when you investigate a department, look for a faculty member whose interests and personality are compatible with yours. Since this single person (your "dream adviser") may not be available, be sure to look for a couple of other professors with whom you might be able to work.

If one of your prime motivations in attending a certain program is to take classes from specific professors, make sure you'll have that opportunity. At the master's level, access to prominent professors is often limited to large, foundation-level lecture courses, where papers and exams are graded by the professor's graduate assistants or tutors. At the doctoral level, professors are generally much more accessible.

Is the department stable or changing? Find out whether the faculty is nearing retirement age. Impending retirements may not affect you in a two-year master's program, but this is a serious consideration in doctoral programs, which can (and often do) stretch on for over five years. If you have hopes of working with a distinguished professor, will she even be available for that time—or longer, if you get delayed? Will the department be large and stable enough to allow you to put together a good thesis or dissertation committee? Also, try to find out whether younger members of the department are established. Do they get sufficient funding? Have they settled in to the institution enough that there are not likely to be political controversies?

Placement

Although some people attend graduate school for the love of knowledge, most want to enhance their career prospects in some way. When you graduate with your hard-won degree, what are your chances of getting your desired job?

You'll want to ask what kind of track record a given program has in placing its alumni. With a highly competitive job market, it's especially important to find out when and where graduates have found work. If you're considering work in business, industry, local agencies, schools, health care facilities, or the government, find out whether these employers visit the campus to recruit. Major industries may visit science programs to interview prospective graduates. Some will even employ graduate students over the summer or part-time. If you're going into academia, find out whether recent grads have been able to find academic posts, how long the search took, and where they're working. Are they getting tenure-track positions, or are they shifting from temporary appointment to temporary appointment with little hope of finding a stable position? Don't just look at the first jobs that a school's graduates take. Where are they in 5, 10, or even 25 years?

Your career is more like a marathon than a sprint. So take the long view. A strong indicator of a program's strength is the accomplishments of its alumni.

Student Body

Some graduate catalogs contain profiles of or statements by current master's and PhD students. Sometimes this is an informal blurb on a few students—it's really marketing material—and sometimes it's a full listing of graduate students. Use this as a resource both to find out what everyone else in the program is up to and to find current students you can interview about the school and the program.

Because much of your learning will come from your classmates, consider the makeup of your class. A school with a geographically, professionally, and ethnically diverse student body will expose you to far more viewpoints than will a school with a more homogeneous group. If you're an older applicant, ask yourself how you'll fit in with a predominantly younger group of students. For many, the fit is terrific, but for others, the transition can be tougher. The answer depends on you, but it's something to consider.

The student body, as well as the faculty, will have varied philosophical and political orientations. The theories and perspectives considered liberal in one program can be deemed conservative in another, and where you fit among your peers can have a lot of influence on your image and your opportunities. If you plan on an academic career, remember that your student colleagues will someday likely be your professional colleagues.

Networking

Forging relationships—with your classmates, your professors, and, in a larger sense, all the alumni—is a big part of the graduate school experience. One of the things you'll take with you when you graduate, aside from an education, a diploma, and debt, is that network. And whether you thrive on networking or tend to shy away from it, it's a necessity. At some point it may help you advance your career, in academia or outside.

Quality of Life

Your graduate school experience will extend far beyond your classroom learning, particularly for full-time students. That's why it's so important to find out as much as you can about the schools that interest you. For example, what activities would you like to participate in? Perhaps convenient recreational facilities or an intramural sports program is appealing. If you'd like to be involved in community activities, perhaps there's a school volunteer organization. Regardless of your interests, your ability to maintain balance in your life in the face of a rigorous academic challenge will help you keep a healthy outlook.

Housing is another quality-of-life issue to consider. Is campus housing available? Is off-campus housing convenient? Is it affordable? Where do most of the students live?

Quality of life is another important consideration for significant others, especially if your school choice requires a move to a new city. When graduate school takes over your life, your partner may feel left out. Find out what kind of groups and activities there are for families and partners. For example, are there any services to help your spouse find employment? Is child care available? What sort of public transportation is available?

Full-Time versus Part-Time

In a full-time program, you can focus your energy on your studies to maximize your learning. You're also likely to meet more people and forge closer relationships with your classmates. Many programs are oriented toward the full-time student, and many top-tier programs don't offer part-time options. A part-time schedule may also make it difficult for you to take classes with the best professors.

There are, however, many compelling reasons for attending part-time. It may not be economically feasible for you to attend full-time. Or you may wish to continue gaining professional experience while earning the degree that will allow you to move on to the next level. If there's a possibility that you'll have to work while you're in school, particularly while you're in the coursework stage, check out the flexibility of any program that interests you. Are there night or weekend classes? When is the library open? What about the lab? Talk to students currently in the program, especially those who work. Part-time programs often take a long time to complete, which can be discouraging, especially when licensure or salary increases are at stake. However, there are some programs, especially master's programs, that are specifically designed for part-time students (for example, many business school and physical therapy programs). In such programs, classes can be taken on weekends or specific nights of the week. It can be worth seeking out these sorts of options.

Although many students in full-time graduate programs support themselves with part-time work, their primary allegiance is to the graduate program. Many students who must work during graduate school are employed by their schools. This is an option worth exploring. Since graduate studies tend to become the focus of your life, if you can manage full-time or nearly full-time studies at the higher levels, do it. You can graduate earlier and start picking up the financial pieces that much sooner—often with a more secure base for your job search in the form of good support from your adviser.

Most master's programs are flexible about part-time studies, but doctoral programs are less so. Many doctoral programs expect a minimum amount of time "in residence"—that is, enrolled as a full-time student for a certain number of consecutive semesters. This requirement is usually listed in the catalog.

Program Costs

Some graduate programs charge per credit or per hour, meaning that your tuition bill is calculated by the number of credits you take each semester. Other programs charge per semester or per year with a minimum and maximum number of credits you can take per semester for that flat fee. In general, per-credit tuition makes sense for part-time students, while per-semester tuition makes sense for full-time students. Generally speaking, the most expensive kind of graduate program (per semester) will be a master's degree at a private school. Loans are available to master's-level students, but grants, scholarships, and other forms of "free" financial assistance are harder to find. Furthermore, most private schools apply the same tuition rate to in-state and out-of-state residents. State colleges and universities usually give in-state residents a tuition break. Other forms of savings can come from finding the cheapest living and housing expenses and from working your way through the program as quickly as possible.

At the doctoral level, tuition remission (you don't pay any of it) and grants or stipends (they pay you) are common. Percentages of doctoral students in a program receiving full tuition remission plus stipend/grant money can range anywhere from 0 percent to 100 percent—every student in the program pays no tuition and receives some grant or stipend. In these programs, the major financial burden will be your living expenses over the years of coursework, language requirements, qualifying and field exams, research, and the dissertation.

WHERE YOU CAN GET IN

Once you've developed a list of schools that meet your needs, take an objective look at your chances of getting into them.

A good way to get a sense of how graduate schools will perceive you is to make up a fact sheet with your GRE scores (or projected scores), your overall grade point average (GPA), your GPA in your major, and your work experience. Outside activities and your personal statement will contribute to the overall "score" that admissions officers will use to evaluate you, but let's stick with the raw data for now.

The next step is to find a current source of information about graduate school programs. There are several guides published every year that provide data about acceptance rates for given years, as well as median GPA and GRE scores. You can also request this information directly from a given department. The school of your dreams may not care very much about your GPA, but it might be very interested in your GRE scores. Make sure you find out what your target school prioritizes in its search for worthy applicants.

One of the best ways to gauge whether you're in contention for a certain program is to compare your numbers to theirs. And remember that you needn't hit the nail on the head. Median is similar to average, so some applicants do better or worse than the GRE scores or GPA cited. And remember all the other factors that add up to make you a desirable applicant. Comparing numbers is merely a good way to get a preliminary estimate of your compatibility with the schools of your choice.

"Safety" Schools

Once you have some idea of where you fall in the applicant pool, you can begin to make decisions about your application strategy. No matter what your circumstances, it's wise to choose at least one school that is likely to accept you, a "safety" school. Make sure it's one that fits your academic goals and your economic circumstances. If your GRE scores and GPA are well above a school's median scores and you don't anticipate any problems with other parts of your record or application, you've probably found your safety school.

"Wishful Thinking" Schools

If your ideal program is one that you don't seem qualified for, apply to your "dream school" anyway. You may be surprised! GPA and GRE scores aren't the only criteria by which applicants are judged, and you may discover that you're admitted in spite of your academic background on the merits of your personal statement, work samples, or other criteria. It's always worth a try. Some people underestimate their potential and apply only to safety schools. This can often lead to disappointment when they end up at one of these schools and discover that it doesn't provide the rigorous training they want.

WHEN TO APPLY

With the number of graduate school applications received by institutions of higher learning on the rise, the issue of when to apply for admission has become very important. There are perfect times to begin and end the application process. You should begin at least a year before you plan to enter school (sooner if you're a nontraditional candidate or are changing fields). Find out the following essential dates as early as possible and incorporate them into your own personal application schedule:

- standardized test registration deadlines
- transcript deadlines (some schools send out transcripts only on particular dates)
- letters-of-recommendation due dates
- application deadlines (submit your application as early as possible to ensure that you get a fair and comprehensive review)
- financial aid forms deadlines (federal/state programs, universities, and independent sources of aid all have definite deadlines)

Setting Up an Application Schedule

We've organized the following "seasonal" schedule to help you understand how to proceed through the admissions process.

Winter (18–20 months prior to start date)

- If you're a nontraditional applicant or plan to switch fields, begin investigating program requirements. Take courses to make up any missing portion of your background.

Spring (16–18 months prior to start date)

- Browse through program catalogs and collect information on different grants and loans. Create your own graduate school library.

Summer

- Request applications from schools. If they're not available yet, ask for last year's so you can get a feel for the questions you'll have to answer.
- Write a draft of your personal statement and show it to trusted friends and/or colleagues for feedback.
- Consider registering for the GRE in the fall. This will give you plenty of time to submit your scores with your application.
- Research your options for test preparation. Take the test included in this book to give you a good idea of where you stand with regard to the GRE.

Early Fall

- Ask for recommendations. Make sure that your recommenders know enough about you to write a meaningful letter. Ask them first if they would be willing to write you recommendations and then ask how much lead time they would need.

Once your recommenders have agreed to write recommendations, make sure to give them clear deadlines so you can avoid any timing conflicts.

Late Fall

- Take the GRE.
- Request applications from schools, if you haven't already done so.
- Request institutional, state, and federal financial aid materials from school aid offices.
- Request information on independent grants and loans.
- Order transcripts from your undergraduate (and any graduate) institution(s).
- Follow up with your recommenders, sending a thank-you note to those who have sent their recommendations in already.

Winter

- Fill out applications. Mail them as early as possible.
- Fill out financial aid applications. Mail these early as well.
- Make sure your recommendation writers have the appropriate forms and directions for mailing. Remind them of deadline dates.

Spring

- Sit back and relax (if you can). Most schools indicate how long it will take to inform you of their decision. This is also a crucial time to solidify your financial plans as you begin to receive offers of aid (with any luck).

The timing described here is approximate, and you needn't follow it exactly. The most important thing for you to do is make yourself aware of strict deadlines well in advance so that you'll be able to devote plenty of quality time to your application. In the next chapter, we'll go over the application process in detail.

CHAPTER 24

How to Apply to Graduate School

You've taken the GRE and you've researched schools that offer programs you want. Your next step in the application process is to get the application forms from the various schools you've selected. Some schools will require you to complete an online application, some will have PDF downloads of the application documents, and yet others will require that you request applications that will then be sent to you. Once you get the applications, you'll notice one thing quickly: no two applications are exactly alike. Some ask you to write one essay or personal statement, and others ask for three or more essays on various subjects. Some have very detailed forms requiring extensive background information; others are satisfied with your name and address and little else.

Despite these differences, most applications follow a general pattern with variations on the same kinds of questions. So read this section with the understanding that, although not all of it is relevant to every application, these guidelines will be valuable for just about any graduate school application you'll encounter.

HOW SCHOOLS EVALUATE APPLICANTS

Each graduate school has its own admissions policies and practices, but all programs evaluate your application based on a range of objective and subjective criteria. Regardless of which schools you are pursuing, understanding how admissions officers judge your candidacy can give you a leg up on the competition.

Generally, all admissions officers use the application process to measure your intellectual abilities, aptitude in your field of study, and personal characteristics. When you submit your application, admissions officers will evaluate the total package. Most admissions officers look for reasons to admit candidates, not reject them. Your challenge, therefore, is to distinguish yourself positively from the other candidates.

INTELLECTUAL ABILITY

To assess your intellectual ability, admissions officers look at two key factors: your academic record and your GRE scores.

Academic Record

Your grade point average (GPA) is important, but it's just part of your academic profile. Admissions officers will consider the reputation of your undergraduate institution and the difficulty of your courses. Admissions officers are well aware that comparing GPAs from different schools and even different majors from the same school is like comparing apples and oranges. So they'll look closely at your transcript. Do your grades show an upward trend? How did you perform in your major? How did you fare in courses related to the program you're applying to?

Admissions officers focus primarily on your undergraduate performance, but they will consider all graduate studies and non-degree coursework that you have completed. Be sure to submit those transcripts. Generally, the undergraduate GPA of an applicant who is about to complete or has recently completed an undergraduate degree is given much more weight than that of an applicant returning to school after several years.

If you have a poor academic record, it will be tougher to get into a top school, but it is by no means impossible. Your challenge is to find other ways to demonstrate your intellectual horsepower. High GRE scores, an intelligently written personal statement, and strong recommendations will help.

The GRE

You are already familiar with the GRE and are armed with strategies to score higher on the test. An integral part of the admissions process at virtually all schools, the GRE measures general verbal, quantitative, and analytical writing skills. Some programs, particularly in psychology and the sciences, require you to take one or more GRE Subject Tests as well. In addition to or instead of the GRE, some programs require the Miller Analogies Test (MAT). Be sure to check with the programs you're considering to see which tests they require.

When admissions officers review your GRE scores, they'll look at your Verbal Reasoning, Quantitative Reasoning, and Analytical Writing scores separately, particularly if they have any questions about your abilities in a certain area. Different programs give varying weight to each score. If you've taken the GRE more than once, schools will generally credit you with your highest score for each section, though some may average the scores or take the most recent.

Used by itself, the GRE may not be a perfect predictor of academic performance, but it is the single best one available. The GRE does not measure your intelligence, nor does it measure the likelihood of your success in your field. The revised GRE has been designed to predict with more certainty your success in graduate school. As with any standardized test, by preparing properly for the GRE, you can boost your score significantly. The strategies you practice and learn will also help you decipher difficult academic text you may encounter in your future studies.

One thing to note is that your essays from the Analytical Writing section are now sent to the schools to which you send a score report. Previously, schools would only receive your score report. Schools will know that these are GRE essays, completed under time limits. Still, it makes the Analytical Writing section even more important to complete well.

Fellowships and Assistantships

Some graduate programs award fellowships and assistantships partly on the basis of GRE scores. Because most programs have limited funds and therefore limited positions to offer, the awards process can be quite competitive. Not only should you take your scores seriously, you should also confirm the submission deadline with your department. The financial aid deadline is usually earlier than the application deadline.

Relevant Experience and Skills

When evaluating your application, admissions officers look at work experience and other activities related to the program in question. In fields like psychology, social work, and health, your research and practical experience will play a role in the admissions decision. If you're applying to film, writing, or other arts programs, you'll be asked to submit samples of your work. And if you're planning on an academic career, your research and publications will be of particular interest to the admissions committee. The way you present yourself and your achievements should be tailored to the programs you're applying to.

You can communicate some of your abilities through the straightforward "data" part of your application. Be sure to describe your job and internship responsibilities. Be aware that your job title alone will not necessarily communicate enough about what you do or the level of your responsibilities. If you are asked to submit a résumé or CV, make sure you illustrate your experience and on-the-job training in a way that highlights skills you already have and those you think will serve you well in your future field of study.

If you are working and applying to a graduate program in the same field, admissions officers will look at your overall career record. How have you progressed? Have you been an outstanding performer? What do your recommendation writers say about your performance? Have you progressed to increasingly higher levels of responsibility? If you have limited work experience, you will not be expected to match the accomplishments of an applicant with 10 years' experience, but you will be expected to demonstrate your abilities.

Extracurricular activities and community involvement also present opportunities for you to highlight your skills. For younger applicants, college activities play a more significant role than for more seasoned applicants. Your activities say a lot about who you are and what's important to you. Were you a campus leader? Did your activities require discipline and commitment? Did you work with a team? What did you learn from your involvement?

Active community involvement provides a way for you to demonstrate your skills and to impress admissions officers with your personal character. In fact, many applications ask directly about community activities. Getting involved in your community is a chance to do something worthwhile and enhance your application in the process.

Personal Characteristics

The third, and most subjective, criterion on which schools evaluate you is your personal character. Admissions officers judge you in this area primarily through your personal statement (and essays, if applicable), recommendations, and personal interview (if applicable). Although different schools emphasize different qualities, most seek candidates who demonstrate maturity, integrity, responsibility, and a clear sense of how they fit into their chosen field. The more competitive programs place special emphasis on these criteria because they have many qualified applicants for each available spot in the class.

WHO EVALUATES APPLICANTS

At most schools, the admissions board includes professional admissions officers and/or faculty from the department to which you're applying. At some schools, the authority to make admissions decisions lies with the graduate school itself—that is, with the central administration. At others, it lies with individual departments.

What Decisions Do They Make?

Upon reviewing your application, the admissions board may make any number of decisions, including the following:

- *Admit:* Congratulations, you're in! But read the letter carefully. The board may recommend or, in some cases, require you to do some preparatory coursework to ensure that your quantitative or language skills are up to speed.
- *Reject:* At the top schools, there are far more qualified applicants than spaces in the class. Even though you were rejected, you can reapply at a later date. However, if you are considering reapplying, you need to understand why you were rejected and whether you have a reasonable chance of being admitted the next time around. Some schools will speak with you about your application, but they often wait until the end of the admissions season, by which time you may have accepted another offer.

- *Waiting list:* Schools use the waiting list to manage class size, leaving the applicant with a mixed message. The good news is that you are a strong enough candidate to have made the list. The bad news is there is no way to know with certainty whether you'll be accepted. Take heart, though, that schools do tend to look kindly upon wait-listed candidates who reapply in a subsequent year. Similar to the waiting list is the *provisional admit.* You may be asked to retake the GRE or resend another part of your application in order to gain admission to your desired school.
- *Request for an interview:* Schools at which an interview is not required may request that you interview prior to making their final decision. Your application may have raised some specific issues that you can address in an interview, or perhaps the board feels your personal statement did not give them a complete enough picture to render a decision. Look at this as a positive opportunity to strengthen your case.

PREPARING YOUR APPLICATION

A key part of getting into the graduate school of your choice is to develop a basic application strategy so you can present yourself in the best light.

YOUR APPLICATION AS A MARKETING TOOL

When it comes to applying to graduate school, you are the product. Your application is your marketing document. Of course, marketing yourself doesn't mean that you should lie or even embellish; it just means that you need to make a tight presentation of the facts. Everything in your application should add up to a coherent whole and underscore the fact that not only are you qualified to be in the program but you should be in it.

Many application forms have a comforting and accepting tone. *Why would you like to come to our program?* they ask. They do want an answer to that question, but what's even more important—the subtext for the whole application process—is the question: *Why should we accept you?* This is the question that your application will answer. And with some effective marketing strategies, your answer will be clear, concise, coherent, and strong.

MAXIMIZING THE VARIOUS PARTS OF YOUR APPLICATION

Let's take a close look at how you should approach the specific parts of your application.

PERSONAL STATEMENT

Your personal statement is a critical part of your application. The personal statement is where you can explain why you're applying to graduate school, what interests you about this program, and what your future goals are. The situations you choose to write about and the manner in which you present them can have a major bearing on the strength of your candidacy.

Writing an effective personal statement requires serious self-examination and sound strategic planning. What major personal and professional events have shaped you? What accomplishments best demonstrate your abilities? Remember, admissions officers are interested in getting to know you as a complete person. What you choose to write about sends clear signals about what's important to you and what your values are. You want the readers to put your essay down and think, "Wow! That was really interesting and memorable," and, "Wow! This person really knows why he's going into this program and has real contributions to make to the field."

Creating Your Statement

Your statement should demonstrate the patterns in your life that have led you to apply to the program. Part of demonstrating why you are right for the program involves demonstrating that you understand what the program is and where it will lead you. A personal statement requires honesty and distinctiveness. If you are heading to graduate school straight from undergraduate school, what has made you so certain that you know what you want to do with your life? If you are returning to school, particularly if you are changing fields, what has led you to this decision? You can use vignettes from your personal history, academic life, work life, and extracurricular activities to explain. If you are applying to a doctoral program, indicate which ideas, fields of research, or problems intrigue you. It's always a good idea to demonstrate familiarity with the field you want to enter.

You should start compiling information for your statement three or four months before you fill out your application. Write a draft once you've narrowed your list of potential topics. Have it edited by someone who knows you well. After rewriting, have someone whose opinion and writing skills you trust read your final draft, make suggestions, and, above all, help you proofread.

General Personal Statement Tips

Once you've determined what you plan to write for your statement, keep the following tips in mind:

- *Length:* Schools are pretty specific about how long they want your statement to be. Adhere to their guidelines.
- *Spelling/typos/grammar:* Remember, your application is your marketing document. What would you think of a product that's promoted with sloppy materials containing typos, spelling errors, and grammatical mistakes?

- *Write in the active voice:* Candidates who write well have an advantage in the application process because they can state their case in a concise, compelling manner. Sentences in the passive voice tend to be unnecessarily wordy. For example:

  Passive voice: *The essays were written by me.*
  Active voice: *I wrote the essays.*

  Strong writing will not compensate for a lack of substance, but poor writing can torpedo an otherwise impressive candidate.

- *Tone:* On the one hand, you want to tout your achievements and present yourself as a poised, self-confident applicant. On the other hand, arrogance and self-importance do not go over well with admissions officers. Before you submit your application, be sure that you're comfortable with the tone as well as the content.
- *Creative approaches:* If you choose to submit a humorous or creative application, you are employing a high-risk, high-reward strategy. If you're confident you can pull it off, go for it. Be aware, though, that what may work for one admissions officer may fall flat with another. Admissions officers who review thousands of essays every year may consider your approach gimmicky or simply find it distracting. Remember, your challenge is to stand out in the applicant pool in a positive way. Don't let your creativity obscure the substance of your application.
- *Answer the question asked:* Schools do not want to receive a personal statement or other essay that seems to have been written generically or perhaps even for another school.

Making Your Statement Distinctive

Depending on the amount of time you have and the amount of effort you're willing to put in, you can write a personal statement that will stand out from the crowd. One of the first mistakes that some applicants make is in thinking that "thorough" and "comprehensive" are sufficient qualities for their personal statement. They try to include as much information as possible, without regard for length limitations or strategic intent. Application readers dread reading these bloated personal statements. So how do you decide what to include? There are usually clear length guidelines, and admissions officers prefer that you adhere to them. So get rid of the idea of "comprehensive" and focus more on "distinctive."

Unless they ask for it, don't dwell on your weak points. A strong personal statement, for example, about how much you learned in your current position and how the experience and knowledge you've gained inspired you to apply to graduate school will give readers what they want—a quick image of who you are, how you got that way, and why you want to go to their school. One of the best ways to be distinctive is to sell your image briefly and accurately, including real-life examples to back up your points.

The admissions team wants to know about you, but there is the potential for including too much personal information. Beware of sharing reasons for applying that include furthering personal relationships, improving finances, or proving someone wrong.

"Distinctive" means that your statement should answer the questions that admissions officers think about while reading personal statements: What's different about this applicant? Why should we pick this applicant over others? Authentic enthusiasm can be a plus, and writing about parts of your life or career that are interesting and relevant helps grab a reader's attention.

The Interview

In some programs, an interview with the department is conducted at the applicant's discretion: if you want one, you're welcome to ask. In other programs, only the most promising applicants are invited to interview. Whether or not a department can pay your travel expenses depends on its financial circumstances. If you have the opportunity, definitely go to interview at your first-choice departments. There's no substitute for face-to-face contact with your potential colleagues, and by visiting the school, you can check out the city or town where it is located. You should investigate cost-of-living and transportation options during your visit.

As you prepare for an interview, here are some tips:

- *Review your application:* If you've submitted your application prior to the interview, your interviewer is likely to use it as a guide and may ask specific questions about it. Be sure you remember what you wrote.
- *Be ready to provide examples and specifics:* Professionally trained interviewers are more likely to ask you about specific situations than to ask broad, open-ended questions. They can learn more by asking what you've done in situations than by asking what you think you'd do. Here are a few situations an interviewer may ask you to discuss: "Tell me about a recent accomplishment." "Discuss a recent situation in which you demonstrated leadership." "Give me an example of a situation where you overcame difficult circumstances." As you think about these situations, be prepared to discuss specifics—what you did and why you did it that way. You do not need to "script" or overrehearse your responses, but you should go into the interview confident that you can field any question.
- *Be open and honest:* Don't struggle to think of "right" answers. The only right answers are those that are right for you. By responding openly and honestly, you'll find the interview less stressful, and you'll come across as a more genuine, attractive candidate.
- *Ask questions:* The interview is as much an opportunity for you to learn about the school as for the school to learn about you. Good questions demonstrate

your knowledge about a particular program and your thoughtfulness about the entire process.

- *Follow proper professional decorum:* Be on time, dress appropriately, and follow up with thank-you letters. Treat the process as you would a job interview, which in many respects it is.
- *Watch your nonverbal cues:* Nonverbal communication is much more important than people realize. Maintain eye contact, keep good posture, sustain positive energy, and avoid nervous fidgeting. It will help you come across as confident, poised, and mature.
- *Be courteous to the administrative staff:* These people are colleagues of the board members, and how you treat them can have an impact, either positive or negative.
- *Relax and have fun*: Interviews are inherently stressful. But by being well prepared, you can enhance your prospects for admission, learn about the school, and enjoy yourself in the process.

Recommendations

Graduate schools will require at least three recommendations. Choose recommenders who can write meaningfully about your strengths. One of the more common mistakes is to sacrifice an insightful recommendation from someone who knows you well for a generic recommendation from a celebrity or a prominent professor. Admissions officers are not impressed by famous names. So unless that individual knows you and can write convincingly on your behalf, it's not a strategy worth pursuing. Good choices for recommenders include current and past supervisors, professors, academic and nonacademic advisers, and people you work with in community activities.

Many schools will specifically request an academic recommendation. Professors in your major are ideal recommenders, as they can vouch for your ability to study at the graduate level. If you don't have a professor who can recommend you, use a TA who knows your work well. Similarly, if requesting a recommendation from your employer would create an awkward situation, look for someone else who can comment on your skills. Your recommendations will confirm your strengths and, in some cases, help you overcome perceived weaknesses in your application.

If you wish to submit an extra recommendation, it's generally not a problem. Most schools will include the letter in your file, and those that don't will not penalize you for it. You should, however, send a note explaining why you have requested an additional recommendation so it does not appear that you disregarded the instructions. It's also a good idea to check with the admissions department before submitting an extra recommendation.

Asking for Recommendations

There are two fundamental rules of requesting recommendations: ask early and ask nicely. As soon as you decide to go to graduate school, you should start sizing up potential recommendation writers and let them know that you may ask them for a recommendation. This will give them plenty of time to think about what to say. Once they've agreed, let them know about deadlines well in advance to avoid potential scheduling conflicts. The more time they have, the better the job they'll do recommending you. As for asking nicely, you should let these people know you think highly of their opinion and you'd be happy and honored if they would consider writing you a letter of recommendation. You can help your recommenders by scheduling brief appointments with them to discuss your background; providing a list of due dates for each application; providing any forms required by the program; listing which recommendations will be submitted in hard copy and which will be submitted online; providing any forms required by the program; supplying stamped, addressed envelopes for hard-copy submissions; and following up with the recommenders.

BEFORE YOU SUBMIT YOUR APPLICATION

When you've completed your personal statement and you're ready to submit your application, take two more steps to ensure that your application is as strong as it can be.

1. Be sure to read your personal statement in the context of your entire application.
    a. Does the total package make sense? Does it represent you favorably? Is everything consistent?
    b. Have you demonstrated your intellectual ability, relevant experience and skills, and personal characteristics?
    c. Most importantly, do you feel good about the application? After all, you don't want to be rejected on the basis of an application that you don't believe represents the real you.
2. Have someone you trust and respect review your application. Someone who has not been involved in writing the application may pick up spelling or grammatical errors that you've overlooked. In addition, because your application is an intensely personal document that requires significant self-examination, you may not be able to remain objective. Someone who knows you and can be frank will tell you whether your application has "captured" you most favorably. Note, however, that some schools prohibit you from using any outside help on your application. A last-minute once-over from a friend or family member is probably within reason, but you may want to directly ask the school what is permissible.

PUTTING IT ALL TOGETHER

There are no magic formulas that automatically admit you to, or reject you from, the school of your choice. Rather, your application is like a jigsaw puzzle. Each component—GPA, GRE scores, professional experience, school activities, recommendations—is a different piece of the puzzle.

Outstanding professional experience and personal characteristics may enable you to overcome a mediocre academic record. Conversely, outstanding academic credentials will not ensure your admission to a top-tier program if you do not demonstrate strong relevant skills and experience, as well as solid personal character. Your challenge in preparing your application is to convince the admissions board that all of the pieces in your background fit together to form a substantial and unique puzzle.

CONGRATULATIONS!

You have all of the tools you need to put together a stand-out application package, including a top GRE score. Best of luck, and remember, your Kaplan training will be with you each step of the way.

A SPECIAL NOTE FOR INTERNATIONAL STUDENTS

About a quarter of a million international students pursue advanced academic degrees at the master's or PhD level at US universities each year. This trend of pursuing higher education in the United States, particularly at the graduate level, is expected to continue. Business, management, engineering, and the physical and life sciences are popular areas of study for students coming to the United States from other countries. Along with these academic options, international students are also taking advantage of opportunities for research grants, teaching assistantships, and practical training or work experience in US graduate departments.

If you are not from the United States but are considering attending a graduate program at a university in the United States, here is what you'll need to get started.

- If English is not your first language, you will probably need to take the Test of English as a Foreign Language (TOEFL) or show some other evidence that you're proficient in English prior to gaining admission to a graduate program. Graduate programs will vary on what is an acceptable TOEFL score. For degrees in business, journalism, management, or the humanities, a minimum TOEFL score of 100 (600 on the paper-based TOEFL) or better is expected. For the hard sciences and computer technology, a TOEFL score of 79 (550 on the paper-based TOEFL) is a common minimum requirement.
- You may also need to take the GRE. The strategies in this book are designed to help you maximize your score on the computer-based GRE. However, many sites outside the United States and Canada offer only the paper-based version of the

GRE. Fortunately, most strategies can be applied to the paper-based version as well. For additional paper-based GRE strategies, see Chapter 2.

- Because admission to many graduate programs is quite competitive, you may want to select three or four programs you would like to attend and complete applications for each program.
- Selecting the correct graduate school is very different from selecting a suitable undergraduate institution. You should research the qualifications and interests of faculty members teaching and doing research in your chosen field. Look for professors who share your specialty.
- You need to begin the application process at least a year in advance. Be aware that many programs offer only August or September start dates. Find out application deadlines and plan accordingly.
- Finally, you will need to obtain an I-20 Certificate of Eligibility in order to obtain an F-1 student visa to study in the United States.

Kaplan English International Centers

If you need more help with the complex process of graduate school admissions, assistance preparing for the TOEFL or GRE, or help building your English language skills in general, you may be interested in Kaplan's English language and test preparation for international students, available at Kaplan's International Centers/Colleges around the world.

Kaplan's English courses have been designed to help students and professionals from outside the United States meet their educational and career goals. At locations throughout the United States, international students take advantage of Kaplan's programs to help them improve their academic and conversational English skills; to raise their scores on the TOEFL, GRE, and other standardized exams; and to gain admission to the schools of their choice. Our staff and instructors give international students the individualized instruction they need to succeed. Here is a brief description of some of Kaplan's programs for international students.

General Intensive English

Kaplan's General Intensive English course is the fastest and most effective way for students to improve their English. This full-time program integrates the four key elements of language learning—listening, speaking, reading, and writing. The challenging curriculum and intensive schedule are designed for both the general language learner and the academically bound student.

TOEFL and Academic English (TAE)

Our world-famous TOEFL course prepares you for the TOEFL and teaches you the academic language and skills needed to succeed in a university. Designed for high-intermediate to proficiency-level English speakers, our course includes TOEFL-focused reading, writing, listening, speaking, vocabulary, and grammar instruction.

General English

Our General English course is a semi-intensive program designed for students who want to improve their listening and speaking skills without the time commitment of an intensive program. With morning or afternoon class times and flexible Structured Study hours throughout the week, our General English course is perfect for every schedule.

GRE for International Students

The GRE is required for admission to many graduate programs in the United States. Nearly a half-million people take the GRE each year. A high score can help you stand out from other test takers. This course, designed especially for nonnative English speakers, includes the skills you need to succeed on each section of the GRE, as well as access to Kaplan's exclusive computer-based practice materials and extra Verbal practice.

Other Kaplan Programs

Since 1938, more than three million students have come to Kaplan to advance their studies, prepare for entry to American universities, and further their careers. In addition to the above programs, Kaplan offers courses to prepare for the SAT, GMAT, LSAT, MCAT, DAT, OAT, PCAT, USMLE, NCLEX, and other standardized exams at locations throughout the United States.

Applying to Kaplan English Programs

To get more information, or to apply for admission to any of Kaplan's programs for international students and professionals, please visit our website at **kaplaninternational.com.**

PART SEVEN

GRE Resources

APPENDIX A

Kaplan's Word Groups

The following lists contain a lot of common GRE words grouped together by meaning. Make flashcards from these lists and look over your cards a few times a week from now until the day of the test. Look over the word group lists once or twice a week every week until the test. If you don't have much time until the exam date, look over your lists more frequently. Then, by the day of the test, you should have a rough idea of what most of the words on your lists mean.

Note: The categories in which these words are listed are *general* and should *not* be interpreted as the exact definitions of the words.

A

Abbreviated Communication
- abridge
- compendium
- cursory
- curtail
- syllabus
- synopsis
- terse

Act Quickly
- abrupt
- apace
- headlong
- impetuous
- precipitate

Assist
- abet
- advocate
- ancillary
- bolster
- corroborate
- countenance
- espouse
- mainstay
- munificent
- proponent
- stalwart
- sustenance

B

Bad Mood
- bilious
- dudgeon
- irascible
- pettish
- petulant
- pique
- querulous
- umbrage
- waspish

Beginner/Amateur
- dilettante
- fledgling
- neophyte
- novitiate
- proselyte
- tyro

Beginning/Young
- burgeoning
- callow
- engender
- inchoate
- incipient
- nascent

Biting (as in wit or temperament)
- acerbic
- acidulous
- acrimonious
- asperity
- caustic
- mordacious
- mordant
- trenchant

Bold
- audacious
- courageous
- dauntless

Boring
- banal
- fatuous
- hackneyed
- insipid
- mundane
- pedestrian
- platitude
- prosaic
- quotidian
- trite

C

Carousal
- bacchanalian
- debauchery
- depraved
- dissipated
- iniquity
- libertine
- libidinous

licentious
reprobate
ribald
salacious
sordid
turpitude

Changing Quickly
capricious
mercurial
volatile

Copy
counterpart
emulate
facsimile
factitious
paradigm
precursor
simulate
vicarious

Criticize/Criticism
aspersion
belittle
berate
calumny
castigate
decry
defame/defamation
denounce
deride/derisive
diatribe
disparage
excoriate
gainsay
harangue
impugn
inveigh
lambaste
objurgate
obloquy
opprobrium
pillory
rebuke
remonstrate
reprehend
reprove
revile
tirade
vituperate

D

Death/Mourning
bereave
cadaver
defunct
demise
dolorous
elegy
knell
lament
macabre
moribund
obsequies
sepulchral
wraith

Denying of Self
abnegate
abstain
ascetic
spartan
stoic
temperate

Dictatorial
authoritarian
despotic
dogmatic
hegemonic/hegemony
imperious
peremptory
tyrannical

Difficult to Understand
abstruse
ambiguous
arcane
bemusing
cryptic
enigmatic
esoteric
inscrutable
obscure
opaque
paradoxical
perplexing
recondite
turbid

Disgusting/Offensive
defile
fetid
invidious
noisome
odious
putrid
rebarbative

E

Easy to Understand
articulate
cogent
eloquent
evident
limpid
lucid
pellucid

Eccentric/Dissimilar
aberrant
anachronism
anomalous
discrete
eclectic
esoteric
iconoclast

Embarrass
abash
chagrin
compunction
contrition
diffidence
expiate
foible
gaucherie
rue

Equal
equitable
equity
tantamount

F

Falsehood
apocryphal
canard
chicanery
dissemble
duplicity
equivocate
erroneous
ersatz
fallacious
feigned
guile
mendacious/mendacity
perfidy
prevaricate
specious
spurious

Family
conjugal
consanguine
distaff
endogamous
filial
fraternal
fratricide
progenitor
scion
sorority

Favoring/Not Impartial
ardent/ardor
doctrinaire
fervid
partisan
tendentious
zealot

Forgive/Make Amends
absolve
acquit
exculpate
exonerate
expiate
palliate
redress
vindicate

Funny
chortle
droll
facetious
flippant
gibe
jocular
levity
ludicrous
raillery

riposte
simper

G

Gaps/Openings
abatement
aperture
fissure
hiatus
interregnum
interstice
lull
orifice
rent
respite
rift

Generous/Kind
altruistic
beneficent
clement
largess
magnanimous
munificent
philanthropic
unstinting

Greedy
avaricious
covetous
mercenary
miserly
penurious
rapacious
venal

H

Hard-Hearted
asperity
baleful
dour
fell
malevolent
mordant
sardonic
scathing
truculent
vitriolic
vituperation

Harmful
baleful
baneful
deleterious
inimical
injurious
insidious
minatory
perfidious
pernicious

Harsh-Sounding
cacophony
din
dissonant
raucous
strident

Hatred
abhorrence
anathema
antagonism
antipathy
detestation
enmity
loathing
malice
odium
rancor

Healthy
beneficial
salubrious
salutary

Hesitate
dither
oscillate
teeter
vacillate
waver

Hostile
antithetic
churlish
curmudgeon
irascible
malevolent
misanthropic
truculent
vindictive

I

Innocent/Inexperienced
credulous
gullible
ingenuous
naive
novitiate
tyro

Insincere
disingenuous
dissemble
fulsome
ostensible
unctuous

Investigate
appraise
ascertain
assay
descry
peruse

L

Lazy/Sluggish
indolent
inert
lackadaisical
languid
lassitude
lethargic
phlegmatic
quiescent
slothful
torpid

Luck
adventitious
amulet
auspicious
fortuitous
kismet
optimum
portentous
propitiate
propitious
providential
serendipity
talisman

N

Nag
admonish
belabor
cavil
enjoin
exhort
harangue
hector
martinet
remonstrate
reproof

Nasty
fetid
noisome
noxious

Not a Straight Line
askance
awry
careen
carom
circuitous
circumvent
gyrate
labyrinth
meander
oblique
serrated
sidle
sinuous
undulating
vortex

O

Overblown/Wordy
bombastic
circumlocution
garrulous
grandiloquent
loquacious
periphrastic
prolix
rhetoric
turgid
verbose

P

Pacify/Satisfy
ameliorate
appease
assuage
defer
mitigate

mollify
placate
propitiate
satiate
slake
soothe

Pleasant-Sounding
euphonious
harmonious
melodious
sonorous

Poor
destitute
esurient
impecunious
indigent

Praise
acclaim
accolade
aggrandize
encomium
eulogize
extol
fawn
laud/laudatory
venerate/veneration

Predict
augur
auspice
fey
harbinger
portentous
precursor
presage
prescient
prognosticate

Prevent/Obstruct
discomfit
encumber
fetter
forfend
hinder
impede
inhibit
occlude

S

Smart/Learned
astute
canny
erudite
perspicacious

Sorrow
disconsolate
doleful
dolor
elegiac
forlorn
lament
lugubrious
melancholy
morose
plaintive
threnody

Stubborn
implacable
inexorable
intractable
intransigent
obdurate
obstinate
recalcitrant
refractory
renitent
untoward
vexing

T

Terse
compendious
curt
laconic
pithy
succinct
taciturn

Time/Order/Duration
anachronism
antecede
antedate
anterior
archaic
diurnal
eon
ephemeral
epoch
fortnight
millennium
penultimate
synchronous
temporal

Timid/Timidity
craven
diffident
pusillanimous
recreant
timorous
trepidation

Truth
candor/candid
fealty
frankness
indisputable
indubitable
legitimate
probity
sincere
veracious
verity

U

Unusual
aberration
anomaly
iconoclast
idiosyncrasy

W

Walking About
ambulatory
itinerant
meander
peripatetic

Wandering
discursive
expatiate
forage
itinerant
peregrination
peripatetic
sojourn

Weaken
adulterate
enervate
exacerbate
inhibit
obviate
stultify
undermine
vitiate

Wisdom
adage
aphorism
apothegm
axiom
bromide
dictum
epigram
platitude
sententious
truism

Withdrawal/Retreat
abeyance
abjure
abnegation
abortive
abrogate
decamp
demur
recant
recidivism
remission
renege
rescind
retrograde

APPENDIX B

Kaplan's Root List

Kaplan's Root List can boost your knowledge of GRE-level words, and that can help you get more questions right. No one can predict exactly which words will show up on your test, but the testmakers favor certain words. The Root List gives you the component parts of many typical GRE words. Knowing these words can help you because you may run across them on your GRE. Also, becoming comfortable with the types of words that pop up will reduce your anxiety about the test.

Knowing roots can help you in two more ways. First, instead of learning one word at a time, you can learn a whole group of words that contain a certain root. They'll be related in meaning, so if you remember one, it will be easier for you to remember others. Second, roots can often help you decode an unknown GRE word. If you recognize a familiar root, you could get a good enough grasp of the word to answer the question.

This list is a starting point and a quick review, not an exhaustive guide. Roots are given in their most common forms, with their most common or broadest definitions; often, other forms and meanings exist. Similarly, the definitions for the words given as examples may be incomplete, and other senses of those words may exist. Get into the habit of looking up unfamiliar words in a good, current dictionary—whether on paper or on the Internet—and be sure to check their etymologies while you're there.

A

A/AN: not, without

agnostic: one who believes the existence of God is not provable
amoral: neither moral nor immoral; having no relation to morality
anomaly: an irregularity
anonymous: of unknown authorship or origin
apathy: lack of interest or emotion
atheist: one who does not believe in God
atrophy: the wasting away of body tissue
atypical: not typical

AB: off, away from, apart, down

abdicate: to renounce or relinquish a throne
abduct: to take away by force
abhor: to hate, detest
abject: cast down; degraded
abnormal: deviating from a standard
abolish: to do away with, make void
abstinence: forbearance from any indulgence of appetite
abstract: conceived apart from concrete realities, specific objects, or actual instances
abstruse: hard to understand; secret, hidden

ABLE/IBLE: capable of, worthy of

changeable: able to be changed
combustible: capable of being burned; easily inflamed
inevitable: impossible to be avoided; certain to happen
presentable: suitable for being presented

AC/ACR: sharp, bitter, sour

acerbic: sour or astringent in taste; harsh in temper
acid: something that is sharp, sour, or ill-natured
acrimonious: caustic, stinging, or bitter in nature
acumen: mental sharpness; quickness of wit
acute: sharp at the end; ending in a point
exacerbate: to increase bitterness or violence; aggravate

ACT/AG: to do, to drive, to force, to lead

agile: quick and well-coordinated in movement; active, lively
agitate: to move or force into violent, irregular action
pedagogue: a teacher
prodigal: wastefully or recklessly extravagant
synagogue: a gathering or congregation of Jews for the purpose of religious worship

ACOU: hearing

acoustic: pertaining to hearing; sound made through mechanical, not electronic, means

AD: to, toward, near

(Often the *d* is dropped and the first letter to which *a* is prefixed is doubled.)
accede: to yield to a demand; to enter office
adapt: adjust or modify fittingly
addict: to give oneself over, as to a habit or pursuit
address: to direct a speech or written statement to
adhere: to stick fast; cleave; cling
adjacent: near, close, or contiguous; adjoining
adjoin: to be close or in contact with
admire: to regard with wonder, pleasure, and approval
advocate: to plead in favor of
attract: to draw either by physical force or by an appeal to emotions or senses

AL/ALI/ALTER: other, another

alias: an assumed name; another name
alibi: the defense by an accused person that he was verifiably elsewhere at the time of the crime with which he is charged
alien: one born in another country; a foreigner
allegory: figurative treatment of one subject under the guise of another
alter ego: the second self; a substitute or deputy
alternative: a possible choice
altruist: a person unselfishly concerned for the welfare of others

AM: love

amateur: a person who engages in an activity for pleasure rather than financial or professional gain
amatory: of or pertaining to lovers or lovemaking
amiable: having or showing agreeable personal qualities
amicable: characterized by exhibiting good will
amity: friendship; peaceful harmony
amorous: inclined to love, esp. sexual love

enamored: inflamed with love; charmed; captivated

inamorata: a female lover

AMBI/AMPHI: both, on both sides, around

ambidextrous: able to use both hands equally well

ambient: moving around freely; circulating

ambiguous: open to various interpretations

amphibian: any cold-blooded vertebrate, the larva of which is aquatic and the adult of which is terrestrial; a person or thing having a twofold nature

AMBL/AMBUL: to go, to walk

ambulance: a vehicle equipped for carrying sick people (from a phrase meaning "walking hospital")

ambulatory: of, pertaining to, or capable of walking

perambulator: one who makes a tour of inspection on foot

preamble: an introductory statement (originally: to walk in front)

ANIM: of the life, mind, soul, breath

animal: a living being

animosity: a feeling of ill will or enmity

equanimity: mental or emotional stability, especially under tension

magnanimous: generous in forgiving an insult or injury

unanimous: of one mind; in complete accord

ANNUI/ENNI: year

annals: a record of events, esp. a yearly record

anniversary: the yearly recurrence of the date of a past event

annual: of, for, or pertaining to a year; yearly

annuity: a specified income payable at stated intervals

perennial: lasting for an indefinite amount of time

ANT/ANTE: before

antebellum: before the war (especially the American Civil War)

antecedent: existing, being, or going before

antedate: precede in time

antediluvian: belonging to the period before the biblical flood; very old or old-fashioned

anterior: placed before

ANTHRO/ANDR: man, human

androgen: any substance that promotes masculine characteristics

androgynous: being both male and female

android: a robot; a mechanical man

anthropocentric: regarding humanity as the central fact of the universe

anthropology: the science that deals with the origins of humankind

misanthrope: one who hates humans or humanity

philanderer: one who carries on flirtations

ANTI: against, opposite

antibody: a protein naturally existing in blood serum that reacts to overcome the toxic effects of an antigen

antidote: a remedy for counteracting the effects of poison, disease, etc.

antipathy: aversion

antipodal: on the opposite side of the globe

antiseptic: free from germs; particularly clean or neat

APO: away

apocalypse: revelation; discovery; disclosure

apocryphal: of doubtful authorship or authenticity

apogee: the highest or most distant point

apology: an expression of one's regret or sorrow for having wronged another

apostasy: a total desertion of one's religion, principles, party, cause, etc.

apostle: one of the 12 disciples sent forth by Jesus to preach the Gospel

AQUA/AQUE: water

aquamarine: a bluish-green color

aquarium: a tank for keeping fish and other underwater creatures

aquatic: having to do with water

aqueduct: a channel for transporting water

subaqueous: underwater

ARCH/ARCHI/ARCHY: chief, principal, ruler

anarchy: a state or society without government or law

archenemy: chief enemy

architect: the devisor, maker, or planner of anything

monarchy: a government in which the supreme power is lodged in a sovereign

oligarchy: a state or society ruled by a select group

ARD: to burn

ardent: burning; fierce; passionate

ardor: flame; passion

arson: the crime of setting property on fire

AUTO: self

autocrat: an absolute ruler

automatic: self-moving or self-acting

autonomy: independence or freedom

B

BE: about, to make, to surround, to affect (often used to transform words into transitive verbs)

belie: to misrepresent; to contradict

belittle: to make small; to make something appear smaller

bemoan: to moan for; to lament

bewilder: to confuse completely (that is, to make one mentally wander)

BEL/BELL: beautiful

belle: a beautiful woman

embellish: to make beautiful; to ornament

BELL: war

antebellum: before the war (especially the American Civil War)

belligerent: warlike, given to waging war

rebel: a person who resists authority, control, or tradition

BEN/BENE: good

benediction: act of uttering a blessing

benefit: anything advantageous to a person or thing

benevolent: desiring to do good to others

benign: having a kindly disposition

BI/BIN: two

biennial: happening every two years

bilateral: pertaining to or affecting two or both sides

bilingual: able to speak one's native language and another with equal facility

binocular: involving two eyes

bipartisan: representing two parties

combination: the joining of two or more things into a whole

BON/BOUN: good, generous

bona fide: in good faith; without fraud

bonus: something given over and above what is due

bountiful: generous

BREV/BRID: short, small

abbreviate: to shorten

abridge: to shorten

brevet: an honorary promotion with no additional pay

breviloquent: laconic; concise in one's speech

brevity: shortness

brief: short

BURS: purse, money

bursar: treasurer

bursary: treasury

disburse: to pay

reimburse: to pay back

C

CAD/CID: to fall, to happen by chance

accident: happening by chance; unexpected

cascade: a waterfall descending over a steep surface

coincidence: a striking occurrence of two or more events at one time, apparently by chance

decadent: decaying; deteriorating

recidivist: one who repeatedly relapses, as into crime

CANT/CENT/CHANT: to sing

accent: prominence of a syllable in terms of pronunciation

chant: a song; singing

enchant: to subject to magical influence; bewitch

incantation: the chanting of words purporting to have magical power

Incentive: that which incites action

recant: to withdraw or disavow a statement

CAP/CIP/CEPT: to take, to get

anticipate: to realize beforehand; foretaste or foresee

capture: to take by force or stratagem

emancipate: to free from restraint

percipient: having perception; discerning; discriminating

precept: a commandment or direction given as a rule of conduct

susceptible: capable of receiving, admitting, undergoing, or being affected by something

CAP/CAPIT/CIPIT: head, headlong

capital: the city or town that is the official seat of government

capitulate: to surrender unconditionally or on stipulated terms

caption: a heading or title

disciple: one who is a pupil of the doctrines of another

precipice: a cliff with a vertical face

precipitate: to hasten the occurrence of; to bring about prematurely

CARD/CORD/COUR: heart

cardiac: pertaining to the heart

concord: agreement; peace, amity

concordance: agreement, concord, harmony

discord: lack of harmony between persons or things

encourage: to inspire with spirit or confidence

CARN: flesh

carnage: the slaughter of a great number of people

carnival: a traveling amusement show

carnivorous: eating flesh

incarnation: a being invested with a bodily form

reincarnation: rebirth of a soul in a new body

CAST/CHAST: to cut

cast: to throw or hurl; fling

caste: a hereditary social group, limited to people of the same rank

castigate: to punish in order to correct

chaste: free from obscenity; decent

chastise: to discipline, esp. by corporal punishment

CAUS/CAUT: to burn

caustic: burning or corrosive

cauterize: to burn or deaden

cautery: an instrument used for branding; branding

holocaust: a burnt offering; complete destruction by fire or other means

CED/CEED/CESS: to go, to yield, to stop

accede: to yield to a demand; to enter office

antecedent: existing, being, or going before

cessation: a temporary or complete discontinuance

concede: to acknowledge as true, just, or proper; admit

incessant: without stop

predecessor: one who comes before another in an office, position, etc.

CELER: speed

accelerant: something used to speed up a process

accelerate: to increase in speed

celerity: speed; quickness

decelerate: to decrease in speed

CENT: hundred, hundredth

bicentennial: two-hundredth anniversary

cent: a hundredth of a dollar

centigrade: a temperature system with one hundred degrees between the freezing and boiling points of water

centimeter: one-hundredth of a meter

centipede: a creature with many legs

century: one hundred years

percent: in every hundred

CENTR: center

centrifuge: an apparatus that rotates at high speed and separates substances of different densities using centrifugal force

centrist: of or pertaining to moderate political or social ideas

concentrate: to bring to a common center; to converge, to direct toward one point

concentric: having a common center, as in circles or spheres

eccentric: off-center

CERN/CERT/CRET/CRIM/CRIT: to separate, to judge, to distinguish, to decide

ascertain: to make sure of; to determine

certitude: freedom from doubt

criterion: a standard of judgment or criticism

discreet: judicious in one's conduct of speech, esp. with regard to maintaining silence about something of a delicate nature

discrete: detached from others, separate

hypocrite: a person who pretends to have beliefs that she does not

CHROM: color
chromatic: having to do with color
chrome: a metallic element (chromium) used to make vivid colors or something plated with chromium
chromosome: genetic material that can be studied by coloring it with dyes
monochromatic: having only one color

CHRON: time
anachronism: something that is out-of-date or belonging to the wrong time
chronic: constant, habitual
chronology: the sequential order in which past events occurred
chronometer: a highly accurate clock or watch
synchronize: to occur at the same time or agree in time

CIRCU/CIRCUM: around
circuit: a line around an area; a racecourse; the path traveled by electrical current
circuitous: roundabout, indirect
circumference: the outer boundary of a circular area
circumspect: cautious; watching all sides
circumstances: the existing conditions or state of affairs surrounding and affecting an agent

CIS: to cut
exorcise: to seek to expel an evil spirit by ceremony
incision: a cut, gash, or notch
incisive: penetrating, cutting
precise: definitely stated or defined
scissors: cutting instrument for paper

CLA/CLO/CLU: to shut, to close
claustrophobia: an abnormal fear of enclosed places
cloister: a courtyard bordered with covered walks, esp. in a religious institution
conclude: to bring to an end; finish; to terminate
disclose: to make known, reveal, or uncover
exclusive: not admitting of something else; shutting out others
preclude: to prevent the presence, existence, or occurrence of

CLAIM/CLAM: to shout, to cry out
clamor: a loud uproar
disclaim: to deny interest in or connection with
exclaim: to cry out or speak suddenly and vehemently
proclaim: to announce or declare in an official way
reclaim: to claim or demand the return of a right or possession

CLI: to lean toward
climax: the most intense point in the development of something
decline: to cause to slope or incline downward
disinclination: aversion, distaste
proclivity: inclination, bias
recline: to lean back

CO/COL/COM/CON: with, together
coerce: to compel by force, intimidation, or authority
collaborate: to work with another, cooperate
collide: to strike one another with a forceful impact
commensurate: suitable in measure, proportionate
compatible: capable of existing together in harmony
conciliate: to placate, win over
connect: to bind or fasten together

COGN/CONN: to know
cognition: the process of knowing
incognito: with one's name or identity concealed
recognize: to identify as already known

CONTRA/CONTRO/COUNTER: against
contradict: to oppose; to speak against
contrary: opposed to; opposite
controversy: a disputation; a quarrel
counterfeit: fake; a false imitation
countermand: to retract an order
encounter: a meeting, often with an opponent

CORP/CORS: body
corporation: a company legally treated as an individual
corps: a body (an organized group) of troops
corpse: a dead body
corpulent: obese; having a lot of flesh
corset: a garment used to give shape and support to the body
incorporation: combining into a single body

COSM: order, universe, world
cosmetic: improving the appearance (making it look better ordered)
cosmic: relating to the universe
cosmology: a theory of the universe as a whole
cosmonaut: an astronaut; an explorer of outer space
cosmopolitan: worldly
cosmos: the universe; an orderly system; order
microcosm: a small system that reflects a larger whole

COUR/CUR: running, a course
concur: to accord in opinion; agree
courier: a messenger traveling in haste who bears news
curriculum: the regular course of study
cursive: handwriting in flowing strokes with the letters joined together
cursory: going rapidly over something; hasty; superficial
excursion: a short journey or trip
incursion: a hostile entrance into a place, esp. suddenly
recur: to happen again

CRE/CRESC/CRET: to grow
accretion: an increase by natural growth
accrue: to be added as a matter of periodic gain
creation: the act of producing or causing to exist
excrescence: an outgrowth
increase: to make greater in any respect
increment: something added or gained; an addition or increase

CRED: to believe, to trust
credentials: anything that provides the basis for belief
credit: trustworthiness
credo: any formula of belief
credulity: willingness to believe or trust too readily
incredible: unbelievable

CRYPT: hidden
apocryphal: of doubtful authorship or authenticity
crypt: a subterranean chamber or vault
cryptography: procedures of making and using secret writing
cryptology: the science of interpreting secret writings, codes, ciphers, and the like

CUB/CUMB: to lie down
cubicle: any small space or compartment that is partitioned off
incubate: to sit upon for the purpose of hatching
incumbent: holding an indicated position
recumbent: lying down; reclining; leaning
succumb: to give away to superior force; yield

CULP: fault, blame
culpable: deserving blame or censure
culprit: a person guilty of an offense
inculpate: to charge with fault
mea culpa: through my fault; my fault

D

DAC/DOC: to teach
didactic: intended for instruction
docile: easily managed or handled; tractable
doctor: someone licensed to practice medicine; a learned person
doctrine: a particular principle advocated, as of a government or religion
indoctrinate: to imbue a person with learning

DE: away, off, down, completely, reversal
decipher: to make out the meaning; to interpret
defame: to attack the good name or reputation of
deferential: respectful; to yield to judgment
defile: to make foul, dirty, or unclean
delineate: to trace the outline of; sketch or trace in outline
descend: to move from a higher to a lower place

DELE: to erase
delete: erase; blot out; remove
indelible: impossible to erase; lasting

DEM: people
democracy: government by the people
demographics: vital and social statistics of populations
endemic: peculiar to a particular people or locality
epidemic: affecting a large number of people at the same time and spreading from person to person
pandemic: general, universal

DEXT: right hand, right side, deft
ambidextrous: equally able to use both hands
dexter: on the right
dexterity: deftness; adroitness

DI: day
dial: a device for seeing the hour of the day; a clock face; rotatable discs or knobs used as a control input
diary: a record of one's days
dismal: gloomy (from "bad days")
diurnal: daily
meridian: a direct line from the North Pole to the South Pole; the highest point reached by the sun; noon
quotidian: everyday; ordinary

DI/DIA: in two, through, across
diagnose: to identify disease or fault from symptoms
dialogue: a conversation between two or more persons
diameter: a line going through a circle, dividing it in two
dichotomy: division into two parts, kinds, etc.

DI/DIF/DIS: away from, apart, reversal, not
diffuse: to pour out and spread, as in a fluid
dilate: to make wider or larger; to cause to expand
dilatory: inclined to delay or procrastinate
disperse: to drive or send off in various directions
disseminate: to scatter or spread widely; promulgate
dissipate: to scatter wastefully
dissuade: to deter by advice or persuasion

DIC/DICT/DIT: to say, to tell, to use words
dictionary: a book containing a selection of the words of a language
interdict: to forbid; prohibit
predict: to tell in advance
verdict: a judgment or decision

DIGN: worth
condign: well deserved; fitting; adequate
deign: to think fit or in accordance with one's dignity
dignitary: a person who holds a high rank or office
dignity: nobility or elevation of character; worthiness
disdain: to look upon or treat with contempt

DOG/DOX: opinion
dogma: a system of tenets, as of a church
orthodox: sound or correct in opinion or doctrine
paradox: an opinion or statement contrary to accepted opinion

DOL: to suffer, to pain, to grieve
condolence: expression of sympathy with one who is suffering
doleful: sorrowful, mournful
dolorous: full of pain or sorrow, grievous
indolence: a state of being lazy or slothful

DON/DOT/DOW: to give
anecdote: a short narrative about an interesting event
antidote: something that prevents or counteracts ill effects
donate: to present as a gift or contribution
endow: to provide with a permanent fund
pardon: kind indulgence, forgiveness

DORM: sleep
dormant: sleeping; inactive
dormitory: a place for sleeping; a residence hall

DORS: back
dorsal: having to do with the back
endorse: to sign on the back; to vouch for

DUB: doubt
dubiety: doubtfulness
dubious: doubtful
indubitable: unquestionable

DUC/DUCT: to lead
abduct: to carry off or lead away
conducive: contributive, helpful
conduct: personal behavior, way of acting
induce: to lead or move by influence
induct: to install in a position with formal ceremonies
produce: to bring into existence; give cause to

DULC: sweet
dulcet: sweet; pleasing
dulcified: sweetened; softened
dulcimer: a musical instrument

DUR: hard, lasting
dour: sullen, gloomy (originally: hard, obstinate)

durable: able to resist decay
duration: the length of time something exists
duress: compulsion by threat, coercion
endure: to hold out against; to sustain without yielding
obdurate: stubborn, resistant to persuasion

DYS: faulty, abnormal
dysfunctional: poorly functioning
dyslexia: an impairment of the ability to read due to a brain defect
dyspepsia: impaired digestion
dystrophy: faulty or inadequate nutrition or development

E

E/EX: out, out of, from, former, completely
efface: to rub or wipe out; surpass, eclipse
evade: to escape from, avoid
exclude: to shut out; to leave out
exonerate: to free or declare free from blame
expire: to breathe out; to breathe one's last; to end
extricate: to disentangle, release

EGO: self
ego: oneself; the part of oneself that is self-aware
egocentric: focused on oneself
egoism/egotism: selfishness; self-absorption

EM/EN: in, into
embrace: to clasp in the arms; to include or contain
enclose: to close in on all sides

EPI: upon
epidemic: affecting a large number of people at the same time and spreading from person to person
epidermis: the outer layer of the skin
epigram: a witty or pointed saying tersely expressed
epilogue: a concluding part added to a literary work
epithet: a word or phrase, used invectively as a term of abuse

EQU: equal, even
adequate: equal to the requirement or occasion
equation: the act of making equal
equidistant: equally distant
iniquity: gross injustice; wickedness

ERR: to wander
arrant: notorious; downright (originally: wandering)
err: to go astray in thought or belief, to be mistaken
erratic: deviating from the proper or usual course in conduct
error: a deviation from accuracy or correctness

ESCE: becoming
adolescent: between childhood and adulthood
convalescent: recovering from illness
incandescent: glowing with heat, shining
obsolescent: becoming obsolete
reminiscent: reminding or suggestive of

EU: good, well
eugenics: improvement of qualities of race by control of inherited characteristics
eulogy: speech or writing in praise or commendation
euphemism: pleasant-sounding term for something unpleasant
euphony: pleasantness of sound
euthanasia: killing a person painlessly, usually one who has an incurable, painful disease

EXTRA: outside, beyond
extract: to take out, obtain against a person's will
extradite: to hand over (person accused of crime) to state where crime was committed
extraordinary: beyond the ordinary
extrapolate: to estimate (unknown facts or values) from known data
extrasensory: derived by means other than known senses

F

FAB/FAM: to speak
affable: friendly, courteous
defame: to attack the good name of
fable: fictional tale, esp. legendary
famous: well known, celebrated
ineffable: too great for description in words; that which must not be uttered

FAC/FIC/FIG/FAIT/FEIT/FY: to do, to make
configuration: manner of arrangement, shape
counterfeit: imitation, forgery

deficient: incomplete or insufficient
effigy: sculpture or model of person
faction: small dissenting group within larger one, esp. in politics
factory: building for manufacture of goods
prolific: producing many offspring or much output
ratify: to confirm or accept by formal consent

FAL: to err, to deceive
default: to fail
fail: to be insufficient; to be unsuccessful; to die out
fallacy: a flawed argument
false: not true; erroneous; lying
faux pas: a false step; a social gaffe
infallible: incapable of being wrong or being deceived

FATU: foolish
fatuity: foolishness; stupidity
fatuous: foolish; stupid
infatuated: swept up in a fit of passion, impairing one's reason

FER: to bring, to carry, to bear
confer: to grant, bestow
offer: to present for acceptance, refusal, or consideration
proffer: to offer
proliferate: to reproduce; produce rapidly
referendum: a vote on a political question open to the entire electorate

FERV: to boil, to bubble
effervescent: with the quality of giving off bubbles of gas
fervid: ardent, intense
fervor: passion, zeal

FI/FID: faith, trust
affidavit: a written statement on oath
confide: to entrust with a secret
fidelity: faithfulness, loyalty
fiduciary: of a trust; held or given in trust
infidel: disbeliever in the supposed true religion

FIN: end
confine: to keep or restrict within certain limits; imprison
definitive: decisive, unconditional, final
final: at the end; coming last
infinite: boundless; endless
infinitesimal: infinitely or very small

FLAGR/FLAM: to burn
conflagration: a large, destructive fire
flagrant: blatant, scandalous
flambeau: a lighted torch
inflame: to set on fire

FLECT/FLEX: to bend, to turn
deflect: to bend or turn aside from a purpose
flexible: able to bend without breaking
genuflect: to bend knee, esp. in worship
inflect: to change or vary pitch of
reflect: to throw back

FLU/FLUX: to flow
confluence: merging into one
effluence: flowing out of (light, electricity, etc.)
fluctuation: something that varies, rising and falling
fluid: a substance, esp. gas or liquid, capable of flowing freely
mellifluous: pleasing, musical

FORE: before
foreshadow: be warning or indication of (future event)
foresight: care or provision for future
forestall: to prevent by advance action
forthright: straightforward, outspoken, decisive

FORT: chance
fortuitous: happening by luck
fortunate: lucky, auspicious
fortune: chance or luck in human affairs

FORT: strength
forte: strong point; something a person does well
fortify: to provide with fortifications; strengthen
fortissimo: very loud

FRA/FRAC/FRAG/FRING: to break
fractious: irritable, peevish
fracture: breakage, esp. of a bone
fragment: a part broken off
infringe: to break or violate (a law, etc.)
refractory: stubborn, unmanageable, rebellious

FUG: to flee, to fly
centrifugal: flying off from the center

fugitive: on the run; someone who flees

fugue: a musical composition in which subsequent parts imitate or pursue the first part; a psychological state in which one flies from one's own identity

refuge: a haven for those fleeing

refugee: a fleeing person who seeks refuge

subterfuge: a deception used to avoid a confrontation

FULG: to shine

effulgent: shining forth

refulgent: radiant; shining

FUM: smoke

fume: smoke; scented vapor; to emit smoke or vapors

fumigate: to treat with smoke or vapors

perfume: scents, from burning incense or other sources of fragrance

FUS: to pour

diffuse: to spread widely or thinly

fusillade: continuous discharge of firearms or outburst of criticism

infusion: the act of permeating or steeping; liquid extract so obtained

profuse: lavish, extravagant, copious

suffuse: to spread throughout or over from within

G

GEN: birth, creation, race, kind

carcinogenic: producing cancer

congenital: existing or as such from birth

gender: classification roughly corresponding to the two sexes and sexlessness

generous: giving or given freely

genetics: the study of heredity and variation among animals and plants

progeny: offspring, descendants

GNI/GNO: to know

agnostic: one who believes that the existence of God is not provable

diagnose: to identify disease or fault from symptoms

ignoramus: a person lacking knowledge, uninformed

ignore: to refuse to take notice of

prognosis: to forecast, especially of disease

GRAD/GRESS: to step

aggressive: given to hostile acts or feelings

degrade: to humiliate, dishonor, reduce to lower rank

digress: to depart from the main subject

egress: going out; way out

progress: forward movement

regress: to move backward, revert to an earlier state

GRAM/GRAPH: to write, to draw

diagram: a figure made by drawing lines; an illustration

epigram: a short poem; a pointed statement

grammar: a system of language and its rules

graph: a diagram used to convey mathematical information

graphite: mineral used for writing, as the "lead" in pencils

photograph: a picture, originally made by exposing chemically treated film to light

GRAT: pleasing

gracious: kindly, esp. to inferiors; merciful

grateful: thankful

gratuity: money given for good service

ingratiate: to bring oneself into favor

GREG: flock

aggregate: a number of things considered as a collective whole

congregate: to come together in a group

egregious: remarkably bad; standing out from the crowd

gregarious: sociable; enjoying spending time with others

segregate: to separate from the crowd

H

HAP: by chance

haphazard: at random

hapless: without luck

happen: occur (originally: to occur by chance)

happily: through good fortune

happy: pleased, as by good fortune

mishap: an unlucky accident

perhaps: a qualifier suggesting something might (or might not) take place

HEMI: half

hemisphere: half a sphere; half of the Earth

hemistich: half a line of poetry

HER/HES: to stick

adherent: able to adhere; believer or advocate of a particular thing

adhesive: tending to remain in memory; sticky; an adhesive substance

coherent: logically consistent; having waves in phase and of one wavelength

inherent: involved in the constitution or essential character of something

(H)ETERO: different, other

heterodox: different from acknowledged standard; holding unorthodox opinions or doctrines

heterogeneous: of other origin; not originating in the body

heterosexual: of or pertaining to sexual orientation toward members of the opposite sex; relating to different sexes

HOL: whole

catholic: universal

holocaust: a burnt offering; complete destruction by fire or other means

hologram: a sort of three-dimensional image

holograph: a document written entirely by the person whose name it's in

holistic: considering something as a unified whole

(H)OM: same

anomaly: deviation from the common rule

homeostasis: a relatively stable state of equilibrium

homogeneous: of the same or a similar kind of nature; of uniform structure of composition throughout

homonym: one of two or more words spelled and pronounced alike but different in meaning

homosexual: of, relating to, or exhibiting sexual desire toward a member of one's own sex

HUM: earth

exhume: unearth

humble: down-to-earth

humility: the state of being humble

HYPER: over, excessive

hyperactive: excessively active

hyperbole: purposeful exaggeration for effect

hyperglycemia: an abnormally high concentration of sugar in the blood

HYPO: under, beneath, less than

hypochondriac: one affected by extreme depression of mind or spirits, often centered on imaginary physical ailments

hypocritical: pretending to have beliefs one does not

hypodermic: relating to the parts beneath the skin

hypothesis: assumption subject to proof

I

ICON: image, idol

icon: a symbolic picture; a statue; something seen as representative of a culture or movement

iconic: being representative of a culture or movement

iconoclast: one who attacks established beliefs; one who tears down images

iconology: symbolism

IDIO: one's own

idiom: a language, dialect, or style of speaking particular to a people

idiosyncrasy: peculiarity of temperament; eccentricity

idiot: an utterly stupid person

IN/IM: not, without

(Often the *m* is dropped and the first letter to which *i* is prefixed is doubled.)

immoral: not moral; evil

impartial: not partial or biased; just

inactive: not active

indigent: poor, needy, lacking in what is needed

indolence: showing a disposition to avoid exertion; slothful

innocuous: not harmful or injurious

IN/IM: in, into

(Often the *m* is dropped and the first letter to which *i* is prefixed is doubled.)

implicit: not expressly stated; implied

incarnate: given a bodily, esp. a human, form

indigenous: native; innate, natural

influx: the act of flowing in; inflow

intrinsic: belonging to a thing by its very nature

INTER: between, among

interim: a temporary or provisional arrangement; meantime

interloper: one who intrudes in the domain of others

intermittent: stopping or ceasing for a time

intersperse: to scatter here and there

interstate: connecting or jointly involving states

INTRA: inside, within

intramural: within a school; inside a city

intrastate: within a state

intravenous: inside the veins

IT/ITER: way, journey

ambition: strong desire to achieve (from "going around" for votes)

circuit: a line around an area; a racecourse; the path traveled by electrical current

itinerant: traveling

itinerary: travel plans

reiterate: to repeat

transit: traveling; means of transportation

J

JECT: to throw, to throw down

abject: utterly hopeless, humiliating, or wretched

conjecture: formation of opinion on incomplete information

dejected: sad, depressed

eject: to throw out, expel

inject: to place (quality, etc.) where needed in something

JOC: joke

jocose: given to joking; playful

jocular: in a joking manner; funny

jocund: merry; cheerful

joke: a witticism; a humorous anecdote; something funny

JOIN/JUG/JUNCT: to meet, to join

adjoin: to be next to and joined with

conjugal: related to marriage

conjunction: joining; occurring together; a connecting word

injunction: a command; an act of enjoining

junction: the act of joining; combining; a place where multiple paths join

junta: a group of military officers who join together to run a country; a council

rejoinder: to reply, retort

subjugate: to make subservient; to place under a yoke

JOUR: day

adjourn: to close a meeting; to put off further proceedings for another day

journal: a record of one's days

journey: a trip (originally: a day's travel)

JUD: to judge

adjudicate: to act as a judge

judiciary: a system of courts; members of a court system

judicious: having good judgment

prejudice: a previous or premature judgment; bias

JUR: law, to swear

abjure: to renounce on oath

adjure: to beg or command

jurisprudence: a system of law; knowledge of law

perjury: willful lying while on oath

JUV: young

juvenile: young; immature

juvenilia: writings or art produced in one's youth

rejuvenate: to refresh; to make young again

L

LANG/LING: tongue

bilingual: speaking two languages

language: a system of (usually spoken) communication

linguistics: the study of language

LAUD: praise, honor

cum laude: with honors

laudable: praiseworthy

laudatory: expressing praise

LAV/LAU/LU: to wash

ablution: act of cleansing

antediluvian: before the biblical flood; extremely old

deluge: a great flood of water

dilute: to make thinner or weaker by the addition of water

laundry: items to be, or that have been, washed
lavatory: a room with equipment for washing hands and face

LAX/LEAS/LES: loose

lax: loose; undisciplined
laxative: medicine or food that loosens the bowels
lease: to rent out (that is, to let something loose for others' use)
leash: a cord used to hold an animal while giving it some freedom to run loose
relax: loosen; be less strict; calm down
release: let go; set free

LEC/LEG/LEX: to read, to speak

dialect: a manner of speaking; a regional variety of a language
lectern: a reading desk
lecture: an instructional speech
legend: a story; a written explanation of a map or illustration
legible: readable
lesson: instruction (originally: part of a book or oral instruction to be studied and repeated to a teacher)
lexicographer: a writer of dictionaries
lexicon: a dictionary

LECT/LEG: to select, to choose

collect: to gather together or assemble
eclectic: selecting ideas, etc. from various sources
elect: to choose; to decide
predilection: preference, liking
select: to choose with care

LEV: to lift, to rise, light (weight)

alleviate: to make easier to endure, lessen
levee: an embankment against river flooding
levitate: to rise in the air or cause to rise
levity: humor, frivolity, gaiety
relevant: bearing on or pertinent to information at hand
relieve: to mitigate; to free from a burden

LI/LIG: to tie, to bind

ally: to unite; one in an alliance
league: an association; a group of nations, teams, etc. that have agreed to work for a common cause
liable: legally responsible; bound by law
liaison: a connection; one who serves to connect
lien: the right to hold a property due to an outstanding debt
ligament: a band holding bones together; a bond
ligature: a connection between two letters; a bond
oblige: to obligate; to make indebted or form personal bonds by doing a favor
rely: to depend upon (originally: to come together; to rally)

LIBER: free

deliver: to set free; to save; to hand over
liberal: generous; giving away freely
liberality: generosity
liberate: set free
libertine: one who follows one's own path, without regard for morals or other restrictions
liberty: freedom
livery: a uniform; an emblem indicating an owner or manufacturer (originally: an allowance of food or other provisions given to servants)

LITH: stone

acrolith: a statue with a stone head and limbs (but a wooden body)
lithography: a printing process that originally involved writing on a flat stone
lithology: the study of rocks and stones
lithotomy: an operation to remove stones from the body
megalith: a very big stone
monolith: a single block of stone, often shaped into a monument

LOC/LOG/LOQU: word, speech, thought

colloquial: of ordinary or familiar conversation
dialogue: a conversation, esp. in a literary work
elocution: art of clear and expressive speaking
eulogy: a speech or writing in praise of someone
grandiloquent: pompous or inflated in language
loquacious: talkative
prologue: introduction to a poem, play, etc.

LUC/LUM/LUS: light (brightness)

illuminate: to supply or brighten with light

illustrate: to make intelligible with examples or analogies
illustrious: highly distinguished
lackluster: lacking brilliance or radiance
lucid: easily understood, intelligible
luminous: bright, brilliant, glowing
translucent: permitting light to pass through

LUD/LUS: to play
allude: to refer casually or indirectly
delude: to mislead the mind or judgment of, deceive
elude: to avoid capture or escape defection by
illusion: something that deceives by producing a false impression of reality
ludicrous: ridiculous, laughable
prelude: a preliminary to an action, event, etc.

M

MACRO: great, long
macro: broad; large; a single computer command that executes a longer set of commands
macrobiotics: a system intended to prolong life
macrocephalous: having a large head
macrocosm: the universe; a large system that is reflected in at least one of its subsets
macroscopic: large enough to be visible to the naked eye

MAG/MAJ/MAX: big, great
magnanimous: generous in forgiving an insult or injury
magnate: a powerful or influential person
magnify: to increase the apparent size of
magnitude: greatness of size, extent, or dimensions
maxim: an expression of general truth or principle
maximum: the highest amount, value, or degree attained

MAL/MALE: bad, ill, evil, wrong
maladroit: clumsy; tactless
malady: a disorder or disease of the body
malapropism: humorous misuse of a word
malediction: a curse
malfeasance: misconduct or wrongdoing often committed by a public official
malfunction: failure to function properly
malicious: full of or showing malice
malign: to speak harmful untruths about, to slander

MAN/MANU: hand
emancipate: to free from bondage
manifest: readily perceived by the eye or the understanding
manual: operated by hand
manufacture: to make by hand or machinery

MAND/MEND: to command, to order, to entrust
command: to order; an order; control
commend: to give something over to the care of another; to praise
countermand: to retract an order
demand: to strongly ask for; to claim; to require
mandatory: commanded; required
recommend: to praise and suggest the use of; to advise
remand: to send back

MEDI: middle
immediate: nearest; having nothing in between
intermediate: in the middle
mean: average; in the middle
mediate: to serve as a go-between; to try to settle an argument
medieval: related to the Middle Ages
mediocre: neither good nor bad; so-so
medium: size between small and large; a substance or agency that things travel through (as, for example, light travels through air, and news is conveyed by television and newspapers)

MEGA: large, great
megalith: a very big stone
megalomania: a mental condition involving delusions of greatness; an obsession with doing great things
megalopolis: a very large city
megaphone: a device for magnifying the sound of one's voice
megaton: explosive power equal to 1,000 tons of T.N.T.

MICRO: very small
microbe: a very small organism
microcosm: a small system that reflects a larger whole

micron: a millionth of a meter
microorganism: a very small organism
microscope: a device that magnifies very small things for viewing

MIN: small
diminish: to lessen
diminution: the act or process of diminishing
miniature: a copy or model that represents something in greatly reduced size
minute: a unit of time equal to one-sixtieth of an hour
minutiae: small or trivial details

MIN: to project, to hang over
eminent: towering above others; projecting
imminent: about to occur; impending
preeminent: superior to or notable above all others
prominent: projecting outward

MIS: bad, wrong, to hate
misadventure: bad luck; an unlucky accident
misanthrope: one who hates people or humanity
misapply: to use something incorrectly
mischance: bad luck; an unlucky accident
mischief: bad or annoying behavior
misconstrue: to take something in a way that wasn't intended; to understand something incorrectly
misfit: somebody or something that doesn't fit in

MIS/MIT: to send
emissary: a messenger or agent sent to represent the interests of another
intermittent: stopping and starting at intervals
remission: a lessening of intensity or degree
remit: to send money
transmit: to send from one person, thing, or place to another

MISC: mixed
miscellaneous: made up of a variety of parts or ingredients
promiscuous: consisting of diverse and unrelated parts or individuals; indiscriminate

MOB/MOM/MOT/MOV: to move
automobile: a vehicle that moves under its own power; a motorized car
demote: to move downward in an organization
immovable: incapable of being moved; unyielding
locomotion: moving from place to place; the ability to do so
mob: the rabble; a disorderly group of people (from the Latin *mobile vulgus*, meaning "the fickle crowd")
mobile: movable
mobilize: to make ready for movement; to assemble
moment: an instant; importance
momentous: of great importance (originally: having the power to move)
momentum: the force driving a moving object to keep moving; a growing force
motion: movement
motive: a reason for action; what moves a person to do something
motor: a device that makes something move
mutiny: rebellion against authority, esp. by sailors
promote: to move to a higher rank in an organization
remove: to take away; to move away

MOLL: soft
emollient: something that softens or soothes (e.g., a lotion)
mild: gentle; kind
mollify: soothe; soften; calm
mollusk: a phylum of invertebrate animals—including octopuses, squids, oysters, clams, and slugs—with soft bodies

MON/MONO: one
monarchy: rule by a single person
monk: a man in a religious order living apart from society (originally: a religious hermit)
monochord: a musical instrument with a single string
monogram: a design combining multiple letters into one
monograph: a scholarly study of a single subject
monologue: a speech or other dramatic composition recited by one person
monomania: an obsession with a single subject
monotonous: boring; spoken using only one tone

MON/MONIT: to remind, to warn

admonish: to counsel against something; caution

monitor: one that admonishes, cautions, or reminds

monument: a structure, such as a building, tower, or sculpture, erected as a memorial

premonition: forewarning, presentiment

remonstrate: to say or plead in protect, objection, or reproof

summon: to call together; convene

MOR/MORT: death

immortal: not subject to death

morbid: susceptible to preoccupation with unwholesome matters

moribund: dying, decaying

MORPH: shape

amorphous: without definite form; lacking a specific shape

anthropomorphism: attribution of human characteristics to inanimate objects, animals, or natural phenomena

metamorphosis: a transformation, as by magic or sorcery

MULT: many

multiple: many, having many parts; a number containing some quantity of a smaller number without remainder

multiplex: having many parts; a movie theater or other building with many separate units

multiply: to increase; to become many

multitudinous: very many; containing very many; having very many forms

MUT: to change

commute: to substitute; exchange; interchange

immutable: unchangeable, invariable

mutation: the process of being changed

permutation: a complete change; transformation

transmute: to change from one form into another

N

NAT/NAS/NAI/GNA: birth

cognate: related by blood; having a common ancestor

naive: lacking worldliness and sophistication; artless

nascent: starting to develop

native: belonging to one by nature; inborn; innate

natural: present due to nature, not to artificial or man-made means

renaissance: rebirth, esp. referring to culture

NAU/NAV: ship, sailor

astronaut: one who travels in outer space

circumnavigate: to sail all the way around

cosmonaut: one who travels in outer space

nauseous: causing a squeamish feeling (originally: seasickness)

nautical: related to sailing or sailors

naval: related to the navy

nave: the central portion of a church (which resembles the shape of a ship)

navy: a military force consisting of ships and sailors

NIHIL: nothing, none

annihilate: wipe out; reduce to nothing

nihilism: denial of all moral beliefs; denial that existence has any meaning

NOC/NOX: harm

innocent: uncorrupted by evil, malice, or wrongdoing

innocuous: not harmful or injurious

noxious: injurious or harmful to health or morals

obnoxious: highly disagreeable or offensive

NOCT/NOX: night

equinox: one of two times in a year when day and night are equal in length

noctambulant: walking at night; sleepwalking

nocturnal: related to the night; active at night

nocturne: a dreamlike piece of music; a painting set at night

NOM: rule, order

astronomy: the scientific study of the universe beyond the Earth

autonomy: independence, self-governance

economy: the careful or thrifty use of resources, as of income, materials, or labor

gastronomy: the art or science of good eating

taxonomy: the science, laws, or principles of classification

NOM/NYM/NOUN/NOWN: name

acronym: a word formed from the initial letters of a name

anonymous: having an unknown or unacknowledged name

nomenclature: a system of names; systematic naming

nominal: existing in name only; negligible

nominate: to propose by name as a candidate

noun: a word that names a person, place, or thing

renown: fame; reputation

synonym: a word having a meaning similar to that of another word of the same language

NON: not

nonconformist: one who does not conform to a church or other societal institution

nonentity: something that doesn't exist; something that is unimportant

nonpareil: something with no equal

nonpartisan: not affiliated with a political party

NOUNC/NUNC: to announce

announce: to proclaim

pronounce: to articulate

renounce: to give up, especially by formal announcement

NOV/NEO/NOU: new

innovate: to begin or introduce something new

neologism: a newly coined word, phrase, or expression

neophyte: a beginner; a new convert; a new worker

neoplasm: a new growth in the body; a tumor

nouveau riche: one who has lately become rich

novice: a person new to any field or activity

renovate: to restore to an earlier condition

NULL: nothing

annul: to cancel; to make into nothing

nullify: to cancel; to make into nothing

nullity: the condition of being nothing

O

OB: toward, to, against, over

obese: extremely fat, corpulent

obfuscate: to render indistinct or dim; darken

oblique: having a slanting or sloping direction

obsequious: overly submissive

obstinate: stubbornly adhering to an idea, inflexible

obstreperous: noisily defiant, unruly

obstruct: to block or fill with obstacles

obtuse: not sharp, pointed, or acute in any form

OMNI: all

omnibus: an anthology of the works of one author or of writings on related subjects

omnipotent: all powerful

omnipresent: everywhere at one time

omniscient: having infinite knowledge

ONER: burden

exonerate: to free from blame (originally: to relieve of a burden)

onerous: burdensome; difficult

onus: a burden; a responsibility

OSS/OSTE: bone

ossify: to become bone; to harden; to become callous

ossuary: a place where bones are kept; a charnel house

osteopathy: a medical system based on the belief that many illnesses can be traced to issues in the skeletal system

P

PAC/PEAC: peace

appease: to bring peace to

pacifier: something or someone that eases the anger or agitation of

pacify: to ease the anger or agitation of

pact: a formal agreement, as between nations

PALP: to feel

palpable: capable of being felt; tangible

palpate: to feel; to examine by feeling

palpitate: to beat quickly, as the heart; to throb

PAN/PANT: all, everyone

pandemic: widespread, general, universal

panegyric: formal or elaborate praise at an assembly

panoply: a wide-ranging and impressive array or display

panorama: an unobstructed and wide view of an extensive area

pantheon: a public building containing tombs or memorials of the illustrious dead of a nation

PAR: equal

apartheid: any system or caste that separates people according to race, etc.

disparage: to belittle, speak disrespectfully about

disparate: essentially different

par: an equality in value or standing

parity: equally, as in amount, status, or character

PARA: next to, beside

parable: a short, allegorical story designed to illustrate a moral lesson or religious principle

paragon: a model of excellence

parallel: extending in the same direction

paranoid: suffering from a baseless distrust of others

parasite: an organism that lives on or within a plant or animal of another species, from which it obtains nutrients

parody: to imitate for purposes of satire

PAS/PAT/PATH: feeling, suffering, disease

compassion: a feeling of deep sympathy for someone struck by misfortune, accompanied by a desire to alleviate suffering

dispassionate: devoid of personal feeling or bias

empathy: the identification with the feelings or thoughts of others

impassive: showing or feeling no emotion

pathogenic: causing disease

sociopath: a person whose behavior is antisocial and who lacks a sense of moral responsibility

sympathy: harmony or agreement in feeling

PAU/PO/POV/PU: few, little, poor

impoverish: to deplete

paucity: smallness of quantity; scarcity; scantiness

pauper: a person without any personal means of support

poverty: the condition of being poor

puerile: childish, immature

pusillanimous: lacking courage or resolution

PEC: money

impecunious: having no money; penniless

peculation: embezzlement

pecuniary: relating to money

PED: child, education

encyclopedia: book or set of books containing articles on various topics, covering all branches of knowledge or of one particular subject

pedagogue: a teacher

pedant: one who displays learning ostentatiously

pediatrician: a doctor who primarily has children as patients

PED/POD: foot

antipodes: places that are diametrically opposite each other on the globe

expedite: to speed up the progress of

impede: to retard progress by means of obstacles or hindrances

pedal: a foot-operated lever or part used to control

pedestrian: a person who travels on foot

podium: a small platform for an orchestra conductor, speaker, etc.

PEL: to drive, to push

compel: to force; to command

dispel: to drive away; to disperse

expel: to drive out; to banish; to eject

impel: to force; to drive forward

propel: to drive forward

PEN/PUN: to pay, to compensate

penal: of or pertaining to punishment, as for crimes

penalty: a punishment imposed for a violation of law or rule

penance: a punishment undergone to express regret for a sin

penitent: contrite

punitive: serving for, concerned with, or inflicting punishment

PEN/PENE: almost

peninsula: a landmass that is mostly surrounded by water, making it almost an island

penultimate: second-to-last

penumbra: a shaded area between pure shadow and pure light

PEND/PENS: to hang, to weight, to pay

appendage: a limb or other subsidiary part that diverges from the central structure

appendix: supplementary material at the end of a text

compensate: to counterbalance, offset

depend: to rely; to place trust in

indispensable: absolutely necessary, essential, or requisite

stipend: a periodic payment; fixed or regular pay

PER: completely

perforate: to make a way through or into something

perfunctory: performed merely as routine duty

perplex: to cause to be puzzled or bewildered over what is not understood

persistent: lasting or enduring tenaciously

perspicacious: shrewd, astute

pertinacious: resolute, persistent

peruse: to read with thoroughness or care

PERI: around

perimeter: the border or outer boundary of a two-dimensional figure

peripatetic: walking or traveling about; itinerant

periscope: an optical instrument for seeing objects in an obstructed field of vision

PET/PIT: to go, to seek, to strive

appetite: a desire for food or drink

centripetal: moving toward the center

compete: to strive to outdo another

impetuous: characterized by sudden or rash action or emotion

petition: a formally drawn request soliciting some benefit

petulant: showing sudden irritation, esp. over some annoyance

PHIL: love

bibliophile: one who loves or collects books

philatelist: one who loves or collects postage stamps

philology: the study of literary texts to establish their authenticity and determine their meaning

philosopher: one who investigates the truths and principles of being, knowledge, or conduct (originally: lover of wisdom)

PHOB: fear

claustrophobia: fear of enclosed places

hydrophobia: fear of water, which is a symptom of rabies; rabies

phobia: fear; an irrational fear

xenophobia: fear of foreigners; hatred of foreigners

PHON: sound

euphony: the quality of sounding good

megaphone: a device for magnifying the sound of one's voice

phonetics: the study of the sounds used in speech

polyphony: the use of simultaneous melodic lines to produce harmonies in musical compositions

telephone: a device for transmitting sound at a distance

PHOTO: light

photograph: a picture, originally made by exposing chemically treated film to light

photon: a packet of light or other electromagnetic radiation

photosynthesis: a process by which plants create carbohydrates when under light

PLAC: to please

complacent: self-satisfied, unconcerned

complaisant: inclined or disposed to please

implacable: unable to be pleased

placebo: a substance with no pharmacological effect that acts to placate a patient who believes it to be a medicine

placid: pleasantly calm or peaceful

PLE/PLEN: to fill, full

complete: having all parts or elements

deplete: to decrease seriously or exhaust the supply of

implement: an instrument, tool, or utensil for accomplishing work

plenitude: fullness

plethora: excess, overabundance

replete: abundantly supplied

supplement: something added to supply a deficiency

PLEX/PLIC/PLY: to fold, twist, tangle, or bend

complex: composed of many interconnected parts

duplicity: deceitfulness in speech or conduct, double-dealing

implicate: to show to be involved, usually in an incriminating manner

implicit: not expressly stated, implied

replica: any close copy or reproduction

supplicate: to make humble and earnest entreaty

POLY: many

polyandry: the practice of having multiple husbands

polygamy: the practice of having multiple wives

polyglot: someone who speaks many languages

polygon: a figure with many sides

polytheism: belief in many gods

PON/POS/POUND: to put, to place

component: a constituent part, elemental ingredient

expose: to lay open to danger, attack, or harm

expound: to set forth in detail

juxtapose: to place close together or side by side

repository: a receptacle or place where things are deposited

PORT: to carry

deportment: conduct, behavior

disport: to divert or amuse oneself

export: to transmit abroad

import: to bring in from a foreign country

importune: to urge or press with excessive persistence

portable: easily carried

POST: behind, after

post facto: after the fact

posterior: situated at the rear

posterity: future generations

posthumous: after death

POT: to drink

potable: drinkable; safe to drink; a drink

potation: drinking; a drink

potion: a drinkable medicine, poison, or other concoction

PRE: before, in front

precarious: dependent on circumstances beyond one's control

precedent: an act that serves as an example for subsequent situations

precept: a commandment given as a rule of action or conduct

precocious: unusually advanced or mature in mental development or talent

premonition: a feeling of anticipation over a future event

presentiment: foreboding

PREHEND/PRISE: to take, to get, to seize

apprehend: to take into custody

comprise: to include or contain

enterprise: a project undertaken

reprehensible: deserving rebuke or censure

reprisals: retaliation against an enemy

surprise: to strike with an unexpected feeling of wonder or astonishment

PRI/PRIM: first

primary: first; most important

primal: original; most important

prime: first in quality; best

primeval: ancient; going back to the first age of the world

pristine: original; like new; unspoiled; pure

PRO: in front, before, much, for

problem: a difficult question (originally: one put before another for solution)

proceed: to go forward

profuse: spending or giving freely

prolific: highly fruitful

propound: to set forth for consideration

proselytize: to convert or attempt to recruit

provident: having or showing foresight

PROB: to prove, to test

approbation: praise, consideration

opprobrium: the disgrace incurred by shameful conduct

probe: to search or examine thoroughly

probity: honesty, high-mindedness

reprobate: a depraved or wicked person

PROP/PROX: near

approximate: very near; close to being accurate

proximate: nearby; coming just before or just after

proximity: nearness; distance

PROT/PROTO: first

protagonist: the main character in a play or story

protocol: diplomatic etiquette; a system of proper conduct; the original record of a treaty or other negotiation

prototype: the first version of an invention, on which later models are based

protozoan: belonging to a group of single-celled animals, which came before more complex animals

PSEUD/PSEUDO: false

pseudonym: a false name; a pen name

pseudopod: part of a single-celled organism that can be stuck out (like a foot) and used to move around

pseudoscience: false science; something believed to be based on the scientific method but that actually is not

PUG: to fight

impugn: to challenge as false

pugilist: a fighter or boxer

pugnacious: to quarrel or fight readily

repugnant: objectionable or offensive

PUNC/PUNG/POIGN: to point, to prick, to pierce

compunction: a feeling of uneasiness for doing wrong

expunge: to erase, eliminate completely

point: a sharp or tapering end

punctilious: strict or exact in the observance of formalities

puncture: the act of piercing

pungent: caustic or sharply expressive

PYR: fire

pyre: a bonfire, usually for burning a dead body

pyromania: an urge to start fires

pyrosis: heartburn

pyrotechnics: fireworks

Q

QUAD/QUAR/QUAT: four

quadrant: a quarter of a circle; a 90-degree arc

quadrille: a square dance involving four couples

quadruple: four times as many

quadruplets: four children born in one birth

quart: one fourth of a gallon

quaternary: the number four; the fourth in a series

QUE/QUIS: to seek

acquire: to come into possession of

conquest: the act gaining control by force

exquisite: of special beauty or charm

inquisitive: given to research, eager for knowledge

perquisite: a gratuity, tip

querulous: full of complaints

query: a question, inquiry

QUIE/QUIT: quiet, rest

acquiesce: to comply, give in

disquiet: lack of calm or peace

quiescence: the condition of being at rest, still, inactive

quiet: making little or no sound

tranquil: free from commotion or tumult

QUIN/QUINT: five

quinquennial: a five-year period; a fifth anniversary

quintessence: the essential part of something (originally: the "fifth essence," which was believed to permeate everything and be what stars and planets were made of)

quintuple: five times as many

R

RACI/RADI: root

deracinate: to uproot

eradicate: to uproot; to wipe out

radical: pertaining to roots; questioning everything, even basic beliefs; going to root causes; thorough

radish: a root vegetable

RAMI: branch

ramification: a branch; an offshoot; a collection of branches; a consequence

ramiform: branchlike

RE: back, again

recline: to lean back; to lie down

regain: to gain again; to take back

remain: to stay behind; to be left; to continue to be

reorganize: to organize again

request: to ask (originally: to seek again)

RECT: straight, right

correct: to set right

direct: to guide; to put straight

erect: upright; starting up straight

rectangle: a four-sided figure in which every angle is a right angle

rectitude: moral uprightness; moral straightness

REG: king, rule

interregnum: a period between kings

realm: a kingdom; a domain

regal: kingly; royal

regent: one who serves on behalf of a king; one who rules

regicide: killing a king; one who kills a king

regiment: a body of troops in an army; to form into such a body; to subject to strict rule

regular: having a structure following some rule; orderly; normally used; average

RETRO: backward

retroactive: extending to things that happened in the past

retrofit: to install newer parts into an older device or structure

retrograde: moving backward; appearing to move backward

retrospective: looking back at the past

RID/RIS: to laugh

derision: the act of mockery

risible: causing laughter

ROG: to ask

abrogate: to abolish by formal means

arrogant: making claims to superior importance or rights

arrogate: to claim unwarrantably or presumptuously

derogatory: belittling, disparaging

interrogate: to ask questions of, esp. formally

surrogate: a person appointed to act for another

RUB/RUD: red

rouge: a red powder used as makeup

rubella: German measles; a disease marked by red spots

rubicund: reddish; rosy-cheeked

rubric: a rule; a guide for scoring tests; a heading in a book set in red letters

russet: reddish-brown; a coarse cloth, usually reddish-brown; a type of apple or pear, typically reddish-brown

RUD: crude

erudite: scholarly; learned (that is, trained out of crudeness)

rude: uncivilized; impolite

rudimentary: undeveloped; related to rudiments

rudiments: first principles; imperfect first step of one's training

S

SACR/SANCT: holy

execrable: abominable

sacrament: something regarded as possessing sacred character

sacred: devoted or dedicated to a deity or religious purpose

sacrifice: the offering of some living or inanimate thing to a deity in homage

sacrilege: the violation of anything sacred

sanctify: to make holy

sanction: authoritative permission or approval

SAG/SAP/SAV: taste, thinking, discerning

insipid: tasteless

sagacious: perceptive; discerning; insightful

sage: wise

sapient: wise

savant: a learned person

savor: taste; to enjoy flavors

SAL/SIL/SAULT/SULT: to leap, to jump

assault: a sudden or violent attack

desultory: at random, unmethodical

exult: to show or feel triumphant joy

insolent: boldly rude or disrespectful

insult: to treat with contemptuous rudeness

resilient: able to spring back to an original form after compression

salient: prominent or conspicuous

somersault: to roll the body end over end, making a complete revolution

SAL: salt

salary: payment for services (originally: money for Roman soldiers to buy salt)

saline: containing salt; salty

SALU: health

salubrious: healthful

salutary: healthful

salute: to greet; a gesture of greeting (originally: to wish good health)

SALV: to save

salvage: to save; something saved or recovered

salvation: being saved

savior: one who saves

SAN: healthy

sane: mentally healthy

sanitarium: a place of healing

sanitary: promoting health; related to conditions that affect health, such as cleanliness

SANG: blood

consanguinity: being related by blood

sanguinary: bloody; bloodthirsty

sanguine: hopeful; confident (from the "sanguine humor," which was believed to be associated with those traits)

SAT: enough

assets: property; possessions (originally: enough property to cover one's debts)

dissatisfied: feeling that one does not have enough

sate: to fill

satisfy: to meet one's desires; to meet an obligation; to provide with enough

saturate: to fill completely; to entirely satisfy

SCI: to know

conscience: the inner sense of what is right or wrong, impelling one toward right action

conscious: aware of one's own existence

omniscient: knowing everything

prescient: having knowledge of things before they happen

unconscionable: unscrupulous

SCRIBE/SCRIPT: to write

ascribe: to credit or assign, as to a cause or course

circumscribe: to draw a line around

conscription: draft

describe: to tell or depict in words

postscript: any addition or supplement

proscribe: to condemn as harmful or odious

scribble: to write hastily or carelessly

script: handwriting

transcript: a written or typed copy

SE: apart, away

secede: to withdraw formally from an association

sedition: incitement of discontent or rebellion against a government

seduce: to lead astray

segregate: to separate or set apart from others

select: to choose in preference to another

separate: to keep apart, divide

sequester: to remove or withdraw into solitude or retirement

SEC/SEQU/SUE/SUI: to follow

non sequitur: an inference or a conclusion that does not follow from the premises

obsequious: fawning

prosecute: to seek to enforce by legal process

pursue: to chase after

second: next after the first

sequence: the following of one thing after another

suite: a series; a set (originally: a train of followers)

SED/SESS/SID: to sit, to settle

assiduous: diligent, persistent, hardworking (literally, "sitting down" to business)

dissident: disagreeing, as in opinion or attitude (literally, "sitting apart")

insidious: intended to entrap or beguile; lying in wait to entrap

preside: to exercise management or control; to sit in the leader's chair

resident: a person who lives in a place

residual: remaining, leftover

sediment: the matter that settles to the bottom of a liquid

session: a meeting at which people sit together in discussion

SEM: seed, to sow

disseminate: to spread; to scatter around

semen: seed (of male animals)

seminary: a school, esp. for religious training (originally: a place for raising plants)

SEMI: half

semicircle: half a circle

semiconscious: only partly conscious; half awake

SEN: old

senate: the highest legislative body (from "council of elders")

senescent: getting old

senile: relating to old age; experiencing memory loss or other age-related mental impairments

sire: a title for a king; a father (originally: an important person, an old man)

SENS/SENT: to feel, to be aware

dissent: to differ in opinion, esp. from the majority

insensate: without feeling or sensitivity

presentiment: a feeling that something is about to happen

resent: to feel or show displeasure

sense: any of the faculties by which humans and animals perceive stimuli originating outside the body

sensory: of or pertaining to the senses or sensation

sentiment: an attitude or feeling toward something

sentinel: a person or thing that stands watch

SIN/SINU: bend, fold, curve

insinuate: to introduce in sneaky or winding ways

sinuous: moving in a bending or wavy manner

sinus: a curved or irregularly shaped cavity in the body, such as those related to the nostrils

SOL: alone

desolate: deserted; laid waste; left alone

isolate: to set apart from others

soliloquize: talk to oneself; talk onstage as if to oneself

solipsism: the belief that the only thing that really exists, or can really be known, is oneself

solitude: the state of being alone

SOL: to loosen, to free

absolution: forgiveness for wrongdoing

dissolute: indifferent to moral restraints

dissolution: the act or process of dissolving into parts or elements

dissolve: to make a solution of, as by mixing in a liquid

resolution: a formal expression of opinion or intention made

soluble: capable of being dissolved or liquefied

SOL: sun

parasol: an umbrella that protects from the sun

solar: related to the sun

solarium: a sunroom; a room with windows for taking in the sun

solstice: one of two days when the sun reaches its highest point at noon and seems to stand still

SOMN: sleep

insomnia: inability to sleep

somnambulist: a sleepwalker

somniferous: sleep-inducing

somniloquist: one who talks while asleep

somnolent: sleep-inducing; sleepy; drowsy

SOPH: wisdom

philosopher: one who studies logic, beauty, truth, etc.; one who seeks wisdom

sophism: a superficially appealing but fallacious argument

sophisticated: complex; worldly; experienced

SOURC/SURG/SURRECT: to rise

insurgent: rising up in revolution; rushing in

insurrection: rising up in armed rebellion

resurrection: coming back to life; rising again

source: where something comes from (such as spring water rising out of the ground)

surge: to rise up forcefully, as ocean waves

SPEC/SPIC: to look, to see

circumspect: watchful and discreet, cautious

conspicuous: easily seen or noticed; readily observable

perspective: one's mental view of facts, ideas, and their interrelationships

perspicacious: having keen mental perception and understanding

retrospective: contemplative of past situations

specious: deceptively attractive

spectrum: a broad range of related things that form a continuous series

speculation: the contemplation or consideration of some subject

SPIR: breath

aspire: to desire; to pant for (originally: to breathe on)

expire: to breathe out; to breathe one's last; to come to an end

spirit: the breath of life; the soul; an incorporeal supernatural being; an outlook; a lively quality

STA/STI: to stand, to be in place

apostasy: renunciation of an object of one's previous loyalty

constitute: to make up

destitute: without means of subsistence

obstinate: stubbornly adhering to a purpose, opinion, or course of action

stasis: the state of equilibrium or inactivity caused by opposing equal forces

static: of bodies or forces at rest or in equilibrium

STRICT/STRING/STRAN: to tighten, to bind

astringent: causing to tighten

constrain: to confine; to bind within certain limits

restriction: a limitation

strangle: to kill by suffocation, usually by tightening a cord or one's hand around the throat

SUA: sweet, pleasing, to urge

assuage: to make less severe, ease, relieve

dissuade: to deter; to advise against

persuade: to encourage; to convince

suave: smoothly agreeable or polite; sweet

SUB/SUP: below, under

subliminal: existing or operating below the threshold of consciousness

submissive: inclined or ready to submit

subsidiary: serving to assist or supplement

subterfuge: an artifice or expedient used to evade a rule

subtle: thin, tenuous, or rarefied

suppose: to put down as a hypothesis; to use as the underlying basis of an argument; to assume

SUMM: highest, total

consummate: highly qualified; complete; perfect

sum: total; amount of money

summary: concise statement of the total findings on a subject; comprehensive

summit: highest point

SUPER/SUR: over, above

supercilious: arrogant, haughty, condescending

superfluous: extra, more than necessary

superlative: the highest kind or order

supersede: to replace in power, as by another person or thing

surmount: to get over or across, to prevail

surpass: to go beyond in amount, extent, or degree

surveillance: a watch kept over someone or something

SYM/SYN: together

symbiosis: living together in a mutually beneficial relationship

symmetry: balanced proportions; having opposite parts that mirror one another

sympathy: affinity; feeling affected by what happens to another

symposium: a meeting at which ideas are discussed (originally: a party at which people drink together)

synonym: a word that means the same thing as another

synthesis: combining things to create a new whole

T

TAC/TIC: to be silent

reticent: disposed to be silent or not to speak freely

tacit: unspoken understanding

taciturn: uncommunicative

TACT/TAG/TAM/TANG: to touch

contact: to touch; to get in touch

contagious: able to spread by contact, as disease

contaminate: to corrupt, taint, or otherwise damage the integrity of something by contact or mixture

contiguous: directly touching; sharing a boundary

intact: untouched; whole

intangible: unable to be touched

tactile: pertaining to touch; touchable

TAIN/TEN/TENT/TIN: to hold
abstention: the act of refraining voluntarily
detain: to keep from proceeding
pertain: to have reference or relation
pertinacious: persistent, stubborn
sustenance: nourishment, means of livelihood
tenable: capable of being held, maintained, or defended
tenacious: holding fast
tenure: the holding or possessing of anything

TEND/TENS/TENT/TENU: to stretch, to thin
attenuate: to weaken or reduce in force
contentious: quarrelsome, disagreeable, belligerent
distend: to expand by stretching
extenuating: making less serious by offering excuses
tendentious: having a predisposition toward a point of view
tension: the act of stretching or straining
tentative: of the nature of, or done as a trial, attempt

TEST: to bear witness
attest: bear witness
contest: to dispute (from bringing a lawsuit by calling witnesses)
detest: to despise; to hate (originally: to curse something by calling upon God to witness it)
protest: a dissent; a declaration, esp. of disagreement
testament: a statement of a person's wishes for the disposal of his or her property after death; a will
testify: bear witness

THEO: god
apotheosis: glorification, glorified ideal
atheist: one who does not believe in a deity or divine system
theocracy: a form of government in which a deity is recognized as the supreme ruler
theology: the study of divine things and the divine faith

THERM: heat
thermal: relating to heat; retaining heat
thermometer: a device for measuring heat
thermonuclear: relating to a nuclear reaction that takes place at high temperatures
thermostat: a device for regulating heat

TIM: fear
intimidate: to strike fear into; to make fearful
timid: fearful; shy

TOR/TORQ/TORT: to twist
contort: to twist; to distort
distort: to pull out of shape, often by twisting; to twist or misrepresent facts
extort: to wring money, property, or services out of somebody using threats or force
torch: a portable flame used for light (perhaps derived from hemp twisted around sticks, then dipped in pitch)
torque: twisting force; a force that creates rotation
tort: a wrongful act (other than breach of contract) that legally entitles one to damages
torture: to inflict pain (including by twisting instruments like the rack or wheel)

TORP: stiff, numb
torpedo: a explosive weapon used to sink ships (originally: a fish—the electric ray—that could shock victims to numbness)
torpid: numbed; sluggish
torpor: numbness; listlessness; apathy

TOX: poison
antitoxin: an antibody that counteracts a given poison
intoxication: being poisoned; drunkenness
toxic: poisonous

TRACT: to drag, to pull, to draw
abstract: to draw or pull away, remove
attract: to draw either by physical force or by an appeal to emotions or senses
contract: a legally binding document
detract: to take away from, esp. a positive thing
protract: to prolong, draw out, extend
tractable: easily managed or controlled
tractor: a powerful vehicle used to pull farm machinery

TRANS: across, beyond
intransigent: refusing to agree or compromise
transaction: the act of carrying on or conduct to a conclusion or settlement
transcendent: going beyond ordinary limits
transgress: to violate a law, command, or moral code

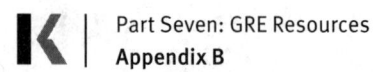

transition: a change from one way of being to another

transparent: easily seen through, recognized, or detected

U

ULT: last, beyond

penultimate: second-to-last

ulterior: beyond what is immediately present; future; beyond what is stated; hidden

ultimate: last; final

ultimatum: final offer; final terms

ultraviolet: beyond the violet end of the spectrum

UMBR: shadow

adumbrate: to foreshadow; to sketch; to overshadow

penumbra: a shaded area between pure shadow and pure light

somber: gloomy; darkened

umbrage: shade; shadow; displeasure; resentment

umbrella: a device providing shade from the sun or protection from rain

UN: not

unseen: not seen

unusual: not usual; exceptional; strange

UND: wave

abound: to be plentiful; to overflow (from water flowing in waves)

inundate: to flood

undulate: to move in a wavelike way

UNI/UN: one

reunion: a meeting that brings people back together

unanimous: of one mind; in complete accord

unicorn: a mythical animal with a single horn

uniform: of one kind; consistent

universe: all things considered as one whole

URB: city

suburb: a residential area just outside a city; an outlying area of a city

urban: relating to a city

urbane: polite; refined; polished (considered characteristic of those in cities)

urbanization: the process of an area becoming more like a city

US/UT: to use

abuse: to use wrongly or improperly

usage: a customary way of doing something

usurp: to seize and hold

utilitarian: efficient, functional, useful

V

VAIL/VAL: strength, use, worth

ambivalent: being caught between contradictory feelings of equal power or worth

avail: to have force; to be useful; to be of value

convalescent: recovering strength; healing

equivalent: of equal worth, strength, or use

evaluate: to determine the worth of

invalid: having no force or strength; void

valediction: a farewell (from wishing that someone be well; i.e., that someone have strength)

valid: having force; legally binding; effective; useful

value: worth

VEN/VENT: to come or to move toward

adventitious: accidental

contravene: to come into conflict with

convene: to assemble for some public purpose

intervene: to come between disputing factions, mediate

venturesome: showing a disposition to undertake risks

VER: truth

aver: to affirm, to declare to be true

veracious: habitually truthful

verdict: a judgment or decision

verisimilitude: the appearance or semblance of truth

verity: truthfulness

VERB: word

proverb: an adage; a byword; a short, commonly known saying

verbatim: exactly as stated; word-for-word

verbose: wordy

verbiage: excessive use of words; diction

VERD: green

verdant: green with vegetation; inexperienced

verdure: fresh, rich vegetation

VERS/VERT: to turn
aversion: dislike
avert: to turn away from
controversy: a public dispute involving a matter of opinion
diverse: of a different kind, form, character
extrovert: an outgoing person
inadvertent: unintentional
introvert: a person concerned primarily with inner thoughts and feelings
revert: to return to a former habit

VI: life
convivial: sociable
joie de vivre: joy of life (French expression)
viable: capable of living
vivacity: the quality of being lively, animated, spirited
vivid: strikingly bright or intense

VID/VIS: to see
adviser: one who gives counsel
evident: plain or clear to the sight or understanding
survey: to view in a general or comprehensive way
video: elements pertaining to the transmission or reception of an image
vista: a view or prospect

VIL: base, mean
revile: to criticize with harsh language
vile: loathsome, unpleasant
vilify: to slander, to defame

VIRU: poison
virulent: acrimonious; very bitter; very poisonous
viruliferous: containing a virus
virus: a submicroscopic agent that infects an organism and causes disease

VOC/VOK: call, word
advocate: to support or urge by argument
avocation: something one does in addition to a principle occupation
convoke: to call together
equivocate: to use ambiguous or unclear expressions
invoke: to call on a deity
vocabulary: the stock of words used by or known to a particular person or group
vocation: a particular occupation
vociferous: crying out noisily

VOL: wish
benevolent: characterized by or expressing goodwill
malevolent: characterized by or expressing bad will
volition: free choice, free will; act of choosing
voluntary: undertaken of one's own accord or by free choice

VOLU/VOLV: to roll, to turn
convolution: a twisting or folding
evolve: to develop naturally; literally, to unfold or unroll
revolt: to rebel; to turn against those in authority
revolve: to rotate; to turn around
voluble: easily turning; fluent; changeable
volume: a book (originally: a scroll); size or dimensions (originally: of a book)

VOR: to eat
carnivorous: meat-eating
omnivorous: eating or absorbing everything
voracious: having a great appetite

Common GRE-Level Words in Context

The GRE tests the same kinds of words over and over again. Here you will find some common GRE-Level words with their definitions in context to help you to remember them. If you see a word that's unfamiliar to you, take a moment to study the definition and, most importantly, reread the sentence with the word's definition in mind.

Remember: learning vocabulary words in context is one of the best ways for your brain to retain the words' meanings. A broader vocabulary will serve you well on all four GRE Verbal question types and will also be extremely helpful in the Analytical Writing section.

A

ABATE: to reduce in amount, degree, or severity
As the hurricane's force ABATED, the winds dropped and the sea became calm.

ABSCOND: to leave secretly
The patron ABSCONDED from the restaurant without paying his bill by sneaking out the back door.

ABSTAIN: to choose not to do something
She ABSTAINED from choosing a mouthwatering dessert from the tray.

ABYSS: an extremely deep hole
The submarine dove into the ABYSS to chart the previously unseen depths.

ADULTERATE: to make impure
The chef made his ketchup last longer by ADULTERATING it with water.

ADVOCATE: to speak in favor of
The vegetarian ADVOCATED a diet containing no meat.

AESTHETIC: concerning the appreciation of beauty
Followers of the AESTHETIC Movement regarded the pursuit of beauty as the only true purpose of art.

AGGRANDIZE: to increase in power, influence, and reputation
The supervisor sought to AGGRANDIZE herself by claiming that the achievements of her staff were actually her own.

ALLEVIATE: to make more bearable
Taking aspirin helps to ALLEVIATE a headache.

AMALGAMATE: to combine; to mix together
Giant Industries AMALGAMATED with Mega Products to form Giant-Mega Products Incorporated.

AMBIGUOUS: doubtful or uncertain; able to be interpreted several ways
The directions she gave were so AMBIGUOUS that we disagreed on which way to turn.

AMELIORATE: to make better; to improve
The doctor was able to AMELIORATE the patient's suffering using painkillers.

ANACHRONISM: something out of place in time
The aged hippie used ANACHRONISTIC phrases, like "groovy" and "far out," that had not been popular for years.

ANALOGOUS: similar or alike in some way; equivalent to
In the Newtonian construct for explaining the existence of God, the universe is ANALOGOUS to a mechanical timepiece, the creation of a divinely intelligent "clockmaker."

ANOMALY: deviation from what is normal
Albino animals may display too great an ANOMALY in their coloring to attract normally colored mates.

ANTAGONIZE: to annoy or provoke to anger
The child discovered that he could ANTAGONIZE the cat by pulling its tail.

ANTIPATHY: extreme dislike
The ANTIPATHY between the French and the English regularly erupted into open warfare.

APATHY: lack of interest or emotion
The APATHY of voters is so great that less than half the people who are eligible to vote actually bother to do so.

ARBITRATE: to judge a dispute between two opposing parties
Since the couple could not come to an agreement, a judge was forced to ARBITRATE their divorce proceedings.

ARCHAIC: ancient, old-fashioned
Her ARCHAIC Commodore computer could not run the latest software.

ARDOR: intense and passionate feeling
Bishop's ARDOR for the landscape was evident when he passionately described the beauty of the scenic Hudson Valley.

ARTICULATE: able to speak clearly and expressively
She is such an ARTICULATE defender of labor that unions are among her strongest supporters.

ASSUAGE: to make something unpleasant less severe
Serena used aspirin to ASSUAGE her pounding headache.

ATTENUATE: to reduce in force or degree; to weaken
The Bill of Rights ATTENUATED the traditional power of governments to change laws at will.

AUDACIOUS: fearless and daring
Her AUDACIOUS nature allowed her to fulfill her dream of skydiving.

AUSTERE: severe or stern in appearance; undecorated

The lack of decoration makes military barracks seem AUSTERE to the civilian eye.

B

BANAL: predictable, clichéd, boring

He used BANAL phrases like "have a nice day" and "another day, another dollar."

BOLSTER: to support; to prop up

The presence of giant footprints BOLSTERED the argument that Sasquatch was in the area.

BOMBASTIC: pompous in speech and manner

The ranting of the radio talk-show host was mostly BOMBASTIC; his boasting and outrageous claims had no basis in fact.

C

CACOPHONY: harsh, jarring noise

The junior high orchestra created an almost unbearable CACOPHONY as they tried to tune their instruments.

CANDID: impartial and honest in speech

The observations of a child can be charming since they are CANDID and unpretentious.

CAPRICIOUS: changing one's mind quickly and often

Queen Elizabeth I was quite CAPRICIOUS; her courtiers could never be sure which of their number would catch her fancy.

CASTIGATE: to punish or criticize harshly

Many Americans are amazed at how harshly the authorities in Singapore CASTIGATE perpetrators of what would be considered minor crimes in the United States.

CATALYST: something that brings about a change in something else

The imposition of harsh taxes was the CATALYST that finally brought on the revolution.

CAUSTIC: biting in wit

Dorothy Parker gained her reputation for CAUSTIC wit from her cutting, yet clever, insults.

CHAOS: great disorder or confusion

In many religious traditions, God created an ordered universe from CHAOS.

CHAUVINIST: someone prejudiced in favor of a group to which he or she belongs

The attitude that men are inherently superior to women and therefore must be obeyed is common among male CHAUVINISTS.

CHICANERY: deception by means of craft or guile

Dishonest used car salespeople often use CHICANERY to sell their beat-up old cars.

COGENT: convincing and well reasoned

Swayed by the COGENT argument of the defense, the jury had no choice but to acquit the defendant.

CONDONE: to overlook, pardon, or disregard

Some theorists believe that failing to prosecute minor crimes is the same as CONDONING an air of lawlessness.

CONVOLUTED: intricate and complicated

Although many people bought *A Brief History of Time,* few could follow its CONVOLUTED ideas and theories.

CORROBORATE: to provide supporting evidence

Fingerprints CORROBORATED the witness's testimony that he saw the defendant in the victim's apartment.

CREDULOUS: too trusting; gullible

Although some four-year-olds believe in the Easter Bunny, only the most CREDULOUS nine-year-olds still believe in him.

CRESCENDO: steadily increasing volume or force

The CRESCENDO of tension became unbearable as Evel Knievel prepared to jump his motorcycle over the school buses.

D

DECORUM: appropriateness of behavior or conduct; propriety

The countess complained that the vulgar peasants lacked the DECORUM appropriate for a visit to the palace.

DEFERENCE: respect, courtesy

The respectful young law clerk treated the Supreme Court justice with the utmost DEFERENCE.

DERIDE: to speak of or treat with contempt; to mock

The awkward child was often DERIDED by his "cooler" peers.

DESICCATE: to dry out thoroughly
After a few weeks of lying on the desert's baking sands, the cow's carcass became completely DESICCATED.

DESULTORY: jumping from one thing to another; disconnected
Diane had a DESULTORY academic record; she had changed majors 12 times in three years.

DIATRIBE: an abusive, condemnatory speech
The trucker bellowed a DIATRIBE at the driver who had cut him off.

DIFFIDENT: lacking self-confidence
Steve's DIFFIDENT manner during the job interview stemmed from his nervous nature and lack of experience in the field.

DILATE: to make larger; to expand
When you enter a darkened room, the pupils of your eyes DILATE to let in more light.

DILATORY: intended to delay
The congressman used DILATORY measures to delay the passage of the bill.

DILETTANTE: someone with an amateurish and superficial interest in a topic
Jerry's friends were such DILETTANTES that they seemed to have new jobs and hobbies every week.

DIRGE: a funeral hymn or mournful speech
Melville wrote the poem "A DIRGE for James McPherson" for the funeral of a Union general who was killed in 1864.

DISABUSE: to set right; to free from error
Galileo's observations DISABUSED scholars of the notion that the Sun revolved around the Earth.

DISCERN: to perceive; to recognize
It is easy to DISCERN the difference between butter and butter-flavored topping.

DISPARATE: fundamentally different; entirely unlike
Although the twins appear to be identical physically, their personalities are DISPARATE.

DISSEMBLE: to present a false appearance; to disguise one's real intentions or character
The villain could DISSEMBLE to the police no longer—he admitted the deed and tore up the floor to reveal the body of the old man.

DISSONANCE: a harsh and disagreeable combination, often of sounds
Cognitive DISSONANCE is the inner conflict produced when long-standing beliefs are contradicted by new evidence.

DOGMA: a firmly held opinion, often a religious belief
Linus's central DOGMA was that children who believed in the Great Pumpkin would be rewarded.

DOGMATIC: dictatorial in one's opinions
The dictator was DOGMATIC—he, and only he, was right.

DUPE: to deceive; a person who is easily deceived
Bugs Bunny was able to DUPE Elmer Fudd by dressing up as a lady rabbit.

E

ECLECTIC: selecting from or made up from a variety of sources
Budapest's architecture is an ECLECTIC mix of Eastern and Western styles.

EFFICACY: effectiveness
The EFFICACY of penicillin was unsurpassed when it was first introduced; the drug completely eliminated almost all bacterial infections for which it was administered.

ELEGY: a sorrowful poem or speech
Although Thomas Gray's "ELEGY Written in a Country Churchyard" is about death and loss, it urges its readers to endure this life and to trust in spirituality.

ELOQUENT: persuasive and moving, especially in speech
The Gettysburg Address is moving not only because of its lofty sentiments but also because of its ELOQUENT words.

EMULATE: to copy; to try to equal or excel
The graduate student sought to EMULATE his professor in every way, copying not only how she taught but also how she conducted herself outside of class.

ENERVATE: to reduce in strength
The guerrillas hoped that a series of surprise attacks would ENERVATE the regular army.

ENGENDER: to produce, cause, or bring about
His fear and hatred of clowns was ENGENDERED when he witnessed the death of his father at the hands of a clown.

ENIGMA: a puzzle; a mystery
Speaking in riddles and dressed in old robes, the artist gained a reputation as something of an ENIGMA.

ENUMERATE: to count, list, or itemize
Moses returned from the mountain with tablets on which the commandments were ENUMERATED.

EPHEMERAL: lasting a short time
The lives of mayflies seem EPHEMERAL to us, since the flies' average life span is a matter of hours.

EQUIVOCAL: open to more than one interpretation; misleading
Asked a pointed question, the politician nevertheless gave an EQUIVOCAL answer.

EQUIVOCATE: to use expressions of double meaning in order to mislead
When faced with criticism of her policies, the politician EQUIVOCATED and left all parties thinking she agreed with them.

ERRATIC: wandering and unpredictable
The plot seemed predictable until it suddenly took a series of ERRATIC turns that surprised the audience.

ERUDITE: learned, scholarly, bookish
The annual meeting of philosophy professors was a gathering of the most ERUDITE, well-published individuals in the field.

ESOTERIC: known or understood by only a few
Only a handful of experts are knowledgeable about the ESOTERIC world of particle physics.

ESTIMABLE: admirable
Most people consider it ESTIMABLE that Mother Teresa spent her life helping the poor of India.

EULOGY: speech in praise of someone
His best friend gave the EULOGY, outlining his many achievements and talents.

EUPHEMISM: use of an inoffensive word or phrase in place of a more distasteful one
The funeral director preferred to use the EUPHEMISM "sleeping" instead of the word "dead."

EXACERBATE: to make worse
It is unwise to take aspirin to try to relieve heartburn; instead of providing relief, the drug will only EXACERBATE the problem.

EXCULPATE: to clear from blame; prove innocent
The adversarial legal system is intended to convict those who are guilty and to EXCULPATE those who are innocent.

EXIGENT: urgent; requiring immediate action
The patient was losing blood so rapidly that it was EXIGENT to stop the source of the bleeding.

EXONERATE: to clear of blame
The fugitive was EXONERATED when another criminal confessed to committing the crime.

EXPLICIT: clearly stated or shown; forthright in expression
The owners of the house left a list of EXPLICIT instructions detailing their house sitter's duties, including a schedule for watering the house plants.

F

FANATICAL: acting excessively enthusiastic; filled with extreme, unquestioned devotion
The stormtroopers were FANATICAL in their devotion to the emperor, readily sacrificing their lives for him.

FAWN: to grovel
The understudy FAWNED over the director in hopes of being cast in the part on a permanent basis.

FERVID: intensely emotional; feverish
The fans of Maria Callas were unusually FERVID, doing anything to catch a glimpse of the great opera singer.

FLORID: excessively decorated or embellished
The palace had been decorated in a FLORID style; every surface had been carved and gilded.

FOMENT: to arouse or incite
The protesters tried to FOMENT feeling against the war through their speeches and demonstrations.

FRUGALITY: a tendency to be thrifty or cheap
Scrooge McDuck's FRUGALITY was so great that he accumulated enough wealth to fill a giant storehouse with money.

G

GARRULOUS: tending to talk a lot
The GARRULOUS parakeet distracted its owner with its continuous talking.

GREGARIOUS: outgoing, sociable
She was so GREGARIOUS that when she found herself alone, she felt quite sad.

GUILE: deceit or trickery
Since he was not fast enough to catch the roadrunner on foot, the coyote resorted to GUILE in an effort to trap his enemy.

GULLIBLE: easily deceived
The con man pretended to be a bank officer so as to fool GULLIBLE bank customers into giving him their account information.

H

HOMOGENEOUS (or HOMOGENOUS): of a similar kind
The class was fairly HOMOGENEOUS, since almost all of the students were senior journalism majors.

I

ICONOCLAST: one who opposes established beliefs, customs, and institutions
His lack of regard for traditional beliefs soon established him as an ICONOCLAST.

IMPERTURBABLE: not capable of being disturbed
The counselor had so much experience dealing with distraught children that she seemed IMPERTURBABLE, even when faced with the wildest tantrums.

IMPERVIOUS: impossible to penetrate; incapable of being affected
A good raincoat will be IMPERVIOUS to moisture.

IMPETUOUS: quick to act without thinking
It is not good for an investment broker to be IMPETUOUS, since much thought should be given to all the possible options.

IMPLACABLE: unable to be calmed down or made peaceful
His rage at the betrayal was so great that he remained IMPLACABLE for weeks.

INCHOATE: not fully formed; disorganized
The ideas expressed in Nietzsche's mature work also appear in an INCHOATE form in his earliest writing.

INGENUOUS: showing innocence or childlike simplicity
She was so INGENUOUS that her friends feared that her innocence and trustfulness would be exploited when she visited the big city.

INIMICAL: hostile, unfriendly
Even though the children had grown up together, they were INIMICAL to each other at school.

INNOCUOUS: harmless
Some snakes are poisonous, but most species are INNOCUOUS and pose no danger to humans.

INSIPID: lacking interest or flavor
The critic claimed that the painting was INSIPID, containing no interesting qualities at all.

INTRANSIGENT: uncompromising; refusing to be reconciled
The professor was INTRANSIGENT on the deadline, insisting that everyone turn the assignment in at the same time.

INUNDATE: to overwhelm; to cover with water
The tidal wave INUNDATED Atlantis, which was lost beneath the water.

IRASCIBLE: easily made angry
Attila the Hun's IRASCIBLE and violent nature made all who dealt with him fear for their lives.

L

LACONIC: using few words
She was a LACONIC poet who built her reputation on using words as sparingly as possible.

LAMENT: to express sorrow; to grieve
The children continued to LAMENT the death of the goldfish weeks after its demise.

LAUD: to give praise; to glorify
Parades and fireworks were staged to LAUD the success of the rebels.

LAVISH: to give unsparingly (v.); extremely generous or extravagant (adj.)
She LAVISHED the puppy with so many treats that it soon became overweight and spoiled.

LETHARGIC: acting in an indifferent or slow, sluggish manner

The clerk was so LETHARGIC that, even when the store was slow, he always had a long line in front of him.

LOQUACIOUS: talkative
She was naturally LOQUACIOUS, which was a problem in situations in which listening was more important than talking.

LUCID: clear and easily understood
The explanations were written in a simple and LUCID manner so that students were immediately able to apply what they learned.

LUMINOUS: bright, brilliant, glowing
The park was bathed in LUMINOUS sunshine, which warmed the bodies and the souls of the visitors.

M

MALINGER: to evade responsibility by pretending to be ill
A common way to avoid the draft was by MALINGERING—pretending to be mentally or physically ill so as to avoid being taken by the Army.

MALLEABLE: capable of being shaped
Gold is the most MALLEABLE of precious metals; it can easily be formed into almost any shape.

METAPHOR: a figure of speech comparing two different things; a symbol
The METAPHOR "a sea of troubles" suggests a lot of troubles by comparing their number to the vastness of the sea.

METICULOUS: extremely careful about details
To find all the clues at the crime scene, the investigators METICULOUSLY examined every inch of the area.

MISANTHROPE: a person who dislikes others
The character Scrooge in *A Christmas Carol* is such a MISANTHROPE that even the sight of children singing makes him angry.

MITIGATE: to soften; to lessen
A judge may MITIGATE a sentence if she decides that a person committed a crime out of need.

MOLLIFY: to calm or make less severe
Their argument was so intense that it was difficult to believe any compromise would MOLLIFY them.

MONOTONY: lack of variation
The MONOTONY of the sound of the dripping faucet almost drove the research assistant crazy.

N

NAIVE: lacking sophistication or experience
Having never traveled before, the elementary school students were more NAIVE than their high school counterparts on the field trip.

O

OBDURATE: hardened in feeling; resistant to persuasion
The president was completely OBDURATE on the issue, and no amount of persuasion would change his mind.

OBSEQUIOUS: overly submissive and eager to please
The OBSEQUIOUS new associate made sure to compliment her supervisor's tie and agree with him on every issue.

OBSTINATE: stubborn, unyielding
The OBSTINATE child could not be made to eat any food that he disliked.

OBVIATE: to prevent; to make unnecessary
The river was shallow enough to wade across at many points, which OBVIATED the need for a bridge.

OCCLUDE: to stop up; to prevent the passage of
A shadow is thrown across the earth's surface during a solar eclipse, when the light from the sun is OCCLUDED by the moon.

ONEROUS: troublesome and oppressive; burdensome
The assignment was so extensive and difficult to manage that it proved ONEROUS to the team in charge of it.

OPAQUE: impossible to see through; preventing the passage of light
The heavy buildup of dirt and grime on the windows almost made them OPAQUE.

OPPROBRIUM: public disgrace
After the scheme to embezzle the elderly was made public, the treasurer resigned in utter OPPROBRIUM.

OSTENTATION: excessive showiness
The OSTENTATION of the Sun King's court is evident in the lavish decoration and luxuriousness of his palace at Versailles.

P

PARADOX: a contradiction or dilemma
It is a PARADOX that those most in need of medical attention are often those least able to obtain it.

PARAGON: model of excellence or perfection
She is the PARAGON of what a judge should be: honest, intelligent, hardworking, and just.

PEDANT: someone who shows off learning
The graduate instructor's tedious and excessive commentary on the subject soon gained her a reputation as a PEDANT.

PERFIDIOUS: willing to betray one's trust
The actress's PERFIDIOUS companion revealed all of her intimate secrets to the gossip columnist.

PERFUNCTORY: done in a routine way; indifferent
The machinelike bank teller processed the transaction and gave the waiting customer a PERFUNCTORY smile.

PERMEATE: to penetrate
This miraculous new cleaning fluid is able to PERMEATE stains and dissolve them in minutes!

PHILANTHROPY: charity; a desire or effort to promote goodness
New York's Metropolitan Museum of Art owes much of its collection to the PHILANTHROPY of private collectors who willed their estates to the museum.

PLACATE: to soothe or pacify
The burglar tried to PLACATE the snarling dog by saying "Nice doggy," and offering it a treat.

PLASTIC: able to be molded, altered, or bent
The new material was very PLASTIC and could be formed into products of vastly different shapes.

PLETHORA: excess
Assuming that more was better, the defendant offered the judge a PLETHORA of excuses.

PRAGMATIC: practical as opposed to idealistic
While daydreaming gamblers think they can get rich by frequenting casinos, PRAGMATIC gamblers realize that the odds are heavily stacked against them.

PRECIPITATE: to throw violently or bring about abruptly; lacking deliberation
Upon learning that the couple married after knowing each other only two months, friends and family members expected such a PRECIPITATE marriage to end in divorce.

PREVARICATE: to lie or deviate from the truth
Rather than admit that he had overslept again, the employee PREVARICATED and claimed that heavy traffic had prevented him from arriving at work on time.

PRISTINE: fresh and clean; uncorrupted
Since concerted measures had been taken to prevent looting, the archeological site was still PRISTINE when researchers arrived.

PRODIGAL: lavish, wasteful
The PRODIGAL son quickly wasted all of his inheritance on a lavish lifestyle devoted to pleasure.

PROLIFERATE: to increase in number quickly
Although she only kept two guinea pigs initially, they PROLIFERATED to such an extent that she soon had dozens.

PROPITIATE: to conciliate; to appease
The management PROPITIATED the irate union by agreeing to raise wages for its members.

PROPRIETY: correct behavior; obedience to rules and customs
The aristocracy maintained a high level of PROPRIETY, adhering to even the most minor social rules.

PRUDENCE: wisdom, caution, or restraint
The college student exhibited PRUDENCE by obtaining practical experience along with her studies, which greatly strengthened her résumé.

PUNGENT: sharp and irritating to the senses
The smoke from the burning tires was extremely PUNGENT.

Q

QUIESCENT: motionless
Many animals are QUIESCENT over the winter months, minimizing activity in order to conserve energy.

R

RAREFY: to make thinner or sparser
Since the atmosphere RAREFIES as altitudes increase, the air at the top of very tall mountains is too thin to breathe.

REPUDIATE: to reject the validity of
The old woman's claim that she was Russian royalty was REPUDIATED when DNA tests showed she was of no relation to them.

RETICENT: silent, reserved
Physically small and RETICENT in her speech, Joan Didion often went unnoticed by those upon whom she was reporting.

RHETORIC: effective writing or speaking
Lincoln's talent for RHETORIC was evident in his beautifully expressed Gettysburg Address.

S

SATIATE: to satisfy fully or overindulge
His desire for power was so great that nothing less than complete control of the country could SATIATE it.

SOPORIFIC: causing sleep or lethargy
The movie proved to be so SOPORIFIC that soon loud snores were heard throughout the theater.

SPECIOUS: deceptively attractive; seemingly plausible but fallacious
The student's SPECIOUS excuse for being late sounded legitimate but was proved otherwise when her teacher called her home.

STIGMA: a mark of shame or discredit
In *The Scarlet Letter*, Hester Prynne was required to wear the letter *A* on her clothes as a public STIGMA for her adultery.

STOLID: unemotional; lacking sensitivity
The prisoner appeared STOLID and unaffected by the judge's harsh sentence.

SUBLIME: lofty or grand
The music was so SUBLIME that it transformed the rude surroundings into a special place.

T

TACIT: done without using words
Although not a word had been said, everyone in the room knew that a TACIT agreement had been made about which course of action to take.

TACITURN: silent, not talkative
The clerk's TACITURN nature earned him the nickname "Silent Bob."

TIRADE: long, harsh speech or verbal attack
Observers were shocked at the manager's TIRADE over such a minor mistake.

TORPOR: extreme mental and physical sluggishness
After surgery, the patient experienced TORPOR until the anesthesia wore off.

TRANSITORY: temporary, lasting a brief time
The reporter lived a TRANSITORY life, staying in one place only long enough to cover the current story.

V

VACILLATE: to sway physically; to be indecisive
The customer held up the line as he VACILLATED between ordering chocolate chip or rocky road ice cream.

VENERATE: to respect deeply
In a traditional Confucian society, the young VENERATE their elders, deferring to the elders' wisdom and experience.

VERACITY: truthfulness; accuracy
She had a reputation for VERACITY, so everyone trusted her description of events.

VERBOSE: wordy
The professor's answer was so VERBOSE that his student forgot what the original question had been.

VEX: to annoy
The old man who loved his peace and quiet was VEXED by his neighbor's loud music.

VOLATILE: easily aroused or changeable; lively or explosive
His VOLATILE personality made it difficult to predict his reaction to anything.

W

WAVER: to fluctuate between choices
If you WAVER too long before making a decision about which testing site to register for, you may not get your first choice.

WHIMSICAL: acting in a fanciful or capricious manner; unpredictable
The ballet was WHIMSICAL, delighting the children with its imaginative characters and unpredictable sets.

Z

ZEAL: passion, excitement
She brought her typical ZEAL to the project, sparking enthusiasm in the other team members.

COMMONLY CONFUSED WORDS

ALREADY: by this or that time, previously
He already completed his work.

ALL READY: completely prepared
The students were all ready to take their exam.

ALTOGETHER: entirely, completely
I am altogether certain that I turned in my homework.

ALL TOGETHER: in the same place
She kept the figurines all together on her mantle.

CAPITAL: a city containing the seat of government; the wealth or funds owned by a business or individual; resources
Atlanta is the capital of Georgia.
The company's capital gains have diminished in recent years.

CAPITOL: the building in which a legislative body meets
Our trip included a visit to the Capitol building in Washington, D.C.

COARSE: rough, not smooth; lacking refinement
The truck's large wheels enabled it to navigate the coarse, rough terrain.
His coarse language prevented him from getting hired for the job.

COURSE: path, series of classes or studies
James's favorite course is biology.
The doctor suggested that Amy rest and let the disease run its course.

HERE: in this location
George Washington used to live here.

HEAR: to listen to or to perceive by the ear
Did you hear the question?

ITS: a personal pronoun that shows possession
Please put the book back in its place.

IT'S: the contraction of "it is" or "it has"
It's snowing outside.
It's been too long.

LEAD: to act as a leader, to go first, or to take a superior position
The guide will lead us through the forest.

LED: past tense of "lead"
The guide led us through the forest.

LEAD: a metal
It is dangerous to inhale fumes from paint containing lead.

LOOSE: free, to set free, not tight
She always wears loose clothing when she does yoga.

LOSE: to become without
Use a bookmark so you don't lose your place in your book.

PASSED: the past tense of pass; a euphemism for someone dying
We passed by her house on Sunday.

PAST: that which has gone by or elapsed in time
In the past, Abby never used to study.
We drove past her house.

PRINCIPAL: the head of a school; main or important
The quarterback's injury is the principal reason the team lost.
The principal of the school meets with parents regularly.

PRINCIPLE: a fundamental law or truth
The laws of motion are among the most important principles in physics.

STATIONARY: fixed, not moving
Thomas rode a stationary bicycle at the gym.

STATIONERY: paper used for letter writing
The principal's stationery has the school's logo on the top.

THEIR: possessive of "they"
Paul and Ben studied for their test together.

THERE: a place; in that matter or respect
There are several question types on the GRE.
Please hang up your jacket over there.

THEY'RE: contraction of "they are"
Be careful of the bushes, as they're filled with thorns.

APPENDIX D

Math Reference

The math on the GRE covers a lot of ground—from number properties and arithmetic to basic algebra and symbol problems to geometry and statistics. Don't let yourself be intimidated.

We've highlighted the 100 most important concepts that you need to know and divided them into three levels. The GRE Quantitative sections test your understanding of a relatively limited number of mathematical concepts, all of which you will be able to master.

Level 1 consists of foundational math topics. Though these topics may seem basic, review this list so that you are aware that these skills may play a part in the questions you will answer on the GRE. Look over the Level 1 list to make sure you're comfortable with the basics.

Level 2 is where most people start their review of math. Level 2 skills and formulas come into play quite frequently on the GRE. If the skills needed to handle Level 1 or 2 topics are keeping you from feeling up to the tasks expected on the GRE Quantitative section, you might consider taking the Kaplan GRE Math Refresher course.

Level 3 represents the most challenging math concepts you'll find on the GRE. Don't spend a lot of time on Level 3 if you still have gaps in Level 2, but once you've mastered Level 2, tackling Level 3 can put you over the top.

LEVEL 1

1. How to add, subtract, multiply, and divide WHOLE NUMBERS

You can check addition with subtraction.

$17 + 5 = 22 \qquad 22 - 5 = 17$

You can check multiplication with division.

$5 \times 28 = 140 \qquad 140 \div 5 = 28$

2. How to add, subtract, multiply, and divide FRACTIONS

Find a common denominator before adding or subtracting fractions.

$$\frac{4}{5} + \frac{3}{10} = \frac{8}{10} + \frac{3}{10} = \frac{11}{10} \text{ or } 1\frac{1}{10}$$
$$2 - \frac{3}{8} = \frac{16}{8} - \frac{3}{8} = \frac{13}{8} \text{ or } 1\frac{5}{8}$$

To multiply fractions, multiply the numerators first and then multiply the denominators. Simplify if necessary.

$$\frac{3}{4} \times \frac{1}{6} = \frac{3}{24} = \frac{1}{8}$$

You can also reduce before multiplying numerators and denominators. This keeps the products small.

$$\frac{5}{8} \times \frac{2}{15} = \frac{{}^{1}\cancel{5}}{{}_{4}\cancel{8}} \times \frac{\cancel{2}^{1}}{\cancel{15}_{3}} = \frac{1}{12}$$

To divide by a fraction, multiply by its reciprocal. To write the reciprocal of a fraction, flip the numerator and the denominator.

$$5 \div \frac{1}{3} = \frac{5}{1} \times \frac{3}{1} = 15 \qquad \frac{1}{3} \div \frac{4}{5} = \frac{1}{3} \times \frac{5}{4} = \frac{5}{12}$$

3. How to add, subtract, multiply, and divide DECIMALS

To add or subtract, align the decimal points and then add or subtract normally. Place the decimal point in the answer directly below existing decimal points.

$$\begin{array}{r} 3.25 \\ +4.4 \\ \hline 7.65 \end{array} \qquad \begin{array}{r} 7.65 \\ -4.4 \\ \hline 3.25 \end{array}$$

To multiply with decimals, multiply the digits normally and count off decimal places (equal to the total number of places in the factors) from the right.

$$2.5 \times 2.5 = 6.25$$
$$0.06 \times 2{,}000 = 120.00 = 120$$

To divide by a decimal, move the decimal point in the divisor to the right to form a whole number; move the decimal point in the dividend the same number of places. Divide as though there were no decimals, then place the decimal point in the quotient.

$$6.25 \div 2.5$$
$$= 62.5 \div 25 = 2.5$$

4. How to convert FRACTIONS TO DECIMALS and DECIMALS TO FRACTIONS

To convert a fraction to a decimal, divide the numerator by the denominator.

$$\frac{4}{5} = 0.8 \quad \frac{4}{50} = 0.08 \quad \frac{4}{500} = 0.008$$

To convert a decimal to a fraction, write the digits in the numerator and use the decimal name in the denominator.

$$0.003 = \frac{3}{1{,}000} \quad 0.03 = \frac{3}{100} \quad 0.3 = \frac{3}{10}$$

5. How to add, subtract, multiply, and divide POSITIVE AND NEGATIVE NUMBERS

When addends (the numbers being added) have the same sign, add their absolute values; the sum has the same sign as the addends. But when addends have different signs, subtract the absolute values; the sum has the sign of the greater absolute value.

$3 + 9 = 12$, but $-3 + (-9) = -12$
$3 + (-9) = -6$, but $-3 + 9 = 6$

In multiplication and division, when the signs are the same, the product/quotient is positive. When the signs are different, the product/quotient is negative.

$6 \times 7 = 42$ and $-6 \times (-7) = 42$
$-6 \times 7 = -42$ and $6 \times (-7) = -42$
$96 \div 8 = 12$ and $-96 \div (-8) = 12$
$-96 \div 8 = -12$ and $96 \div (-8) = -12$

6. How to plot points on the NUMBER LINE

To plot the point 4.5 on the number line, start at 0, go right to 4.5, halfway between 4 and 5.

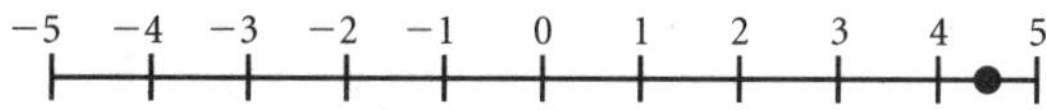

To plot the point −2.5 on the number line, start at 0, go left to −2.5, halfway between −2 and −3.

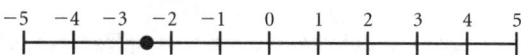

−5 −4 −3 −2 −1 0 1 2 3 4 5

7. How to plug a number into an ALGEBRAIC EXPRESSION

To evaluate an algebraic expression, choose numbers for the variables or use the numbers assigned to the variables.

Evaluate $4np + 1$ when $n = -4$ and $p = 3$.

$4np + 1 = 4(-4)(3) + 1 = -48 + 1 = -47$

8. How to SOLVE a simple LINEAR EQUATION

Use algebra to isolate the variable. Do the same steps to both sides of the equation.

$$
\begin{aligned}
28 &= -3x - 5 \\
28 + 5 &= -3x - 5 + 5 \quad \text{Add 5.} \\
33 &= -3x \\
\frac{33}{-3} &= \frac{-3x}{-3} \quad \text{Divide by } -3. \\
-11 &= x
\end{aligned}
$$

9. How to add and subtract LINE SEGMENTS

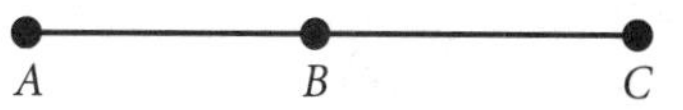

If $AB = 6$ and $BC = 8$, then $AC = 6 + 8 = 14$.
If $AC = 14$ and $BC = 8$, then $AB = 14 - 8 = 6$.

10. How to find the THIRD ANGLE of a TRIANGLE, given the other two angles

Use the fact that the sum of the measures of the interior angles of a triangle always equals 180°.

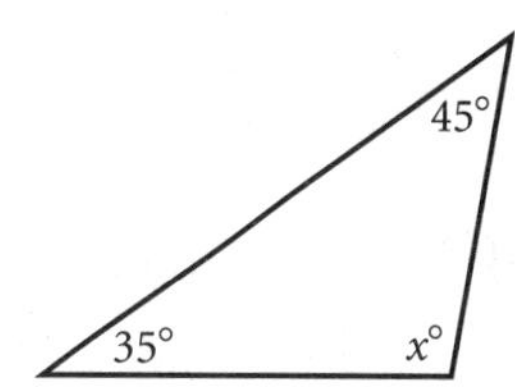

$$
\begin{aligned}
35 + 45 + x &= 180 \\
80 + x &= 180 \\
x &= 100
\end{aligned}
$$

LEVEL 2

11. How to use PEMDAS

When you're given a complex arithmetic expression, it's important to know the order of operations. Just remember PEMDAS (as in "Please Excuse My Dear Aunt Sally"). What PEMDAS means is this: Clean up **Parentheses** first (nested sets of parentheses are worked from the innermost set to the outermost set); then deal with **Exponents** (or **Radicals**); then do the **Multiplication** and **Division** together, going from left to right; and finally do the **Addition** and **Subtraction** together, again going from left to right.

Example:

$$9 - 2 \times (5 - 3)^2 + 6 \div 3 =$$

Begin with the parentheses:

$$9 - 2 \times (2)^2 + 6 \div 3 =$$

Then do the exponent:

$$9 - 2 \times 4 + 6 \div 3 =$$

Now do multiplication and division from left to right:

$$9 - 8 + 2 =$$

Finally, do addition and subtraction from left to right:

$$1 + 2 = 3$$

12. How to use the PERCENT FORMULA

Identify the part, the percent, and the whole.

$$Part = Percent \times Whole$$

Find the part.

Example:

What is 12 percent of 25?

Setup:

$$Part = \frac{12}{100} \times 25 = \frac{300}{100} = 3$$

Find the percent.

Example:

45 is what percent of 9?

Setup:

$$\begin{aligned} 45 &= \frac{\text{Percent}}{100} \times 9 \\ 4{,}500 &= \text{Percent} \times 9 \\ 500 &= \text{Percent} \end{aligned}$$

Find the whole.

Example:

15 is $\frac{3}{5}$ percent of what number?

Setup:

$$15 = \frac{3}{5}\left(\frac{1}{100}\right) \times Whole$$

$$15 = \frac{3}{500} \times Whole$$

$$Whole = 15\left(\frac{500}{3}\right) = \frac{7{,}500}{3} = 2{,}500$$

13. How to use the PERCENT INCREASE/DECREASE FORMULAS

Identify the original whole and the amount of increase/decrease.

$$Percent\ increase = \frac{Amount\ of\ increase}{Original\ whole} \times 100\%$$

$$Percent\ decrease = \frac{Amount\ of\ decrease}{Original\ whole} \times 100\%$$

Example:

The price goes up from \$80 to \$100. What is the percent increase?

Setup:

$$\begin{aligned} Percent\ increase &= \frac{20}{80} \times 100\% \\ &= 0.25 \times 100\% = 25\% \end{aligned}$$

14. How to predict whether a sum, difference, or product will be ODD or EVEN

Don't bother memorizing the rules. Just take simple numbers such as 2 for even numbers and 3 for odd numbers and see what happens.

Example:

If m is even and n is odd, is the product mn odd or even?

Setup:

Say $m = 2$ and $n = 3$.
$2 \times 3 = 6$, which is even, so mn is even.

15. How to recognize MULTIPLES OF 2, 3, 4, 5, 6, 9, 10, and 12

2: Last digit is even.
3: Sum of digits is a multiple of 3.
4: Last two digits are a multiple of 4.
5: Last digit is 5 or 0.
6: Sum of digits is a multiple of 3, and last digit is even.
9: Sum of digits is a multiple of 9.
10: Last digit is 0.
12: Sum of digits is a multiple of 3, and last two digits are a multiple of 4.

16. How to find a COMMON FACTOR of two numbers

Break both numbers down to their prime factors to see which they have in common. Then multiply the shared prime factors to find all common factors.

Example:

What factors greater than 1 do 135 and 225 have in common?

Setup:

First find the prime factors of 135 and 225; $135 = 3 \times 3 \times 3 \times 5$, and $225 = 3 \times 3 \times 5 \times 5$. The numbers share $3 \times 3 \times 5$ in common. Thus, aside from 3 and 5, the remaining common factors can be found by multiplying 3, 3, and 5 in every possible combination: $3 \times 3 = 9$, $3 \times 5 = 15$, and $3 \times 3 \times 5 = 45$. Therefore, the common factors of 135 and 225 are 3, 5, 9, 15, and 45.

17. How to find a COMMON MULTIPLE of two numbers

The product of two numbers is the easiest common multiple to find, but it is not always the least common multiple (LCM).

Example:

What is the least common multiple of 28 and 42?

Setup:

$$\begin{aligned} 28 &= 2 \times 2 \times 7 \\ 42 &= 2 \times 3 \times 7 \end{aligned}$$

The LCM can be found by finding the prime factorization of each number, then seeing the greatest number of times each factor is used. Multiply each prime factor the greatest number of times it appears.

In 28, 2 is used twice. In 42, 2 is used once. In 28, 7 is used once. In 42, 7 is used once, and 3 is used once.

So you multiply each factor the greatest number of times it appears in a prime factorization:

$$\text{LCM} = 2 \times 2 \times 3 \times 7 = 84$$

18. How to find the AVERAGE or ARITHMETIC MEAN

$$\textit{Average} = \frac{\textit{Sum of terms}}{\textit{Number of terms}}$$

Example:

What is the average of 3, 4, and 8?

Setup:

$$\textit{Average} = \frac{3 + 4 + 8}{3} = \frac{15}{3} = 5$$

19. How to use the AVERAGE to find the SUM

$$\textit{Sum} = (\textit{Average}) \times (\textit{Number of terms})$$

Example:

17.5 is the average (arithmetic mean) of 24 numbers.

What is the sum of the 24 numbers?

Setup:

$$\textit{Sum} = 17.5 \times 24 = 420$$

20. How to find the AVERAGE of CONSECUTIVE NUMBERS

The average of evenly spaced numbers is simply the average of the smallest number and the largest number. The average of all the integers from 13 to 77, for example, is the same as the average of 13 and 77:

$$\frac{13 + 77}{2} = \frac{90}{2} = 45$$

21. How to COUNT CONSECUTIVE NUMBERS

The number of integers from A to B inclusive is $B - A + 1$.

Example:

How many integers are there from 73 through 419, inclusive?

Setup:

$$419 - 73 + 1 = 347$$

22. How to find the SUM OF CONSECUTIVE NUMBERS

$$Sum = (Average) \times (Number\ of\ terms)$$

Example:

What is the sum of the integers from 10 through 50, inclusive?

Setup:

Average: $\frac{10 + 50}{2} = 30$

Number of terms: $50 - 10 + 1 = 41$

Sum: $30 \times 41 = 1{,}230$

23. How to find the MEDIAN

Put the numbers in numerical order and take the middle number.

Example:

What is the median of 88, 86, 57, 94, and 73?

Setup:

First, put the numbers in numerical order, then take the middle number:

57, 73, 86, 88, 94

The median is 86.

In a set with an even number of numbers, take the average of the two in the middle.

Example:

What is the median of 88, 86, 57, 73, 94, and 100?

Setup:

First, put the numbers in numerical order.

57, 73, 86, 88, 94, 100

Because 86 and 88 are the two numbers in the middle:

$$\frac{86 + 88}{2} = \frac{174}{2} = 87$$

The median is 87.

24. How to find the MODE

Take the number that appears most often. For example, if your test scores were 88, 57, 68, 85, 98, 93, 93, 84, and 81, the mode of the scores would be 93 because it appears more often than any other score. (If there's a tie for most often, then there's more than one mode. If each number in a set is used equally often, there is no mode.)

25. How to find the RANGE

Take the positive difference between the greatest and least values. Using the example under "How to find the MODE" above, if your test scores were 88, 57, 68, 85, 98, 93, 93, 84, and 81, the range of the scores would be 41, the greatest value minus the least value ($98 - 57 = 41$).

26. How to use actual numbers to determine a RATIO

To find a ratio, put the number associated with *of* on the top and the number associated with *to* on the bottom.

$$Ratio = \frac{of}{to}$$

The ratio of 20 oranges to 12 apples is $\frac{20}{12}$, or $\frac{5}{3}$.

Ratios should always be reduced to lowest terms. Ratios can also be expressed in linear form, such as 5:3.

27. How to use a ratio to determine an ACTUAL NUMBER

Set up a proportion using the given ratio.

Example:

The ratio of boys to girls is 3 to 4. If there are 135 boys, how many girls are there?

Setup:

$$\frac{3}{4} = \frac{135}{g}$$
$$3 \times g = 4 \times 135$$
$$3g = 540$$
$$g = 180$$

28. How to use actual numbers to determine a RATE

Identify the quantities and the units to be compared. Keep the units straight.

Example:

Anders typed 9,450 words in $3\frac{1}{2}$ hours. What was his rate in words per minute?

Setup:

First convert $3\frac{1}{2}$ hours to 210 minutes. Then set up the rate with words on top and minutes on bottom (because "per" means "divided by"):

$$\frac{9{,}450\text{ words}}{210\text{ minutes}} = 45\text{ words per minute}$$

29. How to deal with TABLES, GRAPHS, AND CHARTS

Read the question and all labels carefully. Ignore extraneous information and zero in on what the question asks for. Take advantage of the spread in the answer choices by approximating the answer whenever possible and choosing the answer choice closest to your approximation.

30. How to count the NUMBER OF POSSIBILITIES

You can use multiplication to find the number of possibilities when items can be arranged in various ways.

Example:

How many three-digit numbers can be formed with the digits 1, 3, and 5 each used only once?

Setup:

Look at each digit individually. The first digit (or, the hundreds digit) has three possible numbers to plug in: 1, 3, or 5. The second digit (or, the tens digit) has two possible numbers, since one has already been plugged in. The last digit (or, the ones digit) has only one remaining possible number. Multiply the possibilities together: $3 \times 2 \times 1 = 6$.

31. How to calculate a simple PROBABILITY

$$\textit{Probability} = \frac{\textit{Number of desired outcomes}}{\textit{Number of total possible outcomes}}$$

Example:

What is the probability of throwing a 5 on a fair six-sided die?

Setup:

There is one desired outcome—throwing a 5. There are 6 possible outcomes—one for each side of the die.

$$\textit{Probability} = \frac{1}{6}$$

32. How to work with new SYMBOLS

If you see a symbol you've never seen before, don't be alarmed. It's just a made-up symbol whose operation is uniquely defined by the problem. Everything you need to know is in the question stem. Just follow the instructions.

33. How to SIMPLIFY BINOMIALS

A binomial is a sum or difference of two terms. To simplify two binomials that are multiplied together, use the **FOIL** method. Multiply the **F**irst terms, then the **O**uter terms, followed by the **I**nner terms and the **L**ast terms. Lastly, combine like terms.

Example:

$$\begin{aligned}(3x + 5)(x - 1) &= \\ 3x^2 - 3x + 5x - 5 &= \\ 3x^2 + 2x - 5\end{aligned}$$

34. How to FACTOR certain POLYNOMIALS

A polynomial is an expression consisting of the sum of two or more terms, where at least one of the terms is a variable.

Learn to spot these classic polynomial equations.

$$ab + ac = a(b + c)$$
$$a^2 + 2ab + b^2 = (a + b)^2$$
$$a^2 - 2ab + b^2 = (a - b)^2$$
$$a^2 - b^2 = (a - b)(a + b)$$

35. How to solve for one variable IN TERMS OF ANOTHER

To find x "in terms of" y, isolate x on one side, leaving y as the only variable on the other.

36. How to solve an INEQUALITY

Treat it much like an equation—adding, subtracting, multiplying, and dividing both sides by the same thing. Just remember to reverse the inequality sign if you multiply or divide by a negative quantity.

Example:

Rewrite $7 - 3x > 2$ in its simplest form.

Setup:

$$7 - 3x > 2$$

First, subtract 7 from both sides:

$$7 - 3x - 7 > 2 - 7$$
$$-3x > -5$$

Now divide both sides by -3, remembering to reverse the inequality sign:

$$x < \frac{5}{3}$$

37. How to handle ABSOLUTE VALUES

The *absolute value* of a number n, denoted by $|n|$, is defined as n if $n \geq 0$ and $-n$ if $n < 0$. The absolute value of a number is the distance from zero to the number on the number line. The absolute value of a number or expression is always positive.

$$|-5| = 5$$

If $|x| = 3$, then x could be 3 or -3.

Example:

If $|x - 3| < 2$, what is the range of possible values for x?

Setup:

Represent the possible range for $x - 3$ on a number line.

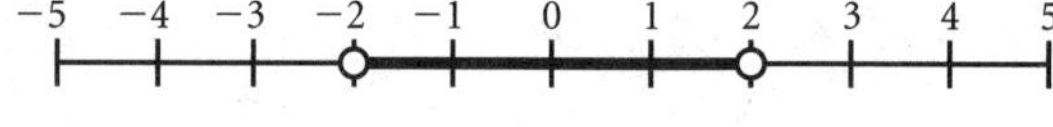

$|x - 3| < 2$, so $(x - 3) < 2$ and $(x - 3) > -2$
$x - 3 < 2$ and $x - 3 > -2$
$x < 2 + 3$ and $x > -2 + 3$
$x < 5$ and $x > 1$
So, $1 < x < 5$.

38. How to TRANSLATE ENGLISH INTO ALGEBRA

Look for the key words and systematically turn phrases into algebraic expressions and sentences into equations.

Here's a table of key words that you may have to translate into mathematical terms:

Operation	Key Words
Addition	sum, plus, and, added to, more than, increased by, combined with, exceeds, total, greater than
Subtraction	difference between, minus, subtracted from, decreased by, diminished by, less than, reduced by
Multiplication	of, product, times, multiplied by, twice, double, triple, half
Division	quotient, divided by, per, out of, ratio of _ to _
Equals	equals, is, was, will be, the result is, adds up to, costs, is the same as

39. How to find an ANGLE formed by INTERSECTING LINES

Vertical angles are equal. Angles along a line add up to 180°.

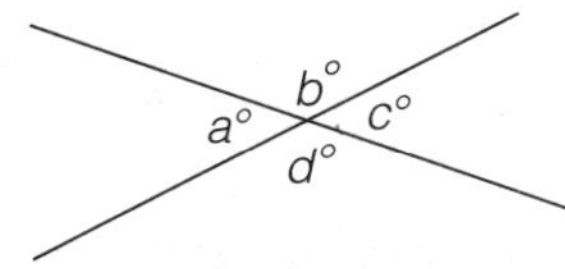

$$\begin{aligned} a^\circ &= c^\circ \\ b^\circ &= d^\circ \\ a^\circ + b^\circ &= 180^\circ \\ a^\circ + b^\circ + c^\circ + d^\circ &= 360^\circ \end{aligned}$$

40. How to find an angle formed by a TRANSVERSAL across PARALLEL LINES

When a transversal crosses parallel lines, all the acute angles formed are equal, and all the obtuse angles formed are equal. Any acute angle plus any obtuse angle equals 180°.

Example:

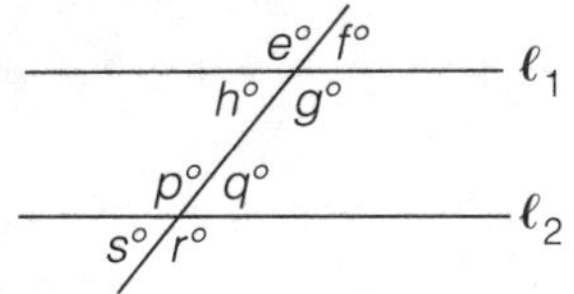

$$\begin{aligned} e^\circ = g^\circ = p^\circ &= r^\circ \\ f^\circ = h^\circ = q^\circ &= s^\circ \\ e^\circ + q^\circ = g^\circ + s^\circ &= 180^\circ \end{aligned}$$

41. How to find the AREA of a TRIANGLE

$$Area = \frac{1}{2}(Base)(Height)$$

Base and height must be perpendicular to each other. Height is measured by drawing a perpendicular line segment from the base—which can be any side of the triangle—to the angle opposite the base.

Example:

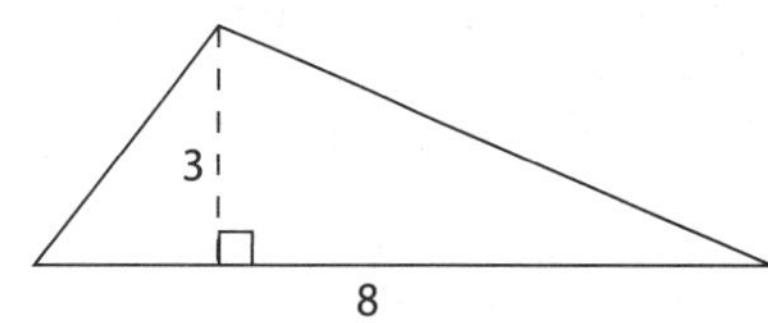

Setup:

$$Area = \frac{1}{2}(8)(3) = 12$$

42. How to work with ISOSCELES TRIANGLES

Isosceles triangles have at least two equal sides and two equal angles. If a GRE question tells you that a triangle is isosceles, you can bet that you'll need to use that information to find the length of a side or a measure of an angle.

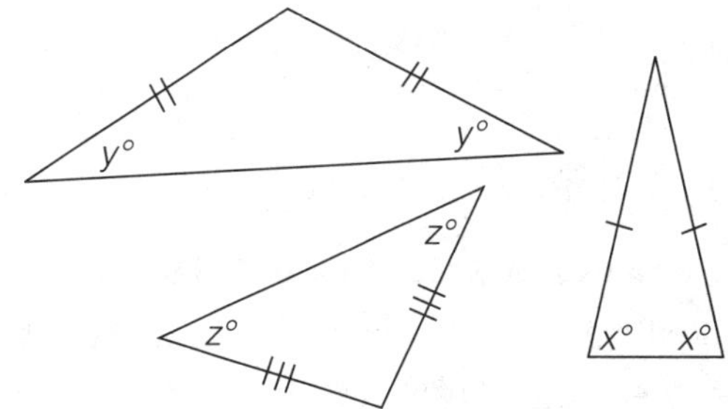

43. How to work with EQUILATERAL TRIANGLES

Equilateral triangles have three equal sides and three 60° angles. If a GRE question tells you that a triangle is equilateral, you can bet that you'll need to use that information to find the length of a side or the measure of an angle.

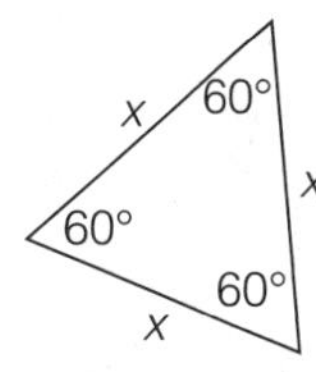

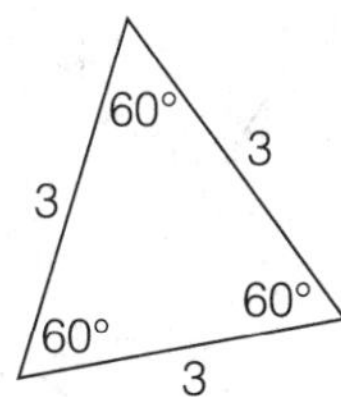

44. How to work with SIMILAR TRIANGLES

In similar triangles, corresponding angles are equal, and corresponding sides are proportional. If a GRE question tells you that triangles are similar, use the properties of similar triangles to find the length of a side or the measure of an angle.

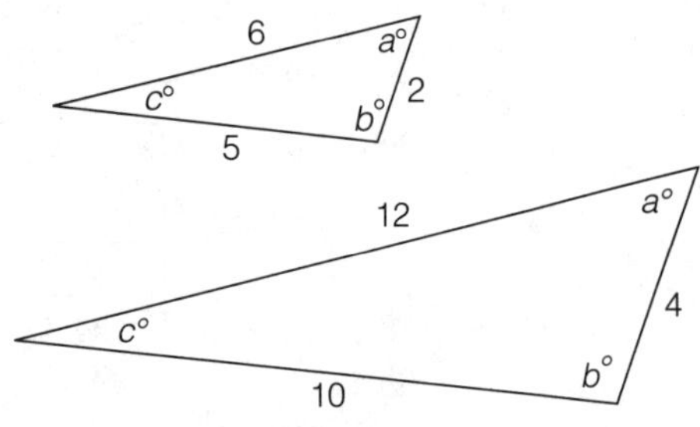

45. How to find the HYPOTENUSE or a LEG of a RIGHT TRIANGLE

For all right triangles, the Pythagorean theorem is $a^2 + b^2 = c^2$, where a and b are the legs and c is the hypotenuse.

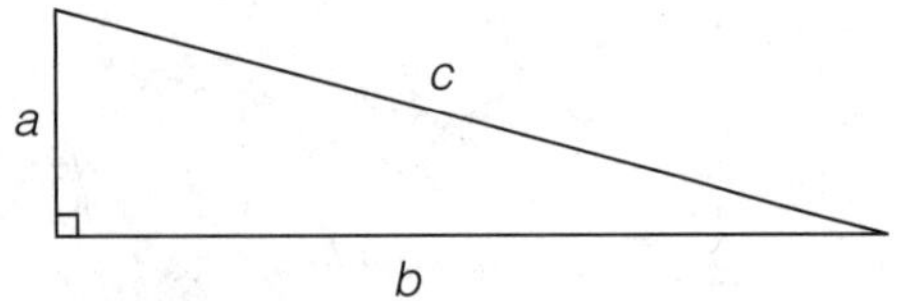

46. How to spot SPECIAL RIGHT TRIANGLES

Special right triangles are ones that are seen on the GRE with frequency. Recognizing them can streamline your problem solving.

3:4:5
5:12:13

These numbers (3, 4, 5 and 5, 12, 13) represent the ratio of the side lengths of these triangles.

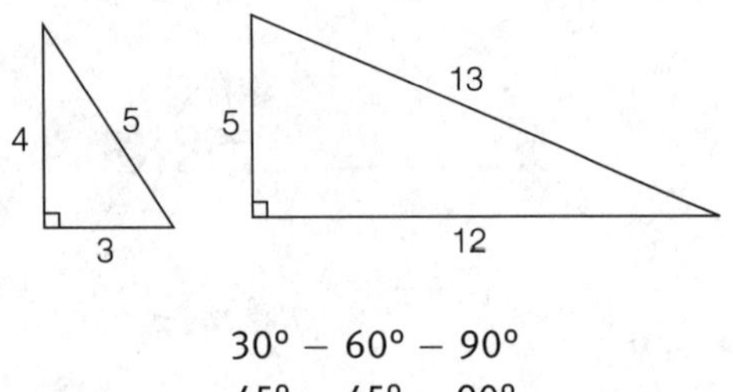

$30° - 60° - 90°$
$45° - 45° - 90°$

In a 30 – 60 – 90 triangle, the side lengths are multiples of 1, $\sqrt{3}$, and 2, respectively. In a 45 – 45 – 90 triangle, the side lengths are multiples of 1, 1, and $\sqrt{2}$, respectfully.

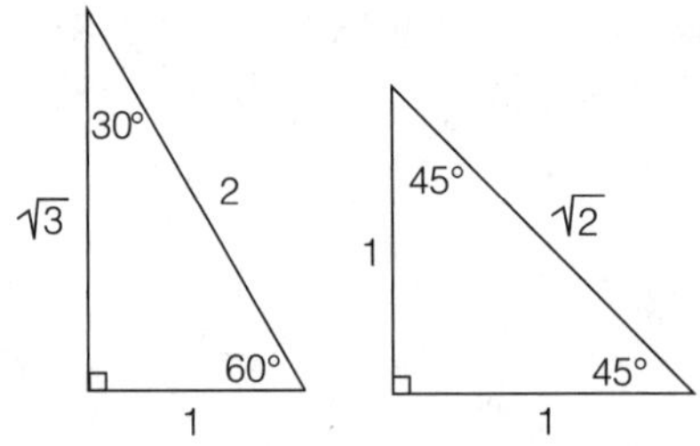

47. How to find the PERIMETER of a RECTANGLE

$$Perimeter = 2(Length + Width)$$

Example:

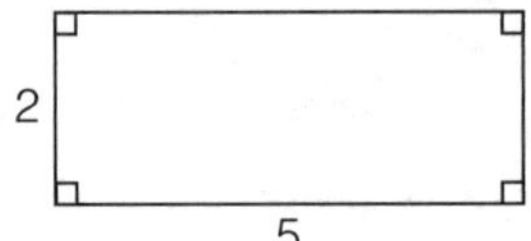

Setup:

$$Perimeter = 2(2 + 5) = 14$$

48. How to find the AREA of a RECTANGLE

$$Area = (Length)(Width)$$

Example:

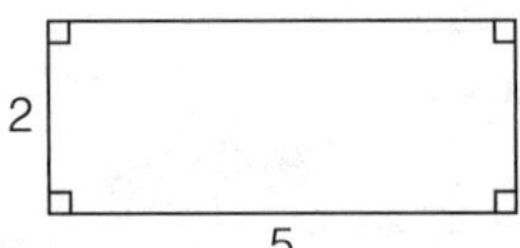

Setup:

$$Area = 2 \times 5 = 10$$

49. How to find the AREA of a SQUARE

$$Area = (Side)^2$$

Example:

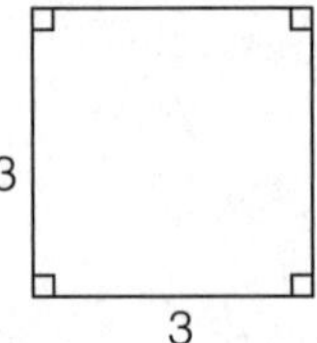

Setup:

$$Area = 3^2 = 9$$

50. How to find the AREA of a PARALLELOGRAM

$$Area = (Base)(Height)$$

Example:

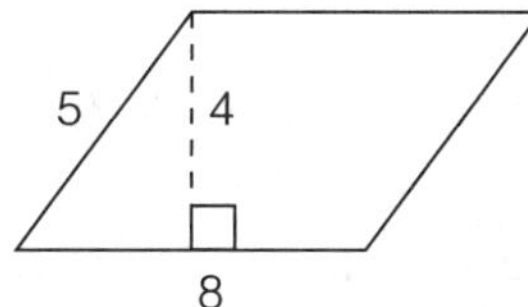

Setup:

$$Area = 8 \times 4 = 32$$

51. How to find the AREA of a TRAPEZOID

A trapezoid is a quadrilateral having only two parallel sides. You can always drop a perpendicular line or two to break the figure into a rectangle and a triangle or two triangles. Use the area formulas for those familiar shapes. Alternatively, you could apply the general formula for the area of a trapezoid:

$$Area = (Average\ of\ parallel\ sides) \times (Height)$$

Example:

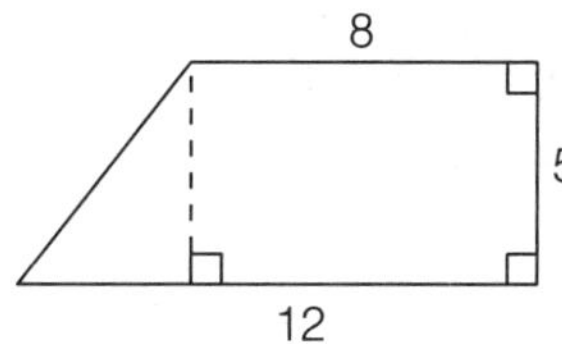

Setup:

$$Area\ of\ rectangle = 8 \times 5 = 40$$

$$Area\ of\ triangle = \frac{1}{2}(4 \times 5) = 10$$

$$Area\ of\ trapezoid = 40 + 10 = 50$$

$$Area\ of\ trapezoid = \left(\frac{8+12}{2}\right) \times 5 = 50$$

52. How to find the CIRCUMFERENCE of a CIRCLE

Circumference = 2 r, *where* r *is the radius*

Circumference = d, *where* d *is the diameter*

Example:

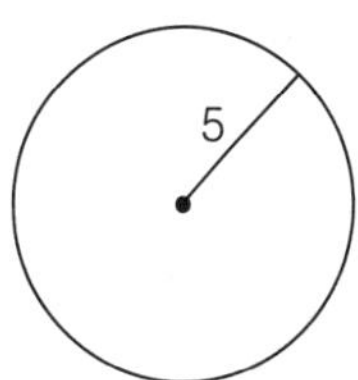

Setup:

$$Circumference = 2\pi(5) = 10\pi$$

53. How to find the AREA of a CIRCLE

$$Area = \pi r^2 \text{ where } r \text{ is the radius}$$

Example:

Setup:

$$Area = \pi \times 5^2 = 25\pi$$

54. How to find the DISTANCE BETWEEN POINTS on the coordinate plane

If two points have the same x-coordinates or the same y-coordinates—that is, they make a line segment that is parallel to an axis—all you have to do is subtract the numbers that are different. Just remember that distance is always positive.

Example:

What is the distance from (2, 3) to (–7, 3)?

Setup:

The y's are the same, so just subtract the x's: $2 - (-7) = 9$.

If the points have different x-coordinates and different y-coordinates, make a right triangle and use the Pythagorean theorem or apply the special right triangle attributes if applicable.

Example:

What is the distance from (2,3) to (–1,–1)?

Setup:

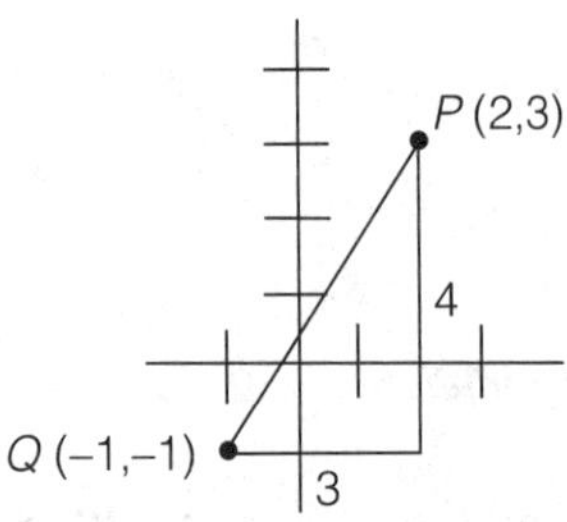

It's a 3:4:5 triangle!

$PQ = 5$

55. How to find the SLOPE of a LINE

$$Slope = \frac{Rise}{Run} = \frac{Change\ in\ y}{Change\ in\ x}$$

Example:

What is the slope of the line that contains the points (1,2) and (4,–5)?

Setup:

$$Slope = \frac{-5-2}{4-1} = \frac{-7}{3} = -\frac{7}{3}$$

LEVEL 3

56 How to determine COMBINED PERCENT INCREASE/DECREASE when no original value is specified

Start with 100 as a starting value.

Example:

A price rises by 10 percent one year and by 20 percent the next. What's the combined percent increase?

Setup:

Say the original price is $100.

Year one:
100 + (10% of 100) = 100 + 10 = 110

Year two:
110 + (20% of 110) = 110 + 22 = 132

From 100 to 132 is a 32 percent increase.

57. How to find the ORIGINAL WHOLE before percent increase/decrease

Think of a 15 percent increase over x as $1.15x$ and set up an equation.

Example:

After decreasing by 5 percent, the population is now 57,000. What was the original population?

Setup:

0.95 × (*Original population*) = 57,000

Divide both sides by 0.95.

Original population = 57,000 ÷ 0.95 = 60,000

58. How to solve a SIMPLE INTEREST problem

With simple interest, the interest is computed on the principal only and is given by

$$Interest = Principle \times rt$$

In this formula, r is defined as the interest rate per payment period, and t is defined as the number of payment periods.

Example:

If $12,000 is invested at 6 percent simple annual interest, how much interest is earned after 9 months?

Setup:

Since the interest rate is annual and we are calculating how much interest accrues after 9 months, we will express the payment period as $\frac{9}{12}$.

$$(12{,}000) \times (0.06) \times \frac{9}{12} = 540$$

59. How to solve a COMPOUND INTEREST problem

If interest is compounded, the interest is computed on the principal as well as on any interest earned. To compute compound interest:

$$(\textit{Final balance}) = (\textit{Principal}) \times \left(1 + \frac{\textit{interest rate}}{c}\right)^{(\textit{time})(c)}$$

where $c =$ the number of times the interest is compounded annually.

Example:

If $10,000 is invested at 8 percent annual interest, compounded semiannually, what is the balance after 1 year?

Setup:

Final balance

$$= (10{,}000) \times \left(1 + \frac{0.08}{2}\right)^{(1)(2)}$$
$$= (10{,}000) \times (1.04)^2$$
$$= 10{,}816$$

Semiannual interest is interest that is distributed twice a year. When an interest rate is given as an annual rate, divide by 2 to find the semiannual interest rate.

60. How to solve a REMAINDERS problem

Pick a number that fits the given conditions and see what happens.

Example:

When n is divided by 7, the remainder is 5. What is the remainder when $2n$ is divided by 7?

Setup:

Find a number that leaves a remainder of 5 when divided by 7. You can find such a number by taking any multiple of 7 and adding 5 to it. A good choice would be 12. If $n = 12$, then $2n = 24$, which when divided by 7 leaves a remainder of 3.

61. How to solve a DIGITS problem

Use a little logic—and some trial and error.

Example:

If A, B, C, and D represent distinct digits in the addition problem below, what is the value of D?

$$\begin{array}{r} AB \\ +\,BA \\ \hline CDC \end{array}$$

Setup:

Two 2-digit numbers will add up to at most something in the 100s, so $C = 1$. B plus A in the units column gives a 1, and since A and B in the tens column don't add up to C, it can't simply be that $B + A = 1$. It must be that $B + A = 11$, and a 1 gets carried. In fact, A and B can be any pair of digits that add up to 11 (3 and 8, 4 and 7, etc.), but it doesn't matter what they are: they always give you the same value for D, which is 2:

$$\begin{array}{r} 47 \\ +\;74 \\ \hline 121 \end{array} \qquad \begin{array}{r} 83 \\ +\;38 \\ \hline 121 \end{array}$$

62. How to find a WEIGHTED AVERAGE

Give each term the appropriate "weight."

Example:

The girls' average score is 30. The boys' average score is 24. If there are twice as many boys as girls, what is the overall average?

Setup:

$$\textit{Weighted avg.} = \frac{(1 \times 30) + (2 \times 24)}{3} = \frac{78}{3} = 26$$

HINT: Don't just average the averages.

63. How to find the NEW AVERAGE when a number is added or deleted

Use the sum of the terms of the old average to help you find the new average.

Example:

Michael's average score after four tests is 80. If he scores 100 on the fifth test, what's his new average?

Setup:

Find the original sum from the original average:

$$\textit{Original sum} = 4 \times 80 = 320$$

Add the fifth score to make the new sum:

$$\textit{New sum} = 320 + 100 = 420$$

Find the new average from the new sum:

$$\textit{New average} = \frac{420}{5} = 84$$

64. How to use the ORIGINAL AVERAGE and NEW AVERAGE to figure out WHAT WAS ADDED OR DELETED

Use the sums.

Number added = (*New sum*) – (*Original sum*)
Number deleted = (*Original sum*) – (*New sum*)

Example:

The average of five numbers is 2. After one number is deleted, the new average is –3. What number was deleted?

Setup:

Find the original sum from the original average:

$$\textit{Original sum} = 5 \times 2 = 10$$

Find the new sum from the new average:

$$\textit{New sum} = 4 \times (-3) = -12$$

The difference between the original sum and the new sum is the answer.

$$\textit{Number deleted} = 10 - (-12) = 22$$

65. How to find an AVERAGE RATE

Convert to totals.

$$\textit{Average A per B} = \frac{\textit{Total A}}{\textit{Total B}}$$

Example:

If the first 500 pages have an average of 150 words per page, and the remaining 100 pages have an average of 450 words per page, what is the average number of words per page for the entire 600 pages?

Setup:

$$\begin{aligned} \textit{Total pages} &= 500 + 100 = 600 \\ \textit{Total words} &= (500 \times 150) + (100 \times 450) \\ &= 75{,}000 + 45{,}00 \\ &= 120{,}000 \end{aligned}$$

$$\textit{Average words per page} = \frac{120{,}000}{600} = 200$$

To find an average speed, you also convert to totals.

$$\textit{Average speed} = \frac{\textit{Total distance}}{\textit{Total time}}$$

Example:

Rosa drove 120 miles one way at an average speed of 40 miles per hour and returned by the same 120-mile route at an average speed of 60 miles per hour. What was Rosa's average speed for the entire 240-mile round trip?

Setup:

To drive 120 miles at 40 mph takes 3 hours. To return at 60 mph takes 2 hours. The total time, then, is 5 hours.

$$\textit{Average speed} = \frac{240 \text{ miles}}{5 \text{ hours}} = 48 \text{ mph}$$

66. How to solve a COMBINED WORK PROBLEM

In a combined work problem, you are given the rate at which people or machines perform work individually and you are asked to compute the rate at which they work together (or vice versa). The work formula states: *The inverse of the time it would take everyone working together equals the sum of the inverses of the times it would take each working individually.* In other words:

$$\frac{1}{r} + \frac{1}{s} = \frac{1}{t}$$

where r and s are, for example, the number of hours it would take Rebecca and Sam, respectively, to complete a job working by themselves, and t is the number of hours it would take the two of them working together. Remember that all these variables must stand for units of *time* and must all refer to the amount of time it takes to do the same task.

Example:

If it takes Joe 4 hours to paint a room and Pete twice as long to paint the same room, how long would it take the two of them, working together, to paint the same room, if each of them works at his respective individual rate?

Setup:

Joe takes 4 hours, so Pete takes 8 hours; thus:

$$\frac{1}{4}+\frac{1}{8} = \frac{1}{t}$$

$$\frac{2}{8}+\frac{1}{8} = \frac{1}{t}$$

$$\frac{3}{8} = \frac{1}{t}$$

$$t = \frac{1}{\left(\frac{3}{8}\right)} = \frac{8}{3}$$

So it would take them $\frac{8}{3}$ hours, or 2 hours and 40 minutes, to paint the room together.

67. How to determine a COMBINED RATIO

Multiply one or both ratios by whatever you need in order to get the terms they have in common to match.

Example:

The ratio of a to b is 7:3. The ratio of b to c is 2:5. What is the ratio of a to c?

Setup:

Multiply each member of $a{:}b$ by 2 and multiply each member of $b{:}c$ by 3, and you get $a{:}b = 14{:}6$ and $b{:}c = 6{:}15$. Now that the values of b match, you can write $a{:}b{:}c = 14{:}6{:}15$ and then say $a{:}c = 14{:}15$.

68. How to solve a DILUTION or MIXTURE problem

In dilution or mixture problems, you have to determine the characteristics of a resulting mixture when different substances are combined. Or, alternatively, you have to determine how to combine different substances to produce a desired mixture. There are two approaches to such problems—the straightforward setup and the balancing method.

Example:

If 5 pounds of raisins that cost \$1 per pound are mixed with 2 pounds of almonds that cost \$2.40 per pound, what is the cost per pound of the resulting mixture?

Setup:

The straightforward setup:

$(\$1)(5) + (\$2.40)(2) = \$9.80 =$ total cost for 7 pounds of the mixture

The cost per pound is $\frac{\$9.80}{7} = \$1.40$.

Example:

How many liters of a solution that is 10 percent alcohol by volume must be added to 2 liters of a solution that is 50 percent alcohol by volume to create a solution that is 15 percent alcohol by volume?

Setup:

The balancing method: Make the weaker and stronger (or cheaper and more expensive, etc.) substances balance. That is, (percent difference between the weaker solution and the desired solution) $\times$ (amount of weaker solution) $=$ (percent difference between the stronger solution and the desired solution) × (amount of stronger solution). Make n the amount, in liters, of the weaker solution.

$$\begin{aligned} n(15 - 10) &= 2(50 - 15) \\ 5n &= 2(35) \\ n &= \frac{70}{5} = 14 \end{aligned}$$

So 14 liters of the 10 percent solution must be added to the original, stronger solution.

69. How to solve an OVERLAPPING SETS problem involving BOTH/NEITHER

Some GRE word problems involve two groups with overlapping members and possibly elements that belong to neither group. It's easy to identify this type of question because the words *both* and/or *neither* appear in the question. These problems are quite workable if you just memorize the following formula:

$$\textit{Group 1} + \textit{Group 2} + \textit{Neither} - \textit{Both} = \textit{Total}$$

Example:

Of the 120 students at a certain language school, 65 are studying French, 51 are studying Spanish, and 53 are studying neither language. How many are studying both French and Spanish?

Setup:

$$\begin{aligned} 65 + 51 + 53 - \textit{Both} &= 120 \\ 169 - \textit{Both} &= 120 \\ \textit{Both} &= 49 \end{aligned}$$

70 How to solve an OVERLAPPING SETS problem involving EITHER/OR CATEGORIES

Other GRE word problems involve groups with distinct "either/or" categories (male/female, blue-collar/white-collar, etc.). The key to solving this type of problem is to organize the information in a grid.

Example:

At a certain professional conference with 130 attendees, 94 of the attendees are doctors, and the rest are dentists. If 48 of the attendees are women and $\frac{1}{4}$ of the dentists in attendance are women, how many of the attendees are male doctors?

Setup:

To complete the grid, use the information in the problem, making each row and column add up to the corresponding total:

	Doctors	Dentists	Total
Male	55	27	82
Female	39	9	48
Total	94	36	130

After you've filled in the information from the question, use simple arithmetic to fill in the remaining boxes until you get the number you are looking for—in this case, that 55 of the attendees are male doctors.

71. How to work with FACTORIALS

You may see a problem involving factorial notation, which is indicated by the ! symbol. If n is an integer greater than 1, then n factorial, denoted by $n!$, is defined as the product of all the integers from 1 to n. For example:

$$\begin{aligned} 2! &= 2 \times 1 = 2 \\ 3! &= 3 \times 2 \times 1 = 6 \\ 4! &= 4 \times 3 \times 2 \times 1 = 24, \text{etc} \end{aligned}$$

By definition, $0! = 1$.

Also note: $6! = 6 \times 5! = 6 \times 5 \times 4!$, etc. Most GRE factorial problems test your ability to factor and/or cancel.

Example:

$$\frac{8!}{6! \times 2!} = \frac{8 \times 7 \times 6!}{6! \times 2 \times 1} = 28$$

72: How to solve a PERMUTATION problem

Factorials are useful for solving questions about permutations (i.e., the number of ways to arrange elements sequentially). For instance, to figure out how many ways there are to arrange 7 items along a shelf, you would multiply the number of possibilities for the first position times the number of possibilities remaining for the second position, and so on—in other words: $7 \times 6 \times 5 \times 4 \times 3 \times 2 \times 1$, or 7!.

If you're asked to find the number of ways to arrange a smaller group that's being drawn from a larger group, you can either apply logic, or you can use the permutation formula:

$${}_nP_k = \frac{n!}{(n-k)!}$$

where n = (the number in the larger group) and
k = (the number you're arranging).

Example:

Five runners run in a race. The runners who come in first, second, and third place will win gold, silver, and bronze medals, respectively. How many possible outcomes for gold, silver, and bronze medal winners are there?

Setup:

Any of the 5 runners could come in first place, leaving 4 runners who could come in second place, leaving 3 runners who could come in third place, for a total of $5 \times 4 \times 3 = 60$ possible outcomes for gold, silver, and bronze medal winners. Or, using the formula:

$$\begin{aligned} {}_5P_3 &= \frac{5!}{(5-3)!} = \frac{5!}{2!} = \frac{5 \times 4 \times 3 \times \cancel{2} \times \cancel{1}}{\cancel{2} \times \cancel{1}} \\ &= 5 \times 4 \times 3 = 60 \end{aligned}$$

73: How to solve a COMBINATION problem

If the order or arrangement of the smaller group that's being drawn from the larger group does *not* matter, you are looking for the numbers of combinations, and a different formula is called for:

$${}_nC_k = \frac{n!}{k!(n-k)!}$$

where n = (the number in the larger group) and
k = (the number you're choosing).

Example:

How many different ways are there to choose 3 delegates from 8 possible candidates?

Setup:

$$\begin{aligned} {}_nC_k &= \frac{8!}{3!(8-3)!} = \frac{8!}{3! \times 5!} \\ &= \frac{8 \times 7 \times \cancel{6} \times \cancel{5} \times \cancel{4} \times \cancel{3} \times \cancel{2} \times \cancel{1}}{\cancel{3} \times \cancel{2} \times 1 \times \cancel{5} \times \cancel{4} \times \cancel{3} \times \cancel{2} \times \cancel{1}} \\ &= 8 \times 7 = 56 \end{aligned}$$

So there are 56 different possible combinations.

74. How to solve PROBABILITY problems where probabilities must be multiplied

Suppose that a random process is performed. Then there is a set of possible outcomes that can occur. An event is a set of possible outcomes. We are concerned with the probability of events.

When all the outcomes are all equally likely, the basic probability formula is this:

$$\textit{Probability} = \frac{\textit{Number of desired outcomes}}{\textit{Number of total possible outcomes}}$$

Many more difficult probability questions involve finding the probability that several events occur. Let's consider first the case of the probability that two events occur. Call these two events A and B. The probability that both events occur is the probability that event A occurs multiplied by the probability that event B occurs given that event A occurred. The probability that B occurs given that

A occurs is called the conditional probability that *B* occurs given that *A* occurs. Except when events *A* and *B* do not depend on one another, the probability that *B* occurs given that *A* occurs is not the same as the probability that *B* occurs.

The probability that three events *A*, *B*, and *C* occur is the probability that *A* occurs multiplied by the conditional probability that *B* occurs given that *A* occurred multiplied by the conditional probability that *C* occurs given that both *A* and *B* have occurred.

This can be generalized to any number of events.

Example:

If 2 students are chosen at random to run an errand from a class with 5 girls and 5 boys, what is the probability that both students chosen will be girls?

Setup:

The probability that the first student chosen will be a girl is $\frac{5}{10} = \frac{1}{2}$, and since there would be 4 girls and 5 boys left out of 9 students, the probability that the second student chosen will be a girl (given that the first student chosen is a girl) is $\frac{4}{9}$. Thus, the probability that both students chosen will be girls is $\frac{1}{2} \times \frac{4}{9} = \frac{2}{9}$. There was conditional probability here because the probability of choosing the second girl was affected by another girl being chosen first. Now let's consider another example where a random process is repeated.

Example:

If a fair coin is tossed 4 times, what's the probability that at least 3 of the 4 tosses will be heads?

Setup:

There are 2 possible outcomes for each toss, so after 4 tosses, there are $2 \times 2 \times 2 \times 2 = 16$ possible outcomes.

We can list the different possible sequences where at least 3 of the 4 tosses are heads. These sequences are

HHHT
HHTH
HTHH
THHH
HHHH

Thus, the probability that at least 3 of the 4 tosses will come up heads is:

$$\frac{\textit{Number of desired outcomes}}{\textit{Number of total possible outcomes}} = \frac{5}{16}$$

We could have also solved this question using the combinations formula. The probability of a head is $\frac{1}{2}$, and the probability of a tail is $\frac{1}{2}$. The probability of any particular sequence of heads and tails resulting from 4 tosses is $\frac{1}{2} \times \frac{1}{2} \times \frac{1}{2} \times \frac{1}{2}$, which is $\frac{1}{16}$.

Suppose that the result of each of the four tosses is recorded in each of the four spaces.

____ ____ ____ ____

Thus, we would record an H for head or a T for tails in each of the 4 spaces.

The number of ways of having exactly 3 heads among the 4 tosses is the number of ways of choosing 3 of the 4 spaces above to record an H for heads.

The number of ways of choosing 3 of the 4 spaces is

$${}_4C_3 = \frac{4!}{3!\,(4-3)!} = \frac{4!}{3!(1)!} = \frac{4 \times 3 \times 2 \times 1}{3 \times 2 \times 1 \times 1} = 4$$

The number of ways of having exactly 4 heads among the 4 tosses is 1.

If we use the combinations formula, using the definition that $0! = 1$, then

$$
\begin{aligned}
{}_4C_4 &= \frac{4!}{4!(4-4)!} = \frac{4!}{4!(0)!} \\
&= \frac{4 \times 3 \times 2 \times 1}{4 \times 3 \times 2 \times 1 \times 1} = 1
\end{aligned}
$$

Thus, ${}_4C_3 = 4$ and ${}_4C_4 = 1$. So the number of different sequences containing at least 3 heads is $4 + 1 = 5$.

The probability of having at least 3 heads is $\frac{5}{16}$.

75. How to deal with STANDARD DEVIATION

Like the terms *mean*, *mode*, *median*, and *range*, *standard deviation* is a term used to describe sets of numbers. Standard deviation is a measure of how spread out a set of numbers is (how much the numbers deviate from the mean). The greater the spread, the higher the standard deviation. You'll rarely have to calculate the standard deviation on Test Day (although this skill may be necessary for some high-difficulty questions). Here's how standard deviation is calculated:

- Find the average (arithmetic mean) of the set.
- Find the differences between the mean and each value in the set.
- Square each of the differences.
- Find the average of the squared differences.
- Take the positive square root of the average.

In addition to the occasional question that asks you to calculate standard deviation, you may also be asked to compare standard deviations between sets of data or otherwise demonstrate that you understand what standard deviation means. You can often handle these questions using estimation.

Example:

High temperatures, in degrees Fahrenheit, in two cities over five days:

September	1	2	3	4	5
City A	54	61	70	49	56
City B	62	56	60	67	65

For the five-day period listed, which city had the greater standard deviation in high temperatures?

Setup:

Even without trying to calculate them out, one can see that City A has the greater spread in temperatures and, therefore, the greater standard deviation in high temperatures. If you were to go ahead and calculate the standard deviations following the steps described above, you would find that the standard deviation in high temperatures for

City A $= \sqrt{\frac{254}{5}} \approx 7.1$ while the standard

deviation for City

B $= \sqrt{\frac{74}{5}} \approx 3.8$.

76. How to MULTIPLY/DIVIDE VALUES WITH EXPONENTS

Add/subtract the exponents.

Example:

$$
\begin{aligned}
x^a \times x^b &= x^{a+b} \\
2^3 \times 2^4 &= 2^7
\end{aligned}
$$

Example:

$$
\begin{aligned}
\frac{x^a}{x^b} &= x^{a-b} \\
\frac{2^8}{2^2} &= 2^{8-2} = 2^6
\end{aligned}
$$

77. How to handle a value with an EXPONENT RAISED TO AN EXPONENT

Multiply the exponents.

Example:

$$
\begin{aligned}
(x^a)^b &= x^{ab} \\
(3^4)^5 &= 3^{20}
\end{aligned}
$$

78. How to handle EXPONENTS with a base of ZERO and BASES with an EXPONENT of ZERO

Zero raised to any nonzero exponent equals zero.

Example:

$$0^4 = 0^{12} = 0^1 = 0$$

Any nonzero number raised to the exponent 0 equals 1.

Example:

$$3^0 = 15^0 = (0.34)^0 = (-345)^0 = \pi^0 = 1$$

The lone exception is 0 raised to the 0 power, which is *undefined.*

79. How to handle NEGATIVE POWERS

A number raised to the exponent $-x$ is the reciprocal of that number raised to the exponent x.

Example:

$$n^{-1} = \frac{1}{n},\ n^{-2} = \frac{1}{n^2}, \text{ and so on.}$$

$$5^{-3} = \frac{1}{5^3} = \frac{1}{5 \times 5 \times 5} = \frac{1}{125}$$

80. How to handle FRACTIONAL POWERS

Fractional exponents relate to roots. For instance, $x^{\frac{1}{2}} = \sqrt{x}$.

Likewise, $x^{\frac{1}{3}} = \sqrt[3]{x}$, $x^{\frac{2}{3}} = \sqrt[3]{x^2}$, and so on.

Example:

$$\sqrt{x^{-2}} = (x^{-2})^{\frac{1}{2}} = x^{(-2)\left(\frac{1}{2}\right)} = x^{-1} = \frac{1}{x}$$

$$4^{\frac{1}{2}} = \sqrt{4} = 2$$

81. How to handle CUBE ROOTS

The cube root of x is just the number that, when used as a factor 3 times (i.e., cubed), gives you x. Both positive and negative numbers have one and only one cube root, denoted by the symbol $\sqrt[3]{\ }$, and the cube root of a number is always the same sign as the number itself.

Example:

$$(-5) \times (-5) \times (-5) = -125, \text{ so } \sqrt[3]{-125} = -5$$

$$\frac{1}{2} \times \frac{1}{2} \times \frac{1}{2} = \frac{1}{8}, \text{ so } \sqrt[3]{\frac{1}{8}} = \frac{1}{2}$$

82. How to ADD, SUBTRACT, MULTIPLY, and DIVIDE ROOTS

You can add/subtract roots only when the parts inside the $\sqrt{\ }$ are identical.

Example:

$$\sqrt{2} + 3\sqrt{2} = 4\sqrt{2}$$

$$\sqrt{2} - 3\sqrt{2} = -2\sqrt{2}$$

$\sqrt{2} + \sqrt{3}$ can not be combined.

To multiply/divide roots, deal with what's inside the $\sqrt{\ }$ and outside the $\sqrt{\ }$ separately.

Example:

$$\left(2\sqrt{3}\right)\left(7\sqrt{5}\right) = (2 \times 7)\left(\sqrt{3 \times 5}\right) = 14\sqrt{15}$$

$$\frac{10\sqrt{21}}{5\sqrt{3}} = \frac{10}{5}\sqrt{\frac{21}{3}} = 2\sqrt{7}$$

83. How to SIMPLIFY A RADICAL

Look for factors of the number under the radical sign that are perfect squares; then find the square root of those perfect squares. Keep simplifying until the term with the square root sign is as simplified as possible, that is, when there are no other perfect square factors (4, 9, 16, 25, 36, . . .) inside the $\sqrt{\ }$. Write the perfect squares as separate factors and "unsquare" them.

Example:

$$\sqrt{48} = \sqrt{16}\ \sqrt{3} = 4\sqrt{3}$$

$$\sqrt{180} = \sqrt{36}\ \sqrt{5} = 6\sqrt{5}$$

84. How to solve certain QUADRATIC EQUATIONS

Manipulate the equation (if necessary) so that it is equal to 0, factor the left side (reverse FOIL by finding two numbers whose product is the constant and whose sum is the coefficient of the term without the exponent), and break the quadratic into two simple expressions. Then find the value(s) for the variable that make either expression = 0.

Example:

$$\begin{aligned} x^2 + 6 &= 5x \\ x^2 - 5x + 6 &= 0 \\ (x - 2)(x - 3) &= 0 \\ x - 2 &= 0 \text{ or } x - 3 = 0 \\ x &= 2 \text{ or } 3 \end{aligned}$$

Example:

$$\begin{aligned} x^2 &= 9 \\ x &= 3 \text{ or } -3 \end{aligned}$$

85. How to solve MULTIPLE EQUATIONS

When you see two equations with two variables on the GRE, they're probably easy to combine in such a way that you get something closer to what you're looking for.

Example:

If $5x - 2y = -9$ and $3y - 4x = 6$, what is the value of $x + y$?

Setup:

The question doesn't ask for x and y separately, so don't solve for them separately if you don't have to. Look what happens if you just rearrange a little and "add" the equations:

$$\begin{aligned} 5x - 2y &= -9 \\ +[-4x + 3y &= 6] \\ \hline x + y &= -3 \end{aligned}$$

86. How to solve a SEQUENCE problem

The notation used in sequence problems scares many test takers, but these problems aren't as bad as they look. In a sequence problem, the nth term in the sequence is generated by performing an operation, which will be defined for you, on either n or on the previous term in the sequence. The term itself is expressed as a_n. For instance, if you are referring to the fourth term in a sequence, it is called a_4 in sequence notation. Familiarize yourself with sequence notation and you should have no problem.

Example:

What is the positive difference between the fifth and fourth terms in the sequence 0, 4, 18, . . . whose nth term is $n^2(n - 1)$?

Setup:

Use the definition given to come up with the values for your terms:

$$\begin{aligned} a_5 &= 5^2(5 - 1) = 25(4) = 100 \\ a_4 &= 4^2(4 - 1) = 16(3) = 48 \end{aligned}$$

So the positive difference between the fifth and fourth terms is $100 - 48 = 52$.

87. How to solve a FUNCTION problem

You may see function notation on the GRE. An algebraic expression of only one variable may be defined as a function, usually symbolized by f or g, of that variable.

Example:

What is the minimum value of x in the function $f(x) = x^2 - 1$?

Setup:

In the function $f(x) = x^2 - 1$, if x is 1, then $f(1) = 1^2 - 1 = 0$. In other words, by inputting 1 into the function, the output $f(x) = 0$. Every number inputted has one and only one output (although the reverse is not necessarily true). You're asked to find the minimum value, so how would you minimize the expression $f(x) = x^2 - 1$? Since x^2 cannot be negative, in this case $f(x)$ is minimized by making $x = 0$: $f(0) = 0^2 - 1 = -1$, so the minimum value of the function is -1.

88. How to handle GRAPHS of FUNCTIONS

You may see a problem that involves a function graphed onto the *xy*-coordinate plane, often called a "rectangular coordinate system" on the GRE. When graphing a function, the output, $f(x)$, becomes the *y*-coordinate. For example, in the previous example, $f(x) = x^2 - 1$, you've already determined 2 points, (1,0) and (0,−1). If you were to keep plugging in numbers to determine more points and then plotted those points on the *xy*-coordinate plane, you would come up with something like this:

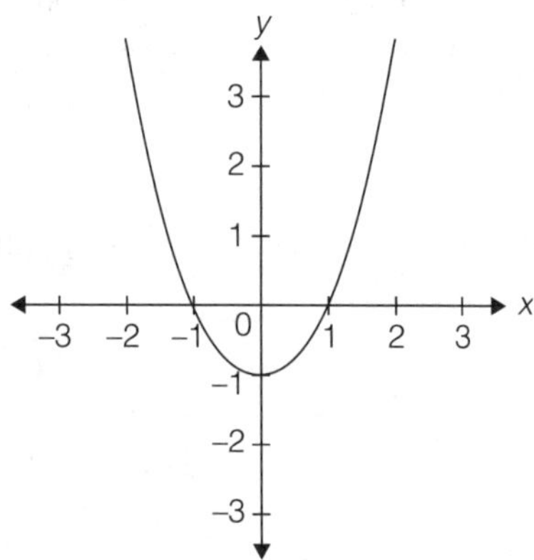

This curved line is called a *parabola*. In the event that you should see a parabola on the GRE (it could be upside down or narrower or wider than the one shown), you will most likely be asked to choose which equation the parabola is describing. These questions can be surprisingly easy to answer. Pick out obvious points on the graph, such as (1,0) and (0,−1) above, plug these values into the answer choices, and eliminate answer choices that don't work with those values until only one answer choice is left.

89. How to handle LINEAR EQUATIONS

You may also encounter linear equations on the GRE. A linear equation is often expressed in the form

$y = mx + b$, where

m = the slope of the line $= \frac{rise}{run}$

b = the *y*-intercept (the point where the line crosses the *y*-axis)

Example:

The graph of the linear equation

$$y = -\frac{3}{4}x + 3 \text{ is this:}$$

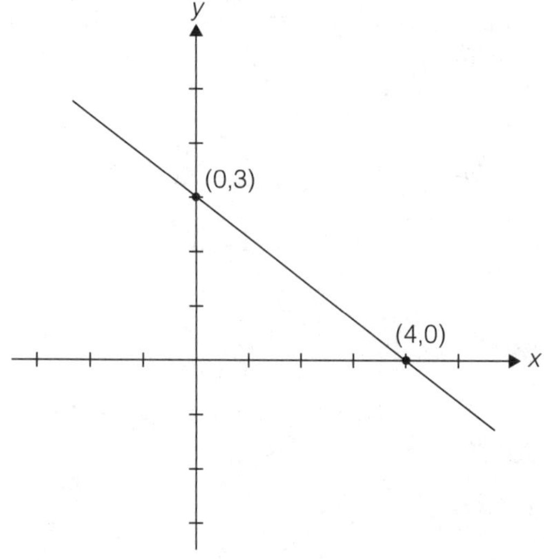

Note:

The equation could also be written in the form $3x + 4y = 12$, but this form does not readily describe the slope and *y*-intercept of the line.

To get a better handle on an equation written in this form, you can solve for *y* to write it in its more familiar form. Or, if you're asked to choose which equation the line is describing, you can pick obvious points, such as (0,3) and (4,0) in this example, and use these values to eliminate answer choices until only one answer is left.

90. How to find the *x*- and *y*-INTERCEPTS of a line

The *x*-intercept of a line is the value of *x* where the line crosses the *x*-axis. In other words, it's the value of *x* when $y = 0$. Likewise, the *y*-intercept is the value of *y* where the line crosses the *y*-axis (i.e., the value of *y* when $x = 0$). The *y*-intercept is also the value *b* when the equation is in the form $y = mx + b$. For instance, in the line shown in the previous example, the *x*-intercept is 4 and the *y*-intercept is 3.

91. How to find the MAXIMUM and MINIMUM lengths for a SIDE of a TRIANGLE

If you know the lengths of two sides of a triangle, you know that the third side is somewhere between the positive difference and the sum of the other two sides.

Example:

The length of one side of a triangle is 7. The length of another side is 3. What is the range of possible lengths for the third side?

Setup:

The third side is greater than the positive difference $(7 - 3 = 4)$ and less than the sum $(7 + 3 = 10)$ of the other two sides.

92. How to find the sum of all the ANGLES of a POLYGON and one angle measure of a REGULAR POLYGON

Sum of the interior angles in a polygon with n sides:

$$(n - 2) \times 180$$

The term *regular* means all angles in the polygon are of equal measure.

Degree measure of one angle in a regular polygon with n sides:

$$\frac{(n - 2) \times 180}{n}$$

Example:

What is the measure of one angle of a regular pentagon?

Setup:

Since a pentagon is a five-sided figure, plug $n = 5$ into the formula:

Degree measure of one angle:

$$\frac{(5 - 2) \times 180}{5} = \frac{540}{5} = 108$$

93. How to find the LENGTH of an ARC

Think of an arc as a fraction of the circle's circumference. Use the measure of an interior angle of a circle, which has 360 degrees around the central point, to determine the length of an arc.

$$\textit{Length of arc} = \frac{n}{360} \times 2\pi r$$

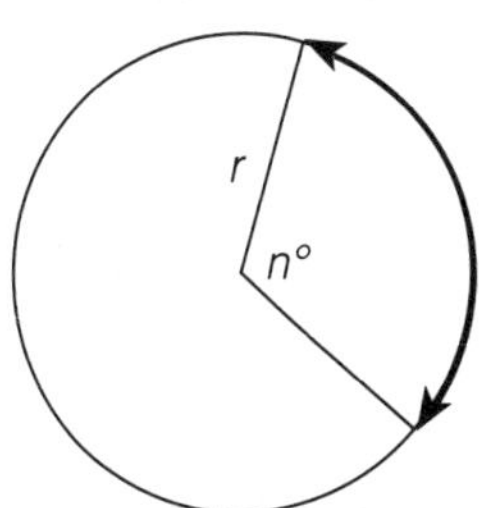

94. How to find the AREA of a SECTOR

Think of a sector as a fraction of the circle's area. Again, set up the interior angle measure as a fraction of 360, which is the degree measure of a circle around the central point.

$$\textit{Area of sector} = \frac{n}{360} \times \pi r^2$$

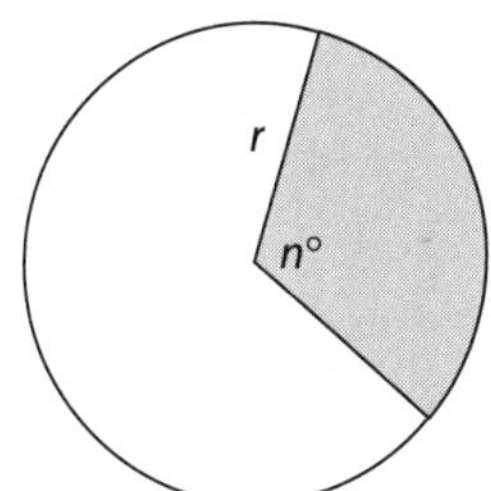

95. How to find the dimensions or area of an INSCRIBED or CIRCUMSCRIBED FIGURE

Look for the connection. Is the diameter the same as a side or a diagonal?

Example:

If the area of the square is 36, what is the circumference of the circle?

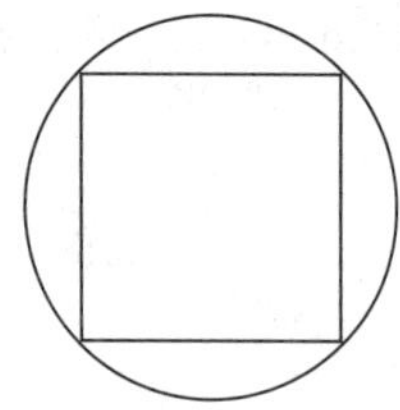

Setup:

To get the circumference, you need the diameter or radius. The circle's diameter is also the square's diagonal. The diagonal of the square is $6\sqrt{2}$. This is because the diagonal of the square transforms it into two separate $45° - 45° - 90°$ triangles (see #46). So, the diameter of the circle is $6\sqrt{2}$.

$$Circumference = \pi(Diameter) = 6\pi\sqrt{2}.$$

96. How to find the VOLUME of a RECTANGULAR SOLID

Volume = *Length* × *Width* × *Height*

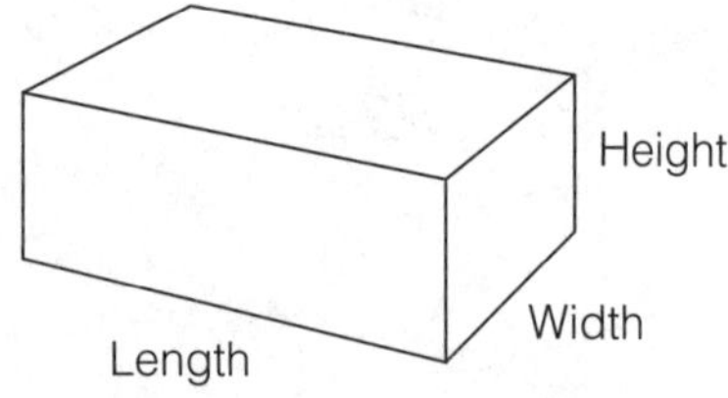

97. How to find the SURFACE AREA of a RECTANGULAR SOLID

To find the surface area of a rectangular solid, you have to find the area of each face and add the areas together. Here's the formula:

Let l = length, w = width, h = height:

$$Surface\ area = 2(lw) + 2(wh) + 2(lh)$$

98. How to find the DIAGONAL of a RECTANGULAR SOLID

Use the Pythagorean theorem twice, unless you spot "special" triangles.

Example:

What is the length of *AG*?

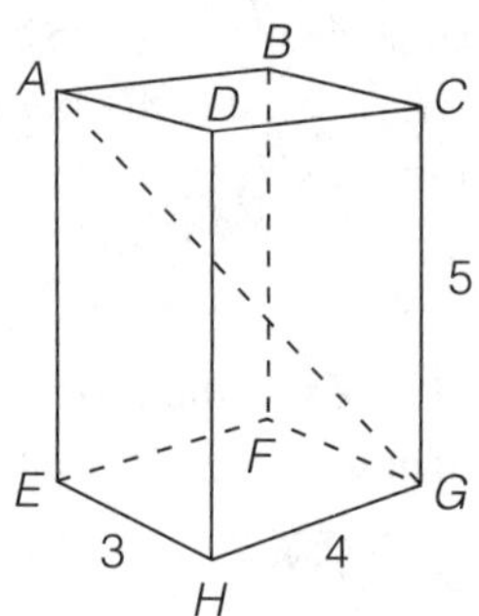

Setup:

Draw diagonal *AC*.

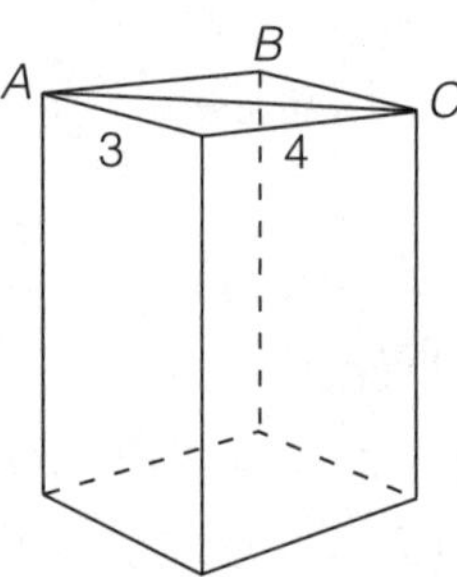

ABC is a 3:4:5 triangle, so *AC* = 5. Now look at triangle *ACG*:

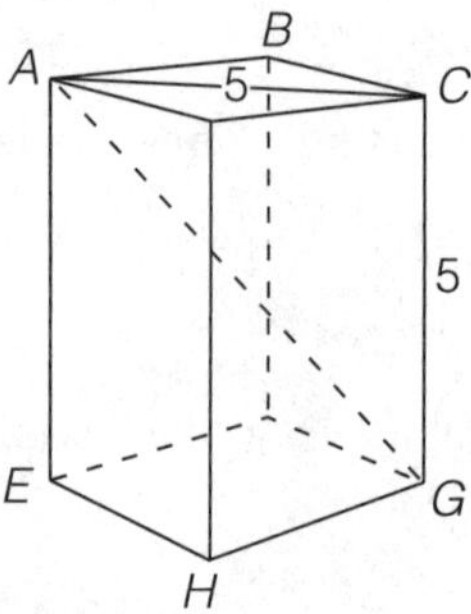

ACG is another special triangle, so you don't need to use the Pythagorean theorem. *ACG* is a $45° - 45° - 90°$ triangle, so $AG = 5\sqrt{2}$.

99. How to find the VOLUME of a CYLINDER

Volume = *Area of the base* × *Height* = $\pi r^2 h$

Example:

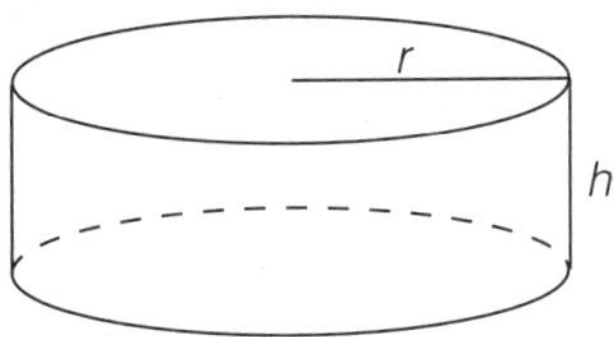

Let $r = 6$ and $h = 3$.

Setup:

Volume = $\pi r^2 h = \pi(6^2)(3) = 108\pi$

100. How to find the SURFACE AREA of a CYLINDER

Surface area = $2\pi r^2 + 2\pi rh$

Example:

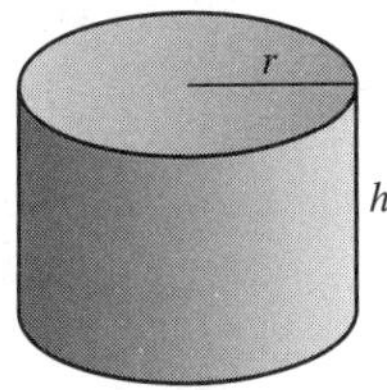

Let $r = 3$ and $h = 4$.

Setup:

$$\begin{aligned} \textit{Surface area} &= 2\pi r^2 + 2\pi rh \\ &= 2\pi(3)^2 + 2\pi(3)(4) \\ &= 18\pi + 24\pi = 42\pi \end{aligned}$$

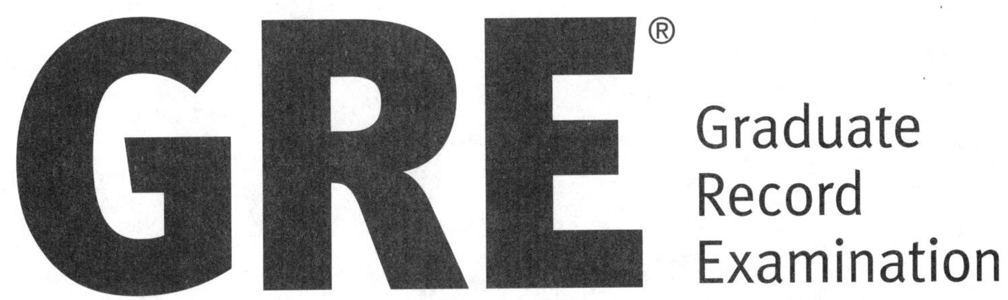

MATH WORKBOOK

Tenth Edition

For more GRE® prep, Kaplan offers a range of print and digital products, available in stores and online, including:

Kaplan GRE® Premier with 6 Practice Tests

Kaplan GRE® Strategies, Practice, and Review with 4 Practice Tests

GRE® Verbal Workbook

Kaplan GRE® Vocabulary Flashcards

To learn more about Kaplan's comprehensive prep courses for the GRE®, please visit **www.kaptest.com/GRE.**

MATH WORKBOOK

Tenth Edition

New York

Published by Kaplan Publishing, a division of Kaplan, Inc.
750 Third Avenue
New York, NY 10017

Printed in the United States of America

10 9 8 7 6 5 4 3 2 1

ISBN: 978-1-62523-299-1

Table of Contents

Acknowledgments

Special thanks to the team that made this book possible:

Arthur Ahn, Matthew Belinkie, Shannon Berning, Lauren T. Bernstein, Kim Bowers, Gerard Cortinez, Elisa Davis, Lola Disparte, Boris Dvorkin, John Evans, Paula Fleming, Darcy Galane, Joanna Graham, Adam Grey, Allison Harm, Jack Hayes, Adam Hinz, Gar Hong, Sunny Hwang, Cinzia Iacono, Avi Lidgi, Kate Lopaze, Keith Lubeley, TJ Mancini, Jennifer Moore, Jason Moss, Walt Niedner, Robert Reiss, Shmuel Ross, Derek Rusnak, Emily Sachar, Stephanie Schrauth, Sheryl Stebbins, Glen Stohr, Sascha Strelka, Gene Suhir, Martha Torres, Liza Weale, Lee A. Weiss, and many others who have contributed materials and advice over the years.

How to Use This Book

Kaplan has prepared students to take standardized tests for more than 75 years. Our team of teachers and researchers knows more about preparation for the GRE than anyone else, and you'll find Kaplan's accumulated knowledge and experience throughout this book. The GRE is a standardized test, so every test covers the same content in roughly the same way. This is good news for you; it means that the best way to prepare is to focus on the sort of questions you are likely to see on Test Day. The main focus of this book is on strategic reviews, exercises, and practice sets with explanations that will help you brush up on any math skills you may have forgotten. There is a lot of math to absorb, and it's hard to do it all at once. Instead, plan out a study schedule and work through this book over the course of several weeks.

Getting Started

In Part 1 of this book, "Getting Started," we'll provide you with background information on the Quantitative Reasoning section of the test, what it covers, and how it's organized.

QUANTITATIVE REASONING SECTION

The Quantitative Reasoning section of the GRE contains three main question types: Quantitative Comparison, Problem Solving, and Data Interpretation. Part 2 of this book covers these types with strategies and sample questions. Your focus here should be to familiarize yourself with the question types so you won't be trying to figure out how to approach them on Test Day. And practice, practice, practice!

MATH CONTENT REVIEW

Once you have the big picture, focus on the content. Part 3 of this book, "Math Content Review," gives you a complete tour of the math that you will see on Test Day. The material in the math content review is divided into particular subjects. Each subject begins with a review, followed by practice exercises organized by level of difficulty. This structure makes it easy for you to pinpoint the math concepts you need to review and quickly get your skills up to speed.

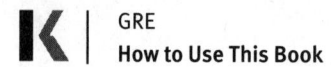

We suggest that you read the content review that introduces a section and then try some of the exercises. After checking your answers to those exercises, decide whether you need to spend more time with the content review before completing the sets of exercises. Keep track of your progress as you proceed with the content review. Not only will this build your skills, it will increase your confidence leading up to Test Day.

If you find that you would like access to more of Kaplan's practice tests and quizzes, as well as in-depth instruction on the question types and strategies, look into the variety of course options available at **www.kaptest.com/GRE**.

If you have questions about what you're studying, ask our expert GRE faculty on our Facebook page: **www.facebook.com/KaplanGradPrep**.

Thanks for choosing Kaplan. We wish you the best of luck on your journey to graduate school.

PART ONE

Getting Started

CHAPTER 1

Introduction to GRE Math

UNDERSTANDING THE GRE QUANTITATIVE REASONING SECTIONS

The Quantitative Reasoning sections of the GRE test your ability to reason quantitatively—to read a math problem, understand what it is asking, and solve it. The basic math disciplines covered on the GRE are arithmetic, algebra, geometry, and data interpretation. In this way, the GRE has topics similar to those covered on the SAT. There is no trigonometry or calculus on the GRE. The aim of the test is to provide an accurate indication of your ability to use your knowledge of the fundamental topics and apply reasoning skills to the various question types. The goal is to make the test a true indicator of your ability to apply given information, think logically, and draw conclusions. These are skills you will need at the graduate level of study.

The GRE contains two math sections, each having 20 questions. The allotted time for each section is 35 minutes. To perform well on the Quantitative Reasoning sections, you want to perform the fundamental math skills efficiently and apply your reasoning skills at the same time to answer as many questions correctly as possible. The various question types will be explained in detail in part 2 of this book. The foundations of arithmetic, algebra, geometry, and data interpretation will be reviewed in part 3 of this book. In every chapter, there will be plenty of opportunities to practice and check your answers.

MST MECHANICS

The GRE is a multi-stage test (MST). While working within a section of the test during the time allotted, you are allowed to skip questions and return to them as long as time remains for the section. The test is computer-based with built-in capabilities such as the "Mark" button to indicate a question you want to examine later (within the time allowed for that section) and the "Review" button to see your progress on the entire set of questions in a section, an optional time display, and an on-screen calculator. As you prepare for Test Day, always consider how you plan to manage your time for each section and how these computer capabilities can help you.

On the GRE, every question has the same value. So you do not want to waste time dwelling on one question while you may be able to answer several others correctly. This is one way the Mark and Review buttons can assist you in managing your time. You can turn the time display *on* or *off* as you wish. Some test takers will find it helpful; others will find it annoying.

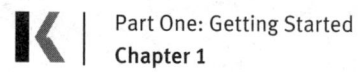

The availability of an on-screen calculator is something you will want to consider as you practice for the test. Questions in the Quantitative Reasoning sections are not designed to be calculator-intensive. If you find yourself doing a long calculation to answer a question, you may be missing the reasoning aspect completely. That means most questions on the GRE are written to be answered without a calculator. You will want to reserve the calculator for an isolated calculation or a quick check of an answer, but not use it as your main resource for the questions. To help you plan for the best use of the on-screen calculator, an image of it is shown below. Notice that it is a simple, four-function calculator with a square root key and change of sign key.

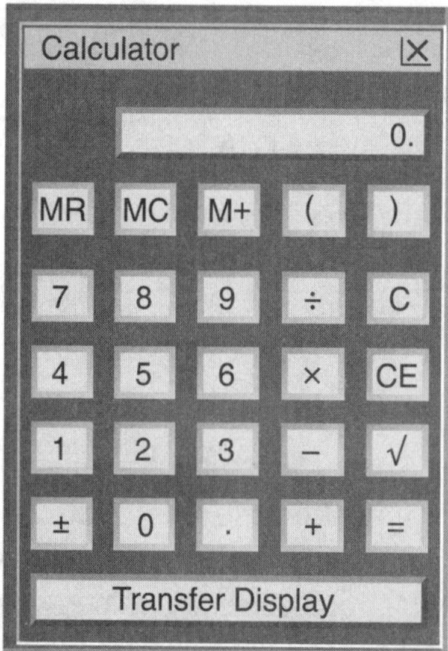

As you review mathematical foundations and practice answering the various question types in this workbook, use your own calculator strategically. This will lead you to rely on your critical thinking skills.

QUESTION TYPES

A Quantitative Reasoning section with 20 questions will be composed of three question types:

- Quantitative Comparison
- Problem Solving
- Data Interpretation

Each question type will require you to draw upon your ability to combine your knowledge of mathematical concepts with your reasoning skills in a particular way. However, the question types are not distributed evenly within a section. The chart below shows how many questions you can expect of each type, as well as the average amount of time you should spend on each question type.

	Quantitative Comparison	**Problem Solving**	**Data Interpretation**
Number of Questions	Approx. 7–8	Approx. 9–10	Approx. 3
Time per Question	1.5 minutes	1.5–2 minutes	2 minutes

QUANTITATIVE COMPARISON

A Quantitative Comparison question will not ask you to identify a particular value as the answer, but it will ask you to make a comparison between two quantities and identify a relationship between them. The four answer choices for a Quantitative Comparison are always the same—same wording, same order. Because the answer choices are consistent, you will become familiar with them quickly and be able to concentrate on the comparison at hand.

The Kaplan Method for answering Quantitative Comparison questions and strategies to help solve them efficiently can be found in chapter 2.

PROBLEM SOLVING

A Problem Solving question may appear as a math problem, or it may appear as a word problem dealing with a real-world situation. These questions deal with percents, ratios, and other proportions; linear and quadratic equations; basic probability and statistics; and two- and three-dimensional geometry.

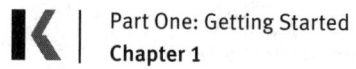

The Kaplan Method for answering Problem Solving questions and strategies to help solve them efficiently can be found in chapter 3.

DATA INTERPRETATION

Questions that require you to interpret data will be based on information located in graphs or tables. You will see a set of three or four questions based on each data presentation. Frequently, you will have to use information from more than one data source to answer a question. Data Interpretation questions need to be answered thoughtfully, only after you have taken time to analyze the contents of each graph or table of data.

The Kaplan Method for answering Data Interpretation questions and strategies to help solve them efficiently can be found in chapter 4.

PART TWO

Quantitative Reasoning

CHAPTER 2

Quantitative Comparison

QUANTITATIVE COMPARISON

A Quantitative Comparison question asks you to compare two mathematical expressions; one is Quantity A, the other Quantity B. Sometimes additional information is given centered above the quantities. The additional information applies to both quantities and is needed to make the comparison. The question asks you to compare the relative values of the quantities or to tell whether there is enough information to make a comparison. This type of question is generally about the *relative* values of the two quantities, so you won't need the on-screen calculator for the most part.

The four answer choices for Quantitative Comparison questions are always the same. Choices (A), (B), and (C) represent definite relationships between the quantities. Choice (D) represents a relationship that cannot be determined, based on the information given. Choice (D) means that more than one relationship is possible, depending on the numbers chosen for the variable(s) in the question. When there is at least one variable in a Quantitative Comparison problem, using the Kaplan Picking Numbers strategy is one way to answer the question quickly. If the numbers chosen demonstrate more than one possible relationship between the quantities, you know that the answer is choice (D).

The directions for Quantitative Comparison questions will look like this:

Directions: Select the correct answer.

QUANTITATIVE COMPARISON QUESTIONS

THE KAPLAN METHOD FOR QUANTITATIVE COMPARISON

STEP 1 Analyze the centered information and quantities.

STEP 2 Approach strategically.

$h > 1$

Quantity A	Quantity B
$\frac{60}{h}$	The number of minutes in h hours

Ⓐ Quantity A is greater.
Ⓑ Quantity B is greater.
Ⓒ The two quantities are equal.
Ⓓ The relationship cannot be determined from the information given.

APPLY THE KAPLAN METHOD FOR QUANTITATIVE COMPARISON

Now let's apply the Kaplan Method to a Quantitative Comparison question:

$h > 1$

Quantity A	Quantity B
$\frac{60}{h}$	The number of minutes in h hours

Ⓐ Quantity A is greater.
Ⓑ Quantity B is greater.
Ⓒ The two quantities are equal.
Ⓓ The relationship cannot be determined from the information given.

STEP 1

Analyze the centered information and quantities.

The centered information tells you that the variable h is greater than 1. In Quantity A, the variable appears in the denominator of a fraction. So, the variable h is a divisor in Quantity A. In Quantity B, you are told that the variable h represents a number of hours. To find the number of minutes in h hours, the variable will be used as a multiplier: the number of minutes in h hours $= 60h$.

STEP 2

Approach strategically.

The restriction that h is greater than 1 is critical to determining the relationship between the quantities. A whole number (60 in this case) divided by a number greater than 1 will always be less than the whole number (60) multiplied by the same number greater than 1. A quick check using the Picking Numbers strategy verifies the reasoning. Let $h = 2 : \frac{60}{h} = \frac{60}{2} = 30$ and $60h = 60 \times 2 = 120$. Quantity B is greater and the answer is **(B)**.

QUANTITATIVE COMPARISON PRACTICE SET

Try the following Quantitative Comparison questions using the Kaplan Method.

Basic

1.

Quantity A	Quantity B
The number of edges on a cube	Twice the number of faces on a cube

- (A) Quantity A is greater.
- (B) Quantity B is greater.
- (C) The two quantities are equal.
- (D) The relationship cannot be determined from the information given.

2.

Quantity A	Quantity B
The length of the hypotenuse of a right triangle with legs of lengths 5 and 12	The length of a leg of a right triangle with a hypotenuse length of 17 and the other leg of length 8

- (A) Quantity A is greater.
- (B) Quantity B is greater.
- (C) The two quantities are equal.
- (D) The relationship cannot be determined from the information given.

3.

Quantity A	Quantity B
The number of degrees in the largest angle of a triangle inscribed in a circle, in which the diameter of the circle is one side of the triangle	The number of degrees in a right angle

- (A) Quantity A is greater.
- (B) Quantity B is greater.
- (C) The two quantities are equal.
- (D) The relationship cannot be determined from the information given.

4. $$\frac{a}{b} = \frac{3}{7} = \frac{c}{d}$$

Quantity A	Quantity B
$a + d$	$b + c$

Ⓐ Quantity A is greater.
Ⓑ Quantity B is greater.
Ⓒ The two quantities are equal.
Ⓓ The relationship cannot be determined from the information given.

5. $$12x - 46 = -18 + 5x$$

Quantity A	Quantity B
x	5

Ⓐ Quantity A is greater.
Ⓑ Quantity B is greater.
Ⓒ The two quantities are equal.
Ⓓ The relationship cannot be determined from the information given.

6. In a three-digit number n, the hundreds digit is 3 times the units digit.

Quantity A	Quantity B
The units digit of n	4

Ⓐ Quantity A is greater.
Ⓑ Quantity B is greater.
Ⓒ The two quantities are equal.
Ⓓ The relationship cannot be determined from the information given.

7.

Quantity A	Quantity B
The number of days in 17 weeks	The number of minutes in 2 hours

Ⓐ Quantity A is greater.
Ⓑ Quantity B is greater.
Ⓒ The two quantities are equal.
Ⓓ The relationship cannot be determined from the information given.

8. $2x + y = z$

Quantity A	Quantity B
The value of z when $x = -1$ and $y = 3$	The value of z when $x = -2$ and $y = 2$

(A) Quantity A is greater.
(B) Quantity B is greater.
(C) The two quantities are equal.
(D) The relationship cannot be determined from the information given.

9. $5p + 6q = 74$

$q = 8$

Quantity A	Quantity B
p	5

(A) Quantity A is greater.
(B) Quantity B is greater.
(C) The two quantities are equal.
(D) The relationship cannot be determined from the information given.

10. $f(x) = 3x + 4$

Quantity A	Quantity B
Slope of $f(x)$	y-intercept of $f(x)$

(A) Quantity A is greater.
(B) Quantity B is greater.
(C) The two quantities are equal.
(D) The relationship cannot be determined from the information given.

Intermediate

11. One marble is randomly selected from a bag that contains only 4 black marbles, 3 red marbles, 5 yellow marbles, and 4 green marbles.

Quantity A	Quantity B
The probability of selecting either a black marble or a red marble	The probability of selecting either a yellow marble or a green marble

Ⓐ Quantity A is greater.
Ⓑ Quantity B is greater.
Ⓒ The two quantities are equal.
Ⓓ The relationship cannot be determined from the information given.

12. $$f(x) = x^2 - 6x + 8$$

Quantity A	Quantity B
$f(-6)$	$f(6)$

Ⓐ Quantity A is greater.
Ⓑ Quantity B is greater.
Ⓒ The two quantities are equal.
Ⓓ The relationship cannot be determined from the information given.

13. A bag has 20 marbles that are either black or white.

Quantity A	Quantity B
The number of times one must randomly draw a marble from the bag, without replacing it, to ensure that at least 4 black marbles are selected	The number of times one must randomly draw a marble from the bag, without replacing it, to ensure that at least 4 white marbles are selected

Ⓐ Quantity A is greater.
Ⓑ Quantity B is greater.
Ⓒ The two quantities are equal.
Ⓓ The relationship cannot be determined from the information given.

14. $$\frac{a}{b} = \frac{3}{4}$$

Quantity A	Quantity B
$\frac{2a - b}{b}$	$\frac{a}{a + b}$

Ⓐ Quantity A is greater.
Ⓑ Quantity B is greater.
Ⓒ The two quantities are equal.
Ⓓ The relationship cannot be determined from the information given.

15. A line is represented by the equation $4x + 3y = 12$.

Quantity A	Quantity B
The value of the x-intercept of the line	The value of the y-intercept of the line

Ⓐ Quantity A is greater.
Ⓑ Quantity B is greater.
Ⓒ The two quantities are equal.
Ⓓ The relationship cannot be determined from the information given.

16. The positive integer x is odd, and the positive integer y is even.

Quantity A	Quantity B
$(-1)^{2x + y}$	$\frac{1}{2}$

Ⓐ Quantity A is greater.
Ⓑ Quantity B is greater.
Ⓒ The two quantities are equal.
Ⓓ The relationship cannot be determined from the information given.

17. Data set $M = \{60, 9, 10, 20, 12, 7, 10, 8\}$

Quantity A	Quantity B
The mode of data set M	The mean of data set M

Ⓐ Quantity A is greater.
Ⓑ Quantity B is greater.
Ⓒ The two quantities are equal.
Ⓓ The relationship cannot be determined from the information given.

18. $$\sqrt{x^2 + 39} = 8$$

Quantity A	Quantity B
x	4

Ⓐ Quantity A is greater.
Ⓑ Quantity B is greater.
Ⓒ The two quantities are equal.
Ⓓ The relationship cannot be determined from the information given.

19.

Quantity A	Quantity B
The sum of the coordinates of a point in the fourth quadrant of an xy-coordinate plane	The product of the coordinates of a point in the first quadrant of an xy-coordinate plane

Ⓐ Quantity A is greater.
Ⓑ Quantity B is greater.
Ⓒ The two quantities are equal.
Ⓓ The relationship cannot be determined from the information given.

20. $$4 < x < 10$$
$$3 < y < 5$$

Quantity A	Quantity B
$x + y$	14

Ⓐ Quantity A is greater.
Ⓑ Quantity B is greater.
Ⓒ The two quantities are equal.
Ⓓ The relationship cannot be determined from the information given.

Advanced

21. The length of a rectangular canvas is increased by x percent, and the width of the canvas is decreased by x percent.

Quantity A	Quantity B
The area of the new canvas if $x = 20$	The area of the new canvas if $x = 40$

Ⓐ Quantity A is greater.
Ⓑ Quantity B is greater.
Ⓒ The two quantities are equal.
Ⓓ The relationship cannot be determined from the information given.

22.

$$|4x + 24| = 96$$
$$|4x| = 120$$

Quantity A	Quantity B
x	18

Ⓐ Quantity A is greater.
Ⓑ Quantity B is greater.
Ⓒ The two quantities are equal.
Ⓓ The relationship cannot be determined from the information given.

23.

Quantity A	Quantity B
The number of miles driven at 50 miles per hour for 2 hours	The shortest distance between the starting point and the ending point of a trip if a vehicle is driven 60 miles north and 80 miles east

Ⓐ Quantity A is greater.
Ⓑ Quantity B is greater.
Ⓒ The two quantities are equal.
Ⓓ The relationship cannot be determined from the information given.

24.

Quantity A	Quantity B
The area of a triangle with sides 6, 8, and 10	The area of an equilateral triangle with side 8

Ⓐ Quantity A is greater.
Ⓑ Quantity B is greater.
Ⓒ The two quantities are equal.
Ⓓ The relationship cannot be determined from the information given.

25.

$$x < 0 < y$$

Quantity A	Quantity B
$-2(x + y)$	$-xy$

Ⓐ Quantity A is greater.
Ⓑ Quantity B is greater.
Ⓒ The two quantities are equal.
Ⓓ The relationship cannot be determined from the information given.

26.

$$f(x) = 2x$$
$$g(x) = \frac{1}{2}x$$

Quantity A	Quantity B
$f(g(3))$	$g(f(3))$

Ⓐ Quantity A is greater.
Ⓑ Quantity B is greater.
Ⓒ The two quantities are equal.
Ⓓ The relationship cannot be determined from the information given.

27.

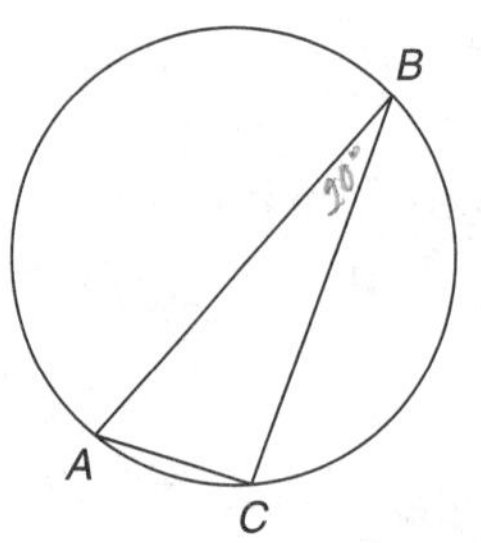

AB is a diameter of the circle.

$\angle ABC = 20°$

Quantity A	Quantity B
The measure of $\angle BAC$	70°

(A) Quantity A is greater.
(B) Quantity B is greater.
(C) The two quantities are equal.
(D) The relationship cannot be determined from the information given.

28. Five consecutive even integers have a sum of –20.

Quantity A	Quantity B
The greatest of the five even integers	0

(A) Quantity A is greater.
(B) Quantity B is greater.
(C) The two quantities are equal.
(D) The relationship cannot be determined from the information given.

29.

$$s = (t + r)^2$$
$$s = 4$$

Quantity A	Quantity B
$2 - r$	t

(A) Quantity A is greater.
(B) Quantity B is greater.
(C) The two quantities are equal.
(D) The relationship cannot be determined from the information given.

30. The numbers in a data set have a mean (arithmetic average) of 0.

Quantity A	Quantity B
Number of data elements below the mean	Number of data elements above the mean

(A) Quantity A is greater.
(B) Quantity B is greater.
(C) The two quantities are equal.
(D) The relationship cannot be determined from the information given.

QUANTITATIVE COMPARISON PRACTICE SET ANSWER KEY

1. C
2. B
3. C
4. D
5. B
6. B
7. B
8. A
9. A
10. B
11. B
12. A
13. D
14. A
15. B
16. A
17. B
18. D
19. D
20. D
21. A
22. B
23. C
24. B
25. D
26. C
27. C
28. C
29. D
30. D

QUANTITATIVE COMPARISON PRACTICE SET ANSWERS AND EXPLANATIONS

Basic

1. C

A question like this one shows the value of spending some time with common solids (cubes/rectangular solids—boxes; right cylinders—soup cans) before Test Day. In this way, you can familiarize yourself with the properties of these solids so you can visualize them when asked a question like this one.

A cube has 12 edges: 4 edges on top, 4 edges on the bottom, and 4 edges connecting the top to the bottom. A cube has 6 faces: top, bottom, back, front, right, and left: $2 \times 6 = 12$. The correct answer is **(C)**.

2. B

Quantity A is a 5:12:13 right triangle. The hypotenuse is 13. Quantity B is a right triangle with hypotenuse 17 and one of the legs 8. You may have this Pythagorean triplet memorized, too; it's an 8:15:17 right triangle. If not, the other leg can be found using the Pythagorean theorem. Let b be the length of the missing leg.

$8^2 + b^2 = 17^2$. Simplifying this equation: $64 + b^2 = 289$. Therefore $b^2 = 225$. Since the question asks for the length, we can disregard the negative value, so $b = 15$.

Quantity B is larger, so the correct answer is **(B)**.

3. C

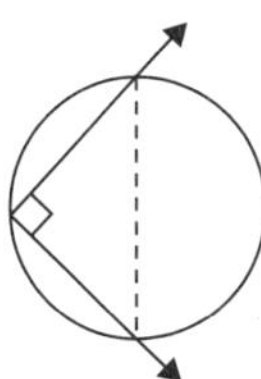

In the figure shown, the dashed line is the diameter of the circle.

When a triangle inscribed in a circle has the circle's diameter as one side, the angle on the circle's circumference intercepts a 180° arc. The measure of such an angle is always half the number of degrees of the intercepted arc, so the angle is a right angle: $180 \div 2 = 90$. Because a triangle has 180° total, the remaining angles have $180 - 90 = 90$ degrees between them; neither can be as large as the angle on the circumference, so it is the largest angle of the triangle. Quantity A equals 90°, which is the number of degrees in a right angle. The correct answer is **(C)**.

4. D

To simplify this Quantitative Comparison, use the strategy of Picking Numbers.

Let $a = 3$ and $b = 7$. Let $c = 3$ and $d = 7$.

$$a + d = 3 + 7 = 10$$
$$b + c = 7 + 3 = 10$$

In this case, the quantities are equal.

Repeat using a different set of numbers. Let $a = -3$ and $b = -7$. Let $c = 3$ and $d = 7$.

$$a + d = -3 + 7 = 4$$
$$b + c = -7 + 3 = -4$$

Now Quantity A is greater. When you pick a second set of numbers in a Quantitative Comparison, always consider the potential role of negatives and nonintegers. The correct answer is **(D)**.

5. B

Solve the equation for x. Subtract $5x$ from both sides:

$$\begin{aligned} 7x - 46 &= -18 \\ 7x &= 28 \\ x &= 4 \end{aligned}$$

Quantity A is 4, and Quantity B is 5. Therefore, the correct answer is **(B)**.

6. B

Start by trying to set the quantities equal. If the units digit of the number is 4, then the hundreds digit must be 3 times 4, based on the centered information in the problem. But that is impossible; the number 12 will not fit in the hundreds place. That means the units digit must be less than 4. Therefore, Quantity A is less than Quantity B. Choose **(B)** as the answer.

7. B

The number of days in 17 weeks is $17 \times 7 = 119$. The number of minutes in 2 hours is $2 \times 60 = 120$. The correct answer is **(B)**.

8. A

Before you take time to calculate, look closely at the equation in the centered information and the values given for x and y in the quantities. The value of z is twice x plus y. The value of x in Quantity A, -1, is greater than the value of x in Quantity B, -2. Therefore, $2x$ in Quantity A is greater than $2x$ in Quantity B. Likewise, the value of y in Quantity A, 3, is greater than the value of y in Quantity B, 2. Both values in Quantity A are greater than the corresponding values in Quantity B. The correct answer is **(A)**.

9. A

Use the two equations to determine the value of the variable p. Substitute 8 for q in the first equation. Then $5p + 6(8) = 74$, $5p = 26$, and $p = \frac{26}{5}$, or $5\frac{1}{5}$. Quantity A is $5\frac{1}{5}$, and Quantity B is 5. The correct answer is **(A)**.

10. B

The function $f(x) = 3x + 4$ is in slope-intercept form, where $y = mx + b$ and m is the slope and b is the y-intercept. $f(x)$ is another way of writing y.

The slope is 3 and the y-intercept is 4. The correct answer is **(B)**.

Intermediate

11. B

Use the probability formula to compare the quantities.

$$Probability = \frac{Number\ of\ desired\ outcomes}{Number\ of\ total\ possible\ outcomes}$$

The number of total possible outcomes is the same for both quantities. You only need to compare the numerators. The number of desired outcomes for Quantity A is $4 + 3 = 7$. The number of desired outcomes for Quantity B is $5 + 4 = 9$. The correct answer is **(B)**.

12. A

Look at the function $f(x) = x^2 - 6x + 8$. No matter what value is plugged in for x, you will add 8 to it; this is the same for both quantities. Also, when you evaluate $f(-6)$ and $f(6)$, $x^2 = 36$ in both cases. But $-6x = 36$ when $x = -6$, and $-6x = -36$ when $x = 6$. The correct answer is **(A)**.

13. D

You can't tell how many marbles you need to draw from the bag to have at least 4 black marbles or 4 white marbles, unless you know how many of each kind there are. The correct answer is **(D)**.

14. A

Try Picking Numbers here, making sure to pick numbers that conform to the centered information ($\frac{a}{b}$ must equal $\frac{3}{4}$). Also, make sure to try two sets of numbers.

Substitute $a = 3$ and $b = 4$ into both expressions:

$$\frac{2a - b}{b} = \frac{2(3) - 4}{4} = \frac{6 - 4}{4} = \frac{2}{4} = \frac{1}{2}$$

$$\frac{a}{a + b} = \frac{3}{3 + 4} = \frac{3}{7}$$

Now, let's try $a = -6$ and $b = -8$:

$$\frac{2a - b}{b} = \frac{2(-6) - (-8)}{-8} = \frac{-4}{-8} = \frac{1}{2}$$

$$\frac{a}{a + b} = \frac{-6}{-6 + -8} = \frac{-6}{-14} = \frac{3}{7}$$

Quantity A will always be larger than Quantity B, so the correct answer is **(A)**.

15. B

The x-intercept is where the line crosses the x-axis; at this point, the value of y is zero. To find the x-intercept, set $y = 0$ and solve for x.

$$\begin{aligned} 4x + 3y &= 12 \\ 4x + (3)(0) &= 12 \\ 4x + 0 &= 12 \\ 4x &= 12 \\ x &= 3 \end{aligned}$$

The y-intercept is where the line crosses the y-axis; at this point the value of x is zero. To find the y-intercept, set $x = 0$ and solve for y.

$$\begin{aligned} 4x + 3y &= 12 \\ (4)(0) + 3y &= 12 \\ 0 + 3y &= 12 \\ 3y &= 12 \\ y &= 4 \end{aligned}$$

The correct answer is **(B)**.

16. A

Since x is an integer, $2x$ must be even because 2 times any integer is even. Since $2x$ is even and y is even, $2x + y$ is even because an even plus an even is even. Then $(-1)^{2x+y} = 1$, because -1 is being raised to an even exponent. Quantity A is greater, so the correct answer is **(A)**.

17. B

Whenever a problem calls for the median or mode, put the numbers in order first: 7, 8, 9, 10, 10, 12, 20, 60. The mode—the number that occurs most often—is 10. Use reasoning, not calculating, to determine that the mean must be more than 10. Reason like this: if the mean were 10, then the sum of all eight numbers would be $8 \times 10 = 80$. However, you know the sum of the numbers is greater than 80 because the sum of just the last three numbers $(12 + 20 + 60)$ is greater than 80. So, the mean is greater than 10. The correct answer is **(B)**.

18. D

Eliminate the square root in the equation by squaring both sides; $x^2 + 39 = 64$. Then $x^2 = 25$. So $x = 5$ or $x = -5$. If $x = 5$, then Quantity A is greater. If $x = -5$, then Quantity B is greater. Because more than one relationship between the quantities is possible, the relationship between the quantities cannot be determined. The correct answer is **(D)**.

19. D

Use the strategy of Picking Numbers.

For Quantity A, pick (10, –2); for Quantity B, pick (1, 2). $10 + (-2) = 8$ and $1 \times 2 = 2$. In this case, Quantity A is greater.

Next, for Quantity A, pick (1, −2); for Quantity B, pick (1, 2). $1 + (-2) = -1$ and $1 \times 2 = 2$. In this case, Quantity B is greater.

The correct answer is **(D)**.

20. D

Since $4 < x$ and $3 < y$, the value of $x + y$ must be greater than 7. Since $x < 10$ and $y < 5$, the value of $x + y$ must be less than 15. So $7 < x + y < 15$. Quantity B is 14. Since $x + y$ can be any value between 7 and 15, it could be less than 14, or greater than 14. You can use Picking Numbers to see this. If $x = 9$ and $y = 4$, Quantity A is $9 + 4 = 13$ and Quantity B is greater. However, if $x = 9.5$ and $y = 4.5$, then Quantity A is $9.5 + 4.5 = 14$ and the quantities are the same. There are different possible relationships between Quantity A and Quantity B, so the correct answer is **(D)**.

Advanced

21. A

First, recall the formula for the area of a rectangle: $A = lw$. Then consider how to express the length after an increase and the width after a decrease. In Quantity A, the value of x is 20. Add 0.20 to l for the increase and subtract 0.20 from w for the decrease. That makes the new length $1.2l$ and the new width $0.8w$. So, if $x = 20$, $Area = (1.2l)(0.8w) = 1.20 \times 0.80(lw)$.

For $x = 40$ under Quantity B, add 0.40 to l and subtract 0.40 from w. That gives you a new length of $1.40l$ and a new width of $0.60w$. For Quantity B, $Area = (1.4l)(0.6w) = 1.40 \times 0.60(lw)$.

To compare the quantities in each column, ignore the piece in each expression that is the same (lw) and just compare the product 1.20×0.80 to the product 1.40×0.60.

Quantity A: $1.20 \times 0.80 = 0.96$

Quantity B: $1.40 \times 0.60 = 0.84$

Because $0.96 > 0.84$, the answer is **(A)**.

Picking Numbers is also a great strategy here. Try picking 10 for both l and w. Then Quantity A is $12 \times 8 = 96$, and Quantity B is $14 \times 6 = 84$. Then try picking 20 for l and 30 for w. Now, Quantity A is $24 \times 24 = 576$ and Quantity B is $28 \times 18 = 504$. Since Quantity A is still bigger than Quantity B, it's probably safe to assume that the relationship is consistent, and the answer is, again, **(A)**.

22. B

If $|4x + 24| = 96$, then $4x + 24$ equals either 96 or −96. If the expression equals 96, then $4x + 24 = 96$, $4x = 72$, and $x = 18$. If the expression equals −96, then $4x + 24 = -96$, $4x = -120$, and $x = -30$. So for the first equation, x is either 18 or −30.

For the second equation, if $|4x| = 120$, then $4x$ equals either 120 or −120. If the expression equals 120, then $4x = 120$, and $x = 30$. If the expression equals −120, then $4x = -120$, and $x = -30$.

Since the same variable x is used in both equations, it must have the same value. Therefore, $x = -30$. Quantity A is -30, and Quantity B is 18. The correct answer is **(B)**.

23. C

A vehicle driven 50 miles per hour for 2 hours travels $2 \times 50 = 100$ miles in that time.

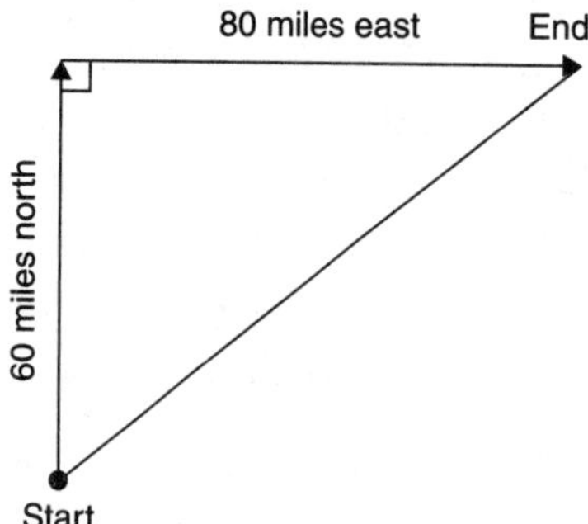

If a vehicle goes 60 miles north and 80 miles east, the distance from the starting point to the ending point is the hypotenuse of a right triangle with sides 60 and 80. The triangle formed is a 3:4:5 triangle because $60 = 3 \times 20$ and $80 = 4 \times 20$. The hypotenuse of the triangle is $5 \times 20 = 100$. Therefore, the quantities are equal. The correct answer is **(C)**.

24. B

A 6:8:10 triangle is a multiple of a 3:4:5 special right triangle. Because this is a right triangle with legs of 6 and 8, the base and height of the triangle are 6 and 8, and you can plug these into the area formula: $A = \frac{1}{2}(6)(8) = 24$. The area of the 6:8:10 right triangle is $A = \frac{1}{2}(6)(8) = 24$.

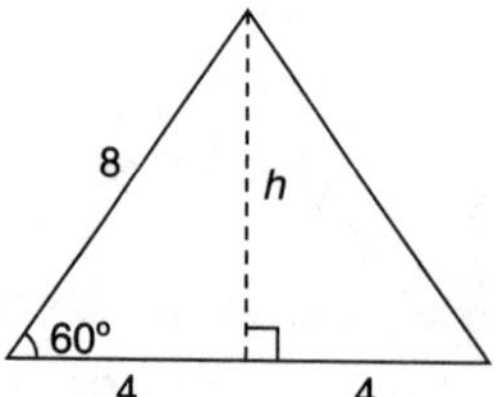

An equilateral triangle has three equal angles of 60 degrees each. Hence, when you drop the height as shown in the figure, you bisect the angle at the top, creating two 30°-60°-90° triangles. The ratios of a 30°-60°-90° triangle are $1:\sqrt{3}:2$, so the height, h, of the equilateral triangle is $4\sqrt{3}$. The area is $A = \frac{1}{2}(8)(4\sqrt{3}) = 16\sqrt{3}$. You can divide both quantities by 8 so that Quantity A is equal to 3 and Quantity B is equal to $2\sqrt{3}$. If you square both sides to make them look more alike, then Quantity A is 3^2, which equals 9. Quantity B is 4×3, which equals 12. Quantity B is larger, so the correct answer is **(B)**.

25. D

The centered information tells you that x is negative and y is positive. That means that Quantity B is always positive because it is the product of -1, a negative number, and a positive number. What about Quantity A? It can be positive or negative depending on the values chosen for x and y. Use the strategy of Picking Numbers to see whether it is possible to demonstrate that more than one relationship is possible, which is often the case when variables appear in both quantities.

Let $x = -1$ and $y = 2$. Then $-2(x + y) = -2(-1 + 2) = -2(1) = -2$ in Quantity A and $-xy = -1(-1)(2) = 2$ in Quantity B. In this case, Quantity B is greater.

Now, use reasoning before picking another set of numbers. What would it take for Quantity A to be greater? You need the sum of x and y to be a negative number with a large absolute value. That is, there must be a large negative difference between x and y.

Let $x = -51$ and $y = 1$. Then $-2(x + y) = -2(-51 + 1) = -2(-50) = 100$ in Quantity A and $-xy = -1(-51)(1) = 51$ in Quantity B. In this case, Quantity A is greater.

Two relationships have been demonstrated and the correct answer is **(D)**.

26. C

Quantity A: Take $g(x)$ first and then plug the result into $f(x)$.

$g(x) = g(3) = \frac{1}{2}(3) = \left(\frac{3}{2}\right)$, and then $f(g(x)) = f\left(\frac{3}{2}\right) = 2\left(\frac{3}{2}\right) = 3.$

Now, Quantity B: Take $f(x)$ first and then plug the result into $g(x)$.

$f(x) = f(3) = 2(3) = 6$, and then $g(f(x)) = g(6) = \frac{1}{2}(6) = 3.$

The result is the same both times. The correct answer is **(C)**.

27. C

At first it may seem that there is not enough information to compare the measure of $\angle BAC$ to $70°$. But the centered information tells you that AB is a diameter of the circle and provides a way to get started with the comparison.

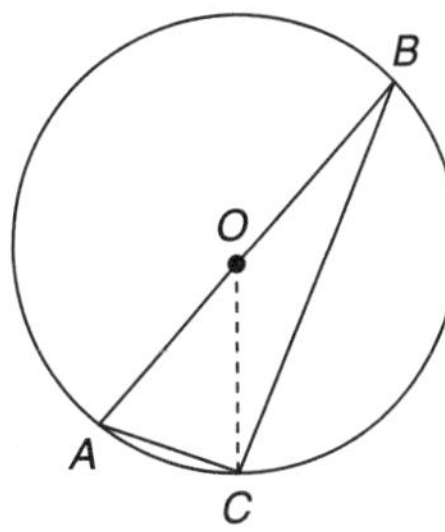

Because one side of the triangle is the diameter of the circle, this is a right triangle with $\angle BCA$ measuring 90 degrees. Since the centered information says that $\angle ABC = 20°$, $\angle BAC$ must equal 70 degrees. The two quantities are equal, so the answer is **(C)**.

28. C

Set x as the largest of the five consecutive even integers. Then, the second-largest even integer will be $x - 2$, the third-largest even integer will be $x - 4$, the fourth-largest will be $x - 6$, and the smallest of the five even integers will be $x - 8$. The sum of these five expressions is $(x) + (x - 2) + (x - 4) + (x - 6) + (x - 8)$, which equals $5x - 20$. Therefore $5x - 20 = -20$ and $x = 0$. This question may have been confusing at first because zero seems like a neutral number that is neither even nor odd, but zero is an even number because it is an integer multiple of 2 ($2 \times 0 = 0$).

Alternatively, use the fact that, for a set of consecutive or evenly-spaced integers, the median is equal to the mean (average); and, as always, the average equals the sum divided by the number of terms. So median (the third term) = mean = $\frac{-20}{5} = -4$. To find the greatest term, just count up by 2s to the fifth term: −4, −2, 0.

The correct answer is **(C)**.

29. D

The question asks for a comparison of $2 - r$ and t. You know that the centered information in a GRE question is important, so begin by plugging the given value for s into the top equation.

If $s = 4$, then $4 = (t + r)^2$, and you now have a quadratic equation with a perfect square on both sides of the equal sign. A quadratic equation can have two solutions, one positive and one negative. So, $(t + r)$ may be +2 or −2. Write out the equations for each case:

If $t + r = 2$, then $t = 2 - r$

If $t + r = -2$, then $t = -2 - r$

There is not enough information to make a comparison, so the answer is **(D)**.

Another way to make short work of this one is to pick numbers that satisfy the centered information. If $t = 3$ and $r = -1$, for example, then the two quantities are equal: $2 - (-1) = 3$. If, on the other hand, $t = -1$ and $r = -1$, then Quantity A has the greater value: $2 - (-1) > -1$. When different sets of numbers satisfy the centered information but produce different relationships between the two quantities, the answer is always **(D)**.

30. D

Be careful when the GRE poses a question like this without telling you the elements in the set. For example, the data set could be {−2, 0, 2} or {−4, 0, 2, 2}. It could also be a set of many more elements. The correct answer is **(D)**.

CHAPTER 3

Problem Solving

PROBLEM SOLVING

You will find about nine Problem Solving questions per Quantitative Reasoning section on the actual GRE. Problem Solving questions may be pure math or they may involve a real-world situation. The GRE tests algebraic, arithmetic, and geometric concepts. The questions will test your ability to reason mathematically using your knowledge of the various topics.

You will see three formats for answering Problem Solving questions on the GRE. You may be required to select one answer from the five choices given, select one or more choices from the choices given, or enter your answer in an on-screen box.

PROBLEM SOLVING QUESTIONS (SINGLE ANSWER)

THE KAPLAN METHOD FOR PROBLEM SOLVING

STEP 1 **Analyze the question.**

STEP 2 **Identify the task.**

STEP 3 **Approach strategically.**

STEP 4 **Confirm your answer.**

The directions for a Problem Solving question requiring a single answer will look like this:

> **Directions:** Select one answer choice.

A Problem Solving question requiring you to select a single answer will look like this:

> A retailer charges 25% more than his purchase price for any appliance he sells. When the retailer has a clearance sale, all appliances are marked 10% off. If the dealer sells a vacuum cleaner during a clearance sale, his profit (selling price minus purchase price) is what percent of his purchase price of the vacuum cleaner?
>
> (A) 10%
> (B) 12.5%
> (C) 15%
> (D) 17.5%
> (E) 20%

Apply the Kaplan Method for Problem Solving

Now let's apply the Kaplan Method to a Problem Solving question requiring a single answer.

A retailer charges 25% more than his purchase price for any appliance he sells. When the retailer has a clearance sale, all appliances are marked 10% off. If the retailer sells a vacuum cleaner during a clearance sale, his profit (selling price minus purchase price) is what percent of his purchase price of the vacuum cleaner?

(A) 10%
(B) 12.5%
(C) 15%
(D) 17.5%
(E) 20%

STEP 1

Analyze the question.

This is a real-world situation involving a retailer's percent markup to obtain a selling price and the retailer's percent markdown of items for a clearance sale. The question asks for the percent profit the retailer makes on an item he sells during a clearance sale. The answer choices are given as percents; however, no specific price is given for the item sold.

STEP 2

Identify the task.

The task is to calculate the percent profit, using the percent markup of 25% and the percent markdown of 10% for every item sold.

STEP 3

Approach strategically.

Although this problem could be solved using algebra, it may not be the fastest way for you to arrive at an answer. Instead, try the strategy of Picking Numbers for the initial purchase price of the vacuum cleaner and go from there. Suppose the retailer purchased the vacuum for $100.

A great number to pick for percent problems when no value is given is 100 because the calculations will be quite manageable.

First, determine the price assigned to the vacuum after a 25% markup:

$$125\% \text{ of } 100 = 1.25 \times 100 = 125$$

So the price assigned to the vacuum was $125, but it did not sell at that price. It was reduced 10%, so take 90% (100 − 10 = 90) of 125 to find the clearance sale price:

$$90\% \text{ of } 125 = 0.90 \times 125 = 112.50$$

When the vacuum sells at this price, the profit for the retailer is $112.50 − $100 = $12.50.

Now you are ready to compare the profit of 12.50 to the original 100:

$$\frac{12.50}{100} = 0.125 = 12.5\%$$

The correct answer is **(B)**, 12.5%.

STEP 4

Confirm your answer.

There are two components to confirming your answer. First, does your answer make sense in the context of the question? In this case, a profit of 12.5% is less than the markup percent and more than the markdown percent, so it seems reasonable. Second, did you answer the question that was asked? In this question, you are asked *his profit is what percent of his purchase price?* Look back at the calculation to see that the correct comparison was made: dollar amount of profit compared to dollar amount of purchase price. Your answer is confirmed.

For more information on percents, see chapter 6.

PROBLEM SOLVING (ALL-THAT-APPLY)

The directions for a Problem Solving question requiring you to select one or more answers will look like this:

Directions: Select one or more answer choices.

A Problem Solving question requiring you to select one or more answers will look like this:

> The product of two integers is 14. Which of the following could be the average (arithmetic mean) of the two integers?
>
> Indicate <u>all</u> such averages.
>
> [A] –7.5
> [B] –6.5
> [C] –4.5
> [D] 4.5
> [E] 6.5

APPLY THE KAPLAN METHOD FOR PROBLEM SOLVING

Now let's apply the Kaplan Method to a Problem Solving question requiring you to select one or more answers.

The product of two integers is 14. Which of the following could be the average (arithmetic mean) of the two integers?

Indicate <u>all</u> such averages.

[A] –7.5
[B] –6.5
[C] –4.5
[D] 4.5
[E] 6.5

STEP 1

Analyze the question.

This is a pure math question involving integers. Whenever you see possible values described as integers, remember that the set of integers could include both positive and negative values and zero. In the question, you are given information about the product of two integers. Notice that the answer choices are not integers, but they do include both negative and positive values.

STEP 2

Identify the task.

The task is to select all the values that could be an average of the integers whose product is 14.

STEP 3

Approach strategically.

The best strategy here is to find all possible answers and then check which ones are given as answer choices. Start by writing the factors of positive 14: $1 \times 14 = 14$ and $2 \times 7 = 14$. Next consider the negative integers whose product is 14: $-1 \times (-14) = 14$ and $-2 \times (-7) = 14$.

Recall that the average of two numbers is the sum of the numbers divided by 2.

$$\frac{1+14}{2} = \frac{15}{2} = 7.5 \qquad \frac{-1+(-14)}{2} = \frac{-15}{2} = -7.5$$

$$\frac{2+7}{2} = \frac{9}{2} = 4.5 \qquad \frac{-2+(-7)}{2} = \frac{-9}{2} = -4.5$$

The correct answers are **(A)**, **(C)**, and **(D)**.

STEP 4

Confirm your answer.

For this question, check that you considered all the possible factors of 14. There were four possibilities because the only factors of 14 are 1 and 14, 2 and 7, –1 and –14, and –2 and –7. Therefore, it was reasonable to do all the calculations. The values chosen are the averages of the sets of factors of 14. The answer is confirmed.

For more information on averages, see chapter 6.

PROBLEM SOLVING QUESTIONS (NUMERIC ENTRY)

The directions for a Problem Solving question requiring you to make a Numeric Entry will look like this:

> **Directions:** Click in the box and type a number. Backspace to erase.

Enter your answer as an integer or decimal if there is one box or as a fraction if there are two boxes.

To enter an integer or decimal, type directly in the box or use the Transfer Display button on the calculator.

- Use backspace to erase.
- Use a hyphen to enter a negative sign; type a hyphen a second time to remove it. The digits will remain.

- Use a period for a decimal point.
- The Transfer Display button will enter your answer directly from the calculator.
- Equivalent forms of decimals are all correct. Example: $.14 = 0.140$.
- Enter the exact answer unless the question asks you to round your answer.

To enter a fraction, type the numerator and denominator in the appropriate boxes.

- Use a hyphen to enter a negative sign.
- The Transfer Display button does not work for fractions.
- Equivalent forms of fractions are all correct. Example: $\frac{25}{15} = \frac{5}{3}$.
- If numbers are large, reduce fractions to fit in boxes.

A Problem Solving question with Numeric Entry will look like this:

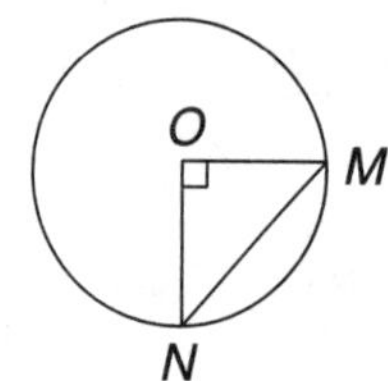

In the figure shown, the area of the circle whose center is *O* is 16π. What is the area of triangle *MNO*?

[ ] square units

Apply the Kaplan Method for Problem Solving

Now let's apply the Kaplan Method to a Problem Solving question involving Numeric Entry.

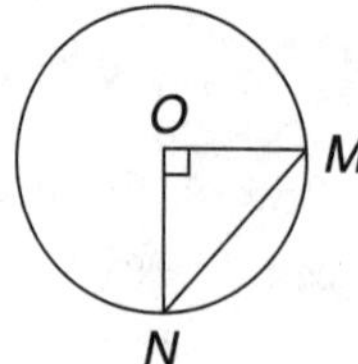

In the figure shown, the area of the circle whose center is *O* is 16π. What is the area of triangle *MNO*?

[ ] square units

STEP 1

Analyze the question.

You must use the figure shown and the information given to answer this geometry question. You have a circle with an inscribed triangle to deal with here. The center of the circle, *O*, is also a vertex of the right triangle. The question indicates that you will fill in a numerical answer for the square units.

STEP 2

Identify the task.

You must find the area of the triangle using the information given. That is, you will use the value given for the area of the circle to determine information about the dimensions of the triangle. Then you will be able to find the area of the triangle.

STEP 3

Approach strategically.

Start with what you know—the area of a circle is given by the equation $A = \pi r^2$. Solve for the length of the radius:

$$\begin{aligned} A &= \pi r^2 \\ 16\pi &= \pi r^2 \\ 16 &= r^2 \\ 4 &= r \end{aligned}$$

In the figure, the radius of the circle is also the base and height of the isosceles right triangle. The area of a triangle is given by the equation

$$A = \frac{1}{2}(\text{base})(\text{height}) = \frac{1}{2} \times 4 \times 4 = 8.$$

The area of the triangle is **8** square units.

STEP 4

Confirm your answer.

Do a quick check to confirm that your answer makes sense. If the area of the complete circle is 16π, then the area of one-fourth of the circle is 4π. Use 3 as an estimate for π and you have 4π is approximately $4 \times 3 = 12$. In the figure, the triangle takes up less than one-fourth of the circle, so the answer of **8** is reasonable.

For more information on circles and triangles, see chapter 8.

PROBLEM SOLVING PRACTICE SET

Try the following Problem Solving questions using the Kaplan Method.

Basic

1. What is the perimeter of a parallelogram with adjacent side lengths measuring $9a$ and $14b$?

   (A) $9a + 14b$
   (B) $18a + 28b$
   (C) $23(a + b)$
   (D) $36a$
   (E) $63ab$

2. What is the value of $-[(s + t)^0]$ if $s + t \neq 0$?

   (A) –1
   (B) 0
   (C) 1
   (D) $s + t$
   (E) $-(s + t)$

3. The data below show the monthly dollar amounts Marco spent on postage over the past 6 months. What is the average (arithmetic mean) of the data set?

   $1.08, $5.43, $2.17, $3.25, $5.95, $1.08

   $ [3.16]

4. What is the sixth term in a sequence in which the nth term is $n(n - 1)^2$?

   (A) 42
   (B) 150
   (C) 900
   (D) 1,225
   (E) 2,592

5. What is the value of $\left(2\sqrt{2}\right)\left(\sqrt{6}\right)+2\sqrt{3}$?

Ⓐ 18
Ⓑ $10\sqrt{3}$
Ⓒ $6\sqrt{6}$
Ⓓ $4\sqrt{2}+2\sqrt{3}$
Ⓔ $6\sqrt{3}$

6. If one of the angle measures of an equilateral triangle is given in degrees as $15n$, what is the value of n?

Ⓐ 3
Ⓑ 4
Ⓒ 6
Ⓓ 12
Ⓔ 15

7. If $3x + y = -1$ and $y - 2x = 4$, what is the value of $x + 2y$?

Ⓐ –5
Ⓑ –3
Ⓒ 0
Ⓓ 3
Ⓔ 5

8. The sum of the interior angles of a regular polygon is less than 540°. Which could be the polygon?

Indicate all such polygons.

Ⓐ triangle
Ⓑ quadrilateral
Ⓒ pentagon
Ⓓ hexagon

9. The ratio of $\frac{1}{2}$ to $\frac{3}{5}$ is the same as which of the following ratios?

   (A) 1:5
   (B) 3:10
   (C) 2:3
   (D) 5:6
   (E) 3:2

10. What is the value of $(-8)^{-3}$?

   (A) –512
   (B) –24
   (C) –2
   (D) $-\frac{1}{2}$
   (E) $-\frac{1}{512}$

Intermediate

11. A computer company's featured laptop cost \$800 last year. This year, the laptop sold for 15% less than it did last year. Next year, after updates are made to the model, there will be a 25% price increase over this year's price. What will be the price next year?

   (A) \$810
   (B) \$825
   (C) \$840
   (D) \$850
   (E) \$880

12. If $x < -3$ and $x^2 + 5x + 12 = 8$, what is the value of $x + 2$?

   (A) –4
   (B) –2
   (C) –1
   (D) 0
   (E) 3

13. What is the probability of rolling a number greater than 2 twice in a row on a fair six-sided die, with each of the numbers 1–6 on each side?

    (A) $\frac{1}{4}$

    (B) $\frac{5}{18}$

    (C) $\frac{4}{9}$

    (D) $\frac{5}{9}$

    (E) $\frac{2}{3}$

14. If $\clubsuit m = 3m$ and $\bullet n = n + 7$, which of the following is the value of $[(\clubsuit(\bullet 4) - 3(\bullet 2)]$?

    (A) −9
    (B) 1
    (C) 6
    (D) 13
    (E) 20

15. A flower shop sells flowers in a ratio of roses to carnations of 5:2. The ratio of carnations to tulips sold is 5:3. What is the ratio of roses to tulips?

    (A) 2:3
    (B) 3:2
    (C) 5:3
    (D) 25:6
    (E) 25:9

16. A principal has four different trophies available for display in his two display cases. If only one trophy can fit in each display case, how many distinct ways are there to display two of the trophies in the cases at any given time?

    (A) 16
    (B) 12
    (C) 9
    (D) 8
    (E) 6

17. Telephone company A charges \$3.00 for the first minute of any long distance call and \$0.50 for each additional minute. Telephone company B charges \$2.00 for the first minute of any long distance call and \$0.70 for each additional minute. If the cost of a call lasting x minutes, where x is a positive integer, is \$15.00 more with telephone company B than with telephone company A, then what is the value of x?

(A) 56
(B) 60
(C) 77
(D) 80
(E) 81

18. Find the measures, in degrees, of angles *GEF* and *DEG*.

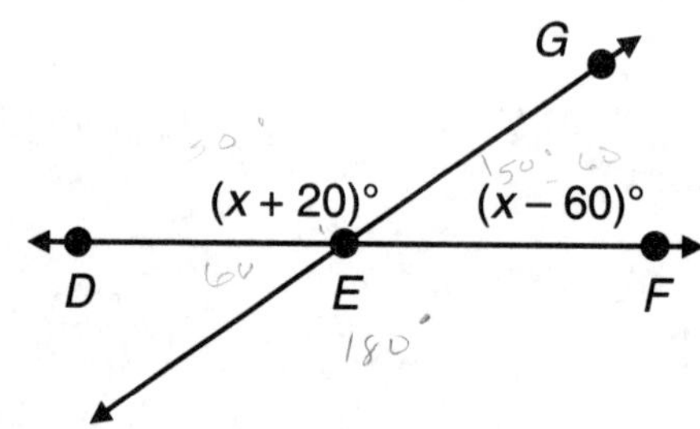

(A) 30 and 150
(B) 50 and 110
(C) 50 and 130
(D) 90 and 170
(E) 110 and 130

19. The average (arithmetic mean) of a, b, and c is 70, and the average (arithmetic mean) of d and e is 120. What is the average (arithmetic mean) of a, b, c, d, and e?

(A) 84
(B) 90
(C) 95
(D) 96
(E) 100

20. The length of one side of a triangle is 12. The length of another side is 18. Which of the following could be the perimeter of the triangle?

Indicate <u>all</u> such perimeters.

- A 30
- B 36
- C 44
- D 48
- E 60

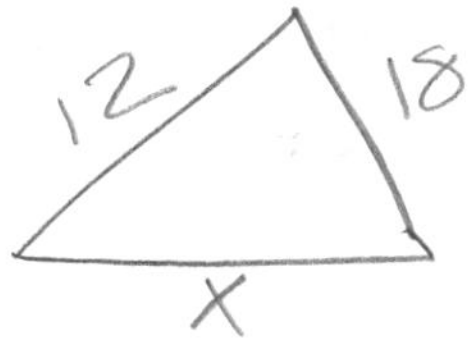

Advanced

21. The average of all the consecutive integers from a to b inclusive is 39. Which of the following could be a and b?

Indicate <u>all</u> such integers.

- A 4 and 74
- B 19 and 39
- C 25 and 53
- D 29 and 59
- E 33 and 45

22. A square is inscribed inside a shaded circle, as shown. The circumference of the circle is $6\pi\sqrt{2}$. What is the area of the shaded region?

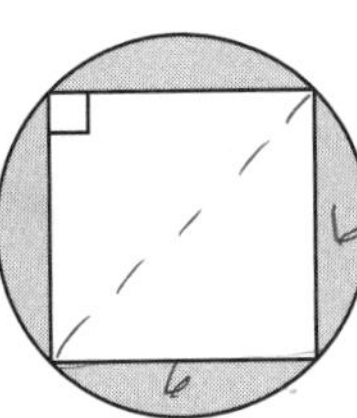

- (A) $12\pi - 6\sqrt{2}$
- (B) $12\pi - 18$
- (C) $18\pi - 6$
- (D) $18\pi - 36$
- (E) $36\pi - 18$

23. Point A (4, 6) lies on a line with slope $-\frac{3}{4}$. Point B lies on the same line and is 5 units from Point A. Which of the following could be the coordinates of Point B?

Indicate all such coordinates.

[A] (−1, 1)
[B] (−4, 12)
[C] (8, 3)
[D] (1, 10)
[E] (0, 9)

24. The surface area of a cube with side length $(x + 4)$ is 294. What is the value of x?

(A) −10
(B) −1
(C) 3
(D) 7
(E) 19

25. Pipe A can fill a tank in 3 hours. If pipe B can fill the same tank in 2 hours, how many minutes will it take both pipes to fill $\frac{2}{3}$ of the tank?

(A) 30
(B) 48
(C) 54
(D) 60
(E) 72

26. If it takes Nathan 4 hours to unload a moving truck and it takes Iris 2 hours longer than Nathan to unload a moving truck, how long would it take the two of them, working together, to unload 2 moving trucks?

(A) 5 hours
(B) 4 hours, 48 minutes
(C) 4 hours
(D) 2 hours 24 minutes
(E) 2 hours

27. The integer y is positive. If $6y$ is a factor of $(2^{14})(3^{24})$, then what is the greatest possible value of y?

(A) 7
(B) 8
(C) 14
(D) 18
(E) 36

28. Phillip has twice as many tropical fish as Jody. If Phillip gave Jody 10 of his tropical fish, he would have half as many as Jody. How many tropical fish do Phillip and Jody have together?

(A) 10
(B) 20
(C) 30
(D) 40
(E) 60

29. When Dahlia's professor eliminated the lowest of her 4 quiz scores, her quiz average rose from 77 to 91. What was the score of the quiz that the professor eliminated?

(A) 14
(B) 21
(C) 35
(D) 42
(E) 56

30. In company X, no employee is both a technician and an accountant. Also, in company X, $\frac{2}{5}$ of the employees are technicians, and $\frac{5}{16}$ of the remaining employees are accountants. What fraction of the total number of employees at company X are neither technicians nor accountants?

Ⓐ $\frac{23}{80}$

Ⓑ $\frac{33}{80}$

Ⓒ $\frac{3}{7}$

Ⓓ $\frac{47}{80}$

Ⓔ $\frac{57}{80}$

X – no tech & acc.

2/5 = tech .4 = 32

5/16 = acc. .3125 25

.7125

.2875

$\frac{2}{5} \cdot \frac{5}{16} = \frac{10}{80}$

PROBLEM SOLVING PRACTICE SET ANSWER KEY

1. B
2. A
3. 3.16
4. B
5. E
6. B
7. D
8. A, B
9. D
10. E
11. D
12. B
13. C
14. C
15. D
16. B
17. E
18. C
19. B
20. C, D
21. A, C, E
22. D
23. C, E
24. C
25. B
26. B
27. C
28. C
29. C
30. B

PROBLEM SOLVING PRACTICE SET ANSWERS AND EXPLANATIONS

Basic

1. B

The perimeter of a parallelogram is the sum of the lengths of all four of its sides. Two side lengths are given, and a parallelogram has two pairs of equal opposite sides. So, the perimeter of the parallelogram is $2(9a) + 2(14b) = 18a + 28b$, and the answer is **(B)**.

2. A

For any non-zero base raised to the zero power, the value is equal to 1. (If the base and exponent are both zero, then the number is undefined.) Since the problem specifies that the base is not zero, it does not matter what *s* or *t* is. Their sum raised to the zero power will be 1. The expression asks for the negation of 1, which is –1, so the answer is **(A)**.

3. 3.16

Use the formula for average:

$$\textit{Average} = \frac{\textit{Sum of terms}}{\textit{Number of terms}} = \frac{1.08 + 5.43 + 2.17 + 3.25 + 5.95 + 1.08}{6}$$

$$= \frac{18.96}{6} = 3.16$$

The answer is \$3.16.

4. B

Use the rule given, substituting in 6 for *n* to find the sixth term. Be sure to follow the order of operations (PEMDAS):

$$6(6-1)^2 =$$
$$6(5)^2 =$$
$$6(25) = 150$$

The correct choice is **(B)**.

5. E

Following PEMDAS, simplify the first part of the expression first. To multiply radical terms, deal with the inside and outside separately. Then, if the radical terms have the same number under the $\sqrt{\ }$, they can be added together.

$$\left(2\sqrt{2}\right)\left(\sqrt{6}\right) + 2\sqrt{3} = \left(2\sqrt{2}\right)\left(\sqrt{2} \times \sqrt{3}\right) + 2\sqrt{3}$$
$$= (2)\left(\sqrt{2} \times \sqrt{2}\right)\left(\sqrt{3}\right) + 2\sqrt{3} = 4\left(\sqrt{3}\right) + 2\sqrt{3}$$
$$= 6\sqrt{3}$$

The answer is **(E)**.

6. B

An equilateral triangle has three equal angles. Since the sum of the angles of a triangle always equals 180°, you can divide 180 by 3 to determine that the angles of an equilateral triangle are each 60°. So, $15n = 60$ and $n = 4$. The answer is **(B)**.

7. D

The question asks for $x + 2y$, but not for x or y individually. In such situations, it is typically unnecessary to solve for the value of x and the value of y. Rearrange the equations so that like terms are on top of each other and then add the equations:

$$\begin{array}{r} 3x + y = -1 \\ +[-2x + y = \ \ 4] \\ \hline x + 2y = \ \ 3 \end{array}$$

Since $x + 2y = 3$, the answer is **(D)**.

8. A, B

In a regular polygon with n sides, the formula for the sum of the interior angles is $(n - 2) \times 180$. This equation can be set up as an inequality to solve for n:

$$(n - 2) \times 180 < 540°$$

Dividing both sides by 180 gives us:

$$n - 2 < 3$$

$$n < 5$$

The polygons listed with fewer than 5 sides are the triangle and quadrilateral, so the answers are **(A)** and **(B)**.

9. D

The ratio of two numbers a and b can be expressed as $\frac{a}{b}$. So the expression is the same as the value of $\frac{1}{2}$ divided by $\frac{3}{5}$. To divide by a fraction, you multiply by the reciprocal, $\frac{1}{2} \times \frac{5}{3} = \frac{5}{6}$. So the ratio of $\frac{1}{2}$ and $\frac{3}{5}$ is the same as $\frac{5}{6}$, which can be written as the ratio of 5:6. The answer is **(D)**.

Alternatively, express both fractions in terms of a common denominator: $\frac{1}{2} = \frac{5}{10}$ and $\frac{3}{5} = \frac{6}{10}$. Now compare $\frac{5}{10}$ to $\frac{6}{10}$ and see that the ratio is 5:6. Again, the answer is **(D)**.

10. E

A number raised to a negative exponent is equal to the reciprocal of that number raised to the positive exponent. So,

$$(-8)^{-3} = \frac{1}{(-8)^3} = \frac{1}{(-8)(-8)(-8)} = -\frac{1}{512}$$

The answer is **(E)**.

Intermediate

11. D

First, calculate the price of the laptop this year. Then, use that price to determine what the price will be next year. After a 15% decrease in price, the system would sell for 85% of $800: $0.85 \times \$800 = \$680$. If there is a 25% increase next year, the system would sell for 125% of this year's price. That would be 125% of $680: $1.25 \times \$680 = \$850$. The answer is **(D)**.

12. B

The equation is quadratic, so all terms should be moved to one side and set equal to zero to solve for x. The equation $x^2 + 5x + 12 = 8$ becomes $x^2 + 5x + 4 = 0$. This can be factored to $(x + 4)(x + 1) = 0$, so either $x + 4 = 0$ or $x + 1 = 0$, and solving for x gives $x = -1$ or $x = -4$. The problem states that $x < -3$, so the only valid solution is $x = -4$. Once the value of x is specified, you can substitute in the value for x to solve: $x + 2 = -4 + 2 = -2$. Always make sure to confirm your answer, because choice (A) is the trap that represents the value of x; but, remember, you're looking for the value of $x + 2$. The answer is **(B)**.

13. C

Use the probability formula:

$$Probability = \frac{Number\ of\ desired\ outcomes}{Number\ of\ total\ possible\ outcomes}$$

There are 6 possible outcomes with each roll of a fair six-sided die, and 4 outcomes are greater than 2. The probability of rolling a number greater than 2 on the first roll is $\frac{4}{6} = \frac{2}{3}$.

The probability of rolling a number greater than 2 on the second roll is the same, $\frac{4}{6} = \frac{2}{3}$.

Multiply the two probabilities to find the chance of both events occurring: $\frac{2}{3} \times \frac{2}{3} = \frac{4}{9}$. The correct choice is **(C)**.

14. C

The symbols represent operations on the numbers. So, to get the answer, apply the operation described in the problem statement each time the symbol appears. Apply PEMDAS and start with the interior parentheses. Since •$n = n + 7$, •$4 = 4 + 7 = 11$ and •$2 = 2 + 7 = 9$. Now the expression is [♣(11) − 3(9)] = (♣(11) − 27). Since ♣$n = 3n$, ♣(11) = 3(11) = 33. Finally, the expression is 33 − 27 = 6. The answer is **(C)**.

15. D

This question is asking about a combined ratio. To compare the ratios, the number for carnations must be the same in each ratio. Since carnations are represented by 2 in one ratio and 5 in the other, convert the ratios so that both have carnations represented by 10. The number 10 is chosen because it is the least common multiple of 2 and 5. The ratio of roses to carnations is $5:2 = 25:10$, and the ratio of carnations to tulips is $5:3 = 10:6$. Now the value for carnations, 10, is the same in both ratios. The ratio of roses to tulips is 25:6, and the answer is **(D)**.

16. B

This is a permutations question. To understand why, first imagine that the two cases are in two different locations, say by the cafeteria and by the gymnasium. In this case, placing the hockey trophy in the cafeteria case and the debate team trophy in the gymnasium case is not the same as putting the debate trophy by the cafeteria and the hockey trophy by the gym. In other words, not only is the principal selecting two of four trophies, but he is also arranging them. Call the trophies A, B, C, and D. There are 3 ways for trophy A to be chosen first: AB, AC, AD. Likewise, there are 3 ways for Trophy B to be chosen first, 3 for trophy C, and 3 for trophy D. There are 12 total ways, so the answer is **(B)**.

You can also use the permutations formula to solve:

$$\frac{n!}{(n-k)!} = \frac{4!}{(4-2)!} = \frac{4 \times 3 \times 2 \times 1}{2 \times 1} = 12$$

17. E

The cost of a telephone call lasting x minutes with telephone company A is \$3.00 for the first minute and \$0.50 for each minute of the additional $x - 1$ minutes. So the cost of this telephone call with telephone company A is $3 + 0.5(x - 1)$ dollars. The cost of a telephone call lasting x minutes with telephone company B is \$2.00 for the first minute and \$0.70 for each minute of the additional $x - 1$ minutes. So the cost of this telephone call with telephone company B is $2 + 0.7(x - 1)$ dollars. Since the cost of a call lasting x minutes with telephone company B is \$15.00 more than the cost of a call lasting x minutes with telephone company A, we have this equation:

$$2 + 0.7(x - 1) = 3 + 0.5(x - 1) + 15$$

We can now solve this equation for x.

$$\begin{aligned} 2 + 0.7x - 0.7 &= 3 + 0.5x - 0.5 + 15 \\ 1.3 + 0.7x &= 17.5 + 0.5x \\ 0.2x &= 16.2 \end{aligned}$$

Therefore, $x = 81$. The answer is **(E)**.

18. C

From the general rules about relationships between angles formed by intersecting lines, you know that the sum of angles along a straight line is 180°. Angles *DEG* and *GEF* lie along a straight line. They are supplementary angles, so you can eliminate answer choices that do not sum to 180°; eliminate (B), (D), and (E). Now write an equation: $(x + 20) + (x - 60) = 180$. Simplify:

$$\begin{aligned} 2x - 40 &= 180 \\ 2x &= 220 \\ x &= 110 \end{aligned}$$

Since x is 110, the angle measures are $(x + 20) = (110 + 20) = 130$ and $(x - 60) = (110 - 60) = 50$, and the answer is **(C)**.

19. B

The average formula is $Average = \frac{Sum\ of\ terms}{Number\ of\ terms}$. Since the average of a, b, and c is 70, $\frac{a + b + c}{3} = 70$. Then $a + b + c = 3 \times 70$, or 210. Similarly, since the average of d and e is given as 120, $\frac{d + e}{2} = 120$. The sum of $d + e = 240$. Adding the corresponding sides of the equations $a + b + c = 210$ and $d + e = 240$, we have $(a + b + c) + (d + e) = 210 + 240$, and then $a + b + c + d + e = 450$. To find the average, divide 450 by 5. So the average of a, b, c, d, and e is 90. The correct answer is **(B)**.

20. C, D

The problem asks for the perimeter of the triangle. The triangle inequality theorem states that the length of the third side of a triangle must be between the positive difference and the sum of the other two sides. So, once you find the range of possible lengths for the third side, you can add the side lengths to find the range of possible perimeters.

The third side must be greater than the difference $18 - 12 = 6$ and less than the sum $12 + 18 = 30$. So, the perimeter must be greater than $12 + 18 + 6 = 36$ and less than $12 + 18 + 30 = 60$. Answer choices **(C)** and **(D)** are the only values that are greater than 36 and less than 60.

Advanced

21. A, C, E

The average of a group of consecutive integers is equal to the average of the smallest and largest integers, so any pair of numbers whose average is 39 could be a and b. Since the average of a and b is equal to their sum divided by 2, any pair of numbers whose sum is $2 \times 39 = 78$ is a valid answer choice. The answer choices with a pair of numbers that sum to 78 are **(A)**, **(C)**, and **(E)**.

22. D

The problem asks for the area of the shaded region, so you need to find the difference between the area of the circle and the area covered by the square.

For the area of the circle, first find the radius. The circumference of a circle is $2\pi r$. Since the circumference is given as $6\pi\sqrt{2}$, $2\pi r = 6\pi\sqrt{2}$, $2r = 6\sqrt{2}$, and $r = 3\sqrt{2}$. The area of the circle, then, is $\pi r^2 = \pi\left(3\sqrt{2}\right)^2 = 18\pi$.

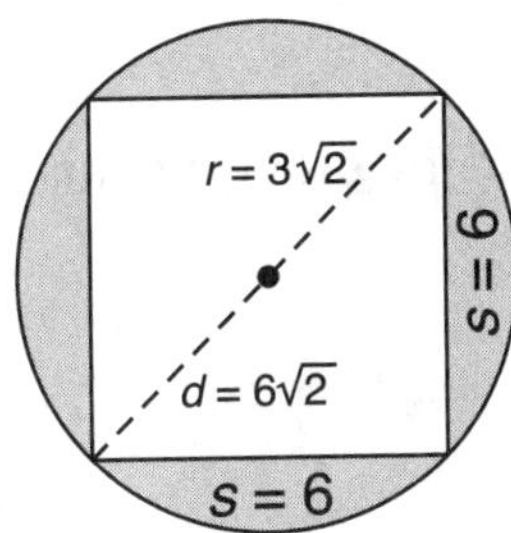

For the area of the square, find the side length. The square is inscribed in the circle, so the diagonal of the square is the diameter of the circle, or $6\sqrt{2}$. Since the diagonal of a square creates two 45°-45°-90° triangles, the sides of the square are the legs of a 45°-45°-90° triangle with a hypotenuse of $6\sqrt{2}$. Therefore, a side length is 6, and the area of the square is $6 \times 6 = 36$.

The difference between the area of the circle and the area of the square is $18\pi - 36$. The correct choice is **(D)**.

23. C, E

Using the definition of slope as $m = \frac{\text{rise}}{\text{run}} = -\frac{3}{4}$, you can plot point *A* and move vertically 3 and horizontally –4 to point $(4 - 4, 6 + 3) = (0, 9)$, which will also lie on the line with slope $-\frac{3}{4}$. This creates a 3:4:5 triangle, so the distance along the line from point *A* to the new point (0, 9) is 5 units, so (E) could be point *B*. You can also move vertically –3 and horizontally 4 to point $(4 + 4, 6 - 3) = (8, 3)$, which lies on the same line. Since the triangle formed is a 3:4:5 triangle again, this distance from point *A* to the new point (8, 3) is also 5. Choice (C) could also be point *B*. So, the answers are **(C)** and **(E)**.

24. C

First, consider that a cube has six faces and all edges of a cube are equal. So the total surface area is comprised of six squares. In this question, you're given the surface area as 294, so the area of one face is $\frac{294}{6} = 49$. The area of a square is equal to the square of its side, which is given as $x + 4$.

$(x + 4)^2 = 49$

$(x + 4)^2 = 7^2$

Remember, we can disregard the negative in this case, since distance won't be negative.

$$x + 4 = 7$$
$$x = 3$$

Remember that you're solving for x, not the length of the side.

The answer is **(C)**.

25. B

Approach the problem strategically: find the number of hours it takes both pipes to fill the entire tank, multiply by $\frac{2}{3}$, and then convert hours to minutes.

To solve a combined work problem where the information is given in hours to complete the work, use the combined work formula. The time it takes pipe A and pipe B to fill the tank together is the product of their individual times to do the work divided by the sum of their individual times. In this case, that is $\left(\frac{2\times3}{2+3}\right) = \frac{6}{5}$. It would take the two pipes $\frac{6}{5}$ hours to fill the entire tank. It will take $\frac{2}{3} \times \frac{6}{5} = \frac{2}{{}_1\cancel{3}} \times \frac{\cancel{6}^2}{5} = \frac{4}{5}$ hour to fill $\frac{2}{3}$ of the tank. The final step is to convert $\frac{4}{5}$ hour to minutes. There are 60 minutes in one hour: $\frac{4}{5} \times 60 = 48$.

The answer is **(B)**.

26. B

According to the combined work formula, the amount of time it takes two people to do a single task together is the product of their individual times to do the task divided by the sum of those times. It takes Nathan 4 hours, so it takes Iris $4 + 2 = 6$ hours. Then:

$$T_{together} = \frac{T_a \times T_b}{T_a + T_b}$$

$$T_{together} = \frac{4 \times 6}{4 + 6}$$

$$T_{together} = \frac{24}{10}$$

$$T_{together} = \frac{12}{5}$$

So it would take $\frac{12}{5}$ hours, or 2 hours 24 minutes, to unload the truck together. However, the question asks how long would it take to unload *two* moving trucks, so the answer is 4 hours 48 minutes, which is **(B)**.

27. C

Let's rewrite $6y$ by using the prime factorization of 6. The prime factorization of 6 is 2×3. We know by the law of exponents that $(ab)n = anbn$. So we have $6y = (2 \times 3)y = 2y \times 3y$.

Since we have 14 factors of two and 24 factors of three, there can be up to 14 factors of 6, since you're limited by the smallest number of possible factors. You cannot have 15 factors of 6, since you would need 15 factors of 2. Therefore, the greatest possible value of y is 14. The answer is **(C)**.

28. C

First, note that since Phillip has twice as many tropical fish as Jody, this can be written as the ratio $p:j = 2:1$, where p represents Phillip's original number of fish and j represents Jody's original number of fish. Then, because there are $2 + 1 = 3$ total parts in this ratio, the total number of fish that Phillip and Jody have must be a multiple of 3. Eliminate choices (A), (B), and (D). With just two possibilities to choose from, Backsolving would be a very efficient strategy here. However, this is also a great exercise in systems of linear equations, so here's the algebraic solution:

If Phillip has twice as many tropical fish as Jody, you can write $p = 2j$.

If Phillip gives Jody 10 fish, then he will have 10 fewer, or $p - 10$, and Jody will have 10 more, or $j + 10$. In this case Phillip would have half as many as Jody, so $p - 10 = \frac{1}{2}(j + 10)$.

Now you have two equations to describe the situation:

$$p = 2j$$
$$p - 10 = \frac{1}{2}(j + 10)$$

Solve this system of equations using substitution. Replace p in the second equation with $2j$ and solve:

$$p - 10 = \frac{1}{2}(j + 10)$$
$$2j - 10 = \frac{1}{2}(j + 10)$$
$$4j - 20 = j + 10 \quad \text{Multiply both sides by 2.}$$
$$3j = 30 \quad \text{Collect like terms.}$$
$$j = 10$$

Jody has 10 fish and Phillip has twice as many, 20. The total they have together is 30 fish. The answer is **(C)**.

29. C

The score that was deleted is equal to the difference between the original sum of the scores and the new sum of the scores. Since the average score is equal to the sum of the scores divided by the number of scores, use the average and number of scores given to find the sum before and after the lowest score was deleted. The original sum is equal to the original average score times the number of scores, or $77 \times 4 = 308$. The new sum is equal to the new average score times the number of scores, which is 3, since one score was eliminated. So, the new sum is $91 \times 3 = 273$. The score that was eliminated is $308 - 273 = 35$. The answer is **(C)**.

30. B

This is a good question for using the strategy of Picking Numbers. Start with picking a number for the total number of employees in the company. Since the denominators that appear in the fractions of the question stem contain the denominators 5 and 16, pick a total number of employees that works for both denominators. Since $5 \times 16 = 80$, start with 80. If $\frac{2}{5}$ of the 80 employees are technicians, then there are 32 technicians. This leaves $80 - 32 = 48$ employees who are not technicians. Then $\frac{5}{16}$ of these remaining 48 employees are accountants: $\frac{5}{16} \times 48 = 15$. Therefore, $48 - 15 = 33$ employees are neither technicians nor accountants. So $\frac{33}{80}$ of the employees are neither technicians nor accountants, and the answer is **(B)**.

CHAPTER 4

Data Interpretation

DATA INTERPRETATION

Data Interpretation questions are based on information presented to you in the form of graphs or tables of data. Typically, the data are presented in more than one graph or table, and you will be required to extract the data needed to answer the question from one or more of them. Questions range from those requiring simple arithmetic calculations to those that are more statistics-oriented. Typically, three or four questions will be associated with each data presentation.

You will see three formats for answering Data Interpretation questions on the GRE. You may be required to select one answer from the five choices given, select one or more choices from the choices given, or enter your answer in an on-screen box. These three formats for Data Interpretation questions are similar to those for Problem Solving questions.

THE KAPLAN METHOD FOR DATA INTERPRETATION

STEP 1 Analyze the tables and graphs.

STEP 2 Approach strategically.

DATA INTERPRETATION QUESTIONS (ONE ANSWER)

A Data Interpretation question requiring you to select a single answer will look like this:

Questions 1–3 are based on the following graphs.

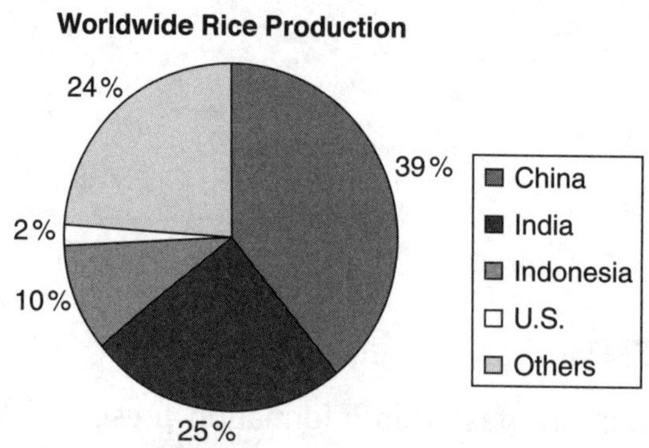

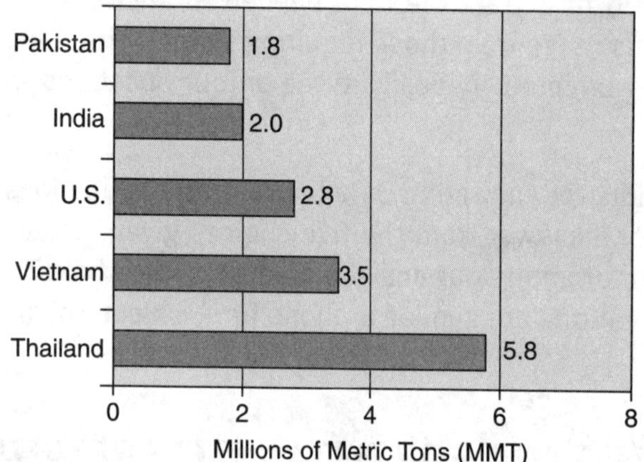

If the U.S. exports 50% of its crop one year, which is the best estimate, in MMT, of total worldwide production for that year?

Ⓐ 56
Ⓑ 112
Ⓒ 200
Ⓓ 280
Ⓔ 400

APPLY THE KAPLAN METHOD FOR DATA INTERPRETATION

Now let's apply the Kaplan Method to a Data Interpretation question requiring a single answer.

If the U.S. exports 50% of its crop one year, which is the best estimate, in MMT, of total worldwide production for that year?

(A) 56
(B) 112
(C) 200
(D) 280
(E) 400

STEP 1

Analyze the tables and graphs.

The top graph is a pie chart showing a breakdown of worldwide rice production by country. Notice that the percents are given for each slice of the pie. The bottom bar graph shows data, given in MMT, concerning exporters of rice.

STEP 2

Approach strategically.

To approach a Data Interpretation question strategically, you must identify the information that is needed to answer the question and the calculation to be done. All other information presented in the data set is "put on hold" until that one question is answered. For this question, the amount 2.8 MMT is given for U.S. exports, and the question states that the number of MMT exported represents 50% of the U.S. production. You must use these pieces of information to estimate worldwide production. That requires going to the pie chart to see the percent assigned to the U.S. That is just 2% of worldwide production.

First, consider the amount exported, 2.8. If 2.8 represents 50% (half) of U.S. production, then the amount produced must be twice 2.8: $2 \times 2.8 = 5.6$.

Now use the percent formula: *Part* = *Percent* × *Whole*. You know the *Part*; it is 5.6. You also know the *Percent*; it is 2%. Set up the formula and solve for the *Whole*.

5.6 is 2% of what number?

$$
\begin{aligned}
5.6 &= 2\left(\frac{1}{100}\right) \times \textit{Whole} \\
5.6 &= \frac{2}{100} \times \textit{Whole} \\
5.6\left(\frac{100}{2}\right) &= \left(\frac{2}{100}\right)\left(\frac{100}{2}\right)\textit{Whole} \\
5.6 \times 50 &= \textit{Whole} \\
280 &= \textit{Whole}
\end{aligned}
$$

The solution to the equation indicates that 280 is the number of MMT produced worldwide. Choice **(D)** is correct.

For more information on percent equations, see chapter 6.

DATA INTERPRETATION QUESTIONS (ALL-THAT-APPLY)

The directions for a Data Interpretation question requiring you to select one or more answers will look like this:

> **Directions:** Select one or more answer choices.

A Data Interpretation question requiring you to select one or more answers will look like this:

Questions 1–3 are based on the following graphs.

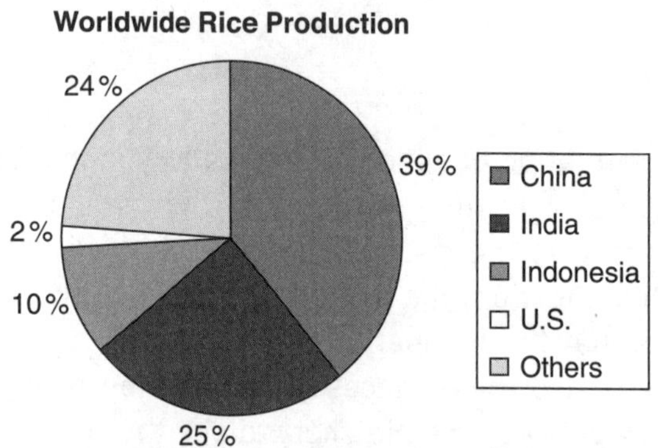

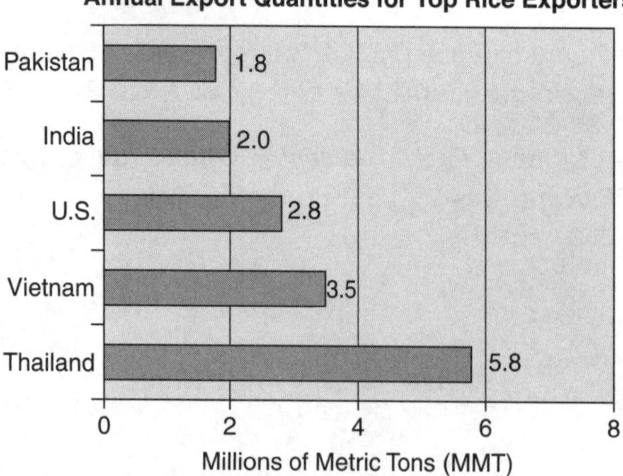

Which countries exported less than the average number of MMT for all exporting countries listed?

Indicate all such countries.

[A] Thailand
[B] Vietnam
[C] U.S.
[D] India
[E] Pakistan

Apply the Kaplan Method for Data Interpretation

Now let's apply the Kaplan Method to a Data Interpretation question requiring you to select one or more answers.

Which countries exported less than the average number of MMT for all exporting countries listed?

Indicate all such countries.

[A] Thailand
[B] Vietnam
[C] U.S.
[D] India
[E] Pakistan

STEP 1

Analyze the tables and graphs.

This question is based on the bottom graph dealing with exports.

STEP 2

Approach strategically.

To answer the question, the average number of MMT per country must be found. Read the export quantities for each country from the graph and use the equation for finding the average (arithmetic mean):

$$Average = \frac{Sum\ of\ terms}{Number\ of\ terms} = \frac{5.8 + 3.5 + 2.8 + 2 + 1.8}{5} = \frac{15.9}{5} \approx 3$$

There is no need to be concerned about decimal places; an estimate of 3 is sufficient to answer the question. The U.S., India, and Pakistan exported less than the average number of MMT. The correct choices are **(C)**, **(D)**, and **(E)**.

For more information on finding an average, see chapter 6.

DATA INTERPRETATION QUESTIONS (NUMERIC ENTRY)

The directions for a Data Interpretation question requiring you to make a Numeric Entry will look like this:

> **Directions:** Click on the box and type a number. Backspace to erase.

Enter your answer as an integer or decimal if there is one box or as a fraction if there are two boxes.

To enter an integer or decimal, type directly in the box or use the Transfer Display button on the calculator.

- Use the backspace to erase.
- Use a hyphen to enter a negative sign; type a hyphen a second time to remove it. The digits will remain.
- Use a period for a decimal point.
- The Transfer Display button will enter your answer directly from the calculator.
- Equivalent forms of decimals are all correct. Example: $.14 = 0.140$.
- Enter the exact answer unless the question asks you to round your answer.

To enter a fraction, type the numerator and denominator in the appropriate boxes.

- Use a hyphen to enter a negative sign.
- The Transfer Display button does *not* work for fractions.
- Equivalent forms of fractions are all correct. Example: $\frac{25}{15} = \frac{5}{3}$.
- If numbers are large, reduce fractions to fit in boxes.

A Data Interpretation question with Numeric Entry will look like this:

Questions 1–3 are based on the following graphs.

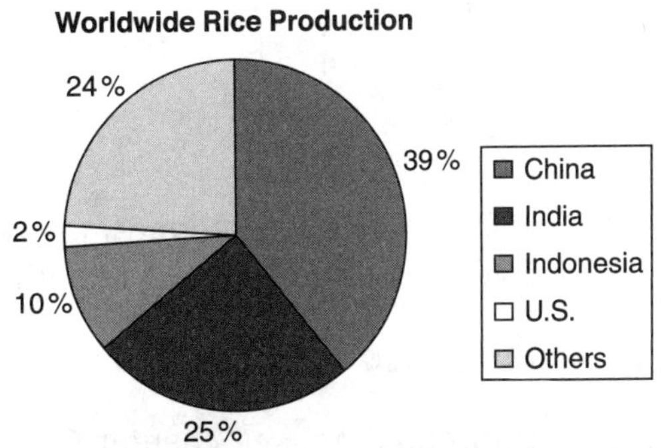

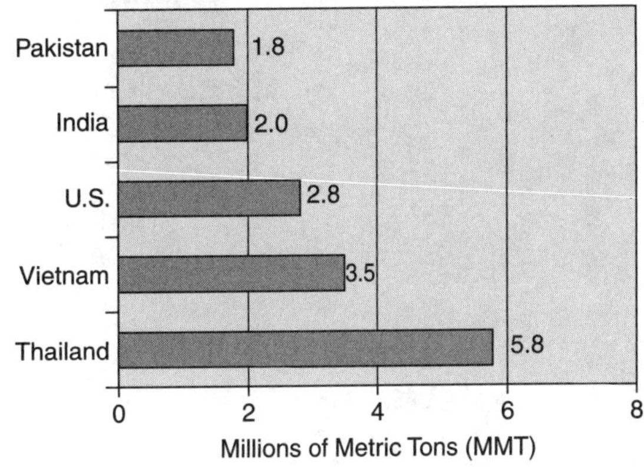

For a certain year, the worldwide production of rice was 600 MMT. Based on the data presented, what would Indonesia's production have been that year?

[ ] MMT

APPLY THE KAPLAN METHOD FOR DATA INTERPRETATION

Now let's apply the Kaplan Method to a Data Interpretation question requiring you to make a Numeric Entry.

For a certain year, the worldwide production of rice was 600 MMT. Based on the data presented, what would Indonesia's production have been that year?

[ ] MMT

STEP 1

Analyze the tables and graphs.

The question requires you to use the top graph and find the percent of worldwide production contributed by Indonesia.

STEP 2

Approach strategically.

Solve a percent equation for the *Part* produced by Indonesia. You know from the pie chart that the percent is 10%, and you know from the question that the *Whole* is 600.

$Part = Percent \times Whole = 0.10 \times 600 = 60$. The answer is **60** MMT.

For more information on the percent equation, see chapter 6.

DATA INTERPRETATION PRACTICE SET

Try the following Data Interpretation questions using the Kaplan Method.

Basic

Questions 1–3 are based on the following graph.

Madagascar's Export Partners 2009

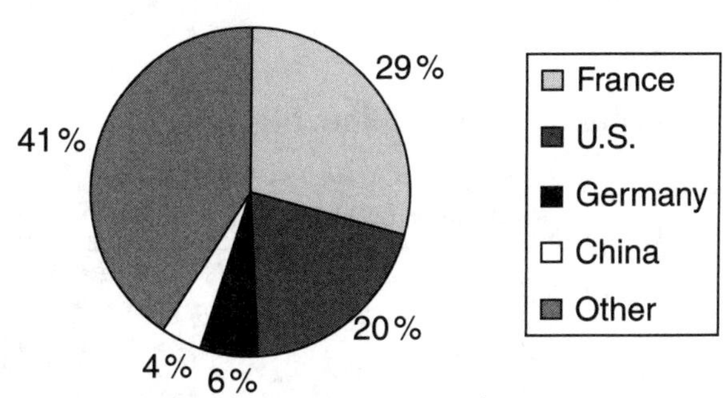

1. If Madagascar's exports totaled 1.3 billion dollars in 2009, approximately what was the value, in millions of dollars, of the country's exports to China?

   (A) 52
   (B) 78
   (C) 100
   (D) 325
   (E) 520

2. What is the approximate ratio of Madagascar's combined total exports to France, the United States, Germany, and China to Madagascar's exports to all other countries?

   (A) $\frac{2}{5}$
   (B) $\frac{1}{2}$
   (C) $\frac{2}{3}$
   (D) $\frac{3}{2}$
   (E) $\frac{2}{1}$

3. If Madagascar's exports to France increased to 33% of Madagascar's total exports in 2010, by approximately what percent did Madagascar's exports to France's increase from 2009–2010?

(A) 4%
(B) 14%
(C) 32%
(D) 88%
(E) 114%

Questions 4–6 are based on the following graph.

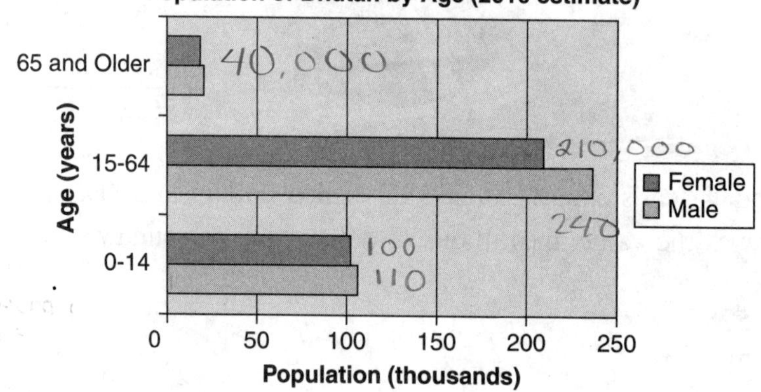

4. Approximately what percent of Bhutan's total population was between the ages of 0 and 14 years in 2010?

(A) 15%
(B) 25%
(C) 30%
(D) 40%
(E) 55%

5. What is the best estimate of the ratio of the female population age 65 and older to the female population age 0 to 14 years?

(A) 1:10
(B) 1:5
(C) 1:3
(D) 3:1
(E) 5:1

6. Which of the following ratios are greater than 1:2?

   Indicate <u>all</u> such ratios.

   [A] Males and females ages 0–14 to total population
   [B] Males ages 0–14 to males and females ages 0–14
   [C] Males ages 15–64 to total population
   [D] Males and females ages 0–14 to males and females ages 15–64
   [E] Males over 65 to males and females ages over 65

Questions 7–10 are based on the following graphs.

Distribution of Students at Shady Brook High School

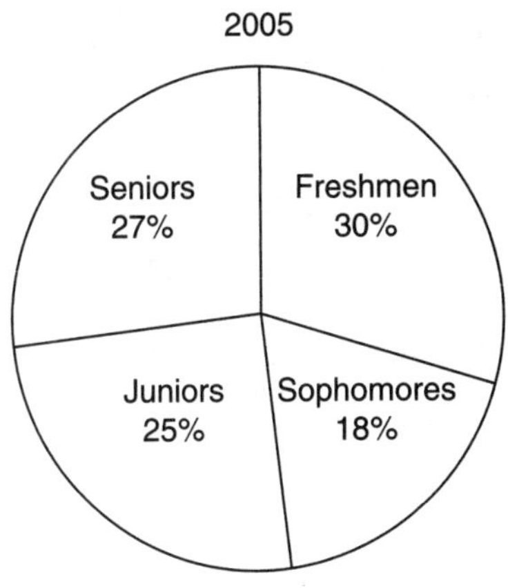

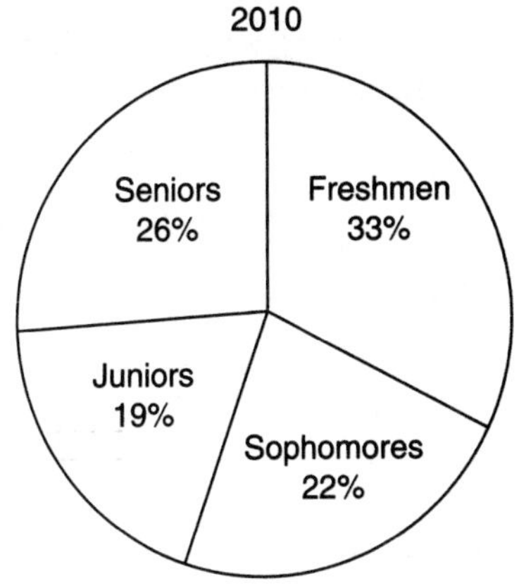

7. Suppose there were 1,100 students at Shady Brook High School in 2005 and 1,300 students in 2010. How many more freshmen attended the school in 2010 than in 2005?

   (A) 429
   (B) 200
   (C) 99
   (D) 33
   (E) 3

8. Suppose 1,100 students attended Shady Brook High School in 2005. If two-thirds of the seniors were female, how many male seniors attended the school in 2005?

(A) 99
(B) 132
(C) 216
(D) 324
(E) 400

9. Suppose 1,300 students attended Shady Brook High School in 2010. If the ratio of faculty assigned to work with underclassmen to underclassmen (freshmen and sophomores) was about 1:14, how many faculty were assigned to work with the underclassmen?

(A) 30
(B) 45
(C) 50
(D) 56
(E) 100

10. If the number of juniors in 2005 and 2010 was the same, which of the following statements could be true?

Indicate all such statements.

[A] There were 988 students in 2005 and 1,300 students in 2010.
[B] There were 952 students in 2005 and 1,300 students in 2010.
[C] There were 987 students in 2005 and 750 students in 2010.
[D] There were 1,158 students in 2005 and 875 students in 2010.
[E] There were 1,064 students in 2005 and 1,400 students in 2010.

Intermediate

Questions 11–13 are based on the following graphs.

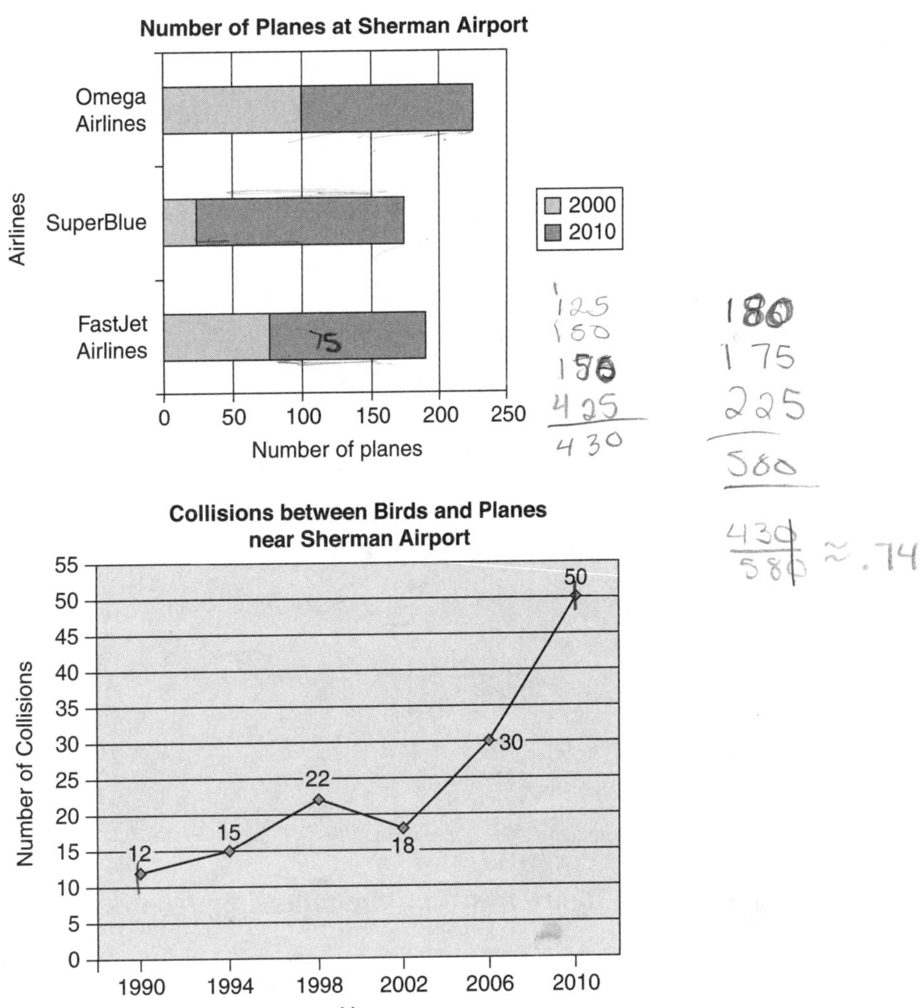

11. The number of collisions between birds and planes near Sherman Airport increased by approximately what percent between 1990 and 2010?

- (A) 3%
- (B) 37%
- (C) 193%
- (D) 245%
- (E) 317%

12. What is the probability that a collision between a bird and a plane in 2010 involved a SuperBlue plane, assuming that collisions between birds and planes involved only Omega, SuperBlue, and FastJet airplanes?

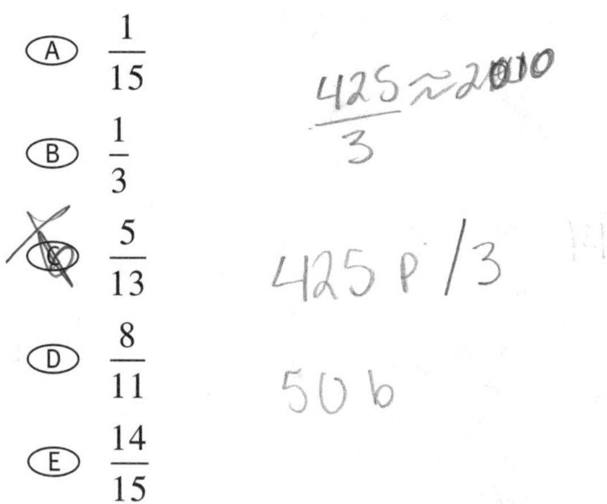

Ⓐ $\frac{1}{15}$

Ⓑ $\frac{1}{3}$

Ⓒ $\frac{5}{13}$

Ⓓ $\frac{8}{11}$

Ⓔ $\frac{14}{15}$

13. Based on the data given in the graph, approximately what percentage of collisions between birds and planes between 1990 and 2010, inclusive, occurred before 2002?

Ⓐ 12%
Ⓑ 20%
Ⓒ 33%
Ⓓ 50%
Ⓔ 67%

Questions 14–16 are based on the following graphs.

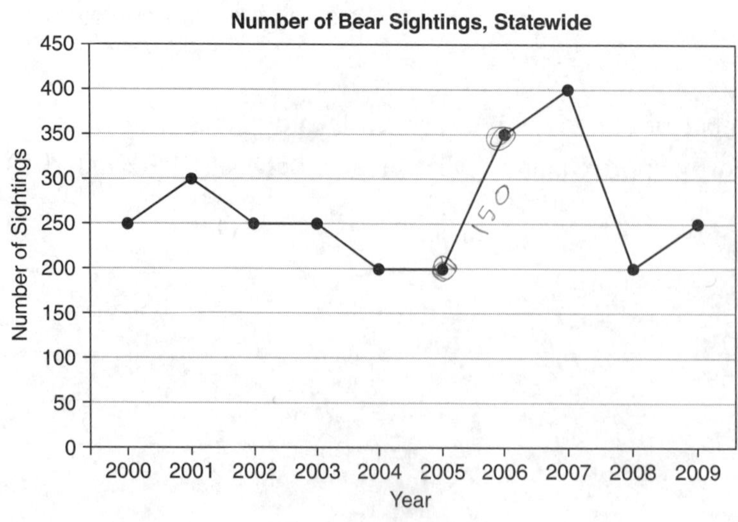

Typical Reasons for Bear Sightings

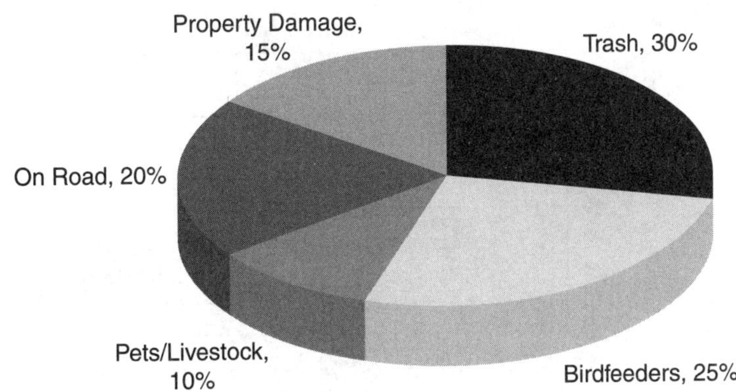

14. If Smithson County reported 20% of the bear sightings in the state in 2000, how many sightings were reported for that location?

Ⓐ 20
Ⓑ 25
Ⓒ 30
Ⓓ 40
Ⓔ 50

15. During the year that had the greatest increase in the number of bear sightings from the previous year, how many "on road" sightings were reported, assuming a typical distribution of bear-sighting types?

Ⓐ 20
Ⓑ 35
Ⓒ 40
Ⓓ 70
Ⓔ 80

16. According to the data given, in which year was there no change in the number of bear sightings from the previous year?

Select <u>all</u> that apply.

[A] 2002
[B] 2003
[C] 2004
[D] 2005
[E] 2006

Questions 17–20 are based on the following graphs.

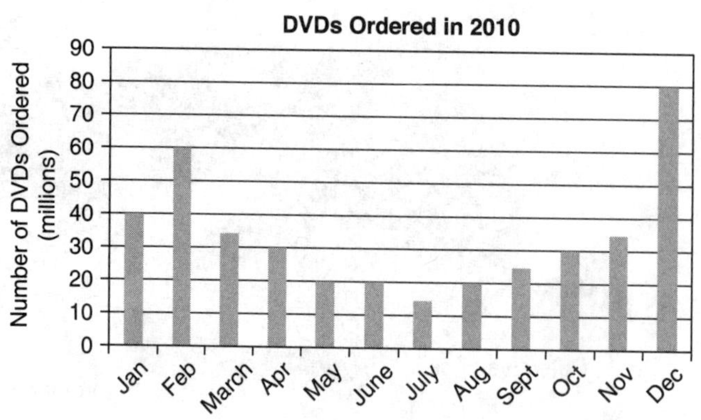

17. There was a $41\frac{2}{3}\%$ change in the number of DVDs ordered between which two consecutive months in 2010?

(A) February to March 58
(B) April to May 64
(C) May to June 0
(D) August to September
(E) November to December

18. Which pairs of months in 2010 have a sales ratio of 2:3?

Select all such months.

- [A] January:February
- [B] April:May
- [C] August:April
- [D] October:November
- [E] May:June

19. In December 2010, how many more comedy DVDs were ordered than drama DVDs?

- Ⓐ 4.2 million
- Ⓑ 6.3 million
- Ⓒ 8 million
- Ⓓ 14.4 million
- Ⓔ 18 million

20. Suppose 15% of the DVDs ordered in October 2010 were horror films. How many more horror films, in millions, were ordered in December than in October?

[1.9] million

Advanced

Questions 21–24 are based on the following graphs.

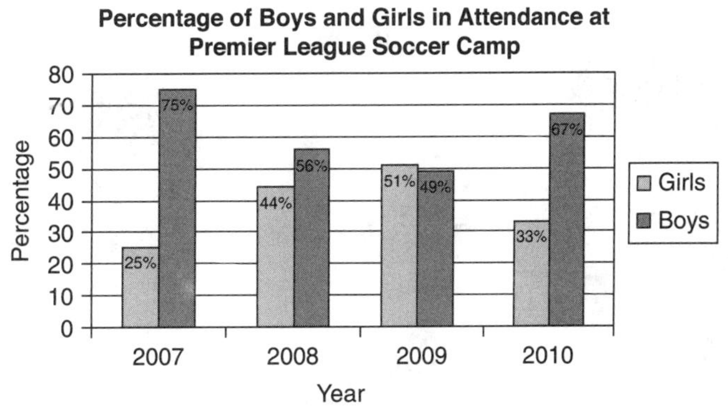

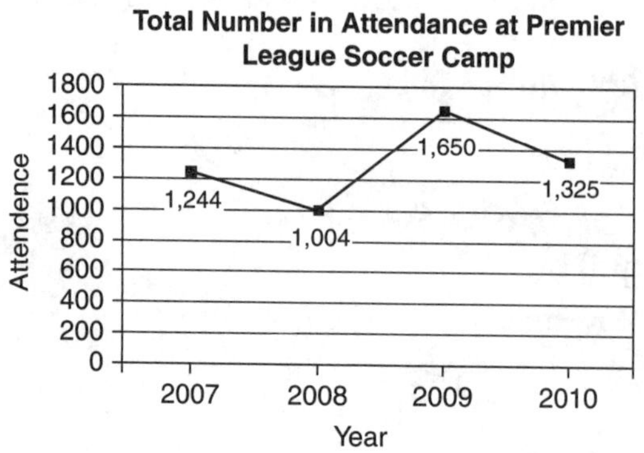

21. Approximately how many girls attended the 2010 Premier League Soccer Camp?

(A) 330
(B) 450
(C) 545
(D) 825
(E) 890

22. In which year(s) shown did approximately the same number of girls and boys attend the camp?

(A) 2007
(B) 2008
(C) 2009
(D) 2007 and 2008
(E) 2008 and 2009

23. Which two years from 2007 to 2010, inclusive, had the lowest numbers of boys in attendance?

(A) 2007 and 2008
(B) 2008 and 2009
(C) 2009 and 2010
(D) 2007 and 2010
(E) 2008 and 2010

24. Which is the best estimate of the total number of girls who attended in the two years that had the lowest total attendance?

(A) 1,500
(B) 1,275
(C) 1,280
(D) 750
(E) 660

Questions 25–27 are based on the following graphs.

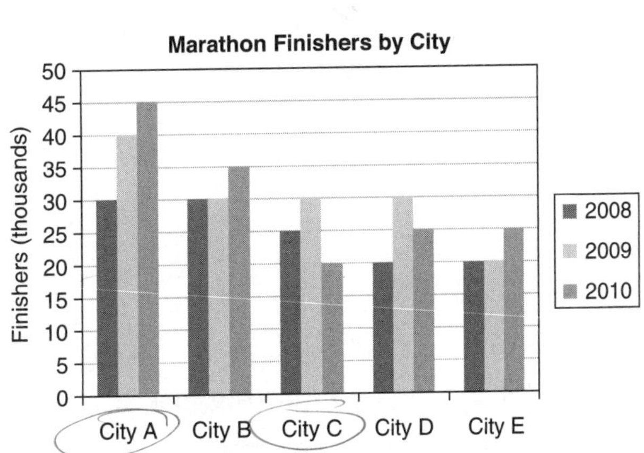

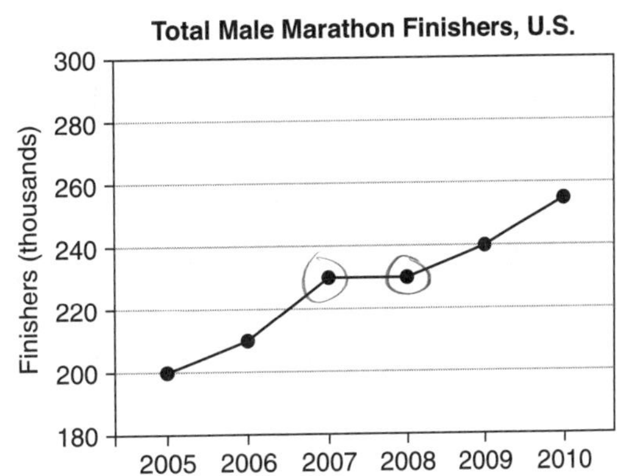

25. Which city showed the greatest percent increase in marathon finishers from 2009 to 2010?

(A) City A
(B) City B
(C) City C
(D) City D
(E) City E

26. During the year in which there was no change in male marathon finishers from the previous year, what was the ratio of finishers in city A to finishers in city C?

Ⓐ 6:5
Ⓑ 4:3
Ⓒ 1:1
Ⓓ 8:5
Ⓔ 14:11

27. If 60% of marathon finishers are male, what percentage of the total 2009 U.S. marathon finishers ran in city A?

Ⓐ 5%
Ⓑ 10%
Ⓒ 25%
Ⓓ 30%
Ⓔ 40%

Questions 28–30 are based on the following graphs.

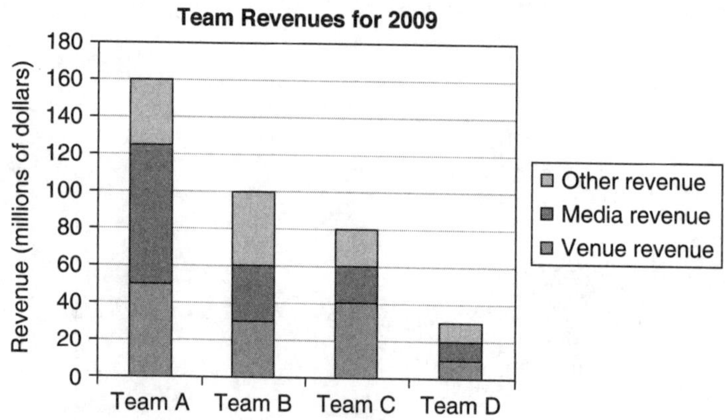

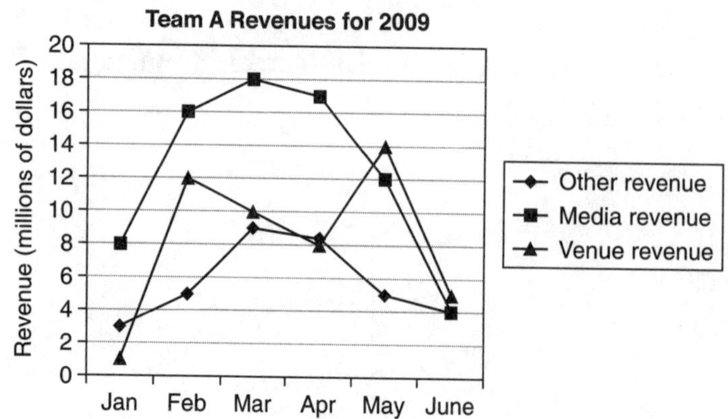

28. For the team that earned $20 million in media revenue in 2009, what percent of total revenue that year came from venue revenue?

[50] percent

29. For the month in which team A showed the greatest media revenue, which statement(s) is (are) true?

Indicate <u>all</u> such statements.

- [A] Team A's venue was about the same as revenue from other sources.
- [B] Team A's revenue from media was more than $120 million.
- [C] Team A's media revenue for that month accounted for about one-fourth of the team's media revenue for the year.
- [D] In the same month, team A's revenue from other sources also showed its greatest amount.
- [E] Total revenues for team A for the month were less than $30 million.

30. What percent change did team A experience in venue revenue from May to June 2009?

- (A) Venue revenue decreased by 35.7%.
- (B) Venue revenue decreased by 64.3%.
- (C) Venue revenue increased by 66.6%.
- (D) Venue revenue increased by 80%.
- (E) Venue revenue stayed the same.

DATA INTERPRETATION PRACTICE SET ANSWER KEY

1. A
2. D
3. B
4. C
5. B
6. B, E
7. C
8. A
9. C
10. A, E
11. E
12. C
13. C
14. E
15. D
16. B, D
17. A
18. A, C
19. D
20. 1.9
21. B
22. C
23. B
24. D
25. E
26. A
27. B
28. 50
29. A, C, D
30. B

DATA INTERPRETATION PRACTICE SET ANSWERS AND EXPLANATIONS

Basic

1. A

Exports to China are 4% of all of Madagascar's exports. The dollar amount for Madagascar's exports is 1.3 billion dollars, but be aware that the question asks for millions of dollars. Multiply 1.3 billion by 1,000 to get the number of millions, or 1,300 million. Then, multiply 1,300 by 0.04 (4%) to get 52 million. The answer is choice **(A)**.

2. D

The percent shown for all other countries is 41%. So the percent for the remaining entries must be 100 − 41 = 59%. Write the ratio and then round:

$$\frac{59}{41} \approx \frac{60}{40} = \frac{3}{2}.$$

The correct answer is **(D)**.

3. B

The percent shown in the graph for France in 2009 is 29%. An increase to 33% would be an increase of 4 percentage points. Use the formula for percent increase:

$$\textit{Percent increase} = \frac{\textit{Amount of increase}}{\textit{Original whole}} \times 100\% = \frac{4}{29} \times 100\% \approx 14\%$$

The correct answer is **(B)**.

4. C

First, combine the approximate figures for males and females between the ages of 0 and 14 years. These are both just a little more than 100,000 for a total of about 210,000. Compare that figure to the total population. The total population is approximately 110,000 + 100,000 + 240,000 + 210,000 + 20,000 + 20,000 = 700,000. So, the percent of the population between 0 and 14 years (ignoring the thousands) is about $\frac{210}{700} = \frac{\overset{3}{\cancel{21}}}{\underset{10}{\cancel{70}}} = \frac{3}{10} = 30\%$. The answer is **(C)**.

5. B

Compare the number of females in the oldest age group to the number of females in the youngest age group. Those numbers are approximately 20,000 and 100,000, respectively: 20:100 = 1:5. The answer is **(B)**.

6. B, E

(A) The population of males and females between 0 and 14 is about 210,000. That's less than half of the total population of about 700,000. Eliminate (A).

(B) For the age group 0–14, the length of the bar for the males is longer than the bar for females. Therefore, the males represent more than 50% of that group. Choice **(B)** is correct.

(C) There are approximately 240,000 males in the 15–64 age group. This is less than half of the total population of about 700,000. Eliminate (C).

(D) Do a quick estimate of the population numbers here: The total in the 0–14 age group is about 210,000. The total in the 15–64 age group is about 450,000. Eliminate (D) because twice 210,000 is less than 450,000.

(E) In the 65 and older age group, the bar for males is longer than the bar for females. Therefore, the males represent more than 50% of that group. Choice **(E)** is correct.

The correct choices are **(B)** and **(E)**.

7. C

Use the first graph to determine the number of freshmen in 2005 and use the second graph to determine the number of freshmen in 2010. Then subtract. The first graph shows that 30% of the students in 2005 were freshmen, so $0.30 \times 1{,}100 = 330$. The second graph shows that 33% of the students in 2010 were freshmen, so $0.33 \times 1{,}300 = 429$. Subtract: $429 - 330 = 99$. The answer is **(C)**.

8. A

Since the problem only involves the year 2005, only the first graph is needed. If two-thirds of the seniors were female, then the remaining one-third of the seniors were male. To find the number of male seniors, find one-third of the number of seniors. To find the number of seniors, find 27% of 1,100: $0.27 \times 1{,}100 = 297$. Then multiply by $\frac{1}{3}$: $297 \times \frac{1}{3} = 99$. The answer is **(A)**.

9. C

The percents given for the freshmen and sophomores in 2010 are 33% and 22% respectively. Use the sum of these percents ($33 + 22 = 55$) to find the number of underclassmen: $0.55 \times 1{,}300 = 715$. Let f represent the number of faculty in the proportion $\frac{1}{14} = \frac{f}{715}$. Cross multiply and solve for f:

$$175 = 14f$$
$$\frac{715}{14} = f \approx 51$$

The closest choice is **(C)**, 50.

10. A, E

In 2005, 25% of all the students were juniors. In 2010, 19% of all the students were juniors. For the number of juniors to be the same for both years, 25% of the 2005 student body must equal 19% of the 2010 student body, or 0.25 (number of students in 2005) = 0.19 (number of students in 2010). For this to be possible, the number of students in 2010 would have to be greater than the number of students in 2005. Eliminate any choices right away where this is not the case—eliminate choices (C) and (D).

Now check to see whether the numbers in choices (A), (B), and (E) make this a true statement. Answer choice **(A)** works: 0.25(988) = 247 and 0.19(1,300) = 247.

However, 0.25(952) = 238, and 0.19(1,300) = 247. Note that, since choice **(A)** works, choice (B) cannot possibly work, since (B) uses the same value for 2010, but a different value for 2005. Eliminate (B).

Try (E) next: 0.25(1,064) = 266 and 0.19(1,400) = 266. Choice **(E)** works.

The answers are **(A)** and **(E)** only.

Intermediate

11. E

The equation for percent increase is $\frac{\textit{Amount of increase}}{\textit{Original whole}} \times 100\%$. There were 50 collisions in 2010 and 12 collisions in 1990; there were 50 − 12 = 38 more collisions in 2010 than there were in 1990. To find the percent increase in collisions, divide 38 (the amount of increase) by 12 (the original whole) and multiply by 100. $\frac{38}{12} \times 100 \approx 317\%$. The answer is **(E)**.

12. C

From the data, in 2010 there were about 150 SuperBlue planes at the airport and a total of 390 planes at the airport. So, the probability that a collision involved a SuperBlue plane is $\frac{150}{390}$, which reduces to $\frac{5}{13}$. The answer is **(C)**.

13. C

In the years 1990, 1994, and 1998, there were about 12 + 15 + 22 = 49 collisions and a total of about 12 + 15 + 22 + 18 + 30 + 50 = 147 collisions during all the years shown on the graph. So, the percentage of collisions that occurred in the years 1990, 1994, and 1998 was $\frac{49}{147} \times 100 \approx 33\%$. The answer is **(C)**.

14. E

The question is asking about a percentage of the total bear sightings in 2000. The first graph shows total bear sightings, and in 2000, there were 250 sightings. Smithson County reported 20% of those, so 20% of 250 is 0.20 × 250 = 50. The answer is **(E)**.

15. D

The second graph shows the "on road" sightings as a percentage of the total sightings. So to find the number of "on road" sightings, you first need the total number of sightings. The year that had the greatest increase in the number of sightings from the previous year is the year with the steepest slope from the previous year on the first graph, which occurs in 2006. This graph shows 350 total sightings in 2006. The second graph shows that "on road" sightings account for 20% of the total: 20% of 350 = 0.20 × 350 = 70. The answer is **(D)**.

16. B, D

This question relates to the first graph. The two horizontal line segments represent no change in bear sightings. They occur from 2002 to 2003 and from 2004 to 2005. The question asks for the years that did not experience a change from the previous year, so choose the second year for each pair. The answers are 2003 and 2005, choices **(B)** and **(D)**.

17. A

This question involves a percent change, so the following formula can be used:

$$\frac{\textit{Amount of change}}{\textit{Original whole}} \times 100\% = \textit{percent change.}$$

Using the bar graph, look to see which answer choices seem unreasonable to avoid needless calculations.

(A) February to March showed a change from 60 to 35. That's a decrease of 25 from 60, which is a 41.67% or $41\frac{2}{3}\%$ change. This seems like the correct answer, but we can check the other answer choices to make sure.

(B) April to May was a change from 30 down to 20. That's a drop of 10 compared to 30. You know 10 divided by 30 is about 33%, so ignore this choice.

(C) May to June showed no real change, certainly not the percent you are looking for. Ignore this choice.

(D) August to September showed a change from 20 up to 25. When you compare 5 to 20, you get 25%. Not the percent you are looking for.

(E) The bar for December is more than twice as high as the bar for November. This increase is too high a percent.

The answer is **(A)**.

18. A, C

First, eliminate any ratios where the first month's sales are higher than or equal to the second month's sales, since you are looking for a ratio of 2:3. Then, for each remaining answer choice, write and simplify the ratio. If the answer choice simplifies to 2:3, then the answer is correct. The sales ratios are as follows:

(A) January:February → 40:60 = 2:3 → Correct.

(B) April:May → 30:20 → April larger than May. Eliminate.

(C) August:April → 20:30 = 2:3 → Correct.

(D) October:November → 30:35 = 6:7 → Incorrect.

(E) May:June → 20:20 → The two months are equal. Eliminate.

The answers are **(A)** and **(C)**.

19. D

To solve this problem, first use the bar graph to determine that 80 million DVDs were sold in December. Then, use the circle graph. To find the difference, subtract the percent of DVDs that were dramas from the percent that were comedies. Then, multiply that times the total number of DVDs to get the actual number of DVDs.

Percent comedies (37%) – *Percent dramas* (19%) = *Number of percentage points greater* (18%)

18% of 80 million = 14.4 million

The answer is **(D)**.

20. 1.9

To solve this problem, first use the bar graph to determine that there were 30 million DVDs sold in October and 80 million DVDs sold in December. From the question, you know that 15% of October's DVDs were horror films. From the circle graph, you know that 8% of December's DVDs were horror films. To find the difference, subtract the number of October horror DVDs from the number of December horror DVDs. In order to do this, you must use the percent formula to calculate each of these numbers.

Number of December horror films: 8% of 80 million = 0.08 × 80 million = 6.4 million

Number of October horror films: 15% of 30 million = 0.15 × 30 million = 4.5 million

Subtract: 6.4 million −4.5 million = 1.9 million.

The answer is 1.9 million. Since the numeric entry field is labeled with the word *million*, you only need to enter 1.9 for the answer.

Advanced

21. B

There were about 1,350 total children in attendance at the camp in 2010. Thirty-three percent of those attending that year were girls. Since 33% is close to $\frac{1}{3}$, divide 1,350 by 3, which equals 450. Therefore, the answer is **(B)**.

22. C

Examine the bar graph to find two bars that are closest to the same height. The bars are very nearly the same height in 2009. Therefore, in 2009, about the same number of boys and girls attended the camp. The answer is **(C)**.

23. B

Examine both graphs to see which years are the most likely years to have the least number of boys in attendance. If the bar that represents boys shows a high percentage and the corresponding year on the line graph shows a high total attendance, that year will have a high number of boys that attended. The opposite is also true:

if the bar that represents boys shows a low percentage and the corresponding year on the line graph shows a low total attendance, that year will have a low number of boys that attended. You can also find the number of boys that attended each year by multiplying the percentage of boys attending (taken from the bar chart) by the total number of children that attended (taken from the line graph). The calculations using rounded numbers would look like this:

Year 2007: $0.75 \times 1{,}250 \approx 938$

Year 2008: $0.55 \times 1{,}000 = 550$

Year 2009: $0.50 \times 1{,}650 = 825$

Year 2010: $0.65 \times 1{,}350 \approx 878$

The years 2008 and 2009 had the lowest numbers of boys attending. Therefore, the answer is **(B)**.

24. D

Estimate the total number of girls that attended in the two lowest years, 2007 and 2008, by multiplying the percentage of girls attending (taken from the bar chart) by the total number of children that attended (taken from the line graph). The answer choices are far enough apart that it is safe to round the numbers taken from the line graph.

$$(0.25 \times 1{,}200) + (0.45 \times 1{,}000) = 300 + 450 = 750$$

Therefore, the answer is **(D)**.

25. E

Only three cities showed an increase in the number of finishers between 2009 and 2010, so you only need to consider the data for cities A, B, and E. All three of these cities had the same increase in finishers, 5,000 more in 2010 than in 2009. You can avoid calculating the percent increase if you recall the percent increase formula:

$$\textit{Percent increase} = \frac{\textit{Amount of increase}}{\textit{Original whole}} \times 100\%$$

In the three options you are considering, the numerator is the same; it is 5,000. So, the city with the smallest number in the denominator will yield the greatest fraction. That is city E, making choice **(E)** the correct answer.

If you do compute the percent increase for each of the three cities, the results will look like this:

City A:

$$\textit{Percent increase} = \frac{\textit{Amount of increase}}{\textit{Original whole}} \times 100\% = \frac{5}{40} \times 100\% = \frac{1}{8} \times 100\% = 12.5\%$$

City B:

$$\text{Percent increase} = \frac{\text{Amount of increase}}{\text{Original whole}} \times 100\% = \frac{5}{30} \times 100\% = \frac{1}{6} \times 100\% = 16.7\%$$

City E:

$$\text{Percent increase} = \frac{\text{Amount of increase}}{\text{Original whole}} \times 100\% = \frac{5}{20} \times 100\% = \frac{1}{4} \times 100\% = 25\%$$

An important takeaway from this question is the property demonstrated about fractions; when the numerators are the same, the fraction with the smallest positive denominator has the greatest value.

26. A

To find the ratio of finishers in city A to finishers in city C, you need to know which year's data to use. The second graph shows the number of male marathon finishers. The year 2008 shows no increase or decrease in the number of male finishers from the previous year. Using the 2008 values, the first graph shows 30,000 city A marathon finishers and 25,000 city C marathon finishers. The ratio is 30:25, or 6:5, and the answer is **(A)**.

27. B

The second graph shows that in 2009 there were 240,000 male marathon finishers. The question states that this represents 60% of the total marathon finishers. Let T be total marathon finishers. Then $0.60 \times T = 240{,}000$. Solve for T by dividing both sides by 0.60 to give $T = 400{,}000$. The first graph shows that in 2009 there were 40,000 marathon finishers in city A. To find the percentage of the total that this represents, use the percent formula:

$$\begin{aligned}\text{Percent} &= \frac{\text{Part}}{\text{Whole}} \times 100\% \\ &= \frac{\text{2009 City A finishers}}{\text{2009 Total finishers}} \times 100\% \\ &= \frac{40{,}000}{400{,}000} \times 100\% \\ &= 10\%\end{aligned}$$

The answer is **(B)**.

28. 50

First, use the bar graph to determine that team C earned $20 million in media revenue in 2009. Then, find the requested percent by writing a fraction and renaming it as a percent. The venue revenue for team C is 40 million, and the total revenue for team C is 80 million. The fraction $\frac{40\text{ million}}{80\text{ million}} = \frac{40}{80} = \frac{1}{2}$, which equals 50%. Since the numeric entry field has the label *percent* after it, a percent sign is not needed.

The answer is **50**.

29. A, C, D

You really have no choice but to test each statement, but you can still approach the question strategically. First, in the bottom graph, locate the month described in the question: the month in which team A received the most revenue from media was March. In that month, the revenue figures (in millions of dollars) were media, 18; venue, 10; and other, 9. A tally of team A's monthly media revenues (in millions of dollars) shows that the total for January through June, inclusive, was $8 + 16 + 18 + 17 + 12 + 4 = 75$. Compare this total to team A's 2009 media revenues from the bar graph: $125 - 50 = 75$ million dollars. Therefore, all of team A's media revenues were generated in the January–June period. Now you are ready to evaluate each statement.

(A) Compare 10 for venue revenue to 9 for other revenue and conclude that these amounts are about the same. This is a true statement.

(B) Don't be fooled by looking at the top graph and reading the value at the top of the part for media. This is a false statement.

(C) Compare the amount given for media in March to the total for the year from media: $\frac{18}{75} = 0.24 = 24\%$. This is a true statement.

(D) The amount from other sources in March, 9, was the greatest amount shown for that category. This is a true statement.

(E) The total revenue (in millions of dollars) for March was $18 + 10 + 9$, which is greater than 30. This is a false statement.

The correct choices are **(A)**, **(C)**, and **(D)**.

30. B

According to the line graph, team A's venue revenue decreased from 14 million to 5 million from May to June, a change of 9 million. To find the percent decrease, you can use this formula:

$$\frac{\textit{Percent decrease}}{100} = \frac{\textit{Amount of decrease}}{\textit{Original whole}}$$

$$\frac{x}{100} = \frac{9}{14}$$

$$14x = 900$$

$$x = 64.3$$

The answer is **(B)**.

CHAPTER 5

Quantitative Reasoning Practice

In this section, you will work on practice sets composed of 20 questions each. This is the same number of questions you will see on each of the two sections of Quantitative Reasoning on the GRE. There is a diagnostic tool at the end of each practice set to help you learn from your mistakes and continue with more confidence as you prepare for the actual GRE.

On Test Day, you will have 35 minutes to complete 20 questions in a Quantitative Reasoning section. Keep the time allowed in mind as you work these practice sets.

QUANTITATIVE REASONING PRACTICE SET 1

Directions: Select the correct answer.

1.

Quantity A	Quantity B
40 percent of 0.75	$\frac{3}{5} \times \frac{3}{4}$

(A) Quantity A is greater.
(B) Quantity B is greater.
(C) The two quantities are equal.
(D) The relationship cannot be determined from the information given.

2.

$m > 8$

Quantity A	Quantity B
$m + \sqrt{51}$	$\sqrt{64} + 7$

(A) Quantity A is greater.
(B) Quantity B is greater.
(C) The two quantities are equal.
(D) The relationship cannot be determined from the information given.

3. The side of equilateral triangle T is the same as the length of a side of square S.

Quantity A	Quantity B
The area of triangle T	The area of square S

(A) Quantity A is greater.
(B) Quantity B is greater.
(C) The two quantities are equal.
(D) The relationship cannot be determined from the information given.

4.

Quantity A	Quantity B
The number of distinct prime factors of 28	The number of distinct prime factors of 36

Ⓐ Quantity A is greater.
Ⓑ Quantity B is greater.
Ⓒ The two quantities are equal.
Ⓓ The relationship cannot be determined from the information given.

5.

$$4^5 = \frac{4^{20}}{4^x}$$

Quantity A	Quantity B
x	4

Ⓐ Quantity A is greater.
Ⓑ Quantity B is greater.
Ⓒ The two quantities are equal.
Ⓓ The relationship cannot be determined from the information given.

6.

$$g > 1$$

Quantity A	Quantity B
$\frac{g}{2g + 3} - 1$	$\frac{1}{g + 3} - 1$

Ⓐ Quantity A is greater.
Ⓑ Quantity B is greater.
Ⓒ The two quantities are equal.
Ⓓ The relationship cannot be determined from the information given.

7. ♣$j = j + 3$ and ◖$j = \dfrac{j^2 + 2}{j}$

Quantity A	Quantity B
◖(♣2)	♣(◖2)

Ⓐ Quantity A is greater.
Ⓑ Quantity B is greater.
Ⓒ The two quantities are equal.
Ⓓ The relationship cannot be determined from the information given.

8. $a = bc \qquad c > 0$

Quantity A	Quantity B
a	b

Ⓐ Quantity A is greater.
Ⓑ Quantity B is greater.
Ⓒ The two quantities are equal.
Ⓓ The relationship cannot be determined from the information given.

9. The value of a certain stock rose by 40 percent from March to April, and then decreased by 30 percent from April to May. The stock's value in May was what percent of its value in March?

Ⓐ 90%
Ⓑ 98%
Ⓒ 110%
Ⓓ 130%
Ⓔ 142%

10.

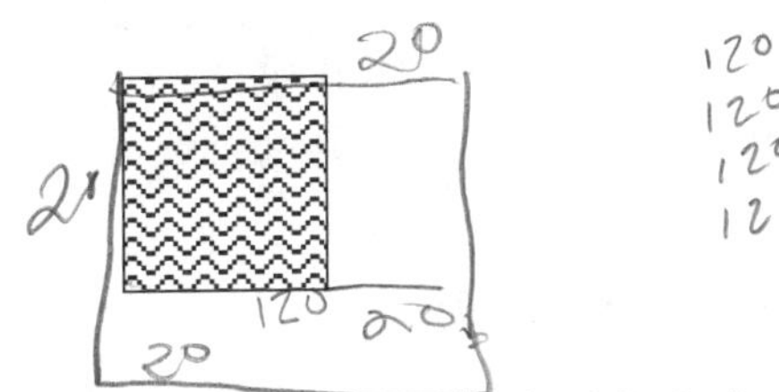

The figure shown represents a square garden. If each side is increased in length by 20 percent, by what percent is the area of the garden increased?

- (A) 44%
- (B) 50%
- (C) 125%
- (D) 144%
- (E) 150%

11. What is the value of a if $\dfrac{a + 1}{a - 3} - \dfrac{a + 2}{a - 4} = 0$?

- (A) −2
- (B) −1
- (C) 0
- (D) 1
- (E) 2

12.

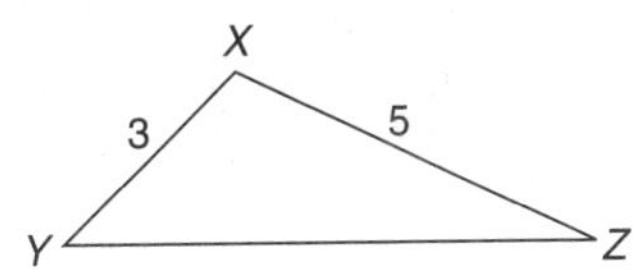

In the figure shown, which of the following could be the length of YZ?

Indicate <u>all</u> such lengths.

- [A] 2
- [B] 3
- [C] 5
- [D] 8
- [E] 9

13. In a certain school, the ratio of boys to girls is 5:13. If there are 72 more girls than boys, how many boys are there?

(A) 27
(B) 36
(C) 45
(D) 72
(E) 117

Questions 14–16 are based on the following graphs.

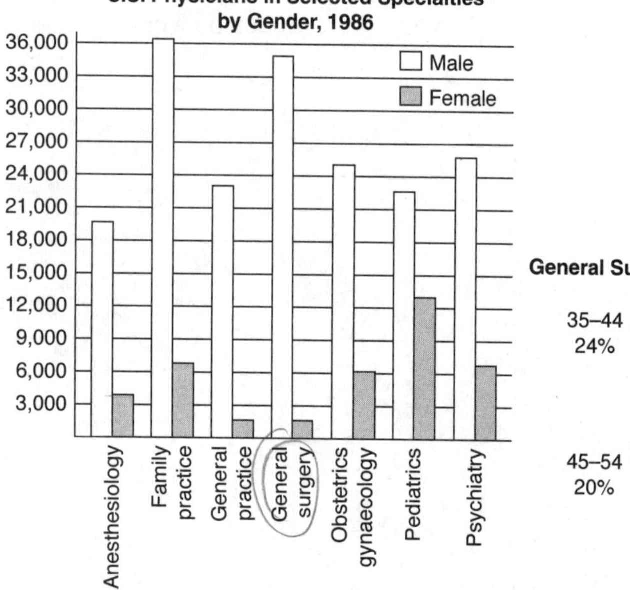

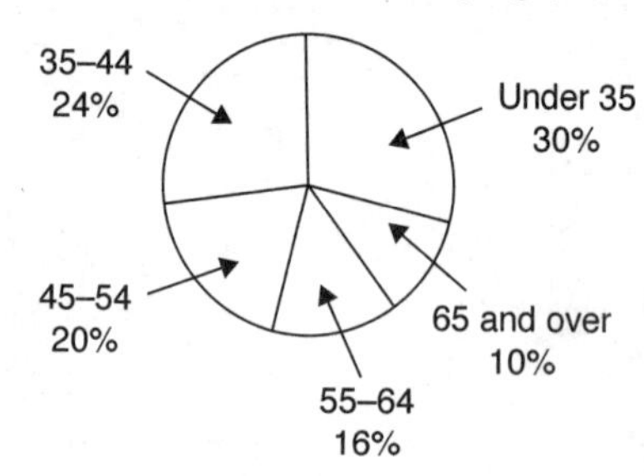

14. Approximately what percent of all general practice physicians in 1986 were female?

(A) 8%
(B) 23%
(C) 75%
(D) 82%
(E) 90%

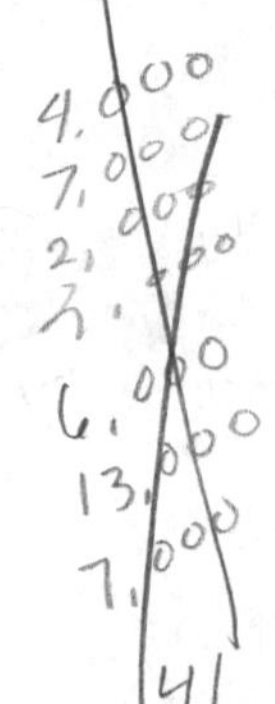

15. In 1986, approximately how many general surgery physicians were between the ages of 35 and 44, inclusive?

Ⓐ 5,440
Ⓑ 6,300
Ⓒ 7,350
Ⓓ 8,880
Ⓔ 10,200

16. If the number of female general surgery physicians in the under-35 category represented 8.5 percent of all the general surgery physicians, approximately how many male general surgery physicians were under 35 years of age?

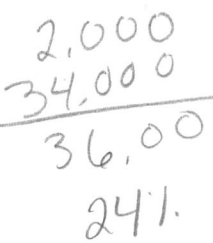

Ⓐ 7,350
Ⓑ 7,960
Ⓒ 9,750
Ⓓ 10,260
Ⓔ 11,980

17.

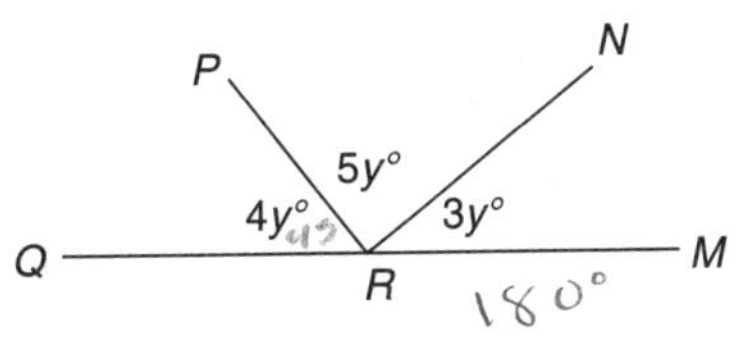

What is the degree measure of angle *PRM* shown?

[ ] degrees

18. Employee X is paid $19.50 an hour no matter how many hours he works per week. Employee Y is paid $18 an hour for the first 40 hours she works in a week and is paid 1.5 times the hourly rate for every additional hour she works. On a certain week, both employees worked the same number of hours and were paid the same amount. How many hours did each employee work that week?

Ⓐ 32
Ⓑ 36
Ⓒ 40
Ⓓ 42
Ⓔ 48

19.

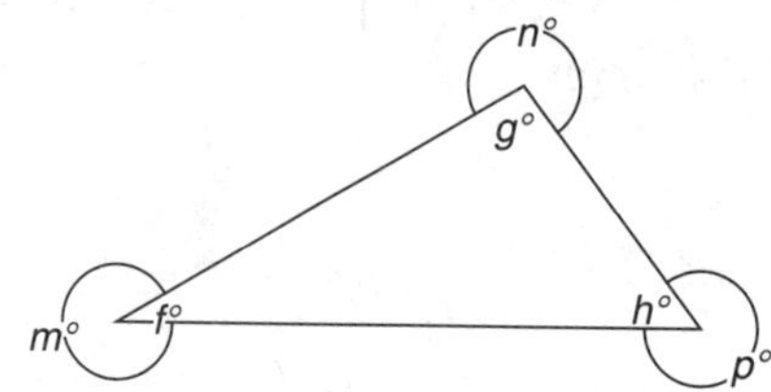

In the figure shown, what is $\dfrac{f + g + h}{m + n + p}$?

Ⓐ $\frac{1}{6}$

Ⓑ $\frac{1}{5}$

Ⓒ $\frac{1}{4}$

Ⓓ $\frac{1}{3}$

Ⓔ It cannot be determined from the information given.

20. Machine A can produce $\frac{1}{6}$ of a ton of paintbrushes in one hour. Machine B can produce $\frac{1}{14}$ of a ton of paintbrushes in one hour. Working together at their individual rates, how long would it take the two machines to produce 2 tons of paintbrushes?

Ⓐ 8 hours

Ⓑ 8 hours 24 minutes

Ⓒ 9 hours

Ⓓ 9 hours 46 minutes

Ⓔ 12 hours

QUANTITATIVE REASONING PRACTICE SET 1 ANSWER KEY

1. B
2. A
3. B
4. C
5. A
6. A
7. B
8. D
9. B
10. A
11. D
12. B, C
13. C
14. A
15. D
16. B
17. 120
18. E
19. B
20. B

QUANTITATIVE REASONING PRACTICE SET 1 ANSWERS AND EXPLANATIONS

1. B

Forty percent as a fraction is $\frac{4}{10}$. The decimal 0.75 as a fraction is $\frac{3}{4}$. We now have $\frac{4}{10} \times \frac{3}{4}$ for Quantity A. You know that $\frac{3}{5}$ is greater than $\frac{4}{10}$ because $\frac{3}{5} = \frac{6}{10}$. Therefore, $\frac{3}{5} \times \frac{3}{4}$ is greater than $\frac{4}{10} \times \frac{3}{4}$. Notice that you don't have to perform the multiplication because both sides are being multiplied by $\frac{3}{4}$. You only need to compare $\frac{3}{5}$ and $\frac{4}{10}$. In this case, Quantity B is greater than Quantity A, so the answer is **(B)**.

2. A

Compare each term in one quantity to see if it is larger than the corresponding term in the other quantity. Look at the first term in each quantity. Because *m* is larger than 8, you know that $m > \sqrt{64}$. Compare the next terms: $\sqrt{51} > 7$, since $\sqrt{49} = 7$. For every term of Quantity B, there is a larger term in Quantity A. Therefore, Quantity A is greater than Quantity B. The correct answer is **(A)**.

3. B

In geometry questions, if you are not given a diagram, then you should quickly sketch one on your scratch paper. If you draw a square where one side is also the side of an equilateral triangle, you should get something like this:

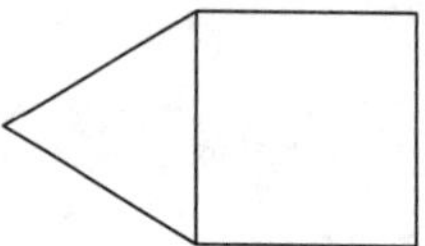

If you move the triangle over, it fits within the square.

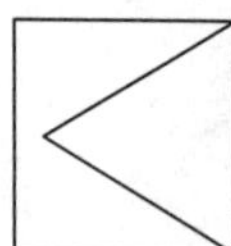

The square, or Quantity B, is larger. So the answer is **(B)**.

4. C

To find the number of distinct prime factors of a number, continue to break down factors of the number until you are left with only prime numbers. Remember that *distinct* simply means to count any repeated value only once. Therefore, 28 factors to 4×7, which further factors to $2 \times 2 \times 7$. The prime factors of 28 are 2, 2, and 7, and the distinct prime factors of 28 are 2 and 7. Likewise, 36 factors to 4×9, which further factors to $2 \times 2 \times 3 \times 3$. The prime factors of 36 are 2, 2, 3, and 3, and the distinct prime factors of 36 are 2 and 3. Each number has two distinct prime factors, so **(C)** is the correct choice.

5. A

When dividing values with the same base, you subtract the exponents. Look at the exponents in the given equation: $4^5 = \frac{4^{20}}{4^x}$. You know that $5 = 20 - x$. Some quick algebra shows you that $x = 15$. Quantity A is greater, so the correct choice is **(A)**.

6. A

Try simplifying each expression one step at a time. First, eliminate the 1 by adding 1 to both expressions:

Quantity A	Quantity B
$\frac{g}{g+3}$	$\frac{1}{g+3}$

Simplify by multiplying both expressions by $g + 3$. Remember, you can multiply both sides by the same positive value, and you know $(g + 3)$ is positive because you're given that $g > 1$.

Quantity A	Quantity B
$\frac{g}{g+3} \times (g+3) = g$	$\frac{1}{g+3} \times (g+3) = 1$

Now, compare g to 1. Given that $g > 1$, Quantity A is greater than Quantity B. The correct answer is **(A)**.

7. B

To compare these quantities, you will be applying the definitions of the symbols to the number 2. So everywhere you see j in the definitions, you will plug in the number 2. It also helps to say the definition of the symbol to yourself. For example, "club j" means to add 3 to j, and "semicircle j" means to square j and add 2 before dividing by j. As with any algebraic expression, work within the parentheses first.

For Quantity A, to calculate ◖(♣2), you do (♣2) first: ♣2 = $2 + 3 = 5$.

Then ◖5 = $\frac{5^2+2}{5} = \frac{25+2}{5} = \frac{27}{5} = 5\frac{2}{5}$.

For Quantity B, to calculate ♣(◖2), you do (◖2) first: ◖2 = $\frac{2^2+2}{2} = \frac{4+2}{2} = \frac{6}{2} = 3$.

Then, ♣3 = $3 + 3 = 6$. The answer is choice **(B)**.

8. D

You are given three variables, so it is an excellent time to use the Picking Numbers strategy. Remember when picking numbers, you must pick numbers that conform to the given information; that is, $a = bc$ and $c > 0$. Because c must be greater than zero, let's pick $c = 1$. If $c = 1$, any values you pick for a and b must be equal.

Because you picked numbers and found that the quantities can be equal, you know the correct answer is either (C) or (D).

Now try to pick values that give you a different relationship. If $c = 2$ and $b = 1$, a must equal 2. In this case, Quantity A is greater. The relationship changes, so **(D)** is correct. Remember, when picking numbers on Quantitative Comparison questions, once you find two different relationships, stop picking numbers and choose **(D)**.

9. B

Notice that even though the situation talks about the value of the stock, that value is never given. If you pick a number for the value of the stock, you can see much more easily what is going on.

Think about what would be a good number to pick for the value of the stock. The best number to pick when dealing with percents is almost always 100 because it is easy to find any percentage of 100.

Apply the percent changes to 100.

Forty percent of 100 is 40. Therefore, if the stock's value rises by 40 percent, its new value is 140.

Next, decrease this number by 30 percent.

Thirty percent of 140 is $0.30 \times 140 = 42$. So a decrease in price of 30 percent is $140 - 42 = 98$.

The original value was 100, and the new value is 98. So the stock is 98 percent of its original value. The correct choice is **(B)**.

10. A

Like almost all percent problems where no actual values are given, this is a great question to solve with the Picking Numbers strategy. Because you are dealing with a square garden, both sides are the same, and the area is side $\times$ side. Make the original dimensions 10 ft $\times$ 10 ft for an area of 100 sq ft. (Always start with 100 in percents questions because it is easy to find any percentage of 100.) Thus, if you increase each side length by 20 percent, the new dimensions would be 12 ft $\times$ 12 ft, for a new area of 144 sq ft. Consequently, the increase is 144 sq ft $-$ 100 sq ft $=$ 44 sq ft, which is 44 percent of 100 sq ft.

(A) is the correct choice.

11. D

Use the Backsolving strategy. Substitute the values in the answer choices into the equation. The one that gives you 0 must be correct.

(B): $\frac{a+1}{a-3} - \frac{a+2}{a-4} = \frac{-1+1}{-1-3} - \frac{-1+2}{-1-4} = \frac{0}{-4} - \frac{1}{-5} \neq 0$. Eliminate this answer choice.

Try another answer choice that is easy to work with.

(D): $\frac{a+1}{a-3} - \frac{a+2}{a-4} = \frac{1+1}{1-3} - \frac{1+2}{1-4} = \frac{2}{-2} - \frac{3}{-3} = -1 - (-1) = 0.$

Because the equation is true for **(D)**, it must be the answer.

12. B, C

In a triangle, each side must be shorter than the sum of the other two sides, and each side must be longer than the difference of the other two sides. Therefore, $(5 - 3) < YZ < (3 + 5)$, or $2 < YZ < 8$. The only possible values for YZ here that fall between 2 and 8 are 3 and 5.

So, **(B)** and **(C)** are the answers.

13. C

Use Backsolving on this one. The correct answer will yield a ratio of boys to girls of 5:13 when there are 72 more girls than boys. Start with (B).

(B): If there are 36 boys, there are $36 + 72 = 108$ girls, so the ratio of boys to girls is $36{:}108 = 1{:}3$. This is not the same as the ratio of 5:13 that you want. Try the next answer choice, (C).

(C): If there are 45 boys, there are $45 + 72 = 117$ girls, so the ratio of boys to girls is $45{:}117 = 5{:}13$, which is just what you want. The answer is **(C)**.

14. A

The bar graph doesn't give you the total number of general practice physicians, but you can find that number by adding the number of males to the number of females. To find the percent that are female, you take the number of females and put it over the total number. There are about 2,000 women and about 23,000 men, making the total about 25,000. If there are around 25,000 general practice physicians altogether and 2,000 of them are female, then 8 percent of the general practice physicians are female. The answer is **(A)**.

15. D

To refer to the ages of physicians, you need to find the slice of the pie that goes from 35 to 44. It's 24 percent, but 24 percent of what? You're not looking for a percent—you're looking for a number of doctors. For general surgery, the male bar goes up to about 35,000, and the female bar goes up to about 2,000—about 37,000 total. So 24 percent of 37,000 is the number of general surgery physicians between ages of 35 and 44, inclusive. That's 0.24 times 37,000, or 8,880. Choice **(D)** is the correct answer.

16. B

How many male general surgery physicians were under the age of 35? The pie chart breaks down general surgery by age, so you'll be working with it. And because you are looking for a number of general surgery physicians, you know that you are going to have to find the total number of general surgery physicians and then break it down according to the percentages on the pie chart.

You are given that the number of female general surgery physicians in the under-35 category represented 8.5 percent of all the general surgery physicians. What this does is break down the under-35 slice into two smaller slices, one for men under 35 and one for women under 35. You know that the whole under-35 slice is 30 percent of the total, and you are given that the number of females under 35 is 8.5 percent of the total. Thus, 30% – 8.5% = 21.5%, the amount you'll need to multiply by the total number of general surgery physicians.

For general surgery, the male bar goes up to about 35,000, and the female bar goes up to about 2,000—about 37,000 total. 21.5 percent of 37,000 is 7,955, which is closest to 7,960, making **(B)** the correct answer.

17. 120

Remember that a straight line has 180 degrees. That means that if you add the measures of angles *QRP*, *PRN*, and *NRM*, you'll get 180. Therefore, $4y + 5y + 3y = 180$, or $12y = 180$. Dividing both sides by 12 yields $y = 15$. Be careful, however; that's not your answer. You need to find the measure of angle *PRM*, which is the sum of the measures of angles *PRN* and *NRM*. That's $5(15) + 3(15) = 8(15) = 120$.

18. E

Use the Backsolving strategy. Note that in order for both employees to make the same amount in a given week, they must work more than 40 hours to allow Employee *Y*'s overtime rate to kick in. That means that choices (A), (B), and (C) are all too small. Start with (D). If (D) works, it's the correct answer; if not, the answer must be (E).

In 42 hours, employee *X* earns 42 × \$19.50 = \$819.

In 42 hours, employee *Y* earns (40 × \$18) + (2 × \$27) = \$774.

(D) is still too small, so **(E)** must be correct.

19. B

Remember that there are 360° around any point and that the interior angles of a triangle add up to 180°. From the first fact, you know that $f + m = g + n = h + p = 360$. Therefore, $m = 360 - f$, $n = 360 - g$, and $p = 360 - h$. From the second fact, you know that $f + g + h = 180$. Substitute these into the given rational expression:

$$\begin{aligned}
\frac{f+g+h}{m+n+p} &= \frac{f+g+h}{360-f+360-g+360-h} \\
&= \frac{f+g+h}{360+360+360-f-g-h} \\
&= \frac{f+g+h}{360+360+360-(f+g+h)} \\
&= \frac{180}{360+360+360-180} \\
&= \frac{180}{900} \\
&= \frac{1}{5}
\end{aligned}$$

The answer is **(B)**.

20. B

First you need to find out how long it will take each machine to produce 2 tons of paintbrushes. If Machine *A* can produce $\frac{1}{6}$ of a ton in one hour, it will take 6 hours for it to produce a full ton and twice that, or 12 hours, to produce 2 tons. If Machine *B* can produce $\frac{1}{14}$ of a ton in one hour, it will take 14 hours for it to produce a full ton and 28 hours to produce 2 tons. Now, use the combined work formula:

$$\frac{1}{r} + \frac{1}{s} = \frac{1}{t}$$

where *r* and *s* are the number of hours it takes Machines *A* and *B*, respectively, to produce 2 tons working by themselves, and *t* is the time it would take them to produce 2 tons working together.

$$\begin{aligned}
\frac{1}{12} + \frac{1}{28} &= \frac{1}{t} \\
\frac{7}{84} + \frac{3}{84} &= \frac{1}{t} \\
\frac{10}{84} &= \frac{1}{t} \\
t &= \frac{84}{10}
\end{aligned}$$

So it would take them $\frac{84}{10}$ or $8\frac{2}{5}$ hours to produce 2 tons of paintbrushes. The answer is **(B)**.

Diagnostic Tool

Tally up your score and write the results below.

Total

Total Correct: ________ out of 20

Percentage Correct: # you got right $\times$ 100 $\div$ 20: ________

By Section:

Quantitative Comparison ________ out of 8

Problem Solving ________ out of 9

Data Interpretation ________ out of 3

Diagnose Your Results

Look back at the questions you got wrong and think about your experience answering them. Were you stymied by a particular question type, or by a certain math topic? If the latter, studying the relevant math content review in Part 3 of this book should help.

QUANTITATIVE REASONING PRACTICE SET 2

Directions: Select the correct answer.

1. $a > 1$

Quantity A	Quantity B
$3 + (-9) - (-7)$	$4a$

(A) Quantity A is greater.
(B) Quantity B is greater.
(C) The two quantities are equal.
(D) The relationship cannot be determined from the information given.

2. 1 foot = 12 inches

Quantity A	Quantity B
The area of a square with a side length of 3 feet	400 square inches

(A) Quantity A is greater.
(B) Quantity B is greater.
(C) The two quantities are equal.
(D) The relationship cannot be determined from the information given.

3.

Quantity A	Quantity B
The number of square units in the area of a circle with a radius of 4	The number of units in the circumference of a circle with a radius of 8

(A) Quantity A is greater.
(B) Quantity B is greater.
(C) The two quantities are equal.
(D) The relationship cannot be determined from the information given.

4. $\square n = 5n$

Quantity A	Quantity B
$15 + \square 3$	$(\square 12) \div 2$

Ⓐ Quantity A is greater.
Ⓑ Quantity B is greater.
Ⓒ The two quantities are equal.
Ⓓ The relationship cannot be determined from the information given.

5. $ab \neq 0$

Quantity A	Quantity B
$(a^{-2}b^{-2})^{-1}$	$(a^{-1}b^{-1})^{-2}$

Ⓐ Quantity A is greater.
Ⓑ Quantity B is greater.
Ⓒ The two quantities are equal.
Ⓓ The relationship cannot be determined from the information given.

6. An integer x is selected at random from the set {17, 21, 23, 25, 27, 30, 33}.

Quantity A	Quantity B
The probability that the average (arithmetic mean) of 8, 16, and x is at least 17	$\frac{1}{2}$

Ⓐ Quantity A is greater.
Ⓑ Quantity B is greater.
Ⓒ The two quantities are equal.
Ⓓ The relationship cannot be determined from the information given.

7. (5, 2), (m, 4), (3, 5), (n, 7) are points on the same line.

Quantity A	Quantity B
m	n

Ⓐ Quantity A is greater.
Ⓑ Quantity B is greater.
Ⓒ The two quantities are equal.
Ⓓ The relationship cannot be determined from the information given.

8. $x \geq 0$

Quantity A	Quantity B
5^{5x}	5^{x+5}

Ⓐ Quantity A is greater.
Ⓑ Quantity B is greater.
Ⓒ The two quantities are equal.
Ⓓ The relationship cannot be determined from the information given.

9. The manager of a local grocery store earns an hourly wage of $21.00. The assistant manager earns 25% less than the manager. The stocker earns 60% less than the assistant manager. How much more does the manager make per hour than the stocker?

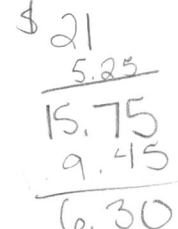

Ⓐ $6.30
Ⓑ $8.40
Ⓒ $9.45
Ⓓ $12.60
Ⓔ $14.70

10. Joe has a collection of 280 sports cards. If 30% of them are baseball cards, 25% of them are football cards, and the rest are basketball cards, how many basketball cards does Joe have?

Ⓐ 70
Ⓑ 84
Ⓒ 126
Ⓓ 154
Ⓔ 196

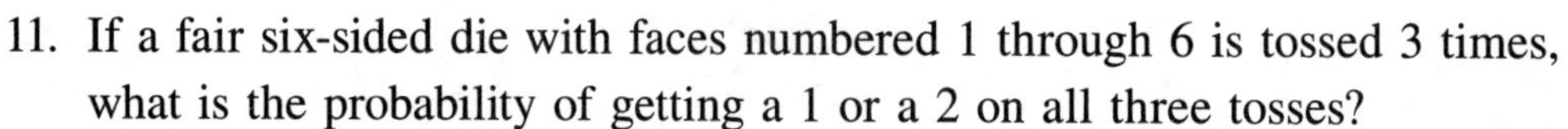

11. If a fair six-sided die with faces numbered 1 through 6 is tossed 3 times, what is the probability of getting a 1 or a 2 on all three tosses?

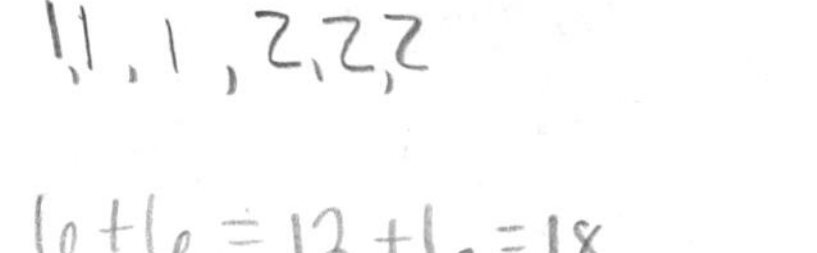

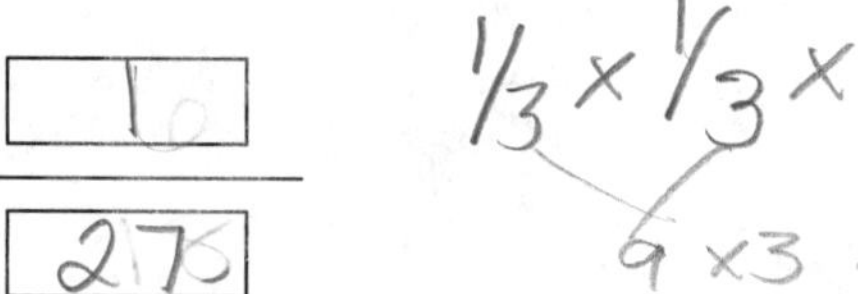

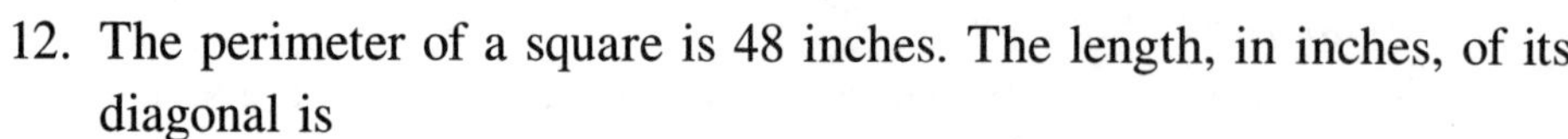

12. The perimeter of a square is 48 inches. The length, in inches, of its diagonal is

Ⓐ $6\sqrt{2}$
Ⓑ $8\sqrt{2}$
Ⓒ $12\sqrt{2}$
Ⓓ $24\sqrt{2}$
Ⓔ $48\sqrt{2}$

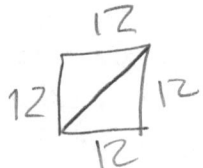

13. During a semester of her U.S. history class, Sophia received quiz scores of 85, 76, 98, 76, 100, and 75. How much greater is Sophia's average (arithmetic mean) quiz score than the mode of the set of scores?

Ⓐ 1
Ⓑ 5
Ⓒ 9
Ⓓ 10
Ⓔ 14

14. The ratio of girls to boys in a class is 6:7. If there are 18 girls, how many total students are in the class?

Ⓐ 18
Ⓑ 21
Ⓒ 27
Ⓓ 28
Ⓔ 39

15. If 12 is x percent of 60, what is 30 percent of x?

(A) 6
(B) 15
(C) 18
(D) 24
(E) 66

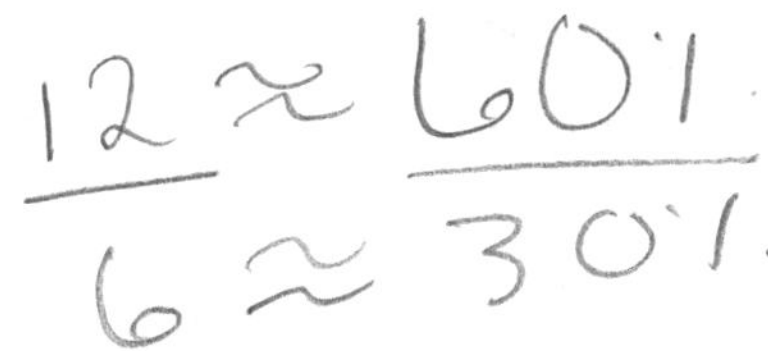

16.

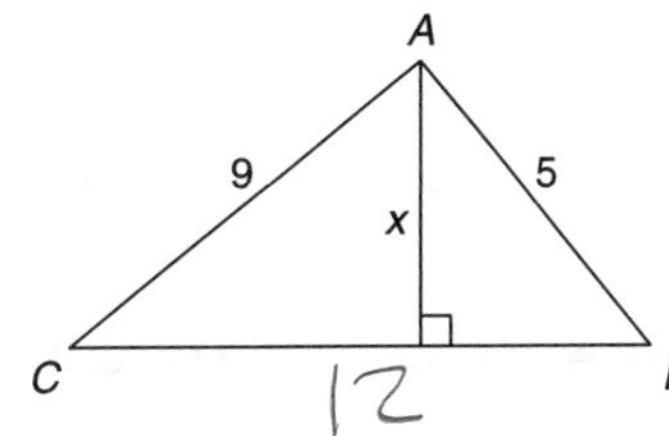

The area of triangle ABC is $6x$. What is the perimeter of triangle ABC?

(A) 12
(B) 17
(C) 20
(D) 25
(E) 26

17. Circle A has an area of 9π. Circle B has an area of 49π. If the circles intersect at exactly one point, which of the following could be the distance from the center of circle A to the center of circle B?

(A) 6
(B) 10
(C) 21
(D) 29
(E) 58

Questions 18–20 are based on the following graphs.

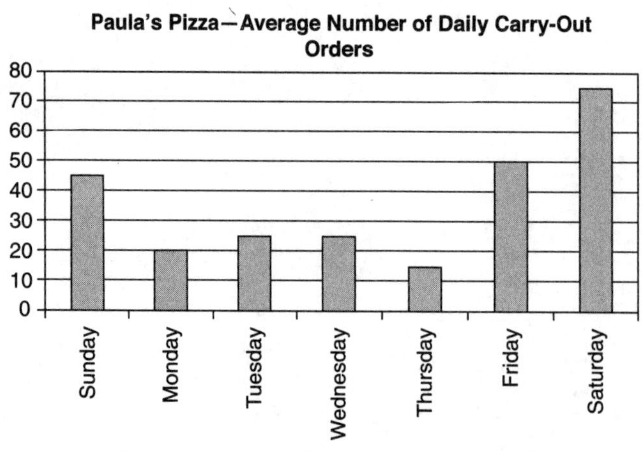

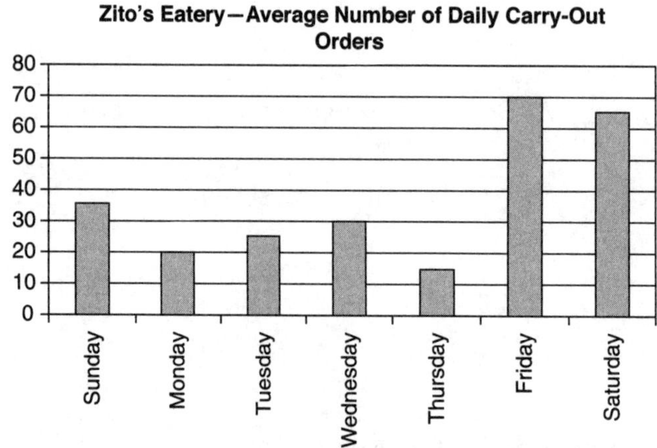

18. On which day of the week is the average number of carry-out orders the same for Paula's Pizza and Zito's Eatery?

Indicate all such days.

[A] Sunday
[B] Monday
[C] Tuesday
[D] Wednesday
[E] Thursday
[F] Friday
[G] Saturday

19. By what percent are Zito's Eatery's total average weekday (Monday through Friday) carry-out orders greater than its total average weekend (Saturday and Sunday) carry-out orders?

- (A) 12%
- (B) 18%
- (C) 50%
- (D) 60%
- (E) 63%

20. Between which two days does Paula's Pizza see the biggest drop in average carry-out orders?

- (A) Sunday to Monday
- (B) Wednesday to Thursday
- (C) Thursday to Friday
- (D) Friday to Saturday
- (E) Saturday to Sunday

QUANTITATIVE REASONING PRACTICE SET 2 ANSWER KEY

1. B
2. A
3. C
4. C
5. C
6. B
7. A
8. D
9. E
10. C
11. $\frac{1}{27}$
12. C
13. C
14. E
15. A
16. E
17. B
18. B, C, E
19. D
20. E

QUANTITATIVE REASONING PRACTICE SET 2 ANSWERS AND EXPLANATIONS

1. B

Quantity A contains all numbers, so it can be evaluated. Adding a negative number is the same as subtracting the positive of that number. So $3 + (-9)$ is the same as $3 - 9$, which is -6. Subtracting a negative number is the same as adding the positive of that number. So $-6 - (-7)$ is the same as $-6 + 7$, which is 1. Quantity B contains a variable, and its value is greater than 1. That means $4a$ is greater than 4 and Quantity B will always be greater than Quantity A. The correct answer is **(B)**.

2. A

There are 12 inches in 1 foot. Therefore, a square that measures 3 feet by 3 feet is the same as a 36-inch by 36-inch square. So Quantity A equals $36 \times 36 = 1{,}296$ square inches, which is greater than 400 square inches. The correct answer is **(A)**.

3. C

The area of a circle can be calculated by the formula $A = \pi r^2$. Quantity A is the area of a circle with a radius of 4, so its area is 16π. The circumference of a circle can be calculated by the formula $C = 2\pi r$. Quantity B is the circumference of a circle with a radius of 8, so its circumference is $2 \times \pi \times 8 = 16\pi$. The quantities are equal and, therefore, choice **(C)** is correct.

4. C

To apply the symbol in the centered information, multiply the number that follows it by 5. You must apply the symbol in both Quantity A and Quantity B. Look at Quantity A first:

$$15 + \square 3 = 15 + (5 \times 3) = 15 + 15 = 30$$

Now evaluate Quantity B:

$$(\square 12) \div 2 = 5 \times 12 \div 2 = 60 \div 2 = 30$$

Both values are the same, and choice **(C)** is correct.

5. C

When one exponent is raised to another, multiply the exponents. Simplifying Quantity A gives:

$$\left(a^{-2}b^{-2}\right)^{-1} = a^2b^2$$

Simplifying Quantity B gives:

$$\left(a^{-1}b^{-1}\right)^{-2} = a^2b^2$$

So the Quantities are equal, and the correct answer is **(C)**.

6. B

The average of 8, 16, and x is $\frac{8 + 16 + x}{3}$. Since the average is to be at least 17, we can say that $\frac{8 + 16 + x}{3} \geq 17$. Solving the inequality for x by first multiplying both sides by 3, we have $24 + x \geq 51$. Subtracting 24 from both sides, we have $x \geq 27$. The set contains seven numbers, three of which are greater than or equal to 27. So the probability of choosing a number greater than or equal to 27 is $\frac{3}{7}$. Quantity A is $\frac{3}{7}$, and Quantity B is $\frac{1}{2}$. Since $\frac{3}{7}$ is a little less than $\frac{1}{2}$, Quantity B is larger. The correct answer is **(B)**.

7. A

Notice in the given points (5, 2) and (3, 5) that as the x-value decreases, the y-value increases. This indicates a line that has a negative slope. In the point $(m, 4)$ the y-value, 4, is between the other given y-values, 2 and 5, so therefore the x-value, m, must be between the other given x-values, 5 and 3. In the other point $(n, 7)$, the y-value, 7, is greater than the given y-value of 5, so therefore the x-value, n, must be less than the other given x-value, 3. So, $5 > m > 3$, and $n < 3$. The correct answer is **(A)**.

8. D

One way of solving this problem is to use the strategy of Picking Numbers for the variable, x. Substitute values in for x to determine if Quantity A or B is greater. Be sure that in doing so, enough values of x are evaluated to present a wide range of possibilities. For example:

If $x = 0$:

Quantity A: $5^{5x} = 5^0 = 1$

Quantity B: $5^{x+5} = 5^5$, which is greater than 1.

So when $x = 0$, Quantity B would be greater.

If $x = 1$:

Quantity A: $5^{5x} = 5^5$.

Quantity B: $5^{x+5} = 5^6$.

So when $x = 1$, Quantity B would still be greater.

If $x = 2$:

Quantity A: $5^{5x} = 5^{10}$.

Quantity B: $5^{x+5} = 5^7$.

So when $x = 2$, Quantity A would be greater.

Since the relationship varies depending on the value of x, the correct answer is **(D)**.

9. E

The manager of a grocery store makes \$21.00 an hour. If the assistant manager makes 25% less than the manager, the assistant manager makes $21.00 \times 0.25 = 5.25$ less, or \$15.75. The stocker makes 60% less than the assistant manager, so he makes $15.75 \times 0.60 = 9.45$ less, or \$6.30. The question asks how much more the manager makes per hour than the stocker. Subtract the stocker's hourly wage from the manager's hourly wage: $\$21.00 - \$6.30 = \$14.70$. The correct answer is **(E)**.

10. C

Joe has 280 sports cards in his collection. Of these, 30% are baseball cards and 25% are football cards. Therefore, 55% of the collection is baseball and football cards, and just a little less than half of the collection—45%—is basketball cards. Calculate 45% of the total: $280 \times 0.45 = 126$. The answer is **(C)**, 126 basketball cards.

11. $\mathbf{\frac{1}{27}}$

Since a die has 6 sides, the probability of getting a 1 or a 2 on the first toss is 2 out of 6, or $\frac{1}{3}$. This would be the same on the next two tosses. Because the probability of getting a 1 or a 2 is $\frac{1}{3}$ on each toss, the probability of getting a 1 or a 2 on all three tosses would be $\frac{1}{3} \times \frac{1}{3} \times \frac{1}{3} = \frac{1}{27}$.

12. C

If the perimeter of the square is 48 inches, each of the 4 sides would be 12 inches in length. The diagonal of the square would form a right triangle, with each of the sides being 12 inches long and the diagonal acting as the hypotenuse. The diagonal would split the right angle in half, forming a 45°-45°-90° triangle. In a 45°-45°-90° triangle, the hypotenuse is $\sqrt{2}$ times the side length. Therefore the answer is **(C)**, $12\sqrt{2}$.

13. C

The average quiz score is calculated by adding the quiz scores and dividing by the number of scores: $(85 + 76 + 98 + 76 + 100 + 75) \div 6 = 510 \div 6 = 85$. The mode of a data set is the value that is listed most often. In this list of U.S. history quiz scores, the score that is listed most often is 76. The difference between the average quiz score and the mode of the data set is $85 - 76 = 9$. The answer is **(C)**.

14. E

The ratio of girls to boys in a class is 6:7. There are 18 girls in the class ($6 \times 3 = 18$), so the number of boys can be determined by $7 \times 3 = 21$. Since there are 18 girls and 21 boys, the total number of students is $18 + 21 = 39$. The correct answer is **(E)**.

15. A

To calculate what percent 12 is of 60, divide: $12 \div 60 = 0.20$, which is 20%. That means $x = 20$. To calculate 30 percent of this value, multiply: $20 \times 0.30 = 6$. Therefore, the answer is **(A)**.

16. E

The area of a triangle can be calculated using the formula $A = \frac{1}{2}(base)(height)$. Given that the area of the triangle is $6x$, and the height of the triangle is x, the base must be 12, since $\frac{1}{2}(x)(12) = 6x$. To find the perimeter of the triangle, simply add the lengths of the three sides: $12 + 9 + 5 = 26$. The answer is **(E)**.

17. B

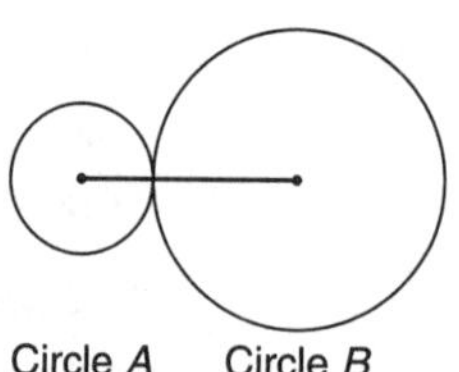

Draw a figure similar to the one shown to help visualize the information given. Recall that the area of a circle is πr^2. The area of circle A is 9π. So, $9 = r^2$, and $r = 3$. So the radius of circle A is 3. The area of circle B is 49π. So, $49 = r^2$, and $r = 7$. So the radius of circle B is 7. If the circles intersect at exactly one point, this means that the two circles are next to each other just touching each other (i.e., they are tangent to each other). To find the distance from the center of circle A to the center of circle B, simply add their radii: $3 + 7 = 10$. The correct answer is **(B)**.

18. B, C, E

Read each graph carefully to choose the days whose bars have the same height for each restaurant. The correct choices are Monday, Tuesday, and Thursday, or **(B)**, **(C)**, and **(E)**.

19. D

The total average number of daily carry-out orders at Zito's Eatery on the weekends is $65 + 35 = 100$. The total average number of daily carry-out orders at Zito's Eatery on the weekdays is $20 + 25 + 30 + 15 + 70 = 160$. So there are 60 more carry-out orders during the week than there are on the weekends. Since the weekend total is 100, it is easy to see that the weekday total is a 60% increase. Therefore, the answer is **(D)**.

20. E

Looking at the graph for Paula's Pizza, the biggest drop in average carry-out orders from one day to the next would either be between Saturday and Sunday or between Sunday and Monday. (The greatest difference is from Thursday to Friday, but that's an increase, and the question asks for a decrease.) From Saturday to Sunday, the average number of carry-out orders fell from 75 to 45, a drop of 30 orders. From Sunday to Monday, the average number of carry-out orders fell from 45 to 20, a drop of 25 orders. So the biggest drop occurs between Saturday and Sunday. Therefore, the answer is **(E)**.

Diagnostic Tool

Tally up your score and write your results below.

Total

Total Correct: ________ out of 20

Percentage Correct: # you got right × 100 ÷ 20: ________

By Section:

Quantitative Comparison ________ out of 8

Problem Solving ________ out of 9

Data Interpretation ________ out of 3

DIAGNOSE YOUR RESULTS

Look back at the questions you got wrong and think about your experience answering them. Were you stymied by a particular question type, or by a certain math topic? If the latter, studying the relevant math content review in Part 3 of this book should help.

QUANTITATIVE REASONING PRACTICE SET 3

Directions: Select the correct answer.

1. $x < 0 < y$

Quantity A	Quantity B
x^2y^2	$(xy)^3$

Ⓐ Quantity A is greater.
Ⓑ Quantity B is greater.
Ⓒ The two quantities are equal.
Ⓓ The relationship cannot be determined from the information given.

2.

Quantity A	Quantity B
The hypotenuse of a right triangle with leg lengths 7 and 24	25

Ⓐ Quantity A is greater.
Ⓑ Quantity B is greater.
Ⓒ The two quantities are equal.
Ⓓ The relationship cannot be determined from the information given.

3.

Quantity A	Quantity B
$10^{-4} \times 10^3$	10^{-12}

Ⓐ Quantity A is greater.
Ⓑ Quantity B is greater.
Ⓒ The two quantities are equal.
Ⓓ The relationship cannot be determined from the information given.

4.

Quantity A	Quantity B
The area of a square with perimeter 36	3^4

Ⓐ Quantity A is greater.
Ⓑ Quantity B is greater.
Ⓒ The two quantities are equal.
Ⓓ The relationship cannot be determined from the information given.

5. a is a positive integer.

Quantity A	Quantity B
$-3a + 15$	$-3(a + 5)$

Ⓐ Quantity A is greater.
Ⓑ Quantity B is greater.
Ⓒ The two quantities are equal.
Ⓓ The relationship cannot be determined from the information given.

6.

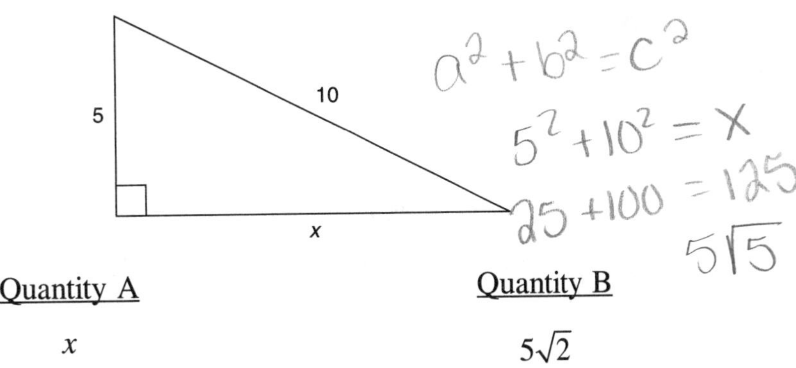

Quantity A	Quantity B
x	$5\sqrt{2}$

Ⓐ Quantity A is greater.
Ⓑ Quantity B is greater.
Ⓒ The two quantities are equal.
Ⓓ The relationship cannot be determined from the information given.

7.

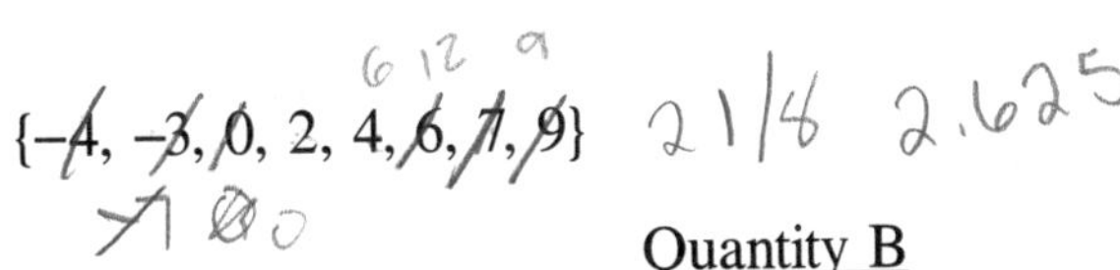

$\{-4, -3, 0, 2, 4, 6, 7, 9\}$

Quantity A	Quantity B
The average (arithmetic mean) of the set of numbers	The median of the set of numbers

Ⓐ Quantity A is greater.
Ⓑ Quantity B is greater.
Ⓒ The two quantities are equal.
Ⓓ The relationship cannot be determined from the information given.

8. $xy < 0$

Quantity A	Quantity B
$x - y$	$\frac{x}{y}$

(A) Quantity A is greater.
(B) Quantity B is greater.
(C) The two quantities are equal.
(D) The relationship cannot be determined from the information given.

9. In an election, 36% of the voters were women. If 48,000 people voted, how many of the voters were men?

(A) 12,000
(B) 17,280
(C) 28,520
(D) 30,720
(E) 35,520

10. If $a = 2b + \frac{1}{2}$ and $4b = 3$, what is the value of a?

(A) 1
(B) $1\frac{1}{2}$
(C) 2
(D) $2\frac{1}{2}$
(E) 3

11. If Sierra's scores on her first three tests were 90, 93, and 98, what must she score on the fourth test to have 95 as her test average?

   (A) 95
   (B) 96
   (C) 97
   (D) 98
   (E) 99

12. If a is an even integer and b is an odd integer, which of the following must be odd?

   Indicate all such expressions.

   [A] $a - b$
   [B] $a + 2b$
   [C] $3a + b$
   [D] $2a - b$
   [E] $a + b$

13. If Eugene can complete a project in 4 hours and Steve can complete the same project in 6 hours, how many hours will it take Eugene and Steve to complete the project if they work together?

   (A) 2
   (B) $2\frac{1}{4}$
   (C) $2\frac{2}{5}$
   (D) $2\frac{3}{4}$
   (E) 3

14. The product of two consecutive positive integers is 156. What is the larger of the two integers?

(A) 11
(B) 12
(C) 13
(D) 14
(E) 15

15. How many milliliters of acid are there in 350 milliliters of a 4% acid solution?

(A) 3.5
(B) 10
(C) 14
(D) 35
(E) 87.5

16. Maia packed three skirts, two hats, and four blouses for a trip. How many different outfits consisting of one skirt, one hat, and one blouse can she make with the clothes she has packed?

[ ] outfits

Questions 17–20 are based on the following graphs.

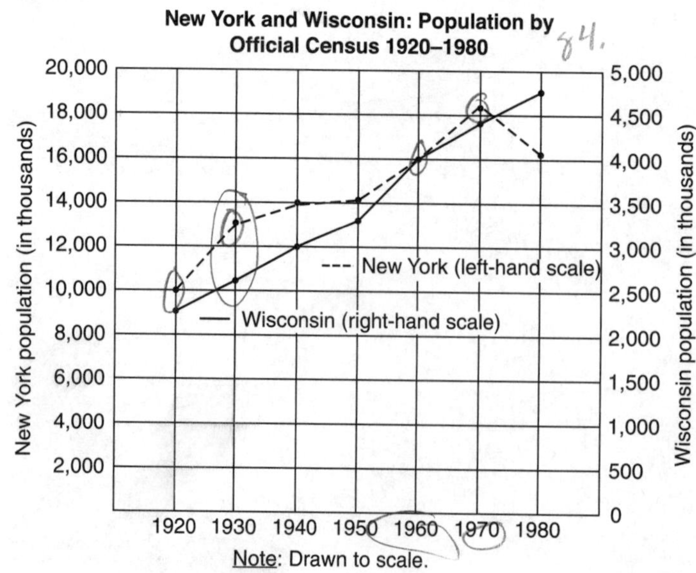

Note: Drawn to scale.

Density of Population by State
(per square mile, land area only)

State	1920	1960	1970	1980
Arkansas	33.4	34.2	37.0	43.9
Illinois	115.7	180.4	199.4	205.3
New York	217.9	350.6	381.3	370.6
Texas	17.8	36.4	42.7	54.3
Wisconsin	47.6	72.6	81.1	86.5

17. What was the least densely populated of the listed states in 1960?

    (A) Arkansas
    (B) Illinois
    (C) New York
    (D) Texas
    (E) Wisconsin

18. In 1930, what was the approximate ratio of the number of people living in Wisconsin to the number of people living in New York?

    (A) 1:6
    (B) 1:5
    (C) 5:6
    (D) 6:5
    (E) 4:1

19. If, in 1830, the population density of New York was 44 people per square mile, and the area of New York has stayed relatively constant since then, approximately what was the population of New York in 1830, in millions?

    (A) 1.2
    (B) 2.0
    (C) 3.5
    (D) 4.0
    (E) 4.8

20. Which of the following statements can be inferred from the information in the graph and table?

Indicate all such statements.

[A] From 1920 through 1980, the population of New York has always been more than twice the population of Wisconsin.

[B] Between 1960 and 1970, the percent increase in Wisconsin's population was greater than its percent increase in population between 1920 and 1930.

[C] Of the five states listed, New York had the greatest increase in population between 1920 and 1960.

[D] For the years 1920, 1960, 1970, and 1980, New York had a greater population density than each of the other states listed.

[E] The population density of Texas decreased between 1960 and 1970.

QUANTITATIVE REASONING PRACTICE SET 3 ANSWER KEY

1. A
2. C
3. A
4. C
5. A
6. A
7. B
8. D
9. D
10. C
11. E
12. A, C, D, E
13. C
14. C
15. C
16. 24
17. A
18. B
19. B
20. A, D

QUANTITATIVE REASONING PRACTICE SET 3 ANSWERS AND EXPLANATIONS

1. A

Even though x is a negative number and y is a positive number, both x^2 and y^2 are positive. Since the product of two positive numbers is positive, x^2y^2 in Quantity A is positive. The product of a negative number and a positive number is negative, so xy is negative. It follows that $(xy)^3$ in Quantity B is negative because a negative number raised to an odd exponent is negative. A positive number is always greater than a negative number, so Quantity A is larger. The answer is **(A)**.

2. C

You can use the Pythagorean theorem, $a^2 + b^2 = c^2$, to find the hypotenuse of the right triangle. The letters a and b represent the legs, so $7^2 + 24^2 = c^2$.

$$\begin{aligned} 49 + 576 &= c^2 \\ 625 &= c^2 \\ 25 &= c \end{aligned}$$

Solving the equation for c, you get $c = 25$. So, Quantity A and Quantity B are equal. The answer is **(C)**.

3. A

Recall the rules for working with exponents to make this comparison. To multiply numbers with the same base, add the exponents:

$10^{-4} \times 10^3 = 10^{-4+3} = 10^{-1}$

That makes Quantity A equal to 10^{-1}. Now compare Quantity A to Quantity B:

$10^{-1} = \frac{1}{10}$ and $10^{-12} = \frac{1}{10^{12}} = \frac{1}{1{,}000{,}000{,}000{,}000}$. So, Quantity A is larger, much larger. The answer is **(A)**.

4. C

If the perimeter of a square is 36, then each side length is 9 because all four sides of a square are equal, and $36 \div 4 = 9$. The area of a square is given by the formula $A = s^2$, making the area of the square $9^2 = 81$. Likewise, $3^4 = 3 \times 3 \times 3 \times 3 = 81$. So, Quantity A and Quantity B are equal. The answer is **(C)**.

5. A

First, make the quantities look the same. Leave Quantity A alone for now and go to the expression in Quantity B. Distribute the –3, making the expression:

$$-3(a - 5) = -3a - 15$$

Now, compare the expressions in both sides of the Quantitative Comparison. Each has $-3a$, so you can eliminate those from each quantity. This leaves you comparing the value 15 under Quantity A with the value -15 in Quantity B. Quantity A is larger, so the answer is **(A)**.

6. A

A right triangle whose shorter leg is 5 and whose hypotenuse is 10 is a 30°-60°-90° right triangle. In a 30°-60°-90° triangle, the sides of the triangle are in the ratio of $x : x\sqrt{3} : 2x$. So, the other side of the triangle must be $5\sqrt{3}$. Quantity B is $5\sqrt{2}$. You do not need to calculate the individual square roots. The square root of 3 is greater than the square root of 2, so Quantity A is larger. The answer is **(A)**.

7. B

The mean of the set is $\frac{-4 + (-3) + 0 + 2 + 4 + 6 + 7 + 9}{8} = \frac{21}{8} = 2\frac{5}{8}$. The median is the middle value in a set of numbers arranged in order—when there is an odd number of terms in the set. This set has an even number of entries, so the median is the average of the two middle numbers, 2 and 4. That makes the median 3 since $(2 + 4) \div 2 = 3$. Quantity B is larger. The answer is **(B)**.

8. D

Because $xy < 0$, either x is positive and y is negative, or x is negative and y is positive. Use the Kaplan strategy of Picking Numbers for x and y to test the values of $x - y$ and $\frac{x}{y}$. If x is positive and y is negative, you can choose $x = 3$ and $y = -1$. Then, $x - y = 3 - (-1) = 3 + 1 = 4$ and $\frac{x}{y} = \frac{3}{-1} = -3$. So, Quantity A is larger. But if x is negative and y is positive, you can choose $x = -3$ and $y = 1$. Then, $x - y = -3 - 1 = -4$ and $\frac{x}{y} = \frac{-3}{1} = -3$. In this case, Quantity B is larger. So, the relationship cannot be determined from the given information. The answer is **(D)**.

9. D

If 36% of the voters were women, then 64% of the voters were men. To find 64% of the total number of voters, change 64% to its decimal form and multiply by 48,000: $0.64 \times 48{,}000 = 30{,}720$. So, 30,720 of the voters were men. This is choice **(D)**.

Alternatively, you can use a strategy to get the answer while lessening your chances of making a computation error—and without having to take the time to pull up the online calculator. If the percent of voters who are women is 36%, that means that a little more than one-third of the voters are women, leaving a little less than two-thirds of the voters to be men. Divide 48,000 by 3 to get 16,000, then double it to get two-thirds (32,000). Looking at the answer choices, only one answer, **(D)** 30,720, is a little less than 32,000, making it the only answer that can be correct. The answer is **(D)**.

10. C

First, solve the equation $4b = 3$ to find b. To solve for b, divide both sides of the equation by 4. So $b = \frac{3}{4}$. Then, substitute $\frac{3}{4}$ for b in the equation $a = 2b + \frac{1}{2}$. Simplify to get the value of a: $a = 2\left(\frac{3}{4}\right) + \frac{1}{2}$; $a = \frac{3}{2} + \frac{1}{2}$. Therefore, a is equal to 2. The answer is **(C)**.

11. E

To figure out what Sierra needs to score on her fourth test, use the variable x to represent the fourth test score. Add up all four test values, including x, and divide by 4. This equals the test average. Set this expression equal to 95 : $\frac{90 + 93 + 98 + x}{4} = 95$. Then, solve the equation for x.

$$\begin{aligned} 90 + 93 + 98 + x &= 4(95) \\ 281 + x &= 380 \\ x &= 380 - 281 \\ x &= 99 \end{aligned}$$

Sierra needs to score 99 on the fourth test to have a test average of 95, which is answer choice **(E)**.

An alternative approach, involving much less computation, is to use the Balancing method. An average is "balanced" in that the surpluses (amounts above the average) are equal to the deficits (amounts below the average). In Sierra's case, she has a 90 that's 5 points below her desired average of 95, a 93 that's 2 points below, and a 98 that's 3 points above. Overall, that's $(-5) + (-2) + (+3) = -4$. To balance that deficit, she needs a surplus of $+4$ on her last test; that's $95 + 4$, or 99: again, answer choice **(E)**.

12. A, C, D, E

Use the Picking Numbers strategy for a and b to test each answer choice. You can choose $a = 4$ and $b = 3$.

Then test each answer choice.

(A) $a - b = 4 - 3 = 1$, which is odd.

(B) $a + 2b = 4 + 2(3) = 4 + 6 = 10$, which is even.

(C) $3a + b = 3(4) + 3 = 12 + 3 = 15$, which is odd.

(D) $2a - b = 2(4) - 3 = 8 - 3 = 5$, which is odd.

(E) $a + b = 4 + 3 = 7$, which is odd.

So, $a - b$, $3a + b$, $2a - b$, and $a + b$ are odd. The answers are **(A)**, **(C)** , **(D)**, and **(E)**.

13. C

This is a combined work problem asking how long it will take two separate people (or machines, or whatever) to complete one job together, if we know how long it will take each person to do the same job separately. If you had no idea how to do this problem, (A) and (E) could still be eliminated straight off, leaving a 33% chance of guessing correctly, because (A) requires Steve to work at Eugene's rate and (E) requires Eugene to work at Steve's rate.

The generic equation for solving such a problem is $\frac{1}{a}+\frac{1}{b}=\frac{1}{t}$, where *a* is the time that it takes one person to complete the job alone, *b* is the the time that it takes the other person to complete the job alone, and *t* is the time the job will take when the two people work on it together.

$$\frac{1}{4}+\frac{1}{6} = \frac{1}{t}$$
$$\frac{3}{12}+\frac{2}{12} = \frac{1}{t}$$
$$\frac{5}{12} = \frac{1}{t}$$

To solve for *t*, find the reciprocal of the fraction on the left: $t=\frac{12}{5}$ or $2\frac{2}{5}$ hours.

Note that this problem is also set up in such a way that you can take advantage of the simpler "time per task" formula: the time it takes two people to complete a task together is equal to the product of their individual times divided by the sum of their individual times.

$$T_{together} = \frac{T_a \times T_b}{T_a + T_b}$$
$$T_{together} = \frac{4 \times 6}{4+6}$$
$$T_{together} = \frac{24}{10}$$
$$T_{together} = \frac{12}{5}$$

No matter how you approach it, the answer is **(C)**.

14. C

Kaplan's Backsolving strategy is a great approach to solving this problem. You are told that two consecutive integers, multiplied together, will produce 156, and you're asked to identify the larger of the two integers. In order to multiply to 156, the units digits of the integers will have to multiply to 6 (or some other number that has a units digit of 6).

Let's test the answer choices, which each represent the larger of the two integers, to see which one(s) multiply to have a units digit of 6:

(A) 11: 0×1 No

(B) 12: 1×2 No

(C) 13: 2×3 Yes!

(D) 14: 3×4 No

(E) 15: 4×5 No

Therefore, the two consecutive numbers end in a 2 and a 3, respectively. The question asks for the larger number, so the larger integer is 13. The answer is **(C)**.

15. C

The volume of acid in 350 milliliters of a 4% acid solution is 4% of 350 milliliters, or $0.04 \times 350 = 14$ milliliters. The answer is **(C)**.

16. 24

Since Maia has 3 skirts, 2 pairs of shoes, and 4 blouses, she can create $3 \times 2 \times 4 = 24$ different outfits. The answer is **24**.

17. A

You only need to use the table; that gives you information on population density. Look down the column for 1960 and find the state with the smallest density. It's Arkansas, with 34.2 people per square mile. The correct answer is **(A)**.

18. B

You need the ratio of the number in Wisconsin in 1930 to the number in New York in 1930. Because of the different scales, you can't estimate the ratios by comparing the respective heights of the two graphs—you need to find the actual figures. Because the populations for each state are shown in the thousands, you can compare the thousands in Wisconsin to the thousands in New York. The ratio of Wisconsin's population in 1930 to that of New York's in the same year is approximately 2,600:13,000, which reduces to a ratio of 1:5.

The answer is **(B)**.

19. B

You have to reason with proportions here while also using the given table. The question gives the population density of New York for 1830. The population density of the state is the ratio of the population to the amount of land; if the amount of land stays constant, then the density will increase at the same rate as the population. Now you could work with any of the four density figures given in the chart, but it's probably easiest to work with 1920's figure: New York's population in 1920 was approximately 10 million people, a nice round number to work with. In addition, the 1830 density was 44 people per square mile—very close to $\frac{1}{5}$ of the 1920 density, 217.9 people per square mile. That means the 1830 population must have been about one-fifth of the 1920 population. The 1920 population was about 10 million, so the 1830 population must have been approximately $\frac{1}{5}$ of 10 million, or 2 million people.

The correct choice is **(B)**.

20. A, D

For a question of this type, you must test each statement.

(A) Rather than calculate the ratio for every year, look at the smallest population for New York, 10 million, and the largest population for Wisconsin, about 4.75 million. Therefore, this statement must be true. Choose **(A)**.

(B) There are two things to consider in order to evaluate this statement about the population changes in Wisconsin for the time periods given. Look at the solid line on the graph for the two periods and notice that the amount of change is the same. Recall the formula for percent change:

$$\textit{Percent change} = \frac{\textit{Amount of change}}{\textit{Original whole}}.$$

Now use logic rather than your calculator. The amount of change for both time periods is the same—that is the numerator of each fraction in the formula. However, the denominators are different. The population in 1920 was less than the population in 1960, so the original amount is smaller in that fraction, making the percent increase greater from 1920 to 1930 than it was from 1960 to 1970, not lesser.

(C) The table gives population density (number of people per square mile) for five states, but it does not give the number of square miles in the state. It is not possible to infer anything about the increase in population numbers of the five states from the table.

(D) This is a true statement and can be verified by reading down each column of the table of population densities. In each of the years shown, New York's population density is the greatest value. Choose **(D)**.

(E) In 1960, Texas's population density was 36.4. In 1970, it was 42.7. That's an increase, not a decrease, so (E) is not a true statement.

The correct answers are **(A)** and **(D)**.

Diagnostic Tool

Tally up your score and write the results below.

Total

Total Correct: ________ out of 20

Percentage Correct: # you got right $\times$ 100 $\div$ 20: ________

By Section:

Quantitative Comparison ________ out of 8

Problem Solving ________ out of 8

Data Interpretation ________ out of 4

Diagnose Your Results

Look back at the questions you got wrong and think about your experience answering them. Were you stymied by a particular question type, or by a certain math topic? If the latter, studying the relevant math content review in Part 3 of this book should help.

QUANTITATIVE REASONING PRACTICE SET 4

Directions: Select the correct answer.

1. $m \neq 1$

Quantity A	Quantity B
m	m^3

(A) Quantity A is greater.
(B) Quantity B is greater.
(C) The two quantities are equal.
(D) The relationship cannot be determined from the information given.

2.

Quantity A	Quantity B
$(3^{-1} + 3^{-2})^{-1}$	1

(A) Quantity A is greater.
(B) Quantity B is greater.
(C) The two quantities are equal.
(D) The relationship cannot be determined from the information given.

3. $x^2 + 5x + 6 = 0$

Quantity A	Quantity B
The square of the sum of the roots of the equation	25

(A) Quantity A is greater.
(B) Quantity B is greater.
(C) The two quantities are equal.
(D) The relationship cannot be determined from the information given.

4.

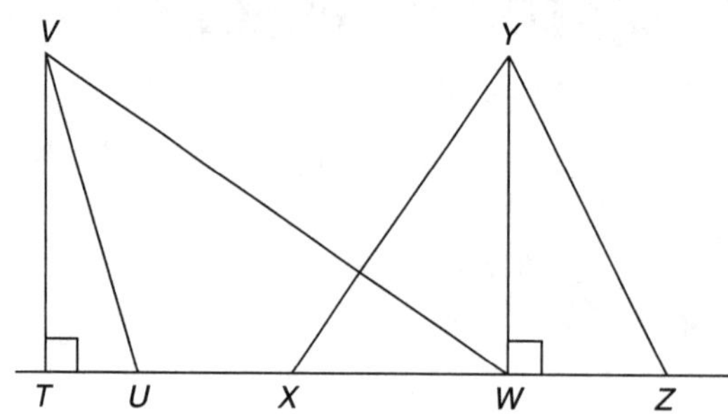

The area of triangle UVW is greater than the area of triangle XYZ.

$$UX = WZ$$

Quantity A	Quantity B
TV	YW

(A) Quantity A is greater.
(B) Quantity B is greater.
(C) The two quantities are equal.
(D) The relationship cannot be determined from the information given.

5.

Three circles have radii of x, y, and $x + y$ units, respectively.

Quantity A	Quantity B
The sum of the areas of the two smaller circles	The area of the largest circle

(A) Quantity A is greater.
(B) Quantity B is greater.
(C) The two quantities are equal.
(D) The relationship cannot be determined from the information given.

6.

A child ate 1 less than 25% of the 28 apples his father purchased.

Quantity A	Quantity B
The number of apples the child ate	8

(A) Quantity A is greater.
(B) Quantity B is greater.
(C) The two quantities are equal.
(D) The relationship cannot be determined from the information given.

7. Line m on a coordinate plane can be defined by the equation $-2x + 3y = 6$.

Quantity A	Quantity B
The slope of a line parallel to line m	The slope of a line perpendicular to line m

Ⓐ Quantity A is greater.
Ⓑ Quantity B is greater.
Ⓒ The two quantities are equal.
Ⓓ The relationship cannot be determined from the information given.

8. The price of a \$240 coat was discounted by 25%. Then the coat was discounted by an additional 30% of the discounted price.

Quantity A	Quantity B
The final price of the coat	\$120

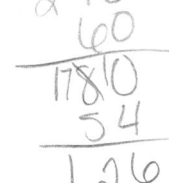

Ⓐ Quantity A is greater.
Ⓑ Quantity B is greater.
Ⓒ The two quantities are equal.
Ⓓ The relationship cannot be determined from the information given.

9. Maria bought a new cell phone, cell phone case, and wall charger. The cell phone cost \$149.99, the case cost \$24.99, and the wall charger cost \$29.99. If tax on each of these items was 9.5%, which of the following is closest to the amount Maria spent?

Ⓐ \$175
Ⓑ \$200
Ⓒ \$210
Ⓓ \$224
Ⓔ \$250

10. Three consecutive even integers have a sum of 102. If x represents the least number in the set, what equation can be used to determine the value of the sum of the integers?

$\frac{102}{3}$ X

Ⓐ $x + (x + 1) + (x + 2) = 102$
Ⓑ $x + (x + 1) + (x + 3) = 102$
Ⓒ $x + (x + 2) + (x + 4) = 102$
Ⓓ $x + 2x + 4x = 102$
Ⓔ $x + x + x = 102$

11. Kourtland and Caleb share an apartment. If each month Caleb pays c dollars and Kourtland pays k dollars, what percent of the total cost does Kourtland pay?

Ⓐ $\frac{k}{c}\%$
Ⓑ $\frac{c}{k}\%$
Ⓒ $\frac{k}{c+k}\%$
Ⓓ $\frac{100k}{c}\%$
Ⓔ $\frac{100k}{c+k}\%$

12. Which of the following is a possible value of k for which $\frac{24}{\sqrt{k}}$ is an integer?

Indicate <u>all</u> possible choices.

[A] 9
[B] 12
[C] 16
[D] 25
[E] 64

13. If $M = \frac{at^2}{h}$ and $M \neq 0$, what is the effect on M of doubling t, tripling a, and quadrupling h?

(A) M is multiplied by 1.5.
(B) M is multiplied by 3.
(C) M is multiplied by 4.
(D) M is multiplied by 4.5.
(E) M is multiplied by 79.

14. If Caroline drove 211 miles between 9:30 a.m. and 12:45 p.m. of the same day, what was her approximate average speed in miles per hour?

(A) 50
(B) 55
(C) 60
(D) 65
(E) 70

15. Each person in a room is a junior or a senior. The number of juniors in the room is 7 times the number of seniors. Which of the following could be the number of people in the room?

Indicate all such numbers.

[A] 14
[B] 26
[C] 35
[D] 48
[E] 49
[F] 63

16. Astrid wrote down all the different three-digit numbers that can be written using each of the numerals 1, 2, and 3 exactly once. What is the median of the numbers Astrid wrote down?

(A) 213
(B) 222
(C) 223
(D) 231
(E) 233

17.

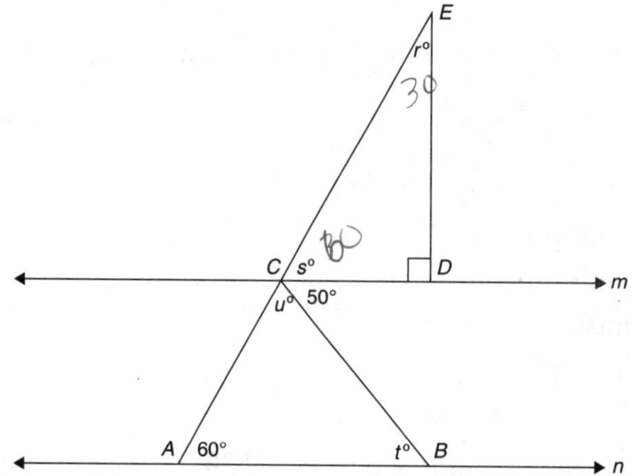

In the figure shown, line m is parallel to line n. What is the value of $s - 2r$?

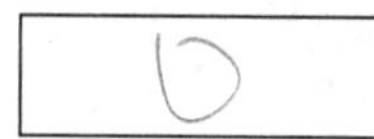

Questions 18–20 refer to the following graphs.

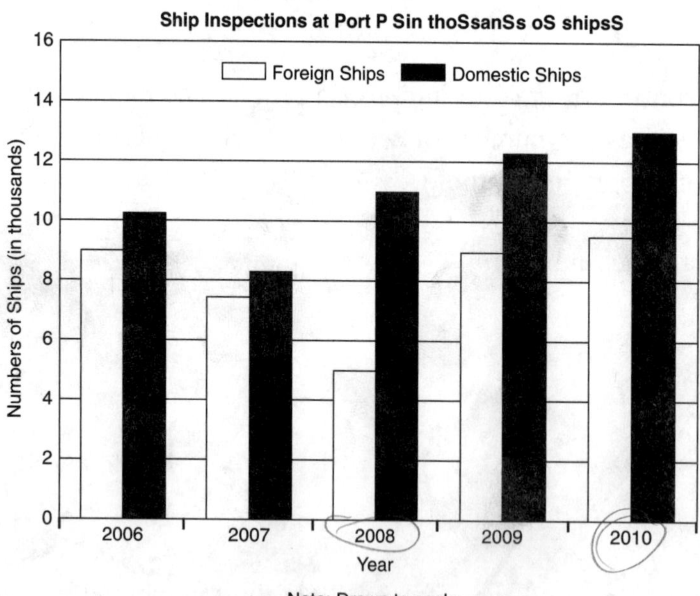

Note: Drawn to scale.

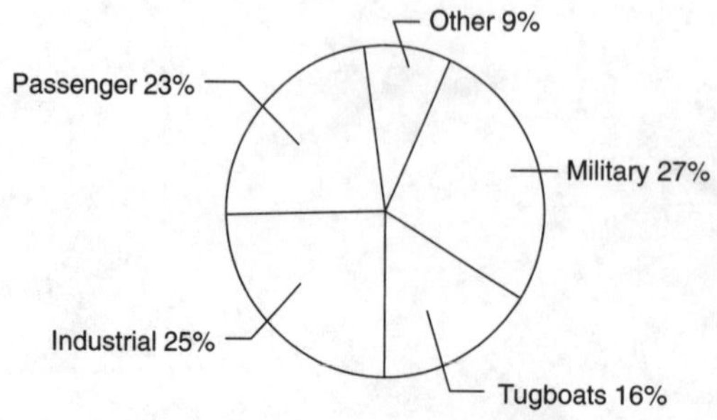

Note: Drawn to scale.

18. In 2009, the ratio of domestic ships inspected to foreign ships inspected was approximately

Ⓐ $\frac{9}{4}$

Ⓑ $\frac{2}{1}$

Ⓒ $\frac{5}{3}$

Ⓓ $\frac{8}{5}$

Ⓔ $\frac{4}{3}$

19. If the average ship carries 500 tons of cargo, which of the following is closest to the number of tons of cargo inspected at Port P in 2008?

Ⓐ 1.0 million
Ⓑ 2.0 million
Ⓒ 4.0 million
Ⓓ 8.0 million
Ⓔ 16.0 million

20. In 2010, approximately how many more domestic passenger ships were inspected than domestic tugboats at Port P?

Ⓐ 820
Ⓑ 855
Ⓒ 890
Ⓓ 910
Ⓔ 955

QUANTITATIVE REASONING PRACTICE SET 4 ANSWER KEY

1. D
2. A
3. C
4. A
5. B
6. B
7. A
8. A
9. D
10. C
11. E
12. A, C, E
13. B
14. D
15. D
16. B
17. 0
18. E
19. D
20. D

QUANTITATIVE REASONING PRACTICE SET 4 ANSWERS AND EXPLANATIONS

1. D

For a question like this, with the variable in both quantities, it is best to use the strategy of Picking Numbers and try several values for the variable. If $m = 0$, both quantities equal 0. If $m = 2$, Quantity B is greater. Just testing these two options is enough to conclude that **(D)** is the answer.

2. A

This question requires that you apply the law of exponents dealing with negative exponents. Recall that $n^{-1} = \frac{1}{n}$ and $n^{-2} = \frac{1}{n^2}$ and so on, provided n does not equal 0. To simplify the expression in Quantity A, work inside the parentheses first.

$$\begin{aligned}\left(3^{-1} + 3^{-2}\right)^{-1} &= \left(\frac{1}{3} + \frac{1}{3^2}\right)^{-1} \\ &= \left(\frac{3}{9} + \frac{1}{9}\right)^{-1} \\ &= \left(\frac{4}{9}\right)^{-1} \\ &= \frac{9}{4}\end{aligned}$$

Notice that in the last step of work shown, the fraction is inverted. The result is a number greater than 1, and the answer is **(A)**.

3. C

Begin by finding the roots of the quadratic equation, using the reverse of the FOIL process. Find two numbers whose product is positive 6 and whose sum is positive 5. The numbers are 2 and 3; use these numbers in the factors and solve the equation.

$$\begin{aligned}x^2 + 5x + 6 &= 0 \\ (x + 2)(x + 3) &= 0 \\ x = -2 \text{ or } x &= -3\end{aligned}$$

To find the value of Quantity A, add the roots and then square the result:

$-2 + -3 = -5$; $(-5)^2 = 25$. Therefore, the quantities are equal. Choose **(C)**.

4. A

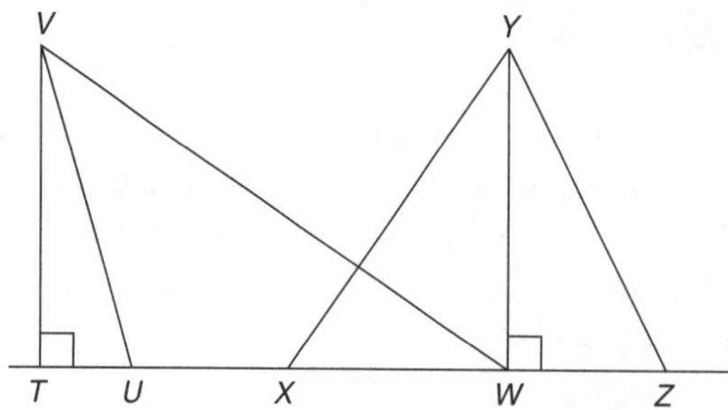

The area of triangle *UVW* is greater than the area of triangle *XYZ*.

$UX = WZ$

You are given that the area of triangle *UVW* is greater than the area of triangle *XYZ*. Make note of the other information conveyed by the diagram. The height of each triangle is indicated by the right angle box in each triangle, but no other information is given about the heights. Notice that the bases of the triangles are overlapping in the diagram; they have segment *XW* in common. Segment *UW* is the base of triangle *UVW*, and segment *XZ* is the base of triangle *XYZ*.

It may be helpful to draw the triangles separately to keep the information given about triangle *UVW* and triangle *XYZ* organized as you apply the area formula to each one.

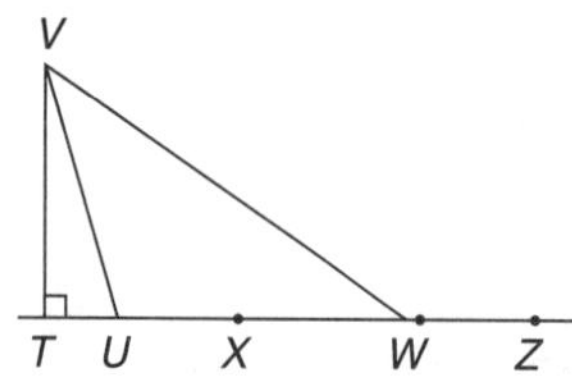

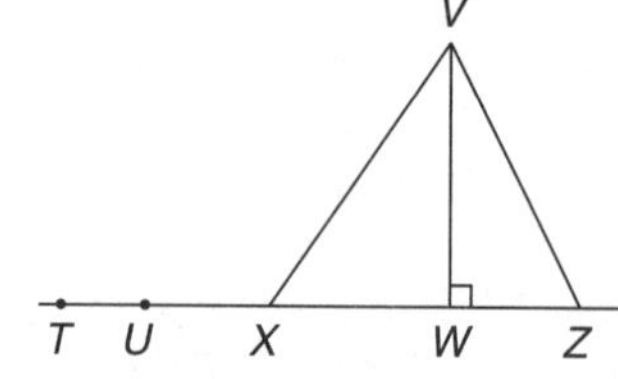

Area (triangle *UVW*)

$= \frac{1}{2}bh$

$= \frac{1}{2}(UW)(TV)$

$= \frac{1}{2}(UX + XW)(TV)$

Area (triangle *XYZ*)

$= \frac{1}{2}bh$

$= \frac{1}{2}(XZ)(WY)$

$= \frac{1}{2}(WZ + XW)(WY)$

The key to making the correct comparison is recognizing that the bases of the triangles are the same length. You are given that $UX = WZ$ and certainly $XW = XW$. If the area of triangle *UVW* is greater, as the question states, it is because its height is greater. Therefore, $TV > YW$ and the answer is **(A)**.

5. B

Use the Picking Numbers strategy to make this question more concrete. Let $x = 2$ and $y = 3$. The two smaller circles will have radii of 2 and 3, and their areas will be 4π and 9π, respectively. Quantity A would be $4\pi + 9\pi = 13\pi$ in this case. Using the same values for *x* and *y*, the radius of the largest circle would be $2 + 3 = 5$, and its area would be 25π. Therefore, Quantity B is greater. The correct choice is **(B)**.

6. B

Find 25% of 28 first and then subtract 1: $0.25 \times 28 = 7$ and $7 - 1 = 6$. The child ate 6 apples. Quantity B is greater. The correct choice is **(B)**.

7. A

To compare these quantities, you need to determine the slope of a parallel and perpendicular line to the linear function $-2x + 3y = 6$. First, solve the equation for y in order to put the equation in the form of $y = mx + b$, where m represents the slope of the line and b represents the y-intercept:

$$\begin{aligned} -2x + 3y &= 6 \\ 3y &= 2x + 6 \\ y &= \frac{2}{3}x + 2 \end{aligned}$$

This is the slope-intercept form of the equation of the line. Parallel lines have the same slope, so the value of Quantity A is $\frac{2}{3}$. The slopes of two perpendicular lines are negative reciprocals of each other, so the value of Quantity B is $-\frac{3}{2}$. Therefore, you can conclude that Quantity A is greater than Quantity B. The correct choice is **(A)**.

8. A

The original price of the coat was \$240. After the first discount of 25%, the coat cost $\$240 - (\$240 \times 0.25) = \$240 - \$60 = \$180$. After the second discount of 30%, the coat cost $\$180 - (\$180 \times 0.30) = \$180 - \$54 = \$126$. Therefore, Quantity A, the final cost of the coat, is \$126. This is larger than Quantity B, \$120. The correct choice is **(A)**.

9. D

First, estimate the total cost: $\$150 + \$25 + \$30 = \$205$. To find the estimated tax, multiply the estimated total by 10%, or 0.1. Ten percent of \$205 is \$20.50. Adding the two amounts together will give the approximate amount she spent: \$225.50, which is closest to \$224. The correct choice is **(D)**.

10. C

The question states that the least number in the set is x. Therefore, the next even number following x will be $x + 2$, and the next even number will be $x + 4$. Since the sum is equal to 102, you set $x + (x + 2) + (x + 4) = 102$. The correct choice is **(C)**.

11. E

The question asks you to find the percent that a part (Kourtland's share) is of a whole (Kourtland and Caleb's total cost). The formula for finding the answer is $\frac{part}{whole} \times 100\%$. In this case, Kourtland's part is k, and the whole is the sum of Kourtland and Caleb's cost, which is $c + k$. $\frac{\textit{Kourtland's share}}{\textit{total amount}} = \frac{k}{c+k} \times 100\% = \frac{100k}{c+k}\%$. The correct choice is **(E)**.

12. A, C, E

The keyword in the question is *integer.* The set of *integers* is composed of all whole numbers: positive, negative, and zero. Therefore, you are looking for $-\frac{24}{\sqrt{k}}$ to equal a whole number. Begin by Backsolving and substituting each answer choice into the expression.

(A) $-\frac{24}{\sqrt{9}} = -\frac{24}{3} = -8$. Since −8 is an integer, choice **(A)** works.

(B) 12 is not a perfect square. Only a perfect square will work here; choice (B) can be eliminated. For the record:

$$-\frac{24}{\sqrt{12}} = -\frac{24}{\sqrt{3 \times 4}} = -\frac{24}{2\sqrt{3}} = -\frac{12}{\sqrt{3}}.$$

(C) $-\frac{24}{\sqrt{16}} = -\frac{24}{4} = -6$. Since −6 is an integer, choice **(C)** works.

(D) $-\frac{24}{\sqrt{25}} = -\frac{24}{5} = -4.8$. Since −4.8 is not an integer, choice (D) can be eliminated.

(E) $-\frac{24}{\sqrt{64}} = -\frac{24}{8} = -3$. Since −3 is an integer, choice **(E)** works.

The correct choices are **(A)**, **(C)**, and **(E)**.

13. B

Doubling t is equal to $2t$, tripling a is equal to $3a$, and quadrupling h is equal to $4h$. Substitute these new terms into the expression and simplify:

$$M = \frac{(3a)(2t)^2}{4h}$$

$$M = \frac{(3a)(4t^2)}{4h}$$

$$M = \frac{3at^2}{h}$$

This expression is 3 times the original expression of $M = \frac{at^2}{h}$. The correct choice is **(B)**.

14. D

The key here is *miles per hour.* You need to determine the time, in hours, between 9:30 a.m. and 12:45 p.m. It is 3 hours and 15 minutes or 3.25 hours. To find miles per hour, divide the miles by the amount of time: $\frac{211 \text{ miles}}{3.25 \text{ hours}} \approx 64.9 \approx 65$ mph.

The correct choice is **(D)**.

15. D

If the number of seniors in the room is x, then the number of juniors is $7x$. The total number of people in the room is $7x + x = 8x$. So the number of people in the room, which is $8x$, must be a multiple of 8. Let's look at the answer choices to see which ones are multiples of 8.

Choice **(D)**, 48, is the only answer choice that is a multiple of 8. The correct answer is **(D)**.

16. B

Start by determining the different three-digit numbers that can be written using 1, 2, and 3. They are 123, 132, 213, 231, 312, and 321.

The *median* of a set is the middle value when the set is listed from least to greatest.

There are two middle values in this set: 213 and 231. To find the median, add them and divide by 2. The correct choice is **(B)**.

17. 0

You are given that lines m and n are parallel. When a transversal cuts across two parallel lines, the corresponding angles formed are congruent. Line AE is a transversal. Therefore, angle ECD is congruent to angle CAB, so $s = 60°$.

You know that angle CDE is 90° and the sum of angles in a triangle is 180°.

$$\begin{aligned} s + r + 90 &= 180 \\ 60 + r + 90 &= 180 \\ r + 150 &= 180 \\ r &= 30 \end{aligned}$$

Since you know the values of s and r, substitute them into the expression:

$$s - 2r = 60 - 2(30) = 60 - 60 = 0$$

The correct answer is 0.

18. E

The bars start at zero on the graph, so it is possible to do some estimation to narrow down the choices. In 2009, more domestic ships were inspected than foreign ships, so the ratio is greater than 1. However, the ratio is not greater than 2 based on the heights of the bars. Choices (A) and (B) can be eliminated. Reading across from the vertical scale to the height of the bar for domestic inspections, you see that a little more than 12,000 domestic ships were inspected and about 9,000 foreign ships were inspected. So the answer is a little more than the ratio of 12 to 9. Since $\frac{12}{9}$ can be simplified to $\frac{4}{3}$, the answer is **(E)**.

19. D

Add the number of domestic ships inspected in 2008 to the number of foreign ships, then multiply the total number of ships by 500 tons to get the total tonnage. There were approximately 11,000 domestic ships inspected and 5,000 foreign ships inspected for a total of 16,000 ships. Multiply that by 500 tons per ship to get an estimate of 8 million tons. The correct answer is **(D)**.

20. D

You need both the graph and the pie chart to answer the question. The simplest approach is this: You are taking the percents of the same whole; therefore, the difference in the two amounts is the same as the difference in the percents, multiplied by the whole. The whole here is the number of 2010 domestic ship inspections, or 13,000 ships. The percents are 23% and 16%, for a difference of 7%. Take 7% of 13,000:

$$0.07 \times 13{,}000 = 910$$

The answer is **(D)**.

Diagnostic Tool

Tally up your score and write the results below.

Total

Total Correct: ________ out of 20

Percentage Correct: # you got right × 100 ÷ 20: ________

By Section:

Quantitative Comparison ________ out of 8

Problem Solving ________ out of 9

Data Interpretation ________ out of 3

Diagnose Your Results

Look back at the questions you got wrong and think about your experience answering them. Were you stymied by a particular question type, or by a certain math topic? If the latter, studying the relevant math content review in Part 3 of this book should help.

QUANTITATIVE REASONING PRACTICE SET 5

Directions: Select the correct answer.

1. $$y = 7x - 14$$
$$x > 4$$

Quantity A	Quantity B
y	14

Ⓐ Quantity A is greater.
Ⓑ Quantity B is greater.
Ⓒ The two quantities are equal.
Ⓓ The relationship cannot be determined from the information given.

2. Lines m and n are parallel lines cut by a transversal, l.

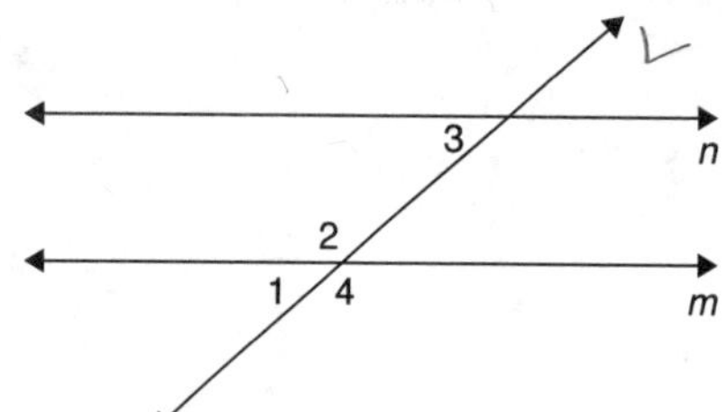

Quantity A	Quantity B
$\angle 1 + \angle 2$	$\angle 3 + \angle 4$

Ⓐ Quantity A is greater.
Ⓑ Quantity B is greater.
Ⓒ The two quantities are equal.
Ⓓ The relationship cannot be determined from the information given.

3.

Quantity A	Quantity B
0.10% of 0.15	1.5×10^{-5}

Ⓐ Quantity A is greater.
Ⓑ Quantity B is greater.
Ⓒ The two quantities are equal.
Ⓓ The relationship cannot be determined from the information given.

4. Use the following data set to answer the question.

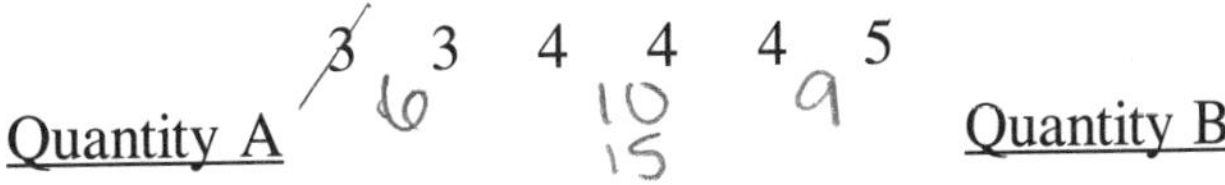

Quantity A	Quantity B
The mode of the data set	The average (arithmetic) mean of the data set

Ⓐ Quantity A is greater.
Ⓑ Quantity B is greater.
Ⓒ The two quantities are equal.
Ⓓ The relationship cannot be determined from the information given.

5. $2 \leq x \leq 10$

$y > 3$

Quantity A	Quantity B
$x - y$	xy

Ⓐ Quantity A is greater.
Ⓑ Quantity B is greater.
Ⓒ The two quantities are equal.
Ⓓ The relationship cannot be determined from the information given.

6.

Quantity A	Quantity B
$\frac{2\sqrt{3}}{6}$	$\frac{1}{\sqrt{3}}$

Ⓐ Quantity A is greater.
Ⓑ Quantity B is greater.
Ⓒ The two quantities are equal.
Ⓓ The relationship cannot be determined from the information given.

7. The ratio of y to c is equal to the ratio of x to b.

x, y, b, and c are positive integers.

$0 < y < 4$ and $x > 4$.

Quantity A	Quantity B
$3c$	$2b$

Ⓐ Quantity A is greater.
Ⓑ Quantity B is greater.
Ⓒ The two quantities are equal.
Ⓓ The relationship cannot be determined from the information given.

8. There are 60% fewer parking spots than cars.
There is one car for every 3 people.

Quantity A	Quantity B
the number of parking spots	the number of people

Ⓐ Quantity A is greater.
Ⓑ Quantity B is greater.
Ⓒ The two quantities are equal.
Ⓓ The relationship cannot be determined from the information given.

9. Which of the following has a value that is greater than 25?

Indicate all such values.

[A] $\sqrt{525}$

[B] $10\sqrt{6}$

[C] $\sqrt{625}$

[D] $2\sqrt{169}$

[E] $10\sqrt{7}$

10. At a sandwich shop, there are 2 breads, 3 kinds of meat, 4 types of cheeses, and 6 different sauces to choose from. Customers can choose only one of each. Assuming a customer has already chosen one kind of bread and one kind of meat for a sandwich, how many different sandwiches can be made from the other ingredients?

Ⓐ 36
Ⓑ 24
Ⓒ 18
Ⓓ 10
Ⓔ 2

11. Which of the following is less than the sum of all the prime factors of 330?

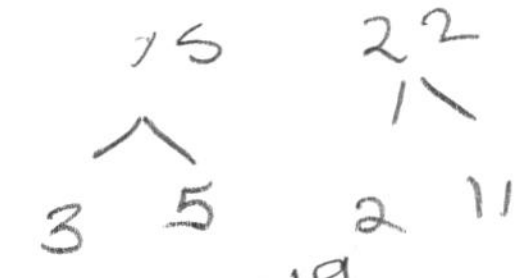

Indicate <u>all</u> such values.

- [A] 15
- [B] 17
- [C] 19
- [D] 21

12. There are at least 150 jars of jelly in a grocery store. The ratio of jars of jelly to jars of peanut butter is 5:6. Which of the following could be the number of jars of peanut butter in the store?

Indicate <u>all</u> such numbers.

- [A] 115
- [B] 125
- [C] 180
- [D] 192
- [E] 225

13.

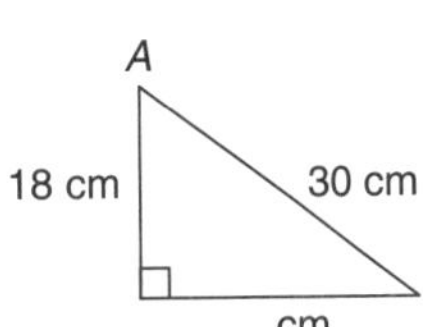

What is the area of triangle *ABC* in square centimeters?

[ ] square centimeters

Questions 14–16 are based on the following data.

Sales Convention Facts	
Total businesses	226
Business Types:	
Sole Proprietorships (single owner)	134
Male owners	61
Female owners	73
Joint Ventures (multiple owners)	92
Two Owners	33
Three Owners	22
Four or more Owners	37
Business Fields:	
Automotive Sales Business	72
Agriculture Sales Business	18
Electronics Sales Business	66
Household Sales Business	39
Other Businesses	31
Revenues:	
\$25,000 – \$49,999	87
\$50,000 – \$99,999	94
\$100,000 – \$249,999	39
\$250,000 or higher	6

14. All electronics sales businesses are conducted as sole proprietorships. If $\frac{1}{3}$ of electronic sales businesses have female owners, how many electronic sales businesses have male owners?

(A) 73
(B) 66
(C) 61
(D) 44
(E) 22

15. Approximately what percentage of the total number of businesses at the sales convention generate less than $100,000 in annual sales?

(A) 80%
(B) 52%
(C) 42%
(D) 20%
(E) 18%

16. Of the household sales businesses present at the convention, there are 7 female-owned sole proprietorships and 4 male-owned sole proprietorships. Approximately what percentage of the household sales businesses are joint ventures?

(A) 12%
(B) 28%
(C) 31%
(D) 42%
(E) 72%

17.

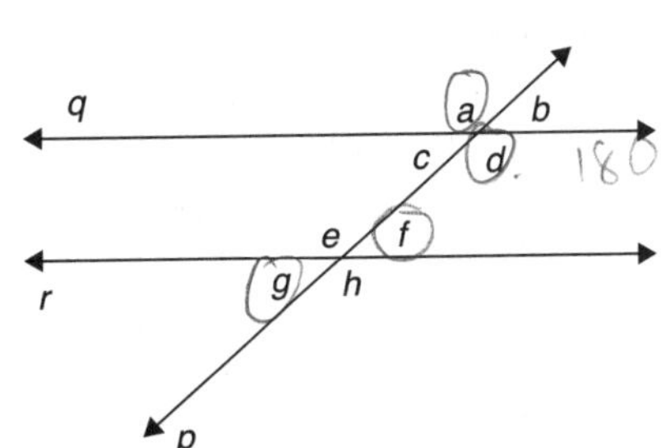

Lines q and r in the figure shown are parallel lines cut by transversal p. What is the sum of the measure of angles a, d, f, and g in degrees?

[ ] degrees

18. The average of John's test scores in his economics class is 80%. Only one test remains, and it is weighted at 25% of the final grade. If his final grade is based entirely on his test scores, what is the lowest percent John can receive on the final to earn an 85% in the class?

   (A) 96%
   (B) 97%
   (C) 98%
   (D) 99%
   (E) 100%

19. What is the total number of unique prime factors of 450?

   (A) 2
   (B) 3
   (C) 4
   (D) 5
   (E) 6

20. Pedro traveled 6,252 kilometers last year. If he continues to travel at the same rate, approximately how many kilometers will he travel in the next 3 months?

   (A) 500
   (B) 1,500
   (C) 2,000
   (D) 2,500
   (E) 3,000

QUANTITATIVE REASONING PRACTICE SET 5 ANSWER KEY

1. A
2. C
3. A
4. A
5. B
6. C
7. B
8. B
9. D, E
10. B
11. A, B, C
12. C, D
13. 216
14. D
15. A
16. E
17. 360
18. E
19. B
20. B

QUANTITATIVE REASONING PRACTICE SET 5 ANSWERS AND EXPLANATIONS

1. A

For y to be less than or equal to 14, x has to be less than or equal to 4. Since x is greater than 4, it follows that y is greater than 14. This relationship can also be determined by using the Picking Numbers strategy. Since x is greater than 4, a substitution of any value greater than 4 for x will result in a value of y that is greater than 14. For example, let $x = 5$. That gives you $y = 7x - 14 = 7(5) - 14 = 35 - 14 = 21$. So, Quantity A is greater; the answer is **(A)**.

2. C

$m\angle 1 + m\angle 2 = 180°$ and $m\angle 1 + m\angle 4 = 180°$ because they are supplementary angles. Lines m and n are parallel lines cut by a transversal, l. They create corresponding angles that are congruent, so $m\angle 1 = m\angle 3$. Substituting $m\angle 3$ for its equivalent angle, $m\angle 1$, results in the equation $m\angle 3 + m\angle 4 = 180°$. Therefore, Quantity A is equal to Quantity B; the answer is **(C)**.

3. A

For Quantity A, write the percent in decimal form and then multiply: $0.10\% = 0.0010$; $0.001 \times 0.15 = 0.00015$. Quantity B $= 1.5 \times 10^{-5} = 1.5 \times 0.00001 = 0.000015$. So, Quantity A is greater than Quantity B; the answer is **(A)**.

4. A

The mode, or data item that occurs most frequently, of 3, 3, 4, 4, 4, 5 is 4. The mean, or average of the data, is $\frac{3 + 3 + 4 + 4 + 4 + 5}{6} = 3.83$. So, Quantity A is greater than Quantity B; the answer is **(A)**.

5. B

In this problem, x can be any number from 2 to 10 inclusive, and y can be any number greater than 3. Substituting possible values for x and y, xy is always greater than $x - y$. For example, let $x = 3$ and $y = 4$. Then $x - y = 3 - 4 = -1$; $xy = 3 \times 4 = 12$. Try a different set of numbers to be certain: let $x = 9$ and $y = 9$. Then $x - y = 9 - 9 = 0$; $xy = 9 \times 9 = 81$. You can conclude that Quantity B is greater than Quantity A; the correct answer is **(B)**.

Note that you could also approach this problem strategically by thinking like this: Because x and y are both positive, $x - y$ will always be less than x. Because x and y are both greater than 1, xy will always be greater than x.

6. C

Quantity A can be simplified as follows: $\frac{2\sqrt{3}}{6} = \frac{\sqrt{3}}{3}$.

Quantity B can be rationalized as follows: $\frac{1}{\sqrt{3}} = \frac{1}{\sqrt{3}} \times \frac{\sqrt{3}}{\sqrt{3}} = \frac{\sqrt{3}}{3}$.

So, Quantity A is equal to Quantity B; the correct answer is **(C)**.

7. B

This problem can be solved by Picking Numbers. You are given that y is less than 4 and greater than 0; x is greater than 4. Since x and y are whole numbers, y cannot be greater than 3. Representative values can be assigned to each variable. For example, $y = 3$ and $x = 5$. The variables c and b are directly related to each other. For example, if c were 7 times the amount of y, then b would be 7 times the amount of x. Using these values, $y = 3$, $x = 5$, $c = 21$ ($y \times 7$), and $b = 35$ ($x \times 7$). Substituting these values into the expressions for Quantity A and Quantity B, $3c = 63$ and $2b = 70$. $2b$ is greater than $3c$. So, Quantity B is greater than Quantity A; the correct answer is **(B)**.

8. B

At a glance, you can see that there are fewer parking spots than cars and that there are fewer cars than people. Thus Quantity B must be larger than Quantity A.

The easiest way to see this is simply to Pick Numbers. If there are 30 people, there are ten cars (one car for every three people). That would mean that there are four parking spots (60% of 10 is 6 and $10 - 6 = 4$).

To see the algebra, let the number of parking spots be represented by s, the number of cars be represented by c, and the number of people be represented by p. s equals c minus 60% of c and c equals $\frac{p}{3}$. Substitute $\frac{p}{3}$ for c in the first equation, $s = c - 0.6c$, resulting in $s = \frac{p}{3} - 0.6\left(\frac{p}{3}\right)$.

Next, simplifying the equation results in $3s = 0.4p$. Dividing each side by 0.4 yields $7.5s = p$. Plug in the numbers from the earlier Picking Numbers approach (four parking spots for every 30 people) and you'll see that this equation is correct. So, the number of people (Quantity B) is greater than the number of parking spots (Quantity A); the answer is **(B)**.

9. D, E

Notice that all the answers involve a square root in one way or another. So, first consider the given number, 25, and its square: $25 \times 25 = 625$. A number greater than 25 must be greater than $\sqrt{625}$. Choices (A) and (C) have values that are less than or equal to 25. In choice (B), $10\sqrt{6}$ is equal to $\sqrt{600}$, which is less than 25. Choice **(D)** is correct because $\sqrt{169}$ is 13 and $13 \times 2 = 26$. Choice **(E)** is also correct because $10\sqrt{7}$ is equal to $\sqrt{700}$. So, the correct choices are **(D)** and **(E)**.

10. B

Since the bread and meat have been decided, the remaining options consist of 4 cheeses and 6 sauces. Remember, each can only be used once. Using the multiplication principle, the 4 cheeses and the 6 sauces allow for 24 different sandwiches ($6 \times 4 = 24$). So, the answer is **(B)**.

11. A, B, C

The prime factorization of 330 is $2 \times 3 \times 5 \times 11$. The sum of the prime factors is $2 + 3 + 5 + 11 = 21$. So, the correct choices are **(A)**, **(B)**, and **(C)**.

12. C, D

Using the ratio of 5:6, having at least 150 jars of jelly indicates that there are at least 180 jars of peanut butter. Since the number of jars of jelly can be 150 or greater, the number of jars of peanut butter can be 180 or greater. Adhering to the ratio of 5:6, the number of jars of peanut butter must be a multiple of 6 greater than or equal to 180. Note that 225 is greater than 180 but it's not divisible by 6; therefore, it cannot form a ratio of 5:6 with the number of jars of jelly. So, 180 and 192 are the only choices that meet those criteria; the correct answers are **(C)** and **(D)**.

13. 216

Triangle *ABC* is a right triangle. Its side lengths consist of three positive integers *a*, *b*, and *c* such that $a^2 + b^2 = c^2$. 18 and 30 are multiples of 6 and the representatives of the 3 and 5 in the 3:4:5 ratio. So, $x = 6 \times 4 = 24$, or 24 cm.

Apply the formula for area: $\frac{1}{2} \times \text{base} \times \text{height} = \frac{1}{2} \times 24 \times 18 = 216$, or 216 cm^2.

This can also be solved using the Pythagorean theorem, $a^2 + b^2 = c^2$. Substitute the values into the equation and simplify.

$$\begin{aligned} (18)^2 + (x)^2 &= (30)^2 \\ 324 + x^2 &= 900 \\ x^2 &= 576 \\ x &= 24 \end{aligned}$$

Use $x = 24$ to find the area of the triangle as shown. The correct answer is **216**.

14. D

One-third of the 66 electronics sales businesses have female owners: $\frac{1}{3} \times 66 = 22$.

The female-owned electronics sales businesses, 22, subtracted from the total electronics sales businesses, 66, leaves 44 male-owned electronics sales businesses. So, the answer is **(D)**.

15. A

There are 87 businesses at the convention that generate less than $50,000 annually and 94 businesses at the convention that generate between $50,000 and $99,999 annually. So, the total number of businesses that generate less than $100,000 is 181.

These 181 businesses account for approximately 80% of the 226 businesses at the convention: $\frac{181}{226} = 80.09\%$. So, the answer is **(A)**.

16. E

There are 39 household sales businesses. Subtracting the 7 female-owned sole proprietorships and 4 male-owned sole proprietorships, the remaining 28 household sales businesses are joint ventures. About 72% of household sales businesses are joint ventures: $\frac{28}{39} = 71.79\%$. So, the answer is **(E)**.

17. 360

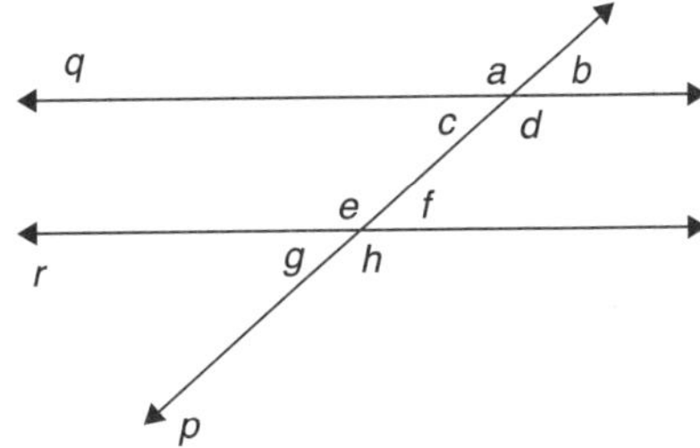

In this problem, every obtuse angle is equal to every other obtuse angle, and every acute angle is equal to every other acute angle. Also, any obtuse angle plus any acute angle equals 180 degrees; *a* and *d* are obtuse angles, and *f* and *g* are acute angles.

So, the correct answer is **360**.

18. E

Use the Picking Numbers strategy here, and start with 100 for the total number of possible points to score in the class. The tests taken so far weigh 75%, or 75 points out of 100 points. John has achieved a score of 80% so far. This means he has earned $0.75 \times 80 = 60$, or 60 points out of 100 points in the class.

To earn 85%, or 85 points, in the class, John needs $85 - 60 = 25$, or 25 points more. John would have to get a score x such that $0.25x = 25$, or $x = 100$, to earn an 85% in the class. Thus, John has to get 100% on his last test to pull his average up to 85% for the class. The correct answer is **(E)**.

19. B

The prime factorization of 450 is $2 \times 3 \times 3 \times 5 \times 5$. This factorization consists of 3 unique prime factors: 2, 3, and 5. So, there are 3 unique prime factors; the answer is **(B)**.

20. B

Three months is one fourth of a year. Thus, Pedro will travel $6{,}252 \div 4 = 1{,}563$ miles in 3 months if he continues traveling at the same rate. The closest answer is 1,500, choice **(B)**.

Diagnostic Tool

Tally up your score and write the results below.

Total

Total Correct: 13 out of 20

Percentage Correct: # you got right × 100 ÷ 20: 65

By Section:

Quantitative Comparison 4 out of 8

Problem Solving 6 out of 9

Data Interpretation 2 out of 3

DIAGNOSE YOUR RESULTS

Look back at the questions you got wrong and think about your experience answering them. Were you stymied by a particular question type, or by a certain math topic? If the latter, studying the relevant math content review in Part 3 of this book should help.

QUANTITATIVE REASONING PRACTICE SET 6

Directions: Select the correct answer.

1.

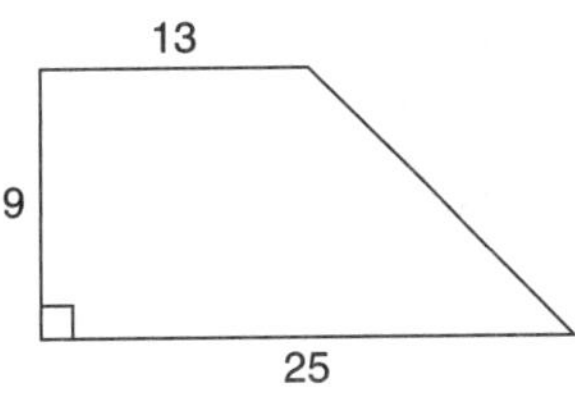

Quantity A	Quantity B
Three times the number of units in the perimeter of the figure	The number of square units in the area of the figure

Ⓐ Quantity A is greater.
Ⓑ Quantity B is greater.
Ⓒ The two quantities are equal.
Ⓓ The relationship cannot be determined from the information given.

2.

$$5 < c < 8$$

$$7 < d < 10$$

Quantity A	Quantity B
$c + d$	16

Ⓐ Quantity A is greater.
Ⓑ Quantity B is greater.
Ⓒ The two quantities are equal.
Ⓓ The relationship cannot be determined from the information given.

3.

The surface area of a cube is 96 square units.

Quantity A	Quantity B
The volume of the cube	256

Ⓐ Quantity A is greater.
Ⓑ Quantity B is greater.
Ⓒ The two quantities are equal.
Ⓓ The relationship cannot be determined from the information given.

4. 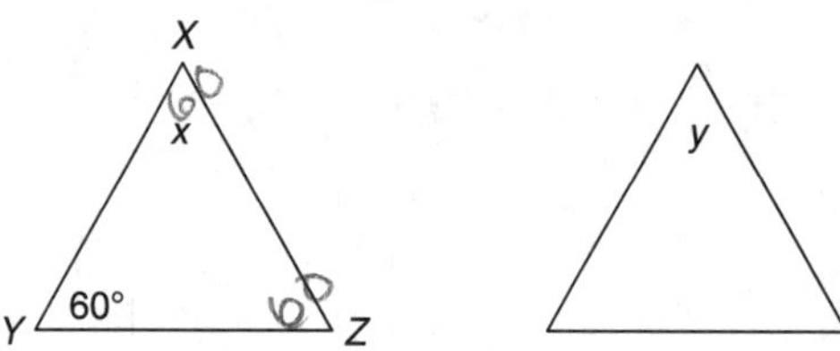

In the triangles above, $XY = XZ$ and $ST = TU = SU$.

Quantity A	Quantity B
x	y

(A) Quantity A is greater.
(B) Quantity B is greater.
(C) The two quantities are equal.
(D) The relationship cannot be determined from the information given.

5. The price of an item was increased by 20 percent. The new price of the item was decreased by x percent, resulting in a final price that is 28 percent less than the original price.

Quantity A	Quantity B
x	43

(A) Quantity A is greater.
(B) Quantity B is greater.
(C) The two quantities are equal.
(D) The relationship cannot be determined from the information given.

6. $$2x^2 + 4x - 30 = 0$$

Quantity A	Quantity B
The product of the roots of the equation	The sum of the roots of the equation

(A) Quantity A is greater.
(B) Quantity B is greater.
(C) The two quantities are equal.
(D) The relationship cannot be determined from the information given.

7. $$⌂c = -c + \frac{1}{c}$$

Quantity A	Quantity B
The value of ⌂ c if $c = 4$	The value of ⌂ c if $c = 3$

Ⓐ Quantity A is greater.
Ⓑ Quantity B is greater.
Ⓒ The two quantities are equal.
Ⓓ The relationship cannot be determined from the information given.

8.

Quantity A	Quantity B
$9^2 + 8^2 + 7^2$	$49 + 63 + 80$

Ⓐ Quantity A is greater.
Ⓑ Quantity B is greater.
Ⓒ The two quantities are equal.
Ⓓ The relationship cannot be determined from the information given.

9. Which of the following is equivalent to the expression $\frac{(ab)^3c^0}{a^3b^4}$, where $abc \neq 0$?

Ⓐ c
Ⓑ ab
Ⓒ abc
Ⓓ $\frac{1}{b}$
Ⓔ $\frac{c}{ab}$

10. Jayson has 172 ounces of sports drink in a cooler. If he pours an equal amount into 8 bottles with 4 ounces left over, approximately what percent of the total does he pour into each bottle?

Ⓐ 4%
Ⓑ 8%
Ⓒ 12%
Ⓓ 20%
Ⓔ 32%

11. Given that $f(x) = (x - 4)^2$ and $g(x) = x^2 - 5$, what is the value of $f(2) - g(2)$?

(A) −1
(B) 1
(C) 3
(D) 5
(E) 9

12. Out of every 500 picture frames shipped, there are always exactly 20 damaged frames. Which of the following could be the number of damaged and undamaged frames, respectively, within a given shipment?

Indicate <u>all</u> such numbers.

[A] 5 and 100
[B] 5 and 120
[C] 10 and 250
[D] 20 and 480
[E] 40 and 800

13. Keep Cool Air-Conditioning charges $60 for the first 30 minutes of every house call and $15 for each additional quarter hour. In addition, the customer has to pay for any required parts needed for repairs. If Mrs. Lewis's bill was $225, which included $90 for parts, how long did the air-conditioning repair technician work?

(A) 1 hour and 15 minutes
(B) 1 hour and 45 minutes
(C) 2 hours
(D) 2 hours and 15 minutes
(E) 3 hours

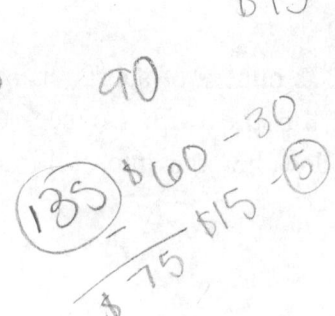

14. Darion has at least one quarter, one dime, one nickel, and one penny in his pocket. He has three times as many pennies as nickels, three times as many nickels as dimes, and three times as many dimes as quarters. If he has 120 coins, how much money does he have?

(A) \$1.20
(B) \$3.81
(C) \$4.06
(D) \$4.07
(E) \$7.75

15.

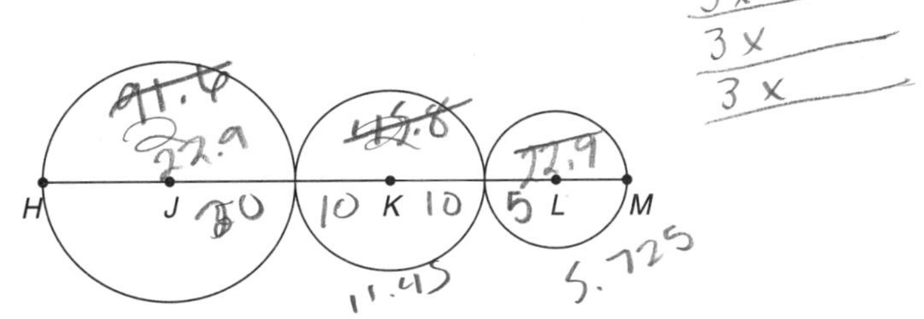

In the figure shown, *J*, *K*, and *L* are the centers of the three circles. The radius of the circle with center *J* is four times the radius of the circle with center *L*, and the radius of the circle with center *J* is two times the radius of the circle with center *K*. If the sum of the areas of the three circles is 525π square units, what is the measure, in units, of *JL*?

(A) 35
(B) 45
(C) 50
(D) 65
(E) 70

16. A line whose slope is $-\frac{1}{4}$ passes through the points (4, 3) and (x, 1). What is the value of x?

(A) −12
(B) −4
(C) 0
(D) 8
(E) 12

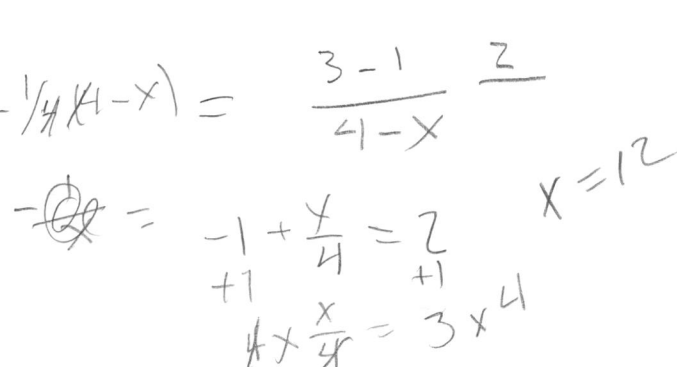

17. Full Force's annual dance recital was attended by 205 people, each of whom purchased a ticket. Children and youth tickets cost \$3.50 and adult tickets cost \$5.00. If Full Force collected \$828.50 in ticket sales, how many adults attended?

	adults

Questions 18–20 are based on the following graph:

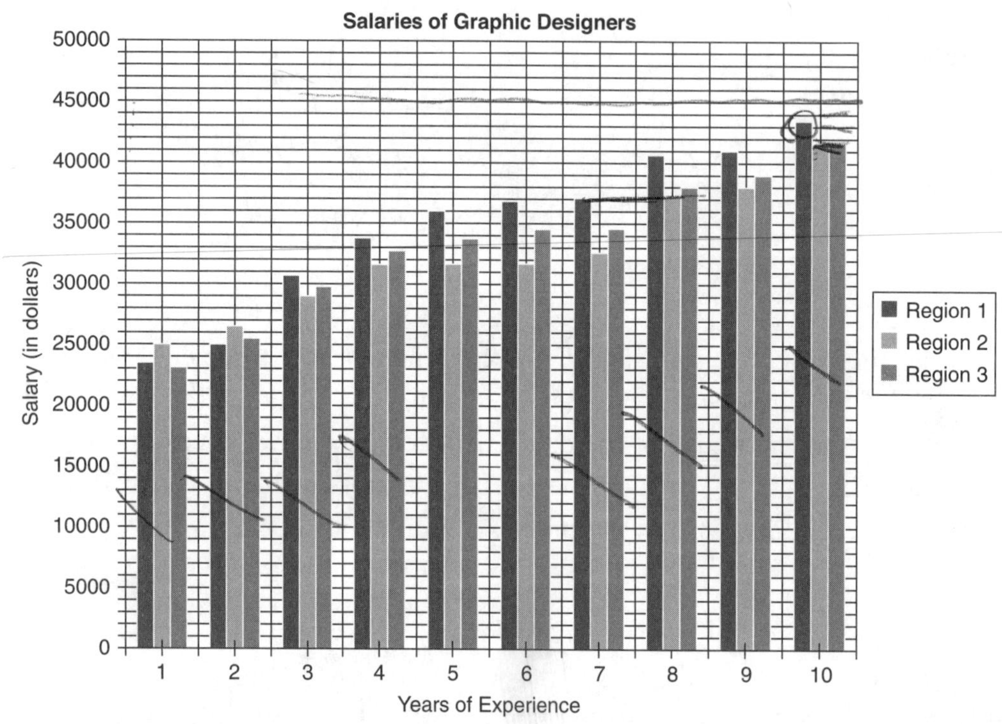

18. How many years of experience does a graphic designer in Region 2 need in order to earn the same salary as a graphic designer in Region 1 with 7 years of experience?

Ⓐ 5
Ⓑ 6
Ⓒ 7
Ⓓ 8
Ⓔ 9

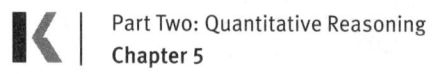

19. Richard, who lives in Region 2, just graduated from college and has zero years of experience. His starting salary is $23,900 per year. Suppose the correlation between experience and pay shown in the graph remains the same over the next 10 years. What is the approximate percent increase in annual pay over his starting salary that he can expect to receive if he works 10 years?

41,500 23,900

(A) 42%
(B) 45%
(C) 55%
(D) 58%
(E) 74%

20. What is the approximate difference, in dollars, between the median of the region with the highest median salary for the ten different possible years shown and the median of the region with the lowest median salary for the ten different possible years shown?

(A) 1,000
(B) 2,000
(C) 2,500
(D) 3,000
(E) 5,000

QUANTITATIVE REASONING PRACTICE SET 6 ANSWER KEY

1. A
2. D
3. B
4. C
5. B
6. B
7. B
8. A
9. D
10. C
11. D
12. B, D
13. B
14. B
15. B
16. E
17. 74
18. D
19. E
20. E

QUANTITATIVE REASONING PRACTICE SET 6 ANSWERS AND EXPLANATIONS

1. A

To compare the quantities, you must first determine the perimeter and the area of the figure. Break up the complex figure into two smaller figures:

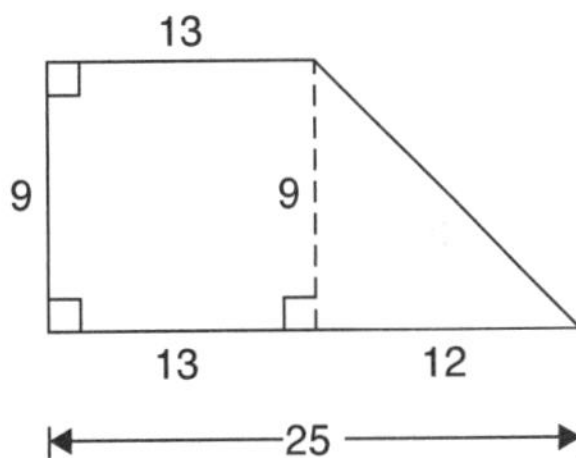

Look at the triangle created by drawing the dashed segment. The dashed segment is both a leg of a right triangle and a side of a 9×13 rectangle. To calculate the perimeter of the entire figure, you have to find the hypotenuse of the triangle created. The legs of the triangle are 9 and 12, so the triangle is a 3:4:5 triangle—$3 \times 3 = 9$, $3 \times 4 = 12$—whose hypotenuse is 15, because $3 \times 5 = 15$.

The perimeter of the figure can be found now: $9 + 13 + 15 + 25 = 62$. That means Quantity A is $3 \times 62 = 186$.

The area of the entire figure is the sum of the area of the rectangle and the area of the triangle:

Rectangle: $A = l \times w = 9 \times 13 = 117$

Triangle: $A = \frac{1}{2}bh = \frac{1}{2}(12 \times 9) = 54$

Complete figure: $117 + 54 = 171$

Compare 186 for Quantity A to 171 for Quantity B. The answer is **(A)**.

2. D

Consider Picking Numbers to test the relationship between $c + d$ and 16. It is not necessary that you choose whole numbers for c and d, but it is easier that way. Suppose $c = 6$ and $d = 8$. Then Quantity A is less: $6 + 8 = 14$; $14 < 16$.

But don't jump to conclusions yet; try another set of values. Suppose $c = 7$ and $d = 9$. Then Quantity A equals Quantity B: $7 + 9 = 16$. So, more than one relationship is possible, and the correct choice is **(D)**.

3. B

The key to solving this problem is knowing the formula for the surface area of a cube, knowing the formula for the volume of a cube, and knowing that all the sides of a cube are equal. The formula for the surface area of a cube is $6s^2$, where s is the side length. To find the side length, solve the equation for s:

$$\begin{aligned} 6s^2 &= 96 \\ s^2 &= 16 \\ s &= 4 \end{aligned}$$

Now, use the formula for the volume of a cube: $V = s^3$, where s is the side length.

$V = s^3 = 4 \times 4 \times 4 = 64$. Quantity B is greater. The answer is **(B)**.

4. C

The sum of the interior angles in a triangle is 180°. The given information indicates that the triangle on the left is isosceles. Since its two top sides are equal, the two base angles are also equal. If the two base angles are equal, then the value of x is also 60°. The given information indicates that the triangle on the right is equilateral. Since all three sides are equal, all three interior angles are also equal, and the value of y is 60°. Therefore, the two quantities are equal, and the correct choice is **(C)**.

5. B

If the original price of the item was 100 dollars and the price was increased by 20%, the new price, in dollars, was $100 + (0.20 \times 100) = 120$. The final price was 28% less than the original price, so the final price, in dollars, was $100 - (0.28 \times 100) = 100 - 28 = 72$.

Use the percent decrease formula to find what x, the percent decrease, is from 120 to 72.

$$\textit{Percent decrease} = \frac{\textit{Amount of decrease}}{\textit{Original whole}} \times \textit{100\%}$$

$\frac{120 - 72}{120} \times 100\% = \frac{48}{120} \times 100\%$. $\frac{48}{120}$ simplifies to $\frac{2}{5}$. So $\frac{2}{5} \times 100\% = 40\%$.
Thus, $x = 40$. Quantity A has a value of 40, and Quantity B has a value of 43. The correct answer is **(B)**.

6. B

To compare the quantities, you have to solve the equation first. Start by factoring out the greatest common factor, 2.

$$\begin{aligned} 2x^2 + 4x - 30 &= 0 \\ 2(x^2 + 2x - 15) &= 0 \end{aligned}$$

Divide both sides by 2 and factor the expression inside the parentheses into two binomials:

$$(x + 5)(x - 3) = 0$$

To solve the equation, set each binomial equal to 0 and solve for x:

$$x + 5 = 0 \qquad x - 3 = 0$$

So $x = -5$ or $x = 3$. The product of the two possible values of x is -15, and the sum of the two possible values of x is -2. The correct choice is **(B)** because $-2 > -15$.

7. B

The operation indicated by the symbol says to take negative c and then add the reciprocal of c. For $c = 4$, you have

$$-4 + \frac{1}{4} = \frac{-16 + 1}{4} = -\frac{15}{4} = -3\frac{3}{4}.$$

For $c = 3$, you have

$$-3 + \frac{1}{3} = \frac{-9 + 1}{3} = -\frac{8}{3} = -2\frac{2}{3}.$$

On a number line, Quantity B would be to the right of Quantity A. Quantity B is greater, so the answer is **(B)**.

8. A

There is no need to do a lot of calculating for this question—use reasoning instead. Compare the pieces in the quantities. On the left there is 7^2, and on the right there is 49. Cross these off because they are the same. Now compare the pieces that are left. Because 9^2 is greater than 80 and 8^2 is greater than 63, Quantity A is greater.

9. D

To simplify the expression, you will use the rules of exponents. $(ab)^3$ can be rewritten as a^3b^3 by applying the power rule, and c^0 should be rewritten as 1 because any nonzero number to the zero power equals 1. That gives you $\frac{a^3b^3}{a^3b^4}$. Although you are not finished simplifying, you can eliminate choices (A), (C), and (E) because they contain c. Next, simplify the expression to $\frac{1}{b}$.

The correct choice is **(D)**.

10. C

If there were 4 ounces left over, then $172 - 4 = 168$ ounces were poured. If 8 bottles were filled, then each bottle got $168 \div 8 = 21$ ounces. Now calculate the percentage that 21 is of the total 172: $\frac{21}{172} \approx 0.12$, or 12%. The correct answer is **(C)**.

11. D

Start by evaluating each function for $x = 2$.

$$f(x) = (x - 4)^2 = (2 - 4)^2 = (-2)^2 = 4$$
$$g(x) = x^2 - 5 = (2)^2 - 5 = 4 - 5 = -1$$

The question asks for the difference: $4 - (-1) = 5$. The correct answer is **(D)**.

12. B, D

The key to determining the ratio is to calculate the number of picture frames that are undamaged, which is $500 - 20 = 480$ for every 500 frames. The ratio of damaged frames to undamaged frames is $\frac{20}{480} = \frac{10}{240} = \frac{5}{120} = \frac{1}{24}$. Choices **(B)** and **(D)** are multiples of this ratio: $\frac{5}{5} \times \frac{1}{24} = \frac{5}{120}$ and $\frac{20}{20} \times \frac{1}{24} = \frac{20}{480}$.

The correct choices are **(B)** and **(D)**.

13. B

One way to solve this problem is to set up an equation, where x represents the number of quarter hours the repair technician worked:

$$\begin{aligned} \$60 + \$15x + \$90 &= \$225 \\ \$150 + \$15x &= \$225 \\ \$15x &= \$75 \\ x &= 5 \end{aligned}$$

The repair technician worked for 5 quarter hours (in addition to the first 30 minutes). A quarter of an hour is 15 minutes, so 5 quarter hours is equal to 1 hour and 15 minutes. Add in the first 30 minutes, and the answer is **(B)**, 1 hour and 45 minutes.

14. B

This problem can be solved with algebra, but it can also be solved by Picking Numbers. The total number of coins is 120, so pick a number for the number of quarters and go from there. The number of coins are all based on the number of quarters as shown. Suppose Darion has 2 quarters:

pennies	$3 \times 18 = 54$
nickels	$3 \times 6 = 18$
dimes	$3 \times 2 = 6$
quarters	2
Total coins	80 (too few)

That is not enough coins, so try 3 quarters:

pennies	$3 \times 27 = 81$
nickels	$3 \times 9 = 27$
dimes	$3 \times 3 = 9$
quarters	3
Total coins	120

Now that you have the correct number of coins, their value may be found:

$0.81 + (27 \times 0.05) + (9 \times 0.10) + (3 \times 0.25) = 3.81$. The correct answer is **(B)**.

15. B

To solve this problem, use the formula for the area of a circle, $A = \pi r^2$, where r is the radius. Before you find the length of JL, you have to find the length of the radius of each circle. Since the radii of circles J and K are four and two times the radius of circle L, respectively, you can set up the equation, where r represents the radius of circle L:

$$\begin{aligned} \pi(4r)^2 + \pi(2r)^2 + \pi(r)^2 &= 525\pi \\ 16r^2\pi + 4r^2\pi + r^2\pi &= 525\pi \\ 21r^2\pi &= 525\pi \\ r^2 &= 25 \\ r &= 5 \end{aligned}$$

If the radius of circle L is 5 units, the radius of circle K is 10 units, and the radius of circle J is 20 units. So the length of line segment JL is composed of the radius of circle L, the diameter of circle K, and the radius of circle J. This equals 20 + 10 + 10 + 5 or 45 units. The correct choice is **(B)**.

16. E

For this question, use the formula for the slope of a line: *Slope* $= \dfrac{y_2 - y_1}{x_2 - x_1}$.

$$\begin{aligned} -\frac{1}{4} &= \frac{3-1}{4-x} \\ -\frac{1}{4}(4-x) &= \frac{3-1}{\cancel{4-x}}\cancel{(4-x)} \\ -1+\frac{x}{4} &= 2 \\ \frac{x}{4} &= 3 \\ x &= 12 \end{aligned}$$

The answer is **(E)**.

17. 74

To solve this problem, set up a system of equations where a represents the number of adults and c represents the number of children and youths:

$$a + c = 205$$
$$3.50c + 5a = \$828.50$$

Solve for a in the first equation and then substitute it into the second equation: $a = 205 - c$.

$$\begin{aligned} 3.50c + 5(205 - c) &= 828.50 \\ 3.50c + 1{,}025 - 5c &= 828.50 \\ -1.50c &= -196.50 \\ c &= 131 \end{aligned}$$

Since there were 131 children and youths, there were $205 - 131 = 74$ adults. The correct answer is **74**.

18. D

First, locate the bar of a graphic designer in Region 1 with 7 years of experience. Since Region 1 remains highest compared to all other bars from 1 to 7 years, you can eliminate any number of years that are 7 or less in the answer choices. Then, locate a bar that has the same height as the bar you found from 7 years and beyond. A graphic designer in Region 2 with 8 years of experience has the same salary. The correct choice is **(D)**.

19. E

The key to finding the percent increase is to compare the increase to the original amount. If Richard works 10 years, he can expect to earn \$41,500 per year at the end of that time. The amount of increase is $\$41{,}500 - \$23{,}900 = \$17{,}600$.

$$\frac{17{,}600}{23{,}900} \times 100\% = 73.6\% \approx 74\%$$

The percent increase is about 74%. The correct choice is **(E)**.

20. E

Start by determining the medians for the regions you'll want to compare. Since there are ten data values in each set, the median for each region will be the average of the fifth and sixth data values. It's clear from the graph that Region 1 will have the highest median value and Region 2 will have the lowest median value, so those are the ones to calculate:

Region 1: $(\$36{,}000 + \$37{,}000) \div 2 = \$36{,}500$
Region 2: $(\$31{,}500 + \$31{,}500) \div 2 = \$31{,}500$

The approximate difference is \$5,000. The correct choice is **(E)**.

Diagnostic Tool

Tally up your score and write the results below.

Total

Total Correct: _______ out of 20

Percentage Correct: # you got right × 100 ÷ 20: _______

By Section:

Quantitative Comparison _______ out of 8

Problem Solving _______ out of 9

Data Interpretation _______ out of 3

Diagnose Your Results

Look back at the questions you got wrong and think about your experience answering them. Were you stymied by a particular question type, or by a certain math topic? If the latter, studying the relevant math content review in Part 3 of this book should help.

PART THREE

Math Content Review

Arithmetic

Most of the problems on the GRE involve arithmetic to some extent. Among the most important topics are number properties, ratios, and percents. You should know most of the definitions of different types of numbers such as what an integer is, what even numbers are, etc.

Not only do arithmetic topics covered in the unit themselves appear on the GRE, but they are also essential for understanding some of the more advanced topics that will be covered later. For instance, many of the rules covering arithmetic operations, such as the commutative law, will be important when we discuss variables and algebraic expressions. In addition, the concepts we cover here will be needed for solving problems.

REAL NUMBERS

Number Types

The set of real numbers consists of all rational and irrational numbers, including integers, fractions, and decimals. This number tree is a visual representation of the types of numbers and their relationships:

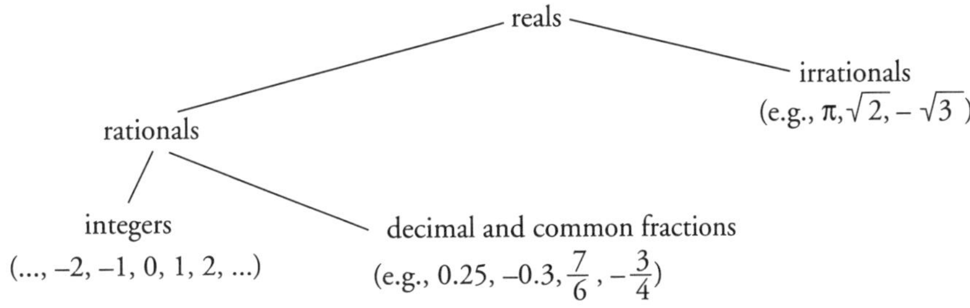

Real Numbers: All numbers on the number line; all the numbers on the GRE are real

Rational Numbers: All numbers that can be expressed as the ratio of two integers (all integers and fractions)

Irrational Numbers: All real numbers that are not rational, both positive and negative (e.g., π, $-\sqrt{3}$)

Integers: All numbers, including zero, with no fractional or decimal parts

A number line can be used to represent the set of real numbers. Every real number corresponds to a point on the number line, and every point on the number line corresponds to a real number. Numbers to the left of 0 on the number line are negative and numbers to the right of 0 are positive. Zero is neither negative nor positive.

$-\sqrt{7}$ -1.3 0.25 $\sqrt{3}$ $\frac{5}{2}$

-3 -2 -1 0 1 2 3

The number line can be used to compare real numbers. For real numbers a and b, if a is to the left of b, then a is less than b, $a < b$. If a is to the right of b, then a is greater than b, $a > b$. So, $-\sqrt{7} < \sqrt{3}$, $\sqrt{3} > -1.3$, and $0.25 < \frac{5}{2}$.

NUMBER OPERATIONS

Working efficiently and confidently with numeric expressions can save you time on the GRE. The following operations may be just one important step in solving a problem.

ORDER OF OPERATIONS

PEMDAS = **P**lease **E**xcuse **M**y **D**ear **A**unt **S**ally—This mnemonic will help you remember the order of operations.

P = Parentheses
E = Exponents
M = Multiplication } in order from left to right
D = Division
A = Addition } in order from left to right
S = Subtraction

Example: $30 - 5 \times 4 + (7 - 3)^2 \div 8$

First perform any operations within **Parentheses**. (If the expression has parentheses within parentheses, work from the innermost out.)	$30 - 5 \times 4 + 4^2 \div 8$

Next, raise to any powers indicated by **Exponents**.	$30 - 5 \times 4 + 16 \div 8$
Then do all **Multiplication** and **Division** in order from left to right.	$30 - 20 + 2$
Last, do all **Addition** and **Subtraction** in order from left to right.	$10 + 2$ 12

Laws of Operations

Commutative law: Addition and multiplication are both **commutative**; it doesn't matter **in what order** the operation is performed.

Example: $5 + 8 = 8 + 5$; $2 \times 6 = 6 \times 2$

Division and subtraction are **not** commutative.

Example: $3 - 2 \neq 2 - 3$; $6 \div 2 \neq 2 \div 6$

Associative law: Addition and multiplication are also **associative**; the terms can be **regrouped** without changing the result.

Example:

$$\begin{aligned}(a + b) + c &= a + (b + c)\\(3 + 5) + 8 &= 3 + (5 + 8)\\8 + 8 &= 3 + 13\\16 &= 16\end{aligned}\qquad\begin{aligned}(a \times b) \times c &= a \times (b \times c)\\(4 \times 5) \times 6 &= 4 \times (5 \times 6)\\20 \times 6 &= 4 \times 30\\120 &= 120\end{aligned}$$

Distributive law: The **distributive law** of multiplication allows us to "distribute" a factor among the terms being added or subtracted. In general, $a(b + c) = ab + ac$.

Example:

$$\begin{aligned}4(3 + 7) &= 4 \times 3 + 4 \times 7\\4 \times 10 &= 12 + 28\\40 &= 40\end{aligned}$$

Division can be distributed in a similar way.

Example:

$$\begin{aligned}\frac{3 + 5}{2} &= \frac{3}{2} + \frac{5}{2}\\\frac{8}{2} &= 1\frac{1}{2} + 2\frac{1}{2}\\4 &= 4\end{aligned}$$

Don't get carried away, though. When the sum or difference is in the **denominator,** no distribution is possible.

Example: $\frac{9}{4+5}$ is NOT equal to $\frac{9}{4} + \frac{9}{5}$.

FRACTIONS

4 ← numerator
— ← fraction bar (means "divided by")
5 ← denominator

Equivalent fractions: The value of a number is unchanged if you multiply the number by 1. In a fraction, multiplying the numerator and denominator by the same nonzero number is the same as multiplying the fraction by 1; the fraction is unchanged. Similarly, dividing the top and bottom by the same nonzero number leaves the fraction unchanged.

Example: $\frac{1}{2} = \frac{1 \times 2}{2 \times 2} = \frac{2}{4}$

$\frac{5}{10} = \frac{5 \div 5}{10 \div 5} = \frac{1}{2}$

Canceling and reducing: Generally speaking, when you work with fractions on the GRE, you'll need to put them in **lowest terms.** That means that the numerator and the denominator are not divisible by any common integer greater than 1. For example, the fraction $\frac{1}{2}$ is in lowest terms, but the fraction $\frac{3}{6}$ is not, since 3 and 6 are both divisible by 3.

The method we use to take such a fraction and put it in lowest terms is called **reducing**. That simply means to divide out any common multiples from both the numerator and denominator. This process is also commonly called **canceling.**

Example: Reduce $\frac{15}{35}$ to lowest terms.

First, determine the largest common factor of the numerator and denominator. Then, divide the top and bottom by that number to reduce.

$\frac{15}{35} = \frac{3 \times 5}{7 \times 5} = \frac{3 \times 5 \div 5}{7 \times 5 \div 5} = \frac{3}{7}$

Addition and subtraction: We can't add or subtract two fractions directly unless they have the same denominator. Therefore, before adding or subtracting, we must find a common denominator. A common denominator is just a **common multiple** of the denominators of the fractions. The **least common denominator** is the **least common multiple** (the smallest positive number that is a multiple of all the terms).

Example: $\frac{3}{5}+\frac{2}{3}-\frac{1}{2}$

Denominators are 5, 3, 2. $\text{LCM} = 5 \times 3 \times 2 = 30 = \text{LCD}$

Multiply numerator and denominator of each fraction by the value that raises each denominator to the LCD.

$$\left(\frac{3}{5}\times\frac{6}{6}\right)+\left(\frac{2}{3}\times\frac{10}{10}\right)-\left(\frac{1}{2}\times\frac{15}{15}\right)$$

$$=\frac{18}{30}+\frac{20}{30}-\frac{15}{30}$$

Combine the numerators by adding or subtracting and keep the LCD as the denominator.

$$=\frac{18+20-15}{30}=\frac{23}{30}$$

Multiplication:

Example: $\frac{10}{9}\times\frac{3}{4}\times\frac{8}{15}$

First, reduce (cancel) diagonally and vertically.

$$\frac{{}^{2}\cancel{10}}{{}_{3}\cancel{9}}\times\frac{{}^{1}\cancel{3}}{{}_{1}\cancel{4}}\times\frac{\cancel{8}^{2}}{\cancel{15}_{3}}$$

Then multiply numerators together and denominators together.

$$\frac{2\times1\times2}{3\times1\times3}=\frac{4}{9}$$

Division: Dividing is the same as multiplying by the **reciprocal** of the divisor. To get the reciprocal of a fraction, just invert it by interchanging the numerator and the denominator. For example, the reciprocal of the fraction $\frac{3}{7}$ is $\frac{7}{3}$.

Example: $\frac{4}{3}\div\frac{4}{9}$

To divide, invert the second term (the divisor), and then multiply as above.

$$\frac{4}{3}\div\frac{4}{9}=\frac{4}{3}\times\frac{9}{4}=\frac{{}^{1}\cancel{4}}{{}_{1}\cancel{3}}\times\frac{\cancel{9}^{3}}{\cancel{4}_{1}}=\frac{1\times3}{1\times1}=3$$

Complex fractions: A complex fraction is a fraction that contains one or more fractions in its numerator or denominator. There are two ways to simplify complex fractions.

Method I: Use the distributive law. Find the least common multiple of all the denominators, and multiply all the terms in the top and bottom of the complex fraction by the LCM. This will eliminate all the denominators, greatly simplifying the calculation.

Example: $\dfrac{\frac{7}{9}-\frac{1}{6}}{\frac{1}{3}+\frac{1}{2}} = \dfrac{18\times\left(\frac{7}{9}-\frac{1}{6}\right)}{18\times\left(\frac{1}{3}+\frac{1}{2}\right)}$ LCM of all the denominators is 18.

$$= \dfrac{\frac{{}^{2}\cancel{18}}{1}\times\frac{7}{\cancel{9}_1}-\frac{{}^{3}\cancel{18}}{1}\times\frac{1}{\cancel{6}_1}}{\frac{{}^{6}\cancel{18}}{1}\times\frac{1}{\cancel{3}_1}+\frac{{}^{9}\cancel{18}}{1}\times\frac{1}{\cancel{2}_1}}$$

$$= \dfrac{2\times 7-3\times 1}{6\times 1+9\times 1}$$

$$= \dfrac{14-3}{6+9} = \dfrac{11}{15}$$

Method II: Treat the numerator and denominator separately. Combine the terms in each to get a single fraction on top and a single fraction on bottom. We are left with the division of two fractions, which we perform by multiplying the top fraction by the reciprocal of the bottom one. This method is preferable when it is difficult to get an LCM for all the denominators.

Example: $\dfrac{\frac{7}{9}-\frac{1}{6}}{\frac{1}{3}+\frac{1}{2}} = \dfrac{\frac{14}{18}-\frac{3}{18}}{\frac{2}{6}+\frac{3}{6}} = \dfrac{\frac{11}{18}}{\frac{5}{6}} = \dfrac{11}{18}\div\dfrac{5}{6} = \dfrac{11}{\cancel{18}_3}\times\dfrac{\cancel{6}^1}{5} = \dfrac{11}{15}$

Example: $\dfrac{\frac{5}{11}-\frac{5}{22}}{\frac{7}{16}+\frac{3}{8}} = \dfrac{\frac{10}{22}-\frac{5}{22}}{\frac{7}{16}+\frac{6}{16}} = \dfrac{\frac{5}{22}}{\frac{13}{16}} = \dfrac{5}{\cancel{22}_{11}}\times\dfrac{\cancel{16}^8}{13} = \dfrac{40}{143}$

Comparing positive fractions: If the numerators are the same, the fraction with the smaller denominator will have the larger value, since the numerator is divided into a smaller number of parts.

Example: $\dfrac{4}{5} > \dfrac{4}{7}$ i.e.: >

If the denominators are the same, the fraction with the larger numerator will have the larger value.

Example: $\dfrac{5}{8} > \dfrac{3}{8}$ i.e.: >

If neither the numerators nor the denominators are the same, express all of the fractions in terms of some common denominator. The fraction with the largest numerator will be the largest.

Example: Compare $\frac{11}{15}$ and $\frac{13}{20}$.

$$\frac{11}{15} = \frac{11 \times 20}{15 \times 20} \qquad \frac{13}{20} = \frac{13 \times 15}{20 \times 15}$$

$$= \frac{220}{15 \times 20} \qquad = \frac{195}{20 \times 15}$$

Since $220 > 195$, $\frac{11}{15} > \frac{13}{20}$.

Notice that it is not necessary to calculate the denominators. A shorter version of this method is to multiply the numerator of the left fraction by the denominator of the right fraction and vice versa (cross multiply). Then compare the products obtained this way. If the left product is greater, then the left fraction was greater to start with.

Example: Compare $\frac{5}{7}$ and $\frac{9}{11}$.

$5 \times 11 \; ? \; 9 \times 7$

$55 < 63$ so $\frac{5}{7} < \frac{9}{11}$

Sometimes it is easier to find a common **numerator**. In this case, the fraction with the **smaller** denominator will be the **larger** fraction.

Example: Compare $\frac{22}{19}$ and $\frac{11}{9}$.

Multiply $\frac{11}{9} \times \frac{2}{2}$ to obtain a common numerator of 22.

$$\frac{11}{9} = \frac{11 \times 22}{9 \times 2} = \frac{22}{18}$$

Since $\frac{22}{19} < \frac{22}{18}$, $\frac{22}{19} < \frac{11}{9}$.

As before, the comparison can also be made by cross multiplying.

$22 \times 9 < 11 \times 19$, so $\frac{22}{19} < \frac{11}{9}$

Mixed Numbers: Mixed numbers are numbers consisting of an integer and a fraction. For example, $3\frac{1}{4}$, $12\frac{2}{5}$, and $5\frac{7}{8}$ are all mixed numbers. Fractions whose numerators are greater than their denominators may be converted into mixed numbers, and vice versa.

Example: Convert $\frac{23}{4}$ to a mixed number.

$$\frac{23}{4} = \frac{20}{4} + \frac{3}{4} = 5\frac{3}{4}$$

Example: Convert $2\frac{3}{7}$ to a fraction.

$$2\frac{3}{7} = 2 + \frac{3}{7} = \frac{14}{7} + \frac{3}{7} = \frac{17}{7}$$

Decimal Fractions

Decimal fractions are just another way of expressing common fractions; they can be converted to common fractions with a power of ten in the denominator.

Example: $0.053 = \frac{53}{10^3}$ or $\frac{53}{1{,}000}$

Each position, or **digit**, in the decimal has a name associated with it. The GRE occasionally contains questions on digits, so you should be familiar with this naming convention:

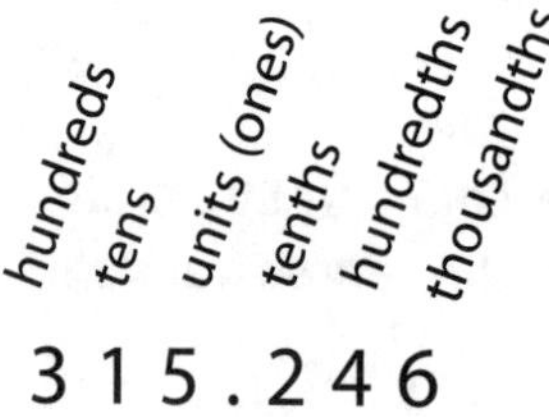

Comparing decimal fractions: To compare decimals, add zeros to the decimals (after the last digit to the right of the decimal point) until all the decimals have the same number of digits. Since the denominators of all the fractions are the same, the numerators determine the order of values.

Example: Arrange in order from smallest to largest: 0.7, 0.77, 0.07, 0.707 and 0.077.

$$0.7 = 0.700 = \frac{700}{1{,}000}$$

$$0.77 = 0.770 = \frac{770}{1{,}000}$$

$$0.07 = 0.070 = \frac{70}{1{,}000}$$

$$0.707 = 0.707 = \frac{707}{1{,}000}$$

$$0.077 = 0.077 = \frac{77}{1{,}000}$$

$70 < 77 < 700 < 707 < 770$; therefore, $0.07 < 0.077 < 0.7 < 0.707 < 0.77$

Addition and subtraction: When adding or subtracting one decimal to or from another, make sure that the decimal points are lined up, one under the other. This will ensure that tenths are added to tenths, hundredths to hundredths, etc.

Example: $0.6 + 0.06 + 0.006 =$

$$\begin{array}{r} 0.6 \\ 0.06 \\ +0.006 \\ \hline 0.666 \end{array}$$

Answer: 0.666

Example: $0.72 - 0.072 =$

$$\begin{array}{r} 0.72 \\ -0.072 \\ \hline \end{array} = \begin{array}{r} 0.720 \\ -0.072 \\ \hline 0.648 \end{array}$$

Answer: 0.648

Multiplication and division: To multiply two decimals, multiply them as you would integers. The number of decimal places in the product will be the total number of decimal places in the factors that are multiplied together.

Example: $0.675 \times 0.42 =$

$$\begin{array}{r} 0.675 \\ \times 0.42 \\ \hline 1350 \\ 2700 \\ \hline 0.28350 \end{array} \qquad \begin{array}{r} \text{(3 decimal places)} \\ +\text{(2 decimal places)} \\ \hline \\ \\ \text{(5 decimal places)} \end{array}$$

Answer: 0.2835

When dividing a decimal by another decimal, multiply each by a power of 10 such that the divisor becomes an integer. (This doesn't change the value of the quotient.) Then carry out the division as you would with integers, placing the decimal point in the quotient directly above the decimal point in the dividend.

Example: $0.675 \div 0.25$

Multiply each decimal by 100 by moving the decimal point two places to the right (since there are two zeros in 100).

$67.5 \div 25$

$$\begin{array}{r} 2.7 \\ 25\overline{)67.5} \\ 50 \\ \hline 175 \\ 175 \\ \hline 0 \end{array}$$

Answer: 2.7

NUMBER OPERATIONS EXERCISES

BASIC

1. Is $6.205 > 6.250$?

2. According to the order of operations, what will be evaluated first?
$3^2 - (6 + 2)$

3. Does $(6 \times 12) \times 8$ equal $6 + (12 \times 8)$?

4. Evaluate and write as a mixed number: $\frac{2}{7} - \frac{3}{21} + 2\frac{4}{14}$.

5. Convert $\frac{17}{4}$ to a mixed number.

6. Reduce $\frac{6}{42}$ to simplest terms.

7. Simplify $\frac{3}{5} \times \frac{3}{8} \times \frac{2}{3}$.

Evaluate Exercises 8-10.

8. $\frac{1}{3} + \frac{1}{5}$

9. $8.84 \div 5.2$

10. 2.67×4.08

INTERMEDIATE

11. Evaluate $\frac{4}{11} + \frac{11}{12}$.

12. Which operation will be evaluated third? $6 \times \left(4.02 - 7^2\right) + 5.15$

13. True or false? $\frac{3}{7 + 10} = \frac{3}{7} + \frac{3}{10}$

14. Write in simplest form: $\frac{3}{8} \times \frac{7}{3} \times 2\frac{1}{4}$.

15. Evaluate $3\frac{2}{7} \div \frac{1}{3}$.

16. Simplify the complex fraction: $\dfrac{\frac{7}{12} - \frac{1}{4}}{\frac{4}{9} + \frac{1}{3}}$.

17. Fill in the box with <, >, or = : $\frac{3}{13} \square \frac{7}{28}$.

Evaluate Exercises 18–20.

18. $4.875 \div 6.5$

19. $\frac{3}{2} - \left(\frac{1}{6}\right)^2$

20. $5\left(\frac{9}{8} - \frac{2}{3}\right)$

ADVANCED

21. Evaluate $7.02^2 + \left(3 - 4.3^2\right) \times \frac{3}{4}$.

22. True or false: $\frac{\frac{1}{5} - \frac{3}{8}}{3} = \frac{3}{5} - \frac{9}{8}$?

23. Evaluate and write in simplest terms: $\frac{2}{5} \times \frac{7}{10} + \left(\frac{11}{5}\right)^2$.

24. Evaluate the expression: $\frac{\frac{3}{8} + \frac{5}{6} - 3}{\frac{9}{2} - \frac{3}{8} + 6}$.

25. Fill in the box with <, >, or =: $\frac{\frac{2}{5}}{\frac{2}{3}} \square \frac{5}{3}$

26. Write 3.067 as a mixed number fraction.

27. Order from least to greatest: 1.085, $1\frac{1}{7}$, 1.850, $\frac{10,805}{10,000}$.

Evaluate Exercises 28–30.

28. $3\frac{2}{7} + 1\frac{1}{5} - \frac{4}{3}$

29. $\frac{(2.2 - 0.3)^2}{0.95} - (1.1 - 7.08)$

30. $(14.08 - 5.78) \times 3.28 \div 1.2$

NUMBER OPERATIONS ANSWER KEY

Basic

1. No

Since both numbers start with 6, you need only compare the decimals. Since 250 is greater than 205, 6.250 is greater than 6.205.

2. (6 + 2)

Actions inside parentheses must be completed first according to the order of operations.

3. No

According to the rules of multiplication, $(a \times b) \times c = a \times (b \times c)$, but plus signs and multiplication signs are not interchangeable. So, $(6 \times 12) \times 8$ is not equal to $6 + (12 \times 8)$.

4. $2\frac{3}{7}$

First, convert to an improper fraction and reduce: $\frac{2}{7} - \frac{1}{7} + \frac{16}{7}$. Then, add and subtract numerators to get $\frac{17}{7}$, and convert to a mixed number, $2\frac{3}{7}$.

5. $4\frac{1}{4}$

Divide 17 by 4 to find the whole number, 4. There is 1 left over. Write the remainder as a fraction, $\frac{1}{4}$.

6. $\frac{1}{7}$

To reduce, find the greatest common factor of 6 and 42, which is 6. Divide both the numerator and the denominator by that common factor. This gives us $\frac{1}{7}$.

7. $\frac{3}{20}$

Multiply across the numerators and the denominators, $\frac{18}{120}$. Then, reduce the result by dividing both by the greatest common factor of 6. However, a much simpler way is to cancel out the common factors on the top and bottom before multiplying: $\frac{3}{5} \times \frac{{}^{1}\cancel{3}}{{}_{4}\cancel{8}} \times \frac{\cancel{2}^{1}}{\cancel{3}_{1}} = \frac{3}{20}$.

8. $\frac{8}{15}$

Since 3 and 5 have no factors in common, multiply them together to find the Least Common Multiple. Then, change each fraction to have a denominator with this common multiple: $\frac{5}{15} + \frac{3}{15}$. Then, add. Since 8 and 15 have no common factors, the result cannot be reduced.

9. 1.7

When dividing by a number with a decimal place, first move the decimal point over by the same number of places in the dividend and divisor. So you are dividing 88.4 by 52:

$$5.2\overline{)8.84} \quad = \quad \begin{array}{r} 1.7 \\ 52\overline{)88.4} \\ \underline{52} \\ 364 \\ \underline{364} \\ 0 \end{array}$$

10. 10.8936

First, multiply the two numbers as though they have no decimals. Then, count the number of decimal places in the two numbers that are multiplied; in this case, there are 4. Count 4 places from the rightmost digit in the product and place the decimal there. In this case, that means putting the decimal between the 0 and the 8, so the answer is 10.8936.

$$\begin{array}{r} 2.67 \\ \times\ 4.08 \\ \hline 21\ 36 \\ \underline{10\ 68} \\ 10.8936 \end{array}$$

Intermediate

11. $\mathbf{1\frac{37}{132}}$

First, find a common denominator. Since 11 and 12 have no common factors, multiply them together to get 132, which is the Least Common Multiple: $\frac{48}{132} + \frac{121}{132}$. Then, add the numerators, $\frac{169}{132}$, and convert to a mixed number, $1\frac{37}{132}$.

12. Multiplication

According to the order of operations, the parentheses must be cleared first, and this includes evaluating the exponent and performing subtraction. Next, this result is multiplied by 6.

13. False

Be careful! If you have addition or subtraction in the numerator, you can split the fraction into two fractions with the same denominator. The same does not hold true if you have addition or subtraction in the denominator. In that situation, you first have to complete the operation(s) in the denominator.

14. $\mathbf{1\frac{31}{32}}$

First, convert to an improper fraction: $\frac{3}{8} \times \frac{7}{3} \times \frac{9}{4}$. Next, cancel common factors in the numerator and denominator wherever possible. In this case, the 3s can be cancelled, giving you a product of $\frac{63}{32}$, which can then be converted to a mixed number, $1\frac{31}{32}$.

15. $\mathbf{9\frac{6}{7}}$

To evaluate, first convert the mixed number to an improper fraction, $\frac{23}{7}$. Next, convert the division to multiplication by multiplying the first fraction by the reciprocal of the second: $\frac{23}{7} \times \frac{3}{1} = \frac{69}{7}$. Convert back to a mixed number by dividing by $7: 9\frac{6}{7}$.

16. $\mathbf{\frac{3}{7}}$

First, evaluate the expression in the numerator, $\frac{7}{12} - \frac{1}{4}$ or $\frac{1}{3}$. Then, evaluate the expression in the denominator: $\frac{4}{9} + \frac{1}{3}$, or $\frac{7}{9}$. Finally, perform the division: $\frac{1}{3} \div \frac{7}{9} = \frac{1}{3} \times \frac{9}{7} = \frac{9}{21} = \frac{3}{7}$.

17. $<$

Express both fractions with common denominators to determine which fraction is greater. The least common denominator of $\frac{3}{13}$ and $\frac{7}{28} = \frac{1}{4}$ is 52 (13×4).

Thus $\frac{3}{13} = \frac{3 \times 4}{13 \times 4} = \frac{12}{52}$ and $\frac{1}{4} = \frac{1 \times 13}{4 \times 13} = \frac{13}{52}$. Then $\frac{12}{52} < \frac{13}{52}$, so $\frac{3}{13}$ is less than $\frac{7}{28}$.

18. 0.75

Dividing 4.875 by 6.5 gives:

$$\begin{array}{r} 0.75 \\ 65\overline{)48.75} \\ \underline{455} \\ 325 \\ \underline{325} \\ 0 \end{array}$$

19. $\mathbf{1\frac{17}{36}}$

First, evaluate $\left(\frac{1}{6}\right)^2$, or $\frac{1}{36}$. Then, convert the fractions using a common denominator of 36 and subtract: $\frac{54}{36} - \frac{1}{36} = \frac{53}{36}$. Finally, convert to a mixed number, $1\frac{17}{36}$.

20. $2\frac{7}{24}$

Begin by converting the fractions in parentheses to a common denominator of 24: $5\left(\frac{27}{24} - \frac{16}{24}\right)$. Evaluate the expression inside the parentheses: $5\left(\frac{11}{24}\right)$. Next, multiply: $\frac{5}{1} \times \frac{11}{24} = \frac{55}{24}$. Finally, convert to a mixed number, $2\frac{7}{24}$.

Advanced

21. 37.6629

First, evaluate the expression inside the parentheses: $7.02^2 + (-15.49) \times \frac{3}{4}$. Next, calculate $7.02^2 = 49.2804$. Multiplying the second term by $\frac{3}{4}$ then gives $49.2804 + (-11.6175)$. Performing the addition gives 37.6629.

22. False

Dividing by 3 is the same as multiplying by $\frac{1}{3}$: $\left(\frac{1}{5} - \frac{3}{8}\right) \times \frac{1}{3}$. Distributing $\frac{1}{3}$ across the parentheses gives $\frac{1}{15} - \frac{3}{24}$ or $\frac{1}{15} - \frac{1}{8}$. Also, $\frac{3}{5} - \frac{9}{8}$ can be restated as $\frac{9}{15} - \frac{9}{8}$. Comparing piece by piece, it can be seen without further calculation that these expressions are not equal.

23. $5\frac{3}{25}$

To evaluate, first clear the exponent: $\left(\frac{11}{5}\right)^2 = \frac{121}{25}$. Then, multiply: $\frac{2}{5} \times \frac{7}{10} = \frac{\cancel{2}^{1}}{5} \times \frac{7}{\cancel{10}_{5}} = \frac{7}{25}$. Since the two terms have the same denominator, you can simply add them together: $\frac{7}{25} + \frac{121}{25} = \frac{128}{25} = 5\frac{3}{25}$.

24. $-\frac{43}{243}$

First, evaluate the expression in the numerator:

$$\frac{3}{8} + \frac{5}{6} - 3 = \frac{9}{24} + \frac{20}{24} - \frac{72}{24} = -\frac{43}{24}.$$

Then, evaluate the expression in the denominator:

$\frac{9}{2} - \frac{3}{8} + 6 = \frac{36}{8} - \frac{3}{8} + \frac{48}{8} = \frac{81}{8}$. Finally, perform the division:

$$-\frac{43}{24} \div \frac{81}{8} = -\frac{43}{24} \times \frac{8}{81} = -\frac{43}{\cancel{24}_{3}} \times \frac{\cancel{8}^{1}}{81} = -\frac{43}{243}.$$

25. $<$

Simplify $\frac{\frac{2}{5}}{\frac{2}{3}}$. Dividing by $\frac{2}{3}$ is the same as multiplying by $\frac{3}{2}$: $\frac{\cancel{2}^{1}}{5} \times \frac{3}{\cancel{2}_{1}} = \frac{3}{5}$.

Finally, compare: $\frac{3}{5} < \frac{5}{3}$.

26. $\mathbf{3\frac{67}{1,000}}$

The decimal part is 67 thousandths. Write as a mixed number. $3 + \frac{67}{1,000} = 3\frac{67}{1,000}$.

27. $\mathbf{\frac{10,805}{10,000}}$**, 1.085,** $\mathbf{1\frac{1}{7}}$**, 1.850**

Convert the fractions to decimals to compare: $\frac{10,805}{10,000} = 1.0805$ and $1\frac{1}{7} = 1.14286$.

Compare the ones place, then the tenths, then the hundredths, and then the thousandths.

28. $\mathbf{3\frac{16}{105}}$

First, convert mixed numbers to improper fractions and find a common denominator: $\frac{345}{105} + \frac{126}{105} - \frac{140}{105}$. Then, add and subtract numerators, $\frac{331}{105}$, and convert to a mixed number, $3\frac{16}{105}$.

29. 9.78

Evaluate the expressions inside the parentheses: $\frac{(1.9)^2}{0.95} - (-5.98)$. Calculate the exponent: $\frac{3.61}{0.95} - (-5.98)$. Divide: 3.8 – (–5.98). Finally, subtract: 9.78.

30. 22.6867

Evaluate the expression inside the parentheses: $(8.3) \times 3.28 \div 1.2$. Then, multiply and divide from left to right: $(8.3) \times 3.28 \div 1.2 = 27.224 \div 1.2 = 22.6867$.

NUMBER PROPERTIES

Number Line and Absolute Value

A **number line** is a straight line that extends infinitely in either direction, on which real numbers are represented as points.

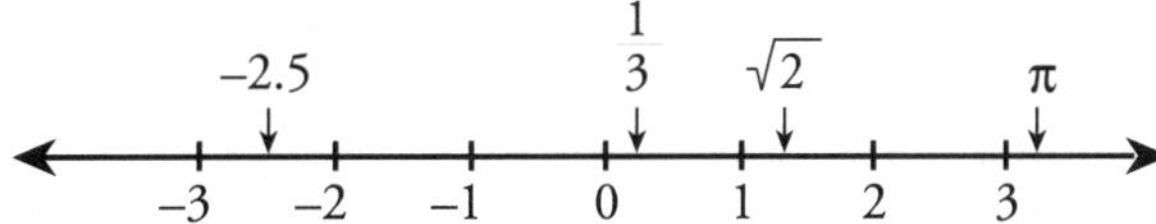

As you move to the right on a number line, the values increase.

Conversely, as you move to the left, the values decrease.

Zero separates the positive numbers (to the right of zero) and the negative numbers (to the left of zero) along the number line. Zero is neither positive nor negative.

The **absolute value** of a number is just the number without its sign. It is written as two vertical lines.

Example: $|-3| = |+3| = 3$

The absolute value can be thought of as the number's distance from zero on the number line; for instance, both +3 and −3 are 3 units from zero, so their absolute values are both 3.

Properties of −1, 0, 1, and Numbers in Between

Properties of zero: Adding or subtracting zero from a number does not change the number.

Example: $0 + x = x$; $2 + 0 = 2$; $4 - 0 = 4$

Any number multiplied by zero equals zero.

Example: $z \times 0 = 0$; $12 \times 0 = 0$

Division by zero is **undefined**. When given an algebraic expression, be sure that the denominator is not zero. $\frac{0}{0}$ is also undefined.

Properties of 1 and −1: Multiplying or dividing a number by 1 does not change the number.

Example: $x \div 1 = x$; $4 \times 1 = 4$; $-3 \times 1 = -3$

Multiplying or dividing a number by –1 changes the sign.

Example: $y \times (-1) = -y$; $6 \times (-1) = -6$; $-2 \div (-1) = -(-2) = 2$; $(x - y) \times (-1) = -x + y$

Note: The sum of a number and –1 times that number is equal to zero.

Example: $a + (-a) = 0$; $8 + (-8) = 0$;

The **reciprocal** of a number is 1 divided by the number. For a fraction, as we've already seen, the reciprocal can be found by just interchanging the denominator and the numerator. The product of a number and its reciprocal is 1. Zero has no reciprocal, since $\frac{1}{0}$ is undefined.

Properties of numbers between –1 and 1: The reciprocal of a number between 0 and 1 is greater than the number.

Example: The reciprocal of $\frac{2}{3} = \frac{1}{\frac{2}{3}} = \frac{3}{2} = 1\frac{1}{2}$, which is greater than $\frac{2}{3}$.

The reciprocal of a number between –1 and 0 is less than the number.

Example: The reciprocal of $-\frac{2}{3} = \frac{1}{\left(-\frac{2}{3}\right)} = -\frac{3}{2} = -1\frac{1}{2}$, which is less than $-\frac{2}{3}$.

The square of a number between 0 and 1 is less than the number.

Example: $\left(\frac{1}{2}\right)^2 = \frac{1}{2} \times \frac{1}{2} = \frac{1}{4}$, which is less than $\frac{1}{2}$.

Multiplying any positive number by a fraction between 0 and 1 gives a product smaller than the original number.

Example: $6 \times \frac{1}{4} = 1\frac{1}{2}$, which is less than 6.

Multiplying any negative number by a fraction between 0 and 1 gives a product greater than the original number.

Example: $-3 \times \frac{1}{6} = -\frac{1}{2}$, which is greater than –3.

All these properties can best be seen by observation rather than by memorization.

Operations with Signed Numbers

The ability to add and subtract signed numbers is best learned by practice and common sense.

Addition: Like signs: Add the absolute values and keep the same sign.

Example: $(-6) + (-3) = -9$

Unlike signs: Take the difference of the absolute values and keep the sign of the number with the larger absolute value.

Example: $(-7) + (+3) = -4$

Subtraction: Subtraction is the inverse operation of addition; subtracting a number is the same as adding its inverse. Subtraction is often easier if you change to addition by changing the sign of the number being subtracted. Then use the rules for addition of signed numbers.

Example: $(-5) - (-10) = (-5) + (+10) = +5$

Multiplication and division: The product or the quotient of two numbers with the same sign is positive.

Example: $(-2) \times (-5) = +10; \frac{-50}{-5} = +10$

The product or the quotient of two numbers with opposite signs is negative.

Example: $(-2)(+3) = -6; \frac{-6}{2} = -3$

Odd and Even

Odd and even apply only to integers. There are no odd or even noninteger numbers. Put simply, even numbers are integers that are divisible by 2, and odd numbers are integers that are not divisible by 2. Another easy way to classify an integer as even or odd is to check its last digit. If an integer's last digit is either 0, 2, 4, 6, or 8, the integer is even; if its last digit is 1, 3, 5, 7, or 9, it is odd. Odd and even numbers may be negative.

A number needs just a single factor of 2 to be even, so the product of an even number and **any** integer will always be even.

Rules for Odds and Evens:

Odd ± Odd = Even	Odd × Odd = Odd
Even ± Even = Even	Even × Even = Even
Odd ± Even = Odd	Odd × Even = Even

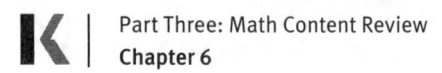

You can easily establish these rules when you need them by picking sample numbers.

Example: $3 + 5 = 8$, so the sum of any two odd numbers is even.

Example: $\frac{4}{2} = 2$, but $\frac{6}{2} = 3$, so the quotient of two even numbers could be odd or even (or a fraction!)

FACTORS, PRIMES, AND DIVISIBILITY

Multiples: An integer that is divisible by another integer is a **multiple** of that integer.

Example: 12 is a multiple of 3, since 12 is divisible by 3; $3 \times 4 = 12$.

Remainders: The remainder is what is left over in a division problem. A remainder is always smaller than the number we are dividing by.

Example: 17 divided by 3 is 5, with a remainder of 2.

Factors: The **factors**, or **divisors**, of a number are the positive integers that evenly divide into that number.

Example: 36 has nine factors: 1, 2, 3, 4, 6, 9, 12, 18, and 36.

We can group these factors in pairs:

$1 \times 36 = 2 \times 18 = 3 \times 12 = 4 \times 9 = 6 \times 6$

The **greatest common factor**, or **greatest common divisor**, of a pair of numbers is the largest factor shared by the two numbers.

Divisibility tests: There are several tests to determine whether a number is divisible by 2, 3, 4, 5, 6, and 9.

A number is divisible by 2 if its last digit is divisible by 2.

Example: 138 is divisible by 2 because 8 is divisible by 2.

A number is divisible by 3 if the **sum** of its digits is divisible by 3.

Example: 4,317 is divisible by 3 because $4 + 3 + 1 + 7 = 15$, and 15 is divisible by 3.

239 is **not** divisible by 3 because $2 + 3 + 9 = 14$, and 14 is not divisible by 3.

A number is divisible by 4 if its last two digits are divisible by 4.

Example: 1,748 is divisible by 4 because 48 is divisible by 4.

A number is divisible by 5 if its last digit is 0 or 5.

Example: 2,635 is divisible by 5. 5,052 is **not** divisible by 5.

A number is divisible by 6 if it is divisible by both 2 and 3.

Example: 4,326 is divisible by 6 because it is divisible by 2 (last digit is 6) and by 3 ($4 + 3 + 2 + 6 = 15$).

A number is divisible by 9 if the sum of its digits is divisible by 9.

Example: 22,428 is divisible by 9 because $2 + 2 + 4 + 2 + 8 = 18$, and 18 is divisible by 9.

A number is divisible by 10 if its last digit is 0.

Example: 790 is divisible by 10. 8,431 is not.

A number is divisible by 12 if it is divisible by both 3 and 4.

Example: 21,528 is divisible by 12 because it is divisible by 3 ($2 + 1 + 5 + 2 + 8 = 18$) and by 4 (last two digits are 28).

Prime number: A **prime** number is an integer greater than 1 that has no factors other than 1 and itself. The number 1 is not considered prime. The number 2 is the first prime number and the only even prime. (Do you see why? Any other even number has 2 as a factor, and therefore is not prime.) The first ten prime numbers are 2, 3, 5, 7, 11, 13, 17, 19, 23, 29.

Prime factorization: The **prime factorization** of a number is the expression of the number as the product of its prime factors. No matter how you factor a number, its prime factors will always be the same.

Example: $36 = 6 \times 6 = 2 \times 3 \times 2 \times 3$ or $2 \times 2 \times 3 \times 3$ or $2^2 \times 3^2$

Example:

$$\begin{aligned} 480 &= 48 \times 10 = 8 \times 6 \times 2 \times 5 \\ &= 2 \times 4 \times 2 \times 3 \times 2 \times 5 \\ &= 2 \times 2 \times 2 \times 2 \times 3 \times 2 \times 5 \\ &= 2^5 \times 3 \times 5 \end{aligned}$$

The easiest way to determine a number's prime factorization is to figure out a pair of factors of the number, and then determine their factors, continuing the process until you're left with only prime numbers. Those primes will be the prime factorization.

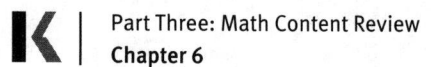

Example: Find the prime factorization of 1,050.

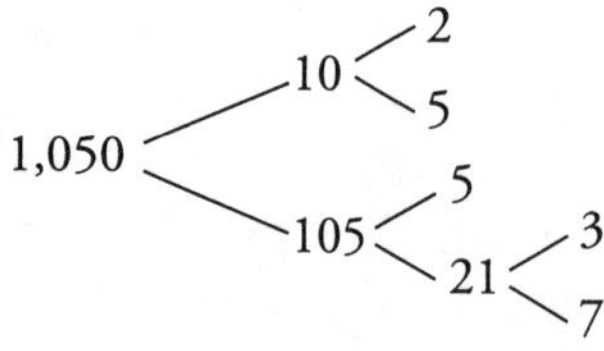

So the prime factorization of 1,050 is $2 \times 3 \times 5^2 \times 7$.

Consecutive Numbers

A list of numbers is **consecutive** if the numbers either occur at a fixed interval, or exhibit a fixed pattern. All the consecutive numbers you will encounter on the GRE are integers. Consecutive numbers could be in ascending **or** descending order.

Example: 1, 2, 3, 4, 5, 6 . . . is a series of consecutive positive integers.

Example: −6, −4, −2, 0, 2, 4 . . . is a series of consecutive even numbers.

Example: 5, 7, 11, 13, 17, 19 . . . is a series of consecutive prime numbers.

NUMBER PROPERTIES EXERCISES

BASIC

1. Evaluate (–7) + (–4 + 3).

2. Which of the following numbers is divisible by 7: 43, 51, 56, 58?

3. Which is greater: |–6| or –6?

For Exercises 4 and 5, use your knowledge of number properties to determine if the values will be odd or even.

4. The product of an even number and an odd number.

5. The sum of two odd numbers.

6. What is the greatest integer that will divide evenly into both 48 and 60?

7. The following list contains all the factors of what number: 1, 2, 3, 5, 6, 10, 15, 30?

8. The prime factorization of a number contains exactly five 2s and one 3 and no other numbers. What is the number?

9. What is the smallest positive integer divisible by both 18 and 7?

10. What are the next 3 consecutive integers in this arithmetic sequence: –5, 5, 15, 25?

INTERMEDIATE

11. Which is greater: |6| or |–7|?

12. Find all numbers between 70 and 90 that are evenly divisible by 8.

For Exercises 13 and 14, use your knowledge of number properties to determine if the values will be odd or even.

13. The sum of four odd numbers.

14. The product of two even numbers multiplied by one odd number.

15. What is the greatest number that is less than 153 and is also divisible by 3 and 7?

16. The sum of a set of 3 consecutive even integers is 102. What is the sum of the 3 consecutive odd integers that precede the lowest number in that set?

17. True or false? If n is an integer, $2n + 2$ will always be even.

18. Which of the following numbers are divisible by 6: 168, 273, 348, 434?

For Exercises 19 and 20, find the number's prime factorization.

19. 208

20. 52^2

ADVANCED

21. Which expression is greater: $|(-6) + (-3)|$ or $(-3)(-3)(-1)$?

22. $200 \leq x \leq 300$. How many values of x are divisible by both 5 and 8?

For Exercises 23 and 24, use your knowledge of number properties to determine if the values will be odd or even.

23. The difference between an even number and an odd number, squared.

24. The sum of two odd numbers plus the product of an even number times an odd number.

25. What number between 70 and 75, inclusive, has the greatest number of factors?

26. What are the smallest three prime numbers greater than 65?

27. What is the smallest number that can be written as the product of three distinct prime factors?

28. True or false? The product of three consecutive integers is always even.

29. How many positive integers between 21 and 59 are equal to the product of a multiple of 4 and an odd number?

30. What is the prime factorization of $18^4 \times 6$?

NUMBER PROPERTIES EXERCISES ANSWER KEY

BASIC

1. –8

First, evaluate the expressions inside parentheses from left to right: $(-7) + (-1)$. Then, add.

2. 56

The product of 7 and 8 is 56, so 56 is divisible by 7.

3. |–6|

The absolute value of -6 is 6. Since 6 is greater than -6, $|-6| > -6$.

4. Even

The product of an even number and an odd number is an even number.

5. Even

The sum of two odd numbers is an even number.

6. 12

Use prime factorization to determine the greatest common factor of two numbers: $48 = 2 \times 2 \times 2 \times 2 \times 3$ and $60 = 2 \times 2 \times 3 \times 5$. Their common factors are 2, 2, and 3, so the greatest common factor is $2 \times 2 \times 3 = 12$.

7. 30

Every number is a factor of itself, and by definition a number itself is its greatest factor. Since this list contains every factor of the number, the largest number in the list must be the right answer to the question. The largest number in this list is 30.

8. 96

The prime factorization is the expression of a number as the product of its prime factors. A prime factorization that contains five 2s and one 3 is the expression $2 \times 2 \times 2 \times 2 \times 2 \times 3$, which equals 96.

9. 126

Find the least common multiple, or LCM, of the numbers. In this case the LCM is the product of the two factors, because 7 is a prime number and it isn't a factor of 18.

10. 35, 45, 55

This sequence is created by adding 10 to the previous number. Following this pattern, the next 3 integers will be 35, 45, and 55.

Intermediate

11. |–7|

The absolute value of 6 is 6, and the absolute value of –7 is 7. Since 7 is greater than 6, $|6| < |-7|$.

12. 72, 80, 88

To be divisible by 8, the quotient must divide evenly. Start at 70 and increase by 2 (as any number evenly divisible by an even number must be even), and determine if the number is divisible by 8. Since 72 is divisible by 8, start here. Then, the next numbers will each be 8 greater than the last: $72 + 8 = 80$, and $80 + 8 = 88$.

13. Even

Two odd numbers added together produce an even number. Twice that amount of odd numbers (or four odd numbers) will also produce an even number. In fact, any even number of odd numbers, added together, will yield an even number.

14. Even

The product of two even numbers is an even number. Then the product of an odd number and an even number will be an even number.

15. 147

A number that is divisible by both 3 and 7 is divisible by $3 \times 7 = 21$. Find the largest number less than 153 that is divisible by 21. It is 147.

16. 87

If numbers are evenly spaced and added together, the average is the median of those numbers. 102 divided by 3 is 34, so the three numbers in the original list are $32 + 34 + 36 = 102$. The three consecutive odd integers that come before 32 are 27, 29 and 31, which add up to 87.

Alternatively, use algebra to find the least of the even integers. If n is the least of the even integers, then the next two even integers are $n + 2$ and $n + 4$. $n + n + 2 + n + 4 = 102$. Combine like terms and solve for n: $3n + 6 = 102$, and $n = 32$.

17. True

The product of an even number and any other number is also even. Therefore, the product of $2n$ will always be even. Then, the sum of two even numbers is even, so adding 2 to that even number will result in an even number.

18. 168, 348

Use the divisibility rules to find the numbers that are divisible by the prime factors of 6: 2 and 3. Of the numbers in the list, 168 and 348 are even numbers, so they are divisible by 2, and the sum of their digits produces a number that is divisible by 3.

19. $2 \times 2 \times 2 \times 2 \times 13$

The prime factorization is the expression of a number as the product of its prime factors.

20. $2 \times 2 \times 13 \times 2 \times 2 \times 13$

First, find the prime factorization of the base number, 52: $52 = 2 \times 2 \times 13$. The question asks for the prime factorization of 52^2, so square the prime factorization (repeat each number in it) to get the final answer.

Advanced

21. $|(-6) + (-3)|$

Evaluate each expression according to the rules of operations with signed numbers. The expression $|(-6) + (-3)| = |-9| = 9$, and the expression $(-3)(-3)(-1) = (9)(-1) = -9$. And 9 is greater than −9, so $|(-6) + (-3)| > (-3)(-3)(-1)$.

22. 3

Any number divisible by 8 and 5 is divisible by 8×5, since 5 is prime and not a factor of 8. Also, $8 \times 5 = 40$ is a factor of 200, the smallest number in *x*'s range. Add 40 to 200 to find the next number in the series, 240, then 40 again for 280. The next number that is a multiple of 40 after 280 is larger than 300, the top of the range. This means 200, 240, and 280 are divisible by 8 and 5.

23. Odd

The difference is an odd number because an even minus an odd is odd, and then an odd number raised to any power remains odd, so the square of an odd number is odd.

24. Even

The sum of two odd numbers is an even number, and the product of an even number and an odd number is an even number. Finally, the sum of two even numbers is an even number.

25. 72

There are 12 factors of 72: 1, 2, 3, 4, 6, 8, 9, 12, 18, 24, 36, and 72. Each of the other numbers in the list has fewer factors than does 72.

70: 1, 2, 5, 7, 10, 14, 35, 70

71: 1, 71

73: 1, 73

74: 1, 2, 37, 74

75: 1, 3, 5, 15, 25, 75

26. 67, 71, 73

A prime number is one that is divisible only by 1 and itself. The smallest three numbers greater than 65 that are prime are 67, 71, and 73.

27. 30

Consider the smallest prime numbers. The number 2 is the smallest (and the only even) prime number. So the smallest prime factors are 2, 3, and 5: $2 \times 3 \times 5 = 30$.

28. True

Three consecutive numbers must include at least one even number. If an even number is multiplied by any other integer, the product must be even. You can also Pick Numbers to see that this will always work.

29. 9

The first few multiples of 4 are 4, 8, 12, 16, and 20. The multiples of 4 that are between 21 and 59 are 24, 28, 32, 36, 40, 44, 48, 52, and 56. These can each be written as the product of a multiple of 4 and an odd number as follows:

$24 = 8 \times 3$

$28 = 4 \times 7$

$32 = 32 \times 1$

$36 = 12 \times 3 = 4 \times 9$

$40 = 8 \times 5$

$44 = 4 \times 11$

$48 = 16 \times 3$

$52 = 4 \times 13$

$56 = 8 \times 7$

30. $2 \times 2 \times 2 \times 2 \times 2 \times 3 \times 3 \times 3 \times 3 \times 3 \times 3 \times 3 \times 3 \times 3$, $2^5 \times 3^9$

The prime factorization of 18 is $2 \times 3 \times 3$. This shows up 4 times in the prime factorization of $18^4 \times 6$ because 18 is raised to the 4th power. Then, multiply this by the prime factorization of 6, 3×2, resulting in $(2 \times 3 \times 3) \times (2 \times 3 \times 3) \times (2 \times 3 \times 3) \times (2 \times 3 \times 3) \times (2 \times 3)$.

AVERAGES (ARITHMETIC MEANS)

The average (arithmetic mean) of a group of numbers is defined as the sum of the values divided by the number of values.

$$\text{Average value} = \frac{\text{Sum of values}}{\text{Number of values}}$$

Example: Henry buys three items costing \$2.00, \$0.75, and \$0.25. What is the average price?

$$\text{Average price} = \frac{\text{Sum of prices}}{\text{Number of prices}} = \frac{\text{Total price}}{\text{Total items}} = \frac{\$2.00 + \$0.75 + \$0.25}{3}$$

$$= \frac{\$3.00}{3} = \$1.00$$

On the GRE you might see a reference to the median. If a group of numbers is arranged in numerical order, the median is the middle value. For instance, the median of the numbers 4, 5, 100, 1, and 6 is 5. The median can be quite different from the average. For instance, in the example shown, the average was \$1.00, while the median is simply the middle of the three prices given, or \$0.75.

If we know the average of a group of numbers, and the number of numbers in the group, we can find the **sum** of the numbers. It's as if all the numbers in the group have the average value.

$$\text{Sum of values} = \text{Average value} \times \text{Number of values}$$

Example: The average daily temperature for the first week in January was 31 degrees. If the average temperature for the first six days was 30 degrees, what was the temperature on the seventh day?

The sum for all 7 days $= 31 \times 7 = 217$ degrees.

The sum of the first six days $= 30 \times 6 = 180$ degrees.

The temperature on the seventh day $= 217 - 180 = 37$ degrees.

For evenly spaced numbers, the average is the middle value. The average of consecutive integers 6, 7, and 8 is 7. The average of 5, 10, 15, and 20 is $12\frac{1}{2}$ (midway between the middle values 10 and 15).

It might be useful to try and think of the average as the "balanced" value. That is, all the numbers below the average are less than the average by an amount that will "balance out" the amount that the numbers above the average are greater than the average. For example, the average of 3, 5, and 10 is 6. 3 is 3 less than 6 and 5 is 1 less than 6. This, in total, is 4, which is the same as the amount that 10 is greater than 6.

Example: The average of 3, 4, 5, and x is 5. What is the value of x?

Think of each value in terms of its position relative to the average, 5.

3 is 2 less than the average.

4 is 1 less than the average.

5 is at the average.

So these 3 terms together are $1 + 2 + 0$, or 3, less than the average. Therefore, x must be 3 **more** than the average, to restore the balance at 5. So x is $3 + 5$ or 8.

AVERAGE RATE (AVERAGE *A* PER *B*)

$$\textbf{Average } A \textbf{ per } B = \frac{\textbf{Total } A}{\textbf{Total } B}$$

Example: John travels 30 miles in 2 hours and then 60 miles in 3 hours. What is his average speed in miles per hour?

$$\begin{aligned}\text{Average miles per hour} &= \frac{\text{Total miles}}{\text{Total hours}}\\ &= \frac{(30 + 60)\text{ miles}}{(2 + 3)\text{ hours}}\\ &= \frac{90\text{ miles}}{5\text{ hours}}\\ &= 18\text{ miles/hour}\end{aligned}$$

AVERAGES (ARITHMETIC MEANS) EXERCISES

Basic

1. What is the average of $\frac{1}{3}$ and $\frac{1}{2}$?

2. What is the average of 5, 10, 50, and 100?

3. What is the value of x if the average of 3, 7, 8, and x is 6?

4. What is the value of x if the average of −6, 4, 10, and x is 2?

5. If the average of 7, 5, 14, 9, and x is 9, what is the value of x?

6. What is the average of $\frac{1}{4}, \frac{1}{5}, \frac{1}{20}$, and $\frac{1}{2}$?

7. The average of six numbers is 8. If 2 is subtracted from three of the numbers, what is the new average?

8. Deonte travels 72 miles in 3 hours and then 84 miles in 3 hours. What is his average speed for the whole trip in miles per hour?

9. What is the average of $\frac{4}{3}, \frac{2}{3}$, and 3?

10. What is the average of −12, 4, 15, and −25?

Intermediate

11. What is the sum of the five consecutive even numbers whose average (arithmetic mean) is 20?

12. What is the average of y, $y + 2$, $y + 4$, and $y + 6$ in terms of y?

13. If the average of 32, 5, 11, and n is 21, then what is the sum of $32 + 5 + 11 + n$?

14. What is the sum of the five consecutive even numbers whose average is 12?

15. Five bakeries sell an average of 300 muffins per bakery per day. If two of the bakeries stop making muffins, but the total number of muffins sold stays the same, what is the average number of muffins sold per bakery among the remaining bakeries?

16. What is the sum of the five consecutive odd numbers whose average is 75?

17. The average of r and s is 40. If $t = 10$, what is the average of r, s, and t?

18. If the average of 5 consecutive integers is 14, what is the sum of the least and greatest of the 5 integers?

19. If the average of 7 consecutive even integers is 44, what is the sum of the integers?

20. On three consecutive passes, a football team gains 5 yards, loses 33 yards, and gains 25 yards. How many yards must the team gain on the next pass to have an average gain of 3 yards?

Advanced

21. If 20 students in one class had an average grade of 94% and 18 students from another class had an average grade of 92%, what is the average grade for all 38 students across both classes? Round to the nearest hundredth.

22. Ashley's scores on five math tests are 84, 100, 88, 95, and 92. What does she need to score on the next test for her final average on all the tests to be at least 92?

23. Rob has received scores of 96, 89, and 85 on 3 quizzes. If the exam is weighted twice as heavily as each of the three quizzes, what is the lowest score Rob can get on the exam to have a final average of at least 90?

24. If the average of 5 consecutive integers is 15, what is the sum of the least and greatest of the 5 integers?

25. The Ryder family traveled at an average rate of 60 miles per hour (mph), and it took 10 hours to complete their trip. If they traveled for 4 of their 10 hours at a constant speed of 70 miles per hour, at what average speed did they travel for the remaining 6 hours to obtain the 60 miles per hour average for the entire trip?

26. If the average of 10 consecutive odd integers is 224, what is the least of these integers?

27. The average of five numbers is 30. After one of the numbers is removed, the average arithmetic mean of the remaining numbers is 32. What number was removed?

28. The table shows the closing price of a stock during one week. If the average (arithmetic mean) closing price for the five days was $32.88, what was the closing price on Friday?

Monday	$32.59
Tuesday	$33.62
Wednesday	$30.78
Thursday	$35.23
Friday	?

29. Two airplanes leave the same airport at the same time, one traveling west and the other east. Their average speeds differ by 10 miles per hour. After 1.5 hours, they are 520 miles apart. What is the approximate average speed of each plane over the 1.5 hours? Round to the nearest tenth.

30. If the average (arithmetic mean) of $a + b$ is n, what is the average of a, b, and c in terms of n and c?

AVERAGES (ARITHMETIC MEANS) EXERCISES ANSWER KEY

BASIC

1. $\mathbf{\frac{5}{12}}$

Find the sum of the values: $\frac{1}{2} + \frac{1}{3} = \frac{3}{6} + \frac{2}{6} = \frac{5}{6}$. Then divide by the number of values: $\frac{5}{6} \div 2 = \frac{5}{6} \times \frac{1}{2} = \frac{5}{12}$.

2. 41.25 or $41\frac{1}{4}$

Find the sum of the values: $5 + 10 + 50 + 100 = 165$. Then divide by the number of values: $165 \div 4 = 41.25$ or $41\frac{1}{4}$.

3. 6

Think of each value in terms of its position relative to the average, 6:

3 is 3 less than the average.
7 is 1 more than the average.
8 is 2 more than the average.

So these 3 terms together are $-3 + 1 + 2$, or 0 more than the average. Therefore x must equal the average. So x is 6.

Alternatively, if the average of the four numbers is 6, then their sum must be $4 \times 6 = 24$. Then $24 - (3 + 7 + 8) = 6$. The unknown value, x, equals 6.

4. 0

Think of each value in terms of its position relative to the average, 2:

−6 is 8 less than the average.
4 is 2 more than the average.
10 is 8 more than the average.

So, these 3 terms together are $-8 + 2 + 8$, or 2 more than the average. Therefore, x must be 2 less than the average to restore the balance at 2. So x is $2 - 2$, or 0.

Alternatively, if the average of the four numbers is 2, then their sum must be $4 \times 2 = 8$. Then $8 - (-6 + 4 + 10) = 0$. The unknown value, x, equals 0.

5. 10

Think of each value in terms of its position relative to the average, 9:

7 is 2 less than the average.
5 is 4 less than the average.

14 is 5 more than the average.

9 is 0 more than the average.

So, these 4 terms together are $-2 + -4 + 5 + 0$, or 1 less than the average. Therefore, x must be 1 more than the average to restore the balance at 9. So x is $1 + 9$ or 10.

Alternatively, if the average of the five numbers is 9, then their sum must be $5 \times 9 = 45$. Then $45 - (7 + 5 + 14 + 9) = 10$. The unknown value, x, equals 10.

6. $\mathbf{\frac{1}{4}}$

Find the sum of the values: $\frac{1}{4} + \frac{1}{5} + \frac{1}{20} + \frac{1}{2} = \frac{5}{20} + \frac{4}{20} + \frac{1}{20} + \frac{10}{20} = \frac{20}{20} = 1$.

Then divide by the number of values: $1 \div 4 = \frac{1}{4}$.

7. 7

The average of six numbers is 8. While we don't know the individual values, we can multiply $6 \times 8 = 48$ to get the original total of the numbers. If 2 is subtracted from each of three numbers, $2 \times 3 = 6$ was subtracted from the original total, leaving $48 - 6 = 42$. The new average is $42 \div 6 = 7$.

8. 26

Use the equation total miles $\div$ total hours $=$ average miles per hour. Total miles $= 72 + 84 = 156$ miles and total hours $= 3 + 3 = 6$ hours. Divide: 156 miles $\div$ 6 hours $=$ 26 miles per hour. Deonte's average speed is 26 miles per hour.

9. $\mathbf{1\frac{2}{3}}$

Find the sum of the values: $\frac{4}{3} + \frac{2}{3} + 3 = \frac{4}{3} + \frac{2}{3} + \frac{9}{3} = \frac{15}{3} = 5$. Then divide 5 by the number of values: $5 \div 3 = \frac{5}{3} = 1\frac{2}{3}$.

10. $\mathbf{-4.5}$ **or** $\mathbf{-4\frac{1}{2}}$

Find the sum of the values: $-12 + 4 + 15 + -25 = -18$. Then divide by the number of values: $-18 \div 4 = -4.5$.

INTERMEDIATE

11. 100

If the average is 20 and there are 5 terms, the sum of the terms is $20 \times 5 = 100$. There is no need to determine all the individual values in the set.

12. $y + 3$

Find the sum of the values: $y + y + 2 + y + 4 + y + 6 = 4y + 12$. Then divide by the number of values: $\frac{4y + 12}{4} = y + 3$.

13. 84

If you know the average of a set of terms and you know how many terms there are, you can multiply the two together to get the total of all the terms: $21 \times 4 = 84$. In this case, the sum of the values is 84.

14. 60

If the average is 12 and there are 5 terms, the sum of the terms is $12 \times 5 = 60$. There is no need to determine all the individual values in the set.

15. 500

Originally, five bakeries sold an average of 300 muffins each day, which equals $5 \times 300 = 1{,}500$ total muffins per day.

If two bakeries drop out but the total number of muffins stays the same, the 1,500 muffins will be made by only $5 - 2 = 3$ bakeries. Divide the 1,500 by 3 to find the average for the 3 bakeries: $1{,}500 \div 3 = 500$.

So the average number of muffins sold per bakery among the remaining bakeries is 500.

16. 375

If the average is 75 and there are 5 terms, the sum of the terms is $75 \times 5 = 375$. There is no need to determine all the individual values in the set.

17. 30

If you know the average of a set of terms and you know how many terms there are, you can multiply the average and the number of terms together to get the total. In this case, the average is 40 and the number of terms is 2, so the total for $r + s$ is $40 \times 2 = 80$. If $t = 10$, then $r + s + t = 80 + 10 = 90$. Therefore, the average of r, s, and t is $\frac{r + s + t}{3} = \frac{90}{3} = 30$.

18. 28

The arithmetic mean of 5 evenly spaced integers is the middle number in the set. The sum of the least and the greatest integers is twice the average, or in this case, $2 \times 14 = 28$. There is no need to know the specific numbers in the set.

19. 308

If the average is 44 and there are 7 terms, the sum of the terms is $44 \times 7 = 308$. There is no need to determine all the individual values in the set.

20. 15

To have an average of 3 yards over 4 plays, the total yards gained must equal 12 yards ($3 \times 4 = 12$). If $y =$ the number of yards gained on the last play, $5 - 33 + 25 + y = 12$. Solving for y, $-3 + y = 12$, and $y = 15$. So the team must gain 15 yards on the next pass to have an average gain of 3 yards.

Alternatively, you can use the balancing method:

To get to the average:

5 yards must lose 2

–33 must gain 36

25 must lose 22

Add ($-2 + 36 - 22$) to the average of 3 to find that the next pass must gain 15 yards to get an average of 3.

Advanced

21. 93.05%

If 20 students averaged 94, then the total number of points they scored is $20 \times 94 = 1{,}880$. If 18 students averaged 92, then the total number of points they scored is $18 \times 92 = 1{,}656$. So, the total number of points scored for the group is $1{,}880 + 1{,}656 = 3{,}536$. Divide the total number of points by the total number of students ($20 + 18 = 38$): $\frac{3{,}536}{38} \approx 93.05\%$. The average, rounded to the nearest hundredth, is 93.05%.

22. 93

The easiest way to solve a problem like this one is to use the balancing method. Determine how many points each of the actual scores must gain or lose to get to the average, then add that to the average to get your solution. In this case:

84 must gain 8

100 must lose 8

88 must gain 4

95 must lose 3

92 doesn't have to gain or lose

Add ($8 - 8 + 4 - 3$) to 92, for a required score of 93 on the next test to have at least a 92 average.

Alternatively, call the missing score x and solve algebraically using the fact that the sum of the tests divided by the number of tests is the average.

$$
\begin{aligned}
\frac{84 + 100 + 88 + 95 + 92 + x}{6} &\geq 92 \\
\frac{459 + x}{6} &\geq 92 \\
(6)\left(\frac{459 + x}{6}\right) &\geq 6(92) \\
459 + x &\geq 552 \\
x &\geq 552 - 459 \\
x &\geq 93
\end{aligned}
$$

Ashley needs to score at least a 93 on the next test to have at least a 92 average overall.

23. 90

The sum of the tests divided by the number of tests is the average. Because the exam counts twice as much as the quizzes, it is included two times.

The easiest way to solve a problem like this one is to use the balancing method. Determine how many points each of the actual scores must gain or lose to get to the average, then add that to the average to get your solution. In this case:

96 must lose 6

89 must gain 1

85 must gain 5

Since $-6 + 1 + 5 = 0$, Rob already has an average of 90, so he can get a score as low as 90 on his final exam to maintain at least that average.

If you prefer to "do the math":

$$
\begin{aligned}
\frac{96 + 89 + 85 + x + x}{5} &= 90 \\
\frac{270 + 2x}{5} &= 90 \\
(5)\left(\frac{270 + 2x}{5}\right) &= 5(90) \\
270 + 2x &= 450 \\
2x &= 450 - 270 \\
2x &= 180 \\
x &= 90
\end{aligned}
$$

Rob needs to score at least 90 on the exam.

24. 30

The sum of two numbers at an equal distance from the middle number will be twice their average. In this case, the average is 15, so the sum of the smallest and largest numbers is $2 \times 15 = 30$. There is no need to know the specific numbers in the set.

25. $53\frac{1}{3}$ mph

Use the distance formula: distance = rate × time. Find how many miles the Ryder family traveled: total distance = 60 mph × 10 hours = 600 miles. Next find how many of the 600 miles were traveled at 70 mph: d = 70 mph × 4 hours = 280 miles. Subtract to find the remaining number of miles traveled at an unknown speed: 600 − 280 = 320. Now, use the rate formula to determine the miles per hour, rate $= \frac{\text{distance}}{\text{time}}$. In this case, mph $= \frac{320 \text{ miles}}{6 \text{ hours}} = 53\frac{1}{3}$ mph.

The Ryder family traveled at an average of $53\frac{1}{3}$ miles per hour for the remaining 6 hours of the trip.

26. 215

For a set of numbers that are evenly spaced, the average is the same as the middle (median) of the numbers. If 224 is the average of an even number of evenly spaced odd numbers, half the terms are less than the average. To find the smallest number in the 10-number set, count down 5 odd numbers below 224: 223, 221, 219, 217, 215.

The least of these integers is 215.

27. 22

While you don't know the individual values, you can multiply the number of values times the average, or 5 × 30 = 150, to get the original total of the numbers. If one of the numbers is removed and the new average is 32, then the new total for the four remaining values is 4 × 32 = 128. Subtract the sum of four numbers from the sum of five numbers to find the value of the number that was removed: 150 − 128 = 22.

28. $32.18

Even with daunting numbers like these, the easiest way to solve a problem like this one is to use the balancing method. Determine how much money each of the prices must gain or lose to get to the average, then add that to the average to get your solution. In this case:

$32.59 must gain $0.29

$33.62 must lose $0.74

$30.78 must gain $2.10

$35.23 must lose $2.35

This means the final closing price must be (0.29 − 0.74 + 2.10 − 2.35) plus the average of $32.88, or $32.18.

To use algebra to solve the problem, let x = Friday's price. The sum of the values ÷ number of days = average price.

$$\frac{32.59 + 33.62 + 30.78 + 35.23 + x}{5} = 32.88$$
$$\frac{132.22 + x}{5} = 32.88$$
$$132.22 + x = 164.4$$
$$x = 32.18$$

The closing price on Friday was $32.18.

29. 168.3 mph, 178.3 mph

To solve this problem, let $x =$ speed of one plane and $x + 10 =$ speed of other plane. To travel the distance the two planes are apart from each other, add the distance traveled by the slow one (1.5 hours times its rate, x) to the distance traveled by the faster plane (1.5 hours times its rate, $x + 10$).

$$1.5x + 1.5(x + 10) = 520$$
$$1.5x + 1.5x + 15 = 520$$
$$3x = 520 - 15$$
$$3x = 505$$
$$x = 168.3 \text{ mph}$$
$$x + 10 = 168.3 + 10 = 178.3 \text{ mph}$$

30. $\mathbf{\dfrac{2n + c}{3}}$

Find the average of a and b, and simplify to find the value of $a + b$:

$$\frac{a + b}{2} = n$$
$$a + b = 2n$$

Find the average of a, b, and c by substituting the value of $a + b$: $\frac{a + b + c}{3} = \frac{2n + c}{3}$.

RATIOS

A ratio is a comparison of two quantities by division.

Ratios may be written with a fraction bar $\left(\frac{x}{y}\right)$, a colon (x:y), or English terms (ratio of x to y). We recommend the first way, since ratios can be treated as fractions for the purposes of computation.

Ratios can (and in most cases, should) be reduced to lowest terms just as fractions are reduced.

Example: Joe is 16 years old and Mary is 12.

The ratio of Joe's age to Mary's age is $\frac{16}{12}$. (Read "16 to 12.")

$\frac{16}{12} = \frac{4}{3}$ or 4:3

In a ratio of two numbers, the numerator is often associated with the word *of*; the denominator with the word *to*.

The ratio **of** 3 **to** 4 is $\frac{\text{of } 3}{\text{to } 4} = \frac{3}{4}$.

$$\textbf{Ratio} = \frac{\textbf{of...}}{\textbf{to...}}$$

Example: In a box of doughnuts, 12 are sugar and 18 are chocolate. What is the ratio of sugar doughnuts to chocolate doughnuts?

$$\text{Ratio} = \frac{\text{of sugar}}{\text{to chocolate}} = \frac{12}{18} = \frac{2}{3}$$

We frequently deal with ratios by working with a **proportion**. A proportion is simply an equation in which two ratios are set equal to one another.

Ratios typically deal with "parts" and "wholes." The whole is the entire set; for instance, all the workers in a factory. The part is a certain section of the whole; for instance, the female workers in the factory.

The ratio of a part to a whole is usually called a fraction. "What fraction of the workers are female?" means the same thing as "What is the ratio of the number of female workers to the total number of workers?"

A fraction can represent the ratio of a part to a whole:

$\frac{\text{Part}}{\text{Whole}}$ or Part : Whole.

Example: There are 15 men and 20 women in a class. What fraction of the students are female?

$$\begin{aligned} \text{Fraction} &= \frac{\text{Part}}{\text{Whole}} \\ &= \frac{\text{Number of female students}}{\text{Total number of students}} \\ &= \frac{20}{15 + 20} \\ &= \frac{\cancel{20}^{4}}{\cancel{35}_{7}} \\ &= \frac{4}{7} \end{aligned}$$

This means that $\frac{4}{7}$ of the students are female, 4 out of every 7 students are female, or the ratio of female students to total students is 4:7.

Part:Part Ratios and Part:Whole Ratios

A ratio can compare either a part to another part or a part to a whole. One type of ratio can readily be converted to the other **if** all the parts together equal the whole and there is no overlap among the parts (that is, if the whole is equal to the sum of its parts).

Example: The ratio of domestic sales to foreign sales of a certain product is 3:5. What fraction of the total sales are domestic sales? (Note: This is the same as asking for the ratio of the amount of domestic sales to the amount of total sales.)

In this case, the whole (total sales) is equal to the sum of the parts (domestic and foreign sales). We can convert from a **part:part** ratio to a **part:whole** ratio.

Of every 8 sales of the product, 3 are domestic and 5 are foreign. The ratio of domestic sales to total sales is $\frac{3}{8}$ or 3:8.

Example: The ratio of domestic to foreign sales of a certain product is 3:5. What is the ratio of domestic sales to European sales?

Here we cannot convert from a **part:whole** ratio (domestic sales:total sales) to a **part:part** ratio (domestic sales:European sales) because we don't know if there are any other sales besides domestic and European sales. The question doesn't say that the product is sold only domestically and in Europe, so we cannot assume there are no African, Australian, Asian, etc., sales, and so the ratio asked for here cannot be determined.

Ratios with more than two terms: Ratios involving more than two terms are governed by the same principles. These ratios contain more relationships, so they convey more information than two-term ratios. Ratios involving more than two terms are usually ratios of various parts, and it is usually the case that the sum of these parts does equal the whole, which makes it possible to find **part:whole** ratios as well.

Example: Given that the ratio of men to women to children in a room is 4:3:2, what other ratios can be determined?

Quite a few. The **whole** here is the number of people in the room, and since every person is either a man, a woman, or a child, we can determine **part:whole** ratios for each of these parts. Of every nine $(4 + 3 + 2)$ people in the room, 4 are men, 3 are women, and 2 are children. This gives us three **part:whole** ratios:

$$\text{Ratio of men:total people} = 4{:}9 \text{ or } \frac{4}{9}$$

$$\text{Ratio of women:total people} = 3{:}9 = 1{:}3 \text{ or } \frac{1}{3}$$

$$\text{Ratio of children:total people} = 2{:}9 \text{ or } \frac{2}{9}$$

In addition, from any ratio of more than two terms, we can determine various two-term ratios among the parts.

$$\text{Ratio of women:men} = 3{:}4$$

$$\text{Ratio of men:children} = 4{:}2 = 2{:}1$$

And finally, if we were asked to establish a relationship between the number of adults in the room and the number of children, we would find that this would be possible as well. For every 2 children there are 4 men and 3 women, which is $4 + 3$ or 7 adults. So:

$$\text{Ratio of children:adults} = 2{:}7 \text{ or}$$

$$\text{Ratio of adults:children} = 7{:}2$$

Naturally, a test question will require you to determine only one or at most two of these ratios, but knowing how much information is contained in a given ratio will help you to determine quickly which questions are solvable and which, if any, are not.

Ratio versus Actual Number

Ratios are always reduced to simplest form. If a team's ratio of wins to losses is 5:3, this does not necessarily mean that the team has won 5 games and lost 3. For instance, if a team has won 30 games and lost 18, the ratio is still 5:3. Unless we know the actual **number** of games played (or the actual number won or lost), we don't know the actual values of the parts in the ratio.

Example: In a classroom of 30 students, the ratio of the boys in the class to students in the class is 2:5. How many are boys?

We are given a part to whole ratio (boys:students). This ratio is a fraction. Multiplying this fraction by the actual whole gives the value of the corresponding part. There are 30 students; $\frac{2}{5}$ of them are boys, so the number of boys must be $\frac{2}{5} \times 30$.

$$\frac{2 \text{ boys}}{{}_1\cancel{5} \ \cancel{\text{students}}} \times \cancel{30}^{6} \ \cancel{\text{students}} = 2 \times 6 = 12 \text{ boys}$$

Picking Numbers

Ratio problems that do not contain any actual values, just ratios, are ideal for solving by Picking Numbers. Just make sure that the numbers you pick are divisible by both the numerator and denominator of the ratio.

Example: A building has $\frac{2}{5}$ of its floors below ground. What is the ratio of the number of floors above ground to the number of floors below ground?

Ⓐ 5:2
Ⓑ 3:2
Ⓒ 4:3
Ⓓ 3:5
Ⓔ 2:5

Pick a value for the total number of floors, one that is divisible by both the numerator and denominator of $\frac{2}{5}$. Let's say 10. Then, since $\frac{2}{5}$ of the floors are below ground, $\frac{2}{5} \times 10$, or 4 floors, are below ground. This leaves 6 floors above ground.

> Therefore, the ratio of the number of floors above ground to the number of floors below ground is 6:4, or 3:2, choice **(B)**.
>
> We'll see more on ratios and how we can pick numbers to simplify things in the Problem Solving chapter.

Rates

A rate is a ratio that relates two different kinds of quantities. Speed, the ratio of distance traveled to time elapsed, is an example of a rate.

When we talk about rates, we usually use the word *per*, as in "miles per hour," "cost per item," etc. Since *per* means "for one" or "for each," we express the rates as ratios reduced to a denominator of 1.

Example: John travels 50 miles in two hours. His average rate is $\frac{\text{50 miles}}{\text{2 hours}}$ or 25 miles per hour.

Note: We frequently speak in terms of "average rate," since it may be improbable (as in the case of speed) that the rate has been constant over the period in question. See the Averages section for more details.

RATIOS EXERCISES

Basic

For exercises 1–5, reduce each ratio to simplest form.

1. 16:172

2. 15.5:3.1

3. $\frac{6}{8}:\frac{1}{4}$

4. 4.8:0.8:1.6

5. 27:3

6. If the ratio of the number of men to the number of women on a committee of 25 members is 2:3, how many members of the committee are women?

7. If the ratio of boys to girls in a class is 4:3 and there are 24 boys, how many girls are in the class?

8. Nicholas has 9 goldfish and 6 guppies in his fish tank. What is the ratio of goldfish to guppies in his fish tank?

9. After spending $\frac{1}{4}$ of her paycheck, Rachelle has $150 left. How much was Rachelle's paycheck?

10. In a local recreation center, votes were cast for a new yoga, spin, or Pilates exercise class in the ratio of 3:4:2. If there were 360 votes total, how many votes did yoga receive?

Intermediate

11. A punch recipe calls for 3 pints of ginger ale for every 2 quarts of juice. How many pints of ginger ale will be needed to mix with 10 quarts of juice?

12. The ratio of the ages of Anna and Emma is 3:5 and the ratio of the ages of Emma and Nicholas is 3:5. What is the ratio of Anna's age to Nicholas's age?

13. Selena collects football, baseball, and basketball cards. If the ratio of football to baseball cards is 4:2 and the ratio of baseball to basketball cards is 4:1, what is the ratio of football to basketball cards?

14. A certain juice is in the ratio of 2 parts concentrate to 1 part water. If there are currently 9 gallons of juice, how much water must be added to make the juice in the ratio of 1 part concentrate to 1 part water?

15. If the ratio of $3x$ to $7y$ is 3:4, what is the ratio of x to y?

16. Lin finishes the first half of an exam in one-third the time it takes her to finish the second half. If the whole exam takes her 60 minutes, how many minutes does she spend on the first half of the exam?

17. Bella's grade in a course is determined by 5 quizzes and 1 exam. If the exam counts twice as much as each of the quizzes, what fraction of the final grade is determined by the exam?

18. If red, blue, and yellow gravels are to be mixed in the ratio 4:5:2 respectively, and 12 pounds of red gravel are available, how many pounds of the colored gravel mixture can be made? Assume there is enough blue and yellow gravel available to use all the red gravel.

19. At a football game with 5,400 fans, two-thirds of the fans are rooting for the home team. If 800 of the home-team fans are students, what fraction of the home-team fans are not students?

20. In a certain year, California produced $\frac{7}{10}$ and South Carolina produced $\frac{1}{10}$ of all fresh peach crops in the United States. If all the other states combined produced 242 million pounds that year, how many million pounds did South Carolina produce?

ADVANCED

21. If the ratio of $2a - b$ to $a + b$ is 2:5, what is the ratio of a to b?

22. A moisturizer has 4 parts aloe for every 1 part glycerin. If 65 ounces of this moisturizer are made, how many ounces of glycerin are required?

23. A sportswear store ordered an equal number of blue and white jerseys. The jersey company delivered 22 extra blue jerseys, making the ratio of blue jerseys to white jerseys 7:5. How many jerseys of each color did the store originally order?

24. In a pet store, the ratio of the number of puppies to kittens is 4:7. When 7 more puppies are received, the ratio of the number of puppies to the number of kittens changes to 5:7. How many puppies does the pet store now have?

25. A soccer field has a total area of 7,700 square yards. If 1,100 pounds of grass seed are spread evenly across the entire field, approximately how many pounds of grass seed, to the nearest whole number, are spread over an area of the field totaling 2,500 square yards?

26. If $\frac{1}{2}$ of the number of white roses in a garden is $\frac{1}{8}$ of the total number of roses, and $\frac{1}{3}$ of the number of red roses is $\frac{1}{9}$ of the total number of roses, then what is the ratio of white roses to red roses?

27. The ratio of $5x$ to $2(x + y)$ is 2:3. What is the ratio of x to y?

28. Liquids A and B are in the ratio 2:1 in the first container, and 1:2 in the second container. In what ratio should the contents of the two containers be mixed to obtain a mixture of A and B in the ratio 1:1?

29. A full soap dispenser contains 400 milliliters of soap. After the first 100 milliliters of soap are used, the missing quantity is replaced with pure water, which is added to the dispenser. What is the ratio of soap to water in the dispenser after the water is added?

30. The ratio of the age of a woman to that of her husband was 5:7 when they were first married. After 20 years of marriage, this ratio will be 5:6. What were the ages of the husband and the wife at the time they were first married?

RATIOS EXERCISES ANSWER KEY

BASIC

1. 4:43

Divide both numbers by their greatest common factor, 4. 16:172 = 4:43

2. 5:1

First, multiply both numbers by ten, to compare whole numbers. Then, divide by their greatest common factor, 31. 155:31 = 5:1

3. 3:1

First, multiply both sides by the lowest common denominator, 8, to convert the fractions to whole numbers. Then, divide both sides by their greatest common factor.

$$8\left(\frac{6}{8}\right):8\left(\frac{1}{4}\right) = 6:2 = 3:1$$

4. 6:1:2

First, multiply all three numbers by 10, to compare whole numbers. Then, divide by their greatest common factor, 8:

$$4.8:0.8:1.6 = 48:8:16 = 6:1:2$$

5. 9:1

Divide both numbers by their greatest common factor, 3. Thus, 27:3 = 9:1.

6. 15

The ratio of men to women is 2:3. Now, convert to a part:whole ratio to find the actual number of women. The proportion of women to the whole is $\frac{3}{(2+3)} = \frac{3}{5}$.

Find $\frac{3}{5}$ of the total to calculate the number of women: $\frac{3}{5}(25) = 15$.

There are 15 women on the committee.

7. 18

The ratio of boys to girls is 4:3. Let x = number of girls. Set up a proportion and solve.

$$\begin{aligned} \frac{4}{3} &= \frac{24}{x} \\ 4x &= 72 \\ x &= 18 \end{aligned}$$

There are 18 girls.

8. 3:2

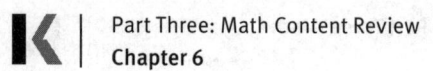

The ratio of goldfish to guppies is 9:6. Divide both numbers by their greatest common factor, 3, to reduce to simplest form, 3:2.

9. $200

Rachelle spent $\frac{1}{4}$ of her paycheck, so $150 is $1 - \frac{1}{4} = \frac{3}{4}$ of her paycheck. Let x equal her total paycheck.

$$\begin{aligned} \text{fraction} &= \frac{\text{part}}{\text{whole}} \\ \frac{3}{4} &= \frac{150}{x} \\ 3x &= 600 \\ x &= 200 \end{aligned}$$

Her paycheck is $200.

10. 120

Yoga accounts for 3 out of every 9 votes ($3 + 4 + 2 = 9$). Let x equal the number of votes for yoga. Set up a proportion and solve for x.

$$\begin{aligned} \frac{3}{9} &= \frac{x}{360} \\ 9x &= 1{,}080 \\ x &= 120 \end{aligned}$$

Yoga received 120 votes.

Intermediate

11. 15

Let x be the number of pints of ginger ale. Set up a proportion and solve for x.

$$\begin{aligned} \frac{\text{3 pints ginger ale}}{\text{2 quarts juice}} &= \frac{x\text{ pints ginger ale}}{\text{10 quarts juice}} \\ \frac{3}{2} &= \frac{x}{10} \\ 2x &= 30 \\ x &= 15 \end{aligned}$$

There will be 15 pints of ginger ale needed for 10 quarts of juice.

12. 9:25

The ratio of the ages of Anna and Emma is 3:5. The ratio of the ages of Emma and Nicholas is 3:5. Emma's age is common to both ratios, so replace Emma's age with the least common multiple of 3 and 5, or 15. Anna's age to Emma's age is 9:15 (multiply both values by 3). Emma's age to Nicholas's age is 15:25 (multiply both values by 5 to get Emma's age to 15, as in the earlier ratio). Now that Emma's age is the same in each ratio, you can combine the two ratios. Anna:Emma:Nicholas = 9:15:25.

The ratio of Anna's age to Nicholas's age is 9:25.

13. 8:1

Baseball cards are common to both ratios. Multiply both ratios by appropriate factors so that the baseball cards are represented by the same number in each ratio. Football:baseball = 4:2 and baseball:basketball = 4:1. Multiply the first ratio by 2. Now, football:baseball = 8:4. So, football:baseball:basketball is 8:4:1; football:basketball is 8:1.

14. 3

The juice is 2 parts of concentrate and 1 part of water. Since there are 9 gallons of juice, there must be 6 gallons of concentrate and 3 gallons of water. In order to have the concentrate and water be the same, you must add 3 gallons of water.

15. 7:4

Set up a proportion using the given ratios and solve.

$$\frac{3x}{7y} = \frac{3}{4}$$

$$\frac{x}{y} = \frac{3}{4} \times \frac{7}{3}$$

$$\frac{x}{y} = \frac{21}{12} = \frac{7}{4}$$

The ratio of x to y is 7:4.

16. 15 minutes

Let x equal the number of minutes it took to complete the first half of the exam. Set up a proportion and solve.

$$\frac{1}{3} = \frac{x}{60 - x}$$

$$3x = 60 - x$$

$$4x = 60$$

$$x = 15$$

Lin finishes the first half of the exam in 15 minutes.

17. $\frac{2}{7}$

Each of the 5 quizzes counts once and the exam counts twice, which means there are $5 + 2 = 7$ total parts. The exam is 2 parts, so it counts as $\frac{2}{7}$ of the final grade.

18. 33 pounds

There are 4 parts of red. $4 \times 3 = 12$, so multiply each element in the ratio 4:5:2 by 3 to determine how many pounds of each color should be used: $(4 \times 3):(5 \times 3):(2 \times 3) = 12:15:6$. Add the amounts together to determine how many pounds of the mixture will be made: $12 + 15 + 6 = 33$.

19. $\frac{7}{9}$

First, find the number of home team fans: $\frac{2}{3} \times 5{,}400 = 3{,}600$ home team fans. Then, subtract the number of those fans who are students to find the number of home-team fans who are not students: 3,600 – 800 students = 2,800. Create a ratio of part to whole, and simplify:

$$\frac{\text{2,800 home-team fans who are not students}}{\text{3,600 home-team fans}} = \frac{7}{9}$$

Thus, $\frac{7}{9}$ of the home-team fans are not students.

20. 121

Together, California and South Carolina produced $\frac{7}{10} + \frac{1}{10}$ or $\frac{8}{10}$ of all the fresh peaches in the country. All the other states combined produced $1 - \frac{8}{10}$ or $\frac{2}{10}$ of all the fresh peaches. So, the ratio of California to South Carolina to other states is 7:1:2. The other states produced 242 million pounds. Let t = total million pounds of peaches. First, solve for t:

$$\begin{aligned} \frac{2}{10}t &= 242 \\ t &= 1{,}210 \end{aligned}$$

South Carolina produced $\frac{1}{10}$ of the total, or $\frac{1}{10}(1{,}210) = 121$.
Therefore, South Carolina produced 121 million pounds of peaches.

ADVANCED

21. 7:8

Set up a proportion using the given ratios and solve:

$$\begin{aligned} \frac{2a-b}{a+b} &= \frac{2}{5} \\ 5(2a-b) &= 2(a+b) \\ 10a-5b &= 2a+2b \\ 10a-2a &= 2b+5b \\ 8a &= 7b \\ \frac{a}{b} &= \frac{7}{8} \end{aligned}$$

The ratio of a to b is 7:8.

22. 13

4 parts aloe + 1 part glycerin = 5 total parts

$$\begin{aligned} \frac{\text{1 part glycerin}}{\text{5 parts}} &= \frac{x \text{ ounces glycerin}}{\text{65 ounces total}} \\ 5x &= 65 \\ x &= 13 \end{aligned}$$

13 ounces of glycerin are required.

23. 55

Let the initial number of each color of blue and white jerseys be x. The jersey company delivered 22 extra blue jerseys, so total blue jerseys $= x + 22$.

$$\begin{aligned} \frac{7}{5} &= \frac{x+22}{x} \\ 5x+110 &= 7x \\ 110 &= 2x \\ 55 &= x \end{aligned}$$

The store originally ordered 55 jerseys of each color.

24. 35

Let x be the initial scale of puppies to kittens: $\frac{4x}{7x}$. Add 7 more puppies: $\frac{4x+7}{7x}$.

The new ratio is 5:7. Use the new ratios to create a proportion and solve for x.

$$\begin{aligned} \frac{4x+7}{7x} &= \frac{5}{7} \\ 28x+49 &= 35x \\ 49 &= 7x \\ 7 &= x \end{aligned}$$

The original number of puppies is $4x$, so the current number of puppies is $4x + 7 = 4(7) + 7 = 35$. So, there are 35 puppies.

25. Approximately 357 pounds

Use the given information to set up a proportion and solve for the unknown.

$$\begin{aligned} \frac{7 \text{ square yards}}{1 \text{ pounds}} &= \frac{2{,}500 \text{ square yards}}{x \text{ pounds}} \\ 2{,}500 &= 7x \\ 357.14 &\approx 357 = x \end{aligned}$$

26. 3:4

Ratio of white roses to total roses: $\frac{1}{\frac{1}{2}}:\frac{1}{\frac{1}{8}} = 1:4 = \frac{1}{4}:1$. So white roses are $\frac{1}{4}$ of total roses.

Ratio of red roses to total roses: $\frac{1}{\frac{1}{3}}:\frac{1}{\frac{1}{9}} = 3:9 = 1:3 = \frac{1}{3}:1$. So red roses are $\frac{1}{3}$ of total roses.

Ratio of white roses to red roses: $\frac{1}{4}:\frac{1}{3} = 12 \times \frac{1}{4}:12 \times \frac{1}{3} = 3:4$.

27. 4:11

Set up a proportion using the given ratios and solve:

$$\begin{aligned} \frac{5x}{2(x+y)} &= \frac{2}{3} \\ 15x &= 4(x+y) \\ 15x &= 4x + 4y \\ 11x &= 4y \\ \frac{x}{y} &= \frac{4}{11} \end{aligned}$$

The ratio of x to y is 4:11.

28. 1:1

In the first container, the ratio of A to total liquid is $\frac{2}{2+1} = \frac{2}{3}$, and the ratio of B to total liquid is $\frac{1}{1+2} = \frac{1}{3}$. In the second container, the ratio of A to total liquid is $\frac{1}{1+2} = \frac{1}{3}$, and the ratio of B to total liquid is $\frac{2}{2+1} = \frac{2}{3}$. So the ratio of A to total liquid in both containers is 3:6 or 1:2, and the ratio of B to total liquid in both containers is 3:6 or 1:2. If equal parts from each container are mixed, the ratio of A to B will be 1:1.

29. 3:1

The amount of soap left is 300 milliliters. The amount of water is 100 milliliters. So the ratio of soap to water is 300:100, which reduces to 3:1.

30. The wife was 20, and the husband was 28.

Let the woman's age at marriage $= 5x$ and the man's age at marriage $= 7x$. Set up a proportion of their ages in 20 years and solve:

$$\begin{aligned}\frac{5x + 20}{7x + 20} &= \frac{5}{6}\\ 6(5x + 20) &= 5(7x + 20)\\ 30x + 120 &= 35x + 100\\ 20 &= 5x\\ 4 &= x\end{aligned}$$

Woman's age at marriage $= 5(4) = 20$.

Man's age at marriage $= 7(4) = 28$.

PERCENTS

Percents are one of the most commonly used math relationships. Percents are also a popular topic on the GRE. *Percent* is just another word for *hundredth.* Therefore, 19% (19 percent) means

19 hundredths

or $\frac{19}{100}$

or 0.19

or 19 out of every 100 things

or 19 parts out of a whole of 100 parts.

They're all just different names for the same thing.

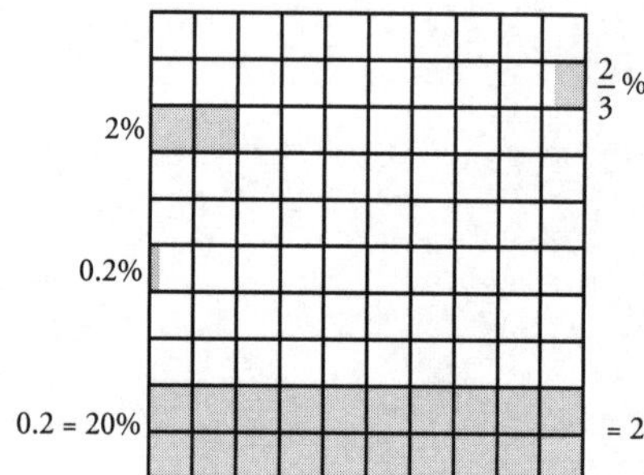

Each box at the left represents 1%. 100 boxes = (100)(1%) = 100% = 1 whole. Note that we have, in increasing order, 0.2%, $\frac{2}{3}$%, 2%, and 20%.

Making and Dropping Percents

To make a percent, multiply by 100%. Since 100% means 100 hundredths or 1, multiplying by 100% will not change the value.

Example: $0.17 = 0.17 \times 100\% = 17.0\%$ *or* 17%

Example: $\frac{1}{4} = \frac{1}{4} \times 100\% = 0.25 \times 100\% = 25\%$

To drop a percent, divide by 100%. Once again, dividing by 100% will not change the value.

Example: $32\% = \frac{32\%}{100\%} = \frac{32}{100} = \frac{8}{25}$

Example: $\frac{1}{2}\% = \frac{\frac{1}{2}\%}{100\%} = \frac{1}{200}$

To change a percent to a decimal, just drop the percent and move the decimal point two places to the left. (This is the same as dividing by 100%.)

Example: $0.8\% = 0.00.8 = 0.008$

Example: $2\frac{1}{4}\% = 2.25\% = 0.02.25 = 0.0225$

Common Percent and Fractional Equivalents

$\frac{1}{20} = 5\%$	$\frac{1}{10} = 10\%$	$\frac{1}{8} = 12\frac{1}{2}\%$	$\frac{1}{6} = 16\frac{2}{3}\%$
$\frac{1}{5} = 20\%$	$\frac{1}{4} = 25\%$	$\frac{1}{3} = 33\frac{1}{3}\%$	$\frac{1}{2} = 50\%$

$10\% = \frac{1}{10}$	$12\frac{1}{2}\% = \frac{1}{8}$	$16\frac{2}{3}\% = \frac{1}{6}$
$20\% = \frac{2}{10} = \frac{1}{5}$	$25\% = \frac{2}{8} = \frac{1}{4}$	
$30\% = \frac{3}{10}$	$37\frac{1}{2}\% = \frac{3}{8}$	$33\frac{1}{3}\% = \frac{2}{6} = \frac{1}{3}$
$40\% = \frac{4}{10} = \frac{2}{5}$		
$50\% = \frac{5}{10} = \frac{1}{2}$	$50\% = \frac{4}{8} = \frac{2}{4} = \frac{1}{2}$	$50\% = \frac{3}{6} = \frac{1}{2}$
$60\% = \frac{6}{10} = \frac{3}{5}$	$62\frac{1}{2}\% = \frac{5}{8}$	$66\frac{2}{3}\% = \frac{4}{6} = \frac{2}{3}$
$70\% = \frac{7}{10}$	$75\% = \frac{6}{8} = \frac{3}{4}$	$83\frac{1}{3}\% = \frac{5}{6}$
$80\% = \frac{8}{10} = \frac{4}{5}$	$87\frac{1}{2}\% = \frac{7}{8}$	
$90\% = \frac{9}{10}$		
$100\% = \frac{10}{10} = 1$		

Being familiar with these equivalents can save you a lot of time on Test Day.

Percent Problems

Most percent problems can be solved by plugging into one formula:

Percent × Whole = Part

This formula has three variables: percent, whole, and part. In percent problems, generally, the **whole** will be associated with the word *of*; the **part** will be associated with the word *is*. The percent can be represented as the ratio of the part to the whole, or the *is* to the *of*.

Percent problems will usually give you two of the variables and ask for the third. See the examples of the three types of problems. On the GRE, it is usually easiest to change the percent to a common fraction and work it out from there.

Example: What is 25% of 36?

Here we are given the percent and the whole. To find the part, change the percent to a fraction, then multiply. Use the formula above.

$$\text{Percent} \times \text{Whole} = \text{Part}$$

Since $25\% = \frac{1}{4}$, we are really asking what one-fourth of 36 is.

$$\frac{1}{4} \times 36 = 9$$

Example: 13 is $33\frac{1}{3}\%$ of what number?

Here we are given the percent and the part and asked for the whole.

If Percent × Whole = Part, then

$$\text{Whole} = \frac{\text{Part}}{\text{Percent}}. \text{ Recall that } 33\frac{1}{3}\% = \frac{1}{3}.$$

$$= \frac{13}{\frac{1}{3}}$$

$$= 13 \times \frac{3}{1} = 39$$

We can avoid all this algebra. All we are asked is "13 is one-third of what number?" And 13 is one-third of 3 × 13 or 39.

Example: 18 is what percent of 3?

Here we are given the whole (3) and the part (18) and asked for the percent. If Percent × Whole = Part, then

$$\text{Percent} = \frac{\text{Part}}{\text{Whole}}$$

Since the part and the whole are both integers and we're looking for a percent, we're going to have to make our result into a percent by multiplying it by 100%.

$$\text{Percent} = \frac{18}{3}(100\%) = 6(100\%) = 600\%$$

Note here that we can find the percent as the "is" part divided by the "of" part:

What percent is 18 of 3?

$$\text{Percent} = \frac{\text{is}}{\text{of}} = \frac{18}{3} = 6 = 600\%$$

Alternative method: The base 3 represents 100%. Since 18 is 6 times as large, the percent equals $6 \times 100\% = 600\%$.

Percent increase and decrease:

$$\textbf{Percent increase} = \frac{\textbf{Amount of increase}}{\textbf{Original whole}} \times (\textbf{100\%})$$

$$\textbf{Percent decrease} = \frac{\textbf{Amount of decrease}}{\textbf{Original whole}} \times (\textbf{100\%})$$

$$\textbf{New whole} = \textbf{Original whole} \pm \textbf{Amount of change}$$

When dealing with percent increase and percent decrease, always be careful to put the amount of increase or decrease over the original whole, not the new whole.

Example: If a \$120 dress is increased in price by 25%, what is the new selling price?

Our original whole here is \$120, and the percent increase is 25%. Change 25% to a fraction, $\frac{1}{4}$, and use the formula.

$$\begin{aligned}\text{Amount of increase} &= \text{Percent increase} \times \text{Original whole} \\ &= 25\% \times \$120 \\ &= \frac{1}{4} \times \$120 \\ &= \$30\end{aligned}$$

To find the **new whole** (the new selling price):

New whole = Original whole + Amount of increase

New whole = \$120 + \$30 = **\$150**

Combining percents: On some problems, you'll need to find more than one percent, or a percent of a percent. Be careful. You can't just add percents, unless you're taking the percents of the same whole. Let's look at an example.

Example: The price of an antique is reduced by 20 percent and then this price is reduced by 10 percent. If the antique originally cost \$200, what is its final price?

First, we know that the price is reduced by 20%. That's the same thing as saying that the price becomes 100% – 20%, or 80% of what it originally was. 80% of \$200 is equal to $\frac{8}{10} \times \$200$, or \$160. Then, *this* price is reduced by 10%. $10\% \times \$160 = \$16$, so the final price of the antique is $\$160 - \$16 = \$144$.

A common error in this kind of problem is to assume that the final price is simply a 30% reduction of the original price. That would mean that the final price is 70% of the original, or $70\% \times \$200 = \$140$. But, as we've just seen, this is *not* correct. Adding or subtracting percents directly only works if those percents are being taken of the same whole. In this example, since we took 20% of the original price, and then 10% of that reduced price, we can't just add the percents together.

For this type of question, the GRE will always provide the answer choice of simply adding or subtracting the percents, so beware of this trap. More practice with percent problems can be found in the Problem Solving chapter.

PERCENTS EXERCISES

BASIC

For Exercises 1–2, convert to a percent:

1. 0.087

2. $\frac{3}{20}$

For Exercises 3–4, convert to a fraction:

3. 65%

4. 232%

5. What is 28% of 70?

6. What is 125% of 48?

7. What percent of 40 is 22?

8. Twenty percent of 60 is 50% of what number?

9. Fifteen percent of 40% of 50 is what number?

10. What is 2.5% of $\frac{1}{4}$?

INTERMEDIATE

For Exercises 11–12, convert to a percent:

11. 1.675

12. 0.101

For Exercises 13–14, convert to a fraction:

13. $\frac{1}{8}\%$

14. 0.7%

15. What is 2.5% of 15?

16. What is $\frac{3}{25}\%$ of 100?

17. Of 25 students in a class, 15 have completed their tests. What percent of students in the class have not completed their tests?

18. Seventy percent of 125 is 80% of what number?

19. 60% of 180% of 40 is what number?

20. The price of a car accessory that originally costs $80 is discounted by 25%. What is the discounted price of the car accessory?

ADVANCED

For Exercises 21–22, convert to a percent:

21. 0.0003

22. 5.035

For Exercises 23–24, convert to a fraction:

23. 6.75%

24. $2\frac{3}{5}\%$

25. What is 0.05% of 5,000?

26. What is $150\frac{2}{5}\%$ of 1,000?

27. A scientist is studying the population change in the number of foxes for a certain area. She observes a 25% increase in the population of foxes for a certain area. If the new population is 45 foxes, what was the previous population?

28. Jeff sold $650,000 in software in the fourth quarter. If this was a 40% increase over his third quarter sales, what were his third quarter sales? Round to the nearest dollar.

29. A hostess at an art gallery makes \$100 for each exhibit that she works. She also receives $2\frac{1}{2}\%$ of the art sales. If she earned \$900 for a single exhibit, how much were the art sales?

30. Gasoline at a certain station has increased from \$2.98 to \$3.07. If it then decreases by half the percent of the percent increase, what is the new price? Round to the nearest tenth of a percent at each step, then round the final price to the nearest cent.

PERCENTS EXERCISES ANSWER KEY

Basic

1. 8.7%

To convert to a percent, multiply by 100%. Move the decimal point two places to the right to reach 8.7.

2. 15%

To convert to a percent, multiply by 100%: $\frac{3}{20} \times 100\% = \frac{300}{20}\% = 15\%$.

3. $\frac{13}{20}$

To convert to a fraction, divide by 100%: $\frac{65\%}{100\%} = \frac{65}{100} = \frac{13}{20}$.

4. $2\frac{8}{25}$

To convert to a fraction, divide by 100%: $\frac{232\%}{100\%} = \frac{232}{100} = 2\frac{32}{100} = 2\frac{8}{25}$.

5. 19.6

Use the formula percent × whole = part: $28\% \times 70 = 0.28 \times 70 = 19.6$.

6. 60

Use the formula percent × whole = part: $125\% \times 48 = 1.25 \times 48 = 60$.

7. 55%

Use the formula percent × whole = part: percent × 40 = 22. Divide both sides by 40: percent = 22 ÷ 40 = 0.55. Multiply by 100 and add the % sign.

8. 24

Use the formula percent × whole = part for both steps. First, find 20% of 60: $0.20 \times 60 = 12$. Then, determine what number 12 is 50% of: $50\% \times x = 12$.

$$0.50 \times x = 12$$

$$x = 12 \div 0.50 = 24$$

9. 3

Use the formula percent × whole = part for both steps. First, find 40% of 50: $0.40 \times 50 = 20$. Then, find 15% of 20: $0.15 \times 20 = 3$.

10. 0.00625

Use the formula percent × whole = part:

$$2.5\% \times \frac{1}{4} = 0.025 \times 0.25 = 0.00625.$$

INTERMEDIATE

11. 167.5%

To convert to a percent, multiply by 100%. Move the decimal point two places to the right to reach 167.5%.

12. 10.1%

To convert to a percent, multiply by 100%. Move the decimal point two places to the right to reach 10.1%.

13. $\mathbf{\frac{1}{800}}$

To convert to a fraction, divide by 100%: $\frac{\frac{1}{8}\%}{100\%} = \frac{1}{8} \times \frac{1}{100} = \frac{1}{800}$.

14. $\mathbf{\frac{7}{1000}}$

To convert to a fraction, divide by 100%: $\frac{0.7\%}{100\%} = \frac{0.7}{100} = \frac{7}{1{,}000}$.

15. 0.375

Use the formula percent × whole = part: $2.5\% \times 15 = 0.025 \times 15 = 0.375$.

16. 0.12

Use the formula percent × whole = part:

$$\frac{3}{25}\% \times 100 = 0.12\% \times 100 = 0.0012 \times 100 = 0.12.$$

17. 40%

First, find the number of students who have not completed the test: $25 - 15 = 10$. Then, divide that number by the total: $10 \div 25 = 0.4$ or 40%.

18. 109.375

Use the formula percent × whole = part for both steps. First, find 70% of 125: $0.70 \times 125 = 87.5$. Then, determine what number 87.5 is 80% of: $80\% \times x = 87.5$

$$x = 87.5 \div 0.80 = 109.375$$

19. 43.2

Use the formula percent × whole = part for both steps. First, find 180% of 40: $1.80 \times 40 = 72$. Then, find 60% of 72: $0.60 \times 72 = 43.2$.

20. $60

First, find the amount of the discount, or 25% of 80: $0.25 \times 80 = 20$. Then subtract the discount amount from the original price: \$80 – \$20 = \$60.

Advanced

21. 0.03%

To convert to a percent, multiply by 100%. Move the decimal point two places to the right to reach 0.03%.

22. 503.5%

To convert to a percent, multiply by 100%. Move the decimal point two places to the right to reach 503.5%.

23. $\mathbf{\frac{27}{400}}$

To convert to a fraction, divide by 100%: $\frac{6.75\%}{100\%} = \frac{6.75}{100} = \frac{675}{10{,}000} = \frac{27}{400}$.

24. $\mathbf{\frac{13}{500}}$

To convert to a fraction, divide by 100%: $\frac{2\frac{3}{5}\%}{100\%} = \frac{13}{5} \times \frac{1}{100} = \frac{13}{500}$.

25. 2.5

Use the formula percent × whole = part: $0.05\% \times 5{,}000 = 0.0005 \times 5{,}000 = 2.5$.

26. 1,504

Use the formula percent × whole = part. Convert $150\frac{2}{5}\%$ to a decimal, 150.4%. Then, multiply. $150.4\% \times 1{,}000 = 1.504 \times 1{,}000 = 1{,}504$.

27. 36

Find the number that sums to 45 when 25% of itself is added to it. Use the formula $x + 0.25x = 45$ and solve for x. $1.25x = 45$, so $x = 36$.

28. $464,286

Find the number that sums to $650,000 when 40% of itself is added to it. Use the formula $x + 0.40x = \$650{,}000$ and solve for x. $1.40x = \$650{,}000$. Divide both sides by 1.40, so $x \approx \$464{,}286$.

29. $32,000

Set up a formula that models the situation, with x being the number of art sales. Convert $2\frac{1}{2}\%$ to a decimal, 0.025. $\$100 + 0.025x = \$900$. Solve for x. $0.025x = \$800$. Divide both sides by 0.025, so $x = \$32{,}000$.

30. $3.02

Set up a formula that models the situation and solve for x, where x = original increase in the price of gasoline. Thus, $\$2.98 + \$2.98x = \$3.07$; $\$3.07 - \$2.98 = \$0.09 = \$2.98x$. Then, divide by $2.98 to get an increase of approximately 0.03 or 3%. If the decrease is half the increase, then the decrease is 1.5%. Find 1.5% of $3.07: $0.015 \times \$3.07 \approx \$0.05$. Subtract: $\$3.07 - \$0.05 = \$3.02$.

POWERS AND ROOTS

RULES OF OPERATION WITH POWERS

In the term $3x^2$, 3 is the **coefficient**, x is the **base**, and 2 is the **exponent**. The exponent refers to the number of times the base is multiplied by itself, or how many times the base is a factor. For instance, in 4^3, there are 3 factors of 4 : $4^3 = 4 \times 4 \times 4 = 64$.

A number multiplied by itself twice is called the **square** of that number (e.g., x^2 is x squared).

A number multiplied by itself three times is called the **cube** of that number (e.g., 4^3 is 4 cubed).

To multiply two terms with the same base, keep the base and add the exponents.

Example: $2^2 \times 2^3 = (2 \times 2)(2 \times 2 \times 2) = (2 \times 2 \times 2 \times 2 \times 2) = 2^5$ or $2^2 \times 2^3 = 2^{2+3} = 2^5$

Example: $x^4 \times x^7 = x^{4+7} = x^{11}$

To divide two terms with the same base, keep the base and subtract the exponent of the denominator from the exponent of the numerator.

Example: $4^4 \div 4^2 = \frac{4 \times 4 \times 4 \times 4}{4 \times 4} = \frac{4 \times 4}{1} = 4^2$ or $4^4 \div 4^2 = 4^{4-2} = 4^2$

To raise a power to another power, multiply the exponents.

Example: $\left(3^2\right)^4 = (3 \times 3)^4 = (3 \times 3)(3 \times 3)(3 \times 3)(3 \times 3) = 3^8$ or $(3^2)^4 = 3^{2 \times 4} = 3^8$

Any nonzero number raised to the zero power is equal to 1. $a^0 = 1$ if $a \neq 0$, but 0^0 is undefined.

A negative exponent indicates a reciprocal. To arrive at an equivalent expression, take the reciprocal of the base and change the sign of the exponent.

$$a^{-n} = \frac{1}{a^n} \text{ or } \left(\frac{1}{a}\right)^n$$

Example: $2^{-3} = \left(\frac{1}{2}\right)^3 = \frac{1}{2^3} = \frac{1}{8}$

A fractional exponent indicates a **root**.

$(a)^{\frac{1}{n}} = \sqrt[n]{a}$ (read "the *n*th root of *a*." If no "*n*" is present, the radical sign means a square root.)

Example: $8^{\frac{1}{3}} = \sqrt[3]{8} = 2$

On the GRE you will probably only see the square root. The square root of a non-negative number *x* is equal to the number which, when multiplied by itself, gives you *x*. Every positive number has two square roots, one positive and one negative. The positive square root of 25 is 5, since $5^2 = 25$ and the negative square root of 25 is –5, since $(-5)^2 = 25$ as well. Other types of roots have appeared on the test (cube root, or $\sqrt[3]{\ }$, is an example), but they tend to be extremely rare.

Note: In the expression $3x^2$, only the *x* is being squared, not the 3. In other words, $3x^2 = 3(x^2)$. If we wanted to square the 3 as well, we would write $(3x)^2$. (Remember that in the order of operations we raise to a power **before** we multiply, so in $3x^2$ we square *x* and **then** multiply by 3.)

Rules of Operations with Roots

By convention, the symbol $\sqrt{\ }$ (radical) means the **positive** square root only.

Example: $\sqrt{9} = +3$; $-\sqrt{9} = -3$

Even though there are two different numbers whose square is 9 (both 3 and –3), we say that $\sqrt{9}$ is the positive number 3 only.

When it comes to the four basic arithmetic operations, we treat radicals in much the same way we would treat variables.

Addition and Subtraction: Only like radicals can be added to or subtracted from one another.

Example:

$$\begin{aligned} 2\sqrt{3} + 4\sqrt{2} - \sqrt{2} - 3\sqrt{3} &= \left(4\sqrt{2} - \sqrt{2}\right) + \left(2\sqrt{3} - 3\sqrt{3}\right) \quad \left[\text{Note: } \sqrt{2} = 1\sqrt{2}\right] \\ &= 3\sqrt{2} + \left(-\sqrt{3}\right) \\ &= 3\sqrt{2} - \sqrt{3} \end{aligned}$$

Multiplication and Division: To multiply or divide one radical by another, multiply or divide the numbers outside the radical signs, then the numbers inside the radical signs.

Example: $\left(6\sqrt{3}\right) \times \left(2\sqrt{5}\right) = (6 \times 2) \times \left(\sqrt{3} \times \sqrt{5}\right) = 12\sqrt{3 \times 5} = 12\sqrt{15}$

Example: $12\sqrt{15} \div 2\sqrt{5} = (12 \div 2) \times \left(\sqrt{15} \div \sqrt{5}\right) = 6\left(\sqrt{\frac{15}{5}}\right) = 6\sqrt{3}$

Example: $\frac{4\sqrt{18}}{2\sqrt{6}} = \left(\frac{4}{2}\right)\left(\frac{\sqrt{18}}{\sqrt{6}}\right) = 2\frac{\sqrt{18}}{\sqrt{6}} = 2\sqrt{3}$

If the number inside the radical is a multiple of a perfect square, the expression can be simplified by factoring out the perfect square.

Example: $\sqrt{72} = \sqrt{36 \times 2} = \sqrt{36} \times \sqrt{2} = 6\sqrt{2}$

Powers of 10

The exponent of a power of 10 tells us how many zeros the number would contain if written out.

Example: $10^6 = 1{,}000{,}000$ (6 zeros) since 10 multiplied by itself six times is equal to 1,000,000.

When multiplying a number by a power of 10, move the decimal point to the right the same number of places as the number of zeros in that power of 10.

Example: $0.029 \times 10^3 = 0.029 \times 1{,}000 = 0.\underbrace{029}_{3\text{ places}}. = 29$

When dividing by a power of 10, move the decimal point the corresponding number of places to the left. (Note that dividing by 10^4 is the same as multiplying by 10^{-4}.)

Example: $416.03 \times 10^{-4} = 416.03 \div 10^4 = 0.\underbrace{0416}_{4\text{ places}}.03 = 0.041603$

Large numbers or small decimal fractions can be expressed more conveniently using scientific notation. Scientific notation means expressing a number as the product of a decimal between 1 and 10, and a power of 10.

Example: $5{,}600{,}000 = 5.6 \times 10^6$ (5.6 million)

Example: $0.00000079 = 7.9 \times 10^{-7}$

Example: $0.00765 \times 10^7 = 7.65 \times 10^4$

POWERS AND ROOTS EXERCISES

BASIC

For Exercises 1–3, evaluate the expression.

1. 3^6

2. 8^3

3. $\sqrt{2}\sqrt{50}$

4. Write the expression 4^{-3} with a positive exponent.

5. Write 0.0028207 in scientific notation.

6. If $t = 4$, then what is the value of $4t^2 + \frac{1}{2}t^3$?

7. Evaluate $\frac{3^5 \times 9^2}{9^4}$.

8. If $5\sqrt{2x} = 20$, then what is the value of $3x^2$?

9. Simplify $2\sqrt{2} - 3\sqrt{5} + \sqrt{2} + 4\sqrt{5} - 2\left(\sqrt{2} - 6\right)$.

10. Find the value of y for $\sqrt{100 - 4y^2} = 0$.

INTERMEDIATE

For Exercises 11–13, evaluate the expression.

11. $(5 + 3)^2$

12. 6×3^3

13. $\sqrt{8}\sqrt{12}$. Do not evaluate any square roots that would result in a noninteger.

14. If $m = 2$ and $n = -2$, what is the value of $m^2n^3 - (3mn)^2$?

15. If $5^n < 2000$, what is the greatest possible integer value of n?

16. Simplify $12\sqrt{18} \div 3\sqrt{2}$.

17. Find the maximum value of r for $\sqrt{18r - 6r^2}$ to be a real number.

18. What positive number when squared is equal to four times the square of –5?

19. Simplify $(4.825 \times 10^6) \div (3.2 \times 10^8)$. Round to the nearest hundredth.

20. If $k = 3$ and $l = -1$, what is the value of $3l^3k^4$?

ADVANCED

For Exercises 21–23, evaluate the expression.

21. $(4^3)^2$

22. $\left(\frac{2}{3}\right)^2 \times 3^4$

23. $\frac{\sqrt{5}\sqrt{60}}{\sqrt{3}}$

24. Write $10{,}843 \times 10^7$ in scientific notation.

25. True or false? 4.809×10^7 is equivalent to 0.0004809×10^{11}.

26. If $a = -1$ and $b = 3$, what is the value of $\frac{4a^3b^2 - 12a^2b^5}{16\left(a^3b^2\right)}$?

27. True or false? Given d, e, and $f \neq 0$, $\frac{d^3ef^5}{2de^3}$ is equal to $\frac{3d^2e^3f^7}{6e^5f^2}$.

28. If x and y are negative odd integers, is the following always, sometimes, or never positive: $4x + 3y - yx + x^3$?

29. Simplify $\frac{4\sqrt{21} \times 5\sqrt{2}}{10\sqrt{7}}$.

30. Simplify $9^{\frac{1}{2}} \times 4^3 \times 2^{-6}$.

POWERS AND ROOTS EXERCISES ANSWER KEY

Basic

1. 729

3^6 is the same as 3 multiplied six times: $3 \times 3 \times 3 \times 3 \times 3 \times 3$, or 729.

2. 512

8^3 is the same as $8 \times 8 \times 8$, or 512.

3. 10

$$\sqrt{2}\sqrt{50} = \sqrt{2 \times 50} = \sqrt{100} = 10$$

4. $\mathbf{\frac{1}{4^3}}$

A negative exponent denotes the reciprocal of a base with a positive exponent.

5. $\mathbf{2.8207 \times 10^{-3}}$

0.0028207 can be written in scientific notation by moving the decimal point 3 places to the right, or 2.8207×10^{-3}.

6. 96

To evaluate, substitute 4 for $t: 4\left(4^2\right) + \frac{1}{2}\left(4^3\right) = 4(16) + \frac{1}{2}(64) = 64 + 32 = 96$.

7. 3

Begin by cancelling any common factors in the numerator and denominator. $\frac{3^5 \times 9^{\cancel{2}}}{9^{\cancel{4}^2}} = \frac{3^5}{9^2}$.

Then, substitute 3^2 for 9 in the denominator and simplify the exponent: $\frac{3^5}{9^2} = \frac{3^5}{\left(3^2\right)^2} = \frac{3^5}{3^4}$.

Finally, cancel any common factors in the numerator and denominator again: $\frac{3^{\cancel{5}^1}}{\cancel{3^4}} = 3$.

8. 192

First, solve $5\sqrt{2x} = 20$ for x. Divide by 5: $\sqrt{2x} = 4$. Square both sides: $2x = 16$. Divide by 2: $x = 8$. Substitute 8 for x in the second equation: $3(8)^2 = 3(64) = 192$.

9. $\mathbf{\sqrt{2} + \sqrt{5} + 12}$

Use the distributive property to multiply. Then use the commutative property to move like square roots together and simplify.

$$2\sqrt{2} - 3\sqrt{5} + \sqrt{2} + 4\sqrt{5} - 2\left(\sqrt{2} - 6\right) =$$
$$2\sqrt{2} - 3\sqrt{5} + \sqrt{2} + 4\sqrt{5} - 2\sqrt{2} + 12 =$$
$$2\sqrt{2} + \sqrt{2} - 2\sqrt{2} - 3\sqrt{5} + 4\sqrt{5} + 12 =$$
$$\sqrt{2} + \sqrt{5} + 12$$

10. 5, –5

First, square both sides so you have the expression $100 - 4y^2 = 0$. Then solve for y. $4y^2 = 100$. Divide both sides by 4 and you get $y^2 = 25$. Finally y must be equal to either 5 or –5.

INTERMEDIATE

11. 64

Begin by evaluating the expression inside the parentheses and then find the square: $(8)^2 = 64$.

12. 162

Evaluate the exponent and then multiply: $6 \times 3^3 = 6 \times (3 \times 3 \times 3) = 6(27) = 162$.

13. $4\sqrt{6}$

Begin by expanding each expression in the square roots to find a perfect square: $\sqrt{2 \times 4}\sqrt{3 \times 4} = \sqrt{2} \times \sqrt{4} \times \sqrt{3} \times \sqrt{4}$. Then, take the square roots: $\sqrt{2} \times 2 \times \sqrt{3} \times 2$. Finally, multiply and combine the square roots again: $4\sqrt{2}\sqrt{3} = 4\sqrt{6}$.

14. –176

Substitute the values for the variables, then use PEMDAS to simplify the expression:

$$m^2n^3 - (3mn)^2$$
$$= 2^2 \times -2^3 - (3 \times 2 \times -2)^2$$
$$= 4 \times -8 - (-12)^2$$
$$= -32 - 144 = -176$$

15. 4

Use a guess-and-check method to find the solution: $5^2 = 25$, $5^3 = 125$, $5^4 = 625$. Since 5^5 will be larger than 2,000, the exponent must be an integer less than 5. Therefore, the answer is 4.

16. 12

Begin by writing as a fraction: $\frac{12\sqrt{18}}{3\sqrt{2}}$. Then, use properties of roots to simplify.

$$4\sqrt{\frac{18}{2}} = 4\sqrt{9} = 4 \times 3 = 12$$

17. 3

For the square root to be real, the value inside the radical must be greater than or equal to 0. Find the value that makes $18r - 6r^2 = 0$, as this is the greatest number that will still produce a real root. $18r = 6r^2$. Divide both sides by r: $18 = 6r$. Divide both sides by 6: $3 = r$. The greatest value that will still produce a real root is 3.

18. 10

First, find the square of –5, or 25. Then, find $4 \times 25 = 100$. Find the (positive) square root of 100, which is 10.

19. 0.02

Write the expression as a fraction.

$$\frac{4.825 \times 10^6}{3.2 \times 10^8} = \frac{4.825 \times \cancel{10^6}}{3.2 \times 10^{\cancel{8}^2}} = \frac{4.825}{3.2 \times 10^2} = \frac{4.825}{320} \approx 0.02$$

20. –243

Substitute the values into the expression: $3(-1)^3(3)^4 = 3(-1)(81) = -3(81) = -243$.

Advanced

21. 4,096

Use the rules of exponents to simplify the expression: $(4^3)^2 = 4^6 = 4{,}096$.

22. 36

Use the rules of exponents to simplify the expression:

$$\left(\frac{2}{3}\right)^2 \times 3^4 = \left(\frac{2^2}{3^2}\right) \times 3^4 = \left(\frac{2^2}{\cancel{3^2}}\right) \times 3^{\cancel{4}^2} = 2^2 \times 3^2 = 4 \times 9 = 36.$$

23. 10

Simplify the square roots:

$$\sqrt{5}\sqrt{\frac{60}{3}} = \sqrt{5}\sqrt{20} = \sqrt{5 \times 20} = \sqrt{100} = 10.$$

24. 1.0843×10^{11}

To be written in scientific notation, the decimal part can have a digit only in the ones place. So, move the decimal point four places to the left. This means we need to add 4 to 7, the power of 10 of the original number.

25. True

Expand both numbers and then compare: $4.809 \times 10^7 = 48{,}090{,}000$. and $0.0004809 \times 10^{11} = 48{,}090{,}000$. The two numbers are equivalent.

26. 20.5

First, factor out the numerator and denominator using the rules of exponents and then simplify:

$\frac{4a^3b^2 - 12a^2b^5}{16\left(a^3b^2\right)} = \frac{4a^2b^2\left(a - 3b^3\right)}{4a^2b^2(4a)} = \frac{a - 3b^3}{4a}$. Then substitute the given values and evaluate:

$$\frac{-1 - 3(3)^3}{4(-1)} = \frac{-1 - 3(27)}{-4} = \frac{-1 - 81}{-4} = \frac{-82}{-4} = 20.5.$$

27. True

Simplify both expressions and see if they are equal.

$$\frac{3d^2e^3f^7}{6e^5f^2} = \frac{d^2f^5}{2e^2}$$

$$\frac{d^3ef^5}{2de^3} = \frac{d^2f^5}{2e^2}$$

Because both expressions simplify to the same expression, they are equal.

28. Never

Reason through each term in the expression. Because x is a negative integer, $4x$ will always be a negative integer. The greatest possible value of $4x$ is -4. Because y is negative, $3y$ will always be a negative integer. The greatest possible value of $3y$ is -3. Then, because x is negative, $-yx$ will be a positive value between 0 and 1, since $-y^x = -\frac{1}{y^{-x}}$. The exponent $-x$ in the denominator will be a positive odd integer, and y raised to a positive odd integer exponent will result in a negative integer in the denominator. Subtracting a negative fraction between -1 and 0 is the same as adding a positive fraction between 0 and 1. Finally, because x is negative, x^3 will always be a negative integer. The greatest possible value of x^3 is -1. Adding these three negative integers and one positive fraction between 0 and 1 will always result in a negative number. It will never be positive.

29. $2\sqrt{6}$

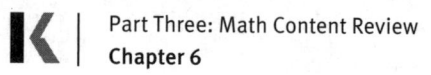

Begin by simplifying the nonroot portions of the expression:

$$\frac{4\sqrt{21} \times 5\sqrt{2}}{10\sqrt{7}} = \frac{20\sqrt{21}\sqrt{2}}{10\sqrt{7}} = \frac{2\sqrt{21}\sqrt{2}}{\sqrt{7}}$$

Then, use the rules of square roots to continue simplifying:

$$\frac{2\sqrt{21}\sqrt{2}}{\sqrt{7}} = \frac{2\sqrt{21 \times 2}}{\sqrt{7}} = \frac{2\sqrt{42}}{\sqrt{7}} = 2\sqrt{\frac{42}{7}} = 2\sqrt{6}$$

30. 3

Remove fractional exponents and change negative exponents to positive exponents: $9^{\frac{1}{2}} \times 4^3 \times 2^{-6} = \sqrt{9} \times 4^3 \times \frac{1}{2^6}$. Then, simplify:

$\sqrt{9} \times 4^3 \times \frac{1}{2^6} = 3 \times 64 \times \frac{1}{64} = 3.$

CHAPTER 7

Algebra

UNDERSTANDING ALGEBRA

The use of variables to represent numbers is what differentiates algebra from arithmetic. Calculations in algebra may involve solving for a value of a variable that makes an equation true, or they may involve substituting different values for a variable in an expression. On the GRE, you will see some questions that are strictly algebra based, but you will also see questions that involve the use of algebra along with reasoning, problem solving, and data interpretation skills. For those reasons, algebra is an important area on which to focus your review. You must understand basic equations and how to solve them.

A good place to start is with a review of algebraic terminology to ensure that you understand directions, questions, and explanations as you go along.

Variable: A letter used to represent a quantity whose value is unknown.

Examples: The letters x, y, n, a, b, and c are used frequently to represent variables.

Term: A term is a numerical constant or the product (or quotient) of a numerical constant and one or more variables.

Examples: $3x$, $4x^2$, and $\frac{2a}{c}$

Expression: An algebraic expression is a combination of one or more terms. Terms in an expression are separated by either addition or subtraction signs.

Examples: $3xy$, $4ab - 5cd$, and $x^2 + x - 1$.

Coefficient: In the term $3xy$, the multiplier 3 is called a coefficient. In a simple term such as z, 1 is the coefficient.

Constant: A value that does not change.

Example: In the expression $x + 7$, the number 7 is a constant.

Monomial: A single term, such as $-6x$ or $2a^2$.

Polynomial: The general name for expressions with more than one term.

Binomial: A polynomial with exactly two terms.

Trinomial: A polynomial with exactly three terms.

OPERATIONS WITH ALGEBRAIC EXPRESSIONS

Working efficiently and confidently with algebraic expressions can save you time on the GRE. The operations shown here may be just one important step in solving a problem.

SUBSTITUTION

Substitution is a method used to evaluate an algebraic expression or to express an algebraic expression in terms of other variables.

Example: Evaluate $3x^2 - 4x$ when $x = 2$.

Replace every x in the expression with 2 and then carry out the designated operations.

Remember to follow the order of operations (PEMDAS).

$$\begin{aligned} 3x^2 - 4x &= 3(2)^2 - 4(2) \\ &= 3 \times 4 - 4 \times 2 \\ &= 12 - 8 \\ &= 4 \end{aligned}$$

Example: Express $\frac{a}{b-a}$ in terms of x and y if $a = 2x$ and $b = 3y$.

Here, replace every a with $2x$ and b with $3y$.

$$\frac{a}{b-a} = \frac{2x}{3y-2x}$$

SYMBOLISM

You are familiar with the operation symbols $+$, $-$, $\times$, and $\div$, but you may also see some unfamiliar symbols in a GRE question. Symbols such as ♦, ❖, or ◘ may be used to describe an operation. These symbols need not confuse you; the question stem in these problems always tells you what a symbol represents. This type of problem may seem odd, but it is really a type of substitution problem.

Example: Let $x \blacklozenge$ be defined by the operation: $x \blacklozenge = \frac{1 - x}{x^2}$, where $x \neq 0$. Evaluate $(-2) \blacklozenge$.

It is helpful to say the meaning of the symbol to yourself as you work the substitution: $x \blacklozenge$ means *the quantity 1 minus the number is then divided by the square of the number.*

For $x = -2$, $x \blacklozenge = \frac{1 - x}{x^2} = \frac{1 - (-2)}{(-2)^2} = \frac{3}{(-2) \times (-2)} = \frac{3}{4}$

Operations with Polynomials

All of the laws of arithmetic operations, such as the commutative, associative, and distributive laws, also apply to polynomials. For polynomials, these laws also make it possible to combine like terms. **Like terms** contain the same variables, and the corresponding variables have the same exponents. For example, $5x^2$ and $-x^2$ are like terms, but $5x^2$ and $4x$ are *not* like terms. The laws for operations with polynomials may be applied one at a time, or they may be combined to simplify expressions.

Commutative law:

$2x + 5y = 5y + 2x$ (for addition)

$5a \times 3b = 3b \times 5a$ (for multiplication)

Associative law:

$2x - 3x + 5y + 2y$

$= (2x - 3x) + (5y + 2y)$ (for addition)

$= -x + 7y$ Combine like terms.

$(7w \times 2a) \times 3a$

$= 7w \times (2a \times 3a)$ (for multiplication)

$= 7w \times 6a^2$ Simplify.

$= 42wa^2$ Simplify.

Distributive law:

$3a(2b - 5c) = (3a \times 2b) - (3a \times 5c)$

$= 6ab - 15ac$ Simplify.

The laws of operations are frequently used in combination to simplify expressions.

Example: $5x(y + 2) - xy + 2x$

$= 5xy + 10x - xy + 2x$ Distributive law

$= 5xy - xy + 10x + 2x$ Commutative law for addition

$= (5xy - xy) + (10x + 2x)$ Associative law for addition

$= 4xy + 12x$ Combine like terms.

The product of two binomials can be found by applying the distributive law twice. Each term in the first binomial is used as a multiplier of the second binomial.

Example: $(x + 5)(x - 2) = x(x - 2) + 5(x - 2)$

$$= x^2 - 2x + 5x - 10$$

$$= x^2 + 3x - 10$$

The mnemonic **FOIL** (**F**irst, **O**uter, **I**nner, **L**ast) describes the multiplication of one binomial by another binomial. The **F**irst terms in $(x + 5)(x - 2)$ are both x; the **L**ast terms are 5 and -2. The **O**uter terms in $(x + 5)(x - 2)$ are x and -2; the **I**nner terms are 5 and x.

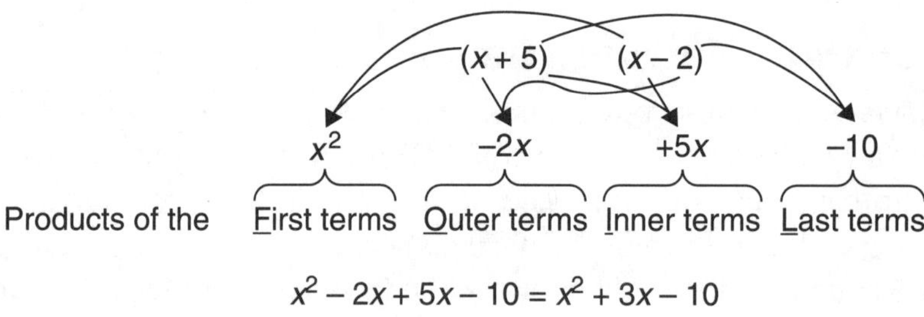

FACTORING

Factoring a polynomial means expressing it as a product of two or more simpler expressions. When there is a monomial factor common to every term in the polynomial, it can be factored out using the distributive law. In the example below, $2a$ is the greatest common factor of $2a$ and $6ac$.

Example: $2a + 6ac = 2a(1 + 3c)$

It is helpful to be able to recognize several classic polynomial equations (Classic Quadratics) because they represent polynomials that can be factored. The factoring, in turn, can lead to simplifying expressions.

Difference of two perfect squares: The difference of two squares can be factored into a product: $a^2 - b^2 = (a - b)(a + b)$. In the example below, $9b^2$ and $4c^2$ are the "squares" and the subtraction sign between them indicates a "difference" is taken.

Example: $9b^2 - 4c^2 = (3b - 2c)(3b + 2c)$

Perfect square trinomials: Any polynomial of the form $a^2 + 2ab + b^2$ is equivalent to the square of a binomial. Notice that $(a + b)^2 = a^2 + 2ab + b^2$ (try FOIL). Factoring such a polynomial is just reversing this procedure.

Example: $x^2 + 6x + 9 = x^2 + 2(3)x + 3^2 = (x + 3)(x + 3)$

Polynomials of the form $a^2 - 2ab + b^2$ can also be factored into two identical binomials. Here, though, the binomial is the difference of two terms: $a^2 - 2ab + b^2 = (a - b)(a - b)$.

Example: $w^2 - 10w + 25 = x^2 - 2(5)x + 5^2 = (w - 5)(w - 5)$

In general, polynomials of the form $x^2 + bx + c$ can be factored into two binomials under these conditions:

- The product of the first terms in each binomial equals the first term of the polynomial.
- The product of the last terms of the binomials equals the third term of the polynomial.
- The sum of the remaining products equals the second term of the polynomial.

Example: $x^2 - 8x - 20 = (x - 10)(x + 2)$

The first term in the polynomial is x^2, so each binomial starts with x. The product of -10 and 2 is -20, the last term in the polynomial, and the sum of -10 and 2 is -8, the coefficient of the middle term. All three conditions for factoring are met. Factoring can be thought of as the FOIL method in reverse, so you can check your factoring by using FOIL to obtain the original polynomial.

OPERATIONS WITH ALGEBRAIC EXPRESSIONS EXERCISES

BASIC

1. If $a = -2$ and $c = 4$, what is the value of $4 - 2a + c$?

2. Factor the expression $5x^2 - 5$.

3. Factor the expression $x^2 - 10x + 25$.

4. If $c \square d = 2c + d - 1$, what is $3 \square 10$?

5. Simplify $(2a - b)(2a + b)$.

6. Which of the following are like terms: $6a$, $6b$, $-a$, $3a^2$?

7. Simplify the expression $-4x + 5 - x + 9$.

8. Factor $x^2 - xy + x$.

9. If $b \neq c$, simplify the expression $\frac{b^2 - c^2}{b - c}$.

10. If $n \bigstar p = \frac{p}{2n}$, what is $7 \bigstar 28$?

INTERMEDIATE

11. If $a = -2$, $b = 1$, and $c = 4$, what is the value of $\frac{-2(b + c)}{2c - a}$?

12. In the equation $mx + 5 = y$, m is a constant. If $x = 2$ when $y = 1$, what is the value of x when $y = -1$?

13. What is the coefficient of the a-term in the product of $(a - 7)(a + 3)$?

14. $5c^2 - 2b = c$, what is b in terms of c?

15. Factor $x^2 + x + \frac{1}{4}$.

16. Simplify $xyz\left(\frac{1}{xy} + \frac{1}{yz} + \frac{1}{xz}\right)$.

17. Express $\frac{2a}{b - 3a}$ in terms of x and y if $a = -x$ and $b = 5y$.

18. If $y \neq z$, what is the simplest form of $\frac{xy - zx}{z - y}$?

19. Simplify $(a^2 + b)^2 - (a^2 - b)^2$.

20. If $x = 0.5$ and $y = -2$, what is the value of $10(2x - y)$?

Advanced

21. If m ❖ n is defined by the equation m ❖ $n = \frac{m^2 - n + 1}{mn}$ for all nonzero m and n, then what is 3 ❖ 1?

22. In the equation $y = -2x + b$, b is a constant. If $y = -5$ when $x = -1$, what is the value of y when $x = 0$?

23. Which of the following are like terms: ab, $-bc$, $\frac{1}{2}bc, ac^2$?

24. What is the common monomial factor in the expression $4c^3d - c^2d^2 + 2cd$?

25. If $p \neq q$, simplify the expression $\frac{p^2 - q^2}{-5(q - p)}$.

26. What is the coefficient of the x^2-term in the product of $(x + 1)(x + 2)(x -1)$?

27. Factor $x^3 - \frac{2}{3}x^2 + \frac{1}{9}x$ completely.

28. If s ❖ $r = \frac{2s^3}{r^2}$, what is -3 ❖ 6?

29. If $m = 0.5$ and $n = -0.25$, what is the value of $(m - n)^2$?

30. What is the value of a if $ab + ac = -21$ and $b + c = 3$?

OPERATIONS WITH ALGEBRAIC EXPRESSIONS ANSWER KEY

BASIC

1. 12

In this problem, plug in the values for the given variables.

$$4 - 2a + c = 4 - 2(-2) + 4 = 4 + 4 + 4 = 12$$

Be careful with the signs of the numbers; $4 - 2(-2)$ is the same as $4 + 4$.

2. $5(x - 1)(x + 1)$

Factor the common factor, 5, and then factor the difference of squares.

$$5x^2 - 5 = 5(x^2 - 1) = 5(x - 1)(x + 1)$$

3. $(x - 5)(x - 5)$ or $(x - 5)^2$

This is one of the Classic Quadratics. $x^2 - 10x + 25 = (x - 5)(x - 5)$.

4. 15

The symbol for the operation says to multiply c by 2, add d, and subtract 1.

$$3\square 10 = 2(3) + 10 - 1 = 6 + 10 - 1 = 15$$

5. $4a^2 - b^2$

This is one of the Classic Quadratics, the difference of two squares, in which $(x + y)(x - y) = x^2 - y^2$. If you recognized this as the difference of two squares, you could have skipped the whole FOIL process. However, using FOIL to simplify:

$$(2a - b)(2a + b) = (2a)(2a) + (2a)b - (2a)b - (b)(b) = 4a^2 - b^2$$

6. $6a, -a$

Only these two terms have the same variable with the same exponent.

7. $-5x + 14$

Combine the x-terms and then combine the constants:

$$-4x + 5 - x + 9 = -5x + 14$$

8. $x(x - y + 1)$

The common factor is x. Use the distributive property to factor out x.

9. $b + c$

Learning to recognize the Classic Quadratics really pays off here. The numerator is a difference of squares, so write the two binomials in the numerator. Then cancel $(b - c)$ in both the numerator and the denominator.

$$\frac{b^2 - c^2}{b - c} = \frac{\cancel{(b - c)}(b + c)}{\cancel{b - c}} = b + c$$

10. 2

The symbol for the operation says to divide p by 2 times n. Substitute for the variables and calculate:

$$\frac{p}{2n} = \frac{28}{2(7)} = \frac{28}{14} = 2$$

Intermediate

11. −1

Substitute for the variables. Evaluate the numerator and the denominator and then write the fraction in its simplest form.

$$\frac{-2(b + c)}{2c - a} = \frac{-2(1 + 4)}{2(4) - (-2)} = \frac{-2(5)}{8 + 2} = \frac{-10}{10} = -1$$

12. 3

Substitute the given values for x and y; solve for m.

$$\begin{aligned} mx + 5 &= y \\ m(2) + 5 &= 1 \\ 2m + 5 - 5 &= 1 - 5 \\ 2m &= -4 \\ m &= \frac{-4}{2} \\ m &= -2 \end{aligned}$$

Now that you know the value of m, you can solve for x when $y = -1$:

$$\begin{aligned} -2x + 5 &= y \\ -2x + 5 &= -1 \\ -2x &= -6 \\ x &= 3 \end{aligned}$$

13. −4

Multiply using FOIL: $(a - 7)(a + 3) = a^2 + 3a - 7a - 21 = a^2 + -4a - 21$. -4 is the coefficient before the a-term.

14. $\mathbf{\frac{5c^2 - c}{2}}$

Isolate the variable b in the equation $5c^2 - 2b = c$.

$$\begin{aligned} 5c^2 - 2b &= c \\ 5c^2 - 2b + 2b - c &= c - c + 2b \\ 5c^2 - c &= 2b \\ \frac{5c^2 - c}{2} &= b \end{aligned}$$

15. $\left(x + \frac{1}{2}\right)\left(x + \frac{1}{2}\right)$

This is a Classic Quadratic. The last term in $x^2 + x + \frac{1}{4}$ is the product $\frac{1}{2} \times \frac{1}{2} = \frac{1}{4}$. The middle term is $(2)\frac{1}{2}x = x$.

16. $z + x + y$

Distribute the term xyz to each fraction inside the parentheses. Then simplify each term.

$$xyz\left(\frac{1}{xy} + \frac{1}{yz} + \frac{1}{xz}\right) = \frac{xyz}{xy} + \frac{xyz}{yz} + \frac{xyz}{xz} = z + x + y$$

17. $\frac{-2x}{5y + 3x}$

Substitute for a and b in the expression: $\frac{2a}{b - 3a} = \frac{2(-x)}{5y - 3(-x)} = \frac{-2x}{5y + 3x}$.

18. $-x$

$$\frac{xy - zx}{z - y} = \frac{x(y - z)}{z - y} = \frac{-x(z - y)}{z - y} = -x$$

When two binomials are the opposite of each other, such as $(y - z)$ and $(z - y)$ here, factor out -1 from one of the binomials to simplify the expression.

19. $4a^2b$

Use FOIL to multiply each Classic Quadratic expression and then combine terms.

$$\begin{aligned}(a^2 + b)^2 - (a^2 - b)^2 &= (a^4 + 2a^2b + b^2) - (a^4 - 2a^2b + b^2)\\ &= a^4 + 2a^2b + b^2 - a^4 + 2a^2b - b^2\\ &= 4a^2b\end{aligned}$$

20. 30

Substitute the given values; watch signs as you evaluate inside the parentheses first.

$$10(2x - y) = 10[2(0.5) - (-2)] = 10[1 - (-2)] = 10(1 + 2) = 30$$

Advanced

21. 3

$$3 \text{ ❖ } 1 = \frac{3^2 - 1 + 1}{3 \times 1} = \frac{9 - 1 + 1}{3} = \frac{9}{3} = 3$$

22. -7

Substitute the given values for x and y in the equation $y = -2x + b$ and solve for b:

$$y = -2x + b;\ -5 = -2(-1) + b;\ -5 = 2 + b;\ b = -7$$

So, $y = -2x - 7$.

Substitute 0 for x:

$$\begin{aligned} y &= -2(0) - 7 \\ y &= 0 - 7 \\ y &= -7 \end{aligned}$$

23. $-bc, \frac{1}{2}bc$

Only these terms have the same variables raised to the same power.

24. cd

Every term contains the common monomial factor cd:

$$4c^3d - c^2d^2 + 2cd = cd(4c^2 - cd + 2)$$

25. $\frac{p+q}{5}$

Factor the difference of squares in the numerator; then factor -1 in the denominator. Simplify as shown.

$$\frac{p^2 - q^2}{-5(q-p)} = \frac{(p-q)(p+q)}{5(-1)(q-p)} = \frac{\cancel{(p-q)}(p+q)}{5\cancel{(p-q)}} = \frac{p+q}{5}$$

26. 2

Use FOIL twice to simplify the expression. Start with $(x + 1)$ and $(x - 1)$ so that you'll end up with the difference of two squares.

$$(x+1)(x+2)(x-1) = (x+2)(x+1)(x-1) = (x+2)(x^2-1) = x^3 + 2x^2 - x - 2$$

The coefficient of the x^2 term is 2.

27. $x\left(x - \frac{1}{3}\right)\left(x - \frac{1}{3}\right)$

First factor out the x, which leaves you with a Classic Quadratic, a perfect square trinomial. Then factor the perfect square:

$$x^3 - \frac{2}{3}x^2 + \frac{1}{9}x = x\left(x^2 - \frac{2}{3}x + \frac{1}{9}\right) = x\left(x - \frac{1}{3}\right)\left(x - \frac{1}{3}\right)$$

28. $-\frac{3}{2}$

If $s ❖ r = \frac{2s^3}{r^2}$, $-3 ❖ 6 = \frac{2(-3)^3}{6^2} = \frac{2(-27)}{36} = -\frac{27}{18} = -\frac{3}{2}$.

29. 0.5625

If $m = 0.5$ and $n = -0.25$, $(m - n)^2 = [0.5 - (-0.25)]^2 = (0.5 + 0.25)^2 = (0.75)^2 = 0.5625$.

30. −7

If $ab + ac = -21$, $a(b + c) = -21$. If $b + c = 3$, then $a(3) = -21$ and $a = -7$.

RULES OF EXPONENTS

The rules of exponents for working with numbers also apply to algebraic expressions. These rules are used to simplify expressions or to make two expressions look more alike. In the expression x^a, the **base** is x and the **exponent** is a. An expression such as x^a is sometimes referred to as a **power.** Consider the rules of exponents, where the bases x and y are nonzero real numbers and the exponents a and b are integers. Note that these restrictions apply to all the rules shown in the table.

Statement of Rule	Meaning and Examples
$x^{-a} = \frac{1}{x^a}$	x^{-a} and x^a are reciprocals of each other. *Examples:* $2^{-3} = \frac{1}{2^3}$, $4^2 = \frac{1}{4^{-2}}$, and $x^{-3} = \frac{1}{x^3}$
$(x^a)(x^b) = x^{a+b}$	When the bases are the same in a product, add the exponents. *Examples:* $(5^3)(5^1) = 5^4 = 625$ and $(x^2)(x^3) = x^5$
$\frac{x^a}{x^b} = x^{a-b}$	When the bases are the same in a quotient, subtract the exponents. *Examples:* $\frac{3^3}{3^{-1}} = 3^{3-(-1)} = 3^4 = 81$ and $\frac{m^2}{m^3} = m^{2-3} = m^{-1} = \frac{1}{m}$
$x^0 = 1$	Any nonzero quantity to the zero power equals 1. However, 0^0 is not defined. *Examples:* $7^0 = 1$, $(-6)^0 = 1$, $(2n)^0 = 1$
$(xy)^a = (x^a)(y^a)$	A product to a power can be written as individual factors to the same power. *Examples:* $(2^2)(5^2) = (10)^2 = 100$ and $(2mn)^3 = (2^3)(m^3)(n^3) = 8m^3n^3$
$\left(\frac{x}{y}\right)^a = \frac{x^a}{y^a}$	A quotient to a power can be written as a numerator and a denominator to the same power. *Examples:* $\left(\frac{4}{5}\right)^3 = \frac{4^3}{5^3}$ and $\left(\frac{3m}{n}\right)^{-2} = \frac{(3m)^{-2}}{n^{-2}} = \frac{n^2}{(3m)^2} = \frac{n^2}{9m^2}$
$(x^a)^b = x^{ab}$	To raise a power to another power, multiply the exponents. *Examples:* $((-3)^2)^3 = (-3)^{2\times 3} = (-3)^6$ and $(m^4)^2 = m^8$

It is a good idea to become familiar with the algebraic form of the exponent rules as well as the wording of the rules. That way, you will not be tempted to simplify expressions incorrectly.

RULES OF EXPONENTS EXERCISES

Basic

Use the rules of exponents to simplify the following. Note: None of the variables are equal to zero.

1. $2^3 \times 2^2$
2. $(3 \times 2)^2$
3. $(rs)^4$
4. $(5b)^0$
5. $\left(\frac{c}{d}\right)^6$
6. $a^2 \times a^8$
7. $(t^4)^3$
8. $(-1)^0$
9. $(28)^1$
10. $\frac{b^7}{b^6}$

Intermediate

Use the rules of exponents to simplify the following.

11. $(-3)^2 \times (-3)^{-1}$
12. $\frac{k^3 \times k^4}{k^2}$
13. $6^3 \times 6^{-2}$
14. $\frac{a^{-1}}{a^5}$
15. $(2a)^4$
16. $(ab^2)^3$
17. $(3b \times 4b^2)^1$
18. $\frac{5^1 - 2^2}{3 \times 3^0}$
19. $(3b^0)^4$
20. $j^3k^2 j^4k$

Advanced

Use the rules of exponents to simplify the following.

21. $\left(\frac{5a}{2b}\right)^2$
22. $\left(\frac{-3}{4st}\right)^3$
23. $\frac{(2b)^{-2}}{(3c)^{-1}}$
24. $\left(\frac{5a}{b}\right)^2 \times \frac{ab}{3}$
25. $\left(\frac{2x}{5}\right)^2 \times \frac{25x}{4}$
26. $\frac{4s^2t}{tv} \times (2v)^3$
27. $\left(\frac{3x}{4}\right)^2 + \left(\frac{y^2}{2}\right)^4$
28. $\frac{x^4y^{-2}}{x^{-3}y^4}$
29. $\frac{r^0s^4}{t} \div \left(\frac{3s}{t}\right)^2$
30. $\left(\frac{-3}{x^2}\right)^3 \times (6xy)^0 \times \left(\frac{x^5}{9}\right)^1$

RULES OF EXPONENTS ANSWER KEY

Basic

1. 32

The powers 2^3 and 2^2 have the same base, 2. To multiply, add the exponents.

$$2^3 \times 2^2 = 2^{3+2} = 2^5 = 32$$

2. 36

PEMDAS [or the Order of Operations] says to do parentheses first, then exponents:

$$(3 \times 2)^2 = 6^2 = 36$$

3. $r^4 s^4$

Apply the exponent 4 to each factor inside the parentheses. (Remember, *rs* means $r \times s$.)

$$(rs)^4 = r^4 s^4$$

4. 1

Any number or expression raised to the 0 power is 1.

$$(5b)^0 = 1$$

5. $\frac{c^6}{d^6}$

To raise a fraction to the sixth power, raise the numerator and denominator each to the sixth power.

$$\left(\frac{c}{d}\right)^6 = \frac{c^6}{d^6}$$

6. a^{10}

The expressions a^2 and a^8 have the same base (a). To multiply the expressions, add the exponents.

$$a^2 \times a^8 = a^{2+8} = a^{10}$$

7. t^{12}

To raise a power to an exponent, multiply the exponents.

$$(t^4)^3 = t^{4 \times 3} = t^{12}$$

8. 1

Any number or expression raised to the 0 power is 1.

$$(-1)^0 = 1$$

9. 28

Any number or expression to the first power is equal to that number or expression.

$$(28)^1 = 28$$

10. *b*

The expressions in the numerator and the denominator have the same base (b). To divide, subtract the exponent in the denominator from the exponent in the numerator. Keep the same base.

$$\frac{b^7}{b^6} = b^{7-6} = b^1 = b$$

INTERMEDIATE

11. –3

The powers being multiplied have the same base, –3. To multiply, add the exponents. Then simplify the power.

$$(-3)^2 \times (-3)^{-1} = (-3)^{2+(-1)} = (-3)^1 = -3$$

12. k^5

First, simplify the numerator using the rule for multiplying powers with the same base. Then use the rule for dividing powers with the same base.

$$\frac{k^3 \times k^4}{k^2} = \frac{k^{3+4}}{k^2} = \frac{k^7}{k^2} = k^{7-2} = k^5$$

13. 6

The powers 6^3 and 6^{-2} have the same base. To multiply the powers, add the exponents.

$$6^3 \times 6^{-2} = 6^{3+(-2)} = 6^1 = 6$$

14. $\frac{1}{a^6}$ or a^{-6}

To divide, subtract the exponents.

$$\frac{a^{-1}}{a^5} = a^{-1-5} = a^{-6} = \frac{1}{a^6}$$

15. $16a^4$

The expression $2a$ is the product of 2 and a. To raise a product to a power, raise each factor to the power.

$$(2a)^4 = 2^4 \times a^4 = 16a^4$$

16. a^3b^6

The expression ab^2 is the product of a and b^2. To raise a product to a power, raise each factor to the power.

$$(ab^2)^3 = a^3 \times (b^2)^3 = a^3b^{2\times 3} = a^3b^6$$

17. $12b^3$

Simplify inside parentheses first. Remember that the variable b has an implied power of 1.

$$(3b \times 4b^2)^1 = (3 \times 4 \times b \times b^2)^1 = (12b^{1+2})^1 = (12b^3)^1$$

Any expression raised to the power of 1 is equal to that expression.

$$(12b^3)^1 = 12b^3$$

18. $\frac{1}{3}$

Apply the rules for powers of 0 and 1.

$$\frac{5^1 - 2^2}{3 \times 3^0} = \frac{5 - 2^2}{3 \times 1}$$

Simplify the remaining power.

$$\frac{5 - 2^2}{3 \times 1} = \frac{5 - 4}{3 \times 1}$$

Simplify the numerator. Simplify the denominator.

$$\frac{5 - 4}{3 \times 1} = \frac{1}{3}$$

19. 81

The exponent 0 applies only to the variable b and NOT to the coefficient 3.

Simplify inside parentheses. Then, apply the exponent 4.

$$(3b^0)^4 = (3 \times 1)^4 = 3^4 = 81$$

20. j^7k^3

Use properties of multiplication to change the order of the factors and group like bases together. Remember that any number or variable without an exponent has an implied exponent of 1. To multiply powers with the same base, add the exponents.

$$j^3 k^2 j^4 k = j^3 j^4 k^2 k^1 = j^{3+4} k^{2+1} = j^7 k^3$$

Advanced

21. $\frac{25a^2}{4b^2}$

Raise the numerator and the denominator to the second power. Then, apply the exponent 2 to each factor inside parentheses.

$$\left(\frac{5a}{2b}\right)^2 = \frac{(5a)^2}{(2b)^2} = \frac{5^2a^2}{2^2b^2} = \frac{25a^2}{4b^2}$$

22. $\dfrac{-27}{64s^3t^3}$

Raise the numerator and the denominator to the third power. Then, apply the exponent 3.

$$\left(\frac{-3}{4st}\right)^3 = \frac{(-3)^3}{(4st)^3} = \frac{-3\times-3\times-3}{4^3s^3t^3} = \frac{-27}{64s^3t^3}$$

23. $\dfrac{3c}{4b^2}$

To apply a negative exponent, which means the reciprocal of a positive one, move the base to the other "level" of the fraction and make the exponent positive. Then, simplify using the rules of exponents.

$$\frac{(2b)^{-2}}{(3c)^{-1}} = \frac{(3c)^1}{(2b)^2} = \frac{3c}{2^2b^2} = \frac{3c}{4b^2}$$

24. $\dfrac{25a^3}{3b}$

Apply the exponent 2:

$$\left(\frac{5a}{b}\right)^2 \times \frac{ab}{3} = \frac{(5a)^2}{b^2} \times \frac{ab}{3} = \frac{5^2a^2}{b^2} \times \frac{ab}{3} = \frac{25a^2}{b^2} \times \frac{ab}{3}$$

Multiply fractions by multiplying across the numerator and across the denominator.

$$\frac{25a^2}{b^2} \times \frac{ab}{3} = \frac{(25a^2)(a^1b^1)}{(b^2)(3)} = \frac{25a^{2+1}b^1}{3b^2} = \frac{25a^3b^1}{3b^2}$$

Simplify further by dividing powers of the same base, b.

$$\frac{25a^3b^1}{3b^2} = \frac{25a^3b^{1-2}}{3} = \frac{25a^3b^{-1}}{3} = \frac{25a^3}{3b}$$

25. x^3

Apply the exponent 2. Then, divide out common factors before multiplying across.

$$\left(\frac{2x}{5}\right)^2 \times \frac{25x}{4} = \frac{\cancel{4}x^2}{\cancel{25}} \times \frac{\cancel{25}x}{\cancel{4}} = \frac{x^2\times x}{1} = \frac{x^{2+1}}{1} = x^3$$

26. $32s^2v^2$

Apply the exponent 3 to $(2v)$. Then, divide out common factors before multiplying across.

$$\frac{4s^2t}{tv}\times(2v)^3 = \frac{4s^2t}{tv}\times\frac{8v^3}{1} = \frac{32s^2\cancel{t^1}v^3}{\cancel{t^1}v^1} = 32s^2v^{3-1} = 32s^2v^2$$

27. $\dfrac{9x^2+y^8}{16}$

Raising each expression inside parentheses to the given power results in a common denominator of 16. To add fractions with the same denominator, add the numerators.

$$\left(\frac{3x}{4}\right)^2 + \left(\frac{y^2}{2}\right)^4 = \frac{(3x)^2}{4^2} + \frac{(y^2)^4}{2^4} = \frac{9x^2}{16} + \frac{y^8}{16} = \frac{9x^2+y^8}{16}$$

28. $\dfrac{x^7}{y^6}$

To apply a negative exponent that appears in the numerator, move the base into the denominator and use a positive exponent. To apply a negative exponent that appears in the denominator, move the base into the numerator and use a positive exponent.

$$\frac{x^4y^{-2}}{x^{-3}y^4} = \frac{x^4x^3}{y^2y^4} = \frac{x^{4+3}}{y^{2+4}} = \frac{x^7}{y^6}$$

29. $\dfrac{s^2t}{9}$

Apply the exponent 2 to the expression $\dfrac{3s}{t}$. Then, divide fractions by multiplying the first fraction by the reciprocal of the second fraction.

$$\frac{r^0s^4}{t} \div \left(\frac{3s}{t}\right)^2 = \frac{s^4}{t} \div \frac{9s^2}{t^2} = \frac{s^4}{t} \times \frac{t^2}{9s^2} = \frac{s^{4-2}t^{2-1}}{9} = \frac{s^2t}{9}$$

30. $\dfrac{-3}{x}$

Apply the rules for exponents 0 and 1.

$$\left(\frac{-3}{x^2}\right)^3 \times (6xy)^0 \times \left(\frac{x^5}{9}\right)^1 = \left(\frac{-3}{x^2}\right)^3 \times 1 \times \frac{x^5}{9} = \left(\frac{-3}{x^2}\right)^3 \times \frac{x^5}{9}$$

Apply the exponent 3.

$$\left(\frac{-3}{x^2}\right)^3 \times \frac{x^5}{9} = \frac{(-3)^3}{(x^2)^3} \times \frac{x^5}{9} = \frac{-27}{x^{2\times 3}} \times \frac{x^5}{9} = \frac{-27}{x^6} \times \frac{x^5}{9}$$

Multiply across.

$$\frac{-27}{x^6} \times \frac{x^5}{9} = \frac{-27x^5}{9x^6}$$

Simplify.

$$\frac{\overset{-3}{\cancel{-27}}\,x^5}{\underset{1}{\cancel{9}}\,x^6} = \frac{-3x^5}{x^6} = -\,3x^{5-6} = -\,3x^{-1} = \frac{-3}{x}$$

SOLVING LINEAR EQUATIONS

An **equation** is an algebraic sentence that says that two expressions are equal to each other. The two expressions consist of numbers, variables, and arithmetic operations to be performed on these numbers and variables. To **solve** for a variable, you can manipulate the equation until you have isolated that variable on one side of the equal sign, leaving any numbers or other variables on the other side. Of course, you must be careful to manipulate the equation only in accordance with the equality postulate: whenever you perform an operation on one side of the equation, you must perform the same operation on the other side. Otherwise, the two sides of the equation will no longer be equal.

Linear Equations with One Variable

A **linear** or first-degree equation is an equation in which all the variables are raised to the first power (there are no squares or cubes). In order to solve such an equation, we'll perform operations on both sides of the equation in order to get the variable we're solving for all alone on one side. The operations that can be performed without upsetting the balance of the equation are addition and subtraction, and multiplication or division by a number other than 0. Typically, at each step in the process, you'll need to use the reverse of the operation that's being applied to the variable in order to isolate the variable.

The equation $n + 6 = -10$ is a linear equation with one variable, in which 6 is added to the variable to get -10. Use the reverse of addition to isolate n; subtract 6 from both sides of the equation:

$$\begin{aligned} n + 6 &= -10 \\ n + 6 - 6 &= -10 - 6 \\ n &= -16 \end{aligned}$$

Alternate version of example above:

$$\begin{array}{rcr} n + 6 &=& -10 \\ -6 & & -6 \\ \hline n &=& -16 \end{array}$$

Here's an example of a linear equation in which the variable appears on both sides of the equation.

Example: If $4x - 7 = 2x + 5$, what is x?

1. Get all the terms with the variable on one side of the equation. Combine like terms.

$$\begin{aligned} 4x - 7 &= 2x + 5 \\ 4x - 2x - 7 &= 2x - 2x + 5 \\ 2x - 7 &= 5 \end{aligned}$$

2. Get all constant terms on the other side of the equation.

$$\begin{aligned} 2x - 7 + 7 &= 5 + 7 \\ 2x &= 12 \end{aligned}$$

3. Isolate the variable by dividing both sides by its coefficient.

$$\begin{aligned} \frac{2x}{2} &= \frac{12}{2} \\ x &= 6 \end{aligned}$$

You can easily check your work when solving this kind of equation. The answer represents the value of the variable that makes the equation true. Therefore, to check that it's correct, substitute the value found for the variable into the original equation. If the equation holds true, you've found the correct answer. In the given example, the answer was $x = 6$. Replacing x with 6 in the original equation gives:

$$\begin{aligned} 4x - 7 &= 2x + 5 \\ 4(6) - 7 &= 2(6) + 5 \\ 24 - 7 &= 12 + 5 \\ 17 &= 17 \checkmark \end{aligned}$$

Substituting 6 for x gives a statement that is true: 17 equals 17. So the answer is correct.

Equations with fractional coefficients can be solved using the same approach—isolate the variable on one side and the constants on the other—but first it is best to multiply to get rid of the fraction format. This will give you an equivalent equation to solve, but you will not have to deal with the fractions. Let's see how to solve such a problem.

Example: If $\frac{x - 2}{3} + \frac{x - 4}{10} = \frac{x}{2}$, what is x?

1. Multiply both sides of the equation by the lowest common denominator (LCD). Here the LCD is 30.

$$\begin{aligned} 30\left(\frac{x - 2}{3}\right) + 30\left(\frac{x - 4}{10}\right) &= 30\left(\frac{x}{2}\right) \\ 10(x - 2) + 3(x - 4) &= 15x \end{aligned}$$

2. Clear parentheses using the distributive property and combine like terms.

$$\begin{aligned} 10x - 20 + 3x - 12 &= 15x \\ 13x - 32 &= 15x \end{aligned}$$

3. Isolate the variable. Again, combine like terms.

$$\begin{aligned} -32 &= 15x - 13x \\ -32 &= 2x \end{aligned}$$

4. Divide both sides by the coefficient of the variable.

$$x = \frac{-32}{2} = -16$$

Literal Equations

If a problem involves more than one variable, we cannot find a specific value for a variable; we can only solve for one variable in terms of the others. To do this, try to get the desired variable alone on one side and all the other variables on the other side.

Example: In the formula $V = \frac{PN}{R + NT}$, solve for N in terms of P, R, T, and V.

1. Clear denominators by cross multiplying.

$$V = \frac{PN}{R + NT}$$

$$V(R + NT) = PN$$

2. Remove parentheses by distributing.

$$VR + VNT = PN$$

3. Put all terms containing N on one side and all other terms on the other side.

$$VNT - PN = -VR$$

4. Factor out the common factor N.

$$N(VT - P) = -VR$$

5. Divide by the coefficient of N to get N alone.

$$N = \frac{-VR}{VT - P}$$

Note: You can reduce the number of negative signs in the fraction by multiplying *both* the numerator and the denominator by -1.

$$N = \frac{VR}{P - VT}$$

Rearranging the terms of an equation to isolate one variable is referred to as *solving a literal equation*. You could also solve the same equation for a different variable.

Simultaneous Equations

Earlier, you solved an equation for one variable and were able to find a numerical value for that variable. In the previous example, you were not able to find a numerical value for N because the equation contained variables other than just N. In general, if you want to find numerical values for all your variables, you will need as many distinct equations as you have variables. Let's say, for example, that you have one equation with two variables: $x - y = 7$. There are an infinite number of solution sets to this equation: for example, $x = 8$ and $y = 1$ (since $8 - 1 = 7$), or $x = 9$ and $y = 2$ (since $9 - 2 = 7$), and so on.

If you are given two different equations with the same two variables, you can solve the equations simultaneously to obtain a unique solution set. Isolate the variable in one equation, then plug that expression into the other equation. This method, called *substitution*, works well when the coefficient of one variable is 1.

Example: Find the values of m and n if $2m + 5n = 7$ and $m + 4n = 2$.

1. Isolate the variable m in the second equation.

$$m + 4n = 2$$
$$m = -4n + 2$$

2. Plug the expression for m into the first equation and solve for n.

$$2m + 5n = 7$$
$$2(-4n + 2) + 5n = 7$$
$$-8n + 4 + 5n = 7$$
$$-3n + 4 = 7$$
$$-3n = 3$$
$$n = -1$$

3. Plug the value for n into the second equation to find the value of m.

$$m + 4n = 2$$
$$m + 4(-1) = 2$$
$$m = 6$$

Be careful to identify the results correctly. The values that make the simultaneous equations true are $m = 6$ and $n = -1$.

It is also possible to solve two equations with two variables using the *combination* method. Let's take a look at how that works.

For the simultaneous equations $8x + 4y = 140$ and $x + 2y = 55$, you cannot eliminate a variable by simply adding or subtracting the equations as they are given. The coefficients of the respective variables are not opposites of each other. But if you multiply both sides of one equation by -2 to make one set of coefficients opposites, then you can solve the system.

Example: Find the values of x and y if $8x + 4y = 140$ and $x + 2y = 55$.

1. Write one equation under the other.

$$8x + 4y = 140$$
$$x + 2y = 55$$

2. Multiply the second equation by -2 to create opposite coefficients for y.

$$8x + 4y = 140$$
$$-2(x + 2y) = -2(55)$$

3. Combine the equations by adding the second one to the first.

$$8x + 4y = 140$$
$$+ (-2x - 4y = -110)$$
$$6x = 30$$

4. Solve for x.

$$x = 5$$

5. To find the value of y, substitute for x in either equation.

$$x + 2y = 55$$
$$5 + 2y = 55$$
$$2y = 50$$
$$y = 25$$

The values that make the simultaneous equations true are $x = 5$ and $y = 25$.

SOLVING LINEAR EQUATIONS EXERCISES

BASIC

Solve each of the following equations for the variable.

1. $2r = 10$
2. $t + 14 = 16$
3. $k - 7 = 4$
4. $\frac{w}{6} = 9$
5. $3x = -12$
6. $2m - 7 = 5$
7. $\frac{y}{2} + 3 = 9$
8. Isolate T: $30R = 4T + B$

Solve each of the following systems of equations for *x* and *y*.

9. $3x = 9$
   $2x + 4y = 22$
10. $x + y = 10$
    $x - y = 2$

INTERMEDIATE

Solve each of the following equations for the variable.

11. $5x + 3 = 4x - 6$
12. $3b = 6b - 2b + 4$
13. $96 - 2b = -18b$
14. $3(x + 2) = 5x + 1$
15. $\frac{2x}{2} + \frac{x}{4} = 10$
16. $\frac{2b}{5} - 6 = 10$
17. Isolate b: $A = \frac{bh}{2}$
18. Isolate t: $A = P(1 + rt)$

Solve each of the following systems of equations for *x* and *y*.

19. $y = 3x$
    $x + y = 8$
20. $y - 2x = -5$
    $y - x = -3$

ADVANCED

Solve each of the following equations for the variable.

21. $3(x + 2) = 14 - 2(3 - 2x)$
22. $5(6 - 3b) = 3b + 3$
23. $6w - 4 - 3w = 8 - 12 - 4w$
24. $\frac{r}{6} - \frac{3r}{5} = \frac{1}{2}$
25. $\frac{2}{3}j - \frac{1}{2} = \frac{1}{6}j + \frac{11}{2}$
26. Isolate F: $C = \frac{5}{9}(F - 32)$
27. Isolate b: $A = \frac{1}{2}(a + b)h$

Solve each of the following systems of equations for both variables.

28. $x - 5y = 2$
    $2x + y = 4$
29. $2c = 14 + 4g$
    $3g = 2 - c$
30. $4x + 3y = 10$
    $3x + 5y = 13$

SOLVING LINEAR EQUATIONS ANSWER KEY

Basic

1. 5

To solve for r, divide both sides by 2.

$$\begin{aligned} 2r &= 10 \\ \frac{2r}{2} &= \frac{10}{2} \\ r &= 5 \end{aligned}$$

2. 12

To solve for t, subtract 4 from both sides.

$$\begin{aligned} t + 4 &= 16 \\ t + 4 - 4 &= 16 - 4 \\ t &= 12 \end{aligned}$$

3. 11

To solve for k, add 7 to both sides.

$$\begin{aligned} k - 7 &= 4 \\ k - 7 + 7 &= 4 + 7 \\ k &= 11 \end{aligned}$$

4. 54

To solve for w, multiply both sides by 6.

$$\begin{aligned} \frac{w}{6} &= 9 \\ \frac{w}{6} \times 6 &= 9 \times 6 \\ w &= 54 \end{aligned}$$

5. −4

To solve for x, divide both sides by 3.

$$\begin{aligned} 3x &= -12 \\ \frac{3x}{3} &= \frac{-12}{3} \\ x &= -4 \end{aligned}$$

6. 6

To solve for m, first isolate the term $2m$ by adding 7 to both sides. Then, isolate m by dividing both sides by 2.

$$\begin{aligned} 2m - 7 &= 5 \\ 2m - 7 + 7 &= 5 + 7 \\ 2m &= 12 \\ \frac{2m}{2} &= \frac{12}{2} \\ m &= 6 \end{aligned}$$

7. 12

To solve for y, first isolate the term $\frac{y}{2}$ by subtracting 3 from both sides. Then, isolate y by multiplying both sides by 2.

$$\begin{aligned} \frac{y}{2} + 3 &= 9 \\ \frac{y}{2} + 3 - 3 &= 9 - 3 \\ \frac{y}{2} &= 6 \\ \frac{y}{2} \times 2 &= 6 \times 2 \\ y &= 12 \end{aligned}$$

8. $\mathbf{T = \dfrac{30R - B}{4}}$

To solve for T, first isolate the term $4T$ on the right side by subtracting B from both sides. Then, isolate T by dividing both sides by 4.

$$\begin{aligned} 30R &= 4T + B \\ 30R - B &= 4T + B - B \\ 30R - B &= 4T \\ \frac{30R - B}{4} &= \frac{4T}{4} \\ \frac{30R - B}{4} &= T \end{aligned}$$

9. $x = 3$ and $y = 4$

The equation $3x = 9$ has only one variable and can therefore be solved independently. Divide both sides by 3.

$$\begin{aligned} 3x &= 9 \\ \frac{3x}{3} &= \frac{9}{3} \\ x &= 3 \end{aligned}$$

Now use $x = 3$ to solve $2x + 4y = 22$. Substitute 3 for x and solve for y.

$$\begin{aligned} 2x + 4y &= 22 \\ 2(3) + 4y &= 22 \\ 6 + 4y &= 22 \\ 6 - 6 + 4y &= 22 - 6 \\ 4y &= 16 \\ \frac{4y}{4} &= \frac{16}{4} \\ y &= 4 \end{aligned}$$

10. $x = 6$ and $y = 4$

In the given equations, the y terms have opposite coefficients. So, combine the equations.

$$\begin{aligned} x + y &= 10 \\ +(x - y &= 2) \\ \hline 2x &= 12 \\ \frac{2x}{2} &= \frac{12}{2} \\ x &= 6 \end{aligned}$$

Now use $x = 6$ to solve for y. Choose either equation and substitute 6 for x to solve for y. We'll choose the first one, but we'd get the same solution with the second.

$$\begin{aligned} x + y &= 10 \\ 6 + y &= 10 \\ y &= 4 \end{aligned}$$

Intermediate

11. $x = -9$

Solve by moving all x terms to the left side and all constant terms to the right side.

$$\begin{aligned} 5x + 3 &= 4x - 6 \\ 5x - 4x + 3 &= 4x - 4x - 6 \\ x + 3 &= -6 \\ x + 3 - 3 &= -6 - 3 \\ x &= -9 \end{aligned}$$

12. $b = -4$

Combine like terms on the right side. Then, move all b terms to the left side.

$$\begin{aligned} 3b &= 6b - 2b + 4 \\ 3b &= 4b + 4 \\ 3b - 4b &= 4b - 4b + 4 \\ -b &= 4 \\ \frac{-b}{-1} &= \frac{4}{-1} \\ b &= -4 \end{aligned}$$

13. $b = -6$

Collect all b terms on the right side and all constant terms on the left side. Then, solve for b by dividing to eliminate the coefficient -16.

$$\begin{aligned} 96 - 2b &= -18b \\ 96 - 2b + 2b &= -18b + 2b \\ 96 &= -16b \\ \frac{96}{-16} &= \frac{-16b}{-16} \\ -6 &= b \end{aligned}$$

14. $x = \frac{5}{2}$

First, simplify the left side using the distributive property. Then, collect *x* terms on one side and constants on the other side.

$$\begin{aligned}
3(x+2) &= 5x+1 \\
3x+6 &= 5x+1 \\
3x-5x+6 &= 5x-5x+1 \\
-2x+6 &= 1 \\
-2x+6-6 &= 1-6 \\
-2x &= -5 \\
\frac{-2x}{-2} &= \frac{-5}{-2} \\
x &= \frac{5}{2}
\end{aligned}$$

15. $x = 8$

Eliminate fractions by multiplying the entire equation by the lowest common multiple of 2 and 4, which is 4.

$$\begin{aligned}
\frac{2x}{2} + \frac{x}{4} &= 10 \\
4\left(\frac{2x}{2} + \frac{x}{4}\right) &= (4)10 \\
2(2x) + x &= 40 \\
4x + x &= 40 \\
5x &= 40 \\
\frac{5x}{5} &= \frac{40}{5} \\
x &= 8
\end{aligned}$$

16. $b = 40$

Isolate the term $\frac{2b}{5}$ on the left side by adding 6 to both sides. Eliminate the fraction by multiplying both sides by 5. Then, divide by 2 to isolate the variable.

$$\begin{aligned}
\frac{2b}{5} - 6 &= 10 \\
\frac{2b}{5} - 6 + 6 &= 10 + 6 \\
\frac{2b}{5} &= 16 \\
\frac{5}{2} \times \frac{2b}{5} &= \frac{5}{2} \times 16 \\
b &= 40
\end{aligned}$$

17. $b = \frac{2A}{h}$

Multiply both sides by 2. Then, divide both sides by *h*.

$$\begin{aligned}
A &= \frac{bh}{2} \\
2 \times A &= \frac{bh}{2} \times 2 \\
2A &= bh \\
\frac{2A}{h} &= b
\end{aligned}$$

18. $t = \frac{\frac{A}{P} - 1}{r}$ **or** $t = \frac{A-P}{Pr}$

Distribute the *P*. Then, put all terms without *t* on one side and all terms with *t* on the other. Divide to isolate *t*.

$$\begin{aligned}
A &= P(1+rt) \\
A &= P + Prt \\
A - P &= Prt \\
\frac{A-P}{Pr} &= t
\end{aligned}$$

19. $x = 2$ **and** $y = 6$

The equation $y = 3x$ tells us that *y* and $3x$ are interchangeable. So, substitute $3x$ for *y* in the other equation.

$$\begin{aligned} x + y &= 8 \\ x + 3x &= 8 \\ 4x &= 8 \\ \frac{4x}{4} &= \frac{8}{4} \\ x &= 2 \end{aligned}$$

If $x = 2$ and $y = 3x$, then $y = 3 \times 2 = 6$.

So, $x = 2$ and $y = 6$.

20. $x = 2$ and $y = -1$

In each equation, y has the coefficient 1. Multiply both sides of the second equation by -1, then combine equations.

$$\begin{aligned} y - 2x = -5 \quad &\rightarrow \quad y - 2x = -5 \\ y - x = -3 \quad &\rightarrow \quad \underline{-y + x = 3} \\ &\qquad\quad -x = -2 \\ &\qquad\quad \frac{-x}{-1} = \frac{-2}{-1} \\ &\qquad\quad x = 2 \end{aligned}$$

Now use $x = 2$ to solve for y.

$$\begin{aligned} y - 2x &= -5 \\ y - 2(2) &= -5 \\ y - 4 &= -5 \\ y - 4 + 4 &= -5 + 4 \\ y &= -1 \end{aligned}$$

ADVANCED

21. $x = -2$

First, simplify each side by distributing and combining like terms. Then, collect x terms on the left side and constants on the right side.

$$\begin{aligned} 3(x + 2) &= 14 - 2(3 - 2x) \\ 3x + 6 &= 14 - 6 + 4x \\ 3x + 6 &= 8 + 4x \\ 3x + 6 - 6 &= 8 + 4x - 6 \\ 3x &= 2 + 4x \\ 3x - 4x &= 2 + 4x - 4x \\ -x &= 2 \\ \frac{-x}{-1} &= \frac{2}{-1} \\ x &= -2 \end{aligned}$$

22. $b = \frac{3}{2}$

Simplify the left side by distributing. Then, collect b terms on one side and constant terms on the other side. Remember to express the final answer in its simplest form.

$$\begin{aligned} 5(6 - 3b) &= 3b + 3 \\ 30 - 15b &= 3b + 3 \\ 30 - 30 - 15b &= 3b + 3 - 30 \\ -15b &= 3b - 27 \\ -15b - 3b &= 3b - 3b - 27 \\ -18b &= -27 \\ \frac{-18b}{-18} &= \frac{-27}{-18} \\ b &= \frac{-27}{-18} \\ b &= \frac{3}{2} \end{aligned}$$

23. $w = 0$

Combine like terms on each side of the equation first. Notice that the term −4 now appears on each side of the equation. When the same term appears on both sides of an equation, you can remove it from each side without upsetting the balance of the equation.

$$\begin{aligned} 6w - 4 - 3w &= 8 - 12 - 4w \\ 3w - 4 &= -4 - 4w \\ 3w &= -4w \\ 7w &= 0 \\ \frac{7w}{7} &= \frac{0}{7} \\ w &= 0 \end{aligned}$$

24. $r = -\frac{15}{13}$

Eliminate fractions by multiplying the entire equation by the least common multiple of 6, 5, and 2.

$$\begin{aligned} 30 \times \left(\frac{r}{6} - \frac{3r}{5}\right) &= \left(\frac{1}{2}\right) \times 30 \\ 5r - 6(3r) &= 15 \\ 5r - 18r &= 15 \\ -13r &= 15 \\ \frac{-13r}{-13} &= \frac{15}{-13} \\ r &= -\frac{15}{13} \end{aligned}$$

25. $j = 12$

Eliminate fractions by multiplying each side of the equation by 6. Then, collect j terms on one side of the equation and constants on the other side.

$$\begin{aligned} 6 \times \left(\frac{2}{3}j - \frac{1}{2}\right) &= 6 \times \left(\frac{1}{6}j + \frac{11}{2}\right) \\ 4j - 3 &= j + 33 \\ 4j - j - 3 &= j - j + 33 \\ 3j - 3 &= 33 \\ 3j - 3 + 3 &= 33 + 3 \\ 3j &= 36 \\ \frac{3j}{3} &= \frac{36}{3} \\ j &= 12 \end{aligned}$$

26. $F = \frac{9}{5}C + 32$

Isolate the expression $F - 32$ by multiplying both sides by the reciprocal of $\frac{5}{9}$, which is $\frac{9}{5}$. Then, isolate F by adding 32 to both sides.

$$\begin{aligned} \frac{9}{5} \times C &= \frac{9}{5} \times \frac{5}{9}(F - 32) \\ \frac{9}{5}C &= F - 32 \\ \frac{9}{5}C + 32 &= F - 32 + 32 \\ \frac{9}{5}C + 32 &= F \end{aligned}$$

27. $b = \frac{2A}{h} - a$ **or** $b = \frac{2A - ah}{h}$

Multiply both sides by 2, and divide both sides by h to isolate the expression $(a + b)$. Then, isolate b.

$$\begin{aligned} A &= \frac{1}{2}(a + b)h \\ 2 \times A &= 2 \times \frac{1}{2}(a + b)h \\ 2A &= (a + b)h \\ \frac{2A}{h} &= \frac{(a + b)h}{h} \\ \frac{2A}{h} &= a + b \\ \frac{2A}{h} - a &= a - a + b \\ \frac{2A}{h} - a &= b \end{aligned}$$

28. $x = 2$ **and** $y = 0$

Create opposite coefficients on x by multiplying the first equation by -2.

$$\begin{aligned} (-2)x - 5y = 2(-2) &\rightarrow -2x + 10y = -4 \\ 2x + y = 4 &\rightarrow \underline{2x + y = 4} \\ & \qquad 11y = 0 \\ & \qquad \frac{11y}{11} = \frac{0}{11} \\ & \qquad y = 0 \end{aligned}$$

Now use $y = 0$ to solve for x.

$$\begin{aligned} 2x + y &= 4 \\ 2x + 0 &= 4 \\ 2x &= 4 \\ \frac{2x}{2} &= \frac{4}{2} \\ x &= 2 \end{aligned}$$

29. $c = 5$ **and** $g = -1$

Solve the first equation for c.

$$\begin{aligned} 2c &= 14 + 4g \\ \frac{2c}{2} &= \frac{14 + 4g}{2} \\ c &= 7 + 2g \end{aligned}$$

Now use $c = 7 + 2g$ to solve for g. Substitute $7 + 2g$ for c in the second equation.

$$\begin{aligned} 3g &= 2 - c \\ 3g &= 2 - (7 + 2g) \\ 3g &= 2 - 7 - 2g \\ 3g &= -5 - 2g \\ 3g + 2g &= -5 - 2g + 2g \\ 5g &= -5 \\ \frac{5g}{5} &= \frac{-5}{5} \\ g &= -1 \end{aligned}$$

Now use $g = -1$ to solve for c.

$$\begin{aligned} c &= 7 + 2g \\ c &= 7 + 2(-1) \\ c &= 7 + (-2) \\ c &= 5 \end{aligned}$$

30. $\mathbf{x = 1}$ **and** $\mathbf{y = 2}$

Multiply to create opposite coefficients on x. Then, combine the equations.

$$\begin{aligned} 3(4x + 3y) &= 3(10) &\rightarrow\quad 12x + 9y &= 30 \\ -4(3x + 5y) &= -4(13) &\rightarrow\quad -12x - 20y &= -52 \\ & & -11y &= -22 \\ & & \frac{-11y}{-11} &= \frac{-22}{-11} \\ & & y &= 2 \end{aligned}$$

Now use $y = 2$ to solve for x. Substitute 2 for y in one of the equations.

$$\begin{aligned} 4x + 3y &= 10 \\ 4x + 3(2) &= 10 \\ 4x + 6 &= 10 \\ 4x + 6 - 6 &= 10 - 6 \\ 4x &= 4 \\ \frac{4x}{4} &= \frac{4}{4} \\ x &= 1 \end{aligned}$$

QUADRATIC EQUATIONS

If you set the polynomial $ax^2 + bx + c$ equal to zero, where a, b, and c are constants and $a \neq 0$, there is a special name for it. It is called a quadratic equation. You can find the value(s) for x that make the equation true.

Example: $x^2 - 3x + 2 = 0$

To find the solutions, also called roots of the equation, start by factoring whenever possible. You can factor $x^2 - 3x + 2$ into $(x - 2)(x - 1)$, making the quadratic equation:

$(x - 2)(x - 1) = 0$

Now you have a product of two binomials that is equal to 0. The only time a product of two factors is equal to 0 is when *at least* one of the factors is equal to 0. If the product of $(x - 2)$ and $(x - 1)$ is equal to 0, that means either the first binomial equals 0 or the second binomial equals 0.

To find the roots, set each binomial equal to 0. That gives you:

$(x - 2) = 0$ or $(x - 1) = 0$

Solving for x, you get $x = 2$ or $x = 1$. As a check, plug in each value into the original equation.

Check:

Let $x = 2$

$$\begin{aligned} x^2 - 3x + 2 &= 0 \\ (2)^2 - 3(2) + 2 &\stackrel{?}{=} 0 \\ 4 - 6 + 2 &\stackrel{?}{=} 0 \\ -2 + 2 &\stackrel{?}{=} 0 \\ 0 &= 0 \checkmark \end{aligned}$$

Let $x = 1$

$$\begin{aligned} x^2 - 3x + 2 &= 0 \\ (1)^2 - 3(1) + 2 &\stackrel{?}{=} 0 \\ 1 - 3 + 2 &\stackrel{?}{=} 0 \\ -2 + 2 &\stackrel{?}{=} 0 \\ 0 &= 0 \checkmark \end{aligned}$$

Both values, $x = 2$ and $x = 1$, are solutions of the quadratic equation $x^2 - 3x + 2 = 0$.

Here is another example of a quadratic that can be factored to determine its solutions. Always make sure the equation is set equal to zero before you start to factor.

Example: Find the solutions of $3x^2 - 5x + 2 = 0$.

1. Factor the equation into two binomials.

$$\begin{aligned} 3x^2 - 5x + 2 &= 0 \\ (3x - 2)(x - 1) &= 0 \end{aligned}$$

2. Set each factor equal to zero and solve for x.

$$\begin{aligned} 3x - 2 &= 0 & x - 1 &= 0 \\ 3x &= 2 & x &= 1 \\ x &= \frac{2}{3} \end{aligned}$$

3. Write the solutions.

$$x = \frac{2}{3} \text{ or } x = 1$$

A quadratic equation that can be factored into the square of a binomial will have only one solution. For example, the equation $x^2 - 14x + 49 = 0$ can be factored like this: $(x - 7)(x - 7) = 0$. Its only solution is $x = 7$.

The solutions to a quadratic equation in the form $ax^2 + bx + c = 0$ can also be found using the **quadratic formula**. Provided a, b, and c are real numbers and $a \neq 0$, then:

$$x = \frac{-b \pm \sqrt{b^2 - 4ac}}{2a}$$

Example: Find the solutions of $2x^2 + 9x + 9 = 0$.

Identify a, b, and c: $a = 2$, $b = 9$, $c = 9$.

$$\begin{aligned} x &= \frac{-b \pm \sqrt{b^2 - 4ac}}{2a} \\ &= \frac{-9 \pm \sqrt{9^2 - 4(2)(9)}}{2(2)} \\ & \frac{-9 \pm \sqrt{9}}{4} \\ &= \frac{-9 \pm 3}{4} \\ &= -3 \text{ or } -\frac{3}{2} \end{aligned}$$

The symbol $\pm$ indicates there are two possible solutions, one found with addition and the other with subtraction, as you saw in this example. If the value under the radical, $b^2 - 4ac$, is negative, the two solutions are complex numbers. This is a situation you will not see on the GRE. If the value of $b^2 - 4ac$ equals 0, there is just one solution to the equation.

QUADRATIC EQUATIONS EXERCISES

Basic

Find the value(s) for the variables.

1. $x^2 = 9$
2. $y^2 = 121$
3. $(x - 4)(x + 5) = 0$
4. $x(x - 2) = 0$
5. $(x - 9)^2 = 0$
6. $(b - 2)(b - 5) = 0$
7. $a^2 + 5a + 6 = 0$
8. $t^2 - 2t - 8 = 0$
9. $m^2 - 10m + 16 = 0$
10. $p^2 + p - 8 = 0$

Intermediate

Solve the quadratic equations below.

11. $y^2 - 7y = 0$
12. $d^2 - 20d + 100 = 0$
13. $3b^2 - 5b - 2 = 0$
14. $x^2 - 5x = 6$
15. $8j^2 - 24j - 32 = 0$
16. $4n^2 + 5 = 9n$
17. $n^2 - 11n + 1 = 0$
18. $x^2 + 3x + 1 = 0$
19. $3g^2 + 9g - 6 = 0$
20. $h^2 = 2h + 8$

Advanced

Solve the quadratic equations below.

21. $6w^2 - w - 15 = 0$
22. $4m^2 - 25 = 0$
23. $3x^2 + 4x = x^2 + 5x + 3$
24. $p^2 - 20p + 96 = 0$
25. $2n^2 - n - 1 = 0$
26. $2n^2 - 3n + 1 = 0$
27. $\frac{1}{6}x^2 - \frac{1}{2}x + \frac{1}{6} = 0$
28. $5x^2 - 35x - 55 = 0$
29. $-5h^2 - 5h = 1$
30. $-3b^2 = -10b - 8$

QUADRATIC EQUATIONS ANSWER KEY

BASIC

1. 3, –3

Think: what number, squared, is equal to 9? Since $3^2 = 9$ and $(-3)^2 = 9$, the equation has two solutions.

2. 11, –11

Solve by taking the square root of both sides. y can be either 11 or –11.

3. 4, –5

The expression $(x - 4)(x + 5)$ equals 0 when one or both factors are equal to 0. Set each factor equal to 0 and solve.

$$x - 4 = 0 \qquad x + 5 = 0$$
$$x = 4 \qquad x = -5$$

4. 0, 2

Set each factor equal to 0 and solve.

$$x = 0 \qquad x - 2 = 0$$
$$x = 2$$

5. 9

The equation $(x - 9)^2 = 0$ is true when $x - 9 = 0$.

$$x - 9 = 0$$
$$x = 9$$

6. 2, 5

The equation is true when $b - 2 = 0$ and when $b - 5 = 0$.

$$b - 2 = 0 \qquad b - 5 = 0$$
$$b = 2 \qquad b = 5$$

7. –2, –3

Factor. Then, set each factor equal to 0.

$$a^2 + 5a + 6 = 0$$
$$(a + 2)(a + 3) = 0$$

Set each factor equal to 0 and solve.

$$a + 2 = 0 \qquad a + 3 = 0$$
$$a = -2 \qquad a = -3$$

8. 4, –2

Factor. Then, set each factor equal to 0.

$$\begin{aligned} t^2 - 2t - 8 &= 0 \\ (t - 4)(t + 2) &= 0 \end{aligned}$$

Set each factor equal to 0 and solve.

$$t - 4 = 0 \qquad t + 2 = 0$$
$$t = 4 \qquad t = -2$$

9. 8, 2

Though the expression on the left-hand side of this equation can be factored, you can also use the quadratic formula with $a = 1$, $b = -10$, and $c = 16$.

$$\begin{aligned} \frac{-b \pm \sqrt{b^2 - 4ac}}{2a} &= \frac{-(-10) \pm \sqrt{(-10)^2 - 4(1)(16)}}{2(1)} \\ &= \frac{10 \pm \sqrt{100 - (64)}}{2} \\ &= \frac{10 \pm \sqrt{36}}{2} \\ &= \frac{10 \pm 6}{2} \end{aligned}$$

Now separate the two solutions.

$$\frac{10 + 6}{2} = \frac{16}{2} = 8 \qquad \frac{10 - 6}{2} = \frac{4}{2} = 2$$

If you use factoring, $m^2 - 10m + 16 = (m - 8)(m - 2) = 0$. Setting each factor equal to 0 and solving for m, you get $m = 8$ and $m = 2$.

10. $\mathbf{\dfrac{-1 + \sqrt{33}}{2}, \dfrac{-1 - \sqrt{33}}{2}}$

Use the quadratic formula with $a = 1$, $b = 1$, and $c = -8$.

$$\begin{aligned} \frac{-b \pm \sqrt{b^2 - 4ac}}{2a} &= \frac{-1 \pm \sqrt{1^2 - 4(1)(-8)}}{2(1)} \\ &= \frac{-1 \pm \sqrt{1 - (-32)}}{2} \\ &= \frac{-1 \pm \sqrt{33}}{2} \end{aligned}$$

INTERMEDIATE

11. 0, 7

Factor the left side. Then, find the value of y that makes each factor equal to 0.

$$y^2 - 7y = 0$$
$$y(y - 7) = 0$$

Set each factor equal to 0 and solve.

$$y = 0 \qquad y - 7 = 0$$
$$y = 7$$

12. 10

Factor.

$$d^2 - 20d + 100 = 0$$
$$(d - 10)(d - 10) = 0$$

The two factors are identical, so set one equal to 0 and solve.

$$d - 10 = 0$$
$$d = 10$$

13. $-\frac{1}{3}$, 2

Factor.

$$3b^2 - 5b - 2 = 0$$
$$(3b + 1)(b - 2) = 0$$

Set each factor equal to 0 and solve.

$$3b + 1 = 0 \qquad b - 2 = 0$$
$$3b = -1 \qquad b = 2$$
$$b = -\frac{1}{3}$$

14. 6, −1

Rearrange the terms so that the equation takes the form $ax^2 + bx + c = 0$. Then, factor to solve.

$$x^2 - 5x = 6$$
$$x^2 - 5x - 6 = 0$$
$$(x - 6)(x + 1) = 0$$

Set each factor equal to 0 and solve.

$$x - 6 = 0 \qquad x + 1 = 0$$
$$x = 6 \qquad x = -1$$

15. 4, −1

First, factor the common factor 8 from each term.

$$8j^2 - 24j - 32 = 0$$
$$8(j^2 - 3j - 4) = 0$$

Continue factoring the quadratic expression.

$$8(j - 4)(j + 1) = 0$$

Set each factor equal to 0 and solve. (The factor 8 is never equal to 0.)

$$j - 4 = 0 \qquad j + 1 = 0$$
$$j = 4 \qquad j = -1$$

16. $\frac{5}{4}$, 1

Rearrange the terms so that the equation takes the form $ax^2 + bx + c = 0$. Then, factor to solve.

$$4n^2 + 5 = 9n$$
$$4n^2 - 9n + 5 = 0$$
$$(4n - 5)(n - 1) = 0$$

Set each factor equal to 0 and solve.

$$4n - 5 = 0$$
$$4n = 5 \qquad n - 1 = 0$$
$$n = \frac{5}{4} \qquad n = 1$$

17. $\frac{11 + \sqrt{117}}{2}, \frac{11 - \sqrt{117}}{2}$

Use the quadratic formula with $a = 1$, $b = -11$, and $c = 1$.

$$\frac{-b \pm \sqrt{b^2 - 4ac}}{2a} = \frac{-(-11) \pm \sqrt{(-11)^2 - 4(1)(1)}}{2(1)}$$
$$= \frac{11 \pm \sqrt{121 - 4}}{2}$$
$$= \frac{11 \pm \sqrt{117}}{2}$$

18. $\mathbf{\frac{-3+\sqrt{5}}{2}, \frac{-3-\sqrt{5}}{2}}$

Solve using the quadratic formula with $a = 1$, $b = 3$, and $c = 1$.

$$\begin{aligned}\frac{-b \pm \sqrt{b^2 - 4ac}}{2a} &= \frac{-3 \pm \sqrt{3^2 - 4(1)(1)}}{2(1)} \\ &= \frac{-3 \pm \sqrt{9-4}}{2} \\ &= \frac{-3 \pm \sqrt{5}}{2}\end{aligned}$$

19. $\mathbf{\frac{-3+\sqrt{17}}{2}, \frac{-3-\sqrt{17}}{2}}$

Solve using the quadratic formula with $a = 3$, $b = 9$, and $c = -6$.

$$\begin{aligned}3g^2 + 9g - 6 &= 0 \\ \frac{-b \pm \sqrt{b^2 - 4ac}}{2a} &= \frac{-9 \pm \sqrt{9^2 - 4(3)(-6)}}{2(3)} \\ &= \frac{-9 \pm \sqrt{81 + 72}}{6} \\ &= \frac{-9 \pm \sqrt{153}}{6} = \frac{-9 \pm \sqrt{9 \times 17}}{6} = \frac{-9 \pm 3\sqrt{17}}{6} = \frac{-3 \pm \sqrt{17}}{2}\end{aligned}$$

20. 4, –2

Rearrange the terms so that the equation takes the form $ax^2 + bx + c = 0$.

$$\begin{aligned}h^2 &= 2h + 8 \\ h^2 - 2h - 8 &= 0\end{aligned}$$

Factor.

$$(h-4)(h+2) = 0$$

Set each factor equal to 0 and solve.

$$\begin{aligned}h - 4 &= 0 \qquad & h + 2 &= 0 \\ h &= 4 & h &= -2\end{aligned}$$

ADVANCED

21. $-\frac{3}{2}, \frac{5}{3}$

Factor.

$$\begin{aligned} 6w^2 - w - 15 &= 0 \\ (2w + 3)(3w - 5) &= 0 \end{aligned}$$

Set each factor equal to 0 and solve.

$$\begin{aligned} 2w + 3 &= 0 & 3w - 5 &= 0 \\ 2w &= -3 & 3w &= 5 \\ w &= -\frac{3}{2} & w &= \frac{5}{3} \end{aligned}$$

22. $-\frac{5}{2}, \frac{5}{2}$

This is a Classic Quadratic: the difference of two squares.

$$\begin{aligned} 4m^2 - 25 &= 0 \\ (2m + 5)(2m - 5) &= 0 \end{aligned}$$

Set each factor equal to 0 and solve.

$$\begin{aligned} 2m + 5 &= 0 & 2m - 5 &= 0 \\ 2m &= -5 & 2m &= 5 \\ m &= -\frac{5}{2} & m &= \frac{5}{2} \end{aligned}$$

23. $\frac{3}{2}, -1$

Get the equation into the standard form. Then, factor.

$$\begin{aligned} 3x^2 + 4x &= x^2 + 5x + 3 \\ 2x^2 - x - 3 &= 0 \\ (2x - 3)(x + 1) &= 0 \end{aligned}$$

Set each factor equal to 0 and solve.

$$\begin{aligned} 2x - 3 &= 0 & x + 1 &= 0 \\ 2x &= 3 & x &= -1 \\ x &= \frac{3}{2} \end{aligned}$$

24. 12, 8

Factor.

$$\begin{aligned} p^2 - 20p + 96 &= 0 \\ (p - 12)(p - 8) &= 0 \end{aligned}$$

Set each factor equal to 0 and solve.

$$\begin{aligned} p - 12 &= 0 \qquad & p - 8 &= 0 \\ p &= 12 & p &= 8 \end{aligned}$$

25. $-\frac{1}{2}$**, 1**

Factor.

$$\begin{aligned} 2n^2 - n - 1 &= 0 \\ (2n + 1)(n - 1) &= 0 \end{aligned}$$

Set each factor equal to 0 and solve.

$$\begin{aligned} 2n + 1 &= 0 \\ 2n &= -1 \\ n &= \frac{-1}{2} \end{aligned} \qquad \begin{aligned} n - 1 &= 0 \\ n &= 1 \end{aligned}$$

26. 1, $\frac{1}{2}$

Use the quadratic formula with $a = 2$, $b = -3$, and $c = 1$.

$$\begin{aligned} \frac{-b \pm \sqrt{b^2 - 4ac}}{2a} &= \frac{-(-3) \pm \sqrt{(-3)^2 - 4(2)(1)}}{2(2)} \\ &= \frac{3 \pm \sqrt{9 - 8}}{4} \\ &= \frac{3 \pm \sqrt{1}}{4} \\ &= \frac{3 \pm 1}{4} \end{aligned}$$

Now separate the two solutions.

$$\frac{3 + 1}{4} = \frac{4}{4} = 1 \qquad \frac{3 - 1}{4} = \frac{2}{4} = \frac{1}{2}$$

You can also solve this problem using factoring. $2n^2 - 3n + 1 = (2n - 1)(n - 1) = 0$. Set each factor equal to 0 and solve for n: $n = 1$ and $n = \frac{1}{2}$.

27. $\frac{3+\sqrt{5}}{2}, \frac{3-\sqrt{5}}{2}$

Clear fractions by multiplying both sides of the equation by 6.

$$\frac{1}{6}x^2 - \frac{1}{2}x + \frac{1}{6} = 0 \rightarrow x^2 - 3x + 1 = 0$$

Use the quadratic formula with $a = 1$, $b = -3$, and $c = 1$.

$$\frac{-b \pm \sqrt{b^2 - 4ac}}{2a} = \frac{-(-3) \pm \sqrt{(-3)^2 - 4(1)(1)}}{2(1)}$$
$$= \frac{3 \pm \sqrt{9-4}}{2}$$
$$= \frac{3 \pm \sqrt{5}}{2}$$

28. $\frac{7+\sqrt{93}}{2}, \frac{7-\sqrt{93}}{2}$

Make a, b, and c easier to work with by dividing both sides of the equation by 5.

$$5x^2 - 35x - 55 = 0 \rightarrow x^2 - 7x - 11 = 0$$

Use the quadratic formula with $a = 1$, $b = -7$, and $c = -11$.

$$\frac{-b \pm \sqrt{b^2 - 4ac}}{2a} = \frac{-(-7) \pm \sqrt{(-7)^2 - 4(1)(-11)}}{2(1)}$$
$$= \frac{7 \pm \sqrt{49 + 44}}{2}$$
$$= \frac{7 \pm \sqrt{93}}{2}$$

29. $\frac{-5+\sqrt{5}}{10}, \frac{-5-\sqrt{5}}{10}$

Get the equation into the standard form.

$$-5h^2 - 5h = 1$$
$$-5h^2 - 5h - 1 = 0$$
$$5h^2 + 5h + 1 = 0$$

Use the quadratic formula with $a = 5$, $b = 5$, and $c = 1$.

$$\frac{-b \pm \sqrt{b^2 - 4ac}}{2a} = \frac{-5 \pm \sqrt{5^2 - 4(5)(1)}}{2(5)}$$
$$= \frac{-5 \pm \sqrt{25 - 20}}{10}$$
$$= \frac{-5 \pm \sqrt{5}}{10}$$

30. $\mathbf{b = -\frac{2}{3}, b = 4}$

Rearrange the equation into the form $ax^2 + bx + c = 0$.

$$-3b^2 + 10b + 8 = 0$$

Factor.

$$3b^2 - 10b - 8 = 0$$
$$(3b + 2)(b - 4) = 0$$

Set each factor equal to 0 and solve.

$$3b + 2 = 0$$
$$3b = -2 \qquad b - 4 = 0$$
$$b = -\frac{2}{3} \qquad b = 4$$

SOLVING INEQUALITIES

Inequalities may be written with the symbols shown here:

$<$ less than	$\leq$ less than or equal to
$>$ greater than	$\geq$ greater than or equal to

Examples: $x > 4$ means all numbers greater than 4.

$x < 0$ means all numbers less than zero (the negative numbers).

$x \geq -2$ means x can be -2 or any number greater than -2.

$x \leq \frac{1}{2}$ means x can be $\frac{1}{2}$ or any number less than $\frac{1}{2}$.

A range of values is often expressed on a number line. Two ranges are shown below.

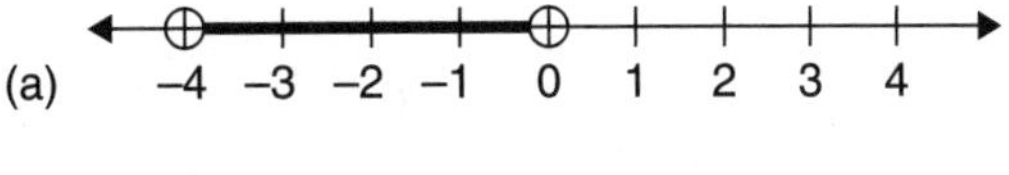

(a) Represents the set of all numbers between –4 and 0 excluding the endpoints –4 and 0, or $-4 < x < 0$.

(b) Represents the set of all numbers greater than –1, up to and including 3, or $-1 < x \leq 3$.

To solve inequalities, use the same methods used in solving equations, with one exception.

If the inequality is multiplied or divided by a negative number, the direction of the inequality is reversed. For instance, if both sides of the inequality $-3x < 2$ are multiplied by -1, the result is $3x > -2$.

Example: Solve for x and represent the solution set on a number line.

$3 - \frac{x}{4} \geq 2$

1. Multiply both sides by 4. $\quad 12 - x \geq 8$
2. Subtract 12 from both sides. $\quad -x \geq -4$
3. Divide both sides by -1 and reverse the direction of the inequality symbol. $\quad x \leq 4$

Note: the solution set to an inequality is not a single number, but a range of possible values. Here the values include 4 and all numbers less than 4. These numbers are located to the left of 4 on the number line.

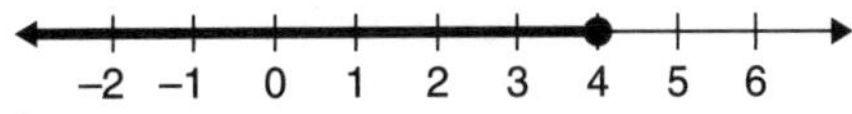

SOLVING INEQUALITIES EXERCISES

Basic

Solve.

1. $x - 3 > 7$
2. $5 \geq x + 3$
3. $x + 5 < 3$
4. $-6x > 18$
5. $9 \leq \frac{x}{5}$
6. $2x + 1 \leq 7$
7. $\frac{1}{2}x + 3 > -2$
8. $-3x > 6$
9. $-8 < -2x$
10. $-x + 3 \geq 5$

Intermediate

11. $2x + 3 > 4x - 9$
12. $\frac{x + 3}{2} \geq 7$
13. $-2(x - 4) < -8$
14. $2x - 3x \leq 6$
15. $6x - 3 > 5x + 2x + 1$
16. $-x + 3 \geq 5$
17. $\frac{3x}{-2} \geq -6$
18. $0.5x + 3 > 7$
19. $-\frac{1}{3}x > 5 - 2x$
20. $2(x + 10) \geq 30$

Advanced

21. $3x + \frac{5}{8} > 2x + \frac{5}{6}$
22. $5(x - 3) + 7 < 2x + 7$
23. $-\frac{3}{4}x \geq -\frac{5}{8}$
24. $5x - 2(x + 3) \geq 12$
25. $\frac{7}{10}x > -\frac{4}{15}$
26. $-5 \geq \frac{10(x - 2)}{-4}$
27. $\frac{1}{4}(8 - 12d) < \frac{2}{5}(10d + 15)$
28. $4 - 3(3 - n) \leq 3(2 - 5n)$
29. $2x - 3(x - 4) > 4 - 2(x - 7)$
30. $\frac{3}{2}x - \frac{3}{4}x < \frac{7}{4}x - 1$

SOLVING INEQUALITIES ANSWER KEY

BASIC

1. $x > 10$

Add 3 to both sides of the inequality.

$$\begin{aligned} x - 3 &> 7 \\ x - 3 + 3 &> 7 + 3 \\ x &> 10 \end{aligned}$$

2. $x \leq 2$

Subtract 3 from both sides of the inequality. Remember that the inequalities $2 \geq x$ and $x \leq 2$ are equivalent.

$$\begin{aligned} 5 &\geq x + 3 \\ 5 - 3 &\geq x + 3 - 3 \\ 2 &\geq x \end{aligned}$$

3. $x < -2$

Subtract 5 from both sides of the inequality.

$$\begin{aligned} x + 5 &< 3 \\ x + 5 - 5 &< 3 - 5 \\ x &< -2 \end{aligned}$$

4. $x < -3$

Divide both sides of the inequality by -6. Remember that you must reverse the inequality symbol (from $>$ to $<$) when dividing by a negative number.

$$\begin{aligned} -6x &> 18 \\ \frac{-6x}{-6} &< \frac{18}{-6} \\ x &< -3 \end{aligned}$$

5. $x \geq 45$

Multiply both sides of the inequality by 5.

$$\begin{aligned} 9 &\leq \frac{x}{5} \\ 5 \times 9 &\leq 5 \times \frac{x}{5} \\ 45 &\leq x \end{aligned}$$

6. $x \leq 3$

First, subtract 1 from both sides of the inequality. Then, divide both sides by 2.

$$\begin{aligned} 2x + 1 &\leq 7 \\ 2x + 1 - 1 &\leq 7 - 1 \\ 2x &\leq 6 \\ \frac{2x}{2} &\leq \frac{6}{2} \\ x &\leq 3 \end{aligned}$$

7. $x > -10$

First, subtract 3 from both sides of the equation. Then, multiply both sides by 2 to eliminate the fraction.

$$\begin{aligned} \frac{1}{2}x + 3 &> -2 \\ \frac{1}{2}x + 3 - 3 &> -2 - 3 \\ \frac{1}{2}x &> -5 \\ 2 \times \frac{1}{2}x &> 2 \times -5 \\ x &> -10 \end{aligned}$$

8. $x < -2$

Divide both sides of the inequality by -3. Remember to reverse the direction of the inequality when you divide by a negative number.

$$\begin{aligned} -3x &> 6 \\ \frac{-3x}{-3} &< \frac{6}{-3} \\ x &< -2 \end{aligned}$$

9. $x < 4$

Divide both sides of the inequality by -2. Remember to reverse the direction of the inequality when you divide by a negative number.

$$\begin{aligned} -8 &< -2x \\ \frac{-8}{-2} &> \frac{-2x}{-2} \\ 4 &> x \end{aligned}$$

10. $x \leq -2$

First, subtract 3 from both sides of the inequality. Then, multiply both sides by –1. Reverse the direction of the inequality when you multiply by a negative number.

$$\begin{aligned} -x + 3 &\geq 5 \\ -x + 3 - 3 &\geq 5 - 3 \\ -x &\geq 2 \\ -1 \times (-x) &\leq -1 \times 2 \\ x &\leq -2 \end{aligned}$$

INTERMEDIATE

11. $x < 6$

Isolate all the x terms on one side of the inequality and all constant terms on the other side.

$$\begin{aligned} 2x + 3 &> 4x - 9 \\ 12 &> 2x \\ 6 &> x \end{aligned}$$

12. $x \geq 11$

First, isolate $x + 3$ by multiplying both sides of the inequality by 2. Then, isolate x by subtracting 3 from both sides.

$$\begin{aligned} \frac{x+3}{2} &\geq 7 \\ x + 3 &\geq 14 \\ x &\geq 11 \end{aligned}$$

13. $x > 8$

First, simplify the left side of the inequality by distributing –2. Then, isolate x. Remember to reverse the direction of the inequality when you divide by a negative number.

$$\begin{aligned} -2(x - 4) &< -8 \\ -2x + 8 &< -8 \\ -2x &< -16 \\ \frac{-2x}{-2} &> \frac{-16}{-2} \\ x &> 8 \end{aligned}$$

14. $x \geq -6$

First, simplify the left side of the inequality by combining like terms. Then, solve for x by dividing both sides by –1. Remember to reverse the direction of the inequality when you divide by a negative number.

$$\begin{aligned} 2x - 3x &\leq 6 \\ -x &\leq 6 \\ \frac{-x}{-1} &\geq \frac{6}{-1} \\ x &\geq -6 \end{aligned}$$

15. $x < -4$

Simplify the right side by combining like terms. Then, isolate x using inverse operations.

$$\begin{aligned} 6x - 3 &> 5x + 2x + 1 \\ 6x - 3 &> 7x + 1 \\ -4 &> x \end{aligned}$$

16. $x \leq -2$

Isolate the x term and then divide by –1. Remember to reverse the direction of the inequality when you divide by a negative number.

$$\begin{aligned} -x + 3 &\geq 5 \\ -x &\geq 2 \\ \frac{-x}{-1} &\leq \frac{2}{-1} \\ x &\leq -2 \end{aligned}$$

17. $x \leq 4$

First isolate $3x$. Then isolate x. Remember to reverse the direction of the inequality when you multiply by a negative number.

$$\begin{aligned} \frac{3x}{-2} &\geq -6 \\ -2 \times \left(\frac{3x}{-2}\right) &\leq -2 \times (-6) \\ 3x &\leq 12 \\ x &\leq 4 \end{aligned}$$

18. $x > 8$

One way to avoid calculations involving a decimal is to replace the decimal 0.5 with the equivalent fraction $\frac{1}{2}$. First, isolate the x term; then, multiply by 2 to solve for x.

$$\begin{aligned} 0.5x + 3 &> 7 \\ \frac{1}{2}x + 3 &> 7 \\ \frac{1}{2}x &> 4 \\ 2 \times \frac{1}{2}x &> 2 \times 4 \\ x &> 8 \end{aligned}$$

19. $x > 3$

You can avoid having to add fractions by eliminating them. Multiply both sides of the inequality by 3. Then isolate x.

$$\begin{aligned} 3 \times \left(-\frac{1}{3}x\right) &> 3 \times (5 - 2x) \\ -x &> 15 - 6x \\ 5x &> 15 \\ x &> 3 \end{aligned}$$

20. $x \geq 5$

Simplify the left side of the inequality by distributing 2 to each term inside the parentheses. Then isolate x.

$$\begin{aligned} 2(x + 10) &\geq 30 \\ 2x + 20 &\geq 30 \\ 2x &\geq 10 \\ x &\geq 5 \end{aligned}$$

Advanced

21. $x > \frac{5}{24}$

Eliminate fractions by multiplying both sides of the inequality by the least common multiple of 8 and 6, 24.

$$\begin{aligned} 3x + \frac{5}{8} &> 2x + \frac{5}{6} \\ 24 \times \left(3x + \frac{5}{8}\right) &> 24 \times \left(2x + \frac{5}{6}\right) \\ 72x + 15 &> 48x + 20 \\ 24x &> 5 \\ x &> \frac{5}{24} \end{aligned}$$

22. $x < 5$

Simplify the left side before attempting to isolate x.

$$\begin{aligned} 5(x - 3) + 7 &< 2x + 7 \\ 5x - 15 + 7 &< 2x + 7 \\ 5x - 8 &< 2x + 7 \\ 3x &< 15 \\ x &< 5 \end{aligned}$$

23. $x \leq \frac{5}{6}$

Eliminate fractions by multiplying both sides of the inequality by 8. Remember to reverse the direction of the inequality when you divide by a negative number.

$$\begin{aligned} 8 \times \left(-\frac{3}{4}x\right) &\geq 8 \times \left(-\frac{5}{8}\right) \\ -6x &\geq -5 \\ \frac{-6x}{-6} &\geq \frac{-5}{-6} \\ x &\leq \frac{5}{6} \end{aligned}$$

24. $x \geq 6$

Simplify the left side before isolating x.

$$\begin{aligned} 5x - 2(x + 3) &\geq 12 \\ 5x - 2x - 6 &\geq 12 \\ 3x - 6 &\geq 12 \\ 3x &\geq 18 \\ x &\geq 6 \end{aligned}$$

25. $x > \frac{-8}{21}$

Multiply both sides by the least common multiple of 10 and 15, 30, to eliminate the fractions.

$$\begin{aligned} 30 \times \left(\frac{7}{10}x\right) &> 30 \times \left(-\frac{4}{15}\right) \\ 21x &> -8 \\ x &> \frac{-8}{21} \end{aligned}$$

26. $x \geq 4$

Begin by multiplying both sides by −4. Remember to reverse the direction of the inequality when you multiply by a negative number. Once the fraction is eliminated, isolate *x*.

$$\begin{aligned} -5 &\geq \frac{10(x-2)}{-4} \\ -4 \times (-5) &\leq -4 \times \left(\frac{10(x-2)}{-4}\right) \\ 20 &\leq 10(x-2) \\ 20 &\leq 10x - 20 \\ 40 &\leq 10x \\ 4 &\leq x \end{aligned}$$

27. $-\frac{4}{7} < d$

Eliminate fractions by multiplying both sides of the inequality by the least common multiple of 4 and 5, 20. Then simplify each side before isolating *x*.

$$\begin{aligned} \frac{1}{4}(8-12d) &< \frac{2}{5}(10d+15) \\ 20 \times \frac{1}{4}(8-12d) &< 20 \times \frac{2}{5}(10d+15) \\ 5(8-12d) &< 8(10d+15) \\ 40 - 60d &< 80d + 120 \\ -80 &< 140d \\ \frac{-80}{140} &< \frac{140d}{140} \\ -\frac{80}{140} &< d \\ -\frac{4}{7} &< d \end{aligned}$$

28. $n \leq \frac{11}{18}$

Simplify each side of the inequality before isolating *n*.

$$\begin{aligned} 4 - 3(3-n) &\leq 3(2-5n) \\ 4 - 9 + 3n &\leq 6 - 15n \\ -5 + 3n &\leq 6 - 15n \\ 18n &\leq 11 \\ n &\leq \frac{11}{18} \end{aligned}$$

29. $x > 6$

Simplify each side of the inequality before isolating *x*.

$$\begin{aligned} 2x - 3(x-4) &> 4 - 2(x-7) \\ 2x - 3x + 12 &> 4 - 2x + 14 \\ -x + 12 &> 18 - 2x \\ x &> 6 \end{aligned}$$

30. $x > 1$

Eliminate fractions by multiplying each term in the inequality by 4. Remember to reverse the direction of the inequality when you divide by a negative number.

$$\begin{aligned} \frac{3}{2}x - \frac{3}{4}x &< \frac{7}{4}x - 1 \\ 4\times(\frac{3}{2}x - \frac{3}{4}x) &< 4 \times (\frac{7}{4}x - 1) \\ 6x - 3x &< 7x - 4 \\ 3x &< 7x - 4 \\ -4x &< -4 \\ \frac{-4x}{-4} &> \frac{-4}{-4} \\ x &> 1 \end{aligned}$$

TRANSLATION INTO ALGEBRA

Identifying information about a situation given in words and translating the words into algebra is often the first step in solving a problem. This involves defining a variable to represent an unknown value and then writing an expression, equation, or inequality.

The Translation Table below lists some common English words and phrases and the corresponding algebraic symbols.

Translation Table

Equals, is, was, will, be, has, costs, adds up to, is the same as	=
Times, of, multiplied by, product of, twice, double, half, triple	• or ×
Divided by, per, out of, each, ratio of __ to __	÷
Plus, added to, sum, combined, and, more than, total	+
Minus, subtracted from, less than, decreased by, difference between	–
What, how much, how many, a number	*x*, *n*, etc.

TRANSLATING TO EXPRESSIONS

To solve some word problems, you will have to translate the information given into algebra. This means representing the unknown value with a variable and then writing an expression. Here are some examples:

Examples: Raul's age is 1 more than twice his sister's age:

Let s represent the sister's age. Then Raul's age is given by $2s + 1$.

The cube of a number is multiplied by 2 and then 1 is subtracted from the product.

Let n represent the number. Then $2n^3 - 1$ represents the result of the operations on n.

A number of chairs, c, is arranged for a banquet so that 10 of the chairs are placed at the head table and the remaining chairs are divided equally among 20 other dining tables.

Then $\frac{c - 10}{20}$ represents the number of chairs at each table other than the head table.

TRANSLATING TO EQUATIONS

For Problem Solving questions, you may have to write an equation to solve the problem. The equation may be unique to the problem, or it may be a formula you are familiar with.

Examples: Company Z spent $\frac{2}{5}$ of its revenues one year on its payroll and $\frac{1}{6}$ of what was left on research. What were the year's original revenues for Company Z if there was \$500,000 left after its payroll and research expenditures?

Let R represent the original revenues.

After $\frac{2}{5}R$ was spent on payroll, there was $\frac{3}{5}R$ left for other uses, including research.

The amount spent on research is given by $\frac{1}{6} \times \frac{3}{5}R = \frac{1}{\cancel{6}_2} \times \frac{\cancel{3}^1}{5}R = \frac{1}{10}R.$

Write the equation and solve for R.

$$
\begin{aligned}
R - \frac{2}{5}R - \frac{1}{10}R &= 500{,}000 \\
R\left(1 - \frac{2}{5} - \frac{1}{10}\right) &= 500{,}000 && \text{Factor } R \text{ from each term.} \\
R\left(\frac{10}{10} - \frac{4}{10} - \frac{1}{10}\right) &= 500{,}000 && \text{Write fractions with a common denominator.} \\
R\left(\frac{5}{10}\right) &= 500{,}000 && \text{Simplify fractions.} \\
R &= 2 \times 500{,}000 \\
R &= 1{,}000{,}000
\end{aligned}
$$

The original revenue for Company Z was \$1,000,000.

The distance formula $d = rt$, where d represents distance, r represents the rate of speed, and t represents time, is frequently the basis for questions on the GRE. To use the formula, the rate and the time must be given in the same units of time, for example, in *miles per hour* and *hours*. Consider this question:

Two cyclists finish a bike course at average speeds of 22 mph and 26 mph, respectively. If it took the first cyclist 38 minutes to finish the course, approximately how long did it take the second cyclist?

The rate for each cyclist is given in mph, so write the time for each one as part of an hour: $38 \text{ minutes} = \frac{38}{60}$ hour, and the unknown time for the second cyclist can be written as $\frac{m}{60}$ hour. Each cyclist rode the same distance, so you can equate the products of rate and time for the two cyclists.

Write the equation and solve for m.

$$\begin{aligned}
\text{Cyclist 1's distance} &= \text{Cyclist 2's distance} \\
r_1 t_1 &= r_2 t_2 \\
22\left(\frac{38}{60}\right) &= 26\left(\frac{m}{60}\right) \\
22(38) &= 26m \\
m &= \frac{22 \times 38}{26} \approx 32
\end{aligned}$$

It took Cyclist 2 about 32 minutes to finish the course.

Translating to Inequalities

Some word problems are solved with an inequality rather than an equation. Key words such as *at least*, *no more than*, or *at most* are clues that an inequality is appropriate.

Example: It costs a manufacturer \$25 to produce a certain phone. Assume that 250 phones are produced, none are defective, and all will be sold to customers. What must the selling price of the phones be if a profit (revenue less production cost) of at least \$2,000 is needed on the order?

Let p represent the selling price of one phone. Then the total profit is $250(p - 25)$.

Write the inequality and solve for p.

$$\begin{aligned}
250(p - 25) &\geq 2{,}000 \\
250p - 6{,}250 &\geq 2{,}000 \\
250p &\geq 8{,}250 \\
p &\geq 33
\end{aligned}$$

The selling price must be at least \$33 per phone to guarantee a profit of \$2,000.

Simple and Compound Interest

Some questions on the GRE involve information about earning interest on an investment or paying interest on a loan. The interest may be **simple interest**, which is computed only on the **principal**—the initial amount invested. Simple interest is usually applied to investments with a time period less than one year. The formula for the computation of simple interest is

$$I = Prt$$

where I is the interest, P is the principal, r is the annual rate expressed as a decimal, and t is the time expressed in years.

To compute the amount, A, of an investment, P, at the end of t years, at annual rate, r, use the formula $A = P(1 + rt)$.

Example: If $3,000 is invested at a simple interest rate of 4%, what is the value of the investment after 9 months?

1. Identify what is given.

$$P = 3{,}000 \qquad r = 4\%$$

$$t = 9 \text{ months} = \frac{3}{4} \text{ year}$$

2. Write the equation and solve for A.

$$\begin{aligned} A &= P(1 + rt) \\ &= 3{,}000\left(1 + 0.04\left(\frac{3}{4}\right)\right) \\ &= 3{,}000(1 + 0.03) \\ &= 3{,}000 \times 1.03 \\ &= 3{,}090 \end{aligned}$$

The value of the investment after 9 months is $3,090.

In the case of compound interest, the interest is computed on the principal as well as any interest earned. To compute the amount of an investment, A, involving compound interest, use this formula: $A = P\left(1 + \frac{r}{C}\right)^{tC}$, where C is the number of times compounded annually, r is the annual rate expressed as a decimal, and t is the time in years.

Example: If $6,000 is invested at 5% annual interest, compounded semiannually, what is the balance after 3 years?

1. Identify what is given.

$$P = 6{,}000 \quad r = 5\%$$

$$t = 3 \text{ years} \quad C = 2 \text{ (semiannually)}$$

2. Write the equation and solve for A.

$$\begin{aligned} A &= P\left(1 + \frac{r}{C}\right)^{tC} \\ &= 6{,}000\left(1 + \frac{0.05}{2}\right)^{3\times 2} \\ &= 6{,}000(1.025)^6 \\ &\approx 6.958.16 \end{aligned}$$

The value of the investment after 3 years is $6,958.16.

TRANSLATION INTO ALGEBRA EXERCISES

Basic

Find an algebraic expression or equation to represent each of the following.

1. Javier is 2 years older than three times his sister's age, s. How old is Javier?

2. The product of 5 and one-half of n.

3. 8 more than k is the same as 2.

4. The sum of the cube of 7 and the value of 1.

5. The quotient of h divided by -11.

6. b is at most the sum of 2 and -1.

Solve.

7. The difference between a number and 4.5 is -1. What is the number?

8. The sum of 18 and a number is at most 10. What could the number be?

9. The quotient of a number divided by -15 is less than 4. What could the number be?

10. Two numbers have a sum of 51. One number is 3 more than the other. What is the greater number?

Intermediate

Find an algebraic expression or equation to represent each of the following.

11. The sum of 4 and b is multiplied by -3, and 0.5 is subtracted from the result.

12. 9 is at least $2\frac{1}{2}$ less than x.

13. The product of 4 less than x and 6 more than x is 20.

Solve.

14. Carla drives for 1.5 hours at 55 miles per hour, then stops for lunch. Then she drives for 2.5 hours at 60 miles per hour. How far does she travel in total?

15. Two consecutive even integers have a sum of 70. What is the lesser integer?

16. The length of a rectangle is 3 less than twice its width. If the perimeter is 36, what are the dimensions of the rectangle?

17. Two numbers have the ratio 4:5. The sum of the numbers is 81. What are the numbers?

18. If $10,800 is invested at a simple interest rate of 4%, what is the value of the investment after 18 months?

19. If $4,500 is invested at a simple interest rate of 6%, what is the value of the investment after 10 months?

20. Two consecutive integers have a sum of –35. What are the integers?

ADVANCED

21. Sixty people attended a concert. Children's tickets sold for $8, and adult tickets sold for $12. If $624 was collected in ticket money, how many children and how many adults attended the concert?

22. Two cars started from the same point and traveled on a straight course in opposite directions for exactly 3 hours, at which time they were 300 miles apart. If one car traveled, on average, 10 miles per hour faster than the other car, what was the average speed of each car for the 3-hour trip?

23. For a given two-digit positive integer, the ones digit is 1 less than the tens digit. The sum of the digits is 15. Find the integer.

24. If the ratio of $3x$ to $5y$ is 4:7, what is the ratio of x to y?

25. At a snack stand, hot dogs cost $3.50, and hamburgers cost $5. If the snack stand sold 27 snacks and had total sales of $118.50, how many hot dogs were sold? How many hamburgers?

26. The sum of x and $\frac{1}{2}$ of y is 10. The value of x minus y is –5. What are the numbers represented by x and y?

27. If $9,500 is invested at 4.5% annual interest, compounded quarterly, what is the balance after 2 years?

28. The length of a rectangle is 5 less than 5 times its width. If the area is 60 square units, what is the length of the rectangle?

29. If $2,300 is invested at $5\frac{1}{2}\%$ annual interest, compounded semiannually, what is the balance after 5 years?

30. Hector invested a total of $6,000. Part of the money was invested in a money market account that paid 9% simple annual interest, and the remainder of the money was invested in a fund that paid 7% simple annual interest. If the interest earned at the end of the first year from these investments was $490, how much did Hector invest at 9%, and how much was invested at 7%?

TRANSLATION INTO ALGEBRA ANSWER KEY

Basic

1. $J = 2 + 3s$

Let J represent Javier's age. Three times s is $3s$, and 2 years older means plus 2. Another correct expression is $J = 3s + 2$.

2. $5\left(\frac{1}{2}n\right)$

"Product" means to multiply. Half of n means $\frac{1}{2}$ times n. A multiplication sign can be used instead of parentheses. Another correct expression is $\frac{5n}{2}$.

3. $8 + k = 2$

"8 more than k" means 8 plus k, and "is" translates to equals. Another correct equation is $k + 8 = 2$.

4. $7^3 + 1$

The "cube" of a number means that number raised to the third power. "Sum" indicates addition.

5. $\frac{h}{-11}$

"Quotient" indicates division. Another correct expression is $h \div -11$.

6. $b \leq 2 + (-1)$

The phrase "at most" means "no more than," which translates to the $\leq$ symbol.

7. $n = 3.5$

"Difference" indicates subtraction, so write the subtraction equation $n - 4.5 = -1$. Then solve by adding 4.5 to both sides.

$$\begin{aligned} n - 4.5 &= -1 \\ n - 4.5 + 4.5 &= -1 + 4.5 \\ n &= 3.5 \end{aligned}$$

8. $x \leq -8$

The phrase "at most" means "no more than." Write and solve $18 + x \leq 10$. Subtract 18 from both sides. The solution includes all numbers less than or equal to -8.

$$\begin{aligned} 18 + x &\leq 10 \\ 18 - 18 + x &\leq 10 - 18 \\ x &\leq -8 \end{aligned}$$

9. $x > -60$

Write the inequality $\frac{x}{-15} < 4$. Solve by multiplying both sides by -15. Whenever you multiply or divide both sides of an inequality by a negative, reverse the symbol.

$$\begin{aligned} \frac{x}{-15} &< 4 \\ -15 \times \frac{x}{-15} &> 4(-15) \\ x &> -60 \end{aligned}$$

10. 27

Let $x =$ the lesser number, and let $x + 3 =$ the greater number. Write the equation $x + x + 3 = 51$. Combine like terms on the left side, and then solve the equation.

$$\begin{aligned} x + x + 3 &= 51 \\ 2x + 3 &= 51 \\ 2x &= 48 \\ x &= 24 \end{aligned}$$

Since $x = 24$, the lesser number is 24 and the greater number is $x + 3 = 24 + 3 = 27$. The question asked for the greater number, so the answer is 27.

INTERMEDIATE

11. $-3(4 + b) - 0.5$

To indicate that a sum is multiplied by a number, use parentheses. If you wrote $-3 \times 4 + b - 0.5$, the multiplication would only apply to 4, and not b.

12. $9 \geq x - 2\frac{1}{2}$

The phrase "at least" indicates an inequality that uses the symbol $\geq$. Note that another way to write this inequality would be $x - 2\frac{1}{2} \leq 9$.

13. $(x - 4)(x + 6) = 20$

Since the factors are binomials, use parentheses to group them. No multiplication sign is needed. Note that "4 less than x" means $x - 4$, not $4 - x$.

14. 232.5 miles

To find distance, use $d = rt$. Add the distances of the two different parts of the trip to find the total.

$$\begin{aligned} d &= r_1t_1 + r_2t_2 \\ d &= 55(1.5) + 60(2.5) \\ d &= 82.5 + 150 \\ d &= 232.5 \end{aligned}$$

15. 34

Let n = the lesser integer. The next even integer would be 2 more than n, so the greater integer is $n + 2$.

$$\begin{aligned} n + n + 2 &= 70 \\ 2n + 2 &= 70 \\ 2n &= 68 \\ n &= 34 \end{aligned}$$

If $n = 34$, then $n + 2 = 36$. Check: $34 + 36 = 70$.

The question asked for the lesser integer, so the answer is 34.

16. 7 and 11

Always make a sketch for polygon problems. Draw a rectangle and label the sides. Since the length is compared to the width, let w = width and $2w - 3$ = length.

w

2w − 3

To find the perimeter of a rectangle, find the sum of all four sides.

$$\begin{aligned} (w) + (2w - 3) + (w) + (2w - 3) &= 36 \\ 6w - 6 &= 36 \\ 6w &= 42 \\ w &= 7 \end{aligned}$$

The width is 7, so the length is $2w - 3 = 2(7) - 3 = 11$.

To check the answer, find the perimeter using the dimensions you found: $7 + 11 + 7 + 11 = 36$, so the answer is correct. The problem asks for the dimensions, so both numbers are needed to answer the question.

17. 36 and 45

Think about numbers that have a ratio of 4:5. Some ratios include $\frac{4}{5}, \frac{8}{10}, \frac{12}{15}$, and $\frac{40}{50}$. Notice that both 4 and 5 are always multiplied by the same number to find the numbers in an equivalent ratio. Think of 4 and 5 both being multiplied by x. Write the equation $4x + 5x = 81$. Combine like terms and use division to find that $x = 9$. The question asks for the two numbers in the ratio. Since $x = 9$, the numbers are $4x = 36$ and $5x = 45$.

18. $11,448

Use the simple interest formula. Since $t =$ the number of years, use $\frac{18}{12}$ for t.

$$\begin{aligned} A &= P(1 + rt) \\ A &= 10{,}800\left(1 + 0.04 \times \frac{18}{12}\right) \\ A &= 10{,}800(1 + 0.04 \times 1.5) \\ A &= 10{,}800(1 + 0.06) \\ A &= 10{,}800(1.06) \\ A &= 11{,}448 \end{aligned}$$

19. $4,725

Use the simple interest formula. Since $t =$ the number of years, use $\frac{10}{12}$ for t.

$$\begin{aligned} A &= P(1 + rt) \\ A &= 4{,}500\left(1 + 0.06 \times \frac{10}{12}\right) \\ A &= 4{,}500\left(1 + \frac{0.6}{12}\right) \\ A &= 4{,}500(1+0.05) \\ A &= 4{,}500(1.05) \\ A &= 4{,}725 \end{aligned}$$

20. −18 and −17

"Consecutive" means in a row. For example, consecutive integers include 4, 5, 6, 7, etc. Each is one more than the previous integer. Let $n =$ the first integer and $n + 1 =$ the greater integer. The sum of these two expressions is −35. Solve $n + n + 1 = -35$.

$$\begin{aligned} n + n + 1 &= -35 \\ 2n + 1 &= -35 \\ 2n &= -36 \\ n &= -18 \end{aligned}$$

The lesser integer is −18, so the greater integer is $n + 1 = -18 + 1 = -17$.

Advanced

21. 24 children, 36 adults

Write and solve a system of equations. Let c = the number of children's tickets and a = the number of adult tickets. Write one equation for the number of tickets sold and another equation for the money earned.

$$\begin{aligned} c + a &= 60 \\ 8c + 12a &= 624 \end{aligned}$$

Then solve the system using substitution. Subtract a from both sides of the first equation to find that $c = 60 - a$. Substitute $60 - a$ for c into the second equation.

$$\begin{aligned} 8(60 - a) + 12a &= 624 \\ 480 - 8a + 12a &= 624 \\ 480 + 4a &= 624 \\ 4a &= 144 \\ a &= 36 \end{aligned}$$

This means that there were 36 adult tickets sold. Substitute this into the first equation to find the number of children's tickets sold.

$$\begin{aligned} c + a &= 60 \\ c + 36 &= 60 \\ c &= 24 \end{aligned}$$

So, 36 adult tickets and 24 children's tickets were sold.

22. 45 miles per hour and 55 miles per hour

Think of two partial distances being added together to form one long distance of 300 miles. Let x = the rate of one car and $x + 10$ = the rate of the faster car. Use the formula distance = rate × time, or $d = rt$.

$$\begin{aligned} d_1 + d_2 &= 300 \\ r_1t_1 + r_2t_2 &= 300 \\ x(3) + (10 + x)3 &= 300 \\ 3x + 30 + 3x &= 300 \\ 6x + 30 &= 300 \\ 6x &= 270 \\ x &= 45 \end{aligned}$$

This means that the slower car was driving 45 miles per hour and $x + 10 = 55$ is the rate of the other car. The question asks for the rate of both cars, so the answer is 45 miles per hour and 55 miles per hour.

23. 87

Write and solve a system of equations. Let $x =$ the tens digit and $y =$ the ones digit. Since the sum of the digits is 15, write the equation $x + y = 15$. Since the ones digit is 1 less than the tens digit, think "ones digit = tens digit minus 1", and write the equation $y = x - 1$. Solve to find both digits of the number. Substitute $x - 1$ for y in the equation $x + y = 15$:

$$\begin{aligned} x + x - 1 &= 15 \\ 2x - 1 &= 15 \\ 2x &= 16 \\ x &= 8 \end{aligned}$$

The tens digit is 8, and the ones digit is $15 - 8 = 7$. Therefore, the number is 87.

24. $\frac{20}{21}$

Write a proportion to show the equivalent ratios. Then multiply both sides of the equation by $\frac{5}{3}$ to isolate $\frac{x}{y}$. Express the answer as a ratio.

$$\begin{aligned} \frac{3x}{5y} &= \frac{4}{7} \\ \frac{5}{3} \times \frac{3x}{5y} &= \frac{4}{7} \times \frac{5}{3} \\ \frac{x}{y} &= \frac{20}{21} \end{aligned}$$

So, the answer is $\frac{20}{21}$.

25. 11 hot dogs and 16 hamburgers

Write and solve a system of equations. Let $h =$ the number of hot dogs sold and $b =$ the number of hamburgers sold. Write one equation for the number of snacks sold and another equation for the money earned.

$$\begin{aligned} h + b &= 27 \\ 3.5h + 5b &= 118.5 \end{aligned}$$

Solve the first equation for b: $b = 27 - h$.

Substitute $27 - h$ for b in the second equation.

$$\begin{aligned} 3.5h + 5(27 - h) &= 118.5 \\ 3.5h + 135 - 5h &= 118.5 \\ -1.5h + 135 &= 118.5 \\ -1.5h &= -16.5 \\ h &= 11 \end{aligned}$$

Substitute 11 for h in the first equation to find b:

$$\begin{aligned} 11 + b &= 27 \\ b &= 16 \end{aligned}$$

There were 11 hot dogs sold and 16 hamburgers sold.

26. $x = 5$ and $y = 10$

Write out the system of equations.

$$\begin{aligned} x + \frac{1}{2}y &= 10 \\ x - y &= -5 \end{aligned}$$

To eliminate the x terms, combine the equations by subtracting the second equation from the first.

$$\begin{aligned} x + \frac{1}{2}y &= 10 \\ -(x - y &= -5) \\ \frac{1}{2}y - (-\ y) &= 10 - (-5) \\ \frac{3}{2}y &= 15 \\ y &= 15 \times \frac{2}{3} \\ y &= 10 \end{aligned}$$

Now, substitute 10 for y in either equation to find x. Since the second equation is easier to work with, use that one:

$$\begin{aligned} x - y &= -5 \\ x - (10) &= -5 \\ x &= 5 \end{aligned}$$

The answer is $x = 5$ and $y = 10$.

27. $10,389.20

Use the compound interest formula. Express the rate 4.5% as 0.045.

$$\begin{aligned} A &= P\left(1 + \frac{r}{C}\right)^{tC} \\ A &= 9{,}500\left(1 + \frac{0.045}{4}\right)^{2\times 4} \\ A &= 9{,}500(1 + 0.01125)^{8} \\ A &= 9{,}500(1.01125)^{8} \\ A &\approx 9{,}500(1.0936) \\ A &\approx 10{,}389.20 \end{aligned}$$

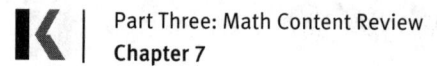

28. $l = 15$

Draw and label a diagram. Since the length is compared to the width, let $w =$ the width.

w

$5w - 5$

Since the area of a rectangle equals *length* × *width*, write an expression with the factors being multiplied and set it equal to the area, which is 60.

$$\begin{aligned} w(5w - 5) &= 60 \\ 5w^2 - 5w &= 60 \\ 5w^2 - 5w - 60 &= 0 \\ 5(w^2 - w - 12) &= 0 \\ 5(w + 3)(w - 4) &= 0 \\ w + 3 &= 0;\ w - 4 = 0 \\ w &= -3;\ w = 4 \end{aligned}$$

Since the rectangle cannot have a negative width, use the solution $w = 4$. Then the length is $5w - 5 = 5(4) - 5 = 15$.

29. $3,016.80

Use the compound interest formula.

$$\begin{aligned} A &= P\left(1 + \frac{r}{C}\right)^{tC} \\ A &= 2{,}300\left(1 + \frac{0.055}{2}\right)^{5\times 2} \\ A &= 2{,}300(1 + 0.0275)^{10} \\ A &= 2{,}300(1.0275)^{10} \\ A &\approx 2{,}300(1.31165) \\ A &\approx 3{,}016.80 \end{aligned}$$

30. $3,500 in the 9% account and $2,500 in the 7% account

Let x = the amount invested in the 9% account. Therefore, $6{,}000 - x$ represents the amount invested in the 7% account. The amounts invested must add up to 6,000. To find each amount of interest, use $I = Prt$. (Note that this formula gives the amount of interest, not the total amount of investment plus interest.) The two amounts of interest add up to 490.

$$\begin{aligned} 0.09(x) + 0.07(6{,}000 - x) &= 490 \\ 0.09x + 420 - 0.07x &= 490 \\ 0.02x + 420 &= 490 \\ 0.02x &= 70 \\ x &= 3{,}500 \end{aligned}$$

Hector invested $3,500 in the 9% account. Subtract this amount from 6,000 to find the amount invested in the 7% account: $6{,}000 - 3{,}500 = 2{,}500$. Hector invested $2,500 in the 7% account.

FUNCTIONS

Classic function notation problems may appear on the test. An algebraic expression of only one variable may be defined as a **function**, usually *f* or *g*, of that variable.

Example: What is the value of the function $f(x) = x^2 - 1$ when $x = 1$?

In the function $f(x) = x^2 - 1$, if x is 1, then $f(1) = 1^2 - 1 = 0$. In other words, when the **input** to the function is 1, the **output** is 0. The set of input numbers for a function is the **domain** and the set of output values is the **range** of the function. Every input value of a function has exactly one output value. However, more than one input value may have the same output value. Consider the function $f(x) = x^2 - 1$ again. If $x = -1$, $f(-1) = (-1)^2 - 1 = 1 - 1 = 0$. So for $f(x) = x^2 - 1$, $f(1) = f(-1) = 0$.

RESTRICTED DOMAIN OF A FUNCTION

A function may be defined for all real numbers or it may be defined only for a subset of the real numbers.

Example: $g(x) = -x^2 + 2$, where $-3 \leq x \leq 3$

The domain of the function $g(x)$ is restricted to values of x between -3 and 3 inclusive. On the GRE you may be asked to find the minimum value of a function or the maximum value of a function. The maximum value of $g(x) = -x^2 + 2$ occurs when $x = 0$; $g(0) = -x^2 + 2 = 0 + 2 = 2$. On the graph, this is represented by the point (0, 2). To find the minimum value of $g(x) = -x^2 + 2$, where $-3 \leq x \leq 3$, find the value when $x = -3$ or $x = 3$.

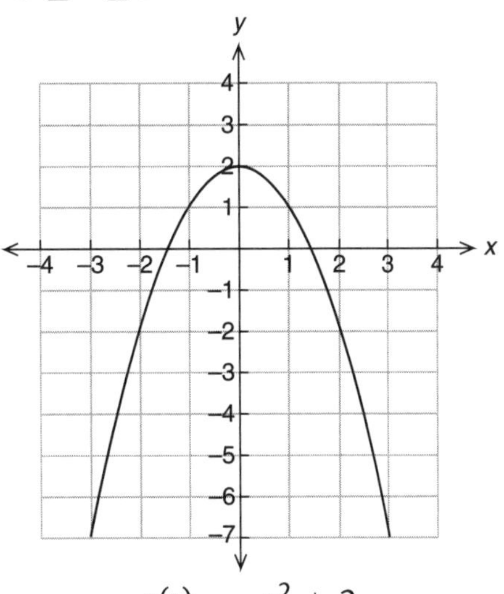

$g(x) = -x^2 + 2$,
$-3 \leq x \leq 3$

$g(-3) = -x^2 + 2 = -(-3)^2 + 2 = -(9) + 2 = -7$ and

$g(3) = -x^2 + 2 = -(3)^2 + 2 = -(9) + 2 = -7$

On the GRE, a minimum (or maximum) value problem can be solved in one of two ways. Either plug the answer choices into the function and find which gives you the least (or greatest) value, or use what you know about number operations. In the case $g(x) = -x^2 + 2$, the function g will be at a maximum when $-x^2$ is as small as possible. This leads you to consider the case where $x = 0$. Conversely, the minimum value occurs when $-x^2$ is as large as possible, considering the restricted domain. This occurs when $x = -3$ or $x = 3$. That value is -7.

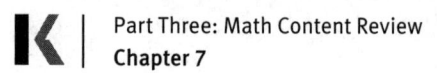

The domain of a function may also be restricted to avoid having a zero in the denominator of a fraction or to avoid taking the square root of a negative number.

Examples: $f(x) = \frac{2x - 5}{x - 3}$, where $x \neq 3$ — Restrict domain of f to avoid $x - 3 = 0$.

$h(x) = \sqrt{x + 10}$, where $x \geq -10$ — Restrict the domain of h to avoid $x + 10 < 0$.

Absolute Value Function

The function $g(x) = |x|$ is called the **absolute value function**. The domain of g is all real numbers—unless it is restricted in a certain problem—and represents the distance between any number x and 0 on the number line. Because the absolute value function represents a distance, its output is always a positive number or zero.

FUNCTIONS EXERCISES

Basic

1. What is the domain of this function? {(–3, 4), (–2, 5), (–1, 6), (0, 7), (1, 8)}

2. What is the range of this function? {(–3, 4), (–2, 5), (–1, 6), (0, 7), (1, 8)}

3. Determine if this table represents a function.

x	*y*
8	4
6	3
4	2
2	1
0	0

4. Does this set of ordered pairs represent a function? {(8, 5), (4, 6), (2, 3), (4, 9), (1, 7)}

5. Write the equation $y = 2x + 7$ using function notation.

6. If $f(x) = 4x + 1$, what is the value of $f(-3)$?

7. If $f(x) = -2(x - 4)$, what is the value of $f(-7)$?

8. What is the range of the function $f(x) = 6 + x$ if the domain is $\{-4, 0, 4\}$?

9. If $g(x) = x^2 + x$, what is the value of $g(9)$?

10. For what value should the domain be restricted for the function $f(x) = \frac{x+2}{x-2}$?

Intermediate

11. What is the minimum value for the function $f(x) = x^2 - 5$?

12. What is the maximum value for the function $g(x) = -2x^2 - 1$?

13. What is the minimum value for the function $f(x) = -x^2 + x + 4$ where $-6 \le x \le 6$?

14. For what values should the domain be restricted for the function $g(x) = \sqrt{x + 8}$?

15. Does the graph below represent a function? Why or why not?

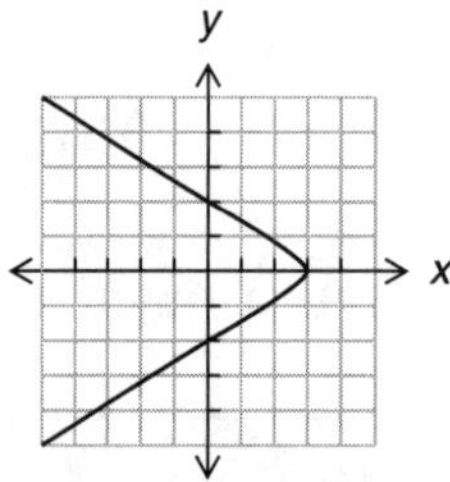

16. Express the relationship between x and $f(x)$ algebraically; x and $f(x)$ have a linear relationship.

x	4	5	6	−4	−5	−6
f(x)	25	31	37	−23	−29	−35

17. Determine the range for this function table.

$g(x) = |x| + 2$

x	**g(x)**
−8.8	
−6.6	
−4.4	
−2.2	
0	

18. What is the range of the function shown in the graph?

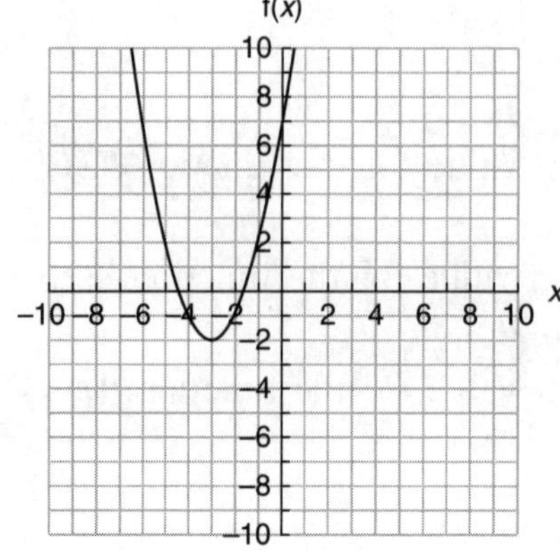

19. What is the domain for the function shown in the graph?

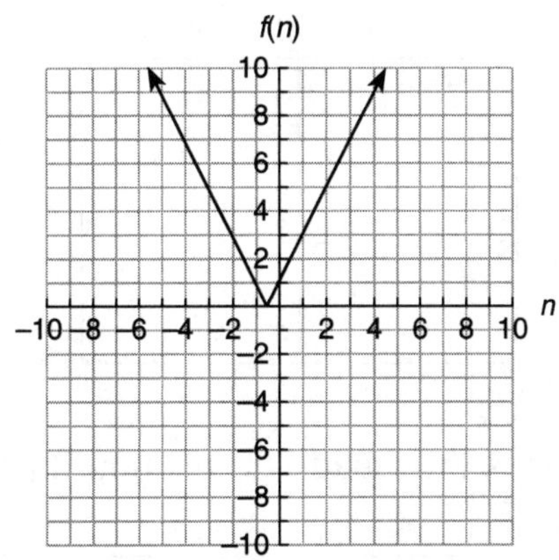

20. If $f(x) = \frac{1}{2}x + 8$, what value of x makes $f(x) = 0$?

Advanced

21. For what values should the domain be restricted for this function?

$$f(n) = \frac{n - 6}{n^2 - 6n}$$

22. What is the domain of the function shown below?

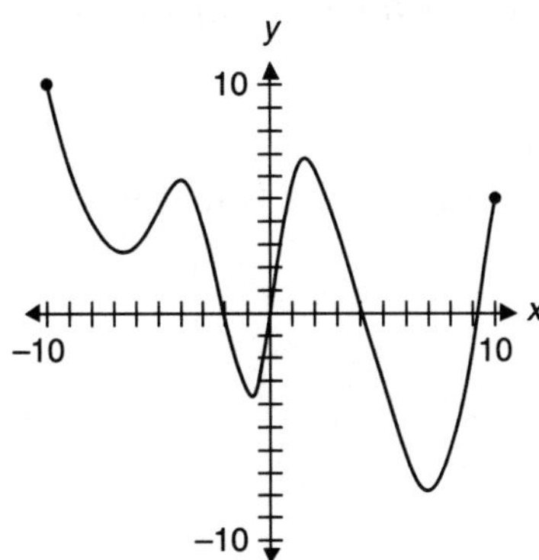

23. What is $h(-4)$ if $h(x) = h^3 + 3h^2 + h$?

24. If $g(a) = a^2 - 1$ and $f(a) = a + 4$, what is $g(f(-4))$?

25. What is the domain for this function?

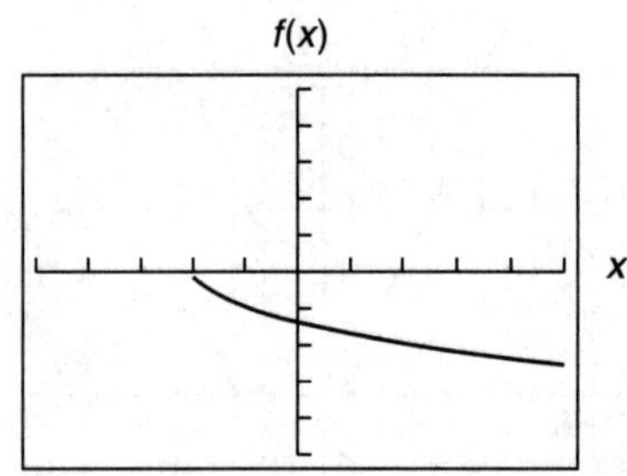

26. What equation describes this quadratic relationship?

x	$f(x)$
3	10
6	37
9	82
12	145

27. If $f(x) = \dfrac{2x + 6}{4}$ and $g(x) = 2x - 1$, what is $f(g(x))$?

28. What is the minimum value for the function $f(x) = -x^2 - x + 1$ where $-6 \leq x \leq 6$?

29. What is the maximum value for the function $g(x) = -2x^2 + 5$ where $-5 < x < 5$?

30. What is the minimum value for the function $|x| + 3 = g(x)$?

FUNCTIONS ANSWER KEY

Basic

1. {–3, –2, –1, 0, 1}

The domain of a function is the set of *x*-values in a set of ordered pairs. In the set {(–3, 4), (–2, 5), (–1, 6), (0, 7), (1, 8)} the *x*-values (domain) are listed first in each pair.

2. {4, 5, 6, 7, 8}

The range of a function is the set of *y*-values in a set of ordered pairs. In the set {(–3, 4), (–2, 5), (–1, 6), (0, 7), (1, 8)} the *y*-values (range) are listed second in each pair.

3. Yes, this table represents a function.

Each element of the domain is paired with exactly one element of the range.

4. No, this set of ordered pairs does not represent a function.

The *x*-value of 4 is paired with two different *y*-values; therefore, it is not a function.

5. $f(x) = 2x + 7$

In a function, x represents the domain, and $f(x)$ represents the range.

6. –11

Replace x with –3 in $f(x) = 4x + 1$ to find the value of $f(-3)$:

$$\begin{aligned} f(-3) &= 4(-3) + 1 \\ f(-3) &= -12 + 1 \\ f(-3) &= -11 \end{aligned}$$

7. 22

Replace x with –7 in $f(x) = -2(x - 4)$ to find the value of $f(-7)$:

$$\begin{aligned} f(-7) &= -2(-7 - 4) \\ f(-7) &= -2(-11) \\ f(-7) &= 22 \end{aligned}$$

8. {2, 6, 10}

Replace x with each value of the domain and solve for the range.

Replace x with –4 in $f(x) = 6 + x$. $\quad f(x) = 6 + -4 = 2$

Replace x with 0 in $f(x) = 6 + x$. $\quad f(x) = 6 + 0 = 6$

Replace x with 4 in $f(x) = 6 + x$. $\quad f(x) = 6 + 4 = 10$

9. 90

Replace x with 9 in $g(x) = x^2 + x$ to find the value of $g(9)$.

$$\begin{aligned} g(9) &= 9^2 + 9 \\ g(9) &= 81 + 9 \\ g(9) &= 90 \end{aligned}$$

10. $x = 2$

Restrict the domain of x to avoid $x - 2 = 0$; 0 is not permissible as a divisor.

INTERMEDIATE

11. −5

The minimum value for the function $f(x) = x^2 - 5$ is found by replacing x with 0; $0^2 - 5 = 0 - 5 = -5$. Because the value of any number squared (besides 0) is positive, the value of x^2 is always positive; replacing x with 0 gives the minimum of the function.

12. −1

The maximum value for the function $g(x) = -2x^2 - 1$ is found by replacing x with 0; $-2(0)^2 - 1 = 0 - 1 = -1$. Because the coefficient of x^2 is negative, replacing x with 0 gives the maximum of the function.

13. −38

The minimum value for the function $f(x) = -x^2 + x + 4$ where $-6 \leq x \leq 6$ is found by replacing x with -6; $f(-6) = -(-6)^2 + (-6) + 4 = -36 - 6 + 4 = -38$. Replacing x with any other value of the domain results in a value greater than -38.

14. All values less than −8; $x < -8$

Restrict the domain of x to avoid $x + 8 < 0$; the square root of a negative number is nonreal.

15. Yes

We're used to thinking of functions as $y = f(x)$; that is, given a particular x-value, we can find a single value for y. There are multiple (indeed, infinite) points on this graph at which two different y-values exist for the same x-value. Therefore, this graph does not represent a function in the sense that you might be used to. However, it is a function expressed as $x = f(y)$: for a given y value, there is a single x value. Therefore, this is a function.

16. $f(x) = 6x + 1$

Because you are told that this is a linear relationship, try to express the relationship in the slope-intercept form of a line, $f(x) = y = mx + b$, where m is the slope and b is the y-intercept. First, find the slope using the equation $m = \frac{\text{change in } y}{\text{change in } x} = \frac{31 - 25}{5 - 4} = \frac{6}{1} = 6$.

Next, plug in values of m, x, and y into the slope-intercept form to find b.

$$\begin{aligned} y &= mx + b \\ 25 &= (6)(4) + b \\ 25 &= 24 + b \\ b &= 1 \end{aligned}$$

Finally, use function notation to express the relationship between x and $f(x)$:

$$f(x) = 6x + 1$$

Plug in the values of x to make sure the values of $f(x)$ correspond with your chosen rule.

17. {10.8, 8.6, 6.4, 4.2, 2}

Replace x in the function with each value of the domain to find the range.

18. $f(x) \geq -2$

To determine the range of the function, look at all the values of $f(x)$. The values are greater than or equal to -2, so the range is $f(x) \geq -2$.

19. The domain of the function is the set of all real numbers.

The domain represents all the values for n. Since there are no constraints on what n can be, the domain is the set of all real numbers.

20. $x = -16$

Replace $f(x)$ with 0 and then solve for x.

$$\begin{aligned} \frac{1}{2}x + 8 &= 0 \\ \frac{1}{2}x &= -8 \\ x &= -16 \end{aligned}$$

Advanced

21. 6 and 0

Factor the denominator: $n^2 - 6n = n(n - 6)$; the value of n cannot be 6 or 0, as a denominator of 0 is not permissible.

22. $-10 \leq x \leq 10$

The x-values on the graph range from -10 to 10, so the domain includes all of the values between these numbers.

23. −20

Replace h with -4 in $h(x) = h^3 + 3h^2 + h$ to find the value of $h(-4)$.

$$\begin{aligned} h(-4) &= (-4)^3 + 3(-4)^2 + (-4) \\ h(-4) &= -64 + 3(16) + (-4) \\ h(-4) &= -64 + 48 - 4 \\ h(-4) &= -20 \end{aligned}$$

24. −1

Replace a in $f(a)$ with -4: $f(-4) = -4 + 4 = 0$. Then replace a in $g(a)$ with the value of $f(-4)$, or 0: $g(f(-4)) = g(0) = (0)^2 - 1 = -1$.

25. $x \geq -2$

Notice the values on the x-axis. For this function, x begins at -2 and increases, so the domain of this function is any value greater than or equal to -2.

26. $f(x) = x^2 + 1$

Because you are told that this is a quadratic relationship, try to express the relationship in the general form of a quadratic equation, $f(x) = y = ax^2 + bx + c$. Before setting up a complicated series of three equations to solve for a, b, and c, look at the values of x and $f(x)$ that are given. You know that $f(x)$ is related to x^2, so square the given values of x and see how they relate to $f(x)$.

x	x^2	$f(x)$	$f(x) - x^2$
3	9	10	1
6	36	37	1
9	81	82	1
12	144	145	1

Since $f(x) - x^2$ is a constant for all values of x and $f(x)$ given, $f(x) - x^2 = 1 = c$, so b must equal 0. Finally, use function notation to express the relationship between x and $f(x)$:

$$f(x) = x^2 + 1$$

Plug in the values of x to make sure the values of $f(x)$ correspond with your chosen rule.

27. $x + 1$

To find $f(g(x))$, replace the variable in $f(x)$ with $g(x)$, or $2x - 1$.

$$f(x) = \frac{2x + 6}{4}$$

$$f(g(x)) = \frac{2(g(x)) + 6}{4} = \frac{2(2x - 1) + 6}{4} = \frac{4x - 2 + 6}{4} = \frac{4x + 4}{4} = x + 1$$

28. -41

To determine the minimum value of the function $f(x) = -x^2 - x + 1$ where $-6 \leq x \leq 6$, find the value of $x = 6$, which yields the least value of $f(x)$ in the domain.

$$-(6)^2 - 6 + 1 = -36 - 6 + 1 = -41$$

29. 5

The maximum value for the function $g(x) = -2x^2 + 5$ where $-5 < x < 5$ is found when $x = 0$.

$$-2(0)^2 + 5 = 0 + 5 = 5$$

30. 3

The minimum for this function occurs at the least possible value for the absolute value of x, which is $x = 0$.

$$|0| + 3 = 3$$

COORDINATE GEOMETRY

Questions on the GRE sometimes refer to lines or curves graphed on a coordinate plane. An ***xy*-coordinate plane** is formed by two number lines at right angles to each other, intersecting at their zero points. The intersecting lines form four quadrants, named by the Roman numerals, I, II, III, and IV. The horizontal number line is the ***x*-axis**, the vertical number line is the ***y*-axis** and the point of intersection is the **origin** (*O*). Every point on the plane is named by its *x*- and *y*-coordinates, (*x*, *y*).

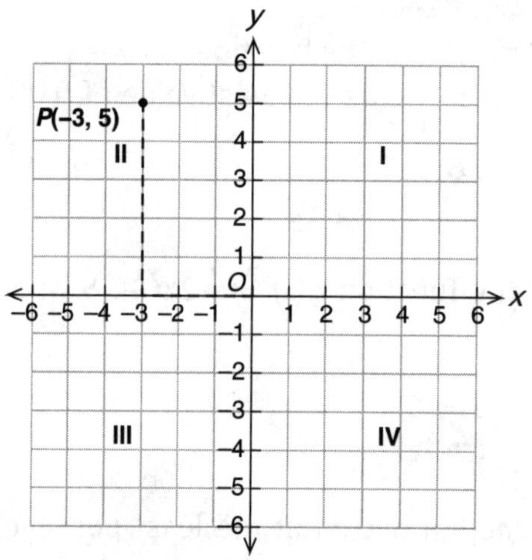

To graph point *P*, whose coordinates are (−3, 5), start at the origin, go left 3 units or spaces, and then go up 5 units or spaces. To reflect point *P*:

- across the *x*-axis, change the sign of the *y*-coordinate.
- across the *y*-axis, change the sign of the *x*-coordinate.
- about the origin, change the sign of both the *x*- and *y*-coordinate.

The reflections of point *P* are shown on the following graph.

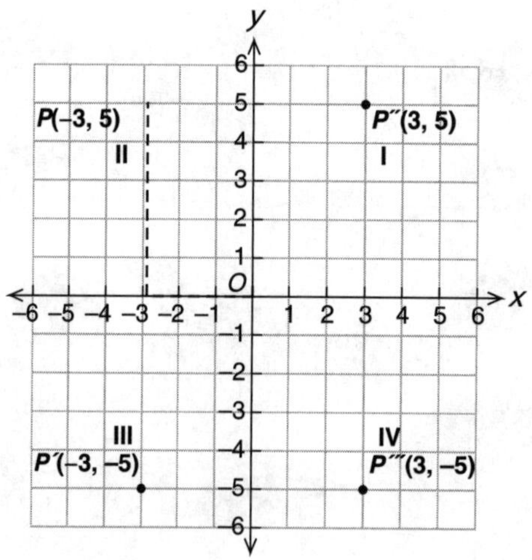

Distance between Points

There are several ways to find the distance between two points in the *xy*-plane, depending on the location of the points. If two points lie on the same horizontal or vertical grid line, just count the units or spaces between them. The distance from C to A below is $5 + 3 = 8$ units or spaces. Likewise, the distance from A to B is 4 units or spaces.

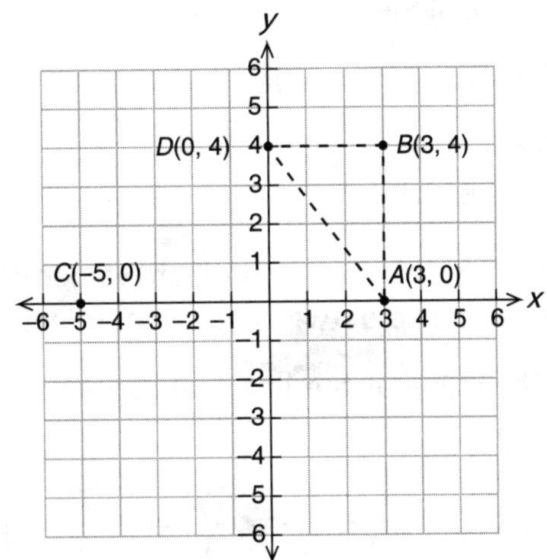

To find the distance from A to D, consider the line segment AD as the hypotenuse of a right triangle, whose legs are segments AB and BD. Because triangle ABD has legs of 3 and 4, it is a 3:4:5 triangle. So the distance from A to D is the same as the length of the hypotenuse of the triangle, which is 5. You will see special triangles such as this frequently on the GRE. For more discussion of special right triangles, see chapter 8.

The distance between two points in the *xy*-plane can also be found using the Pythagorean theorem. To find the distance between the points C and B in the figure shown, use the fact that the length of CA is 8 and the length of AB is 4. Plug these numbers into the Pythagorean theorem:

$$\begin{aligned} CB^2 &= CA^2 + AB^2 \\ CB^2 &= 8^2 + 4^2 \\ CB^2 &= 64 + 16 \\ CB^2 &= 80 \\ CB &= \sqrt{80} \approx 9 \end{aligned}$$

The distance between the points C and B is about 9 units or spaces.

Slope of a Line

The graph of an equation in the variables x and y is the set of all points (x, y) whose coordinates satisfy the equation. The graph of a linear equation in the form $y = mx + b$ is a straight line in the *xy*-plane with slope m and y-intercept b. This form of the equation of a line is known as **slope-intercept form**.

The ***y*-intercepts** of a graph are the *y*-values of the points where the graph crosses the *y*-axis. The graph of a linear function has only one *y*-intercept. The ***x*-intercepts** of a graph are the *x*-values of the points where the graph crosses the *x*-axis. The graph of a linear function has at most one *x*-intercept.

The **slope** of a line tells you how steeply that line goes up or down. If a line gets higher as you move to the right, it has a positive slope. If it goes down as you move to the right, it has a negative slope.

To find the slope of a line, use this formula:

$$\text{Slope} = \frac{\text{rise}}{\text{run}} = \frac{\text{change in } y}{\text{change in } x}$$

Rise means the difference between the *y*-coordinate values of any two points on the line, and *run* means the difference between the *x*-coordinate values.

Example: What is the slope of the line that contains the points (1, 2) and (4, −5)?

$$\text{Slope} = \frac{-5 - 2}{4 - 1} = \frac{-7}{3} = -\frac{7}{3}$$

To determine the slope of a line from an equation, put the equation into the slope-intercept form.

Example: What is the slope of the line represented by the equation $3x + 2y = 4$?

$$3x + 2y = 4$$
$$2y = -3x + 4$$
$$y = -\frac{3}{2}x + 2, \text{ so } m \text{ is } -\frac{3}{2}$$

The larger the absolute value of the slope, the steeper the slope. The slope of any horizontal line is 0 because the *rise* (the numerator of the slope formula) is 0. The slope of any vertical line is undefined because the *run*, (the denominator of the slope formula) is 0.

Parallel lines have the same slope. **Perpendicular** lines have slopes that are negative reciprocals of each other. For example, all lines parallel to $y = -\frac{3}{2}x + 2$ have a slope of $-\frac{3}{2}$, and all lines perpendicular to $y = -\frac{3}{2}x + 2$ have a slope of $\frac{2}{3}$.

Graphing Systems of Equations and Inequalities

A graph can be used to show the solutions of systems of equations or systems of inequalities. Let's look at the graph of a system of two equations first.

Example: What is the solution of the system of linear equations shown below?

$$y = -x + 8$$
$$y = 4x - 7$$

The graphs of the two equations are shown below. The point of intersection, (3, 5), is the solution to the system.

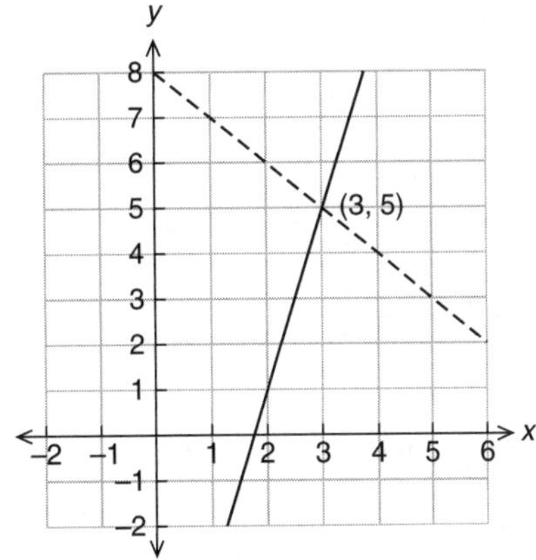

Example: What is the solution of the system of inequalities shown?

$$y \leq x + 2$$
$$y \geq -x$$

The graphs of the two inequalities are shown. The solutions to the inequality $y \leq x + 2$ are all the points on and below the line $y = x + 2$. The solutions to the inequality $y \geq -x$ are all the points on and above the line $y = -x$. The solution to the system includes all the points in the region that is double-shaded.

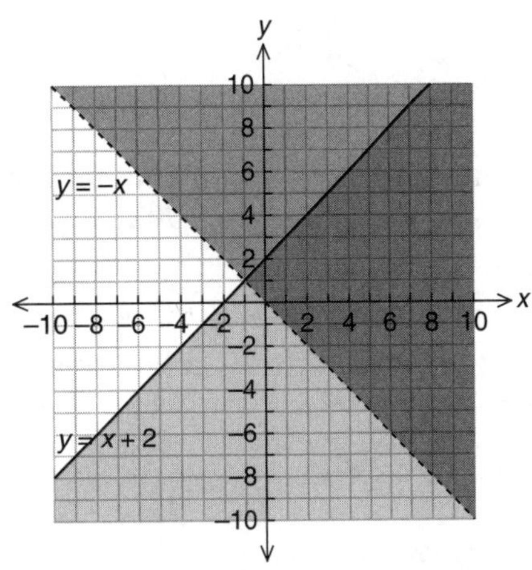

SYMMETRY

A point whose coordinates are (a, b) can be reflected across the line $y = x$ in the coordinate plane. The coordinates of the reflected point will be (b, a). To say it another way, the points (a, b) and (b, a) are symmetric about the line $y = x$.

The line $y = x$ is graphed below. Consider the line $y = 4x + 2$. The equation of the reflection of the line $y = 4x + 2$ is found by interchanging y and x in the equation and then solving for y:

$$\begin{aligned} x &= 4y + 2 \\ -4y &= -x + 2 \\ y &= \frac{-1}{-4}x - \frac{2}{4} \\ y &= \frac{1}{4}x - \frac{1}{2} \end{aligned}$$

Both lines are shown on the graph that follows. Notice that when point $A(1, 6)$ is reflected across the line $y = x$, the coordinates are reversed and you have $A'(6, 1)$.

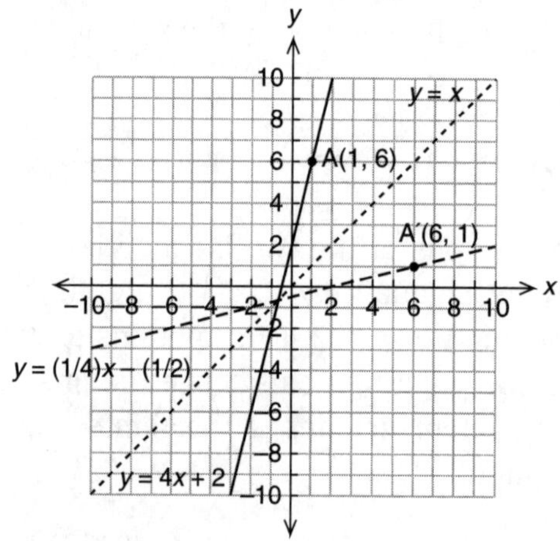

PARABOLAS

The graph of a quadratic equation of the form $ax^2 + bx + c$, where a, b, and c are constants and $a \neq 0$, is a parabola. When a is positive, the parabola opens upward and the **vertex** is the minimum point on its graph. Conversely, when a is negative, the parabola opens downward and the **vertex** is the maximum point on its graph. A vertical line through the vertex is a line of symmetry of the parabola. An example of each case is shown.

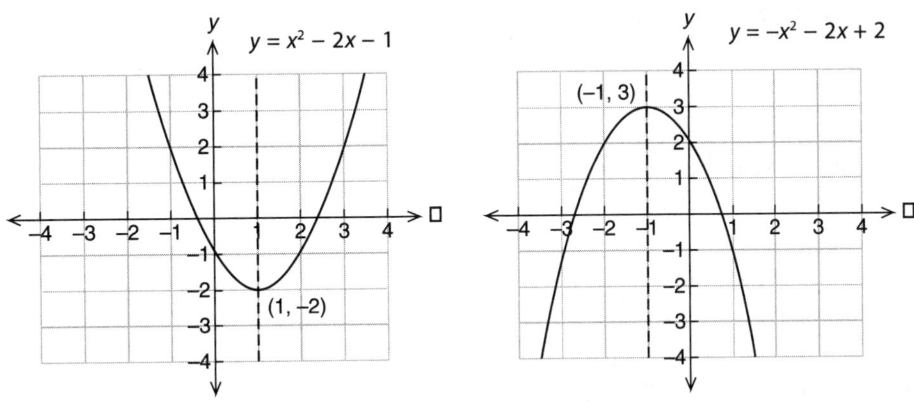

Circles

The graph of $x^2 + y^2 = 64$ is a circle centered at the origin with radius 8. It is the larger circle on the following graph. The smaller circle on the graph is centered at (−2, −2) with radius 3. The equation of the smaller circle is $(x + 2)^2 + (y + 2)^2 = 9$.

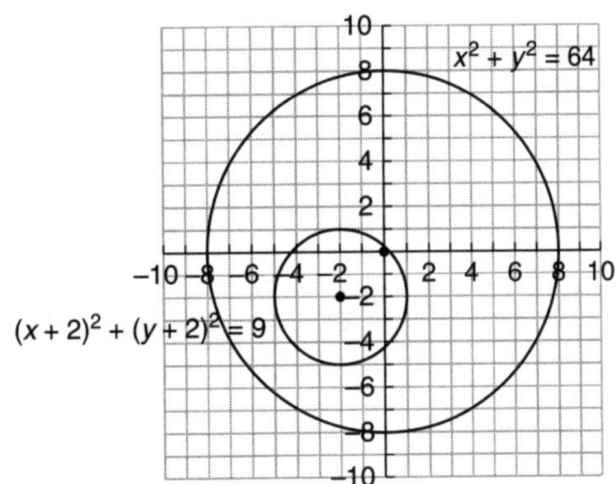

COORDINATE GEOMETRY EXERCISES

BASIC

Use this coordinate plane to answer the following.

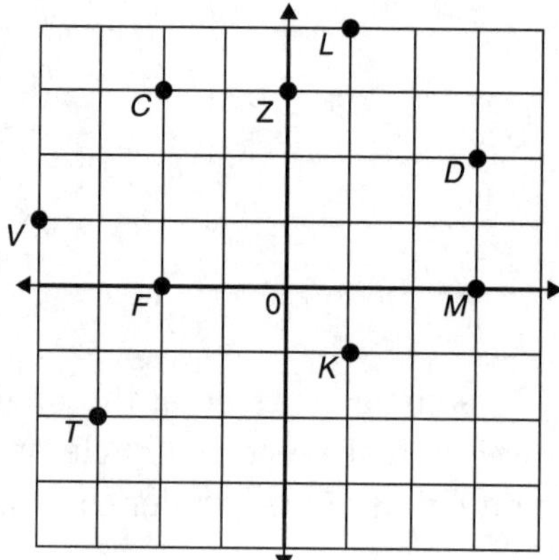

1. What are the coordinates of point *C*?
2. What are the coordinates of point *M*?
3. What are the coordinates of point *T*?
4. What quadrant do points *V* and *C* lie in?
5. What is the distance between points *K* and *L*?
6. What point lies at (0, 3)?
7. What are the coordinates of point *D* if it is reflected over the *x*-axis?
8. What are the coordinates of point *V* if it is reflected over the *y*-axis?
9. What are the coordinates of point *K* if it is reflected about the origin?
10. What is the approximate distance between point *C* and point *M*?

INTERMEDIATE

11. What is the slope of the line that contains the points (4, 8) and (–1, –2)?

12. What is the slope of the line represented by the equation $y = 8x + 3$?

13. What is the slope of the line represented by the equation $4x + 3y = 12$?

14. What is the slope of a line that is parallel to $y = -2x - 4$?

15. What is the slope of a line that is perpendicular to $y = \frac{1}{3}x - 7$?

16. What is the slope of the line that contains the points (–4, 5) and (2, 5)?

17. What is the slope of the line that contains the points (6, 3) and (6, –2)?

18. What is the slope of the line that is represented by the equation $3y = -\frac{1}{2}x$?

19. What is the length of $\overline{CD}$?

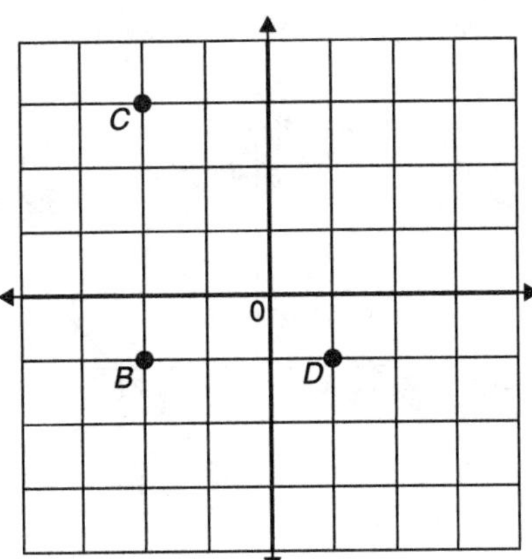

20. What is the solution to the system shown on the coordinate plane?

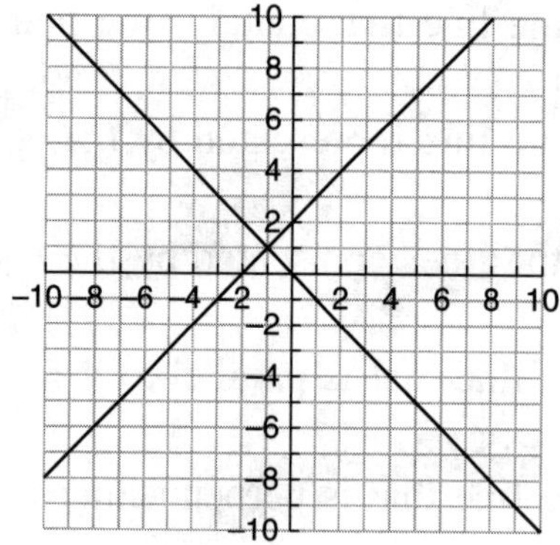

ADVANCED

21. What is the slope of a line parallel to a line that contains the points (–3, 7) and (–3, –2)?

22. What is the slope of a line perpendicular to a line that contains the points (5, –1) and (–2, –1)?

23. Will these two lines have a point of intersection?

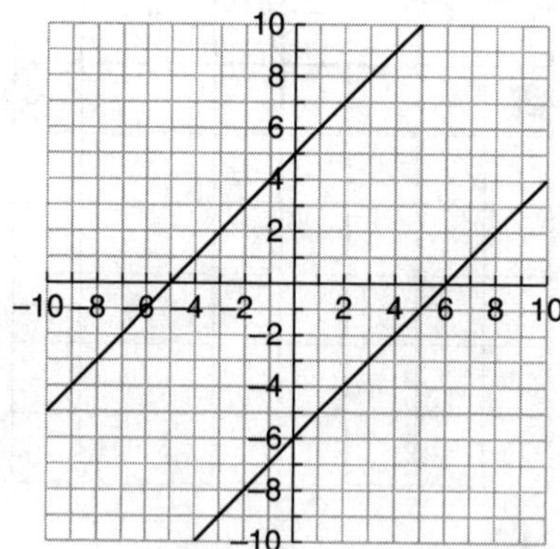

24. What is the solution to this system of inequalities?

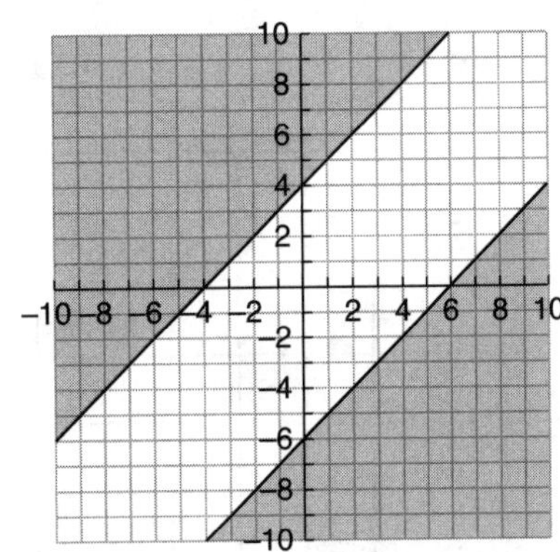

25. What is the slope of a line that is perpendicular to $2x - 5y = 20$?

26. What is the x-intercept of the line represented by $y = 4x - 8$?

27. Determine if the point $(-2, 12)$ lies on the graph of $y = -2.5x + 7$.

28. Which line is steeper?

$y = -3x + 4$
$4x - 3y = 9$

29. Is the origin part of the solution for this system of inequalities?

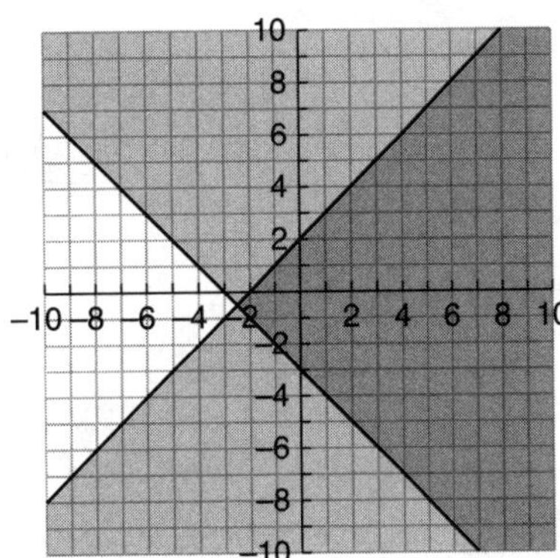

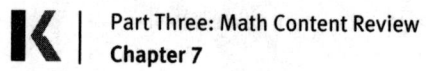

30. What transformation occurs if point C is reflected over the x-axis and then over the y-axis?

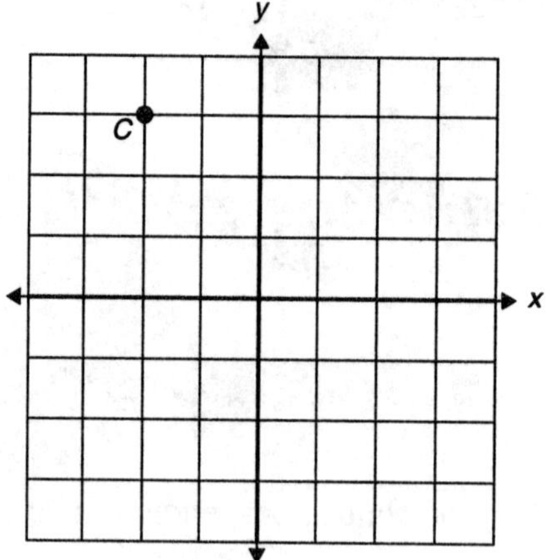

COORDINATE GEOMETRY ANSWER KEY

Basic

1. (–2, 3)

To find the location of point *C*, start at the origin and count two spaces to the left and then count up three spaces.

2. (3, 0)

To find the location of point *M*, start at the origin and count three spaces to the right. When a point is located on the *x*-axis, it will have 0 as a *y*-coordinate.

3. (–3, –2)

To find the location of point *T*, start at the origin and count three spaces to the left and then count down two spaces.

4. Quadrant II

The location of an ordered pair with a negative *x*-coordinate and a positive *y*-coordinate is in Quadrant II.

5. 5 units

Points *K* and *L* are on the same vertical line, so count the number of spaces between points *K* and *L* to determine the distance.

6. Point *Z*

From the origin, count three units up. Point *Z* is located at (0, 3). Any point that lies on the *y*-axis will have 0 as the *x*-coordinate.

7. (3, –2)

The original location of point *D* is (3, 2). To reflect a point over the *x*-axis, change the sign of the *y*-coordinate.

8. (4, 1)

The original location of point *V* is (–4, 1). To reflect a point over the *y*-axis, change the sign of the *x*-coordinate.

9. (–1, 1)

The original location of point *K* is (1, –1). To reflect a point about the origin, change the sign of both the *x*- and *y*-coordinates.

10. A little less than 6

Points *C*, *F*, and *M* form a right triangle. To find the distance from *C* to *M*, use the Pythagorean theorem.

$$\begin{aligned} CM^2 &= CF^2 + FM^2 \\ CM^2 &= 3^2 + 5^2 \\ CM^2 &= 9 + 25 \\ CM^2 &= 34 \\ CM &= \sqrt{34} \approx \text{a little less than 6} \end{aligned}$$

INTERMEDIATE

11. 2

Substitute the coordinates of each point in the slope formula:

$\text{slope} = \frac{\text{change in } y}{\text{change in } x} = \frac{y_2 - y_1}{x_2 - x_1}$.

$$\text{slope} = \frac{-2 - 8}{-1 - 4} = \frac{-10}{-5} = 2$$

12. 8

This equation is written in slope-intercept form, $y = mx + b$, so the slope is the coefficient of the x-term.

13. $m = -\frac{4}{3}$

To find the slope m of the line $4x + 3y = 12$, rewrite it in slope-intercept form $y = mx + b$.

$$\begin{aligned} 4x + 3y &= 12 \\ 3y &= -4x + 12 \\ y &= -\frac{4}{3}x + \frac{12}{3} \\ y &= -\frac{4}{3}x + 4 \end{aligned}$$

14. –2

The slope of the line $y = -2x - 4$ is -2. Parallel lines have the same slope, so the slope of any line parallel to $y = -2x - 4$ is -2.

15. –3

The slope of the line $y = \frac{1}{3}x - 7$ is $\frac{1}{3}$. To find the slope, of a line that is perpendicular, find the negative reciprocal of the slope. The negative reciprocal of $\frac{1}{3}$ is -3.

16. 0

Substitute the coordinates of each point in the slope formula:

$$\text{slope} = \frac{5 - 5}{4 - (-2)} = \frac{0}{6} = 0$$

17. Undefined

Substitute the coordinates of each point in the slope formula:

$$\text{slope} = \frac{-2 - 3}{6 - 6} = \frac{-5}{0}$$

You cannot divide by 0, so the slope is undefined. This line is vertical.

18. $-\frac{1}{6}$

To find the slope of the line $3y = -\frac{1}{2}x$, it needs to be in slope-intercept form.

$$\begin{aligned} 3y &= -\frac{1}{2}x \\ y &= \frac{-\frac{1}{2}x}{3} \\ y &= -\frac{1}{2}x\left(\frac{1}{3}\right) \\ y &= -\frac{1}{6}x \end{aligned}$$

19. 5

Lines *BD* and *BC* are the legs of a right triangle and line *CD* is the hypotenuse. The hypotenuse of a right triangle with leg lengths of 3 and 4 (lines *BD* and *BC* respectively) is 5. (This is the common 3:4:5 Pythagorean triple.)

20. (–1, 1), or $x = -1$, $y = 1$

The point of intersection of the two lines is the solution to the system.

Advanced

21. Undefined

Substitute the coordinates of each point in the slope formula:

$$\text{slope} = \frac{-2 - 7}{-3 - (-3)} = \frac{-9}{0}$$

You cannot divide by 0, so the slope of this line is undefined. The slopes of parallel lines are equal, so the slope of a parallel line is also undefined.

22. Undefined

Substitute the coordinates of each point in the slope formula:

$$\text{slope} = \frac{-1 - (-1)}{-2 - 5} = \frac{0}{-7} = 0$$

The given line has a slope of 0, which means it is horizontal, so a perpendicular line would be vertical. The slope of a vertical line is undefined.

23. No

The lines shown on this graph are parallel. This can be verified by determining that the slope of both lines equals 1. Parallel lines, by definition, do not intersect.

24. No solution

The two regions representing the inequalities do not have any points of intersection. Since no points are in the shaded regions of both inequalities, there is no solution to this system.

25. $-\frac{5}{2}$

First, find the slope of the line represented by $2x - 5y = 20$ by writing it in slope-intercept form:

$$\begin{aligned} 2x - 5y &= 20 \\ -5y &= -2x + 20 \\ y &= \frac{2}{5}x - \frac{20}{5} \\ y &= \frac{2}{5}x - 4 \end{aligned}$$

The slope of this line is $\frac{2}{5}$. So the slope of a line perpendicular to this line would be the negative reciprocal, or a slope of $-\frac{5}{2}$.

26. 2

The *x*-intercept(s) of a graph are the *x*-value(s) of the point(s) where the graph crosses the *x*-axis. This means the *y*-coordinate is 0. Replace *y* with 0 in the equation and solve for *x*.

$$\begin{aligned} y &= 4x - 8 \\ 0 &= 4x - 8 \\ 8 &= 4x \\ 2 &= x \end{aligned}$$

The *x*-intercept is 2.

27. Yes

If the point (–2, 12) lies on the graph of $y = -2.5x + 7$, then replacing *x* and *y* with the ordered pair will make a true equation.

$$\begin{aligned} y &= -2.5x + 7 \\ 12 &= -2.5(-2) + 7 \\ 12 &= 5 + 7 \\ 12 &= 12 \end{aligned}$$

28. $\mathbf{y = -3x + 4}$

The equation $4x - 3y = 9$ needs to be written in slope-intercept form so that the slopes can be compared.

$$\begin{aligned} 4x - 3y &= 9 \\ -3y &= -4x + 9 \\ y &= \frac{4}{3}x - 3 \end{aligned}$$

The slope of $y = -3x + 4$ is -3 and the slope of $4x - 3y = 9$ is $\frac{4}{3}$. The absolute value of -3 is greater than the absolute value of $\frac{4}{3}$. Therefore, the slope of $y = -3x + 4$ is steeper.

29. Yes

The point (0, 0) is the origin and is included in the section that shows shading for both inequalities.

30. A reflection about the origin

The original location of point C is $(-2, 3)$. To reflect a point over the x-axis, change the sign of the y-coordinate. The first reflection has point C at $(-2, -3)$. To reflect a point over the y-axis, change the sign of the x-coordinate. The new location of point C is $(2, -3)$. The original ordered pair was $(-2, 3)$. The sign of both coordinates changed, which indicates a reflection about the origin.

GRAPHS OF FUNCTIONS

To graph a function in the *xy*-plane, use the *x*-axis for the input and the *y*-axis for the output. You can represent every input value, *x*, and its corresponding output value, *y*, as an ordered pair (x, y). The output of a function may also be referred to as $f(x)$, so you can write $y = f(x)$.

Two functions are graphed here. The first is a linear function $f(x) = 2x - 1$ and the second is a quadratic function $g(x) = x^2 - 1$.

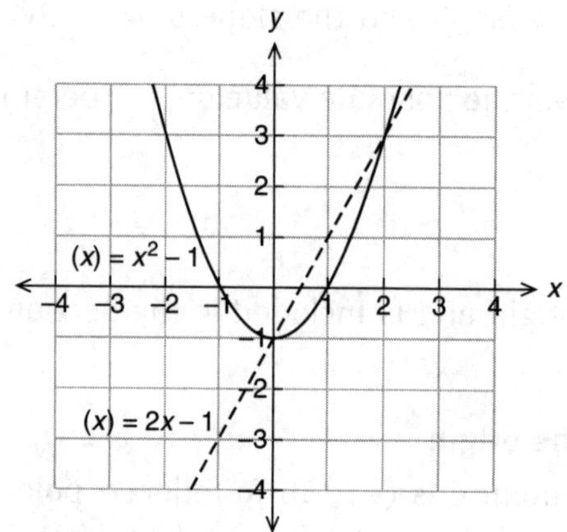

The graphs of the functions intersect at two points. These are the points for which $f(x) = g(x)$. To find the points using algebra, set $f(x) = g(x)$ and solve for *x*.

$$\begin{aligned} x^2 - 1 &= 2x - 1 \\ x^2 - 2x &= -1 + 1 \\ x^2 - 2x &= 0 \\ x(x - 2) &= 0 \\ x &= 0 \text{ or } 2 \end{aligned}$$

Use either function to find the corresponding *y*-value for each point.

For example, if $x = 0$, $f(0) = 2x - 1 = 2(0) - 1 = -1$ and if
$x = 2$, $f(2) = 2x - 1 = 2(2) - 1 = 3$. The points of intersection are $(0, -1)$ and $(2, 3)$.

PIECEWISE FUNCTION

A **piecewise function** is defined by more than one equation, where each equation applies to a different part of the domain of the function. The absolute value function is an example of a piecewise function. Two "pieces" are needed in the definition of the function; these are $y = -x$ for all *x* less than 0 and $y = x$ for all $x \geq 0$. A piecewise function is usually described as shown for $f(x) = |x|$:

$$f(x) = \begin{cases} -2x, \text{ where } x < 0 \\ 2x, \text{ where } x \geq 0 \end{cases}$$

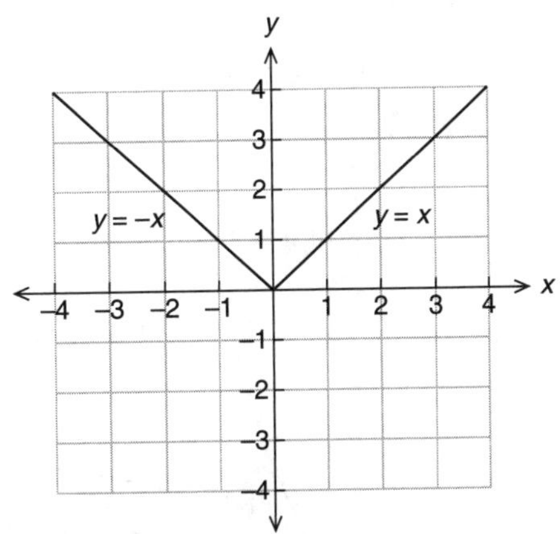

The graph of a function may also be shifted horizontally or vertically c units, where c is a positive number. For example, to shift the graph of $f(x) = |x|$, follow these rules:

- The graph of $f(x) + c$ is the graph of $f(x)$ shifted **upward** c units or spaces.
- The graph of $f(x) - c$ is the graph of $f(x)$ shifted **downward** c units or spaces.
- The graph of $f(x + c)$ is the graph of $f(x)$ shifted **to the left** c units or spaces.
- The graph of $f(x - c)$ is the graph of $f(x)$ shifted **to the right** c units or spaces.

Notice the placement of the constant in each description. To verify the direction of a shift of a function, plot several points of the original function and several points of the shifted function.

Consider the graph of $f(x) = x^2$ for $x > 0$ and the graph of $g(x) = \sqrt{x}$ for $x > 0$ shown. Because the domain is restricted for this graph, only part of the parabola is shown for $f(x) = x^2$.

Notice that these graphs are symmetric about the line $y = x$.

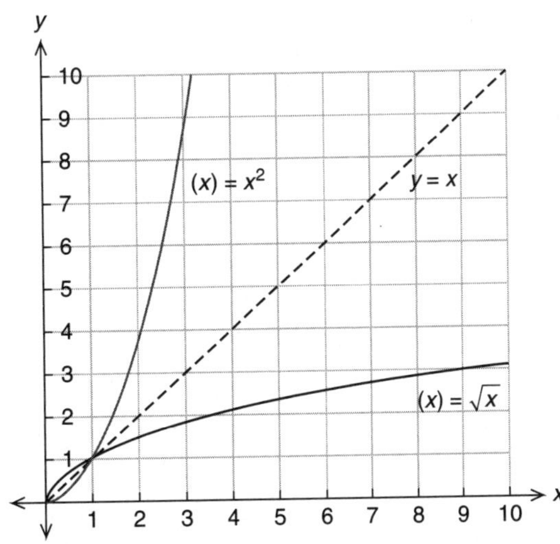

To shift the graphs of $f(x) = x^2$ and $g(x) = \sqrt{x}$ three units or spaces upward, graph $f(x) = x^2 + 3$ and $g(x) = \sqrt{x} + 3$.

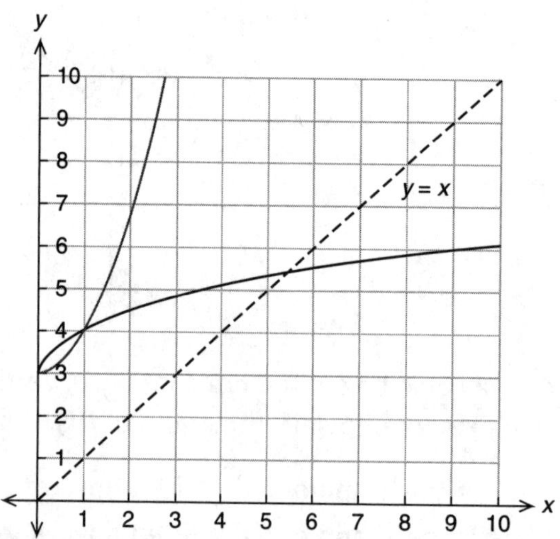

Notice that the graphs still have the same position **relative** to each other, but they are no longer symmetric across the line $y = x$.

The graph of a function may also be vertically stretched away or compressed toward the x-axis by a factor of c, where c is a positive number. That is, you can stretch the graph by making the slope larger and steeper, or you can compress the graph by making the slope smaller and less steep. To change the vertical shape of the graph of $f(x)$, follow these rules:

- The graph of $c \times f(x)$ is the graph of $f(x)$ stretched away from the x-axis by a factor of c.
- The graph of $\frac{1}{c} \times f(x)$ is the graph of $f(x)$ compressed toward the x-axis by a factor of c.

GRAPHS OF FUNCTIONS EXERCISES

BASIC

1. If the point (2, y) lies on the graph of $f(x) = x^2 + 3$, what is y?

2. If the point (x, 0) lies on the graph of $f(x) = 3x - 12$, what is x?

3. Complete the following ordered pairs for the function $f(x) = x^2 - 2x + 1$.

   (0, ___) (–1, ___) (4, ___)

4. Describe the graph of $y = 7$.

5. Describe the graph of $x = -3$

6. The graphs of $f(x) = 3x$ and $g(x) = 2x + 4$ intersect at the point (x, y). What is the value of x at the point of intersection?

7. The graphs of $f(x) = x^2$ and $g(x) = 5x - 6$ intersect at two points. Find the x-coordinate of each point of intersection.

8. The graph of $f(x) = x^2$ is shown. How is the graph of the function $g(x) = x^2 - 4$ related to the graph of $f(x)$?

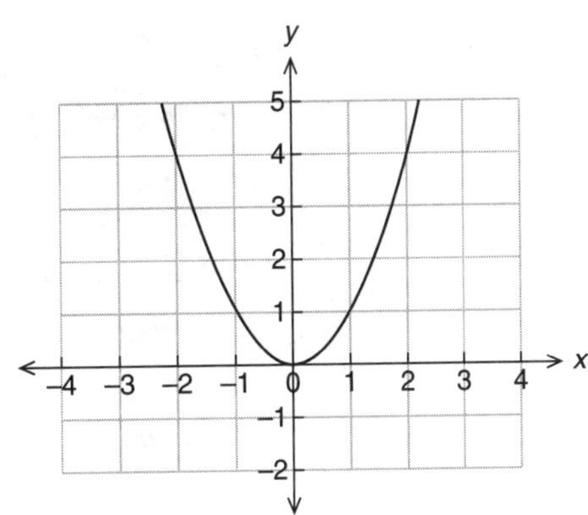

9. The graph of $h(x) = |x|$ is shown. How is the graph of the function $k(x) = |x - 5|$ related to the graph of $h(x)$?

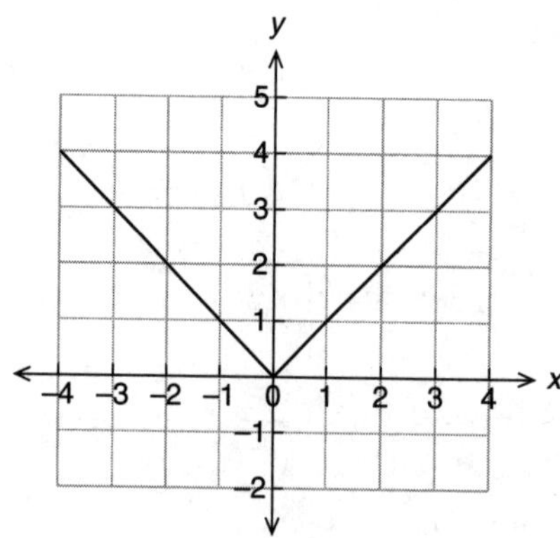

10. Sketch the graph of the piecewise function $f(x)$ on the coordinate plane provided.

$$f(x) = \begin{cases} -2x, \text{ where } x < 0 \\ 2x, \text{ where } x \geq 0 \end{cases}$$

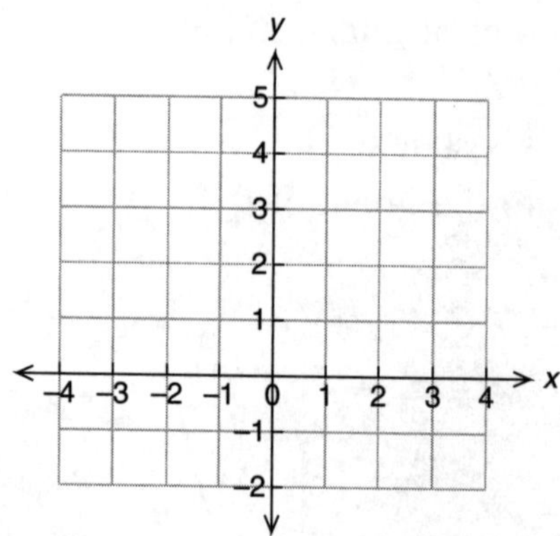

INTERMEDIATE

For Exercises 11–14, use the function $f(x) = 2x + 4$.

11. Complete the following ordered pairs for $f(x)$.

(–1, ___) (0, ___) (___, 0) (___, 6)

12. On the coordinate plane provided, graph the ordered pairs found in Question 11. Describe the graph of $f(x)$.

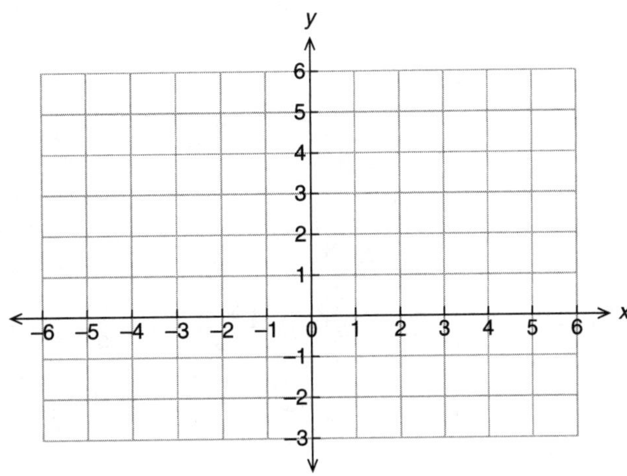

13. Suppose $g(x) = 3x - 2$. At what point(s) do $f(x)$ and $g(x)$ intersect?

14. Suppose $h(x) = x^2 + 1$. At what point(s) do $f(x)$ and $h(x)$ intersect?

15. Describe the relationship between the graphs of $f(x) = 3x^2$ and $g(x) = 3(x - 1)^2$.

16. Describe the relationship between the graphs of $f(x) = x^2$ and $g(x) = \frac{1}{2}x^2$.

17. The graph of $f(x) = 2|x|$ is shown. On the coordinate plane provided, sketch the graph of $g(x) = 2|x + 4|$.

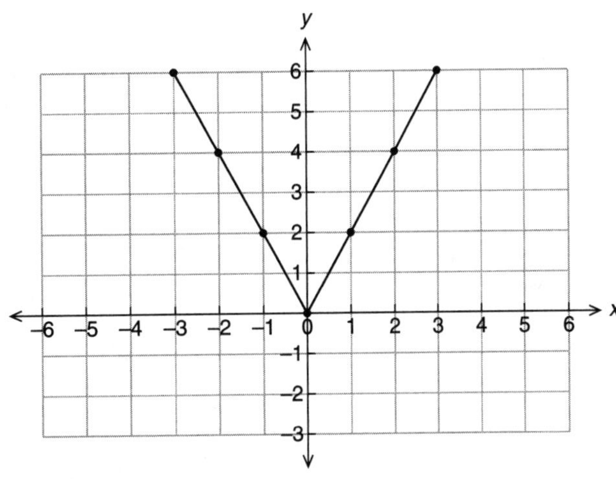

18. The graph of $f(x) = 2|x|$ is shown. On the coordinate plane provided, sketch the graph of $g(x) = 2|x| - 2$.

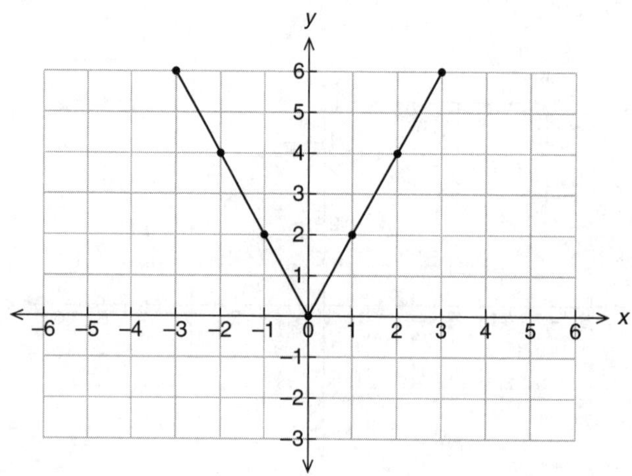

19. Sketch the graph of the piecewise function $f(x)$ on the coordinate plane provided.

$$f(x) = \begin{cases} -x, \text{ where } x < 0 \\ 3x, \text{ where } x \geq 0 \end{cases}$$

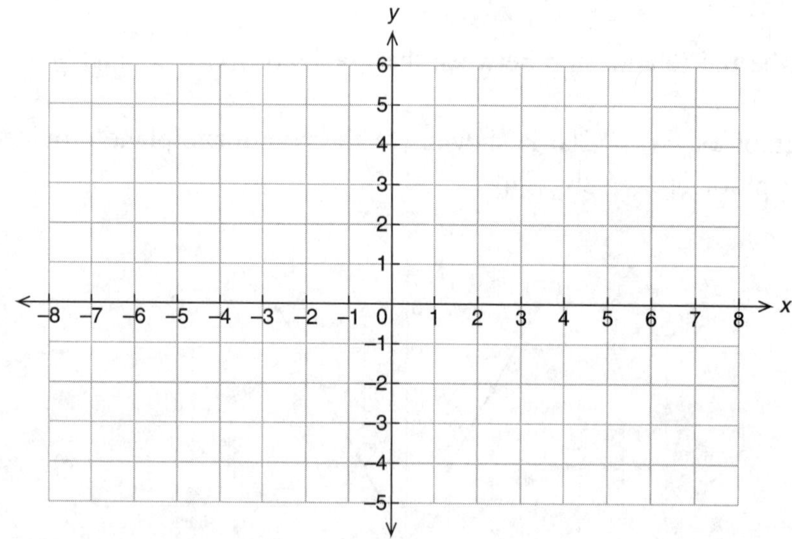

20. At what point(s) do the graphs of $f(x) = x^2 - 4$ and $g(x) = x^2 + 2x$ intersect?

Advanced

For Exercises 21–24, use the graph of $f(x) = -x - 2$ shown.

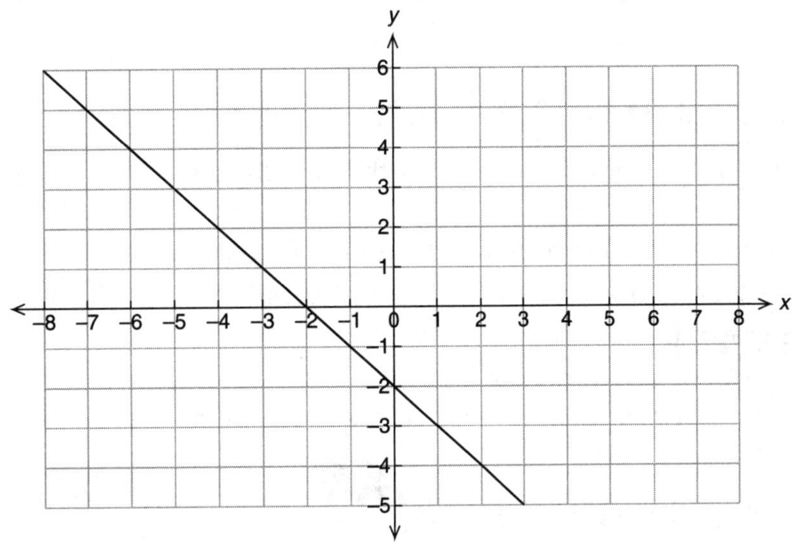

21. If $g(x) = f(x) + 4$, what is the y-intercept of $g(x)$?

22. If $h(x) = f(x - 4)$, what is the x-intercept of $h(x)$?

23. On the following coordinate plane, sketch the graph of $j(x) = x^2$ to show that the graphs of $f(x)$ and $j(x)$ do not intersect.

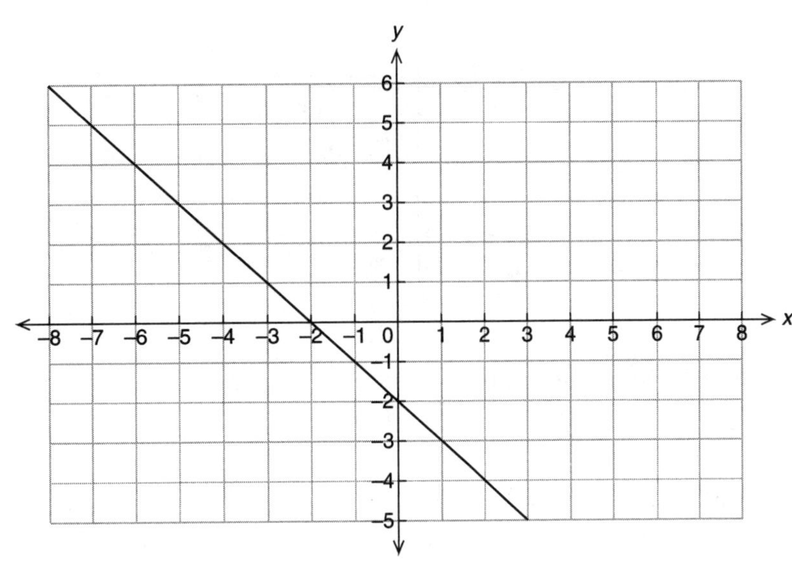

24. Show algebraically that the graph of $f(x)$ does not intersect the graph of $j(x) = x^2$.

25. Suppose that the graph of $f(x)$ is the result of sliding the graph of $y = 2x^2$ down 3 units or spaces. What is the new equation for the graph $f(x)$?

26. Suppose that the graph of $f(x)$ is the result of sliding the graph of $y = \frac{1}{2}x$ to the left 7 units or spaces. What is the new equation for the graph $f(x)$?

27. Suppose that the graph of $f(x)$ is the result of stretching the graph of $y = x + 5$ away from the x-axis by a factor of 2. What is the new equation for the graph $f(x)$?

28. Sketch the graph of the piecewise function $f(x)$ on the coordinate plane provided.

$$f(x) = \begin{cases} x^2, \text{ where } x < 0 \\ x, \text{ where } x \geq 0 \end{cases}$$

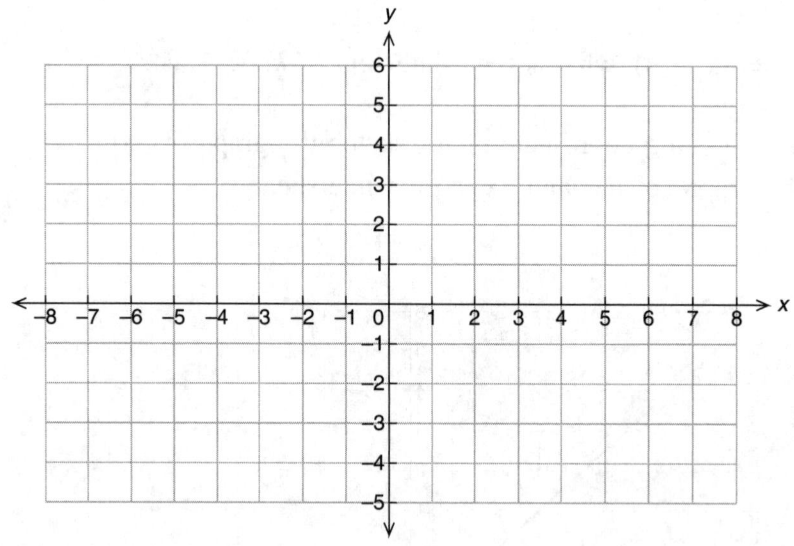

29. At what point(s) does the graph of $f(x) = x^2 + 3x + 11$ intersect the graph of $g(x) = 2x^2 - 3x + 4$?

30. The graph of $f(x) = 2x^2 - 5$ intersects the graph of $g(x) = x^2 + a$ when $x = 3$. What is a?

GRAPHS OF FUNCTIONS ANSWER KEY

BASIC

1. 7

The function $f(x) = x^2 + 3$ can be written $y = x^2 + 3$. To find y when x is 2, substitute 2 for x and solve.

$$\begin{aligned} y &= x^2 + 3 \\ y &= (2)^2 + 3 \\ y &= 4 + 3 \\ y &= 7 \end{aligned}$$

2. 4

The function $f(x) = 3x - 12$ can be written $y = 3x - 12$. To find x when $y = 0$, substitute 0 for y and solve.

$$\begin{aligned} y &= 3x - 12 \\ 0 &= 3x - 12 \\ 12 &= 3x \\ 4 &= x \end{aligned}$$

3. (0, 1) (–1, 4) (4, 9)

Write the function $f(x) = x^2 - 2x + 1$ in the form $y = x^2 - 2x + 1$. Complete each ordered pair by substituting the given value of x, then solving for y.

when $x = 0$	when $x = -1$	when $x = 4$
$y = x^2 - 2x + 1$	$y = x^2 - 2x + 1$	$y = x^2 - 2x + 1$
$y = 0^2 - 2 \times 0 + 1$	$y = (-1)^2 - 2 \times (-1) + 1$	$y = 4^2 - 2 \times 4 + 1$
$y = 0 - 0 + 1$	$y = 1 + 2 + 1$	$y = 16 - 8 + 1$
$y = 1$	$y = 4$	$y = 9$
(0, 1)	(–1, 4)	(4, 9)

4. **The graph of $y = 7$ is a horizontal line that lies 7 units or spaces above the x-axis. Each point on the line $y = 7$ has y-coordinate 7.**

5. **The graph of $x = -3$ is a vertical line that lies 3 units to the left of the y-axis. Each point on the line $x = -3$ has x-coordinate –3.**

6. 4

To find the *x*-coordinate of the point of intersection, set the function rules equal and solve for *x*.

$$\begin{aligned} f(x) &= g(x) \\ 3x &= 2x + 4 \\ x &= 4 \end{aligned}$$

7. $x = 2, x = 3$

To find the *x*-coordinate of each point of intersection, set the function rules equal and solve for *x*.

$$\begin{aligned} f(x) &= g(x) \\ x^2 &= 5x - 6 \\ x^2 - 5x + 6 &= 0 \\ (x - 2)(x - 3) &= 0 \end{aligned}$$

$$\begin{aligned} x - 2 &= 0 \\ x &= 2 \end{aligned} \quad \text{or} \quad \begin{aligned} x - 3 &= 0 \\ x &= 3 \end{aligned}$$

8. **The graph of $g(x) = x^2 - 4$ is a translation (shift) of the graph of $f(x) = x^2$ four units or spaces downward.**

9. **The graph of $k(x) = |x - 5|$ is a translation (shift) of the graph of $h(x) = |x|$ five units or spaces to the right.**

10. The correct graph is shown. Be sure your graph comes to a point at (0, 0) and passes through the points (1, 2) and (2, 4) on the right side and the points (–1, 2) and (–2, 4) on the left side.

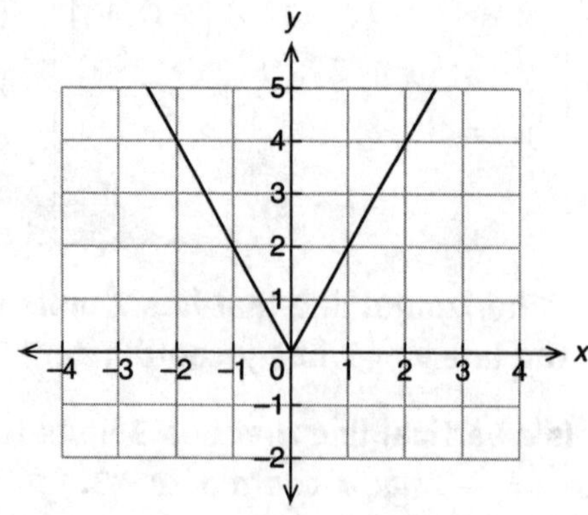

INTERMEDIATE

11. (–1, 2) (0, 4) (–2, 0) (1, 6)

Write the function $f(x) = 2x + 4$ in the form $y = 2x + 4$. Complete each ordered pair by substituting the given coordinate, then solving for the missing coordinate.

when $x = -1$	when $x = 0$	when $y = 0$	when $y = 6$
$y = 2x + 4$	$y = 2x + 4$	$y = 2x + 4$	$y = 2x + 4$
$y = 2(-1) + 4$	$y = 2(0) + 4$	$0 = 2x + 4$	$6 = 2x + 4$
$y = -2 + 4$	$y = 0 + 4$	$-4 = 2x$	$2 = 2x$
$y = 2$	$y = 4$	$-2 = x$	$1 = x$
(–1, 2)	(0, 4)	(–2, 0)	(1, 6)

12. The graph of $f(x)$ is a line with x-intercept at (–2, 0) and y-intercept at (0, 4) and a slope of 2.

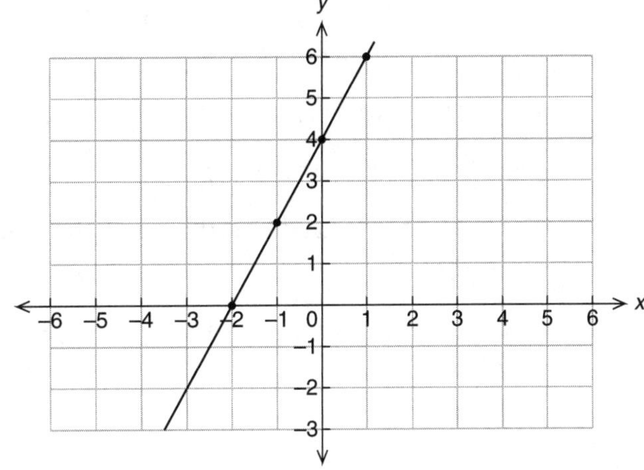

13. (6, 16)

To find the x-coordinate(s) of the point(s) of intersection, set the functions equal and solve for x.

$$\begin{aligned} f(x) &= g(x) \\ 2x + 4 &= 3x - 2 \\ 6 &= x \end{aligned}$$

To find y when $x = 6$, substitute 6 for x in one of the functions.

$$\begin{aligned} y &= 2x + 4 \\ y &= 2(6) + 4 \\ y &= 12 + 4 \\ y &= 16 \end{aligned}$$

When $x = 6$, $y = 16$. So, the graphs intersect at the point (6, 16).

14. (3, 10), (–1, 2)

To find the *x*-coordinate(s) of the point(s) of intersection, set the functions equal and solve for *x*.

$$f(x) = h(x)$$
$$2x + 4 = x^2 + 1$$
$$0 = x^2 - 2x - 3$$
$$0 = (x - 3)(x + 1)$$

$$x - 3 = 0 \quad \text{or} \quad x + 1 = 0$$
$$x = 3 \qquad\qquad x = -1$$

Now find the *y*-coordinate for each point of intersection.

when $x = 3$	when $x = -1$
$y = 2x + 4$	$y = 2x + 4$
$y = 2(3) + 4$	$y = 2(-1) + 4$
$y = 6 + 4$	$y = -2 + 4$
$y = 10$	$y = 2$
(3, 10)	(–1, 2)

15. The graph of $g(x) = 3(x - 1)^2$ is a translation (shift) of the graph of $f(x) = 3x^2$ one unit or space to the right.

16. The graph of $g(x) = \frac{1}{2}x^2$ is the graph of $f(x) = x^2$, compressed vertically toward the *x*-axis by a factor of $\frac{1}{2}$.

17. To sketch the graph of $g(x) = 2|x + 4|$, shift the graph of $f(x) = 2|x|$ to the left four units or spaces. The correct graph of $g(x) = 2|x + 4|$ is shown.

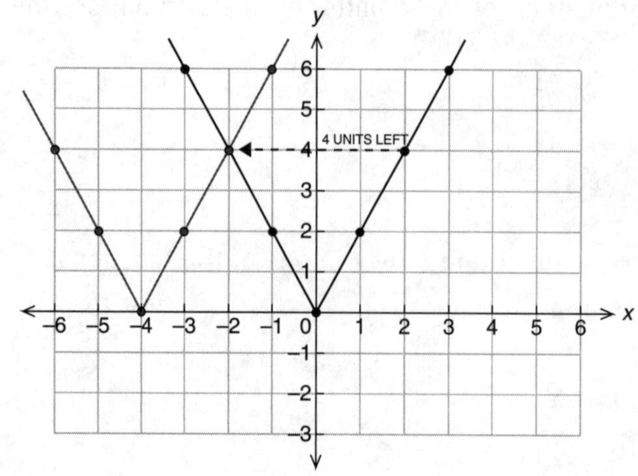

18. To graph $g(x) = 2|x| - 2$, shift the graph of $f(x) = 2|x|$ down 2 units or spaces. The correct graph of $g(x) = 2|x| - 2$ is shown.

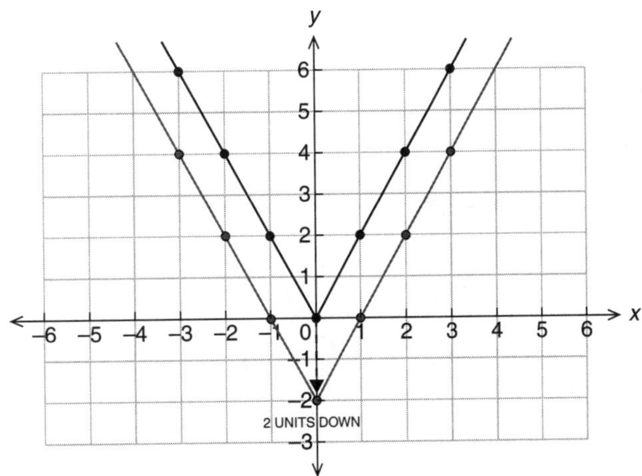

19. The graph of $f(x)$ has two parts. When $x < 0$, sketch the graph of the line $y = -x$. When $x \geq 0$, sketch the graph of the line $y = 3x$. The correct graph of $f(x)$ is shown.

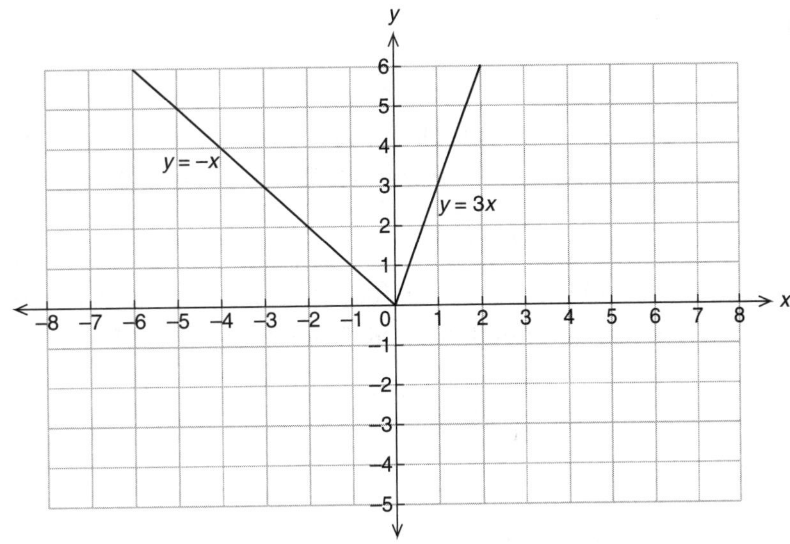

20. (−2, 0)

To find the x-coordinate(s) of the point(s) of intersection, set the functions equal and solve for x.

$$\begin{aligned} f(x) &= g(x) \\ x^2 - 4 &= x^2 + 2x \\ \cancel{x^2} - 4 &= \cancel{x^2} + 2x \\ -4 &= 2x \\ -2 &= x \end{aligned}$$

When $x = -2$,

$$\begin{aligned} y &= x^2 - 4 \\ y &= (-2)^2 - 4 \\ y &= 4 - 4 \\ y &= 0 \end{aligned}$$

ADVANCED

21. 2

The graph of $g(x) = f(x) + 4$ is the graph of $f(x)$, shifted up 4 units or spaces. Since $f(x)$ has y-intercept at -2, $g(x)$ will have y-intercept at $-2 + 4$, or 2.

22. 2

The graph of $h(x) = f(x - 4)$ is the graph of $f(x)$, shifted right 4 units or spaces. Since $f(x)$ has x-intercept at -2, $h(x)$ will have x-intercept at $-2 + 4$, or 2.

23. The correct graph is shown. The graph of $j(x) = x^2$ is a parabola that opens upward with vertex at the origin. The graphs of $f(x)$ and $j(x)$ do not intersect.

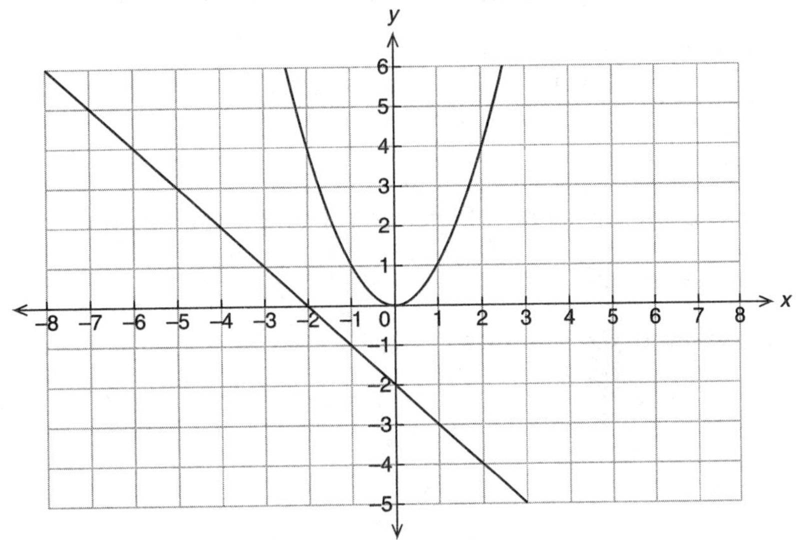

24. To show that the graph of $f(x)$ does not intersect the graph of $j(x) = x^2$, set the functions equal and show that the equation has no solutions.

$$\begin{aligned} f(x) &= g(x) \\ -x - 2 &= x^2 \\ 0 &= x^2 + x + 2 \\ x &= \frac{-1 \pm \sqrt{1^2 - 4(1)(2)}}{2(1)} \\ x &= \frac{-1 \pm \sqrt{1 - 8}}{2} \\ x &= \frac{-1 \pm \sqrt{-7}}{2} \end{aligned}$$

The square root of a negative number is not defined. Therefore, the equation has no solution in the real numbers. Since the equation has no solution, the graphs have no points of intersection.

25. $\mathbf{y = 2x^2 - 3}$

To shift a function downward 3 units or spaces, subtract 3 from the function.

$$y = 2x^2 \rightarrow y = (2x^2) - 3$$

26. $\mathbf{y = \frac{1}{2}(x + 7)}$

To shift a function to the left 7 units or spaces, replace x with $x + 7$ in the function.

$$y = \frac{1}{2}x \rightarrow y = \frac{1}{2}(x + 7)$$

27. $\mathbf{y = 2(x + 5)}$

To stretch a function vertically by a factor of 2, multiply the function by 2.

$$y = x + 5 \rightarrow y = 2(x + 5)$$

28. The correct graph of $f(x)$ is shown.

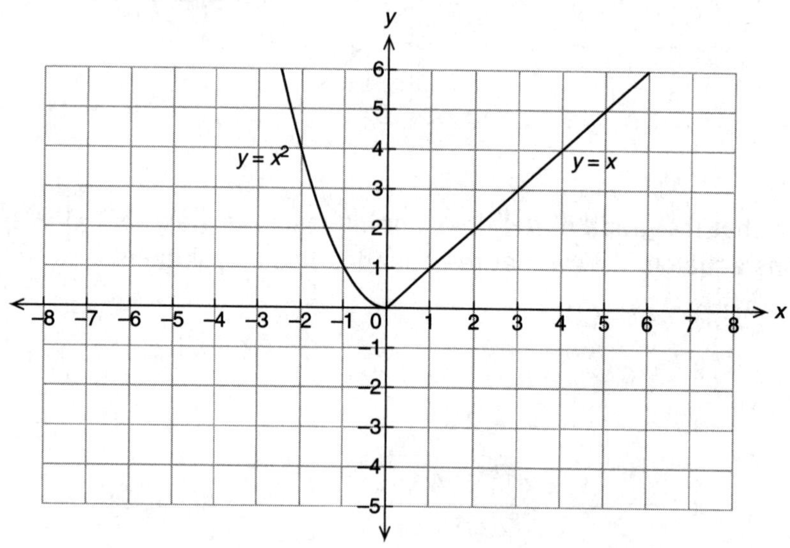

29. (7, 81), (–1, 9)

Set the function rules equal and solve.

$$\begin{aligned} f(x) &= g(x) \\ x^2 + 3x + 11 &= 2x^2 - 3x + 4 \\ 0 &= x^2 - 6x - 7 \\ 0 &= (x - 7)(x + 1) \end{aligned}$$

$$\begin{aligned} x - 7 &= 0 \\ x &= 7 \end{aligned} \quad \text{or} \quad \begin{aligned} x + 1 &= 0 \\ x &= -1 \end{aligned}$$

Now find the y-coordinate for each point of intersection.

when $x = 7$	when $x = -1$
$y = x^2 + 3x + 11$	$y = x^2 + 3x + 11$
$y = 7^2 + 3 \times 7 + 11$	$y = (-1)^2 + 3 \times (-1) + 11$
$y = 49 + 21 + 11$	$y = 1 - 3 + 11$
$y = 81$	$y = 9$
(7, 81)	(−1, 9)

30. 4

If the graphs of $f(x)$ and $g(x)$ intersect when $x = 3$, then the function rules must be equal when $x = 3$. Set the function rules equal. Then substitute 3 for x and solve to find a.

$$\begin{aligned} f(x) &= g(x) \\ 2x^2 - 5 &= x^2 + a \\ 2(3)^2 - 5 &= 3^2 + a \\ 2(9) - 5 &= 9 + a \\ 18 - 5 &= 9 + a \\ 13 &= 9 + a \\ 4 &= a \end{aligned}$$

CHAPTER 8

Geometry

UNDERSTANDING GEOMETRY

Geometry topics include lines and angles, triangles—including isosceles, equilateral, and special right triangles—polygons, circles, multiple figures, three-dimensional figures (uniform solids), area, perimeter, and volume. You do not need to know how to do geometry proofs for the test.

The geometry tested on the GRE is basic. There are only a few fundamental definitions and formulas you need to know. The GRE emphasizes new ways of applying these elementary rules.

DIAGRAMS

Pay a lot of attention to diagrams. There can be a lot of information "hidden" in a diagram. If a diagram of an equilateral triangle gives you the length of one side, for instance, it actually gives the length of all sides. Similarly, if you are given the measure of one of the angles formed by the intersection of two lines, you can easily find the measure of all four angles. In fact, many geometry questions specifically test your ability to determine what additional information is implied by the information you are given in the diagram.

The diagrams provide basic information such as what kind of figure you are dealing with (is it a triangle? a quadrilateral?), the order of the points on lines, etc. However, the figures on the GRE are not drawn to scale unless otherwise stated. Because they are not drawn to scale, you can't rely on how figures are drawn to conclude anything about the size of the figure. If a line looks straight in the diagram, you can assume it is straight. But you must be careful when using the diagram to judge relative lengths, angles, sizes, etc., since these may not be drawn accurately. A square that looks twice as big as another is not necessarily twice as big. If an angle looks like a right angle, you cannot assume it is one, unless it is marked as such. If one side of a triangle looks longer than another, you cannot assume it is unless some other information tells you that it is. If a figure looks like a square, you don't know it is a square; you only know it is a quadrilateral. This is especially important to bear in mind in the Quantitative Comparison section, where the diagram may lead you to believe that one column is greater, but logic will prove that you need more information.

You can also, on occasion, use the diagram to your advantage by looking at the question logically. For instance:

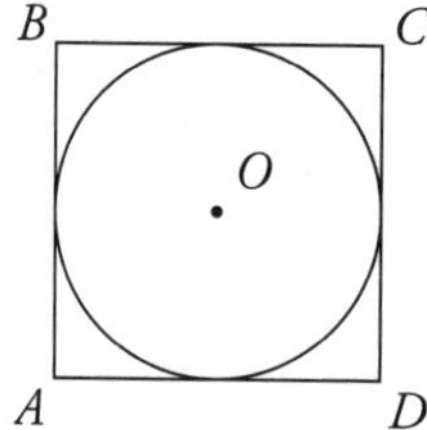

In the figure shown, the circle with center O has area 4π. What is the area of square $ABCD$?

Ⓐ 4
Ⓑ 2π
Ⓒ 12
Ⓓ 16
Ⓔ 8π

We know from the question stem that we have a square and a circle, and we can see from the diagram that the circle is inscribed in the square—that is, it touches the square on all four sides. Whatever the area of the circle, we can see that the square's area must be bigger; otherwise the circle wouldn't fit inside it. So the right answer must be larger than the area of the circle, or larger than 4π. Now we can approximate 4π to a little more than 12. Since the correct answer is larger than 12, it must be either choice (D) or (E). And since you would expect to see π in the area of the circle, as it is here, that means π will not be in the area of the surrounding square. (The correct answer is 16.)

This example highlights an important point: π appears very often on geometry problems, so you should have some idea of its value. It is approximately equal to 3.14, but for most purposes you only need remember that it is slightly greater than 3.

LINES AND ANGLES

A line is a one-dimensional, geometrical abstraction—infinitely long with no width. It is not physically possible to draw a line; any physical line would have a finite length and some width, no matter how long and thin we tried to make it. Two points determine a straight line; given any two points, there is exactly one straight line that passes through them.

Lines: A **line segment** is a section of a straight line, of finite length, with two end-points. A line segment is named by its endpoints, as in segment *AB*. The **midpoint** is the point that divides a line segment into two equal parts.

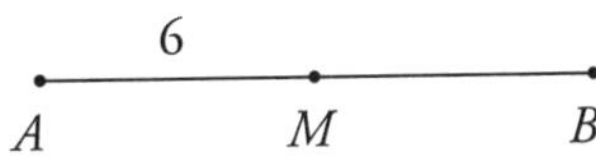

Example: In the figure shown, *A* and *B* are the endpoints of the line segment *AB* and *M* is the midpoint ($AM = MB$). What is the length of *AB*?

Since *AM* is 6, *MB* is also 6, and so *AB* is $6 + 6$, or 12.

Two lines are **parallel** if they lie in the same plane and never intersect each other regardless of how far they are extended. If line ℓ_1 is parallel to line ℓ_2, we write $\ell_1 \parallel \ell_2$.

Angles: An **angle** is formed by two lines or line segments intersecting at a point. The point of intersection is called the **vertex** of the angle. Angles are measured in degrees (°).

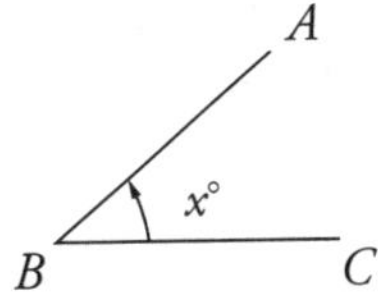

Angle *x*, $\angle ABC$, and $\angle B$ all denote the same angle shown in the diagram.

An **acute angle** is an angle whose degree measure is between 0° and 90°. A **right angle** is an angle whose degree measure is exactly 90°. An **obtuse angle** is an angle whose degree measure is between 90° and 180°. A **straight angle** is an angle whose degree measure is exactly 180°.

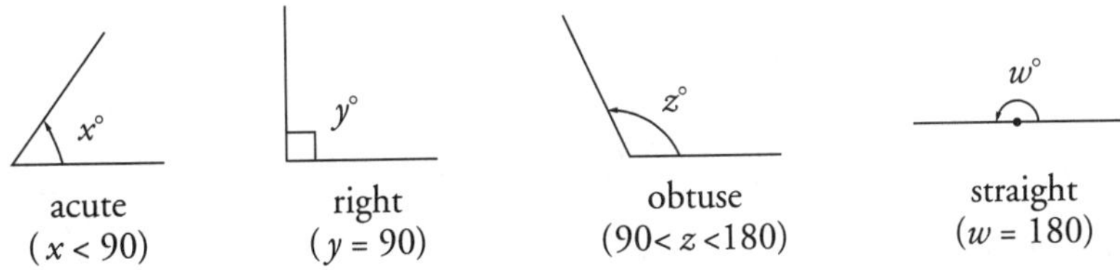

The sum of the measures of the angles on one side of a straight line is 180°.

x° y° z°

straight
($x + y + z = 180$)

The sum of the measures of the angles around a point is 360°.

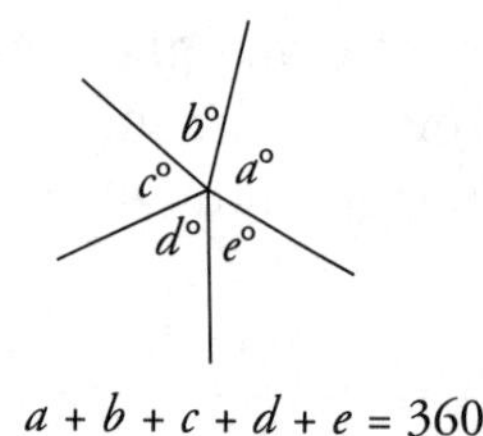

$a + b + c + d + e = 360$

Two lines are **perpendicular** if they intersect at a 90° angle. The shortest distance from a point to a line is the line segment drawn from the point to the line such that it is perpendicular to the line. If line ℓ_1 is perpendicular to line ℓ_2, we write $\ell_1 \perp \ell_2$. If $\ell_1 \perp \ell_2$ and $\ell_2 \perp \ell_3$, then $\ell_1 \parallel \ell_3$.

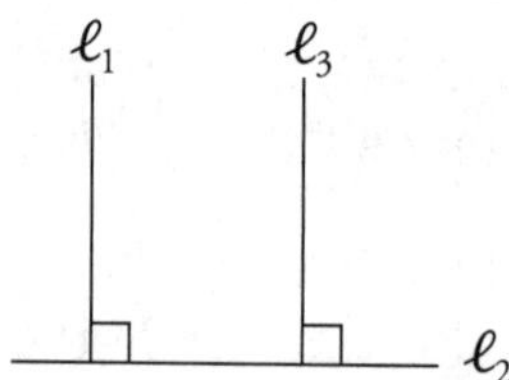

Two angles are **supplementary** if the sum of their measures is 180°. Two angles are **complementary** if together they make up a right angle (i.e., if the sum of their measures is 90°). Angles *c* and *d* below are supplementary; angles *a* and *b* are complementary.

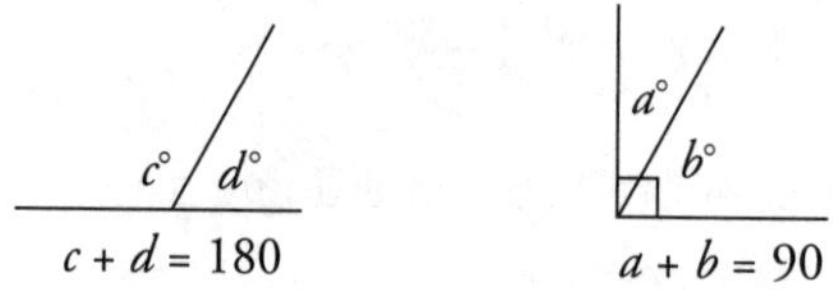

A line or line segment bisects an angle if it splits the angle into two smaller, equal angles. If line segment *BD* below bisects $\angle ABC$, then $\angle ABD$ has the same measure as $\angle DBC$. The two smaller angles are each half the size of $\angle ABC$.

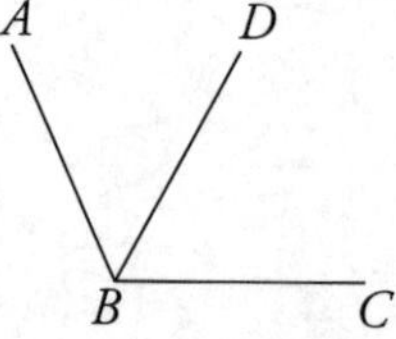

Vertical angles are a pair of opposite angles formed by two intersecting line segments. At the point of intersection, two pairs of vertical angles are formed. Angles *a* and *c* below are vertical angles, as are *b* and *d*.

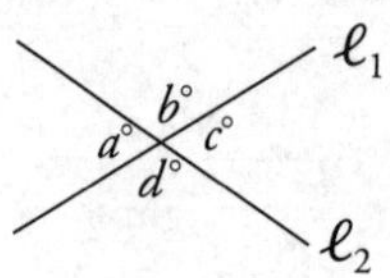

The two angles in a pair of vertical angles have the same degree measure. In the diagram above, $a = c$ and $b = d$. In addition, since ℓ_1 and ℓ_2 are straight lines,

$$a + b = c + d = a + d = b + c = 180^\circ$$

In other words, each angle is supplementary to each of its two adjacent angles.

If two parallel lines intersect with a third line (called a *transversal*), each of the parallel lines will intersect the third line at the same angle. In the figure below, $a = e$. Since a and e are equal, and $c = a$ and $e = g$ (vertical angles), we know that $a = c = e = g$. Similarly, $b = d = f = h$.

If $\ell_1 \parallel \ell_2$, then
$a = c = e = g$ and
$b = d = f = h$.

In other words, when two parallel lines intersect with a third line, all acute angles formed are equal, all obtuse angles formed are equal, and any acute angle is supplementary to any obtuse angle.

Points in the Coordinate Plane

Questions on the GRE sometimes refer to lines or curves graphed on a coordinate plane. An ***xy*-coordinate plane** is formed by two number lines at right angles to each other, intersecting at their zero points. The intersecting lines divide the plane into four quadrants, named counterclockwise by the Roman numerals I, II, III, and IV. The horizontal number line is the ***x*-axis,** the vertical number line is the ***y*-axis,** and the point of intersection is the **origin**. Every point on the plane is named by its *x*- and *y*-coordinates, (*x*, *y*).

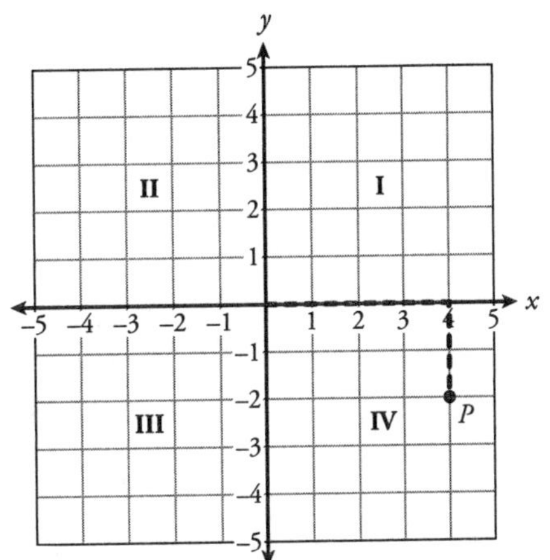

To graph point *P*, whose coordinates are (4, –2), start at the origin, go right 4 units or spaces and then go down 2 units or spaces.

SLOPE

The slope of a line tells you how steeply that line goes up or down from a horizontal position. If a line gets higher as you move to the right, it has a positive slope. If it goes down as you move to the right, it has a negative slope.

To find the slope of a line, use the following formula:

$$\textbf{Slope} = \frac{\textbf{rise}}{\textbf{run}} = \frac{\textbf{change in } y}{\textbf{change in } x}$$

Rise means the difference between the y-coordinate values of the two points on the line, and *run* means the difference between the x-coordinate values.

The slope-intercept equation of a line is $y = mx + b$, where m is the slope and b is the y-intercept. The y-intercept is the value of y where the line crosses the y-axis, in other words, the value of y when $x = 0$.

Example: What is the slope of the line represented by the equation $y = 2x - 5$?

The equation is in slope-intercept form, so the slope is 2 because 2 is the coefficient of x.

Example: What is the slope of the line that contains the points (1, 2) and (4, −5)?

$$Slope = \frac{-5 - 2}{4 - 1} = \frac{-7}{3} = -\frac{7}{3}$$

To determine the slope of a line from an equation, put the equation into the slope-intercept form.

Example: What is the slope of the line represented by the equation $3x + 2y = 4$?

$$3x + 2y = 4$$
$$2y = -3x + 4$$
$$y = -\frac{3}{2}x + 2, \text{ so } m \text{ is } -\frac{3}{2}.$$

LINES AND ANGLES EXERCISES

BASIC

In Exercises 1–4, classify each angle *x* as acute, right, obtuse, or straight.

1. $x = 180°$

2. $x = 90°$

3. $x = 25°$

4. $x = 130°$

5. What is the value of x in the figure shown?

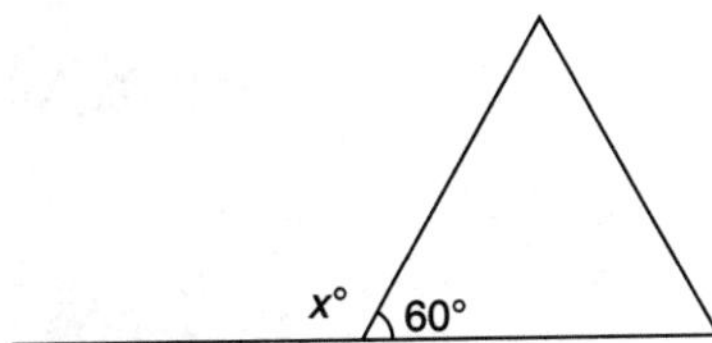

Use the figure shown for Exercises 6–8.

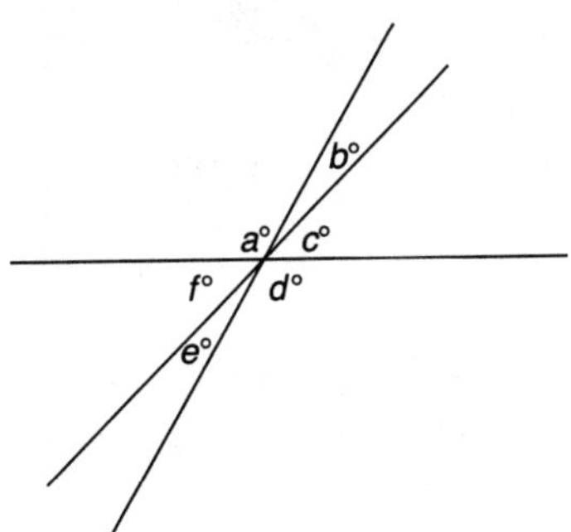

6. If $a = 60°$ and $c = 45°$, what is the value of b?

7. What is the value of $a + f + b$?

8. What is the value of $a + b + c + d + e + f$?

9. If angle x has a measure of 90°, what is the measure of its supplement?

10. If angle x has a measure of 36°, what is the measure of its complement?

INTERMEDIATE

11. The four angles around a point measure y, $2y$, 35°, and 55°, respectively. What is the value of y?

12. In the figure shown, ℓ_1, ℓ_2, and ℓ_3 are parallel. What is the value of $a + 2c + e$?

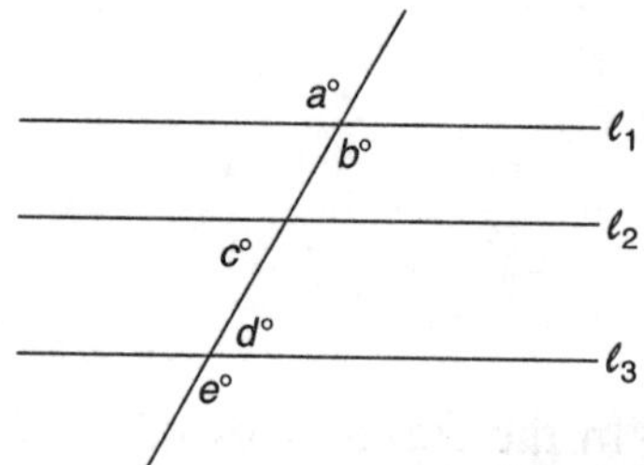

13. In the figure shown, $a = d$ and $b + c = 100°$. What is the value of a?

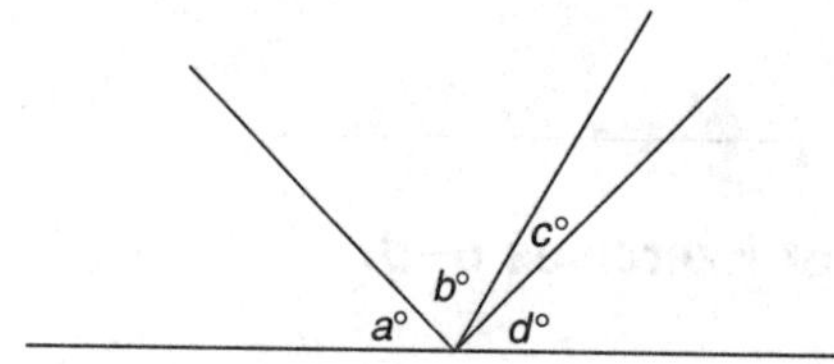

14. If an angle is twice as large as its complement, what is the measure of the larger angle?

15. $\angle A$ and $\angle B$ are supplementary. The measure of $\angle A$ is $(3x + 50)°$. The measure of $\angle B$ is $(7x + 90)°$. What are the measures of $\angle A$ and $\angle B$?

16. In the figure shown, M is the midpoint of segment AB. What is the length of AB?

$4x + 9$ $6x + 5$
A M B

17. What is the slope of the line whose equation is $3x + 5y + 4 = 0$?

18. $\angle A$ and $\angle B$ are vertical angles. The measure of $\angle A$ is $(4x - 35)°$. The measure of $\angle B$ is $(x + 10)°$. What is the measure of $\angle A$?

19. Point X is between points A and B on a line. $AB = 45$, $AX = 2x$, and $XB = 2x + 5$. What is the value of x?

20. In the figure shown, ℓ_1 and ℓ_2 are parallel. What is the value of x?

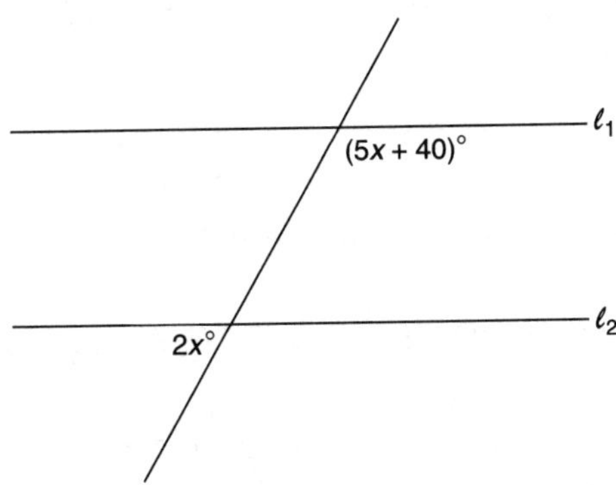

ADVANCED

Use the figure shown for Exercises 21–22.

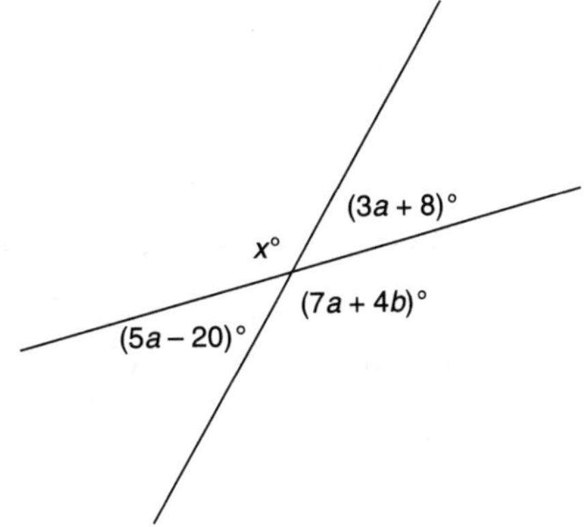

21. What are the values of a and b?

22. What is the measure of $\angle x$?

23. If the ratio of x:y:z in the figure shown is 1:2:3, what are the values of x, y, and z?

$y°$
$x°$ $z°$
straight

24. $\angle A$ and $\angle B$ are supplementary. The measure of $\frac{1}{2}$ $\angle A$ equals the measure of $2\angle B$. What are the measures of $\angle A$ and $\angle B$?

25. The measure of an angle is 48 more than the measure of its complement. What is the measure of the angle?

26. Point X lies on a line segment RS. The length of segment RX is 2 more than half of the length of segment XS. If the length of XS is 10, what is the length of segment RS?

27. $\angle J$ and $\angle K$ are complementary. The measure of $\angle K$ is 15 more than twice the measure of $\angle J$. What are the measures of $\angle J$ and $\angle K$?

28. If the length of segment AD shown is $9x + 7$, what is the length of AD?

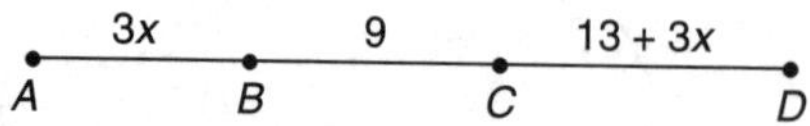

Use the figure shown for Exercises 29–30.

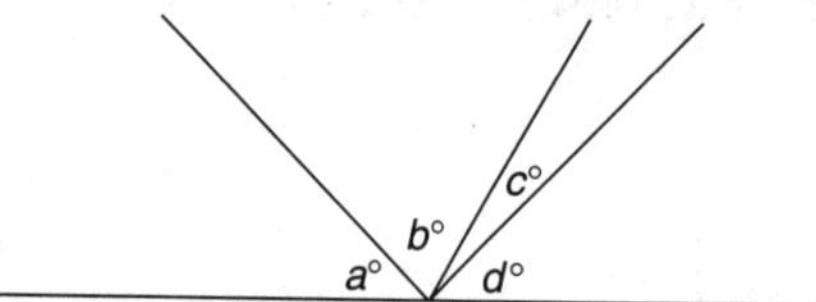

29. If $b = \frac{a}{2}$, $c = \frac{b}{2}$, and $d = 3c$, what is the value of d?

30. If $a = b - 5$, $b = 2c$, and $d = a + 1$, what is the value of c?

LINES AND ANGLES ANSWER KEY

BASIC

1. Straight

A straight angle is 180°.

2. Right

A right angle is 90°.

3. Acute

An acute angle is between 0° and 90°.

4. Obtuse

An obtuse angle is between 90° and 180°.

5. 120°

Angle x is supplementary to the 60° angle. $x + 60° = 180°$ so $x = 120°$.

6. 75°

$a + b + c = 180°$ because they are all angles on the same side of a line. $60° + b + 45° = 180°$. $105° + b = 180°$ so $b = 75°$.

7. 180°

$a + f + b = 180°$ because the three angles together form a straight line.

8. 360°

$a + b + c + d + e + f = 360°$ because the six angles together are all possible angles around a single point.

9. 90°

Supplementary angles sum to 180°. Because $90° + x = 180°$, $x = 90°$.

10. 54°

Complementary angles sum to 90°. Because $36° + x = 90°$, $x = 54°$.

INTERMEDIATE

11. 90°

The angles around a point sum to 360. Therefore, $y + 2y + 35° + 55° = 360°$; $3y + 90° = 360°$; $3y = 270°$, so $y = 90°$.

12. 360°

When two parallel lines intersect with a third line, any acute angle is supplementary to any obtuse angle. Angle a is obtuse, angle c is acute, and angle e is obtuse. $a + c = 180°$ and $c + e = 180°$. $a + c + c + e = 180° + 180° = 360°$.

13. 40°

$a + b + c + d = 180°$ because the four angles together compose a straight line. We know $b + c = 100°$ and $a = d$, so $a + 100° + a = 180°$. Thus, $2a + 100° = 180°$; $2a = 80°$, so $a = 40°$.

14. 60°

Let $2x$ = the larger angle and x = the complement of that angle. Then $2x + x = 90°$ because the angles are complementary. Thus, $3x = 90°$; $x = 30°$, so $2x = 60°$.

15. $\angle A = 62°$ and $\angle B = 118°$

The sum of the measures of angles A and B must be 180° because they are supplementary. Therefore, $3x + 50 + 7x + 90 = 180$.

$$\begin{aligned} 10x + 140 &= 180 \\ 10x &= 40 \\ x &= 4 \end{aligned}$$

The measure of $\angle A = (3x + 50)° = (3(4) + 50)° = 12° + 50° = 62°$.
The measure of $\angle B = (7x + 90)° = (7(4) + 90)° = 28° + 90° = 118°$.

16. 34

$4x + 9 = 6x + 5$ because M is the midpoint. Thus, $4x + 4 = 6x$; $4 = 2x$, so $2 = x$. Substitute 2 for x and add the length of the segments together to find the total length:

$$\begin{aligned} &4x + 9 + 6x + 5 \\ &= 4(2) + 9 + 6(2) + 5 \\ &= 8 + 9 + 12 + 5 \\ &= 34 \end{aligned}$$

17. $-\frac{3}{5}$

Put the equation $3x + 5y + 4 = 0$ in slope-intercept form: $3x + 5y + 4 = 0$; $5y = -3x - 4$. Divide both sides by 5: $y = -\frac{3}{5}x - \frac{4}{5}$. The slope m is the coefficient of x, or $-\frac{3}{5}$.

18. 25°

$\angle A = \angle B$ because vertical angles are equal. Therefore, $4x - 35 = x + 10$; $3x = 45$; $x = 15$. Substitute the value of x to find the measure of $\angle A$: $4x - 35 = 4(15) - 35 = 60 - 35 = 25$.

19. 10

$AX + XB = AB$ because X is between A and B. Therefore, $2x + 2x + 5 = 45$; $4x + 5 = 45$; $4x = 40$; $x = 10$.

20. 20

Angle $2x$ and angle $5x + 40$ are supplementary because when two parallel lines intersect with a third line, any acute angle is supplementary to any obtuse angle. So, $2x + 5x + 40 = 180$; $7x + 40 = 180$; $7x = 140$; $x = 20$.

ADVANCED

21. $a = 14, b = 8$

Vertical angles are equal, so $5a - 20 = 3a + 8$; $2a = 28$; $a = 14$. Angle $(3a + 8)$ and angle $(7a + 4b)$ are supplementary because together they form a straight line. Therefore, $3a + 8 + 7a + 4b = 180$. Substitute 14 for a: $3(14) + 8 + 7(14) + 4b = 180$; $42 + 8 + 98 + 4b = 180$; $148 + 4b = 180$; $4b = 32$; $b = 8$.

22. 130°

Vertical angles are equal, so the measure of $\angle x = 7a + 4b$. Substitute the values of $a = 14$ and $b = 8$ to solve: $\angle x = 7a + 4b = 7(14) + 4(8) = 98 + 32 = 130$.

23. $x = 30°, y = 60°, z = 90°$

The ratio of $x{:}y{:}z$ is 1:2:3, so let $x = 1a$, $y = 2a$, and $z = 3a$. x, y, and z together compose a straight line. $x + y + z = 180$; $1a + 2a + 3a = 180$; $6a = 180$; $a = 30$. Then $x = 1a = 1(30) = 30$; $y = 2a = 2(30) = 60$; $z = 3a = 3(30) = 90$.

24. $\angle A = 144°, \angle B = 36°$

Because $\frac{1}{2}\angle A = 2\angle B$, $\angle A = 4\angle B$. $\angle A$ and $\angle B$ are supplementary. Therefore, $\angle A + \angle B = 180$. Substituting, $4\angle B + \angle B = 180$; $5\angle B = 180$; $\angle B = 36$. $\angle A + \angle B = 180$; $\angle A + 36 = 180$; $\angle A = 144$.

25. 69°

Let $x =$ the angle. Its complement equals $x - 48°$. $x + x - 48° = 90°$; $2x - 48° = 90°$; $2x = 138°$; $x = 69°$.

26. 17

If point X lies on segment RS, then $RX + XS = RS$. If the length of segment RX is 2 more than half of the length of segment XS, then $RX = \frac{1}{2}XS + 2$. Because $XS = 10$, $RX = \frac{1}{2}(10) + 2 = 5 + 2 = 7$. $RX + XS = RS$, so $7 + 10 = 17 = RS$.

27. $\angle J = 25°, \angle K = 65°$

$\angle K = 2\angle J + 15$. $\angle J$ and $\angle K$ are complementary, so $\angle J + \angle K = 90$. Substituting, $\angle J + (2\angle J + 15) = 90$; $3\angle J + 15 = 90$; $3\angle J = 75$; $\angle J = 25$. So, $\angle K = 2\angle J + 15 = 2(25) + 15 = 50 + 15 = 65$.

28. 52

$$\begin{aligned} AD &= AB + BC + CD \\ 9x + 7 &= 3x + 9 + (13 + 3x) \\ 9x + 7 &= 6x + 22 \\ 3x + 7 &= 22 \\ 3x &= 15 \\ x &= 5 \\ AD &= 9x + 7 = 9(5) + 7 = 45 + 7 = 52 \end{aligned}$$

29. 54°

Express a, b, and d in terms of c.

$$c = \frac{b}{2}, \text{ so } b = 2c. \; b = \frac{a}{2}, \text{ so } a = 2b = 2(2c) = 4c. \; d = 3c.$$

Because the four angles together compose a straight line, $a + b + c + d = 180$. Substituting,

$$\begin{aligned} 4c + 2c + c + 3c &= 180^\circ \\ 10c &= 180^\circ \\ c &= 18^\circ \\ d &= 3c = 3(18^\circ) = 54^\circ \end{aligned}$$

30. $c = 27°$

Express a, b, and d in terms of c.

$$\begin{aligned} &b = 2c \text{ so } a = 2c - 5 \\ &d = 2c - 5 + 1 = 2c - 4 \end{aligned}$$

Because the four angles together compose a straight line, $a + b + c + d = 180$. Substituting,

$$\begin{aligned} 2c - 5 + 2c + c + 2c - 4 &= 180^\circ \\ 7c - 9 &= 180^\circ \\ 7c &= 189^\circ \\ c &= 27^\circ \end{aligned}$$

TRIANGLES AND PYTHAGOREAN THEOREM

General Triangles

A **triangle** is a closed figure with three angles and three straight sides.

The sum of the **interior angles** of any triangle is 180 degrees.

Each interior angle is supplementary to an adjacent **exterior angle**. The degree measure of an exterior angle is equal to the sum of the measures of the two nonadjacent (remote) interior angles, or 180° minus the measure of the adjacent interior angle.

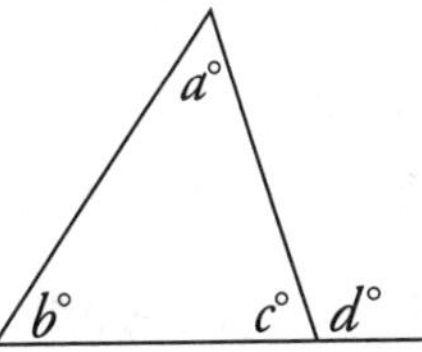

The **height** of a triangle is the perpendicular distance from a vertex to the side opposite the vertex. The height, or altitude, can fall inside the triangle, outside the triangle, or on one of the sides.

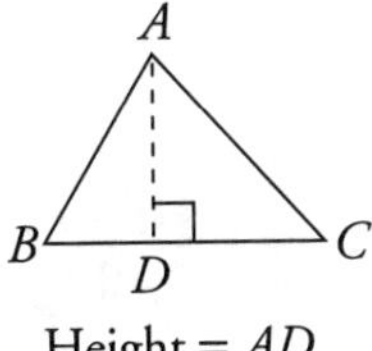

Height = AD

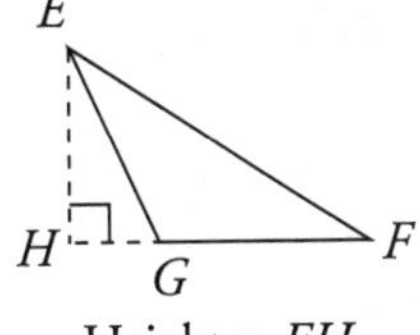

Height = EH

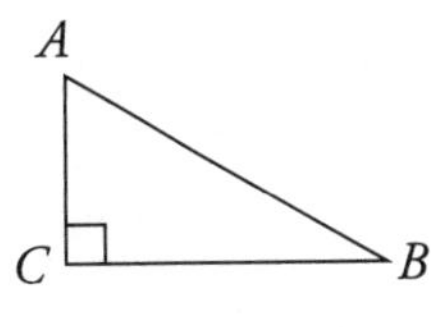

Height = AC

Sides and angles: The length of any side of a triangle is less than the sum of the lengths of the other two sides, and it is greater than the positive difference of the lengths of the other two sides.

$$b + c > a > b - c$$
$$a + b > c > a - b$$
$$a + c > b > a - c$$

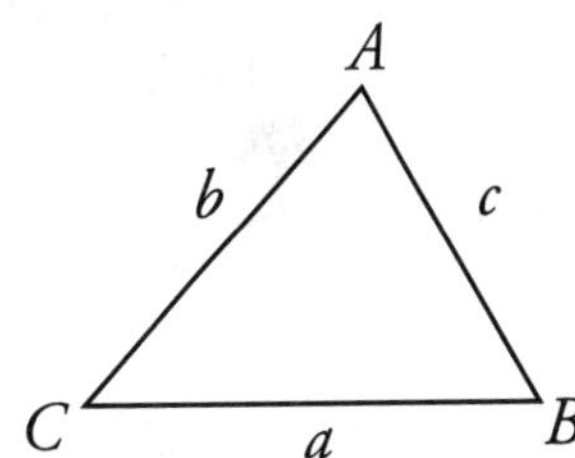

If the lengths of two sides of a triangle are unequal, the **greater angle** lies **opposite the longer side** and vice versa. In the figure shown, if $\angle A > \angle B > \angle C$, then $a > b > c$.

Example: In the diagram shown, what is an inequality that shows the relationship between the sides of the triangle?

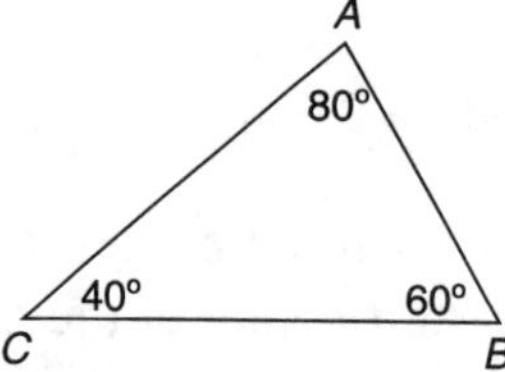

Because $\angle A > \angle B > \angle C$, $BC > AC > AB$.

Area of a triangle: The area of a triangle is the number of square units inside the triangle. A formula for the area of a triangle is $A = \frac{1}{2}bh$, where b is the length of the base of the triangle and h is the corresponding height.

Example: In the diagram shown, the base has length 4 and the height has length 3. What is the area of the triangle?

> The area of a triangle is $\frac{1}{2}$ base $\times$ height.

$$A = \frac{1}{2}bh$$
$$= \frac{1}{2} \times 4 \times 3 = 6$$

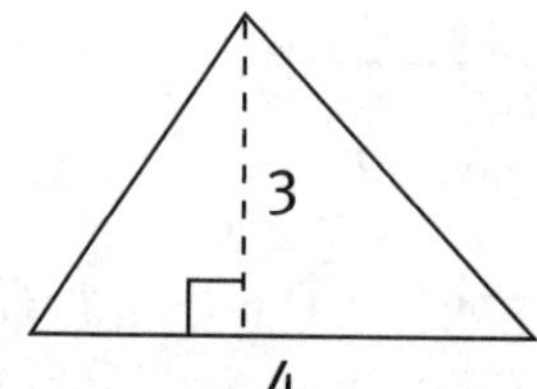

Remember that the height is perpendicular to the base. Therefore, when two sides of a triangle are perpendicular to each other, the area is easy to find. In a right triangle, we call the two sides that form the 90° angle the **legs**. The easiest base and height are always the two legs, and it doesn't matter which is called the base and which is called the height. Then the area is one-half the product of the legs, or

$$A = \frac{1}{2}bh$$
$$A = \frac{1}{2}ab$$

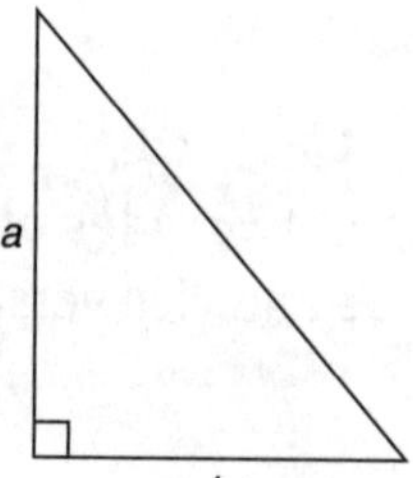

Example: What is the area of a right triangle with legs 6 and 8?

$$A = \frac{1}{2}\ell_1 \times \ell_2$$
$$= \frac{1}{2} \times 6 \times 8 = 24$$

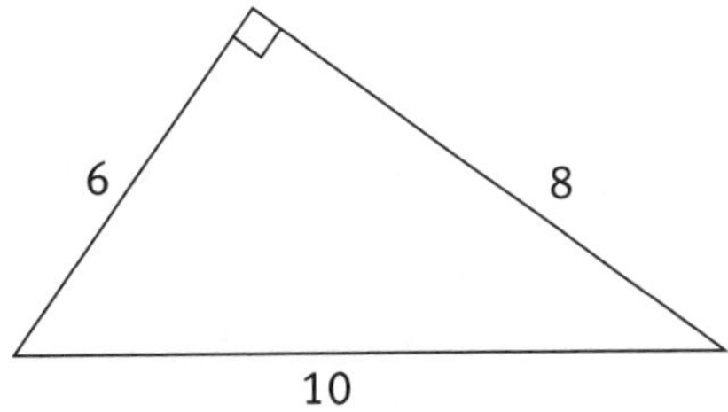

Perimeter of a triangle: The **perimeter** of a triangle is the distance around the triangle. In other words, the perimeter is equal to the sum of the lengths of the sides.

Example: In the triangle shown, the sides are of length 5, 6, and 8. What is the perimeter?

The perimeter is the sum of the sides: $5 + 6 + 8$, or 19.

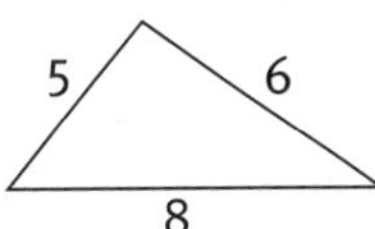

Isosceles triangles: An **isosceles triangle** is a triangle that has two sides of equal length. The two equal sides are called **legs**, and the third side is called the **base**.

Since the two legs have the same length, the two angles opposite the legs must have the same measure. In the figure shown, $PQ = PR$, and $\angle R = \angle Q$.

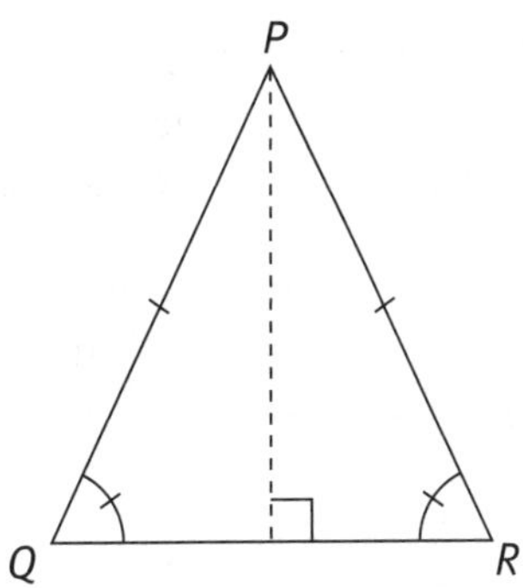

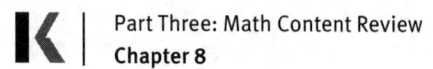

Equilateral triangles: An **equilateral triangle** has three sides of equal length and three 60° angles.

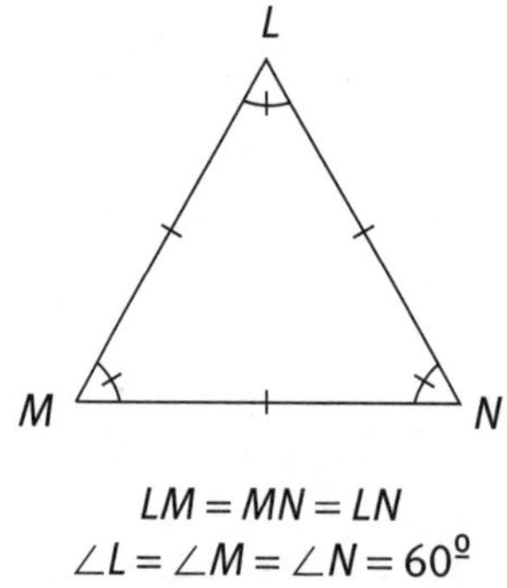

Similar triangles: Triangles are **similar** if they have the same shape—if corresponding angles have the same measure. For instance, any two triangles whose angles measure 30°, 60°, and 90° are similar. In similar triangles, corresponding sides are in the same ratio. Triangles are **congruent** if corresponding angles have the same measure and corresponding sides have the same length.

Example: What is the perimeter of $\triangle DEF$ below?

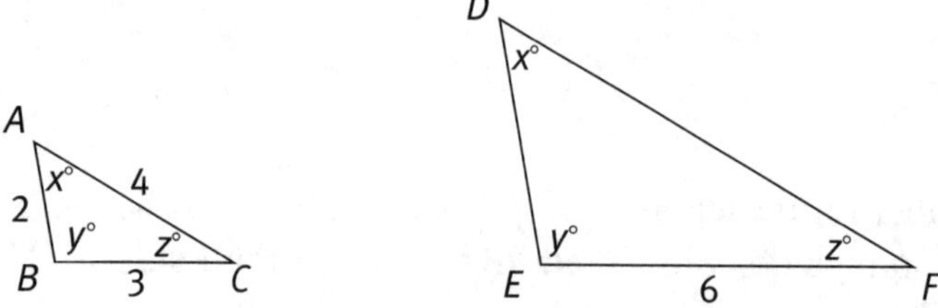

Each triangle has an $x°$ angle, a $y°$ angle, and a $z°$ angle; therefore, they are similar, and corresponding sides are in the same ratio. *BC* and *EF* are corresponding sides; each is opposite the $x°$ angle. Since *EF* is twice the length of *BC*, each side of *DEF* will be twice the length of the corresponding side of *ABC*. Therefore $DE = 2(AB)$ or 4, and $DF = 2(AC)$ or 8. The perimeter of *DEF* is $4 + 6 + 8 = 18$.

The ratio of the areas of two similar triangles is the square of the ratio of corresponding lengths. For instance, in the example shown, since each side of *DEF* is 2 times the length of the corresponding side of *ABC*, *DEF* must have 2^2 or 4 times the area of *ABC*.

$$\frac{\text{Area } \triangle DEF}{\text{Area } \triangle ABC} = \left(\frac{DE}{AB}\right)^2 = \left(\frac{2}{1}\right)^2 = 4$$

Right Triangles and the Pythagorean Theorem

A right triangle has one interior angle of 90°. The longest side (which lies opposite the right angle, the largest angle of a right triangle) is called the **hypotenuse**. As mentioned before, the other two sides are called the **legs**.

Pythagorean Theorem

The Pythagorean theorem holds for all right triangles and states that the square of the hypotenuse is equal to the sum of the squares of the legs.

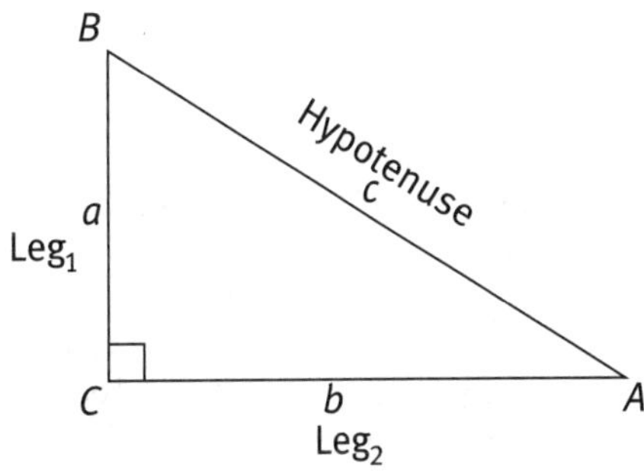

$$(\text{Leg}_1)^2 + (\text{Leg}_2)^2 = (\text{Hypotenuse})^2$$

or

$$a^2 + b^2 = c^2$$

Some sets of integers happen to satisfy the Pythagorean theorem. These sets of integers are commonly referred to as "Pythagorean triples." One very common set that you might remember is 3, 4, and 5. Since $3^2 + 4^2 = 5^2$, you can have a right triangle with legs of lengths 3 and 4 and hypotenuse of length 5. This is probably the most common kind of right triangle on the GRE. You should be familiar with the numbers so that whenever you see a right triangle with legs of 3 and 4, you will immediately know the hypotenuse must have length 5. In addition, any multiple of these lengths makes another Pythagorean triple; for instance, $6^2 + 8^2 = 10^2$, so 6, 8, and 10 also make a right triangle. One other triple that is seen frequently is 5, 12, and 13. The Pythagorean theorem is very useful; whenever you're given the lengths of two sides of a right triangle, you can find the length of the third side with the Pythagorean theorem.

Example: What is the length of the hypotenuse of a right triangle with legs of length 9 and 10?

Use the Pythagorean theorem: the square of the length of the hypotenuse equals the sum of the squares of the lengths of the legs. Here the legs are 9 and 10, so we have

$$\begin{aligned}\text{Hypotenuse}^2 &= 9^2 + 10^2\\ &= 81 + 100\\ &= 181\\ \text{Hypotenuse} &= \sqrt{181}\end{aligned}$$

Example: What is the length of the hypotenuse of an isosceles right triangle with legs of length 4?

Since we're told the triangle is isosceles, we know two of the sides have the same length. We know the hypotenuse can't be the same length as one of the legs (the hypotenuse must be the longest side), so it must be the two legs that are equal. Therefore, in this example, the two legs have length 4, and we can use the Pythagorean theorem to find the hypotenuse.

$$\begin{aligned}\text{Hypotenuse}^2 &= 4^2 + 4^2\\ &= 16 + 16\\ &= 32\\ \text{Hypotenuse} &= \sqrt{32} = 4\sqrt{2}\end{aligned}$$

An isosceles right triangle is a special right triangle. The ratio of its sides is $1:1:\sqrt{2}$.

You can always use the Pythagorean theorem to find the lengths of the sides in a right triangle. There are two frequently-tested special right triangles, though, that always have the same ratios. They are:

$1:1:\sqrt{2}$ (for isosceles 45°–45°–90° right triangles)

$1:\sqrt{3}:2$ (for 30°–60°–90° right triangles)

Thus, special right triangles include those with the following side ratios:

- 3:4:5
- 5:12:13
- $1:1:\sqrt{2}$
- $1:\sqrt{3}:2$

Example: What is the hypotenuse of a right triangle if the legs are 5 and 5?

This is a multiple of a $1:1:\sqrt{2}$ triangle, so the sides are $5:5:5\sqrt{2}$. The hypotenuse is $5\sqrt{2}$.

Example: What is the hypotenuse of a right triangle if the legs are 12 and 16?

This is a multiple of a 3:4:5, so the sides are 12:16:20. The hypotenuse is 20.

Example: The hypotenuse of a right triangle is 4 and one leg is 2. What is the other leg?

This is a multiple of $1:\sqrt{3}:2$, so the sides are $2:2\sqrt{3}:4$. The other leg is $2\sqrt{3}$.

If you don't remember the special right triangles, you can still use the Pythagorean theorem to calculate the length of a side, as we did in examples on the previous page.

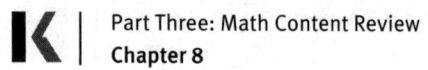

TRIANGLES AND PYTHAGOREAN THEOREM EXERCISES

BASIC

1. The angles of a triangle are 50°, 60°, and x°. What is the value of x?
2. What is the area of a triangle with a height of 8 and a base of 10?
3. What is the perimeter of a triangle with sides of lengths 6, 7, and 9?
4. What is the perimeter of a right triangle with legs of lengths 3 and 4?
5. What is the area of a right triangle with legs of lengths 12 and 16?
6. Angle x is an exterior angle of a triangle with remote interior angles 50° and 80°. What is the value of x in degrees?
7. The measure of an angle across from one of the legs of an isosceles triangle is 40°. What are the measures of the other two angles?
8. For two similar triangles, the ratio of their corresponding sides is 2:3. What is the ratio of their perimeters?
9. What is the ratio of the areas of two congruent triangles?
10. The legs of a right triangle are of length 1 and $\sqrt{3}$. What is the hypotenuse?

INTERMEDIATE

11. The sides of a triangle are of length 5, 8, and c. What is the range of the possible values of c?
12. The hypotenuse of an isosceles right triangle is 16. What is the area of the triangle?
13. What is the length of a diagonal of the rectangle shown?

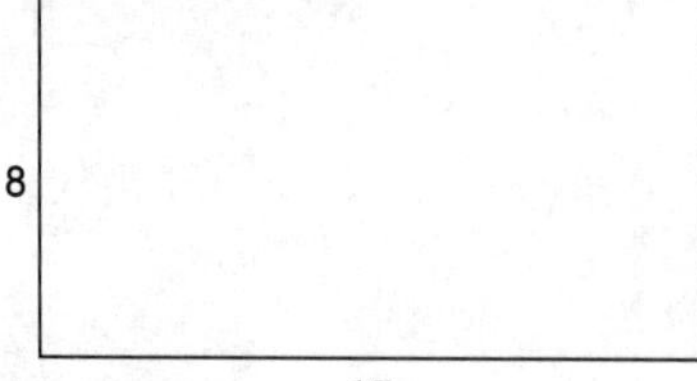

14. A square has a diagonal of length 5. What is the length of a side of the square?

15. A triangle has sides with lengths 4, 6, and 9. A larger similar triangle's shortest side has length 12. What is the perimeter of the larger triangle?

16. Triangle ABC is congruent to triangle DEF, $AC = 8$, $AB = 10$, and $BC = 15$. What is EF?

17. For similar triangles, the ratio of their corresponding sides is 2:3. What is the ratio of their areas?

18. The area of a triangle with a base of length 6 is equal to 12. What is the height of the triangle?

19. Triangle ABC is similar to triangle DEF, $AC = 9$, $AB = 6$, $DF = 18$, $DE = 12$, and $BC = 12$. What is EF?

20. What is the value of x in the triangle shown?

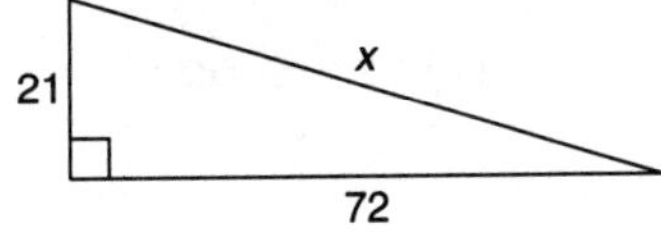

ADVANCED

21. What is the area of the triangle shown?

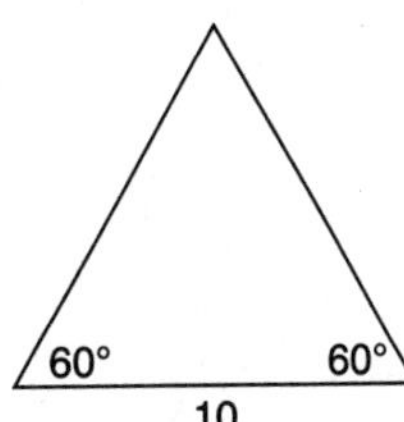

22. The sides of a triangle are of length 4, 8, and $4\sqrt{3}$. What is the area of the triangle?

23. What is the area of the triangle shown?

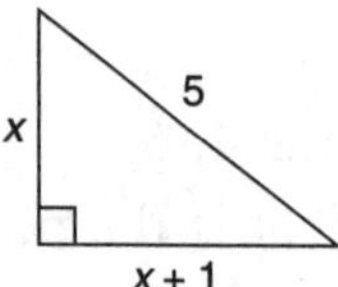

24. A 25-foot ladder rests against the side of a house. If the base of the ladder is 7 feet away from the house, how high off the ground is the top of the ladder?

25. A rectangle inscribed in a circle has a length of 8 and a width of 6. What is the area of the circle in terms of π?

26. What is the area of a right triangle with hypotenuse 61 and one leg 11?

27. The lengths of the legs of a right triangle are $3x$ and $x + 1$. The hypotenuse is $3x + 1$. What is the value of x ?

28. What is the side length of an equilateral triangle with an altitude of 6?

29. What is the value of x in the triangle shown?

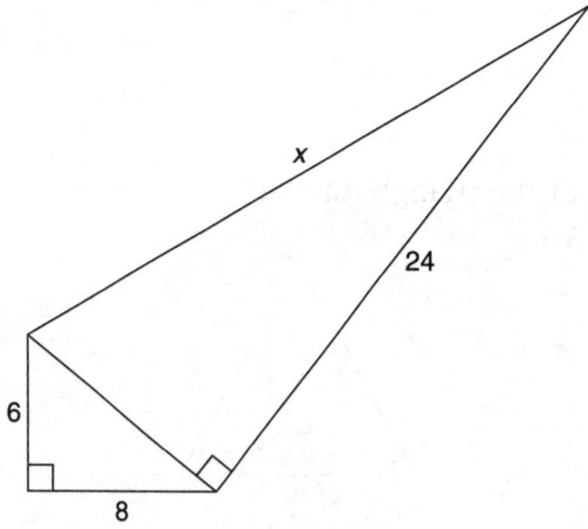

30. What is the value of x in the triangle shown?

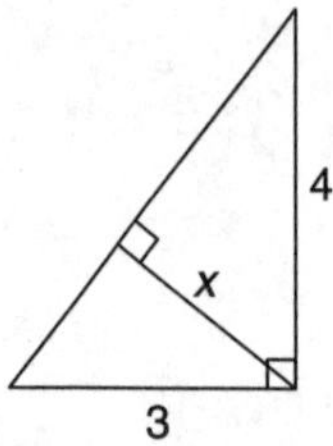

TRIANGLES AND PYTHAGOREAN THEOREM ANSWER KEY

BASIC

1. 70°

The sum of the interior angles of a triangle is 180°. Therefore, $50° + 60° + x = 180°$; $110° + x = 180°$; $x = 70°$.

2. 40

The formula for the area of a triangle is $A = \frac{1}{2}bh$. $A = \frac{1}{2}(10)(8) = 40$.

3. 22

The perimeter is equal to the sum of the lengths of the sides. $P = 6 + 7 + 9 = 22$.

4. 12

A right triangle with legs 3 and 4 has a hypotenuse of 5. It is a special right triangle. $P = 3 + 4 + 5 = 12$.

5. 6

The legs of a right triangle are the base and height of the triangle.

$$A = \frac{1}{2}bh.\ A = \frac{1}{2}(12)(16) = 96.$$

6. 130°

An exterior angle of a triangle is equal to the sum of the remote interior angles.

Thus, $50° + 80° = 130°$.

7. 40°, 100°

Base angles of an isosceles triangle are equal, so the other base angle is 40°. The sum of all the angles is 180°. Solve to find the measure of the remaining angle x: $40° + 40° + x = 180°$; $80° + x = 180°$; $x = 100°$.

8. 2:3

The ratio of the perimeters of two similar triangles equals the ratio of the corresponding sides, 2:3.

9. 1:1

Corresponding sides of congruent triangles are equal, so the areas will be the same; they will have a ratio of 1:1.

10. 2

If the legs of a right triangle are 1 and $\sqrt{3}$, the right triangle is a 30°-60°-90° right triangle and the hypotenuse is 2. You can also use the Pythagorean theorem: $c^2 = 1^2 + (\sqrt{3})^2 = 1 + 3 = 4$. $c = \pm 2$. Since c is a side of a triangle, it must be positive, and $c = 2$.

Intermediate

11. $3 < c < 13$

The third side of a triangle is greater than the difference of the two sides but less than the sum of the two sides.

$$a - b < c < a + b$$
$$8 - 5 < c < 8 + 5$$
$$3 < c < 13$$

12. 64

The sides of an isosceles right triangle are in the ratio $1:1:\sqrt{2}$. So, divide the hypotenuse by $\sqrt{2}$ to get the length of a leg: $\frac{16}{\sqrt{2}} = \frac{16\sqrt{2}}{\sqrt{2} \times \sqrt{2}} = \frac{16\sqrt{2}}{2} = 8\sqrt{2}$. The legs of a right triangle are the base and height of the triangle. $A = \frac{1}{2}bh$. $A = \frac{1}{2}(8\sqrt{2})(8\sqrt{2}) = 64$.

13. 17

The diagonal of a rectangle is the hypotenuse of a right triangle whose legs are the length and the width of the rectangle. $c^2 = 8^2 + 15^2 = 64 + 225 = 289$; $c = 17$. 8:15:17 is a Pythagorean triple.

14. $\frac{5\sqrt{2}}{2}$

The diagonal of a square is the hypotenuse of an isosceles right triangle whose legs are sides of the square. The sides of an isosceles right triangle are in the ratio $1:1:\sqrt{2}$. So, divide the hypotenuse by $\sqrt{2}$ to get the length of a leg: $\frac{5}{\sqrt{2}} = \frac{5\sqrt{2}}{\sqrt{2} \times \sqrt{2}} = \frac{5\sqrt{2}}{2}$.

15. 57

The triangles are similar. The shortest side of the smaller triangle is 4. The shortest side of the larger triangle is 12. The ratio of corresponding sides is 4:12 or 1:3. So the sides of the larger triangle are $4(3) = 12$, $6(3) = 18$, and $9(3) = 27$. $P = 12 + 18 + 27 = 57$.

16. 15

Triangle *ABC* is congruent to triangle *DEF*. The corresponding sides are *AB* and *DE*, *AC* and *DF*, and *BC* and *EF*. Because the two triangles are congruent, the sides are in the ratio 1:1. So, if $BC = 15$, $EF = 15$.

17. 4:9

The ratio of the areas of two similar triangles equals the square of the ratio of the corresponding sides: $2^2:3^2 = 4:9$.

18. 4

$$A = \frac{1}{2}bh.\ 12 = \frac{1}{2}(6)(h); 12 = 3h; 4 = h.$$

19. 24

Triangle *ABC* is similar to triangle *DEF*. The corresponding sides are *AB* and *DE*, *AC* and *DF*, and *BC* and *EF*. $\frac{AB}{DE} = \frac{AC}{DF} = \frac{BC}{EF}$. $\frac{6}{12} = \frac{9}{18} = \frac{12}{EF}$. The scale factor is 1:2. So $EF = 24$.

20. 75

Use the Pythagorean theorem. $x^2 = 21^2 + 72^2 = 441 + 5{,}184 = 5{,}625$. $x = 75$. This is a multiple of the Pythagorean triple 7:24:25.

Advanced

21. $25\sqrt{3}$

If two angles of a triangle are each 60°, the third angle must also be 60°. So the triangle is equilateral with side length 10. Draw an altitude. It is the side opposite the 60° angle in a 30°-60°-90° triangle. Its length is one-half the hypotenuse times the square root of 3.

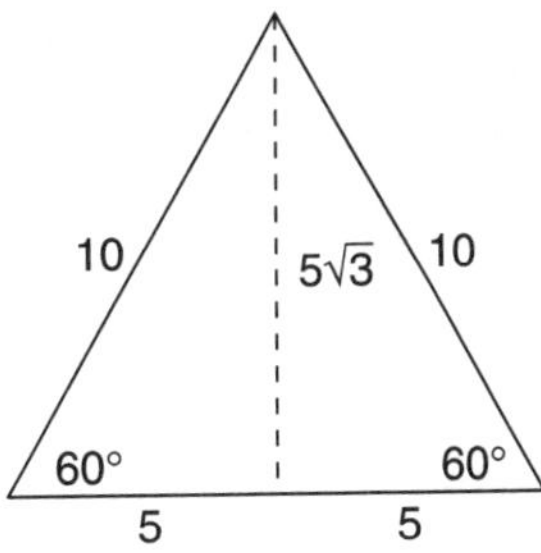

$$A = \frac{1}{2}bh.\ A = \frac{1}{2}(10)(5\sqrt{3}) = 25\sqrt{3}.$$

22. $8\sqrt{3}$

The ratio of the sides is $4:4\sqrt{3}:8$. So, the triangle is a 30°-60°-90° triangle with legs 4 and $4\sqrt{3}$. The area of a right triangle is one-half the product of the legs: $A = \frac{1}{2}bh$. Thus, $A = \frac{1}{2}(4)(4\sqrt{3}) = 8\sqrt{3}$.

23. 6

The triangle is a special right triangle. It is a 3:4:5 triangle.

The area of a right triangle is one-half the product of the legs: $A = \frac{1}{2}bh$. $A = \frac{1}{2}(3)(4) = 6$.

24. 24 feet

The ladder, the ground, and the house form a right triangle with hypotenuse 25 and leg 7.

If you notice that this is a 7:24:25 Pythagorean triple, you're done. Alternatively, use the Pythagorean theorem: $25^2 = 7^2 + x^2$; $625 = 49 + x^2$; $576 = x^2$; $x = 24$.

25. 25π

The diagonal of a rectangle inscribed in a circle is the diameter of the circle. The diagonal of the rectangle is equal to the hypotenuse of a right triangle with legs 6 and 8. Therefore, the hypotenuse is 10 because it is a multiple of a 3:4:5 right triangle. The area of a circle is $A = \pi r^2$. The diameter of a circle is $2r$, so $r = 5$. The area of the circle is $A = \pi r^2 = \pi(5)^2 = 25\pi$.

26. 330

You can use the Pythagorean theorem to find the other leg. Thus, $61^2 = 11^2 + x^2$; $3{,}721 = 121 + x^2$; $3{,}600 = x^2$; $x = 60$. The area of a right triangle is one-half the product of the legs: $A = \frac{1}{2}bh$. $A = \frac{1}{2}(60)(11) = 330$.

27. 4

Use the Pythagorean theorem.

$$\begin{aligned}(3x + 1)^2 &= (3x)^2 + (x + 1)^2 \\ 9x^2 + 6x + 1 &= 9x^2 + x^2 + 2x + 1 \\ 6x &= x^2 + 2x \\ 4x &= x^2 \\ 4 &= x\end{aligned}$$

28. $4\sqrt{3}$

The altitude of this equilateral triangle divides the triangle into two 30°-60°-90° triangles with side lengths x, 6, and $2x$, where $2x$ is the hypotenuse of the 30°-60°-90° triangles and side length of the equilateral triangle. You can use the Pythagorean theorem, but since 6 is the longer leg of the 30°-60°-90° triangle and a 30°-60°-90° triangle has sides of ratio $1:\sqrt{3}:2$, you can say that $\mathbf{6 = x\sqrt{3}}$. From here,

$$x = \frac{6}{\sqrt{3}}$$

$$x = \frac{6\sqrt{3}}{\sqrt{3}\sqrt{3}} = \frac{6\sqrt{3}}{3} = 2\sqrt{3}$$

However, the question asks for the length of the side of the equilateral triangle, which is $2x$, so we need to double the value of x.

$$2 \times 2\sqrt{3} = 4\sqrt{3}$$

The answer is $4\sqrt{3}$.

29. 26

The right triangle with legs 6 and 8 has hypotenuse 10 because it is a double 3:4:5 triangle. The other triangle has legs 10 and 24, which are doubles of 5 and 12. A 5:12:13 right triangle has hypotenuse 13. So, the hypotenuse of a right triangle with legs of length 10 and 24 is $2(13) = 26$.

30. 2.4

If the legs of a right triangle are of length 3 and 4, the hypotenuse is 5. We also know the area of the triangle is one-half times the product of the lengths of the two legs. Therefore,

$$A = \frac{1}{2}(3)(4) = 6$$

The line segment marked by x can also be used as the height when the hypotenuse is used as the base, since the hypotenuse and the line marked by x are perpendicular. Since the area of the triangle is 6,

$$6 = \frac{1}{2}(5)(x)$$
$$6 = 2.5x$$
$$\frac{6}{2.5} = x$$
$$2.4 = x$$

Therefore, x is equal to 2.4.

POLYGONS

A **polygon** is a closed figure whose sides are straight line segments.

The **perimeter** of a polygon is the sum of the lengths of the sides.

A **vertex** of a polygon is the point where two adjacent sides meet.

A **diagonal** of a polygon is a line segment connecting two nonadjacent vertices.

A **regular polygon** has sides of equal length and interior angles of equal measure.

The number of sides determines the specific name of the polygon. A **triangle** has three sides, a **quadrilateral** has four sides, a **pentagon** has five sides, and a **hexagon** has six sides. Triangles and quadrilaterals are by far the most important polygons on the GRE.

Interior and exterior angles: A polygon can be divided into triangles by drawing diagonals from a given vertex to all other nonadjacent vertices. For instance, the pentagon shown can be divided into 3 triangles. Since the sum of the interior angles of each triangle is 180°, the sum of the interior angles of a pentagon is $3 \times 180° = 540°$.

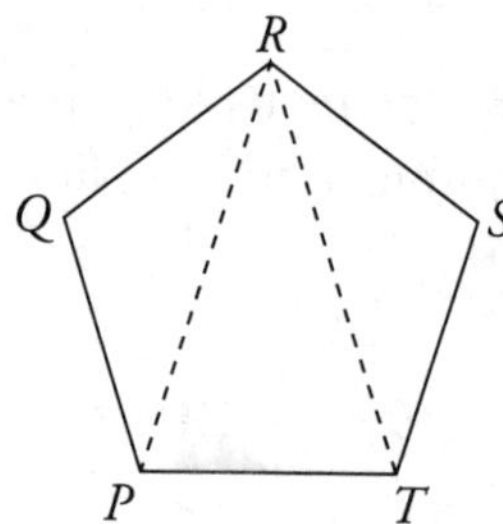

Example: What is the measure of one interior angle of the regular hexagon shown?

Find the sum of the interior angles and divide by the number of interior angles, or 6. (Since all angles are equal, each of them is equal to one-sixth of the sum.)

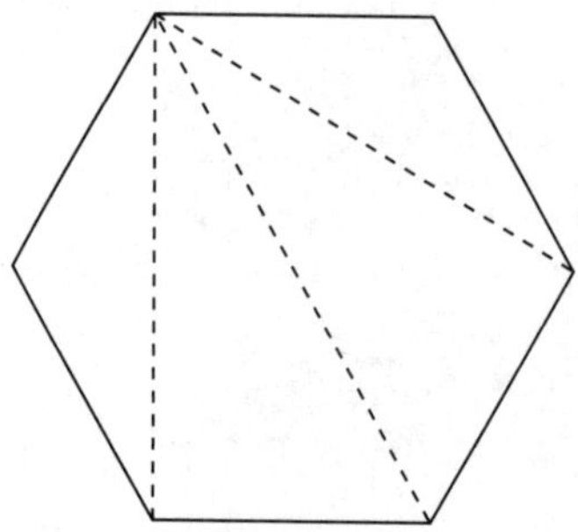

Since we can draw 4 triangles in a 6-sided figure, the sum of the interior angles will be $4 \times 180°$, or $720°$. Therefore, each of the six interior angles has measure $\frac{720}{6}$, or 120 degrees.

In general, the sum of the interior angles of a polygon equals $180°(n - 2)$, where n is the number of sides in the polygon.

QUADRILATERALS

The most important quadrilaterals to know for the GRE are the rectangle and square. Any quadrilateral could show up on the test, but concentrate on the most important figures and principles as they will yield you the most points.

Quadrilateral: A four-sided polygon. The sum of its four interior angles is 360°.

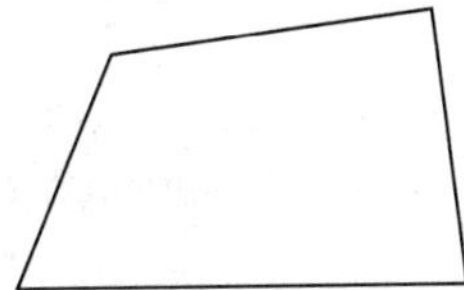

Parallelogram: A quadrilateral with two pairs of parallel sides.

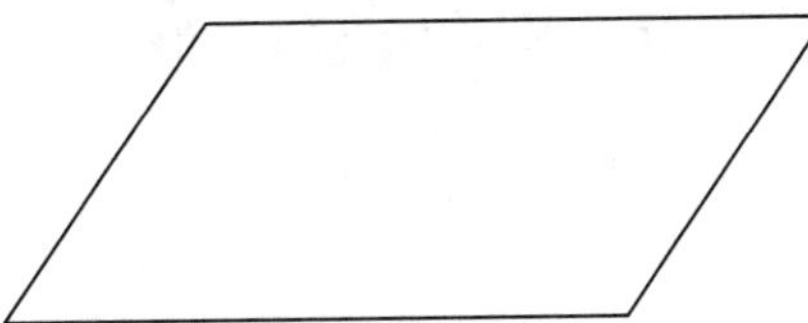

Rectangle: A parallelogram with four equal angles, each a right angle.

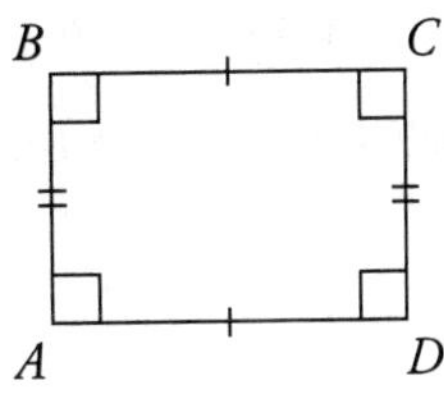

$AB = CD \qquad AD = CB$

The opposite sides of a rectangle are equal in length. Also, the diagonals of a rectangle have equal length.

Square: A rectangle with four equal sides.

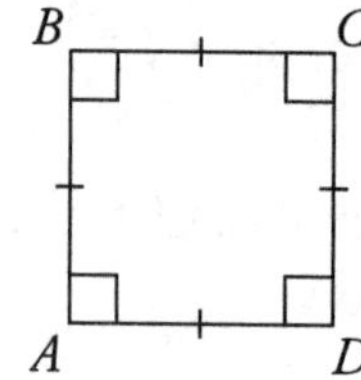

$$AB = BC = CD = DA$$

Trapezoid: A quadrilateral having only two parallel sides.

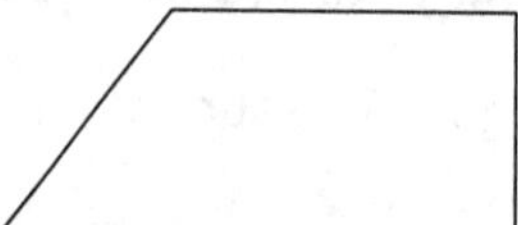

Areas of quadrilaterals: All formulas are based on common sense, observation, and deductions. Memorizing the formulas will save you time.

For the case of a rectangle, we multiply the lengths of any two adjacent sides, called the length and width, or:

Area of rectangle = lw

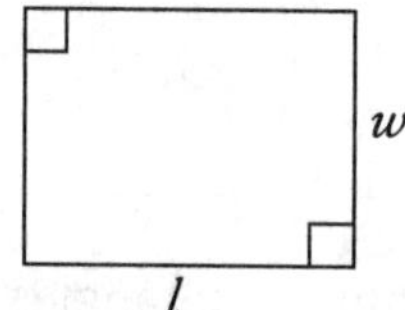

For the case of a square, since length and width are equal, we say:

Area of a square = $(\text{side})^2 = s^2$

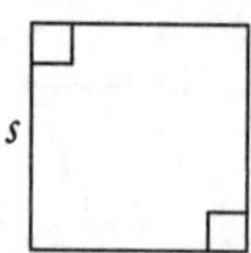

Area of a parallelogram = bh

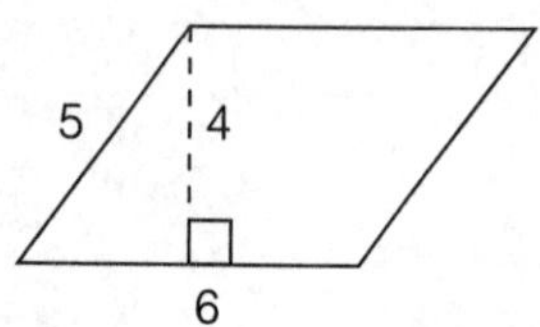

$$\text{Area} = 6 \times 4 = 24$$

Area of a trapezoid = (average of parallel sides)(height)

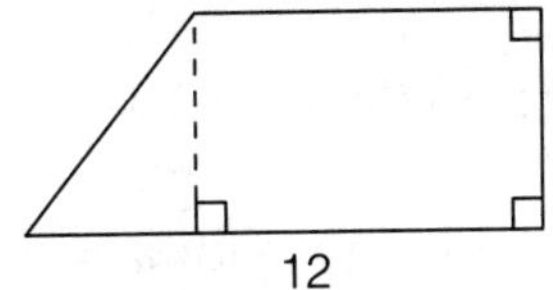

$$\text{Area} = \left(\frac{8 + 12}{2}\right) \times 5 = 50$$

The areas of other figures can usually be found using the methods we'll discuss later in the Multiple Figures section.

POLYGONS EXERCISES

Basic

1. The angles of a pentagon are 50°, 60°, 70°, $x°$, and $2x°$. What is the value of x?

2. What is the area of a parallelogram with a height of 6 and a base of 8?

3. What is the perimeter of a quadrilateral with sides 6, 7, 8, and 9?

4. What is the sum of the interior angles of a heptagon, or seven-sided polygon?

5. What is the measure of one interior angle of a regular octagon?

6. What is the measure of an exterior angle of a regular pentagon?

7. What is the perimeter of a square with a side of length 6?

8. If a triangle has two sides of length 4 and 6, what is the range of possible values for the length of the third side x?

9. What is the perimeter of a regular hexagon with a side of length 8?

10. What is the area of a rectangle with a length of 6 and a width of 4?

Intermediate

11. The length of a rectangle is $2x - 1$. The width is $3x + 5$. The perimeter is 38. What is the value of x?

12. The following figure shows three squares and a triangle. What is the area of square A?

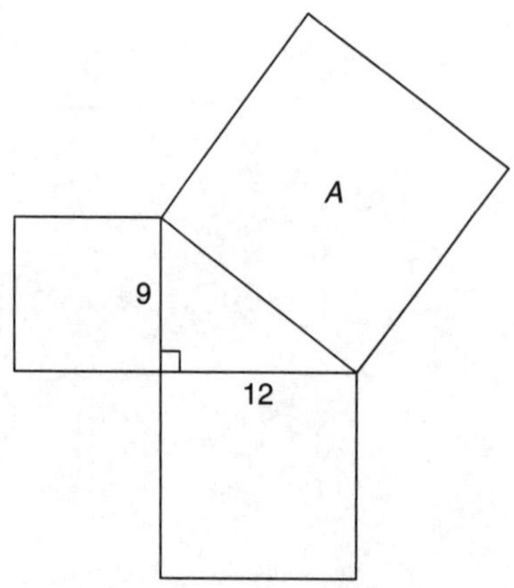

13. What is the area of the rectangle shown?

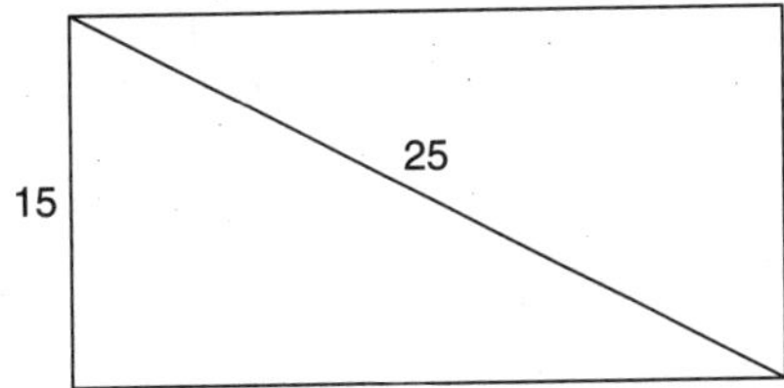

14. The area of a rectangle is 588 square feet, and its length is three times its width. What are the measures of the length and the width?

15. Regular pentagon *ABCDE* has a side length of 28. Regular pentagon *FGHIJ* has a perimeter of 60 and an area of about 248. What is the ratio of the area of *ABCDE* to the area of *FGHIJ*?

16. What is the area of the quadrilateral shown?

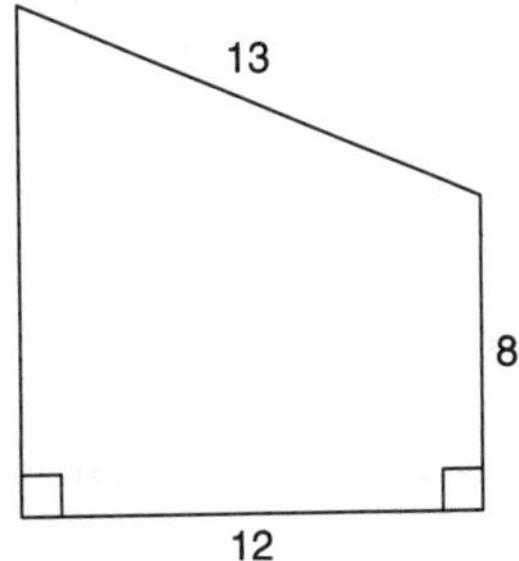

17. In similar hexagons, the ratio of the areas is 16:25. What is the ratio of their corresponding sides?

18. What is the perimeter of the square shown?

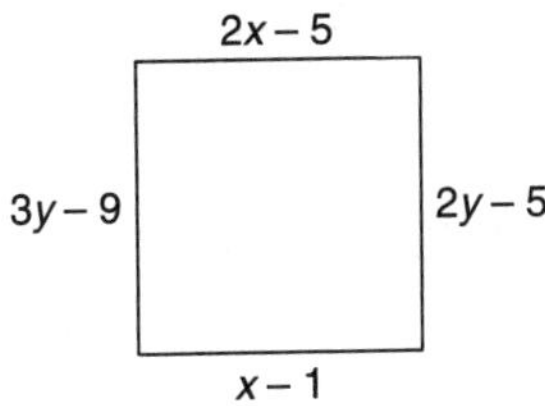

19. What are the values of x and y in the figure shown?

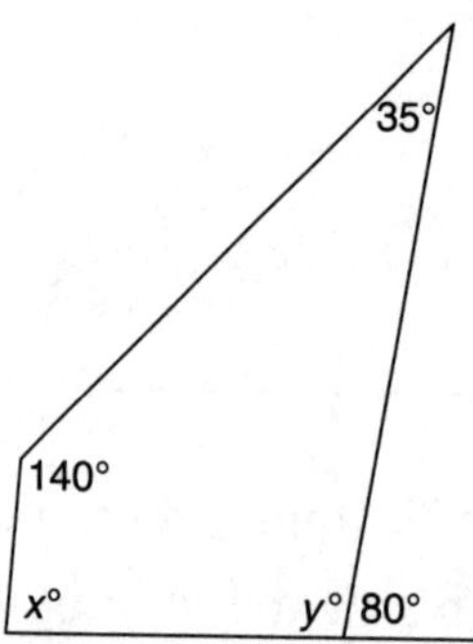

20. Four congruent squares are joined together in the figure shown. What is the ratio of the nonshaded area to the shaded area?

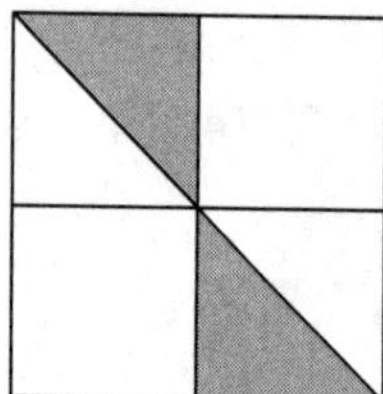

ADVANCED

21. What is the area of the quadrilateral shown?

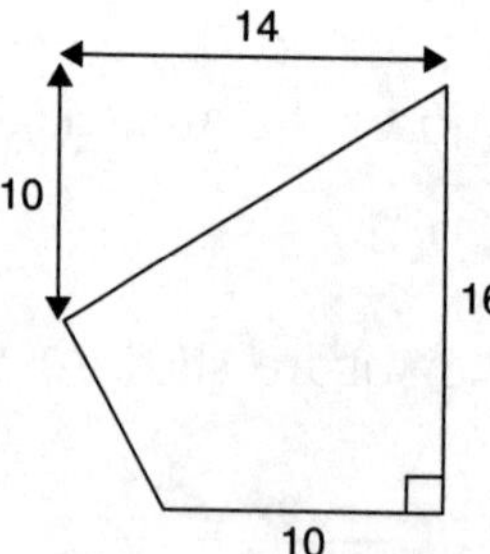

22. The area of a rectangle can be represented by the expression $2x^2 + 9x + 10$. The length is $2x + 5$ and the width is 6. What is the value of the area of the rectangle?

23. A rectangle with an area of 18 has a length that is 3 more than its width. What are the length and width of the rectangle?

24. A ceiling has a length of 30 feet and a width of 30 feet. The ceiling is going to be tiled with 24-inch by 36-inch tiles. How many tiles are needed to cover the ceiling?

25. What is the area of quadrilateral *ABCD* shown?

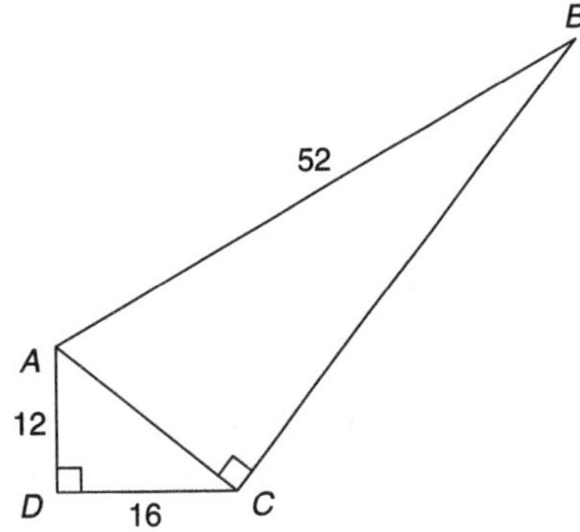

26. In the figure shown, *ABCD* is a rectangle, $AB = 8$, and $BC = 6$. *R*, *S*, *T*, and *Q* are midpoints of the sides of *ABCD*. What is the perimeter of *RSTQ*?

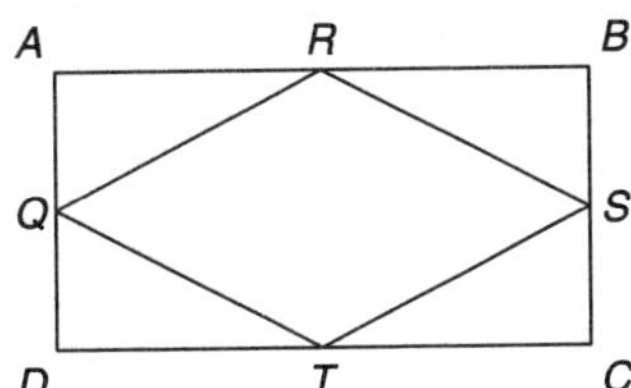

27. In the figure shown, the small square divides the diagonal of the large square into three equal parts. What is the ratio of the area of the large square to the area of the small square?

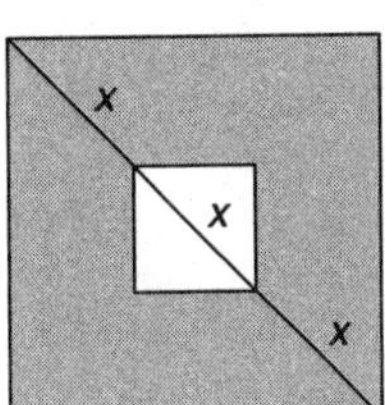

28. In the figure shown, $ABCD$ is a square with a side length of 16. R, S, T, and Q are midpoints of the sides of $ABCD$. What is the area of $RSTQ$?

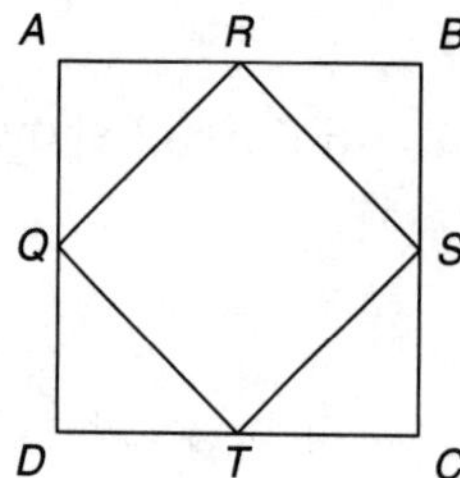

29. What is the area of a regular hexagon with sides of length 6?

30. In the figure shown, squares A and B are in rectangle R. The area of rectangle R is 216. The width (vertical dimension) of rectangle R is 12. The area of square A is 4 times the area of square B. The sum of the areas of squares A and B is 80. What is the value of x ?

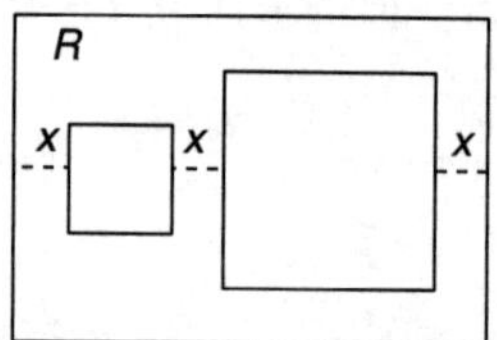

POLYGONS EXERCISES ANSWER KEY

BASIC

1. 120

The sum of the interior angles of a pentagon is $(5 - 2)180 = 3(180) = 540$. Thus, $50 + 60 + 70 + x + 2x = 540$; $3x + 180 = 540$; $3x = 360$; $x = 120$.

2. 48

The formula for the area of a parallelogram is $A = bh$. $A = (6)(8) = 48$.

3. 30

The perimeter is equal to the sum of the lengths of the sides. $P = 6 + 7 + 8 + 9 = 30$.

4. 900

The sum of the interior angles of a seven-sided polygon is $(7 - 2)180 = 5(180) = 900$.

5. 135

An octagon is an eight-sided figure. The sum of the interior angles of an octagon is $(8 - 2)180 = 6(180) = 1{,}080$. Divide by 8 to get the measure of one interior angle: $1{,}080 \div 8 = 135$.

6. 72

The sum of the interior angles of a pentagon is $(5 - 2)180 = 3(180) = 540$. Divide by 5 to get the measure of one interior angle: $540 \div 5 = 108$. An exterior angle is supplementary to an interior angle: $x + 108 = 180$; $x = 72$.

7. 24

The perimeter of a square is $P = 4s$. $P = 4(6) = 24$.

8. $2 < x < 10$

For any triangle, the length of any side must be greater than the difference and less than the sum of the lengths of the other two sides. Since the two sides given here are 4 and 6, the third side of length x can be expressed as follows:

$$6 - 4 < x < 6 + 4$$
$$2 < x < 10$$

The length of the third side must be between 2 and 10.

9. 48

The perimeter of a regular hexagon is $P = 6s$. $P = 6(8) = 48$.

10. 24

The area of a rectangle is $A = lw$. $A = (6)(4) = 24$.

Intermediate

11. 3

The perimeter is the sum of all the sides. Therefore, $(2x - 1) + (3x + 5) + (2x - 1) + (3x + 5) = 38$; $10x + 8 = 38$; $10x = 30$; $x = 3$.

12. 225

The triangle is a 9:12:15 triangle, a multiple of a 3:4:5 triangle. The triangle's hypotenuse, 15, is also the side length of the square. $A = s^2 = 15^2 = 225$.

13. 300

The triangle is a 15:20:25 triangle, a multiple of a 3:4:5 triangle. The length of the rectangle is 20, the width is 15. $A = lw = (20)(15) = 300$.

14. Width = 14, Length = 42

Let w = the width. The length equals $3w$. $A = (3w)(w) = 3w^2$; $3w^2 = 588$; $w^2 = 196$; $w = 14$. Thus, $3w = 3(14) = 42$.

15. 49:9

The regular pentagons are similar. The length of one of the sides of *ABCDE* is 28. The perimeter of *FGHIJ* is 60. Since there are 5 sides, the length of one side can be found by dividing the perimeter, in this case 60, by the number of sides, in this case, 5. Each side has a length of 12. The ratio of the areas of two similar polygons equals the square of the ratios of the corresponding sides. The ratio of the sides is 28:12 or 7:3. The ratio of the areas is $7^2:3^2$ or 49:9.

16. 126

Divide the quadrilateral into a right triangle and a rectangle.

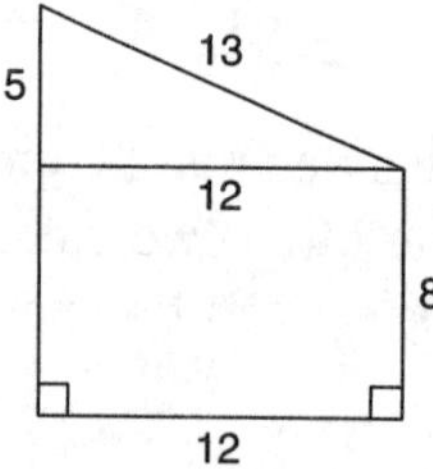

The triangle is a 5:12:13 triangle. For the triangle, $A = \frac{1}{2}bh$. $A = \frac{1}{2}(12)(5) = 30$.

For the rectangle, $A = lw$. $A = (12)(8) = 96$. Add the areas: $30 + 96 = 126$.

17. 4:5

The ratio of the areas of two similar polygons equals the square of the ratio of the corresponding sides. In this case, the ratio of the areas, 16:25, is the same as $4^2:5^2$. So, the ratio of the corresponding sides is 4:5.

18. 12

All sides of a square are equal. In this case, $2x - 5 = x - 1$; $2x = x + 4$; $x = 4$. One of the sides of the square is $x - 1 = 4 - 1 = 3$, so the other three sides also have length 3. The perimeter is $P = 4s = 4(3) = 12$.

19. $x = 85$, $y = 100$

The 80° angle and y are supplementary. Therefore, $y + 80 = 180$; $y = 100$. The sum of the interior angles of a quadrilateral is 360. $x + y + 140 + 35 = 360$; $x + 100 + 140 + 35 = 360$; $x + 275 = 360$; $x = 85$.

20. 3:1

If diagonals are drawn in all the squares, 8 congruent triangles are formed, 2 of which are shaded. There are 6 nonshaded triangles. The ratio is 6:2 or 3:1.

Advanced

21. 142

Divide the quadrilateral into two right triangles and a rectangle.

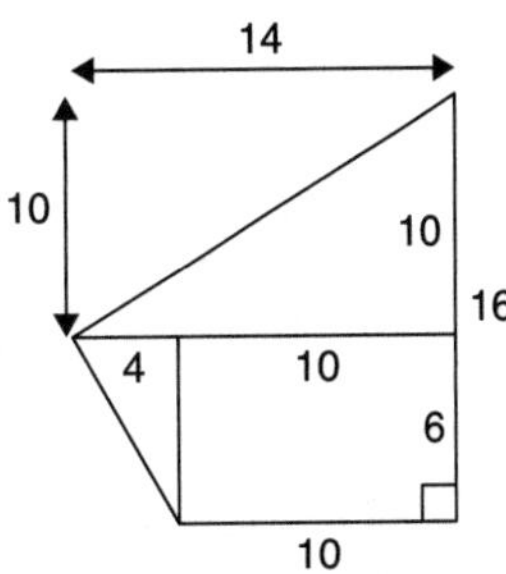

Area of small triangle: $A = \frac{1}{2}bh$. $A = \frac{1}{2}(4)(6) = 12$.

Area of large triangle: $A = \frac{1}{2}bh$. $A = \frac{1}{2}(14)(10) = 70$.

Area of rectangle: $A = lw$. $A = (10)(6) = 60$.

Add the areas: $A = 12 + 70 + 60 = 142$.

22. 78

To find the width in terms of x, divide the area by the length in terms of x:

$$\frac{2x^2 + 9x + 10}{2x + 5} = \frac{(2x + 5)(x + 2)}{(2x + 5)} = x + 2$$

So, $x + 2 = 6$ and $x = 4$. The area is then $2x^2 + 9x + 10 = 2(4)^2 + 9(4) + 10 = 32 + 36 + 10 = 78$. Alternately, length $= 2x + 5 = 2(4) + 5 = 13$, and width $= 6$. $A = lw$. $A = (13)(6) = 78$.

23. Length = 6, Width = 3

Let $w =$ the width. The length equals $w + 3$. Then $18 = (w)(w + 3)$; $18 = w^2 + 3w$; $0 = w^2 + 3w - 18$; $0 = (w + 6)(w - 3)$; $0 = w + 6$, or $0 = w - 3$. So, $w = -6$, or $w = 3$. Width is a distance and cannot be negative, so the width is 3. The length is $w + 3 = 3 + 3 = 6$.

24. 150

The area of the ceiling is $A = (30)(30) = 900$ square feet. The tiles are 24 inches, which is 2 feet, by 36 inches, which is 3 feet. The area of a tile is $A = (2)(3) = 6$ square feet. Divide the area of the ceiling by the area of a tile to get the number of tiles needed.

$900 \div 6 = 150$

25. 576

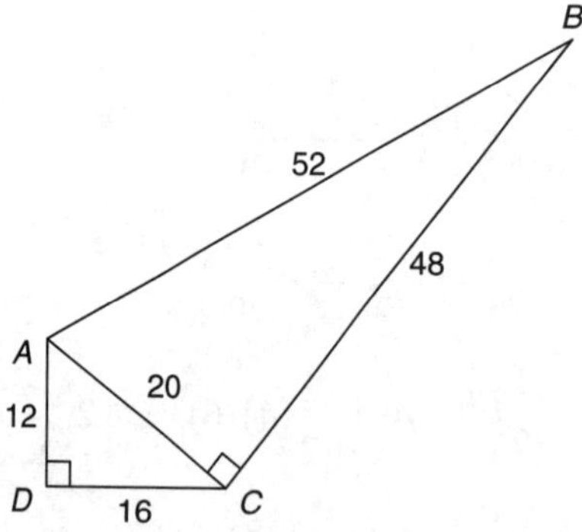

The triangles are multiples of a 3:4:5 right triangle and a 5:12:13 right triangle. The hypotenuse of the triangle with legs 12 and 16 is 20. The missing leg in the other triangle is 48.

Area of small triangle: $A = \frac{1}{2}bh$. $A = \frac{1}{2}(12)(16) = 96$.

Area of large triangle: $A = \frac{1}{2}bh$. $A = \frac{1}{2}(20)(48) = 480$.

$A = 96 + 480 = 576$.

26. 20

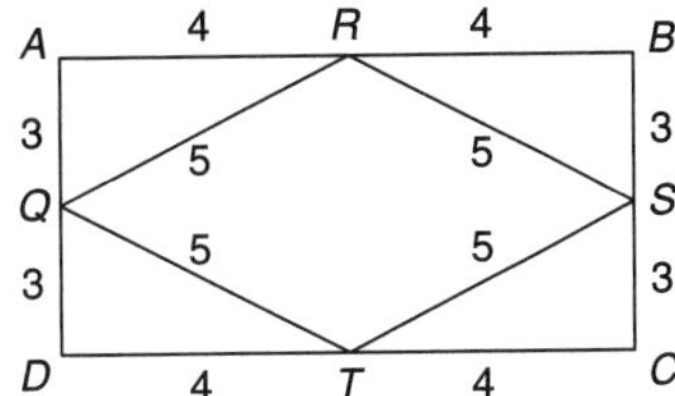

$AR = RB = DT = TC = 4$

$AQ = QD = BS = SC = 3$

The triangles formed are congruent 3:4:5 right triangles. The perimeter of *RSTQ* is 20.

27. 9:1

We can use Picking Numbers for this question. Let a side of the large square be 6. The diagonal of the large square is $6\sqrt{2}$, because a diagonal divides a square into two congruent isosceles right triangles. In addition, $6\sqrt{2} = 3x$. Therefore, $2\sqrt{2} = x =$ diagonal of small square. So, a side of the small square is 2. The ratio of the sides of the large square to the small square is 6:2 or 3:1. The ratio of their areas is $3^2{:}1^3$, or 9:1.

28. 128

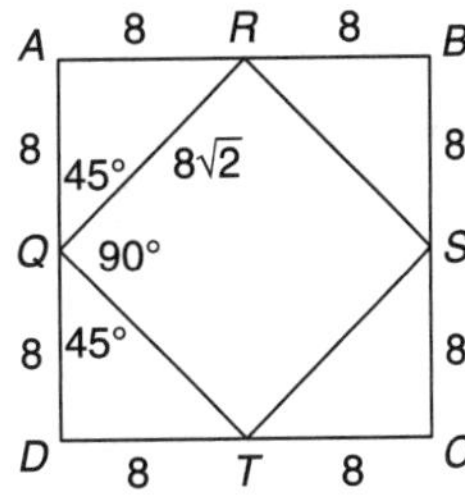

The triangles formed are all isosceles right triangles with legs of length 8. *RSTQ* is a square because all the angles are 90° as shown in the figure above, and its sides are the hypotenuses of four identical right triangles; each side measures $8\sqrt{2}$, as shown. $A = s^2$. $A = (8\sqrt{2})^2 = 128$.

29. $54\sqrt{3}$

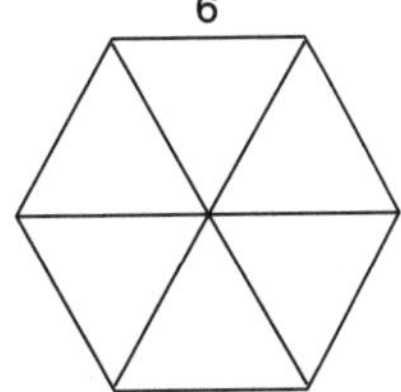

A regular hexagon can be divided into 6 congruent equilateral triangles. Find the area of one of the triangles and multiply by 6.

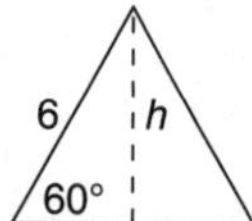

The altitude h is the side opposite a 60° angle in a 30°-60°-90° triangle; h is equal to one-half the hypotenuse times the square root of 3, or $3\sqrt{3}$. The area of one of the triangles, then, is:

$$A = \frac{1}{2}(6)(3\sqrt{3}) = 9\sqrt{3}$$

The area of the hexagon is $A = 6(9\sqrt{3}) = 54\sqrt{3}$.

30. 2

$$\begin{aligned} \text{Area of } A + \text{Area of } B &= 80 \\ \text{Area of } A &= 4(\text{Area of } B) \end{aligned}$$

$$\begin{aligned} 4(\text{Area of } B) + \text{Area of } B &= 80 \\ 5(\text{Area of } B) &= 80 \\ \text{Area of } B &= 16 \\ \text{Area of } A &= 4(16) = 64 \end{aligned}$$

$$\begin{aligned} \text{Area of } R &= lw \\ 216 &= 12l \\ 18 &= l \end{aligned}$$

The length of the rectangle is 18. A side of square A is $\sqrt{64} = 8$, and a side of square B is $\sqrt{16} = 4$.

$$\begin{aligned} 18 &= x + 4 + x + 8 + x \\ 18 &= 3x + 12 \\ 6 &= 3x \\ 2 &= x \end{aligned}$$

CIRCLES

A **circle** is labeled by its center point: circle O means the circle with center point O.

Diameter: A line segment, generally denoted by the variable d, that connects two points on the circle and passes through the center of the circle.

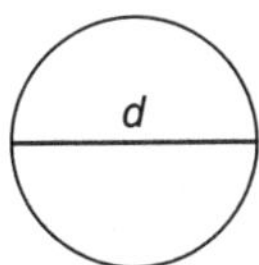

Radius: A line segment, generally denoted by the variable r, from the center of the circle to any point on the circle. The radius of a circle is one-half the length of the diameter.

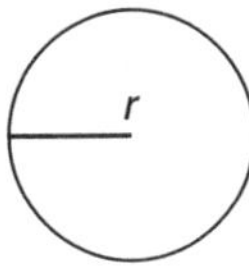

Chord: A line segment joining two points on the circle. Segment c is a chord.

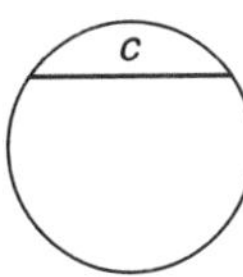

Central angle: An angle formed by two radii. Angle x is a central angle.

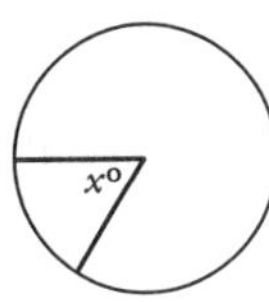

Tangent: A line that touches only one point on the circumference of the circle. A line drawn tangent to a circle is perpendicular to the radius at the point of tangency. Line t is tangent to circle O at point T.

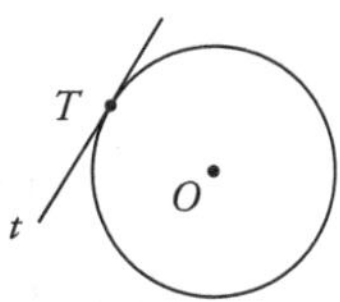

Circumference and arc length: The distance around a circle is called the circumference.

The number π (pi) is the ratio of a circle's circumference C to its diameter d.

$$\pi = \frac{C}{d}$$

$$C = \pi d$$

or

$$C = 2\pi r$$

The value of π is a never-ending decimal that starts with 3.1415926 but is usually approximated 3.14. For the GRE, it is usually sufficient to remember that π is a little more than 3.

An **arc** is a portion of the circumference of a circle. In the figure shown, *AB* is an arc of the circle, with the same degree measure as central angle *AOB*. The shorter distance between *A* and *B* along the circle is called the **minor arc**; the longer distance *AXB* is the **major arc**. An arc that is exactly half the circumference of the circle is called a **semicircle** (in other words, half a circle).

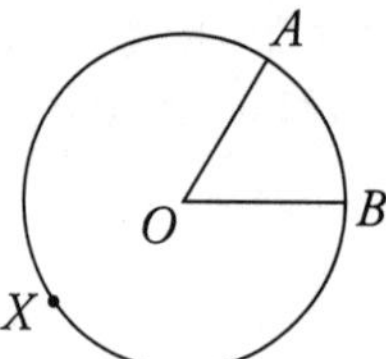

The length of an arc is the same fraction of a circle's circumference as its degree measure is of the degree measure of the circle (360°). For an arc with a central angle measuring *n* degrees:

$$\text{Arc length} = \left(\frac{n}{360}\right)(\text{circumference})$$
$$= \frac{n}{360} \times 2\pi r$$

Example: What is the length of arc *ABC* of the circle with center *O* shown?

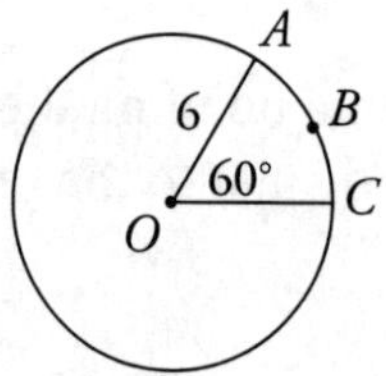

Since $C = 2\pi r$, if the radius is 6, the circumference is $2 \times \pi \times 6 = 12\pi$.

Since $\angle AOC$ measures 60°, the arc is $\frac{60°}{360°}$, or one-sixth, of the circumference.

Therefore, the length of the arc is one-sixth of 12π, which is $\frac{12\pi}{6}$ or 2π.

Area of a circle: The area of a circle is given by the formula

$$\boxed{A = \pi r^2}$$

A **sector** is a portion of the circle that is bounded by two radii and an arc. In the circle shown with center *O*, *OAB* is a sector. To determine the area of a sector of a circle, use the same method we used to find the length of an arc. Determine what fraction of 360° is in the degree measure of the central angle of the sector, then multiply that fraction by the area of the circle. In a sector whose central angle measures *n* degrees:

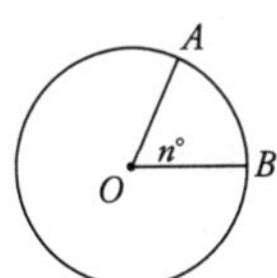

$$\text{Area of sector} = \left(\frac{n}{360}\right) \times (\text{Area of circle})$$
$$= \left(\frac{n}{360}\right) \times \pi r^2$$

Example: What is the area of sector *AOC* in the circle with center *O* shown?

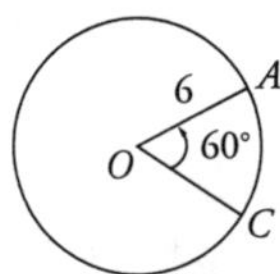

Since $\angle AOC$ measures 60°, a 60° "slice" is $\frac{60°}{360°}$, or one-sixth, of the circle.

So the sector has area $\frac{1}{6} \times \pi r^2 = \frac{1}{6} \times 36\pi = 6\pi$.

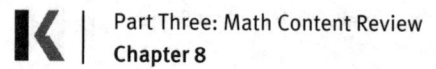

CIRCLES EXERCISES

BASIC

1. The radius of a circle is 4 centimeters. What is the diameter of the circle?

2. The diameter of a circle is 7 inches. What is the circumference of the circle?

3. The radius of a circle is 6 meters. What is the circumference of the circle?

4. The circumference of a circle is 10π centimeters. What is the length of the diameter of the circle?

5. The radius of a circle is 5 inches. What is the area of the circle?

6. The diameter of a circle is 12 feet. What is the area of the circle?

7. The area of a circle is 64π square centimeters. What is the radius?

8. The distance around a circular fountain is 38π meters. What is the radius of the fountain?

9. If the radius of a circle is tripled, the circle's area is multiplied by what amount?

10. Find the measure of the smaller angle made by the hands of a clock at 12:30.

INTERMEDIATE

For Exercises 11–13, use the following information:

The circle with center O shown has radius 4. Find the following:

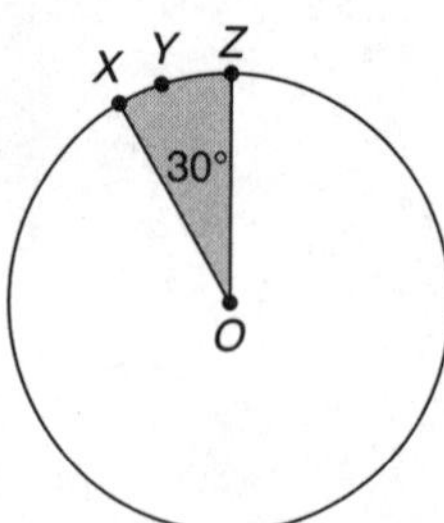

11. Circumference of the circle

12. Length of minor arc XYZ

13. Area of the shaded region

For Exercises 14–16, use the following information:

The figure shows two concentric circles, each with center C. Given that the larger circle has radius 14 and the smaller circle has radius 6, find the following:

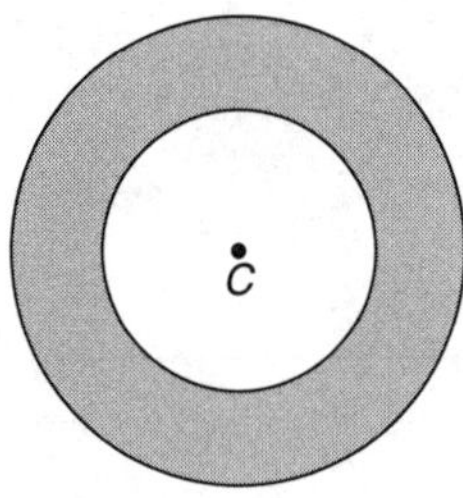

14. Circumference of the larger circle

15. Area of the smaller circle

16. Area of the shaded region

17. If the radius of circle C is 12, then what is the area of sector CED?

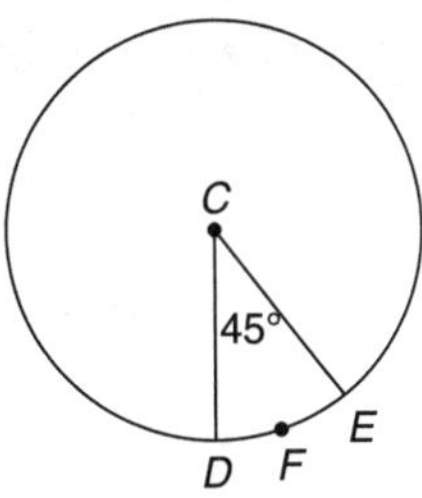

18. If the radius of the circle with center C is 6 and the measure of angle ACB is 120, what is the length of the minor arc from A to B?

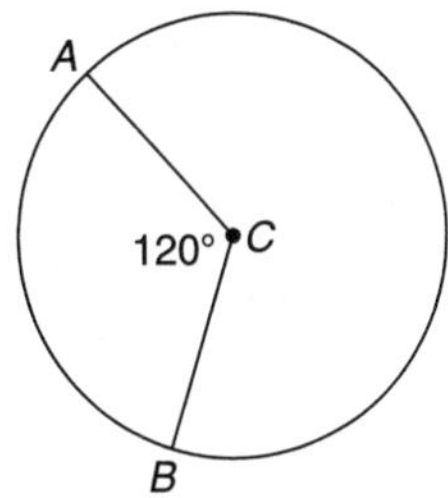

19. What is the number of degrees that the hour hand of a clock moves between noon and 2:30 in the afternoon of the same day?

20. Rectangle *RSTU* has a perimeter of 42. The half circle with diameter *RS* has an area of 8π. What is the area of the unshaded part of the figure?

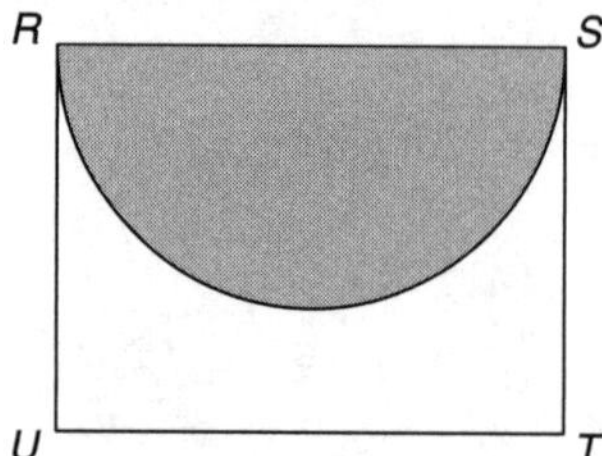

ADVANCED

21. A circular image is to be enlarged. The new radius will be 25 percent larger than the original. What is the ratio of the area of the current image to the area of the new image?

22. The diameter of a circle is formed by the line joining points (5, –2) and (–5, 3). Find the circumference of the circle.

23. What is the area of a circle if its center is at (3, 0) and the circle passes through (–1, –3)?

24. A 5 by 12 rectangle is inscribed in a circle. What is the circumference of the circle?

25. In the figure shown, if the radius of circle *P* is 3 times the radius of circle *A*, $\angle BAC = \angle QPR$, and the shaded area of circle *A* is 3π square units, then what is the area of the shaded part of circle *P*?

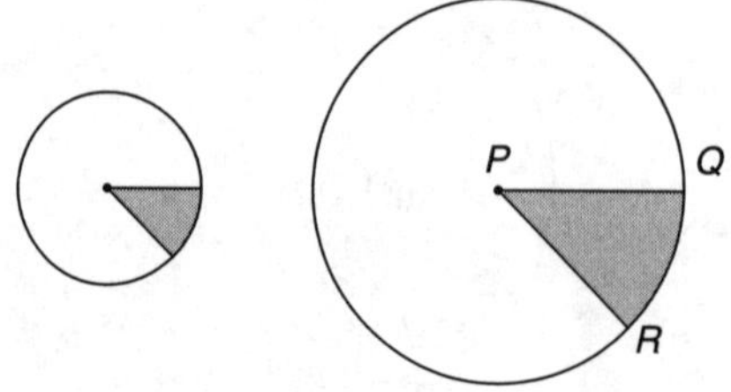

26. An 8-by-6 rectangle is inscribed in a circle. What is the circumference of the circle?

27. In the figure, the square has two sides that are tangent to the circle. If the area of the circle is $16x^2\pi$, what is the area of the square, in terms of x?

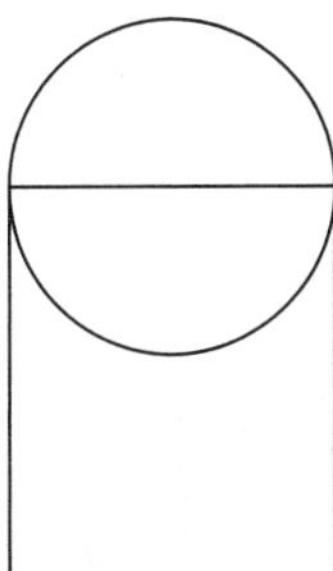

28. Two congruent, adjacent circles are cut out of a 16-by-8 rectangle. The circles have the maximum diameter possible. What is the area of the paper remaining after the circles have been cut out?

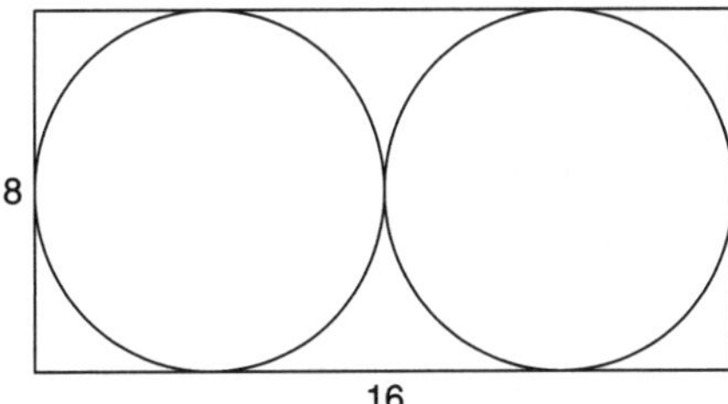

29. Points C and D are equidistant from the line l, and line segment CD intersects line l at a 45-degree angle. If the shortest straight-line distance between point C and line l is 5 units, what is the area of a circle drawn with its center on line l and line segment CD as its diameter?

30. A wheel has a diameter of x centimeters, and a second wheel has a diameter of y centimeters. The first wheel covers a distance of d meters in 200 revolutions. In terms of x and y, how many revolutions does the second wheel make in covering d meters?

CIRCLES EXERCISES ANSWER KEY

Basic

1. 8cm

$$\begin{aligned} d &= 2r \\ d &= 2 \times 4 \\ d &= 8\,\text{cm} \end{aligned}$$

2. 7π or about 21.98in.

$$\begin{aligned} C &= \pi d \\ C &= 7\pi \approx 3.14 \times 7 \\ C &= 21.98\,\text{inches} \end{aligned}$$

3. 12πm or 37.68m

$$\begin{aligned} C &= 2\pi r \\ C &= 2(\pi)(6) = 12\pi \approx 12(3.14) \\ C &= 37.68\,\text{m} \end{aligned}$$

4. 10cm

$$\begin{aligned} C &= \pi d \\ 10\pi &= \pi d \\ d &= 10\,\text{cm} \end{aligned}$$

5. 25πin.^{2} or 78.5in.^{2}

$$\begin{aligned} A &= \pi r^2 \\ A &= 5^2(\pi) = 25\pi \approx 3.14 \times 25 \\ A &\approx 78.5\,\text{in.}^2 \end{aligned}$$

6. 36πft^2

First, find the radius.

$$\begin{aligned} r &= \frac{1}{2}d \\ r &= \frac{1}{2}(12) \\ r &= 6 \end{aligned}$$

Now find the area.

$$\begin{aligned} A &= \pi r^2 \\ A &= \pi \times 6^2 \\ A &= 36\pi\,\text{ft}^2 \end{aligned}$$

7. 8

$$\begin{aligned} A &= \pi r^2 \\ 64\pi &= \pi r^2 \\ \frac{64\pi}{\pi} &= \frac{\pi r^2}{\pi} \\ 64 &= r^2 \\ \sqrt{64} &= \sqrt{r^2} \\ r &= 8\,\text{cm} \end{aligned}$$

8. 19

The distance around the circular fountain is the circumference of a circle.

$$\begin{aligned} 38\pi &= 2\pi r \\ \frac{38\pi}{2\pi} &= \frac{2\pi r}{2\pi} \\ r &= 19\,\text{m} \end{aligned}$$

9. 9

Area is $\pi \times r^2$, so area would be $\pi(3r)^2 = \pi \times 3^2 \times r^2 = 9\pi r^2$ for triple the radius. The area is 9 times bigger than it was before the tripling.

10. 165°

Each hour represents $\frac{1}{12}$ of a rotation, or $\frac{1}{12}$ of the degrees of a circle, which has 360 degrees. Therefore the degree measure between each number on the clock is:

$$360^\circ \times \frac{1}{12} = 30^\circ$$

The time 12:30 will put the hour hand between the positions of 12 o'clock and 1 o'clock, half of the distance between them. Half of 30 degrees equals 15 degrees. So the hour hand will be 15 degrees away from the "12" (for 12 o'clock). The minute hand will be at "6" (for 6 o'clock) at 12:30, so you almost have a straight line, except that the hour hand is rotated 15 degrees from the vertical, shrinking the angle between the hands. So, find the angle measurement: $180^\circ - 15^\circ = 165^\circ$.

Intermediate

11. 8π

$$C = 2\pi r$$
$$C = 2\pi \times 4 = 8\pi$$

12. $\frac{2\pi}{3}$

$$\frac{\text{measure of angle}}{360} = \frac{\text{length of arc}}{\text{circumference}}$$
$$\frac{30}{360} = \frac{\text{length of arc}}{8\pi}$$
$$\frac{1}{12} = \frac{l}{8\pi}$$
$$8\pi = 12l$$
$$\frac{8\pi}{12} = l$$
$$\frac{2\pi}{3} = l$$

13. $\frac{4\pi}{3}$

Area of a circle: $A = \pi r^2 = \pi(4^2) = 16\pi$

Shaded region: $\frac{30°}{360°} \times \pi(4^2) = \frac{1}{12} \times 16\pi = \frac{4\pi}{3}$

14. 28π

$$C = 2\pi r$$
$$C = 2 \times \pi \times 14$$
$$C = 28\pi$$

15. 36π

$$A = \pi\, r^2 = \pi(6^2) = 36\pi$$

16. 160π

Area of larger circle: $A = \pi r^2 = \pi(14^2) = 196\pi$

Area of shaded region = area of larger circle − area of smaller circle.

$196\pi - 36\pi = 160\pi$

17. 18π

$$\text{Area of sector} = \frac{n°}{360°} \times \pi r^2$$

$$= \frac{45°}{360°} \times \pi(12)^2$$

$$= \frac{1}{8} \times 144\pi$$

$$= \frac{144}{8}\pi$$

$$= 18\pi$$

18. 4π

$C = 2\pi r$, so the circumference $= 12\pi$

The length of the arc is $\frac{120}{360}$, or $\frac{1}{3}$ of the circumference.

$$\frac{1}{3} \times 12\pi = 4\pi$$

19. 75

The hour hand starts at 12 and moves until it is halfway between 2 and 3. The angle covered between each hour on the clock is $\frac{360}{12} = 30$. The hour hand has covered 2.5 of these divisions, so $30 \times 2.5 = 75$.

20. 104 – 8π

The total perimeter of the unshaded part is made up of three sides of the rectangle and the perimeter of the half circle.

The area of a half circle $= \frac{1}{2}\pi r^2$.

$8\pi = \frac{1}{2}\pi r^2$; therefore, $r = 4$, and the diameter of the semicircle is 8. This is also the length of the rectangle. Since the perimeter is 42, calculate the width of the rectangle:

$$P = 2l + 2w$$
$$42 = 2(8) + 2(w)$$
$$42 = 16 + 2w$$
$$2w = 26$$
$$w = 13$$

Find the area of the rectangle:

$$A = lw$$
$$A = (8)(13) = 104$$

The unshaded area is the area of the rectangle minus the area of the semicircle. So the area is $104 - 8\pi$.

ADVANCED

21. 16:25

Picking Numbers is a great strategy to use here. If the diameter of the old image is 4, the radius of the new image will be 5, since 25% of 4 = 1. The area of the old image is 16π, and the area of the new image is 25π.

The areas of the images are in the ratio $16\pi:25\pi$, or 16:25.

22. $5\pi\sqrt{5}$

If you draw the distance from (5, –2) to (–5, 3) on a coordinate plane, you are also drawing a right triangle, where the leg that runs parallel to the *x*-axis has a length of 10, and the leg that runs parallel to the *y*-axis has a length of 5. Use the Pythagorean theorem to find the diameter, represented by *c*:

$$(10)^2 + (5)^2 = c^2$$

$$100 + 25 = c^2$$

$$125 = c^2, \text{so } c = \sqrt{125} = \sqrt{25}\sqrt{5} = 5\sqrt{5}$$

The diameter is $5\sqrt{5}$, so the circumference is $5\pi\sqrt{5}$.

23. 25π

If you draw the distance from (3, 0) to (–1, –3) on a coordinate plane, you are also drawing a right triangle, where the leg that runs parallel to the *x*-axis has a length of 4 and the leg that runs parallel to the *y*-axis has a length of 3. The hypotenuse of the triangle is 5 because this is a 3:4:5 right triangle, and it also represents the radius of the circle. Alternatively, use the Pythagorean theorem to find the radius, here represented by *c*:

$$(3)^2 + (4)^2 = c^2$$

$$9 + 16 = c^2$$

$$25 = c^2, \text{ so } c = 5$$

The radius is 5, so the area is $5^2\pi = 25\pi$.

24. 13π

The diagonal of the rectangle is the diameter of the circle. The diagonal is the hypotenuse of a 5:12:13 triangle and is therefore 13. Circumference $= \pi d = 13\pi$.

25. 27π

If the radii of the two circles are in the ratio 1:3, then the areas of the circles will be in the ratio $(1)^2:(3)^2$, which is 1:9. So the areas of the shaded parts are also in the ratio 1:9. Since $\angle BAC$ is congruent to $\angle QPR$, if the shaded area of the smaller circle is 3π, then the shaded area of the larger circle will be 27π.

26. 10π

The diagonal of the rectangle inscribed in a circle is the same as the diameter of the circle. The diagonal is the hypotenuse of a 6:8:10 triangle, a multiple of a 3:4:5 triangle, and is therefore 10. Circumference $= \pi d = 10\pi$.

27. $64x^2$

Note that figures on the GRE are not necessarily drawn to scale. The quadrilateral in the figure looks like a rectangle, not a square, but the question stem calls it a square, so that's how you have to treat it. If the area of the circle is $16x^2\pi$, the radius will be the square root of $16x^2$ (or $4x$). The diameter will be $8x$. The diameter is also the side of the square. Area of the square is $(8x)^2 = 64x^2$.

28. $128 - 32\pi$

The area remaining is the area of the rectangle – (2 × area of a circle). The area of the rectangle is found by multiplying the length times the width.

$$A = lw$$
$$A = (16)(8) = 128$$

For the circles, the diameter of the circle is the same as the width of the rectangle. The radius is one-half of the diameter. Therefore the radius for these circles is 4, and the area of one circle is $\pi(4)^2 = 16\pi$. The sum of the areas of the two circles is $16\pi + 16\pi = 32\pi$.

The area of the paper remaining is $128 - 32\pi$.

29. 50π

If O is the point at the center of the circle that lies on line l, and CD is the diameter of that circle, then point O must be the point of intersection between line segment CD and line l. Since points C and D are equidistant from line l, $CO = DO =$ radius of circle O.

The shortest straight-line distance from point C to line l is specified in the question as 5 units. Since line segment CD intersects line l at a 45-degree angle, a 45°-45°-90° right triangle is formed by the following three line segments: line segment CO, the line segment that represents the shortest straight-line distance between point C and line l, and line l itself. Since the shortest straight-line distance between point C and line l (a leg of the right triangle) is 5 units, the hypotenuse of that triangle, which is line segment CO, is equal to $5\sqrt{2}$. Since $CO = DO =$ radius of circle O, the area of the circle with a radius of $5\sqrt{2}$ is equal to πr^2, which here is $\pi\left(5\sqrt{2}\right)^2$, or $\pi(5)^2\left(\sqrt{2}\right)^2 = \pi(25)(2) = 50\pi$.

30. $200\frac{x}{y}$

Total distance covered by the first wheel $= d$, which is equivalent to 200 × circumference. Circumference $= x\pi$.

Circumference of the second wheel $= y\pi$.

Revolutions covered by the second wheel $= r$.

Total distance covered by the second wheel $= d =$ total distance covered by the first wheel.

Therefore, $ry\pi = 200x\pi$, and $r = \frac{200x}{y} = 200\frac{x}{y}$.

MULTIPLE FIGURES

You can expect to see some problems on the GRE that involve several different types of figures. They test your understanding of various geometrical concepts and relationships, not just your ability to memorize a few formulas. For instance, the hypotenuse of a right triangle may be the side of a neighboring rectangle or the diameter of a circumscribed circle. Keep looking for the relationships between the different figures until you find one that leads you to the correct answer.

One common kind of multiple-figures question involves irregularly shaped regions formed by two or more overlapping figures, often with one region shaded. When you are asked to find the area of such a region, any or all of the following methods may work:

(1) Break up that shaded area into smaller pieces. Find the area of each piece using an appropriate formula. Add those areas together.

(2) Find the area of the whole figure and the area of the unshaded region, then subtract the unshaded area from the total area.

Example: Rectangle *ABCD* has an area of 72 and is composed of 8 equal squares. Find the area of the shaded region.

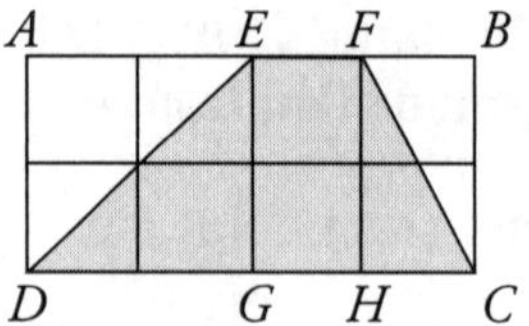

For this problem, you can use either of the two approaches described above or a third approach. First, divide 8 into 72 to get the area of each square, which is 9. Since the area of a square equals its side squared, each side of the small squares must have length 3. Now you have a choice of methods.

(1) You can break up the trapezoid into right triangle *DEG*, rectangle *EFHG*, and right triangle *FHC*.

The area of triangle *DEG* is $\frac{1}{2} \times 6 \times 6$, or 18. The area of rectangle *EFHG* is 3×6, or 18. The area of triangle *FHC* is $\frac{1}{2} \times 6 \times 3$, or 9. The total area is $18 + 18 + 9$, or 45.

(2) The area of the whole rectangle *ABCD* is 72. The area of unshaded triangle *AED* is $\frac{1}{2} \times 6 \times 6,$ or 18. The area of unshaded triangle *FBC* is $\frac{1}{2} \times 6 \times 3,$ or 9. Therefore, the total unshaded area is $18 + 9 = 27$. The area of the shaded region is the area of the rectangle minus the unshaded area, or $72 - 27 = 45$.

(3) Count shaded squares. There are 8 equal squares in total. One is completely blank, two are half shaded (which means that those two blocks equal one shaded block), and two make a rectangle that is half shaded, again making for two blocks equaling one shaded one. Each block has an area of 9. Multiply 9 by 5, the equivalent number of shaded blocks, to get a shaded area of 45.

Inscribed and circumscribed figures: A polygon is **inscribed** in a circle if all the vertices of the polygon lie on the circle. A polygon is **circumscribed** about a circle if all the sides of the polygon are tangent to the circle.

When a rectangle is inscribed in a circle, a diagonal of the rectangle is a diameter of the circle. In the figure, *DB* is the diameter of circle *O* and a diagonal of *ABCD*.

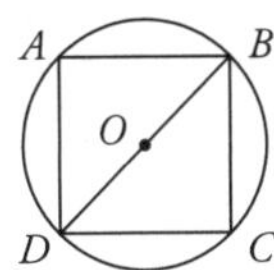

When a square is circumscribed about a circle, a diagonal of the rectangle passes through a diameter of the circle. Moreover, a side of the square is equal in length to the length of the circle's diameter.

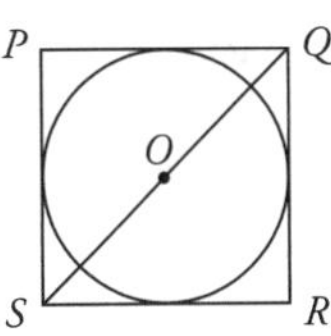

Square *ABCD* is inscribed in circle *O*.

(We can also say that circle *O* is circumscribed about square *ABCD*.)

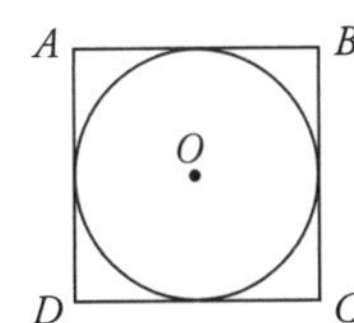

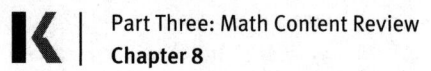

Square *PQRS* is circumscribed about circle *O*.

(We can also say that circle *O* is inscribed in square *PQRS*.)

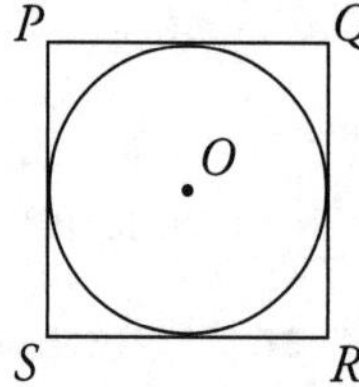

A triangle inscribed in a semicircle such that one side of the triangle coincides with the diameter of the semicircle is a right triangle.

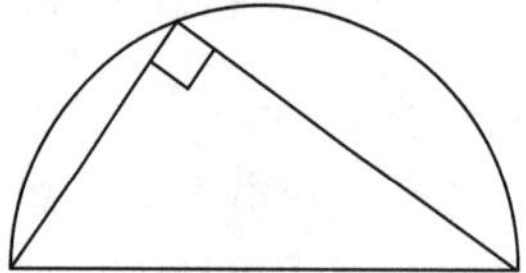

MULTIPLE FIGURES EXERCISES

BASIC

1. In the figure shown, the square is inscribed in a circle, and the area of the circle is 9π. What is the length of the diagonal of the square?

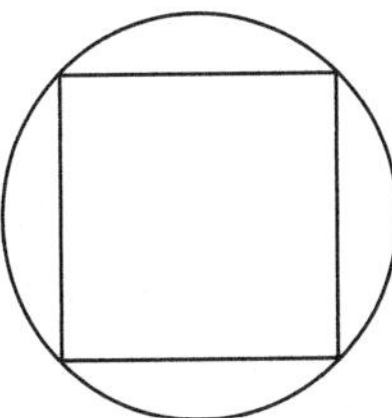

2. In the figure shown, the circle is inscribed in the square. The area of the circle is 100π. What is the area of the square?

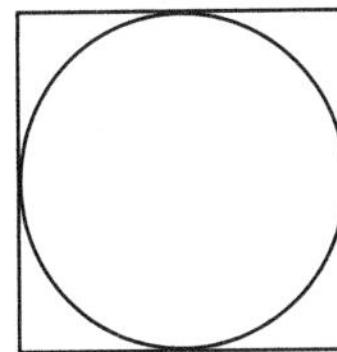

3. In the figure shown, the square is inscribed in a circle, and each side of the square is 10. What is the area of the circle?

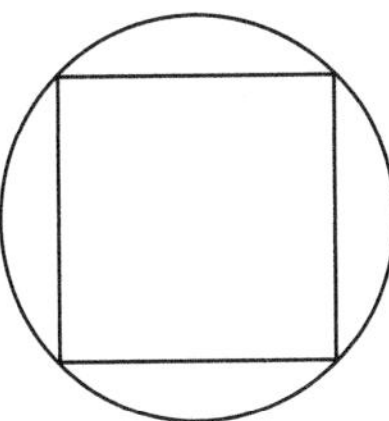

4. In the figure shown, the circle is inscribed in a square, and each side of the square is 4. What is the circumference of the circle?

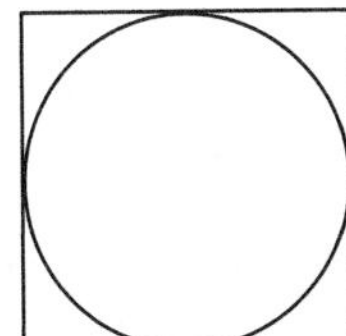

5. In the figure shown, the rectangle is inscribed in the circle. The length of the diagonal of the rectangle is 12. What is the circumference of the circle?

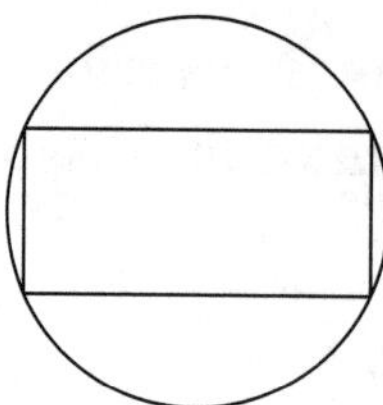

6. In the figure shown, AB is the base of isosceles triangle ABR and a side of rectangle $ABCD$. What is the area of rectangle $ABCD$?

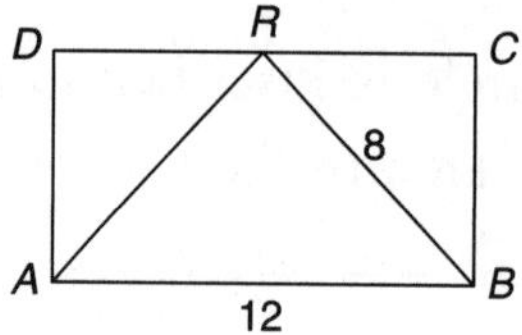

7. What is the value of x?

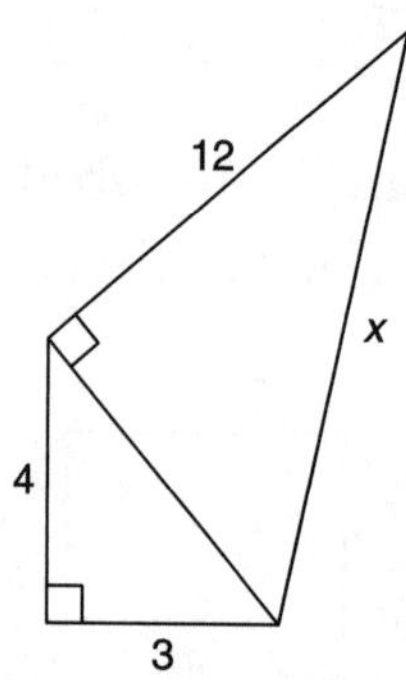

8. A rectangle and a circle have the same area. If the radius of the circle and the length of the rectangle are each 12, what is the width of the rectangle?

9. What is the area of the figure shown?

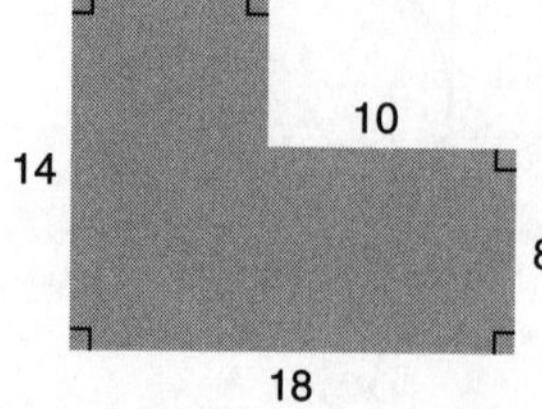

10. A certain manufacturing belt is shown in the following diagram. If the height of each gear is 18 and the length of the horizontal portion of the belt is 28, what is the total length of the belt?

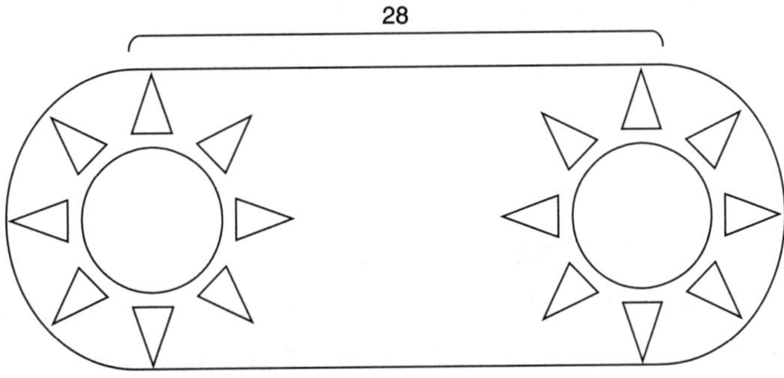

INTERMEDIATE

11. The figure shown is composed of 3 squares and 2 semicircles. Each square has a side of length 8. What is the perimeter of the entire figure?

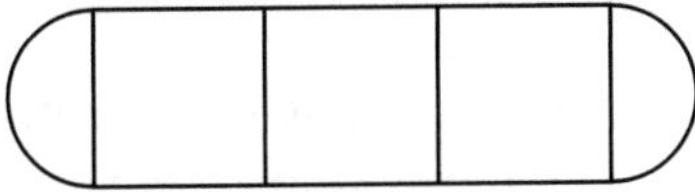

12. In the figure shown, what is the value of y?

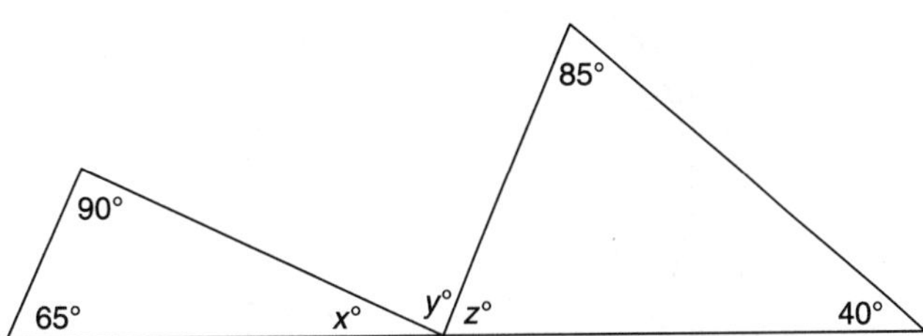

13. The arc in the figure shown is a quarter-circle with endpoints at the vertices of a square. If the area of the quarter circle is 4π, what is the area of the square?

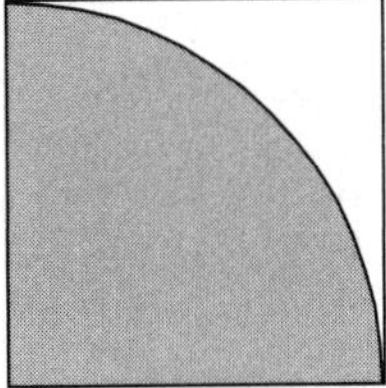

14. In the figure shown, the hypotenuse of the triangle coincides with the diameter of the semicircle. What is the circumference of the semicircle?

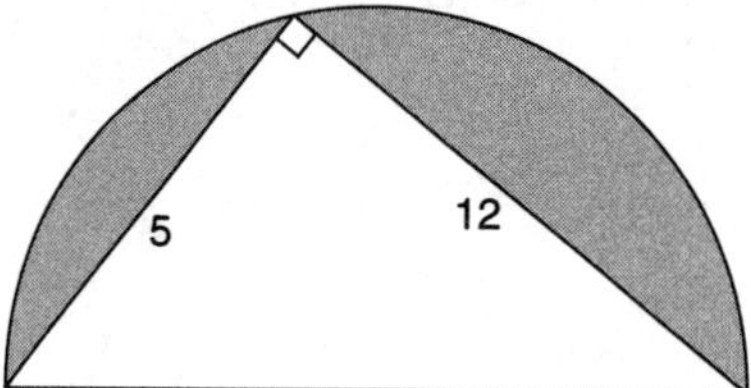

15. Equilateral triangle *RMT* has one vertex at the center of a circle. Its other vertices lie on the circle. The radius of the circle is 10. What is the ratio of the length of minor arc *TM* to the length of segment *TM*?

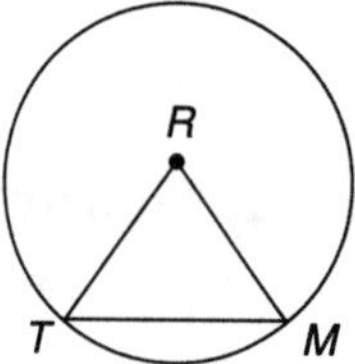

16. A circle is inscribed in a square. What is the ratio of the perimeter of the square to the circumference of the circle?

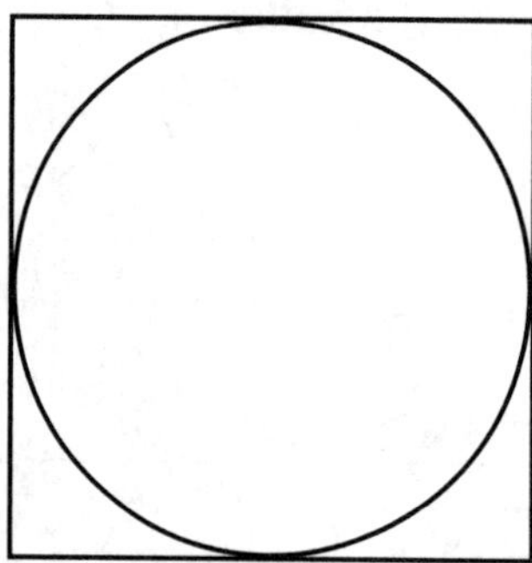

17. The following figure shows concentric circles. What is the area of the shaded region?

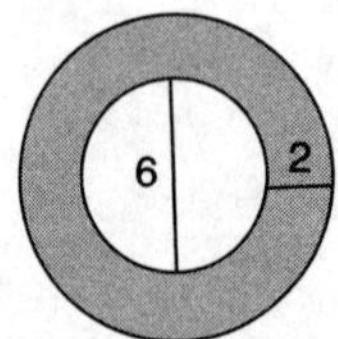

18. A company's logo consists of semicircles constructed on the sides of a right isosceles triangle. What is the total perimeter of the logo?

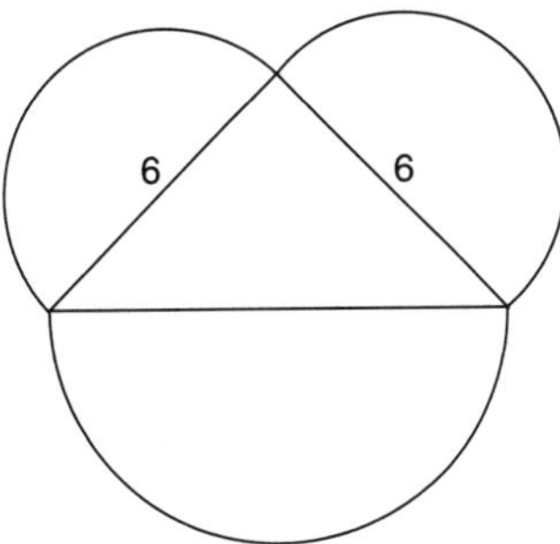

19. An equilateral triangle is constructed on each side of a square. What is the sum of the measures of the angles marked?

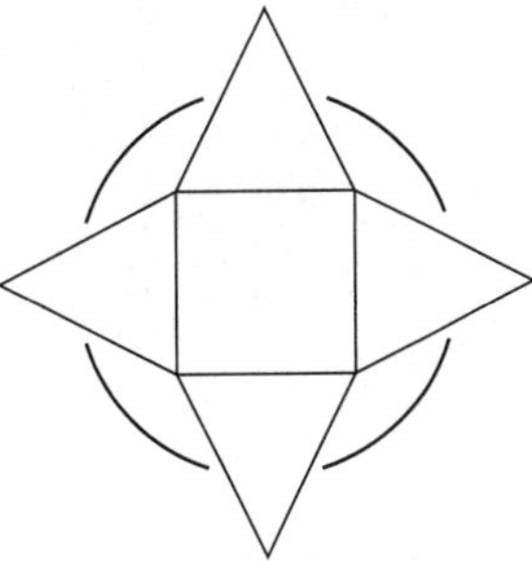

20. Each circle in the figure shown has a diameter of 10. What is the area of the shaded region?

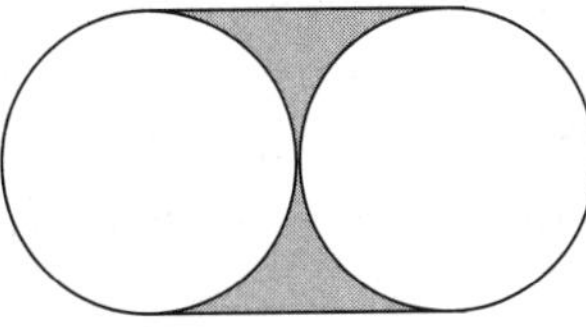

Advanced

21. The figure shows an equilateral triangle where each vertex is the center of a circle. Each circle has a radius of 20. What is the area of the shaded region?

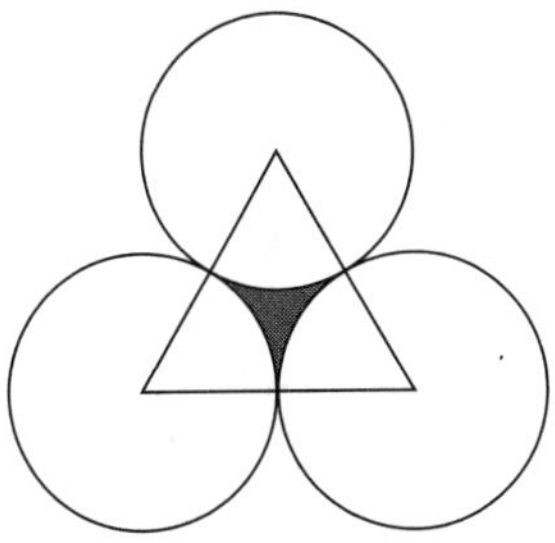

22. What is the circumference of the semicircle in the figure shown?

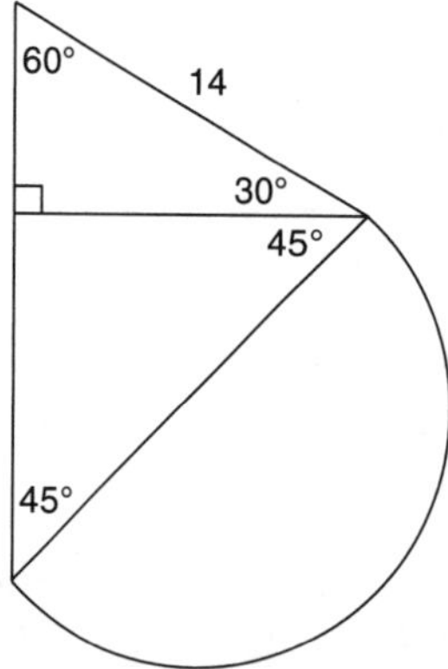

23. The hypotenuse of right triangle ABC is the diameter of the circle. If the diameter of the circle is 18, what is the area of the shaded region?

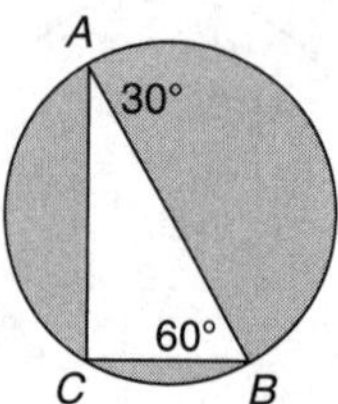

24. The shaded area in the figure shown consists of quarter circles. If each quarter circle has radius r, what is the area of the unshaded region in terms of r?

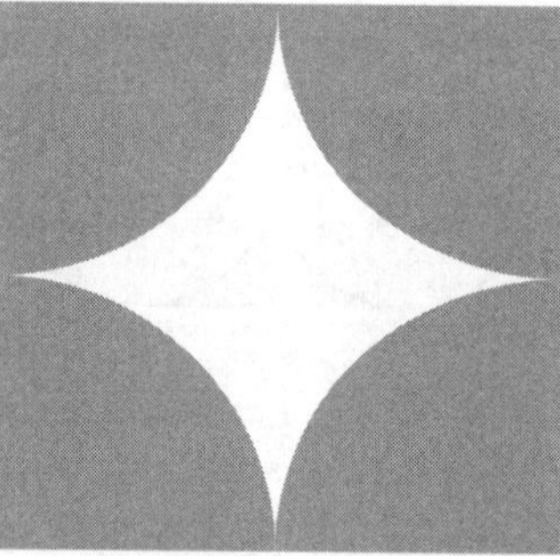

25. A circle is inscribed in an equilateral triangle. Radii to two of the points of tangency are shown. What is x?

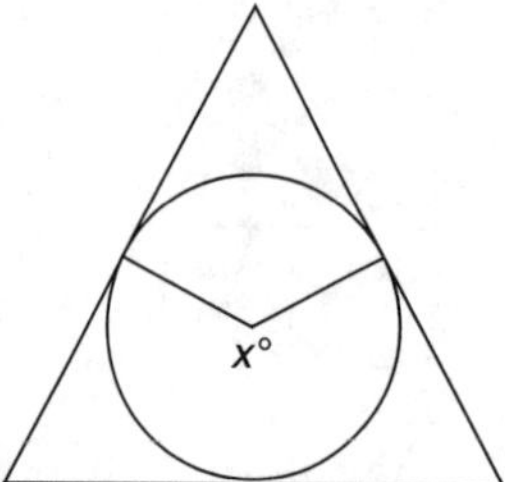

26. The length of the arc PQ in the quarter circle shown is 10π. If RS is 12, what is the area of the rectangle?

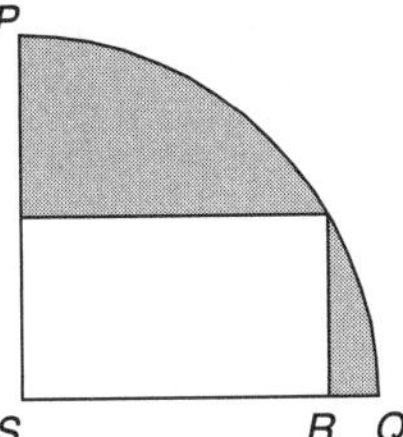

27. In the figure shown, H is the center of the semicircle. Triangles DHF and GHF each have two vertices on the circle. The measure of $\angle DHG$ is 120°. What is the measure of $\angle FHG$?

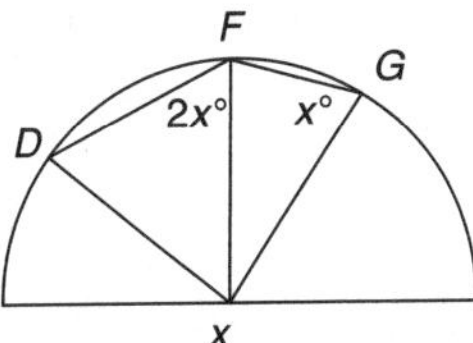

28. A cube with a side of length 4 has the same volume as a rectangular solid with a length of 6 and width of 2. What is the height of the rectangular solid?

29. In the figure shown, the arc of the quarter circle has length 6π. The rectangle has a perimeter of 60. What is the perimeter of the shaded region?

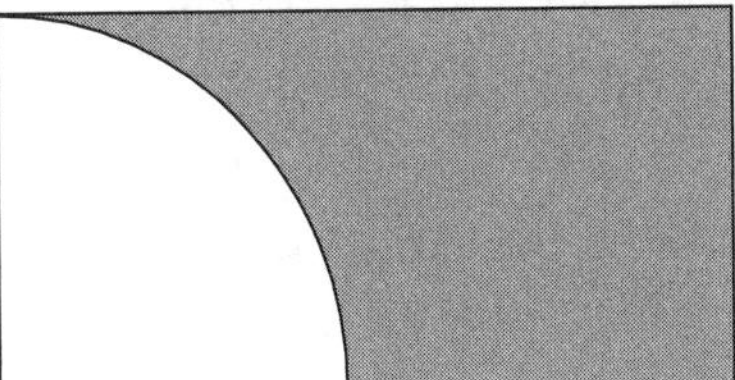

30. In the figure shown, a square is inscribed in a circle. Within the square are four circles, each with two points of tangency on the square and with two points of tangency with two other circles. The diameter of each smaller circle is $2x$. What is the circumference of the outer circle in terms of x?

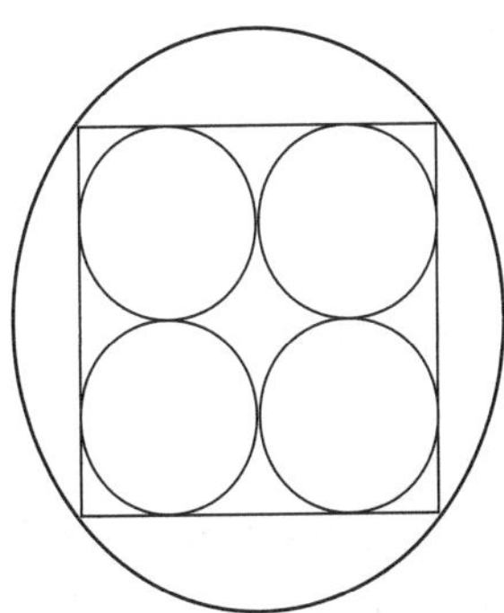

MULTIPLE FIGURES EXERCISES ANSWER KEY

Basic

1. 6

If the area of the circle is 9π, then $r^2 = 9$ and $r = 3$. The diagonal of the square is a diameter of the circle and therefore has a length of 6.

2. 400

If $A = \pi r^2 = 100\pi$, then $r^2 = 100$ and $r = 10$. The length of each side of the square is the same as the diameter of the circle, so $s = 20$. The area of the square is $A = s^2 = 20^2 = 400$.

3. 50π

Use the 45°-45°-90° relationship to find the diagonal of the square (which is also the diameter of the circle). The diagonal is $10\sqrt{2}$, and therefore the radius of the circle is $5\sqrt{2}$. The area of the circle is $\pi(5\sqrt{2})^2 = \pi(5)^2(\sqrt{2})^2 = \pi(25)(2) = 50\pi$.

4. 4π

The diameter of the circle is the same as the side of the square. The diameter of the circle is 4. Therefore, its circumference is $C = \pi d = \pi(4) = 4\pi$.

5. 12π

The diagonal of the rectangle is the diameter of the circle. If the diameter is 12, then the circumference is $C = \pi d = \pi(12) = 12\pi$.

6. $24\sqrt{7}$

Since triangle ABR is isosceles, R must be the midpoint of DC.

$$RC = \frac{1}{2}DC = \frac{1}{2}AB = \frac{1}{2}(12) = 6.$$

Use the Pythagorean theorem to find the length of BC, which is also the height of the rectangle.

$$RC^2 + BC^2 = RB^2$$
$$6^2 + BC^2 = 8^2$$
$$36 + BC^2 = 64$$
$$BC^2 = 28$$
$$BC = \sqrt{28} = \sqrt{4}\sqrt{7} = 2\sqrt{7}$$

The area of the rectangle $= AB \times BC = 12 \times 2\sqrt{7} = 24\sqrt{7}$.

7. 13

Use your knowledge of the Pythagorean triples. The smaller triangle has two legs of lengths 3 and 4. Because this is a 3:4:5 triangle, the hypotenuse must equal 5. The hypotenuse of the smaller triangle is also one of the legs of the larger triangle. The larger triangle has another leg of length 12. Therefore, the larger triangle is a 5:12:13 triangle. Since x represents the hypotenuse of the larger triangle, $x = 13$.

8. 12π

The area of the circle is $A = \pi r^2 = \pi(12)^2 = 144\pi$. If the area of the rectangle is 144π, then

$$\begin{aligned} A &= lw \\ 144\pi &= 12w \\ \frac{144\pi}{12} &= \frac{12w}{12} \\ 12\pi &= w \end{aligned}$$

The question asks for the width, so the answer is 12π.

9. 192

First, find the area of the larger outlined rectangle. Then, subtract the unshaded area.

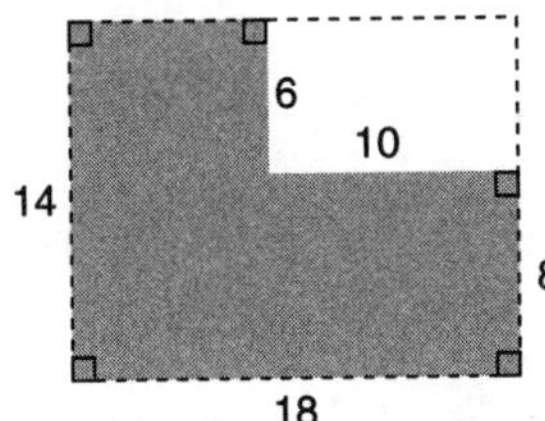

The area of the larger outlined rectangle is the product of its length and its width.

$$14 \times 18 = 252$$

The area of the unshaded region is $6 \times 10 = 60$.

The area of the figure is $252 - 60 = 192$.

10. $56 + 18\pi$

The belt can be thought of as consisting of two horizontal portions and two semicircular portions. The length of each horizontal portion is 28. Each gear has diameter 18; therefore, the length of each semicircular portion is $\frac{1}{2}(\pi d) = \frac{1}{2}(18\pi) = 9\pi$. The total length of the four portions is $28 + 28 + 9\pi + 9\pi = 56 + 18\pi$.

Intermediate

11. $48 + 8\pi$

The perimeter consists of 6 segments (each with length 8) and two semicircles (each with diameter 8). The perimeter is $6 \times 8 + 2 \times \frac{1}{2}(\pi d) = 48 + \pi(8) = 48 + 8\pi$.

12. 100°

The sum of the three angles in any triangle is 180°, and the sum of three angles forming a straight line must also be 180°. Find x and z and then use them to find y.

$$\begin{aligned} 65 + 90 + x &= 180 & 85 + 40 + z &= 180 & 25 + y + 55 &= 180 \\ 155 + x &= 180 & 125 + z &= 180 & y + 80 &= 180 \\ x &= 25 & z &= 55 & y &= 100 \end{aligned}$$

13. 16

The area of the quarter-circle is 4π. Therefore, the area of the entire circle would be $4 \times 4\pi = 16\pi$. If $16\pi = \pi r^2$, then $r^2 = 16$ and $r = 4$. The radius of the quarter-circle coincides with one side of the square, so each side of the square is 4. The area of the square is $A = 4 \times 4 = 16$.

14. $\frac{13\pi}{2}$

The inscribed right triangle is a 5:12:13 triangle. Therefore, the diameter is 13. The circumference of the semicircle is: $\frac{1}{2}\pi d = \frac{1}{2}\pi(13) = \frac{13\pi}{2}$.

15. π**:3**

Because the triangle is equilateral, it has three 60° angles, and all sides have length 10. The length of minor arc *TM* is $\frac{60}{360}$ of the circumference of the entire circle. So, minor arc *TM* has length $\frac{60}{360} \times 2\pi r = \frac{1}{6} \times 2\pi(10) = \frac{10\pi}{3}$. The length of segment *TM* is 10. The ratio of the length of arc *TM* to the length of segment *TM* is $\frac{\frac{10\pi}{3}}{10} = \frac{10\pi}{3} \times \frac{1}{10} = \frac{\pi}{3}$.

16. 4:π

Call the radius of the circle *r*. The perimeter of the square is $2r + 2r + 2r + 2r = 8r$. The circumference of the circle is $2\pi r$. The ratio is $\frac{8r}{2\pi r}$, or $\frac{4}{\pi}$.

17. 16π

The shaded region is the area of the outer circle (diameter 10, radius 5) minus the area of the inner circle (diameter 6, radius 3): $\pi(5)^2 - \pi(3)^2 = 25\pi - 9\pi = 16\pi$.

18. $6\pi + 3\pi\sqrt{2}$

Use the 45°-45°-90° relationship to find that the hypotenuse of the triangle has length $6\sqrt{2}$. Each smaller semicircle has circumference $\frac{1}{2}\pi d = \frac{1}{2}\pi(6) = 3\pi$. The larger semicircle has circumference $\frac{1}{2}\pi d = \frac{1}{2}\pi(6\sqrt{2}) = 3\pi\sqrt{2}$. Therefore, the total perimeter is $3\pi + 3\pi + 3\pi\sqrt{2} = 6\pi + 3\pi\sqrt{2}$.

19. 600°

Label each interior angle of each square and triangle using polygon properties: 90° for interior angles of a square and 60° for interior angles of an equilateral triangle. At each marked angle, the sum of the four angles must be 360°. Therefore, each marked angle measures 360°– 60°– 60°– 90° = 150°. The sum of the measures of the four marked angles is 4 × 150° = 600°.

20. $100 - 25\pi$

Imagine a rectangle whose top and bottom coincide with those of the figure and whose left and right sides are diameters of the circles. This rectangle is a square because its length and width are each 10. The shaded area is the area of the square minus the area of the two semicircles: $(10 \times 10) - 2 \times \frac{1}{2}\pi(5)^2 = 100 - 25\pi$.

ADVANCED

21. $400\sqrt{3} - 200\pi$

The shaded area is the area of the equilateral triangle minus the areas of three 60° sectors. The area of the triangle is $\frac{1}{2}bh = \frac{1}{2}(40)(20\sqrt{3}) = 400\sqrt{3}$ (use the 30°-60°-90° relationship to find the height of the triangle). The area of each sector is $\frac{60}{360} \times \pi r^2 = \frac{1}{6}\pi(20)^2 = \frac{400\pi}{6}$. The total area of the three sectors is $3 \times \frac{400\pi}{6} = 200\pi$. Therefore, the shaded area is $400\sqrt{3} - 200\pi$.

22. $\frac{7\pi\sqrt{6}}{2}$

Use 30°-60°-90° and 45°-45°-90° relationships to find the diameter. The diameter is $7\sqrt{6}$, so the circumference of the semicircle is $\frac{1}{2} \times \pi d = \pi\left(\frac{7\sqrt{6}}{2}\right) = \frac{7\pi\sqrt{6}}{2}$.

23. $81\pi - \frac{81\sqrt{3}}{2}$

The shaded region is the area of the circle minus the area of the triangle. The radius of the circle is 9. Therefore, the area of the circle is $\pi(9)^2 = 81\pi$. Use the 30°-60°-90° relationship to find all sides of the triangle so you can find its area. The area of the triangle is $\frac{1}{2} \times 9 \times 9\sqrt{3} = \frac{81\sqrt{3}}{2}$.

The shaded area is $81\pi - \frac{81\sqrt{3}}{2}$.

24. $4r^2 - \pi r^2$

The unshaded region is the area of the square minus the area of four quarter-circles. The area of the square is $2r \times 2r = 4r^2$. The area of each quarter circle is $\frac{1}{4}\pi r^2$; the sum of the areas of four quarter circles is πr^2. The difference is $4r^2 - \pi r^2$.

25. 240°

The radii are two sides of a quadrilateral. A line tangent to a circle meets a radius at the point of tangency at a 90° angle. Each angle of the equilateral triangle is 60°. Therefore, the remaining angle of the quadrilateral measures 120°. A circle has 360°. So, the measure of $\angle x$ can be found using subtraction: 360° – 120° = 240°.

26. 192

The quarter circle has arc length 10π, so the entire circle has circumference 40π, diameter 40, and radius 20. The unshaded rectangle has base (*RS*) 12 units. Its diagonal is a radius of the quarter circle and, therefore, has length 20. Find the height of the rectangle using the Pythagorean triple 12:16:20 (a multiple of 3:4:5). The area of the rectangle is $12 \times 16 = 192$.

27. 100°

Radii *HD*, *HF*, and *HG* have the same length and form isosceles triangles *DHF* and *GHF*. Isosceles triangles have congruent base angles, so $\angle HFG = x°$ and $\angle HDF = 2x°$. The sum of the four angles of quadrilateral *HDFG* must be 360°. So:

$$\begin{aligned} 2x + 2x + x + x + 120 &= 360 \\ 6x + 120 &= 360 \\ 6x &= 240 \\ x &= 40 \end{aligned}$$

Triangle *FHG* has two 40° angles. Since a triangle has three angles that sum to 180°, the third angle must be 100°. So, the measure of $\angle FHG$ is 100°.

28. $\frac{16}{3}$

The volume of a cube can be found by s^3, in which *s* represents the length of one side, since cubes have the same length for all edges. The cube has a length of 4, so the volume is $4^3 = 4 \times 4 \times 4 = 64$. This is also the volume of the rectangular solid with the length 6 and width 2. To find the height, plug in the numbers into the formula for the volume of a rectangular solid:

$$\begin{aligned} V &= l \times w \times h \\ 64 &= 6 \times 2 \times h \\ 64 &= 12h \\ \frac{64}{12} &= h \\ \frac{16}{3} &= h \end{aligned}$$

29. $36 + 6\pi$

If the quarter circle arc has length 6π, then the entire circle would have a circumference of 24π. Since $C = 2\pi r = 24\pi$, $r = 12$. The radius of the quarter circle is the height of the rectangle. Since the perimeter of the rectangle is 60, the length of the rectangle must be 18. And the bottom portion of the shaded area will have a length of 18 minus the circle's radius, or 6. So, the perimeter of the shaded area is $6 + 12 + 18 + 6\pi$, or $36 + 6\pi$.

30. $4\pi x\sqrt{2}$

If the diameter of each smaller circle is $2x$, then the side of the square is $2x + 2x = 4x$.

Use the 45°-45°-90° relationship to find the diagonal of the square, which is $4x\sqrt{2}$. The diagonal of the square is equal to the diameter of the outer circle.

The circumference of the outer circle is $4\pi x\sqrt{2}$.

THREE-DIMENSIONAL FIGURES (UNIFORM SOLIDS)

A **solid** is a three-dimensional figure (a figure having length, width, and height) and therefore may be rather difficult to represent accurately on a two-dimensional page. Figures are drawn "in perspective," giving them the appearance of depth. If a diagram represents a three-dimensional figure, it will be specified in the accompanying text.

Fortunately, only a few types of solids appear with any frequency on the GRE: rectangular solids (including cubes) and cylinders. You can help your understanding of such figures by spending some time with solids that you can find around your home, such as boxes for rectangular solids and soup cans for cylinders. This will help you visualize what the problems are describing and asking.

Other types, such as spheres, cones, and pyramids, may appear, but these questions typically will only involve understanding the solid's properties. Here are the terms used to describe the common solids:

Vertex: The vertices of a solid are the points at its corners. For example, a cube has eight vertices.

Edge: The edges of a solid are the line segments that connect the vertices and form the sides of each face of the solid. A cube has twelve edges.

Face: The faces of a solid are the polygons that form the outside of the solid. A rectangular prism has six faces, all rectangles. A cube (which is a rectangular prism) has six faces, all squares.

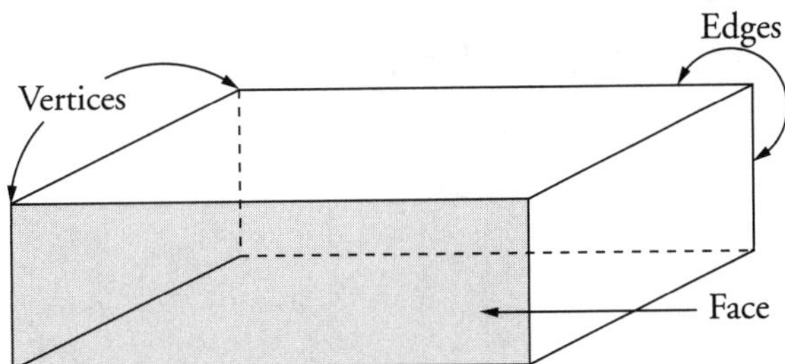

Volume: The volume of a solid is the amount of space enclosed by that solid. The volume of any uniform solid is equal to the area of its base times its height. Volume is expressed in cubic units.

Surface area: In general, the surface area of a solid is equal to the sum of the areas of the solid's faces.

Rectangular solid: A solid with six rectangular faces (all edges meet at right angles). Examples are cereal boxes, bricks, etc.

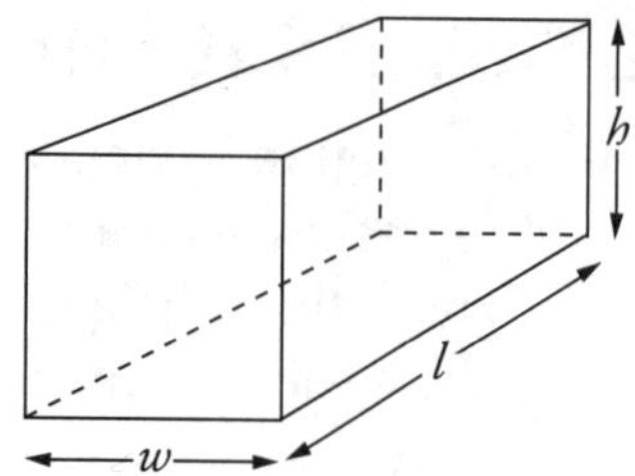

Volume = area of base × height = length × width × height = $l \times w \times h$

Surface area = sum of areas of faces = $2lw + 2lh + 2wh$

Cube: A special rectangular solid with all edges equal ($l = w = h$), such as a die. All faces of a cube are squares. Because each edge is of equal length, the edge is generally known as the variable e, as in the example shown.

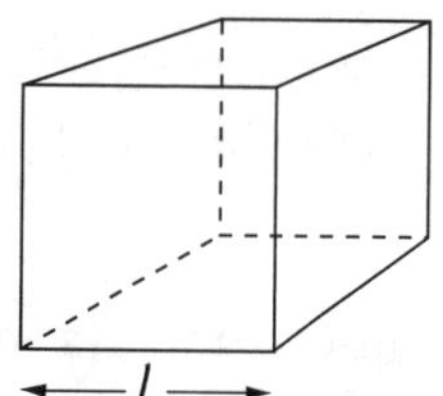

Volume = area of base × height = $l \times w \times h = e^3$

Surface area = sum of areas of faces = $6e^2$

Cylinder: A uniform solid whose base is a circle; for example, a classic soup can. To calculate the volume or surface area, we need two pieces of information for a cylinder: the radius of the base, and the height.

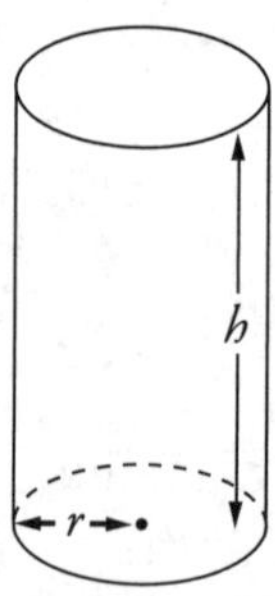

Volume = area of base × height = $\pi r^2 h$

Total surface area = 2 × area of base + area of rest of shell (lateral surface area)

Total surface area = $2(\pi r^2) + 2\pi rh$

You can think of the surface area of a cylinder as having two parts: one part is the top and bottom (the circles), and the other part is the lateral surface. In a can, for example, the area of both the top and the bottom is just the area of the circle, or lid, which represents the top; hence, πr^2 for the top and πr^2 for the bottom, yielding a total of $2\pi r^2$. For the lateral surface, the area around the can, think of removing the can's label. When unrolled, it's actually in the shape of a rectangle. One side is the height of the can, and the other side is the distance around the circle, or circumference. Hence, its area is $h \times (2\pi r)$, or $2\pi rh$. And so, the total surface area is $2\pi r^2 + 2\pi rh$.

Sphere: Occasionally, a question might require you to understand what a sphere is. A sphere is made up of all the points in space a certain distance from a center point; it's like a three-dimensional circle. The distance from the center to a point on the sphere is the radius of the sphere. A basketball is a good example of a sphere. A sphere is not a uniform solid; the cross sections are all circles, but they are of different sizes. (In other words, a slice of a basketball from the middle is bigger than a slice from the top.)

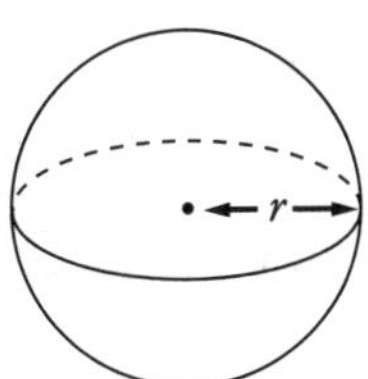

THREE-DIMENSIONAL FIGURES (UNIFORM SOLIDS) EXERCISES

Basic

1. Find the volume of a rectangular solid with dimensions 10, 4, and 9.

2. Find the surface area of a rectangular solid with dimensions $\frac{1}{2}$, 6, and 12.

3. Find the volume of a cube with an edge of 8.

4. Find the surface area of a cube with an edge of 1.5.

5. Find the volume of a cylinder with a radius of 10 and a height of 4.

6. Find the surface area of a cylinder with a radius of 3 and a height of 12.

7. Find the volume of a cylinder with a diameter of 12 and a height of 3.

8. A rectangular solid has a volume of 72. Its width is 3 and its height is 4. What is the length?

9. A cube has a volume of 27. What is the length of one edge?

10. A cube with an edge of 4 has the same volume as a rectangular solid with a length and width of 2. What is the height of the rectangular solid?

Intermediate

11. What is the surface area of a cylinder with a radius of 5 and a height of 8?

12. The dimensions of a cube are each doubled, from 2 to 4. By what factor is the surface area of the cube increased?

13. The dimensions of the rectangular solid shown are each tripled. By what factor is the volume of the rectangular solid increased?

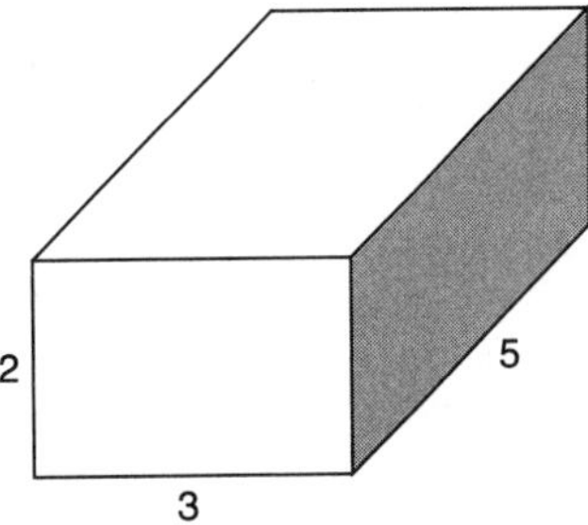

14. A cylinder has a surface area of 22π. If the cylinder has a height of 10, what is its radius?

15. What is the ratio of the surface area of a cube with an edge of 10 to the surface area of a rectangular solid with dimensions 2, 4, and 6?

16. What is the length of segment *AR*?

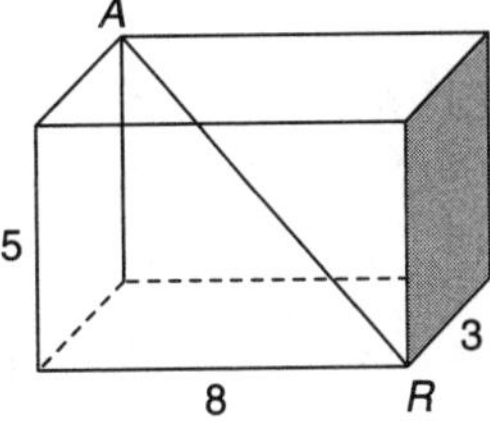

17. How many times can a cube-shaped container with an edge of 2 be emptied into a rectangular prism container with dimensions 4, 8, and 15?

18. The cylinders in the figure shown have the same volume. What is *h*?

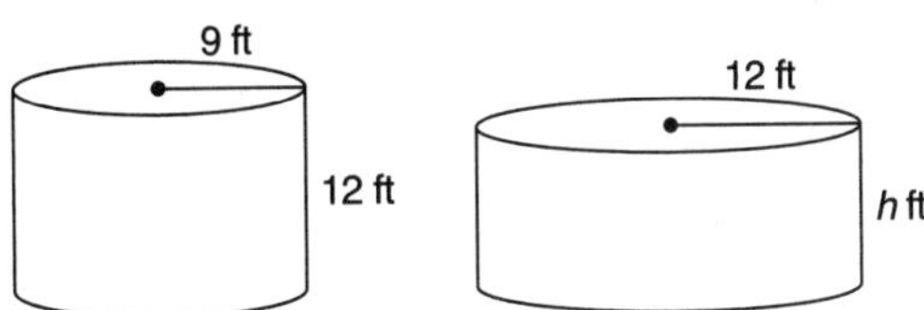

19. The length and width of a rectangular solid are reduced by 10%. The new volume is what percent of the original volume?

20. The solid shown is half a rectangular solid. What is the volume of the solid shown?

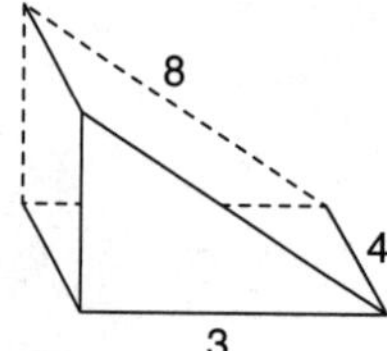

ADVANCED

21. A container in the shape of a rectangular solid with dimensions 5, 5, and 12 has four times the volume of a cylindrical container with a radius of 3. What is the height of the cylinder?

22. A brick with dimensions 10, 15, and 25 weighs 1.5 kg. A second brick (with the same density) has dimensions 12, 18, and 30. Given that weight is proportional to volume in objects of equivalent density, what is the weight of the second brick?

23. Water is poured from a full cylindrical container with a radius of 3 and a height of 5 into a different empty cylindrical container with a radius of 5. The water will not overflow the second container. How many inches high will the water reach when all of it has been poured?

24. Each dimension of a rectangular solid is an integer less than 11. The volume of the solid is 30. If the height of the solid is 10, what is the surface area of the solid?

25. The height of a cylinder is twice its radius. If the volume of the cylinder is 128π, what is the radius?

26. The diagonal AC of the rectangular solid forms a 60° angle with the diagonal of its base. Given the dimensions in the figure, what is the volume of the rectangular solid?

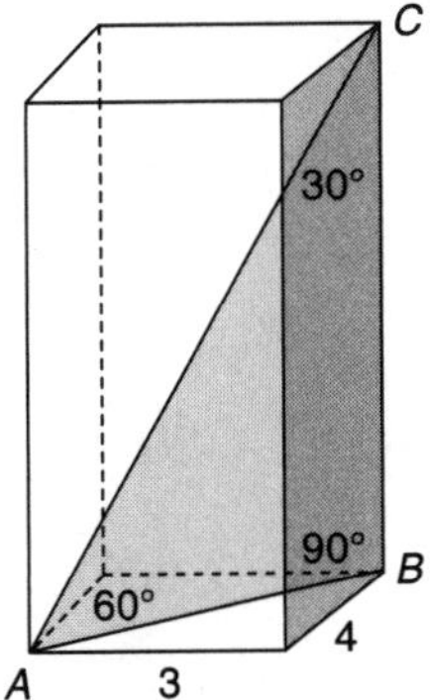

27. Cylinder A has twice the radius but half the height of Cylinder B. What is the ratio of the volume of Cylinder A to the volume of Cylinder B?

28. A cube of ice has edges of length 10. What is the volume of the largest cylinder that can be carved from the cube?

29. A brick with dimensions 3, 4, and 9 has three holes bored completely through it as shown. Each hole has a diameter of 2. What is the net volume of the brick?

30. A solid metal cylinder with a radius of 6 and a height of 3 is melted down, and all of the metal is used to recast a new solid cylinder with a radius of 3. What is the height of the new cylinder?

THREE-DIMENSIONAL FIGURES (UNIFORM SOLIDS) EXERCISES ANSWER KEY

Basic

1. 360

$$V = lwh = 10 \times 4 \times 9 = 360$$

2. 162

$$\begin{aligned} SA &= 2(lw) + 2(wh) + 2(lh) \\ &= 2\left(\frac{1}{2} \times 6\right) + 2(6 \times 12) + 2\left(\frac{1}{2} \times 12\right) \\ &= 2(3) + 2(72) + 2(6) \\ &= 6 + 144 + 12 \\ &= 162 \end{aligned}$$

3. 512

$$\begin{aligned} V &= lwh \\ &= 8 \times 8 \times 8 \\ &= 512 \end{aligned}$$

4. 13.5

The surface area is the sum of the areas of all six faces. Each face is a square with area $A = lw = (1.5)(1.5) = 2.25$. Therefore the surface area of the cube is $6(2.25) = 13.5$.

5. 400π

$$\begin{aligned} V &= \pi r^2 h \\ &= \pi(10)^2(4) \\ &= \pi(100)(4) \\ &= 400\pi \end{aligned}$$

6. 90π

$$\begin{aligned} SA &= 2\pi r^2 + 2\pi rh \\ &= 2\pi(3)^2 + 2\pi(3)(12) \\ &= 2\pi(9) + 2\pi(36) \\ &= 18\pi + 72\pi \\ &= 90\pi \end{aligned}$$

7. 108π

If the diameter is 12, then the radius is 6.

$$\begin{aligned} V &= \pi r^2 h \\ &= \pi(6)^2(3) \\ &= \pi(36)(3) \\ &= 108\pi \end{aligned}$$

8. 6

$$\begin{aligned} V &= lwh \\ 72 &= l(3)(4) \\ 72 &= 12l \\ 6 &= l \end{aligned}$$

9. 3

$$\begin{aligned} V &= e^3 \\ 27 &= e^3 \\ 3 &= e \end{aligned}$$

10. 16

The cube has volume $V = e^3 = 4^3 = 64$. Use the volume 64 to solve for the height of the rectangular solid.

$$\begin{aligned} V &= lwh \\ 64 &= 2 \times 2 \times h \\ 64 &= 4h \\ 16 &= h \end{aligned}$$

INTERMEDIATE

11. 130π

$$\begin{aligned} SA &= 2\pi r^2 + 2\pi rh \\ &= 2\pi(5)^2 + 2\pi(5)(8) \\ &= 2\pi(25) + 2\pi(40) \\ &= 50\pi + 80\pi \\ &= 130\pi \end{aligned}$$

12. 4

The original surface area is $6e^2 = 6(2)^2 = 6 \times 4 = 24$. The new surface area is $6 \times e^2 = 6 \times 4^2 = 6 \times 16 = 96$. Since $96 \div 24 = 4$, the surface area is increased by a factor of 4.

13. 27

The original volume is $V = lwh = 3 \times 2 \times 5 = 30$. The new volume is $V = 9 \times 6 \times 15 = 810$. Since $810 \div 30 = 27$, the volume has increased by a factor of 27.

14. 1

Use the surface area formula:

$$\begin{aligned} SA &= 2\pi r^2 + 2\pi rh \\ 22\pi &= 2\pi r^2 + 2\pi r(10) \\ 22\pi &= 2\pi r^2 + 20\pi r \end{aligned}$$

Look closely at the last equation. The equation is true only when $r = 1$.

$$\begin{aligned} 22\pi &= 2\pi(1)^2 + 20\pi(1) \\ 22\pi &= 2\pi(1) + 20\pi(1) \\ 22\pi &= 2\pi + 20\pi \end{aligned}$$

15. 75:11

The cube has surface area $SA = 6e^2 = 6(10)^2 = 6 \times 100 = 600$.

The rectangular solid has surface area

$$\begin{aligned} SA &= 2(lw) + 2(wh) + 2(lh) \\ &= 2(2 \times 4) + 2(4 \times 6) + 2(2 \times 6) \\ &= 2(8) + 2(24) + 2(12) \\ &= 16 + 48 + 24 \\ &= 88 \end{aligned}$$

The ratio of the cube's surface area to the rectangular solid's surface area is $\frac{600}{88} = \frac{75}{11}$.

16. $7\sqrt{2}$

Segment *AR* is the hypotenuse of a right triangle with height 5. The base of the right triangle is also a diagonal of the base of the rectangular solid. The base has length 8 and width 3, so the diagonal has length $\sqrt{3^2 + 8^2} = \sqrt{9 + 64} = \sqrt{73}$.

Therefore the length of segment *AR* is $\sqrt{\left(\sqrt{73}\right)^2 + 5^2} = \sqrt{73 + 25} = \sqrt{98} = 7\sqrt{2}$.

17. 60

The rectangular container has volume $V = lwh = 4 \times 8 \times 15 = 480$. The cube has volume $V = e^3 = 2^3 = 8$. Since $\frac{480}{8} = 60$, the cubical container can be emptied 60 times into the rectangular prism container.

18. 6.75 or $6\frac{3}{4}$

The volume of the known cylinder is $V = \pi r^2 h = \pi(9)^2\,(12) = \pi(81)(12) = 972\pi$. Now use 972π to find h in the unknown cylinder.

$$\begin{aligned} V &= \pi r^2 h \\ 972\pi &= \pi(12)^2 h \\ 972\pi &= 144\pi h \\ 972 &= 144h \\ 6.75 &= h \end{aligned}$$

19. 81%

The volume of the original solid is $V = lwh$. The volume of the solid with reduced length and width is $V = (0.9l)(0.9w)(h) = (0.81)lwh$. Therefore the solid with reduced length and width has 81% of the volume of the original solid.

20. $6\sqrt{55}$

The rectangular solid has a front face with a width of 3 and a diagonal of 8. The height of the front face can be found using the Pythagorean theorem:

$$\begin{aligned} a^2 + b^2 &= c^2 \\ 3^2 + b^2 &= 8^2 \\ 9 + b^2 &= 64 \\ b^2 &= 55 \\ b &= \sqrt{55} \end{aligned}$$

The whole rectangular solid has dimensions 3, 4, and $\sqrt{55}$. Its volume is $V = lwh = 3 \times 4 \times \sqrt{55} = 12\sqrt{55}$. Half its volume is $6\sqrt{55}$.

Advanced

21. $\frac{25}{3\pi}$

The volume of the rectangular prism is $V = lwh = 5 \times 5 \times 12 = 300$. Therefore, the volume of the cylinder is $300 \div 4 = 75$. Use $V = 75$ to find the height.

$$\begin{aligned} V &= \pi r^2 h \\ 75 &= \pi(3)^2 h \\ 75 &= 9\pi h \\ \frac{75}{9\pi} &= h \\ \frac{25}{3\pi} &= h \end{aligned}$$

22. 2.592 kg

Use the fact that weight is proportional to volume. The volume of the first brick is $V = lwh = 10 \times 15 \times 25 = 3{,}750$. The volume of the second brick is $V = lwh = 12 \times 18 \times 30 = 6{,}480$.

Write and solve a proportion to find the weight of the second brick.

$$\begin{aligned} \frac{3{,}750}{1.5} &= \frac{6{,}480}{x} \\ 3{,}750x &= (6{,}480)(1.5) \\ 3{,}750x &= 9{,}720 \\ x &= 2.592 \end{aligned}$$

23. $\frac{9}{5}$ or 1.8

The volume of water poured is $V = \pi r^2 h = \pi(3)^2\ (5) = \pi(9)(5) = 45\pi$.

Use 45π to find the height of a cylinder with that volume and a radius of 5.

$$\begin{aligned} V &= \pi r^2 h \\ 45\pi &= \pi(5)^2 h \\ 45\pi &= 25\pi h \\ 45 &= 25h \\ \frac{45}{25} &= h \\ \frac{9}{5} &= h\text{, or } 1.8 \end{aligned}$$

24. 86

The volume is 30 and height is 10. Using the volume formula,

$$\begin{aligned} 30 &= lw(10) \\ 3 &= lw \end{aligned}$$

If the product of length and width is 3 and each dimension is an integer, then these two dimensions must be 1 and 3. Therefore the dimensions of the solid are 1, 3, and 10.

$$\begin{aligned} SA &= 2(lw) + 2(wh) + 2(lh) \\ &= 2(1 \times 3) + 2(3 \times 10) + 2(1 \times 10) \\ &= 2(3) + 2(30) + 2(10) \\ &= 6 + 60 + 20 \\ &= 86 \end{aligned}$$

25. 4

Let $h = 2r$.

$$\begin{aligned} V &= \pi r^2 h \\ 128\pi &= \pi r^2(2r) \\ 128 &= 2r^3 \\ 64 &= r^3 \\ 4 &= r \end{aligned}$$

26. $60\sqrt{3}$

The diagonal of the base of the solid is the hypotenuse of a 3:4:5 triangle. Use the 30°-60°-90° relationship to find the height of the shaded triangle. Since the leg with a length of 5 is across from the angle that is 30 degrees, the leg across from the 60 degree angle is $5\sqrt{3}$, which is also the height of the solid. The solid has dimensions 3, 4, and $5\sqrt{3}$, so the volume is $V = lwh = 3 \times 4 \times 5\sqrt{3} = 60\sqrt{3}$.

27. $\frac{2}{1}$

If Cylinder *B* has radius *r* and height *h*, then Cylinder *A* has radius 2*r* and height $\frac{1}{2}h$.

The volume of Cylinder *B* is $V_B = \pi r^2 h$.

The volume of Cylinder *A* is $V_A = \pi(2r)^2\left(\frac{1}{2}h\right) = \pi(4r^2)\left(\frac{1}{2}h\right) = 2\pi r^2 h$.

The ratio is $\frac{V_A}{V_B} = \frac{2\pi r^2 h}{\pi r^2 h} = \frac{2}{1}$.

Picking Numbers would also be a great strategy here. Let the radius and height of Cylinder *B* be 2 and 4, respectively. Then the radius and height of Cylinder *A* are 4 and 2, respectively. $V_B = \pi r^2 h = 16\pi$. $V_A = \pi r^2 h = 32\pi$. The volume of Cylinder *A* is twice that of Cylinder *B*, and the ratio is 2:1.

28. 250π

The largest cylinder would have diameter 10 and height 10 (each equal to the edge of the cube). When diameter is 10, radius is 5. Therefore, the volume is $V = \pi r^2 h = \pi(5)^2\,(10) = \pi(25)(10) = 250\pi$.

29. $108 - 9\pi$

The net volume is the volume of the rectangular solid minus the volume of the three cylindrical holes. The volume of the rectangular solid is $V = lwh = 3 \times 4 \times 9 = 108$. The volume of each hole is $V = \pi r^2 h = \pi(1)^2(3) = 3\pi$.

The net volume is $108 - 3(3\pi) = 108 - 9\pi$.

30. 12

The volume of metal melted down is $V = \pi r^2 h = \pi(6)^2\,(3) = \pi(36)(3) = 108\pi$. Use 108π to find h in the recast cylinder.

$$\begin{aligned} V &= \pi r^2 h \\ 108\pi &= \pi(3)^2 h \\ 108\pi &= 9\pi h \\ 108 &= 9h \\ 12 &= h \end{aligned}$$

CHAPTER 9

Data Interpretation

UNDERSTANDING DATA ANALYSIS

The GRE will test your ability to draw conclusions about sets of objects or data. This chapter explores selecting and arranging members of a group, using statistics to describe the behavior of data, evaluating various presentations of data, and calculating the likelihood of events occurring based on specified manipulations of objects or data.

COUNTING METHODS

Whether counting the number of members in a set or determining the number of possible selections or arrangements that can be made from the set, understanding counting methods is a key element in data analysis. When a data set is too large for you to simply list and count its objects, the objects can often be arranged systematically. There are several counting methods you can then apply to determine the number of elements in the set or the number of possible selections from the set.

Before considering the details of counting data sets, it is helpful to understand the nature of the data. A data set is a group of objects, such as all prime numbers or players on a basketball team, that are presented together regardless of order. The objects in the set are called **members** or **elements**. A set can be either **finite**, with a number of elements that can be counted, or **infinite**. A **subset** is a grouping of the members within the set based on a shared characteristic. For example, the set of digits {0, 1, 2, 3, 4, 5, 6, 7, 8, and 9} is a finite subset of the set of real numbers. The **empty** set, a set with no members, is denoted by the symbol $\varnothing$.

Inclusion-Exclusion Principle

When you consider the relationship between two data sets, a **Venn diagram** can be useful. The following diagram represents three data sets, *A*, *B*, and *C*.

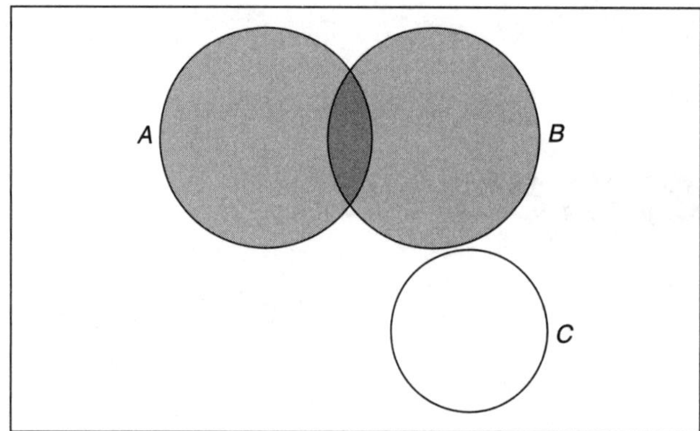

The shaded circles represent the set of elements that are found in *either A or B*. This is the **union** of A and B, or $A \cup B$. The dark shading of the overlapping section of the two circles A and B represents the set of elements that is found in *both A and B*. This is the **intersection** of A and B, or $A \cap B$. Since A and C do not overlap, $A \cap C$ is the empty set, and A and C are considered **mutually exclusive**.

The **inclusion-exclusion principle** for two finite sets states that the number of elements in $A \cup B$ equals the sum of the number of elements in A and the number of elements in B minus the number of elements in $A \cap B$. The principle is written as follows:

$$|A \cup B| = |A| + |B| - |A \cap B|$$

Subtracting the intersection accounts for the double-counting of the overlapping section of A and B when all of the elements within A are added to all of the elements within B.

Multiplication Principle

When two events occur sequentially, and the first does not influence the second, the **multiplication principle** states that the number of possible outcomes is $m \times n$, where m is the number of possible outcomes for the first event, and n is the number of possible outcomes for the second event. Similarly, the probability of two independent events occurring is $P(A \cap B) = P(A) \times P(B)$. The probability of the intersection of A and B—that is, of both A and B occurring—is equal to the product of the probability of A occurring by itself and the probability of B occurring by itself.

Example: How many possible outcomes are there if a fair six-sided die is rolled three times?

Each roll has 6 possible outcomes. So, there are $(6)(6)(6) = 216$ possible outcomes.

Example: Two cards are chosen sequentially from a standard deck of 52 distinct cards. The first card is not returned to the deck before drawing the second card. What is the number of possible outcomes?

The first selection has 52 possible outcomes. Since the first selection is not returned to the deck, the choices are not independent, but the multiplication principle can still be applied. In this case, the second selection only has 51 possible outcomes. There are $(52)(51) = 2{,}652$ possible outcomes.

Permutations

Suppose you have a set of n objects and you want to determine the number of possible orders, or **permutations**, of all of the objects. When the first object is assigned to its position, there are n possibilities. For the second object, there are $n - 1$ remaining positions. For the third, there are $n - 2$, and so on. The number of permutations can be found by applying the multiplication principle. The number of possible orders of n objects is as follows:

$$n\,(n-1)(n-2)\ \dots\ (2)(1)$$

This product is written as $n!$ and pronounced ***n* factorial**.

Example: You are arranging 4 trophies in a row on a shelf. How many distinct ways are there to arrange the trophies?

In this case, $n = 4$. When you place the first trophy, there are 4 possible positions. For the second trophy, there are only 3 remaining positions. Once the second trophy is placed and you are placing the third trophy, there are only 2 positions left. For the last trophy, there is only one possible position. Therefore, there are $n! = 4! = (4)(3)(2)(1) = 24$ possible arrangements for 4 trophies.

Now suppose you have a set of n objects, but you only want to order some of them. Let the number of objects you are choosing for the subset be k. Again, there are n possibilities for the first selection, $n - 1$ for the second, $n - 2$ for the third, and so on. The difference here is that this only continues k times. The formula for the number of **permutations of *n* objects taken *k* at a time** is this:

$$P(n,k) = {}_nP_k = \frac{n!}{(n-k)!}$$

Example: Five runners are in a race. A gold, silver, and bronze medal will be awarded to the first, second, and third place winners. How many different ways could the medals be awarded to the runners?

For three different medals, there are 5 possible winners for the gold medal, 4 possible winners for the silver medal, and 3 possible winners for the bronze medal. There are (5)(4)(3) = 60 possible arrangements of the medals. Using the formula gives the same result:

$$P(5,3) = \frac{5!}{(5-3)!} = \frac{5!}{2!} = \frac{5 \times 4 \times 3 \times \cancel{2 \times 1}}{\cancel{2 \times 1}} = 5 \times 4 \times 3 = 60.$$

Note that when all objects are included in the arrangement, then $k = n$. The denominator of the formula becomes 0!, which is defined as 1. The formula then becomes the formula used for the previous example:

$$P(n,n) = \frac{n!}{0!} = n!$$

Combinations

Now suppose you have a set of n objects and you still want to select some number, k, of them, but their order does not matter. The number of possible groups chosen is called the number of **combinations of *n* objects taken *k* at a time** and is given by the formula:

$$C(n,k) = {}_nC_k = \frac{n!}{k!(n-k)!}$$

Combinations are often referenced as ***n* choose *k*.**

Example: A choir director randomly selects 3 of his 6 members to form a group. How many possible groups of 3 members are there?

$${}_6C_3 = \frac{6!}{3!(6-3)!} = \frac{6!}{3!3!} = \frac{6 \times 5 \times 4 \times \cancel{3 \times 2 \times 1}}{3 \times 2 \times 1 \times \cancel{3 \times 2 \times 1}} = \frac{6 \times 5 \times 4}{3 \times 2 \times 1} = 20$$

COUNTING METHODS EXERCISES

BASIC

1. In how many different ways can the letters in the word DANCE be ordered?
2. Jake went to a football game with 4 of his friends. There are 120 different ways in which they can sit together in a row of 5 seats, with one person per seat. In how many of those ways is Jake sitting in the middle seat?
3. How many 3-digit positive integers are even and do not contain the digit 4?
4. From a box of 12 candles, you are to remove 5. How many different sets of 5 candles could you remove?

For Exercises 5 and 6, use the following information:

There are 10 finalists for the school spelling bee. A first, second, and third place trophy will be awarded with no ties or duplications.

5. In how many different ways can the judges award the three prizes?
6. How many different groups of 3 people can get prizes?
7. If you toss a fair coin 6 times, what is the number of total possible outcomes?
8. What is the value of 4! equal to?
9. In how many different ways can the letters of the word MEXICO be arranged?
10. Evaluate the following: $\frac{7!}{5!}$

INTERMEDIATE

11. There are 6 doors leading into a library. How many different ways could a student enter the room by one door and then leave it using a different door?
12. In how many distinct ways can the letters of the word METHODS be rearranged such that M and S occupy the first and last position respectively?

13. A quiz has 10 true/false questions. If each question is answered with "true" or "false" and none of them are left blank, in how many ways can the quiz be answered?

14. A pizza place offers a dinner combo consisting of pizza, salad, dessert, and a drink from the following menu.

    Pizza: cheese, pepperoni, vegetable
    Salad: Caesar, house
    Dessert: brownie, cookie
    Drink: tea, coffee, soda, lemonade

    How many possible dinner combos are there that include all four choices?

15. A company places a 6-symbol code on each product. The code consists of the letter T, followed by 3 numerical digits, and then 2 consonants. How many different codes are possible? (Consider Y a consonant.)

16. Gloria has 7 shirts to display on 7 possible mannequins in her boutique. If she has already placed the first shirt on mannequin 1, how many different ways can she display the rest of the shirts?

17. If $P(A) = 0.3$, $P(A \cap B) = 0.12$, and the events A and B are independent, then find $P(B)$.

18. There are 7 routes from Springfield to London and 12 routes from London to Fairview. The road a driver takes into London has no effect on the roads that driver can take out of London, and vice versa. Find the number of different ways to travel from Springfield to Fairview that pass through London.

19. If $P(A) = 0.8$, $P(A \cap B) = 0.16$, and the events A and B are independent, what is the value of $P(B)$?

20. Nine coins are tossed simultaneously. In how many of the outcomes will the fourth coin tossed show heads?

Advanced

21. In how many ways can 4 students be selected from a group of 12 students to represent a school in a swimming competition?

22. A student has 3 different science classes, 4 different math classes, 2 different history classes, 2 different English classes, and 5 different electives to choose from. How many different 5-course selections can she make if she needs to enroll in one of each type of class?

23. During practice, a basketball player can successfully complete a foul shot once in 3 throws on average. If the basketball player throws 3 balls in succession, what is the probability that the basketball player will be unsuccessful in all three attempts?

24. How many 4-digit codes can be made using the following digits: 1, 2, 3, 4, 5, 6, 7, 8, 9? (Repetition of a digit is allowed.)

25. If a coin is tossed twice, what is the probability that the coin lands tails up on both tosses?

26. A test has 2 sections, each containing 5 multiple-choice questions. Each question of the first section has 4 answer options, and each question of the second section has 3 answer options. In how many different ways can the test be answered without leaving any questions blank?

27. How many distinct combinations of 3 socks could be made by randomly selecting socks from a drawer containing 8 differently colored socks?

28. At a high school, 300 students are members of the band, chess club, or both. If 200 students are members of the band only and 50 students are members of the band and chess club, what is the probability that a student chosen at random is a member of only the chess club?

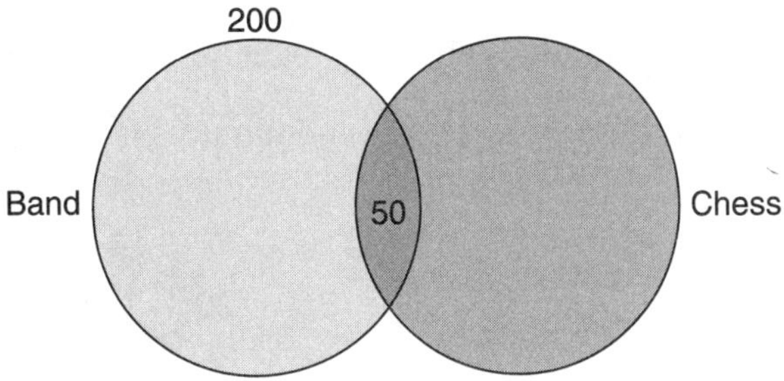

29. Two six-sided dice and one quarter are tossed. How many results are possible?

30. If 8 schools are all in the same conference, how many soccer games are played during the season if the teams all play each other exactly once?

COUNTING METHODS ANSWERS KEY

BASIC

1. 120

Any 5-letter word with none of its letters repeating can be rearranged in 5! ways.

$$5 \times 4 \times 3 \times 2 \times 1 = 120$$

There are 120 ways.

2. 24

If Jake is in the middle, then that removes him from the permutation equation. You're really looking for the number of ways to arrange four people into four seats. So there are 4! ways, with Jake in the middle: $4 \times 3 \times 2 \times 1 = 24$.

3. 288

There are three events to consider: digit 1, digit 2, and digit 3.

There are eight possibilities for the first digit, since you can't use 0 or 4. There are nine possibilities for the second digit, since you can't use the digit 4. There are only four possibilities for the third digit, since you can only use even digits (the final 3-digit number must be even) and not the digit 4.

$$8 \times 9 \times 4 = 288$$

There are 288 possibilities.

4. 792

The order in the sets of 5 candles doesn't matter, so the number of possible 5-candle sets you can remove from a box of 12 equals $\frac{12!}{5!(12-5)!} = \frac{12!}{5!7!} = \frac{12 \times 11 \times 10 \times 9 \times 8}{5 \times 4 \times 3 \times 2 \times 1}$. Divide out the 12 in the numerator with the 4×3 in the denominator, and divide out the 10 in the numerator with the 5×2 in the denominator. The result is $\frac{11 \times 9 \times 8}{1} = 792$.

5. 720

$$\frac{10!}{(10-3)!} = \frac{10!}{7!} = 10 \times 9 \times 8 = 720$$

6. 120

$$\frac{10!}{3!(10-3)!} = \frac{10!}{3!7!} = \frac{10 \times 9 \times 8}{3 \times 2 \times 1} = 120$$

7. 64

There are 2 possible outcomes for each toss, so after 6 tosses there is a total of $2^6 = 64$ possible outcomes.

8. 24

$$4! = 4 \times 3 \times 2 \times 1 = 24$$

9. 720

Any 6-letter word with none of its letters repeating can be rearranged in 6! ways.

$$6 \times 5 \times 4 \times 3 \times 2 \times 1 = 720$$

10. 42

$$\frac{7 \times 6 \times 5 \times 4 \times 3 \times 2 \times 1}{5 \times 4 \times 3 \times 2 \times 1} = \frac{7 \times 6}{1} = 42$$

Intermediate

11. 30

There are 6 doors to the library. The student needs to enter the library using one of those 6 doors. If the student has to leave the library using a different door, then the student has to take one of the remaining 5 doors. Therefore, the total number of ways a student could enter the library and leave using a different door is $6 \times 5 = 30$ ways.

12. 120

The word METHODS is a 7-letter word with none of the letters repeating. Any 7-letter word with none of its letters repeating can be rearranged in 7! ways. However, M and S must occupy the first and last position respectively, so the first and last positions can each be filled in only one way. The remaining 5 positions between M and S can be filled with the 5 other letters in $5! = 120$ ways.

13. 1,024

There are 10 events: question 1, question 2, question 3, question 4, question 5, question 6, question 7, question 8, question 9, and question 10.

There are 2 choices for each question.

$$2 \times 2 \times 2 \times 2 \times 2 \times 2 \times 2 \times 2 \times 2 \times 2 \text{ or } 2^{10} = 1{,}024$$

14. 48

There are 4 events: choosing a pizza, choosing a salad, choosing a dessert, and choosing a drink. There are 3 choices for the pizza, 2 choices for the salad, 2 choices for the dessert, and 4 choices for the drink.

$$3 \times 2 \times 2 \times 4 = 48$$

There are 48 dinner combos available.

15. 441,000

There are 6 events: letter 1, digit 1, digit 2, digit 3, letter 2, and letter 3.

We start with letter 1. Letter 1 is limited to the letter T, so there is only one possibility for letter 1. There are no restrictions on digits 1 through 3, so digit 1, digit 2, and digit 3 have

10 possibilities each. Letter 2 and letter 3 have to be consonants, so there are 21 possible letters for each.

$$1 \times 10 \times 10 \times 10 \times 21 \times 21 = 441{,}000$$

16. 720

There are 7 events: shirt 1, shirt 2, shirt 3, shirt 4, shirt 5, shirt 6, and shirt 7. There is only one possibility for the first shirt. That leaves 6 possibilities for shirt 2, 5 for shirt 3, 4 for shirt 4, 3 for shirt 5, 2 for shirt 6, and 1 for shirt 7.

$$1 \times 6 \times 5 \times 4 \times 3 \times 2 \times 1 = 720$$

17. 0.4

$$P(A \cap B) = P(A) \times P(B)$$
$$0.12 = 0.3 \times P(B)$$
$$0.4 = P(B)$$

18. 84

The number of different ways to reach Fairview from Springfield by passing through London $= 7 \times 12 = 84$.

19. 0.2

$$P(A \cap B) = P(A) \times P(B)$$
$$0.16 = 0.8 \times P(B)$$
$$0.2 = P(B)$$

20. 256

When a coin is tossed once, there are two outcomes, heads or tails. When 9 coins are tossed simultaneously, the total number of outcomes $= 2^9$. If the fourth coin has to show heads, then the number of possibilities for the fourth coin is only 1. So the number of outcomes where the fourth coin would show heads would be: $2 \times 2 \times 2 \times 1 \times 2 \times 2 \times 2 \times 2 \times 2$ or $2^8 = 256$.

Advanced

21. 495

The number of ways to select 4 students out of 12 students is an instance of selecting without replacement and without ordering. So, one can select 4 students out of 12 students in ${}_{12}C_4$ ways.

$$\frac{12!}{4!(12-4)!} = \frac{12!}{4! \times 8!}$$
$$= \frac{12 \times 11 \times 10 \times 9 \times 8!}{4 \times 3 \times 2 \times 1 \times 8!} = \frac{12 \times 11 \times 10 \times 9}{4 \times 3 \times 2 \times 1}$$

Cancel out common factors.

$$\frac{11 \times 5 \times 9}{1} = 495$$

22. 240

Since the student selects one of each type of class, you multiply the number of possibilities for each class. There are 3 different science classes, 4 different math classes, 2 different history classes, 2 different English classes, and 5 different electives to pick from: $3 \times 4 \times 2 \times 2 \times 5 = 240$.

23. $\mathbf{\frac{8}{27}}$

The basketball player throws the ball 3 times. It is possible that he could be successful one, two, or three times in those three throws. The probability that he will not make the foul shot in one throw $= 1 - \frac{1}{3} = \frac{2}{3}$. The probability that he will not make the foul shot in all three attempts $= \frac{2}{3} \times \frac{2}{3} \times \frac{2}{3} = \frac{8}{27}$.

24. 6,561

The number of permutations of 9 digits taken 4 at a time, if repetition of digits is allowed, is $9 \times 9 \times 9 \times 9$ or $9^4 = 6{,}561$.

25. $\mathbf{\frac{1}{4}}$

$$P(A \text{ and } B) = P(A) \times P(B): \frac{1}{2} \times \frac{1}{2} = \frac{1}{4}.$$

26. 248,832

The 5 questions on the first section have 4 answer options each. These can be answered in 4^5 different ways. The 5 questions on the second section have 3 answer options each. These can be answered in 3^5 different ways. The test can be completed in $4^5 \times 3^5 = 1{,}024 \times 243 = 248{,}832$ different ways.

27. 56

n is the number of different socks to choose from, so $n = 8$. k is the number of socks in each possible combination, so $k = 3$.

$$\begin{aligned}
{}_nC_k &= \frac{n!}{k!(n-k)!} \\
{}_8C_3 &= \frac{8!}{3!(8-3)!} \\
&= \frac{8 \times 7 \times 6 \times \cancel{5 \times 4 \times 3 \times 2 \times 1}}{(3 \times 2 \times 1)(\cancel{5 \times 4 \times 3 \times 2 \times 1})} \\
&= \frac{8 \times 7 \times \cancel{6}}{\cancel{3 \times 2} \times 1} \\
&= 8 \times 7 \\
&= 56
\end{aligned}$$

There are 56 different possible combinations.

28. $\frac{1}{6}$

If 200 students are in the band only, then the total number of students in the chess club is 300 − 200 = 100, since there are 300 students who are members of the band, chess club, or both. The number of students who are only in the chess club is 100 − 50 = 50, since there are 50 students who are in both the band and chess club. Therefore, the probability that a student chosen at random from the 300 students is a member of only the chess club is as follows:

$$\frac{50}{300} = \frac{1}{6}$$

29. 72

There are 3 stages or events: two dice and one quarter. Each die has 6 possible outcomes. The quarter has 2 possible outcomes, either tails or heads.

$$6 \times 6 \times 2 = 72$$

30. 28

n is the number of teams, so $n = 8$.

k is the number of teams at a time, so $k = 2$.

$$\begin{aligned} {}_nC_k &= \frac{n!}{(n-k)!k!} \\ {}_8C_2 &= \frac{8!}{(8-2)!2!} \\ &= \frac{8!}{6!2!} \\ &= \frac{8 \times 7 \times 6!}{6!2!} \\ &= \frac{8 \times 7}{2 \times 1} \\ &= \frac{56}{2} \\ &= 28 \end{aligned}$$

DESCRIPTIVE STATISTICS

Statistics is a way to describe and characterize a set of data. Most data sets can be described using measures of central tendency and measures of dispersion.

Measures of Central Tendency

The main measures of central tendency are the arithmetic mean, median, and mode. These values characterize where a data set is centered. Let's review the definitions of mean and median found in chapter 6 on Arithmetic.

The average (arithmetic mean) of a group of numbers is defined as the sum of the values divided by the number of values.

$$\textit{Average value} = \frac{\textit{Sum of values}}{\textit{Number of values}}$$

The median of a set is the middle term when all the terms in the set are listed in sequential order. When there is an even number of terms in a set, the median is the average of the two middle terms.

Since the mean incorporates every data value into a sum, it can be shifted up or down significantly when one or several data values, called **outliers,** are extremely high or extremely low compared to the rest of the values. In these cases, the median is often a more descriptive characteristic of what is typical in the data set.

The third measure of central tendency, **mode**, is the number that appears most frequently in a list of numbers.

Example: For the list of numbers—5, 2, 6, 2, 3, 5, 21, 4—the measures of central tendency are all different.

The mean is 6:

$$\frac{5 + 2 + 6 + 2 + 3 + 5 + 21 + 4}{8} = \frac{48}{8} = 6.$$

The median is 4.5: 2, 2, 3, 4, 5, 5, 6, 21 (The average of the middle two numbers, 4 and 5, is 4.5.)

The list has 2 modes: 2 and 5, because they both appear twice.

Measures of Dispersion

The main measures of dispersion are the range, interquartile range, and standard deviation. These values characterize the spread of a data set.

The **range** of a data set is the difference between the greatest number and the least number.

The **interquartile range** describes the spread of the middle half of the data. Finding the interquartile range involves dividing the data set into four sections, or quartiles. The **first quartile,** Q_1, is the median of all of the numbers below the median. The **second quartile,** Q_2, is the median of the entire data set. The **third quartile,** Q_3, is the median of all of the numbers above Q_2. The **interquartile range** is the difference between Q_3 and Q_1.

The range and interquartile range are often displayed on a **box-and-whisker plot,** also called a **box plot.**

Let's look at an example of the measures of dispersion considered so far.

Example: 2, 2, 3, 4, 5, 5, 6, 21

The median calculated previously, is 4.5. This is also Q_2.

The range is $21 - 2 = 19$.

Q_1 is the median of 2, 2, 3, and 4, which is 2.5.

Q_3 is the median of 5, 5, 6, and 21, which is 5.5.

The interquartile range is $5.5 - 2.5 = 3$. Notice how much larger the range is than the interquartile range because the range is affected by the outlier, 21.

A box-and-whisker-plot of the data is shown below.

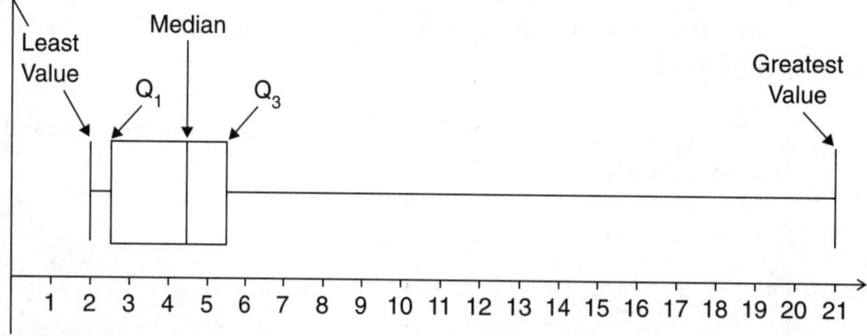

The third measure of dispersion on the GRE is the **standard deviation.** It is a measure of how spread out a set of numbers is (how much the numbers deviate from the mean). The greater the spread, the higher the standard deviation. You will rarely have to calculate the standard deviation on Test Day (although this skill may be necessary for some high-difficulty questions), but you will need a general understanding of what standard deviation is, so here's how it's calculated:

- Find the average (arithmetic mean) of the set.
- Find the differences between the mean and each value in the set.
- Square each of the differences.
- Find the average of the squared differences.
- Take the positive square root of the average.

Here's what the formula looks like if you follow the above steps to calculate the standard deviation of a set of *n* elements, in which *x* is the mean:

$$\text{Standard deviation} = \sqrt{\frac{(n_1 - x)^2 + (n_2 - x)^2 + \ldots + (n_n - x)^2}{n}}$$

Example: For the 5-day listing that follows, which city had the greater standard deviation in high temperatures?

High temperatures, in °F, in 2 cities over 5 days

September	1	2	3	4	5
City A	54	61	70	49	56
City B	62	56	60	67	65

Even without calculating, you can see that City A has the greater spread in temperatures and, therefore, the greater standard deviation in high temperatures. If you were to calculate the standard deviations for each city following the steps described above, you would find that the standard deviation in high temperatures for City A $= \sqrt{\frac{254}{5}} \approx 7.1$, while the same for City B $= \sqrt{\frac{74}{5}} \approx 3.8$.

Standard deviation is a critical measurement in normal distributions, sometimes referred to as "bell curves" because of their shape. In normal distributions, data points tend to cluster around the mean. At one standard deviation away from the mean, there are significantly fewer data points, and at two standard deviations away from the mean, there are fewer still. The GRE will likely refer to the standard deviation as *d* and the mean as *m*.

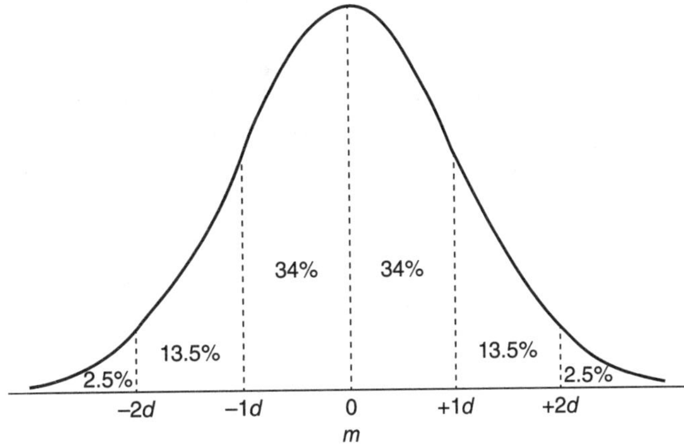

Any normal distribution is defined by its mean and standard deviation, so knowing good estimates for these values is critical to solving problems involving normal distribution. The mean is at the center and highest point on the curve, and because the distribution is symmetrical about the mean, the mean is also the median and mode. The standard deviation, since it is a measure of dispersion, determines the width of the normal distribution: the greater the standard deviation, the wider and flatter the curve. There are many real-world examples of variables that can be approximated by normal distribution: measurement errors, heights of homogeneous populations, random short term movements of stock prices, and standardized test scores.

Some problems that you encounter may deal with areas beneath a normal distribution curve, which are often expressed as percentages of the total area. The values shown in the diagram above for the various key areas of the curve are approximate, but they are sufficiently accurate for the questions you are likely to see on the GRE. To find the approximate number of data points that fall within one standard deviation above the mean, for instance, you would multiply the total number of data points by 34%. Moreover, note that the percentages of the area beneath the curve equate to probabilities. For example, the probability of a data point falling within one standard deviation above the mean is 34%. The actual formula for computing a normal distribution will not be tested, but you should familiarize yourself with the key values shown in the figure. Use those values to work through this example:

Example: A food manufacturer produces energy bars that have a mean weight of 50.0 grams. All bars are weighed before they are wrapped and shipped, and 68 percent of the bars weigh between 49.5 and 50.5 grams. If a given day's production is 10,000 energy bars, how many of those bars would be expected to weigh between 49.0 and 49.5 grams? (Assume that the weights are normally distributed.)

The problem provides the mean, 50 g, and states that 68% of the bars are between 49.5 and 50.5 g. Since 68% corresponds to the area represented by $\pm\ 1d$, the standard deviation is 0.5 g. So 49.0 g is $2d$ below the mean and 49.5 g is $1d$ below the mean. The question asks for the predicted number of bars between 49.0 and 49.5 g, that is, the predicted number of bars between $-2d$ and $-1d$ from the mean. The area between those two numbers is 13.5%. Since 10,000 bars are produced, the company could expect that about $0.135 \times 10{,}000 = 1{,}350$ bars with a weight in that range would be made that day.

DESCRIPTIVE STATISTICS EXERCISES

BASIC

For Exercises 1–4, use the following set of data:

8, 11, 12, 36, 45, 21, 9, 8, 7, 4

1. Find the average (arithmetic mean).
2. Find the median.
3. Find the mode.
4. Find the range.
5. Find the median for the following data set, which shows the scores of 11 students in Ms. Evans's class: 85, 78, 95, 92, 74, 98, 64, 99, 72, 88, 95.
6. The following table gives the ages of students in a class at a high school. Find the mean.

Age	14	15	16	17	18
Number of students	4	8	7	1	2

7. Of the following data set, which number, if any, is an outlier: 81, 73, 85, 79, 90, 155, 76, 89?
8. The sum of 30 measurements of data is 1,680. What is the average (arithmetic mean) of these measurements?
9. What is the third quartile of the following data set: 63, 68, 70, 63, 82, 58, 44?
10. Javier's test scores are 78, 89, 44, 98, 85, 72, 71, and 92. What is the range of his scores?

INTERMEDIATE

11. The average weight of 10 packages increases by 2 ounces when the weight of a book is added to one of them. If the average weight of the packages, after including the weight of the book, is 34 ounces, what is the weight of the book in ounces?

12. Bianca's average wage for 11 days was $110 per day. During the first 5 days, her average wage was $90 per day, and her average wage during the last 5 days was $120 per day. What was her wage on the sixth day?

13. The average of five numbers is 8. The average of three of the numbers is 7. What is the average of the remaining two numbers?

For Exercises 14–16, use the following information:

The numbers of books on each of 7 shelves were 13, 5, 11, 8, 19, 7, and 10.

14. Find the mean, median, mode, range, and interquartile range of the numbers.

15. If each bookshelf had 3 times as many books, what would be the mean, median, range, and interquartile range?

16. If each shelf had 3 fewer books than the initial numbers, what would be the interquartile range?

17. The daily attendance of an art exhibit for the past 8 days was 90, 95, 77, 78, 87, 81, 85, and 93. What are the mean, median, and mode of these attendance numbers?

For Exercises 18 and 19, use the following information:

The daily temperatures, in degrees Fahrenheit, for 9 days in June were 68, 73, 75, 76, 78, 81, 72, 83, and 81.

18. Find the mean, median, mode, and range of the temperatures.

19. If each day had been 6 degrees warmer, what would have been the mean, median, mode, and range of those 9 temperatures?

20. For one week, eight students recorded the numbers of hours they each studied. The mean of their data is 6 hours. If an outlier data value of 18 is removed from the set, what is the mean of the new data set, to the nearest hundredth?

ADVANCED

For Exercises 21 and 22 use the following information:

Test Scores							
Class A	89	92	78	96	86	80	90
Class B	98	86	70	82	92	89	88

21. Which is greater, the mean for Class A or the median of Class B?

22. If Class C has a mean of 86.5, order the classes' means from greatest to least.

23. For five consecutive days, the number of hours a student spends on schoolwork per day is 6, 8, 10, 6, and 7. Find the range, first quartile, and third quartile.

24. If a student's scores for the first four tests are 77, 98, 82, and 93, what is the minimum possible score on the fifth test that will allow his overall mean to be at least 90?

25. If the mean of numbers 18, x, 45, 79, and 98 is 56, then what is the mean of 148, 155, 232, 99, and x?

26. The sale prices of 8 houses are listed below. What is the range of the prices of the 8 houses?

$399,900	$289,500	$650,000	$399,900
$218,000	$250,000	$241,850	$189,000

For Exercises 27 and 28, use the following information:

The temperatures for 365 days were recorded and summarized in the following box plot.

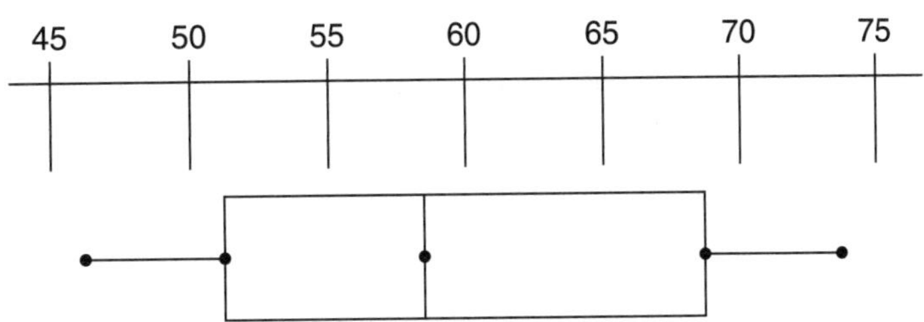

27. What are the range, the three quartiles, and the interquartile range of the measurements?

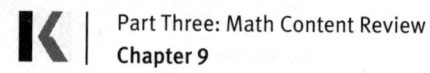

28. If the 80th percentile of the measurements is 72°, about how many measurements are between 69° and 72°? (Round your answer to the nearest whole number.)

29. A group of 40 data points has a mean of 34.7. Another group of 50 points has a mean of 42.1. What is the mean of the 90 points together, to the nearest tenth?

30. Fly With Us Airline keeps track of the deviations from scheduled departure times. If a flight leaves early, the deviation is negative. If a flight is late, the deviation is positive. Each employee gets a $2,000 bonus for every whole number below zero for the mean *and* the median of the deviation data. Given the following deviation values, would a bonus be given, and if so, what would it be per employee? {−3, 2, 0, 0, −4, 8, −6, −2, −5, 0}

DESCRIPTIVE STATISTICS ANSWERS KEY

Basic

1. 16.1

$$\frac{8 + 11 + 12 + 36 + 45 + 21 + 9 + 8 + 7 + 4}{10} = \frac{161}{10} = 16.1$$

2. 10

Arrange the numbers in ascending order: 4, 7, 8, 8, 9, 11, 12, 21, 36, 45. Find the average of the two middle numbers. $\frac{9 + 11}{2} = 10$.

3. 8

The mode is the number that occurs the most frequently. In this case, that is 8.

4. 41

The range is the largest number minus the smallest number: $45 - 4 = 41$.

5. 88

Place the data in ascending order: 64, 72, 74, 78, 85, **88**, 92, 95, 95, 98, 99. The median is the middle number, which here is 88.

6. 15.5

There are four 14s, eight 15s, seven 16s, one 17, and two 18s in the set. Instead of writing out all of the individual numbers, you can evaluate the following:

$4(14) + 8(15) + 7(16) + 1(17) + 2(18) = 341$

There are 22 numbers, so the mean is $\frac{341}{22}$, which equals 15.5.

The mean age is 15.5.

7. 155

The number 155 is much higher than the other numbers in the data set; it is an outlier.

8. 56

$$Mean = \frac{Sum\ of\ values}{Number\ of\ values} = \frac{1{,}680}{30} = 56$$

The mean is 56.

9. 70

Put the numbers in ascending order. Find the median, or second quartile: 44, 58, 63, **63**, 68, 70, 82. Q_2 is 63. The third quartile is the median of all the numbers above Q_2. The third quartile is 70.

10. 54

The range is the positive difference between the highest and the lowest numbers in a set. The highest score is 98, and the lowest score is 44, so the range is $98 - 44$, which equals 54.

Intermediate

11. 20

The new average weight of the packages after including the book is 34 ounces. The new average is 2 ounces more than the old average. The old average without including the book is 32 ounces. The total weight of the 10 packages, without including the weight of the book, is $10 \times 32 = 320$. After adding the book to one package, the average weight of the packages increases to 34 ounces. The total weight of the packages after including the weight of the book is $10 \times 34 = 340$ ounces. So, the book weighs $340 - 320 = 20$ ounces.

Another way to think of it is this: If the average is increased by 2 when the book is added and there are 10 packages total, the weight of the book is $2 \times 10 = 20$.

12. $160

Total wages $= 11 \times \$110 = \$1{,}210$.

The total wages for the first 5 days $= 5 \times 90 = \$450$.

The total wages for the last 5 days $= 5 \times 120 = \$600$.

Total wages earned during the 11 days = wages during first 5 days + wage on 6th day + wages during the last 5 days.

1,210 = 450 + wage on 6th day + 600.

Wage on 6th day $= 1210 - 450 - 600 = \$160$.

13. 9.5

The average of 5 quantities is 8. The sum of the 5 quantities is $5 \times 8 = 40$. The average of 3 of these 5 quantities is 7. The sum of these 3 quantities $= 3 \times 7 = 21$. The sum of the remaining two quantities $= 40 - 21 = 19$.

$$\text{Average of these two quantities} = \frac{19}{2} = 9.5.$$

14. Mean: 10.4286
Median: 10
Mode: none
Range: 14
Interquartile range: 6

Put the data values in order: 5, 7, 8, 10, 11, 13, 19.

$$Mean = \frac{\textit{Sum of values}}{\textit{Number of values}} = \frac{5 + 7 + 8 + 10 + 11 + 13 + 19}{7} = \frac{73}{7} \approx 10.4286$$

There is an odd number of data values, so the median is the middle value when the values are arranged in numerical order: 5, 7, 8, **10**, 11, 13, 19. The median is 10. The range is the difference between the greatest number and the least number: $19 - 5 = 14$.

The interquartile range is the difference between Q_3 and Q_1: $13 - 7 = 6$.

15. Mean: 31.2857
Median: 30
Range: 42
Interquartile range: 18

New numbers with 3 times as many books: 39, 15, 33, 24, 57, 21, 30

Numbers in order: 15, 21, 24, 30, 33, 39, 57

$$Mean = \frac{Sum\ of\ values}{Number\ of\ values} = \frac{15 + 21 + 24 + 30 + 33 + 39 + 57}{7} = \frac{219}{7} \approx 31.2857$$

There is an odd number of data values, so the median is the middle value when the values are arranged in numerical order: 15, 21, 24, **30**, 33, 39, 57. The median is 30.

The range is the difference between the greatest number and the least number: $57 - 15 = 42$.

The interquartile range is the difference between Q_3 and Q_1: $39 - 21 = 18$.

16. 6

New numbers with 3 fewer books on each shelf: 10, 2, 8, 5, 16, 4, 7

Numbers in order: 2, 4, 5, 7, 8, 10, 16

Interquartile range: $Q_3 - Q_1 = 10 - 4 = 6$

Note that the interquartile range will stay the same if the same value is added to or subtracted from all of the data points in the set because the distance between the data points does not change.

17. Mean: 85.75
Median: 86
Mode: none

Numbers in order: 77, 78, 81, 85, 87, 90, 93, 95

$$Mean = \frac{Sum\ of\ values}{Number\ of\ values} = \frac{77 + 78 + 81 + 85 + 87 + 90 + 93 + 95}{8} = \frac{686}{8} = 85.75$$

There is an even number of data values, so the median is the average of the middle two values when they are arranged in numerical order: 77, 78, 81, **85**, **87**, 90, 93, 95. Then $(85 + 87) \div 2 = 86$. The median is 86.

All of the numbers appear with equal frequency, so there is no mode for this data set.

18. Mean: $76.3\overline{3}$
Median: 76
Mode: 81
Range: 15

Numbers in order: 68, 72, 73, 75, 76, 78, 81, 81, 83

$$Mean = \frac{Sum\ of\ values}{Number\ of\ values} = \frac{68+72+73+75+76+78+81+81+83}{9} = \frac{687}{9} = 76.3\bar{3}$$

There is an odd number of data values, so the median is the middle value when the values are arranged in numerical order: 68, 72, 73, 75, **76**, 78, 81, 81, 83. The median is 76. The number 81 occurs twice, which is more frequently than any other number in the data set, so the mode is 81.

The range is the difference between the greatest number and the least number: 83 − 68 = 15.

19. Mean: 82.3$\bar{3}$
Median: 82
Mode: 87
Range: 15

Note that because the entire data set has essentially been shifted 6 places to the right, the mean, median, and mode will all increase by 6, and the range will not change.

New numbers at 6 degrees warmer in order: 74, 78, 79, 81, 82, 84, 87, 87, 89

$$Mean = \frac{Sum\ of\ values}{Number\ of\ values} = \frac{74+78+79+81+82+84+87+87+89}{9} = \frac{741}{9} = 82.3\bar{3}$$

There is an odd number of data values, so the median is the middle value when the values are arranged in numerical order: 74, 78, 79, 81, **82**, 84, 87, 87, 89. The median is 82.

The number 87 occurs twice, which is more frequently than any other number in the data set, so the mode is 87.

The range is the difference between the greatest number and the least number: 89 − 74 = 15.

20. 4.29
To find the new mean, you must first determine what the sum of the original data values was based on the information given.

$$Original\ mean = \frac{Sum\ of\ values}{Number\ of\ values} = \frac{?}{8} = 6$$
$$Sum\ of\ values = 6 \times 8 = 48$$

The original sum of values was 48. Now, you know that a data value has been removed (18), so reduce the sum of values by 18 and the number of values by 1.

$$New\ mean = \frac{Sum\ of\ values}{Number\ of\ values} = \frac{48-18}{8-1} = \frac{30}{7} \approx 4.29$$

ADVANCED

21. Median of Class B

The mean of Class A is

$$\frac{\textit{Sum of values}}{\textit{Number of values}} = \frac{89 + 92 + 78 + 96 + 86 + 80 + 90}{7} = \frac{611}{7} \approx 87.29$$

There is an odd number of data values, so the median of Class B is the middle value when the values are arranged in numerical order: 70, 82, 86, **88**, 89, 92, 98. The median of Class B is 88. So the median of Class B is greater.

22. Class A, Class C, Class B

The mean of Class C is 86.5. The mean of Class A to the nearest hundredth is 87.29. The mean of Class B is

$$\frac{98 + 86 + 70 + 82 + 92 + 89 + 88}{7} = \frac{605}{7} \approx 86.43.$$

So, the mean of Class A is greatest, and then Class C, and finally Class B.

23. Range: 4
Q_1: 6
Q_2: 9

Numbers in order: 6, 6, 7, 8, 10

Range = highest number − lowest number = 10 − 6 = 4

The median of the data is 7, so the first quartile is 6 and the third quartile is 9.

24. 100

$$\begin{aligned}
90 &= \frac{77 + 98 + 82 + 93 + x}{5} \\
90 &= \frac{350 + x}{5} \\
(5)90 &= \frac{350 + x}{5}(5) \\
450 &= 350 + x \\
450 - 350 &= 350 - 350 + x \\
100 &= x
\end{aligned}$$

The student needs a score of 100 on the fifth test for his overall mean to be at least a 90.

25. 134.8

The average (arithmetic mean) of the 5 numbers 18, *x*, 45, 79, and 98 is 56.

Therefore, the sum of these 5 numbers is $56 \times 5 = 280$.
$18 + 45 + 79 + 98 = 240$
So, $x = 280 - 240 = 40$.

The average of 148, 155, 232, 99, and *x* is $\frac{148 + 155 + 232 + 99 + 40}{5} = \frac{674}{5} = 134.8$.

26. 461,000

The range is the positive difference between the highest and the lowest number in a set. The highest value is 650,000, and the lowest value is 189,000. To find the range, subtract the lowest from the highest.

$650{,}000 - 189{,}000 = 461{,}000$

27. Range: 74 – 46 = 28
Q_1: 52
Q_2: 59
Q_3: 69
Interquartile range: 69 – 52 = 17

28. 18

Because 69° represents the 75th percentile, from 69° to 72° is 5% of the measurements. Then $5\% \times 365 = 18.25$, which rounds to 18.

29. 38.8

The mean of the 90 data points together is $\frac{40(34.7) + 50(42.1)}{90} = \frac{3493}{90} = 38.8\bar{1}$.

30. Yes; $4,000

Data values in order: −6, −5, −4, −3, −2, 0, 0, 0, 2, 8

The mean of the data is

$$\frac{(-6) + (-5) + (-4) + (-3) + (-2) + 0 + 0 + 0 + 2 + 8}{10} = \frac{-10}{10} = -1.$$

The median is also −1. This means the employees get $2,000 for being 1 below 0 for the mean and an additional $2,000 for the median being 1 below 0. So, each employee would receive a $4,000 bonus.

DATA GRAPHS AND TABLES

There are several different kinds of charts and graphs that can show up on the test. The most common kinds are tables, bar graphs, line graphs, and pie charts.

Tables

Tables share many of the characteristics of graphs, except for the visual advantages—you can estimate values from a graph, but not from a table. Tables can be enormous and complicated, but the basic structure is always the same: columns and rows. Here's an example of a simple one (much simpler than those that appear on the GRE):

JOHN'S INCOME, 2004–2008	
YEAR	INCOME
2004	$20,000
2005	$22,000
2006	$18,000
2007	$15,000
2008	$28,080

An easy question on this table might ask for the sum of the three lowest incomes. In this case, you would simply look up the amounts and then add. A harder question might ask for John's average income per year over the five given years; then you would have to add up the five incomes, and divide to find the average.

Bar Graphs

These can be used to display the information that would otherwise appear in a table. On a bar graph, the *height* of each column shows its value. Here's the information from the table above presented as a bar graph:

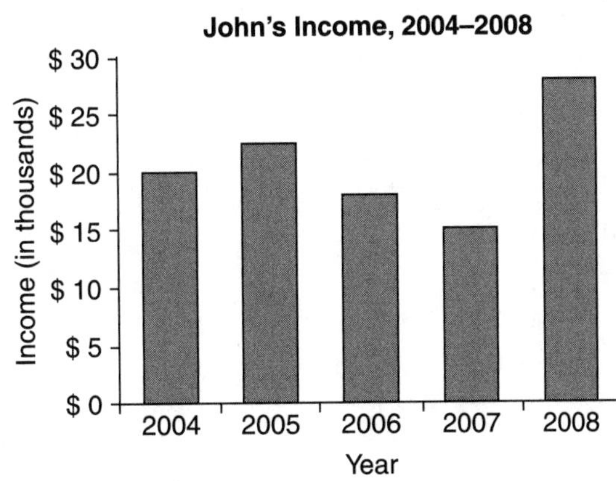

What's handy about a bar graph is that you can see the relative values by looking at their heights. By glancing at the graph shown, for example, it's easy to see that John's income in 2008 was almost double his income in 2007. But you can see this only because the scale starts at zero; the scale could just as easily start somewhere *other* than zero.

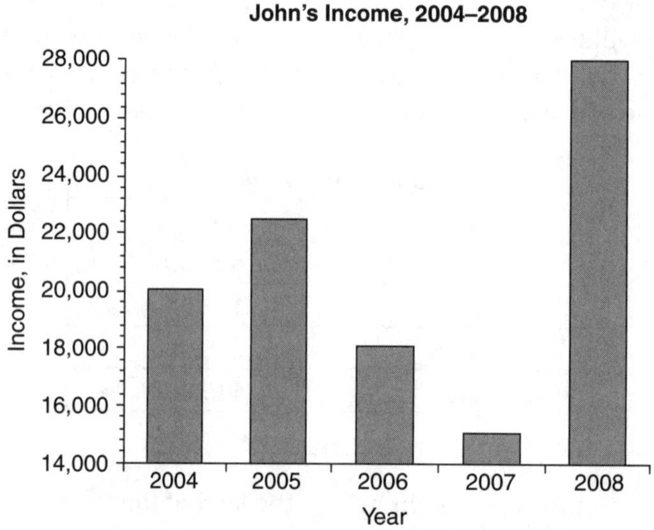

This graph presents the same information, but now you cannot estimate as simply as you did before. You can still tell at a glance that his 2008 income exceeded 2007, but you cannot quickly estimate the ratio.

In order to find some numerical value from a bar graph, find the correct bar (such as 2008 income) and move horizontally across from the top of the bar to the value on the scale on the left or, sometimes, on the right. Don't worry about getting too precise a value; usually, a close approximation will be good enough. For example, John's 2008 income was approximately $28,000. Notice that this is different from the table, where John's *exact* income was given.

Line Graphs

Line graphs follow the same principle as bar graphs, except the values are presented as points, rather than bars.

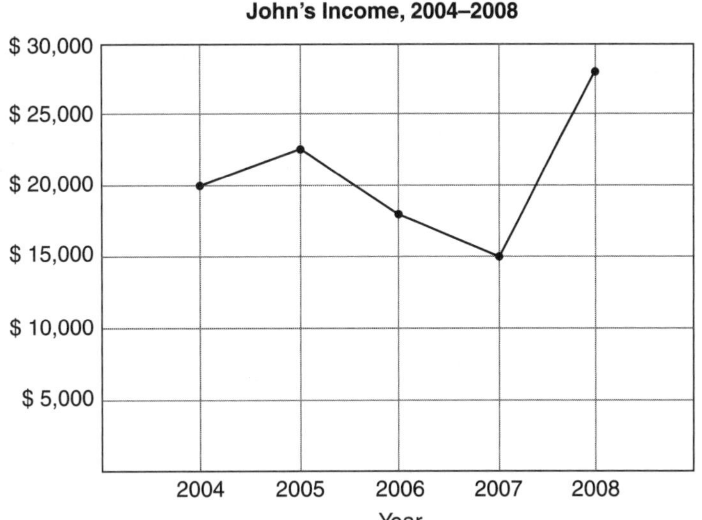

As with bar graphs, the value of a particular year is the vertical distance from the bottom of the graph to the line. And also as with bar graphs, you can see the relative value of the described amounts by looking at their heights—with the caution we mentioned before, that the base must be zero in order to estimate ratios.

Pie Charts

A pie chart shows how things are distributed; the fraction of a circle occupied by each piece of the "pie" indicates what fraction of the whole it represents. Usually, the pie chart will identify what percent of the whole each piece represents, with the whole being 100 percent.

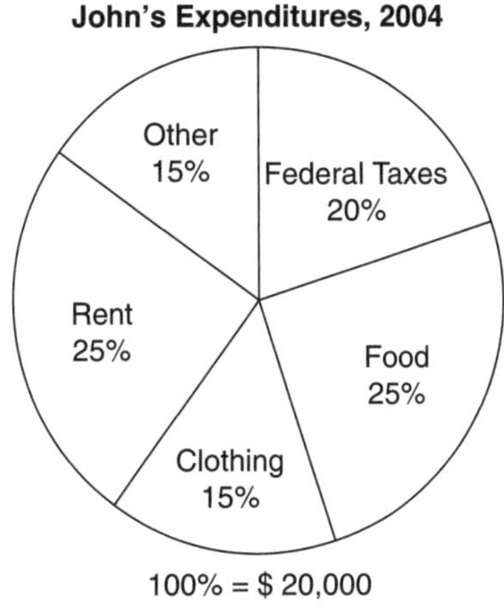

The total size of the whole pie is usually given as "TOTAL = $3,547" or "100% = $5.9 billion" or something of that nature. If we were asked to find the approximate value of a particular piece of the pie, we would multiply the appropriate percent by the whole. For instance, to find the amount John paid in federal taxes in 2004, we find the slice labeled "Federal Taxes," and we see that federal taxes represented 20% of his expenditures. Since the whole is \$20,000, we find that John's federal taxes for 2004 were 20% of \$20,000 or $\frac{1}{5} \times \$20{,}000 = \$4{,}000$.

Pie charts sometimes travel in pairs. If so, be sure that you do not attempt to compare slices from one chart with slices from another. For instance, suppose we were given another pie chart for John's expenditures, this one covering 2008.

John's Expenditures, 2008

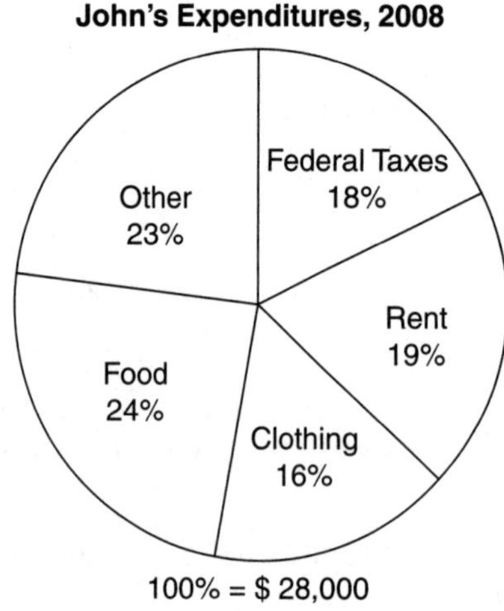

100% = \$ 28,000

A careless glance might suggest that John paid less in federal taxes in 2008 than in 2004. Not true! His 2004 taxes were a greater percentage of his income than were his 2008 taxes, but his 2008 income was much greater than his 2004 income. In fact, he paid about \$1,000 *more* in taxes in 2008 than in 2004. Since the totals for the two charts are different, the pieces of the pie are not directly comparable.

Double Graphs

Very often the GRE will present two graphs for the same set of questions, or one graph and a table. The two charts or graphs will be related in some way.

Stuck Elevators in Country X

Year	Stuck Elevators
2009	432
2010	459
2011	621
2012	645

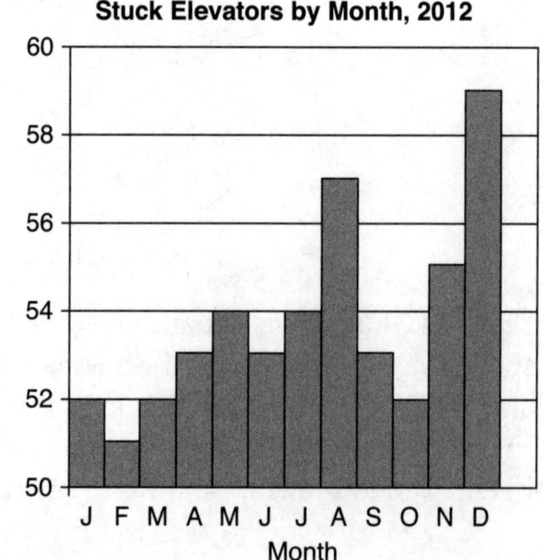

Here, the table covers stuck elevators for four years, while the accompanying bar graph breaks the information down by month for just one year, 2012.

What can be more complex is when the testmaker gives you two graphs (either two line graphs or two bar graphs) occupying the same space. Sometimes both graphs will refer to the same vertical scale; other times, one graph will refer to a scale on the left, the other graph to a scale on the right.

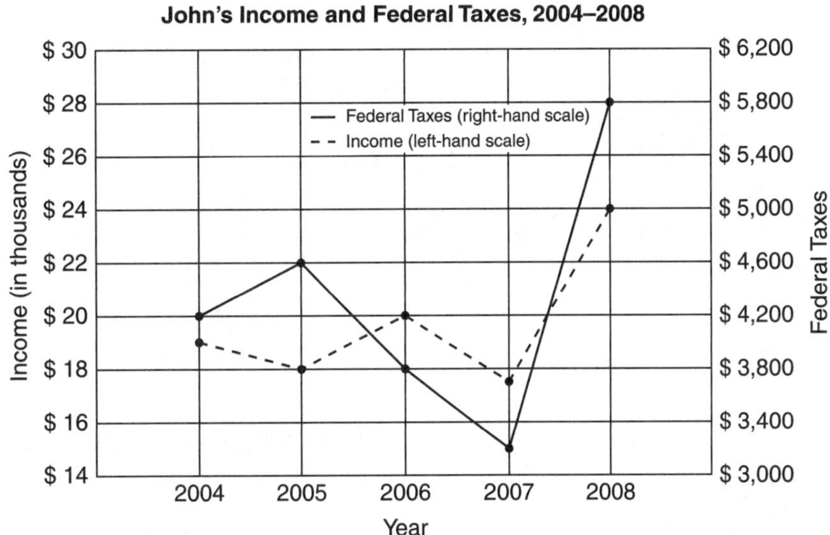

Here is the same graph of John's income, but with new information added. You now see at a glance not only John's income for a given year, but also the amount of federal taxes for that year. The income refers to the left-hand scale; the taxes to the right-hand scale. At this point, the number of potential questions that may be asked of the test taker has risen dramatically.

Double graphs are not really any more difficult than single graphs as long as you don't mix up the scales. Learn to double-check that you're using the correct scale when working with double graphs. If you find yourself getting confused, slow down and give yourself a chance to sort things out.

DATA GRAPHS AND TABLES EXERCISES

BASIC

Use the following graphs to answer Exercises 1–2.

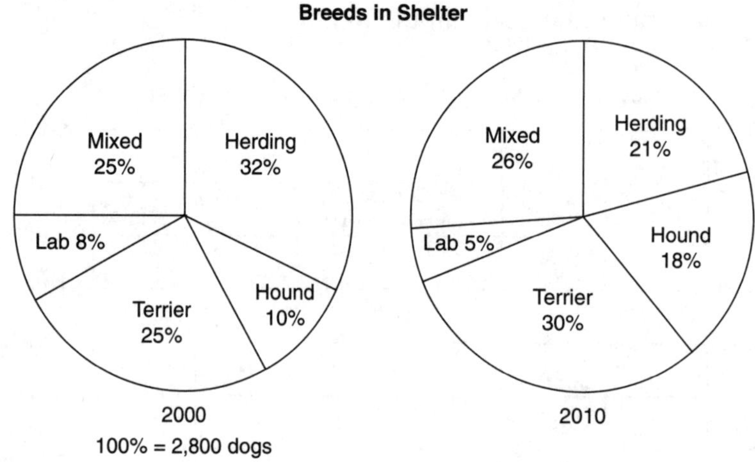

1. Of the total number of dogs in the shelter in 2000, how many were mixed or terrier breed?

2. In 2010, which two types of dogs together equaled the closest approximation of half of the total number of dogs that entered the shelter in 2010?

Use the following graph to answer Exercises 3–4.

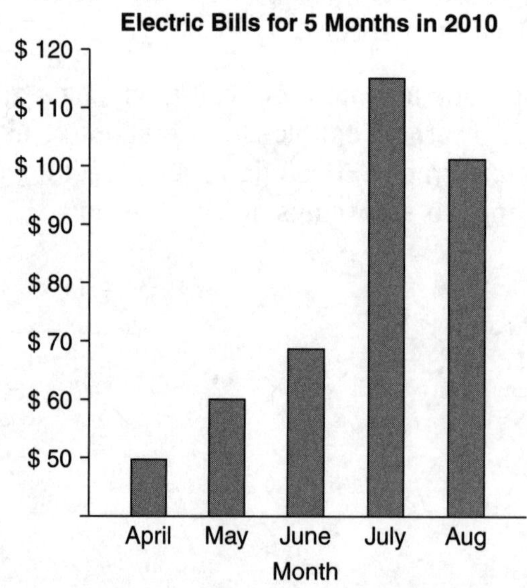

3. If the electric bill in September is half of the bill in August, will it be more or less than the bill in May?

4. How much greater was the July bill than the May bill?

Use the following graph to answer Exercises 5–6.

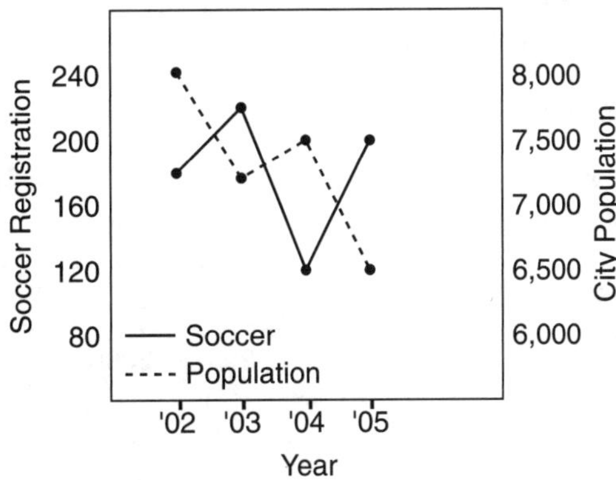

5. Did the number of soccer registrations increase or decrease from 2003 to 2004?

6. What was the approximate change in the city population from 2002 to 2004?

Use the following graph to answer Exercises 7–8.

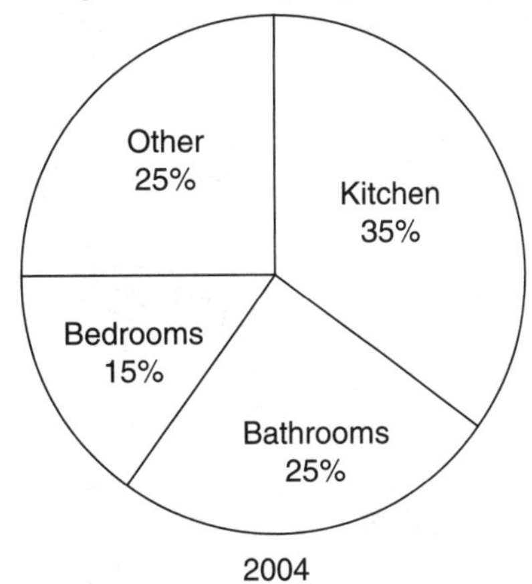

7. How much greater, as a percent of total expenditures, was the percent spent on remodeling kitchens than the percent spent on bedrooms?

8. If an average homeowner spends a total of $10,000 on remodeling and allocates the money according to the expenditure chart shown, how much was spent remodeling the bathrooms?

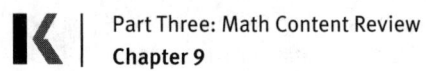

Use the following graph to answer Exercises 9–10.

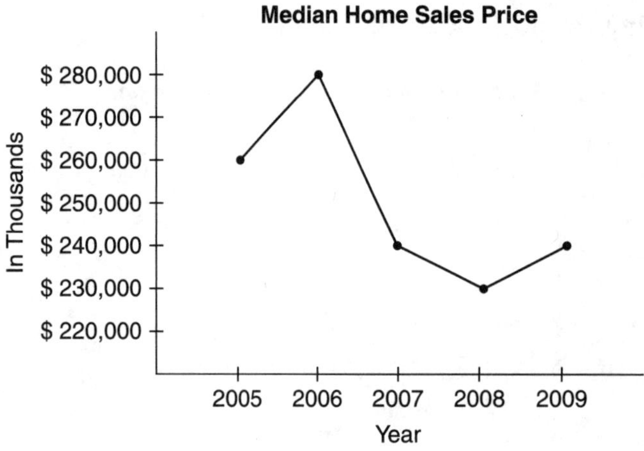

9. What was the difference in the median sales price between 2006 and 2007?

10. What was the percent increase in median sales prices from 2008 to 2009?

INTERMEDIATE

Use the following graphs to answer Exercises 11–12.

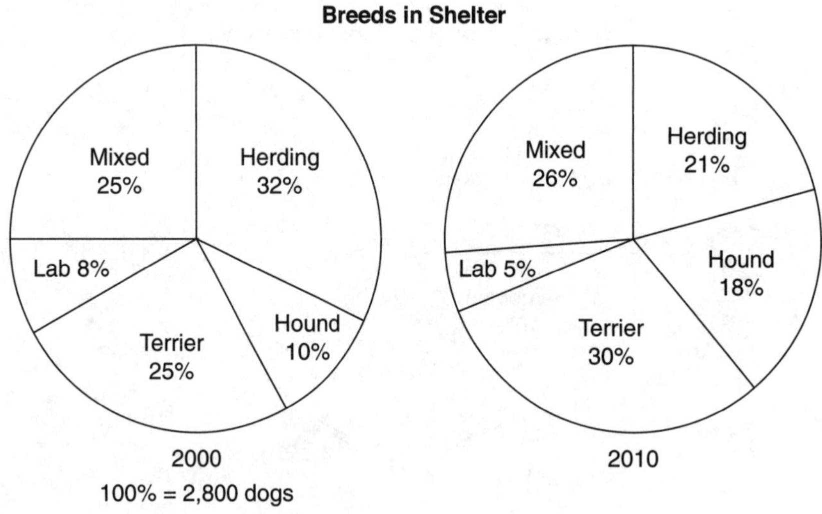

11. In 2000, how much greater of a percentage did labs and terriers represent than herding breeds? Express your answer as a percent of the total number of dogs in the shelter that year.

12. In 2010, if there were 850 herding dogs in the shelter, was this more or less than the number of herding dogs that entered the shelter in 2000?

Use the following graph to answer Exercises 13–14.

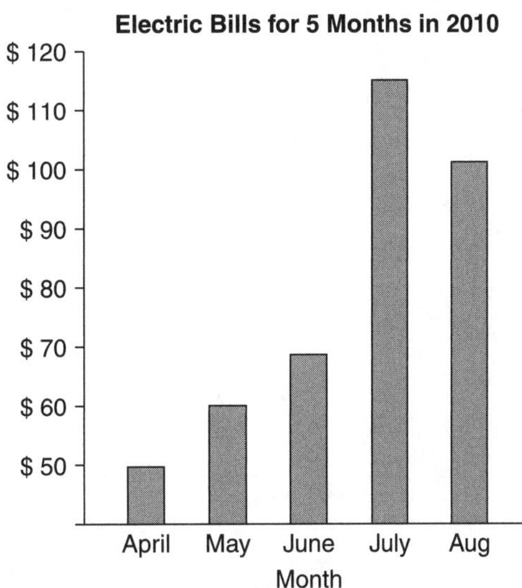

13. The bills shown represent 65% of the customer's total cost of electricity for the year. What was the total cost for the year, to the nearest dollar?

14. What is the percentage change of the cost of the electric bills from June to July?

Use the following graph to answer Exercises 15–16.

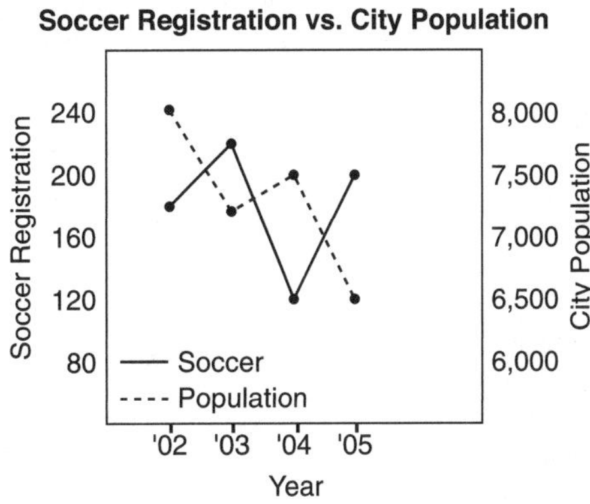

15. Between which two years did the greatest change in soccer registrations occur?

16. If the city population grew in 2006 and the yearly relationship between soccer registration and city population remained the same as it had been since 2002, would the number of soccer registrations in 2006 likely be greater than or less than it was in 2005?

Use the following graph to answer Exercises 17–18.

Average Remodeling Expenditures (%)

Other 25%
Kitchen 35%
Bedrooms 15%
Bathrooms 25%

2004

17. Remodeling media rooms accounts for about 40% of the "Other" section, accounting for $500,000 in expenditures. What is the total amount spent on remodeling "Other" rooms?

18. In a given year, if 12% of the total expenditures allocated to kitchen remodeling in 2004 were reallocated evenly across the remaining three categories, what would be the new percentage amounts for each category?

Use the following graph to answer Exercises 19–20.

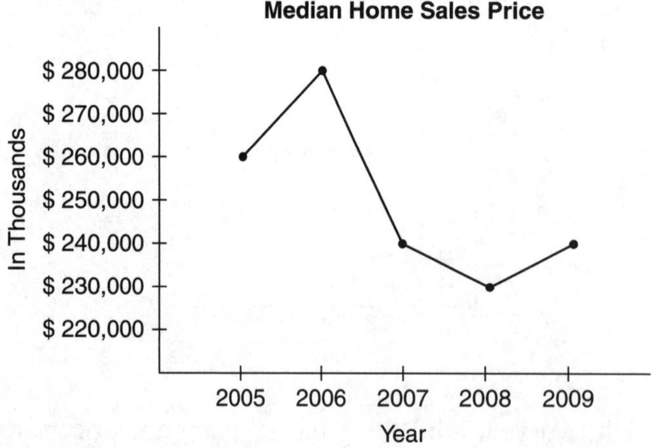

19. What is the percent decrease, to the nearest tenth, of the median home sales price from 2007 to 2008?

20. If the same price increase from 2008 to 2009 happened between 2009 and 2010, what was the median sales price in 2010?

Advanced

Use the following graph to answer Exercises 21–22.

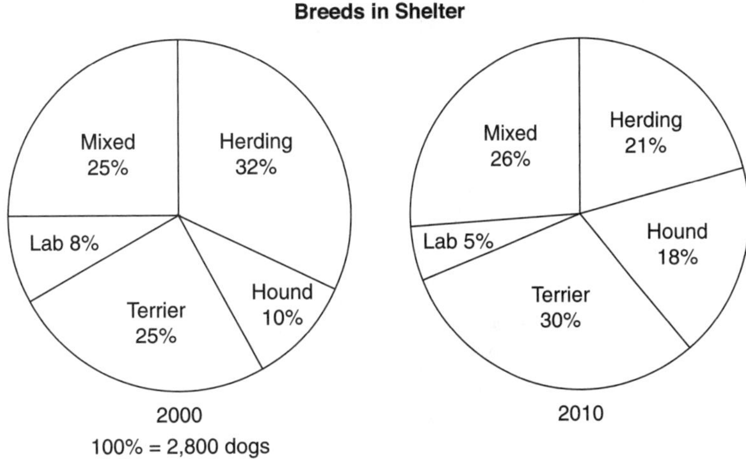

21. In 2010, if there were 850 herding dogs in the shelter, what was the total number of hound breed dogs that entered the shelter in 2000 and 2010 combined?

22. In 2010, there were 850 herding dogs in the shelter. If 40% of the mixed-breed dogs that entered the shelter in 2010 were smaller than 15 pounds, how many mixed-breed dogs were over 15 pounds?

Use the following graph to answer Exercises 23–24.

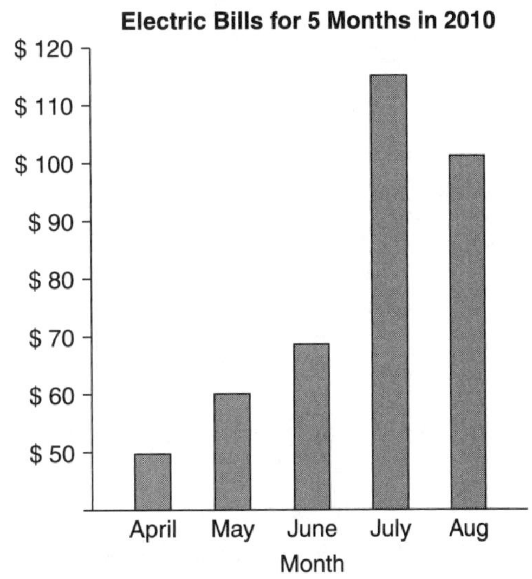

23. After the July electric bill, the homeowner increased the average temperature for the air conditioner by 2 degrees from 76 to 78 degrees. His electric company claims that every 2-degree increase will decrease the electric bill by 4%. Assuming the electric company's claim is correct, what would the electric bill in August have been without this change (to the nearest dollar)?

24. Some electric companies offer a billing option where you pay an average monthly bill. If this customer were paying an average of the five months listed, what would each month's bill have been?

Use the following graph to answer Exercises 25–26.

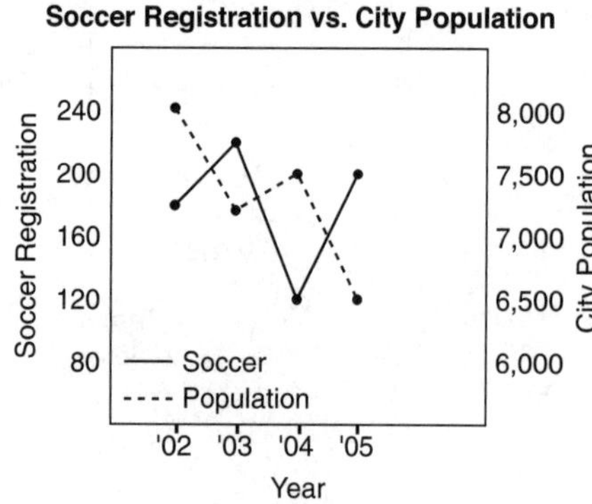

25. During the year that soccer registrations increased by approximately 80, what was the concomitant change in population?

26. During the only year in which the city population increased, what was the percent decrease in soccer registrations, rounded to the nearest whole number?

Use the following graph to answer Exercises 27–28.

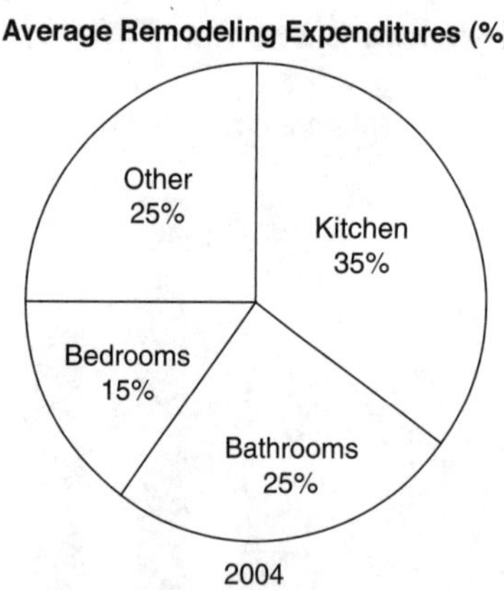

27. If \$720 million was spent on remodeling bedrooms in 2004, how much was spent remodeling kitchens?

28. On average, a homeowner will see a 75 percent return on investment for kitchen remodels. One homeowner increased the value of her home by \$6,000 by remodeling her kitchen. Assuming that she gets the same percent return for bathroom remodels and that her spending follows 2004 averages, how much more would her home increase in value (to the nearest dollar) if she also remodeled the bathrooms?

Use the following graph to answer Exercises 29–30.

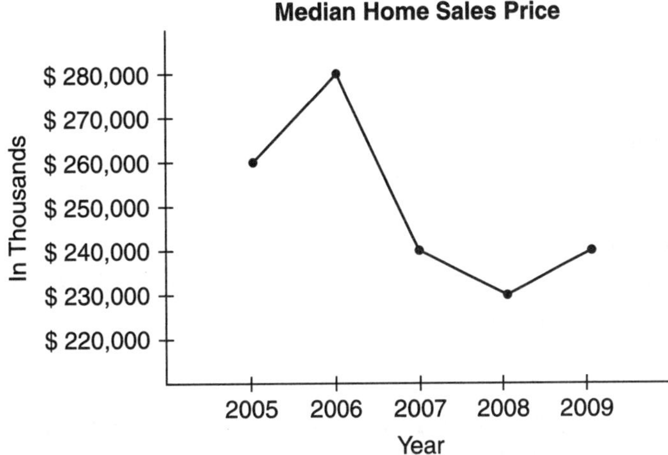

29. In 2009, a homeowner put his house on the market. If the average drop from listing price to sales price is 6%, what was the minimum price (in whole dollars) that the house could have been listed at so that it sold at the price greater than or equal to the median price?

30. A real estate agent says the percent change between 2007 and 2008 is the same as between 2008 and 2009. Is this true or false?

DATA GRAPHS AND TABLES ANSWERS KEY

BASIC

1. 1,400

There were a total of 2,800 dogs and 50% (25% mixed and 25% terrier) belong to the two desired breeds. $2,800 \times 0.50 = 1,400$.

2. Herding and terrier

Half of the dogs in 2010 would be 50%. The two categories whose sum is closest to 50% are herding (21%) and terrier (30%), which make up 51% of the total.

3. Less

The August bill is a little over $100. The September bill will be about $50 if it is half of the August bill. This is less than the May bill of $60.

4. $55

To find how much greater the July bill was, subtract: $\$115 - \$60 = \$55$.

5. Decrease

The solid line represents soccer registrations, and it decreased from 2003 to 2004.

6. Decrease of 500

The population in 2002 was about 8,000, and the population in 2004 was about 7,500. Subtracting, we find the change in population was a decrease of 500.

7. 20%

Kitchen remodels accounted for 35% of the total money spent, while bedrooms accounted for 15%. Subtract to find how much more money was spent remodeling kitchens: $35\% - 15\% = 20\%$.

8. $2,500

Since the graph shows the average way money was spent, we can find the average amount spent on bathroom remodeling by multiplying the total spent by the percent typically spent on bathrooms: $\$10,000 \times 25\% = \$2,500$.

9. $40,000 price drop

The median sales price changed from $280,000 in 2006 to $240,000 in 2007, so there was a $40,000 drop.

10. 4.3%

The percent increase can be found using the formula $\frac{\textit{Amount of increase}}{\textit{Original whole}}$; substitute the known values and solve: $\frac{(240 - 230)}{230}$ or 4.3%.

Intermediate

11. 1%

The labs and terriers represented 33% (25% + 8%), and the herding breeds represented 32% of the total. Subtract: 33% − 32% = 1%. Of the total, 1 percent more labs and terriers entered the shelter in 2000 than herding breeds.

12. Less

In 2000, a total of 2,800 dogs were admitted to the shelter. Of that number, 32% were herding breed dogs: 2,800 × 0.32 = 896. The 850 herding breed dogs admitted in 2010 were less than the 896 admitted in 2000.

13. $603

You know that the total amount of the bills for April through August represents 65% of the total electricity costs for the year. Then 48 + 60 + 67 + 115 + 102 = 392, and $392 is equal to 65% of the total. Divide $392 by 65% to find the total cost for the year: $392 ÷ 0.65 ≈ $603.

14. 72%

To find percent change, use the formula $\frac{\textit{Amount of change}}{\textit{Original whole}}$.

Evaluating, this gives $\frac{(115-67)}{67}=\frac{48}{67}\approx 0.72$

15. 2003 and 2004

The greatest change in the solid line (soccer registrations) happened between 2003 and 2004.

16. Less

Given the relationship between population and soccer registration shown on the graph, if the population increases in 2006, the number of soccer registrations would likely have decreased.

17. $1,250,000

If $500,000 is 40% of the total "Other" remodeling, then dividing $500,000 by 40% will give the total for the "Other" section: $500,000 ÷ 0.40 = $1,250,000.

18. Kitchens: 23%; Bathrooms: 29%; Bedrooms: 19%; Other: 29%

Subtract 12 percent from Kitchens to get 23 percent. Then, divide the 12 percent evenly among the other three categories, which means adding 4 percent to each category's percentage.

19. 4.2%

In 2007, the median sales price was $240,000, and in 2008, the median sales price was $230,000. The difference in price is $10,000, and the original price is $240,000. To find the percent change, take the change in price, divide by the original, and multiply by 100%:

$$\frac{10{,}000}{240{,}000}\times 100\% = \frac{1}{24}\times 100\% = \frac{100}{24}\% \approx 4.2\%$$

20. \$250,000

From 2008 to 2009, the median sales price increased \$10,000. If this same increase occurs from 2009 to 2010, then the median sales price will be \$240,000 + \$10,000, or \$250,000.

ADVANCED

21. 1,009

First, you need to find the total number of dogs that entered the shelter in 2010: $850 \div 0.21 \approx 4{,}048$. The hound breed made up 18% of that number: $4{,}048 \times 0.18 \approx 729$. In 2000, you know that 10% of the 2,800 dogs that entered were hound breed dogs: $2{,}800 \times 0.1 = 280$. Now add the two totals together: $729 + 280 = 1{,}009$ total hound breed dogs.

22. 631

First, you need to find the total number of dogs that entered the shelter in 2010: $850 \div 0.21 \approx 4{,}048$. Of that total, 26% were mixed breed dogs: $4{,}048 \times 0.26 = 1{,}052$. If 40% of those dogs weighed less than 15 pounds, then 60% of them weighed more than 15 pounds: $1{,}052 \times 0.60 \approx 631$.

23. \$106

The current August bill, \$102, is 4% less than what the bill would have been without the adjustment. So if the bill would have been x, then $x - 0.04x = 102$. Solving this equation for x yields $x = 106.25$, which is \$106 rounded to the nearest dollar.

24. \$78.40

The sum of the bills is approximately \$392. Divide by 5 months to get about \$78.40.

25. 1,000

There was about an 80-person increase in soccer registrations from 2004-2005. During that same year, the population decreased by about 1,000.

26. 45%.

City population increased between 2003 and 2004. During that same period, soccer registrations dropped from about 220 to about 120, for an actual decrease of $220 - 120 = 100$. Because 100 is a bit less than half of 220, that's a percent decrease of just under 50%. Apply the percent change formula to find the actual value:

$$\textit{Percent change} = \frac{\textit{change}}{\textit{original}} \times 100\%$$

$$\textit{Percent change} = \frac{100}{220} \times 100\% \approx 45\%$$

27. \$1.68 Billion

\$720 million was 15% of the total. To find the total, use the formula *Percent* × *Whole* = *Part.* 15% × *Whole* = \$720 million.

\$720 million ÷ 0.15 = \$4.8 billion. Now you need to find 35% of this total: 35% × \$4.8 billion = \$1.68 billion.

28. $4,286

Use the formula *Percent* $\times$ *Whole* $=$ *Part* to find the total investment in the kitchen. If $6,000 is 75% of the total, substitute the known values and find the whole: 75% $\times$ *Whole* $=$ $6,000, so the total investment was $8,000. According to the chart, the ratio of money spent on bathrooms to money spent on kitchens is 25:35, or 5:7. So the homeowner spent $\$8{,}000 \times \frac{5}{7} = \$5{,}714$. Multiply by .75 to get $4,286.

It's not really necessary to calculate the amount of money the homeowner spent on bathroom remodeling, though. If returns are identical for different types of remodeling, then the returns will also be in a ratio of 5:7. Thus, $\$6{,}000 \times \frac{5}{7} = \$4{,}286$.

29. $255,320

To find the list price, we need to find the price that when 6% of it is subtracted will equal $240,000, the median price in 2009. Call the listing price *L*. Then 0.94*L* $=$ $240,000. Divide both sides by 0.94 to get a listing price of approximately $255,319.15. Since the question asks for the minimum whole dollar amount for the asking price that, when reduced by 6%, will yield a value greater than or equal to $240,000, the asking price must be rounded up to the nearest whole dollar, $255,320.

30. False

Use the formula $\frac{\textit{Amount of change}}{\textit{Original amount}}$ to compare the changes.

Change from 2007 to 2008: $\frac{(230 - 240)}{240} = -4.17\%$.

Change from 2008 to 2009: $\frac{(240 - 230)}{230} = 4.35\%$. Because $4.35 \neq 4.17$, the statement is false. The percent increase from 2008 to 2009 is actually more than the percent decrease in the previous year.

You don't need to do all the calculations for this problem to see that the real estate agent's statement is false. The numerators in the percent change equations for both sets of years have the same absolute value, but the denominators are different, so you know right away that the percent change for the two sets of years cannot be the same.

PROBABILITY

Probability involves situations that have a finite number of outcomes.

$$\textit{Probability} = \frac{\textit{Number of desired outcomes}}{\textit{Number of total possible outcomes}}$$

Example: If you have 12 shirts in a drawer and 9 of them are white, the probability of picking a white shirt at random is $\frac{9}{12} = \frac{3}{4}$. The probability can also be expressed as 0.75 or 75%.

Many probability questions involve finding the probability of a certain outcome after multiple repetitions of the same experiment or different experiments (a coin being tossed several times, etc.). These questions come in two forms: those in which each individual event must occur a certain way, and those in which individual events can have different outcomes.

To determine multiple-event probability where each individual event must occur a certain way:

- Figure out the probability for each individual event.
- Multiply the individual probabilities.

Example: If 2 students are chosen at random from a class with 5 girls and 5 boys, what's the probability that both students chosen will be girls? The probability that the first student chosen will be a girl is $\frac{5}{10} = \frac{1}{2}$, and since there would be 4 girls left out of 9 students, the probability that the second student chosen will be a girl is $\frac{4}{9}$. So the probability that both students chosen will be girls is $\frac{1}{2} \times \frac{4}{9} = \frac{1}{{}_1\not{2}} \times \frac{\not{4}^2}{9} = \frac{2}{9}$.

To determine multiple-event probability where individual events can have different types of outcomes, find the *total number of possible outcomes*. Do that by determining the number of possible outcomes for each individual event and multiplying these numbers together. Find the *number of desired outcomes* by listing out the possibilities.

Example: If a fair coin is tossed 4 times, what is the probability that at least 3 of the 4 tosses will come up heads?

There are 2 possible outcomes for each toss, so after 4 tosses there is a total of $2 \times 2 \times 2 \times 2 = 16$ possible outcomes. List all the possibilities where at least 3 of the 4 tosses come up heads:

H, H, H, T	H, T, H, H	H, H, H, H
H, H, T, H	T, H, H, H	

There's a total of 5 possible desired outcomes. So the probability that at least 3 of the 4 tosses will come up heads is $\frac{5}{16}$.

Probabilities range from 0, for an event that will certainly not occur, to 1, for an event that is certain to occur.

The sum of the probability that an event will occur and the probability that it will not occur is always equal to 1. Sometimes it is simpler to determine the probability of an event occurring by calculating the probability that an event will not occur and subtracting it from 1.

Example: What is the probability that at least 1 of the 4 coin tosses from the previous example will come up heads?

In this case, to list the desired outcomes, you would have to include all the ways to get 1 head, 2 heads, 3 heads, and 4 heads. That is a lot to consider, would become quite time-consuming, and could risk your overlooking one of the desired outcomes. Instead, by finding the probability that at least 1 of the coin tosses will *not* land on heads, you only need to list ways to get 0 heads. Only one outcome has 0 heads (T, T, T, T). Therefore, out of 16 total possible outcomes, as determined in the previous example, 1 outcome is not the desired outcome. So, the answer is:

$$1 - \frac{1}{16} = \frac{15}{16}$$

PROBABILITY EXERCISES

BASIC

Use this information to answer Exercises 1–2:

In a bag there are 6 red marbles, 7 blue marbles, and 3 black marbles.

1. What is the probability of drawing a blue marble?

2. What is the probability of drawing a red or black marble?

3. Find the probability of tossing at least 1 tail with 2 tosses of a fair coin.

4. Find the probability of randomly selecting 2 blue socks, one at a time without replacement, from a drawer with 14 white and 8 blue socks.

5. If there are 8 people (3 women and 5 men) under consideration for 2 positions on the city council, what is the probability of both positions being filled by women if the people to fill the positions are chosen randomly?

6. If an integer is randomly selected from all positive 2-digit integers, what is the probability that the integer chosen has a 3 in the tens place?

7. Charles says the probability of tossing 3 heads in a row is $\frac{3}{2}$, or $3\left(\frac{1}{2}\right)$. Is he correct?

8. Write the probability 0.80 as a reduced fraction.

9. The weather forecast says there's a 40% chance of rain tomorrow. What is the probability of it raining?

10. Colorado is said to have about 300 days of sunshine per year. If a day is randomly selected, what is the probability that it will be sunny? (Assume 365 days in a year.)

INTERMEDIATE

Use this information to answer Exercises 11–12:

In a bag there are 6 red marbles, 7 blue marbles, and 3 black marbles.

11. What is the probability of NOT drawing a black marble?

12. If two marbles are drawn without replacing the first, what is the probability of drawing a blue and then a red marble?

13. In a pet store, there are 8 puppies and 12 kittens. If a staff member randomly chooses 3 pets for this Saturday's adoption time, what is the probability that all 3 will be puppies?

14. A fair coin is tossed 3 times. What is the probability of NOT getting zero tails across all the three tosses?

15. What is the probability of rolling a 1, 2, or 3 when tossing one fair 6-sided die?

16. Find the probability of getting a sum of 6 when tossing 2 fair 6-sided dice.

17. Teri's work cafeteria offers a lunch with an entrée and a side. If there are 3 entrees (spaghetti, turkey, and pizza) and 4 sides (potatoes, French fries, broccoli, and salad), what is the probability of Teri randomly choosing pizza and salad?

18. A basketball player shoots two free throws, and each free throw is worth 1 point. If the team needs 2 points to win and the probability of the player making a basket is $\frac{1}{2}$, what is the probability that the team will win?

19. Each of 48 employees has entered for a chance to win 3 prizes. If the probability of drawing any given employee is the same, and if winning a prize makes the employee ineligible for the remaining prizes, what is the probability of any given employee winning a prize?

20. Twelve people—3 men and 9 women—want to attend a conference. If 4 people are chosen at random from this group, what is the probability that no men will attend the conference?

Advanced

Use this information to answer Exercises 21 and 22:

A bag has only 6 red marbles, 7 blue marbles, and 3 black marbles.

21. What is the probability of NOT drawing a red marble?

22. What is the probability of NOT drawing any red marble in three draws, when the marbles are replaced after each is drawn?

23. A spinner has the following six colored sections of equal size: 1 red, 1 green, 3 blue, and 1 white. With two spins, what is the probability of the spinner landing on white twice?

24. A fair 12-sided die is rolled once. What is the probability of it landing on 5, 7, or 9?

25. If a fair coin is tossed 3 times, what is the probability that the coin will land heads up exactly 2 times?

26. If there is a 30% chance of rain on Tuesday and a 40% chance of rain on Wednesday, what is the probability that there will be NO rain on both Tuesday and Wednesday?

27. In the game of bingo, each of the numbers from 1 to 60 is written on a ball and placed in a round cage. What is the probability that the first 2 balls that are drawn out of the cage will be 1 even and then 1 odd number, assuming that the balls are not replaced until the next game's drawing?

28. Julia is picking 4 books randomly from a bookshelf. If she has 18 science fiction books, 6 drama books, and 8 how-to books, what is the probability that she will pick 3 science fiction books and then 1 how-to book?

29. A mechanic has 4 metric, 6 standard, and 3 dual wrenches in his pail. If 3 wrenches are grabbed at random and not replaced, what is the probability that one metric, then one standard, and then one dual wrench will be picked?

30. Ten people, 3 women and 7 men, are running for 4 school board positions. If all candidates have an equal chance to win any of the 4 positions, what is the probability that NO women will get a position?

PROBABILITY ANSWERS KEY

Basic

1. $\frac{7}{16}$

$$\text{Probability} = \frac{\text{Number of desired outcomes}}{\text{Number of total possible outcomes}}$$

There are 7 blue marbles, or 7 desired outcomes, and 16 marbles in all, or 16 total possible outcomes. This means the probability of selecting a blue marble is $\frac{7}{16}$.

2. $\frac{9}{16}$

$$\text{Probability} = \frac{\text{Number of desired outcomes}}{\text{Number of total possible outcomes}}$$

There are 6 red marbles and 3 black marbles for a total of 9 desired outcomes, and 16 marbles in all, or 16 total possible outcomes. This means the probability of selecting a red or black marble is $\frac{9}{16}$.

3. $\frac{3}{4}$

There are 2 possible outcomes for each toss, so after 2 tosses there is a total of $2 \times 2 = 4$ total possible outcomes. List the possibilities where at least one of the coins comes up tails:

TT

TH

HT

There are 3 possible outcomes where there is at least 1 tail. So, the probability that at least one of the tosses will come up tails is $\frac{3}{4}$.

4. $\frac{4}{33}$

$$\text{Probability} = \frac{\text{Number of desired outcomes}}{\text{Number of total possible outcomes}}$$

There is a total of 22 socks, so the total number of possible outcomes is 22 for the first sock picked. The first draw has a probability of $\frac{8}{22}$. Since there would then be 7 blue socks remaining out of 21 left in the drawer, the probability that the second sock selected would be blue is $\frac{7}{21}$. Because the selections of socks are independent events, to find the combined probability, multiply the two together: $\frac{8}{22} \times \frac{7}{21} = \frac{56}{462} = \frac{4}{33}$.

5. $\mathbf{\frac{3}{28}}$

The probability of a woman randomly getting the first position is $\frac{3}{8}$. The probability of a woman randomly getting the second position, given that the first position has also been filled by a woman, is $\frac{2}{7}$. To find the probability of both events happening, multiply the two probabilities: $\frac{3}{\cancel{8}_4} \times \frac{\cancel{2}^1}{7} = \frac{3}{28}$.

6. $\mathbf{\frac{1}{9}}$

There can be 9 different digits in the tens place. So, the probability of the integer chosen being a 3 is $\frac{1}{9}$.

7. No

Remember that probability is never less than zero or greater than 1. The probability would actually be $\frac{1}{2} \times \frac{1}{2} \times \frac{1}{2} = \frac{1}{8}$.

8. $\mathbf{\frac{4}{5}}$

To write the probability as a fraction, convert the decimal 0.80 to a fraction, $\frac{8}{10}$, and reduce.

9. $\mathbf{\frac{2}{5}}$ **or 0.4**

If there is a 40% chance of rain, this is the same as a probability of $\frac{40}{100}$ or $\frac{2}{5}$ or 0.4.

10. $\mathbf{\frac{60}{73}}$

The number of desired outcomes is 300. The total number of possible outcomes is 365. So, the probability of the desired outcome is $\frac{300}{365}$ or $\frac{60}{73}$.

Intermediate

11. $\mathbf{\frac{13}{16}}$

$$\textit{Probability} = \frac{\textit{Number of desired outcomes}}{\textit{Number of total possible outcomes}}$$

Because $6 + 7 = 13$ of the marbles in the bag are not black, there are 13 desired outcomes. There are $6 + 7 + 3 = 16$ marbles in all, or 16 total possible outcomes. This means the probability of NOT selecting a black marble is $\frac{13}{16}$.

12. $\mathbf{\frac{7}{40}}$

The probability of drawing a blue marble in the first draw is $\frac{7}{16}$. Since that blue marble is not returned to the bag, there are only 15 marbles remaining, but all 6 red marbles are still there as possible desired outcomes for the second draw. That means the probably of selecting a red marble on the second draw is $\frac{6}{15}$. To find the probability of both happening, multiply the probabilities:

$$\frac{7}{\cancel{16}_8} \times \frac{\cancel{6}^3}{15} = \frac{21}{120} = \frac{7}{40}$$

13. $\mathbf{\frac{14}{285}}$

The probability of getting a puppy on the first selection is $\frac{8}{20}$ or $\frac{2}{5}$. Since there are 7 puppies out of 19 pets left, the probability of getting a puppy on the second selection is $\frac{7}{19}$. Now for the third selection there are 6 puppies out of 18 pets left, so the probability of getting a puppy on this selection is $\frac{6}{18}$ or $\frac{1}{3}$. To find the total probability, multiply the 3 fractions together: $\frac{2}{5} \times \frac{7}{19} \times \frac{1}{3} = \frac{14}{285}$.

14. $\mathbf{\frac{7}{8}}$

The question essentially asks for the probability of not getting all heads. The probability of getting a head on the first toss is $\frac{1}{2}$. In fact, the probability of getting a head on any of the 3 tosses is $\frac{1}{2}$, so the probability of getting 3 heads (or no tails) is $\frac{1}{2} \times \frac{1}{2} \times \frac{1}{2} = \frac{1}{8}$. Since the question asks for the probability that the coin does NOT land on heads for all three tosses, subtract the probability of the non-desired outcome (all heads, no tails) from 1: $1 - \frac{1}{8} = \frac{7}{8}$.

15. $\mathbf{\frac{1}{2}}$

$$\textit{Probability} = \frac{\textit{Number of desired outcomes}}{\textit{Number of total possible outcomes}}$$

There are six total possible outcomes when rolling a 6-sided die. The number of desired outcomes in this case is 3: rolling a 1, a 2, or a 3. So, the probability of rolling a 1, 2, or 3 is $\frac{3}{6}$ or $\frac{1}{2}$.

16. $\frac{5}{36}$

There are six possible outcomes for each die that is rolled. Since there are 2 dice, there are $6 \times 6 = 36$ total possible outcomes. List the possibilities where the sum of the 2 dice would add up to 6:

$1 + 5$

$2 + 4$

$3 + 3$

$4 + 2$

$5 + 1$

There are 5 possible outcomes where the sum of the 2 dice is 6, so the probability of rolling 2 dice whose sum is 6 is $\frac{5}{36}$.

17. $\frac{1}{12}$

The probability of randomly selecting pizza (or any given entrée) is $\frac{1}{3}$. The probability of randomly selecting salad (or any given side) is $\frac{1}{4}$. To find the total probability, multiply the two fractions together: $\frac{1}{3} \times \frac{1}{4} = \frac{1}{12}$.

18. $\frac{1}{4}$

There are 2 possible outcomes for each shot, successful or unsuccessful. The probability of the player making the first shot is $\frac{1}{2}$, and the probability of making the second shot is also $\frac{1}{2}$. To find the probability of both events occurring, multiply the two fractions together: $\frac{1}{2} \times \frac{1}{2} = \frac{1}{4}$.

19. $\frac{1}{16}$

The best way to find the probability that any given employee will win one of the prizes is to find the probability that he or she wins *none* of the prizes, then subtract that from 1. The probability of not winning the first prize is $\frac{47}{48}$. Then, since the winner of each prize is made ineligible, the chances of not winning the second and third prizes are $\frac{46}{47}$ and $\frac{45}{46}$, respectively. To combine these probabilities, multiply them:

$$\frac{47}{48} \times \frac{46}{47} \times \frac{45}{46} = \frac{\cancel{47}}{48} \times \frac{\cancel{46}}{\cancel{47}} \times \frac{45}{\cancel{46}} = \frac{45}{48} = \frac{15}{16}$$

Because the probability of losing all three prizes is $\frac{15}{16}$, the probability of winning one of them is $1 - \frac{15}{16} = \frac{1}{16}$.

20. $\frac{14}{55}$

The probability of no men attending is the same as that of 4 women attending. The probability of a woman being randomly selected for the first spot is $\frac{9}{12}$. Then the probabilities for a woman to be chosen for the second, third, and fourth spots are $\frac{8}{11}$, $\frac{7}{10}$, and $\frac{6}{9}$, respectively. Multiply the fractions together to find the total probability: $\frac{9}{12} \times \frac{8}{11} \times \frac{7}{10} \times \frac{6}{9} = \frac{14}{55}$.

Advanced

21. $\frac{5}{8}$

There are 16 total marbles in the bag. Of these 16, 7 are blue and 3 are black; the rest are red. The probability of drawing a marble that is NOT red is $\frac{7+3}{16} = \frac{10}{16} = \frac{5}{8}$.

22. $\frac{125}{512}$

The probability of NOT drawing a red on the first draw is $\frac{10}{16}$, which can be simplified to $\frac{5}{8}$. Then, since the marble is placed back in the bag after each draw, the probability of not drawing a red on the second and third draws remain $\frac{5}{8}$ for each. Multiply the fractions together: $\frac{5}{8} \times \frac{5}{8} \times \frac{5}{8} = \frac{125}{512}$.

23. $\frac{1}{36}$

The probability of landing on white with the first spin is $\frac{1}{6}$. Then, the probability of landing on white again is $\frac{1}{6}$. Multiply the fractions to find the total probability: $\frac{1}{36}$.

24. $\frac{1}{4}$

There are 3 desired outcomes: rolling a 5, a 7, or a 9. There are 12 total possible outcomes. The probability is then $\frac{3}{12}$, or $\frac{1}{4}$.

25. $\frac{3}{8}$

There are 2 possible outcomes for each toss, so after 3 tosses there are $2 \times 2 \times 2 = 8$ total possible outcomes. To determine how many combinations exist where there are exactly 2 heads, use the combination formula: $\frac{3!}{2!(3-2)!} = \frac{3 \times 2 \times 1}{2 \times 1 \times 1} = \frac{6}{2} = 3$. So there are 3 ways of obtaining exactly 2 heads (shown below) out of 8 total possible arrangements. The probability is $\frac{3}{8}$.

HTH

HHT

THH

26. 42%

Since there is a 30% chance of rain on Tuesday, there is a 70% chance of NO rain on Tuesday. Similarly, if there is a 40% chance of rain on Wednesday, there is a 60% chance of NO rain on Wednesday. To find the probability that there will be no rain for *both* days, multiply the two probabilities together: $70\% \times 60\% = 0.7 \times 0.6 = 0.42 = 42\%$.

27. $\frac{15}{59}$

The probability of the first ball being even is $\frac{30}{60}$ or $\frac{1}{2}$. Then, the probability of the second ball being odd is $\frac{30}{59}$. So, the total probability is $\frac{1}{2} \times \frac{30}{59}$, or $\frac{15}{59}$.

28. $\frac{204}{4495}$

The probability of the first book being a science fiction book is $\frac{18}{32}$. Then, the subsequent probabilities are $\frac{17}{31}$ and $\frac{16}{30}$ for selecting science fiction books. Then, the probability of selecting a how-to book is $\frac{8}{29}$. Multiplying them together and reducing gives $\frac{204}{4495}$.

29. $\frac{6}{143}$

The probability of the first wrench being metric is $\frac{4}{13}$. Then, the probability of the next being standard is $\frac{6}{12}$ or $\frac{1}{2}$, and then the probability of the next being dual is $\frac{3}{11}$. Multiplying them together and reducing gives $\frac{6}{143}$.

30. $\frac{1}{6}$

No woman getting a position is the same as all the positions being filled by men. The probability of the first position being filled by a man is $\frac{7}{10}$, and the probabilities that the subsequent 3 positions would be filled by men are $\frac{6}{9}$ or $\frac{2}{3}$, $\frac{5}{8}$, and $\frac{4}{7}$, respectively. To find the total probability of 4 men being randomly selected to fill the positions, multiply the fractions: $\frac{7}{10} \times \frac{2}{3} \times \frac{5}{8} \times \frac{4}{7} = \frac{1}{6}$.

PART FOUR

Advanced Math Practice

CHAPTER 10

High-Difficulty Question Sets

INTRODUCTION

In this chapter, you'll find four 20-question practice sets consisting entirely of questions most test takers find challenging. Following each practice set, you'll find the answer key, as well as complete explanations for every question.

Remember that because the GRE is a Multi-Stage Test (MST), a strong performance on the first scored Quantitative section will cause you to see a high-difficulty second section. This high-difficulty section will likely include a mix of medium- and high-difficulty questions, with a few on the very high end of the difficulty scale. If you are aiming for an exceptionally high score on the Quantitative part of the exam, then you will want to be sure you can handle even these very toughest questions.

That's exactly what the four practice sets in this chapter are for: to help you prepare for the most advanced math questions the GRE may present to you on Test Day. Many of the questions in these practice sets ask you to combine multiple concepts in order to arrive at a solution, and many may take longer than two minutes to answer. Again, on Test Day, even a high-difficulty Quantitative section will not consist entirely of questions like the ones here; many will be less challenging. Therefore, we suggest that you work through these practice sets without timing yourself. Instead, focus on mastering the various ways the GRE can present math content to make questions more difficult.

If you are not yet comfortable with at least some of the exercises marked "advanced" in the preceding chapters of this book, then continue to review the arithmetic, algebra, geometry, and other topics presented there until you are finding the correct answers to at least half of those advanced exercises. Then you'll be ready to tackle the tougher questions here.

As always, be sure to ***review the explanation*** to every problem you do in this chapter. There is often more than one path to the correct answer; with that in mind, we've included multiple solutions to a number of these questions. Noting a different way to work through a problem, even if you got that problem right, is a powerful way to enhance your critical thinking skills—and it's ultimately those skills that you will be relying on in order to achieve a very high score on Test Day.

Ready to take your Quantitative score to the next level? Then turn the page and begin work!

ADVANCED MATH QUESTIONS PRACTICE SET 1

1.

$$bc < 0$$
$$ab > 0$$
$$cd < 0$$

Quantity A	Quantity B
ac	bd

Ⓐ Quantity A is greater.
Ⓑ Quantity B is greater.
Ⓒ The two quantities are equal.
Ⓓ The relationship cannot be determined from the information given.

2.

$$x > 0$$

The probability that event A will occur is x, and the probability that event A will not occur is y, where $y > 3x$.

Quantity A	Quantity B
x	$\frac{1}{5}$

Ⓐ Quantity A is greater.
Ⓑ Quantity B is greater.
Ⓒ The two quantities are equal.
Ⓓ The relationship cannot be determined from the information given.

3. List A contains 7 consecutive multiples of 4 and nothing else. The average (arithmetic mean) of the 3 greatest integers in list A is 80.

Quantity A	Quantity B
The average (arithmetic mean) of the 5 smallest integers in list A	68

Ⓐ Quantity A is greater.
Ⓑ Quantity B is greater.
Ⓒ The two quantities are equal.
Ⓓ The relationship cannot be determined from the information given.

4.

$$b > 1$$

$$\frac{\left(b^4\right)^x\left(b^{30}\right)}{\left(b^2\right)^7} < \left(b^x\right)\left(b^{37}\right)$$

Quantity A	Quantity B
x	8

Ⓐ Quantity A is greater.
Ⓑ Quantity B is greater.
Ⓒ The two quantities are equal.
Ⓓ The relationship cannot be determined from the information given.

5. The random variable X has a normal distribution with a mean of 70.

Quantity A	Quantity B
The probability that $-30 \leq X \leq 150$	The probability that $-60 \leq X \leq 120$

Ⓐ Quantity A is greater.
Ⓑ Quantity B is greater.
Ⓒ The two quantities are equal.
Ⓓ The relationship cannot be determined from the information given.

6. z is a positive integer.

$$x = 12y + 25$$
$$y = 7z + 5$$

Quantity A	Quantity B
The remainder when x is divided by 42	The remainder when y is divided by 2

Ⓐ Quantity A is greater.
Ⓑ Quantity B is greater.
Ⓒ The two quantities are equal.
Ⓓ The relationship cannot be determined from the information given.

7.

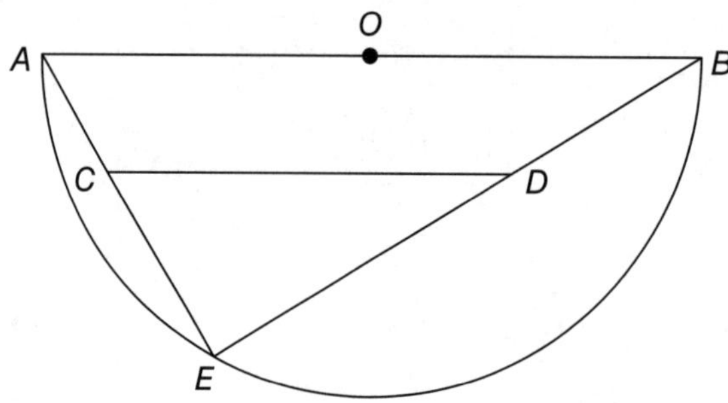

The area of semicircle O is 16π.

$$\angle CDE = \angle ABE = 30^\circ$$
$$AC = \sqrt{2}$$

Quantity A	Quantity B
DE	$3\sqrt{5}$

Ⓐ Quantity A is greater.
Ⓑ Quantity B is greater.
Ⓒ The two quantities are equal.
Ⓓ The relationship cannot be determined from the information given.

8. $a:b = 3:1$ $a:d = 15:2$ $c:e = 7:9$ $c:d = 10:3$

If $e = 60$, what is the value of b?

Ⓐ 20
Ⓑ 35
Ⓒ 70
Ⓓ 180
Ⓔ The value cannot be determined from the information given.

9. What is the area of the figure bounded by lines described by the following equations?

$$y + 2 = 2x$$
$$\frac{x^3 - 5}{11} = 2$$
$$\frac{y - 5}{2} = x$$
$$(x + 2)^5 = 0$$

Ⓐ 6
Ⓑ 12
Ⓒ 17
Ⓓ 35
Ⓔ 56

10. Both x and y are integers. Which of the following expressions must be the square of an integer?

Indicate <u>all</u> such expressions.

[A] $(x + y)(x - y) + 8xy + 17y^2$

[B] $9x^4 - 12x^2y^2 + 4y^4$

[C] $x^6 + 2x^3y^3 + y^6$

11. Sequence S is the sequence of numbers $a_1, a_2, a_3, \ldots, a_n$. For each positive integer n, the nth number a_n is defined by $a_n = \frac{n+1}{3n}$. What is the product of the first 53 numbers in sequence S?

   (A) $\frac{2}{3^{53}}$
   (B) $\frac{2}{3^{50}}$
   (C) $\frac{2}{3^{49}}$
   (D) $\frac{3}{2^{50}}$
   (E) $\frac{2}{3^{25}}$

12. A group of 8 machines that work at the same constant rate can complete 14 jobs in 7 hours. How many hours would it take 17 of these machines to complete 34 of these jobs?

   (A) 4
   (B) 6
   (C) 8
   (D) 12
   (E) 16

13. Let $M = 10!$ and let $N = M^3$. If a is the greatest integer value of x such that 2^x is a factor of N, and b is the greatest integer value of y such that 3^y is a factor of N, then what is the value of $a + b$?

   (A) 18
   (B) 24
   (C) 33
   (D) 36
   (E) 54

14.

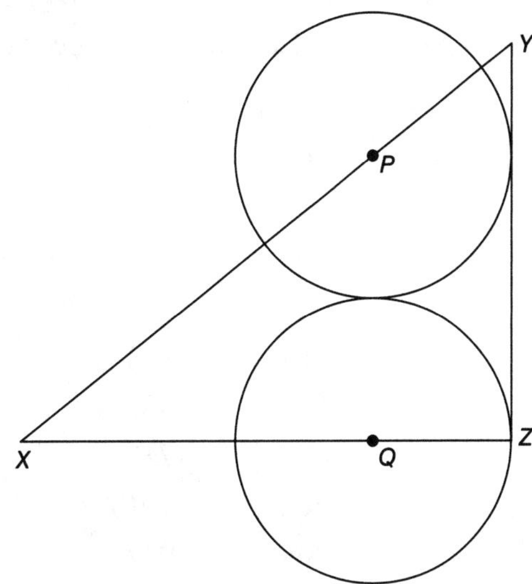

Circles P and Q each have a circumference of 10π and are each tangent to YZ. If $XZ = 17$, then $YZ =$

Ⓐ 10

Ⓑ $\frac{85}{6}$

Ⓒ $\frac{43}{3}$

Ⓓ 15

Ⓔ 17

15. A furniture company has warehouses in two cities: Madison and York. The Madison warehouse stocks desks, tables, and chairs in a ratio of 5:9:15. If all the desks and tables are transferred from the Madison warehouse to the York warehouse, increasing that warehouse's inventory of items by 20 percent, which of the following could be the number of items in the York warehouse after the transfer?

Indicate all such numbers.

[A] 168
[B] 280
[C] 290
[D] 336
[E] 504
[F] 600

16. The U.S. Weather Bureau has provided the following information about the total annual number of reported tornadoes in the United States for the years 1956 to 1975:

505	585
856	926
564	660
604	608
616	653
697	888
657	741
464	1,102
704	947
906	918

The average number of tornadoes per reported year is 730, and the standard deviation of the set is 168.

If one of the numbers in the data set is chosen at random, what is the probability that the number is less than the median and is not within one standard deviation of the mean?

Ⓐ 10%
Ⓑ 15%
Ⓒ 25%
Ⓓ 30%
Ⓔ 40%

17. Liquid A is 32 percent iodine and the rest water. Liquid B is 17 percent iodine and the rest water.

Quantity A	Quantity B
The percentage of a 23 percent iodine mixture of liquid A and liquid B that is liquid A	38%

Ⓐ Quantity A is greater.
Ⓑ Quantity B is greater.
Ⓒ The two quantities are equal.
Ⓓ The relationship cannot be determined from the information given.

Questions 18–20 refer to the following graphs.

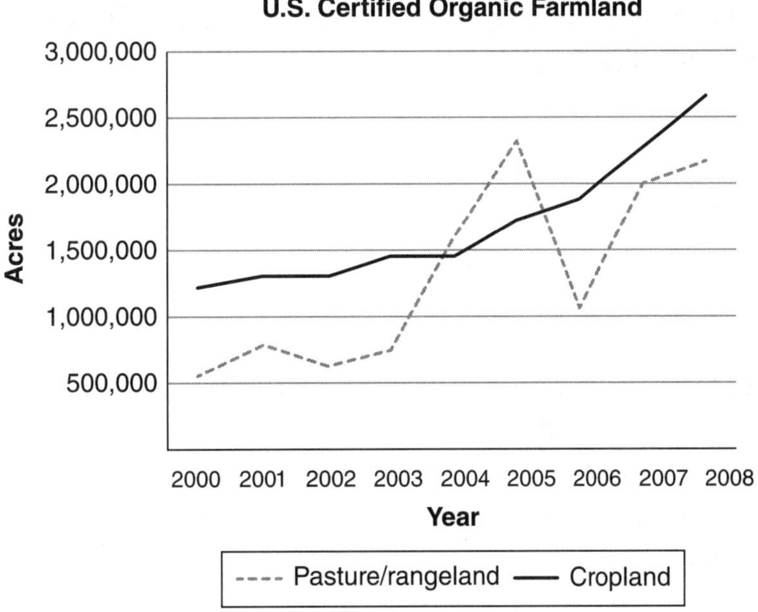

Source: U.S. Department of Agriculture, Economic Research Service, Table 2—U.S. certified organic farmland acreage, livestock numbers, and farm operations, 1992–2011 (based on information from USDA-accredited state and private organic certifiers), http://www.ers.usda.gov/data-products/organic-production.aspx

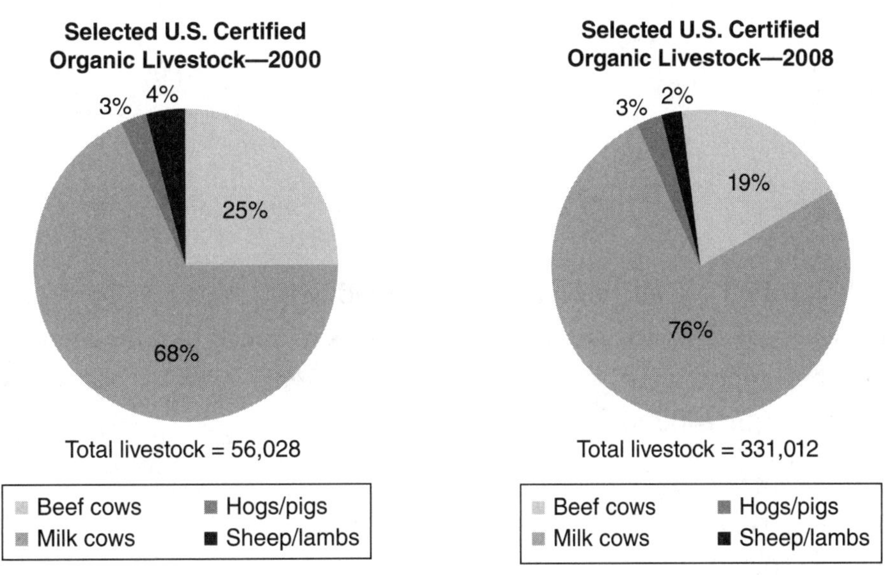

18. If U.S. certified organic farmland acreage increased 42 percent from 1997 to 2002, and the ratio of certified pasture to cropland was the same in 1997 as in 2006, what was the approximate percent increase in certified pasture between 1997 and 2008?

(A) 75%
(B) 155%
(C) 200%
(D) 260%
(E) 355%

19. In 2000, the ratio of U.S. certified organic sheep/lambs to certified organic turkeys was 1 to 4. If that year before Thanksgiving, a national organic retailers' association randomly selected an animal out of all of the hogs/pigs and turkeys as a seasonal mascot, what is the probability that a turkey was selected?

(A) $\frac{16}{3}$
(B) $\frac{19}{16}$
(C) $\frac{16}{19}$
(D) $\frac{3}{4}$
(E) $\frac{8}{11}$

20. If all certified organic pasture in the United States was used by beef cows and sheep, and if each sheep used four times as much pasture as each beef cow, then approximately how much did the acreage used by beef cows increase from 2000 to 2008?

(A) 475,000
(B) 1,200,000
(C) 1,550,000
(D) 2,100,000
(D) 2,500,000

ADVANCED MATH QUESTIONS PRACTICE SET 1 ANSWER KEY

1. B
2. D
3. C
4. B
5. A
6. D
7. A
8. B
9. D
10. A, B, C
11. B
12. C
13. D
14. B
15. A, D, E
16. A
17. A
18. E
19. C
20. B

ADVANCED MATH QUESTIONS PRACTICE SET 1 ANSWERS AND EXPLANATIONS

1. B

Start by analyzing the centered information. None of the individual variables can be isolated in a way that establishes its sign definitively. However, as ab is positive, there are only two possibilities: a and b are either both positive or both negative.

If both a and b are positive, then c must be negative in order to make $bc < 0$, in which case d must be positive so that $cd < 0$. Given those signs, Quantity A, ac, must be negative, and Quantity B, bd, must be positive.

If both a and b are negative, then c must be positive so that $bc < 0$, in which case d must be negative so that $cd < 0$. In this case, Quantity A, ac, is still negative, and Quantity B, bd, is still positive. Thus, in both cases, Quantity B is greater, and the correct answer is **(B)**.

2. D

The sum of the probability that an event will occur and the probability that the event will not occur is 1. So here, $x + y = 1$. Since $y > 3x$, you know that $x + y > x + 3x$, or, simplified, $x + y > 4x$. Since $x + y = 1$, you also know that $1 > 4x$, or $4x < 1$. Dividing both sides of this inequality by 4, you get $x < \frac{1}{4}$. Since $x > 0$, you know that $0 < x < \frac{1}{4}$. This is the range of values that Quantity A must fall into. Quantity B is $\frac{1}{5}$, which is within the range of values that Quantity A can be equal to; there are values in that range that are both smaller and larger than $\frac{1}{5}$. Since more than one relationship between the quantities is possible, the relationship between them cannot be determined.

Choice **(D)** is correct.

3. C

Start with the centered information: a list of 7 consecutive multiples of 4. Draw seven dashes to represent the numbers in the list, with a view to filling in what you know:

_ _ _ _ _ _ _

The last three numbers in the list are the greatest, and their average is 80. Because they are evenly spaced, 80 is not just the average of the three, but also their median. Because the three numbers are multiples of 4, the other two are 76 and 84:

_ _ _ _ 76 80 84

Now fill in the rest of List *A*, going backward from 76, with consecutive multiples of 4. The result looks like this:

60 64 68 72 76 80 84

Again, the average of an evenly spaced list is also its median. So to find Quantity A, just take the middle number of the first five elements in the list, which are

60 64 68 72 76

The median, which is also the average, is 68.

Quantity A is 68 and Quantity B is 68. The quantities are equal, and choice **(C)** is correct.

4. B

Use these exponent rules to solve this problem:

(i) $(a^c)^d = a^{cd}$

(ii) $a^c a^d = a^{c+d}$

(iii) $\frac{a^c}{a^d} = a^{c-d}$

Start by simplifying the inequality:

$$\frac{(b^4)^x(b^{30})}{(b^2)^7} < (b^x)(b^{37})$$

$$\frac{(b^{4x})(b^{30})}{b^{14}} < b^{x+37}$$

$$\frac{b^{4x+30}}{b^{14}} < b^{x+37}$$

$$b^{4x+30-14} < b^{x+37}$$

$$b^{4x+16} < b^{x+37}$$

Because $b > 1$, the exponent on the left side of the inequality must be less than the one on the right, so you can conclude that $4x + 16 < x + 37$. Subtracting 16 from both sides of the inequality produces $4x < x + 21$. Subtracting x from both sides of this inequality, you have $3x < 21$. Dividing both sides by 3 yields $x < 7$. Quantity A, which is x, is less than 7. Quantity B is 8. So Quantity B is greater. Choice **(B)** is correct.

5. A

The range of the variables in Quantity A is 150 − (−30) = 180. This is the same as the range of the variables in Quantity B, 120 − (−60) = 180. The mean of the distribution, 70, falls within both of those ranges. However, the range for Quantity B lies farther to the left side of the bell curve, therefore encompassing more of the tail of the normal distribution. Since values in the tail occur much less frequently than those closer to the mean, the probability that a random value of X falls within the range associated with Quantity B is less than the probability that X will fall within the range associated with Quantity A.

Choice **(A)** is correct.

6. D

To evaluate Quantity A, start by substituting $7z + 5$ for y in the equation $x = 12y + 25$ to produce $x = 12(7z + 5) + 25 = 84z + 60 + 25 = 84z + 85$. Because 84 is a multiple of 42, and because z is a positive integer, $84z$ is also a multiple of 42. So when $84z$ is divided by 42, there is no remainder. When 85 is divided by 42, the quotient is 2 and the remainder is 1. So when x, which equals $84z + 85$, is divided by 42, the remainder is $0 + 1 = 1$.

Evaluating Quantity B is a bit simpler. If an even integer is divided by 2, the remainder is zero. If an odd integer is divided by 2, the remainder is 1. So is y even or odd? It depends on z. If z is even, then $7z$ is also even and $7z + 5$ is odd, since an even plus an odd is an odd. But if z is odd, then $7z$ is also odd and $7z + 5$ is even, since an odd plus an odd is an even. Because you don't know the value of z, there's no way to tell whether the remainder when y is divided by 2 will be 0 or 1.

Quantity A is 1 and Quantity B is either 0 or 1. So the two quantities could be equal, or alternatively, Quantity A could be greater. Because more than one relationship is possible, choice **(D)** is correct.

7. A

If you're not sure how to solve a complex geometry problem, a good first step is to fill in as many deductions as you can and then reassess the situation. First, note that any triangle formed by the diameter of a circle and a point on the circle will always be a right triangle. Because triangles AEB and CED each have a right angle and a 30 degree angle, it follows that they are both 30-60-90 right triangles. Next, since you're given the area of the semicircle, you can find the diameter of semicircle O—which is also the hypotenuse of ΔABE.

If the area of half a circle is 16π, then the area of the whole circle is 32π:

$$\begin{aligned} A &= \pi r^2 \\ 32\pi &= \pi r^2 \\ 32 &= r^2 \\ r &= \sqrt{32} = 4\sqrt{2} \end{aligned}$$

This is the radius. The diameter is double the radius, or $8\sqrt{2}$, which is also the hypotenuse of ΔABE. Recall that the sides of a 30-60-90 triangle are in the proportion $x:x\sqrt{3}:2x$. Since the hypotenuse is $8\sqrt{2}$, it follows that the short leg (AE) is $4\sqrt{2}$ and the long leg (BE) is $4\sqrt{6}$.

The last piece of information you haven't used yet is the fact that $AC = \sqrt{2}$. Subtracting this from AE gives CE:

$$CE = AE - AC = 4\sqrt{2} - \sqrt{2} = 3\sqrt{2}$$

CE is the shorter leg of a 30-60-90 triangle, and DE (the value in Quantity A) is the longer leg. Thus,

$$DE = CE\sqrt{3} = 3\sqrt{2}\sqrt{3} = 3\sqrt{6}$$

This is greater than Quantity B, so choice **(A)** is the answer.

8. B

The problem provides a series of 4 ratios pertaining to 5 different variables and also gives the value of one of the variables (e), so there will be enough information to solve for the values of every variable, and (E) will not be the correct answer. However, the question only requires that you find the value of one variable, b. You could try calculating variables one by one until you arrive at a value for b, but that could become cumbersome very quickly; you would start with the proportion $\frac{c}{60} = \frac{7}{9}$, which would leave you with a fraction if you solved for c. Backsolving would be similarly difficult. Often the most efficient way to solve problems such as this is to chain the given ratios algebraically, multiplying the appropriate ones until you are left with a ratio that is either $e{:}b$ or $b{:}e$.

The variables b and e are each contained in only one of the given ratios, but they are both in the denominator, so one of the ratios needs to be inverted to allow the formation of a chain of ratios in which everything except b and e will cancel out. Start with this: $\left(\frac{a}{b}\right)\left(\frac{e}{c}\right) = \frac{a \times e}{b \times c}$. The a in the numerator can be eliminated by multiplying this expression by $\frac{d}{a}$, and the c in the denominator will be eliminated if the expression is multiplied by $\frac{c}{d}$, like this: $\frac{a \times e \times d \times c}{b \times c \times a \times d}$. Everything but $\frac{e}{b}$ cancels out, so $\left(\frac{a}{b}\right)\left(\frac{e}{c}\right)\left(\frac{d}{a}\right)\left(\frac{c}{d}\right) = \frac{e}{b}$. Now substitute the known values:

$$\left(\frac{3}{1}\right) \times \left(\frac{9}{7}\right) \times \left(\frac{2}{15}\right) \times \left(\frac{10}{3}\right) = \frac{12}{7} = \frac{e}{b}$$

Plug in 60 for e:

$$\frac{12}{7} = \frac{60}{b}$$

Cross multiply to get $12b = 420$ and divide both sides by 12 to get $b = 35$, or think like this: $5(12) = 60$, so $b = 5(7) = 35$.

The correct answer is **(B).**

9. D

A couple of the equations have exponents, but it turns out that all four equations describe straight lines, so this problem isn't as scary as it looks at first glance. Start by simplifying, with the $y = mx + b$ form as your goal. The first and third equations become $y = 2x - 2$ and $y = 2x + 5$, respectively. The second and fourth equations present a bit more of a challenge. Here are the algebraic steps to simplify the second equation:

$$\begin{aligned} \frac{x^3 - 5}{11} &= 2 \\ x^3 - 5 &= 22 \\ x^3 &= 27 \\ x &= 3 \end{aligned}$$

Here are the steps to simplify the fourth equation:

$$\begin{aligned} (x + 2)^5 &= 0 \\ (x + 2)(x + 2)(x + 2)(x + 2)(x + 2) &= 0 \end{aligned}$$

The only way for all five identical factors to multiply to zero is for each factor to equal zero, so:

$$\begin{aligned} x + 2 &= 0 \\ x &= -2 \end{aligned}$$

With the four equations in these forms, you can now see that $y = 2x - 2$ and $y = 2x + 5$ have the same slope and are therefore parallel. Moreover, $x = 3$ and $x = -2$ are both parallel to the y-axis and thus parallel to each other. Since the opposite sides of this four-sided polygon are parallel, it is a parallelogram. The area of a parallelogram is base times height.

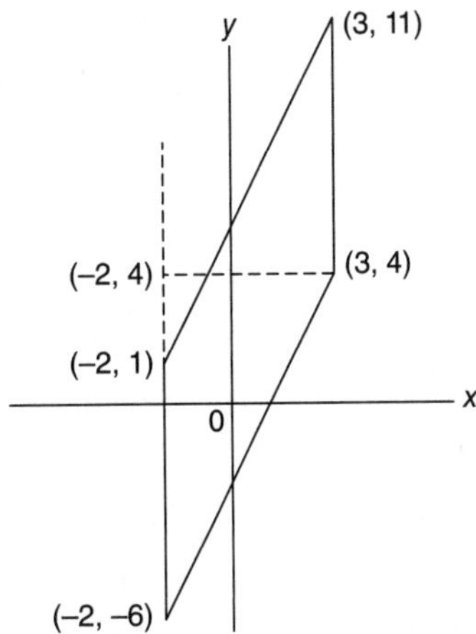

You would have to use the Pythagorean theorem to calculate the lengths of the non-vertical sides and the vertical height between those sides. However, if you consider the vertical sides as the bases, then you can calculate the height easily by constructing a perpendicular to the extension of one of those bases, as shown above. The length of each vertical base is $1 + |-6| = 7$. The horizontal height is the distance between the two vertical bases: $3 + |-2| = 5$.

Plug into the area formula for a parallelogram: base x height $= 7 \times 5 = 35$. Choice **(D)** is correct.

10. A, B, C

First, evaluate expression A: $(x + y)(x - y) + 8xy + 17y^2$.

Multiply the first two terms together:

$$(x + y)(x - y) = x^2 - y^2$$

Plug this into the initial equation and simplify:

$$x^2 - y^2 + 8xy + 17y^2 = x^2 + 8xy + 16y^2$$

Reverse FOIL the equation:

$$x^2 + 8xy + 16y^2 = (x + 4y)(x + 4y) = (x + 4y)^2$$

Since y is an integer, $4y$ is an integer. Since x and $4y$ are both integers, $x + 4y$ is an integer. So $(x + 4y)^2$ is the square of an integer, and it follows that expression A must be the square of an integer.

Next, consider expression B: $9x^4 - 12x^2y^2 + 4y^4$.

Reverse FOIL the equation:

$$9x^4 - 12x^2y^2 + 4y^4 = (3x^2 - 2y^2)(3x^2 - 2y^2) = (3x^2 - 2y^2)^2$$

Since x is an integer, x^2 is an integer, as is $3x^2$. Since y is an integer, y^2 is an integer, as is $2y^2$. Since $3x^2$ and $2y^2$ are integers, $3x^2 - 2y^2$ is also an integer. Thus, $(3x^2 - 2y^2)^2$ is the square of an integer. Therefore, expression B must also be the square of an integer.

Lastly, evaluate expression C: $x^6 + 2x^3y^3 + y^6$.

Reverse FOIL the equation:

$$(x^3)^2 + 2(x^3)(y^3) + (y^3)^2 = (x^3 + y^3)(x^3 + y^3) = (x^3 + y^3)^2$$

Since x is an integer, x^3 is an integer. Since y is an integer, y^3 is an integer. Since x^3 and y^3 are integers, $x^3 + y^3$ is an integer. Thus, $(x^3 + y^3)^2$ is the square of an integer. So it turns out that expression C must also be the square of an integer.

Choices **(A), (B),** and **(C)** are all correct.

11. B

Write out a description of the product of the first 53 numbers of sequence S. Call the product P. There's no need to write out every term; just write out enough to recognize the pattern:

$$\begin{aligned} P &= \left[\frac{1+1}{3(1)}\right] \times \left[\frac{2+1}{3(2)}\right] \times \left[\frac{3+1}{3(3)}\right] \times \left[\frac{4+1}{3(4)}\right] \times \ldots \times \left[\frac{51+1}{3(51)}\right] \times \left[\frac{52+1}{3(52)}\right] \times \left[\frac{53+1}{3(53)}\right] \\ &= \left[\frac{2}{3(1)}\right] \times \left[\frac{3}{3(2)}\right] \times \left[\frac{4}{3(3)}\right] \times \left[\frac{5}{3(4)}\right] \times \ldots \times \left[\frac{52}{3(51)}\right] \times \left[\frac{53}{3(52)}\right] \times \left[\frac{54}{3(53)}\right] \\ &= \left(\frac{1}{3^{53}}\right) \times \left(\frac{2}{1}\right) \times \left(\frac{3}{2}\right) \times \left(\frac{4}{3}\right) \times \left(\frac{5}{4}\right) \times \ldots \times \left(\frac{52}{51}\right) \times \left(\frac{53}{52}\right) \times \left(\frac{54}{53}\right) \\ &= \left(\frac{1}{3^{53}}\right) \times 54 \\ &= \frac{54}{3^{53}} \end{aligned}$$

None of the answer choices is written as $\frac{54}{3^{53}}$. Note that instead, every answer choice has a 2 in the numerator. So rewrite $\frac{54}{3^{53}}$ using prime factorization:

$$54 = 2 \times 27 = 2 \times 3 \times 9 = 2 \times 3 \times 3 \times 3$$

The prime factorization of 54 is $2 \times 3 \times 3 \times 3$, or 2×3^3.

Rewrite the answer as $\frac{54}{3^{53}} = \frac{2 \times 3^3}{3^{53}}$. Cancel the three 3s in the numerator with three 3s in the denominator to get $\frac{2}{3^{50}}$. Or, think like this: if $b \neq 0$, then $\frac{b^a}{b^c} = b^{a-c}$. So:

$$\frac{2 \times 3^3}{3^{53}} = 2 \times \frac{3^3}{3^{53}} = 2 \times 3^{3-53} = 2 \times 3^{-50} = 2 \times \frac{1}{3^{50}} = \frac{2}{3^{50}}.$$

Choice **(B)** is correct.

12. C

Work = Rate × Time.

If each machine works at the rate of r jobs per hour, then together, 8 machines work at the rate of $8r$ jobs per hour.

Using the information given in the question, set up an equation and solve for r.

$$\begin{aligned} \frac{8r \text{ jobs}}{\text{hour}} \times 7 \text{ hours} &= 14 \text{ jobs} \\ 56r &= 14 \\ r &= \frac{1}{4} \end{aligned}$$

Thus, each machine works at the rate of $\frac{1}{4}$ jobs per hour. The question asks how many hours it takes 17 machines to do something. Since one machine works at the rate of $\frac{1}{4}$ jobs per hour, 17 machines work at the rate of $17 \times \frac{1}{4} = \frac{17}{4}$ jobs per hour.

Use the work formula again, with t representing the time in hours, to solve for t.

$$\begin{aligned} \frac{17 \text{ jobs}}{4 \text{ hours}} \times t \text{ hours} &= 34 \text{ jobs} \\ t \text{ hours} &= 34 \text{ jobs} \times \frac{4 \text{ hours}}{17 \text{ jobs}} \\ t &= 34 \div 17 \times 4 = 2 \times 4 = 8 \end{aligned}$$

The correct answer is **(C)**.

13. D

When you see a problem that looks as if it is going to involve manipulation of very large numbers, using prime factors is often an efficient strategy.

First write out the prime factorization of 10!:

$$\begin{array}{lcccccccc} & (1)(2)(3) & (4) & (5) & (6) & (7) & (8) & (9) & (10) \\ = & (1)(2)(3) & [(2)(2)] & (5) & [(2)(3)] & (7) & [(2)(2)(2)] & [(3)(3)] & [(2)(5)] \end{array}$$

Count the number of times each number (greater than 1) appears in the prime factorization.

2 = 8 times

3 = 4 times

5 = 2 times

7 = 1 time

So you can write 10! like this: $10! = (2^8)(3^4)(5^2)(7^1)$

And you can write N like this:

$$\begin{aligned} N &= M^3 = (10!)^3 \\ &= \left[(2^8)(3^4)(5^2)(7^1)\right]^3 \\ &= \left[(2^8)^3\right]\left[(3^4)^3\right]\left[(5^2)^3\right]\left[(7^1)^3\right] \\ &= \left(2^{8(3)}\right)\left(3^{4(3)}\right)\left(5^{2(3)}\right)\left(7^{1(3)}\right) \\ &= \left(2^{24}\right)\left(3^{12}\right)\left(5^{6}\right)\left(7^{3}\right) \end{aligned}$$

Since the factor with the base of 2 is 2^{24}, the greatest possible value of x such that 2^x is a factor of $(10!)^3$ is 24. (Remember that the greatest factor of any number is that number itself.) So $a = 24$.

By the same logic, since the factor with the base of 3 is 3^{12}, the greatest possible value of y such that 3^y is a factor is $(10!)^3$ is 12. So $b = 12$.

Finally, add a and b to get to the answer: $a + b = 24 + 12 = 36$.

Choice **(D)** is correct.

14. B

Take a moment to analyze the figure and write in whatever information you have. You know the circumference of both circles, so you can easily find their radii:

$$\begin{aligned} C &= 2\pi r = 10\pi \\ 2r &= 10 \\ r &= 5 \end{aligned}$$

Next, you know that *YZ* is tangent to both circles. This means that angle *Z* is a right angle, so triangle *XYZ* is a right triangle. This leaves a lot of unknowns in the diagram, however. Whenever a complex figure seems to be missing a lot of information, a good strategy is to look for hidden right triangles. Here, it's natural to add line segment *PQ* to create right triangle *PQX*:

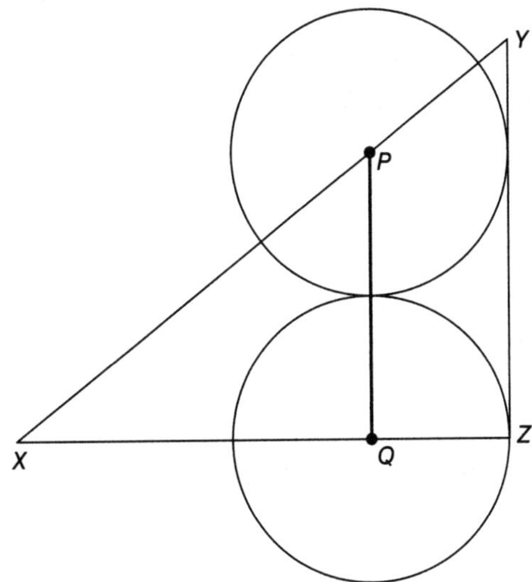

Consider the dimensions of this new right triangle. Leg *PQ* is equal to two radii of the circles, or $2 \times 5 = 10$. Leg *XQ* is equal to $XZ - QZ$. The question states that $XZ = 17$, and you know that *QZ* is a radius, so it's 5. Thus, $XQ = 17 - 5 = 12$. Now, since triangles *XPQ* and *XYZ* are similar (they're both right triangles and they share angle *X*), their sides must be proportional. Set up a proportion and solve:

$$\begin{aligned} \frac{YZ}{PQ} &= \frac{XZ}{XQ} \\ \frac{YZ}{10} &= \frac{17}{12} \end{aligned}$$

$$YZ = \frac{17 \times 10}{12} = \frac{170}{12} = \frac{85}{6}.$$

Choice **(B)** is correct.

15. A, D, E

While it would be possible to Backsolve, the fact that this is an "all that apply" question makes that approach considerably less efficient—you'd have to check every answer choice (unless your Backsolving work helped you to recognize what pattern is at play in the problem). So solve this one using straightforward math and reasoning.

First, note that the only types of furniture being moved are desks and tables, so these are the ratio elements of interest. Since the ratio of the number of desks to the number of tables is 5 to 9, you can say that the number of desks is $5x$ and the number of tables is $9x$, where x is a positive integer. So the total number of desks and tables transferred to the York warehouse is $5x + 9x = 14x$, where x is a positive integer. In other words, the total number of desks and tables transferred to York is a multiple of 14.

Using the second piece of information in the question stem, you know that $14x$ represents 20% of the York warehouse's original inventory. So, if Y_o represents the original inventory in the York warehouse, and Y_f represents the final inventory in the York warehouse (that is, the value that you're looking for), you can set up the following equation to solve for Y_o:

$$\begin{aligned} \frac{1}{5}Y_o &= 14x \\ Y_o &= 70x \end{aligned}$$

The final inventory is 20% greater than the initial inventory, so:

$$Y_f = 1.2Y_o = 84x$$

Hence, the number of items in the York warehouse after the transfer must be a multiple of 84.

Rather than dividing all the answers by 84, eliminate as many as possible by checking for divisibility by 3, since 84 is evenly divisible by 3. That quick process eliminates choices (B) and (C) merely by summing their digits and noting that the sums are not divisible by 3. Choice (A) is readily identifiable as 2×84, (D) is 2×168, and (E) is the sum of (A) and (D), so those numbers are all divisible by 84. Since 504 is divisible by 84 and $504 + 84 = 588$, it's clear that 600 is not divisible by 84. Only choices **(A)**, **(D)**, and **(E)** are correct. Going through a quick analysis such as this eliminates the need to open up the calculator and enter several numbers, but that alternative is always available as well.

16. A

Because the question mentions the median, write the numbers in ascending order to make the median easy to spot:

464	505	564	585	604	608	616	653	657	660
697	704	741	856	888	906	918	926	947	1,102

The list contains an even number of numbers, so the median is the average of the middle two: $(660 + 697) \div 2 = 1{,}357 \div 2 = 678.5$.

The standard deviation is a measure of the absolute value of the distance from the mean. Therefore, the range of all terms within one standard deviation of the mean goes from $730 - 168 = 562$ to $730 + 168 = 898$. The numbers less than the median that are *not* within this range are the following:

464 505

That's 2 numbers out of 20, so the probability is $2 \div 20$, or 10%, which is choice **(A)**.

17. A

The trickiest part of this question is translating Quantity A. There is a mixture of liquids *A* and *B* that is 23% iodine. Quantity A essentially asks, "What percent of this mixture is liquid *A*?" To figure this out, imagine pouring equal parts (ounces, liters, tablespoons—it doesn't matter) of liquid *A* and liquid *B* into an empty flask until you reach the correct percentage of iodine. Each part of liquid *A* that you pour adds $32\% - 23\% = 9\%$ *more* iodine than you're looking for. Each part of liquid *B* that you pour into the flask adds $23\% - 17\% = 6\%$ *less* iodine than you're looking for. The key is to get the +9s and the −6s to cancel out to 0; it's at that point that you'll know you've got the percent of iodine just right. To do this, keep adding parts of liquid *A* (+9s) until you hit a multiple of 6, then add as many parts of liquid *B* (−6s) as needed to reach 0.

$$+9 + 9 - 6 - 6 - 6 = +18 - 18 = 0$$

Thus, there are three parts of liquid *B* for every two parts of Liquid *A* in a 23% iodine mixture. This means that the ratio of liquid *A* to liquid *B* is 2:3, so $\frac{2}{2+3} = \frac{2}{5} = 40\%$ of the mixture is liquid *A*. This is greater than Quantity B, 38%, so the answer is **(A)**.

18. E

This question asks about acres of certified organic farmland, so consult the line graph.

You're told that certified farmland increased 42 percent from 1997 to 2002. The graph shows that in 2002, there were about 600,000 acres of pasture and 1,300,000 acres of cropland, for a total of about 1,900,000 acres. That's 42 percent more than in 1997: $1{,}900{,}000 = 1.42x$; $x = 1{,}338{,}028$ acres in 1997.

The ratio of pasture to cropland was the same in 1997 as in 2006. In 2006, there were just a little over 1,000,000 acres of pasture—call it about 1,050,000 acres—and 1,900,000 acres of cropland, for a ratio of 10.5 to 19 or, eliminating the decimal, 21 to 38. Therefore, the ratio of pasture to all acreage is 21:(21 + 38) or 21:59. That can also be expressed as $\frac{21}{59}$ or about 0.36. Total acreage in 1997 was 1,338,028. Multiply: $1{,}338{,}028 \times 0.36 = 481{,}690$.

For ease of calculation, round this to 500,000. The answer choices are far enough apart that rounding will not lead you to an incorrect answer. According to the graph, there were about 2,200,000 acres of pasture in 2008. Your final step is to calculate the percent increase from 1997 to 2008:

$$\text{Percent change} = 100 \times \frac{\text{Difference in values}}{\text{Original value}}$$

$$100 \times \frac{2{,}200{,}000 - 500{,}000}{500{,}000} = 340\%$$

The denominator has been rounded up, so the actual percent change will be slightly greater than 340. The correct answer is **(E).**

19. C

This question concerns livestock in 2000, so look at the pie chart for that year.

According to the question, the ratio of sheep to turkeys is 1:4. In the pie chart, 4% of all the livestock represented is sheep, and 3% of the same total is hogs. Therefore, the ratio of hogs to sheep is 3:4. The two ratios both contain sheep, so set the number of units of sheep equal to compare hogs to turkeys:

$$\frac{\text{Hogs}}{\text{Sheep}} = \frac{3}{4}; \frac{\text{Sheep}}{\text{Turkeys}} = \frac{1}{4} \rightarrow \frac{4}{16}$$

$$\frac{\text{Hogs}}{\text{Turkeys}} = \frac{3}{16}$$

The association is selecting an animal from among hogs and turkeys, and you are asked for the probability that the selected animal is a turkey. Probability is expressed as a fraction, number of desired outcomes over the total number of outcomes, in its most reduced form—in other words, a ratio. The ratio of turkeys to hogs plus turkeys is 16:(3 + 16), or 16:19. Thus, the correct answer is **(C).**

20. B

This question asks about pasture acreage, which is in the line graph. It also involves cows and sheep in 2000 and 2008, so you'll also use data about livestock in the two pie charts.

In 2000, beef cows represented 25% of all livestock in the pie chart. For purposes of setting up a ratio, think of this as 25 parts of the whole. Sheep were 4% of the livestock, or 4 parts of the whole. However, sheep use four times as much pasture as beef cows. To weight the sheep's pasture acreage accordingly, multiply their 4 parts by 4 to get 16 parts. You now have a total of $25 + 16 = 41$ parts, of which the beef cows used 25 parts. Put another way, the beef cows used $\frac{25}{41}$ of the pasture, or about 61%.

In 2000, there were about 550,000 acres of pasture, so beef cows used about $550{,}000 \times 0.61 = 335{,}500$ acres.

Now do the same calculations for 2008. Beef cows were 19% of the livestock (19 parts of the whole), and sheep were 2%. Again, sheep use four times as much pasture, so multiply their 2 parts of the whole by 4 to get 8 parts. There was a total of $19 + 8 = 27$ parts, and the beef cows used 19 parts. So the beef cows used $\frac{19}{27}$ of the pasture, or about 70%.

In 2008, there were about 2,200,000 acres of pasture, so beef cows used about $2{,}200{,}000 \times 0.7 = 1{,}540{,}000$ acres.

Finally, the question asks for the approximate increase from 2000 to 2008: $1{,}540{,}000 - 335{,}500 = 1{,}204{,}500$. The correct answer is **(B).**

ADVANCED MATH QUESTIONS PRACTICE SET 2

1.

$$\frac{x^2 + 4}{5} = \frac{x + 8}{3}$$

Quantity A	Quantity B
x	x^2

(A) Quantity A is greater.
(B) Quantity B is greater.
(C) The two quantities are equal.
(D) The relationship cannot be determined from the information given.

2. Five sixth-grade classes are competing against one another in an effort to raise money for a local charity. No class raised less than \$60, and one class raised at least five times as much money as all the other classes combined.

Quantity A	Quantity B
The minimum average (arithmetic mean) amount raised by the five classes	\$240

(A) Quantity A is greater.
(B) Quantity B is greater.
(C) The two quantities are equal.
(D) The relationship cannot be determined from the information given.

3.

Weight (kg)	Percent of sample
7	5%
8	10%
9	20%
10	10%
11	10%
12	5%
13	25%
14	10%
15	5%

A veterinarian is working with a dog breeders' association to analyze the weights of a sample of 240 healthy two-year-old purebred dachshunds. The veterinarian collects the above data.

Quantity A	Quantity B
median weight of the dogs in this sample	mean weight of the dogs in this sample

(A) Quantity A is greater.
(B) Quantity B is greater.
(C) The two quantities are equal.
(D) The relationship cannot be determined from the information given.

4.

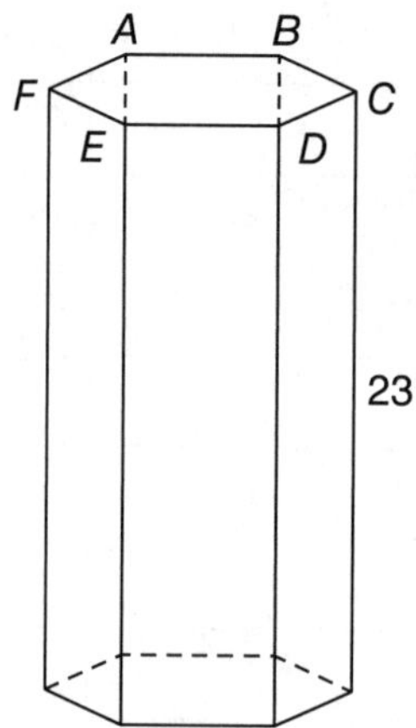

Hexagon *ABCDEF* is a regular hexagon with a perimeter of 48. What is the volume of the uniform prism shown?

(A) 96
(B) $96\sqrt{3}$
(C) 1,104
(D) $1{,}472\sqrt{3}$
(E) $2{,}208\sqrt{3}$

5.

$$3x^{\frac{2}{3}} + 2\sqrt[3]{x} - 8 = 0$$

Quantity A	Quantity B
x	$\frac{64}{25}$

(A) Quantity A is greater.
(B) Quantity B is greater.
(C) The two quantities are equal.
(D) The relationship cannot be determined from the information given.

6. Top-Notch Landscaping must mow sixteen 0.75-acre lots and twelve 1.5-acre lots to complete a certain job. Each of the company's landscapers can mow at a rate of 20 minutes per 0.5 acre.

Quantity A	Quantity B
The minimum number of landscapers needed to complete the job in 6 hours	4

Ⓐ Quantity A is greater.
Ⓑ Quantity B is greater.
Ⓒ The two quantities are equal.
Ⓓ The relationship cannot be determined from the information given.

7.

$$abcd \neq 0$$
$$ad > bc$$
$$bd < 0$$

Quantity A	Quantity B
$\frac{b}{a}$	$\frac{d}{c}$

Ⓐ Quantity A is greater.
Ⓑ Quantity B is greater.
Ⓒ The two quantities are equal.
Ⓓ The relationship cannot be determined from the information given.

8. The perimeters of rectangle Y and rectangle Z are equal. The lengths of the sides of rectangle Y are $x^2 + 21$ and $7x - 5$. The lengths of the sides of rectangle Z are 41 and 5. What is the area of rectangle Y?

Ⓐ 245
Ⓑ 480
Ⓒ 540
Ⓓ 578
Ⓔ 720

9. The average (arithmetic mean) of a, b, c, and d is 12. The average of b, c, d, and e is 17. What is the value of $3(e - a)$?

Ⓐ $\frac{240}{7}$
Ⓑ 48
Ⓒ 54
Ⓓ 58
Ⓔ 60

10. The student population of a certain school increased $a\%$ from 1995 to 2005 and $b\%$ from 2005 to 2015. If the student population increased by 80% from 1995 to 2015 and the increase in the number of students in the second decade was three times the increase in the number of students in the first decade, what is the value of b?

Ⓐ 20
Ⓑ $26\frac{2}{3}$
Ⓒ 50
Ⓓ 60
Ⓔ 75

11. The only items on a shelf are 8 green bins and 4 orange bins. If 3 bins are to be selected from the shelf, one after the other, at random and without replacement, what is the probability that at least one green bin is selected?

Give your answer as a fraction.

12. A store calls the original price of an item the X-level price. The store reduces the X-level price of an item by 30%, resulting in what the store calls the Y-level price of the item. The store then reduces the Y-level price of the item by 20%, resulting in what the store calls the Z-level price of the item. The Z-level price of the item is less than \$49. Which of the following statements must be true?

    Indicate all such statements.

    [A] The X-level price of the item is less than \$86.00.
    [B] When the Z-level price of the item is subtracted from the Y-level price of the item, the result is less than \$16.00.
    [C] The Y-level price of the item is a percent greater than the Z-level price of the item, where $0 < a < 30$.

13. The ratio of w to x is 5:4. The ratio of x to y is 8:1. If the ratio of y:z is 1:3, what is the ratio of $w + x$ to z ?

    (A) 13:3
    (B) 6:1
    (C) 13:2
    (D) 12:1
    (E) 18:1

14. ♥ x ♥ y ♥ $= (2x - y)^2$ and ☻a☻b☻ $= (a + 2b)^2$. If ☻ 5 ☻ $(n-1)$ ☻ $= 5n^2 + 4n$ and $n < 6$, then ♥ $2n$ ♥ 2 ♥ =

    (A) 4
    (B) 9
    (C) 16
    (D) 36
    (E) 49

15.

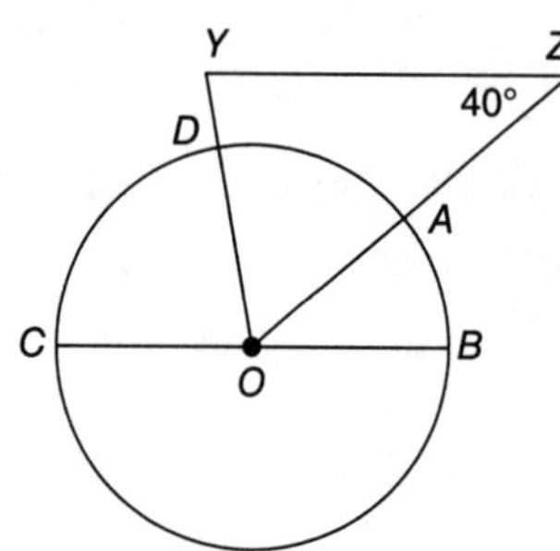

$\overline{BC}$ is a diameter of circle O and is parallel to $\overline{YZ}$. If the length of arc ABC is 22π and the length of minor arc CD is 11π, then what is the positive difference between the degree measures of $\angle OYZ$ and $\angle YOZ$?

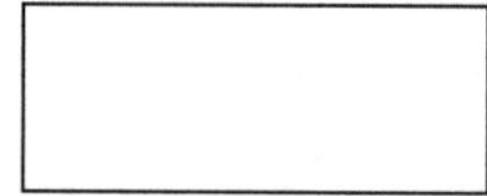

16. In the sequence $a_1, a_2, a_3, \ldots, a_n, \ldots$, each term after the first is equal to r times the previous term, where $a_1 > 0$ and $r > 1$. If $a_1 + a_2 + a_3 = 21$ and $a_2 + a_3 = 18$, what is the value of $a_3 + a_4 + a_5$?

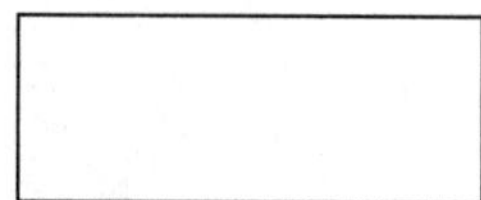

17. Blanca took a non-stop car trip that encompassed three different sections of roadways. Each of the three sections covered the same distance. Blanca averaged 45 miles per hour over the first section, 60 miles per hour over the second section, and 54 miles per hour for the entire trip. What was her average speed for the third section to the nearest mile per hour?

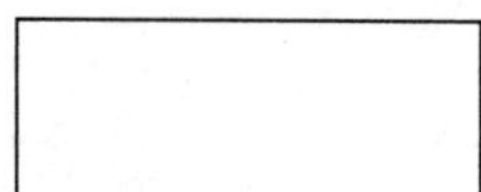

Questions 18–20 refer to the following data.

Percent of Housing Units by Year Built

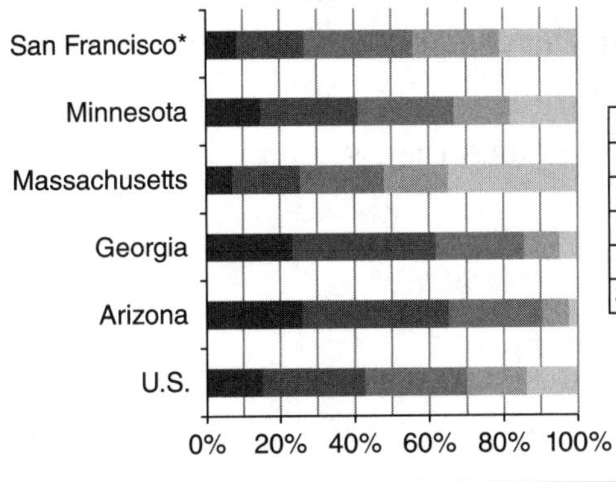

Total Housing Units

U.S.	132,057,804
Arizona	2,859,768
Georgia	4,094,812
Massachusetts	2,808,549
Minnesota	2,353,932
San Francisco area	1,747,506

■ Built 2000 or later ■ Built 1940 to 1959
■ Built 1980 to 1999 ■ Built 1939 or earlier
■ Built 1960 to 1979

Source: 2009–2013 American Community Survey 5-Year Estimates, DP04: Selected Housing Characteristics, census.gov

U.S. Housing Cost as a Percent of Income: Owners with a Mortgage

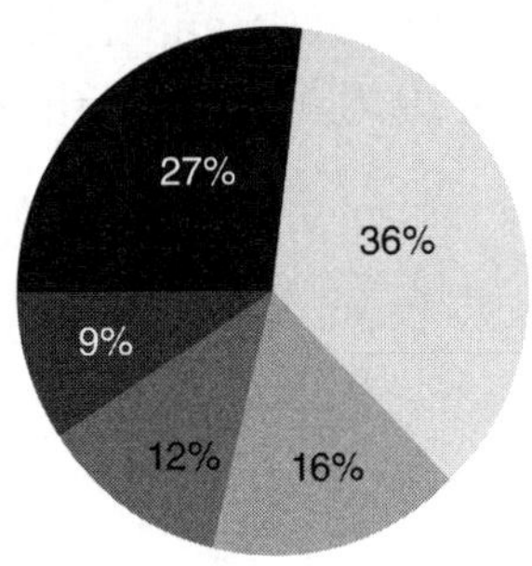

Total: 49.5 million

■ < 20.0% ■ 30.0% to 34.9%
■ 20.0% to 24.9% ■ ≥ 35.0%
■ 25.0% to 29.9%

U.S. Housing Cost as a Percent of Income: Renters

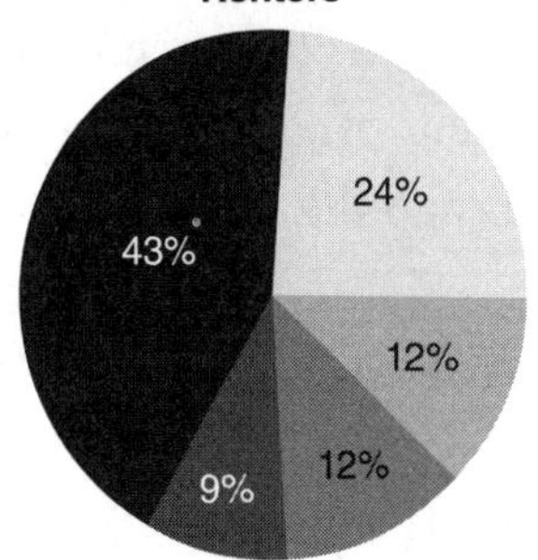

Total: 37.5 million

■ < 20.0% ■ 30.0% to 34.9%
■ 20.0% to 24.9% ■ ≥ 35.0%
■ 25.0% to 29.9%

18. Family A earns \$60,000 and rents its residence, and this family is in the category of housing cost as a percent of income that contains about 3.5 million renters. Family B makes \$85,000 and owns its residence with a mortgage, and this family is in the category of housing cost as a percent of income that contains about 8 million owners. Which of the following could be the difference between the amounts the two families pay for housing?

Indicate <u>all</u> such values.

[A] \$14,500
[B] \$8,200
[C] \$4,000
[D] \$3,700
[E] \$3,165
[F] \$0

19. A real estate investment firm is evaluating housing units built after 1939 and before 1980 for their suitability for profitable renovation and resale. Of the markets within the United States shown, where are there the least such units, if 20 percent of all housing built in the 1940s and 1950s and 60 percent of all housing built in the 1960s and 1970s is not within the price range the firm is considering?

(A) Arizona
(B) Georgia
(C) Massachusetts
(D) Minnesota
(E) San Francisco

20. A national survey conducted in 2014 randomly selected participants who either rent or have a mortgage and asked them: "Do you pay 30 percent or more of your income on housing?" Participants who responded yes completed survey A. Those who responded no completed survey B. Then a prize winner was drawn randomly from all survey participants. What is the approximate ratio of the probability that the prize winner completed survey A and lived in a residence more than 75 years old at the time of the survey to the probability that the prize winner completed survey B and lived in a residence built in the previous 15 years? Assume that percent of income spent on housing is proportionally distributed across residents of housing of varying ages.

Ⓐ $\frac{9}{20}$

Ⓑ $\frac{2}{3}$

Ⓒ $\frac{9}{10}$

Ⓓ $\frac{13}{10}$

Ⓔ $\frac{3}{2}$

ADVANCED MATH QUESTIONS PRACTICE SET 2 ANSWER KEY

1. B
2. A
3. B
4. E
5. B
6. C
7. D
8. B
9. E
10. C
11. $\frac{54}{55}$
12. B, C
13. B
14. D
15. 80
16. 84
17. 60
18. D, E, F
19. A
20. B

ADVANCED MATH QUESTIONS PRACTICE SET 2 ANSWERS AND EXPLANATIONS

1. B

Begin by solving the equation $\frac{x^2 + 4}{5} = \frac{x + 8}{3}$ for the possible values of x.

Cross-multiply to get $3(x^2 + 4) = 5(x + 8)$. Multiplying out each side produces $3x^2 + 12 = 5x + 40$.

Subtracting $5x$ from both sides, you have $3x^2 - 5x + 12 = 40$. Subtracting 40 from both sides gives $3x^2 - 5x - 28 = 0$.

Now factor $3x^2 - 5x - 28$ into a product of binomials of the form $(x + a)(3x + b)$, where a and b are constants. With some testing, it turns out that $3x^2 - 5x - 28 = (x - 4)(3x + 7)$.

So $(x - 4)(3x + 7) = 0$. When the product of a group of factors is 0, at least one of the factors must be 0, so either $x - 4 = 0$ or $3x + 7 = 0$. If $x - 4 = 0$, then $x = 4$. If $3x + 7 = 0$, then $3x = -7$, and $x = -\frac{7}{3}$.

Quantity A could be 4 or $-\frac{7}{3}$. Quantity B could be 16 or $\frac{49}{9} = 5.\bar{4}$. Because the smallest possible value for Quantity B is greater than the largest possible value for Quantity A, Choice **(B)** is correct.

2. A

From the centered information, you know that four of the five classes—excluding the high-performing class—raised at least \$240 altogether. The high-performing class raised at least five times as much as that. So to find the minimum amount raised by the high-performing class, multiply \$240 by 5.

To calculate the value of Quantity A, you'll simply find the minimum total amount raised by all five classes and divide by 5. That's

$$\frac{\$240 + (5)(\$240)}{5} = \$288$$

Note that a bit of critical thinking obviates this final calculation, though. Once you recognize that you'll be multiplying \$240 by 6 to get the total amount raised, then dividing by 5 to get the average, you know that the average must be greater than \$240. Compare, don't calculate!

The correct answer is **(A)**.

3. B

The question presents data about the relative frequency of 240 dogs' weights.

Quantity A, the median weight of this sample, is the average weight of the 120th and 121st dogs when their weights are in order from least to greatest. The table is already in order from least to greatest, so add the percentages until you find where the midpoint of the sample, 50%, falls. That's $5 + 10 + 20 + 10 = 45\%$—not there yet. So keep going: $45 + 10 = 55\%$. That's over the midpoint, so the dogs whose weights you'd average to get the median weight are in the last category added, which is the 11 kg category. The median weight of dogs in this sample is 11 kg.

Calculating Quantity B, the mean weight, requires calculating a weighted average. Instead of working with the percentages of 240 dogs given, which would take a lot of time, remember that percentages represent ratios out of a whole of 100. Thus, $5\% = \frac{5}{100} = \frac{1}{20}$. Every 5% is 1 part out of 20, so represent 5% as 1, 10% as 2, 15% as 3, 20% as 4, and 25% as 5 parts. This approach maintains the proportionality of the categories while making the numbers easier to work with. In your weighted average formula, divide by the total of 20 parts.

$$\frac{1 \times 7 + 2 \times 8 + 4 \times 9 + 2 \times 10 + 2 \times 11 + 1 \times 12 + 5 \times 13 + 2 \times 14 + 1 \times 15}{20} = \frac{7 + 16 + 36 + 20 + 22 + 12 + 65 + 28 + 15}{20} = \frac{221}{20}$$

You can easily estimate that this fraction is slightly over 11 (since $\frac{220}{20} = 11$). Quantity A is exactly 11, so Quantity B is greater.

The correct answer is **(B).**

4. E

The solid shown is a uniform hexagonal prism. While this is certainly an unusual shape, the volume formula is the same for all uniform solids: *Volume* = *Area of Base* × *height.* (Note: a uniform solid is one whose dimensions do not change over the height of the solid. An example of a *non*-uniform solid would be a pyramid or a cone, which is wide at the base and narrow at the top.) For this question, then, if you knew the area of hexagon *ABCDEF*, you could multiply it by 23 to find the volume of the solid.

The question states that *ABCDEF* is regular, which means that all its angles are equal and all its sides are the same length. Since the perimeter is 48, each side must have a length $48 \div 6 = 8$. To find the area of *ABCDEF*, note that a regular hexagon divides into 6 congruent equilateral triangles, like this:

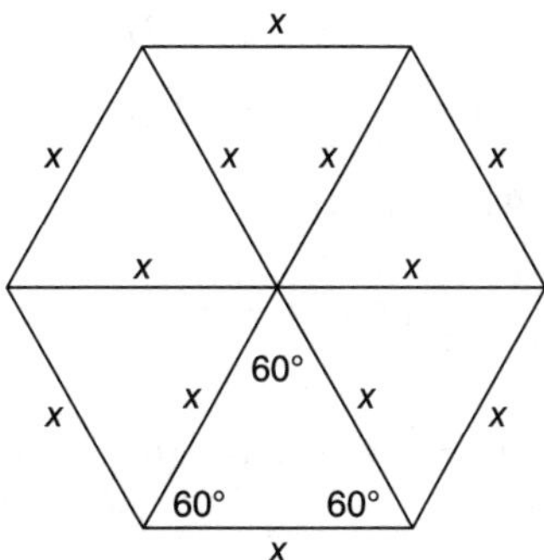

To find the area of the whole hexagon, find the area of one of the triangles and multiply it by 6 (since there are six triangles and they're all the same). In this question, each triangle looks like this:

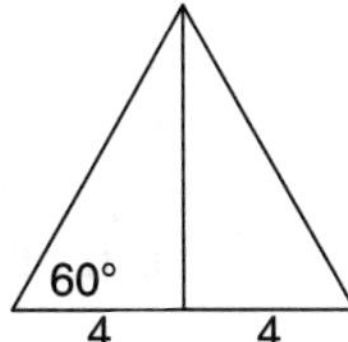

By the properties of 30-60-90 triangles, the height must be $4\sqrt{3}$, so the area of each triangle is $\frac{1}{2}(8)(4\sqrt{3}) = 16\sqrt{3}$. Multiply by 6 to get the total area of the hexagon: $6 \times 16\sqrt{3} = 96\sqrt{3}$.

To find the volume of the solid, multiply by 23:

$$\text{Volume} = 23 \times 96\sqrt{3} = 2{,}208\sqrt{3}$$

Choice **(E)** is correct.

5. B

Strange-looking equations on the GRE are often quadratics in disguise. Note that $x^{\frac{2}{3}}$ is actually just $\sqrt[3]{x}$ squared. To make the equation look more manageable, try letting $\sqrt[3]{x} = m$. Then the equation becomes $3m^2 + 2m - 8 = 0$. Factoring this equation is made more challenging by the coefficient in front of the m^2 term. To factor an expression of the form $ax^2 + bx + c$, look for two numbers that multiply to ac and sum to b. In this case, the two numbers that multiply to $(3)(-8) = -24$ and sum to 2 are 6 and -4. Rewrite the equation, substituting $6m - 4m$ for $2m$. Then factor and solve for m:

$$\begin{aligned} 3m^2 + 2m - 8 &= 0 \\ 3m^2 + 6m - 4m - 8 &= 0 \\ 3m(m + 2) - 4(m + 2) &= 0 \\ (3m - 4)(m + 2) &= 0 \\ m = \frac{4}{3} \text{ or } m &= -2 \end{aligned}$$

At this point, substitute $\sqrt[3]{x}$ back in for m and cube each equation to find the possible values of x:

$$\begin{aligned} \sqrt[3]{x} &= \frac{4}{3} \text{ or } \sqrt[3]{x} = -2 \\ x &= \left(\frac{4}{3}\right)^3 \text{ or } x = (-2)^3 \\ x &= \frac{64}{27} \text{ or } x = -8 \end{aligned}$$

Because Quantity B, $\frac{64}{25}$, is greater than both of the possible values of x, **(B)** is the correct answer.

6. C

This is a combined work problem—the fact that several people are working together to complete a task tells you that. So you need to know how big the task is, and at what rate the workers can tackle it. The first sentence tells you that the landscapers have to mow a total of $16(0.75) + 12(1.5) = 12 + 18 = 30$ acres, and the second sentence provides each landscaper's mowing rate.

One way to figure out how many landscapers are needed is to find out how long it would take a single landscaper to complete the task. There are various ways to do that calculation. You might think like this: 20 minutes per 0.5 acre = 40 minutes per 1 acre, so the entire task takes 40 minutes times 30 acres, or 1,200 minutes, which is 20 hours.

Alternatively, you could convert the given rate to its inverse. The inverse of 20 minutes per half-acre is three half-acres per hour. If you consider one "job" to be a half-acre of mowing, then there are 60 "jobs" that must be completed:

$$\frac{60 \text{ jobs}}{\frac{3 \text{ jobs}}{1 \text{ hour}}} = 60 \text{ jobs}\left(\frac{1 \text{ hour}}{3 \text{ jobs}}\right) = 20 \text{ hours}$$

From here, you can simply test Quantity B to see whether it's too small, too big, or just right. If one landscaper could finish the job in 20 hours, then 4 landscapers working together at the same rate could finish the job in 5 hours; that's a bit faster than needed, so it might look as though the answer is (B). But what happens if you reduce the number of landscapers to 3?

$$\frac{20\text{ hours}}{3} = 6\frac{2}{3}\text{ hours}$$

...so 3 landscapers is too few. At least 4 landscapers are needed to finish the job in 6 hours or less, so the correct answer is **(C).**

7. D

The first line of the centered information indicates that none of the variables is equal to 0. The second line shows a relationship between *ad* and *bc*, but neither of those is one of the expressions being compared. The third line provides the additional information that *b* and *d* must have different signs since their product is negative. Because the compared quantities are given as fractions, you will need to use division in your calculations. And since you're dealing with inequalities, when you divide, you must take into account whether you are dividing by a positive or a negative number because the latter will "flip" the inequality.

Since you know that $bd < 0$, you can divide $ad > bc$ by that term, flipping the inequality accordingly, so that $\frac{ad}{bd} < \frac{bc}{bd}$ and $\frac{a}{b} < \frac{c}{d}$. That's starting to look a lot like the values in the two columns.

But there's one more complication here: the question asks for the relationship between $\frac{b}{a}$ and $\frac{d}{c}$. As long as both fractions have the same sign, taking the reciprocal of both sides of an inequality changes the relationship. For instance, $\frac{1}{2} < \frac{3}{2}$, but of course $\frac{2}{1} > \frac{2}{3}$. If both fractions are negative, the same relationship still holds: $-\frac{2}{3} < -\frac{2}{5}$, but $-\frac{3}{2} > -\frac{5}{2}$. Before you choose (A), though, consider that one fraction might be negative and the other positive: say $a = 1$, $b = -2$, $c = 1$ and $d = 1$. Now, $\frac{b}{a} = -2$ and $\frac{d}{c} = 1$, making Quantity B greater. In fact, as long as the fraction on the left is negative and the fraction on the right is positive, taking the reciprocal will not alter the relationship. So more than one relationship is possible, and the answer is **(D).**

Note: Another way to see that multiple relationships are possible is to divide both sides of the centered inequality by a and c:

$$ad > bc$$
$$\frac{d}{c} \; ? \; \frac{b}{a}$$

The centered information tells you that b and d have opposite signs, but it's silent about the signs of a and c. Thus, after dividing both sides of the inequality by ac, you don't know whether or not you should flip the inequality sign. This is another way to determine that it's impossible to tell which of Quantity A or B is greater, and the correct answer must be **(D).**

8. B

The question states that the perimeters of rectangles Y and Z are equal. You can calculate the perimeter of rectangle Z given that the sides are 41 and 5:

$$\begin{aligned} \text{Perimeter } Z &= 2(41) + 2(5) \\ &= 82 + 10 \\ &= 92 \end{aligned}$$

Thus, the perimeter of rectangle Y must also equal 92. Set up the equation for the perimeter and simplify.

$$\begin{aligned} 2\left[\left(x^2 + 21\right) + \left(7x - 5\right)\right] &= 92 \\ 2\left(x^2 + 21 + 7x - 5\right) &= 92 \\ 2\left(x^2 + 7x + 16\right) &= 92 \\ x^2 + 7x + 16 &= 46 \\ x^2 + 7x - 30 &= 0 \end{aligned}$$

Factoring the equation yields $(x - 3)(x + 10)$. So x comes out to -10 or 3. The lengths of the sides of rectangle Y are $x^2 + 21$ and $7x - 5$.

If $x = 3$, then the lengths of the sides of rectangle Y are $x^2 + 21 = 3^2 + 21 = 9 + 21 = 30$ and $7x - 5 = 7(3) - 5 = 21 - 5 = 16$

If $x = -10$, then the lengths of the sides of rectangle Y are $x^2 + 21 = (-10)^2 + 21 = 100 + 21 = 121$ and $7x - 5 = 7(-10) - 5 = -70 - 5 = -75$

So if $x = -10$, the length of one of the sides would be negative, which is not possible. It follows that x must equal 3 and the lengths of the sides of rectangle Y must be 30 and 16.

The area of any rectangle is length times width. The area of rectangle Y is $30 \times 16 = 480$. The correct answer is **(B).**

9. E

The average formula is: Average $= \dfrac{\text{Sum of terms}}{\text{Number of terms}}$.

Since the average of a, b, c, and d is 12, you can write the following equation: $\dfrac{a+b+c+d}{4} = 12$. Eliminate the fraction by multiplying both sides of this equation by 4 to yield $a + b + c + d = 48$.

Use the fact that the average of b, c, d, and e is 17 to write another equation: $\dfrac{b+c+d+e}{4} = 17$. Again, eliminate the fraction by multiplying both sides of this equation by the 4 in the denominator: $b + c + d + e = 68$.

You now have the two equations $a + b + c + d = 48$ and $b + c + d + e = 68$. The fastest way to the correct answer at this point is to use combination. Subtract the first equation from the second equation: $(b + c + d + e) - (a + b + c + d) = 68 - 48$. That yields $e - a = 20$. Since the question asks for the value of 3(e − a), multiply 20 by 3. That's 60. Choice **(E)** is correct.

10. C

Since you're starting with an unknown value and taking percent increases, this problem represents an excellent opportunity to Pick Numbers. If the starting population (1995) were 100, then the final population (2015) would be 180, since there's an overall percent increase of 80%. Now, the second population increase was three times the first population increase, so the total increase of 80 students would equal the population increase from 1995 to 2005 plus three times that increase:

$x + 3x = 80$, where $x =$ the increase from 1995 to 2005.

So if x, the first population increase, is 20, then the increase from 2005 to 2015 is 3 times that, or 60. Apply the percent change formula (be careful to use the appropriate original value—the population in 2005—in the denominator):

$$\frac{180 - 120}{120} \times 100\% = \frac{60}{120} \times 100\% = 50\%$$

Double check that this represents the value that you're looking for—the second percent increase—before moving on.

You could certainly also solve this using algebra, though it would very likely take longer:

Let p represent the initial population. There are two population increases such that the second is three times the first, and the sum of the two population increases is equal to 80% of p. Use $\dfrac{a}{100}$ to represent the first percent increase. That means that the first population increase is $\frac{pa}{100}$. The second population increase is 3 times the first, or $\frac{3pa}{100}$. The first and second population increases sum to 80% of *p*, so you can set up this equation:

$$\frac{pa}{100} + \frac{3pa}{100} = \frac{80p}{100}$$

This equation simplifies to $a + 3a = 80$ (note the similarity to the first equation in the solution above), allowing you to solve for *a*, the first percent increase. Now that you know that $a = 20$, you can write an equation that represents the change in school population from 2005 to 2015:

$$1.2p + 1.2p\left(\frac{b}{100}\right) = 1.8p$$

Divide all terms by *p* and then subtract 1.2 from both sides of the equation to simplify: $\frac{1.2b}{100} = 0.6$, so $1.2b = 60$, and $b = 50$.

Choice **(C)** is correct.

11. $\mathbf{\frac{54}{55}}$

The sum of the probability that an event occurs and the probability that it doesn't occur is equal to 1.

In this case, it is easier to find the probability of the opposite of what the question is asking for, and then subtract that probability from 1. The opposite of at least one green bin being selected is that no green bins are selected. That is, all selected bins are orange.

There are 4 orange bins out of a total of $8 + 4 = 12$ bins. The probability that the first bin selected is orange is $\frac{4}{12} = \frac{1}{3}$.

If the first bin selected is orange, there are 8 green bins and 3 orange bins left on the shelf. The probability that the second bin selected is also orange is $\frac{3}{11}$.

If the first two bins selected are orange, the probability that the third bin is also orange is $\frac{2}{10} = \frac{1}{5}$.

To find the probability that all 3 bins selected are orange, multiply these three probabilities:

$$\frac{1}{\cancel{3}} \times \frac{\cancel{3}}{11} \times \frac{1}{5} = \frac{1}{1} \times \frac{1}{11} \times \frac{1}{5} = \frac{1}{55}.$$

Since that is the opposite of the event the question asks for, subtract this probability from 1 to get the answer:

$$1 - \frac{1}{55} = \frac{55}{55} - \frac{1}{55} = \frac{55 - 1}{55} = \frac{54}{55}$$

The correct answer is $\mathbf{\frac{54}{55}}$.

12. B, C

Set a variable for the original price, the X-level price, such as T.

After the reduction of the X-level price by 30% to the Y-level price, the Y-level price of the item, in dollars, is $T - 0.3T = 0.7T$.

After the reduction of the Y-level price by 20% to the Z-level price, the Z-level price of the item, in dollars, is $0.7T - 0.2(0.7T) = 0.7T - 0.14T = 0.56T$.

Thus, the prices can be written as follows

$$\begin{aligned} \text{X-level} &= T \text{ dollars} \\ \text{Y-level} &= 0.7\ T \text{ dollars} \\ \text{Z-level} &= 0.56\ T \text{ dollars} \end{aligned}$$

Consider statement A.

The question stem says that the Z-level price of the item is less than 49 dollars. Using $0.56T$ for the Z-level price, $0.56T < 49$.

$T < \frac{49}{0.56}$; since $\frac{49}{0.56} = 87.50$, it follows that $T < 87.50$.

So the original price was less than \$87.50. However, the original price was not necessarily less than \$86.00. Statement A is not necessarily true.

Next, consider statement B.

Find the result of subtracting the Z-level price from the Y-level price, in terms of T:

$0.7T - 0.56T = 0.14T$

Since the Z-level price of the item is less than \$49, you know that $0.56T < 49$. Notice that 0.14 is exactly $\frac{1}{4}$ of 0.56.

Divide both sides of the inequality $0.56\,T < 49$ by 4:

$$\frac{0.56\,T}{4} < \frac{49}{4}$$
$$0.14\,T < 12.25$$

So the the result of subtracting the Z-level price from the Y-level price is less than \$12.25. That means it's certainly less than \$16. Statement B must be true.

Finally, consider statement C.

Use the percent change formula to determine what percent greater than the Z-level price the Y-level price is (the calculation is identical to finding the percent increase from the Z-level price to the Y-level price):

$$\frac{0.7\,T - 0.56\,T}{0.56\,T} \times 100\% = \frac{0.14\,T}{0.56\,T} \times 100\% = \frac{14}{56} \times 100\% = \frac{1}{4} \times 100\% = 25\%.$$

So $a = 25$, and it is true that $0 < a < 30$. Statement C must be true.

(B) and **(C)** are the correct answers.

13. B

You are given 3 ratios of various combinations of *w*, *x*, *y*, and *z* and asked to manipulate them in some manner to determine the value of $\frac{w + x}{z}$. One way to approach this task would be to find the ratios of *w*:*z* and *x*:*z* individually, then combine them. Note that $\left(\frac{w}{x}\right)\left(\frac{x}{y}\right)\left(\frac{y}{z}\right) = \frac{w}{z}$ because the *x* and *y* terms cancel out. Substituting the known values, $\left(\frac{5}{4}\right)\left(\frac{8}{1}\right)\left(\frac{1}{3}\right) = \frac{10}{3}$. Similarly, $\left(\frac{x}{y}\right)\left(\frac{y}{z}\right) = \frac{x}{z} = \left(\frac{8}{1}\right)\left(\frac{1}{3}\right) = \frac{8}{3}$.

The fraction $\frac{w + x}{z}$ can be expressed as $\frac{w}{z} + \frac{x}{z} = \frac{10}{3} + \frac{8}{3} = \frac{18}{3} = \frac{6}{1}$.

Another approach to solving this problem would be to look for commonalities among the given ratios. Since *x*:*y* is 8:1 and *z*:*y* is 3:1, it follows that *x*:*y*:*z* = 8:1:3. The ratio of *w* to *x* is stated to be 5:4. That's the same as 10:8, which results in a common value for *x*. Therefore, *w*:*x*:*y*:*z* = 10:8:1:3, and $\frac{w + x}{z} = \frac{10 + 8}{3} = \frac{18}{3} = \frac{6}{1}$.

Finally, you might consider Picking Numbers. Say $y = 1$. Then $x = 8$, $z = 3$, and $w = 10$. Then the answer is, again, $\frac{w + x}{z} = \frac{10 + 8}{3} = \frac{18}{3} = \frac{6}{1}$.

Choice **(B)** is correct.

14. D

Symbolism questions frighten a lot of students, but symbols are just odd-looking functions, and questions featuring them are typically best solved by substitution. Start by replacing the wacky shapes with simple function notation. Use an "*h*" for the hearts and an "*s*" for the smileys:

$$\begin{aligned} h(x,y) &= (2x - y)^2 \\ s(a,b) &= (a + 2b)^2 \end{aligned}$$

Now the question becomes: given that $s(5, n - 1) = 5n^2 + 4n$ and $n < 6$, what is $h(2n, 2)$? Begin by plugging 5 and $n - 1$, respectively, into function s:

$$s(5, n - 1) = [5 + 2(n - 1)]^2 = (5 + 2n - 2)^2 = (2n + 3)^2 = 4n^2 + 12n + 9$$

The question says that this equals $5n^2 + 4n$, so set the quantities equal and solve the quadratic:

$$\begin{aligned} 4n^2 + 12n + 9 &= 5n^2 + 4n \\ n^2 - 8n - 9 &= 0 \\ (n - 9)(n + 1) &= 0 \\ n &= 9 \text{ or } n = -1 \end{aligned}$$

The question states that $n < 6$, so n must equal -1. Now that you know that $n = -1$, you can find $h(2n, 2)$:

$$\begin{aligned} h(2n,2) &= h[(2)(-1),2] = h(-2,2) \\ h(-2,2) &= [2(-2) - 2]^2 = (-4 - 2)^2 = (-6)^2 = 36 \end{aligned}$$

The correct answer is **(D)**.

15. 80

The key to beating a complex figures problem like this one is to take a deep breath and start filling in what you know. It follows from the properties of parallel lines crossed by a transversal that $\angle AOB$ must be 40°. This is a handy fact because it means that arc *ABC* spans $180° + 40° = 220°$ of the circle. You now know arc *ABC* and its corresponding central angle. The question provides the length of arc *CD* (11π), which means that you can set up a proportion to solve for arc *CD*'s central angle (*COD*):

$$\begin{aligned} \frac{\angle COD}{11\pi} &= \frac{220}{22\pi} \\ \angle COD &= \frac{220 \times 11\pi}{22\pi} = 220 \div 2 = 110 \end{aligned}$$

Since $\angle COD = 110°$, it follows from the properties of parallel lines crossed by a transversal that $\angle OYZ = 110°$ as well. The final angle of the triangle, $\angle YOZ$, is therefore $180° - 40° - 110° = 30°$. After doing all this work, take care to answer the right question! You need the positive difference between $\angle OYZ$ and $\angle YOZ$, which is $110 - 30 = 80$. The correct answer is **80.**

Note: Remember that GRE figures are not necessarily drawn to scale. The one in this question isn't. If you tried to estimate based on the appearance of the figure, you most probably did not get the correct answer. Remember to use geometric reasoning to arrive at your answers on Test Day rather than estimation.

16. 84

Each term after the first term is r times the previous term, so:

$$\begin{aligned} a_2 &= ra_1 \\ a_3 &= r(ra_1) = r^2a_1 \\ a_4 &= r\left(r^2a_1\right) = r^3a_1 \\ a_5 &= r\left(r^3a_1\right) = r^4a_1 \end{aligned}$$

Subtract the second equation given in the problem from the first equation to solve for a_1:

$$\begin{array}{rcl} a_1 + a_2 + a_3 &=& 21 \\ -(a_2 + a_3 &=& 18) \\ \hline a &=& 3 \end{array}$$

The next four terms are as follows:

$$\begin{aligned} a_2 &= 3r \\ a_3 &= 3r^2 \\ a_4 &= 3r^3 \\ a_5 &= 3r^4 \end{aligned}$$

Next, solve for r using the equation $a_1 + a_2 + a_3 = 21$.

$$\begin{aligned} 3 + 3r + 3r^2 &= 21 \\ 3\left(1 + r + r^2\right) &= 21 \\ 1 + r + r^2 &= 7 \\ -6 + r + r^2 &= 0 \\ (r + 3)(r - 2) &= 0 \\ r &= -3 \text{ or } 2 \end{aligned}$$

The question states that $r > 1$, so $r = 2$.

Thus,

$$\begin{aligned} a_2 &= 6 \\ a_3 &= 12 \\ a_4 &= 24 \\ a_5 &= 48 \end{aligned}$$

The value of $a_3 + a_4 + a_5 = 12 + 24 + 48 =$ **84.**

Alternatively, once you've figured out that $a_1 = 3$, you can find r very quickly by trial and error. The first three terms sum to 21, so r can't be all that big, and the fact that both 18 and 21 are integers suggests that r is probably also an integer. It has to be greater than 1, so try $r = 2$. That produces $a_2 = 6$ and $a_3 = 12$. Score! The fact that $3 + 6 + 12 = 21$ confirms that $r = 2$, and now it's just a matter of calculating two more terms and adding $a_3 + a_4 + a_5$, as above.

17. 60

When solving multi-part journey problems, creating a DiRT box table (D = *distance*, R = *rate of speed*, T = *time spent traveling*) with the known variables filled in can greatly simplify the problem. This particular problem provides very little directly quantifiable information, but fill in what's given, as shown in this table:

	Distance	Rate	Time
Section 1		45 mph	
Section 2		60 mph	
Section 3		?	
Total		54 mph	

Since the distance is the same for each section, simply pick a number for a distance that will work efficiently with the numbers provided in the problem. The most convenient number for the distance will be the least common multiple (LCM) of the given rates on the legs of the journey. The LCM of 45 and 60 is 180. Plugging 180 in as the distance for each of the sections yields:

	Distance	Rate	Time
Section 1	180 m	45 mph	
Section 2	180 m	60 mph	
Section 3	180 m	?	
Total	540 m	54 mph	

Using the Distance formula, D = RT, allows easy calculation of the time for each leg of the journey as well as the cumulative time for the total journey:

	Distance	Rate	Time
Section 1	180 m	45 mph	4 h
Section 2	180 m	60 mph	3 h
Section 3	180 m	?	?
Total	540 m	54 mph	10 h

Since the total time is 10 hours, solving for the time it takes to complete the Section 3 leg simply means subtracting the time of the first two legs from the total time: $10 - 4 - 3 = 3$ hours.

Now use D = RT to find that the 180 miles traveled in the third section's 3 hours yields an average rate for that section of 180 miles ÷ 3 hours = **60 mph**.

Algebraic Explanation

The problem can also be solved algebraically, by use of the same helpful table for establishing a firm basis to find the unknown x:

	Distance	Rate	Time
Section 1		45 mph	
Section 2		60 mph	
Section 3		x	
Total		54 mph	

Since the distance is the same for each section, but is not identified, use a variable to stand in for that distance. Using y for each section's distance yields:

	Distance	Rate	Time
Section 1	y	45 mph	
Section 2	y	60 mph	
Section 3	y	x	
Total	$3y$	54 mph	

The time column is still blank, but the times for each section can be calculated using the formula $\text{Time} = \dfrac{\text{Distance}}{\text{Rate}}$.

	Distance	Rate	Time
Section 1	y	45 mph	$y/45$
Section 2	y	60 mph	$y/60$
Section 3	y	x	y/x
Total	$3y$	54 mph	

Since the Time column of the DiRT box is cumulative, the total time for the trip is the sum of the 3 individual sections' times, and that total will satisfy the **Average Rate = Total Distance ÷ Total Time** equation, so you can write the following equation:

$$\frac{y}{45} + \frac{y}{60} + \frac{y}{x} = \frac{3y}{54}$$

Divide both sides by y and reduce:

$$\frac{1}{45} + \frac{1}{60} + \frac{1}{x} = \frac{3}{54} = \frac{1}{18}$$

Multiply both sides by the LCM, $180x$:

$$\frac{180x}{45} + \frac{180x}{60} = \frac{180x}{x} = \frac{180x}{18}$$

Simplify:

$$\begin{aligned} 4x + 3x + 180 &= 10x \\ 7x + 180 &= 10x \\ 180 &= 3x \end{aligned}$$

So x, which represents the average rate of speed for the third section in miles per hour, equals **60.**

18. D, E, F

This question concerns housing cost as a percent of income, so look at the pie charts.

Family A rents—look at the pie chart that represents renters. This family is in the category that contains about 3.5 million people. Total renters are 37.5 million, and 3.5 million is a little less than 10% of that total. Only one category fits, the category with 9% of renters. Therefore, family A pays 30.0% to 34.9% of its income on housing. Family A earns \$60,000, so it pays between $0.30 \times \$60{,}000 = \$18{,}000$ and (round 34.9% to 35%) $0.35 \times \$60{,}000 = \$21{,}000$ on housing.

Family B owns a home with a mortgage—look at the pie chart that represents owners. This family is in the category that contains about 8 million people. The total of owners with a mortgage is 49.5 million. To make the calculation easy, round that to 50 million and set up a proportion to find what percent 8 million is of the total:

$$\frac{8}{50} = \frac{x}{100}$$

You double 50 to turn it into 100, so double 8 to find that $x = 16$.

Family B is in the category that contains about 16% of owners with a mortgage, so it pays 20.0% to 24.9% of income on housing. This family earns \$85,000, so it pays between 0.20 × \$85,000 = \$17,000 and (round 24.9% to 25%) 0.25 × \$85,000 = \$21,250 on housing.

The ranges of the two families' housing costs overlap, so it's possible that there is no difference between what the families pay for housing. The maximum difference occurs when family A pays the greatest amount (\$21,000) and family B pays the least amount (\$17,000): \$21,000 – \$17,000 = \$4,000. Remember that you rounded 34.9% up a little to calculate the \$21,000, so the actual possible difference is a little less than \$4,000 (if you didn't round, you know it's \$3,940). The correct answers are from \$0 to a little less than \$4,000. That's **(D)**, **(E)**, and **(F)**.

19. A

This question concerns the year housing units were built, so look at the stacked bar graph for information. The question asks about units built between 1940 and 1979, inclusive, so look at the third and fourth segments of the bars. You need to find the area with the least units in this date range that also meet the price range criterion, meaning you will consider only 100 – 20 = 80% of the 1940–1959 units and 100 – 60 = 40% of the 1960–1979 units.

Note that Arizona and Massachusetts have very similar total units. However, Massachusetts has a much greater percentage of its units in the relevant decades (about 40% to Arizona's 30%), and of those a much greater proportion are in the more heavily weighted 1940–1959 category. Therefore, without doing any calculations, you can eliminate **(C)** Massachusetts; Arizona must have fewer units.

Also consider Georgia and Arizona, which have very similar percentages of their housing units built in the decades of interest. Georgia, however, has many more total housing units, so **(B)** Georgia can be eliminated.

Do the calculations for Arizona, Minnesota, and San Francisco:

Arizona:

1940–1959: 0.80 × 8% = 6.4%
1960–1979: 0.40 × 25% = 10.0%

Total % of units: 6.4% + 10.0% = 16.4%

0.164 × 2.86 million units = 469,040 units

Minnesota:

1940–1959: 0.80 × 15% = 12.0%

1960–1979: 0.40 × 26% = 10.4 %

Total % of units: 12.0% + 10.4% = 22.4%

0.224 × 2,353,932 units = 527,281 units

So far, Arizona is the clear winner with fewer units.

San Francisco:

1940–1959: 0.80 × 23% = 18.4%

1960–1979: 0.40 × 29% = 11.6%

Total % of units: 18.4% + 11.6% = 30%

0.30 × 1,747,506 units = 524,252 units

Arizona still has the fewest number of units of interest to the real estate firm. The correct answer is **(A).**

20. B

This question concerns the percent of income spent on housing as well as the age of that housing. Use information from the stacked bar graph and both pie charts to calculate your answer. Probability is the ratio of the number of desired outcomes over the total possible outcomes. The question asks for the approximate ratio and the answer choices are relatively far apart, so rounding is a good strategy to make calculations easier.

There are a total of 49.5 + 37.5 = 87 million people who either rent or have a mortgage. Of the 49.5 million mortgage holders, 9% + 27% = 36% spend 30% or more of their income on housing; that's 0.36 × 49.5 = 17.82 million (round to 18 million). Of the 37.5 million renters, 9% + 43% = 52% pay 30% of more of their income on housing; that's 0.52 × 37.5 = 19.5 million. Therefore, the probability that a survey participant completed survey A is $\frac{18 + 19.5}{87} = \frac{37.5}{87} \approx 43\%$.

This was a national survey, so look at the bottommost bar on the bar chart to find percent ownership by age of housing in the United States. "More than 75 years old" in 2014 means the housing was built before 1940. About 13% of U.S. housing was built before 1940. So multiply: 0.13 × 0.43 ≈ 0.056. So 5.6% of the survey participants completed survey A and lived in a unit more than 75 years old. Stated differently, there is a 5.6% probability that a survey participant completed survey A and lived in a unit more than 75 years old.

The probability that a survey participant completed survey B is about 100% − 43% = 57%. In 2014, "built in the previous 15 years" means built in 2000 or later. About 15% of U.S. housing was built in or after 2000, so multiply: $0.15 \times 0.57 \approx 0.086$. So 8.6% of the survey participants completed survey B and lived in a unit no more than 15 years old. Stated differently, there is an 8.6% probability that a survey participant completed survey B and lived in a unit no more than 15 years old.

The ratio of the probabilities is $\frac{5.6\%}{8.6\%}$ or approximately $\frac{2}{3}$. The correct answer is **(B).** Note that because the total of 87 million remains the same throughout the problem, you are really being asked for the ratio of $\frac{\frac{\text{Group A}}{\text{Total}}}{\frac{\text{Group B}}{\text{Total}}}$. That means that you could have also solved for the ratio of the *number* of those who took survey A and lived in a unit more than 75 years old to the *number* of those who took survey B and lived in a unit no more than 15 years old. That ratio is about 4.9 million to 7.4 million, or about $\frac{2}{3}$.

ADVANCED MATH QUESTIONS PRACTICE SET 3

1. a is a prime number

b is a positive factor of $a - 1$

Quantity A	Quantity B
a^2	The product of b and the least non-prime integer greater than a

Ⓐ Quantity A is greater.
Ⓑ Quantity B is greater.
Ⓒ The two quantities are equal.
Ⓓ The relationship cannot be determined from the information given.

2. In rectangle A, the ratio of the length to the width is 3:1. In rectangle B, the ratio of the length to the width is 4:1. The area of rectangle A is 27 percent of the area of rectangle B. The perimeter of rectangle A is v percent of the perimeter of rectangle B.

Quantity A	Quantity B
v	54

Ⓐ Quantity A is greater.
Ⓑ Quantity B is greater.
Ⓒ The two quantities are equal.
Ⓓ The relationship cannot be determined from the information given.

3. The probability that event A occurs and event B does not occur is greater than $\frac{1}{4}$. The probability that event B occurs and event A does not occur is greater than $\frac{1}{4}$. The probability that neither of the events A and B occurs is greater than $\frac{1}{8}$.

Quantity A	Quantity B
The probability that both of the events *A* and *B* occur	$\frac{1}{4}$

- (A) Quantity A is greater.
- (B) Quantity B is greater.
- (C) The two quantities are equal.
- (D) The relationship cannot be determined from the information given.

4.

$$\frac{x - 1}{(x - 2)^2 + 25} = \frac{2}{17}$$

Quantity A	Quantity B
x	8

- (A) Quantity A is greater.
- (B) Quantity B is greater.
- (C) The two quantities are equal.
- (D) The relationship cannot be determined from the information given.

5. The arithmetic mean of {6, 1, 11, x, 2} is x.
   The median of {2, y, 11, 1, 5} is y.

Quantity A	Quantity B
x	y

- (A) Quantity A is greater.
- (B) Quantity B is greater.
- (C) The two quantities are equal.
- (D) The relationship cannot be determined from the information given.

6. A survey measures the heights of 900 people, which are found to be normally distributed. The mean height is 5' 5", and 150 people in the survey have a height between 5' 1" and 5' 3".

Quantity A	Quantity B
The number of people in the survey who are taller than 5' 9"	The number of people in the survey who are more than 2 standard deviations above the mean

Ⓐ Quantity A is greater.
Ⓑ Quantity B is greater.
Ⓒ The two quantities are equal.
Ⓓ The relationship cannot be determined from the information given.

7. $$0 < p < 1$$

When an experiment is conducted, events A, B, and C are all independent of one another. Each of events A, B, and C has a probability p of occurring.

Quantity A	Quantity B
The probability that events A and B occur and event C does not occur	$p(1 - p)$

8. Both of the points $P(17, -20)$ and $Q(25, t)$ are in the xy-plane. Which of the following statements alone give(s) sufficient additional information to determine whether $t > -18$?

Indicate all such statements.

[A] The slope of the line that goes through the points $P(17, -20)$ and $Q(25, t)$ is $\frac{3}{4}$.
[B] The distance between the points $P(17, -20)$ and $Q(25, t)$ is 10.
[C] The point $Q(25, t)$ is the midpoint of the line segment whose endpoints are $P(17, -20)$ and $R(33, 3t + 34)$.

9. If $x = (3^8)(81^5)$ and $y = (9^7)(27^{12})$, then $xy =$

Ⓐ 3^{48}
Ⓑ 3^{54}
Ⓒ 3^{61}
Ⓓ 3^{68}
Ⓔ 3^{78}

10. What is the area of a triangle that has two sides that each have a length of 10, and whose perimeter is equal to that of a square whose area is 81?

    (A) 30
    (B) 36
    (C) 42
    (D) 48
    (E) 60

11. How many different committees of 2 men and 2 women can be formed from a group of 12 people, half of whom are men?

    (A) 225
    (B) 450
    (C) 495
    (D) 900
    (E) 2,970

12. Yaire had 50 pieces of candy, 64% of which were gummy worms. She has eaten several gummy worms, and no other candies, so that now her gummy worms make up 60% of her candies. How many pieces of candy does she have left?

    (A) 48
    (B) 46
    (C) 45
    (D) 36
    (E) 32

13. Water can be pumped from a 100,000 gallon tank at a uniform rate by opening valve *V*, valve *W*, or both. The rate at which water is pumped out by opening valve *V* is 10,000 gallons per hour. If the tank is completely full and both valves are opened, the tank can be drained in 6 hours. How long would it take to empty the tank if it were 80% full and only valve *W* were opened?

    (A) 6 hours
    (B) 8 hours
    (C) 12 hours
    (D) 15 hours
    (E) 18 hours

14. For which of the following sets of integers is the difference between the range and the interquartile range greater than or equal to 10?

Select all such sets of integers.

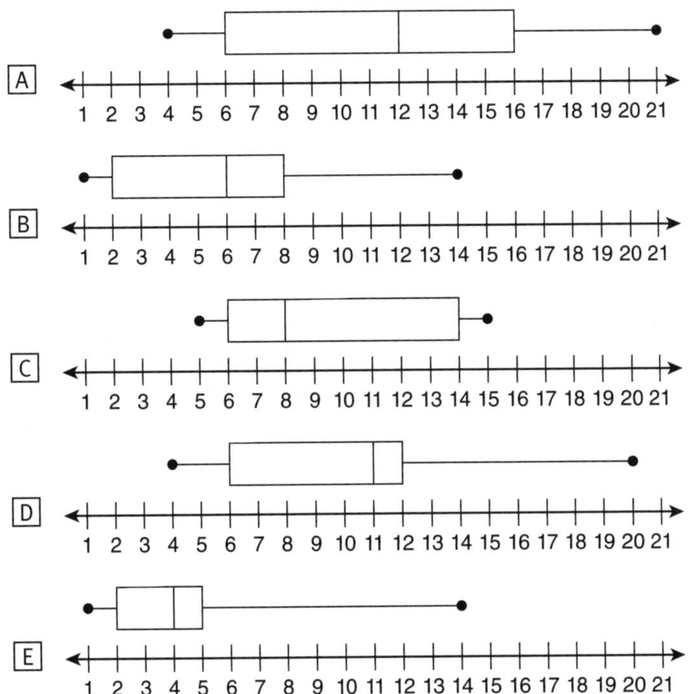

15. The ratio of five-dollar bills to one-dollar bills in Armando's wallet is 2:3. When he made a \$7 purchase, he paid for that purchase with only five-dollar bills, and with the smallest possible number of five-dollar bills. He received his change in one-dollar bills. After completing that transaction, the ratio of five-dollar bills to one-dollar bills was 1:3. How many one-dollar bills did Armando have before his purchase?

16. If Juanita gives half of her bitcoins in a 1:2 ratio to Pat and Svetlana, respectively, then Pat will have one fourth as many bitcoins as will Svetlana, who will in turn have twice as many bitcoins as will Juanita. If Pat currently has 2 bitcoins, then how many more bitcoins does Juanita currently have than Svetlana?

(A) 8
(B) 12
(C) 20
(D) 22
(E) 24

17. Uwe wants to split his rhombus-shaped garden into two triangular plots, one for planting strawberries and one for planting vegetables, by erecting a fence from one corner of the garden to the opposite corner. If one angle of the garden measures 60 degrees and one side of the garden measures x meters, which of the following could be the area of the vegetable plot?

Indicate all such values.

[A] $\frac{x^2\sqrt{3}}{2}$

[B] $\frac{x^2\sqrt{3}}{4}$

[C] $\frac{x^2\sqrt{3}}{8}$

[D] $\frac{x^2}{4}$

[E] $\frac{x^2}{2}$

Questions 18–20 refer to the following graphs.

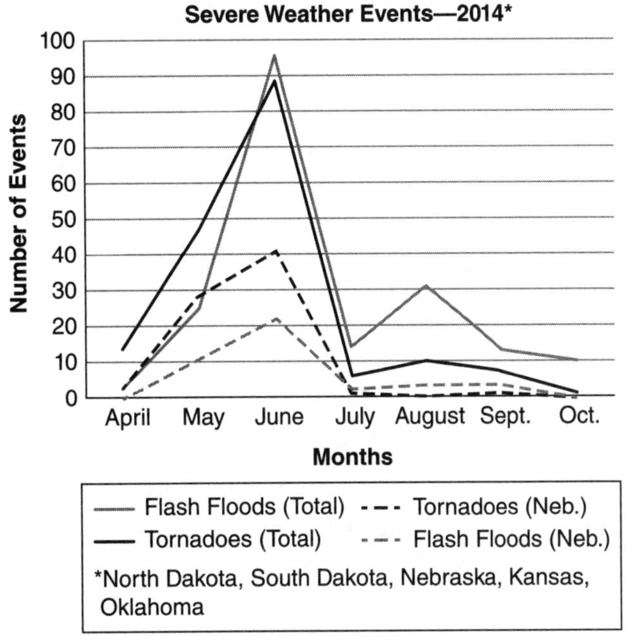

Source: National Atmospheric and Oceanic Administration (NOAA) National Climactic Data Center, Storm Events Database, http://www.ncdc.noaa.gov/stormevents/

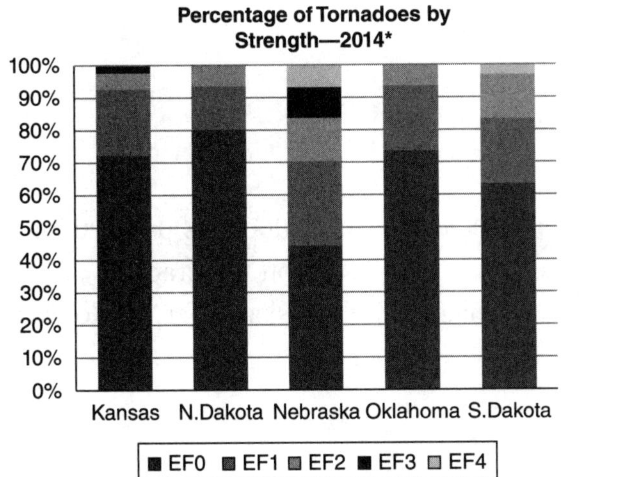

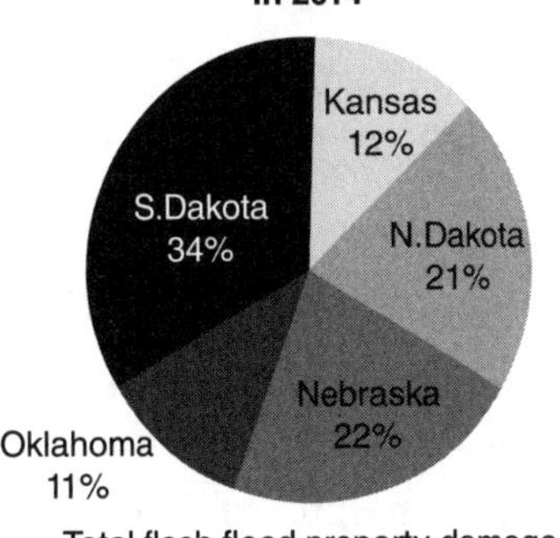

*As measured by the Enhanced Fujita (EF) Scale.

18. If in the years 2013, 2014, and 2015, in the five states shown, the number of severe weather events followed the same pattern as in 2014, but there were 25 percent more flash floods and tornadoes in 2014 than in 2013 and, from 2014 to 2015, the number of flash floods increased by one-third, and the number of tornadoes increased by about one-half, about how many more severe weather events occurred in August 2015 than in August 2013?

Ⓐ 5
Ⓑ 23
Ⓒ 27
Ⓓ 33
Ⓔ 56

19. Based on the information in the graphs, which of the following could have been the numbers of EF1 tornadoes in North Dakota, South Dakota, and Nebraska, respectively, in 2014?

Indicate all such numbers.

[A] 2, 6, 19
[B] 4, 3, 26
[C] 6, 3, 19
[D] 6, 18, 19
[E] 13, 20, 26
[F] 39, 60, 78

20. If the amount of property damage inflicted by flash floods is proportional to the number of flash floods that occur, then based on the graphs, approximately how much property damage did Nebraska suffer due to flash floods in June of 2014?

Ⓐ $65,000
Ⓑ $320,000
Ⓒ $450,000
Ⓓ $735,000
Ⓔ $2,158,296

ADVANCED MATH QUESTIONS PRACTICE SET 3 ANSWER KEY

1. D
2. B
3. D
4. B
5. D
6. A
7. B
8. A, C
9. E
10. D
11. A
12. C
13. C
14. D, E
15. 9
16. A
17. B
18. B
19. A, C
20. C

ADVANCED MATH QUESTIONS PRACTICE SET 3 ANSWERS AND EXPLANATIONS

1. D

From the centered information, you can determine that the greatest number b can be is $a - 1$, as the greatest factor of any number is the number itself. So to make Quantity B as large as possible, substitute $a - 1$ for b, and multiply by the next non-prime greater than a. As the only consecutive prime numbers are 2 and 3, in nearly all cases, the least non-prime integer greater than a will be $a + 1$. Quantity B would thus be $(a - 1)(a + 1) = a^2 - 1$, making Quantity A, which is a^2, greater. However, consider the special case mentioned of the consecutive prime numbers 2 and 3. If a is 2, $a - 1 = 1$, and the next non-prime greater than a would be 4. In this specific case, Quantity A, a^2, would be 4 and Quantity B would also be 4. Since two relationships are possible between the quantities, the answer is **(D).**

Note that you could also solve this problem by Picking Numbers for a and b. The smallest prime number is 2, so try that first. In that case, b has to equal $2 - 1 = 1$, and the least non-prime integer greater than a is 4. So Quantity A equals $a^2 = 2^2 = 4$, and Quantity B equals $1 \times 4 = 4$. With these numbers, the two quantities are equal. However, they cannot always be equal, because for greater values of a, there will be many possibilities for b. For example, if $a = 5$ and $b = 4$, then Quantity A equals $5 \times 5 = 25$ and Quantity B equals $4 \times 6 = 24$. More than one relationship is possible, so again, the answer is **(D).**

2. B

Since the problem is stated in terms of ratios rather than actual dimensions, use variables and algebra to find the solution for the value of v. Set the width of rectangle A equal to x and the length to $3x$. By the same logic, the width and length of rectangle B can be represented by y and $4y$. The area of a rectangle is $l \times w$, so the areas of rectangles A and B, respectively, are $3x \times x = 3x^2$ and $4y \times y = 4y^2$. From the information given in the problem, $3x^2 = 0.27 \times 4y^2$, which means that $\frac{3x^2}{4y^2} = \frac{27}{100}$.

Divide both sides of the equation by 3 and multiply by 4 to obtain $\frac{x^2}{y^2} = \frac{9}{25}$. Take the square root of both sides, and voila, $\frac{x}{y} = \frac{3}{5}$. (Because the problem deals with geometric figures, you do not need to worry about the negative roots.)

The perimeter of a rectangle with length l and width w is $2(l + w)$. The perimeter of rectangle A is $2(3x + x) = 2(4x) = 8x$. The perimeter of rectangle B is $2(4y + y) = 2(5y) = 10y$. So the ratio of the perimeter of rectangle A to the perimeter of rectangle B is $\frac{8x}{10y} = \frac{4x}{5y}$.

Since there are now two independent variables, x and y, and two distinct linear equations, solve for the value of v. Use the fact that

$$Perimeter\ A = \left(\frac{v}{100}\right) Perimeter\ B$$

to set up the proportion $\frac{Perimeter\ A}{Perimeter\ B} = \frac{v}{100}$. From earlier calculations:

$$\frac{Perimeter\ A}{Perimeter\ B} = \frac{4x}{5y} = \left(\frac{4}{5}\right)\left(\frac{x}{y}\right).$$

Furthermore, $\frac{x}{y} = \frac{3}{5}$, so $\left(\frac{4}{5}\right)\left(\frac{3}{5}\right) = \frac{v}{100}$. Multiply both sides of the equation by 25 to get $\frac{4 \times 3}{1} = \frac{v}{4}$. Cross multiply to find that $v = 48$. So Quantity A is 48. Quantity B is given as 54. Quantity B is greater and choice **(B)** is correct.

3. D

There are four possibilities, of which exactly one can occur:

(i) Event A occurs and event B does not occur.
(ii) Event B occurs and event A does not occur.
(iii) Neither event A nor event B occurs.
(iv) Both events A and B occur.

The centered information provides a lower limit for the probabilities for each of the first three of the above possibilities. Sum these three known lower limits:

$$\frac{1}{4} + \frac{1}{4} + \frac{1}{8} = \frac{2}{8} + \frac{2}{8} + \frac{1}{8} = \frac{5}{8}.$$

Because this is a sum of lower limits, the probability that one of the first three possibilities occurs must be $> \frac{5}{8}$ and the unknown probability that both events A and B occur must be $< \frac{3}{8}$, since the total of the four probabilities must equal 1. Therefore, the range of the probability that both events A and B occur is $0 \leq P_{A\ and\ B} < \frac{3}{8}$. Since the probability that both occur could be either greater or less than $\frac{1}{4}$, answer choice **(D)** is correct.

4. B

To solve the equation $\frac{x-1}{(x-2)^2+25}=\frac{2}{17}$ for the possible values of x, start by applying FOIL to the $(x-2)^2$ term in the left-hand denominator and combining like terms:

$$\frac{x-1}{x^2-4x+4+25}=\frac{2}{17}$$
$$\frac{x-1}{x^2-4x+29}=\frac{2}{17}$$

Now cross multiply:

$$(17)(x-1)=2\left(x^2-4x+29\right)$$
$$17x-17=2x^2-8x+58$$

Subtract $17x - 17$ from both sides of the equation to produce a quadratic set equal to zero:

$$17x-17-(17x-17)=2x^2-8x+58-(17x-17)$$
$$0=2x^2-25x+75$$

In order to reverse FOIL this equation, look for combinations of factors of 2 and 75 that will produce a sum of –25 when both factors of 75 have the same sign.

$$2(-5)=-10 \text{ and } 1(-15)=-15$$
$$-10+(-15)=-25$$

So the factored equation is $(2x - 15)(x - 5) = 0$, and x must be either $7\frac{1}{2}$ or 5. Since Quantity B is 8, that quantity is greater than either possible value of x, and the correct answer is **(B).**

5. D

In order to determine the value of *x*, use the average formula:

$$\text{Average} = \frac{\text{Sum of Values}}{\text{Number of Values}}.$$

Using the values given in the centered information, you can see that

$$x = \frac{(6 + 1 + 11 + x + 2)}{5} = \frac{20 + x}{5}.$$

Multiply both sides of the equation by 5 to get $5x = 20 + x$, then subtract *x* from both sides to get $4x = 20$. Divide both sides by 4 to obtain $x = 5$.

Since *y* is the median of the set, put the elements of the set in order, with *y* as the middle term: {1, 2, *y*, 5, 11}. Because of its position in the set, $2 \leq y \leq 5$.

Comparing *x* to *y*, given the allowable range, *y* could be either less than 5 or equal to 5 (the known value for *x*). Therefore, more than one relationship between the quantities is possible. The correct answer must be **(D).**

6. A

As with all Quantitative Comparison questions, you need the two values to be expressed in comparable terms, so think of Quantity A in terms of standard deviations above the mean. Because this is a standard deviation question, you might not be able to calculate the exact number of people who are taller than a certain height, but you should be able to approximate it as a percentage of the total.

The question stem states that the data are normally distributed, which means that about 68% of the heights of those involved in the study fall within 1 standard deviation of the mean. It also means that about 95% of those heights fall within 2 standard deviations of the mean. The question stem also says that 150 of the 900 people surveyed were between 5' 1" and 5' 3".

You don't know how great one standard deviation is, but you do know that a certain percentage of the total data lies between two points. Assume for a moment that one standard deviation is 2" in height. In that case, the people whose heights are between 5' 1" and 5' 3" would fall between 1 and 2 standard deviations below the mean of 5' 5". Half of 68% is 34%, which is the amount of data that falls between the mean and 1 standard deviation below the mean. Half of 95% is 47.5%, which is the amount of data that falls between the mean and 2 standard deviations below the mean. Use this information to calculate the percentage of data that would fall between 1 and 2 standard deviations below the mean: 47.5% – 34% = 13.5%.

However, the actual number of people whose heights fall between 5' 1" and 5' 3" is 150/900, or about 16.7%, which is more than 13.5%. Normal distribution means that data points are grouped more densely near the mean than farther away from it. Because more than 13.5% of the data falls between 5' 1" and 5' 3", you know this data selection is closer to the mean than the data selection between 1 and 2 standard deviations below the mean. In other words, you don't know exactly what the standard deviation is for this data set, but you do know it is greater than 2". That means that two standard deviations above the mean will be greater than 5' 9"; therefore, there are more people who are taller than 5' 9" than people who are 2 standard deviations above the mean.

Quantity A is greater, and the correct answer is **(A).**

Note: If you memorize 68%, 95%, 99.7%, and other common numbers for data sets with normal distribution, standard deviation problems will be much easier. For example, if you have memorized that about 13.5% of the data in a normal distribution falls between the 1 and 2 standard deviations below the mean, you don't need to calculate that number. Also note that you don't really need to calculate 150/900. 13.5% of 1,000 would be 135, and you can see at a glance that 150/900 is going to be larger than 135/1000.

7. B

The probability that an event does not occur is equal to 1 minus the probability that the event does occur. Since the probability that event C occurs is p, the probability that event C does not occur is $1 - p$. Since the events A, B, and C are independent of one another, the probability that event A occurs, event B occurs, and event C does not occur is equal to $p \times p \times (1 - p) = p^2(1 - p)$.

So Quantity A is $p^2(1 - p)$ and Quantity B is defined as $p(1 - p)$. The centered information that $0 < p < 1$ defines p as a positive fraction. It follows that $(1 - p)$ must also be a positive fraction. In Quantity A, three positive factors are multiplied; in Quantity B, two positive factors are multiplied. So both Quantities represent positive values. More specifically, Quantity A is Quantity B multiplied by p. In other words, Quantity A is Quantity B multiplied by a positive fraction less than 1.

It follows that Quantity B is greater than Quantity A, and the correct answer is **(B).**

Here's another way to see the answer: Because p and $(1 - p)$ are both positive, you can divide both quantities by p and $(1 - p)$, leaving p in Quantity A and 1 in Quantity B. Because $p < 1$, Quantity B is greater.

8. A, C

Consider statement A:

Plug into the slope formula for a line with a slope of $\frac{3}{4}$ that goes through the points $P(17, -20)$ and $Q(25, t)$:

$$\frac{t-(-20)}{25-17}=\frac{3}{4}$$

Based on this equation, there is just one value for t. So statement A gives sufficient additional information to determine whether $t > -18$.

For the record:

$$\begin{aligned}\frac{t-(-20)}{25-17} &= \frac{3}{4}\\ \frac{t+20}{8} &= \frac{3}{4}\\ t+20 &= 6\\ t &= -14\end{aligned}$$

Keep in mind that this additional calculation is not necessary. To use your time efficiently on Test Day, you would not actually need to solve for t.

Next, consider statement B:

Use the distance formula to try to solve for t, given the fact that the distance between the points $P(17, -20)$ and $Q(25, t)$ is equal to 10:

$$\begin{aligned}\sqrt{(25-17)^2+(t-(-20))^2} &= 10\\ \sqrt{8^2+(t+20)^2} &= 10\\ \sqrt{64+(t+20)^2} &= 10\\ \left(\sqrt{64+(t+20)^2}\right)^2 &= 10^2\\ 64+(t+20)^2 &= 100\\ (t+20)^2 &= 36\end{aligned}$$

Since $(t+20)^2 = 36$, $t + 20 = 6$ or $t + 20 = -6$.

If $t + 20 = 6$, then $t = -14$ and $t > -18$.

If $t + 20 = -6$, then $t = -26$ and $t < -18$.

Statement B does not give sufficient additional information to determine whether or not $t > -18$.

Finally, consider statement C:

The midpoint of the line segment whose endpoints are $P(17, -20)$ and $R(33, 3t + 34)$ is the point

$$\left(\frac{17 + 33}{2}, \frac{-20 + (3t + 34)}{2}\right).$$

This simplifies to

$$\left(\frac{50}{2}, \frac{-20 + 3t + 34}{2}\right).$$

Simplify further and recognize that the point $Q\left(25, \frac{3t + 14}{2}\right)$ is the point $Q(25, t)$.

Set the y-coordinates equal to find that $\frac{3t + 14}{2} = t$.

Solve for t:

$$\begin{aligned} 3t + 14 &= 2t \\ t + 14 &= 0 \\ t &= -14. \end{aligned}$$

Statement C gives sufficient additional information to determine that $t > -18$. As was the case for statement A, you could have stopped after the first equation in the explanation because that equation was sufficient to solve for one value of t.

The correct answers are **(A)** and **(C).**

9. E

Problems involving multiple bases are typically best solved by first converting all the terms to the same base. Here, 3 can be conveniently used as the base for each term:

$9 = 3 \times 3 = 3^2$
$27 = 3 \times 3 \times 3 = 3^3$
$81 = 3 \times 3 \times 3 \times 3 = 3^4$

Substitute 3^2 for 9, 3^3 for 27, and 3^4 for 81 to yield the following:

$x = (3^8)[(3^4)^5]$
$y = [(3^2)^7][(3^3)^{12}]$

Use the laws of exponents $(b^a)^c = b^{ac}$ and $b^a\,b^c = b^{a+c}$ to simplify:

$x = (3^8)(3^{4 \times 5}) = (3^8)(3^{20}) = 3^{8+20} = 3^{28}$
$y = (3^{2 \times 7})(3^{3 \times 12}) = (3^{14})(3^{36}) = 3^{14+36} = 3^{50}$

Finally, multiply x times y:

$xy = (3^{28})(3^{50}) = 3^{28+50} = 3^{78}$

Choice **(E)** is correct.

10. D

The area of a square is its side length squared. Since the area of this square is 81, each side is equal to $\sqrt{81}$ or 9. The perimeter of a square is 4 times the length of its side—in this case, 36. Since the perimeter of the triangle is equal to that of the square, subtract the two existing sides, 10 and 10, from 36, to get 16 for the third side. Here's a labeled diagram; remember to draw one if a problem doesn't provide it:

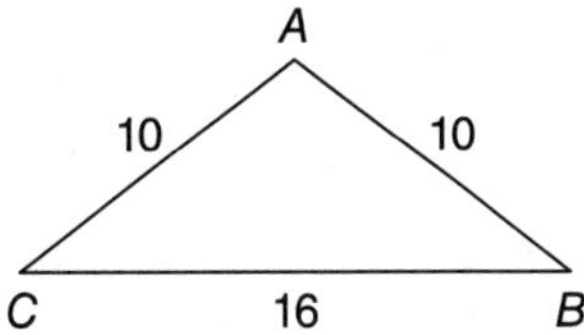

This triangle has two equal sides of length 10. Any triangle that has two equal sides is an isosceles triangle. Drop a perpendicular to divide it into 2 identical right triangles:

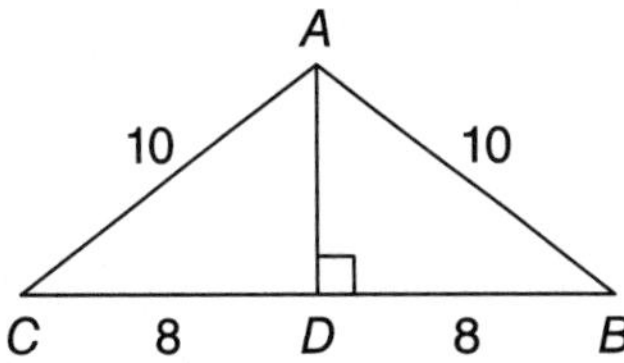

Here, point D divides side BC of the triangle into the two equal segments BD and DC, each equal to 8. To find the area of this triangle, you need the length of AD. Consider triangle ABD. Since the length of hypotenuse AB is 10 and the length of leg BD is 8, the side lengths of right triangle ABD are multiples of the 3-4-5 Pythagorean triple, with each part of the 3 to 4 to 5 ratio multiplied by 2, so $AD = 6$.

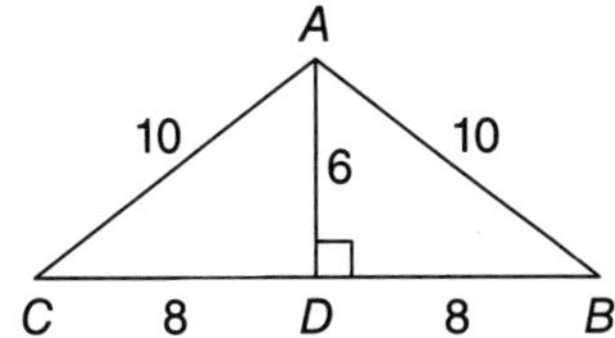

BC is the base of triangle *ABC* and *AD* is the height of the triangle drawn to base *BC*. The area of any triangle is one-half times base times height. Therefore, the area of triangle *ABC* is

$$\frac{1}{2} \times BC \times AD = \frac{1}{2} \times 16 \times 6 = 48.$$

Choice **(D)** is correct.

11. A

Split the group of 12 people into two groups of 6 men and 6 women each. Find the number of ways to choose 2 men from 6, and the number of ways to choose 2 women from 6, and multiply those two results together to find the answer.

Fortunately, the numbers are the same both times, so you'll need to apply the combination formula, ${}_nC_k = \frac{n!}{k!(n-k)!}$, just once:

$${}_6C_2 = \frac{6 \times 5 \times 4 \times 3 \times 2 \times 1}{2 \times 1 \times 4 \times 3 \times 2 \times 1} = \frac{30}{2} = 15.$$

So there are 15 ways to select 2 men from 6, and also 15 ways to select 2 women from 6. $15 \times 15 = 225$. Choice **(A)** is correct.

12. C

This is a variation on the classic mixture problem in which one element of the mixture changes, while the other element stays the same. You can simplify the solution of these problems by focusing on the element that stays the same; here, that's the other kind(s) of candy.

To start, you know that Yaire has (64%)(50) = (50%)(64) = 32 gummy worms. So she must have 18 candies that aren't gummy worms. Once she's eaten some of her worms, those 18 other candies now make up 100% – 60% = 40% of the new total number of candies. So:

$18 = (0.4)(T_n)$, where T_n is the new total. Solving for T_n gives you the answer: 45 pieces of candy.

Alternatively, you could Backsolve this one. Answer choice (D) would give you a gummy worm percentage of 50%, and answer choice (B) would give you a gummy worm percentage of just over 60%, so answer choice **(C)** must be correct. However, there's an even faster way to solve this problem. Since the answer choices are all integers, you can deduce that Yaire didn't eat any partial gummy worms. So you know that 60% of the correct answer—her new number of gummy worms—must be an integer. And since 60% is equivalent to $\frac{3}{5}$, the only potentially correct answers would have to be divisible by 5.

Choice **(C)** is correct.

13. C

A quick way to answer this question is to use the simplified formula for calculating combined work, $T = \frac{AB}{A + B}$, where T represents the total time to do a defined task, and A and B represent the amount of time each person or machine or, in this case, valve takes to do the task. Since the task is to empty a 100,000 gallon tank and opening valve V results in the tank draining at 10,000 gallons per hour, opening V only would empty the tank in 10 hours. Filling in the known values, you get $6 = \frac{10W}{10 + W}$.

$$\begin{aligned} 6(10 + W) &= \frac{10W(10 + W)}{10 + W} \\ 60 + 6W &= 10W \\ 60 &= 4W \\ 15 &= W \end{aligned}$$

Opening only valve W empties the tank in 15 hours when the tank is <u>full</u>. However, the question asks how long it would take to drain the tank from 80% full. That's 0.8×15 hrs $= 12$ hrs. Choice **(C)** is correct.

14. D, E

The range is the difference between the highest point and the lowest point, which are represented by the furthest points on the plots.

The interquartile range is the difference between the third quartile and the first quartile, which are represented by the two vertical edges of the rectangle on the plot.

First, calculate the range and the interquartile range, then take difference between the two. The question is asking for all choices that have a result greater than or equal to 10.

A. Range $= 21 - 4 = 17$
   Interquartile Range $= 16 - 6 = 10$
   Difference $= 17 - 10 = 7$

B. Range $= 14 - 1 = 13$
   Interquartile Range $= 8 - 2 = 6$
   Difference $= 13 - 6 = 7$

C. Range = 15 − 5 = 10
Interquartile Range = 14 − 6 = 8
Difference = 10 − 8 = 2

(Note that the moment you notice the range is 10, there's no need to check the interquartile range, since 10 minus anything will be less than 10.)

D. Range = 20 − 4 = 16
Interquartile Range = 12 − 6 = 6
Difference = 16 − 6 = **10**

E. Range = 14 − 1 = 13
Interquartile Range = 5 − 2 = 3
Difference = 13 − 3 = **10**

Only answer choices **(D)** and **(E)** have a difference greater than or equal to 10; therefore, they are the only two correct answers.

15. 9

The 2:3 ratio of bills does not necessarily mean that Armando starts with 2 five-dollar bills and 3 one-dollar bills; he could have any multiple of 2 and 3—such as 4 and 6, 20 and 30, etc. Therefore, the ratio can be expressed, using a common multiplier, as $\frac{2x}{3x}$. After using 2 five-dollar bills for the transaction, Armando will have $2x - 2$ five dollar bills and, with the 3 one-dollar bills he receives in change, $3x + 3$ one dollar bills. Since the final ratio is 1:3, you can set up a proportion to find $\frac{1}{3} = \frac{2x - 2}{3x + 3}$. Multiply both sides by the denominators to get $1(3x + 3) = 3(2x - 2)$. Simplify to $3x + 3 = 6x - 6$ and solve: $9 = 3x$, so $x = 3$. However, x is not the answer to the question asked, but merely the common multiplier used in the initial ratio. Since Armando started with $3x$ dollar bills, and since $x = 3$, it follows that he had $3(3) = 9$ one-dollar bills initially.

16. A

If the question asked for one value (say, Juanita's number of bitcoins), then Backsolving would be a terrific way to bypass most of the work on this complex translation question. Unfortunately, the question asks for the difference between two values, so backsolving won't work. Algebra it is!

Let J, P, and S represent the number of bitcoins currently in the hands of Juanita, Pat, and Svetlana, respectively. (For simplicity's sake, we'll refer to bitcoins as "coins" from here on out.) If Juanita gives half of her coins away, she'll have $\frac{J}{2}$ coins left. Next, consider the ratio. If Pat and Svetlana receive Juanita's coins in a 1:2 ratio,

that means Pat will receive one third of those coins and Svetlana will receive the remaining two thirds. Thus, Pat will receive one third of one half, or one sixth, of Juanita's coins, or $\frac{J}{6}$. Svetlana will receive two thirds of one half, or $\frac{2}{3} \times \frac{1}{2} = \frac{1}{3}$ of Juanita's coins, or $\frac{J}{3}$. After Juanita makes the gift, she will have $\frac{J}{2}$ coins, Pat will have $P + \frac{J}{6}$, and Svetlana will have $S + \frac{J}{3}$. You're told that Pat's total will be one fourth of Svetlana's. Thus:

$$P + \frac{J}{6} = \frac{1}{4}\left(S + \frac{J}{3}\right)$$

Multiply this equation by 12 to eliminate the fractions, then simplify as much as you can:

$$\begin{aligned} 12P + 2J &= 3\left(S + \frac{J}{3}\right) \\ 12P + 2J &= 3S + J \\ 12P &= 3S - J \end{aligned}$$

You're also told that, after the gift, Svetlana's total will be double Juanita's. Thus:

$$\begin{aligned} S + \frac{J}{3} = 2\left(\frac{J}{2}\right) &= J \\ 3S + J &= 3J \\ 3S &= 2J \end{aligned}$$

Substitute $2J$ in place of $3S$ in the earlier equation to get:

$$\begin{aligned} &12P = 3S - J = 2J - J = J \\ &12P = J \end{aligned}$$

Finally, you can make use of the fact that Pat has 2 coins. This means that Juanita has $12(2) = 24$ coins. Because $3S = 2J$, it follows that $S = \frac{2}{3}J$, and Svetlana has $\frac{2(24)}{3} = 2(8) = 16$ coins. The question asks how many more coins Juanita has than Svetlana, so the answer is $24 - 16 = 8$, choice **(A)**.

17. B

Whenever a geometry problem comes without a figure, start by drawing one yourself:

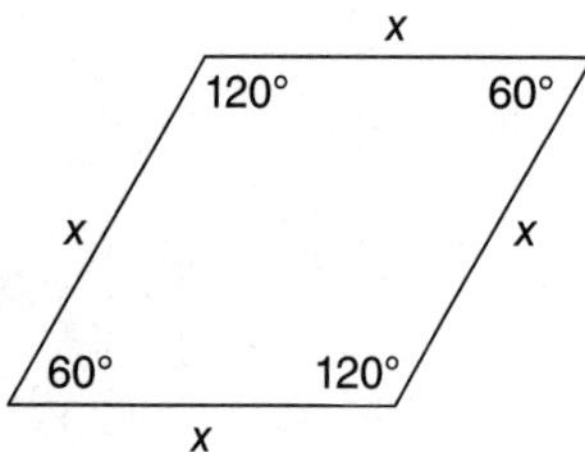

Uwe wants to split this garden into two triangles. What makes this question tricky is that there are two ways to split a rhombus into two triangles. Try it this way first:

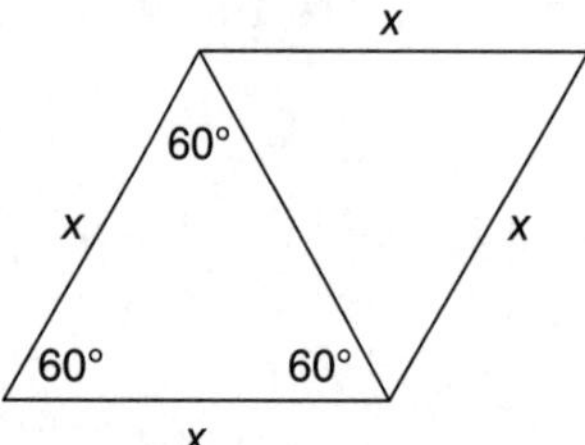

The area of one plot would then be the area of an equilateral triangle with side x. Use the properties of 30-60-90 triangles to deduce that the height of such a triangle must be $\frac{x\sqrt{3}}{2}$, which allows you to calculate the area as follows:

$$\text{Area} = \frac{1}{2}bh = \left(\frac{1}{2}\right)(x)\left(\frac{x\sqrt{3}}{2}\right) = \frac{x^2\sqrt{3}}{4}$$

This is one of the choices, but the garden might be split the other way:

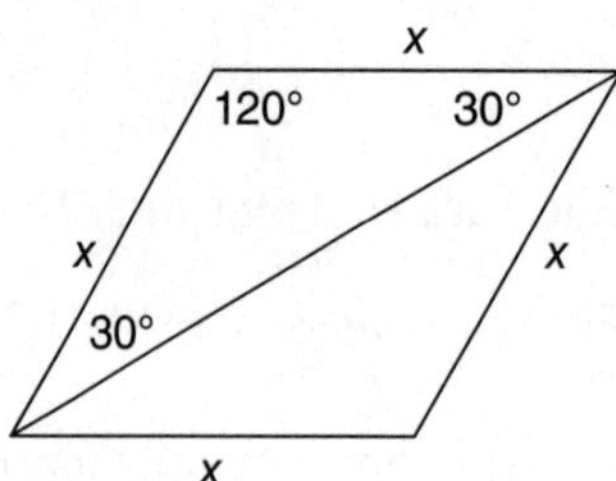

To find the area of one of these triangles, further subdivide it into two right triangles and use again the properties of 30-60-90 right triangles:

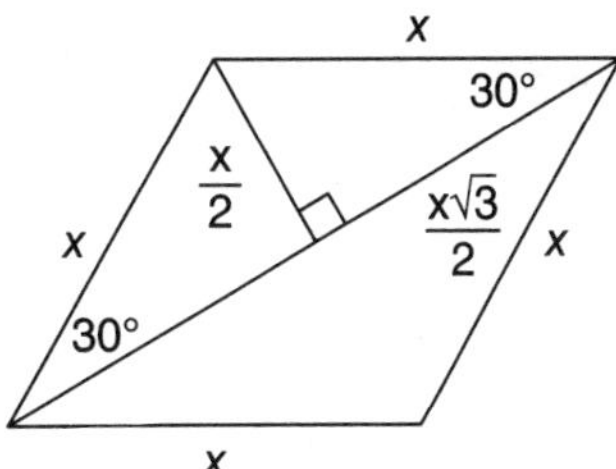

The base of the big triangle is therefore twice $\frac{x\sqrt{3}}{2}$, or $x\sqrt{3}$. The height is $\frac{x}{2}$, and the area is found as follows:

$$Area = \frac{1}{2}bh = \frac{1}{2}(x\sqrt{3})\left(\frac{x}{2}\right) = \frac{x^2\sqrt{3}}{4}$$

This is the same as the previous area, so only one answer choice is correct: **(B).**

Note that you can save some time by using critical thinking to deduce up front that there must only be one correct answer. Imagine breaking up a rhombus into four triangles rather than two:

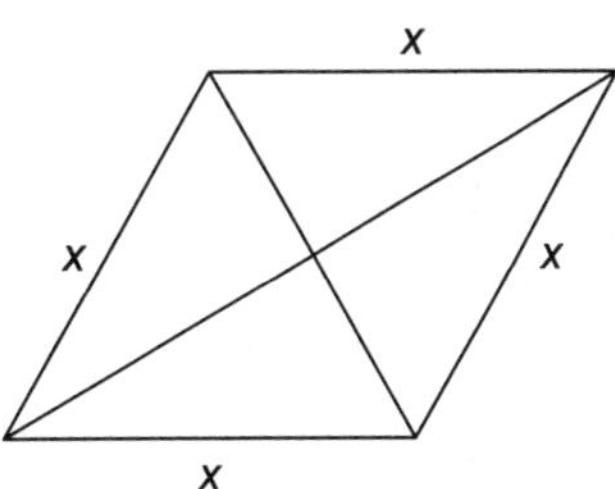

Because the starting shape is a rhombus, all four triangles are congruent. No matter which two triangles you combine to make a big triangle—be it the left and bottom triangle as we tried first, or the left and top triangle as we tried second—the total area will be the same.

18. B

This question refers to the number of flash floods and tornadoes for all five states, so read the line graph, specifically looking at August. The line graph tells you only about events in 2014, so you will need to calculate the number of events in 2013 and 2015. Since the question tells you that events followed the same pattern each year, you can infer that the percent increases in the question affect each month the same way.

In August 2014, there were about 30 flash floods and 10 tornadoes. Both numbers are a 25 percent increase over the previous year, so calculate the number of events in August 2013:

$$\text{Floods} + \text{Tornadoes} = 30 + 10 = 40$$

$$40 = e + 0.25e;\ 40 = 1.25e;\ e = 32$$

There were about 32 severe weather events in August 2013.

Now calculate the numbers in 2015, starting from 2014 as a base and increasing the floods by one-third and the tornadoes by one-half:

Floods:

$$f = 30 + \frac{1}{3}(30);\ f = 40$$

Tornadoes:

$$t = 10 + \frac{1}{2}(10);\ t = 15$$

Add to find that there were about 40 + 15 = 55 severe weather events in August 2015. The question asks how many more events occurred in August 2015 than in August 2013, so subtract: 55 − 32 = 23. The correct answer is **(B).**

19. A, C

This question asks about EF1 tornadoes, so look at the stacked bar graph, which tells you the proportion of tornadoes by intensity for each state. The question is asking for possible actual numbers of tornadoes, so also look at the line graph, which gives you some information about numbers of events.

The line graph gives you the number of tornadoes in Nebraska in 2014, so start there.

April	3
May	28
June	41
July	1
August	0
Sept	1
Oct	0
	74

Your reading of the graph may vary slightly due to estimating the numbers, but you should have a number reasonably close to 74. Then in the stacked bar graph, the

EF1 tornadoes are represented by the second bar from the bottom. For Nebraska, about 25% of the tornadoes were EF1, so $0.25 \times 74 \approx 19$ EF1 tornadoes. The correct answer must have a last number that is close to 19. Again, depending on your estimates from the graphs, you might have arrived at a slightly different number, but choices (B), (E), and (F) clearly do not have the right number for Nebraska and can be eliminated.

Now you can use Backsolving to see which answer choices fit the data. If you add up the tornadoes for all five states, there are 174 (again, your estimate may vary slightly but should be close enough to solve this problem). The stacked bar graph tells you that about 13% of North Dakota's tornadoes and 20% of South Dakota's tornadoes were EF1. According to choice (D), there were 6 EF1 tornadoes in North Dakota, representing about 13% of all North Dakota tornadoes: $6 = 0.13x$; $x \approx 46$ North Dakota tornadoes. Choice (D) also says there were 18 EF1 tornadoes in South Dakota, which would represent 20% of all the tornadoes in South Dakota: $18 = 0.2x$; $x = 90$. Add these to the 74 Nebraska tornadoes: $46 + 90 + 74 = 210$. That's too many total tornadoes, so eliminate choice (D).

Now keep in mind that this all-that-apply question asks what *could have been* the numbers of EF1 tornadoes in 2014. The stacked bar graph tells you what percent of North and South Dakota's tornadoes were EF1—13% of North Dakota's and 20% of South Dakota's tornadoes. However, nowhere are you told how many total tornadoes those states had. (You can deduce only that together they had fewer than 100 tornadoes, to allow for Nebraska's 74 and those occurring in Kansas and Oklahoma). North Dakota could have had more, or South Dakota could have had more. Therefore, a wide range of numbers are possible values. Choice **(A)** works if North Dakota had 15 tornadoes and South Dakota had 30, and choice **(C)** works if North Dakota had 45 tornadoes and South Dakota had 15. Choices **(A)** and **(C)** are correct.

20. C

This question concerns the amount of property damage due to flash floods (look at the pie chart) and the number of flash floods that occur (look at the line graph). The answer choices are far apart, so approximation is an efficient strategy for this question.

Of all the damage accounted for in the pie chart ($3,854,100), 22% was in Nebraska, so calculate Nebraska's share of the damage: $0.22 \times \$3,854,100 = \$847,902$. For ease of calculation, round this to $850,000.

Next, figure out how much of that damage occurred in June. The total number of flash floods in Nebraska was as follows:

Month	Floods
April	0
May	11
June	22
July	2
August	3
Sept	3
Oct	0
	41

Your reading of the graph may vary slightly due to estimating the numbers, but you should have a number close to 40. The number of floods in June was 22, or a little over half the total. You are told that the amount of damage is proportional to the number of events, so a bit more than half the damage in Nebraska happened in June. Half the damage is $850,000 ÷ 2 = $425,000, so the correct answer is the one that is a little more than that. (If you did the calculations precisely, you should have arrived at $454,972.) The correct answer is **(C).**

ADVANCED MATH QUESTIONS PRACTICE SET 4

1. Set S is the set of all positive integers that are less than 100 that are the square of an integer. Set T is the set of all positive integers that are less than 100 that are equal to the cube of an integer.

Quantity A	Quantity B
The number of integers that are in at least one of the sets S and T	12

Ⓐ Quantity A is greater.
Ⓑ Quantity B is greater.
Ⓒ The two quantities are equal.
Ⓓ The relationship cannot be determined from the information given.

2. $$2x - 3y = 7$$

Quantity A	Quantity B
$4x^2 - 12xy + 9y^2 + 18$	70

Ⓐ Quantity A is greater.
Ⓑ Quantity B is greater.
Ⓒ The two quantities are equal.
Ⓓ The relationship cannot be determined from the information given.

3. The integer n is greater than or equal to 40. When the integer n is divided by 28, the remainder is 12.

Quantity A	Quantity B
The remainder when $2n$ is divided by 14	The remainder when $3n$ is divided by 14

Ⓐ Quantity A is greater.
Ⓑ Quantity B is greater.
Ⓒ The two quantities are equal.
Ⓓ The relationship cannot be determined from the information given.

4.

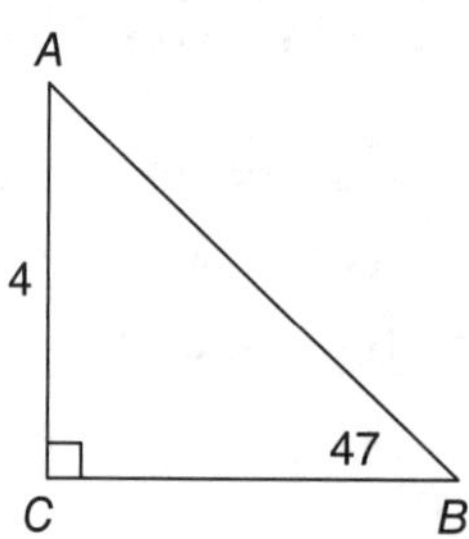

Quantity A	Quantity B
The area of triangle ABC	8

Ⓐ Quantity A is greater.
Ⓑ Quantity B is greater.
Ⓒ The two quantities are equal.
Ⓓ The relationship cannot be determined from the information given.

5. A certain pregnancy test comes back positive for 95 percent of pregnant women who take it. However, it also comes back positive for 5 percent of non-pregnant women who take it. Two percent of the female population of city A is pregnant. Marisa, a resident of city A, takes the pregnancy test and gets a positive result.

Quantity A	Quantity B
The probability that Marisa is pregnant	75%

Ⓐ Quantity A is greater.
Ⓑ Quantity B is greater.
Ⓒ The two quantities are equal.
Ⓓ The relationship cannot be determined from the information given.

6. Clarice, Yolanta, and Albert have among them some chocolates. One of them has triple the chocolates of another. Yolanta has 24 percent of the chocolates.

Quantity A	Quantity B
The number of chocolates Albert has if Clarice has more chocolates than Yolanta	The number of chocolates Clarice has if Yolanta has more chocolates than Albert

(A) Quantity A is greater.
(B) Quantity B is greater.
(C) The two quantities are equal.
(D) The relationship cannot be determined from the information given.

7. Researchers measured the incubation times of 100 emperor penguin eggs. The researchers' analysis showed that the data followed normal distribution, the mean was 64 days, and the standard deviation was 1 day. After recounting, the researchers found more eggs and added them to the original data set: 4 eggs took 64 days to hatch, 2 took 61 days, and 2 took 67 days.

Quantity A	Quantity B
1 day	1 standard deviation of the data set that includes all 108 eggs

(A) Quantity A is greater.
(B) Quantity B is greater.
(C) The two quantities are equal.
(D) The relationship cannot be determined from the information given.

8. The median of the 35 numbers in list L is 18. The mode of list L is not 18 and not 19.

Quantity A	Quantity B
The arithmetic mean of the 17 greatest numbers in list L	19

Ⓐ Quantity A is greater.
Ⓑ Quantity B is greater.
Ⓒ The two quantities are equal.
Ⓓ The relationship cannot be determined from the information given.

9. Lorenzo traveled 120 miles by automobile to visit his brother. The first segment of the trip required Lorenzo to drive on 10 miles of city roads before he reached the interstate highway and accelerated to a constant speed of 60 mph. The last segment of the trip was a 10 mile journey over country roads on which Lorenzo averaged 50 miles per hour. If the entire trip took Lorenzo 2 hours and 22 minutes, what was his average speed in miles per hour for the portion of the route between his home and the interstate highway?

[ ]

10. If $\frac{x}{3}$ is a positive odd integer and $x \leq 15$, which values could be the median of the list of numbers 1, 3, 5, 7, 9, 11, 13, 15, 17, x, $\frac{x}{3}$?

Indicate <u>all</u> such values.

[A] 5
[B] 6
[C] 7
[D] 9
[E] 11

11. Olga's swimming pool has three pipes connected to it. If the pool is empty, pipe A can fill it in 3 hours and pipe B can fill it in 4 hours. If the pool is at capacity, pipe C can empty it in 2 hours. The capacity of Olga's pool is 2,400 cubic meters. If all three pipes are activated when the pool is empty, how many hours will it take for the pool to be filled to 60 percent of capacity?

(A) 7.0
(B) 7.2
(C) 8.0
(D) 8.6
(E) 12.0

12. If $|8x - 7| > 3x + 8$, then each of the following could be true EXCEPT:

(A) $1 < x < 3$
(B) $-1 < x < 0$
(C) $2 < x < 4$
(D) $x = 3.5$
(E) $x = -1$

13. A fair coin is tossed six times. What is the probability that the result will be exactly three heads and three tails?

(A) $\frac{1}{6}$
(B) $\frac{1}{4}$
(C) $\frac{5}{16}$
(D) $\frac{1}{2}$
(E) $\frac{13}{24}$

14. The ratio of cranberry to apple to orange juice in a certain cocktail containing no other liquids is x:5:3. After 6 gallons of water are added to the cocktail, the ratio of orange juice to total liquid becomes 1:4. After another 24 gallons of water are added to the cocktail, the ratio of apple juice to total liquid becomes 1:4. What fraction of the original cocktail is cranberry juice?

(A) $\frac{1}{5}$

(B) $\frac{1}{4}$

(C) $\frac{1}{3}$

(D) $\frac{1}{2}$

(E) $\frac{2}{3}$

15. What is the probability of rolling a number less than 3 at least 3 times in 5 rolls of a six-sided die?

(A) $\frac{2}{15}$

(B) $\frac{17}{81}$

(C) $\frac{1}{3}$

(D) $\frac{2}{5}$

(E) $\frac{15}{32}$

16 Juliana has three options to invest her money for one year. Option A is discounted notes that she can buy for \$98 and cash in for a face value of \$100 a year later. Option B is a savings account that pays a 2% annual interest rate compounded semi-annually. Option C is an account that pays 2.03% simple interest for one year. Which of the answer choices represents the percent returns from the three choices in order from lowest to highest?

(A) A, B, C
(B) A, C, B
(C) B, C, A
(D) C, A, B
(E) C, B, A

17. Rick's Sandwich Shop lets customers create their own sandwiches by choosing from among a certain number of ingredients. When ordering Rick's Rockin' Sandwich, the customer must choose 1 of 3 breads, 1 of 6 meats, and 1 of 4 cheeses. The customer can also add up to 3 of 8 different veggies. How many unique Rick's Rockin' Sandwiches could a customer order?

(A) 4,032
(B) 6,624
(C) 6,696
(D) 24,192
(E) 28,932

Questions 18–20 refer to the following charts.

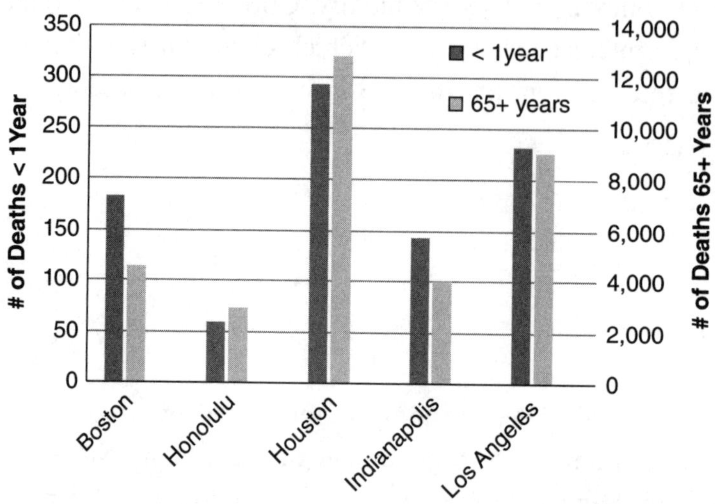

Source: Centers for Disease Control and Prevention, *Morbidity and Mortality Weekly Report* (*MMWR*), Table III: Mortality in 122 U.S. cities, data provided by National Notifiable Diseases Surveillance System (NNDSS), http://wonder.cdc.gov/mmwr/mmwrmort.asp.

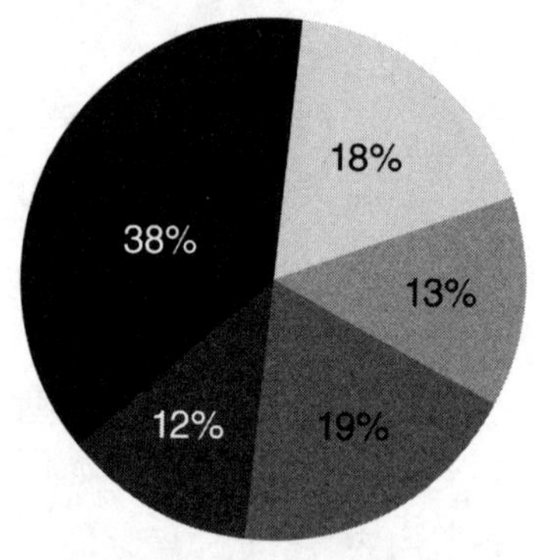

Total deaths from pneumonia/influenza for selected cities: 3,532

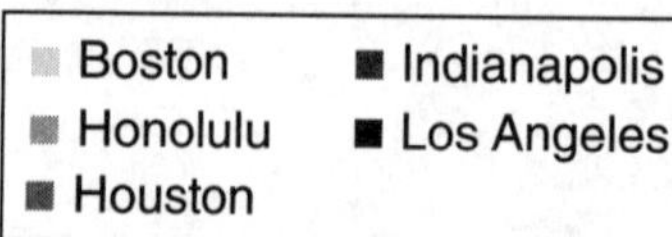

18. Imagine that at the beginning of 2014, Boston and Los Angeles implemented a public health program that reduced deaths of infants less than 1 year old by 20 percent, while the cities of Honolulu and Indianapolis terminated an identical program. What would have been the approximate total impact of these program changes on the number of infant deaths in these cities?

    (A) There would have been 600 more deaths.
    (B) There would have been 70 more deaths.
    (C) There would have been 30 fewer deaths.
    (D) There would have been 65 fewer deaths.
    (E) There would have been 150 fewer deaths.

19. If in 2014, the population of Los Angeles was 75 percent greater than the population of Houston, what is the ratio of the incidence of pneumonia- and influenza-related deaths (expressed as a percent of the city's population) in Houston to the incidence in Los Angeles in that year?

    (A) $\frac{1}{2}$
    (B) $\frac{7}{8}$
    (C) $\frac{15}{16}$
    (D) $\frac{8}{7}$
    (E) $\frac{4}{3}$

20. Assuming that 80 percent of all deaths due to pneumonia or influenza occur among the elderly, defined as those age 65 and over, in which city was the least proportion of all deaths among the elderly attributed to pneumonia or influenza?

    (A) Houston
    (B) Indianapolis
    (C) Honolulu
    (D) Boston
    (E) Los Angeles

ADVANCED MATH QUESTIONS PRACTICE SET 4 ANSWER KEY

1. B
2. B
3. A
4. B
5. B
6. B
7. B
8. D
9. 20
10. C, D
11. B
12. A
13. C
14. A
15. B
16. C
17. C
18. C
19. B
20. A

ADVANCED MATH QUESTIONS PRACTICE SET 4 ANSWERS AND EXPLANATIONS

1. B

Start by determining all the integers in each of sets *S* and *T*. These are the integers in set *S*:

$1^2 = 1 \times 1 = 1$
$2^2 = 2 \times 2 = 4$
$3^2 = 3 \times 3 = 9$
$4^2 = 4 \times 4 = 16$
$5^2 = 5 \times 5 = 25$
$6^2 = 6 \times 6 = 36$
$7^2 = 7 \times 7 = 49$
$8^2 = 8 \times 8 = 64$
$9^2 = 9 \times 9 = 81$

$10^2 = 10 \times 10 = 100$, but this is not included since the centered information specifies less than 100.

These are the integers in set *T*:

$1^3 = 1 \times 1 \times 1 = 1$
$2^3 = 2 \times 2 \times 2 = 4 \times 2 = 8$
$3^3 = 3 \times 3 \times 3 = 9 \times 3 = 27$
$4^3 = 4 \times 4 \times 4 = 16 \times 4 = 64$

Thus, the numbers in set *S* are the 9 integers 1, 4, 9, 16, 25, 36, 49, 64, and 81.

The numbers in set *T* are 1, 8, 27, and 64.

Two of the numbers in set *T*, 1 and 64, are also in set *S*, so don't count those.

It turns out that there are $9 + 2 = 11$ integers in at least one of sets *S* and *T*. Quantity A is 11 and Quantity B is 12. Choice **(B)** is correct.

2. B

You need to compare a quadratic to 70, and the only centered information is a linear equation. Try squaring both sides of the centered equation to see if you get anything similar to Quantity A. Squaring both sides of $2x - 3y = 7$ gives you $(2x - 3y)^2 = 49$. Using the identity $(a - b)^2 = a^2 - 2ab + b^2$, the equation $(2x - 3y)^2 = 49$ becomes $4x^2 - 12xy + 9y^2 = 49$. That looks awfully similar to Quantity A. In fact, Quantity

A is just the result of adding 18 to $4x^2 - 12xy + 9y^2$, which is one side of the equation $4x^2 - 12xy + 9y^2 = 49$. Adding 18 to both sides of this equation produces $4x^2 - 12xy + 9y^2 + 18 = 67$. The left side of this equation is Quantity A, so Quantity A equals 67. Quantity B is 70. Quantity B is greater, and **(B)** is correct.

3. A

The centered information says that when the integer n is divided by 28, the remainder is 12. This means that $n = 28m + 12$, where m is an integer such that $m \geq 1$.

Consider Quantity A. Since $n = 28m + 12$, $2n = 56m + 24$. Since 56 is a multiple of 14 ($56 = 4 \times 14$), and m is a positive integer, the remainder when $56m$ is divided by 14 is 0. When 24 is divided by 14, the quotient is 1 and the remainder is 10. Thus, the remainder when $2n$, which equals $56m + 24$, is divided by 14 is $0 + 10 = 10$. Quantity A is 10.

Now consider Quantity B. Since $n = 28m + 12$, $3n = 84m + 36$. Since 84 is a multiple of 14 ($84 = 6 \times 14$), and m is a positive integer, the remainder when $84m$ is divided by 14 is 0. When 36 is divided by 14, the quotient is 2 and the remainder is 8. You can conclude that the remainder when $3n$, or $84m + 36$, is divided by 14 is $0 + 8 = 8$. Quantity B is 8.

Quantity A is 10 and Quantity B is 8. Quantity A is greater and the correct answer is **(A)**.

4. B

The area of any triangle is $\frac{1}{2} \times \text{base} \times \text{height}$. The area of triangle ABC is $\frac{1}{2} \times AC \times BC$. Since $AC = 4$, the area of right triangle ABC is $\frac{1}{2} \times 4 \times BC = 2 \times BC$. To determine the value of Quantity A, you would need to know the length of BC, but there's no way to calculate that without using trigonometry. Fortunately, you can often answer Quantitative Comparison questions speedily without knowing precise values.

Consider what is known about triangle ABC. In any triangle, the sum of the measures of the 3 interior angles is 180°. You know that the measure of angle ACB is 90° and the measure of angle ABC is 47°. Subtract these two values from 180° to find that angle CAB thus equals 43°. Now in any triangle, a side that is opposite a greater angle is longer than a side that is opposite a smaller angle. So side AC, which is across from a 47° angle, is longer than side BC, which is across from a 43° angle. Since $AC = 4$, it must be that $BC < 4$.

The area of triangle ABC is $2(BC)$. Since $BC < 4$, the area of triangle ABC must be less than $2(4) = 8$. Quantity A is less than 8, and Quantity B is equal to 8. Quantity B is greater and choice **(B)** is correct.

5. B

This question succumbs quickly to Kaplan's Picking Numbers strategy. Although this is one of the hardest GRE questions you're ever likely to see, it's surprisingly straightforward if you apply the Picking Numbers strategy to it.

Suppose 1,000 women take the test. The question states that 2 percent, or $1{,}000 \times 0.02 = 20$, of those women are pregnant. It follows that $1000 - 20 = 980$ women are not pregnant. Of the 20 pregnant women who take the test, 95%, or $20 \times 0.95 = 19$, will see a positive result. Of the 980 non-pregnant women who take the test, 5%, or $980 \times 0.05 = 49$ will see a positive result.

Take a moment to paraphrase Quantity A. It asks, in essence, "If a woman takes the test and gets a positive result, what is the probability that she is actually pregnant?" You know that a total of $19 + 49 = 68$ women will have a positive test, only 19 of whom are in fact pregnant. You can stop here: there is no need to calculate the precise probability, because 19 out of 68 is clearly less than 75%. The correct answer is **(B).** (For the record, the probability is $\frac{19}{68} \approx 28\%$.)

6. B

Before diving into the quantities, consider the possible scenarios. There are three:

Scenario 1: Yolanta has triple the chocolates of someone else. In this case, Yolanta has 24% of the chocolates, someone else has $24\% \div 3 = 8\%$, and the third person has $100\% - 24\% - 8\% = 68\%$.

Scenario 2: Someone has triple the chocolates of Yolanta. In this case, Yolanta has 24% of the chocolates, someone else has $24\% \times 3 = 72\%$, and the third person has $100\% - 24\% - 72\% = 4\%$.

Scenario 3: Yolanta is not involved in the triple scenario. In that case, Clarice and Albert share the remaining $100\% - 24\% = 76\%$ of the chocolates in a ratio of 3:1.

$$\begin{aligned} 3x + x &= 76\% \\ 4x &= 76\% \\ x = 76\% \div 4 &= 19\% \\ 3x = 19\% \times 3 &= 57\% \end{aligned}$$

Thus, in Scenario 3, Yolanta has 24% of the chocolates, someone else has 19%, and the third person has 57%.

The key to this question is that in all three cases, Yolanta has the median number of chocolates. This insight allows you to conclude that in Quantity A, where Clarice has more chocolates than Yolanta, Albert has the fewest. Thus, Quantity A refers to the person with the fewest chocolates (i.e., less than the median of 24%). In Quantity B, where Yolanta has more chocolates than Albert, Clarice must have the most. Thus,

Quantity B refers to the person with the most chocolates (i.e., more than the median of 24%). Paraphrasing, the quantities say:

Quantity A	Quantity B
The number of chocolates the person with the fewest chocolates (less than 24%) has.	The number of chocolates the person with the most chocolates (greater than 24%) has.

The answer is **(B)**.

7. B

First, recognize that the mean does not change. The data added is symmetrical around the original mean of 64 days. The 4 new eggs with a 64-day incubation period will not affect the average. There are 2 new eggs with a 61-day incubation period and 2 new eggs with a 67-day incubation period. Both 61 and 67 are the same distance from the mean (3 days) and the number added is the same at both data points (2 eggs), so they will not change the average either.

Another way to confirm this is to find the average of the new eggs:

$$\begin{aligned}\text{Average} &= \frac{((64 \times 4) + (61 \times 2) + (67 \times 2))}{8} \\ &= \frac{256 + 122 + 134}{8} \\ &= \frac{512}{8} = 64\end{aligned}$$

Next, consider the original data set and how it changes with the addition of the 8 new eggs. If the standard deviation were to remain the same, the distribution of the new data added would have to mirror the normal distribution of the original data set. In other words, about 68% would be within 1 day, 95% within 2 days, and 99.7% within 3 days. The new data added, however, is more spread out. The new data set's standard deviation will be greater than the original data set's of 1 day; therefore, the correct answer is **(B)**.

Note: if you'd like to use this question to learn more about how normal distribution works, you can estimate how many eggs had a 64-day incubation period in the original data set. In the normal distribution, about 68% of the data is within one standard deviation of the mean. That means that of the 100 original eggs, about 68 had an incubation period greater than 63 days and less than 65 days. The new total of 64-day eggs is $68 + 4 = 72$. The new total number of eggs is $100 + 8 = 108$. The new percent of eggs within 1 day of the mean is $72/108 = 66.7\%$. This is less than 68%, which means that compared to the original data set, slightly more data is farther from the mean. The standard deviation would need to become greater in order to include 68% of the data; therefore, the new standard deviation will be more than 1 day.

8. D

The numbers in list *L* could be anything, as long as 18 is the median but not the mode and 19 is also not the mode. For example, imagine that each of the 17 greatest numbers in list *L* is 100, the median is 18, and each of the other 17 numbers is 0. This would be a permissible list because the median (but not the mode) would indeed be 18. Quantity A, the average of the 17 greatest numbers in list *L*, would then be 100, making it greater than Quantity B.

But it is also entirely possible that many of the 35 numbers in list *L* are very close to, but not quite equal to, 18. For example, imagine that each of the 17 greatest numbers is 18.01, the median is 18, and each of the other 17 numbers is 0. (Note that the question never stated that the numbers in List L had to be integers.) In this case, Quantity A would be 18.01, and Quantity B would be greater. Since more than one relationship between the quantities is possible, choice **(D)** is correct.

9. 20

The question describes a three-segment trip and provides the distances for the first and third segments, the average speeds for the second and third segments, the total distance traveled, and the total duration for the trip. The question asks you to calculate the average speed for the first segment. The formula to use is $\text{Speed} = \frac{\text{Distance}}{\text{Time}}$. The distance of the first segment is given in the problem, but you need to calculate time. You can do this by calculating the time required for the second and third segments of the trip and subtracting them from the total time.

For the interstate portion of the trip you know that Lorenzo's speed was 60 mph, but the problem does not give you the distance covered. Since the total distance was 120 miles and the first and third legs were 10 miles each, the distance covered driving on the interstate must have been 120 – 10 – 10 = 100 miles. Rearrange the speed formula to obtain

$$\text{Time} = \frac{\text{Distance}}{\text{Speed}} = \frac{100 \text{ miles}}{\left(60\frac{\text{miles}}{\text{hour}}\right)} = 1\frac{2}{3} \text{ hours,}$$

which converts to 100 minutes. Use this same formula to calculate the time it took Lorenzo to drive the third segment:

$$\text{Time} = \frac{10 \text{ miles}}{\left(50\frac{\text{miles}}{\text{hour}}\right)} = \frac{1}{5} \text{ hour} = 12 \text{ minutes.}$$

Since the entire trip took 2 hours and 22 minutes, or 142 minutes, Lorenzo drove the first segment in $142 - 100 - 12 = 30$ minutes. Now you have known values for both distance and time (convert 30 minutes to 0.5 hour) for the first segment:

$$\text{Speed} = \frac{10 \text{ miles}}{0.5 \text{ hours}} = 20 \text{ miles per hour.}$$

10. C, D

You are given a list with 9 integers and two terms containing a variable, for a total of 11 terms. The median will be the middle, or sixth, term in the list when the terms are ordered from least to greatest.

Because $\frac{x}{3}$ is known to be a positive integer, x must be a positive multiple of 3.

Because $\frac{x}{3}$ is odd, x must be odd. Moreover, because $0 < x \leq 15$, there are limited possible values for x. It could be that $x = 3$ and $\frac{x}{3} = 1$, or that $x = 9$ and $\frac{x}{3} = 3$, or that $x = 15$ and $\frac{x}{3} = 5$.

If $x = 3$ and $\frac{x}{3} = 1$, then the list is 1, 1, 3, 3, 5, 7, 9, 11, 13, 15, 17, and the median is 7.

If $x = 9$ and $\frac{x}{3} = 3$, then the list is 1, 3, 3, 5, 7, 9, 9, 11, 13, 15, 17, and the median is 9.

If $x = 15$ and $\frac{x}{3} = 5$, then the list is 1, 3, 5, 5, 7, 9, 11, 13, 15, 15, 17, and the median is 9.

The median is 7 or 9, so only **(C)** and **(D)** are correct.

11. B

Solving this question takes a lot of steps, but none of the steps are all that difficult. The key to beating questions like this is to stay calm and be methodical.

Pipe A can fill a 2,400 cubic meter pool in 3 hours. This means that pipe A's rate is $\frac{2{,}400}{3} = 800\,m^3$ per hour. Similarly, pipe B can fill the pool in 4 hours, so pipe B's rate is $\frac{2{,}400}{4} = 600\,m^3$ per hour. Since pipe C empties rather than fills the pool, you need to make sure its rate is negative, but you can find this rate just as easily as the other two: $-\frac{2{,}400}{2} = -1{,}200\,m^3$ per hour.

The easiest way to solve a question that has multiple rates is simply to add them up. In this case, the three pipes working together fill the pool at a rate of 800 + 600

– 1,200 = 200 m^3 per hour. The question asks how long it will take to fill 60 percent of the pool. Sixty percent of 2,400 is 2,400 × 0.6 = 1,440 m^3. So 1,440 m^3 need to be filled at a total rate of 200 m^3 per hour. Set up a proportion: $\frac{200}{1\text{ hr}} = \frac{1{,}440}{x\text{ hrs}}$. So 1,440 = 200$x$. Do the final division to get the answer: $\frac{1{,}440}{200} = 7.2$ hours, choice **(B)**.

12. A

To solve an absolute value inequality (or equation), write out two possibilities: one in which the absolute value expression is positive, and one in which it's negative. Case 1 (positive): $(8x - 7) > 3x + 8$, so $5x > 15$, and $x > 3$.

Case 2 (negative): $-(8x - 7) > 3x + 8$, so $-8x + 7 > 3x + 8$, which means that $-1 > 11x$ and $x < -\frac{1}{11}$.

This means that the inequality holds true as long as either $x > 3$ or $x < -\frac{1}{11}$. Now consider the choices. The question asks for the choice that CAN'T be true, and that's choice **(A)**. If x is between 1 and 3, then it is neither greater than 3 nor less than $-\frac{1}{11}$.

13. C

Since probability is defined as $\frac{\text{Number of desired outcomes}}{\text{Number of possible outcomes}}$, a good place to start is to determine the total number of outcomes (that is, with the denominator). Each coin toss has two possible outcomes (heads or tails). Since the coin is tossed six times in this problem, the total number of possible outcomes is $2 \times 2 \times 2 \times 2 \times 2 \times 2 = 2^6 = 64$.

In order to determine how many of those outcomes have exactly 3 heads and 3 tails, use the combinations formula. Think of it as choosing those spaces, between 1 and 6, where the three heads will show up. Order doesn't matter because heads in 1, 2, and 5 is the same as heads in 5, 1, and 2. Calculating ${}_6C_3$ produces $\frac{6 \times 5 \times 4 \times 3 \times 2 \times 1}{3 \times 2 \times 1 \times 3 \times 2 \times 1}$.

The $3 \times 2 \times 1$ in the numerator and denominator of the fraction cancel. The additional $3 \times 2 \times 1$ in the denominator cancels with the 6 in the numerator, leaving $\frac{5 \times 4}{1} = 20$.

Returning to the probability formula, $\frac{20\text{ desired outcomes}}{64\text{ total outcomes}} = \frac{5}{16}$. Choice **(C)** is correct.

14. A

This problem tests your fundamental understanding of ratios. If the ratio of cranberry to apple to orange juice is x:5:3, what that means is that the volume of cranberry juice is a multiple of x, the volume of apple juice is that same multiple of 5, and the volume of orange juice is that same multiple of 3. You're not told what this multiple is, so call it n. Thus, there is a total of $xn + 5n + 3n = xn + 8n$ gallons of juice in the cocktail.

After 6 gallons of water are added, the amount of orange juice ($3n$) doesn't change. Since this amount, as a fraction of the total, is given as 1:4, you can set up a proportion:

$$\frac{3n}{xn + 8n + 6} = \frac{1}{4}$$

Cross multiply and simplify:

$$\begin{aligned} 12n &= xn + 8n + 6 \\ xn - 4n &= -6 \end{aligned}$$

Next, you learn that adding another 24 gallons to the cocktail (so, 30 gallons total) makes the ratio of apple juice to total liquid 1:4. The amount of apple juice ($5n$), like the amount of orange juice, hasn't changed, so you can again set up a proportion and solve:

$$\begin{aligned} \frac{5n}{xn + 8n + 30} &= \frac{1}{4} \\ 20n &= xn + 8n + 30 \\ xn - 12n &= -30 \end{aligned}$$

You now have a system of equations with two variables (x and n), so use combination to solve:

$$\begin{aligned} (xn - 4n &= -6) \\ -(xn - 12n &= -30) \\ \hline 0 + 8n &= 24 \\ n &= 3 \end{aligned}$$

Plug this value for n into one of the original equations to find x:

$$\begin{aligned} xn - 4n &= -6 \\ 3x - 4(3) &= -6 \\ 3x = -6 + 12 &= 6 \\ x &= 2 \end{aligned}$$

In this problem, x represents the portion of the ratio that corresponds to cranberry juice. Thus, the ratio of cranberry to apple to orange juice is 2:5:3, and the ratio of cranberry juice to total liquid is $\frac{2}{2+5+3} = \frac{2}{10} = \frac{1}{5}$, choice **(A)**.

15. B

Before performing any calculations, think through your strategic approach. Since 3 or 4 or 5 rolls coming up less than 3 is a favorable event, you will need to calculate all three of those probabilities and add them to get the final answer.

The probability of rolling a 1 or 2 on a single roll is $\frac{2}{6} = \frac{1}{3}$, so the probability of not rolling a number less than 3 is $1 - \frac{1}{3} = \frac{2}{3}$.

Start with the most straightforward event, 5 rolls all coming up less than 3. The probability of that occurring is $\left(\frac{1}{3}\right)^5 = \frac{1}{243}$, since the first roll and all subsequent rolls must be less than 3.

Any one particular set of 4 favorable and 1 unfavorable outcomes has a probability of $\left(\frac{1}{3}\right)^4\left(\frac{2}{3}\right)^1 = \frac{2}{243}$. However, there are 5 ways to obtain this result (the unfavorable outcome could be any one of the five rolls), so the probability of 4 favorable rolls is $5 \times \left(\frac{2}{243}\right) = \frac{10}{243}$.

Calculating the probability of 3 favorable rolls gets a bit trickier. The probability of any one set of outcomes producing that result is $\left(\frac{1}{3}\right)^3\left(\frac{2}{3}\right)^2 = \frac{4}{243}$. In order to determine how many different ways 5 rolls would result in 3 favorable outcomes, you can use the combinations formula:

$$\frac{n!}{k!(n-k)!} = \frac{5!}{3!(5-3)!} = \frac{5!}{3!2!} = \frac{5 \times 4 \times 3 \times 2 \times 1}{3 \times 2 \times 1 \times 2 \times 1} = 10.$$

Therefore, the probability of 3 favorable outcomes is

$$10 \times \left(\frac{4}{243}\right) = \frac{40}{243}.$$

Add these three probabilities to obtain $\frac{1 + 10 + 40}{243} = \frac{51}{243} = \frac{17}{81}$.

Choice **(B)** is correct.

16. C

Option A results in an increase in value of \$2, but Juliana only has to invest \$98, so the percent return is

$$\frac{\$2}{\$98} \approx 0.0204 \times 100\% = 2.04\%$$

per year. (At this point, if you're short on time, you can eliminate choices (A) and (B) because you know option A gives a better return than option C (a flat 2.03%)).

In option B, you can calculate the compound interest using the formula

$$\text{Final balance} = \text{Principal} \times \left(1 + \frac{\text{Interest rate}}{n}\right)^{(t)(n)}.$$

In this case $t = 1$ (because Juliana invests for 1 year) and $n = 2$, the number of times compounding occurs per year. Pick \$100 for the principal to make things as simple as possible:

$$\begin{aligned}\text{Final balance} &= \$100 \times \left(1 + \frac{.02}{2}\right)^2 = \$100 \times 1.01^2 \\ \text{Final balance} &= \$100 \times 1.01 \times 1.01 = \$102.01\end{aligned}$$

Since the initial investment of \$100 earned \$2.01 in interest, the rate of return is 2.01% for one year.

Option C is given as 2.03% annually.

Therefore, the correct order from lowest to highest percent returns is B, C, A. The correct answer is **(C).**

17. C

This question asks about the number of ways you can combine certain ingredients, which means it is a permutation/combination problem. The customer must choose 1 of 3 breads, 1 of 6 meats, and 1 of 4 cheeses. Multiply these together to find the number of possibilities for those three ingredients: $3 \times 6 \times 4 = 72$. The veggies create several more possibilities because the customer can choose up to 3 of 8 veggies. Start by considering the case when a customer chooses the maximum

of 3 veggies. Since there is no difference between choosing lettuce, tomato, onion and choosing lettuce, onion, tomato, order does not matter; therefore, use the combination formula:

$$_nC_k = \frac{n!}{k!(n-k)!}$$

In this case, we are selecting 3 out of 8, so $k = 3$ and $n = 8$:

$$\begin{aligned} _8C_3 &= \frac{8!}{3!(8-3)!} \\ &= \frac{8!}{3! \times 5!} \\ &= \frac{8 \times 7 \times 6}{3 \times 2 \times 1} \\ &= 8 \times 7 \\ &= 56 \end{aligned}$$

Now, to find the number of total sandwich possibilities, multiply the number of combinations of 3 veggies by the number of combinations of the other ingredients: $56 \times 72 = 4{,}032$.

There are, however, three more possibilities. The customer might select only 2 of 8 veggies or 1 of 8 veggies, or the customer may select none. Add these possibilities to the total. If the customer chooses 2 of the 8 veggies, $k = 2$ and $n = 8$:

$$\frac{8!}{2!(8-2)!} = \frac{8 \times 7}{2!} = \frac{8 \times 7}{2} = 28$$

Again, multiply the number of combinations of veggies by the number of combinations of the other ingredients: $28 \times 72 = 2{,}016$.

If the customer chooses only 1 of the 8 veggies, there will be 8 possibilities. You can plug the numbers $k = 1$ and $n = 8$ into the combination formula, but it is faster to recognize that there are only 8 ways to select 1 out of 8 veggies. Yet again, multiply the number of combinations of veggies by the number of combinations of the other ingredients: $8 \times 72 = 576$.

And finally, you need to consider what happens if the customer does not choose any veggies. You can plug $k = 0$ and $n = 8$ into the combination formula (remembering that $0! = 1$), but this is unnecessary if you recognize that there is only 1 possibility: no veggies! One last time, multiply the number of combinations of veggies (or lack thereof) by the number of combinations of the other ingredients: $1 \times 72 = 72$.

The last step is to sum all of these possibilities:
$4,032 + 2,016 + 576 + 72 = 6,696$. The correct answer is **(C).**

18. C

This question asks about deaths of infants under age 1 year in certain cities. That information is found in the bar graph, specifically in the left bar of each cluster. Note that this graph has two *y*-axes, one on the left and one on the right. Deaths that occur before age 1 year are plotted against the *y*-axis on the left; be sure to read the correct bars against the correct axis.

Boston is represented by the bars on the far left and Los Angeles by the bars on the far right. Honolulu and Indianapolis are represented by the second and fourth pairs of bars, respectively.

Before doing any calculations, you might note that the numbers of infant deaths in both Boston and Los Angeles are significantly higher than in either Honolulu or Indianapolis. Therefore, the effect of introducing public health programs in Boston and Los Angeles will be greater than the effect of terminating programs in the other two cities. In other words, more deaths will be prevented than not prevented, and you can eliminate choices (A) and (B). On Test Day, even if you had no more time to invest in this problem, by using your critical thinking skills to eliminate answer choices, you would improve your odds of guessing the correct answer.

In 2014, Boston had just under 200 infant deaths, and Los Angeles had just over 200. That's about 400 infant deaths total for these cities. The question wants you to imagine that a public health program was introduced in these cities, dropping infant deaths by 20%. In that case, there would be $(0.2)(400) = 80$ fewer infant deaths in those two cities, or 320 infant deaths instead of the actual 400.

Honolulu had about 60 infant deaths, and Indianapolis had not quite 150—call it 140. That's $60 + 140 = 200$ deaths, and you're told to imagine what would have happened had a program reducing infant deaths by 20% been terminated. Without such a program acting to reduce infant deaths, the number would go up, but by how much? Call the number of infant deaths in Honolulu and Indianapolis d. The current 200 infant deaths represent 80% of what the number would be without the program, so you can write the following equation and solve: $0.8d = 200$; $d = 250$. There would have been 50 more deaths.

Therefore, had the stated program changes occurred, there would have been about $320 + 250 = 570$ deaths. There were actually about $400 + 200 = 600$ deaths. That means about 30 fewer deaths would have occurred. Alternatively, you could add the differences in the two cities to get the net difference: $-80 + 50 = 30$. Either way, the correct answer is **(C).**

19. B

This question concerns deaths from pneumonia/influenza, which you find in the pie chart.

The pie chart represents the 3,532 pneumonia/influenza deaths that occurred in five cities. Of these, 19% occurred in Houston, and 38% occurred in Los Angeles. That's a ratio of 19:38 or 1:2. However, the question is asking for the ratio of the *rate of incidence* of these deaths.

If Los Angeles's population were twice the size of Houston's, then the rate of incidence in the two cities would be the same, giving a ratio of 1:1. Because Los Angeles's population is less than twice Houston's, you know that the rate of incidence is higher in Los Angeles than in Houston. The ratio of Houston to Los Angeles must be less than 1. On the basis of this critical thinking, you can eliminate (D) and (E).

The question does not give you the actual populations of the cities, but it does tell you their relative populations. If you call the population of Houston p, then the population of Los Angeles is $1.75p$ or $\frac{7}{4}p$. As shown in the pie chart, for every 1 death from pneumonia/influenza in Houston, there were 2 in Los Angeles. In Houston, therefore, the rate of incidence of deaths can be represented by the ratio of 1 to p, or $\frac{1}{p}$. In Los Angeles, the rate of deaths can be represented as 2 to $\frac{7}{4}p$, or

$$\frac{2}{\frac{7p}{4}} = 2 \times \frac{4}{7p} = \frac{8}{7p}.$$

Now find the ratio of the rates of incidence:

$$\frac{\frac{1}{p}}{\frac{8}{7p}} = \frac{1}{p} \times \frac{7p}{8} = \frac{7}{8}$$

The correct answer is **(B)**, $\frac{7}{8}$.

20. A

This question asks about deaths due to pneumonia/influenza, so look at the pie chart for those data. It also concerns people who died at age 65 or over, and that information is in the bar graph, specifically in the right-hand bar of each pair of bars. Remember that the deaths occurring at age 65 and over are plotted against the *y*-axis on the right side of the bar graph.

Only 80% of the pneumonia/influenza deaths occurred among the elderly. However, because this 80% applies equally to each city, you do not have to take it into account as you compare the percentages of deaths in each city attributed to pneumonia/influenza. If a city has the most such deaths when 100% of pneumonia/influenza deaths are counted, then it will also have the most such deaths when the number of pneumonia/influenza deaths is reduced by 20% for all cities.

If you compare cities using estimation, your thinking might go like this: Boston and Houston have about the same number of P/I deaths, making them easy to compare. Houston has far more deaths from all causes, so Houston's proportion of P/I deaths is lower than Boston's. Houston has about 50% more P/I deaths than Honolulu or Indianapolis, and it has more than four times (Honolulu) and three times (Indianapolis) the deaths from all causes. Therefore, Houston's proportion of P/I deaths is lower than Honolulu's or Indianapolis's. Finally, compare Houston to Los Angeles. Houston has more total deaths and far fewer P/I deaths than Los Angeles has, so its proportion of P/I deaths is definitely lower than Los Angeles's. Houston is the winner; choice **(A)** is correct.

You can also solve using calculation. The pie chart represents a total of 3,532 deaths, and it gives the percentage distribution among the five cities. Determine the number of pneumonia/influenza deaths for each city:

	Deaths from P/I
Boston	$3{,}532 \times 0.18 = 636$
Honolulu	$3{,}532 \times 0.13 = 459$
Houston	$3{,}532 \times 0.19 = 671$
Indianapolis	$3{,}532 \times 0.12 = 424$
Los Angeles	$3{,}532 \times 0.38 = 1{,}342$

Now find the number of deaths among the elderly from the bar graph. Boston is between 4,000 and 5,000, so say 4,500. Honolulu is at about 3,000, Houston is the tallest bar at about 13,000, Indianapolis is at 4,000, and the bar for Los Angeles is at about 9,000.

	Deaths from P/I	Deaths 65+
Boston	$3{,}532 \times 0.18 = 636$	4,500
Honolulu	$3{,}532 \times 0.13 = 459$	3,000
Houston	$3{,}532 \times 0.19 = 671$	13,000
Indianapolis	$3{,}532 \times 0.12 = 424$	4,000
Los Angeles	$3{,}532 \times 0.38 = 1{,}342$	9,000

You can perform calculations to determine the city with the lowest proportion of deaths from P/I, or you can compare cities using estimation. If you calculate the proportions, the result looks like this:

	Deaths from P/I	Deaths 65+	Proportion
Boston	$3{,}532 \times 0.18 = 636$	4,500	14%
Honolulu	$3{,}532 \times 0.13 = 459$	3,000	15%
Houston	$3{,}532 \times 0.19 = 671$	13,000	5%
Indianapolis	$3{,}532 \times 0.12 = 424$	4,000	11%
Los Angeles	$3{,}532 \times 0.38 = 1{,}342$	9,000	15%

The winner is Houston, and answer choice **(A)** is correct.

PART FIVE

GRE Resources

APPENDIX

Math Reference

The math on the GRE covers a lot of ground—from number properties and arithmetic to basic algebra and symbol problems to geometry and statistics. Don't let yourself be intimidated.

We've highlighted the 100 most important concepts that you need to know and divided them into three levels. The GRE Quantitative sections test your understanding of a relatively limited number of mathematical concepts, all of which you will be able to master.

Level 1 consists of foundational math topics. Though these topics may seem basic, review this list so that you are aware that these skills may play a part in the questions you will answer on the GRE. Look over the Level 1 list to make sure you're comfortable with the basics.

Level 2 is where most people start their review of math. Level 2 skills and formulas come into play quite frequently on the GRE. If the skills needed to handle Level 1 or 2 topics are keeping you from feeling up to the tasks expected on the GRE Quantitative section, you might consider taking the Kaplan GRE Math Refresher course.

Level 3 represents the most challenging math concepts you'll find on the GRE. Don't spend a lot of time on Level 3 if you still have gaps in Level 2, but once you've mastered Level 2, tackling Level 3 can put you over the top.

LEVEL 1

1. How to add, subtract, multiply, and divide WHOLE NUMBERS

You can check addition with subtraction.

$$17 + 5 = 22 \qquad 22 - 5 = 17$$

You can check multiplication with division.

$$5 \times 28 = 140 \qquad 140 \div 5 = 28$$

2. How to add, subtract, multiply, and divide FRACTIONS

Find a common denominator before adding or subtracting fractions.

$$\frac{4}{5} + \frac{3}{10} = \frac{8}{10} + \frac{3}{10} = \frac{11}{10} \text{ or } 1\frac{1}{10}$$

$$2 - \frac{3}{8} = \frac{16}{8} - \frac{3}{8} = \frac{13}{8} \text{ or } 1\frac{5}{8}$$

To multiply fractions, multiply the numerators first and then multiply the denominators. Simplify if necessary.

$$\frac{3}{4} \times \frac{1}{6} = \frac{3}{24} = \frac{1}{8}$$

You can also reduce before multiplying numerators and denominators. This keeps the products small.

$$\frac{5}{8} \times \frac{2}{15} = \frac{{}^{1}\cancel{5}}{{}_{4}\cancel{8}} \times \frac{\cancel{2}^{1}}{\cancel{15}_{3}} = \frac{1}{12}$$

To divide by a fraction, multiply by its reciprocal. To write the reciprocal of a fraction, flip the numerator and the denominator.

$$5 \div \frac{1}{3} = \frac{5}{1} \times \frac{3}{1} = 15 \qquad \frac{1}{3} \div \frac{4}{5} = \frac{1}{3} \times \frac{5}{4} = \frac{5}{12}$$

3. How to add, subtract, multiply, and divide DECIMALS

To add or subtract, align the decimal points and then add or subtract normally. Place the decimal point in the answer directly below existing decimal points.

$$\begin{array}{r} 3.25 \\ +4.4 \\ \hline 7.65 \end{array} \qquad \begin{array}{r} 7.65 \\ -4.4 \\ \hline 3.25 \end{array}$$

To multiply with decimals, multiply the digits normally and count off decimal places (equal to the total number of places in the factors) from the right.

$$2.5 \times 2.5 = 6.25$$

$$0.06 \times 2{,}000 = 120.00 = 120$$

To divide by a decimal, move the decimal point in the divisor to the right to form a whole number; move the decimal point in the dividend the same number of places. Divide as though there were no decimals, then place the decimal point in the quotient.

$$6.25 \div 2.5$$

$$= 62.5 \div 25 = 2.5$$

4. How to convert FRACTIONS TO DECIMALS and DECIMALS TO FRACTIONS

To convert a fraction to a decimal, divide the numerator by the denominator.

$$\frac{4}{5} = 0.8 \quad \frac{4}{50} = 0.08 \quad \frac{4}{500} = 0.008$$

To convert a decimal to a fraction, write the digits in the numerator and use the decimal name in the denominator.

$$0.003 = \frac{3}{1{,}000} \quad 0.03 = \frac{3}{100} \quad 0.3 = \frac{3}{10}$$

5. How to add, subtract, multiply, and divide POSITIVE AND NEGATIVE NUMBERS

When addends (the numbers being added) have the same sign, add their absolute values; the sum has the same sign as the addends. But when addends have different signs, subtract the absolute values; the sum has the sign of the greater absolute value.

$3 + 9 = 12$, but $-3 + (-9) = -12$
$3 + (-9) = -6$, but $-3 + 9 = 6$

In multiplication and division, when the signs are the same, the product/quotient is positive. When the signs are different, the product/quotient is negative.

$6 \times 7 = 42$ and $-6 \times (-7) = 42$
$-6 \times 7 = -42$ and $6 \times (-7) = -42$
$96 \div 8 = 12$ and $-96 \div (-8) = 12$
$-96 \div 8 = -12$ and $96 \div (-8) = -12$

6. How to plot points on the NUMBER LINE

To plot the point 4.5 on the number line, start at 0, go right to 4.5, halfway between 4 and 5.

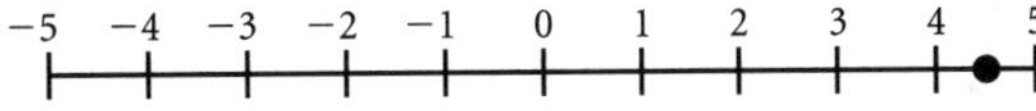

To plot the point −2.5 on the number line, start at 0, go left to −2.5, halfway between −2 and −3.

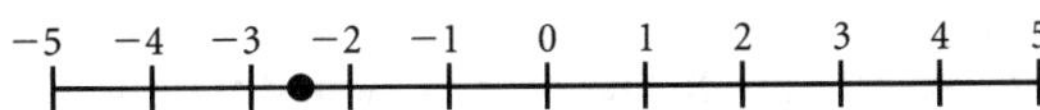

7. How to plug a number into an ALGEBRAIC EXPRESSION

To evaluate an algebraic expression, choose numbers for the variables or use the numbers assigned to the variables.

Evaluate $4np + 1$ when $n = -4$ and $p = 3$.

$4np + 1 = 4(-4)(3) + 1 = -48 + 1 = -47$

8. How to SOLVE a simple LINEAR EQUATION

Use algebra to isolate the variable. Do the same steps to both sides of the equation.

$$28 = -3x - 5$$
$$28 + 5 = -3x - 5 + 5 \quad \text{Add 5.}$$
$$33 = -3x$$
$$\frac{33}{-3} = \frac{-3x}{-3} \quad \text{Divide by } -3.$$
$$-11 = x$$

9. How to add and subtract LINE SEGMENTS

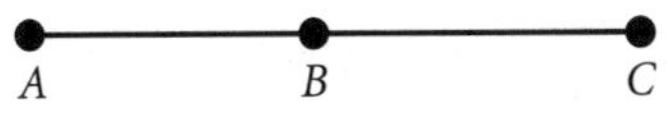

If $AB = 6$ and $BC = 8$, then $AC = 6 + 8 = 14$.
If $AC = 14$ and $BC = 8$, then $AB = 14 - 8 = 6$.

10. How to find the THIRD ANGLE of a TRIANGLE, given the other two angles

Use the fact that the sum of the measures of the interior angles of a triangle always equals 180°.

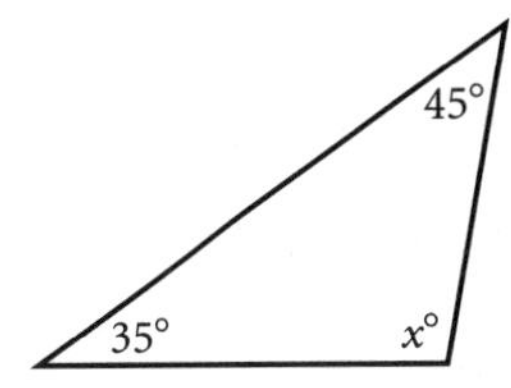

$$35 + 45 + x = 180$$
$$80 + x = 180$$
$$x = 100$$

LEVEL 2

11. How to use PEMDAS

When you're given a complex arithmetic expression, it's important to know the order of operations. Just remember PEMDAS (as in "Please Excuse My Dear Aunt Sally"). What PEMDAS means is this: Clean up **Parentheses** first (nested sets of parentheses are worked from the innermost set to the outermost set); then deal with **Exponents** (or **Radicals**); then do the **Multiplication** and **Division** together, going from left to right; and finally do the **Addition** and **Subtraction** together, again going from left to right.

Example:

$$9 - 2 \times (5 - 3)^2 + 6 \div 3 =$$

Begin with the parentheses:

$$9 - 2 \times (2)^2 + 6 \div 3 =$$

Then do the exponent:

$$9 - 2 \times 4 + 6 \div 3 =$$

Now do multiplication and division from left to right:

$$9 - 8 + 2 =$$

Finally, do addition and subtraction from left to right:

$$1 + 2 = 3$$

12. How to use the PERCENT FORMULA

Identify the part, the percent, and the whole.

$$\textit{Part} = \textit{Percent} \times \textit{Whole}$$

Find the part.

Example:

What is 12 percent of 25?

Setup:

$$\textit{Part} = \frac{12}{100} \times 25 = \frac{300}{100} = 3$$

Find the percent.

Example:

45 is what percent of 9?

Setup:

$$\begin{aligned} 45 &= \frac{\text{Percent}}{100} \times 9 \\ 4{,}500 &= \text{Percent} \times 9 \\ 500 &= \text{Percent} \end{aligned}$$

Find the whole.

Example:

15 is $\frac{3}{5}$ percent of what number?

Setup:

$$\begin{aligned} 15 &= \frac{3}{5}\left(\frac{1}{100}\right) \times \textit{Whole} \\ 15 &= \frac{3}{500} \times \textit{Whole} \\ \textit{Whole} &= 15\left(\frac{500}{3}\right) = \frac{7{,}500}{3} = 2{,}500 \end{aligned}$$

13. How to use the PERCENT INCREASE/DECREASE FORMULAS

Identify the original whole and the amount of increase/decrease.

$$\textit{Percent increase} = \frac{\textit{Amount of increase}}{\textit{Original whole}} \times 100\%$$

$$\textit{Percent decrease} = \frac{\textit{Amount of decrease}}{\textit{Original whole}} \times 100\%$$

Example:

The price goes up from \$80 to \$100. What is the percent increase?

Setup:

$$\begin{aligned} \textit{Percent increase} &= \frac{20}{80} \times 100\% \\ &= 0.25 \times 100\% = 25\% \end{aligned}$$

14. How to predict whether a sum, difference, or product will be ODD or EVEN

Don't bother memorizing the rules. Just take simple numbers such as 2 for even numbers and 3 for odd numbers and see what happens.

Example:

If m is even and n is odd, is the product mn odd or even?

Setup:

Say $m = 2$ and $n = 3$.
$2 \times 3 = 6$, which is even, so mn is even.

15. How to recognize MULTIPLES OF 2, 3, 4, 5, 6, 9, 10, and 12

2: Last digit is even.
3: Sum of digits is a multiple of 3.
4: Last two digits are a multiple of 4.
5: Last digit is 5 or 0.
6: Sum of digits is a multiple of 3, and last digit is even.
9: Sum of digits is a multiple of 9.
10: Last digit is 0.
12: Sum of digits is a multiple of 3, and last two digits are a multiple of 4.

16. How to find a COMMON FACTOR of two numbers

Break both numbers down to their prime factors to see which they have in common. Then multiply the shared prime factors to find all common factors.

Example:

What factors greater than 1 do 135 and 225 have in common?

Setup:

First find the prime factors of 135 and 225; $135 = 3 \times 3 \times 3 \times 5$, and $225 = 3 \times 3 \times 5 \times 5$. The numbers share $3 \times 3 \times 5$ in common. Thus, aside from 3 and 5, the remaining common factors can be found by multiplying 3, 3, and 5 in every possible combination: $3 \times 3 = 9$, $3 \times 5 = 15$, and $3 \times 3 \times 5 = 45$. Therefore, the common factors of 135 and 225 are 3, 5, 9, 15, and 45.

17. How to find a COMMON MULTIPLE of two numbers

The product of two numbers is the easiest common multiple to find, but it is not always the least common multiple (LCM).

Example:

What is the least common multiple of 28 and 42?

Setup:

$$\begin{aligned} 28 &= 2 \times 2 \times 7 \\ 42 &= 2 \times 3 \times 7 \end{aligned}$$

The LCM can be found by finding the prime factorization of each number, then seeing the greatest number of times each factor is used. Multiply each prime factor the greatest number of times it appears.

In 28, 2 is used twice. In 42, 2 is used once. In 28, 7 is used once. In 42, 7 is used once, and 3 is used once.

So you multiply each factor the greatest number of times it appears in a prime factorization:

$$\text{LCM} = 2 \times 2 \times 3 \times 7 = 84$$

18. How to find the AVERAGE or ARITHMETIC MEAN

$$\textit{Average} = \frac{\textit{Sum of terms}}{\textit{Number of terms}}$$

Example:

What is the average of 3, 4, and 8?

Setup:

$$\textit{Average} = \frac{3 + 4 + 8}{3} = \frac{15}{3} = 5$$

19. How to use the AVERAGE to find the SUM

$$\textit{Sum} = (\textit{Average}) \times (\textit{Number of terms})$$

Example:

17.5 is the average (arithmetic mean) of 24 numbers.

What is the sum of the 24 numbers?

Setup:

$$\textit{Sum} = 17.5 \times 24 = 420$$

20. How to find the AVERAGE of CONSECUTIVE NUMBERS

The average of evenly spaced numbers is simply the average of the smallest number and the largest number. The average of all the integers from 13 to 77, for example, is the same as the average of 13 and 77:

$$\frac{13 + 77}{2} = \frac{90}{2} = 45$$

21. How to COUNT CONSECUTIVE NUMBERS

The number of integers from A to B inclusive is $B - A + 1$.

Example:

How many integers are there from 73 through 419, inclusive?

Setup:

$$419 - 73 + 1 = 347$$

22. How to find the SUM OF CONSECUTIVE NUMBERS

$$Sum = (Average) \times (Number\ of\ terms)$$

Example:

What is the sum of the integers from 10 through 50, inclusive?

Setup:

Average: $\frac{10 + 50}{2} = 30$

Number of terms: $50 - 10 + 1 = 41$
Sum: $30 \times 41 = 1{,}230$

23. How to find the MEDIAN

Put the numbers in numerical order and take the middle number.

Example:

What is the median of 88, 86, 57, 94, and 73?

Setup:

First, put the numbers in numerical order, then take the middle number:

57, 73, 86, 88, 94

The median is 86.

In a set with an even number of numbers, take the average of the two in the middle.

Example:

What is the median of 88, 86, 57, 73, 94, and 100?

Setup:

First, put the numbers in numerical order.

57, 73, 86, 88, 94, 100

Because 86 and 88 are the two numbers in the middle:

$$\frac{86 + 88}{2} = \frac{174}{2} = 87$$

The median is 87.

24. How to find the MODE

Take the number that appears most often. For example, if your test scores were 88, 57, 68, 85, 98, 93, 93, 84, and 81, the mode of the scores would be 93 because it appears more often than any other score. (If there's a tie for most often, then there's more than one mode. If each number in a set is used equally often, there is no mode.)

25. How to find the RANGE

Take the positive difference between the greatest and least values. Using the example under "How to find the MODE" above, if your test scores were 88, 57, 68, 85, 98, 93, 93, 84, and 81, the range of the scores would be 41, the greatest value minus the least value ($98 - 57 = 41$).

26. How to use actual numbers to determine a RATIO

To find a ratio, put the number associated with *of* on the top and the number associated with *to* on the bottom.

$$Ratio = \frac{of}{to}$$

The ratio of 20 oranges to 12 apples is $\frac{20}{12}$, or $\frac{5}{3}$.

Ratios should always be reduced to lowest terms. Ratios can also be expressed in linear form, such as 5:3.

27. How to use a ratio to determine an ACTUAL NUMBER

Set up a proportion using the given ratio.

Example:

The ratio of boys to girls is 3 to 4. If there are 135 boys, how many girls are there?

Setup:

$$\frac{3}{4} = \frac{135}{g}$$
$$3 \times g = 4 \times 135$$
$$3g = 540$$
$$g = 180$$

28. How to use actual numbers to determine a RATE

Identify the quantities and the units to be compared. Keep the units straight.

Example:

Anders typed 9,450 words in $3\frac{1}{2}$ hours. What was his rate in words per minute?

Setup:

First convert $3\frac{1}{2}$ hours to 210 minutes. Then set up the rate with words on top and minutes on bottom (because "per" means "divided by"):

$$\frac{9{,}450 \text{ words}}{210 \text{ minutes}} = 45 \text{ words per minute}$$

29. How to deal with TABLES, GRAPHS, AND CHARTS

Read the question and all labels carefully. Ignore extraneous information and zero in on what the question asks for. Take advantage of the spread in the answer choices by approximating the answer whenever possible and choosing the answer choice closest to your approximation.

30. How to count the NUMBER OF POSSIBILITIES

You can use multiplication to find the number of possibilities when items can be arranged in various ways.

Example:

How many three-digit numbers can be formed with the digits 1, 3, and 5 each used only once?

Setup:

Look at each digit individually. The first digit (or, the hundreds digit) has three possible numbers to plug in: 1, 3, or 5. The second digit (or, the tens digit) has two possible numbers, since one has already been plugged in. The last digit (or, the ones digit) has only one remaining possible number. Multiply the possibilities together: $3 \times 2 \times 1 = 6$.

31. How to calculate a simple PROBABILITY

$$\textit{Probability} = \frac{\textit{Number of desired outcomes}}{\textit{Number of total possible outcomes}}$$

Example:

What is the probability of throwing a 5 on a fair six-sided die?

Setup:

There is one desired outcome—throwing a 5. There are 6 possible outcomes—one for each side of the die.

$$\textit{Probability} = \frac{1}{6}$$

32. How to work with new SYMBOLS

If you see a symbol you've never seen before, don't be alarmed. It's just a made-up symbol whose operation is uniquely defined by the problem. Everything you need to know is in the question stem. Just follow the instructions.

33. How to SIMPLIFY BINOMIALS

A binomial is a sum or difference of two terms. To simplify two binomials that are multiplied together, use the **FOIL** method. Multiply the **F**irst terms, then the **O**uter terms, followed by the **I**nner terms and the **L**ast terms. Lastly, combine like terms.

Example:

$$\begin{aligned}(3x + 5)(x - 1) &= \\ 3x^2 - 3x + 5x - 5 &= \\ 3x^2 + 2x - 5\end{aligned}$$

34. How to FACTOR certain POLYNOMIALS

A polynomial is an expression consisting of the sum of two or more terms, where at least one of the terms is a variable.

Learn to spot these classic polynomial equations.

$$ab + ac = a(b + c)$$
$$a^2 + 2ab + b^2 = (a + b)^2$$
$$a^2 - 2ab + b^2 = (a - b)^2$$
$$a^2 - b^2 = (a - b)(a + b)$$

35. How to solve for one variable IN TERMS OF ANOTHER

To find x "in terms of" y, isolate x on one side, leaving y as the only variable on the other.

36. How to solve an INEQUALITY

Treat it much like an equation—adding, subtracting, multiplying, and dividing both sides by the same thing. Just remember to reverse the inequality sign if you multiply or divide by a negative quantity.

Example:

Rewrite $7 - 3x > 2$ in its simplest form.

Setup:

$$7 - 3x > 2$$

First, subtract 7 from both sides:

$$7 - 3x - 7 > 2 - 7$$
$$-3x > -5$$

Now divide both sides by −3, remembering to reverse the inequality sign:

$$x < \frac{5}{3}$$

37. How to handle ABSOLUTE VALUES

The *absolute value* of a number n, denoted by $|n|$, is defined as n if $n \geq 0$ and $-n$ if $n < 0$. The absolute value of a number is the distance from zero to the number on the number line. The absolute value of a number or expression is always positive.

$$|-5| = 5$$

If $|x| = 3$, then x could be 3 or −3.

Example:

If $|x - 3| < 2$, what is the range of possible values for x?

Setup:

Represent the possible range for $x - 3$ on a number line.

−5 −4 −3 −2 −1 0 1 2 3 4 5

$|x - 3| < 2$, so $(x - 3) < 2$ and $(x - 3) > -2$
$x - 3 < 2$ and $x - 3 > -2$
$x < 2 + 3$ and $x > -2 + 3$
$x < 5$ and $x > 1$
So, $1 < x < 5$.

38. How to TRANSLATE ENGLISH INTO ALGEBRA

Look for the key words and systematically turn phrases into algebraic expressions and sentences into equations.

Here's a table of key words that you may have to translate into mathematical terms:

Operation	Key Words
Addition	sum, plus, and, added to, more than, increased by, combined with, exceeds, total, greater than
Subtraction	difference between, minus, subtracted from, decreased by, diminished by, less than, reduced by
Multiplication	of, product, times, multiplied by, twice, double, triple, half
Division	quotient, divided by, per, out of, ratio of _ to _
Equals	equals, is, was, will be, the result is, adds up to, costs, is the same as

39. How to find an ANGLE formed by INTERSECTING LINES

Vertical angles are equal. Angles along a line add up to 180°.

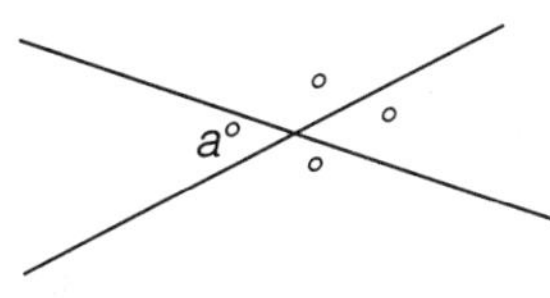

$$a^\circ = c^\circ$$
$$b^\circ = d^\circ$$
$$a^\circ + b^\circ = 180^\circ$$
$$a^\circ + b^\circ + c^\circ + d^\circ = 360^\circ$$

40. How to find an angle formed by a TRANSVERSAL across PARALLEL LINES

When a transversal crosses parallel lines, all the acute angles formed are equal, and all the obtuse angles formed are equal. Any acute angle plus any obtuse angle equals 180°.

Example:

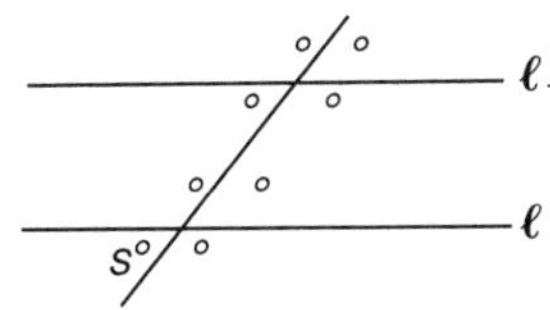

$$e^\circ = g^\circ = p^\circ = r^\circ$$
$$f^\circ = h^\circ = q^\circ = s^\circ$$
$$e^\circ + q^\circ = g^\circ + s^\circ = 180^\circ$$

41. How to find the AREA of a TRIANGLE

$$Area = \frac{1}{2}(Base)(Height)$$

Base and height must be perpendicular to each other. Height is measured by drawing a perpendicular line segment from the base—which can be any side of the triangle—to the angle opposite the base.

Example:

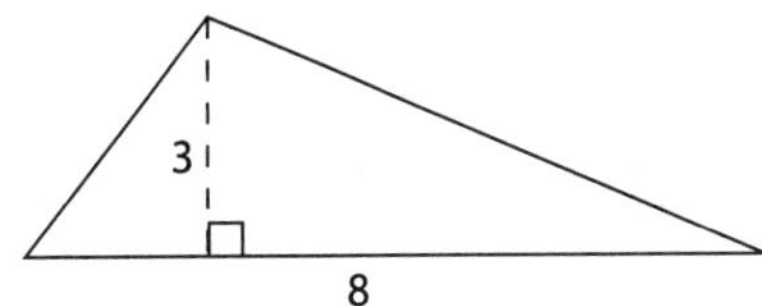

Setup:

$$Area = \frac{1}{2}(8)(3) = 12$$

42. How to work with ISOSCELES TRIANGLES

Isosceles triangles have at least two equal sides and two equal angles. If a GRE question tells you that a triangle is isosceles, you can bet that you'll need to use that information to find the length of a side or a measure of an angle.

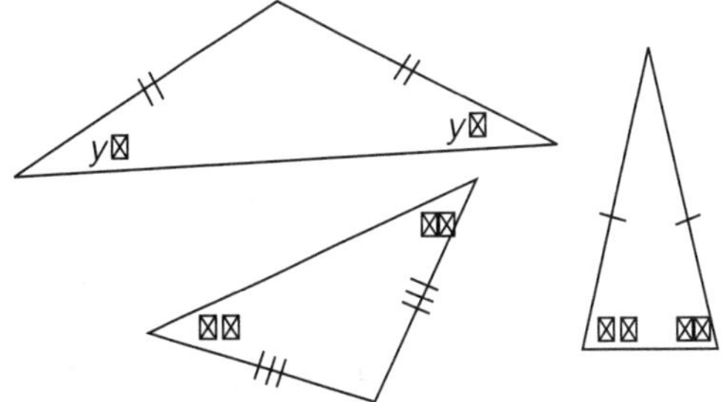

43. How to work with EQUILATERAL TRIANGLES

Equilateral triangles have three equal sides and three 60° angles. If a GRE question tells you that a triangle is equilateral, you can bet that you'll need to use that information to find the length of a side or the measure of an angle.

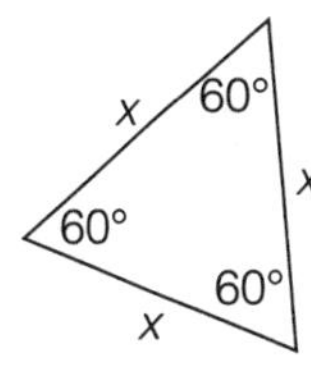

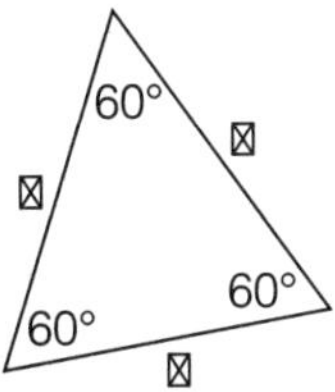

44. How to work with SIMILAR TRIANGLES

In similar triangles, corresponding angles are equal, and corresponding sides are proportional. If a GRE question tells you that triangles are similar, use the properties of similar triangles to find the length of a side or the measure of an angle.

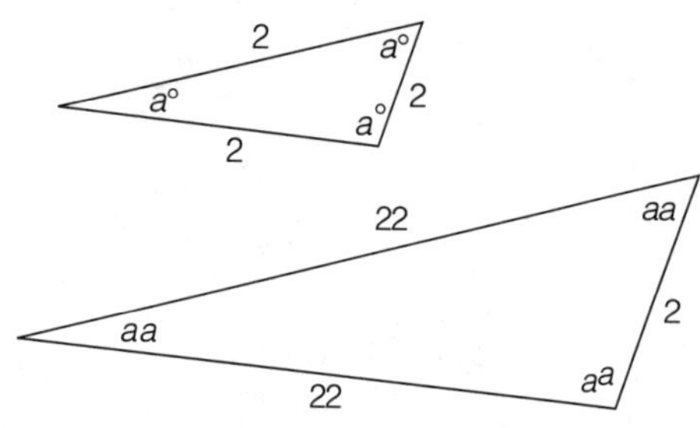

45. How to find the HYPOTENUSE or a LEG of a RIGHT TRIANGLE

For all right triangles, the Pythagorean theorem is $a^2 + b^2 = c^2$, where a and b are the legs and c is the hypotenuse.

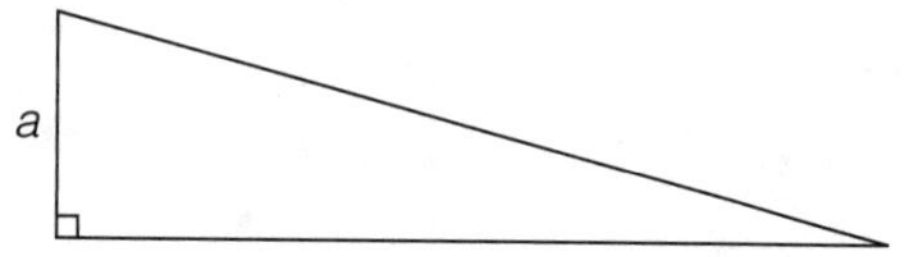

46. How to spot SPECIAL RIGHT TRIANGLES

Special right triangles are ones that are seen on the GRE with frequency. Recognizing them can streamline your problem solving.

3:4:5
5:12:13

These numbers (3, 4, 5 and 5, 12, 13) represent the ratio of the side lengths of these triangles.

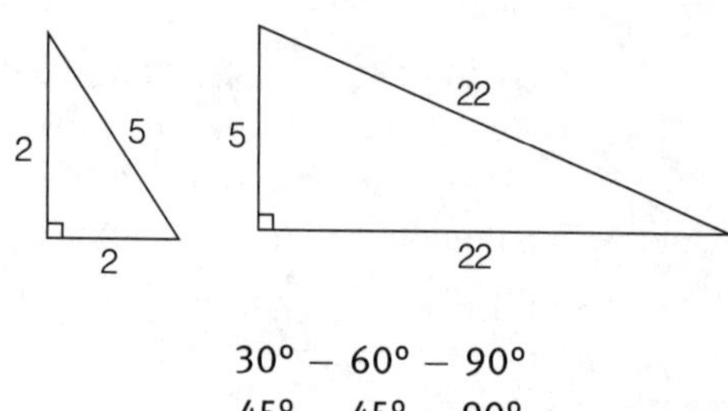

$30^\circ - 60^\circ - 90^\circ$
$45^\circ - 45^\circ - 90^\circ$

In a $30 - 60 - 90$ triangle, the side lengths are multiples of 1, $\sqrt{3}$, and 2, respectively. In a $45 - 45 - 90$ triangle, the side lengths are multiples of 1, 1, and $\sqrt{2}$, respectfully.

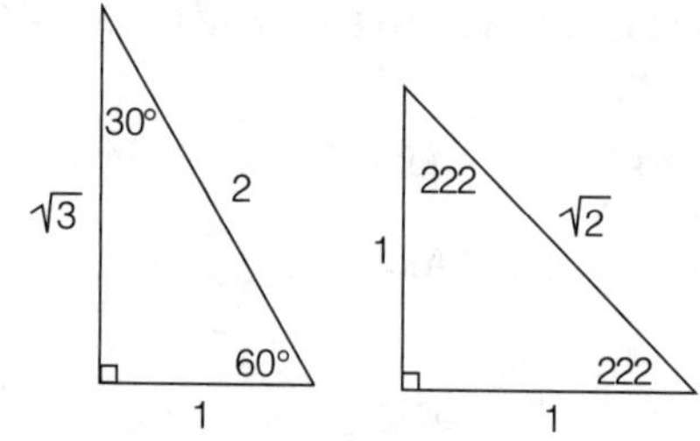

47. How to find the PERIMETER of a RECTANGLE

$$Perimeter = 2(Length + Width)$$

Example:

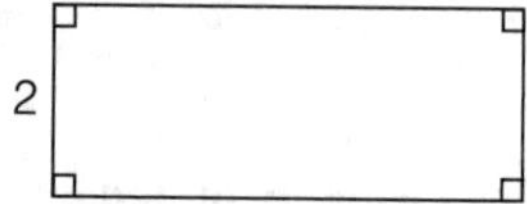

Setup:

$$Perimeter = 2(2 + 5) = 14$$

48. How to find the AREA of a RECTANGLE

$$Area = (Length)(Width)$$

Example:

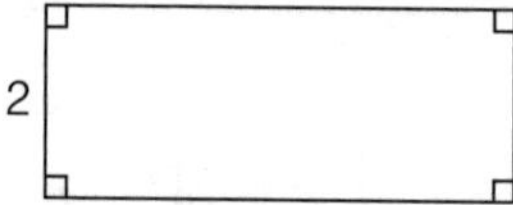

Setup:

$$Area = 2 \times 5 = 10$$

49. How to find the AREA of a SQUARE

$$Area = (Side)^2$$

Example:

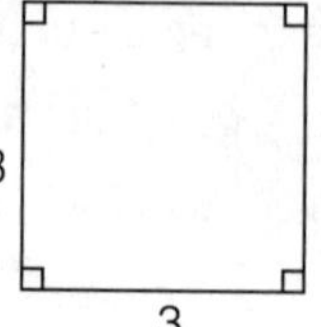

Setup:

$$Area = 3^2 = 9$$

50. How to find the AREA of a PARALLELOGRAM

$$Area = (Base)(Height)$$

Example:

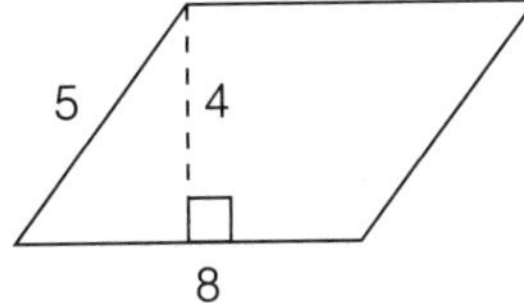

Setup:

$$Area = 8 \times 4 = 32$$

51. How to find the AREA of a TRAPEZOID

A trapezoid is a quadrilateral having only two parallel sides. You can always drop a perpendicular line or two to break the figure into a rectangle and a triangle or two triangles. Use the area formulas for those familiar shapes. Alternatively, you could apply the general formula for the area of a trapezoid:

$$Area = (Average\ of\ parallel\ sides) \times (Height)$$

Example:

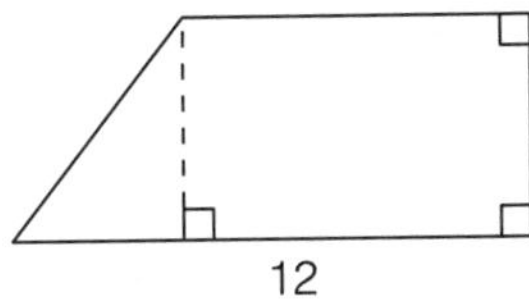

Setup:

$$Area\ of\ rectangle = 8 \times 5 = 40$$

$$Area\ of\ triangle = \frac{1}{2}(4 \times 5) = 10$$

$$Area\ of\ trapezoid = 40 + 10 = 50$$

$$Area\ of\ trapezoid = \left(\frac{8+12}{2}\right) \times 5 = 50$$

52. How to find the CIRCUMFERENCE of a CIRCLE

Circumference = 2□r, *where* r *is the radius*
Circumference = □d, *where* d *is the diameter*

Example:

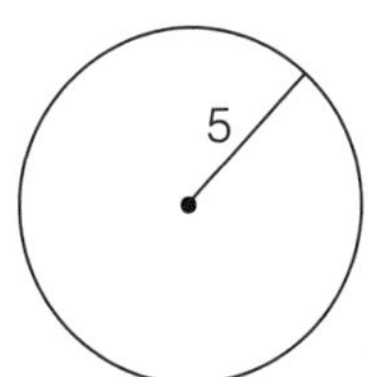

Setup:

$$Circumference = 2\pi(5) = 10\pi$$

53. How to find the AREA of a CIRCLE

$$Area = \pi r^2 \text{ where r is the radius}$$

Example:

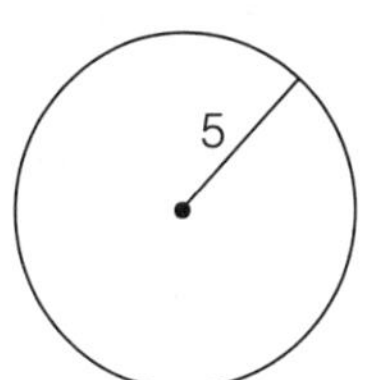

Setup:

$$Area = \pi \times 5^2 = 25\pi$$

54. How to find the DISTANCE BETWEEN POINTS on the coordinate plane

If two points have the same *x*-coordinates or the same *y*-coordinates—that is, they make a line segment that is parallel to an axis—all you have to do is subtract the numbers that are different. Just remember that distance is always positive.

Example:

What is the distance from (2, 3) to (−7, 3)?

Setup:

The *y*'s are the same, so just subtract the *x*'s: $2 - (-7) = 9$.

If the points have different x-coordinates and different y-coordinates, make a right triangle and use the Pythagorean theorem or apply the special right triangle attributes if applicable.

Example:

What is the distance from (2,3) to (–1,–1)?

Setup:

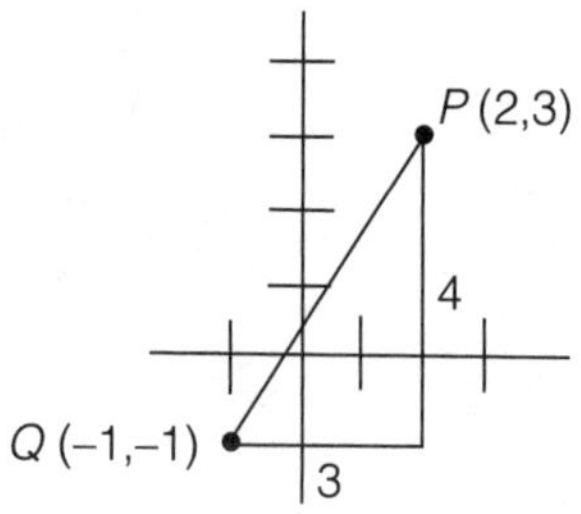

It's a 3:4:5 triangle!
$PQ = 5$

55. How to find the SLOPE of a LINE

$$Slope = \frac{Rise}{Run} = \frac{Change\ in\ y}{Change\ in\ x}$$

Example:

What is the slope of the line that contains the points (1,2) and (4,–5)?

Setup:

$$Slope = \frac{-5-2}{4-1} = \frac{-7}{3} = -\frac{7}{3}$$

LEVEL 3

56 How to determine COMBINED PERCENT INCREASE/DECREASE when no original value is specified

Start with 100 as a starting value.

Example:

A price rises by 10 percent one year and by 20 percent the next. What's the combined percent increase?

Setup:

Say the original price is \$100.

Year one:
\$100 + (10% of 100) = 100 + 10 = 110

Year two:
110 + (20% of 110) = 110 + 22 = 132

From 100 to 132 is a 32 percent increase.

57. How to find the ORIGINAL WHOLE before percent increase/decrease

Think of a 15 percent increase over x as $1.15x$ and set up an equation.

Example:

After decreasing by 5 percent, the population is now 57,000. What was the original population?

Setup:

0.95 × (*Original population*) = 57,000
Divide both sides by 0.95.
Original population = 57,000 ÷ 0.95 = 60,000

58. How to solve a SIMPLE INTEREST problem

With simple interest, the interest is computed on the principal only and is given by

Interest = *Principle* × *rt*

In this formula, r is defined as the interest rate per payment period, and t is defined as the number of payment periods.

Example:

If \$12,000 is invested at 6 percent simple annual interest, how much interest is earned after 9 months?

Setup:

Since the interest rate is annual and we are calculating how much interest accrues after 9 months, we will express the payment period as $\frac{9}{12}$.

$$(12{,}000) \times (0.06) \times \frac{9}{12} = \$540$$

59. How to solve a COMPOUND INTEREST problem

If interest is compounded, the interest is computed on the principal as well as on any interest earned. To compute compound interest:

$$(\textit{Final balance}) = (\textit{Principal}) \times \left(1 + \frac{\textit{interest rate}}{c}\right)^{(\textit{time})(c)}$$

where c = the number of times the interest is compounded annually.

Example:

If $10,000 is invested at 8 percent annual interest, compounded semiannually, what is the balance after 1 year?

Setup:

Final balance

$$= (10{,}000) \times \left(1 + \frac{0.08}{2}\right)^{(1)(2)}$$
$$= (10{,}000) \times (1.04)^2$$
$$= \$10{,}816$$

Semiannual interest is interest that is distributed twice a year. When an interest rate is given as an annual rate, divide by 2 to find the semiannual interest rate.

60. How to solve a REMAINDERS problem

Pick a number that fits the given conditions and see what happens.

Example:

When n is divided by 7, the remainder is 5. What is the remainder when $2n$ is divided by 7?

Setup:

Find a number that leaves a remainder of 5 when divided by 7. You can find such a number by taking any multiple of 7 and adding 5 to it. A good choice would be 12. If $n = 12$, then $2n = 24$, which when divided by 7 leaves a remainder of 3.

61. How to solve a DIGITS problem

Use a little logic—and some trial and error.

Example:

If A, B, C, and D represent distinct digits in the addition problem below, what is the value of D?

$$\begin{array}{r} AB \\ +\,BA \\ \hline CDC \end{array}$$

Setup:

Two 2-digit numbers will add up to at most something in the 100s, so $C = 1$. B plus A in the units column gives a 1, and since A and B in the tens column don't add up to C, it can't simply be that $B + A = 1$. It must be that $B + A = 11$, and a 1 gets carried. In fact, A and B can be any pair of digits that add up to 11 (3 and 8, 4 and 7, etc.), but it doesn't matter what they are: they always give you the same value for D, which is 2:

$$\begin{array}{r} 47 \\ +\ 74 \\ \hline 121 \end{array} \qquad \begin{array}{r} 83 \\ +\ 38 \\ \hline 121 \end{array}$$

62. How to find a WEIGHTED AVERAGE

Give each term the appropriate "weight."

Example:

The girls' average score is 30. The boys' average score is 24. If there are twice as many boys as girls, what is the overall average?

Setup:

$$\textit{Weighted avg.} = \frac{(1 \times 30) + (2 \times 24)}{3} = \frac{78}{3} = 26$$

HINT: Don't just average the averages.

63. How to find the NEW AVERAGE when a number is added or deleted

Use the sum of the terms of the old average to help you find the new average.

Example:

Michael's average score after four tests is 80. If he scores 100 on the fifth test, what's his new average?

Setup:

Find the original sum from the original average:

$$\textit{Original sum} = 4 \times 80 = 320$$

Add the fifth score to make the new sum:

$$\textit{New sum} = 320 + 100 = 420$$

Find the new average from the new sum:

$$\textit{New average} = \frac{420}{5} = 84$$

64. How to use the ORIGINAL AVERAGE and NEW AVERAGE to figure out WHAT WAS ADDED OR DELETED

Use the sums.

Number added = (*New sum*) − (*Original sum*)
Number deleted = (*Original sum*) − (*New sum*)

Example:

The average of five numbers is 2. After one number is deleted, the new average is −3. What number was deleted?

Setup:

Find the original sum from the original average:

$$\textit{Original sum} = 5 \times 2 = 10$$

Find the new sum from the new average:

$$\textit{New sum} = 4 \times (-3) = -12$$

The difference between the original sum and the new sum is the answer.

$$\textit{Number deleted} = 10 - (-12) = 22$$

65. How to find an AVERAGE RATE

Convert to totals.

$$\textit{Average A per B} = \frac{\textit{Total A}}{\textit{Total B}}$$

Example:

If the first 500 pages have an average of 150 words per page, and the remaining 100 pages have an average of 450 words per page, what is the average number of words per page for the entire 600 pages?

Setup:

$$\begin{aligned} \textit{Total pages} &= 500 + 100 = 600 \\ \textit{Total words} &= (500 \times 150) + (100 \times 450) \\ &= 75{,}000 + 45{,}00 \\ &= 120{,}000 \end{aligned}$$

$$\textit{Average words per page} = \frac{120{,}000}{600} = 200$$

To find an average speed, you also convert to totals.

$$\textit{Average speed} = \frac{\textit{Total distance}}{\textit{Total time}}$$

Example:

Rosa drove 120 miles one way at an average speed of 40 miles per hour and returned by the same 120-mile route at an average speed of 60 miles per hour. What was Rosa's average speed for the entire 240-mile round trip?

Setup:

To drive 120 miles at 40 mph takes 3 hours. To return at 60 mph takes 2 hours. The total time, then, is 5 hours.

$$\textit{Average speed} = \frac{240 \text{ miles}}{5 \text{ hours}} = 48 \text{ mph}$$

66. How to solve a COMBINED WORK PROBLEM

In a combined work problem, you are given the rate at which people or machines perform work individually and you are asked to compute the rate at which they work together (or vice versa). The work formula states: *The inverse of the time it would take everyone working together equals the sum of the inverses of the times it would take each working individually.* In other words:

$$\frac{1}{r} + \frac{1}{s} = \frac{1}{t}$$

where r and s are, for example, the number of hours it would take Rebecca and Sam, respectively, to complete a job working by themselves, and t is the number of hours it would take the two of them working together. Remember that all these variables must stand for units of TIME and must all refer to the amount of time it takes to do the same task.

Example:

If it takes Joe 4 hours to paint a room and Pete twice as long to paint the same room, how long would it take the two of them, working together, to paint the same room, if each of them works at his respective individual rate?

Setup:

Joe takes 4 hours, so Pete takes 8 hours; thus:

$$\frac{1}{4}+\frac{1}{8} = \frac{1}{t}$$

$$\frac{2}{8}+\frac{1}{8} = \frac{1}{t}$$

$$\frac{3}{8} = \frac{1}{t}$$

$$t = \frac{1}{\left(\frac{3}{8}\right)} = \frac{8}{3}$$

So it would take them $\frac{8}{3}$ hours, or 2 hours and 40 minutes, to paint the room together.

67. How to determine a COMBINED RATIO

Multiply one or both ratios by whatever you need in order to get the terms they have in common to match.

Example:

The ratio of a to b is 7:3. The ratio of b to c is 2:5. What is the ratio of a to c?

Setup:

Multiply each member of $a{:}b$ by 2 and multiply each member of $b{:}c$ by 3, and you get $a{:}b = 14{:}6$ and $b{:}c = 6{:}15$. Now that the values of b match, you can write $a{:}b{:}c = 14{:}6{:}15$ and then say $a{:}c = 14{:}15$.

68. How to solve a DILUTION or MIXTURE problem

In dilution or mixture problems, you have to determine the characteristics of a resulting mixture when different substances are combined. Or, alternatively, you have to determine how to combine different substances to produce a desired mixture. There are two approaches to such problems—the straightforward setup and the balancing method.

Example:

If 5 pounds of raisins that cost \$1 per pound are mixed with 2 pounds of almonds that cost \$2.40 per pound, what is the cost per pound of the resulting mixture?

Setup:

The straightforward setup:

$(\$1)(5) + (\$2.40)(2) = \$9.80 =$ total cost for 7 pounds of the mixture

The cost per pound is $\frac{\$9.80}{7} = \$1.40$.

Example:

How many liters of a solution that is 10 percent alcohol by volume must be added to 2 liters of a solution that is 50 percent alcohol by volume to create a solution that is 15 percent alcohol by volume?

Setup:

The balancing method: Make the weaker and stronger (or cheaper and more expensive, etc.) substances balance. That is, (percent difference between the weaker solution and the desired solution) $\times$ (amount of weaker solution) $=$ (percent difference between the stronger solution and the desired solution) × (amount of stronger solution). Make n the amount, in liters, of the weaker solution.

$$\begin{aligned} n(15-10) &= 2(50-15) \\ 5n &= 2(35) \\ n &= \frac{70}{5} = 14 \end{aligned}$$

So 14 liters of the 10 percent solution must be added to the original, stronger solution.

69. How to solve an OVERLAPPING SETS problem involving BOTH/NEITHER

Some GRE word problems involve two groups with overlapping members and possibly elements that belong to neither group. It's easy to identify this type of question because the words *both* and/or *neither* appear in the question. These problems are quite workable if you just memorize the following formula:

Group 1 + Group 2 + Neither – Both = Total

Example:

Of the 120 students at a certain language school, 65 are studying French, 51 are studying Spanish, and 53 are studying neither language. How many are studying both French and Spanish?

Setup:

$$\begin{aligned} 65+51+53-\textit{Both} &= 120 \\ 169-\textit{Both} &= 120 \\ \textit{Both} &= 49 \end{aligned}$$

70 How to solve an OVERLAPPING SETS problem involving EITHER/OR CATEGORIES

Other GRE word problems involve groups with distinct "either/or" categories (male/female, blue-collar/white-collar, etc.). The key to solving this type of problem is to organize the information in a grid.

Example:

At a certain professional conference with 130 attendees, 94 of the attendees are doctors, and the rest are dentists. If 48 of the attendees are women and $\frac{1}{4}$ of the dentists in attendance are women, how many of the attendees are male doctors?

Setup:

To complete the grid, use the information in the problem, making each row and column add up to the corresponding total:

	Doctors	Dentists	Total
Male	55	27	82
Female	39	9	48
Total	94	36	130

After you've filled in the information from the question, use simple arithmetic to fill in the remaining boxes until you get the number you are looking for—in this case, that 55 of the attendees are male doctors.

71. How to work with FACTORIALS

You may see a problem involving factorial notation, which is indicated by the ! symbol. If n is an integer greater than 1, then n factorial, denoted by $n!$, is defined as the product of all the integers from 1 to n. For example:

$$\begin{aligned} 2! &= 2\times 1 = 2 \\ 3! &= 3\times 2\times 1 = 6 \\ 4! &= 4\times 3\times 2\times 1 = 24, \text{etc} \end{aligned}$$

By definition, $0! = 1$.

Also note: $6! = 6 \times 5! = 6 \times 5 \times 4!$, etc. Most GRE factorial problems test your ability to factor and/or cancel.

Example:

$$\frac{8!}{6! \times 2!} = \frac{8 \times 7 \times 6!}{6! \times 2 \times 1} = 28$$

72: How to solve a PERMUTATION problem

Factorials are useful for solving questions about permutations (i.e., the number of ways to arrange elements sequentially). For instance, to figure out how many ways there are to arrange 7 items along a shelf, you would multiply the number of possibilities for the first position times the number of possibilities remaining for the second position, and so on—in other words: $7 \times 6 \times 5 \times 4 \times 3 \times 2 \times 1$, or 7!.

If you're asked to find the number of ways to arrange a smaller group that's being drawn from a larger group, you can either apply logic, or you can use the permutation formula:

$${}_nP_k = \frac{n!}{(n-k)!}$$

where n = (the number in the larger group) and
k = (the number you're arranging).

Example:

Five runners run in a race. The runners who come in first, second, and third place will win gold, silver, and bronze medals, respectively. How many possible outcomes for gold, silver, and bronze medal winners are there?

Setup:

Any of the 5 runners could come in first place, leaving 4 runners who could come in second place, leaving 3 runners who could come in third place, for a total of $5 \times 4 \times 3 = 60$ possible outcomes for gold, silver, and bronze medal winners. Or, using the formula:

$${}_5P_3 = \frac{5!}{(5-3)!} = \frac{5!}{2!} = \frac{5 \times 4 \times 3 \times \cancel{2} \times \cancel{1}}{\cancel{2} \times \cancel{1}}$$
$$= 5 \times 4 \times 3 = 60$$

73: How to solve a COMBINATION problem

If the order or arrangement of the smaller group that's being drawn from the larger group does NOT matter, you are looking for the numbers of combinations, and a different formula is called for:

$${}_nC_k = \frac{n!}{k!(n-k)!}$$

where n = (the number in the larger group) and
k = (the number you're choosing).

Example:

How many different ways are there to choose 3 delegates from 8 possible candidates?

Setup:

$${}_nC_k = \frac{8!}{3!(8-3)!} = \frac{8!}{3! \times 5!}$$
$$= \frac{8 \times 7 \times \cancel{6} \times \cancel{5} \times \cancel{4} \times \cancel{3} \times \cancel{2} \times \cancel{1}}{\cancel{3} \times \cancel{2} \times 1 \times \cancel{5} \times \cancel{4} \times \cancel{3} \times \cancel{2} \times \cancel{1}}$$
$$= 8 \times 7 = 56$$

So there are 56 different possible combinations.

74. How to solve PROBABILITY problems where probabilities must be multiplied

Suppose that a random process is performed. Then there is a set of possible outcomes that can occur. An event is a set of possible outcomes. We are concerned with the probability of events.

When all the outcomes are all equally likely, the basic probability formula is this:

$$\textit{Probability} = \frac{\textit{Number of desired outcomes}}{\textit{Number of total possible outcomes}}$$

Many more difficult probability questions involve finding the probability that several events occur. Let's consider first the case of the probability that two events occur. Call these two events A and B. The probability that both events occur is the probability that event A occurs multiplied by the probability that event B occurs given that event A occurred. The probability that B occurs given that

A occurs is called the conditional probability that B occurs given that A occurs. Except when events A and B do not depend on one another, the probability that B occurs given that A occurs is not the same as the probability that B occurs.

The probability that three events A, B, and C occur is the probability that A occurs multiplied by the conditional probability that B occurs given that A occurred multiplied by the conditional probability that C occurs given that both A and B have occurred.

This can be generalized to any number of events.

Example:

If 2 students are chosen at random to run an errand from a class with 5 girls and 5 boys, what is the probability that both students chosen will be girls?

Setup:

The probability that the first student chosen will be a girl is $\frac{5}{10} = \frac{1}{2}$, and since there would be 4 girls and 5 boys left out of 9 students, the probability that the second student chosen will be a girl (given that the first student chosen is a girl) is $\frac{4}{9}$. Thus, the probability that both students chosen will be girls is $\frac{1}{2} \times \frac{4}{9} = \frac{2}{9}$. There was conditional probability here because the probability of choosing the second girl was affected by another girl being chosen first. Now let's consider another example where a random process is repeated.

Example:

If a fair coin is tossed 4 times, what's the probability that at least 3 of the 4 tosses will be heads?

Setup:

There are 2 possible outcomes for each toss, so after 4 tosses, there are $2 \times 2 \times 2 \times 2 = 16$ possible outcomes.

We can list the different possible sequences where at least 3 of the 4 tosses are heads. These sequences are

HHHT
HHTH
HTHH
THHH
HHHH

Thus, the probability that at least 3 of the 4 tosses will come up heads is:

$$\frac{\textit{Number of desired outcomes}}{\textit{Number of total possible outcomes}} = \frac{5}{16}$$

We could have also solved this question using the combinations formula. The probability of a head is $\frac{1}{2}$, and the probability of a tail is $\frac{1}{2}$. The probability of any particular sequence of heads and tails resulting from 4 tosses is $\frac{1}{2} \times \frac{1}{2} \times \frac{1}{2} \times \frac{1}{2}$, which is $\frac{1}{16}$.

Suppose that the result of each of the four tosses is recorded in each of the four spaces.

____ ____ ____ ____

Thus, we would record an H for head or a T for tails in each of the 4 spaces.

The number of ways of having exactly 3 heads among the 4 tosses is the number of ways of choosing 3 of the 4 spaces above to record an H for heads.

The number of ways of choosing 3 of the 4 spaces is

$${}_4C_3 = \frac{4!}{3!\,(4-3)!} = \frac{4!}{3!(1)!} = \frac{4 \times 3 \times 2 \times 1}{3 \times 2 \times 1 \times 1} = 4$$

The number of ways of having exactly 4 heads among the 4 tosses is 1.

If we use the combinations formula, using the definition that $0! = 1$, then

$$_4C_4 = \frac{4!}{4!(4-4)!} = \frac{4!}{4!(0)!} = \frac{4 \times 3 \times 2 \times 1}{4 \times 3 \times 2 \times 1 \times 1} = 1$$

Thus, $_4C_3 = 4$ and $_4C_4 = 1$. So the number of different sequences containing at least 3 heads is $4 + 1 = 5$.

The probability of having at least 3 heads is $\frac{5}{16}$.

75. How to deal with STANDARD DEVIATION

Like the terms *mean*, *mode*, *median*, and *range*, *standard deviation* is a term used to describe sets of numbers. Standard deviation is a measure of how spread out a set of numbers is (how much the numbers deviate from the mean). The greater the spread, the higher the standard deviation. You'll rarely have to calculate the standard deviation on Test Day (although this skill may be necessary for some high-difficulty questions). Here's how standard deviation is calculated:

- Find the average (arithmetic mean) of the set.
- Find the differences between the mean and each value in the set.
- Square each of the differences.
- Find the average of the squared differences.
- Take the positive square root of the average.

In addition to the occasional question that asks you to calculate standard deviation, you may also be asked to compare standard deviations between sets of data or otherwise demonstrate that you understand what standard deviation means. You can often handle these questions using estimation.

Example:

High temperatures, in degrees Fahrenheit, in two cities over five days:

September	**1**	**2**	**3**	**4**	**5**
City A	54	61	70	49	56
City B	62	56	60	67	65

For the five-day period listed, which city had the greater standard deviation in high temperatures?

Setup:

Even without trying to calculate them out, one can see that City A has the greater spread in temperatures and, therefore, the greater standard deviation in high temperatures. If you were to go ahead and calculate the standard deviations following the steps described above, you would find that the standard deviation in high temperatures for

City A $= \sqrt{\frac{254}{5}} \approx 7.1$ while the standard

deviation for City

B $= \sqrt{\frac{74}{5}} \approx 3.8$.

76. How to MULTIPLY/DIVIDE VALUES WITH EXPONENTS

Add/subtract the exponents.

Example:

$x^a \times x^b = x^{a+b}$

$2^3 \times 2^4 = 2^7$

Example:

$\frac{x^a}{x^b} = x^{a-b}$

$\frac{2^8}{2^2} = 2^{8-2} = 2^6$

77. How to handle a value with an EXPONENT RAISED TO AN EXPONENT

Multiply the exponents.

Example:

$(x^a)^b = x^{ab}$

$(3^4)^5 = 3^{20}$

78. How to handle EXPONENTS with a base of ZERO and BASES with an EXPONENT of ZERO

Zero raised to any nonzero exponent equals zero.

Example:

$$0^4 = 0^{12} = 0^1 = 0$$

Any nonzero number raised to the exponent 0 equals 1.

Example:

$$3^0 = 15^0 = (0.34)^0 = (-345)^0 = \pi^0 = 1$$

The lone exception is 0 raised to the 0 power, which is *undefined.*

79. How to handle NEGATIVE POWERS

A number raised to the exponent $-x$ is the reciprocal of that number raised to the exponent x.

Example:

$$n^{-1} = \frac{1}{n},\ n^{-2} = \frac{1}{n^2},\ \text{and so on.}$$

$$5^{-3} = \frac{1}{5^3} = \frac{1}{5 \times 5 \times 5} = \frac{1}{125}$$

80. How to handle FRACTIONAL POWERS

Fractional exponents relate to roots. For instance, $x^{\frac{1}{2}} = \sqrt{x}$.

Likewise, $x^{\frac{1}{3}} = \sqrt[3]{x}$, $x^{\frac{2}{3}} = \sqrt[3]{x^2}$, and so on.

Example:

$$\sqrt{x^{-2}} = (x^{-2})^{\frac{1}{2}} = x^{(-2)\left(\frac{1}{2}\right)} = x^{-1} = \frac{1}{x}$$

$$4^{\frac{1}{2}} = \sqrt{4} = 2$$

81. How to handle CUBE ROOTS

The cube root of x is just the number that, when used as a factor 3 times (i.e., cubed), gives you x. Both positive and negative numbers have one and only one cube root, denoted by the symbol $\sqrt[3]{\ }$, and the cube root of a number is always the same sign as the number itself.

Example:

$$(-5) \times (-5) \times (-5) = -125, \text{ so } \sqrt[3]{-125} = -5$$

$$\frac{1}{2} \times \frac{1}{2} \times \frac{1}{2} = \frac{1}{8}, \text{ so } \sqrt[3]{\frac{1}{8}} = \frac{1}{2}$$

82. How to ADD, SUBTRACT, MULTIPLY, and DIVIDE ROOTS

You can add/subtract roots only when the parts inside the $\sqrt{\ }$ are identical.

Example:

$$\sqrt{2} + 3\sqrt{2} = 4\sqrt{2}$$

$$\sqrt{2} - 3\sqrt{2} = -2\sqrt{2}$$

$\sqrt{2} + \sqrt{3}$ can not be combined.

To multiply/divide roots, deal with what's inside the $\sqrt{\ }$ and outside the $\sqrt{\ }$ separately.

Example:

$$\left(2\sqrt{3}\right)\left(7\sqrt{5}\right) = (2 \times 7)\left(\sqrt{3 \times 5}\right) = 14\sqrt{15}$$

$$\frac{10\sqrt{21}}{5\sqrt{3}} = \frac{10}{5}\sqrt{\frac{21}{3}} = 2\sqrt{7}$$

83. How to SIMPLIFY A RADICAL

Look for factors of the number under the radical sign that are perfect squares; then find the square root of those perfect squares. Keep simplifying until the term with the square root sign is as simplified as possible, that is, when there are no other perfect square factors (4, 9, 16, 25, 36, . . .) inside the $\sqrt{\ }$. Write the perfect squares as separate factors and "unsquare" them.

Example:

$$\sqrt{48} = \sqrt{16}\,\sqrt{3} = 4\sqrt{3}$$

$$\sqrt{180} = \sqrt{36}\,\sqrt{5} = 6\sqrt{5}$$

84. How to solve certain QUADRATIC EQUATIONS

Manipulate the equation (if necessary) so that it is equal to 0, factor the left side (reverse FOIL by finding two numbers whose product is the constant and whose sum is the coefficient of the term without the exponent), and break the quadratic into two simple expressions. Then find the value(s) for the variable that make either expression = 0.

Example:

$$\begin{aligned} x^2 + 6 &= 5x \\ x^2 - 5x + 6 &= 0 \\ (x - 2)(x - 3) &= 0 \\ x - 2 &= 0 \text{ or } x - 3 = 0 \\ x &= 2 \text{ or } 3 \end{aligned}$$

Example:

$$\begin{aligned} x^2 &= 9 \\ x &= 3 \text{ or } -3 \end{aligned}$$

85. How to solve MULTIPLE EQUATIONS

When you see two equations with two variables on the GRE, they're probably easy to combine in such a way that you get something closer to what you're looking for.

Example:

If $5x - 2y = -9$ and $3y - 4x = 6$, what is the value of $x + y$?

Setup:

The question doesn't ask for x and y separately, so don't solve for them separately if you don't have to. Look what happens if you just rearrange a little and "add" the equations:

$$\begin{aligned} 5x - 2y &= -9 \\ +[-4x + 3y &= 6] \\ \hline x + y &= -3 \end{aligned}$$

86. How to solve a SEQUENCE problem

The notation used in sequence problems scares many test takers, but these problems aren't as bad as they look. In a sequence problem, the nth term in the sequence is generated by performing an operation, which will be defined for you, on either n or on the previous term in the sequence. The term itself is expressed as a_n. For instance, if you are referring to the fourth term in a sequence, it is called a_4 in sequence notation. Familiarize yourself with sequence notation and you should have no problem.

Example:

What is the positive difference between the fifth and fourth terms in the sequence 0, 4, 18, . . . whose nth term is $n^2(n - 1)$?

Setup:

Use the definition given to come up with the values for your terms:

$$\begin{aligned} a_5 &= 5^2(5 - 1) = 25(4) = 100 \\ a_4 &= 4^2(4 - 1) = 16(3) = 48 \end{aligned}$$

So the positive difference between the fifth and fourth terms is $100 - 48 = 52$.

87. How to solve a FUNCTION problem

You may see function notation on the GRE. An algebraic expression of only one variable may be defined as a function, usually symbolized by f or g, of that variable.

Example:

What is the minimum value of x in the function $f(x) = x^2 - 1$?

Setup:

In the function $f(x) = x^2 - 1$, if x is 1, then $f(1) = 1^2 - 1 = 0$. In other words, by inputting 1 into the function, the output $f(x) = 0$. Every number inputted has one and only one output (although the reverse is not necessarily true). You're asked to find the minimum value, so how would you minimize the expression $f(x) = x^2 - 1$? Since x^2 cannot be negative, in this case $f(x)$ is minimized by making $x = 0$: $f(0) = 0^2 - 1 = -1$, so the minimum value of the function is -1.

88. How to handle GRAPHS of FUNCTIONS

You may see a problem that involves a function graphed onto the xy-coordinate plane, often called a "rectangular coordinate system" on the GRE. When graphing a function, the output, $f(x)$, becomes the y-coordinate. For example, in the previous example, $f(x) = x^2 - 1$, you've already determined 2 points, (1,0) and (0,−1). If you were to keep plugging in numbers to determine more points and then plotted those points on the xy-coordinate plane, you would come up with something like this:

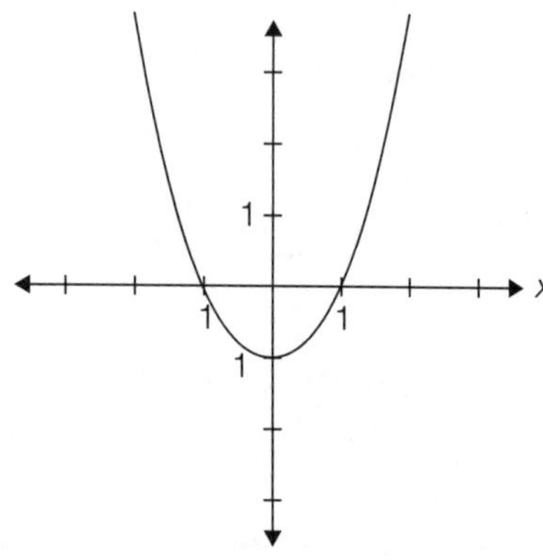

This curved line is called a *parabola*. In the event that you should see a parabola on the GRE (it could be upside down or narrower or wider than the one shown), you will most likely be asked to choose which equation the parabola is describing. These questions can be surprisingly easy to answer. Pick out obvious points on the graph, such as (1,0) and (0,−1) above, plug these values into the answer choices, and eliminate answer choices that don't work with those values until only one answer choice is left.

89. How to handle LINEAR EQUATIONS

You may also encounter linear equations on the GRE. A linear equation is often expressed in the form

$y = mx + b$, where

m = the slope of the line $= \frac{rise}{run}$

b = the y-intercept (the point where the line crosses the y-axis)

Example:

The graph of the linear equation

$y = -\frac{3}{4}x + 3$ is this:

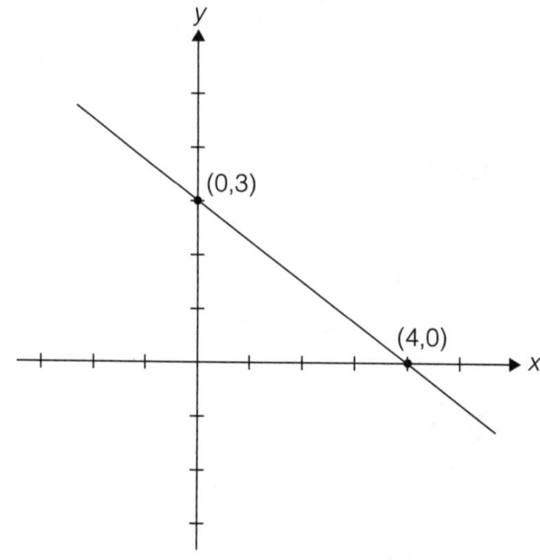

Note:

The equation could also be written in the form $3x + 4y = 12$, but this form does not readily describe the slope and y-intercept of the line.

To get a better handle on an equation written in this form, you can solve for y to write it in its more familiar form. Or, if you're asked to choose which equation the line is describing, you can pick obvious points, such as (0,3) and (4,0) in this example, and use these values to eliminate answer choices until only one answer is left.

90. How to find the x- and y-INTERCEPTS of a line

The x-intercept of a line is the value of x where the line crosses the x-axis. In other words, it's the value of x when $y = 0$. Likewise, the y-intercept is the value of y where the line crosses the y-axis (i.e., the value of y when $x = 0$). The y-intercept is also the value b when the equation is in the form $y = mx + b$. For instance, in the line shown in the previous example, the x-intercept is 4 and the y-intercept is 3.

91. How to find the MAXIMUM and MINIMUM lengths for a SIDE of a TRIANGLE

If you know the lengths of two sides of a triangle, you know that the third side is somewhere between the positive difference and the sum of the other two sides.

Example:

The length of one side of a triangle is 7. The length of another side is 3. What is the range of possible lengths for the third side?

Setup:

The third side is greater than the positive difference ($7 - 3 = 4$) and less than the sum ($7 + 3 = 10$) of the other two sides.

92. How to find the sum of all the ANGLES of a POLYGON and one angle measure of a REGULAR POLYGON

Sum of the interior angles in a polygon with n sides:

$$(n - 2) \times 180$$

The term *regular* means all angles in the polygon are of equal measure.

Degree measure of one angle in a regular polygon with n sides:

$$\frac{(n - 2) \times 180}{n}$$

Example:

What is the measure of one angle of a regular pentagon?

Setup:

Since a pentagon is a five-sided figure, plug $n = 5$ into the formula:

Degree measure of one angle:

$$\frac{(5 - 2) \times 180}{5} = \frac{540}{5} = 108$$

93. How to find the LENGTH of an ARC

Think of an arc as a fraction of the circle's circumference. Use the measure of an interior angle of a circle, which has 360 degrees around the central point, to determine the length of an arc.

$$\textit{Length of arc} = \frac{n}{360} \times 2\pi r$$

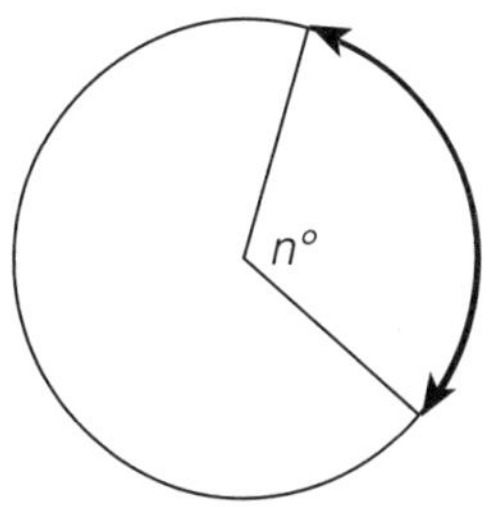

94. How to find the AREA of a SECTOR

Think of a sector as a fraction of the circle's area. Again, set up the interior angle measure as a fraction of 360, which is the degree measure of a circle around the central point.

$$\textit{Area of sector} = \frac{n}{360} \times \pi r^2$$

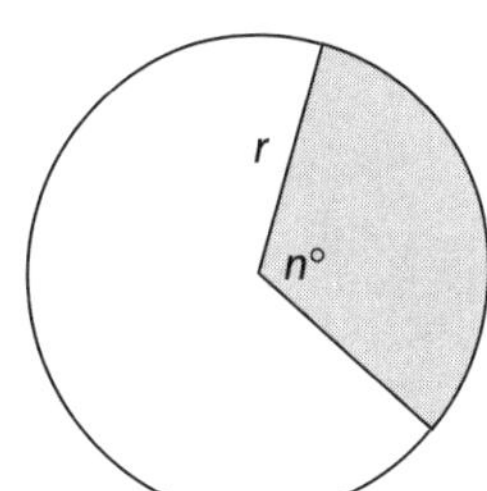

95. How to find the dimensions or area of an INSCRIBED or CIRCUMSCRIBED FIGURE

Look for the connection. Is the diameter the same as a side or a diagonal?

Example:

If the area of the square is 36, what is the circumference of the circle?

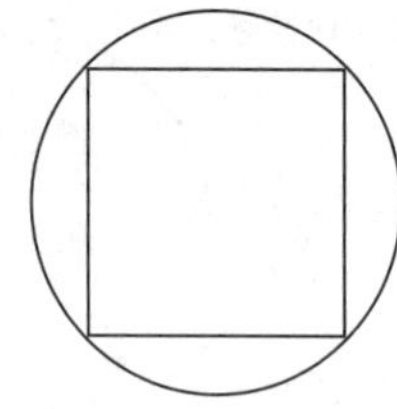

Setup:

To get the circumference, you need the diameter or radius. The circle's diameter is also the square's diagonal. The diagonal of the square is $6\sqrt{2}$. This is because the diagonal of the square transforms it into two separate $45° - 45° - 90°$ triangles (see #46). So, the diameter of the circle is $6\sqrt{2}$.

$$Circumference = \pi(Diameter) = 6\pi\sqrt{2}.$$

96. How to find the VOLUME of a RECTANGULAR SOLID

$$Volume = Length \times Width \times Height$$

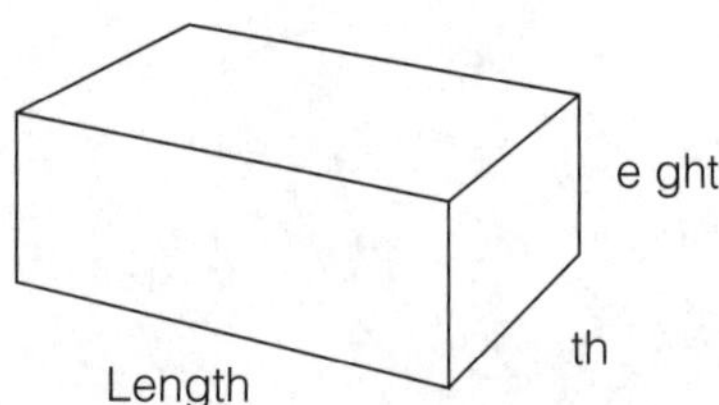

97. How to find the SURFACE AREA of a RECTANGULAR SOLID

To find the surface area of a rectangular solid, you have to find the area of each face and add the areas together. Here's the formula:

Let l = length, w = width, h = height:

$$Surface\ area = 2(lw) + 2(wh) + 2(lh)$$

98. How to find the DIAGONAL of a RECTANGULAR SOLID

Use the Pythagorean theorem twice, unless you spot "special" triangles.

Example:

What is the length of *AG*?

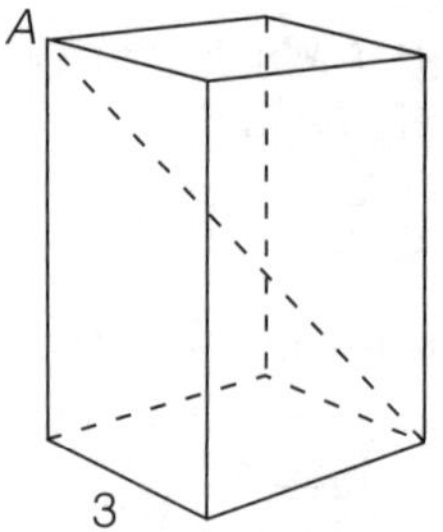

Setup:

Draw diagonal *AC*.

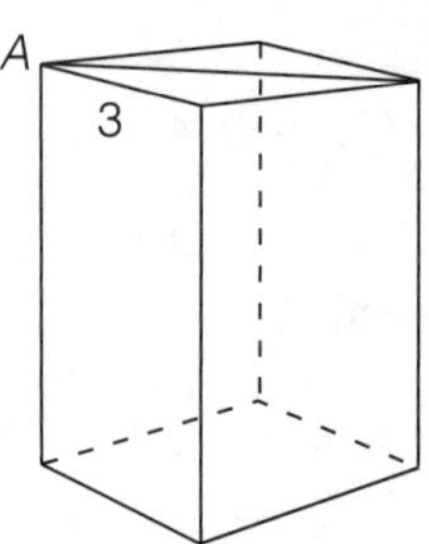

ABC is a 3:4:5 triangle, so $AC = 5$. Now look at triangle *ACG*:

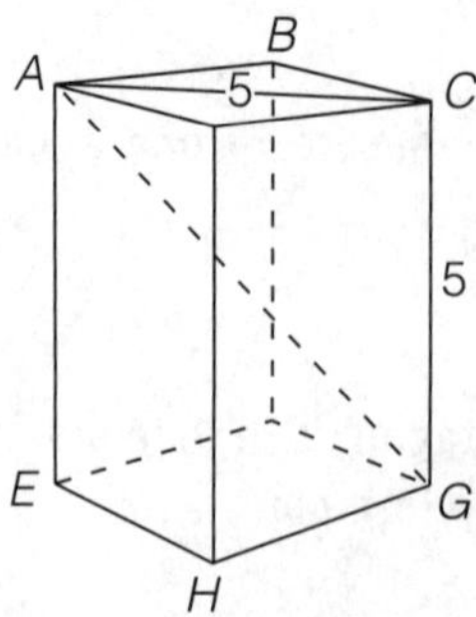

ACG is another special triangle, so you don't need to use the Pythagorean theorem. *ACG* is a $45° - 45° - 90°$ triangle, so $AG = 5\sqrt{2}$.

99. How to find the VOLUME of a CYLINDER

Volume = *Area of the base* × *Height* = $\pi r^2 h$

Example:

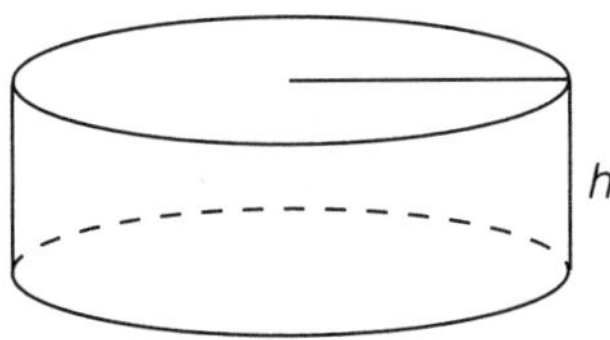

Let $r = 6$ and $h = 3$.

Setup:

$$Volume = \pi r^2 h = \pi(6^2)(3) = 108\pi$$

100. How to find the SURFACE AREA of a CYLINDER

Surface area = $2\pi r^2 + 2\pi rh$

Example:

Let $r = 3$ and $h = 4$.

Setup:

$$\begin{aligned} Surface\ area &= 2\pi r^2 + 2\pi rh \\ &= 2\pi(3)^2 + 2\pi(3)(4) \\ &= 18\pi + 24\pi = 42\pi \end{aligned}$$

10.1

15.1

21.6

7.8

29.4

13.5

19.9

8.9

22.8

7.5

30.3

B

9.7

3.5

13.2

4.1

17.3

4.9

22.2

C

30.3

34

13.470

100

.10

10

5.1

8.0

6.5

7.8

.84

6.9

7.5

92

4.1

4.9

10.6

6.9

17.5

7.8

7.5

15.3

4.9

20.2

GRE®

Graduate
Record
Examination

VERBAL WORKBOOK

Ninth Edition

New York

For more GRE® prep, Kaplan offers a range of print and digital products, available in stores and online:

Kaplan GRE® Premier with 6 Practice Tests
Kaplan GRE® Strategies, Practice, and Review with 4 Practice Tests
GRE® Math Workbook
Kaplan GRE® Vocabulary Flashcards

To learn more about Kaplan's comprehensive prep courses for the GRE®, please visit **www.kaptest.com/GRE**.

GRE®

Graduate Record Examination

VERBAL WORKBOOK

Ninth Edition

New York

Published by Kaplan Publishing, a division of Kaplan, Inc.
750 Third Avenue
New York, NY 10017

Printed in the United States of America

10 9 8 7 6 5 4 3 2 1
ISBN: 978-1-62523-298-4

Table of Contents

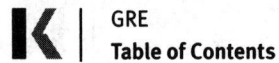

Acknowledgments

Special thanks to the team that made this book possible:

Arthur Ahn, Matthew Belinkie, Shannon Berning, Lauren T. Bernstein, Kim Bowers, Gerard Cortinez, Elisa Davis, Lola Disparte, Boris Dvorkin, John Evans, Paula Fleming, Darcy Galane, Joanna Graham, Adam Grey, Allison Harm, Jack Hayes, Adam Hinz, Gar Hong, Sunny Hwang, Cinzia Iacono, Avi Lidgi, Kate Lopaze, Keith Lubeley, TJ Mancini, Jennifer Moore, Jason Moss, Walt Niedner, Robert Reiss, Shmuel Ross, Derek Rusnak, Emily Sachar, Stephanie Schrauth, Sheryl Stebbins, Glen Stohr, Sascha Strelka, Gene Suhir, Martha Torres, Liza Weale, Lee A. Weiss, and many others who have contributed materials and advice over the years.

How to Use This Book

Kaplan has prepared students to take standardized tests for more than 75 years. Our team of teachers and researchers knows more about preparation for the GRE than anyone else, and you'll find Kaplan's accumulated knowledge and experience throughout this book. The GRE is a standardized test, so every administration covers the same content in roughly the same way. This is good news for you; it means that the best way to prepare is to focus on the sort of questions you are likely to see on Test Day. The main focus of this book is on strategic reviews, exercises, and practice tests with explanations that will help you brush up on your vocabulary, reading comprehension, and writing skills. If possible, work through this book a little at a time over the course of several weeks. There is a lot of material to absorb, and it's hard to do all at once.

Getting Started

Part 1 of this book, "Getting Started," provides you with background information on the Verbal Reasoning section of the test, what it covers, and how it's organized.

Verbal Reasoning Section

The Verbal Reasoning section of the GRE contains three main question types: Text Completion, Sentence Equivalence, and Reading Comprehension. Part 3 of this book covers these types with strategies and sample questions. Your focus here should be to familiarize yourself with the question types so you won't be trying to figure out how to approach them on Test Day.

Read the explanations to all the questions—even those you got right. Often the explanations will contain strategies that show you how you could have gotten to the answer more quickly and efficiently.

Analytical Writing Section

The analytical writing content review covers grammar, mechanics, and style, as well as strategies for writing effective paragraphs and essays. The final chapters of this workbook cover sample GRE prompts. Using these prompts, you can practice the skills you have learned to write strong essays. In addition to sample prompts, we've also included sample top-scoring essays so you can review the qualities that earn an essay a high score.

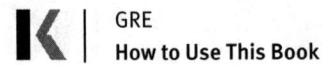

Verbal Content Review

Once you have the big picture, focus on the content. Part 2 of this book, "Verbal Content Review," gives you a complete tour of the vocabulary that you will see on Test Day. The material in the verbal content review is divided into particular subjects. Each subject begins with a review, followed by practice questions. This structure makes it easy for you to pinpoint the vocabulary concepts you need to review and quickly get your skills up to speed.

If you find that you would like access to more of Kaplan's practice tests and quizzes, as well as in-depth instruction on the question types and strategies, look into the variety of course options available at **www.kaptest.com/GRE**.

If you have questions about what you're studying, ask our expert GRE faculty on our Facebook page: **www.facebook.com/KaplanGradPrep**.

Thanks for choosing Kaplan. We wish you the best of luck on your journey to graduate school.

PART ONE

Getting Started

CHAPTER 1

Introduction to GRE Verbal

UNDERSTANDING THE GRE VERBAL REASONING SECTION

The Verbal Reasoning sections of the Graduate Record Exam (GRE) emphasize complex reasoning skills and reward your ability to analyze the relationships among words and sentences as they are used in context. The exam tests vocabulary contextually, and the reading passages are both dense and written with a sophisticated level of diction. The goal of the test's content and emphasis on analytical skills is to provide an accurate indication of your ability to understand what you're reading and to apply reasoning skills to the text's premises and arguments. These are all skills you will need at the graduate level.

To perform well on the Verbal Reasoning section—to answer correctly as many questions as possible—you need to have a good grasp of vocabulary and the ability to apply reasoning skills. Part 2 of this book explains the various question types in detail. Part 3 reviews the foundations of vocabulary. Every chapter offers plenty of opportunities to practice and review your answers.

MST MECHANICS

The GRE is a multi-stage test (MST). While working within a section of the test, you may skip questions and return to them as long as time remains for the section. The test is computer based, presented in an interface with tools such as a Mark button (to indicate a question you want to examine later within the time allowed for that section), a Review button (to see your progress on the entire set of questions in a section), and an optional time display. As you prepare for Test Day, consider how these computer capabilities may help you manage your time for each section.

As best you can, approach the exam as you would a paper-based one. After all, the idea behind the MST is that it will feel more comfortable and familiar than some other computer-based or adaptive tests, on which you cannot move about freely within a section. Use the MST's design to your advantage. If a question looks too daunting, skip it. Use the Mark button to remind you to come back to the question when you have time at the end of that section. By doing so, you can better organize your time by keeping track of which questions you are done with and which ones need a second look.

Finally, having an on-screen timer (which appears in the corner of the display) works to your advantage, helping you keep track of the time remaining in the section. But if you find yourself looking at it so frequently that it becomes a distraction, turn it off for a few minutes and refocus your attention on the test. Use the timer to help you make good decisions about how to spend your time within the section, but don't let it prevent you from concentrating on the questions.

VERBAL REASONING QUESTION TYPES

The GRE MST contains two Verbal Reasoning sections with 20 questions each. Each section lasts 30 minutes and contains a selection of the following question types:

- Text Completion
- Sentence Equivalence
- Reading Comprehension

The Verbal Reasoning portion of the GRE rewards a strong, university-level vocabulary and facility with understanding and analyzing written material. Specifically, it evaluates your ability to do the following:

- accurately paraphrase sentences and paragraphs
- derive a word's meaning based on its context
- detect relationships among words
- understand the logic of sentences and paragraphs
- draw inferences
- recognize major, minor, and irrelevant points
- summarize ideas
- understand passage and paragraph structure
- recognize an author's tone, purpose, and perspective

The GRE assesses those skills with an assortment of Text Completion, Sentence Equivalence, and Reading Comprehension items. The following chart shows how many questions of each type you can expect, as well as the average amount of time you should spend per question.

	Text Completion	Sentence Equivalence	Reading Comprehension
Number of Questions	Approx. 6	Approx. 4	Approx. 10
Time per Question	1–1.5 minutes	1 minute	1–3 minutes, depending on the length, to read the passage and 1 minute to answer each question

TEXT COMPLETION

You will find about six Text Completion questions in each Verbal Reasoning section. These questions consist of single sentences or short paragraphs of two or three sentences. The text has blanks replacing one, two, or three words. Your task is to select one word for each blank from a column of corresponding choices to complete the text logically. This question type tests your ability to read strategically—to recognize the point of a sentence and find the best word(s) to fit its meaning.

Chapter 2 presents the Kaplan Method for answering Text Completion questions and strategies to help you solve them efficiently.

SENTENCE EQUIVALENCE

Each Verbal Reasoning section features approximately four Sentence Equivalence questions. These questions provide a single sentence with one missing word. You must identify two correct words, either of which would complete the sentence. The correct answer choices, when inserted into the blank, will give the same meaning to *both* resulting sentences. These questions test your ability to determine a sentence's meaning and to use vocabulary in context.

You'll find the Kaplan Method for Sentence Equivalence questions and strategies to help solve them efficiently in chapter 3.

READING COMPREHENSION

Reading Comprehension is the only question type that appears on all major standardized tests, and with good reason. No matter what academic discipline you pursue, you'll have to make sense of dense, complex written material. Being able to understand and assess such material is a crucial skill for every graduate student.

To make the test broadly relevant, and to better evaluate your ability to understand comparable material, the testmaker, Educational Testing Service (ETS), adapts Reading Comprehension content from "real-world" graduate-level documents. GRE passages come from four disciplines: social sciences, biological sciences, physical sciences, and the arts and humanities.

The GRE includes roughly ten reading passages between the two Verbal Reasoning sections. Many of these passages are one paragraph in length, although a few are longer. Each passage is accompanied by one to six questions. These questions reward you for ascertaining the author's purpose and meaning, determining what can be validly inferred from the passage, researching details in the text, and understanding the meaning of words and the function of sentences in context.

Chapter 4 contains the Kaplan Method for answering Reading Comprehension questions and strategies to help solve them efficiently.

ANALYTICAL WRITING

The Analytical Writing section assesses not only how well you write, but also the thought processes you employ in formulating and articulating a position. In response to short, descriptive prompts, you produce two essays, one in which you evaluate an argument and one in which you make an argument of your own. Specifically, the Analytical Writing tasks measure your ability to do the following:

- articulate and defend a position
- deconstruct and evaluate a complex argument
- develop a cogent argument
- assess the fundamental soundness of an argument
- recognize major, minor, and irrelevant points
- provide evidence and support for an argument
- detect the flaws in an unsound argument
- write articulately and effectively at a high level

Regardless of your field, you will need these critical thinking skills to perform well in a graduate program.

ANALYTICAL WRITING ESSAY TYPES

The GRE's Analytical Writing section contains two different essay types. You'll be given 30 minutes for each essay. Here are your tasks:

- The Issue Essay Task provides a brief quotation on an issue of general interest and instructions on how to respond to the issue. You can discuss the issue from any perspective, making use of your own educational and personal background, examples from current or historical events, things you've read, or even relevant hypothetical situations. In this task, you develop your own argument in response to the prompt.
- The Argument Essay Task contains a short argument that may or may not be complete and specific instructions on how to evaluate the argument's strength. You will assess the argument's cogency, analyze the author's reasoning, and evaluate the use (or lack) of evidence. In this task, you critique the argument presented in the prompt.

You'll write the essays on the computer, using a simple word processing program with functions allowing you to cut, paste, delete, and insert text but with no spelling or grammar checker. Graders score the Analytical Writing essays based on your ability to plan and compose a logical, well-reasoned essay, one that's responsive to the test's instructions, under timed conditions. Only a score report is sent to the schools to which you apply.

PART TWO

Verbal Reasoning

CHAPTER 2

Text Completion

TEXT COMPLETION: OVERVIEW AND METHOD

You will find about six Text Completion questions per Verbal Reasoning section on the GRE. In each Text Completion question, one, two, or three words from the sentence(s) will be missing. This question type tests your ability to recognize the point of the passage and find the best word(s) to fit its meaning. In addition to testing vocabulary, Text Completion questions require you to read actively and strategically for context. Even an answer choice that "sounds good" when read into the sentence will be incorrect if it does not closely fit the meaning. For Text Completion questions with two or three blanks, all of the blanks must be filled in correctly to earn the point. As elsewhere on the GRE, *no partial credit is given.*

The directions for Text Completion questions will look like this:

> For each blank select one entry from the corresponding column of choices. Fill all blanks in the way that best completes the text.

A Text Completion question with one blank will look like this:

> Although the city's public mass transportation system has been _______ from active service, traces of its presence may be seen in the train stations that have been converted into shopping centers.
>
> (A) dilated
> (B) retired
> (C) metastasized
> (D) frozen
> (E) waxed

THE KAPLAN METHOD FOR TEXT COMPLETION (ONE-BLANK)

STEP 1 Read the sentence, looking for clues.

STEP 2 Predict an answer.

STEP 3 Select the choice that most closely matches your prediction.

STEP 4 Check your answer.

How the Kaplan Method for Text Completion (One-Blank) Works

Here's how the Kaplan Method for Text Completion (One-Blank) works.

STEP 1

Read the sentence, looking for clues.

There are always clues in the sentence that will point you to the right answer. The missing words in Text Completion questions will usually be similar or opposite to key words in the sentence.

Key words and *key phrases* give context clues that will help you predict the meaning of the missing word(s).

A *road sign* is a structural key word that signals the connection between ideas. Road signs indicate the sentence's direction. Some road signs tell you the sentence is going *straight ahead*—the next idea follows from what has come before. Other road signs, *detour* road signs, indicate that the sentence is changing direction, with the next idea contrasting with what has come before.

Straight-ahead road signs—*and, additionally, moreover, so*—are used when one part of the sentence supports or elaborates on the other part. They continue the sentence in the same direction. The positive or negative connotation of what follows is not changed by these clues.

Detour road signs—*but, however, on the other hand, to the contrary*—change the direction of the sentence. They indicate that one part of the sentence contradicts or qualifies the other part. The positive or negative connotation of an answer is changed by these clues.

On the GRE, a semicolon always connects two closely related independent clauses. If it is not accompanied by a detour road sign, the semicolon functions as a straight-ahead road sign.

Recognizing road signs will help you determine which way a Text Completion sentence is going and predict what word(s) will be used to fill in the blank(s). Here are some examples.

Straight-ahead road signs:	**Detour road signs:**
And	*But*
Since	*Despite*
Also	*Yet*
Thus	*However*
Because	*Unless*
: (colon)	*Rather*
Likewise	*Although*
Moreover	*While*
Similarly	*On the other hand*
In addition	*Unfortunately*
Consequently	*Nonetheless*
Therefore	*Conversely*

STEP 2

Predict an answer.

Once you've found the road sign and the key word(s) relevant to the blank, use them to predict an answer for the blank. Your prediction does not have to be a sophisticated or complex word or phrase, simply a paraphrase that fits logically into the sentence. By predicting, you will know what kind of word you are looking for and be able to efficiently eliminate words that are not a match. This will save you time and help you avoid the trap answers.

STEP 3

Select the answer choice that most closely matches your prediction.

Quickly go through the choices and select the one that most closely matches your prediction of the correct answer. Eliminate choices that do not fit your prediction. If none of the choices matches your prediction, reread the question and revisit Steps 1 and 2.

STEP 4

Check your answer.

Check that your answer choice makes sense in context. Read the sentence to yourself with your choice(s) in the blanks. If the sentence makes sense, confirm your answer(s) and move on. If the sentence does not make sense or just doesn't "sound right," reread the question and revisit Steps 1 through 3.

Apply the Kaplan Method for Text Completion (One-Blank)

Now, apply the Kaplan Method to a Text Completion (One-Blank) question:

Although the city's public mass transportation system has been ________ from active service, traces of its presence may be seen in the train stations that have been converted into shopping centers.

Ⓐ dilated
Ⓑ retired
Ⓒ metastasized
Ⓓ frozen
Ⓔ waxed

STEP 1

Read the sentence, looking for clues.

Begin by paraphrasing the sentence's main idea: The city's transportation system has not disappeared entirely, because traces of it may still be seen. The detour road sign "although" indicates that the verb that will fill the blank will contrast with the second half of the sentence.

STEP 2

Predict an answer.

Based on that paraphrase, you can predict that the correct answer will have a meaning similar to "removed" or "quit."

STEP 3

Select the answer choice that most closely matches your prediction.

Answer choice **(B)** *retired* matches the meaning of your prediction. The system has been "retired" from active service. Choices **(A)** *dilated* and **(E)** *waxed* mean "increased" or "widened"; they are the opposite of your prediction. Similarly, choice **(C)** *metastasized* means something has spread. Choice **(D)** *frozen* makes little sense in this context.

STEP 4

Check your answer.

To make sure your answer is right, simply plug it back into the original sentence:

"Although the city's public mass transportation system has been *retired* from active service, traces of its presence may be seen in the train stations that have been converted into shopping centers."

The sentence is logical, and the answer choice matches your prediction; it's the correct answer.

TEXT COMPLETION (ONE-BLANK) PRACTICE SET

Try the following Text Completion questions using the Kaplan Method:

1. The director is normally lauded for his exciting science-fiction films, but his latest effort is marred by its _______ special effects.

   (A) electrifying
   (B) piquant
   (C) bland
   (D) emotive
   (E) sophisticated

2. Despite her long battle with illness, the dancer displayed astonishing _______ of motion on stage.

   (A) indolence
   (B) hesitancy
   (C) extension
   (D) queasiness
   (E) fluency

3. Having established his competence as a playwright with his first play, the author went on to show greater _______ with his second.

   (A) characterization
   (B) mastery
   (C) understanding
   (D) perception
   (E) insufficiency

4. Such a _______ response to a client is not consistent with the high standards of customer service this company demands.

   (A) politic
   (B) cloying
   (C) meticulous
   (D) boastful
   (E) disrespectful

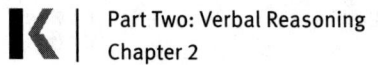

5. Difficult as it may sometimes be, in all our dealings with both clients and competitors, we must be seen to be above ______.

   (A) profit
   (B) integrity
   (C) ambivalence
   (D) reproach
   (E) scruples

TEXT COMPLETION (ONE-BLANK) PRACTICE SET ANSWERS AND EXPLANATIONS

1. C

Reading this sentence all the way through reveals that "but" is a detour road sign, indicating that the sentence will change direction. So, while the director is normally "lauded," which means "praised," for his exciting films, his newest one is "marred" by its special effects. Therefore, the word that goes in the blank must be a negatively charged adjective that contrasts with "exciting." You can predict that the correct answer is a word that means "unexciting" or "dull." The answer that fits this prediction is choice **(C)** *bland*. Choices **(A)** *electrifying*, **(B)** *piquant*, and **(D)** *emotive* are related in meaning to "exciting" or "engaging." Choice **(E)** *sophisticated*, meaning "complex" or "refined," also does not logically contrast with "exciting." Sophisticated special effects would tend to make a science-fiction film more exciting, not less so. *Bland*, on the other hand, is a direct opposite of "exciting," making **(C)** the correct answer.

2. E

"Despite" is a detour road sign indicating that the correct answer will contrast with the fact that the dancer has endured a long battle with illness. A reasonable prediction is *gracefulness*, which you would not expect from a dancer who has been seriously ill. The best choice is **(E)** *fluency*. "Fluency of motion" has a meaning similar to "gracefulness," so it matches your prediction. Choice **(D)** *queasiness* does not describe movement and also does not follow the detour road sign; there is nothing "astonishing" about nausea in a dancer who has been ill. The same applies for **(B)** *hesitancy*, as you might expect the dancer to be tentative in her movements after an illness. Choice **(A)** *indolence*, which means "laziness," doesn't fit because there would be nothing astonishing about that, either. Choice **(C)** *extension* might have been tempting if you were thinking of ballet or another dance style in which extension of the body is emphasized, but "extension" describes body posture, not movement. Moreover, the sentence is not limited to a particular style of dance, so this choice is too specific for the context.

3. B

The first clause in this sentence describes the playwright as "competent" in his first play, while the second clause asserts that he has progressed beyond mere competence in his second. *Skill* is an excellent prediction. Choice **(B)** *mastery* fits perfectly; the playwright no longer is merely *competent*, but is now *masterful*. You can reject **(E)** *insufficiency* as the opposite of what the sentence needs. Choices **(A)** *characterization*, **(C)** *understanding*, and **(D)** *perception* are all elements of writing that the playwright may have improved upon, but you're looking for a more general word. Nothing in the sentence leads logically to a specific area of improvement.

4. E

The word "not" is a detour road sign indicating that the adjective in the blank (which describes the word "response") must be inconsistent with "high standards of customer service." High customer service standards imply proper etiquette, responsiveness, and professionalism. A simple, accurate prediction of the opposite of those is *rude*. Choice **(E)** *disrespectful* is the answer choice closest to that prediction. Choice **(A)** *politic* has a couple of meanings: "shrewd" and "tactful." Both could describe someone who is good at customer service. Choice **(C)** *meticulous* means "attentive to detail," another good trait in someone who serves customers. Choice **(B)** *cloying* means "too sweet" or "too sentimental." While potentially annoying, this quality does not relate to the context clue of "customer service." Choice **(D)** *boastful* means "full of excessive pride," which does not necessarily make someone rude or inhospitable.

5. D

To unlock this question, recognize that the term in the blank must be a negatively charged word with which a reputable business would not wish to be associated. *Suspicion* works nicely. Choice **(D)** *reproach,* meaning "blame," is the best fit for the context and is the correct answer. You can immediately eliminate **(B)** *integrity* and **(E)** *scruples,* which mean "adherence to ethical principles" and "moral considerations," respectively. These qualities are desirable in a business or company. In context, choice **(A)** *profit* makes little sense; it's not logical to say a company appears to be "above profit," since one of the primary purposes of a business is to make a profit. Similarly, choice **(C)** *ambivalence,* meaning "undecided" or "uncertain," makes little sense in context; indecision is not a quality that would make a company appear disreputable.

THE KAPLAN METHOD FOR TEXT COMPLETION (TWO-BLANK AND THREE-BLANK)

STEP 1 **Read the sentence, looking for clues.**

STEP 2 **Predict the answer for the easier/easiest blank.**

STEP 3 **Select the answer choice that most closely matches your prediction.**

STEP 4 **Predict and select for the remaining blanks.**

STEP 5 **Check your answers.**

A Text Completion question with two blanks will look like this:

Even when faced with continuing (i) _______, the recalcitrant graduate student persisted in her spendthrift ways; she abjured any thought of self-(ii) _______ and spent prodigally.

Blank (i)		Blank (ii)	
A	lucre	D	adumbration
B	penury	E	aggrandizement
C	avarice	F	abnegation

A Text Completion question with three blanks will look like this:

Though scientific discoveries are often (i) _______ shortly after they've been accepted as fact, scientists still seem to leap to hasty conclusions, (ii) _______ that the (iii) _______ nature of what can be called "fact" has not eroded their confidence.

Blank (i)		Blank (ii)		Blank (iii)	
A	validated	D	denying	G	predictable
B	published	E	refuting	H	incendiary
C	disproved	F	demonstrating	I	illusory

HOW THE KAPLAN METHOD FOR TEXT COMPLETION (TWO-BLANK AND THREE-BLANK) WORKS

Here's how the Kaplan Method for Text Completion (Two-Blank and Three-Blank) works.

STEP 1

Read the sentence, looking for clues.

Just as with one-blank Text Completion questions, the sentence(s) will contain key words and road signs that point you to the right answer. In particular, the missing words will usually have a meaning either similar or opposite to that of key words or phrases in the sentence(s). Therefore, pay attention to the road signs, which tell you whether there is a straight-ahead relationship or a detour relationship between words. In addition, when there are multiple blanks, a sentence is likely to contain both detour and straight-ahead road signs, indicating different relationships between the different blanks and their context. Pay attention to these relationships as you untangle the sentence(s). You may want to refer to the list of example road signs in the previous section to refresh your memory.

Remember, you must select the correct answer choice for *each* blank for the question to be scored as correct. No partial credit is given.

STEP 2

Predict an answer for the easier/easiest blank.

You do not need to tackle the blanks in order. Instead, identify the easier/easiest blank to work with. This is often one with key words and road signs that help you make a clear prediction. As with one-blank Text Completions, your prediction does not have to be a sophisticated or complex word or phrase. Just come up with a term that logically fits into the sentence at that point. Again, by making a prediction, you can zero in on the choice that matches your prediction, saving time and avoiding trap answers.

When you have correctly filled in one blank, that answer often becomes a key word that provides a clue to another blank(s).

STEP 3

Select the answer choice that most closely matches your prediction.

Quickly go through the choices and see which one matches your prediction.

Simultaneously, eliminate whichever answer choices do not fit your prediction. If none of the choices match your prediction, reread the question and revisit Steps 1 and 2. If one does match, you should proceed to Step 4.

STEP 4

Predict and select for the remaining blanks.

Filling in the easier/easiest blank provides additional context for the remaining blanks.

For two-blank Text Completion questions, use the context to help you choose the answer for the remaining blank. If the answers for the second blank are not working out, you need to go back to Step 2.

For three-blank Text Completion questions, select the easier of the two remaining blanks and predict which choice will most logically complete the sentence. You now have two blanks to provide context for the last, most difficult blank. This approach to two- and three-blank questions is just a logical extension of the Kaplan Method as it applies to one-blank questions.

STEP 5

Check your answers.

Double-check that your answer choices make sense in context by reading the sentence to yourself with your answers plugged in. If the sentence makes sense when you read your choices back into it, confirm your answers and move on. If the sentence doesn't make sense when read with your choices, reread the question and revisit Steps 1 through 4.

Apply the Kaplan Method for Text Completion (Two-Blank)

Now, apply the Kaplan Method to a Text Completion (Two-Blank) question:

Even when faced with continuing (i) ________, the recalcitrant graduate student persisted in her spendthrift ways; she abjured any thought of self-(ii) ________ and spent prodigally.

Blank (i)		Blank (ii)	
A	lucre	D	adumbration
B	penury	E	aggrandizement
C	avarice	F	abnegation

STEP 1

Read the sentence, looking for clues.

This is a fairly straightforward question, once you wade through all the polysyllabic words. Look at the end of the second clause; you'll notice that the student "spent prodigally," which means "wastefully." Even if you don't know the meaning of the word "prodigally," you can tell from the word "spendthrift" that this is a student who isn't careful with the way she spends her money. If the student is poor at managing money, she likely doesn't have much of it.

STEP 2

Predict the answer for the easier/easiest blank.

Start with the first blank. As noted above, the student is poor at managing money. That means whatever goes in the first blank has a meaning roughly synonymous with "poverty."

STEP 3

Select the answer choice that most closely matches your prediction.

Look at the answer choices for the first blank. Choice **(B)** *penury*, which means "poverty," matches the prediction precisely. You can eliminate **(A)** *lucre* and **(C)** *avarice*, as those mean "wealth" and "greed," respectively.

STEP 4

Predict and select for the remaining blanks.

For the second blank, recall that the student is described as "recalcitrant," which is a term for "stubborn." Also, the student "persisted" in her money-wasting ways. Therefore, she continued to waste money. To "abjure" is to "renounce or repudiate," so she repudiated spending wisely. Thus, "self-________" must carry the meaning of restraint or self-denial, since she is renouncing any thought of restraint or temperance. That points to **(F)** *abnegation*, which means "denial." The root—"negate"—provides a helpful vocabulary clue. Choice **(D)** *adumbration* means a "foreshadowing," or "image of things to come," which makes no sense in this context. Choice **(E)** *aggrandizement* is wrong, as it means "an increase in wealth, power, or rank," and you know she did not shy away from such things if she indulged in overspending.

STEP 5

Check your answers.

Putting both answers back into the sentence, you'll get:

Even when faced with continuing *penury*, the recalcitrant graduate student persisted in her spendthrift ways; she abjured any thought of self-*abnegation* and spent prodigally.

This sentence makes perfect sense.

Apply the Kaplan Method for Text Completion (Three-Blank)

Now, apply the Kaplan Method to a Text Completion (Three-Blank) question:

Though scientific discoveries are often (i) ______ shortly after they've been accepted as fact, scientists still seem to leap to hasty conclusions, (ii) ______ that the (iii) ______ nature of what can be called "fact" has not eroded their confidence.

Blank (i)	Blank (ii)	Blank (iii)
A validated	D denying	G predictable
B published	E refuting	H incendiary
C disproved	F demonstrating	I illusory

STEP 1

Read the sentence, looking for clues.

Paraphrasing long sentences boils them down to their essentials. Here, you learn that something happens to discoveries shortly after they're accepted as fact; even so, scientists still jump to conclusions.

STEP 2

Predict the answer for the easier/easiest blank.

Because the last part of the sentence refers to "what can be called 'fact,'" you can predict for the first blank that some discoveries are *invalidated* after their acceptance.

STEP 3

Select the answer choice that most closely matches your prediction.

The best match for the prediction is choice **(C)** *disproved*. Choice **(A)** *validated* is the opposite of your prediction, and whether these facts are *published*, choice **(B)**, is irrelevant to their validation.

STEP 4

Predict and select for the remaining blanks.

Now, for the second blank, the only choice that works is **(F)** *demonstrating*. You can see from the sentence structure that the author intends for the scientists' continuing haste to *show* or *demonstrate* a further conclusion. Both choice **(D)** *denying* and choice **(E)** *refuting* are the opposite of what's needed.

Since the sentence posits that some "facts" turn out not to be facts at all, you can predict for the third blank that their nature is *changeable*.

Although it's not an exact match for your prediction, the best choice is **(I)** *illusory*. If the nature of facts was *predictable*, choice **(G)**, they wouldn't get disproved as often. And **(H)** *incendiary* literally refers to setting something on fire but is often used figuratively to describe something that is harmfully provocative or arouses agitation. While the changing nature of fact can no doubt be troubling, the connotation of this word is far too extreme for the context.

STEP 5

Check your answers.

Now, plug your choices into their respective blanks: "Though scientific discoveries are often *disproved* shortly after they've been accepted as fact, scientists still seem to leap to hasty conclusions, *demonstrating* that the *illusory* nature of what can be called 'fact' has not eroded their confidence." These choices fit perfectly, creating a logical, sensible statement.

TEXT COMPLETION (TWO-BLANK AND THREE-BLANK) PRACTICE SET

Try the following Text Completion questions using the Kaplan Method:

1. Despite his insistence to the contrary, the author's (i) _______ hostility was evinced in the tone he used when describing the senator's qualifications; he did not (ii) _______ using words like "craven" and "ill-conceived" liberally when writing about the legislator's voting record.

Blank (i)	Blank (ii)
A manifest	D demur at
B dubious	E relish
C obscure	F hasten to

2. Given the (i) _______ nature of the evidence, the authorities are unlikely to present a (ii) _______ case against the accused.

Blank (i)	Blank (ii)
A abstract	D weak
B flimsy	E convincing
C rakish	F tepid

3. Every effort by the bank to determine the origin of the funds met with (i) _______ resulting from the web of (ii) _______ created by the account holder.

Blank (i)	Blank (ii)
A exuberance	D deceit
B apathy	E conviviality
C frustration	F temerity

4. The (i) _______ genius of the late Glenn Gould is (ii) _______ in his imaginative (iii) _______ for piano of Wagner's *Siegfried Idyll*, which the composer originally scored for full orchestra and presented to his wife Cosima on her birthday.

Blank (i)	Blank (ii)	Blank (iii)
A unexceptional	D apparent	G diminution
B overrated	E ineluctable	H homage
C unmistakable	F incommensurate	I adaptation

5. Although the European Economic Community was established to (i) _______ the economic growth of all its member nations (ii) _______, some express (iii) _______ at what they claim is their unfair burden in maintaining the organization.

Blank (i)	Blank (ii)	Blank (iii)
A retard	D inequitably	G enthusiasm
B promote	E vigorously	H ennui
C measure	F equally	I resentment

TEXT COMPLETION (TWO-BLANK AND THREE-BLANK) PRACTICE SET ANSWERS AND EXPLANATIONS

1. A, D

Take this question one blank at a time. "Despite" is a standard detour road sign, so you know the sentence will change direction. You know that the author's hostility was evinced (made evident) despite his insisting otherwise. So, whatever goes in the first blank will have a meaning similar to "obvious" or "evident." Choice **(A)** *manifest*, meaning "apparent," works perfectly. Choices **(B)** *dubious* and **(C)** *obscure*, meaning "doubtful" and "unclear," respectively, are the opposite of what you need. For the second blank, remember that if the author were openly hostile, he would be inclined to use negative terms like "craven" and "ill-conceived." Since "not" appears in front of the blank, you're looking for something that means "refrain from." Choice **(D)** *demur at* means to "shy away from." That fits perfectly; if the author was obviously hostile, he would *not* shy away from using strongly negative terms such as "craven" or "ill-conceived." You can rule out **(E)** *relish* and **(F)** *hasten to* straight away. To "relish" is to strongly like something, and to "hasten" is to hurry to do something; these terms produce the wrong meaning in the sentence following the qualifier "not."

2. B, E

This one may be more difficult than it appears at first glance. The word "unlikely" is a detour road sign, indicating that the two correct answers will be opposite in meaning to one another. Since the quality of evidence is directly related to the strength of the case the prosecutors can make against the accused, you can infer that "good" evidence will make them unlikely to present a "bad" case, and "poor" evidence will make them unlikely to present a "good" case. Thus, the correct answers must be oppositely charged. Start with the first blank. You'll notice that **(B)** *flimsy*, meaning "insubstantial," has a negative connotation, while **(A)** *abstract* is neutral and can therefore be ruled out. Choice **(C)** *rakish* means "jaunty" or "dashing"; it makes no sense to describe evidence this way. That leaves **(B)** *flimsy*; the evidence was, therefore, weak. Based on your initial reading of the sentence, you know that the second blank will have to mean "strong." With flimsy evidence, the prosecutors are unlikely to succeed. Choices **(D)** *weak* and **(F)** *tepid* are both negatively charged, while **(E)** *convincing* is positively charged and is a synonym for "strong" when describing a court case. "Given the *flimsy* nature of the evidence, the authorities are unlikely to present a *convincing* case against the accused."

3. C, D

Take this question apart by looking for contextual clues. The phrase "web of ________" is always used in a negative fashion (you're unlikely to ever hear "caught in a web of virtue and delight!"). Start with the second blank, then. The best choice is **(D)** *deceit*, meaning "lies." That makes perfect sense in this context. A web of lies would make it very difficult to determine the origin of the funds. You can immediately rule out **(E)** *conviviality*, as this means "friendliness" or "agreeableness." Choice **(F)** *temerity* means "rashness" or "recklessness." This might, in some cases, be a negative attribute, but the problem in this sentence lies in determining the origin of the funds, which is unlikely to be obscured by the account holder's boldness.

Moving to the first blank, you're looking for a word to characterize the result of an effort that has met with a web of deceit. A good prediction would be *irritation.* Looking at the answer choices, **(C)** *frustration* is a perfect candidate, as it can be a synonym for irritation. Choice **(A)** *exuberance* has a strong positive charge, and it's therefore wrong. Choice **(B)** *apathy,* meaning "indifference," has a neutral charge, so it does not work in this context where you need a negatively charged answer.

4. C, D, I

There are several good clues to work with in this sentence, but the most important word is "imaginative," used to describe a work of Gould's. That helps you predict the first and second blanks. In such an imaginative piece, a *fertile* or *monumental* or *obvious* (blank i) genius would be *on display* or *revealed* (blank ii).

For the first blank the best match for your prediction is choice **(C)** *unmistakable.* Choice **(A)** *unexceptional* is inconsistent with the idea of genius, and nothing in the sentence supports the idea that Gould's genius was *overrated*, choice **(B).**

For the second blank, choice **(D)** *apparent* matches your prediction best. Choice **(E)** *ineluctable* means "unavoidable," which is not the same as being *obvious*, and choice **(F)** *incommensurate* means "disproportionate." Nothing in the sentence supports the idea of Gould's genius being too large or too small.

The third blank is a noun appropriate to the piece itself. The adjective that precedes the blank is no longer of help; presumably, any type of musical piece could be "imaginative." However, the GRE never creates a blank without clues. This is a piece for piano that was "originally" for full orchestra and is now "for piano." So, it must be a word meaning "reworking" or "rearrangement." Choice **(I)** *adaptation* works perfectly in this context. Choice **(G)** *diminution* does indicate a change, but it means "making physically smaller or decreasing stature or importance," which is not the same as reworking a piece of music for fewer instruments. Choice **(H)** *homage* means "reverence," which does not imply that a change was made to the composition. Also, it implies a motive on Gould's part—to pay homage to Wagner—that is not indicated by the sentence. "The *unmistakable* genius of the late Glenn Gould is *apparent* in his imaginative *adaptation* for piano of Wagner's *Siegfried Idyll*, which the composer originally scored for full orchestra and presented to his wife Cosima on her birthday."

5. B, F, I

The word "Although" at the beginning of this sentence is a detour road sign. It signals a change in direction between the first and second clauses. In the first clause, you're told that the European Economic Community's goal is to do something to the growth of all of the member nations. No doubt this is a positive word; an organization would not be established to hinder the growth of the members of the group. Predict a word meaning "support" for the first blank.

The second clause tells you that some nations believe they unfairly bear a greater burden for running the organization and are expressing some type of feeling about this. Since the two clauses are in contrast, you can predict that this support was supposed to be provided to all members *fairly* or *evenly* and, for the third blank, predict that they "express *discontent*" about the fact that it is not.

For the first blank, the best match is choice **(B)** *promote*. Choice **(A)** *retard* means "delay," a negative action inconsistent with the context of the sentence. It's not illogical to imagine an organization founded simply to **(C)** *measure* countries' economic growth, but it doesn't make sense in contrast with a feeling that some countries bear an unfair share of the organization's maintenance.

For the second blank, the best match for your prediction is choice **(F)** *equally*. Choice **(D)** *inequitably*, or "unequally," is the opposite of your prediction. While members might have expected the commission to act **(E)** *vigorously*, or "with strength," this word doesn't create the necessary contrast with "unfair burden."

For the third blank, choice **(I)** *resentment* is closest to the prediction *discontent* and the best fit for the sentence as well. Neither choice **(G)** *enthusiasm* nor choice **(H)** *ennui*, which means "boredom," fits the logic of the sentence: "Although the European Economic Community was established to *promote* the economic growth of all its member nations *equally*, some express *resentment* at what they claim is their unfair burden in maintaining the organization."

KAPLAN'S ADDITIONAL TIPS FOR TEXT COMPLETION QUESTIONS

Look for What's Directly Implied and Not an Ambiguous Interpretation

The questions you'll encounter are written in sophisticated but still logical and straightforward prose. Therefore, the correct answer is the one most directly implied by the meanings of the words in the sentence. These sentences are constructed to allow you to identify the answer using the inferential strategies you just practiced.

Don't Be Too Creative

Read the sentence literally, not imaginatively. Pay attention to the meaning of the words instead of any associations or feelings that might come up for you.

Paraphrase Long or Complex Sentences

You may encounter a sentence that, because of its length or structure, is hard to get a handle on. When faced with a complex sentence, slow down and put it in your own words. Break long, complicated sentences into pieces and tackle one phrase at a time.

Use Word Roots

Use the Resources section of this book to learn the Latin and Greek roots of many common GRE words. If you don't know the meaning of a word, take a look at its root to get close to its meaning or understand what it must refer to. Etymology often provides clues to meaning, especially when you couple a root definition with the word in context.

TEXT COMPLETION PRACTICE SET

Try the following Text Completion questions using the Kaplan Method for Text Completion.

Basic

1. The diffident toddler was so uncomfortable at the birthday party that he constantly _______ his mother's side.

   (A) strayed from
   (B) fled
   (C) abjured
   (D) cleaved to
   (E) avoided

2. Having test-driven this car in a variety of realistic conditions and found its performance lackluster at best, I have to say that its maker's sanguine claims are _______.

   (A) understated
   (B) impeccable
   (C) unfounded
   (D) plausible
   (E) mediocre

3. In the world of professional team sports, individual prowess has its place, but ultimately the players are valued chiefly for their _______ qualities.

   (A) ethical
   (B) inspirational
   (C) dispersive
   (D) singular
   (E) collaborative

4. Although subjected to endless ________, she was unwavering in advocating her theory, claiming to be untroubled by the raillery.

   (A) rebuttal
   (B) approbation
   (C) disavowal
   (D) japery
   (E) consent

5. After a destructive, summer-long drought, during which the crops ________, Midwestern farmers did not know whether to welcome or curse the heavy, late-August rains that finally swept through the region, washing away critical topsoil.

   (A) acclimated
   (B) persevered
   (C) languished
   (D) plundered
   (E) retracted

6. The idea that the Internet is not a (i) ________ place has become ingrained in popular culture. Because of the increasing number of users, it has become more complicated for authorities to (ii) ________ the breaches of privacy that proliferate on a regular basis. The average user should remain (iii) ________ the exchange of personal data over the Internet.

Blank (i)	Blank (ii)	Blank (iii)
A sensible	D castigate	G indignant about
B secure	E relinquish	H skeptical of
C reliable	F constrain	I prudent in

Intermediate

7. Now that the message of the underground, counterculture youth movement is being (i) ______ by the mass media, many of the movement's followers, once loyal to the cause, have (ii) ______.

Blank (i)	Blank (ii)
A reported on	D defected
B contradicted	E retaliated
C promulgated	F acquiesced

8. Although he founded an entire magazine about the art of the interview, Warhol was himself a (i) ______ interview subject, revealing little about his life and work and often supplying (ii) ______ answers to straightforward questions.

Blank (i)	Blank (ii)
A definitive	D ominous
B callow	E meticulous
C laconic	F enigmatic

9. Despite the widespread popularity of soy products among American consumers, discussion about the effects of soy on human health remains ______.

Ⓐ conclusive
Ⓑ contentious
Ⓒ preposterous
Ⓓ enlightening
Ⓔ fraudulent

10. Although the chairman's new policies cut costs at the time, his strategy was ultimately revealed to be ______, and his lack of foresight crippled the department in the long run.

    (A) vacuous
    (B) myopic
    (C) prescient
    (D) ingenuous
    (E) ingenious

11. In conversation, people usually adjust the register, or (i) ______, of their speech according to the circumstances in which they find themselves. For example, they will be less (ii) ______ in their use of vocabulary and (iii) ______ when relaxing with friends than when they are speaking with clergy or legal officials.

Blank (i)	Blank (ii)	Blank (iii)
A meaning	D thoughtful	G lexicon
B significance	E interested	H grammar
C style	F formal	I verbiage

12. In the writer's view, now and then in the (i) ______ of politics, a person of observable integrity and moral strength appears in a way that draws public attention to the central rather than the (ii) ______ matters that affect our lives. Such a person is vital for a number of reasons: he or she cuts through the natural (iii) ______ of competing interests, focuses on key issues, posits realistic solutions, and brings together opponents who might otherwise never agree.

Blank (i)	Blank (ii)	Blank (iii)
A existence	D weaker	G usefulness
B hurly-burly	E confidential	H distractions
C practice	F peripheral	I succession

13. In the United Kingdom, a "stately home" is usually a large and impressive (i) _______, often centuries old, composed of many magnificent rooms worthy of noble occupation. Such houses are generally set in (ii) _______, well-tended grounds and are likely to look out over (iii) _______ of breathtaking beauty. Luckily, as a by-product of an ever-changing economy, stately homes are now often open to the public.

Blank (i)	Blank (ii)	Blank (iii)
A edifice	D confined	G fields
B architecture	E mown	H hills
C apartment	F expansive	I vistas

14. A dictionary that provides the (i) _______ of words—that is, the origin and development of their meanings—offers proof of a (ii) _______ language. Over time, words not only change but sometimes even (iii) _______ their meanings. "Nice," for example, is an instance of such a word. Today it means "agreeable" or "pleasant," whereas in Middle English it meant "stupid" or "ignorant."

Blank (i)	Blank (ii)	Blank (iii)
A toxicology	D nascent	G reverse
B etymology	E living	H amend
C taxonomy	F faltering	I exchange

15. The development of drama over the centuries has been a (i) _______ journey, from the open-air stylized performances of Greek and Roman tragedies and comedies to the more recent "three-walled" room of indoor theater. Yet, much has remained unchanged—actors in costume still (ii) _______ the stage before audiences who willingly suspend their (iii) _______ in order to enter into the "reality" of events created for them.

Blank (i)	Blank (ii)	Blank (iii)
A remarkable	D strut	G interest
B modest	E stalk	H concern
C implacable	F straddle	I disbelief

Advanced

16. In the workplace, it is important that employees (i) ______ the (ii) ______ of the company rather than the other way around.

Blank (i)		Blank (ii)	
A	object to	D	standards
B	conform to	E	idiosyncrasies
C	balk at	F	peccadilloes

17. It is hard to believe that the highly (i) ______ game of soccer began many centuries ago as a rowdy (ii) ______ without rules, fought cross-country by entire villages determined to get possession of an inflated pig's bladder.

Blank (i)		Blank (ii)	
A	structured	D	séance
B	pell-mell	E	massacre
C	helter-skelter	F	brawl

18. Although good writing is an art, it is also a (i) ______ skill that most people can master by following the principle that (ii) ______ and economy of language are good.

Blank (i)		Blank (ii)	
A	superfluous	D	simplicity
B	fundamental	E	preponderance
C	nugatory	F	prolixity

19. Ambition is a useful (i) ______ that leads people to great achievement, but it can also be (ii) ______ force, as Shakespeare showed in his tragedy *Macbeth.*

Blank (i)		Blank (ii)	
A	tenet	D	an ersatz
B	indicator	E	a pulsating
C	motivator	F	a destructive

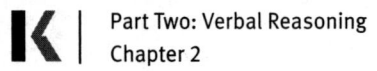

20. Lacking members with a sound sense of (i) _______ knowledge, the explorers were almost certainly (ii) _______ to failure from the start.

Blank (i)	Blank (ii)
A geographical	D doomed
B general	E accustomed
C abstruse	F immune

TEXT COMPLETION PRACTICE SET ANSWER KEY

1. D
2. C
3. E
4. D
5. C
6. B, F, I
7. C, D
8. C, F
9. B
10. B
11. C, F, H
12. B, F, H
13. A, F, I
14. B, E, G
15. A, D, I
16. B, D
17. A, F
18. B, D
19. C, F
20. A, D

TEXT COMPLETION PRACTICE SET ANSWERS AND EXPLANATIONS

1. D

"Diffident" means shy or timid. Coupling that with the toddler's discomfort, you can reasonably infer that the child must have stayed near his mother's side. So, the answer choice must mean something like "clung to." *Cleaved* might strike you as having the opposite meaning, but the verb "to cleave" is interesting in that it can mean both "to cut away" and "to adhere to." When the word "cleave" is followed by the preposition "to," it means "adhere to." In this context, **(D)** *cleaved to* is the right answer. Choices **(A)** *strayed from*, **(B)** *fled*, and **(E)** *avoided* can be eliminated, as they mean essentially the opposite. Choice **(C)** *abjured* means "shunned" or "renounced," so that can't be right.

2. C

The author characterizes the car's performance as "lackluster," so you know that the word that will go in the blank will say that the maker's "sanguine," or optimistic, claims about the car are groundless. A good, simple prediction is *untrue*. Looking at the answer choices, **(C)** *unfounded* means "baseless," and that's the answer. You can throw out **(A)** *understated,* **(B)** *impeccable,* and **(D)** *plausible. Understated* means "restrained," and that is not a negative characterization. *Impeccable* means "flawless," which is far too positive. *Plausible* means "possible," and the author is expressing doubt, not trust. Choice **(E)** *mediocre* does have a negative charge, but while the car in question is medicore, the maker's claims need a word that speaks to their truthfulness, not their general quality.

3. E

The word "but" is a detour road sign. So, start there. "Individual" is contrasted with whatever will go in the blank. A good prediction is *group*. The sentence would then mean something like "Individual prowess has its place, but players are chiefly valued for their group abilities." Looking at the answer choices, **(E)** *collaborative* means "working together." Collaborative qualities are a direct contrast to individual abilities. Perfect! You can reject **(A)** *ethical* and **(B)** *inspirational*; these are both admirable qualities but do not contrast with "individual" at all. Choice **(C)** *dispersive*, meaning "tending to spread apart," makes little sense in context and is, at any rate, an undesirable quality in a teammate. Choice **(D)** *singular* means "unique" or "individual" and is not at all opposed to "individual."

4. D

The detour road sign "Although" tells you that this person holds to her ideas despite whatever she is subjected to. Therefore, the word in the blank must be negative. A further key to this sentence is the word "raillery," meaning "mockery" or "ridicule." The subject of the sentence is "untroubled by the raillery," so you can determine that what she has been subjected to is a synonym for "raillery." Only **(D)** *japery*, also meaning "mockery," fits this description. Choices **(B)** *approbation* and **(E)** *consent* both mean "approval," so you can eliminate those immediately. Choice **(A)** *rebuttal* is a responding argument, and **(C)** *disavowal* is a rejection; while these terms might be related in idea to the sentence, they are not synonymous with "raillery."

5. C

"Destructive" is a key word that suggests a negative outcome, so predict a word with a negative meaning for the blank. In addition, even though the rains washed away topsoil, the farmers did not feel entirely bad about the rain, indicating that the drought had been very hard on the crops. The correct answer is **(C)** *languished*, or "became weak." Choices **(A)** *acclimated* and **(B)** *persevered* suggest a more positive outcome than the sentence implies, so eliminate these choices. Choice **(E)** *retracted* doesn't make sense and can also be eliminated. The word *plundered*, choice **(D)**, means "to take something wrongfully," which doesn't fit the tone of the sentence.

6. B, F, I

Since all of the three answer choices fit the first blank, you must read the entire passage first, for context. The phrase "breaches of privacy" suggests that the Internet is a place where unauthorized third parties can obtain data. Choice **(C)** *reliable* doesn't quite fit this context, so you can rule it out. And while it may be true that content posted on the Internet is not always **(A)** *sensible*, there is no context in the sentence to support this idea. Choice **(B)** *secure* is most applicable to the issue at hand, so it is the correct choice.

For the second blank, choice **(F)** *constrain* means "to get under control," **(D)** *castigate* means "to criticize or punish," and **(E)** *relinquish* means "to surrender." *Relinquish* doesn't make sense, and while authorities might try to castigate the people who hack into Internet users' private information, officials do not punish the privacy violations themselves. So **(D)** and **(E)** can be ruled out, and **(F)** is the correct answer.

While one could be **(G)** *indignant about* (angry about) a loss of privacy and **(H)** *skeptical of* (doubtful of) the security of one's data online, the only choice that makes sense relative to "the exchange of personal data" is **(I)** *prudent in*. Given the difficulty in maintaining Internet security, one must indeed be careful about transmitting personal data.

7. C, D

The detour road sign "now that" signals a change; something new and different is happening. The missing word in the first blank suggests a change in the youth movement's underground, counterculture status. Since the movement's followers were "once loyal," the detour road sign indicates that is no longer the case. Think about how the movement may have changed. Based on what's known, **(C)** *promulgated* is the best choice—something that was once underground and counterculture is now being not only exposed but supported by the established media. While members of an underground movement might resent being *reported on,* it would not have nearly the same effect. That eliminates choice **(A)**. The word *contradicted*, choice **(B)**, is plausible, but the context makes it more likely that this would reinforce the movement's oppositional stance. You can fill the second blank using a similar strategy—look for a word that suggests the opposite of "once loyal." When somebody defects, that person abandons something to go to the other side. Choice **(D)** *defected* is correct. If you *acquiesce*, you give in, which is not likely here since the sentence implies a reaction to being loyal. Throw out choice **(F)**. Choice **(E)** *retaliated* might seem tempting, but to infer that the movement's followers are now seeking revenge would require more information than the sentence gives; instead they are simply no longer loyal, and *defected* provides the best contrast.

8. C, F

For the first blank, you can use the key words "revealing little" to predict a word that describes Warhol. Predict a word like *terse.* Choice **(C)** *laconic,* which means "short and abrupt," is a match. Choice **(A)** *definitive* means "final" or "the best," and Warhol is far from the best interview subject. Choice **(B)** *callow* means "immature" or "inexperienced." While it might be immature to withhold information during an interview, this choice requires more information about Warhol than you are given; he may have had other reasons for responding the way he did.

For the second blank, look for a word or phrase that means the opposite of "straightforward," something like *hard to read* or *evasive.* An *enigmatic* person says or does mysterious things, so **(F)** is a good fit. Choice **(E)** *meticulous,* which suggests great care and detail, is the opposite of what you want. Choice **(D)** *ominous,* meaning "threatening," is too negative for the context.

9. B

"Despite" is a detour road sign that directs you to look for a contrast. If the popularity of soy is widespread, that means many people like to consume it. Because of the detour road sign, you can surmise that the effects of soy on health may be an issue people do not agree on. The correct answer is **(B)** *contentious,* which means "likely to cause disagreement." That choice is perfect for the context of describing a "discussion." Go ahead and rule out choices **(A)** *conclusive* and **(D)** *enlightening,* since they both suggest agreement. Choices **(C)** *preposterous* and **(E)** *fraudulent* are too extreme for the context.

10. B

The detour road sign "although" will help you with this sentence. You are told that the policies were initially effective at cutting costs, but that "his lack of foresight crippled the department in the long run." The straight-ahead road sign "and" connects this "lack of foresight" with the blank, so you can predict an answer meaning "shortsighted." Choice **(B)** *myopic* means "shortsighted," and it is the right answer. Choice **(A)** *vacuous* would mean the plans lacked intelligence or importance. While you know the plans did not turn out well eventually, they did accomplish some good (they cut costs), so to describe them as "vacuous" does not correctly identify the problem. Choice **(C)** *prescient* means "farsighted," the opposite of what you are looking for. Choice **(D)** *ingenuous* means "sincere" or "guileless," and **(E)** *ingenious* means "brilliant." Neither of these fits the sentence.

11. C, F, H

Use the clues in these sentences to determine which words fit in the blanks. The word for the first blank must be an attribute of speech that is roughly synonymous with "register." Speakers are unlikely to change the **(A)** *meaning* or **(B)** *significance* of their speech to fit the circumstances, but **(C)** *style* fits well as a partner for "register."

The second blank, preceded by "less," suggests a descriptive word in opposition to the phrase "when relaxing with friends." Neither **(D)** *thoughtful* nor **(E)** *interested* works here, because these qualities of speech do not necessarily change depending on whom one is with. In this case, the remaining word

(F) *formal* matches the contrast between "friends" and "officials."

You may be able to identify quickly that both **(G)** *lexicon* and **(I)** *verbiage* refer to the specific words used, so both of these terms are redundant as a partner to "vocabulary." Instead, **(H)** *grammar* is the correct choice.

12. B, F, H

Use the key words in these sentences as clues to the blanks. The first choice here requires a word that contrasts with a good person who brings order and direction to a situation that lacks them. Only **(B)** *hurly-burly*, meaning "commotion" or "disorder," matches the sense of the sentence. The words **(A)** *existence* and **(C)** *practice* are too general, and neither implies a chaotic situation.

The detour road sign "rather than" indicates that the adjective in the blank describing the "matters that affect our lives" is the opposite of "central." Choices **(D)** *weaker* and **(E)** *confidential* do not contrast with "central." Choice **(F)** *peripheral*, which means "at the edge of," is the opposite of "central" and is correct.

The second sentence lists achievements of the good politician, so the "competing interests" that "he or she cuts through" would not have the characteristic of **(G)** *usefulness*. As the word "focuses" suggests, it is the **(H)** *distractions* of competing interests that prevent political progress, making this the correct choice for the third blank. There might be a **(I)** *succession* of competing interests, but "cutting through" it doesn't make sense.

13. A, F, I

In these sentences, key words lead to the correct choices. The term "stately home" suggests that a word meaning "building" would fit best in the first blank. Choice **(A)** *edifice* is another word for "building" and has the connotation of size or importance. It is the correct choice here. Choice **(B)** *architecture* is a profession or an abstract quality, and **(C)** *apartment* is a portion of a building.

The grounds surrounding a "large and impressive" home are likely to be of great extent, which eliminates **(D)** *confined*. With its meaning of "abundant" or "sizeable," **(F)** *expansive* is the logical choice for the second blank. The grounds may or may not be **(E)** *mown*, but "well-tended" already covers this possibility.

Such a great house may or may not "look out over" **(G)** *fields* or **(H)** *hills*, but it would definitely look out over scenic "views," which is the meaning of **(I)** *vistas*, the correct choice.

14. B, E, G

The word choice for the first blank is defined in the phrase "the origin and development" of word meanings. The definition that determines the blank applies only to **(B)** *etymology*, the correct answer. The word **(A)** *toxicology* refers to the study of poisons and is therefore inappropriate. A **(C)** *taxonomy* is a system of scientific classifications.

The sense of the first sentence is that a dictionary showing the development of word meanings "offers proof" of a certain type of language, one in which words "change."

A language that is **(E)** *living* is one that changes and develops, which makes that the correct answer here. A **(D)** *nascent* language is one that has just been born, so rule that out. A language that is **(F)** *faltering* is "hesitant" or "unsteady," which makes no sense in the context.

The second sentence includes the construction "not only . . . but," which serves as a clue that you need a word that is more extreme than "change." The word **(G)** *reverse* is correct here because it carries the right weight and matches the example. The word **(H)** *amend* is synonymous with the word "change" and is therefore inappropriate. Choice **(I)** *exchange* makes some sense, since words might exchange meanings. However, this answer doesn't carry the idea of an extreme change, nor does it fit the example of "nice," used to illustrate it.

15. A, D, I

Key words are important in evaluating the answer choices in this passage. The first sentence suggests that the "journey" of drama over the centuries has been substantial. The word **(A)** *remarkable*, meaning "extraordinary" or "very noteworthy," is true to the nature of the journey and is the correct choice. **(B)** *modest* is the opposite of what's needed for the blank. The meaning of **(C)** *implacable*, "incapable of being appeased or changed," makes no sense in this context.

In the second blank, the word must describe the common movements of actors on the stage. To **(D)** *strut*, to "walk proudly or pompously," is the best choice because it is more general and suggests the natural confidence of a performer. Actors may occasionally **(E)** *stalk* around the stage, but the word is too limited to fit the meaning here. The word **(F)** *straddle* has the specific meaning of standing with legs wide apart, which does not fit this situation.

The choice for the third blank is dictated by the phrase "in order to enter into the 'reality' of events created for them." Members of any audience know that a stage performance is not "real," but they put aside that knowledge in order to enjoy the play. Choice **(I)** *disbelief* is therefore correct; people often use the phrase "willing suspension of disbelief" to describe an audience's acceptance of the events in a play. Audiences do not put aside their **(G)** *interest*, which rules out that choice. The word **(H)** *concern*, which can also mean "interest" or "sense of unease," is also illogical in this context.

16. B, D

Reading this question through, you can see that it hinges on the relationship between the company and its employees. Employees must follow the rules of their employers, so for the first blank, you can reasonably predict that it will require a word with a meaning similar to "obey." Looking at the options, choice **(B)** *conform to* makes sense. Choices **(A)** *object to* and **(C)** *balk at* are wrong, as it is important that employees *not* do those things. For the second blank, you have already predicted that employees must obey rules, so predict "rules" for this blank. Choice **(D)** *standards* are practices to which companies would want their employees to conform, and it is the correct answer. Choice **(E)** *idiosyncrasies* means "quirks," and **(F)** *peccadilloes* means "minor faults," neither of which employees would be expected to imitate.

17. A, F

This question has a detour road sign that's a bit longer than usual. The phrase "It is hard to believe" indicates that the answer choices will contrast with one another. The second blank is a term described as "rowdy," so you can safely predict that the first blank will have the meaning of "calm" or "orderly" to describe early soccer.

The second blank is easier. With the context clue of "rowdy," **(F)** *brawl* works well. You can eliminate **(D)** *séance* because this is a ritual to speak with the dead. A séance would never be described as rowdy, nor would it describe a contest over an inflated pig's bladder. Choice **(E)** *massacre* does not fit because it is too extreme: while people fought over the pig's bladder, nothing indicates that they fought until they had killed each other in large numbers.

You can now answer the first blank with certainty. Choice **(A)** *structured* fits the prediction and contrasts with the rowdy brawl described in the second part of the sentence. Both **(B)** *pell-mell* and **(C)** *helter-skelter* describe unstructured situations, so they cannot be correct.

18. B, D

"Although" is a detour road sign, so you know that the first blank will detour in meaning from "art," as it is used to describe writing. Something less than "artistic" could be called *basic*. That's a good prediction for the first blank. Choice **(B)** *fundamental* fits perfectly. You can rule out **(A)** *superfluous*, as it means "unnecessary," while you're looking for a term that describes writing at its bare essence. You can also reject choice **(C)** *nugatory,* which means "trifling," since nothing in the sentence indicates that good writing is not important. Moving to the second blank, the straight-ahead road sign "and" tells you that the blank will agree with "economy of language," or short, compact writing without ornamentation. Choice **(D)** *simplicity* is a perfect way to describe basic, fundamental writing. Choice **(E)** *preponderance* and **(F)** *prolixity* both have a meaning related to "excess" and thus are the opposite of what you need.

19. C, F

The conjunction "but" is a detour road sign, signaling a change in direction between the two blanks. For the first blank, ambition is described as being useful in leading people to achievement. A good prediction is *inducement*. Looking at the options, **(C)** *motivator* fits perfectly; ambition *motivates* people to great achievement. Choice **(B)** *indicator* is a passive word, not an agent that effects action. Choice **(A)** *tenet*, a component of a philosophy, does not work in this context because it does not "induce" action—it works more as a guide than as an impetus.

The second blank must contrast with "useful" and "achievement" and therefore has a negative charge. Choice **(F)** *destructive* fits perfectly; it's strongly negative, and "destructive force" contrasts perfectly with "useful motivator" as a description of ambition. Choice **(D)** *ersatz*, which means "artificial," is too neutral to contrast with "motivator." Choice **(E)** *pulsating,* meaning "throbbing," makes no sense in this context.

20. A, D

The phrase "almost certainly" is a straight-ahead road sign, indicating that the second clause in the sentence will continue the direction of the first. Reading the sentence, you can infer that the lack of a certain kind of knowledge affected the explorers' chances of success. A lack of knowledge would not prevent failure, so you can reasonably assume that it "led to" failure. This provides a good prediction for the second blank, so start there. Choice **(D)** *doomed* makes sense. A lack of knowledge *doomed* the explorers. A lack of knowledge would be unlikely to make an expedition **(F)** *immune* to, meaning unaffected by, failure, so **(F)** is wrong. You can also reject choice **(E)** *accustomed*; you have no idea whether the explorers have failed in the past.

For the first blank, you're asked to find the word that characterizes this knowledge. Choice **(A)** *geographical* fits perfectly. It is precisely the type of knowledge an explorer would need and would be doomed without. Choice **(B)** *general* can be rejected; it's not specific enough to indicate why the explorers would be doomed. You can reject choice **(C)** *abstruse*, meaning "obscure" or "hard to understand," since this type of knowledge is not of importance to explorers per se.

CHAPTER 3

Sentence Equivalence

SENTENCE EQUIVALENCE: OVERVIEW AND METHOD

You will find about four Sentence Equivalence questions per Verbal Reasoning section on the GRE. Each consists of a single sentence with one word missing. They differ from Text Completion questions in that there will be six answer choices, two of which are correct. Your job is to identify the two answer choices that, when inserted into the sentence, correctly complete the sentence and produce sentences of similar meaning. These questions are similar to Text Completion questions, as both ask you to deduce the meaning of a missing word in a passage on the basis of incomplete information.

One very important thing to bear in mind when working out a Sentence Equivalence question is that the correct answer choices are often, *but are not necessarily*, synonyms. You must pay close attention to the differing shades of meaning that words have and understand that the key to unlocking the correct answer is to look for choices that create sentences with similar meanings. You must select both correct choices in order to receive credit for the question; no partial credit is given for selecting one of the correct choices.

The directions for Sentence Equivalence questions will look like this:

> Select the two answer choices that, when used to complete the sentence, fit the meaning of the sentence as a whole and produce completed sentences that are alike in meaning.

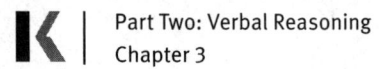

A Sentence Equivalence question will look like this:

> Cora was not known for her reticence; regardless, she only ________ acquiesced to calls to speak at the conference.
>
> [A] jejunely
> [B] exuberantly
> [C] willfully
> [D] grudgingly
> [E] candidly
> [F] timidly

THE KAPLAN METHOD FOR SENTENCE EQUIVALENCE

STEP 1 **Read the sentence, looking for clues.**

STEP 2 **Predict the answer.**

STEP 3 **Select the two answer choices that most closely match your prediction.**

STEP 4 **Check your answers to see if the sentence retains the same meaning.**

How the Kaplan Method for Sentence Equivalence Works

Here's how the Kaplan Method for Sentence Equivalence works:

STEP 1

Read the sentence, looking for clues.

As you read the sentence, look for specific words in the sentence that will help you understand its meaning. As mentioned in chapter 2, these are key words or phrases, which provide context clues, and road signs, which are structural clues. Use key words and road signs to help you predict the words that go in the blank.

As a reminder, words that show that the second part of a sentence continues or builds on the meaning of the first—"straight-ahead" road signs—include the following:

And	*Because*	*Similarly*
Since	*: (colon)*	*In addition*
Also	*Likewise*	*Consequently*
Thus	*Moreover*	*Therefore*

Words that show that one part of the sentence contradicts or contrasts with the other part—"detour" road signs—include these:

But	*Unless*	*On the other hand*
Despite	*Rather*	*Unfortunately*
Yet	*Although*	*Nonetheless*
However	*While*	*Conversely*

STEP 2

Predict the answer.

Once you have read the sentence and identified clues to words that will complete the sentence, predict an answer. Your prediction should be a simple word that logically completes the sentence. Predict the right answer *before* you look at the answer choices. Characterizing the correct answer before evaluating the choices will help you efficiently eliminate those that don't match your prediction and avoid trap answers.

STEP 3

Select the two answer choices that most closely match your prediction.

Quickly review the six answer choices and choose the two words that, when plugged into the sentence, most closely match its intended meaning and thus, your prediction. Eliminate the answer choices that do not fit your prediction. Sometimes you will need to adjust your prediction—often by making it more or less specific—in order to find two answer choices that match it.

STEP 4

Check your answers to see if the sentence retains the same meaning.

Read the sentence with each answer choice to check that you have selected the correct answers. Ensure that both answer choices make sense in the context of the sentence and produce resulting sentences with similar meanings. Pay close attention to the charge of a word's meaning. For example, *dislike* and *despise* both mean the same thing, but *despise* has a much stronger degree of charge to that meaning. If one or both of your answers do not make sense when you reread the sentence, revisit the question and repeat Steps 1, 2, and 3.

Apply the Kaplan Method for Sentence Equivalence

Now let's apply the Kaplan Method to a Sentence Equivalence question:

> Cora was not known for her reticence; regardless, she only _______ acquiesced to calls to speak at the conference.
>
> [A] jejunely
> [B] exuberantly
> [C] willfully
> [D] grudgingly
> [E] candidly
> [F] timidly

STEP 1

Read the sentence, looking for clues.

The first thing you should notice is the structural road sign "regardless," which functions as a detour road sign. Therefore, the clause after the semicolon will depart from the meaning of the first clause. You're told in the first clause that Cora is "not known for her reticence," so the second will indicate hesitance or reluctance.

STEP 2

Predict the answer.

The blank will be an adverb that describes "acquiesced," which means to "give in" or "relent." Since you're looking for a word that shows Cora being uncharacteristically reticent, a good prediction is *reluctantly.*

STEP 3

Select the two choices that most closely match your prediction.

Evaluating the answer choices, you can immediately reject **(A)** *jejunely,* "childishly," which doesn't make sense, and **(B)** *exuberantly,* "gleefully," which implies Cora was anything but reluctant to speak at the conference. You can eliminate **(C)** *willfully,* since it implies that she was headstrong, which does not harmonize with *reluctant.* Choice **(E)** *candidly,* "openly", doesn't have a meaning close to *reluctant.* That leaves **(D)** *grudgingly,* meaning "resentfully unwilling," and **(F)** *timidly,* which means "in an easily frightened way." These two are the best matches.

STEP 4

Check your answers to see if the sentence retains the same meaning.

If you check your answers in the context of the original sentence, you'll arrive at two sentences that mean: "Cora was not known for being hesitant, but she only reluctantly agreed to speak at the conference." Notice that the two answer choices are not precise synonyms. Both connote reluctance, but with different shades of meaning. *Grudgingly* has an undertone of resentfulness, while *timidly* implies that one is fearfully shy. However, both produce sentences with similar meanings, and they're the correct answers.

KAPLAN'S ADDITIONAL TIPS FOR SENTENCE EQUIVALENCE QUESTIONS

Consider All Answer Choices

Make sure to read and check all answer choices in the sentence before making your final choice. An answer may fit well in the sentence and closely match your prediction, but if there is no other answer choice that also completes the sentence with the same meaning, it isn't correct.

Paraphrase the Question

If you rephrase a difficult or longer sentence in your own words, it will be easier to predict the right answer. Paraphrasing will also ensure that you understand the meaning of the sentence.

Look Beyond Synonyms

Simply finding a synonym pair in the answer choices will not always lead you to the correct answer. Answer choices may include a pair of synonyms that do not fit the context of the sentence. Both of those choices are incorrect. The meanings of both resultant sentences must be the same and correct. Be sure to try both words in the sentence, checking that each sentence has the same meaning, before making your final choice.

Use Prefixes, Suffixes, and Roots

If you are struggling to figure out the meaning of a word, think about the meaning of any prefix, suffix, or root that you find in the word. These word parts can provide important clues to the word's definition.

SENTENCE EQUIVALENCE PRACTICE SET

Try the following Sentence Equivalence questions using the Kaplan Method.

Basic

1. Although the report indicated a disturbing rise in obesity, many people, by choosing junk food over nutrition, continue to _______ the problem.

   [A] exacerbate
   [B] extort
   [C] abhor
   [D] compound
   [E] attenuate
   [F] mitigate

2. A notoriously private figure, the actor remained _______ when the paparazzi confronted him about recent rumors that his longtime marriage was on the brink of collapse.

   [A] ambivalent
   [B] reticent
   [C] gregarious
   [D] taciturn
   [E] pompous
   [F] imperious

3. Following up on a sizable lead in the polls, the gubernatorial candidate established _______ advantage over his incumbent opponent on election night and ultimately gained victory.

   [A] an inequitable
   [B] a negligible
   [C] a decisive
   [D] a disconcerting
   [E] a patent
   [F] an ignominious

4. Although the band received a glowing reception during its exhaustive world tour, the much-anticipated debut album met with uniformly _______ reviews.

   [A] deprecating
   [B] deferential
   [C] obsequious
   [D] unorthodox
   [E] eloquent
   [F] disparaging

5. The residents, who for many years relished the safe, idyllic surroundings of their suburban neighborhood, have in recent months faced _______ of vandalism.

   A a deficiency
   B an epidemic
   C a backlash
   D a scourge
   E an abatement
   F a revelry

6. In her laudatory _______, the food columnist captured the spirit of the hotel dining room.

   A homage
   B paean
   C banter
   D denunciation
   E rebuff
   F examination

7. After losing his entire fortune on Wall Street, the investor abandoned New York City and began a pilgrimage across Europe; in addition, he gave away most of his possessions and _______ materialism.

   A espoused
   B renounced
   C disregarded
   D initiated
   E spurned
   F aggrandized

8. The _______ entourage accompanied Elvis everywhere he went, and they fetched the singer anything he requested—however challenging or ridiculous—at a moment's notice.

   A avaricious
   B obsequious
   C humble
   D belligerent
   E jubilant
   F fawning

9. The CEO felt she should keep the court case under cover so as not to cause alarm, but to do so would contradict her usually _______ management style.

   A transparent
   B pusillanimous
   C aggressive
   D forthright
   E slipshod
   F negligent

10. As a child, he was often lost in thought, a habit that persisted throughout his life, with the result that his contemporaries described him as _______.

   A surly
   B pensive
   C meditative
   D indigenous
   E arcane
   F livid

Intermediate

11. Although the suburban townhouse seemed like a good value, the buyer _______ when the real estate agent asked for a commitment.

    A elaborated
    B ambled
    C vacillated
    D groveled
    E lamented
    F dawdled

12. Despite the senator's blatant lies about her role in the scandal, many voters showed their _______ when it came time for reelection.

    A resilience
    B fortitude
    C ignominy
    D constancy
    E ambivalence
    F allegiance

13. Within hours the hurricane weakened considerably, serving to _______ the fears of hundreds of residents who had refused to evacuate.

    A assuage
    B emblazon
    C ignite
    D annihilate
    E mediate
    F allay

14. Despite being known by the moniker "the accidental president," Gerald Ford was _______ posthumously for actions he took to address both the Vietnam War and the Watergate scandal.

    A emancipated
    B extolled
    C indemnified
    D lauded
    E denigrated
    F belittled

15. The movie—adapted from a well-known story—was supposedly intended for all audiences, but many parents felt the content was too _______.

    A ribald
    B arcane
    C superfluous
    D pervasive
    E lascivious
    F esoteric

16. Not wanting to be caught _______, the graduate student spent hours frantically preparing for every possible question that the faculty committee might pose during his thesis defense.

    A unaware
    B easily
    C quickly
    D unrehearsed
    E early
    F red-handed

17. One of the most _______ events of the transition from Late Antiquity to the Early Middle Ages was the diaspora of Germanic tribes into lands that were once held securely by the Roman Empire, giving the time period the name "Migration Era."

    A seminal
    B abstract
    C momentous
    D gratuitous
    E diluvial
    F trifling

18. Only in response to the _______ of the ambassador did the magistrate relent and agree to drop the charges against the tourist.

    A approbation
    B behest
    C ingenuousness
    D delight
    E circumlocution
    F urging

19. The singer was renowned for being _______; consequently, anecdotes about her tantrums grew to mythic proportions.

    A captious
    B dissolute
    C irascible
    D profligate
    E smug
    F nettlesome

20. The warriors didn't expect an assault on their olfactory senses; however, they were confronted with such a _______ group of opponents that they decided to beat a hasty retreat.

    A cloying
    B saccharine
    C repulsive
    D dejected
    E fetid
    F malodorous

Advanced

21. In contradistinction to the _______ cat, the dog is the quintessential pack animal.

    A transparent
    B supercilious
    C solitary
    D forthright
    E maladroit
    F aloof

22. Mozart manifested the signs of _______ genius when he began composing music at the precocious age of five.

    A refined
    B incipient
    C staggering
    D nascent
    E fathomless
    F piddling

23. Without more robust funding, the charity's goals will go unfulfilled; furthermore, thousands of _______ children will want for basic necessities.

    A prodigal
    B malnourished
    C vagrant
    D impecunious
    E indigent
    F overindulged

24. When the patron requested books by an amusing author to help lift her spirits, the librarian suggested Wodehouse, claiming him likely to induce _______ in most readers.

    A lugubriousness
    B mirth
    C poignancy
    D gravity
    E merriment
    F solemnity

25. Not only was the author's prose _______, but also his well-known penchant for dissembling colored the way that reviewers read his texts.

    A fulsome
    B effulgent
    C effusive
    D unctuous
    E cryptic
    F vulgar

26. Nigel was usually a model of equanimity, so his _______ demeanor during the attorney's cross-examination left many surprised.

    A staid
    B equanimous
    C testy
    D placid
    E discomposed
    F jubilant

27. The unchecked _______ of state secrets is a source of great concern to intelligence agencies.

    A proliferation
    B retention
    C lassitude
    D acquisition
    E dissemination
    F quality

28. Although the celebrity _______ vociferously on political issues as a guest on several talk shows, her lack of experience in the area led many to ignore her.

    A inveighed
    B declaimed
    C conceded
    D demurred
    E abstained
    F acceded

29. Reginald's _______ aunt was spry for her age but nonetheless required help in ascending the staircase.

    A acrobatic
    B dexterous
    C caustic
    D genial
    E septuagenarian
    F hoary

30. _______, he decided to pass on the project, his professed support notwithstanding.

    A Counterintuitively
    B Unexpectedly
    C Self-indulgently
    D Obscurely
    E Pusillanimously
    F Punctiliously

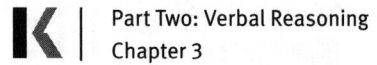

SENTENCE EQUIVALENCE PRACTICE SET ANSWER KEY

1. A, D
2. B, D
3. C, E
4. A, F
5. B, D
6. A, B
7. B, E
8. B, F
9. A, D
10. B, C
11. C, F
12. D, F
13. A, F
14. B, D
15. A, E
16. A, D
17. A, C
18. B, F
19. A, C
20. E, F
21. C, F
22. B, D
23. D, E
24. B, E
25. A, D
26. C, E
27. A, E
28. A, B
29. E, F
30. A, B

SENTENCE EQUIVALENCE PRACTICE SET ANSWERS AND EXPLANATIONS

Advanced

1. A, D

The word "although" is a detour road sign that suggests contrasting ideas. Try paraphrasing the sentence to clarify this relationship. "People ________ the obesity problem by eating junk food." So, although the problem is clear, people are making it worse. Make *to worsen* your prediction and look for two words that reflect this. Choices **(A)** *exacerbate* and **(D)** *compound* both mean "to make worse." These make sense in context. By eating junk food, people are doing the opposite of solving the problem. Choice **(B)** *extort* means "to take by force or threat." This doesn't make sense in the context of the sentence, so eliminate it. Choice **(C)** *abhor* means "to hate." The sentence suggests that people are ignoring the problem of obesity, not hating it. Choices **(E)** *attenuate* and **(F)** *mitigate* mean "to reduce." While these words have a similar meaning, it is the opposite of the meaning that fits the context, so you can rule out these answer choices.

2. B, D

The phrase "A notoriously private figure" provides the key description of the actor. An actor who is "private" probably doesn't share much information. Since he "remained" this way, you're looking for a word that suggests keeping to oneself or disclosing little about oneself. Choice **(B)** *reticent* means "silent" or "not revealing much." This is one of the correct answers. Choice **(D)** *taciturn* has a similar meaning to choice **(B)** *reticent*; both words mean "reserved in expression." These are the two correct answers. Review the other choices to see why each is incorrect. *Ambivalent*, choice **(A)**, means "having mixed feelings." The actor did not have mixed feelings about talking to the paparazzi. He really did not want to talk to them, so eliminate this choice. Choice **(C)** *gregarious* means "sociable." It is doubtful that a private person would be sociable with the press, so eliminate this word. A *pompous* (choice **(E)**) person is arrogant. Pomposity is unrelated to a person's desire for privacy, however. Choice **(F)** *imperious* has a meaning similar to *pompous*. Although these words would produce sentences with similar meanings, the synonyms *reticent* and *taciturn* fit the context and are the correct answers.

3. C, E

The straight-ahead road sign "following up on" indicates that the remainder of the sentence will match the first part. Since the candidate's advantage followed a sizable lead in the polls, it was likely as strong or stronger by election night. You want two words that complement the word "sizable." If something is *decisive*, there can be no doubt about it, so choice **(C)** is one of the correct answer choices. Choice **(E)** *patent* means "clear" or "obvious." An obvious advantage is roughly the same thing as a decisive advantage, so this is the second correct answer. If something is *inequitable*, choice **(A)**, it is not equal, which you may deduce from the word parts *in–* and *equi–*. At first glance, this word may seem to fit. However, it suggests unfairness, and no clues in the sentence imply that the candidate acted unfairly. Choice **(B)** *negligible* means "slight" or "inconsequential in size," so that doesn't agree with the "sizable lead" described earlier. Choice **(D)** *disconcerting* means "upsetting" or "embarrassing," and there is nothing in the sentence to suggest that anyone was upset by the candidate's lead or ultimate victory. The prefix *ig–* in choice **(F)** *ignominious* tells you that, like "ignoble" or "ignorant," this is a negatively charged word. In fact, it means "shameful" and therefore doesn't fit the sentence.

4. A, F

"Although" suggests a contrast, so read the remainder of the opening clause to find out what will be contrasted in the second part of the sentence where the blank is located. The band received a "glowing reception" during its tour, so the album's reviews must have turned out to be quite negative. Choice **(A)** *deprecating* means "showing disapproval," so it is correct. You might have heard of people making "disparaging remarks" about each other. The word *disparaging* conveys a negative tone, so choice **(F)** completes the synonym pair. You may know the words *unorthodox*, meaning "odd," and *eloquent*, meaning "expressive." Neither word contrasts with "glowing," so eliminate choices **(D)** and **(E)**. Choice **(B)** *deferential* means "showing respect." This is the opposite of what you are looking for, as is choice **(C)** *obsequious*, which means "fawning."

5. B, D

Read this sentence closely to uncover clues suggesting the direction the sentence is taking (whether the blank will continue or contradict the thoughts that come before). The phrases "for many years" and "in recent months" suggest a change of events. After many years of "safe, idyllic" life, people faced vandalism, which means there probably was not much vandalism before. Look for words that suggest a spike in vandalism. *Epidemic*, choice **(B)**, is a word you have probably heard used to describe outbreaks of disease. It fits the context of a sudden increase in vandalism. The word *scourge*, choice **(D)**, can refer to a cause of widespread suffering. That's the other correct choice. Choice **(A)** *deficiency* does not fit. There is no shortage of vandalism. Choice **(C)** *backlash* may seem like a possible fit, but it is not. A backlash, or sudden reaction, comes after an action or development, and there is nothing in the sentence to indicate that anything happened beforehand to prompt such a response. Eliminate it. *Abatement* is a reduction, the opposite of an increase, so rule out choice **(E)**. Choice **(F)** *revelry* suggests a party atmosphere. That makes no sense, so eliminate it.

6. A, B

"Laudatory," which means "expressing praise," is your key word. You need to find two words that mean "positive review" and rule out any negative trap answers. Choice **(A)** *homage* is an expression of respect and is correct. Choice **(B)** *paean* is a synonym of *homage*. If you didn't know the definition of *paean,* you could still eliminate the remaining choices. Choice **(C)** *banter* is idle chat; this doesn't make sense in context. Choices **(D)** *denunciation* (from *denounce*) and **(E)** *rebuff* both mean "to criticize." That is the opposite of the meaning you want. Choice **(F)** *examination* sounds formal and scientific, and it is netural in tone, not positive; you can rule out this answer.

7. B, E

Paraphrase this sentence to make the contrasting ideas more obvious: "He gave away his possessions and ________ materialism." Someone who gave away possessions would reject material things. Choice **(B)** *renounced* means "gave up," and choice **(E)** *spurned* means "scornfully rejected"; although not exact synonyms, both of these words function similarly in the context of the sentence. Choice **(C)** *disregarded* means "ignored," which is not strong enough for this context, given that the investor is turning his back on his former life. What separates **(B)** and **(E)**, the correct answers, from **(C)** is the intent; the first two suggest using a change in behavior to make a statement, which matches the mood of the sentence. Just as importantly, the words match one another. Choice **(A)** *espoused* means "supported," and choice **(D)** *initiated* means "began"; both are the opposite of the meaning you need, so eliminate them. Choice **(F)** *aggrandized* means "made something look greater or stronger." Aggrandizing materialism is the last thing the investor was trying to do by getting rid of possessions.

8. B, F

You can tell by the straight-ahead road sign "and" that the second half will expand on or clarify the first part. Think about the type of person who would fetch anything another person wanted. In this case, you're looking for words that describe a "yes-man" or "toady." Choice **(B)** *obsequious* describes somebody who will, as a form of flattery, do anything another person says. This is a correct answer choice. See if you can find another word like it. Choice **(C)** *humble* means "modest," which does not explain why the entourage would do absolutely anything for the singer. Choice **(F)** *fawning* means "showing extreme flattery," so it's the other correct answer. You might recall that avarice is greed; you can toss out **(A)** *avaricious*, which describes a greedy person, since the entourage is looking out for Elvis, not themselves. Choice **(D)** *belligerent* contains the root *belli* (meaning "war"), like another more common word, *rebellion*. You can deduce that a *belligerent* person challenges others, which is not the case with those in the entourage. That rules out choice **(D)**. Choice **(E)** *jubilant* is used to describe somebody who is joyfully excited. This might describe Elvis's entourage, but it's not a synonym of *obsequious*, nor does it effectively describe the actions reported in the second half of the sentence.

9. A, D

The detour road sign "but" indicates a turning point in the sentence. You can predict that the words that fill the blank mean the opposite of keeping something under cover. Choice **(A)** *transparent* means "obvious, straightforward" and is correct. Choice **(D)** *forthright* means "straightforward" and is the other correct answer. Choice **(B)** *pusillanimous* means "timid, cowardly in nature," which doesn't fit the sentence. Neither does choice **(C)** *aggressive*. Although one could characterize someone's management style as "aggressive," you need a word meaning "open" or "straightforward" to fit the sentence clues. Choices **(E)** and **(F)**, *slipshod* and *negligent*, mean virtually the same thing, "careless." Neither makes sense in context. The correct pair is choices **(A)** and **(D)**.

10. B, C

The straight-ahead road sign "with the result" signals that the sentence will continue its direction. To understand this sentence, focus on the phrase "lost in thought." What feeling does this bring to mind? Typically, such a person is wistful, curious, or reflective. You want a word that continues this feeling. Choice **(B)** *pensive*, meaning "deep in thought," complements the phrase and is a correct answer. The next word, choice **(C)** *meditative*, is a synonym for *pensive* and is likely the other correct answer. Evaluate the remaining words just to be sure. Choices **(A)** and **(F)** are related words that differ in degree, *surly* being "irritable" and *livid* being "very angry." Neither works because they both carry a negative charge. Choice **(D)** *indigenous* means "native," which doesn't make sense in this sentence. The last choice, **(E)** *arcane*, means "secret" or "mysterious," and it typically is not used to refer to people, nor is there a second choice that would give the sentence the same meaning, so it is incorrect. Choices **(B)** and **(C)** are the correct answers.

11. C, F

The detour road sign "although" signifies a contrast. In the first clause, the homebuyer thinks a townhouse is "decent," so look for the opposite tone after the comma. Find a pair of words that suggest doubt or indecision on the part of the homebuyer. It's important to understand the subtle difference between choices **(B)** *ambled* and **(F)** *dawdled*. To *amble* is "to walk leisurely," while *dawdle* means "to waste time or delay in a decision." Both words suggest taking one's time, but *dawdled* better fits the context and is one of the correct answers. Put *ambled* aside and try to find a better match for *dawdled*. Choice **(C)** *vacillated* also means "wavered." The word *elaborated* **(A)** means "expanded on a subject" and does not make sense in this context. Choice **(D)** *groveled* means "humbled oneself out of fear or service to another." This does not explain the homebuyer's unexpectedly hesitant response to the real estate agent. A person who **(E)** *lamented* mourned or expressed deep regret. Like *groveled*, the word *lamented* is inappropriate in this scenario. The correct answers are choices **(C)** *vacillated* and **(F)** *dawdled*.

12. D, F

You can use the detour road sign "despite" to conclude that one event happened despite another. Focus on the key words "lies" and "voters." How might voters act toward a candidate *despite* her lies? You're looking for a positive word, one meaning that the voters continued to support the untruthful legislator. You may know that choice **(A)** *resilience* means "the ability to recover from adversity." There's nothing in the sentence to indicate that the voters had to face any sort of adversity, so eliminate this one. Choice **(D)** *constancy* means "faithfulness" and is a correct answer. Choice **(F)** *allegiance* means something similar. Those two answers match your prediction. The word **(B)** *fortitude* is related to stamina and survival. It fits with *resilience* but not with the sentence, so eliminate it. Choice **(C)** *ignominy* means "disgrace" and, with its negative connotation, fits the senator but not her loyal voters. Finally, choice **(E)** *ambivalence* suggests uncertainty about what to do. That would be a natural response to the senator's lying and therefore doesn't fit with the detour road sign "despite." The correct answers are **(D)** *constancy* and **(F)** *allegiance*.

13. A, F

Look at the key phrase "hurricane weakened considerably." This phrase suggests a positive outcome for residents, so the correct answers will reflect this. Choice **(A)** *assuage* means "to lessen or relieve." It makes sense that people's fears were relieved. Choice **(F)** *allay* also means "to lessen or relieve." Only **(A)** and **(F)** give the sentence the same meaning, so they're correct. Even if you didn't know the meaning of either correct answer, you could use the process of elimination to rule out the words you know don't fit. Choice **(D)** *annihilate*, meaning "destroy," is a very negative word, and you need a positive one. Choice **(B)** *emblazon* means "to adorn, decorate, or celebrate." This doesn't work in the sentence. Choice **(C)** *ignite* means "to light a fire" or "to arouse one's passions." This would imply that the residents' fears grew more intense, and you need the opposite meaning. Choice **(E)** *mediate* shares its root with the word *medium*, which means "in the middle." That doesn't make sense in the context of people who've just received news that a threatening storm is abating.

14. B, D

The thoughts in this sentence contrast with one another as evidenced by the detour road sign "Despite." Think about the connotation of the phrase "the accidental president." It's negative, so the sentence will shift to a positive tone; what was said about Ford after his death must have contrasted with how he was popularly regarded while in office. Look for adjectives that express praise for Ford's accomplishments. Choice **(B)** *extolled* means "praised" and is a correct answer. The root comes from the Latin for "lift up" or "raise." It's shared by the word *tolerate*, meaning "to bear or sustain." You may be familiar with the word **(D)** *lauded* from book or music reviews (and from the word "applause"); it also means "praised." *Lauded* also matches your prediction and is correct. Choice **(A)** *emancipated* or "liberated" is often used to describe freedom from slavery. It wouldn't make sense to say that Ford was "emancipated" after his death; moreover, this word does not connote praise. Eliminate. Choice **(C)** *indemnified* means "gave security against future loss," which doesn't fit and can be eliminated. Choices **(E)** *denigrated* and **(F)** *belittled* are synonyms meaning "to attack one's reputation." This is the opposite of the meaning you need, so you can rule out this pair.

15. A, E

The road sign "but" indicates a contrast. The use of the word "parents" is another clue. Think about what kind of movie might concern parents, especially if children are in the audience. Choice **(A)** *ribald* is another word for "vulgar." This makes perfect sense in context, so hold on to it and find its match. Something *lascivious*, choice **(E)**, is obscene or vulgar, which matches closely the meaning of *ribald*. Don't be tempted to choose **(B)** and **(F)**, even though they are synonyms. *Arcane* means "mysterious" or "hard to understand." This doesn't fit the tone of the sentence. Something hard to understand might not appeal to all audiences, but it is unlikely to cause concern among parents in particular. Choice **(C)** *superfluous* means "more than needed." As with *arcane*, when you look at the sentence as a whole, this word is not the best fit. Something *pervasive*, choice **(D)**, covers a lot of space. This doesn't make sense in the sentence.

16. A, D

This question contains a subtle detour road sign, "not." The student spent hours preparing, so you're looking for something similar in meaning to "unprepared." Choice **(A)** *unaware* is pretty close, so hold on to that one. Choice **(D)** *unrehearsed* works perfectly, since it would imply he hadn't prepared properly. Choices **(B)** *easily,* **(C)** *quickly,* and **(E)** *early* all give the sentence the same meaning. None of these words captures the idea that the student wants to be prepared "for every possible question." Preparing just a little would prevent him from being caught in an error right away. Eliminate both of these. Choice **(F)** *red-handed* is a trap answer. The subject is a graduate student, not a thief, so "caught red-handed" doesn't work in this context.

17. A, C

The blank describes an event that gave an era or epoch its name. So the blank must be filled with words indicating "great importance." Choice **(C)** *momentous* means "very significant," as does choice **(A)** *seminal*, in the sense of something being influential or original. Choice **(B)** *abstract* means "theoretical" or "complex." Choice **(D)** *gratuitous* means "excessive." Choice **(E)** *diluvial* means "related to a flood." Choice **(F)** *trifling* means "insignificant." None of those fits the context of the sentence at all.

18. B, F

You're told that the magistrate "relented" (gave in) as a result of some action that the ambassador took. It's unclear whether the ambassador used power or persuasion, so consider words such as *insistence* or *plea*. Both are good predictions. Both correct choices will mean one or the other. Choice **(B)** *behest*, "a strongly worded request," works very well; a strongly worded request could induce someone to relent. Choice **(F)** *urging* creates a sentence similar to the one created by **(B)** *behest*. Those two are the correct answers. Choice **(A)** *approbation* means "approval," which doesn't make sense given that the ambassador seems to disapprove of the charges. Choice **(C)** *ingenuousness* means "frankness" or "naïvité" and does not fit the context of the sentence. Choice **(D)** *delight* also does not make sense in this context. Choice **(E)** *circumlocution* means "roundabout speech," which is not typically very persuasive.

19. A, C

The hard part about this question is that all of the choices are undesirable traits that could lead to unflattering stories about a performer. However, only two of these answer choices will make sense given the context of the sentence. You're told that the anecdotes (stories) are about the singer's "tantrums," so the correct answers will relate to her irritability. A reasonable prediction for the correct answers is *irritable*. Choice **(A)** *captious*, "easily displeased", and is pretty close to your prediction, and it makes sense; if she's difficult to please, she's likely to throw tantrums. Choice **(C)** *irascible*, which means "easily angered," is also worth hanging on to. Someone who's easily angered will throw tantrums. Just as important, the sentence created with *irascible* has a meaning similar to the one created with *captious*. You can immediately reject choices **(B)** *dissolute* and **(D)** *profligate*. Both mean "morally corrupt"; that's negative, but it wouldn't incline someone toward tantrums. Choice **(E)** *smug*, "haughty", is another unpleasant trait, but not one that describes someone who loses her temper. Choice **(F)** *nettlesome*, "annoying", would mean that she is irritating, not that she's easily irritated. The correct answers are **(A)** and **(C)**.

20. E, F

The word "however" is a road sign indicating that the direction of the second clause will take a detour from that of the first. The first clause tells you that the warriors did not expect to encounter an "assault" on their olfactory senses (sense of smell). Since the road sign "however" signals a detour, you can infer that they did indeed encounter something quite smelly. *Smelly* is a simple, serviceable prediction; keep it in mind and scan the answer choices. Choices **(E)** *fetid* and **(F)** *malodorous* both specifically refer to disgusting aromas. They produce sentences with similar meanings and are the correct answers. You can reject **(A)** *cloying* and **(B)** *saccharine*; both mean "excessively sweet," which is the opposite of what you need. Choice **(D)** *dejected* is wrong because *dejected* means "sad" and has nothing to do with smell. Choice **(C)** *repulsive* is more difficult to eliminate (you might say, "That smells repulsive," after all), but the word has too broad a meaning to create a sentence equivalent to either *fetid* or *malodorous*.

21. C, F

Your first reaction here should be to notice the rather unusual word "contradistinction," which means "distinction by contrast." You can infer from the root *contra*, which means "in contrast to," that "contradistinction" is acting as a detour road sign. In this sentence, the dog is described as being a "pack animal," which means it is social and communal. Because the cat is in "contradistinction" to the dog, the word in the blank describing the cat must contrast with "pack animal," so predict something like *isolated*. Choice **(C)** *solitary* certainly works well as a contrast to "pack animal." Keep that one. Choice **(F)** *aloof*, meaning "standoffish," fits just as well; those who are standoffish are solitary and dislike company. Choice **(A)** *transparent* doesn't make sense as a way to describe cats. Choice **(B)** *supercilious* may be tempting; it describes a popular view of cats (it means "haughty"), but it does not contrast as strongly with "pack animals." Choice **(D)** *forthright* (candid) is not necessarily characteristic of someone or something that prefers solitude. The same can be said for choice **(E)** *maladroit*, which means "awkward or clumsy."

22. B, D

You're told that Mozart's genius manifested itself at the "precocious" age of five. "Precocious" means "prematurely developed," an accurate description of a child prodigy. The blank describes such a genius, so the correct answer must mean "early" or "budding." Choice **(B)** *incipient* "at an early stage" works, since Mozart's genius was just beginning to blossom if he was five years old. Choice **(D)** *nascent* "beginning to exist or develop" creates a sentence nearly identical to the one created by *incipient*. Reject choice **(A)** *refined*, since, by definition, refinement comes with time while this sentence describes Mozart's beginnings. Choice **(C)** *staggering* is harder to eliminate, since the genius of a five-year-old who composes symphonies is certainly staggering, but that doesn't dovetail with "precocious," and no other answer choice creates a sentence with similar meaning. Choice **(E)** *fathomless* (incomprehensible) can also describe genius, but it doesn't create a sentence similar to one created by another answer choice. Choice **(F)** *piddling* can be rejected outright, since it means "negligible" and certainly doesn't describe Mozart's genius.

23. D, E

In this question, "furthermore" is a straight-ahead road sign. The sentence will continue in the same direction in which it starts, connecting a lack of funding with the needs of children, who will go wanting without assistance. The blank describes the children. A simple, accurate prediction is *needy*. The sentence doesn't imply specifically what it is the children lack (food, shelter, education), and *needy* is broad enough to cover all contingencies. Choices **(D)** *impecunious* and **(E)** *indigent* both mean "impoverished" and thus create sentences with similar meanings. They both match your prediction, too. Reject choice **(A)** *prodigal* (wasteful) right off the bat; by definition, needy children can't be prodigal. The same logic applies to choice **(F)** *overindulged* (spoiled); the children here are needy, not spoiled. While needy children could certainly be **(B)** *malnourished,* "underfed," or **(C)** *vagrant,* "homeless," these characterizations are too specific to create sentences similar to any others created by the answer choices. Choices **(D)** and **(E)** are the correct answers.

24. B, E

The sentence opens with the word "When," which functions as a straight-ahead road sign. The missing word will be in accord with the key words in the first half of the sentence. The patron wants an "amusing" and uplifting author. Predict something like "laughter" or "joy." Choices **(B)** *mirth* and **(E)** *merriment* both mean "gladness" or "hilarity," and are the correct answers. Choices **(A)** *lugubriousness* and **(C)** *poignancy* both mean "sadness," and are the opposite of what you're looking for. Finally, choices **(D)** *gravity* and **(F)** *solemnity* both mean "dignity" or "seriousness," and are likewise the opposite of what you want.

25. A, D

"Not only" is a straight-ahead road sign. Always paired with "but also," it indicates that the sentence will continue in its original direction. You're told that the author has a penchant for "dissembling," which means "to speak or act hypocritically." Since he dissembles when he writes, his prose can be described as "insincere." That's a good prediction, so start checking the answer choices. Choice **(A)** *fulsome* means "excessive" or "over-the-top." That's an excellent way to characterize insincere prose, so hang on to it. Choice **(D)** *unctuous* means "excessively smug," which is certainly insincere in its tenor. Choice **(B)** *effulgent,* meaning "radiant" or "shining," doesn't make sense in this context. Choice **(C)** *effusive,* which means "gushing" or "enthusiastic," would describe the emotional tenor of the prose but not the author's sincerity. Choice **(E)** *cryptic,* or "mysterious," is not supported by the context; there is nothing in the sentence to indicate that the author's work was hard to understand. Also, no other answer choice creates a similar sentence. Choice **(F)** *vulgar* can be rejected for the same reason; it also has nothing to do with "dissembling."

26. C, E

The key to this question is the context key word "surprised." Since Nigel is typically a model of "equanimity" (calm), the correct answer choices, describing surprising behavior on his part, must mean something like "unsettled." Choices **(C)** *testy,* "irritable," and **(E)** *discomposed,*"out of sorts," create sentences that indicate that Nigel lost his cool and failed to remain calm. These are the correct answers. You can eliminate **(A)** *staid,* **(B)** *equanimous,* and **(D)** *placid,* as those are all synonyms for "calm," from which the sentence detours. Choice **(F)** *jubilant,* "overjoyed," can also be rejected; although excessive joy does depart from "calm," no other word in the answer choices would create an equivalent sentence.

27. A, E

The blank in this sentence takes a verb that describes an action that would concern "intelligence agencies." Since the object of concern is state secrets, it's a good bet the agencies are alarmed by their "spread" or "leaking." Choices **(A)** *proliferation* and

(E) *dissemination*, both of which are synonymous with "spreading," create similar sentences that make sense: intelligence agencies would be highly concerned about the spread of state secrets. Choices **(B)** *retention* and **(D)** *acquisition* can be ruled out, as intelligence agencies would be keen to both *retain* and *acquire* state secrets. Choice **(C)** *lassitude,* "laziness," doesn't make sense in this context (state secrets can't be "lazy"). Choice **(F)** *quality* might be tempting, but no other answer choice produces a similar sentence.

28. A, B

The celebrity in the sentence has done something "vociferously." "Vociferously" means "clamorously" and describes speech, so you know she spoke ardently and loudly. She must also have been trying to convince her audience of something, since her action is contrasted with being ignored. A good prediction is *lectured* or *orated*. When you look at the answer choices, there's nothing that precisely matches your prediction, but **(A)** *inveighed* and **(B)** *declaimed* come close. Both have a connotation of oratory, typically arguing against something. That harmonizes very well with "vociferously." Choices **(C)** *conceded,* "gave in," **(E)** *abstained,* "declined to participate," and **(F)** *acceded,* "agreed," can all be rejected as being too passive and therefore opposite to what you need. Choice **(D)** *demurred* "raised an objection" is wrong because it isn't strong enough.

29. E, F

This question obliges you to find an adjective to describe Reginald's aunt, who you are told is "spry" (nimble) for her age. The key words "for her age" imply that Reginald's aunt is of an age at which it is unusual to be spry. You can therefore predict answers similar to *elderly*. Choice **(E)** *septuagenarian*, which is a term for someone in her seventies, works well. Choice **(F)** *hoary* means "very old." These are the correct answers. You can reject choices **(A)** *acrobatic* and **(B)** *dexterous*, as these are both synonymous with "agile," in which case she would not need help getting up the stairs. Choices **(C)** *caustic,* "sarcastic or corrosive," and **(D)** *genial,* "pleasant," are also wrong, because they describe her personality, not her fitness.

30. A, B

The fact that the blank is the word that begins the sentence may make this question more challenging than a typical Sentence Equivalence question. The first clause is fairly direct; he passed on the project, and the blank will contain an adverb to describe this decision. The second clause contains the detour road sign "notwithstanding," which means "despite." "Professed," which describes his support, means "stated," so you know he passed on the project despite his vocal support. Therefore, you can predict the first blank to be something like *surprisingly* or *paradoxically.* Choices **(A)** *counterintuitively,* "contrary to intuition," and **(B)** *unexpectedly* both match that prediction quite well. They both create sentences pointing out the subject's seeming inconsistency. Three of the other choices could work on their own in this context: **(C)** *self-indulgently,* "to indulge one's own desires," **(D)** *obscurely,* "vaguely," and **(E)** *pusillanimously,* "cowardly," all characterize the way in which one could decline a project, but none logically contrast with "professed support." Choice **(F)** *punctiliously,* "attentive to detail," does not make sense in this context. Only **(A)** and **(B)** logically complete similar sentences.

CHAPTER 4

Reading Comprehension

READING COMPREHENSION: OVERVIEW AND METHOD

Even though reading is a skill that you've been developing and practicing for most of your life, navigating the often verbose and detailed language of academia can be a challenge. While the GRE tests your ability to assess ideas and information, the greater test of the skills involved will come in the field of higher learning you pursue. Regardless of academic discipline, you will almost certainly be presented with written material at least as difficult to penetrate as the practice set questions to follow.

So that the GRE reflects the real-world nature of postgraduate reading, the passages are drawn from four standard disciplines of higher learning—social sciences, biological sciences, physical sciences, and arts and humanities.

The types of questions the GRE uses fall into three categories, distinguished by the answer choices: standard multiple-choice questions with one correct answer, multiple-choice questions in which one or more of the choices is correct, and questions that ask you to select the sentence from the passage that best answers the question. These different question formats reward a wide range of analytical skills, from determining the best definition of a specific word in context or identifying details that support a main idea to evaluating the author's perspective or drawing inferences from the evidence presented.

A Reading Comprehension passage and question will look like this:

Questions 1–3 are based on the following passage.

A pioneering figure in modern sociology, French social theorist Emile Durkheim examined the effect of societal cohesion on emotional well-being. Believing that scientific methods should be applied to the study of society, Durkheim studied the levels of integration in various social formations and the impact that such cohesion had on individuals within the group. He postulated that social groups with high levels of integration serve to buffer their members from frustrations and tragedies that could otherwise lead to desperation and self-destruction. Integration, in Durkheim's view, generally arises through shared activities and values. Durkheim distinguished between mechanical solidarity and organic solidarity in classifying integrated groups. *Mechanical solidarity* dominates in groups in which individual differences are minimized and group devotion to a common goal is high. Durkheim identified mechanical solidarity among groups with little division of labor and high degrees of cultural similarity, such as among more traditional and geographically isolated groups. *Organic solidarity*, in contrast, prevails in groups with high levels of individual differences, such as those with a highly specialized division of labor. In such groups, individual differences are a powerful source of connection rather than of division. Because people engage in highly differentiated ways of life, they are by necessity interdependent. In these societies, there is greater freedom from some external controls, but such freedom occurs in concert with the interdependence of individuals, not in conflict with it. Durkheim realized that societies may take many forms and, consequently, that group allegiance can manifest itself in a variety of ways. In both types of societies outlined previously, however, Durkheim stressed that adherence to a common set of assumptions about the world was a necessary prerequisite for maintaining group integrity and avoiding social decay.

1. Which of the following is NOT a feature of an organic societal formation, according to Emile Durkheim?

   (A) Members are buffered from individual frustration that would lead the individual to cease being a productive member of society.
   (B) Citizens operate independently in their daily lives, but toward a common overall goal.
   (C) Each person must come to accept a series of assumptions that form a collective worldview shared by the formation.
   (D) Workers have an even division of labor and share the work of common tasks.
   (E) Individual differences are celebrated, and have a strengthening effect on the society.

The GRE features three types of Reading Comprehension questions: Select One, Select One or More, and Select-in-Passage. You will review all three types in this chapter.

THE KAPLAN METHOD FOR READING COMPREHENSION

STEP 1 Read the passage strategically.

STEP 2 Analyze the question stem.

STEP 3 Research the relevant text in the passage.

STEP 4 Make a prediction.

STEP 5 Evaluate the answer choices.

How the Kaplan Method for Reading Comprehension Works

Here's how the Kaplan Method for Reading Comprehension works.

STEP 1

Read the passage strategically.

Reading strategically means identifying the topic, scope, and purpose of a passage, as well as noting the passage's structure and main points. The *topic* is the general subject matter, and the *scope* is the specific aspect of the topic that the author focuses on. In order to identify the topic, scope, and purpose, you should target the passage's main ideas, primary arguments, secondary arguments, supporting statements or evidence, and conclusions. Take notes on scratch paper about the points discussed above to create a "passage map" that will be useful to you in answering the questions. For each paragraph, jot down a one- to two-line summary highlighting the main points. For any given passage, you should be able to both summarize the text and identify the main points in your own words before proceeding. It's also important to use the key words and phrases connected to the sentences to identify the important ideas and statements.

With each passage, you need to look for the purpose of the text: Why did the author write it? While there will be numerous facts provided in any given piece, not all passages are purely informative. There will be persuasive elements in each passage, even if designed only to convince you of the subject's importance. Identify early on whether the piece is primarily informative or argumentative, and to what degree. You do this by recognizing the author's tone, which reflects the author's attitude towards her subject. Tone is indispensable in identifying an author's purpose, especially if her purpose is not entirely explicit. If the author makes use of comparisons (*better, more effective*) or recommendations (*should, must, need to*), the author is trying to persuade. If the author writes in a more straightforward style with no persuasive or judgmental terminology, the piece is more purely informative. Pieces written in that tone are more likely to have the purpose of explanation or description. Purpose is important for Inference questions, which reward you for identifying the author's opinion on the subject matter.

In general, a social sciences piece is likely to argue a position because the complex nature of human behavior and interaction is open to wide interpretation. Likewise, a discussion of a piece of art or literature will likely contain arguments because the author asserts an interpretation of these art forms. Scientific articles, on the other hand, will be mainly informative, seeking primarily to explain a scientific concept or discovery. Still, there may be arguments or conclusions drawn about the importance of these discoveries or principles in daily application. Pay close attention to the author's tone; it is inseparable from her argument.

STEP 2

Analyze the question stem.

Most GRE Reading Comprehension passages are accompanied by one to three questions. Above the passage on the computer screen, you'll see a note that indicates the number of questions: "Question 11. . ." or "Questions 4–6. . ." Not surprisingly, passages with only one question tend to be shorter (usually one paragraph), while those with several questions may be longer.

When a passage has only one question, it makes sense to read the question stem before reading the passage. You can target the text that answers the specific question. When multiple questions accompany a passage, however, you're better off reading the passage strategically before concerning yourself with the question stems.

When a passage has multiple questions, one stem may be concerned with the author's tone, another focused on a vocabulary term, and still another designed to reward your analytical reasoning skills. Reading with multiple questions in mind makes it difficult to discern the main ideas of the passage. It's usually more valuable to use the question stem to guide research for details in the passage than to try to read for several alternative details at the outset. Your passage map or notes will allow you to find the correct answer(s) quickly while still reading for the big points and main idea. You'll have the answers to general questions—"Which of the following best states the main idea/primary purpose of the passage?"—and the notes to research more specific questions. Likewise, by knowing the author's attitude and purpose, you'll be prepared for questions that ask what an author is most likely or least likely to agree with.

STEP 3

Research the relevant text in the passage.

Notice that this step tells you to *research* the passage, not *reread* it. Once you have analyzed and understood the question stem, you should already have an idea of where in the passage you'll find the answer. Use your passage map or notes, the product of Step 1's strategic reading, to target this research step. Don't consider more text from the passage than is necessary to answer the question. If the question rewards your understanding of vocabulary in context, for example, you need not look further than the sentence in which it appears, and possibly the preceding sentence, to derive the answer.

STEP 4

Make a prediction.

GRE questions will, by design, test your comprehension of what you have read and not just your ability to go into a passage and mine for details. As such, you will often need the ability to formulate a prediction as to the answers of many questions that deal with the main idea, conclusions, arguments, author's meaning, tone, and implications of the information provided. Before moving on to the answer choices, try to either form a response to the stem in your own mind or target the section of the passage that will contain the answer.

At times, you will have to infer an answer based on clues provided in the text, but the test will not ask you for outside information. In these Inference questions, research the relevant sections of the passage, those that provide evidence or details to support (or refute) the opinion or conclusion in question. When you find it difficult to make a specific, word-for-word prediction for the correct answer, remember that the correct answer will be supported by the passage. Use your research to evaluate the answer choices.

STEP 5

Evaluate the answer choices.

You'll take this step a little differently depending on the Reading Comprehension question type you're answering. For a multiple-choice question with one correct answer, look to match your prediction and eliminate violators. When you find the unequivocally correct choice, select it. Time permitting, check the remaining choices and confirm that each is demonstrably incorrect. Eliminating incorrect answers not only helps narrow down options for questions that are hard to answer, it also validates the selection you are considering.

For a multiple-choice question in which multiple answer choices may be correct (a Select One or More question, indicated by "select all that apply"), you must check all of the choices. You receive credit only if you choose all of (and only) the applicable choices. For a Select-in-Passage question, place your cursor over the correct sentence and click. Only one sentence from the passage will be credited as the correct answer.

When you're uncertain about the correct answer, begin by eliminating answers that are demonstrably wrong. Use the same steps as you would for finding the right answer: Weigh the choices against the passage text and eliminate choices that contradict, distort, or fall outside the scope of the passage. Determine the criteria for the correct answer and eliminate choices that violate them. Don't compare answer choices to one another; compare them to the standard of what the correct choice must contain.

APPLY THE KAPLAN METHOD FOR READING COMPREHENSION

Now, apply the Kaplan Method to a Reading Comprehension (Select One) question:

Question 1 is based on the following passage.

A pioneering figure in modern sociology, French social theorist Emile Durkheim examined the effect of societal cohesion on emotional well-being. Believing that scientific methods should be applied to the study of society, Durkheim studied the levels of integration in various social formations and the impact that such cohesion had on individuals within the group. He postulated that social groups with high levels of integration serve to buffer their members from frustrations and tragedies that could otherwise lead to desperation and self-destruction. Integration, in Durkheim's view, generally arises through shared activities and values. Durkheim distinguished between mechanical solidarity and organic solidarity in classifying integrated groups. *Mechanical solidarity* dominates in groups in which individual differences are minimized and group devotion to a common goal is high. Durkheim identified mechanical solidarity among groups with little division of labor and high degrees of cultural similarity, such as among more traditional and geographically isolated groups. *Organic solidarity*, in contrast, prevails in groups with high levels of individual differences, such as those with a highly specialized division of labor. In such groups, individual differences are a powerful source of connection rather than of division. Because people engage in highly differentiated ways of life, they are by necessity interdependent. In these societies, there is greater freedom from some external controls, but such freedom occurs in concert with the interdependence of individuals, not in conflict with it. Durkheim realized that societies may take many forms and, consequently, that group allegiance can manifest itself in a variety of ways. In both types of societies outlined previously, however, Durkheim stressed that adherence to a common set of assumptions about the world was a necessary prerequisite for maintaining group integrity and avoiding social decay.

1. Which of the following is NOT a feature of an organic societal formation, according to Emile Durkheim?

   (A) Members are buffered from individual frustration that would lead the individual to cease being a productive member of society.
   (B) Citizens operate independently in their daily lives, but toward a common overall goal.
   (C) Each person must come to accept a series of assumptions that form a collective worldview shared by the formation.
   (D) Workers have an even division of labor and share the work of common tasks.
   (E) Individual differences are celebrated, and have a strengthening effect on the society.

The most common standardized test question—multiple-choice—has a strong presence on the GRE. Most often, the multiple-choice question asks you to select the best answer from a set of five choices. Only one choice is credited as the right answer; the other four options will either be incorrect or less complete than the correct selection.

STEP 1

Read the passage strategically.

As the author sets forth the criteria for Emile Durkheim's theory of social cohesion, he defines two models of social solidarity by introducing qualities that are common to both constructs before addressing the differences between the two. The passage concludes with a prerequisite for social cohesion common to both models. The two models have similarities, but note that the author is contrasting them with one another.

STEP 2

Analyze the question stem.

This question asks which choice is NOT a feature of the organic solidarity model. Normally, you would approach this question type by researching what the passage says *are* features of the organic solidarity model and eliminating answers that mention them. In this case, since the passage contrasts two models of societal formation, the correct answer will likely be a feature of the opposed mechanical solidarity model.

STEP 3

Research the relevant text in the passage.

The relevant text is the part of the passage that discusses the features of the two types of societal formation. Since the question asks you to find what is *not* common to the organic solidarity model, research the portion that defines the mechanical solidarity model as well. The author emphasizes one distinction between the models: the lack of a specialized labor force in the mechanical solidarity model versus the presence of a specialized division of labor in the organic solidarity model.

STEP 4

Make a prediction.

Apply your research to the "call" of the question stem. The correct answer here is a feature not found in organic solidarity groups. Since the author highlights the organic solidarity model's highly specialized division of labor, predict that the correct answer will describe a case in which labor is not differentiated. Now, check the answers to find the choice that matches this prediction.

STEP 5

Evaluate the answer choices.

Choice **(D)** matches your prediction quite well. Societies that distribute labor evenly and parcel out common tasks among everyone are not using a specialized labor force. They fit the mechanical solidaritymodel, not the organic solidarity one. Choice **(A)** and choice **(C)** are found among the descriptions for both forms of Durkheim's societal formations, the first early in the paragraph and the other toward the end, so they are wrong. Within the section discussing organic solidarity societies, you can find, as part of the definition, differently worded forms of both choice **(B)** and choice **(E)**.

Apply the Kaplan Method for Reading Comprehension

Now, apply the Kaplan Method to a Reading Comprehension (Select One or More) question:

Question 2 is based on the following passage.

A pioneering figure in modern sociology, French social theorist Emile Durkheim examined the effect of societal cohesion on emotional well-being. Believing that scientific methods should be applied to the study of society, Durkheim studied the levels of integration in various social formations and the impact that such cohesion had on individuals within the group. He postulated that social groups with high levels of integration serve to buffer their members from frustrations and tragedies that could otherwise lead to desperation and self-destruction. Integration, in Durkheim's view, generally arises through shared activities and values. Durkheim distinguished between mechanical solidarity and organic solidarity in classifying integrated groups. *Mechanical solidarity* dominates in groups in which individual differences are minimized and group devotion to a common goal is high. Durkheim identified mechanical solidarity among groups with little division of labor and high degrees of cultural similarity, such as among more traditional and geographically isolated groups. *Organic solidarity*, in contrast, prevails in groups with high levels of individual differences, such as those with a highly specialized division of labor. In such groups, individual differences are a powerful source of connection rather than of division. Because people engage in highly differentiated ways of life, they are by necessity interdependent. In these societies, there is greater freedom from some external controls, but such freedom occurs in concert with the interdependence of individuals, not in conflict with it. Durkheim realized that societies may take many forms and, consequently, that group allegiance can manifest itself in a variety of ways. In both types of societies outlined previously, however, Durkheim stressed that adherence to a common set of assumptions about the world was a necessary prerequisite for maintaining group integrity and avoiding social decay.

Consider each of the following choices separately and select all that apply.

2. Which of the following might be examples of a mechanical solidarity societal formation as explained by the passage?

   [A] A religious order living in a monastery with an evenly distributed division of labor

   [B] A company comprised of a group of architects, carpenters, plumbers, and construction workers who can design and complete all facets of a building project from start to finish

   [C] A xenophobic tribe living in an isolated fishing village amid an uncolonized set of islands

The second form of multiple-choice question offers three choices, but any combination of them could be the correct answer, from a single choice to all three being correct. In order to get the question correct on the test, you must identify all of (and only) the correct choices.

STEP 1

Read the passage strategically.

You've already read the passage strategically, of course. It will come as no surprise that the questions continue to reward you for noting the contrast between Durkheim's two models.

STEP 2

Analyze the question stem.

This question asks you to identify which of three examples meet the criteria supplied by the text to qualify as a society displaying "mechanical solidarity." Notice that the author divides societal formation into "mechanical" and "organic," and the question is only concerned with the former. In a Select One question, once you're confident that you have the correct choice, you can move on. You need not give the remaining choices equal consideration. In Select One or More questions, on the other hand, don't stop once you spot a correct answer. Evaluate all of the choices. More than one may be correct.

STEP 3

Research the relevant text in the passage.

This question rewards you for identifying which of the three examples meet the criteria supplied by the text to qualify as a mechanical solidarity social formation. The author cites "more traditional and geographically isolated groups" as examples of this sort of group. You also know that the author distinguishes mechanical from organic solidarity on the basis of labor specialization.

STEP 4

Make a prediction.

Now, apply your research. You noted the author's illustration of mechanical solidarity groups: "such as more traditional and geographically isolated groups." Make this your prediction.

STEP 5

Evaluate the answer choices.

Your prediction makes choice **(C)** easy to select; it uses much of the same terminology. Knowing that *xenophobic* means "fearful of outsiders" helps, but is not necessary for answering that portion of the question. Keep choice **(C)** as an answer, but check the others as well. Choice **(A)** also meets the criteria. A monastic religious order (such as monks) in which the members do all the same tasks without specialization meets the non-specialized distribution of labor portion of the author's definition as well. Only choice **(B)** fails to meet the definition; even though the workers listed may share a singular goal (of creating a house or building), each worker has very specific specialties and abilities—a feature associated with organic solidarity groups.

Apply the Kaplan Method for Reading Comprehension

Now, apply the Kaplan Method to a Reading Comprehension (Select-in-Passage) question:

Question 3 is based on the following passage.

A pioneering figure in modern sociology, French social theorist Emile Durkheim examined the role of societal cohesion on emotional well-being. Believing that scientific methods should be applied to the study of society, Durkheim studied the levels of integration in various social formations and the impact that such cohesion had on individuals within the group. He postulated that social groups with high levels of integration serve to buffer their members from frustrations and tragedies that could otherwise lead to desperation and self-destruction. Integration, in Durkheim's view, generally arises through shared activities and values. Durkheim distinguished between mechanical solidarity and organic solidarity in classifying integrated groups. *Mechanical solidarity* dominates in groups in which individual differences are minimized and Durkheim distinguished between mechanical solidarity and organic solidarity in classifying integrated groups. *Mechanical solidarity* dominates in groups in which individual differences are minimized and groups with high levels of individual differences, such as those with a highly specialized division of labor. In such groups, individual differences are a powerful source of connection rather than of division. Because people engage in highly differentiated ways of life, they are by necessity interdependent. In these societies, there is greater freedom from some external controls, but such freedom occurs in concert with the interdependence of individuals, not in conflict with it. Durkheim realized that societies may take many forms and, consequently, that group allegiance can manifest itself in a variety of ways. In both types of societies outlined previously, however, Durkheim stressed that adherence to a common set of assumptions about the world was a necessary prerequisite for maintaining group integrity and avoiding social decay.

3. Select the sentence in the passage that explains why a society displaying organic solidarity tends more toward social codependence than does a mechanical societal formation.

This question type asks you to click on the sentence that meets the criteria or provides the information solicited by the question stem.

STEP 1

Read the passage strategically.

You know from having analyzed the text already that the correct answer will be found somewhere after the introduction of the two forms of societal formations. Keep that in mind.

STEP 2

Analyze the question stem.

This question rewards you for distinguishing the ways in which societies displaying the two forms of solidarity manifest codependence.

STEP 3

Research the relevant text in the passage.

Since the question centers on the organic solidarity model, the best place to start looking is in the part of the passage where the author defines and illustrates organic solidarity. There, you find this cause-and-effect statement: "Because people engage in highly differentiated ways of life, they are by necessity interdependent."

STEP 4

Make a prediction.

Make that sentence your prediction.

STEP 5

Evaluate the answer choices.

The sentence is the right answer; it explains that because the members of an organic society do not have the same skill sets, they are forced to rely on others for those things they are unable to do or do not have the skill for. Click it and confirm your answer.

KAPLAN'S ADDITIONAL TIPS FOR READING COMPREHENSION QUESTIONS

Express the Main Idea in Your Own Words

Summarizing the main idea of the passage not only forms the foundation of your comprehension of the passage, it's also the starting point for your evaluation of the questions. While not every passage has a specific main idea, each passage does have a topic and scope, both of which you should discern by the end of the first paragraph. If you are halfway through a passage and still have not identified these elements, you may be reading too fast and not outlining or identifying key words and phrases in the text.

Focus on Retaining Ideas, Not Facts

Unlike university coursework, you do not have to memorize or retain any of the dates, details, or minutiae of a GRE passage. If you are asked a question about a specific term or detail within the text, such as a date or place, the question will likely ask *why* or *how* the author used the detail rather than what's true about it. You have the text there to refer back to. In that sense, the GRE is an open-book test. Concern yourself with the ideas, arguments, and conclusions the author presents in order to assess the questions accurately and examine them within the context of the passage.

Concentrate on Using Only What the Passage Gives You

As a smart test taker, you can benefit from a passage about a topic completely foreign to you. Whatever the passage is about, it is still presented using familiar patterns of expository and persuasive writing.

A danger occurs when you encounter topics about which you have pre-existing knowledge. Such knowledge can confuse or muddle your ability to answer a question by clouding or expanding the scope of the piece beyond what's written. To best handle the questions, you must be concerned only with the text itself and not be influenced by outside knowledge that may be at odds with the answer as defined by the passage and the question stem. When it comes to answering GRE Reading Comprehension questions, the passage is your "universe."

While you've no doubt honed an ability to question and critique text, on the GRE you should accept the information given in informative passages as true. The questions reward you for determining correct answers "based on the passage" or "according to the passage," not for answers true in the world at large. Even with persuasive passages, and regardless of your own opinions on the author's subject or point of view, correct answers follow from the evidence and arguments given as the groundwork for the passage.

Do Not Approach Highlighted Statement Questions Differently

From time to time, the GRE will highlight words, phrases, clauses, or sentences in the passage in order to ask you about the logic, function, or meaning of the highlighted portion. In the most complex of these—which Kaplan designates as Highlighted Statement questions—the test highlights two portions of text (clauses or sentences) in the passage. It then asks you to determine the functions of both statements or their relationship to one another. Some of the functions a sentence might serve are these:

- development of an argument
- conclusion of an argument
- evidence supporting a conclusion
- evidence supporting part of a conclusion
- evidence supporting an objection to the conclusion
- a secondary argument or support for a secondary argument
- illustration or example of a point
- a principle underlying an argument

While it's natural to focus primarily or exclusively on the highlighted sentences, you may need the entire passage in order to determine the roles played by the highlighted portions. As you read the passage, read strategically to determine the position taken by the author. Identify the argument and its conclusion and note how the author supports them or refutes opposing views. While the highlighted lines are central to the correct answer, the surrounding material provides key context.

Predict the correct answer. Then, move on to evaluating the choices and eliminating obviously incorrect answers. In Highlighted Statement questions, each answer has two parts, one for each highlighted sentence; both must be correct in order for the answer to be correct. If you are unable to predict an answer, or if your prediction is not among the answer choices, eliminate wrong answer choices by looking carefully at the two parts. Get rid of choices in which you find a mischaracterization of the role of a sentence, a reversal of the sentences' roles, a reference to a sentence not highlighted, or a description of something that does not appear in the passage. Once you've eliminated the obviously incorrect answers, you'll more easily be able to identify the answer that best describes the roles of the sentences.

Do Not Get Misled by Variations on Standard Question Stems

While most questions concern themselves with what is stated in or follows from the passage, some questions will ask you to find an answer that is *not* supported by the passage. Don't confuse "true" with correct. Characterize the choices before you evaluate them. Consider a question stem like this one, for example:

According to the passage, each of the following is commonly associated with inflation EXCEPT:

This question has four answers that are "true" according to the passage, but wrong (because of the call of the question stem). The one correct choice is the "false" answer, the one that does not follow from the text. While you should assume passages to be true, veracity is irrelevant to evaluating the answers. Choices are correct because they follow from the passage and answer the question. They're incorrect when they do not. From time to time, the testmakers will ask "Which of the following, if TRUE, most strengthens the argument?" In such cases, treat the five answer choices as facts, but distinguish the correct answer from the incorrect ones based on the effect they have on the reasoning.

Now try the following section of practice passages and questions to drill and strengthen your Reading Comprehension skills. The following passages are representative in terms of length and number of questions associated with passages on the GRE. Complete the thirty questions and use the explanations that follow to gauge your thinking and refine your test-taking skills.

READING COMPREHENSION PRACTICE SET

Basic

Questions 1–3 are based on the following passage.

Could any comic book superheroes exist in real life? According to a physics professor who studies the way science concepts are applied in comics, Superman is a surprising nominee as one who might actually have a chance. Not the flying, heat-vision-using version we know today, says Dr. James Kakalios of the University of Minnesota, but rather the Superman who first appeared in 1938. Jerry Siegel and Joe Shuster imagined a rocket-borne infant refugee whose alien physiology gave him bullet-resistant skin, the strength of 15 strong men, and the ability to leap (not fly) over "tall buildings in a single bound." Whereas today's Superman gets his strength from our "yellow sun," the original Superman's power derived from his planet of origin. According to Kakalios, a compact planet with extreme gravity could produce a being who, as a result of adaptation to environmental factors, would have superhuman strength in Earth's lesser gravity. But that planet's ability to bring forth such a being would ultimately result in the planet's own destruction. Its gravitational collapse would be very similar to the planetary death that resulted, fictionally of course, in Superman being sent to our world in the first place.

1. Which of the following is TRUE according to the passage?

   (A) The author believes that a superhuman being might really exist somewhere on Earth.
   (B) The character of Superman is more likely to exist in reality than the character of Batman.
   (C) Superman as he is portrayed today is more powerful than the Superman of 1938.
   (D) Dr. James Kakalios has a large comic book collection.
   (E) Looking for a planet with beings of superhuman strength is pointless because any such planets would have been destroyed.

2. Select the sentence in the passage that identifies the scientific rationale for the possibility of a superhuman being.

Consider each of the following choices separately and select all that apply.

3. According to Dr. Kakalios, which of the following abilities would be possible in a superhuman being?

   [A] The ability to travel unaided through outer space
   [B] The ability to bench-press many times more weight than a normal man
   [C] The ability to jump over a house

Question 4 is based on the following passage.

Richard Wagner's *The Ring of the Nibelung* is perhaps the epitome of a *magnum opus.* If the entire work were to be performed beginning at seven o'clock in the morning, it might not conclude until close to midnight! Despite its immensity, Wagner's epic cycle of four music dramas, filled with familiar melodies such as "Ride of the Valkyries," is still performed and celebrated today. This daunting work is usually divided into a cycle of its four component pieces, which are often performed on successive nights because of the long and arduous level of singing over the course of a full cycle. The performance requirements of *The Ring of the Nibelung* also occasioned a specially constructed opera house in which the orchestra was placed in a covered pit under the stage. This ensured that the size and volume of the orchestra did not drown out the voices of the chorus. This innovation is still in use today. That opera companies are still willing to perform and enthusiasts are still willing to pay for what amounts to multiple consecutive shows is a testament to what some have called the greatest piece of operatic theater ever written.

Consider each of the following choices separately and select all that apply.

4. With which of the following statements would the author be likely to agree?

   [A] Wagner's *Ring of the Nibelung* cycle is too demanding and logistically difficult to be performed.
   [B] An enduring effect of Wagner's *Ring of the Nibelung* cycle is the innovation made to the opera house to accommodate the large orchestra.
   [C] Mammoth works such as *Ring of the Nibelung* are better performed on one day to preserve their full effect.

Questions 5 and 6 are based on the following passage.

Discovered in 2001, the mimic octopus is a creature whose survival abilities are as unique as they are versatile. This talented cephalopod is capable of imitating several different species of creatures found in its environment, and it does so for different purposes. It imitates a crab to get close enough to catch and eat one, it imitates toxic fish to avoid being eaten itself, and it can imitate a predatory sea snake to scare off trespassers. The shape-shifting creature's conscious selection from among multiple forms is an exceptionally rare trait among animals, and one that adds a wrinkle to the more commonly expressed forms of singularly limited camouflage seen in nature. Many species exist that survive in part by resembling sticks, leaves, or other animals. Scientists have suggested that, within these species, members showing adaptive coloring or designs were overlooked by predators while the differently marked members were consumed. The survivors were then left to mate and to pass on their beneficial forms as a natural defense. The mimic octopus's intelligent use of selective disguise suggests a creative and adaptive survival mechanism, more versatile and intriguing than that arising from appearance alone.

5. Select the sentence in the passage that distinguishes how the mimic octopus's camouflage exceeds that of most forms found in nature.

6. The author would most likely agree with which of the following sentences?

   Ⓐ The mimic octopus was probably discovered only recently because of its incredible ability to camouflage itself.
   Ⓑ The mimic octopus's method of conscious and situational disguise discredits current evolutionary theory.
   Ⓒ Mimic octopuses can only imitate the forms of creatures they can see.
   Ⓓ Octopuses must be nearly as intelligent as humans.
   Ⓔ Animal mimicry throughout nature is primarily a defensive mechanism as opposed to a means of attracting food.

Questions 7 and 8 are based on the following passage.

Few today would argue that including women in modern productions of Shakespeare's plays, a practice almost universally forbidden in Shakespeare's time, detracts from the presentation as a whole. However, in realizing gender equality through the assignment of women to female roles, a layer of both added humor and dramatic challenge is removed from several of the Bard's works, including a light comedy (*Twelfth Night*), a dark comedy (*The Merchant of Venice*), and a romance (*As You Like It*). In each, a female character, whom Shakespeare would have imagined played by a man, disguises herself as a man. A male actor of Shakespeare's age would have had to move beyond instilling feminine qualities in his character and into sustaining a feminine undercurrent beneath a superficial masculine pretension within an obviously masculine form. To the historic audience of *As You Like It*, the spectacle of a young man pretending to be young Rosalind pretending to be an old man brought additional "fourth wall" humor to the event. That humorous presentation may be lost on today's audiences, for whom assigning one gender to play another within a gender-mixed cast might come across more as a surprising distraction than as an added laugh.

Consider each of the following choices separately and select all that apply.

7. Which of the following options would reflect a modern return to the same gender humor the author describes in the passage?

   [A] Changing a male character to a female character and having the role played by a woman
   [B] Casting a male actor to play the part of Rosalind in *As You Like It*
   [C] Casting a female actor in the role of a male servant in *The Taming of the Shrew*, who disguises himself as a woman

8. Select in the passage the sentence that expresses the author's overall thesis.

Questions 9 and 10 are based on the following passage.

In some key ways, a zoologist's orderly method for identifying and classifying a subject species is at odds with the multi-millennial chaos of adaptive development that led to the species as it is embodied today. If the laws of nature were as rigid as we want our classification system to be, famous taxonomic rebels such as the platypus would be forced, as mammals, to gestate and give birth to live young even if the risk to both parent and child were increased to the point of bringing about the end of the species. We are thus fortunate that the rigid biological nomenclature of science makes concessions for such an unusual marvel, one that not only scorns the basic tenets of its class, but brings new and mystifying qualities to the whole branch of its kingdom. It is hard enough to believe in the existence of a furry, duck-billed, egg-laying, venomous mammal that senses its prey through disturbances in a surrounding electromagnetic field without an unassailable checklist stating that the creature cannot by definition exist.

9. Select the sentence that explicitly states one of the traditional zoological characteristics of a species of mammal.

Consider each of the following choices separately and select all that apply.

10. Which of the following accurately describes the author's intent in writing the passage?

    [A] To indicate the shortcomings of using a highly structured classification system to define radically adaptive animals

    [B] To express admiration for the unusual abilities of the platypus

    [C] To make an argument in favor of changing how scientists classify animals with atypical traits

INTERMEDIATE

Question 11 is based on the following passage.

A healthy national economy is normally in oscillation between a period of freely flowing dollars driving the economy to expansion and a more tightly controlled release of money stabilizing it. All of these actions are initiated by the Federal Reserve (the Fed). When the Fed unleashes money into the system with low interest rates, consumer confidence rises, spending increases, business expands, and the economy itself grows. As wealth accumulates, the pricing of goods and services rises rapidly, creating inflation. The Fed neutralizes inflation by clamping down on the flow of money by setting higher interest rates. With less money available, spending and demand diminishes, usually curtailing or lowering prices. Unfortunately, this balance of control can only operate perfectly in a closed system. In the world economy, external, universal demands for food and oil fuel create an internal inflationary resonance. Increased flow of money is offset by unchecked inflation, and the economy remains flat. When that happens, the Fed is faced with the no-win condition of *stagflation*: it must attempt to increase the flow of dollars into the economy and see inflation skyrocket disproportionately against economic growth, or restrain spending to control inflation, forcing Americans to see their cumulative wealth dissipate.

11. What roles do the highlighted sentences play in the passage?

    (A) The first sentence establishes the author's primary argument, and the second sentence is a detail supporting the argument.
    (B) The first sentence identifies the two subjects of the passage, and the second sentence describes a point of comparison.
    (C) The first sentence states a premise, and the second sentence supplies a criticism of that premise.
    (D) The first sentence defines the primary idea of the passage, and the second sentence states the secondary idea.
    (E) The first sentence provides a definition for the subject of the passage, and the second sentence is an example of the subject.

Questions 12 and 13 are based on the following passage.

After a successful digital grassroots movement resulted in a hosting appearance by accomplished actress Betty White on the sketch comedy show *Saturday Night Live* (or *SNL*), a second movement appeared to get the revered stateswoman of comedy Carol Burnett to host an episode as well. If successful, it would mark an ironic full circle for the show that imagined itself in the 1970s as a counteragent to the supposedly hackneyed antics of Burnett's own successful sketch comedy show. As *SNL* embarked on a path toward the irreverent humor that continues today, the accessible and sentimental *Carol Burnett Show*, which ended every evening with Burnett giving a gentle tug on her ear in symbolic reverence to her grandmother, had already cultivated an audience with an intimate familiarity and genuine appreciation for the unassuming comedienne. Should such a convergence of these shows finally come to pass, will the current show's stars, whose fan bases combined are probably eclipsed by Burnett's own, encourage the show business legend to engage completely in their particular populist stylings? Or will the show that once denounced Burnett's style be willing at last to give a wink, nod, and ear tug to Burnett's highly regarded comedic sensibilities?

12. Select the sentence that most strongly suggests that *The Carol Burnett Show* had been on television prior to *Saturday Night Live*.

13. Which of the following would be the most appropriate title for the passage?

    (A) "The Demise and Return of Classic Comedy"
    (B) "Saturday Night Success"
    (C) "Burnett and *SNL*—Together at Last?"
    (D) "The Internet Brings Back a Laughing Legend"
    (E) "Carol Burnett: The Mother of Sketch Comedy"

Question 14 is based on the following passage.

For the past year, a network television talk-show host has been making fun of the name of a particular brand of chainsaw, the Tree Toppler. The ridicule is obviously taking its toll: in the past 12 months, sales of the Tree Toppler have declined by 15 percent, while the sales of other chainsaws have increased.

14. Which of the following, if true, casts the most serious doubt on the conclusion drawn above?

    (A) The talk-show host who is ridiculing the Tree Toppler name actually owns a Tree Toppler.
    (B) The number of product complaints from owners of the Tree Toppler has not increased in the past year.
    (C) The average price of all chainsaws has increased by 10 percent in the past year.
    (D) The number of stores that sell the Tree Toppler has remained steady for the past year.
    (E) A year ago, a leading consumer magazine rated the Tree Toppler as "intolerably unsafe."

Question 15 is based on the following passage.

With the rise of community file-sharing programs that facilitated the easy distribution of data, which initially were used almost exclusively to disseminate music, artists and recording companies faced the possibility of a massive decrease in album sales. While record labels were unified in calling for swift legal crackdowns against file sharing, artists themselves were divided. No one was excited about the prospect of losing royalties, yet a few musicians imagined that the circumstances might lead to a return of the "bardic tradition," in which a musician's living was made through live performances. With large increases in the number of people with access to an artist's music, it was hoped that a potentially larger fan base would translate into better attended shows and concerts. Talented musicians or acts with entertaining showmanship would thrive while contrived or manufactured music groups would disappear, improving the overall quality of music. To date, that imagined future has failed to appear, in part due to rising ticket costs.

Consider each of the following choices separately and select all that apply.

15. Which of the following statements is suggested by the passage?

[A] Regardless of the ultimate impact of file sharing on the music industry, two certainties will be a decrease in album sales for musicians and an increase in concert tours.

[B] A subset of musicians would prefer to make their living as touring performers.

[C] A musician's profits from concert tours are usually greater than that from record sales.

Question 16 is based on the following passage.

Between 1997 and 2002, the incidence of peanut allergies in young children doubled, according to studies by medical allergists. The sharp rise in peanut and other food allergies in adolescents led scientists and doctors to look for possible causes and contributing factors. One idea gaining support is the "hygiene hypothesis," which suggests that the human immune system requires contact with a wide range of environmental pathogens in order to strengthen itself. In a home environment that is kept largely sterile, particularly through the use of antibacterial soaps and sprays, the body does not learn to recognize and later combat some harmful viruses and bacteria. The absence of germs to fight, some theorize, leads the immune system to begin focusing on other, more innocuous substances such as peanuts, milk, and eggs. As a result of the overly clean environment, the developing autoimmune reaction becomes too sensitive to other organisms. Unfortunately, even if there is sufficient evidence to support the hygiene hypothesis, the benefits of that knowledge are mixed. Few people would want to resort to introducing germs, avoiding vaccines, or purposely living less sanitary lives in hopes of preventing a mere possibility of food allergies.

16. In the passage, what purpose do the highlighted sentences serve?

(A) The first sentence states the main idea of the paragraph, and the second sentence states the secondary idea.

(B) The first sentence states a counterargument to the author's argument, and the second sentence provides a supporting detail.

(C) The first sentence identifies a problem, and the second sentence argues a solution.

(D) The first sentence introduces the main idea of the paragraph, and the second sentence is a supporting statement for the conclusion.

(E) The first sentence is the primary argument, and the second sentence is a secondary argument.

Questions 17 and 18 are based on the following passage.

It is possible for a product to become a victim of its own success. When a product is so new, so innovative, or so well marketed that it dominates the marketplace and the mindset of the consumer, it can be easy to associate the product's brand name with the product itself. When a type of product is nearly universally known or referred to by the brand name of one version of the product, the brand name becomes a victim of "genericism." Aspirin (acetylsalicylic acid), the escalator (moving stair), and the pogo stick (hopping toy) are all former brand names whose success and popularity led to such general and widespread use of the name that the inventors or parent companies were unable to maintain their trademark protections and even lost their competitive advantage against similar products described with the term that had once been a definitive brand name. All it takes is one court ruling for a term that has shifted away from its identity as a trusted brand name to become forever identified as a generic product. When this happens, a company is likely to lose a profitable beachhead within the consumer consciousness. Therefore, companies are highly motivated to use lawsuits and advertisements to dissuade others from making product identifications, such as a permutation of the original brand name, that even passingly resemble their trademarks.

The loss of revenue due to a shift to genericism is compounded by the large amounts of money companies may spend in an attempt to keep it from happening. Despite spending millions of dollars in legal and public relations campaigns, the company Kimberly-Clark has been fighting an uphill battle to keep people from referring to all forms of tissues as *Kleenex*. Google has laid heavy pressure on dictionary publishers that include the term *googled* to define the word as a Web search using the Google search engine instead of any Web search. The risk for a company facing a genericized trademark is not only the loss of a profitable brand's trademark but also the sense of superiority that comes with that brand name. Once, people seeking to keep their coffee hot or milk cold for hours would only depend on a Thermos brand vacuum flask. Unfortunately, the product was so successful and in such high demand that the other companies' vacuum flasks became colloquially known as Thermoses as well. The term became so general that any such product is usually identified as a *thermos*, and the Thermos company lost U.S. protections for the trademark. Now, instead of spending to protect its brand name, the company that first created the product, Thermos, LLC, spends its marketing dollars to make sure that, when people "Google" the term *thermos*, pages for their company's stores and products are the first to appear.

17. According to the above passage, which of these statements is NOT true:

    (A) Only one company can refer to its product as "aspirin."
    (B) Kimberly-Clark would prefer that people refer to its product as "Kleenex brand tissues."
    (C) Companies that lose U.S. protection of their trademarks also stand to lose money on the brands associated with those trademarks.
    (D) Genericism is a by-product of a company's successful positioning of a product so that it assumes a place of dominance with the general public.
    (E) Americans' awareness of the distinction between a product and its brand name is key to preventing a trademark from becoming genericized.

18. Select the sentence in the passage that identifies what ultimately is required for a trademark to become fully "genericized."

Question 19 is based on the following passage.

Thousands who suffer heart attacks each year die before reaching a hospital or clinic where they can benefit from the drugs that dissolve clots found in coronary arteries. The Food and Drug Administration recently approved a new blood clot dissolving agent, which a spokesman claimed could save the lives of many people who would otherwise join this group of heart attack victims.

19. Which of the following statements, if true, would most weaken the argument above?

    (A) The new agent must be administered by a team of doctors in a hospital or clinic setting.
    (B) Many heart attack victims die unnecessarily even though they reach a hospital or clinic in time.
    (C) The new agent can be effectively administered prior to the victim's arrival at a hospital or clinic.
    (D) The Food and Drug Administration has already approved agents that are at least as effective as the new drug in dissolving blood clots.
    (E) The new blood clot dissolving agent causes kidney damage and irregular heart rates in some patients.

Advanced

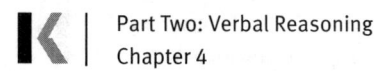

Questions 20 and 21 are based on the following passage.

With computer access for work, education, and personal use reaching near universal saturation, and with many people logging time on more than one networked machine, a vast array of online computers are operated by largely untrained users. These operators' lack of network security awareness presents a large opportunity for hackers and cybercriminals to gain access to sensitive business and personal data. Ironically, it is not these users' computing inexperience that represents the vulnerability. A very small percentage of malicious computer attacks are caused by a "traditional" external attack. Instead of kicking in the door, so to speak, the perpetrators usually convince computer users to open it for them. Through targeted links and ads from dubious websites or fake emails to anonymous contacts made through instant messaging services or social networking sites, cybercriminals rely on people's trusting nature to provide them with the means to infect or gain access to the victims' computers. In some cases, creative criminals will even initiate their attack in the real world, placing advertisements or fake parking tickets on cars that ask the owners to visit a website for more information. The website usually contains invasive software that users then download to their computers.

Consider each of the following choices separately and select all that apply.

20. According to the passage, which of the following are means that the passage suggests cybercriminals can use to illegitimately access another's computer?

- [A] Engage in an external attack over a network
- [B] Get users to click on a link contained in a deceitful email
- [C] Use a seemingly innocuous object to get a person to voluntarily visit a specifically created attack site

21. With which of the following sentences would the author most likely agree?

- (A) Since nearly everyone uses computers, the sheer number of computers in use makes the odds of any one computer being hacked too low to merit concern about security.
- (B) One way to combat cybercrime is to become more suspicious of anonymous requests or messages sent over social networks.
- (C) In order to prevent illegal access to data, only trained personnel should be allowed to use computers.
- (D) If a cybercriminal is unable to trick users into giving access to their machines, the criminal will likely attack the users' machines directly.
- (E) In order to protect their computers, people should refrain from using instant messaging services and social networks.

Questions 22 and 23 are based on the following passage.

One of the strategic principles for success in the stock market is to refrain from having knee-jerk reactions to possibly deceptive fluctuations in the market's or a particular stock's performance. Before reinvesting in a rapidly falling stock, analysts and investors will often wait for the passing of one or more small upward bumps, referred to as "dead cat bounces." The term reflects the somewhat crude idea that even a dead cat will bounce if it falls from a great height. Upticks in a plummeting stock can be caused by short selling, triggered sell-offs, or overly optimistic reactions to changes made by the company, such as replacing an unpopular CEO. Such a small, unimpressive rise is usually followed by another drop-off that surpasses the previous low. While almost exclusively related to the stock market, the term has found occasional use in describing other areas of misleading improvement. Poll numbers for a candidate losing ground near an election sometimes make a brief, illusory surge. In sports, losing teams that make midseason coaching changes sometimes experience a mild surge of energy that translates to one or more wins before the team reverts to form.

22. According to the passage, each of the following is TRUE of a "dead cat bounce" EXCEPT:

    Ⓐ It occurs when a stock shows a small improvement followed by a much greater decline in performance.
    Ⓑ It only occurs in instances where performance is already showing a rapid decline.
    Ⓒ It provides a good opportunity to sell stock at the peak of the "dead cat bounce" before the stock plummets even further.
    Ⓓ It is a term that primarily exists to explain a regularly occurring feature of the stock market.
    Ⓔ It is capable of occurring multiple times within the same stock's downward collapse before the stock's improvement becomes sustainable.

23. Select the sentence in the passage that demonstrates the traditional investment strategy in regard to a stock experiencing or expected to experience a "dead cat bounce."

Questions 24–26 are based on the following passage.

The barely edible rarity known as *casu marzu* is a cheese so dangerous that it has been illegal to sell, serve, or in some cases even possess in its native Italy. And yet, it is one of the most sought-after dishes for weddings there. What starts out as a firm hunk of cheese made from sheep's milk is soaked in brine, smoked, and left in a cellar to age. The step that infringes European food and hygiene laws comes next, when holes are drilled into the cheese so that cheese flies and fly larvae can be inserted into the center of the cheese. The flies are then free to spawn thousands upon thousands of maggots that consume, digest, and expel a fermented cheese by-product. The result is an extremely runny and flowing substance that, live maggots and all, is spread over dry bread or crackers and consumed. In fact, the Italians who produce and eat the cheese today, and do so with the same delight and confidence that their ancestors did hundreds of years ago, insist that the maggots must be alive within the cheese. If they are not, they warn, the cheese has clearly ripened too much and become too toxic for consumption.

This makes the maggots a considerable factor in preparing the cheese. The agile and nimble creatures are said to jump as high as six inches from the cheese with considerable precision, often targeting a potential new host's eyes. They are also quite hardy and, if not thoroughly masticated during eating, might survive passage through the stomach and live on as an internal parasite. As if the danger of fly larvae taking up residence in one's intestines isn't troublesome enough, the liquid excretions from the cheese are capable of burning the skin, eyes, and tongue. Even the cheese itself, properly formed, can cause a burning, itching skin irritation that can last for a week after eating.

All of these gastronomic hazards, some of which can be lethal, belie the fact that the cheese is still a considerable black market item, consumed in sizable amounts in the Sardinia region of Italy, but very little by even the most curious outsiders who must ask why people, particularly people in celebration, would subject themselves to such a concoction. The answer for this, as with many other seemingly unpalatable foods such as raw fish eggs and ground cockroach eaten in other parts of the world, is that the dish has traditionally been seen as an aphrodisiac, thus making it sought after not just for the aforementioned weddings, but also for the bachelor parties that precede them.

24. Based on the preceding passage, with which of the following statements would the author most likely agree?

    Ⓐ Despite the process *casu marzu* goes through in order to be formed, the end product must taste delicious, or else people would not make it.

    Ⓑ Some people are willing to eat foods with potential health risks based on traditional claims about those foods.

    Ⓒ The popularity of *casu marzu* in Sardinia suggests that the laws regarding food and hygiene making the food illegal are not enforced there.

    Ⓓ Long-standing traditions, such as *casu marzu*, should, based on their cultural importance, be given some degree of exemption from legal regulation.

    Ⓔ *Casu marzu*'s continued popularity as a wedding food probably means that claims regarding its effects have a basis in fact.

25. Select the sentence that best explains the violations that have resulted in *casu marzu* being unavailable through traditional outlets.

Consider each of the following choices separately and select all that apply.

26. According to the passage, which of the following are potential health effects of eating *casu marzu*?

[A] Larval parasitic infection caused by live maggots passing through the stomach into the intestines
[B] Mild intoxication caused by the fermentation process of the cheese
[C] Caustic burns to the surface of the tongue caused by the liquid issued by the cheese

Question 27 is based on the following passage.

Archaeologists found the ruins of a Mayan city they named X near the site of another Mayan city that is known to have been destroyed by a major earthquake in 950 c.e. The archaeologists hypothesized that the same earthquake destroyed both cities.

27. All of the following, if true, would strengthen the archaeologists' hypothesis EXCEPT:

(A) The Mayans built all of their cities primarily of masonry, which provides little stability in case of earth tremors.
(B) Records of another society that came to control the region in approximately 1000 c.e. contain no records of either city.
(C) City X does not lie on a fault line, as the neighboring city does.
(D) Archaeologists found no inscriptions written after 950 c.e. in city X, but many written before that date.
(E) The pattern of collapsed buildings in city X is consistent with earthquake damage in other cities destroyed by earthquake.

Question 28 is based on the following passage.

A study of children's television-watching habits by the federal Department of Education found that children aged 7–10 who watched more than 25 hours of television per week performed worse in school than children of the same age who watched fewer than 25 hours of television per week. Therefore, parents of children aged 7–10 should prohibit their children from watching more than 25 hours of television per week.

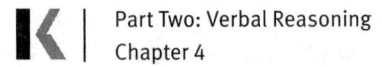

28. Which of the following, if true, would best strengthen the argument above?

Ⓐ A separate study, by a renowned graduate school of education, found that when parents prohibited their children from watching any television, the children's reading scores increased rapidly and significantly, and stayed high indefinitely.

Ⓑ Children who watched more than 25 hours of television per week also performed worse on measures of physical fitness than children who watched fewer than 25 hours per week.

Ⓒ The television shows that children aged 7–10 are most likely to watch are saturated with advertisements for products, such as toys and candy, of little educational value.

Ⓓ The Department of Education study gave appropriate weight to children of backgrounds representative of children nationwide.

Ⓔ Children who develop a habit of extensive television watching are more likely than others to maintain that habit as an adult.

Questions 29 and 30 are based on the following passage.

Decompression sickness, colloquially known as "the bends," occurs when inert gas bubbles are formed and expelled from organic tissue during rapid ascent following an extended period of prolonged intensive atmospheric pressure. This is most commonly experienced during deepwater dives. Surface divers capable of descending to sufficient depth, or scuba divers using air tanks, supersaturate their lungs with air, which diffuses throughout the body. When a diver remains at high pressure for a sufficiently long time, nitrogen, a gas present in the air and breathed into the body, is driven into the muscle tissue in elevated amounts and subsequently released again as pressure subsides. When pressure on the body decreases as the diver nears the surface, the diver must take care to rise gradually and expel excess gas through the mouth, nose, and ears. Without these pressure balances, the gas bubbles that form in the tissue can disrupt the joints and organs. In mild cases, the diver suffers from painful sensations in the knees, elbows, hips, and shoulders. In extreme cases, the bubbles can impede or rupture blood vessels in the brain or spine, which can lead to paralysis or even death.

29. Select the sentence that identifies the preventative process for circumventing decompression sickness during the conclusion of a deepwater dive.

Consider each of the following choices separately and select all that apply.

30. Which of the following must have occurred in order to initiate a case of decompression sickness in a diver according to the passage?

    [A] The person suffering decompression sickness must have experienced a decrease in atmospheric pressure.
    [B] A supply of nitrogen sufficient to form high levels of gas bubbles must be present in the muscle tissue of the person suffering decompression sickness.
    [C] The person suffering decompression sickness must have used a breathing apparatus, such as a scuba tank that supplies air to a diver.

READING COMPREHENSION PRACTICE SET ANSWER KEY

1. C
2. *"According to Kakalios, a compact planet with extreme gravity could produce a being who, as a result of adaptation to environmental factors, would have superhuman strength in Earth's lesser gravity."*
3. B, C
4. B
5. *"The shape-shifting creature's conscious selection from among multiple forms is an exceptionally rare trait among animals, and one that adds a wrinkle to the more commonly expressed forms of singularly limited camouflage seen in nature."*
6. E
7. B, C
8. *"However, in realizing gender equality through the assignment of women to female roles, a layer of both added humor and dramatic challenge are removed from several of the Bard's works, including a light comedy (Twelfth Night), a dark comedy (The Merchant of Venice), and a romance (As You Like It)."*
9. *"If the laws of nature were as rigid as we want our classification system to be, famous taxonomic rebels such as the platypus would be forced, as mammals, to gestate and give birth to live young even if the risk to both parent and child were increased to the point of bringing about the end of the species."*
10. *A, B*
11. *D*
12. *"As SNL embarked on a path toward the irreverent humor that continues today, the accessible and sentimental Carol Burnett Show, which ended every evening with Burnett giving a gentle tug on her ear in symbolic reverence to her grandmother, had already cultivated an audience with an intimate familiarity and genuine appreciation for the unassuming comedienne."*
13. *C*
14. *E*
15. *B*
16. *D*
17. *A*
18. *"All it takes is one court ruling for a term that has shifted away from its identity as a trusted brand name to become forever identified as a generic product."*
19. *A*
20. *A, B, C*
21. *B*
22. *C*

23. *"Before reinvesting in a rapidly falling stock, analysts and investors will often wait for the passing of one or more small upward bumps, referred to as 'dead cat bounces.'"*
24. *B*
25. *"The step that infringes European food and hygiene laws comes next, when holes are drilled into the cheese so that cheese flies and fly larvae can be inserted into the center of the cheese."*
26. *A, C*
27. *C*
28. *D*
29. *"When pressure on the body decreases as the diver nears the surface, the diver must take care to rise gradually and expel excess gas through the mouth, nose, and ears."*
30. *A, B*

READING COMPREHENSION PRACTICE SET ANSWERS AND EXPLANATIONS

Advanced

1. C

You can quickly eliminate choices **(B)** and **(D)** because neither one of these is addressed in the text. Choice **(A)** requires slightly more attentive reading; though the passage explains why Dr. Kakalios believes a superhuman being is plausible, nothing in the passage suggests that he believes one exists on Earth. Similarly, in eliminating choice **(E)**, note that the passage states that a planet capable of producing a superman would eventually be destroyed; it does not state that such planets could not exist now, in a pre-collapse state. Choice **(C)** is easy to defend, because it makes specific comparisons between the original Superman, who could only leap and had super strength, and the modern version, who has developed greater additional powers.

2. *"According to Kakalios, a compact planet with extreme gravity could produce a being who, as a result of adaptation to environmental factors, would have superhuman strength in Earth's lesser gravity."*

Only a few sentences discuss scientific principles. Of those, the correct answer is the one that defines how a superhuman's powers could result from his home environment. The sentence immediately prior attributes Superman's powers to his "planet of origin," but is devoid of any *rationale* explaining "how" or "why" the exceptional physiology came about. The sentence following the correct one describes a scientific analysis of how the high-gravity planet would end but doesn't discuss the possibility of a superhuman being.

3. B, C

Choice **(C)** is a portion of the right answer, because the text reinforces the supposed ability of Superman to leap over a tall building, which would certainly enable him to clear a house. Choice **(A)** can comfortably be ruled out because the passage discusses a "rocket-borne infant" and distinguishes the plausible "Superman" from the character who is able to fly. There is nothing in the text to suggest that Dr. Kakalios imagines a being that could survive unaided in space. Choice **(B)**, on the other hand, is a viable option. The text states that the being Dr. Kakalios considers possible had the strength of 15 strong men. It is therefore reasonable that Superman's strength would allow him to lift much more weight than a normal man, making **(B)** a correct choice as well.

4. B

The correct answer to this question can be discerned from one key detail in the text, in which the passage explains that the performance requirements for the *Ring of the Nibelung* necessitated the construction of a newly designed opera house, and that this innovation is still in use today. With that knowledge, you know that **(B)** applies, because that is the only effect mentioned that is still in use today. You can reject **(A)** because the author explains the technical innovations that have allowed such a work to be performed on a regular basis. Choice **(C)** is incorrect because the author nowhere implies that he disapproves of the multi-night performances, and notes the logistical difficulties of a single-day performance.

5. *"The shape-shifting creature's conscious selection from among multiple forms is an exceptionally rare trait among animals, and one that adds a wrinkle to the more commonly expressed forms of singularly limited camouflage seen in nature."*

This sentence best meets the criterion of describing how the camouflage of the mimic octopus exceeds that of other creatures. The sentence asserts that the creature's ability is rare and elaborates that the mimic octopus's ability to take multiple forms is a step above that of most other camouflaging creatures, which possess only a single form of disguise.

6. E

With five-choice questions that are not specific enough for you to make a prediction, it is better to eliminate than attempt to recognize the correct answer initially. Walking down the list of choices, **(A)** doesn't stand up because no details are given concerning the nature of the mimic octopus's discovery, only its year. The most that the passage asserts regarding the mimic octopus's abilities within the scheme of evolutionary theory is that it "adds a wrinkle." The wording of choice **(B)** is too extreme to follow from the passage. As with **(A)**, choice **(C)** makes an inference without any supporting details in the passage. The passage lists three creatures that the octopus mimics and explains how it uses each of those disguises. Nothing suggests that these are the only creatures it imitates or that sight is required for the mimicking process. Choice **(D)**, which acknowledges the mimic octopus's intelligence, falls outside the scope of the passage, which gives no grounds for comparing it to that of humans. Choice **(E)** is the correct answer, not just because it is left standing after the process of elimination, but also because the passage gives us ample discussion of animal camouflage, describing it primarily as defensive. Only the mimic octopus is described as using camouflage to catch prey.

7. B, C

The aspect of gender humor specified in the text by the author involves an actor of one gender playing the role of the other gender who is then disguised in the form of the actor's original gender. Modern versions of this can be accomplished by a man playing a woman's role disguised as a man, or a woman playing a man's role disguised as a woman. These versions are the ones contained in choices **(B)** and **(C)**. Simply changing the part from its original gender, as in **(A)**, is insufficient.

8. *"However, in realizing gender equality through the assignment of women to female roles, a layer of both added humor and dramatic challenge are removed from several of the Bard's works, including a light comedy* (Twelfth Night), *a dark comedy* (The Merchant of Venice), *and a romance* (As You Like It)."

The task here is the most fundamental in all of Reading Comprehension: find the topic sentence. That sentence, initially identified by the transition "however" clearly outlines the premise of the paragraph: modern productions, which tend to assign roles to actors who are the same gender as their characters, have removed an aspect of humor that was intended in Shakespeare's time. Keep in mind that the author does not argue that such a loss is negative or positive, only that it exists. This is why the passage's initial, evaluative sentence is not correct.

9. ***"If the laws of nature were as rigid as we want our classification system to be, famous taxonomic rebels such as the platypus would be forced, as mammals, to gestate and give birth to live young even if the risk to both parent and child were increased to the point of bringing about the end of the species."***

With a four-sentence passage, your odds of getting this question right are one in four, just on a blind guess. Those odds are better than on a "one right, four wrong" multiple-choice question, but you can do better. Only two sentences—the second and the fourth—discuss mammals. The fourth describes the traits that make the platypus unlike most mammals. You can infer the standard mammalian traits from that, but the question asks for a sentence in which qualities are "explicitly" listed. The second sentence, however, states that, to fit properly within the definition of a "mammal," a creature must produce live young.

10. A, B

Reading strategically, you likely discerned the author's dual purposes. They're indicated by key words indicating her opinion and emphases. The passage centers on the limitations of the standard method of zoological classification, which the author chides for being too rigid to accommodate species that don't fall precisely within certain families. That fits choice **(A)**; the author, indeed, "indicate(s) the shortcomings" of the biological taxonomy. Choice **(C)**, on the other hand, goes too far; the author does not suggest an alternative classification system. The author illustrates her point through a discussion of the platypus. In addition to describing its category-defying traits, the author considers it a "marvel," one we're "fortunate" to experience because it's difficult to define. Attending to the author's tone enables you to discern her admiration for the platypus. That tells you to include choice **(B)** as part of the correct answer.

11. D

In Highlighted Statement questions, in which the sentences to be analyzed are pointed out, you are best served by forming a prediction for the correct answer before you consider the choices. You should look for the main idea or argument and then determine how the highlighted sentences apply. By predicting the correct answer, you're less likely to let the choices influence you into thinking a sentence does something it does not. Here, for instance, the passage is informative, not persuasive. This means that choices **(A)** and **(C)**—which use the words "argument" and "criticism" to imply that the author expresses a strong opinion on the issue—are incorrect. Even without reading the second highlighted sentence, you can dismiss choice **(B)** because the description of the first sentence, which introduces a single subject, is inaccurate. You might be able to make an argument for the first part of **(E)**, if you see the explanation of the state of a healthy U.S. economy as a definition. But the second part of choice **(E)** is derailed by the word "unfortunately" at the onset of the second highlighted sentence, which suggests not a supporting example but a separate and contrasting idea. Indeed, the second highlighted sentence contains a secondary idea that further refines the main idea. That matches the correct answer, choice **(D)**.

12. ***"As* SNL *embarked on a path toward the irreverent humor that continues today, the accessible and sentimental* Carol Burnett Show, *which ended every evening with Burnett giving a gentle tug on her ear in symbolic reverence to her grandmother, had already cultivated an audience with an intimate familiarity and genuine appreciation for the unassuming comedienne."***

It's easy to presume that the second sentence in the passage, which outlines how *SNL* planned to position itself against the *Carol Burnett Show*, would suffice for this question, but it does not assure that the two shows did not arise simultaneously or even that Burnett's show wasn't following in the footsteps but competing for an audience. Only in the third sentence (the correct answer to this question) do the combined statements of "As *SNL* embarked" and "had already cultivated an audience" guarantee us that Burnett had preceded *SNL* into the sketch comedy arena.

13. C

Titles can be difficult to judge. We've all experienced articles and stories with titles at odds with their content. For the purposes of defining a passage such as this, there are qualifiers you should keep in mind. First, the possible title cannot introduce or fixate on some element of discussion that does not appear in the text. Choice **(E)** fails on that standard; nowhere does the passage posit that Burnett invented sketch comedy. Choice **(A)** stumbles on this point as well; you're never told of a "demise" or death of any form of comedy or of any show. You can tell that Burnett's show no longer runs today, but you get no explanation of the conditions under which that occurred. A title must also be an accurate summary of the main subject or idea. Choice **(B)** is not only too bland, but too general, missing the comparison central to the passage. Choice **(D)** misses the boat by targeting an introductory detail rather than the main idea. Choice **(C)**, which most correctly identifies both the longevity and disparate comedy careers of Burnett and *Saturday Night Live* elaborated on in the passage, is the clear choice.

14. E

This question asks you to cast doubt on the author's conclusion that the talk-show host's ridicule of the Tree Toppler is damaging the chainsaw's sales. To weaken this conclusion, you want an answer choice that presents new information that goes against the stimulus—something that suggests the talk-show host *has not* had undue influence on the sales figures stated by the author.

Choice **(A)** suggests that the host might be engaging in some hypocrisy, but fails to address the Tree Toppler's sales directly, so it is incorrect. Choice **(B)**, if anything, actually *strengthens* the connection between the host's criticism and chainsaw sales, by suggesting that consumers are not otherwise dissatisfied with the Tree Toppler. Choice **(C)** may seem tempting at first, but an increase in the price of *all* chainsaws would not account for the last piece of evidence in the stimulus: Tree Toppler sales have gone down while *sales of other chainsaws have increased*. Choice **(D)** is incorrect on the same grounds as **(B)**: a "steady" level of market penetration, if anything, strengthens the argument. But choice **(E)** does what you want. If the Tree Toppler is "intolerably unsafe," then it is reasonable to assume that sales might decrease, talk-show host or no. Since choice **(E)** introduces a non-talk-show host explanation for the drop in Tree Toppler sales, it weakens the connection and is thus correct.

15. B

As always, each statement needs to be considered on its own merits, using only evidence stated in the passage. Remember that you only have to discredit one aspect of a choice to show that it's invalid. Option **(A)** has multiple parts, and none is supported by the text. Whether or not you agree that the end result of music file sharing can't be determined, the passage does not establish that either the decrease in album sales (which the music industry fears) or an increase in the number of concerts (which some musicians anticipate) has or will come to pass. Option **(B)** has merit, and is a correct answer. Indeed, the passage's main idea is that, with the onset of music file sharing, some musicians were optimistic that they could engage in and support themselves through live performance. Option **(C)**, similarly to **(A)**, has multiple undemonstrated aspects. The passage does not compare the profitability of albums and concerts, either before or after the influence of file sharing. There is no basis in the text for this claim.

16. D

The topic of this passage, introduced in the first two sentences, is food allergies and the search for a possible cause. The next sentence presents the main idea; it defines the "hygiene hypothesis" and asserts that it might explain the rise in adolescent food allergies. Once you have recognized that, you can pass over all choices that do not acknowledge that role for the first highlighted sentence, meaning **(B)**, **(C)**, and **(E)** are out. Your understanding of the passage's structure is important, because the conclusion, "Unfortunately, even if there is sufficient evidence to support the hygiene hypothesis, the benefits of that knowledge are mixed," is not one of the highlighted sentences. The final, highlighted sentence supports that conclusion. This puts choice **(A)** by the wayside and indicates **(D)** as the correct choice.

17. A

You should immediately identify choice **(A)** as correct, not because general knowledge suggests that more than one brand sells aspirin (don't bring in outside knowledge), but because the text specifically identifies aspirin as a product that lost its brand name protections in the United States. However, this choice is clear-cut only if you read the question stem properly to see that the question asks you to find the choice that is *not* true. The other four choices are defended by the text. The section detailing Kimberly-Clark's battle to retain its control over Kleenex brand tissues supports choice **(B)**, and choice **(C)** is identified in the section that states, "When [genericization] happens, a company is likely to lose a profitable beachhead within the consumer consciousness." The opening sentences state the crux of the premise of choice **(D)**. The hardest to demonstrate to be true is choice **(E)**, but the supporting details for the main idea of the passage illustrate that the key to whether or not a product reaches a state of genericization hinges on the public perception as interpreted by a court of law. Keeping the brand name separate from the product seems to be the overall key to protecting a brand.

18. *"All it takes is one court ruling for a term that has shifted away from its identity as a trusted brand name to become forever identified as a generic product."*

This can be a tricky question to answer, because an early introduction to the term "genericization" provides a cursory explanation of its cause: "When a type of product is nearly universally known or referred to by the brand name of one version of the product, the brand name becomes a victim of 'genericism.'" However, keeping in mind the Kaplan strategy of analyzing the question stem, you need to take into account that the question demands that you identify what *ultimately* is required. The shift in public consciousness regarding a brand name must, as the passage indicates, be ruled into fact by a court. That ruling, which negates U.S. trademark protections, completes the process of genericization. That makes the statement indicated at the beginning of this answer explanation the correct one.

19. A

This question asks you to weaken the argument in the stimulus. In the last sentence of the stimulus, a spokesperson says that this dissolving agent will save the lives of many people who would otherwise join "this group of heart attack victims." Which group of heart attack victims? Those who die before reaching a hospital or clinic, who are mentioned earlier in the stimulus.

To weaken the spokesperson's conclusion, you need to find an answer choice that goes against this specific argument. In other words, you want a choice that says people who would die before reaching a hospital *will not be saved* by this drug. Answer Choice **(A)** does this, and it is correct; if the new agent can't be administered outside a hospital or clinic setting, it's not going to make a shred of difference for those who die before they get there.

Choice **(B)** is outside the scope of this argument, as this argument only cares about those who die before they hit the hospital. Choice **(C)** actually *strengthens* the argument, attesting to the agent's ability to save pre-hospital patients. And choices **(D)** and **(E)** both begin suggesting reasons why this new drug might not make a difference, but there is too much uncertainty in each of them: for **(D)**, perhaps the more-effective drugs are not yet in wide usage or have some other caveat; for **(E)**, maybe the lives saved would outweigh those endangered by the side effects.

20. A, B, C

This is a tough Select One or More question. For the untrained test taker, the difficulty is compounded by the fact that, here, all three choices are correct. Remember not to assume that one of the answers must be wrong. The testmakers may write one, two, or all three of the choices to be applicable to the question stem. In this question, select any answer that lists a way in which the passage tells you a cybercriminal might attack a personal computer. The passage states that direct attack over the network, choice **(A)**, is unlikely, but still a possibility. Likewise, the passage explicitly cites "dubious websites or fake emails," choice **(B)**. The use of "advertisements or fake parking tickets" cited near the end of the passage matches choice **(C)**'s "seemingly innocuous object" reference.

21. B

This question asks for a choice with which the author would agree. Rule out the choices that are not supported in the text. Choice **(A)** contradicts the author; he states that near-universal computer use increases the security risk. You can infer that the author would agree with choice **(B)**; he cites fraudulent requests and messages from unknown sources on social networks and instant messaging systems as a significant source of cyber-vulnerability. This makes **(B)** the correct answer. In this predominantly informative paragraph, the author makes no claims that come close to either of the controversial suggestions in choices **(C)** and **(E)**. Choice **(D)** receives no support from the passage. The author says indirect attack is more common than direct attack, but doesn't state or suggest that criminals turn to direct attack when their indirect schemes fail.

22. C

This is a question that asks for the answer choice that is *not* supported by the passage. That means that the four wrong answers will contain statements you can infer from the text. A solid reading of the text gives you all you need to know about the definition and characteristics of a "dead cat bounce" in order to eliminate choices **(A)** "usually followed by another drop-off that surpasses the previous low," **(B)** "before reinvesting in a rapidly falling stock," **(D)** "occasional use in describing other areas," and **(E)** "one or more small upward bumps." Choice **(C)**, on the other hand, is out of scope and is therefore the correct answer. Nowhere in the passage does the author discuss the strategies that sellers should use to take advantage of a "dead cat bounce."

23. *"Before reinvesting in a rapidly falling stock, analysts and investors will often wait for the passing of one or more small upward bumps, referred to as 'dead cat bounces.'"*

Here, the sentence that provides the definition for a "dead cat bounce" also gives you the conventional wisdom investors use in response: wait out the deceptive event before finding a more opportune time to reinvest.

24. B

This is an open-ended Inference question. The stem doesn't direct you to a particular detail or piece of text. You know the author's high-level evaluation of *casu marzu* from your passage map and topic, scope, and purpose summaries. The author describes the food as "barely edible," cites its health risks, and tells you that the claims about its aphrodisiacal qualities are the reason for its continued popularity. Use those broad summaries to eliminate any clearly wrong answer choices. If more than one answer choice remains, use the choices to research the passage. Confirm the correct answer or eliminate the remaining incorrect choices. The author directly contradicts choice **(A)**. Eliminate it. Choice **(B)** may sound overly generic, but read it carefully. Combining the author's list of potential health hazards from eating *casu marzu* with her conclusion about the reasons for its popularity, you can conclude beyond any doubt that the author would agree with choice **(B)**. Eliminate the remaining choices. The author tells you that those seeking *casu marzu* buy it on the black market, suggesting that she would not agree with choice **(C)**. The author offers no recommendations about policies or regulations on traditional or culturally significant foods. So, choice **(D)** is out. The author tells you that *casu marzu* shares its claim as an aphrodisiac with other traditional foods, but makes no assessment of the claim's validity. Choice **(E)** can be eliminated, too.

25. *"The step that infringes European food and hygiene laws comes next, when holes are drilled into the cheese so that cheese flies and fly larvae can be inserted into the center of the cheese."*

In the passage's first sentence, you learn that *casu marzu* is illegal to make, sell, and possess. That explains why the cheese is available only on the black market. But this question asks for the sentence that best explains the violations that lead to its illegality. Only in this sentence, highlighting a step in the cheese's creation that violates regulatory standards, does the author explicitly address the reasons that the cheese runs afoul of the regulatory process.

26. A, C

The author lists many potential health risks to *casu marzu*, so you must be diligent in locating and filing them away as you research the passage. The danger of parasitic infection in the intestines is stated explicitly in the second paragraph, confirming choice **(A)** as a correct answer. The passage also points out that the liquid that comes from the cheese is capable of burning the skin, eyes, and tongue, which confirms **(C)**. Drunkenness, however, is not mentioned as an effect of the cheese. *Casu marzu* is fermented, but the author makes no mention of an intoxicant byproduct to that process. Choice **(B)**, therefore, is not a part of the answer.

27. C

In this question, we are asked to identify statements that would strengthen the archaeologists' hypothesis, which is outlined above: the same earthquake destroyed both cities in question—City X and its neighbor. However, since this is an EXCEPT question, all the answer choices that match up with the question stem and strengthen the argument will be *incorrect*. The one choice that either weakens the argument or stays neutral on the issue will be our correct answer.

It's a good idea to have a predictive framework before we go to the answer choices here. The best way to support the assertion that both cities were destroyed by the same earthquake is to outline key similarities between them, especially similarities that would predispose them to being destroyed by earthquakes, or evidence that they disappeared at the same time. So anything that makes them look more similar will be *incorrect*.

Choices **(A)**, **(B)**, **(D)**, and **(E)** all fall in line with the fact that the two cities are analogous and were both destroyed around 950 c.e. Answer Choice **(C)**, however, shares a key difference: City X is not on a fault line. Since City X's not being on a fault line would make it undoubtedly *less* likely to be destroyed by an earthquake, Answer choice **(C)** actually *weakens* the argument, making it the correct answer to this EXCEPT question.

28. D

We need to strengthen the argument in the stimulus here by finding an answer choice that goes along with the last sentence in the stimulus: children aged 7–10 shouldn't watch more than 25 hours of TV per week. Since the author uses a study as his evidence, the most likely way this argument will be strengthened is by bolstering the legitimacy of this evidence. We also want to quickly eliminate answers that are outside the scope of the issue; this will be a particularly large trap because the conclusion here is so specific.

Choice **(A)** might sound very official, but it errs on two crucial details: first, the cited study in **(A)** is about children who are *prohibited* from watching television, not just kept down to 25 hours. It also only mentions "children" as its subjects rather than the age range given by the stimulus. While this choice does toe the line of "less TV equals better grades," it does not strengthen the argument's specific conclusion and doesn't consider the original argument's evidence at all. It is incorrect. Choice **(B)** is out of scope because it ventures into measures of physical fitness rather than performance in school. It is incorrect as well. Choice **(C)** is out of scope and incorrect; it offers a possible *explanation* for why TV doesn't educate children, but avoids strengthening this author's specific argument.

Choice **(D)** is correct. If the Department of Education study—the one cited in the stimulus—was appropriately weighted and the sample was representative, then it legitimizes the author's evidence and strengthens her argument.

Choice **(E)**, while perhaps interesting in its own right, joins **(B)** and **(C)** in venturing outside the scope of scholastic achievement.

29. *"When pressure on the body decreases as the diver nears the surface, the diver must take care to rise gradually and expel excess gas through the mouth, nose, and ears."*

The phrase "the diver must . . ." indicates that this sentence gives instructions for how to avoid a case of decompression sickness.

30. A, B

The passage outlines the two things necessary for a diver to get a case of the bends: the external cause found in the rapid change in atmospheric pressure caused by a quick ascent from a deep location—that covers choice **(A)**—and the effect in the form of the nitrogen gas bubbles forming too large and too quickly, which must therefore have to be present, as choice **(B)** states, to begin with. The main detail to catch regarding **(C)** is that the author provides an exception for "surface divers capable of descending to sufficient depth," which means that a scuba tank is not a prerequisite for a diver to get the bends.

CHAPTER 5

Verbal Reasoning Practice

VERBAL REASONING PRACTICE SET 1

Directions: For each sentence, choose one word for each set of blanks. Select the word or words that best fit(s) the meaning of the sentence as a whole.

1. Despite much informed (i) _______ and a great deal of scientific interest and money invested in research on the subject, the precise nature of the relationship between sunspot cycles and the weather on Earth remains (ii) _______.

Blank (i)		Blank (ii)	
A	confusion	D	decisive
B	conjecture	E	elusive
C	evidence	F	clear

2. (i) _______ in crimes committed by juveniles has been noted in recent years. This trend has occurred despite the fact that, over the same period of time, increased attention has been (ii) _______ juvenile delinquency by law enforcement.

Blank (i)		Blank (ii)	
A	A decrease	D	given to
B	An escalation	E	withdrawn from
C	A decline	F	requested for

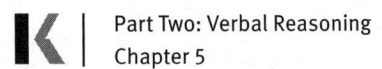

3. The Strait of Bab-el-Mandeb has earned itself the _______ "Gates of Tears" for the large number of fatal disasters that have befallen those attempting its navigation.

   (A) sobriquet
   (B) veneration
   (C) machination
   (D) syncopation
   (E) condemnation

4. Although intended as only a white lie to avoid conflict, the _______, when discovered, stirred the same resentment the original falsehood sought to avoid.

   (A) euphemism
   (B) guile
   (C) candor
   (D) sophism
   (E) mendacity

5. When the vitamin and supplement company issued the report, even the company's most (i) _______ customers questioned it, calling it (ii) _______ used to lure buyers. Within three months, the company (iii) _______ as much in a public announcement, confirming the suspicion.

Blank (i)	Blank (ii)	Blank (iii)
A devout	D a sanction	G conceded
B incredulous	E an artifice	H retaliated
C obtuse	F an enigma	I recuperated

6. While (i) _______ the public outcry for a new approach, the panel encouraged consumers to (ii) _______ current measures to stabilize the problem. These measures, the panel emphasized, had (iii) _______ unemployment in the past.

Blank (i)	Blank (ii)	Blank (iii)
A dismissing	D steadfastly support	G curtailed
B acknowledging	E vehemently oppose	H confirmed
C explicating	F carefully question	I imparted

Questions 7 and 8 are based on the following passage.

The psychoactive herb salvia has garnered a great deal of attention for its use among adolescents. Thousands of online videos have sprung up of teenagers filming their hallucinogenic experiences. Most of this footage is uninspired: it shows the subjects losing focus for approximately seven to ten minutes, followed by enthusiastic claims regarding the transformative experience they underwent. These videos serve to compound parents' fear of neurological damage with the more real horrors of compromised personal privacy, documentation of potentially illegal activities, and a seemingly open invitation to online predators.

7. The author would most likely agree with which of the following sentences?

   Ⓐ salvia is a highly dangerous and addictive substance that causes neurological damage.
   Ⓑ An important protection for our young people is to regulate herbal substances such as salvia.
   Ⓒ Online video sites should require people posting videos of themselves using salvia to prove they are 18 or older.
   Ⓓ People who post salvia videos should be more explicit about the hallucinations they experienced when they come out of the high.
   Ⓔ The videos of teenagers using salvia exemplify multiple concerns faced by today's parents.

Consider each of the following choices separately and select all that apply.

8. Which of the following statements is suggested by the passage?

   [A] The effects of smoking salvia are short-lived, but intense.
   [B] Posting a public video of oneself engaging in the use of mind-altering substances is a cry for help.
   [C] Young people who expose their private drug use could open themselves to being targeted by pushers of more dangerous drugs.

Questions 9 is based on the following passage.

According to recent research, during the final days of planet formation but before planets had fully formed, planetesimals, which were itinerant objects as large as Pluto, may have collided with Earth, Mars, and the moon. It is hypothesized that they deposited siderophiles (elements such as gold, platinum, and palladium) into Earth's crust. Siderophiles are typically drawn to iron, which forms much of the inner core of Earth. Logically, during planet formation, most of these elements would have been drawn into the center of Earth; however, their abundance in Earth's crust has long perplexed scientists. These collisions may also have caused Earth's axis to tilt by 10 degrees and deposited water on the moon.

9. Based on the information in the passage, which of the following best describes planetesimals?

   (A) Free-roaming proto-planets
   (B) Planets that collided with Earth and bounced out of the galaxy
   (C) Objects embedded in Earth's crust
   (D) Highly magnetic bodies that helped form planets
   (E) Large rocks composed of siderophiles

Question 10 is based on the following passage.

Attempts to blame the mayor's policies for the growing inequality of wages are misguided. The sharp growth in the gap in earnings between college and high school graduates in this city during the past decade resulted from overall technological trends that favored the skills of more educated workers. The mayor's response to this problem cannot be criticized, as it would hardly be reasonable to expect him to attempt to slow the forces of technology.

10. Which of the following, if true, casts the most serious doubt on the conclusion drawn in the last sentence in the passage?

   (A) The mayor could have initiated policies that would have made it easier for less-educated workers to receive the education necessary for better-paying jobs.
   (B) Rather than cutting the education budget, the mayor could have increased the amount of staff and funding devoted to locating employment for graduating high school seniors.
   (C) The mayor could have attempted to generate more demand for products from industries that paid high blue-collar wages.
   (D) Instead of reducing the tax rate on the wealthiest earners, the mayor could have ensured that they shouldered a greater share of the total tax burden.
   (E) The mayor could have attempted to protect the earnings of city workers by instituting policies designed to reduce competition from foreign industries.

Directions: Select the <u>two</u> answer choices that, when inserted into the sentence, fit the meaning of the sentence as a whole <u>and</u> yield complete sentences that are similar in meaning.

11. She was _______ spender, as evidenced by her life of luxury, which included a collection of fine wines and jewelry from around the world.

    [A] an exorbitant
    [B] an expedient
    [C] an erratic
    [D] a lavish
    [E] a penitent
    [F] a desultory

12. Although the candidate was warned repeatedly by his campaign staff that he had a congenial public image to uphold, he continued to release _______ campaign ads.

    [A] polemical
    [B] hackneyed
    [C] amiable
    [D] riveting
    [E] gripping
    [F] contentious

13. American consumers responded to a surge in the economy with an increase in spending, countering last year's trend toward _______.

    [A] ambiguity
    [B] parsimony
    [C] benevolence
    [D] opulence
    [E] abundance
    [F] frugality

14. The defendant, charged with conspiring to defraud investors, steered clear of the public eye; nonetheless, the press _______ each day outside the courthouse, hoping to stop him for an interview.

    [A] skulked
    [B] disseminated
    [C] amassed
    [D] languished
    [E] convened
    [F] dispersed

Question 15 is based on the following passage.

The Stone of Scone, originally a Scottish coronation stone, had been held in Westminster Abbey in London from 1296 until Christmas Day 1950, when a quartet of Scottish university students and nationalists liberated the stone. After first hiding it in England, they smuggled it past English roadblocks and brought the stone back to Scotland. The British government initiated a hunt but was unable to locate the stone until its presence at a Scottish Abbey was made known over a year later. The stone was promptly taken back to London, but Scottish protests eventually triumphed, and in 1996 the stone was moved to Scotland. However, despite its position as a national treasure of Scotland, the English consider it to be on loan and expect the Scots to return it when needed for English coronations.

15. Based on the passage's content, what is the author's opinion of the ownership of the Stone of Scone?

    (A) It is the rightful property of England.
    (B) It is the rightful property of Scotland.
    (C) Both countries are part of the British Empire, and therefore it belongs to both.
    (D) Both countries have used it for coronations, and therefore it belongs to both.
    (E) Both countries have legitimate claims, and therefore it is unclear.

Question 16 is based on the following passage.

The word *atom* is derived from the Greek *atomos*, meaning "uncuttable," and was popularized by Democritus as a fundamental, indivisible building block of natural matter around the turn of the fourth century b.c.e. Although other philosophers across the world developed similar theories, it was not until the turn of the 19th century that the existence of atoms was definitively proved by science. However, at the turn of the 20th century, J.J. Thompson demonstrated the existence of subatomic particles, and these were in turn found to be reducible into elementary (or fundamental) particles. These discoveries, dividing what was previously considered indivisible, have revolutionized physics and spawned a number of subfields. In 2010, the Large Hadron Collider (a hadron being a type of subatomic particle) gained international attention for creating the highest-energy man-made particle collisions. It is the hope of particle physicists that experiments using the collider will be able to shed light on a number of fundamental questions about the laws of nature.

16. Which of the following statements is NOT supported by the passage?

    (A) The theory of atoms was proposed long before it was proved.
    (B) The hadron is not the smallest type of particle.
    (C) Students of particle physics hope to answer questions about the laws of nature.
    (D) The atom was first discovered by Democritus.
    (E) The theory of atoms was proposed by multiple philosophers.

Questions 17–20 are based on the following passage.

Cinematic renditions of historic pieces of literature provide an informative glimpse into the cultural and social context in which the films were made. Shakespeare's *Henry V* is a prime example, as it has been in circulation within the English-speaking world for over 400 years and has been reinterpreted in a number of different milieus. Since the source material has not changed, the way in which different artists and directors treat the play indicates not only the predispositions of the interpreter, but also the prevailing social and political views of the audience. This is acutely noticeable in a play like *Henry V,* which is highly charged with nationalistic concerns.

The play was written during the reign of Elizabeth I, when English national identity (and the modern English language) had begun to crystallize and the language and culture we know today approached their present form. It is a historical biography of King Henry V of England, who waged a bloody campaign during The Hundred Years War with the aim of conquering France. The introduction of the play features an adviser to the King explaining, in a confusing and nearly incomprehensible fashion, the justification for Henry's claim to the French throne. The text of the play itself has been interpreted as being ambiguous in its treatment of Henry's character. Henry has a number of rousing, heroic speeches, but he is also shown to be coldly unmerciful, as in the case of his refusal to pardon petty thieves.

Shakespeare's play has been adapted in two famous film versions. The first, directed by Laurence Olivier, was made during the Second World War, immediately before the invasion of Normandy was launched in 1944. Critics of the film have emphasized the pageantry, bravado, and nationalistic undertones of this version. The battle scenes in the film are understated and tame, with little of the carnage that would be expected of a medieval melee. They are shot in beautiful weather, and the actors are clad in radiant colors. The scene with Henry's harsh justice is omitted. The film was funded, in part, by the British government and is widely understood to have been intended as a propaganda film, made in anticipation of D-day. The second version, directed by Kenneth Branagh, was made in 1989, only a few years after the Falklands War, and was much harsher in tone. The battle scenes are gory and are shot in gray, dismal weather. The actors wear muddy, blood-smeared costumes reflective of the period. The scene with Henry's harsh justice is included.

17. The primary purpose of this passage is to

(A) describe Shakespeare's *Henry V*.
(B) denounce the intrusion of government involvement with the arts.
(C) describe cinematic interpretation of literature.
(D) teach the reader about cinematic versions of theater.
(E) explain the effect of contemporary situations upon interpretation of literature.

Consider each of the following choices separately and select all that apply.

18. The author would most likely agree with which of the following?

[A] Original works of art are more reflective of their societal contexts than are cinematic adaptations of such works.
[B] Contemporary events influence the adaptation of historical source material.
[C] War is likely to produce good cinema.

19. Which of the following most accurately describes the relationship between the highlighted sentences?

    (A) The first is an example of an argument; the second is a counterexample.
    (B) The first is a synthesis of disparate ideas; the second is one of the components of that synthesis.
    (C) The first is the topic of the passage; the second is an argument in support of it.
    (D) The first presents an assertion; the second provides an example to support that assertion.
    (E) The first is a thesis; the second is the antithesis.

20. It can be inferred that the author

    (A) regards texts as being open to interpretation.
    (B) prefers the Olivier version.
    (C) dislikes Henry.
    (D) prefers Branagh's version.
    (E) believes directors should remain as faithful to the original as possible.

VERBAL REASONING PRACTICE SET 1 ANSWER KEY

1. B, E
2. B, D
3. A
4. E
5. A, E, G
6. B, D, G
7. E
8. A
9. A
10. A
11. A, D
12. A, F
13. B, F
14. C, E
15. B
16. D
17. E
18. B
19. D
20. A

VERBAL REASONING PRACTICE SET 1 ANSWERS AND EXPLANATIONS

1. B, E

"Despite" is a road sign that tells you there will be a contrast between the first blank, which is described as "informed," and the description of the state of our knowledge of the sunspot cycle. You can predict that, even if the topic had "much informed *discussion*," the relationship might still "remain *unclear*." Now move on to the answer choices. Choice **(B)** *conjecture* is a good match for *discussion*, but if you didn't see that right away, you could have eliminated the wrong answers. It doesn't make sense to talk about "informed *confusion*," choice **(A)** or "informed *evidence*," choice **(C)**, so **(B)** is the best choice here. For the second blank, the best match for your prediction is choice **(E)** *elusive*. Both choices **(D)** *decisive* and **(F)** *clear* are the opposite of your prediction. Now, plug your choices back into the sentence: "Despite much informed *conjecture*, . . . the relationship between sunspot cycles and the weather on Earth remains *elusive*." That makes sense and is the correct answer.

2. B, D

The detour road sign "despite" in the middle of the sentence helps you to figure this one out. You know that something has happened "despite" increased attention to the issue. Start with the second blank. Predict *shown to* or *paid to*. Since you would expect that, with increased attention, there would be fewer crimes committed by juveniles, predict *an increase* for the first blank. For the second blank, choice **(D)** *given to* matches your prediction. Choice **(E)** *withdrawn from* is the opposite of your prediction, and you wouldn't expect any results from attention that was just **(F)** *requested for* a problem. For the first blank, choice **(B)** *escalation* matches your prediction. Choices **(A)** *decrease* and **(C)** *decline* are the opposite of your prediction. The resulting sentence is logical: "*An escalation* in crimes committed by juveniles has been noted in recent years. This trend has occurred despite the fact that, over the same period of time, increased attention has been *given to* juvenile delinquency by law enforcement."

3. A

Reading through the sentence, you can see that "Gates of Tears" is a *nickname* or *title* given to the strait; that's sufficient to predict the right answer. Choice **(A)** *sobriquet* means just that—a given name or title. Choice **(B)** *veneration*, meaning "reverence," **(C)** *machination*, meaning "scheme," and **(D)** *syncopation*, meaning "metronomic irregularity," are all words unrelated to the sentence. Choice **(E)** *condemnation* might be tempting because of the negative sense of the name "Gates of Tears"; however, the name itself is not a condemnation, so you should also reject **(E)**.

4. E

This sentence contains two synonyms for the correct answer: *lie* and *falsehood*. Based on them, you can eliminate wrong answers. Choice **(A)** *euphemism* is a word or phrase used to replace a more offensive word or phrase of the same meaning. While euphemisms are intended to avoid offensive expression, they aren't lies or falsehoods. Reject **(A)**. Choice **(B)** *guile* means "cleverness" or "wit," with a connotation of being sly or deceitful. Although this choice may be tempting, it is not a direct synonym for "falsehood." Choice

(C) *candor* means "frank truth." This is the opposite of what the correct answer must mean. Choice **(D)** *sophism* is a deceptively incorrect argument, one that appears true or appealing, masking a falsehood. Again, there may be some similarities, but you are looking for a word that simply means "falsehood," which choice **(E)** *mendacity* does; that is the correct answer.

5. A, E, G

The signal word "even" suggests a contrast. What type of customers would you *not* expect to question a company's actions? Choice **(A)** *devout* is often used in a religious context. It means "dedicated," and it is the strongest choice. Choice **(B)** *incredulous* means "skeptical," the opposite of what you want, though *obtuse*, **(C)**, meaning "dim-witted," seems plausible. If you can't choose between *devout* and *obtuse*, fill in the second blank first. Customers would likely question a company's motives if they suspect dishonesty. Choice **(E)** *artifice*, or "ploy," is the only word that works here. If you weren't sure of *artifice*, think of the word *artificial*, which brings to mind something fake. Neither **(D)** *sanction*, which means "authorization," nor **(F)** *enigma*, which means "puzzle" or "mystery," makes sense. You can now see that *devout* is the only choice that fits the first blank. An obtuse customer is not likely to detect an artifice. The sentence ends with a key phrase: "confirming the suspicion." The correct answer for the third blank describes an action taken by the company that would produce that result. Choice **(G)** *conceded* does just that. Choice **(H)** *retaliated* means "got revenge," and **(I)** *recuperated* means "recovered." Neither makes sense in context.

6. B, D, G

The detour road sign "While" at the beginning of the sentence tells you that the first two blanks will produce opposing phrases. The best combination of choices is **(B)** *acknowledging* the public outcry for a new approach and to **(D)** *steadfastly support* current measures. Choice **(C)** *explicating*, meaning "explaining," doesn't make sense; the panel reacts to public outcry rather than explaining it. Choice **(A)** *dismissing* may seem plausible, but it doesn't logically follow a contrast signal in a sentence in which the panel encourages continued support for the current measure. Likewise, in the second blank, neither choice **(E)** *vehemently oppose* nor **(F)** *carefully question* fits the logic of the sentence's construction. Follow the logic of the sentence to fill the last blank. The panel must believe that the current measures have had a positive effect. Only choice **(G)** *curtailed* fits, and it is correct. Choices **(H)** *confirmed* and **(I)** *imparted* suggest—awkwardly—that the measures have caused unemployment.

7. E

In this Inference question, you are asked to identify the statement that follows from the author's point of view as it's expressed in the passage. The author offers two opinionated statements. He finds the video footage "uninspired" and states that it "serve(s) to compound" parental fears. One of those two statements will be paraphrased in the correct answer. The claim in **(A)** is not actually made in the passage. The author suggests that parents may fear possible neurological damage from salvia but suggests that the other "horrors" are "more real," undermining this statement. Choices **(B)** and **(C)** both go beyond the scope of the passage; the author stops short of recommending solutions for the salvia problem. You can also dismiss choice **(D)** because, although the author does intimate that the videos are rather dull, there is no evidence that the author wants more detail about the experience. Choice **(E)** matches your prediction. It is strongly suggested in the passage's final sentence and therefore is the correct answer.

8. A

Here is another Inference question, this time with the potential for multiple correct answers. You can infer choice **(A)** because the text states that the "spaced out" part only lasts a few minutes but that the experience is intense enough that young people describe it in great detail. There is no evidence for choice **(B)**; the author doesn't opine on the psychological state of salvia users. Choice **(C)** is not suggested by the passage; "online predators," not "drug pushers," are cited as the threat, and salvia is not compared to other drugs.

9. A

Though it is not explicitly stated in the passage, you can, from a few clues, determine that a planetesimal was (1) an object that moved—a sort of wandering body—since they are described as "itinerant," and (2) an object that existed during "planet formation." Choice **(A)** follows from those two inferences and is correct. There is no support for choice **(B)**; the passage makes no mention of objects leaving or bouncing out of the galaxy. You can eliminate choice **(C)** because the passage tells you that components of the planetesimals (the siderophiles) remained in Earth's crust after impact but doesn't say that whole planetesimals did so. Choice **(D)** is beyond the scope of the passage, which doesn't contain information about planetesimals' magnetic characteristics. You can also cross off **(E)** because the passage doesn't describe planetesimals as "rocks," nor does it claim that they are always made up of (or necessarily even contain) siderophiles.

10. A

When asked to cast doubt on a conclusion, as you are here, first locate the author's conclusion. Then, find an answer choice that contradicts it in some way. This question stem explicitly directs you to the last sentence of the passage, where the author is defending the mayor from criticism, asserting that the growing inequality of wages is beyond his control. Since the passage is saying, "This isn't the mayor's fault," predict a correct answer that says, "No, this *is* the mayor's fault."

Choice **(A)** should stand out immediately as going against the passage. If the mayor *could* have initiated policies that would have educated those who are now earning less, then his policies—to be precise, his policy of inaction—*is* at least partially to blame for the problem of wage inequality. This is exactly the sort of additional evidence you want, and choice **(A)** is correct.

The wrong choices largely focus on misleading shifts in terminology from the passage. Choice **(B)** sidesteps the wage issue, as more employment of high school graduates would not necessarily raise their wages. Choice **(C)**'s logic requires that we assume "blue-collar" equals "less-educated," which is too large a shift in terminology. Choice **(D)** only discusses taxes and avoids wages altogether. Choice **(E)** only mentions protection of "city workers," again avoiding the education issue from the passage.

11. A, D

Focus on the straight-ahead road sign "as," which alerts you that the sentence will continue in the same direction. How would you describe a person who spends money on a collection of fine wines? Choice **(A)** *exorbitant* means "excessive" and fits the context. See if you can find a similar word. Choice **(B)** *expedient* looks similar to *expedite*, a word you have likely seen. It means "practical" or "efficient." That might or might not describe the wine connoisseur, and it certainly doesn't match *exorbitant*. Eliminate it. Choice **(C)** *erratic* and choice **(F)** *desultory* are synonyms meaning "inconsistent or unfocused." That doesn't describe a person who collects fine wines. Rule out both of these choices. Choice **(D)** *lavish* means "done in excess"; that matches *exorbitant*, and is the second correct answer. The sentence describes the wine and jewelry collection in a way that suggests excessive spending. Choice **(E)** *penitent* may remind you of the word *repent*. Both words describe regret or remorse, which doesn't make sense in context. That leaves you with choices **(A)** and **(D)**, which create equivalent sentences.

12. A, F

"Although" serves as a detour road sign, indicating a contrast between the desired public image and the ads. The correct answers will mean the opposite of "congenial," which means "agreeable." A word similar to "controversial" would be a good prediction. Choice **(A)** *polemical* means "argumentative." This word fits your prediction and the context of the sentence. Something that is *hackneyed*, choice **(B)**, lacks originality. The ads might be unoriginal, but that wouldn't contrast with "congenial." Choice **(C)** *amiable* means "friendly" and is the opposite of what you need. Choices **(D)** *riveting* and **(E)** *gripping* both mean "fascinating," and while the ads may in fact be fascinating, whether they are or not has no bearing on how controversial they are. Choice **(F)** *contentious* is a perfect match for *polemical* and is the second correct answer.

13. B, F

The word "countering" is a clue that the increase in spending is different from "last year's trend." Predict the correct answers to mean "saving" or "being economical." Choice **(A)** *ambiguity* means "uncertainty." This word does not logically fit the context of the sentence. Choice **(B)** *parsimony* means "thrift" or "frugality." This makes sense in context and is a correct answer. Choice **(C)** *benevolence* means "kindness" or "generosity." This doesn't describe people who are spending little money. Choice **(D)** *opulence* and **(E)** *abundance* describe an excess, the opposite of what you are looking for. Choice **(F)** *frugality* means economical. This forms the correct synonym pair along with choice **(B)**.

14. C, E

Rearrange and simplify this sentence to make it easier to see the contrast. Try this paraphrase: "The defendant avoided the public, yet the press sought him daily, hoping to interview him." Look for words that suggest what a group of people trying to get somebody's attention would do. Choice **(A)** *skulked* means "moved secretly." The press might do this when trying to catch off-guard someone who is avoiding an interview, but there's no second choice that gives the sentence the same meaning. Choices **(B)** *disseminated* and **(F)** *dispersed* are similar, containing the same prefix *dis–*. Since this prefix means "apart," you can deduce that these two choices are incorrect. In fact, you need two words that mean the opposite of "came apart." Choice **(C)** *amassed* means "gathered." Note that it contains the word *mass*; knowing the root, you can guess the meaning closely enough to pick this as a correct answer. Choice **(D)** *languished* means "weaken," which doesn't make sense in context. Choice **(E)** *convened* means "came together" or "assembled." This is synonymous with *amassed* and is the other correct answer. This question really brings home the power of word roots. *Con–* means "together," and *–vene* comes from the root VEN meaning "to come or move toward."

15. B

The author uses several terms that indicate her point of view in the passage. Although this is not an argumentative passage, the tone clearly supports choice **(B)**. Words such as "liberated" (indicating the stone was being held unfairly) and phrases such as "national treasure of Scotland" indicate that the author believes the stone to be rightfully Scottish. Choice **(A)** is the opposite of the author's opinion, while choices **(C)**, **(D)**, and **(E)** are simply unsupported in the text.

16. D

The correct answer to this question is *not* supported in the passage, meaning it either contradicts the passage or falls outside the scope. The four wrong answers *are* supported. The first two sentences of the passage describe the origin of the theory of atoms prior to their scientific discovery, which allows you to eliminate choice **(A)**; furthermore, the author mentions that "philosophers across the world developed similar theories," which supports—and thus eliminates—choice **(E)**. However, the author describes Democritus as having "popularized" the theory of atoms, which is not the same as first discovering the atom; based on this, choice **(D)** is correct. Choices **(B)** and **(C)** both relate to the discussion of subatomic particles, but because elementary particles are smaller than subatomic particles (an example of the latter being the hadron), you may eliminate **(B)**. The conclusion of the passage rules out choice **(C)** in the description of the importance of experiments using the Large Hadron Collider.

17. E

The correct answer to a primary purpose question summarizes what the author is trying to do in the passage. Here, the author uses cinematic depictions of *Henry V* to illustrate how contemporary culture influences the interpretation of art. Choice **(A)** misses the point; the author uses Shakespeare's *Henry V* as an illustration, not for the purpose of describing the play itself. **(B)** distorts the author's purpose, which is to illustrate the cultural influence, not to judge which influences are positive or negative. **(C)** is too broad; the passage isn't about cinematic interpretations of literature writ large. **(D)** is too general in the same way as choice **(C)**. So, choice **(E)** is the correct answer. It cites the effect of contemporary situations on the interpretation of literature, striking at the heart of what the author explores in the passage.

18. B

Questions of this type have three options, but any or all of them could be correct. You can't stop when you come across one correct answer. Evaluate the choices in light of this author's scope and purpose. Choice **(A)** makes an irrelevant comparison. The author discusses the influence of historical and societal context on both Shakespeare's play and the later film adaptations of it but never implies that one is more reflective of its societal context than the other. Choice **(B)** is correct; this paraphrases the author's primary purpose, so he's certain to agree with it. Choice **(C)** is incorrect. The author makes no effort to argue about what makes *good* cinema, only what influences it when it's involved in interpreting classic literary works.

19. D

Questions of this type reward you for understanding the logic of a passage. In this case, the first highlighted sentence is an assertion that lays out the topic and scope of the passage. The second highlighted sentence is a specific example that the author offers to illustrate his main point. Choice **(D)**, the correct answer, hits this prediction squarely. Choice **(A)** is incorrect because the second sentence does not contradict the first. You can reject **(B)** as it mischaracterizes the first sentence; there is nothing disparate about its components. You can reject **(C)** because it gets the second sentence wrong; the second sentence is an example, not an argument (which would need a conclusion supported by evidence). Choice **(E)** distorts the relationship between the two sentences; the second doesn't contradict the first.

20. A

This is another question that asks you to put yourself in the author's shoes and try to reason from his perspective. The tone of the passage is neutral; even when describing Henry's darker moments, the author passes no judgment. You can therefore reject choice **(C)**, as the author is not doing a character study. Though choices **(B)** and **(D)** are mutually exclusive, they are both incorrect. The author states no preference for either of the film versions he describes. Choice **(E)** is incorrect because the author states no preference for cinematic versions that maintain greater fidelity to the source material. Choice **(A)** is correct; it matches the author's purpose for the passage. In order for cultural events to influence the interpretation of classic literature, such literature must be interpretable.

Diagnostic Tool

Tally up your score and write your results in the space provided.

Total

Total Correct: ________ out of 20 correct

Percentage Correct: # you got right × 100 ÷ 20: ________

By Question Type

Text Completion ________ out of 6 correct

Sentence Equivalence ________ out of 4 correct

Reading Comprehension ________ out of 10 correct

DIAGNOSE YOUR RESULTS

Look back at the questions you got wrong and think about your experience answering them.

VERBAL REASONING PRACTICE SET 2

Directions: For each sentence, choose one word for each set of blanks. Select the word or words that best fit(s) the meaning of the sentence as a whole.

1. Many felt the rules for the scholarship competition had been unfairly administered to the applicant pool and that, furthermore, the judges were ________.

   (A) biased
   (B) adequate
   (C) inept
   (D) impartial
   (E) objective

2. We will face the idea of old age with ________ as long as we believe that it invariably brings poverty, isolation, and illness.

   (A) regret
   (B) apprehension
   (C) enlightenment
   (D) veneration
   (E) reverence

3. Usually an articulate speaker, as he had given many public addresses over the years, the doctor (i) ________ the keynote speech at the oncology convention. It was clear from their expressions that the audience members were overcome with (ii) ________ by the end.

Blank (i)	Blank (ii)
A flubbed	D rapture
B perfected	E repulsion
C rescinded	F bewilderment

4. The author's agent approached the contract signing with (i) ________, as she knew full well the reputation of the publisher. The author, finally recognized after years of rejection, was more (ii) ________ by the event.

Blank (i)	
A	incertitude
B	hubris
C	cordiality

Blank (ii)	
D	enraptured
E	humiliated
F	mortified

5. The hikers were eager to summit Mount Everest and (i) ________ warnings about the dangerous storm approaching the camp. It was only when disaster struck that the (ii) ________ of the situation took hold. By this time, however, the descent was (iii) ________, and the survivors fought for their lives.

Blank (i)	
A	recollected
B	scrutinized
C	flouted

Blank (ii)	
D	gravity
E	hypocrisy
F	prestige

Blank (iii)	
G	galvanizing
H	fortuitous
I	baleful

6. The fact that Mark Twain gave orders for his memoir to remain unpublished for 100 years reflects the author's (i) ________ about its contents. Indeed, releasing his more (ii) ________ observations about the world during his own time would have spurred a public response, one that Twain must have foreseen as (iii) ________.

Blank (i)	
A	trepidation
B	buoyancy
C	insouciance

Blank (ii)	
D	quixotic
E	utopian
F	vitriolic

Blank (iii)	
G	enigmatic
H	detrimental
I	salubrious

Questions 7 and 8 are based on the following passage.

Pancreatic beta cells are responsible within a body for monitoring homeostatic cues from a wide variety of hormonal inputs and in turn regulate the insulin needed to maintain balance in the blood sugar. Researchers studying this signaling system have located three key proteins that relay signals. Understanding how these proteins function within the context of the signaling system can help scientists gain more insight into how diabetes compromises the healthy functioning of the system and how to counteract the impact of diabetes once it is identified.

7. The passage implies which of the following about diabetes research?

    Ⓐ When scientists fully understand how these key proteins work, rates of Type II diabetes will be greatly reduced.
    Ⓑ Researchers hope to understand the signaling system of pancreatic beta cells in order to replicate an artificial system.
    Ⓒ Without a complete understanding of these key proteins, diabetes research is at a standstill.
    Ⓓ Future medications for diabetes may include or simulate some of the hormonal cues that pancreatic beta cells monitor.
    Ⓔ One way researchers hope to fight diabetes is by stopping the relay signal system in the pancreas by cutting off the proteins.

8. According to the passage, each of the following is true EXCEPT:

    Ⓐ The pancreas helps a body to maintain homeostasis.
    Ⓑ Diabetes controls the functioning of pancreatic beta cells.
    Ⓒ When the pancreas is stimulated, it releases varying amounts of insulin that help to balance blood sugar.
    Ⓓ Pancreatic beta cells must interpret a wide array of hormonal information.
    Ⓔ Blood sugar can be controlled by insulin.

Question 9 is based on the following passage.

Named after the notorious confidence trickster Charles Ponzi (though not originated by him), the term "Ponzi scheme" describes a particular type of fraud in which individual investors are promised extremely high returns, which are then paid either out of their own money or the money of other investors, creating the appearance of an extremely profitable investment. The entire scheme relies on encouraging investors to donate large amounts of money long-term by offering them the enticement of impossibly high short-term returns. As time progresses, investors who have been paid returns contribute even more money, and new investors are drawn into the scheme. New payments are used to pay off new investors. Excess money is then kept as profit for the creator of the fraud, rather than to create any tangible profits for the investment itself.

9. According to the passage, which is necessary for a Ponzi scheme to be successful?

(A) Investors should be tempted into long-term investment by large initial returns.
(B) The investment plan should demonstrate sustainability over the long term.
(C) The percentage of the investment's profits going to the creator of the scam should be concealed.
(D) There should be no paper trails of the fraud.
(E) The culpability for the fraud should be shared among the confidence trickster and investors.

Question 10 is based on the following passage.

Hay-on-Wye is a small town in Wales, just over the border from England. While once a relatively unknown town, the town rose to fame in the second half of the 20th century as a literary hot spot. Influenced by Richard Booth's opening of a secondhand bookshop in a converted fire station, a number of other entrepreneurs followed suit, until the tiny town held over 30 used bookshops; by the 1970s, it became known around the world as the "Town of Books." Aided by Booth's publicity efforts, Hay-on-Wye was turned from a sleepy market town with fewer than 2,000 inhabitants to a thriving tourist destination. The town now boasts half a million tourists per year and hosts a popular annual literary festival. Booth himself was inducted into the Order of the British Empire for his efforts to encourage tourism.

10. Which of the following is the primary purpose of the passage?

(A) To argue for the importance of secondhand bookshops
(B) To describe the life of Richard Booth
(C) To explain the development of Hay-on-Wye as a literary center
(D) To highlight Richard Booth's publicity efforts to encourage tourism
(E) To depict the town of Hay-on-Wye

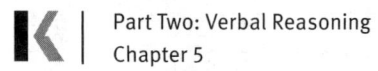

Directions: Select the <u>two</u> answer choices that, when inserted into the sentence, fit the meaning of the sentence as a whole <u>and</u> yield complete sentences that are similar in meaning.

11. The fashion designer's silk scarf wasn't popular initially; the public found it gaudy until a model discovered the accessory and ______ it.

A vilipended
B disavowed
C engendered
D indulged
E championed
F espoused

12. One of the most commonly perpetuated myths about Einstein is that he failed math; on the contrary, he excelled at the subject, developing ______ it at a young age.

A a predilection for
B an enmity toward
C an acquiescence to
D an antipathy toward
E a penchant for
F a reminiscence about

13. The pundits agreed that the speech was both deeply profound and ______ in its delivery, and it was well received by audiences.

A pellucid
B affable
C militant
D asinine
E perspicuous
F magisterial

14. The two boxers battled toe-to-toe until the final round, when the longtime champion of the ring was finally _______ by his young opponent's stamina.

   [A] exiled
   [B] thwarted
   [C] decimated
   [D] galvanized
   [E] annihilated
   [F] stymied

Questions 15–17 are based on the following passage.

Characterized as half zebra and half horse, the quagga sounds like a mythical creature, but at one time, it was a very real animal. Only 150 years ago, a great number of quaggas were found in South Africa. Unlike the common zebra, which has black and white stripes that cover its entire body, the quagga has yellow-brown stripes only on its head, neck, and forebody, which gave it its half-horse facade. Its unique appearance caused early explorers to think the quagga was a separate species from the common zebra when it was discovered around 1760, but DNA analysis later revealed that the animal is a subspecies of the zebra. In the 100 years following its discovery, the quagga population diminished. It was frequently hunted for its meat and hide, and settlers who considered the animal a competitor for the grazing of their livestock also callously killed the quagga in great numbers. By 1870, the quagga was no longer found in the wild. The last captive quagga died in 1880 in an Amsterdam zoo. Today, the quagga is categorized as an extinct animal, but researchers in Africa hope to resurrect the native subspecies through genetic modification and selective breeding.

Select only one answer choice.

15. What does the author designate as the primary reason for the quagga going extinct?

   (A) DNA analysis revealed that the quagga was susceptible to diseases brought by domesticated animals.
   (B) The quagga did not have enough grazing land.
   (C) The quagga was unable to survive in captivity.
   (D) Settlers eliminated the species through hunting and extermination.
   (E) The quagga did not breed as successfully as the common zebra.

16. With which of the following statements would the author of the passage most likely agree?

    Ⓐ The zebra is a type of quagga.
    Ⓑ Researchers hope to restore the quagga using scientific technology.
    Ⓒ Settlers humanely killed quaggas in an effort to protect their livestock.
    Ⓓ Shortly after the quagga was discovered, its population grew.
    Ⓔ Settlers saw the quagga as a competitor for the prey of their livestock.

Consider each of the following choices separately and select all that apply.

17. Based on the information in the passage, which conclusion can be drawn?

    [A] If it were not for the human influence, the quagga would be a surviving species.
    [B] DNA analysis can help humans better understand the origins of certain species.
    [C] The extinction of species should not be a concern as scientists are able to bring back extinct species through genetic modification.

Questions 18–20 are based on the following passage.

According to a recent survey from the National Institute for Drug Abuse, more U.S. adolescents smoke marijuana than cigarettes. The organization's annual survey revealed an increase in marijuana use among all teen groups and a slight decrease in tobacco use among high-school seniors compared to past years. Federal officials speculate that teens are starting to listen to the warnings about the risks of tobacco use but are receiving mixed messages about the safety of marijuana use. While antidrug organizations such as Drug-Free America maintain their message that marijuana impairs judgment and hampers brain development, clinical studies support the medicinal benefits of marijuana, particularly for those suffering from certain cancers and Crohn's disease. These studies have sparked a national debate about the legalization of marijuana. More than a dozen states and the District of Columbia have legalized the use of medical marijuana, and there is a push for the nationwide legalization of the drug. The White House Office of National Drug Control Policy asserts that the message that marijuana use is okay for some is dangerous. The office insists that both policy makers and the general public should be aware of the effect the debate over the legalization of marijuana has on teens' perception of the drug's risk.

Select only one answer choice.

18. The passage implies which of the following about teen drug use?

    (A) The Office of National Drug Control is concerned about teen tobacco use.
    (B) Marijuana has many health benefits for teens.
    (C) Teens are aware of health risks associated with smoking.
    (D) Drug-Free America suspects that teen marijuana use will continue to rise.
    (E) Teens support legislation to legalize marijuana.

19. The passage predicts which of the following would follow the legalization of marijuana?

    (A) It may increase the use of illegal street drugs.
    (B) It may decrease the frequency of teen tobacco use.
    (C) It may cause teens to believe that marijuana use is harmless.
    (D) It may change antidrug organizations' stance on the drug's use.
    (E) It may increase the safety of the drug's use.

20. According to the passage, what is the "mixed message" that teens are receiving about marijuana?

    (A) Its use is acceptable for individuals older than age 18, but not for individuals younger than age 18.
    (B) It has legitimate health benefits for the ill, but it has serious health risks.
    (C) Its use is acceptable in some states, but not acceptable in other states.
    (D) It is safer to use than tobacco, but it is still an unsafe drug.
    (E) Its use is approved by the government, but not by teens' parents.

VERBAL REASONING PRACTICE SET 2 ANSWER KEY

1. A
2. B
3. A, F
4. A, D
5. C, D, I
6. A, F, H
7. D
8. B
9. A
10. C
11. E, F
12. A, E
13. A, E
14. B, F
15. D
16. B
17. B
18. C
19. C
20. B

VERBAL REASONING PRACTICE SET 2 ANSWERS AND EXPLANATIONS

1. A

Here, "furthermore" indicates that the charge of the word in the blank will be consistent with "unfair." Choice **(A)** *biased* is a good synonym for "unfair," and is the correct answer. Choices **(B)**, **(D)**, and **(E)** all list traits one would want in judges. Choice **(C)** *inept* provides a negative trait, but one that challenges the judges' competence, not their fairness.

2. B

First, read the sentence through, noting any structural road signs and/or key words. Here, "as long as" is a structural clue: we view old age in the same way we do poverty, isolation, and illness. Predict that the correct answer matches a word like *fear* or *despair.* Choice **(B)** *apprehension* is a good match. Check the other answers, to confirm that each is incorrect. Choice **(A)** *regret* is tempting, but it applies to something that has already happened, not what you will face in the future. Choice **(C)** *enlightenment* doesn't match the sentence's list of negative conditions. Choices **(D)** *veneration* and **(E)** *reverence* both mean "great respect"; that's a positive way to face old age, but not one that matches the way one would face something likely to bring "poverty, isolation, and illness." That confirms that **(B)** is the right answer. Now, plug the answer into the sentence: "We will face the idea of old age with *apprehension* as long as we believe that it invariably brings poverty, isolation, and illness." This certainly makes sense.

3. A, F

Consider the logic of the sentences before approaching the first blank. It might be tempting to choose a positive word, but the structure and tone suggest a contrast from the "usual." It might help to put the word *while* in front of *usually.* The only word that suggests the opposite of "articulate speaker" is choice **(A)** *flubbed*, which means "to make a mess of." Choice **(B)** *perfected* means "made no errors" and choice **(C)** *rescind* means "took back." These words don't fit the context of the clause. How might an audience subjected to a flubbed speech feel? You can rule out choice **(D)** *rapture* since it means "extreme joy." That leaves choice **(E)** *repulsion* or "disgust" and choice **(F)** *bewilderment* or "deep confusion." Consider the shades of meaning here: the audience is not likely to respond with an emotion as strong as disgust, especially if the doctor is normally a great speaker. *Bewilderment* is correct.

4. A, D

You can infer that the author must be "happy" to be published after years of rejection, so start with the second blank. The correct answer is choice **(D)** *enraptured*, which means "full of delight." It wouldn't make sense for the author to feel **(E)** *humiliated* or **(F)** *mortified*; she's finally received some recognition, after all. Now for the first blank. The word "more" functions as a subtle detour road sign in this sentence. The author is "more" happy than the agent, so predict something like "skepticism" on the part of the agent. Only choice **(A)** *incertitude*, which means "uncertainty," fits this context. Choices **(B)** *hubris* and **(C)** *cordiality*, meaning "pride" and "friendliness," respectively, are too positive to work.

5. C, D, I

The words "and," "only," and "however" are road signs that help you determine the direction of each sentence and choose the appropriate missing words. Overly eager hikers are unlikely to heed warnings, and choice **(C)** *flouted,* which means "defied" or "ignored," captures this relationship best. Neither choice **(A)** *recollected* nor **(B)** *scrutinized,* both of which suggest examining an issue, fits the context. The second blank will contain a word consistent with one's attitude after a disaster. Choice **(E)** *hypocrisy* refers to insincerity; that might describe the hikers (who'd just flouted the warnings), but not the situation they now find themselves in. Choice **(F)** *prestige*, meaning "status" or "consideration," is inappropriate to the context as well. Only choice **(D)** *gravity*, or "seriousness," makes sense here. While the descent may have been **(G)** *galvanizing*, or "exciting," on some level, it was in the context of a dire situation, so keep looking for a better choice. Choice **(H)** *fortuitous* means "lucky." (If you didn't know its definition, notice that it shares the root of "fortune.") You can infer that it doesn't fit logically in the paragraph. Something **(I)** *baleful* appears threatening, or even deadly; this is the correct answer.

6. A, F, H

To complete this sentence, look for key words or phrases that give hints about the context. For instance, "gave orders" in the first sentence indicates a strong feeling, perhaps a concern, so try to find a term that plays off this sentiment. Only choice **(A)** *trepidation*, which means "unease," supports the first sentence. Choice **(B)** *buoyancy* means "quick to recover" (think of the buoy floating in the ocean) and **(C)** *insouciance* means "lightheartedness." Both words suggest unconcern, the opposite of how Twain must have felt when ordering his memoirs to remain sealed for a century. The word in the second blank must describe writing that the author wants to keep private for a long time after his death. Choices **(D)** *quixotic* and **(E)** *utopian* have a similar meaning—"idealistic"—and neither fits the context. Choice **(F)** *vitriolic*, meaning "acidic" or "corrosive," is the best fit. For the third blank, you need a negative word. Choice **(G)** *enigmatic*, or "mysterious," doesn't make sense. Choice **(H)** *detrimental* means "damaging." That is the right answer. Finally, choice **(I)** *salubrious* means "health-promoting," which is too positive and does not fit the context.

7. D

The correct answer follows from the passage, though it may not be stated explicitly. Choice **(A)** is not implied. Although researchers probably hope to stem the occurrence of diabetes, the passage speaks only of combating the disease's impact. There is also no suggestion in the passage of the hope, expressed in choice **(B)**, of creating an artificial system. Choice **(C)** is too extreme. The passage doesn't imply a "standstill" absent "complete" understanding of the proteins. The wording in choice **(D)** is dense, but it's also broad enough to follow from the passage. Researchers may well use their understanding of the hormonal cues monitored by the proteins to develop the treatments mentioned in the final sentence of the passage. Indeed, **(D)** is the correct response. Finally, **(E)** runs counter to the passage. The researchers hope to understand how to help the relay system work, not how to cut it off. You can eliminate **(E)** confidently.

8. B

The four wrong answers to this Detail question are found in the passage. The correct answer will either contradict or distort the passage, or fall outside its scope altogether. Choice **(A)** is true; it is stated in the first sentence of the passage. Choice **(B)** seems like it might be true, but reading carefully, it overstates the role of diabetes as described in the passage: diabetes compromises or impairs the ability of the pancreatic beta cells to function, but you're not told that it *controls* those functions. Choice **(C)** is true and is also stated in the passage's first sentence. Choice **(D)** paraphrases the first main claim of the passage. Choice **(E)** comes from the end of the first sentence.

9. A

The correct answer to this Detail question must paraphrase something stated explicitly in the passage. Choice **(A)** restates the author's definition of Ponzi schemes: the use of short-term payoffs to attract long-term investments. That's the correct answer. Choice **(D)** is incorrect because the passage mentions nothing about paper trails; likewise, it does not address who should share the culpability, ruling out choice **(E)**. Choice **(C)** is initially tempting, but be careful; the final sentence of the passage explicitly states that the investment does not create any real profits, so **(C)**'s recommendations for how to divvy them up must be incorrect. Choice **(B)** is tempting because the schemes attempt to sucker investors into long-term commitments, but the schemes needn't be "sustainable" in any case.

10. C

By the time you begin to look at questions accompanying a passage, you should have already determined the scope and purpose of the passage. In this case, the author is purely expository; she just wants to relate or explain how Hay-on-Wye became known for books and literature. Choices **(A)**, **(B)**, and **(D)** are related to the passage's subject matter but don't describe the overall purpose of the passage. Choices **(C)** and **(E)** look relatively similar, and the fact that the passage is about Hay-on-Wye makes **(E)** tempting. But the passage focuses on a specific aspect of the town, rather than the town as a whole. This aspect is its rise to fame as the "Town of Books," and thus choice **(C)** is your answer.

11. E, F

In this sentence, the words "initially" and "until" function as detour signs, informing you that the idea changes. Since there is a positive change of events, search for a term with a more hopeful meaning. Even if you've never seen choice **(A)** *vilipended*, you've probably seen similar-looking words like *vile*, *revile*, and *vilify*. Given the negative connotation of these words, you can rule out *vilipend*, which means "to dismiss or treat with contempt." Choice **(B)** *disavowed* means "refused to acknowledge or accept." You can tell by the prefix *dis–* ("apart") that the word does not fit the meaning you are looking for. Choice **(C)** *engendered* means "created." Although this word has a positive slant, it doesn't make sense in context. Choices **(D)**, **(E)**, and **(F)** are all possible answers. Consider the shades of meaning and then decide which two words make the most sense. To *champion* or *espouse* means "to support," like a cause. If you *indulge* something, you don't support it as much as yield to it. Choices **(E)** and **(F)** are correct.

12. A, E

The phrase "on the contrary" is a clear turning point in this sentence. Look for a word to fill the blank that suggests a fondness or strong attraction to something. Ask yourself if you know any words that look like choice **(A)** *predilection*. It comes from the same Latin root as *diligent*, which means "attentive" or "careful." Indeed, *predilection* suggests a strong attraction to something, and this fits the meaning you're looking for. You can use a similar strategy to test choices **(B)** *enmity* and **(D)** *antipathy*, two synonyms that have a negative meaning. *Enmity* looks like it's related to the word *enemy*, and *antipathy* contains the word parts *anti–*, meaning "against," and *pathos*, meaning "feeling." Both answer choices mean "hatred," and can be ruled out. Choice **(C)** *acquiescence* means "passive acceptance." This is too soft to work in the sentence or in conjunction with *predilection*. Keep searching for a synonym for choice **(A)**. Choice **(E)** *penchant* means "a strong liking" and is the other correct answer. If you didn't know the word *penchant*, you could deduce that choice **(F)** *reminiscence*, or "fond remembrance," doesn't make sense in context. That leaves **(A)** and **(E)** as the best choices.

13. A, E

The words "both" and "and" alert you that the missing word will have a positive meaning, consonant with "deeply profound" but related to the speech's delivery. Think about what other qualities you would look for in an insightful speech. You may not have seen choice **(A)** *pellucid* before, but it is related to *lucid* and *luminous*. The shared roots, *luc* and *lum*, mean "light." *Pellucid* means "clear in expression," which bears the correct relationship to the word *profound*; you'd want an insightful speech to be clear and understandable. This seems like a strong choice. Choice **(B)** *affable* means "pleasant." This word has a positive connotation but doesn't match *pellucid* at all. Keep this word for now, but only with reservations. Choice **(C)** *militant* has a negative connotation and doesn't fit the tone of the sentence. Choice **(D)** *asinine*, which means "silly" or "stupid," is completely wrong for this sentence. Choice **(E)** *perspicuous* may be unknown to you, but it may look familiar because it comes from the same root as *perspective*. Much like *pellucid*, it means "clear," especially in expression or understanding. Since choices **(A)** and **(E)** create truly equivalent sentences, you can rule out **(B)** *affable* with certainty. You can also rule out **(F)** *magisterial*, which means "weighty" or "authoritative." While this word could describe a speech delivered in a particularly grand manner, it has no match among the other answer choices.

14. B, F

This sentence has no obvious road signs, so look for key descriptive words that might help you. The sentence describes a long, closely fought match in which the young challenger finally prevails. The correct answer is a verb that tells you what happened to the champion at the end. Choice **(A)** *exiled* means "forced out," as from one's country. This doesn't make sense in context. Choice **(B)** *thwarted* means "successfully opposed." This word accurately reflects the outcome of the match. Choices **(C)** *decimated* and **(E)** *annihilated* both mean "destroyed." Given that the two boxers fought "toe-to-toe" until the final round, it doesn't make sense to say that either one destroyed the other. Choice **(D)** *galvanized* means "stimulated." This is a tempting option (the champ could have been inspired by the challenger), but no other answer choice creates a sentence of similar meaning. You need a better fit. Choice **(F)** *stymied* is a synonym for *thwarted* and is the other correct answer.

15. D

This question asks you to identify a major point in the passage, the *primary* reason for the quagga's extinction. Research leads you to the sentence between those asserting the quagga's decline and its extinction. The quagga was hunted and "callously" exterminated by ranchers who considered it a competitor for their livestock. Choice **(A)** distorts the passage. Settlers considered the quagga a competitor with their herds, but there's nothing to suggest that the domestic species infected the wild animals. Choice **(C)** distorts the passage, which states that the last quagga died in captivity but not that the species' extinction was a result of captivity. Similarly, choice **(E)** distorts that portion of the passage stating that researchers want to revive the quagga using selective breeding of existing, related species. It does not link the quagga's extinction to its breeding habits. Choices **(B)** and **(D)** are both, in a way, related to grazing. Choice **(B)** is incorrect because it ascribes the problem to the quagga's loss of grazing habitat. You never learn that the quagga was left with an insufficient range. The quagga competed with livestock for grazing, which caused settlers to hunt the species to extinction. Choice **(D)** best reflects what the passage states as the primary reason for the quagga's extinction.

16. B

The correct answer may not be stated explicitly in the passage, but it must follow directly from something that is stated there. The passage states that the quagga is a subspecies of the zebra, not the other way around. That makes choice **(A)** incorrect. The passage also contradicts choice **(D)**; its population "diminished" after discovery. Choice **(C)**, which states that settlers "humanely" killed quaggas, contradicts the passage more subtly but just as fatally. In fact, according to the passage, settlers "callously" killed quaggas. Choice **(E)** distorts the passage. The quagga was a competitor for the pasture of settlers' livestock, not their prey. Indeed, grazing animals have no prey. Choice **(B)** is the correct answer, as the last sentence of the passage states that scientists are hoping to spark the species' return.

17. B

This question asks you to evaluate the statement and identify what conclusions you can draw using the information from the passage. Choice **(A)** overstates the passage. Humans were historically responsible for the quagga's extinction. There's no way to deduce what would have happened absent human contact. Choice **(B)** follows from the portion of the passage in which you learn that DNA analysis helped determine that the quagga is a subspecies of the zebra and not a unique species. That's enough to make the broadly worded choice **(B)** a viable conclusion. Choice **(C)** does not provide a viable answer; it assumes too much information. The passage states that researchers are trying to bring back the extinct quagga, but it doesn't say how likely these efforts are to be successful, nor does it opine on how much concern extinctions should provoke.

18. C

Examine the answer choices one at a time and choose the one that follows from the passage. Choice **(A)** states that the Office of National Drug Control is concerned about teen tobacco use. While you may assume this to be a true statement, the passage doesn't state this directly, commenting only on the office's concern about teen marijuana use. Similarly, it is reasonable to think that choice **(D)** is true, but the passage only addresses Drug-Free America's stance on the risks of marijuana, not the organization's predictions of future use. The passage mentions claimed health benefits of marijuana, but it does not imply choice **(B)**, that marijuana has health benefits for teens. Choice **(C)** is the correct answer. The passage states that officials believe teens to be acting, in part, in response to anti-tobacco warnings. Choice **(E)** may seem reasonable because the passage makes implications about teen perception of the risks of marijuana, but it contains no statements about teens' feelings on the issue of legalization.

19. C

This question asks you to evaluate the possible connections and compare them to the information in the passage. Choice **(A)** seems possible, but the passage contains no information about drug use beyond marijuana and tobacco. Choice **(B)** makes a reference to information about tobacco use, but it distorts the passage, which states that teen tobacco use is down because teens seem to understand the risk of smoking, not because marijuana has been legalized in some states. Choice **(C)** is the most viable choice. The passage states that research on the medical uses of marijuana and the decision to legalize medical marijuana in some states contribute to the message that marijuana is not harmful. Choice **(D)** addresses antidrug organizations' message on marijuana use. This is not a viable choice because the passage states that antidrug organizations maintain their message that marijuana is harmful and gives you no reason to think they would change their views upon legalization. Choice **(E)** is out of scope; the passage does not give any information on how legalizing marijuana will affect the risks of the drug's use.

20. B

This question asks you to identify a detail in the passage. The "mixed message" referred to in the stem is found in the passage's fourth sentence, introduced with the contrast key word "While." That sentence outlines the contrast between antidrug messages (marijuana impairs judgment and hampers brain development) and research about possible health benefits. That matches choice **(B)** to a T. Choice **(E)** misses the scope of the passage by including a statement about the opinions of teens' parents, who aren't mentioned. Choice **(A)** brings in information about the age-appropriateness of marijuana use, another topic that isn't considered in this passage. Choice **(D)** states that marijuana use is safer than tobacco use, but the passage never makes that comparison. Choice **(C)** accurately states the inconsistent legal status of marijuana, but it doesn't answer the question. The mixed message teens receive is about the health effects—not the legality—of marijuana use.

Diagnostic Tool

Tally up your score and write your results in the space provided.

Total

Total Correct: ________ out of 20 correct

Percentage Correct: # you got right × 100 ÷ 20: ________

By Question Type

Text Completion ________ out of 6 correct

Sentence Equivalence ________ out of 4 correct

Reading Comprehension ________ out of 10 correct

Diagnose Your Results

Look back at the questions you got wrong and think about your experience answering them.

VERBAL REASONING PRACTICE SET 3

Directions: For each sentence, choose one word for each set of blanks. Select the word or words that best fit(s) the meaning of the sentence as a whole.

1. While most of the crowd was elated at the _______ promises that the politicians made, more cynical observers remained skeptical.

   (A) stolid
   (B) verbose
   (C) whimsical
   (D) extravagant
   (E) diffident

2. In mythology, rarely is a hero completely (i) _______ to any harm; even the greatest heroes have some (ii) _______ part of their body, such as Samson's hair or Achilles's heel.

Blank (i)	
A	obdurate
B	impervious
C	oblivious

Blank (ii)	
D	gullible
E	impotent
F	susceptible

3. Pedagogical studies tend to overlook students' motivation and focus instead on differences in learning styles. However, a teacher's ability to (i) _______ students' passion for a subject is paramount to students' learning. The well-intentioned efforts by (ii) _______ scholars with little teaching experience who design intricate strategies intended to (iii) _______ students' specific struggles are woefully insufficient: they cannot instill enthusiasm.

Blank (i)	
A	aggrandize
B	foster
C	enervate

Blank (ii)	
D	saprophytic
E	gregarious
F	unseasoned

Blank (iii)	
G	mitigate
H	exacerbate
I	aggravate

4. The ongoing salmon crisis is the result of (i) _______ of problems, among them pollution, introduction of nonnative species, and pesticide use. Such issues speak to decades of (ii) _______ management at the political level. At this point, (iii) _______ solution will require both an understanding of history and foresight of future challenges.

Blank (i)	Blank (ii)	Blank (iii)
A a reclamation	D methodical	G a sustainable
B a multitude	E rudimentary	H an exigent
C an exhibition	F paltry	I a conspicuous

5. Such a (i) _______ manuscript must be approached with (ii) _______. Only the most seasoned editor should be considered for the job.

Blank (i)	Blank (ii)
A poignant	D circumspection
B frivolous	E creativity
C labyrinthine	F fecundity

6. The Perito Moreno Glacier, located inside Glaciers National Park in Patagonia, houses the so-called Curve of the Sighs. This (i) _______ is earned due to the (ii) _______ view of snow-tipped mountains above and icy, slate-hued waters and the foot of the glacier below.

Blank (i)	Blank (ii)
A appellation	D bucolic
B aphorism	E calorific
C benediction	F panoramic

Question 7 is based on the following passage.

Parents of high-school students argue that poor attendance is the result of poor motivation. If students' attitudes improve, regular attendance will result. The administration, they believe, should concentrate less on making stricter attendance policies and more on increasing students' learning.

7. Which of the following, if true, would most effectively weaken the parents' argument?

   (A) Motivation to learn can be improved at home, during time spent with parents.
   (B) The degree of interest in learning that a student develops is a direct result of the amount of time he or she spends in the classroom.
   (C) Making attendance policies stricter will merely increase students' motivation to attend classes, not their interest in learning.
   (D) Showing a student how to be motivated is insufficient; the student must also accept responsibility for his or her decisions.
   (E) Unmotivated students do not perform as well in school as other students.

Questions 8–10 are based on the following passage.

The National Aeronautics and Space Administration (NASA) recently discovered a new species of bacteria that has changed our understanding of how living things survive. Deep in the waters of Mono Lake in California, NASA scientists discovered a form of bacteria that uses arsenic to make DNA and proteins. Most life forms are made from six main building blocks: carbon, hydrogen, nitrogen, oxygen, sulfur, and phosphorus. The newfound bacteria, called the *GFAJ-1* strain, can substitute arsenic for phosphorus. This discovery is remarkable because arsenic is toxic to most known organisms. What's more, the *GFAJ-1* strain can tolerate high concentrations of arsenic, and it can incorporate the chemical into its cells. Scientists suggest that this discovery has cracked open a new door to what is possible for life elsewhere in the universe, as the new *GFAJ-1* strain has shown that organisms can exist in chemical environments that scientists may not have considered.

Select only one answer choice.

8. Which of the following statements best summarizes the passage?

   Ⓐ The presence of arsenic-based bacteria proves that there is life on other planets.
   Ⓑ Scientists have discovered that arsenic is not toxic to most known organisms.
   Ⓒ The *GFAJ-1* strain is a unique type of bacteria that has changed scientists' perception of how living organisms survive.
   Ⓓ Scientists need to add a seventh element, arsenic, to the six main building blocks of life.
   Ⓔ Mono Lake is a scientific phenomenon that scientists will be studying for years.

9. According to the information in the passage, the *GFAJ-1* strain is which of the following?

   Ⓐ A water-based bacteria that has a high tolerance for toxins
   Ⓑ One of the six building blocks of life
   Ⓒ A form of arsenic that is toxic to most living organisms
   Ⓓ A strain of bacteria that incorporates arsenic into its cells
   Ⓔ A form of DNA that does not need phosphorus to grow

Consider each of the following choices separately and select all that apply.

10. Based on the information in the passage, what reasonable conclusion can be drawn?

   [A] If a species of bacteria can use arsenic in cell development, it is possible that planets that have high levels of arsenic might be able to support living organisms.
   [B] If the *GFAJ-1* strain's chemical processes do not follow the same patterns as those of other organisms, the strain must have originated on another planet.
   [C] If scientists have discovered a living organism that uses arsenic in place of one of the six building blocks of life, it is possible that there may be other chemicals in addition to arsenic that can support life.

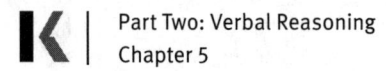

Directions: Select the <u>two</u> answer choices that, when inserted into the sentence, fit the meaning of the sentence as a whole <u>and</u> yield complete sentences that are similar in meaning.

11. After repeated attempts to resolve grievances, 500 sanitation workers went on strike; consequently, city leaders _______ measures to address the issue.

A flouted
B concerted
C contrived
D consecrated
E spurned
F levied

12. By the fifth sequel, the director had become _______ in his delivery; even the most die-hard fans of the series lost interest.

A convoluted
B cautious
C remedial
D perfunctory
E unpleasant
F mundane

13. Within a few short years, the young city council member was able to rise in the political ranks due to her _______ supporters, savvy and skillful team, and incandescent wit.

A intelligent
B ardent
C lenient
D intrepid
E zealous
F recalcitrant

14. In any economy, the success of a business is dependent on two things: the degree to which it can ______ borrowed money and its ability to withstand fluctuations in the market.

[A] invert
[B] capitalize
[C] expound
[D] conjure
[E] repudiate
[F] leverage

Questions 15 and 16 are based on the following passage.

All artists are reputed to suffer to some degree for their art, but some may physically suffer more than others. As part of *The 3rd I* project, a performance artist agreed to have a camera surgically implanted into the back of his head and the footage gathered from the experiment to be uploaded hourly into a website. The surgery involves slicing and lifting folds of skin and implanting the camera into the back of the skull and is excruciating for the artist. Some critics claim that the visceral reaction of hearing about the camera or its insertion may be orchestrated to shock viewers into learning more about the art or the project. Although the camera can be fitted with a lens cap to protect the privacy of those who request it, every single detail of the artist's life is recorded and open for all to view. One might conclude that this project is an extreme example of the Modernists' tendency to take the creation of art as its subject.

15. This passage implies which of the following about performance art?

(A) At least some performance art is Modernist in origin.
(B) Modern technology affords performance artists a wider audience for conveying political messages.
(C) Critics prefer static visual art to performance art because it typically relies less on shock value.
(D) By becoming part of the art, a performance artist can convey a powerful message within the art.
(E) Performance artists suffer more greatly than other types of artists.

Consider each of the following choices separately and select all that apply.

16. The passage implies that the power of the message of the artwork described in the passage would be substantially weakened if which of the following were to happen?

   [A] The content of the video is difficult to make out on-screen.

   [B] Most people who see the video on the website don't know how it was made.

   [C] Certain shots of the video "go viral" and become something that people across the world discuss in real time.

Questions 17 and 18 are based on the following passage.

To poets of the Modern era, 1910–1940, the Romantic verses of previous generations failed to express the chaos of industrialism and devastation of World War I. Modern poets found new influences when "The International Exhibition of Modern Art" opened at New York's Armory building in February 1913. The Armory Show, as it came to be known, exposed Americans to Modern European artists like Kandinsky, Picasso, and Munch. The show also shattered traditional notions of art and introduced techniques such as abstract cubism, in which objects are fragmented and reassembled. The public was shocked, and the press criticized the show, ridiculing one abstract painting in particular, "Nude Descending a Staircase," by Marcel Duchamp, in which a single figure is captured taking successive steps. Most Modern poets, however, loved the show. William Carlos Williams reportedly burst into laughter when he viewed Duchamp's controversial painting. Williams observed motion in an art form previously limited to still-life. He understood that words no longer had to be static. He began infusing movement into his imagery. New poetic styles sprang to life as other poets applied the techniques of visual art to poetry.

17. The main point of the passage is best stated in which of the following sentences?

   (A) Marcel Duchamp gave Modern American poets a way to express the effects of industrialism and war.

   (B) The general public and the press hated the Armory Show because the pieces did not follow conventional, traditional artistic techniques.

   (C) Using words instead of paint, Modern American poets applied the abstract and cubist techniques of Modern European visual art to poetry.

   (D) One form of art can easily influence and shape another.

   (E) William Carlos Williams was influenced by Marcel Duchamp to apply cubist techniques to his poetry.

Consider each of the following choices separately and select all that apply.

18. Which of the following conclusions is supported by the passage?

[A] Cubism was too abstract for anyone except other artists to understand.
[B] Traditional forms of artistic expression were rejected by artists in 1913.
[C] Artistic forms of expression are shaped by world events, social and political.

Questions 19 and 20 are based on the following passage.

Willa Cather (1873–1947) lived in Nebraska and set her novels *O Pioneers!* and *My Ántonia* in the state, describing the land as intricately as she would a main character. However, Nebraska might not have featured so heavily in Cather's work if she had not grown up in the Shenandoah Valley of Virginia. Until she was nine, she lived in the quaint charm of Willow Shade, her grandfather's 300-acre farm. Amid the lush, wooded vegetation, a rustic bridge covered a creek. Box hedges surrounded the house. Willow trees grew large. In 1883, following the lure of fertile farmland in the West, Cather's family left Willow Shade and crossed six states to reach a new farm in Webster County, Nebraska. The new landscape shocked Cather to the core. She felt erased by flat prairies stretching to the horizon, swallowed by the enormous sky. The stark contrast to the mountains of Virginia etched its influence onto her soul. She grew to love the new land, but never forgot the old. Perhaps that is why she identified with immigrants homesick for Czechoslovakia, Norway, and Sweden, the people she wrote about in *O Pioneers!* and *My Ántonia*. She knew how transplanted they felt.

19. Based on the information in the passage, which assumption MOST likely underlies the passage?

(A) Cather's novels would have been much different if her family had not moved to Nebraska.
(B) Cather would not have become an author if her family had not moved to Nebraska.
(C) Cather did not truly remember or value Virginia because she did not use the state as the setting of her most famous novels.
(D) It was Cather's compassion for immigrant people, rather than her passion for landscape, that inspired her novels.
(E) The shock Cather felt in Nebraska and her grief for Virginia deepened her soul and made her an artist.

20. Which best states the author's use of rhetorical structure in the passage?

(A) The passage is a comparison between the different landscapes of Virginia and Nebraska.

(B) The passage compares Willa Cather's response to the different landscapes of Virginia and Nebraska.

(C) The author compares the different landscapes of Virginia and Nebraska as a way to emphasize Willa Cather's experience when she first set eyes on Nebraska.

(D) The author describes how Willa Cather compared the different landscapes of Virginia and Nebraska when she first set eyes on Nebraska.

(E) The author compares Willa Cather's use of landscapes in her two most famous novels.

VERBAL REASONING PRACTICE SET 3 ANSWER KEY

1. D
2. B, F
3. B, F, G
4. B, F, G
5. C, D
6. A, F
7. B
8. C
9. D
10. A, C
11. B, C
12. D, F
13. B, E
14. B, F
15. A
16. B
17. C
18. C
19. A
20. C

VERBAL REASONING PRACTICE SET 3 ANSWERS AND EXPLANATIONS

1. D

The key to this question is the contrast between the "elated," or excited, crowd, and the "skeptical," or doubting, cynics. We are looking for a word that would cause the crowd to be excited, but would cast doubt among skeptics. We can immediately eliminate choice **(A)** *stolid,* "unemotional," choice **(B)** *verbose,* "talkative," and choice **(E)** *diffident,* "lacking self-confidence," as these are all negative adjectives for a political speech and would not invoke the excitement of the crowd. Choice **(C)** *whimsical,* "fanciful," seems plausible: the crowd may like a fanciful, idealistic promise, while cynics would remain doubtful of its veracity. However, choice **(D)** *extravagant* is a better choice, as it implies an attractive promise that may not be realistic.

2. B, F

Based on the context, you can assume that the blank will describe a hero's ability to be harmed, so you can predict *resistant*, or *unable*, to describe the hero's relationship to harm. Choice **(A)** *obdurate* has a meaning related to your prediction, but its connotations are more emotional than physical—it means "resistant to persuasion" or "unmoved by pity" and is therefore not appropriate in this context. Choice **(C)** *oblivious* may be tempting, but the second part of the sentence is clearly discussing actual bodily harm, not awareness of harm. Choice **(B)** *impervious* means "unable to be pierced" and is the best choice.

For the second blank, you could use the examples of Achilles's heel and Samson's hair to help you along. But whether or not you are familiar with these stories, you can use the straight-ahead road sign of the semicolon: the second part of the sentence carries the same ideas as the first. Since the first part of the sentence suggests that heroes all have some sort of flaw or problem, predict a word that means "open to harm." Choice **(D)** *gullible* refers to someone who is easily tricked. This adjective does not make sense to describe a part of the body and is therefore incorrect. Choice **(E)** *impotent* describes what might become of a hero who has been harmed, but it does not work as the predicted meaning itself. Only choice **(F)** *susceptible* carries the correct meaning, "open to harm," and is your answer.

3. B, F, G

The word "however" in the second sentence serves as a detour road sign. The author begins by saying that pedagogical studies focus primarily on learning styles rather than motivation. The word "however" indicates that she takes issue with the focus of the studies; presumably, she would like to see a greater emphasis on motivation or "students' passion." Predict something like "increase" for the first blank. That's choice **(B)** *foster,* which means "to generate" or "to encourage." Choice **(A)** *aggrandize* means "to make more important," so that does not work in this context. Choice **(C)** *enervate* means "to weaken" and is the opposite of what you want.

For the second blank, note that the scholars, while they are "well-intentioned," themselves have little teaching experience, so predict something like "inexperienced." That's choice **(F)** *unseasoned.* For the record, choice **(D)** *saprophytic* means "feeding on dead plant matter" and generally refers to bacteria or fungi. Choice **(F)** *gregarious* means "sociable" or "outgoing," and there is no context clue to indicate that the scholars have this quality.

For the third blank, predict a word that means "improve" or "alleviate" because "well-intentioned efforts" should bring a positive outcome. Choice **(G)** *mitigate* is correct as it means to "to lessen" or "to soften." Choices **(H)** *exacerbate* and **(I)** *aggravate* both mean "to worsen," so they are the opposite of what you are looking for.

4. B, F, G

Try reading the passage and filling in the blanks with words you already know. Then see which answer choices make the most sense in context. The first blank in this sentence is easiest to fill because of the examples given at the end of the sentence. Choice **(B)** *multitude* means "many" or "a great number," which makes sense given that the list that follows includes only some of the problems, as signaled by the phrase "among them." Even though this makes sense, remember to check the other choices for plausibility. Choice **(A)** *reclamation* means "reformation" and choice **(C)** *exhibition* is a public showing. Neither choice works.

Given the information in the first sentence, you need to locate a word for the second blank that implies a problem. Choice **(F)** *paltry* is the only option with a clearly negative tone, meaning "almost worthless." Choice **(D)** *methodical* means "done by routine," which doesn't fit. Choice **(E)** *rudimentary* means "basic" and suggests imperfection. However, it's not a strong enough word to meet the tone of the sentence.

A *sustainable* solution is one that will last a long time, so choice **(G)** makes the most sense in the third sentence. Choice **(H)** *exigent,* which means "requiring immediate help," suggests a meaning opposite of what you want, and choice **(I)** *conspicuous*, meaning "obvious," makes sense but is not the best fit for the context.

5. C, D

Before filling in the two blanks, you need to understand how the second sentence elaborates on the first. Think of what type of manuscript should be approached by a "seasoned editor" and how that editor should conduct his work. **(A)** *poignant* means "emotional." While this makes sense, it doesn't explain why a seasoned editor would be needed. **(B)** *frivolous* means "playful." Choice **(C)** *labyrinthine* means "intricate, complex," like a labyrinth or maze. This is the best fit.

Think about how a complex manuscript should be approached. Skip choice **(D)** *circumspection* for now, if you're unfamiliar with it. Choice **(E)** *creativity* is not quite right—look for an option suggesting attention to detail. Choice **(F)** *fecundity* means "fruitfulness," which doesn't make sense. Going back to *circumspect*, break it down to *circum–*, "around," and *spect*, "to look." *Circumspection* is thoughtfulness around a subject, a metaphorical "looking" around a problem. This is the correct answer.

6. A, F

The first blank refers to the name "Curve of the Sighs." Each of the answer choices listed could refer to the name, so you must take each singly. Choice **(A)** *appellation* means "nickname," and this is a strong choice. Choice **(B)** *aphorism* refers to a pithy phrase that gives a general truth. It is tempting but doesn't quite fit this meaning. Choice **(C)** *benediction* is a blessing, which does not makes sense here. So **(A)** is the correct choice here.

It is easier to predict the second blank because the view seen at the Curve of the Sighs is described in images just after the blank: the answer must have something to do with viewing a wide, dramatic space. Choice **(F)** *panoramic* makes sense in this blank because it means "wide in scope." This is the right answer. Choice **(D)** *bucolic* may be tempting, but it refers to an area that is fertile or where sheepherding is done—not a glacier. Choice **(E)** *calorific* has the opposite meaning: it means "producing heat."

7. B

You are asked here to weaken the parents' argument, which is outlined in the first sentence of the stimulus: parents believe that poor attendance results from poor motivation. This sets up a cause-and-effect relationship between "poor attendance" and "poor motivation," with poor motivation as the cause and poor attendance as the effect. The parents go on to elaborate on their theory and suggest a plan of action, but this cause-and-effect argument is the central issue.

Since you need to *weaken* this argument, you need to find an answer choice that contradicts or otherwise introduces doubt into this assertion. Choice **(B)** does just this by stating that "the degree of interest in learning that a student develops" (i.e., a student's motivation) is a result of "the amount of time he or she spends in the classroom" (his or her attendance). Choice **(B)** establishes a new cause-and-effect relationship with *attendance* as the cause and *motivation* as the effect. Since this reverses the causality from the initial argument, it weakens the stimulus and is the correct answer.

Wrong choices **(A)**, **(D)**, and **(E)** fail to mention both attendance and motivation and therefore sidestep the issue. Choice **(C)** does mention both concepts, but its stance of decrying strict attendance policies is right in line with the last sentence of the stimulus and would thus *strengthen* rather than weaken the argument.

8. C

This question asks you to identify the most accurate summary of the passage. Use your summary of the topic, scope, and purpose of the passage as a prediction of the correct answer. This author is writing to inform his reader about an exciting discovery: Scientists have discovered a new bacterium whose remarkable ability to use arsenic challenges assumptions about the building blocks of life. That matches the correct answer, choice **(C)**. Choice **(A)** is too extreme; the passage states that the new discovery introduces new possibilities for life in other parts of our universe, but it does not state that this discovery *proves* that there is life in other parts of our universe. Choice **(B)** contradicts the passage; the *GFAJ-1* strain is "remarkable because arsenic is toxic to most known organisms." Choice **(D)** goes too far; the new bacteria substitute arsenic for phosphorous, but that doesn't mean arsenic should be considered a new "building block." This is, at any rate, far from the passage's main point. Choice **(E)** misses the boat by focusing on the wrong subject and making a prediction that is not supported by information in the passage.

9. D

The correct answer to this question is directly stated in the passage. *GFAJ-1* is a "newfound bacteria" that can tolerate arsenic and even "incorporate the chemical into its cells." Eliminate choice **(B)** because it states that the *GFAJ-1* strain is a building block of life, not a bacteria strain that uses some of the building blocks of life as the passage suggests. Eliminate **(C)** because it states that the *GFAJ-1* strain is a form of arsenic, not a bacteria strain that is arsenic-based, as the passage suggests. Similarly, eliminate **(E)** because it states that the *GFAJ-1* strain is a form of DNA, whereas the passage suggests that it develops DNA from arsenic. Choices

(A) and **(D)** both state that the *GFAJ-1* strain is a form of bacteria. However, choice **(A)** states that it is a water-based bacteria, which is not supported by information in the passage. Choice **(D)** states that the *GFAJ-1* strain is a type of bacteria that incorporates arsenic into its cells, which (as noted above) is directly stated in the passage.

10. A, C

This question asks you to evaluate the statement and identify the conclusions you can validly draw using the information from the passage. Choice **(A)** is a reasonable conclusion because it is based on the statement in the passage that suggests that the discovery of an arsenic-based bacteria has "cracked open a new door to what is possible for life elsewhere in the universe." Choice **(B)** is not based on any information stated in the passage. The passage suggests that the discovery of this new bacteria will lead to the examination of life on other planets, but it does not suggest that the bacteria came from another planet. Choice **(C)** is a reasonable conclusion because the passage states that *GFAJ-1* has shown that "organisms can exist in chemical environments that scientists may not have considered."

11. B, C

The word "*consequently*" means "as a result." Considering the tone of the sentence, think about how city leaders might have responded. Choice **(A)** *flouted* means "disregarded." It's unlikely that city leaders disregarded the issues after such extreme measures by the workers. Look for a word that suggests a more proactive response. Choice **(B)** *concerted* and choice **(C)** *contrived* mean "devised or planned" and fit the context of the sentence. Although these are likely the correct answers, check the remaining choices just to be sure. Choice **(D)** *consecrated* means "declared sacred," which doesn't make sense and can be eliminated. Choice **(E)** *spurned* has a meaning similar to *flouted.* Like *flouted,* this is opposite to the response that is likely to have occurred. You may be familiar with choice **(F)** *levied* from historical contexts, as in "a tax was levied." The word *levied* means "collected" and doesn't make sense in context. Stick with options **(B)** and **(C)**; they are synonyms and create sentences with similar meanings.

12. D, F

Use the key phrase "lost interest" to determine the tone of the word in the blank. The semicolon separating the two clauses acts as a straight-ahead road sign. You need a negative word to describe the director's work, which has become rote or boring. Choice **(A)** *convoluted* means "intricate." Depending on the type of story, an "intricate" film might be boring or very interesting. There's not enough context to make this choice a logical certainty. **(B)** *cautious* is another choice that could go either way. A "cautious" delivery might make for a better or worse fifth film. Choice **(C)** *remedial* contains the word *remedy,* which means "cure." This does not fit the context of the sentence. Choices **(D)** *perfunctory* and **(F)** *mundane* are synonyms meaning "in a routine manner." They fit the tone of the sentence. You can also rule out choice **(E)** *unpleasant.* Even though the film may be unpleasant, the phrase "by the fifth sequel" suggests fatigue or boredom on the part of the director. Choices **(D)** and **(F)** are correct.

13. B, E

Ask yourself what kind of supporters a young politician would need in order to move up quickly in local government. Choice **(A)** *intelligent* fits in the sentence, so hold on to it for now. Choice **(B)** *ardent* means "eager, full of passion." This word is more precise in context than choice **(A)**, so see if you can find a synonym for it. Choice **(C)** *lenient* is not the best fit for the context. *Lenient* is similar to "tolerant," but it has a negative connotation, implying that a lenient person may allow people to do things they are not supposed to. *Intrepid*, choice **(D)**, means "fearless." This choice is possible as well, so we'll keep it under consideration as we move on to the final choices. Somebody who is **(F)** *recalcitrant* is stubborn and resists authority, which doesn't apply here. Choice **(E)** *zealous* is a synonym for *ardent*. Since both *ardent* and *zealous* fit the sentence and are synonyms, you can get rid of *intelligent* and *intrepid*. Even though they would fit, no other word matches either to create a sentence with the same meaning.

14. B, F

The straightforward road sign "and" means that the verb for the blank matches "ability" in the accompanying phrase. You're looking for a word that means "use" and that fits with "borrowed money." Choice **(A)** *invert* means "to put upside down or inside out," which doesn't make sense, so eliminate it. Choice **(B)** *capitalize* means "to take advantage of." This describes a business strategy and fits in context. Choice **(C)** *expound* is "to explain." A business will most likely not have to explain its borrowed money as a business strategy—unless it gets into trouble! Choice **(D)** *conjure* means "to imagine or make up." This doesn't work in context. Choice **(E)** *repudiate* means "to reject." Move on to the last choice, **(F)** *leverage*, which is the synonym you needed; like *capitalize*, it means "to take advantage of." Choices **(B)** and **(F)** are the correct answers. This is a good example of a situation where the answers are not quite synonyms, but the words affect the meaning of the sentence similarly.

15. A

The correct answer to this question will be true based on the passage. With this in mind, **(A)** is the correct answer. If this performance art project is an "example of" Modernist art, it must be the case that at least some performance art is Modernist in origin. Although choice **(B)** may be true in the real world, it is not an implication of the passage. The author says nothing about the political dimensions of the performance. Consider choice **(C)** carefully: critics do comment on this aspect of this project's shock value, but nowhere is it suggested that critics prefer visual art to performance art. This passage doesn't make any assessment of how "powerful" the piece is, so choice **(D)** is incorrect. Choice **(E)** is too vague; the artist described here may suffer more *physically*, but that doesn't translate to a generalized statement that performance artists suffer more than artists of other genres.

16. B

This Inference question asks you for any and all answers that follow from the passage. According to the critics mentioned in the passage, knowing how the art was created is potentially related to the audience's interest in it. Choice **(A)** doesn't follow from the passage. Nothing suggests that the beauty or clarity of the images produced affects the success of the project. The message is mainly reliant on the concept, not the product, of the art. Thus, choice **(B)** is correct. If the audience doesn't appreciate how the art was made, they may be less interested in it. If choice **(C)** were true, it would likely increase the popularity of the performance and get people thinking about it. This has the opposite effect called for by the question stem.

17. C

In this question, you are asked to identify the statement that expresses the main point of the passage. The author begins with large concepts and narrows the information to a single specific event and the influence it had on one person. The claim in choice **(A)** is lopsided. The author suggests that poets found new influences in art, not only that of Marcel Duchamp and not only on the subjects of war and industry. The statement in choice **(B)** is supported by the passage, but the reason why the general public reacted negatively to the show is an aside intended to provide context for Williams's response. Choice **(C)** best states the connection made in the paragraph and is the correct response. You can disregard choice **(D)** as too vague and too broad; nothing implies that influence across genres of art is "easy." Choice **(E)** merely states the specific example given to support the main point.

18. C

This question asks you to evaluate the veracity of the general statements by making inferences using evidence from the passage. The claim in choice **(A)** cannot be supported as there is no proof that all viewers other than artists disliked cubism or that cubism was disliked because it was misunderstood. There is also no evidence to suggest that choice **(B)** is correct. Because artists invented new styles that "shattered traditional notions" does not necessarily mean the artists rejected old styles. Choice **(C)** is supported, as the author of the paragraph directly correlates world events with new forms of artistic expression.

19. A

This question asks you to make inferences based on the information in the passage. You will need to evaluate each response one by one and weigh its merits. Choices **(A)** and **(B)** are similar in that they refer to Cather's motives in becoming an author. The passage does not prove, however, that she wouldn't have become an author at all if she had stayed in Virginia. Choice **(B)** is not the correct answer. You can also rule out choice **(C)**; the author tells you explicitly that Cather remembered Virginia. The fact that she was influenced by Nebraska doesn't mean that she devalued her former home. To support the claim in choice **(D)**, the passage would have to offer summaries of each novel and more information about Cather's relationship to communities of people. You can't draw this inference from the passage. In a literary analysis, an author could possibly support a claim such as the one stated in choice **(E)**. However, based on this passage, **(E)** is emotional hyperbole. Choice **(A)** is the most feasible assumption. According to the passage, Cather certainly would not have written the specific novels she did write if she hadn't moved to Nebraska as a child.

20. C

The correct answer to this Global question summarizes the passage's structure. The passage certainly compares two landscapes, but to correctly answer this question, you must determine *why* the comparison is made. You can eliminate choice **(A)** because it does not provide a reason for the comparison. Rule out choice **(B)** because prior to seeing Nebraska, Cather had nothing to compare to Virginia. We do not know how she "responded" to her home state. Choice **(C)** includes the main point of the passage—Cather's shock upon first seeing Nebraska and its influence on her writing. Choice **(D)** is not reasonable as you don't know Cather's thought process when she first saw Nebraska. You can also cross off choice **(E)** as there is little to no information about the novels in the passage. Therefore, **(C)** is the correct answer.

Diagnostic Tool

Tally up your score and write your results in the space provided.

Total

Total Correct: _______ out of 20 correct

Percentage Correct: # you got right × 100 ÷ 20: _______

By Question Type

Text Completion _______ out of 6 correct

Sentence Equivalence _______ out of 4 correct

Reading Comprehension _______ out of 10 correct

DIAGNOSE YOUR RESULTS

Look back at the questions you got wrong and think about your experience answering them.

VERBAL REASONING PRACTICE SET 4

Directions: For each sentence, choose one word for each set of blanks. Select the word or words that best fit(s) the meaning of the sentence as a whole.

1. It was apparent that the recordings were _______ remastered, as the vocals were barely audible through the wave of noise.

   (A) maladroitly
   (B) copiously
   (C) ingeniously
   (D) shrewdly
   (E) maliciously

2. He cited financial difficulty as his primary motive in the lucrative robbery; nonetheless, even his own family _______ him.

   (A) deluded
   (B) chastised
   (C) absolved
   (D) venerated
   (D) engulfed

3. The (i) _______ young children were a top priority for their mother and commanded most of her attention. They had such (ii) _______ level of volatile energy that ordinary activities were not enough to keep them occupied for an extended period of time. She devoted herself to channeling their energy into (iii) _______ pursuits

Blank (i)	Blank (ii)	Blank (iii)
A earthy	**D** an eclectic	**G** salutary
B froward	**E** a pedestrian	**H** provocative
C limpid	**F** a robust	**I** dour

4. The punctilious wine aficionado was a consummate purist when it came to his tastes. He immediately rejected the (i) ______ of two wines. As an alternative, and as a general rule, he preferred a simple, (ii) ______ wine.

Blank (i)	Blank (ii)
A amalgamation	D pragmatic
B dissonance	E unadulterated
C enigma	F opaque

5. The belligerent student did everything in her power to (i) ______ the other students with her behavior and classroom conduct. However, the teacher's calm yet stern discipline, acquired through years of dealing with similar situations, quickly (ii) ______ their reactions.

Blank (i)	Blank (ii)
A satiate	D exacerbated
B antagonize	E vacillated
C repudiate	F assuaged

6. The ______ alumni donors for the university's English department is well documented and acknowledged. It creates ______ in the allocation of university funds when the time comes to decide the annual budget. As things stand now, the available money goes to other university departments, which are not always the most underfunded or ______.

Blank (i)	Blank (ii)	Blank (iii)
A paucity of	D an irritation	G widespread
B preponderance of	E a paradox	H needy
C utility of	F a disparity	I newsworthy

Questions 7 and 8 are based on the following passage.

British Naval Officer Robert Scott (1868–1912) made his intent to discover the South Pole public, but that did not stop Norwegian explorer Roald Amundsen (1872–1928) from trying to beat him to it. In 1910, Amundsen raced to Antarctica and headed for the pole with 4 crewmen and 52 sled dogs. Scott's party left base camp ten days later with 17 men, 2 motorized sleds, 10 ponies, and 34 dogs. Scott's motor sleds broke down, the ponies had to be shot, and Scott sent all but four men back to base camp. The remaining crewmen hauled the sleds the rest of the way. Amundsen planted the Norwegian flag on the South Pole on December 14, 1911. A demoralized Scott raised the British flag on January 17, 1912. Amundsen and crew skied back to camp in good health. Scott's team, however, walked in temperatures that reached –30°F, losing two men along the way. A blizzard trapped the remaining three in a tent, which became their grave on March 29, 1912. A search party, discovering the tent, built a cairn, or monument of stones, marking the spot with a cross made of skis. When news of Scott's death reached civilization, England fell into mourning. The cross and cairn honoring Robert Scott still stand today.

7. Which conclusion about the competition between the two explorers does the passage steer the reader toward?

   (A) Scott would not have died if Amundsen had not forced him to compete.
   (B) Scott never should have tried for the South Pole because he was not a good explorer.
   (C) Amundsen was destined to win the historic conquest of the South Pole.
   (D) The English public followed the race to the South Pole with more interest than the Norwegian public did.
   (E) Despite losing the race to the South Pole, Scott's efforts were heroic.

8. With which of the following statements is the author most likely to agree?

   (A) Amundsen's conquest seems anticlimactic compared to Scott's disastrous defeat.
   (B) Scott wanted to conquer the South Pole more than Amundsen did.
   (C) Amundsen was better prepared to discover the South Pole by using commonsense skills suited to Antarctica.
   (D) Amundsen exploited Scott's preparations and ruined his expedition; Scott's defeat was Amundsen's fault.
   (E) Amundsen and Scott both viewed the discovery of the South Pole in part as a competitive race.

Question 9 is based on the following passage.

In the results of a long-term medical study, babies exposed to Mozart's music from the age of four weeks developed into young adults who were, on average, not only better performing scholastically, but also physically more adept than young adults who had not been exposed to Mozart's music from an early age. Therefore, parents who wish to improve the strength and scholastic performance of their children should expose their infants to classical music from the age of four weeks.

Select only one answer choice.

9. Which of the following, if true, best supports the argument above?

Ⓐ Children who were exposed to Mozart starting at the age of eight weeks also exhibited better scholastic performance as young adults.

Ⓑ High-school students who study music tend to be better at math than those students who do not.

Ⓒ Long-term medical studies are difficult to undertake and require large amounts of outside funding.

Ⓓ When infants listen to Mozart's music, it stimulates their brains and increases the rate of brain cell growth.

Ⓔ Babies who listen to classical music from composers other than Mozart also tend to develop into young adults with greater strength and better scholastic performance than other young adults.

Question 10 is based on the following passage.

A social worker surveyed 200 women, each of whom had recently given birth to her first child. Half of the women surveyed had chosen to give birth in a hospital or obstetrics clinic; the other half had chosen to give birth at home under the care of certified midwives. Of the 100 births that occurred at home, only 5 presented substantial complications, whereas 17 of the hospital births presented substantial complications. The social worker concluded from the survey that the home is actually a safer environment in which to give birth than a hospital or clinic.

Select only one answer choice.

10. Which of the following, if true, most seriously calls the social worker's conclusion into question?

Ⓐ Women who give birth in hospitals and clinics often have shorter periods of labor than do women who give birth at home.

Ⓑ Many obstetricians discourage patients from giving birth at home.

Ⓒ All of the women in the study who had been diagnosed as having a high possibility of delivery complications elected to give birth in a hospital.

Ⓓ Women who give birth at home tend to experience less stress during labor than women who deliver in hospitals.

Ⓔ Pregnant doctors prefer giving birth in a hospital.

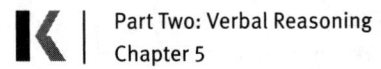

Directions: Select the two answer choices that, when inserted into the sentence, fit the meaning of the sentence as a whole and yield complete sentences that are similar in meaning.

11. Caligula, one of the great ______ of history, is best remembered for his lavish, bacchanalian feasts, in which participants indulged in every form of excess.

[A] gadflies
[B] sybarites
[C] philanthropists
[D] puritans
[E] wantons
[F] ascetics

12. Arthur looked positively ______; as he hadn't seen his wife, Deirdre, in weeks, the mere sight of her filled him with elation.

[A] ebullient
[B] esurient
[C] peevish
[D] pensive
[E] ecstatic
[F] execrable

13. For all his ______ in chatting with his friends and coworkers, when Cedric actually had a good reason to speak up in a serious conversation, he became taciturn.

[A] oratories
[B] declamations
[C] palaver
[D] blather
[E] epigrams
[F] opining

14. Despite the falling temperature and the inclement weather that lasted for most of the expedition, the hunting party was in a ______ mood.

   [A] disconcerted
   [B] jocund
   [C] garrulous
   [D] genial
   [E] histrionic
   [F] sententious

Questions 15–17 are based on the following passage.

The reversal of the Chicago River in 1900 is considered one of the greatest engineering feats of all time. The project involved building a deep channel through miles of solid bedrock in an effort to make the waters of the Chicago River—and its associated untreated sewage—flow out of Chicago and away from Lake Michigan, which was the source of the city's water supply. The project seemed impossible at the time, but it was deemed necessary after a flood in 1885 caused the Chicago River to foul the city's water supply and subsequently killed almost 12 percent of the population as a result of exposure to cholera and other water-borne diseases. In 1889, engineers started construction on the 28-mile channel that would connect Lake Michigan at Chicago with the Des Plaines River at Lockport, Illinois. This complex task gave workers the ability to isolate and reverse the flow of the Chicago River. At the end of the yearlong project, the city's water supply became safer and the river's new mouth at Lake Michigan became a major port that served thousands of ships each year.

Select only one answer choice.

15. Which one of the following statements reflects a major point of the passage?

   (A) Sewage disposal was a serious problem in Chicago during the late 1800s.
   (B) Water-borne diseases can spread easily and kill large populations.
   (C) The reversal of the Chicago River is a tremendous accomplishment in the field of engineering.
   (D) The reversal of the Chicago River opened the river's mouth to Lake Michigan.
   (E) Connecting Lake Michigan to the Des Plaines River was a key component of plans to reverse the flow of the Chicago River.

Consider each of the following choices separately and select all that apply.

16. Using the details from the passage, what can one infer about why the reversal of the Chicago River is considered one of the greatest engineering feats of all time?

    [A] The logistics of drilling through 28 miles of bedrock and connecting rivers was extremely difficult.

    [B] The river-reversal project in Chicago was successful, whereas similar projects were unsuccessful in several other cities.

    [C] The project proved that strong engineering can make things that seem impossible possible.

Select only one answer choice.

17. Which one of the following was NOT a benefit of reversing the Chicago River?

    (A) Engineers created a cure for water-borne illnesses.
    (B) The city's engineers gained recognition for completing an impressive project.
    (C) Citizens received safer drinking water.
    (D) The city became a major port for industry.
    (E) Lake Michigan became a cleaner body of water.

Question 18 is based on the following passage.

The Hague Convention for the Protection of Cultural Property in the Event of Armed Conflict (1954) was an international response to the destruction of cultural artifacts during World War II. Overseen by the United Nations Educational, Scientific, and Cultural Organization (UNESCO), the parties that participated in the convention (numbering over 100) pledged to safeguard locations and items of cultural significance during armed conflict, as well as preempt possible threats to the preservation of culture during times of peace. The Hague Convention is significant in that it formally established in its preamble that "damage to cultural property belonging to any people whatsoever means damage to the cultural heritage of all mankind, since each people makes its contribution to the culture of the world." However, it is difficult to enforce, particularly in the case of pieces of cultural heritage that are claimed by multiple States. An example of this is the possession of some of the Dead Sea Scrolls in the aftermath of the Six Day War (1967), a hotly debated topic between Jordan and Israel today. Both countries are signatories to the convention, but both claim their efforts to hold the scrolls amount to rightful possession, rather than theft as forbidden in the convention.

18. Which of the following statements about the Hague Convention of 1954 is NOT supported by the passage?

    (A) It was a reaction to despoliation and destruction of cultural heritage during World War II.
    (B) It asserted the international significance of all cultural heritage.
    (C) It is the focus of controversy in some cases even to this day.
    (D) It is overseen by a division of the United Nations.
    (E) It included strong and effective measures for enforcement.

Questions 19 and 20 are based on the following passage.

An idea that has gained renewed currency in recent years is that the proliferation of information technology has a deleterious effect on interpersonal relationships. Neil Postman, in his book *Amusing Ourselves to Death*, asserted that television, as a medium, was incapable of fostering intelligent, meaningful discourse around a given subject. Postman wrote his book in the 1980s, when cable television was first becoming widely available. In it, he discusses the way that putatively "serious" news programs are inherently trite. Terse reports on serious, weighty issues such as the war in Iraq are juxtaposed with trivial information, such as celebrity gossip. Often the two are linked, one after another, by the phrase "and now . . ." This leaves the viewer unable to emotionally respond to something traumatic, as he is bombarded with disparate pieces of information in rapid succession. Instant access to a glut of information impoverishes genuine experiences, as it deprives the information of a meaningful context for interpretation.

19. Select the sentence in the passage in which the author cites a concrete example of how mass media has a desensitizing effect.

Consider each of the following choices separately and select all that apply.

20. Based on his views as they're expressed in the passage, Postman would likely agree with which of the following statements?

    [A] Information technologies such as smartphones are unlikely to provide meaningful contexts in which to interpret information.
    [B] Television programs inherently lack intelligent, meaningful discourse.
    [C] The medium in which factual content is delivered can be an important factor in how that content is interpreted.

VERBAL REASONING PRACTICE SET 4 ANSWER KEY

1. A
2. B
3. B, F, G
4. A, E
5. B, F
6. A, F, H
7. E
8. E
9. E
10. C
11. B, E
12. A, E
13. C, D
14. B, D
15. C
16. A, C
17. A
18. E
19. *"Terse reports on serious, weighty issues such as the war in Iraq are juxtaposed with trivial information, such as celebrity gossip."*
20. A, C

VERBAL REASONING PRACTICE SET 4 ANSWERS AND EXPLANATIONS

1. A

The word *as* signals a continuation of ideas—the vocals were hard to hear because of the way the recordings were mastered. The answer is **(A)** *maladroitly*, which means "unskillfully" or "bunglingly." Choices **(B)** *copiously*, **(C)** *ingeniously*, and **(D)** *shrewdly* are not in line with what you're looking for—these words suggest more time and care than was spent. Choice **(E)** *maliciously* is too harsh. It's doubtful the recordings were mastered with intent to harm.

2. B

Even with the road sign *nonetheless*, a contrast is not immediately clear. Consider the tone of the phrase "even his own family," which suggests an element of surprise at the family's response. Choice **(A)** *deluded* means "misled," which doesn't fit the context. Choice **(B)** *chastised* means "scolded," which makes sense, since the robber would expect his family's support, not scolding. Choices **(C)** *absolved* and **(D)** *venerated* imply support—rule these out. The last choice, **(E)** *engulfed*, doesn't make sense in context.

3. B, F, G

It's difficult to predict for the first blank, as all you're told is that the children were time-consuming for their mother. You need more contextual clues, so move on to the second blank. Here, you're looking for something to describe the children's energy level. Their energy is characterized as "volatile" ("explosive"), so they must have an *intense* level of energy. Make that your prediction. Choice **(F)** *robust* ("vigorous") fits perfectly. Choices **(D)** *eclectic* ("varied") and **(E)** *pedestrian* ("ordinary") don't make sense. Now that you know the children are high-energy, you can predict something like "unruly" for the first blank, since that blank describes the children. Looking at the answer choices, choice **(B)** *froward*, meaning "not easily controlled," works perfectly. Choice **(A)** *earthy* means "crude," so that is wrong, and **(C)** *limpid*, which means "calm or untroubled," is the opposite of what you need. For the final blank, remember that the mother is trying to direct the children's energy towards something "constructive" so that they will make productive use of their time. This is close to choice **(G)** *salutary*, which means "beneficial" or "useful," and that's your answer. Choice **(H)** *provocative* ("provoking to anger or desire") and **(I)** *dour* ("gloomy") do not make sense in this context, as they do not describe pursuits that parents would encourage for their children.

4. A, E

The key to this sentence is the description of the wine aficionado (or expert) as a "purist," or someone who insists on the purity of things. Since he rejects the first blank, you can assume it will be an antonym of *pure*. You can predict *mixture*, which fits in the context. However, he prefers the second blank, so this should be a synonym of *pure* and the contextual word, "simple."

For the first blank, the best match for your prediction is choice **(A)** *amalgamation*. This is an exact synonym of your prediction, *mixture*. Choice **(B)** *dissonance*, which means "a disagreeable combination," seems plausible. A purist would definitely find a mixture of two wines to be dissonant. However, we need a word that states this mixture has occurred for the sentence to make sense. Similarly, choice **(C)** *enigma* means "puzzle," which may also be applicable to such a mixture but, again, lacks the necessary meaning of "mixture." For the second blank, choice **(E)** *unadulterated* matches your prediction best. Choice **(D)** *pragmatic* means "practical" and does not fit as well as *unadulterated* in context. The wine aficionado does not prefer something for its practicality but for the taste; therefore, this choice would be misleading in the sentence. Choice **(F)** *opaque*, which means "impossible to see through," may similarly be applicable to the wine; however, nowhere in the sentence is the color implied or relevant.

5. B, F

Since the student is described as "belligerent," meaning "aggressive," you can assume she will be attempting to provoke the other students. Later in the sentence, the road sign "however" appears, which indicates a turn of events when the teacher takes over. You can predict *aggravate* for the first blank and *calmed* or *lessened* for the second blank. For the first blank, the best match for your prediction is **(B)** *antagonize*, which means "provoke." Choice **(A)** *satiate* means "to satisfy," which is inconsistent with the idea of belligerence. Choice **(C)** *repudiate* means "to reject the validity of," which, although it may antagonize the students, lacks the direct connotation of *aggravate*. For the second blank, choice **(F)** *assuaged* is the best match to your prediction. Choice **(D)** *exacerbated*, which means "worsened," is the exact opposite of what you are looking for. Choice **(E)** *vacillated* means "to be indecisive," which sounds plausible but does not match the prediction as well as *assuaged,* or "calmed."

6. A, F, H

Start tackling this question by looking at the last sentence. You know that the money is going to other departments, which are not necessarily the most underfunded. Therefore, you know there aren't enough donors to the English department, or they aren't generous enough. You can predict something that means "lack of" for the first blank. Choice **(A)** *paucity of*, which means "shortage," works perfectly. Hang on to that one. For the second blank, you need something that contrasts how much the English department gets with how much the other ones get. *Discrepancy* works nicely. That eliminates choice **(E)** *paradox*—this is not contrary to what might be expected. Choice **(D)** *irritation* is very tempting but wrong. Although this situation is certainly irritating, choice **(F)** *disparity* better matches your prediction of "discrepancy." The final blank will describe the department in a manner similar to "underfunded," with which it is paired. You can therefore reject choices **(G)** *widespread* and **(I)** *newsworthy* as being incorrect. That leaves **(H)** *needy*, which matches well with "underfunded."

7. E

This is an Inference question. The correct answer, though not directly stated in the passage, must follow from the text. Take the choices one by one and ask what the author is trying to persuade you to believe. Choice **(A)** is not implied. Historians may speculate, but no one can know whether Scott's expedition would have gone any differently without Amundsen in the race. The passage does not support choice **(B)**; it doesn't evaluate Scott's abilities as an explorer. You can cross **(C)** off the list: there is no evidence that the author subscribes to fate or destiny. Cross off **(D)**, too. Though the race was of national significance, the author does not describe Norway's response to victory. Choice **(E)** matches the tone of the passage, which portrays Scott's struggles in a heroic light despite his failure to reach the South Pole first. Choice **(E)** is the correct answer.

8. E

The correct answer to this question will follow from the passage. While the reader may or may not come to the conclusion expressed in choice **(A)**, the author makes no evaluation of which expedition was more "climactic." Choice **(B)** is an irrelevant comparison; the author says nothing to imply which explorer had greater desire or motivation. Choice **(C)** seems reasonable but misses the scope of the passage. The author doesn't attribute Amundsen's success or Scott's failure to "preparation" or "common sense." Choice **(D)** is too harsh to find support in this passage. The author doesn't attribute any sinister motives to either explorer. That leaves choice **(E)**, which you know is the correct answer. While the author never makes this statement directly, he tells you that Amundsen was "trying to beat" Scott and that Scott was "demoralized" to have arrived at the pole after Amundsen.

9. E

A question stem that asks us to "support" an argument is asking you to *strengthen* the argument, which means you want an answer choice that makes the author's conclusion *more likely* to come about, either by introducing additional evidence or shoring up potential flaws in the author's argument.

So what potential flaws does this author have? Well, the author employs a subtle shift in terminology. Her main piece of evidence is a study about babies that listened to Mozart from a very young age; however, her conclusion in the last sentence recommends the broader category of "classical music." Someone looking to criticize this argument could easily say, "Perhaps Mozart's music has some special educational qualities, and other classical music would not produce the same effects." Therefore, since you are asked to strengthen the argument, the best way to do so would be to shore up this flaw and find an answer choice that says other classical music will produce the same proven results as Mozart.

Choice **(E)** matches that prediction perfectly, citing similar results from other classical composers. It is correct.

The wrong answer choices all step outside the scope in various ways: choices **(A)** and **(D)** continue to sing the praises of Mozart, but don't bring in those other classical composers we were looking for; choice **(B)** discusses development of high-school students rather than young children; and choice **(C)** is completely off base, as the viability of these studies is not a point at issue here.

10. C

To call the social worker's conclusion into question, the first step is to find it, which is easily located here by using the key word "concluded" in the last sentence of the stimulus. Since the social worker concludes that the home is safer than the hospital (for giving birth, at least), you'll want to find an answer choice that gives some reason why the home might *not* be as safe as it seems.

The extensive information in this question stem is fertile ground in which to make a solid prediction: The social worker's study showed that substantial complications arose in a larger proportion of hospital births than home births. But what if the women who gave birth in hospitals were otherwise predisposed to complications in some way? If there were such a factor, the extra complications in the hospital births could be explained by non-location-related reasons, and the social worker's argument would be weakened.

Choice **(C)** matches the prediction well: if women in the study who knew they might have complications *chose* to give birth in hospitals, then one could use that information to argue that the hospital is not necessarily more dangerous than the home.

Although choices **(A)**, **(B)**, **(D)**, and **(E)** all place speculations on home and/or hospital births one way or the other, none of them so directly attacks the social worker's evidence—none even mentions the study—and so all are incorrect.

11. B, E

You don't need to know who Caligula was to be able to answer this question: you simply need to recognize how he is being described, and be able to follow the direction the sentence is taking. Caligula is characterized as being remembered for "bacchanalian feasts," which are basically parties involving a great deal of food and alcoholic beverages. This is reinforced by the fact that the participants indulged in "every form of excess." Therefore, you can predict that the blank, which describes Caligula, will mean something like "glutton." Choices **(D)** *puritans* (morally strict persons) and **(F)** *ascetics* (those who renounce worldly indulgences) can both be rejected. Choice **(A)** *gadflies* are "irritating people," so that doesn't fit in this context. Choice **(B)** *sybarites* are people devoted to luxury and pleasure, so that one certainly works. That leaves choices **(C)** *philanthropists* ("humanitarians") and **(E)** *wantons* ("those who live luxuriantly"). Humanitarians aren't necessarily people who indulge in excess, and *wantons* creates a sentence with a meaning similar to the one created by *sybarites*. They're your answers.

12. A, E

The word "as," after the semicolon, is a straight-ahead road sign, indicating that the sentence will continue its original direction. You have to figure out how Arthur looked upon seeing his wife, based on the fact that seeing her filled him with "elation." "Elation" means "exultant gladness," so a good prediction for the blank would be *happy*. That allows you to get rid of choice **(B)** *esurient*, which means "hungry," and **(D)** *pensive*, which means "thoughtful," as those don't work in this context. Choices **(C)** *peevish* ("annoyed") and **(F)** *execrable* ("detestable") have strongly negative meanings, so they're the opposite of what you need. Choices **(A)** *ebullient* ("high-spirited") and **(E)** *ecstatic* ("delighted") both create sentences that say Arthur was happy when he saw his wife.

13. C, D

The phrase "for all his" that begins the sentence is a detour road sign that sets up a contrast between Cedric's behavior in informal vs. serious conversation. He becomes taciturn ("quiet") in serious conversation. In informal chats with friends and coworkers, then, he probably talks a great deal, and probably not very seriously. You can therefore reject choices that describe meaningful, articulate, or pithy speech. Choices **(A)** *oratories* and **(B)** *declamations* are both "eloquent public speeches," so they do not match the context of chats with friends. Choice **(E)** *epigrams* are witty sayings, so you can reject that as well. Choice **(F)** *opining* means "stating an opinion." This choice might be tempting, but there is no second choice that would give the sentence the same meaning. Choices **(C)** *palaver* and **(D)** *blather* are both words that describe meaningless chatter. They're the correct answers.

14. B, D

"Despite" is a classic detour road sign indicating that the sentence will change direction. You're told that the weather is bad, which normally puts people in a "foul" mood, so the blank must have a meaning opposite of that because of the detour road sign. "Happy" works well. Based on that prediction, you can reject **(A)** *disconcerted*, as that means "upset," and **(E)** *histrionic*, as that means "melodramatic." Choice **(C)** *garrulous* means "chatty," so that does work in this context, but no other answer choice creates a similar sentence. Choice **(F)** *sententious* means "given to excessive moralizing," so that doesn't work in this context. Choice **(B)** *jocund*, meaning "jolly," works and creates a sentence similar to the one created by **(D)** *genial* (warm and friendly). They're your answers.

15. C

This Global question asks you to identify the main point of the passage. To determine the correct answer, you will need to examine each choice one by one. While **(A)** refers to one of the major reasons for the reversal of the Chicago River, it is not a major point of the passage because it does not address the main subject of the passage, which is the Chicago River itself. Similarly, **(B)** does not reference the main subject. It refers to one of the issues that helped launch the project to reverse the river, but not the actual river. Choices **(C)**, **(D)**, and **(E)** each reference the Chicago River, but only **(C)** mentions it as a major engineering feat, making **(C)** the best choice. **(D)** and **(E)** reference only minor components of the passage (specific details of the project).

16. A, C

This Function question asks you to evaluate the statements and identify the one(s) that states *why* the river-reversal project was considered a great engineering feat. Choice **(A)** can be inferred because the passage uses words such as "solid" to describe the bedrock and "complex" to describe the process of connecting the rivers. These words suggest that the job was difficult. Choice **(B)** cannot be inferred because the passage does not compare the Chicago River project to any others. Choice **(C)** can be inferred because the statement references a section of the passage that states that the project seemed impossible but in the end it was successful.

17. A

This is an Evaluation question that rewards you for identifying the statement that does *not* follow from the passage. That means that each of the four wrong answers is stated or implied in the text. Choice **(E)** is a benefit of the project implied by the section of the passage that states that untreated sewage no longer flowed into Lake Michigan after the river was reversed. Choice **(D)** is a result of the project stated directly in the passage. Choice **(C)** also paraphrases the passage, which stated directly that the city's water became "safer." Choice **(B)** follows from the passage's first sentence: the Chicago project "is considered one of the greatest engineering feats." Choice **(A)** distorts the passage. Engineers didn't "cure" the diseases mentioned in the passage; they made it possible to prevent them in Chicago's drinking water.

18. E

To answer this question, you must reexamine the passage and determine which of the choices is *not* supported by the passage—often these questions require very careful thinking. Choice **(A)** is the first one you can eliminate because it directly paraphrases the statement in the first sentence of the paragraph about the reason the Hague Convention was adopted. Likewise for choice **(B)**, which is confirmed by the quote taken from the convention's preamble, stating that "each people makes its contribution to the culture of the world." Choice **(C)** refers to the example of the dispute over ownership of the Dead Sea Scrolls following the Six Day War. Choice **(D)** follows from the second sentence of the passage. The Hague Convention is overseen by UNESCO, which, as the name implies, is a division of the United Nations. Choice **(E)**, however, directly contradicts the latter portion of the passage, which states that the Hague Convention is difficult to enforce. Therefore, this is the correct answer.

19. *"Terse reports on serious, weighty issues such as the war in Iraq are juxtaposed with trivial information, such as celebrity gossip."*

This sentence is the only one in the passage that offers a concrete example. The other likely candidate, "This leaves the viewer unable to emotionally respond to something traumatic, as he is bombarded with disparate pieces of information in rapid succession," describes the result. That doesn't answer the question, which calls for a sentence that illustrates *how* mass media has such an effect.

20. A, C

This question is asking you to infer Postman's position from what the brief selection tells you about his views. Choice **(A)** is correct because the author noted that Postman thought "instant access to a glut of information" reduced meaningful context for that information. Thus, he would likely apply this reasoning to newer information technology that has the same effect. Choice **(B)** is subtly wrong. Postman, you're told, thought television incapable of *fostering* intelligent discourse among its viewers; you cannot conclude that he therefore thinks that no intelligent discourse *appears in* any television program. In fact, part of Postman's problem with the medium is that serious topics are juxtaposed with frivolous items. Postman would definitely agree with the statement in choice **(C)**. Given his views on television, as a medium, and those in the final sentence of the passage, you can infer that he believes that media influence how information is interpreted.

Diagnostic Tool

Tally up your score and write your results in the space provided.

Total

Total Correct: ________ out of 20 correct

Percentage Correct: # you got right × 100 ÷ 20: ________

By Question Type

Text Completion ________ out of 6 correct

Sentence Equivalence ________ out of 4 correct

Reading Comprehension ________ out of 10 correct

Diagnose Your Results

Look back at the questions you got wrong and think about your experience answering them.

VERBAL REASONING PRACTICE SET 5

Directions: For each sentence, choose one word for each set of blanks. Select the word or words that best fit(s) the meaning of the sentence as a whole.

1. A responsible business owner may easily feel _______ between her concern for the well-being of her employees and the challenges of financial shortfalls.

   Ⓐ affinity
   Ⓑ tension
   Ⓒ uneasiness
   Ⓓ trepidation
   Ⓔ dejection

2. The controversy surrounding the election dragged on for months, and the lack of a definite victor _______ governance and left people anxious about the future of their leadership.

   Ⓐ facilitated
   Ⓑ augmented
   Ⓒ forestalled
   Ⓓ lowed
   Ⓔ abetted

3. The busboy was known for his diligence rather than his celerity. During his shifts, he worked (i) _______ when cleaning up after customers. Though the chef initially found it annoying, she came to appreciate having things done thoroughly rather than (ii) _______.

Blank (i)		Blank (ii)	
A	perfunctorily	**D**	haphazardly
B	sedulously	**E**	expediently
C	desperately	**F**	disingenuously

4. The middle school principal believed that even a minor (i) _______ the rules demanded his attention. Such a thing could not go (ii) _______ if he were to maintain discipline. In his eyes, obedience and order were of the utmost importance.

Blank (i)	
A	adherence to
B	respect for
C	infraction of

Blank (ii)	
D	unappreciated
E	unobserved
F	unpunished

5. Jurisprudence requires a dispassionate approach on the part of the judge or arbiter. Law and custom require that a definite (i) _______ be made in every case, regardless of how strong the winning argument seems. Therefore, a judge is forced to behave as if a verdict is (ii) _______. This is true even when, in fact, the evidence may not be (iii) _______.

Blank (i)	
A	deadlock
B	dispute
C	determination

Blank (ii)	
D	negotiable
E	irrelevant
F	self-evident

Blank (iii)	
G	conclusive
H	accessible
I	substantiated

6. As a result of poor planning and disorganization, the young team (i) _______ attacking the root of the problem. This went on until there was no other recourse left to them. They were obliged to (ii) _______ a (iii) _______, last-minute solution to the problem.

Blank (i)	
A	expedited
B	postponed
C	accelerated

Blank (ii)	
D	implement
E	envision
F	reject

Blank (iii)	
G	measured
H	premeditated
I	desperate

Questions 7–9 are based on the following passage.

Painting is a process that is ordinarily associated with a brush and a palette, but as an artist who was far from ordinary, Jackson Pollock used neither when creating some of his most famous works. Pollock (1912–1956) is one of the most influential figures in American painting. His unique style of painting and artistic point of view made him stand out from his contemporaries. Pollack painted in an entirely abstract manner. Instead of using an easel, he placed his canvases on the floor or against a wall. Employing a "drip and splash" method, Pollack poured and dripped his paint from the can onto the canvas. Instead of brushes, he manipulated the paint with sticks and knives. Pollack's works created a new, "all-over" style of painting in which there is no focal point and no differentiation is made among areas of the painted surface. His scattered painting style may be a reflection of his unstable mental state, as he was known to battle depression and alcoholism. While his volatile personality may have contributed to his legacy, Pollock will primarily be remembered for his tremendous contributions to the art world.

Select only one answer choice.

7. The primary purpose of this passage is to address which of the following issues related to Pollock as an artist?

   (A) How he developed his unique style
   (B) How his methods influenced future artists
   (C) Whether his personal life affected his work
   (D) How his influential style represented a significant departure from more conventional art
   (E) Whether he should be revered for his work

8. The passage states each of the following EXCEPT:

   (A) Pollock's work was similar to that of his peers.
   (B) The all-over painting method placed no importance on any particular piece of the painting.
   (C) Pollock suffered from mental health issues.
   (D) Pollock's "drip and splash" method created art without the use of conventional painting tools.
   (E) Pollock's legacy will reflect his artistic ability.

9. Based on the information in the passage, which word best describes Pollock as an artist?

   (A) Plain
   (B) Gloomy
   (C) Inventive
   (D) Literal
   (E) Traditional

Question 10 is based on the following passage.

In the field of Kafka studies and its various related subfields, perhaps the most controversial figure is Max Brod, Franz Kafka's publisher, biographer, and closest friend. Although it is thanks to Brod that we possess any of

Kafka's writing—Kafka only allowed his writing to be published at Brod's insistence and had asked Brod to burn all his writing upon his death, which Brod did not do—Brod is considered by many Kafka specialists and enthusiasts to have possessed a meager understanding of his friend's writing and importance. A prolific writer, Brod's writing has in time been greatly overshadowed by Kafka's, and many find his compositions to be blunt and crude when compared to Kafka's abstruse elegance; this contrast was further emphasized by their personalities, with Brod being gregarious and a notorious womanizer, whereas Kafka was withdrawn and shy. Based on this contrast, many in the field of Kafka studies feel that Brod—being the only channel through which we know Kafka—in some ways tainted the "pure" Kafka in the editorial process, and the search for unpublished manuscripts of Kafka (free of Brod's influence) has become for many an obsession.

10. According to the passage, why is Max Brod described as a "controversial figure"?

    (A) Although Brod was Kafka's closest friend, many wonder if Kafka objected to Brod's editorial alterations of his writing.
    (B) Because of the divergence of their upbringings, Brod and Kafka had difficulty seeing eye to eye with one another.
    (C) Although he is the only source of Kafka's writings, Brod is thought to have poorly understood Kafka's writing.
    (D) Brod's lascivious behavior repulsed Kafka, who wished for someone more refined to edit his work.
    (E) Upon Kafka's death, Brod burned all of Kafka's remaining writings, suggesting that he did not properly recognize his friend's incredible talent.

Directions: Select the two answer choices that, when inserted into the sentence, fit the meaning of the sentence as a whole and yield complete sentences that are similar in meaning.

11. Terrance was _______ student, always eager to participate and try his best; unfortunately, his low test scores did not reflect his efforts.

    [A] a pedantic
    [B] an animated
    [C] an apathetic
    [D] a pragmatic
    [E] an assiduous
    [F] a prudent

12. In addition to having sharp teeth and claws, the maned wolf emits _______ musk, which acts as a defense mechanism in the wild.

    A a malodorous
    B a pristine
    C a soporific
    D a pungent
    E an estimable
    F a charming

13. The first baseman and shortstop were both talented players with Hall of Fame credentials, but their _______ relationship exacerbated the chaos in the locker room.

    A venerable
    B prudent
    C volatile
    D stolid
    E inimical
    F stoic

14. Although the old woman had lived through the Great Depression, she _______ spent her money on her grandchildren, giving them everything she didn't have growing up.

    A liberally
    B scrupulously
    C capriciously
    D meticulously
    E lavishly
    F flintily

Questions 15 and 16 are based on the following passage.

Few babies born to HIV-infected mothers carry the disease *in utero*, even though HIV is a blood-borne virus and there is a constant flow of blood through the umbilical cord that could infect the growing fetus. As genetic testing has demonstrated, this is because the human fetal immune system may develop separately from the adult immune system, and it may provide a measure of protection. When exposed to foreign cells, immune cells "activate" to become T-cells, which defend the organism. Fetal T-cells seem to be more tolerant of HIV and do not cause the reactions typically seen in HIV infection; these cells recognize the foreign cells but do not fight them, and the virus is not stimulated to destroy the T-cells, as happens when an individual has full-blown AIDS.

15. Which sentence provides the best summary of the passage?

   (A) Foreign cells cannot enter fetuses' bloodstreams as easily as they can enter the bloodstreams of adults.
   (B) The reason few fetuses contract HIV from infected mothers is that their mothers' T-cells protect them.
   (C) The fetal immune system may not be similar to the adult immune system.
   (D) T-cells affected by HIV are not activated in the fetal immune response and therefore remain more tolerant of foreign cells.
   (E) Fetuses rarely contract HIV *in utero* because the fetal immune system operates differently than the adult system.

Consider each of the following choices separately and select all that apply.

16. Which of the following statements are suggested by the passage?

   [A] Fetuses are better protected from HIV than their mothers because of their respective immune systems.
   [B] If researchers could find a way to stop T-cells in adults from activating, adults would have the same health benefit as fetuses.
   [C] Fetal immune systems are more complicated than those of adults.

Questions 17 and 18 are based on the following passage.

While days of the chain gang are long gone, the effects of meaningful labor during imprisonment demonstrate marked benefits to both the prisoner and society. Some of these benefits take the forms of reduced recidivism, increased job skills and employability, and improved quality of life. In fact, corporations have hired jails to have their inmates perform work from manufacturing to telemarketing. However, some critics argue that prisoners who work are little more than bonded slaves, earning nothing for their labor and forced to do work that may be beyond their physical or mental capacity. Others are more concerned about the economic factors of cheap, noncompetitive labor or issues involved in giving inmates responsibility for critical components of products or providing them with lists of addresses and telephone numbers.

17. The author would most likely agree with which of the following sentences?

    (A) Working may offset deleterious psychological conditions to which prisoners are exposed.
    (B) Too many lawsuits filed against jails involve prisoners being forced to perform work they are not physically equipped to handle.
    (C) Telemarketing corporations are the main entities that stand to profit from inmates working for free or at low cost.
    (D) People in jail lack the mental skill needed to perform more challenging work.
    (E) Adjusting the current model of inmate labor to have prisoners work for money or reduced sentences would improve the penal system.

18. Choose the sentence in the passage that provides support for the main argument.

Questions 19 and 20 are based on the following passage.

The current worldwide economic recession has forced state governments to reevaluate how tax dollars should be spent. A recent statement from the Iowa State legislature indicated that they were considering cutting state-funded sabbaticals for professors working within the publicly funded Iowa University system. The justification has been that this is an inefficient use of funds, which could be better allocated elsewhere or cut out of the tax code. Critics cited the high cost of paying a professor's salary for the entire year in which they do not work. They also suggested that taxpayers should not pay for professors to take time off from teaching to write a book on a subject such as ancient mythology. There is a strong counterargument, however, which points out that not all faculty sabbaticals are, by necessity, unprofitable. Aside from the benefit of the increase of knowledge, it is not entirely clear how a sabbatical may, ultimately, return on its investment. A genetics professor who, during her sabbatical, discovers a new drug treatment methodology, for example, could potentially generate millions of dollars in grant money for the university's research department.

19. Which of the following is likely to be an opinion of the author of this passage?

    (A) Public funding for sabbaticals should be cut.
    (B) The value produced by a faculty sabbatical cannot be determined prior to the sabbatical.
    (C) Professors should only teach, not engage in outside research.
    (D) The goal of a university should be to conduct abstract research that leads to practical applications.
    (E) The study of genetics is a more worthwhile pursuit than that of mythology.

Consider each of the following choices separately and select all that apply.

20. Which of the following statements is suggested by the passage?

    [A] As a result of the sabbatical system, universities are doing less meaningful research than they once did.
    [B] As a state, Iowa has a lower percentage of professors whose primary responsibility is teaching.
    [C] Some state legislators feel that taxpayers should not have to indirectly pay for research that will not benefit them.

VERBAL REASONING PRACTICE SET 5 ANSWER KEY

1. B
2. C
3. B, E
4. C, F
5. C, F, G
6. B, D, I
7. D
8. A
9. C
10. C
11. B, E
12. A, D
13. C, E
14. A, E
15. E
16. A
17. A
18. *"Some of these benefits take the forms of reduced recidivism, increased job skills and employability, and improved quality of life."*
19. B
20. C

VERBAL REASONING PRACTICE SET 5 ANSWERS AND EXPLANATIONS

1. B

The sentence tells you that a relationship exists between concerns for the well-being of employees and the challenges of financial shortfalls. The two are being contrasted, so a reasonable prediction would be *stress*. Scanning the answers, you'll notice choice **(B)** *tension*, which is a synonym for stress, fits perfectly. Choice **(A)** *affinity* is the opposite of the prediction. Choice **(C)** *uneasiness* is close but does not address the conflict between the two concerns as well as *tension*. Choices **(D)** *trepidation* and **(E)** *dejection* are too negatively charged for this context; nothing in the sentence indicates that the business owner is frightened or sad, respectively.

2. C

The people are anxious because they do not know who will be leading them, which will *limit* or *hinder* leadership or governance; your answer will reflect this. Choices **(A)** *facilitated*, **(B)** *augmented*, and **(E)** *abetted* all have meanings of "strengthened" or "increased." Choice **(D)** *lowed* might be tempting because it resembles "lowered," but the verb "low" means to make the sound of a cow. Choice **(C)** *forestalled* is the only option that means "restricted" or "slowed down."

3. B, E

The detour road sign "rather than" indicates that the busboy has one of two contrasting qualities: "diligence" ("thoroughness") rather than "celerity" ("speed"). He is not quick, yet he is thorough. The chef initially disliked the busboy's work habits, but the detour road sign "though" indicates that she has come to like them, since thoroughness can be more important than rapidity. For the first blank, you need a word that means something like *thoroughly*. Choice **(B)** *sedulously*, which means "perseveringly," works well. Choice **(A)** *perfunctorily* "superficial" is the opposite of what you need, and **(C)** *desperately* doesn't make any sense in this context. There is more information available for the second blank. The word "rather" appears again as a detour road sign. The sentence mirrors the earlier contrast in the question. The chef has come to appreciate the busboy's thoroughness even though the busboy isn't fast. Choice **(E)** *expediently* means "quickly," and matches the prediction perfectly. Choice **(D)** *haphazardly* means "sloppily," which is not a quality the chef would want. Choice **(F)** *disingenuously* means "insincerely," which makes no sense here.

4. C, F

You read that the principal wants to "maintain discipline" and that order is of paramount importance to him. From that context, you can determine that a *breaking of* the rules will not be tolerated. Make this your prediction for the first blank. For the second, predict that breaking rules could not go *unpunished*. For the first blank, the best match is choice **(C)** *infraction of*. Both choices **(A)** *adherence to* and **(B)** *respect for* are the opposite of your prediction. The best fit for the second blank is choice **(F)** *unpunished*. Choice **(D)** *unappreciated* doesn't make sense in context, and if the infraction was *unobserved*, choice **(E)**, the principal wouldn't know about it.

5. C, F, G

Here, "law and custom" require that something definite be made in a courtroom—predict *verdict* for the first blank. If a verdict must be reached, predict that the judge may have to assume that a verdict is *always possible* when, in fact, the evidence might not be *compelling*.

For the first blank, choice **(A)** *deadlock* might have sounded tempting, since you often hear about "deadlocked juries," but this is the opposite of what you need. A *dispute*, choice **(B)**, is what is settled in a courtroom, not what is reached there. The best choice here is choice **(C)** *determination*. For the second blank, you can rule out choice **(E)** *irrelevant* immediately, since the verdict is the most relevant thing in a courtroom. You might have initially liked choice **(D)** *negotiable* because sometimes the outcomes of trials are negotiated, but once a verdict is reached, it might be appealed but it cannot be negotiated. Choice **(F)** *self-evident* is the best choice for the second blank. For the third blank, while it's not an exact match to your prediction, the most logical choice is **(G)** *conclusive*. It's illogical to say that the evidence may not be *accessible*, choice **(H)**, or *substantiated*, choice **(I)**; without at least some evidence, there generally wouldn't even be a trial. "[Because] law and custom require that a definite *determination* be made . . . a judge is forced to behave as if a verdict is *self-evident* . . . when in fact, the evidence may not be *conclusive*."

6. B, D, I

The sentences provide context clues to the missing words. You learn that they did something until only one option remained open to them, something consistent with "a . . . last-minute solution." You're also told that the team was disorganized and that they planned poorly. Since the solution was last-minute, predict that they must have *put off their work* until they had no other recourse than to *attempt* a *frantic* last-minute solution. For the first blank, the best match for your prediction is choice **(B)** *postponed*. Choices **(A)** *expedited* and **(C)** *accelerated* are both inconsistent with needing "a . . . last-minute solution." For the second blank, the closest match to your prediction is choice **(D)** *implement*. Choice **(E)** *envision* might have been tempting, but if all they had to do was *envision* a solution, it doesn't seem that time would have been an issue. And since they waited until the last minute, it isn't likely they'd *reject* a solution, choice **(F)**. For the third blank, the best match for your prediction is choice **(I)** *desperate*. Choice **(G)** *measured* is inconsistent with waiting until the last minute to find a solution, and *premeditated*, choice **(H)**, is the opposite of last minute. "[They] *postponed* . . . until there was no . . . recourse [but to] *implement* a *desperate*, last-minute solution to the problem."

7. D

The correct answer states the passage's primary purpose. The wrong answers will, therefore, miss the main point, either by distorting the scope of the passage or by concentrating on a specific detail from the text. Choice **(A)** is not directly addressed in this passage. While the passage speculates that Pollock's scattered style could be the result of his personality, how the style was originally developed is not addressed. There is also no mention of choice **(B)**; the author doesn't describe *how* Pollack's methods influenced future artists, just *that* they did. Choice **(C)** is mentioned in the passage but is not the primary purpose of the passage; it is only a secondary issue. The primary purpose of this passage is to address choice **(D)**, how radically unconventional and influential Pollack's methods were. The passage describes Pollock's style as "unique" and "new" and states that it differed greatly from the style of his contemporaries. Choice **(E)** is incorrect because the author does not address how Pollock should be evaluated by art critics, and certainly not whether he should be revered for his work.

8. A

The correct answer to this Detail EXCEPT question is the one with a statement *not* listed in the passage. When describing Pollock's painting methods, the author mentions that Pollock did not use paintbrushes or an easel when employing his "drip and splash" method. As paintbrushes and easels are conventional painting tools, you can determine that **(D)** is true based on the passage and therefore not the correct choice. The author also mentions that the "all-over" style of painting makes no differentiation among areas of the painted surface; therefore, choice **(B)** follows from the passage and is incorrect. Near the end of the passage, the author mentions Pollock's problems with depression and an "unstable mental state" and that he is remembered for his artistic contributions. That makes **(C)** and **(E)** incorrect choices. Choice **(A)** actually contradicts the passage. The author states that Pollock's unique style of painting and artistic point of view made him stand out from his contemporaries, implying that Pollock did not mirror his peers or contemporaries. Thus, **(A)** is the correct choice.

9. C

None of these words is in the passage, so you will have to base your choice on context clues. In the beginning of the passage, the author states that Pollock was "far from ordinary," had a "unique style," and created a "new" way of painting. That makes choices **(A)** and **(E)** clearly incorrect. When describing Pollock's artistic point of view, the author states that he paints in an abstract manner. Because "abstract" is an antonym for "literal," **(D)** is not the correct choice. The passage indicates that inventing a new style and new techniques of painting is what Pollock is best known for, making **(C)** the best choice. Choice **(B)** is probably the trickiest wrong answer. The passage mentions that Pollock was depressed, but the question asked how the passage described Pollock *as an artist*, not as a person. The passage doesn't suggest that Pollack's art is "gloomy." Therefore, **(B)** is not a viable choice.

10. C

The reasons Brod is described as a controversial figure are a major focus of this passage, so researching this question should give you little trouble. The correct answer comes from the sentence in which the author tells you what "many in the field" feel about Brod: He was incapable of appreciating Kafka's work despite being its sole caretaker. Choice **(A)**, while saying nothing that directly contradicts the passage, is not supported by the passage, either. No mention is made of Kafka's feelings towards Brod's editing. That's the first choice you can eliminate. Choices **(B)** and **(D)** both possess language not contained in the passage. The passage does not discuss Kafka's and Brod's upbringings or Kafka being "repulsed" by Brod's lifestyle. Choice **(E)** sounds reminiscent of the passage, but the passage describes Kafka's wish to have his writing burned, a wish Brod denies. Choice **(E)** misstates this situation and is, thus, also incorrect. Choice **(C)**, however, paraphrases the concern of those in the field who believe that Brod did not really comprehend Kafka's writing (although he saw its importance). That is the correct answer.

11. B, E

The key to this question is the detour road sign "unfortunately." Terrance's low test scores are the exact opposite of what you would expect from a student such as him. You know he is an eager student who always tries his best and participates in class; any of these positive associations could fit in the blank. This allows you to immediately eliminate choice **(A)** *pedantic*, "stodgy," and **(F)** *prudent*, "restrained," which are direct opposites of our predictions. Choice **(C)** *apathetic* can be rejected for the same reason. Contrasting Terrance's ability with his idealistic actions eliminates choice **(D)** *pragmatic*, which means "realistic as opposed to idealistic." The remaining two answer choices, **(B)** *animated*, "lively," and **(E)** *assiduous*, "persistent," both create sentences that describe the type of student who would continue to participate in class when he is not experiencing success.

12. A, D

If the maned wolf's musk acts as a "defense mechanism," it probably smells pretty bad. So you can predict *foul-smelling* for the blank. For this reason, you can eliminate choice **(B)** *pristine,* "fresh," "uncorrupted," which suggests the exact opposite of a foul musk, and choice **(E)** *estimable,* "admirable," which suggests only a positive attitude toward the smell. Choice **(F)** *charming* can be rejected for similar reasons. While a **(C)** *soporific* or "sleep-inducing" musk could conceivably serve as a defense, there is no match for it among the other choices. Choices **(A)** *malodorous,* "bad-smelling," and **(D)** *pungent,* "sharp-smelling," best fit your original prediction of *foul-smelling.*

13. C, E

Reading this sentence all the way through reveals that the missing word describes a relationship that "exacerbates," or "worsens," a chaotic situation. For this reason, you can immediately eliminate choices **(A)** *venerable* and **(B)** *prudent,* as they characterize a relationship as respectful and restrained, the opposite of the relationship described here. Choice **(D)** *stolid,* "unemotional, lacking sensitivity," seems plausible at first glance, as it suggests a negative relationship. Likewise for choice **(F)** *stoic,* "indifferent to pleasure or pain." However, the context key word "chaos" suggests an emotional (albeit negative) relationship. Therefore, choice **(C)** *volatile,* "easily aroused," and **(E)** *inimical,* "hostile," are the best choices. They indicate the hostile, chaotic relationship that the sentence suggests.

14. A, E

"Although" is a detour road sign, indicating that the sentence will change direction. So, although the woman lived through the Great Depression, she can now give her grandchildren the things she couldn't afford growing up. Choice **(F)** *flintily* is wrong, as this implies she was not kindly disposed to spending money. This reasoning also eliminates choices **(B)** *scrupulously* and **(D)** *meticulously* as these imply a restraint with money. Choice **(C)** *capriciously* is plausible, but implies a carelessness that is not evidenced in the passage. Therefore, choice **(A)** *liberally* and choice **(E)** *lavishly* are the best choices, as they indicate exuberant spending, opposite of the frugality typical of the Depression.

15. E

In this question, you are asked to select the best summary of the passage. The main idea of the passage is that fetal immune systems do not operate in the same way as adult immune systems, and that provides protection from HIV to the developing fetus. Choice **(E)** paraphrases that summary and is indeed the answer. Choice **(A)** is not true according to the passage; HIV can enter the bloodstream, but the T-cells are tolerant and don't activate, which allows the HIV to pass through without attacking the T-cells. Choice **(B)** is outside the scope; nothing is said in the passage about the mothers' T-cells. Choice **(C)** is true according to the passage, but it is not a complete summary. The critical component of HIV resistance is not included in this choice. Choice **(D)** gets the facts from the passage wrong. According to the passage, T-cells activate in the fetal immune system but do not fight HIV in the typical way.

16. A

This question asks you to evaluate the statements and select those that can be validly inferred from the passage. Choice **(A)** summarizes the passage's main point. It's one correct answer. Choice **(B)** seems reasonable, but the passage doesn't go this far. Differences between the adult and fetal immune systems beyond their respective responses to HIV may make this statement untrue. There is nothing in the passage to suggest that choice **(C)** is a valid inference. The passage does not compare the complexity of the adult and fetal immune systems.

17. A

This question asks you to evaluate possible explanations and compare them to your understanding of the information in the passage. Choice **(A)** follows from that portion of the passage in which the author tells you that prisoners see "quality of life" improvements as the result of working. Choice **(B)** falls completely outside the scope of the passage. The author says nothing about lawsuits challenging prison work programs. Choice **(C)** distorts the passage. Telemarketing is one of the jobs prisoners perform, but so is manufacturing (and maybe others). Nothing suggests that telemarketing firms have the most to gain from using prison labor. Choice **(D)** is cited as a concern of some critics, but nothing suggests that the author agrees with them. Nor can you determine whether the author would agree with choice **(E)**. The suggestion in **(E)** might address the concerns of some critics, but again, you don't know that the author shares those concerns.

18. *"Some of these benefits take the forms of reduced recidivism, increased job skills and employability, and improved quality of life."*

This sentence supports the main claim that is set up in the first sentence: "While days of the chain gang are long gone, the effects of meaningful labor during imprisonment demonstrate marked benefits to both the prisoner and society." The remainder of the passage contains counterarguments and their supporting evidence.

19. B

This question rewards you for paying attention to the author's attitude and opinions. For the most part, this author takes a neutral tone. He states facts and reports the debate over sabbaticals, but doesn't appear to take a side in that debate. Choice **(A)** is one of the sides in the debate. Nothing in the passage suggests that the author agrees with the anti-sabbatical crowd. Choice **(B)** is the correct answer. The author points out that it is not clear, prior to a sabbatical, whether the result will be profitable. He offers the biotechnology example to illustrate this point. Choice **(C)** is wrong because the author doesn't opine on this issue; he suggests a defense of research through his inclusion of the biotechnology example. Choice **(D)** is the flip side of **(C)**; while the author is positively disposed to research, nothing suggests that he considers it the sole (or even primary) mission of universities. You can reject choice **(E)** as a comparison irrelevant to the scope of this passage.

20. C

This question asks you to evaluate the statements and identify which you can infer from the passage. Choice **(A)** is incorrect because it goes beyond the scope of what the passage implies; nowhere does the author say that there is insufficient research being done within the university system or ascribe blame to the sabbatical system. Choice **(B)** may be tempting, but it is wrong. The passage employs the Iowa debate to illustrate the point, but it doesn't provide any information that compares Iowa to other states. Choice **(C)** is the only correct answer. The author mentions the example of a professor writing a book on ancient mythology during sabbatical to imply that some legislators may not consider that an adequately beneficial work product.

Diagnostic Tool

Tally up your score and write your results in the space provided.

Total

Total Correct: ________ out of 20 correct

Percentage Correct: # you got right × 100 ÷ 20: ________

By Question Type

Text Completion ________ out of 6 correct

Sentence Equivalence ________ out of 4 correct

Reading Comprehension ________ out of 10 correct

Diagnose Your Results

Look back at the questions you got wrong and think about your experience answering them.

VERBAL REASONING PRACTICE SET 6

Directions: For each sentence, choose one word for each set of blanks. Select the word or words that best fit(s) the meaning of the sentence as a whole.

1. After getting expelled from school, Patricia refused to attend any future family functions, petrified that her stern family would _______ her.

   (A) venerate
   (B) deride
   (C) vex
   (D) emulate
   (E) provoke

2. The filmmaker's highly controversial work was _______ in bringing the style of Dogme 95 to the forefront of the film industry.

   (A) a lament
   (B) an anachronism
   (C) a catalyst
   (D) an anomaly
   (E) a paradox

3. Male sperm whales, recognizable by their astonishing size, are normally (i) _______ creatures; however, when they are jealously guarding their territory, they have been known to (ii) _______ ships that they feel have encroached too far.

Blank (i)	Blank (ii)
A docile	D ignore
B aggressive	E follow
C powerful	F attack

4. Opponents of affirmative action by quota, the practice of hiring on the basis of race or sex as well as (i) _______, maintain that both the hired and the rejected suffer (ii) _______ when not judged on their abilities alone.

Blank (i)	Blank (ii)
A status	D nepotism
B creed	E parity
C competence	F injustice

5. Ancient Greek philosophers tried to (i) ________ contemporary notions of change and stability in the physical composition of the world around them. They did so by (ii) ________ the existence of the atom. For them, the atom was (iii) ________ particle from which all varieties of matter are formed.

Blank (i)	Blank (ii)	Blank (iii)
A reconcile	D denying	G a mythical
B eliminate	E ignoring	H an indivisible
C confirm	F postulating	I a munificent

6. As a general rule, feuds between individuals or groups tend to arise in societies that (i) ________ centralized government, because public justice, such as the kind meted out by a strong, centralized authority or sophisticated judicial system, is difficult to (ii) ________. In such societies, it is therefore not surprising that private recourse is more (iii) ________.

Blank (i)	Blank (ii)	Blank (iii)
A espouse	D identify	G objectionable
B lack	E enforce	H prevalent
C affirm	F recognize	I brutal

Questions 7 and 8 are based on the following passage.

Ludwig Wittgenstein asserted that with the publication of his *Tractatus Logico-Philosophicus* he had solved all philosophical problems and retired to teach mathematics at the secondary level. He believed he had achieved this through his exploration of the logic of language, which he referred to as his "picture theory" of language. Wittgenstein's contention was that the world consisted of a collection of interconnected "facts" that created "pictures" of the world through propositions. These propositions are meaningful if they picture matters of empirical fact, such as "Meri is six feet tall." In order for these linguistic pictures to accurately represent facts, they must have the same logical structure as matters of empirical fact.

The problem is that philosophical propositions, such as "truth is beauty," are not matters of empirical fact. Since language itself is based on this relationship, philosophers cannot extricate themselves from the realm of language in order to actually *say* anything about whether or not the "pictures" have the same logical structure as the facts. One important consequence of this argument is that it is nonsensical to discuss philosophical problems. The propositions that philosophers commonly make are not technically wrong but nonsensical. For Wittgenstein, the ultimate goal of philosophy itself is not the actual study or pursuit of "truth." Philosophy has more to do with clarifying the relationship between language and truth than truth itself. The *Tractatus* ends up subverting its own claims by concluding that the kind of propositions of which it is composed are senseless. The most commonly quoted excerpt from the book is the proposition "What we cannot speak about we must pass over in silence."

7. The author believes Wittgenstein would likely agree with which of the following statements?

   (A) The truth is not beautiful.
   (B) Beauty is not truthful.
   (C) Something cannot be both truthful and beautiful.
   (D) The proposition "truth is beauty" is nonsensical.
   (E) Beauty is the same as truth.

8. Based on the context of the passage, the author's use of the word "empirical" most nearly means which of the following?

   (A) verifiable by experimentation
   (B) true
   (C) subjective
   (D) nonsensical
   (E) typical

Question 9 is based on the following passage.

According to a recent study, advertisements in medical journals often contain misleading information about the effectiveness and safety of new prescription drugs. The medical researchers who wrote the study concluded that the advertisements could result in doctors prescribing inappropriate drugs to their patients.

9. The researchers' conclusion would be most strengthened if which of the following were true?

   Ⓐ Advertisements for new prescription drugs are an important source of revenue for medical journals.
   Ⓑ Editors of medical journals are often unable to evaluate the claims made in advertisements for new prescription drugs.
   Ⓒ Doctors rely on the advertisements as a source of information about new prescription drugs.
   Ⓓ Advertisements for new prescription drugs are typically less accurate than medical journal articles evaluating those same drugs.
   Ⓔ The Food and Drug Administration, the government agency responsible for drug regulation, reviews advertisements for new drugs only after the ads have already been printed.

Question 10 is based on the following passage.

Marcus Tullius Cicero was a Roman statesman and philosopher in the final years of the Republic and remains one of the greatest and most influential orators in Western history. Among his many famous tracts and speeches, one of the most remarkable remains the First Catilinarian Oration, a condemnation of the senator Lucius Sergius Catiline for his role in a conspiracy against the Republic. Enraged at having lost the election for consulship the previous year to Cicero, his political rival, Cataline wove a plot to assassinate Cicero and several other senators to ensure his victory in the election of 63 b.c.e. When the plot was uncovered and foiled, the election was postponed, and the Senate meeting moved to a more secure location the following day to discuss the conspiracy. Cataline arrived at the Senate, shocking the entire Senate, but Cicero quickly recovered and delivered the First Catilinarian Oration, a masterpiece of oratory skill, which prompted the rest of the Senate to denounce Cataline as a traitor. Cataline fled the city with his conspirators and was killed a year later in battle with Republican soldiers.

10. What is the topic of this passage?

   Ⓐ The works of Marcus Tullius Cicero
   Ⓑ The effects of the First Catilinarian Oration
   Ⓒ The Catilinarian conspiracy
   Ⓓ The First Catilinarian Oration
   Ⓔ Famous orations

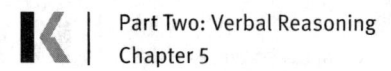

Directions: Select the two answer choices that, when inserted into the sentence, fit the meaning of the sentence as a whole and yield complete sentences that are similar in meaning.

11. Many Americans in the 1950s may have found the idea of a black president _______, but societal changes since then have made this idea a reality.

[A] farcical
[B] puerile
[C] superannuated
[D] implausible
[E] perfidious
[F] fastidious

12. Located in what is perhaps the most geographically remote state in the Union, Hawaii's isolated Molokai Island is known for its hidden, untouched, and _______ beaches.

[A] morose
[B] immaculate
[C] dilapidated
[D] placid
[E] pristine
[F] imperturbable

13. Hot yoga, a practice that takes place in a 95-degree-plus room, clears toxins out of the body through perspiration, leaving a practitioner with a sense of _______.

[A] disarray
[B] turbulence
[C] purgation
[D] quintessence
[E] ablution
[F] exhilaration

14. The doctor told Joe he needed to lose weight, so he began to make more _______ choices when going out to dinner.

    [A] abstemious
    [B] detrimental
    [C] gluttonous
    [D] acerbic
    [E] loquacious
    [F] austere

Question 15 is based on the following passage.

One of the most famous and influential music theorists of the latter half of the 20th century, John Cage is remembered for being to music what Marcel Duchamp was to art—someone who constantly questioned what defined music. One of his best-known interests was in removing the creator, the personal influence, from music and instead creating music based on natural patterns and chance (aleatory music). One of his famous works involved music created by laying musical bars over astrological maps and assigning notes based on the location of the stars and planets. Another famous work (perhaps his most famous), 4′33″, consisted of three movements all entirely of rests: the music, rather, was created by the ambient sounds of and around the performance hall. His stated goal was to remove personal agency and purpose from music and let music act as a reflection of the natural chaos of the world, rather than as an effort to organize and improve nature.

15. According to the passage, which of the following best paraphrases John Cage's philosophy of music?

    (A) Music must be radically changed from our current notions.
    (B) Music should be based in nature rather than on individual purpose.
    (C) Music is not really anything, but rather whatever we wish it to be.
    (D) Music is a reflection of the personal agency of the composer.
    (E) Music is inherently without meaning.

Questions 16–18 are based on the following passage.

Coffee has long been the subject of research due to its popularity as an early-morning pick-me-up and its distinct taste and aroma. Although it has often been laden with a reputation for being potentially unhealthy, many studies have shown that the opposite is true; in fact, coffee has been tied to a wide range of benefits. The acid in coffee can contribute to heartburn, and the caffeine can raise blood pressure, but when consumed in moderation (a few regular cups a day), these disadvantages are minimized.

Although coffee was once linked to cancer, that association has long been dispelled. Instead, coffee may contribute to the prevention of certain types of cancers due to its high volume of antioxidants. Minerals found in coffee, like magnesium and chromium, help the body control blood sugar by influencing insulin, and this may contribute to preventing diabetes. Similarly, although researchers aren't sure why, coffee drinkers seem to have a better chance than do non–coffee drinkers of fighting off Parkinson's disease and dementia as they age. In the short term, coffee is low in calories, stimulates alertness and concentration, and, for some people, lengthens their attention spans.

16. Which statement best summarizes the reading passage?

(A) The more coffee a person consumes, the healthier he or she will be.
(B) The benefits of drinking coffee appear to outweigh the disadvantages.
(C) Drinking coffee can prevent Parkinson's disease and dementia.
(D) Coffee consumption is unrelated to the incidence of cancer.
(E) Caffeine is the cause of high blood pressure.

Consider each of the following choices separately and select all that apply.

17. What can you infer from the passage?

[A] Decaffeinated coffee offers the same benefits as caffeinated coffee.
[B] If berries are high in antioxidants, they may help prevent cancer.
[C] Insulin has an effect on diabetes.

Consider each of the following choices separately and select all that apply.

18. The author would most likely disagree with which of the following statements?

[A] Stimulants are inherently bad for the human body.
[B] It is possible for coffee to be a part of a healthy diet.
[C] Decaffeinated coffee does not have the same benefits as caffeinated coffee.

Questions 19 and 20 are based on the following passage.

In December 2010, the Federation Internationale de Football Association (FIFA), the global governing body of soccer, announced that the 2022 World Cup would be held in Qatar. Immediately, a swirl of controversy surrounded the decision, which followed previous allegations that certain FIFA members had accepted monetary bribes in exchange for their bid votes. Soccer fans questioned how Qatar was able to win the bidding process over other bidders, such as the United States, Australia, South Korea, and Japan. In addition to the logistical problem of oppressive heat during the summer months in which the World Cup is traditionally held, Qatar is a controversial choice because of allegedly discriminatory legislation and its restrictive alcohol policy, which some claim is at odds with the activities typical of a sporting event. Additionally, Qatar would have to build venues for the event from scratch. Nonetheless, FIFA officials insist that this furthers the goal of spreading soccer to new places.

19. Which of the following is likely to be an opinion of the author of this passage?

    Ⓐ FIFA is a corrupt and unethical organization.
    Ⓑ It is improbable that Qatar will be adequately prepared for the 2022 World Cup.
    Ⓒ Japan was most deserving of winning the 2022 World Cup bid.
    Ⓓ Qatar is a controversial choice to host the 2022 World Cup.
    Ⓔ Soccer fans will be unlikely to travel to Qatar for the 2022 World Cup.

Consider each of the following choices separately and select all that apply.

20. Which of the following statements is suggested by the passage?

    [A] FIFA is likely to face criticism and come under scrutiny in the following months.
    [B] The country of Qatar is likely to change in some ways as a result of hosting the 2022 World Cup.
    [C] The choice of Qatar to host the 2022 World Cup is enough evidence to abolish FIFA and replace it.

VERBAL REASONING PRACTICE SET 6 ANSWER KEY

1. B
2. C
3. A, F
4. C, F
5. A, F, H
6. B, E, H
7. D
8. A
9. C
10. D
11. A, D
12. B, E
13. C, E
14. A, F
15. B
16. B
17. B, C
18. A
19. D
20. A, B

VERBAL REASONING PRACTICE SET 6 ANSWERS AND EXPLANATIONS

1. B

Using what you know about the "stern family" and their feelings toward failure, you can predict that the blank will be filled by word with a negative charge. You can also deduce this negative connotation by Patricia's fear (she is "petrified") of seeing her family. This eliminates choices **(A)** *venerate* and **(D)** *emulate*, as they both indicate positive feelings. Choice **(C)** *vex*, "annoy," can also be eliminated, as it indicates Patricia's irritation toward her family, which is not evidenced by the context. Choice **(E)** *provoke* can be eliminated for similar reasons. Choice **(B)** *deride*, "to speak ill of," is the correct answer.

2. C

The key to this sentence is the relationship of the film to the film style of Dogme 95. We can predict the word *start* for the blank. For that reason, you can eliminate choice **(A)** *lament*, "expresses grief," as it directs attention to the past, not the future as is the case in this sentence. Similarly, you can eliminate choice **(E)** *paradox*, "a contradiction," which is irrelevant to the beginning of a new fad. Choices **(B)** *anachronism* and **(D)** *anomaly* are both plausible, as a controversial work is likely to be out of place. However, choice **(C)** *catalyst*, "something that brings about a change in something else," is the correct answer; it best fits your predicted word *start*, and it directly describes the relationship between the film and the change in the film industry.

3. A, F

The first word here will describe what type of creatures male sperm whales normally are. The detour road sign "however" between the clauses indicates that a contrasting point will be made. In the second clause, we learn that something happens when the whales "are jealously guarding their territory." Predict that the whales *attack* ships when they're guarding their territory and are *gentle* when they're not. For the first blank, choice **(A)** *docile* is the best match for your prediction; choices **(B)** *aggressive* and **(C)** *powerful* are more descriptive of the whales when they're guarding their territory. For the second blank, choice **(D)** *ignore* is the opposite of what we expect the whales to do. Choice **(E)** *follow* is possible, but choice **(F)** *attack* is a perfect match for our prediction: "Male sperm whales . . . are normally *docile* creatures; however, when they are jealously guarding their territory, they have been known to *attack* ships."

4. C, F

For the first blank, there are a few clues to pay attention to. The phrase set off with commas will define "affirmative action by quota." The road sign "as well as" directly before the blank tells us that there is a basis upon which people are being hired other than race or sex. Because the rest of the sentence states that people suffer when they are not judged on their abilities alone, the missing word in the first blank must mean *abilities*. The second blank will have a negative connotation, since the opponents believe that people "suffer" from it. For the first blank, the best match is choice **(C)** *competence*. Choice **(A)** *status* and choice **(B)** *creed* have no necessary connection to the idea of ability. For the second blank, choice **(D)** *nepotism* means "favoritism for family members," which, while it might have a negative connotation, is not related to affirmative action by quota. Choice **(E)** *parity* means "equality," which has a positive connotation. The best choice for the second blank is choice **(F)** *injustice*: "Opponents of affirmative action by quota, the practice of hiring on the basis of race or sex as well as *competence*, maintain that both the hired and the rejected suffer *injustice* when not judged on their abilities alone."

5. A, F, H

These philosophers were trying to do something with the notions of "change and stability." The first thing you should notice is that change and stability are starkly opposing ideas, so predict that they were trying to *harmonize* the two ideas. The way they tried to do this was to do something concerning the existence of a particle that could explain both change and stability—predict *hypothesizing*. You're told that this particle is the atom from which all varieties of matter are formed, which would include both changing and stable things. The third blank will describe the atom in some way. This blank is difficult to predict, so you'll need to evaluate the answer choices in context. For the first blank, choice **(A)** *reconcile* is a good match for your prediction. Neither choice **(B)** *eliminate*, nor choice **(C)** *confirm*, takes into account the opposing forces of change and stability. In the second blank, choice **(F)** *postulating* matches your prediction. Neither choice **(D)** *denying* the existence of the atom, nor choice **(E)** *ignoring* it, would have helped the philosophers reconcile the concepts of change and stability. Moving on to the third blank, choice **(G)** *mythical* doesn't work—these philosophers didn't see atoms as the stuff of myth, but rather as a plausible hypothesis. Choice **(H)** *indivisible* seems promising—although you now know that atoms can be split, this was not known at the time of the Greek philosophers—but check choice **(I)** just in case. *Munificent* means "generous" or "bountiful"; this wouldn't be a logical way to describe a particle.

6. B, E, H

The word "because" is a straight-ahead road sign that indicates a close connection between the first two clauses. The first clause tells you that feuds tend to arise in societies that have a certain relationship with centralized government. In the second clause, you learn more about these societies—there is something difficult about public justice in them. The second sentence, in turn, tells you that this difficulty has an effect on the concept of "private recourse." These must be societies that *don't have* strong, centralized governments—because "public justice is difficult to *obtain*," private recourse becomes "more *common*." For the first blank, choice **(B)** *lack* matches your prediction. Societies that *espouse*, choice **(A)**, or *affirm*, choice **(C)**, central governments are the opposite of what you're looking for. For the second blank, the best fit is choice **(E)** *enforce*. It doesn't make sense to say that "public justice is difficult to *identify*," choice **(D)**, or *recognize*, choice **(F)**. For the third blank, *prevalent*, choice **(H)**, matches the prediction and is correct. Choice **(G)** *objectionable* is the opposite of what you need here: you may find the concept of "private recourse" objectionable, but those in the societies referred to in the sentence would not. Choice **(I)** *brutal* is not supported by the information in the sentence.

7. D

The passage itself is largely concerned with the philosophical relationship between logical reasoning and language. The author notes that Wittgenstein distinguishes between propositions that are "pictures" of empirical fact, and those that are not. The statement "truth is beauty" falls into the latter category. Since it is not a matter of empirical fact, you cannot determine if the linguistic picture (the proposition "truth is beauty") has the same logical structure as the fact itself. Therefore, it is nonsensical. Choice **(D)** is your answer.

8. A

The word "empirical" has the meaning of "measurable." That's close to choice **(A)** *verifiable by experimentation*, which makes sense in the context of the passage. You can't measure truth or beauty, but you can measure how tall someone is, which is cited as an example of an empirical fact.

9. C

This question stem asks you to find an answer choice that would strengthen the researchers' conclusion outlined in the second sentence of the stimulus: the researchers believe that misleading drug advertisements in medical journals might lead doctors to prescribe the wrong drugs. Any answer choice that makes this *more* likely will be correct; therefore, look for a choice that further suggests doctors will end up prescribing inappropriate drugs based on misleading ads.

Choice **(C)** does this perfectly. By asserting that doctors actually depend on the advertisements for information, it strengthens the bond between the researchers' evidence and their conclusion and therefore strengthens their argument. Choice **(A)** is outside the scope of this issue—the journals' revenues have no direct connection to the prescribing of drugs. Choice **(B)** critiques the wrong party—even if *editors of medical journals* can't discern true claims from false, maybe doctors still can. Neither choice **(D)** nor **(E)** tells you anything new. Both support the notion that advertisements are inaccurate or misleading, but the falsehood of the ads is already established in the passage, so neither **(D)** nor **(E)** will further strengthen the researchers' argument regarding actual prescriptions.

10. D

Remember: the topic is the general area of the passage, while the scope is the specific purpose or focus of the passage—you should have already determined these before you began attacking the question or questions following the passage. In the case of this passage, some of the choices are *too* broad to be the topic—choice **(A)** is too broad because only one of Cicero's works is discussed, and likewise for **(E)** because only one oration is discussed. Choice **(C)** relates to the passage, but it is the setting of the passage, not the topic. Choices **(B)** and **(D)** may look similar, but you should be able to choose between them—**(B)** is too narrow to be the topic and is more akin to a possible scope. Choice **(D)** is the correct answer because it describes the general topic of the passage (the First Catilinarian Oration) rather than specific aspects of it.

11. A, D

You can use the word "but" in the sentence to deduce that the environment in the 1950s was not the same as it is now. In other words, the second half of the sentence tells us that "societal changes" have led to the reality of a black president, implying that Americans in the 1950s would not have expected such an occurrence. Choice **(E)** *perfidious*, "faithless," "disloyal," "untrustworthy," and **(F)** *fastidious*, "careful with details," can both be ruled out. These are words more likely to be used to describe people than events and ideas and would thus not make sense in this context. While **(B)** *puerile*, which means "childish, immature, or silly," could be used to describe an occurrence or event, it wouldn't make sense to describe an election of a president. Choice **(C)** *superannuated* describes something that is out-of-date or obsolete, which would be in conflict with the idea of social progress. That leaves choice **(A)** *farcical*, "absurd" or "ludicrous," and **(D)** *implausible*, "improbable" or "inconceivable." Both these words render a sentence that means about the same thing. At the beginning of the Civil Rights Movement, people would have found the idea of a black president farfetched, rendering it both absurd and inconceivable during that era.

12. B, E

You can infer from the words "isolated," "hidden," and "untouched" that the blank must be in line with these adjectives. It wouldn't make sense for a beach to be hidden, untouched, and **(A)** *morose,* "gloomy and sullen," or **(C)** *dilapidated,* "in disrepair or run-down," so you can eliminate these choices. Choices **(D)** *placid,* "calm," and **(F)** *imperturbable,* "incapable of being disturbed," are both tempting options because it is possible that an isolated beach would be both of these things. But the sentence doesn't rule out the possibility that the beaches could be less than placid, and just because a beach hasn't been touched yet doesn't mean it is immune from being disturbed in the future. You are left with choice **(B)** *immaculate,* "without stain or flaw," and **(E)** *pristine,* "untouched" or "uncorrupted," which are both synonyms of the adjectives used elsewhere in the sentence and therefore the correct answers.

13. C, E

If your body has been cleared of toxins through sweating from exercise, there is no reason to believe that you would feel a sense of **(A)** *disarray* or **(B)** *turbulence*, which are both terms for disorder. Additionally, choice **(D)** *quintessence*, doesn't make sense in this context, since it is a word for a most typical example or concentrated essence. **(F)** *exhilaration* may seem like a plausible choice if you or a friend has ever described yoga as leaving you in a state of being energetic or filled with happiness. But nothing from this particular sentence implies that a person would feel especially happy after finishing a hot yoga session. Rather, this sentence highlights the fact that sweating plays a role in cleansing a person's body. Therefore, the correct choices are **(C)** *purgation,* "the process of cleansing or purification," and **(E)** *ablution,* "the act of cleansing."

14. A, F

If Joe is making an effort to lose weight, it would be in his best interest to make healthy choices when going out to dine. Therefore, making a **(C)** *gluttonous,* "tending to eat and drink excessively," or a **(B)** *detrimental,* "causing harm or injury," choice for dinner would be the opposite of what he should be doing. He may choose an **(D)** *acerbic,* "bitter" or "sharp in taste" dish for dinner, but there's no telling if that would be a healthy or unhealthy choice. Because the adjective in question applies to food, choice **(E)** *loquacious* makes no sense since it means "talkative." This leaves choices **(A)** *abstemious,* "moderate in appetite," and **(F)** *austere,* "stern" or "strict," which make sense when describing a selection that someone on a diet would make.

15. B

The key to understanding this question is to determine how the author of the passage describes John Cage's approach to music. In the passage, the author describes Cage as being concerned with "removing the creator, the personal influence, from music and instead creating music based on natural patterns." This points immediately to choice **(B)**, a paraphrase of this statement. That answer is correct, but you should take care to eliminate the other options to ensure your correct response. Choice **(A)** may seem to describe Cage's radical departure from traditional music, but the departure itself is not described as his motivation. Choices **(C)** and **(E)** are, in essence, paraphrases of one another, claiming that music has no real definition. While this relates to Cage's question of what defined music, neither choice correctly describes his philosophy of music. Choice **(D)** is clearly incorrect because it directly contradicts the paraphrase of the passage seen in **(B)**. Choice **(B)** is the correct answer.

16. B

While the general sentiment of this passage appears to be in support of coffee, it does not state that the benefits are proportionate to consumption as outlined in choice **(A)**. In fact, it recognizes that there are downsides to drinking coffee and implies that drinking it to excess could exacerbate these problems by saying that the disadvantages are minimized when coffee is consumed in moderation. Instead, choice **(B)** is the statement that most closely aligns with the message of the passage. The use of the word "appear" acknowledges the fact that there are still unknowns about coffee that researchers are studying. Although the passage states that coffee may help a person fight off Parkinson's disease and dementia, you can infer from the passage that the link is merely a correlation and not necessarily a cause-and-effect relationship, rendering **(C)** inaccurate. The passage states that coffee does not *cause* cancer, as was once believed, but that it's now known to have some properties that help fight cancer, which means choice **(D)** is false. Choice **(E)** isn't correct because, although caffeine can be a cause of high blood pressure, it is certainly possible that someone who doesn't consume caffeine can have high blood pressure as well.

17. B, C

This question asks you to evaluate the statements and identify what you can infer using material from the passage. Taking each individually, choice **(A)** may be true, but this particular passage does not address research done on both varieties of coffee. Because the antioxidants in coffee help contribute to fighting cancer, it can be inferred that choice **(B)** is correct because any other food or drink that contains antioxidants would carry the same properties. Similarly, you may deduce that if blood sugar impacts diabetes, and the magnesium and chromium in coffee interact with a person's insulin, thereby changing a person's blood sugar, choice **(C)** *insulin has an effect on diabetes* is correct.

18. A

While the passage does recognize one downside of caffeine as a stimulant (high blood pressure), it also points out a handful of benefits (higher levels of alertness and concentration as well as longer attention spans.) Therefore, the author is likely to disagree with choice **(A)**. It is likely that the author would agree with choice **(B)**, since coffee has been "tied to a wide range of benefits." Although there is no evidence to say that the author would agree with choice **(C)**, because the author doesn't address research on different types of coffee, you can't infer anything about whether or not the author would disagree with that statement.

19. D

This question rewards you for correctly summarizing the author's scope and purpose in writing the passage. For the most part, this author remains objective despite reporting a controversial decision. Choice **(A)** is the attitude of some critics of the decision to have Qatar as host, but the author doesn't express agreement with the critics. The passage claims that Qatar will need to build facilities, but the author doesn't assess the likelihood that the country will or will not be ready for the World Cup by 2022; thus, choice **(B)** is incorrect. The author cites other countries that some felt were deserving, but doesn't state a preference for who should host the Cup; that knocks out choice **(C)**. Choice **(D)** is the correct answer. Without acknowledging whether the criticism is warranted, the author states that Qatar is a controversial choice. Choice **(E)** is out of scope; the likelihood that fans will attend the World Cup in Qatar simply isn't addressed in the passage.

20. A, B

This question asks you to evaluate the statements and identify any and all that you can infer, using material from the passage. Choice **(A)** follows from the passage, which reports that FIFA has already been criticized for its decision. Choice **(B)**, too, follows from the passage. Whether there are cultural or political changes as a result of hosting this global event, Qatar will at least have new stadiums and infrastructure, which the passage says must be built in anticipation of 2022. Choice **(C)** is far too extreme to qualify as a correct answer. The most rabid critics may feel this way, but nothing in the passage offers such a strong opinion.

Diagnostic Tool

Tally up your score and write your results in the space provided.

Total

Total Correct: ________ out of 20 correct

Percentage Correct: # you got right × 100 ÷ 20: ________

By Question Type

Text Completion ________ out of 6 correct

Sentence Equivalence ________ out of 4 correct

Reading Comprehension ________ out of 10 correct

Diagnose Your Results

Look back at the questions you got wrong and think about your experience answering them.

PART THREE

Verbal Content Review

CHAPTER 6

Vocabulary

UNDERSTANDING VOCABULARY

OVERVIEW

A strong vocabulary is the greatest asset you can bring to the GRE Verbal Reasoning sections. Text Completion and Sentence Equivalence questions reward you for knowing the meanings of a large number of words. Similarly, the passages in the Reading Comprehension section contain dense, complex passages and are accompanied by questions that require you to determine the meaning of words and sentences from context.

Building a good vocabulary takes time—a lifetime for most people. However, you can increase your GRE vocabulary quickly. There are a few reasons for this:

1. The GRE tests the same words repeatedly.

Knowing the words that the GRE testmakers love to use gives you a big head start in increasing your GRE vocabulary. We have included the words that appear most often on the GRE in this chapter in the "Words in Context" section. Start learning the meanings of these words as soon as you can.

2. The GRE does not test the exact definitions of words. If you have some idea of what the word means, you can usually determine the correct answer.

You don't need to know the exact definitions of words to achieve a good verbal score on the GRE. It's better to know something about ten words than everything about one word. This is why learning words in groups is a powerful technique. We have included common word groups found on the GRE in this chapter.

Knowing the meanings of common word roots can be helpful in two ways. First, knowing the meaning of word roots can help you guess at the meanings of unfamiliar words you encounter on the GRE. Second, when you're learning new vocabulary, it's more effective to study words in groups rather than individually. Learning several words that are related by a common root will help you to learn more words faster. We have included a list of common GRE word roots in this chapter.

Once you've looked over the top GRE words and the sections on word groups, roots, and words in context, you can hone your skills using the exercises that follow each section.

Basics of Vocabulary Building

The way most people build their vocabularies is by reading words in context. Reading is ultimately the best way to increase your vocabulary, although it also takes the most time. Of course, some types of reading material contain more GRE vocabulary words than others. You should get into the habit of reading high-level publications, such as the *Wall Street Journal*, the *Economist*, and the *New York Times*. (Because you'll have to read from the computer screen on Test Day, we recommend you read these publications online, if possible. And if you read lengthy articles that require scrolling, so much the better.)

WORD GROUPS

Learning words in groups is an efficient way of increasing your GRE vocabulary, since the GRE often tests only the general sense of a word. Imagine you saw the following Sentence Equivalence question on the test:

> The prime minister _______ the actions of the cabinet member; her sanctimonious tone indicated that she wanted to put distance between herself and the lurid implications of the scandal.
>
> [A] denounced
> [B] rephrased
> [C] extirpated
> [D] maligned
> [E] impugned
> [F] exculpated

Let's say that you immediately recognized *denounced* as an answer choice that fits in this blank but weren't sure which other word shares this same basic meaning. If you were to look up *denounce* in a dictionary, you'd see something like this:

de•nounce (dî-nouns') *transitive verb,* de•nounced, de•nounc•ing, de•nounc•es [Middle English: *denouncen, denounsen,* fr. Latin *denoncier,* fr. *de* + *nuntiare* to report, announce, fr. *nuntius* messenger]

1. To declare (a person, an idea, behavior, a philosophy) to be censurable or evil; stigmatize or accuse, especially publicly and indignantly; inveigh against openly
2. *archaic* to announce in a public, formal, and solemn manner: to declare or publish something disastrous
3. to inform against: declare or expose a lawbreaker to the authorities

4a. *obsolete* to indicate or portend

4b. *archaic* to announce in a warning or threatening manner

5. to proclaim formally and publicly the ending of a treaty or pact
6. *Mexican Law* to offer for record legal notice of a claim for a mining concession on land held by the government

Synonym see CRITICIZE

Do you need to know all this to answer the question? No—all you need to know is that *denounce* means something like "criticize." And in the time it took you to learn the meaning of *denounce* from the dictionary, you could have memorized a whole list of other words that also mean something like "criticize": *aspersion*, *berate*, *calumny*, *castigate*, *decry*, *defame/defamation*, *deride/derisive*, *diatribe*, *impugn*, *rebuke*, and others. Note that the answer choice *impugn* is in this list: this Sentence Equivalence question is made dramatically easier! This is why learning words in groups is a better general strategy for beefing up your GRE vocabulary than working slowly through the dictionary.

Just remember, the categories in which these words are listed are *general* and not to be taken for the exact definitions of the words. The words in the list may be different parts of speech than the words in the headers.

BOLD

audacious	courageous	dauntless

CHANGING QUICKLY

capricious	mercurial	volatile

HESITATE

dither	oscillate	teeter
vacillate	waver	

ACT QUICKLY

abrupt	apace	headlong
impetuous	precipitate	

INNOCENT/INEXPERIENCED

credulous	gullible	ingenuous
naive	novitiate	tyro

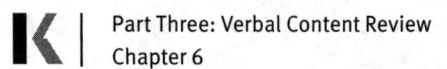

DIFFICULT TO UNDERSTAND

abstruse	ambiguous	arcane
bemusing	cryptic	enigmatic
esoteric	inscrutable	obscure
opaque	paradoxical	perplexing
recondite	turbid	

EASY TO UNDERSTAND

articulate	cogent	eloquent
evident	limpid	lucid
pellucid		

SMART/LEARNED

astute	canny	erudite
perspicacious		

CRITICIZE/CRITICISM

aspersion	belittle	berate
calumny	castigate	decry
defame/defamation	denounce	deride/derisive
diatribe	disparage	excoriate
gainsay	harangue	impugn
inveigh	lambaste	objurgate
obloquy	opprobrium	pillory
rebuke	remonstrate	reprehend
reprove	revile	tirade
vituperate		

CAROUSAL

bacchanalian	debauchery	depraved
dissipated	iniquity	libertine
libidinous	licentious	reprobate
ribald	salacious	sordid
turpitude		

TRUTH

candor/candid	fealty	frankness
indisputable	indubitable	legitimate
probity	sincere	veracious
verity		

FALSEHOOD

apocryphal, canard, chicanery
dissemble, duplicity, equivocate
erroneous, ersatz, fallacious
feigned, guile, mendacious/mendacity
perfidy, prevaricate, specious
spurious

BITING (as in wit or temperament)

acerbic, acidulous, acrimonious
asperity, caustic, mordacious
mordant, trenchant

PRAISE

acclaim, accolade, aggrandize
encomium, eulogize, extol
fawn, laud/laudatory, venerate/veneration

HARMFUL

baleful, baneful, deleterious
inimical, injurious, insidious
minatory, perfidious, pernicious

TIMID/TIMIDITY

craven, diffident, pusillanimous
recreant, timorous, trepidation

BORING

banal, fatuous, hackneyed
insipid, mundane, pedestrian
platitude, prosaic, quotidian
trite

WEAKEN

adulterate, enervate, exacerbate
inhibit, obviate, stultify
undermine, vitiate

ASSIST

abet, advocate, ancillary
bolster, corroborate, countenance
espouse, mainstay, munificent
proponent, stalwart, sustenance

HOSTILE

antithetic	churlish	curmudgeon
irascible	malevolent	misanthropic
truculent	vindictive	

STUBBORN

implacable	inexorable	intractable
intransigent	obdurate	obstinate
recalcitrant	refractory	renitent
untoward	vexing	

BEGINNING/YOUNG

burgeoning	callow	engender
inchoate	incipient	nascent

GENEROUS/KIND

altruistic	beneficent	clement
largess	magnanimous	munificent
philanthropic	unstinting	

GREEDY

avaricious	covetous	mercenary
miserly	penurious	rapacious
venal		

TERSE

compendious	curt	laconic
pithy	succinct	taciturn

OVERBLOWN/WORDY

bombastic	circumlocution	garrulous
grandiloquent	loquacious	periphrastic
prolix	rhetoric	turgid
verbose		

DICTATORIAL

authoritarian	despotic	dogmatic
hegemonic/hegemony	imperious	peremptory
tyrannical		

DEATH/MOURNING

bereave	cadaver	defunct
demise	dolorous	elegy
knell	lament	macabre
moribund	obsequies	sepulchral
wraith		

COPY

counterpart	emulate	facsimile
factitious	paradigm	precursor
simulate	vicarious	

EQUAL

equitable	equity	tantamount

UNUSUAL

aberration	anomaly	iconoclast
idiosyncrasy		

WANDERING

discursive	expatiate	forage
itinerant	peregrination	peripatetic
sojourn		

GAPS/OPENINGS

abatement	aperture	fissure
hiatus	interregnum	interstice
lull	orifice	rent
respite	rift	

HEALTHY

beneficial	salubrious	salutary

ABBREVIATED

abridge	compendium	cursory
curtail	syllabus	synopsis
terse		

WISDOM

adage	aphorism	apothegm
axiom	bromide	dictum
epigram	platitude	sententious
truism		

FAMILY

conjugal	consanguine	distaff
endogamous	filial	fraternal
progenitor	scion	

NOT A STRAIGHT LINE

askance	awry	careen
carom	circuitous	circumvent
gyrate	labyrinth	meander
oblique	serrated	sidle
sinuous	undulating	vortex

INVESTIGATE

appraise	ascertain	assay
descry	peruse	

TIME/ORDER/DURATION

anachronism	antecede	antedate
anterior	archaic	diurnal
eon	ephemeral	epoch
fortnight	millennium	penultimate
synchronous	temporal	

BAD MOOD

bilious	dudgeon	irascible
pettish	petulant	pique
querulous	umbrage	waspish

EMBARRASS

abash	chagrin	compunction
contrition	diffidence	expiate
foible	gaucherie	rue

HARD-HEARTED

asperity	baleful	dour
fell	malevolent	mordant
sardonic	scathing	truculent
vitriolic	vituperation	

NAG

admonish	belabor	cavil
enjoin	exhort	harangue
hector	martinet	remonstrate
reproof		

PREDICT

augur	auspice	fey
harbinger	portentous	precursor
presage	prescient	prognosticate

LUCK

adventitious	amulet	auspicious
fortuitous	kismet	optimum
portentous	propitiate	propitious
providential	serendipity	talisman

NASTY

fetid	noisome	noxious

HARSH-SOUNDING

cacophony	din	dissonant
raucous	strident	

PLEASANT-SOUNDING

euphonious	harmonious	melodious
sonorous		

For ease of study, these lists can also be found in Appendix A.

WORD GROUPS EXERCISE

Directions: Choose the TWO synonyms that can correctly complete the sentence.

[NOTE: While the questions in this exercise are not in GRE format, the task of choosing synonyms is good practice for the kind of thinking rewarded by Sentence Equivalence questions.]

1. The incoming freshman found the 300-level Intermediate Macroeconomic Analysis course ______; he simply did not possess the necessary background knowledge.

   (A) recondite
   (B) ardent
   (C) enigmatic
   (D) noxious
   (E) salubrious

2. The man encountered a series of ______ events on his way to work, from finding $20 on the ground to winning concert tickets off the radio.

   (A) lugubrious
   (B) fortuitous
   (C) gibe
   (D) din
   (E) propitious

3. The accountant became more ______ after she failed to save the company from bankruptcy.

   (A) volatile
   (B) torpid
   (C) lackadaisical
   (D) munificent
   (E) acrimonious

4. Generally, parents punish bad behavior and _______ good behavior in order to teach their children.

   (A) ameliorate
   (B) exculpate
   (C) ribald
   (D) laud
   (E) extol

5. A child may find jokes about bodily functions humorous while an adult finds them _______.

   (A) caustic
   (B) noisome
   (C) pernicious
   (D) odious
   (E) credulous

6. After spending 15 years teaching in the inner city and volunteering at homeless shelters on the weekends, it was clear the teacher was _______.

   (A) beneficent
   (B) disingenuous
   (C) penurious
   (D) rapacious
   (E) altruistic

7. A _______ melody filled the band room the first time the fourth graders played their chosen instruments.

   (A) sonorous
   (B) strident
   (C) jocular
   (D) diffident
   (E) raucous

8. My sister often found her friend's conversations about celebrities and fashion _______; she was more interested in politics and science.

   (A) hackneyed
   (B) banal
   (C) limpid
   (D) trenchant
   (E) perspicacious

9. The student was able to reduce wordiness and rewrite the paper in such a _______ manner that the page count fell from 20 to 12.

   (A) garrulous
   (B) succinct
   (C) mordacious
   (D) compendious
   (E) arcane

10. After feeding the stray cat every day for a week, I watched the once _______ animal develop the audacity to walk up to my door and wait for food.

   (A) craven
   (B) churlish
   (C) iconoclastic
   (D) truculent
   (E) timorous

11. While the author swore her novel was not intended to _______ a classic work of fiction, their syntax, diction, and plot were identical.

   (A) abridge
   (B) bereave
   (C) emulate
   (D) simulate
   (E) rescind

12. The professor answered the question in such a _______ way that the student was left confused and without a straightforward explanation.

   (A) respite
   (B) circuitous
   (C) sententious
   (D) oblique
   (E) presage

13. Instead of taking one piece of candy from the bowl, the _______ child took five.

   (A) avaricious
   (B) ingenuous
   (C) salubrious
   (D) dour
   (E) rapacious

14. In order to _______ her crying baby, the mother gently rocked the infant and sang a lullaby.

   (A) abet
   (B) dither
   (C) mollify
   (D) obviate
   (E) placate

15. The biologist was _______ when he spoke about the characteristics of the red-eyed tree frog, because he had spent nine years studying the animal in its natural habitat.

   (A) perspicacious
   (B) libidinous
   (C) ersatz
   (D) erudite
   (E) acidulous

16. The executive regretted her _______ action when it later became clear that she had approved the proposal without having access to complete information.

Ⓐ precipitate
Ⓑ impecunious
Ⓒ discursive
Ⓓ impetuous
Ⓔ mordacious

17. The _______ side effects of chocolate ingestion can be extremely detrimental for dogs.

Ⓐ insipid
Ⓑ deleterious
Ⓒ injurious
Ⓓ irascible
Ⓔ vexing

18. Adam's bout of bronchitis _______ his ability to get into peak shape for the outdoor track season.

Ⓐ admonished
Ⓑ inhibited
Ⓒ ameliorated
Ⓓ stultified
Ⓔ exhorted

19. Being denied a partial scholarship from her dream school proved _______ for Katie because she received a full scholarship to a different school, where she met her future husband.

Ⓐ providential
Ⓑ serendipitous
Ⓒ raucous
Ⓓ scathing
Ⓔ temporal

20. Her constantly_______ demeanor eventually discouraged Kara's friends from inviting her to social functions.

    (A) irascible
    (B) propitious
    (C) euphonious
    (D) salutary
    (E) querulous

21. The failing economy led the company into an extended _______, resulting in substantial financial losses.

    (A) demise
    (B) precursor
    (C) hiatus
    (D) lull
    (E) recant

22. The teacher's _______ response to the girl's question deterred the student from raising her hand for the rest of the semester.

    (A) caustic
    (B) indigent
    (C) fulsome
    (D) droll
    (E) acerbic

23. Although I've been to her house several times, I've never seen her _______ little cat because he is constantly hiding.

    (A) venal
    (B) insipid
    (C) torpid
    (D) timorous
    (E) diffident

24. It wasn't a surprise that with Kristen's creativity and _______ tastes, her new restaurant was praised as "truly original."

Ⓐ eclectic
Ⓑ noxious
Ⓒ iconoclastic
Ⓓ morose
Ⓔ vitriolic

25. Sick of being continually _______ by her mother, Erica decided it was finally time to move out of the house and into her own apartment.

Ⓐ ascertained
Ⓑ harangued
Ⓒ abashed
Ⓓ admonished
Ⓔ lulled

26. One of the most simple but _______ things we can do is drink lots of water and stay hydrated.

Ⓐ lugubrious
Ⓑ beneficial
Ⓒ salubrious
Ⓓ sinuous
Ⓔ ludicrous

27. Once he realized the inconvenience entailed by holding up his end of the deal, Aaron tried to _______ his promise to help his friend move.

Ⓐ recant
Ⓑ lament
Ⓒ renege on
Ⓓ curtail
Ⓔ descry

28. Although many _______ can seem trite and jaded, there is a lot of truth to most of them.

(A) aphorisms
(B) scions
(C) labyrinths
(D) advocates
(E) adages

29. Despite her dreams of exploring South America after graduating college, Caroline settled into a less-than-satisfying office job to _______ her parents.

(A) abet
(B) appease
(C) placate
(D) stultify
(E) inhibit

30. Because of the capabilities resulting from scientific advancements, identical twin births are far less of an _______ than they were 50 years ago.

(A) aberration
(B) abatement
(C) ancillary
(D) anomaly
(E) accolade

WORD GROUPS EXERCISE ANSWER KEY

1. A, C
2. B, E
3. B, C
4. D, E
5. B, D
6. A, E
7. B, E
8. A, B
9. B, D
10. A, E
11. C, D
12. B, D
13. A, E
14. C, E
15. A, D
16. A, D
17. B, C
18. B, D
19. A, B
20. A, E
21. C, D
22. A, E
23. D, E
24. A, C
25. B, D
26. B, C
27. A, C
28. A, E
29. B, C
30. A, D

WORD GROUPS EXERCISE ANSWERS AND EXPLANATIONS

1. A, C

Recondite and *enigmatic* are both related to "difficult to understand." *Ardent* is "favoring/not impartial." Something *noxious* is "nasty," and something *salubrious* is "healthy."

2. B, E

Fortuitous and *propitious* are both related to "luck." *Lugubrious* refers to "sorrow." A *gibe* is something "funny," and a *din* is "harsh-sounding."

3. B, C

Torpid and *lackadaisical* are both in the "lazy/sluggish" category. *Volatile* means "changing quickly." *Munificent* can be found under "assist," and *acrimonious* under "biting (as in wit or temperament)."

4. D, E

Laud and *extol* both mean "praise." *Ameliorate* is related to "pacify/satisfy." *Exculpate* means "forgive," and *ribald* is related to "carousal."

5. B, D

Noisome and *odious* both mean "disgusting/offensive." *Caustic* means "biting (as in wit or temperament)." *Pernicious* means "harmful," and *credulous* is related to "innocent/inexperienced."

6. A, E

Beneficent and *altruistic* are both related to "generous/kind." *Disingenuous* means "insincere." *Penurious* and *rapacious* are both related to "greedy."

7. B, E

Strident and *raucous* are both on the "harsh-sounding" list. *Sonorous* means "pleasant-sounding." *Jocular* is related to "funny," and *diffident* falls under "timid/timidity."

8. A, B

Hackneyed and *banal* are both related to "boring." *Limpid* is related to "easy to understand." *Trenchant* means "biting (as in wit or temperament)," and *perspicacious* is related to "smart/learned."

9. B, D

Succinct and *compendious* both fall into the "terse" category. *Garrulous* relates to "overblown/wordy." *Mordacious* means "biting (as in wit or temperament)," and *arcane* falls under "difficult to understand."

10. A, E

Craven and *timorous* are both listed under "timid/timidity." *Churlish* is related to "hostile." *Iconoclastic* is related to "eccentric/dissimilar" and "unusual," and *truculent* is related to "hard-hearted" and "hostile."

11. C, D

Emulate and *simulate* are both related to "copy." *Abridge* falls under "abbreviated communication." *Bereave* is related to "death/mourning," and *rescind* is related to "withdrawal/retreat."

12. B, D

Circuitous and *oblique* are both in the "not a straight line" category. *Respite* falls under "gap/opening." *Sententious* is related to "wisdom," and *presage* is related to "predict."

13. A, E

Avaricious and *rapacious* are both related to "greedy." *Ingenuous* can be found under "innocent/inexperienced." *Salubrious* means "healthy," and *dour* is related to "hard-hearted."

14. C, E

Mollify and *placate* both fall under "pacify/satisfy." *Abet* means "assist." *Dither* is related to "hesitate," and *obviate* is related to "weaken."

15. A, D

Perspicacious and *erudite* are both related to "smart/learned." *Libidinous* falls under "carousal." *Ersatz* is related to "falsehood," and *acidulous* is related to "biting (as in wit or temperament)."

16. A, D

Precipitate and *impetuous* are both related to "act quickly." *Impecunious* means "poor," and *discursive* is related to "wandering." *Mordacious* falls under "biting (as in wit or temperament)."

17. B, C

Deleterious and *injurious* are both related to "harmful." *Insipid* is related to "boring." *Irascible* falls under "hostile," and *vexing* falls under "stubborn."

18. B, D

Inhibited and *stultified* are both related to "weaken." *Admonished* and *exhorted* are related to "nag." *Ameliorated* is related to "pacify/satisfy."

19. A, B

Providential and *serendipitous* both refer to "luck." *Raucous* means "harsh-sounding." *Scathing* is related to "hard-hearted." *Temporal* falls under "time/order/duration."

20. A, E

Irascible and *querulous* both refer to "bad mood." *Propitious* is related to "luck." *Euphonious* means "pleasant-sounding," and *salutary* means "healthy."

21. C, D

Hiatus and *lull* are both related to "gaps/openings." *Demise* relates to "death/mourning." *Precursor* is related to "copy," and *recant* falls under "withdrawal/retreat."

22. A, E

Caustic and *acerbic* both refer to "biting (as in wit or temperament)." *Indigent* means "poor." *Fulsome* is related to "insincere," and *droll* means "funny."

23. D, E

Timorous and *diffident* both relate to "timid/timidity." *Venal* is associated with "greedy." *Insipid* is related to "boring," and *torpid* falls under "lazy/sluggish."

24. A, C

Eclectic and *iconoclastic* are both in the "eccentric/dissimilar" group. *Noxious* is related to "nasty." *Morose* relates to "sorrow," and *vitriolic* falls under "hard-hearted."

25. B, D

Harangued and *admonished* are both related to "nag." *Ascertained* is related to "investigate." *Abashed* refers to "embarrass." *Lulled* falls under "gaps/openings."

26. B, C

Beneficial and *salubrious* both refer to "healthy." *Lugubrious* relates to "sorrow." *Sinuous* falls under "not a straight line," and *ludicrous* is related to "funny."

27. A, C

Recant and *renege* are both related to "withdraw/retreat." *Lament* refers to "sorrow." *Curtail* is related to "abbreviated communication," and *descry* refers to "investigate."

28. A, E

Aphorisms and *adages* both relate to "wisdom." *Scions* are related to "family." *Labyrinths* are related to "not a straight line," and *advocates* are related to "assist."

29. B, C

Appease and *placate* are both related to "pacify/satisfy." *Abet* means "assist." *Stultify* means "weaken," and *inhibit* means "prevent/obstruct."

30. A, D

Aberration and *anomaly* are both related to "unusual." *Abatement* relates to "gaps/openings." *Ancillary* is related to "assist." *Accolade* refers to "praise."

WORD ROOTS

INTRODUCTION TO THE WORD ROOT LIST

The following list presents some of the most common word roots—mostly Greek and Latin—that appear in English. Learning to recognize these word roots is a great help in expanding your vocabulary. Many seemingly difficult words yield their meanings easily when you recognize the word roots that make them up. *Excrescence*, for example, contains the roots *ex–*, meaning "out or out of," and *cresc–*, meaning "to grow"; once you know this, the meaning of *excrescence*, an outgrowth (whether normal, such as hair, or abnormal, such as a wart), is easily deduced.

The list concentrates on Latin and Greek roots because these are the most frequently used to form compound words in English and because they tend not to be self-explanatory to the average reader. Each entry gives the root in the most common form or forms in which it appears in English, with a brief definition. (The definition does not cover all the shades of meaning of the given root, only the most important or the most broadly applicable.) The rest of the entry is a list of some of the common English words derived from this root; this list is intended only to provide a few examples of such words, not to be exhaustive. Some words are naturally found under more than one entry. The words themselves are not defined. A longer list, including these roots and more, can be found in Appendix B. We hope these lists will encourage you to look up unfamiliar words in a dictionary.

A/AN — **NOT, WITHOUT**

agnostic, amoral, anomaly, anonymous, apathy, atheist, atrophy, atypical

AB — **OFF, AWAY FROM, APART, DOWN**

abdicate, abduct, abhor, abject, abnormal, abolish, abstinence, abstract, abstruse

ABLE/IBLE — **CAPABLE OF, WORTHY OF**

changeable, combustible, durable, indubitable, inevitable, laudable, tolerable, variable

AC/ACR — **SHARP, BITTER, SOUR**

acerbic, acid, acrid, acrimonious, acumen, acute, exacerbate

AD — **TO, TOWARD, NEAR**

(Often the *d* is dropped and the first letter after the *a* is doubled.) accede, adapt, addict, address, adequate, adhere, adjacent, adjoin, admire, advocate, accede, affiliate, aggregate, allocate, annunciation, appall, arrest, assiduous, attract

AMBI/AMPHI **BOTH, ON BOTH SIDES, AROUND**
ambidextrous, ambient, ambiguous, amphibian, amphitheater

AMBL/AMBUL **TO GO, TO WALK**
amble, ambulance, ambulatory, perambulator, preamble

ANIM **OF THE LIFE, MIND, SOUL, BREATH**
animadversion, animal, animate, animosity, equanimity, magnanimous, pusillanimous, unanimous

ANT/ANTE **BEFORE**
ancient, antebellum, antecedent, antechamber, antedate, antediluvian, anterior, anticipate, antiquity

ANTI **AGAINST, OPPOSITE**
antagonism, antibody, anticlimax, antidote, antipathy, antiphony, antipodal, antiseptic, antithesis

AQUA/AQUE **WATER**
aquamarine, aquarium, aquatic, aquatint, aqueduct, subaqueous

AUTO **SELF**
autism, autobiography, autocrat, autograph, automatic, automaton, autonomy

BELL **WAR**
antebellum, bellicose, belligerent, rebel, rebellion

BEN/BENE **GOOD**
benediction, benefactor, benefit, benevolent, benign

BI/BIN **TWO**
biennial, bifocals, bifurcate, bilateral, bilingual, binocular, binomial, bipartisan, biped, combination

BON/BOUN **GOOD, GENEROUS**
bona fide, bonus, bountiful, bounty, debonair

BREV/BRID **SHORT, SMALL**
abbreviate, abridge, brevet, breviary, breviloquent, brevity, brief

BURS **PURSE, MONEY**
bursar, bursary, disburse, reimburse

CARD/CORD/ COUR	**HEART** accord, cardiac, cardiograph, cardiology, concord, concordance, cordial, discord, encourage, record
CARN	**FLESH** carnage, carnal, carnival, carnivorous, incarnation, reincarnation
CAUS/CAUT	**TO BURN** caustic, cauterize, cautery, encaustic, holocaust
CED/CEED/ CESS	**TO GO, TO YIELD, TO STOP** abscess, accede, antecedent, cessation, concede, exceed, incessant, precede, predecessor, proceed, recede, recess, secede, succeed
CELER	**SPEED** accelerant, accelerate, celerity, decelerate
CENT	**HUNDRED, HUNDREDTH** bicentennial, cent, centennial, centigrade, centigram, centiliter, centimeter, centipede, century, percent
CHROM	**COLOR** chromatic, chrome, chromosome, monochromatic
CHRON	**TIME** anachronism, chronic, chronicle, chronology, chronometer, synchronize
CIRCU/CIRCUM	**AROUND** circuit, circuitous, circumference, circumlocution, circumnavigate, circumspect, circumstances
CO/COL/COM/ CON	**WITH, TOGETHER** coerce, collaborate, collide, commensurate, communicate, compare, compatible, conciliate, connect
COGN/CONN	**TO KNOW** cognition, cognizance, incognito, recognize, reconnaissance, reconnoiter
CONTRA/CONTRO/ COUNTER	**AGAINST** contradict, contrary, controversy, counter, counteract, counterattack, counterfeit, countermand, counterpart, counterpoint, encounter

CORP/CORS	**BODY** corporation, corps, corpse, corpulent, corpus, corpuscle, corset, incorporation
COSM	**ORDER, UNIVERSE, WORLD** cosmetic, cosmic, cosmology, cosmonaut, cosmopolitan, cosmos, microcosm
CRE/CRESC/CRET	**TO GROW** accretion, accrue, creation, excrescence, increase, increment
CRED	**TO BELIEVE, TO TRUST** accredit, credentials, credible, credit, creditable, credo, credulity, creed, incredible, incredulous
CRYPT	**HIDDEN** apocryphal, crypt, cryptic, cryptography, cryptology
CUB/CUMB	**TO LIE DOWN** concubine, cubicle, incubate, incubus, incumbent, recumbent, succubus, succumb
CULP	**FAULT, BLAME** culpable, culprit, exculpate, inculpate, mea culpa
DE	**AWAY, OFF, DOWN, COMPLETELY, REVERSAL** decipher, defame, deferential, defile, delineate, descend
DEXT	**RIGHT HAND, RIGHT SIDE, DEFT** ambidextrous, dexter, dexterity, dexterous
DI	**DAY** dial, diary, dismal, diurnal, meridian, quotidian
DI/DIA	**IN TWO, THROUGH, ACROSS** diagnose, diagonal, diagram, dialect, dialogue, diameter, diaphanous, diaphragm, diarrhea, diatribe, dichotomy
DI/DIF/DIS	**AWAY FROM, APART, REVERSAL, NOT** diffuse, dilate, dilatory, disperse, disseminate, dissipate, dissuade, distant, diverge

DIC/DICT/DIT	**TO SAY, TO TELL, TO USE WORDS** abdicate, benediction, contradict, dedicate, dictate, dictator, diction, dictionary, dictum, edict, indicate, indict, interdict, malediction, predicate, predict, valedictorian, verdict
DOL	**TO SUFFER, TO PAIN, TO GRIEVE** condole, condolence, doleful, dolorous, indolence
DORM	**SLEEP** dormant, dormitory
DORS	**BACK** dorsal, endorse
DUC/DUCT	**TO LEAD** abduct, conducive, conduct, conduit, induce, induct, produce
DULC	**SWEET** dulcet, dulcified, dulcimer
DUR	**HARD, LASTING** dour, durable, duration, duress, during, endure, obdurate, perdurable
E/EX	**OUT, OUT OF, FROM, FORMER, COMPLETELY** efface, eliminate, emanate, eradicate, evade, evict, evince, excavate, except, excerpt, exclude, execute, exhale, exile, exit, exonerate, expire, extricate
EGO	**SELF** ego, egocentric, egoism, egotist
EQU	**EQUAL, EVEN** adequate, equable, equation, equator, equidistant, equilibrium, equinox, equivocate, iniquity
ERR	**TO WANDER** aberration, arrant, err, errant, erratic, erroneous, error
EU	**GOOD, WELL** eugenics, eulogy, euphemism, euphony, euphoria, euthanasia
FAL	**TO ERR, TO DECEIVE** default, fail, fallacy, false, faux pas, infallible

FATU	**FOOLISH** fatuity, fatuous, infatuated
FERV	**TO BOIL, TO BUBBLE** effervescent, fervent, fervid, fervor
FI/FID	**FAITH, TRUST** affiance, affidavit, confide, fealty, fidelity, fiduciary, infidel
FLAGR/FLAM	**TO BURN** conflagration, flagrant, flambeau, inflame
FLECT/FLEX	**TO BEND, TO TURN** circumflex, deflect, flex, flexible, genuflect, inflect, reflect
FUG	**TO FLEE, TO FLY** centrifugal, fugitive, fugue, refuge, refugee, subterfuge
FUM	**SMOKE** fume, fumigate, perfume
GEN	**BIRTH, CREATION, RACE, KIND** carcinogenic, congenital, degenerate, engender, eugenics, gender, gene, general, generation, generous, genesis, genetics, genial, genital, genius, gentility, gentle, ingenuity, progeny, regenerate
GNI/GNO	**TO KNOW** agnostic, diagnose, ignoramus, ignore, prognosis, recognize
GRAM/GRAPH	**TO WRITE, TO DRAW** anagram, diagram, epigram, epigraph, grammar, graph, graphic, graphite, photograph, program, telegram
GREG	**FLOCK** aggregate, congregate, egregious, gregarious, segregate
HAP	**BY CHANCE** haphazard, hapless, happen, happily, happy, mishap, perhaps
HEMI	**HALF** hemicycle, hemisphere, hemistich
(H)ETERO	**DIFFERENT, OTHER** heterodox, heterodyne, heterogeneous, heterosexual

HOL	**WHOLE** catholic, holocaust, hologram, holograph, holistic
(H)OM	**SAME** anomaly, homeostasis, homogeneous, homogenize, homogenous, homologue, homonym, homophone, homosexual, homotype
HUM	**EARTH** exhume, humble, humility
ICON	**IMAGE, IDOL** icon, iconic, iconoclast, iconography, iconology
IN/IM	**NOT, WITHOUT** (Often the *n* is dropped and the first letter after the *i* is doubled.) illogical, immoral, impartial, inactive, indigent, indolence, innocuous, irrelevant
IN/IM	**IN, INTO** (Often the *n* is dropped and the first letter after the *i* is doubled.) illuminate, implicit, incarnate, indigenous, influx, intrinsic, irrigate
INTER	**BETWEEN, AMONG** interim, interloper, intermittent, intersperse, interstate, interval
INTRA	**INSIDE, WITHIN** intramural, intrastate, intravenous
IT/ITER	**WAY, JOURNEY** ambition, circuit, itinerant, itinerary, reiterate, transit
JOC	**JOKE** jocose, jocular, jocularity, jocund, joke
JOIN/JUG/JUNCT	**TO MEET, TO JOIN** adjoin, conjugal, conjunction, injunction, junction, junta, rejoin, subjugate
JOUR	**DAY** adjourn, journal, journey
JUD	**TO JUDGE** adjudicate, judiciary, judicious, prejudice

JUR	**LAW, TO SWEAR** abjure, adjure, conjure, injure, juridical, jurisdiction, jurisprudence, jurist, jury, perjury
JUV	**YOUNG** juvenile, juvenilia, rejuvenate
LANG/LING	**TONGUE** bilingual, language, linguistics
LAUD	**PRAISE, HONOR** cum laude, laud, laudable, laudatory
LAV/LAU/LU	**TO WASH** ablution, antediluvian, deluge, dilute, laundry, lavatory, lave
LAX/LEAS/LES	**LOOSE** lax, laxative, laxity, lease, leash, lessee, lessor, relax, release
LEC/LEG/LEX	**TO READ, TO SPEAK** dialect, lectern, lecture, legend, legible, lesson, lexicographer, lexicon
LEV	**TO LIFT, TO RISE, LIGHT (WEIGHT)** alleviate, elevate, leaven, levee, lever, levitate, levity, levy, relevant, relieve
LI/LIG	**TO TIE, TO BIND** ally, league, liable, liaison, lien, ligament, ligature, oblige, religion, rely
LIBER	**FREE** deliver, illiberal, liberal, liberality, liberate, libertine, liberty, livery
LITH	**STONE** acrolith, lithography, lithoid, lithology, lithotomy, megalith, monolith
LOC/LOG/LOQU	**WORD, SPEECH, THOUGHT** biology, circumlocution, colloquial, dialogue, elocution, eloquent, eulogy, geology, grandiloquent, interlocutor, locution, logic, loquacious, monologue, prologue, soliloquy, ventriloquism
LUC/LUM/LUS	**LIGHT (BRIGHTNESS)** illuminate, illustrate, illustrious, lackluster, lucid, luminous, translucent

MACRO — **GREAT, LONG**
macro, macrobiotics, macrocephalous, macrocosm, macroscopic

MAG/MAJ/MAX — **BIG, GREAT**
magistrate, magnanimous, magnate, magnificent, magnify, magniloquent, magnitude, majesty, major, majority, master, maxim, maximum, mistress

MAL/MALE — **BAD, ILL, EVIL, WRONG**
maladroit, malady, malapropism, malediction, malefactor, malfeasance, malfunction, malevolence, malicious, malign, malinger

MAN/MANU — **HAND**
amanuensis, emancipate, manacle, manage, maneuver, manifest, manipulate, manner, manual, manufacture, manuscript

MAND/MEND — **TO COMMAND, TO ORDER, TO ENTRUST**
command, commend, countermand, demand, mandate, mandatory, recommend, remand, reprimand

MEDI — **MIDDLE**
immediate, intermediate, mean, media, median, mediate, medieval, mediocre, medium

MEGA — **LARGE, GREAT**
megalith, megalomania, megalopolis, megaphone, megaton

MICRO — **VERY SMALL**
microbe, microcosm, micron, microorganism, microscope

MIS — **BAD, WRONG, TO HATE**
misadventure, misanthrope, misapply, miscarry, mischance, mischief, misconstrue, miscount, misfit, misinterpret

MOB/MOM/MOT/MOV — **TO MOVE**
automobile, demote, immovable, locomotion, mob, mobile, mobility, mobilize, moment, momentous, momentum, motion, motive, motor, move, mutiny, promote, remove

MOLL — **SOFT**
emollient, mild, mollify, mollusk

MON/MONO — **ONE**
monarchy, monism, monk, monochord, monogram, monograph, monolithic, monologue, monomania, monotonous

MOR/MORT	**DEATH** amortize, immortal, morbid, moribund, mortality, mortify, mortuary
MULT	**MANY** multiple, multiplex, multiply, multitudinous
MUT	**TO CHANGE** commute, immutable, mutation, mutual, permutation, transmute
NAT/NAS/ NAI/GNA	**BIRTH** cognate, innate, naive, nascent, natal, native, natural, nature, pregnant, renaissance
NAU/NAV	**SHIP, SAILOR** astronaut, circumnavigate, cosmonaut, nauseous, nautical, naval, nave, navy
NIHIL	**NOTHING, NONE** annihilate, nihilism
NOC/NOX	**HARM** innocent, innocuous, internecine, noxious, nuisance, obnoxious, pernicious
NOCT/NOX	**NIGHT** equinox, noctambulant, nocturnal, nocturne
NOM/NYM/ NOUN/NOWN	**NAME** acronym, anonymous, misnomer, nomenclature, nominal, nominate, noun, pronoun, pseudonym, renown, synonym
NON	**NOT** nonconformist, nonentity, nonpareil, nonpartisan
NOV/NEO/NOU	**NEW** innovate, neologism, neophyte, neoplasm, nouveau riche, novel, novice, renovate
NULL	**NOTHING** annul, null, nullify, nullity
OB	**TOWARD, TO, AGAINST, OVER** obese, obfuscate, oblique, obsequious, obstinate, obstreperous, obstruct, obtuse

OMNI — **ALL**
omnibus, omnipotent, omnipresent, omniscient, omnivorous

ONER — **BURDEN**
exonerate, onerous, onus

OSS/OSTE — **BONE**
osseous, ossicle, ossiferous, ossify, ossuary, ostectomy, osteopathy

PALP — **TO FEEL**
palpable, palpate, palpitate, palpitation

PAN/PANT — **ALL, EVERYONE**
panacea, pandemic, panegyric, panoply, panorama, pantheon

PAS/PAT/PATH — **FEELING, SUFFERING, DISEASE**
compassion, dispassionate, empathy, impassive, pathogenic, sociopath, sympathy

PEC — **MONEY**
impecunious, peculation, pecuniary

PED — **CHILD, EDUCATION**
encyclopedia, pedagogue, pedant, pediatrician

PED/POD — **FOOT**
antipodes, arthropod, expedite, impede, pedal, pedestal, pedestrian, pedigree, pediment, podium, tripod

PEL — **TO DRIVE, TO PUSH**
compel, dispel, expel, impel, propel

PEN/PENE — **ALMOST**
antepenult, peninsula, penult, penultimate, penumbra

PERI — **AROUND**
perihelion, perimeter, perineum, peripatetic, periphery, periscope

PHIL — **LOVE**
bibliophile, necrophilia, philanthropy, philatelist, philharmonic, philogyny, philology, philosopher

PHOB — **FEAR**
claustrophobia, hydrophobia, phobia, phobic, xenophobia

PHON	**SOUND** antiphony, euphony, megaphone, phonetics, phonograph, polyphony, saxophone, symphony, telephone
PLAC	**TO PLEASE** complacent, complaisant, implacable, placate, placebo, placid
PLE/PLEN	**TO FILL, FULL** accomplishment, complement, complete, deplete, implement, plenipotentiary, plenitude, plenty, plethora, replenish, replete, supplement
POLY	**MANY** polyandry, polygamy, polyglot, polygon, polyhedron, polynomial, polysyllable, polytechnic, polytheism
PORT	**TO CARRY** comport, deportment, disport, export, import, important, importune, portable, portage, porter, portfolio, portly, purport, rapport, reporter, supportive, transport
POST	**BEHIND, AFTER** post facto, posterior, posterity, postern, posthumous, postmeridian, postmortem, postscript, preposterous
POT	**TO DRINK** potable, potation, potion
PRE	**BEFORE, IN FRONT** preamble, precarious, precedent, precept, precocious, precursor, predict, preface, premonition, prescribe, presentiment, president
PRI/PRIM	**FIRST** primary, primal, prime, primeval, primordial, pristine
PRO	**IN FRONT, BEFORE, MUCH, FOR** problem, proceed, proclaim, procure, profuse, prolific, propound, prostrate, proselytize, protest, provident
PROP/PROX	**NEAR** approximate, propinquity, proximate, proximity
PROT/PROTO	**FIRST** protagonist, protocol, prototype, protozoan

PSEUD/PSEUDO **FALSE**
pseudepigrapha, pseudoclassic, pseudomorph, pseudonym, pseudopod, pseudoscience

PUG **TO FIGHT**
impugn, pugilist, pugnacious, repugnant

PUNC/PUNG/POIGN **TO POINT, TO PRICK, TO PIERCE**
compunction, expunge, poignant, point, punch, punctilious, punctual, punctuate, puncture, pungent

PYR **FIRE**
pyre, pyromania, pyrometer, pyrosis, pyrotechnics

QUAD/QUAR/QUAT **FOUR**
quadrant, quadrille, quadrinomial, quadruple, quadruplets, quart, quarter, quaternary

QUIE/QUIT **QUIET, REST**
acquiesce, acquit, coy, disquiet, quiescence, quiet, quietude, quietus, quit, requiem, requital, tranquil

QUIN/QUINT **FIVE**
quincunx, quinquennial, quintessence, quintile, quintillion, quintuple

RACI/RADI **ROOT**
deracinate, eradicate, radical, radish

RAMI **BRANCH**
ramification, ramiform, ramify

RE **BACK, AGAIN**
recline, refer, regain, remain, reorganize, repent, request

RECT **STRAIGHT, RIGHT**
correct, direct, erect, rectangle, rectify, rectilinear, rectitude, rector

REG **KING, RULE**
interregnum, realm, regal, regent, regicide, regime, regiment, region, regular, regulate

RETRO **BACKWARD**
retroactive, retrofit, retrograde, retrospective

RUB/RUD	**RED** rouge, rubella, rubicund, rubric, ruby, ruddy, russet
RUD	**CRUDE** erudite, rude, rudimentary, rudiments
SACR/SANCT	**HOLY** consecration, desecrate, execrable, sacerdotal, sacrament, sacred, sacrifice, sacrilege, sacristy, sacrosanct, saint, sanctify, sanctimonious, sanction, sanctity, sanctuary, sanctum
SAG/SAP/SAV	**TASTE, THINKING, DISCERNING** insipid, sagacious, sagacity, sage, sapient, savant, savor
SALU	**HEALTH** salubrious, salutary, salute
SALV	**TO SAVE** safe, salvage, salvation, savior
SAN	**HEALTHY** sane, sanitarium, sanitary, sanitation, sanity
SANG	**BLOOD** consanguinity, sanguinary, sanguine
SAT	**ENOUGH** assets, dissatisfied, insatiable, sate, satiate, satisfy, saturate
SCRIBE/SCRIPT	**TO WRITE** ascribe, circumscribe, conscription, describe, indescribable, inscription, postscript, prescribe, proscribe, scribble, scribe, script, scripture, scrivener, subscribe, transcript
SE	**APART, AWAY** secede, sedition, seduce, segregate, select, separate, sequester
SEC/SEQU/ SUE/SUI	**TO FOLLOW** consecutive, consequent, execute, executive, non sequitur, obsequious, obsequy, persecution, prosecute, pursue, second, sequel, sequence, sue, suitable, suite, suitor

SED/SESS/SID — **TO SIT, TO SETTLE**
assiduous, dissident, insidious, preside, resident, residual, séance, sedate, sedative, sedentary, sediment, sedulous, session, siege, subside, supersede

SEM — **SEED, TO SOW**
disseminate, semen, seminal, seminar, seminary

SEMI — **HALF**
semicircle, semicolon, semiconscious, semifluid

SEN — **OLD**
senate, senescent, senile, senior, sire

SIN/SINU — **BEND, FOLD, CURVE**
cosine, insinuate, sine, sinuous, sinus

SOL — **ALONE**
desolate, isolate, sole, soliloquize, solipsism, solitude, solo

SOL — **SUN**
parasol, solar, solarium, solstice

SOMN — **SLEEP**
insomnia, somnambulist, somniferous, somniloquist, somnolent

SOPH — **WISDOM**
philosopher, sophism, sophist, sophisticated, sophistry

SOURC/SURG/SURRECT — **TO RISE**
insurgent, insurrection, resource, resurge, resurrection, source, surge

SPEC/SPIC — **TO LOOK, TO SEE**
circumspect, conspicuous, despicable, inspect, perspective, perspicacious, retrospective, specious, spectrum, speculation

SPIR — **BREATH**
aspire, conspire, expire, inspire, perspire, respirator, spirit, spiritual, sprightly, sprite, suspire, transpire

STRICT/STRING/ STRAN	**TO TIGHTEN, TO BIND** astringent, constrain, constrict, district, restriction, strain, strait, strangle, strict, stringent
SUA	**SWEET, PLEASING, TO URGE** assuage, dissuade, persuade, persuasive, suasion, suave, sweet
SUB/SUP	**BELOW, UNDER** subliminal, submissive, subsidiary, subterfuge, subtle, suppose
SUMM	**HIGHEST, TOTAL** consummate, sum, summary, summit
SUPER/SUR	**OVER, ABOVE** insuperable, superb, supercilious, superficial, superfluous, superior, superlative, supernatural, supersede, supervise, surmount, surpass, surrealism, surveillance, survey
SYM/SYN	**TOGETHER** symbiosis, symmetry, sympathy, symposium, synonym, synthesis
TAC/TIC	**TO BE SILENT** reticent, tacit, taciturn
TACT/TAG/ TAM/TANG	**TO TOUCH** contact, contagious, contaminate, contiguous, cotangent, intact, intangible, integral, tact, tactile, tangent, tangential
TEST	**TO BEAR WITNESS** attest, contest, detest, intestate, protest, testament, testify, testimonial
THERM	**HEAT** diathermy, thermal, thermesthesia, thermometer, thermonuclear, thermophilic, thermostat
TIM	**FEAR** intimidate, timid, timidity, timorous
TOR/TORQ/ TORT	**TO TWIST** contort, distort, extort, retort, torch, torment, torque, torsion, tort, tortuous, torture

TORP	**STIFF, NUMB** torpedo, torpid, torpor
TOX	**POISON** antitoxin, intoxication, toxemia, toxic, toxicology, toxin
TRANS	**ACROSS, BEYOND** intransigent, transaction, transcendent, transcribe, transgress, transient, transition, transmit, transparent, transport
ULT	**LAST, BEYOND** penultimate, ulterior, ultimate, ultimatum, ultramarine, ultramontane, ultraviolet
UMBR	**SHADOW** adumbrate, penumbra, somber, umber, umbrage, umbrella
UN	**NOT** unaccustomed, unruly, unseen, untold, unusual
UND	**WAVE** abound, abundance, inundate, redundant, undulant, undulate
UNI/UN	**ONE** reunion, unanimous, unicorn, uniform, union, unison, unit, unite, unity, universe
URB	**CITY** exurbanite, suburb, urban, urbane, urbanity, urbanization
VAIL/VAL	**STRENGTH, USE, WORTH** ambivalent, avail, convalescent, countervailing, equivalent, evaluate, invalid, prevalent, valediction, valiant, valid, valor, value
VER	**TRUTH** aver, veracious, verdict, verify, verily, verisimilitude, verity, very
VERB	**WORD** adverb, proverb, verb, verbal, verbalize, verbatim, verbose, verbiage
VERD	**GREEN** verdant, verdigris, verdure

VI	**LIFE** convivial, joie de vivre, revival, revive, survive, viable, vital, vitality, vivacity, vivid, viviparous, vivisection
VIL	**BASE, MEAN** revile, vile, vilify, vilification
VIRU	**POISON** virulence, virulent, viruliferous, virus
VOC/VOK	**CALL, WORD** advocate, avocation, avow, convocation, convoke, equivocate, evoke, invoke, provoke, revoke, vocabulary, vocal, vocation, vociferous
VOL	**WISH** benevolent, malevolent, volant, volatile, volition, volley, voluntary
VOLU/VOLV	**TO ROLL, TO TURN** circumvolve, convolution, devolve, evolve, involution, revolt, revolution, revolve, voluble, volume, voluminous, volute

WORD ROOTS EXERCISE

Choose the word that correctly completes the sentence. Make sure to pay attention to structural road signs and key words and use familiar roots to guide your choice.

1. The play's theme was interesting; however, the (*animated, acerbic*) monologues dampened our appreciation of the author's skills.

2. Although poets are stereotypically considered contemplative and gentle souls, composing dulcet rhymes about the vagaries of life, some of our most famous poets have been (*belligerent, breviloquent*), frequently drunk, or even criminal.

3. The intern was a delight; she completed her tasks with professionalism, (*celerity, cautery*), and good sense.

4. Flemish primitive painters such as Jan Van Eyck used a greenish substance called (*micron, verdigris*) in their portraits.

5. The math professor wrote a formula to calculate every (*neologism, permutation*) of a certain set of numbers.

6. Some behaviors are learned, while others are (*innocuous, innate*).

7. Because they had been old friends, the general shook the diplomat's hand with a (*somnolent, sanguine*) air.

8. You can easily recognize (*rubella, toxemia*) because of the raised red spots on the skin.

9. Some people consider desecration of the American flag to be treasonous or even an act of terrorism, but others refuse to treat what they consider a mere symbol as (*sacrosanct, sagacious*).

10. In frog anatomy, the major muscles of the shoulder extend from the (*dorsal, quadriceps*) area, across the shoulder joint, and into the arms.

11. At the end of the service, the general's wife gave an impromptu (*convocation, valediction*), which truly venerated his memory and profoundly moved many attendees.

12. Some families organized an effort to bring about the (*restriction, euphemism*) of the sales of illegal fireworks at the neighborhood convenience store.

13. The dog still enjoyed its vigorous morning romps through the park, but its stiff joints and patchy fur betrayed signs of (*dexterity, senescence*).

14. Around dinner time, a delicious smell (*emanated, adjourned*) from the kitchen.

15. The monorail train arrived at the station in 20-minute (*conduits, intervals*).

16. A military (*fealty, junta*) was set up to determine which party ruled, now that the old, corrupt regime had been deposed.

17. I tried to compliment my boss, but I must have overdone it; she told me to stop being so (*obsequious, salubrious*).

18. My brother was the intrepid one in the family; though I was by no means (*ambivalent, pusillanimous*), he always managed to outdo me in daredevilry.

19. The teacher was so (*peripatetic, philharmonic*) in class that when the maintenance department removed the chair at his desk, he didn't notice for weeks.

20. It was (*indubitable, laudatory*) that Inez would earn the scholarship because she clearly had the best grades and most experience.

21. I felt I had to (*succumb, intercede*) when I saw the child struggling to swim to the side of the pool and the lifeguard failed to respond.

22. The mad scientist in the movie attached a special (*diathermy, chronometer*) to the time machine so that the passengers could control the year to which they would travel.

23. We were afraid that the (*perspicuous, taciturn*) visitor did not like the presentation because she sat quietly and asked no questions.

24. Although we often remember breakthrough artists such as LL Cool J and Run-D.M.C. as the originators of rap, (*seminal, pedantic*) artists such as the Sugarhill Gang and the Fatback Band remind us that rap really started on the street and not in a studio.

25. As much as he practiced and tried to improve, Jack remained (*maladroit, pellucid*) at swimming.

26. While (*jocularity, gentility*) is appreciated in informal conversations with coworkers and colleagues, it is best not to overdo it in formal meetings such as interviews.

27. The appraiser thought she discovered an (*aberrant, indolent*) design in the antique carpet, but after further research, she determined that the pattern was actually consistent with designs in contemporaneous fashions and ornaments.

28. Since many toddlers go through a phase of independence, caregivers should be prepared to deal with frustrated, (*obdurate, dismal*) two-year-olds and provide patient support for this developmental process.

29. The princess arrived in plain clothes; the young ladies who had hoped to espy a beautiful woman with a flowing gown and full (*regalia, heterodoxy*) were bewildered.

30. Whenever she is nervous, my sister becomes very (*liberal, loquacious*), so when she chatted away as we were walking through the woods, I suspected she thought we might be lost.

WORD ROOTS EXERCISE ANSWER KEY

1. acerbic
2. belligerent
3. celerity
4. verdigris
5. permutation
6. innate
7. sanguine
8. rubella
9. sacrosanct
10. dorsal
11. valediction
12. restriction
13. senescence
14. emanated
15. intervals
16. junta
17. obsequious
18. pusillanimous
19. peripatetic
20. indubitable
21. intercede
22. chronometer
23. taciturn
24. seminal
25. maladroit
26. jocularity
27. aberrant
28. obdurate
29. regalia
30. loquacious

WORD ROOTS EXERCISE ANSWERS AND EXPLANATIONS

1. ACERBIC

The root ANIM in *animated* should clue you in to its meaning: "active or living." The root of *acerbic,* AC, provides a clue to its meaning: "sharp or sour."

2. BELLIGERENT

The root BELL relates to war and fighting, and *belligerent* refers to someone who is quick to get into a fight. You may recognize the roots BREV ("short") and LOQU ("speech") in *breviloquent,* which means "terse" or "brief."

3. CELERITY

The root CELER relates to speed, and *celerity* means "alacrity" or "briskness." The word *cautery* contains the root CAUT, which refers to burning. A *cautery* is an instrument used for branding (burning a mark into flesh).

4. VERDIGRIS

The root VERD is the clue to the right answer. VERD refers to green, and *verdigris* is a green pigment used by artists. The root MICRO means "very small," and a *micron* is a millionth of a meter.

5. PERMUTATION

The root MUT is the clue in this word, which refers to a change or transformation. A *permutation* is one of the possible changes or elements in a set. NEO means "new," and LOG refers to words. A *neologism* is a new word.

6. INNATE

The answer to this one is a little complicated: the prefix IN has a different meaning in each option. NAT refers to birth, and the prefix IN means "internal" or "inside." Something *innate* is born into you. The word *innocuous* contains the root NOX, meaning "harm". The prefix IN negates the meaning: an *innocuous* substance is one that will not harm you.

7. SANGUINE

In this sentence, the friendly handshake is the clue. SANG in the word *sanguine* refers to blood. In the Middle Ages, blood was considered to be the humor (or fluid) that led to a hopeful disposition, and a *sanguine* handshake is a confident one. On the other hand, SOMN refers to sleep, so a *somnolent* general would likely be yawning as he shook hands.

8. RUBELLA

Although *toxemia* contains the root TOX, which means "poison," the rash's signature red bumps suggest the answer *rubella,* which contains the root RUB, meaning "red."

9. SACROSANCT

Sacrosanct means "extremely sacred"; you may have guessed this because it contains both SACR and SANCT, both of which mean "holy." *Sagacious* means "wise" and contains the root SAG, which refers to having discernment.

10. DORSAL

If you know anatomy or you spend time at the gym, this may have been an easy one. *Dorsal* contains the root DORS, which relates to an organism's back. The *quadriceps* is a group of four (QUAD means "four") muscles in the legs.

11. VALEDICTION

A *valediction* contains the roots VAL ("strength" or "worth") and DICT ("to say"). A *valediction* is a speech given to commemorate someone or speak of his or her worth. The root CON means "together," and the root VOC means "call"; a *convocation* is a group of people who have been called together. The gathering was a *convocation*, but the speech was a *valediction*.

12. RESTRICTION

Restriction contains the root STRICT, which means "tighten." *Euphemism* contains the root EU ("good") and refers to using a pleasant term for something unpleasant. Since the families wanted to tighten the laws regarding sales of illegal fireworks, *restriction* is your answer.

13. SENESCENCE

Senescence contains the root SEN, which refers to aging or growing old. *Senescence* is the same as maturity or old age. *Dexterity* contains the root DEXT, which refers to the right side of an organism. Because most people in the world are right-handed and are therefore more agile with their right hands, *dexterity* has come to mean the same as *agility*. (If you're a lefty, remember this point of contention, and the root and word will stick with you on the test!)

14. EMANATED

Emanated contains the root E meaning "out," and indeed, it means "coming out," as does a smell. *Adjourned* contains the roots AD, which means "to," and JOUR, which means "day." *Adjourned* means "put off to another day," or finished for now.

15. INTERVALS

The root INTER means "between" or "among," and an *interval* is the time that passes between two or more repeating events. The word *conduits* contains the roots CON ("together") and DUC ("to lead"). *Conduits* are ways to get from one place to another.

16. JUNTA

The root in *junta*, JUNCT, means "join," and a *junta* is a group of people who come together for a specific purpose. The root in *fealty* is harder to see—FID or FI—and means "faith" or "loyalty."

17. OBSEQUIOUS

Obsequious comes from the roots OB, meaning "over," and SEQU, meaning "to follow." It has the sense of overdoing being a follower, or "fawning." *Salubrious* has the root SALU, meaning "health," and it means "healthy."

18. PUSILLANIMOUS

The root in *pusillanimous* is ANIM, which means "life." The other root, not given in the list, is PUSIL, which means "weak." Someone who is *pusillanimous* is "craven" or "cowardly." The word *ambivalent* contains the prefix AMBI ("both") and the root VAL ("strength") and means "pulled with equal force by two choices."

19. PERIPATETIC

The roots PERI ("around") and PED ("foot") provide the strongest clues as to the meaning of *peripatetic*, "given to walking around." *Philharmonic* contains PHIL ("love"); it means "a lover of music" and is often short for *philharmonic society* ("a group of music lovers"). Neither sense of the latter relates to this sentence.

20. INDUBITABLE

The root DUB (not given in the list, but in Appendix B) refers to doubt, and something that is *indubitable* cannot be doubted (the root IN means "not"). The root LAUD means "praise" or "honor." A *laudatory* celebration is one that is in honor of the guest.

21. INTERCEDE

The root INTER ("between") and CEDE ("go") give the meaning of *intercede* plainly: "to go between or go into a situation." The root CUMB refers to lying down or giving in, which is the meaning of *succumb*.

22. CHRONOMETER

The roots CHRON ("time") and METER ("measure") should give you the meaning of *chronometer*: "a clock." Similarly DIA ("through") and THERM ("heat"), the roots in *diathermy*, clue you into that meaning: "heating inside a body, usually through electricity."

23. TACITURN

The root TACIT means "silent," and a *taciturn* person does not speak very much. The root SPIC ("look" or "see") is a clue to the meaning of *perspicuous*: "clear or lucid."

24. SEMINAL

The root SEM refers to seeds or sowing. A *seminal* work is one that influences others (think of a seminal work as sowing creative seeds). The word *pedantic* contains the root PED (the same root as in *pediatric*), which means "child" or "education." A *pedantic* person is a teacher (and the word carries the connotation of being too much of a know-it-all!).

25. MALADROIT

The root MAL ("bad") and the word *adroit* should give you an idea of the meaning of *maladroit*: "clumsy." You may recognize the root in *pellucid*, LUC, meaning "light." Follow those instincts: *pellucid* means "translucent" or "clear."

26. JOCULARITY

You may notice the root JOC ("joke") in the word *jocularity*. *Jocularity* is "joking around" or "having a sense of humor." The word *gentility* contains the root GEN, which refers to birth or class. *Gentility*, or good manners, has been historically expected of the upper classes in society. It does not mean that only the well-off have such manners, but you can remember this connection for the exam.

27. ABERRANT

The root AB ("from") and the root ERR ("to wander") provide strong clues to the word *aberrant*, which means "different" or "off." The word *indolent* contains the root IN ("not") and DOL ("grieve"). If you think of someone who does not grieve (and possibly does not care) when something or someone is lost, you can see how the word *indolent* means "lazy" or "irresponsible."

28. OBDURATE

The roots in *obdurate*, OB ("against") and DUR ("strong") give away the meaning: "stubborn." The roots in *dismal* are actually DI ("day") and MAL ("bad"). Indeed, a *dismal* day is usually pretty lousy.

29. REGALIA

Remember that the root REG means "king" or "rule." *Regalia* thus refers to the crown, scepter, and other symbols of royalty. A *heterodoxy* is a belief or opinion (DOX, not listed here but listed in Appendix B) that is different from or at odds with (HETERO) the norm. Its antonym is "orthodoxy."

30. LOQUACIOUS

The root in *loquacious*, LOQU, refers to speech. A *loquacious* person is a talker. The root in *liberal* refers to freedom (LIBER), and those who hold *liberal* or *libertarian* ideas tend to allow more freedom to individuals to make their own choices in life.

WORDS IN CONTEXT

Some words are tested on the GRE more than others. The following words all turn up regularly on the test. You should start by learning these words, and the groups of words that have similar meanings to them.

Start by learning these 12 words:

ANOMALY	ASSUAGE	ENIGMA
EQUIVOCAL	ERUDITE	FERVID
LUCID	OPAQUE	PLACATE
PRECIPITATE	PRODIGAL	ZEAL

Then learn these:

ABSTAIN	ADULTERATE	APATHY
AUDACIOUS	CAPRICIOUS	CORROBORATE
DESICCATE	ENGENDER	EPHEMERAL
GULLIBLE	HOMOGENEOUS	LACONIC
LAUDABLE	LOQUACIOUS	MITIGATE
PEDANT	PRAGMATIC	PROPRIETY
VACILLATE	VOLATILE	

Then learn these . . . and keep adding to your vocabulary using the longer list that starts at the bottom of this page:

ADVOCATE	ANTIPATHY	BOLSTER	CACOPHONY
DERIDE	DISSONANCE	ENERVATE	EULOGY
GARRULOUS	INGENUOUS	LETHARGIC	MALLEABLE
MISANTHROPE	OBDURATE	OSTENTATION	PARADOX
PHILANTHROPIC	PREVARICATE	VENERATE	WAVER

180 COMMON GRE WORDS IN CONTEXT

ABATE: to reduce in amount, degree, or severity

As the hurricane's force ABATED, the winds dropped and the sea became calm.

Words with similar meanings:

EBB	LAPSE	LET UP
MODERATE	RELENT	SLACKEN
SUBSIDE	WANE	

ABSCOND: to leave secretly

The patron ABSCONDED from the restaurant by sneaking out the back door without paying his bill.

Words with similar meanings:

FLEE DECAMP ESCAPE

ABSTAIN: to choose not to do something

During Lent, practicing Catholics ABSTAIN from eating meat.

Words with similar meanings:

FORBEAR REFRAIN WITHHOLD

ABYSS: an extremely deep hole

The submarine dove into the ABYSS to chart the previously unseen depths.

Related words:

ABYSSAL: pertaining to great depth
ABYSMAL: extremely bad

Words with similar meanings:

CHASM VOID

ADULTERATE: to make impure

The restaurateur made his ketchup last longer by ADULTERATING it with water.

Related words:

UNADULTERATED: pure
ADULTERY: an illicit relationship; an affair

Words with similar meanings:

DOCTOR

ADVOCATE: to speak in favor of

The vegetarian ADVOCATED a diet containing no meat.

Related words:

ADVOCACY: active support for

Words with similar meanings:

BACK CHAMPION SUPPORT

AESTHETIC: concerning the appreciation of beauty

Followers of the AESTHETIC Movement regarded the pursuit of beauty as the only true purpose of art.

Related words:

AESTHETE: someone unusually sensitive to beauty

AESTHETICISM: concern with beauty

Words with similar meanings:

ARTISTIC	TASTEFUL

AGGRANDIZE: to increase in power, influence, and reputation

The supervisor sought to AGGRANDIZE himself by claiming that the achievements of his staff were actually his own.

Words with similar meanings:

AMPLIFY	APOTHEOSIZE	AUGMENT
DIGNIFY	ELEVATE	ENLARGE
ENNOBLE	EXALT	GLORIFY
MAGNIFY	SWELL	UPLIFT
WAX		

ALLEVIATE: to make more bearable

Taking aspirin helps to ALLEVIATE a headache.

Words with similar meanings:

ALLAY	ASSUAGE	COMFORT
EASE	LESSEN	LIGHTEN
MITIGATE	PALLIATE	RELIEVE

AMALGAMATE: to combine; to mix together

Giant Industries AMALGAMATED with Mega Products to form Giant-Mega Products Incorporated.

Related words:

AMALGAM: a mixture, especially of two metals

Words with similar meanings:

ADMIX	BLEND	COMBINE
COMMINGLE	COMMIX	COMPOUND
FUSE	INTERMINGLE	INTERMIX
MERGE	MINGLE	MIX

AMBIGUOUS: doubtful or uncertain; able to be interpreted several ways

The directions he gave were so AMBIGUOUS that we disagreed on which way to turn.

Related words:

AMBIGUITY: the quality of being ambiguous

Words with similar meanings:

CLOUDY	DOUBTFUL	DUBIOUS
EQUIVOCAL	INDETERMINATE	NEBULOUS
OBSCURE	UNCLEAR	VAGUE

AMELIORATE: to make better; to improve

The doctor was able to AMELIORATE the patient's suffering using painkillers.

Words with similar meanings:

AMEND	BETTER	IMPROVE
PACIFY	UPGRADE	

ANACHRONISM: something out of place in time

The aged hippie used ANACHRONISTIC phrases, like "groovy" and "far out," that had not been popular for years.

Words with similar meanings:

ARCHAISM	INCONGRUITY

ANALOGOUS: similar or alike in some way; equivalent to

In a famous argument for the existence of God, the universe is ANALOGOUS to a mechanical timepiece, the creation of a divinely intelligent "clockmaker."

Related words:

ANALOGY: a similarity between things that are otherwise dissimilar

ANALOGUE: something that is similar in some way to something else

Words with similar meanings:

ALIKE	COMPARABLE	CORRESPONDING
EQUIVALENT	HOMOGENEOUS	PARALLEL
SIMILAR		

ANOMALY: deviation from what is normal

Albino animals may display too great an ANOMALY in their coloring to attract normally colored mates.

Related words:

ANOMALOUS: deviating from what is normal

Words with similar meanings:

ABERRANCE	ABERRATION	ABNORMALITY
DEVIANCE	DEVIATION	IRREGULARITY
PRETERNATURALNESS		

ANTAGONIZE: to annoy or provoke to anger

The child discovered that he could ANTAGONIZE the cat by pulling its tail.

Related words:

ANTAGONISTIC: tending to provoke conflict

ANTAGONIST: someone who fights another

Words with similar meanings

CLASH	CONFLICT	INCITE
IRRITATE	OPPOSE	PESTER
PROVOKE	VEX	

ANTIPATHY: extreme dislike

The ANTIPATHY between the French and the English regularly erupted into open warfare.

Words with similar meanings:

ANIMOSITY	ANIMUS	ANTAGONISM
AVERSION	ENMITY	HOSTILITY
REPELLENCE		

APATHY: lack of interest or emotion

The APATHY of voters is so great that less than half the people who are eligible to vote actually bother to do so.

Words with similar meanings:

COOLNESS	DISINTEREST	DISREGARD
IMPASSIVITY	INDIFFERENCE	INSENSIBILITY
LASSITUDE	LETHARGY	LISTLESSNESS
PHLEGM	STOLIDITY	UNCONCERN
UNRESPONSIVENESS		

ARBITRATE: to judge a dispute between two opposing parties

Since the couple could not come to an agreement, a judge was forced to ARBITRATE their divorce proceedings.

Related words:

ARBITRATION: a process by which a conflict is resolved

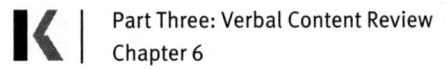

ARBITRATOR: a judge

Words with similar meanings:

ADJUDGE	ADJUDICATE	DECIDE
DETERMINE	JUDGE	MODERATE
REFEREE	RULE	

ARCHAIC: ancient, old-fashioned

Her ARCHAIC Commodore computer could not run the latest software.

Related words:

ARCHAISM: an outdated word or phrase

Words with similar meanings:

ANCIENT	ANTEDILUVIAN	ANTIQUE
BYGONE	DATED	DOWDY
FUSTY	OBSOLETE	OLD-FASHIONED
OUTDATED	OUTMODED	PASSÉ
PREHISTORIC	STALE	SUPERANNUATED
SUPERSEDED	VINTAGE	

ARDOR: intense and passionate feeling

Bishop's ARDOR for landscape was evident when he passionately described the beauty of the scenic Hudson Valley.

Related words:

ARDENT: expressing ardor; passionate

Words with similar meanings:

DEVOTION	ENTHUSIASM	FERVENCY
FERVIDITY	FERVIDNESS	FERVOR
FIRE	PASSION	ZEAL
ZEALOUSNESS		

ARTICULATE: able to speak clearly and expressively

She is such an ARTICULATE defender of labor that unions are among her strongest supporters.

Words with similar meanings:

ELOQUENT	EXPRESSIVE	FLUENT
LUCID	SILVER-TONGUED	SMOOTH-SPOKEN

ASSUAGE: to make something unpleasant less severe

Like many people, Philip Larkin used alcohol to ASSUAGE his sense of meaninglessness and despair.

Words with similar meanings:

ALLAY	ALLEVIATE	APPEASE
COMFORT	CONCILIATE	EASE
LIGHTEN	MITIGATE	MOLLIFY
PACIFY	PALLIATE	PLACATE
PROPITIATE	RELIEVE	SOOTHE
SWEETEN		

ATTENUATE: to reduce in force or degree; to weaken

The Bill of Rights ATTENUATED the traditional power of government to change laws at will.

Words with similar meanings:

DEBILITATE	DEVITALIZE	DILUTE
ENERVATE	ENFEEBLE	RAREFY
SAP	THIN	UNDERMINE
UNDO	UNNERVE	WATER
WEAKEN		

AUDACIOUS: fearless and daring

"And you, your majesty, may kiss my bum!" replied the AUDACIOUS peasant.

Related words:

AUDACITY: the quality of being audacious

Words with similar meanings:

ADVENTURESOME	AGGRESSIVE	ASSERTIVE
BOLD	BRAVE	COURAGEOUS
DARING	DAUNTLESS	DOUGHTY
FEARLESS	GALLANT	GAME
HEROIC	INTREPID	METTLESOME
PLUCKY	STOUT	STOUTHEARTED
UNAFRAID	UNDAUNTED	VALIANT
VALOROUS	VENTURESOME	VENTUROUS

AUSTERE: severe or stern in appearance; undecorated

The lack of decoration makes Zen temples seem AUSTERE to the untrained eye.

Related words:

AUSTERITY: severity, especially poverty

Words with similar meanings:

BLEAK	DOUR	GRIM
HARD	HARSH	SEVERE

BANAL: predictable, clichéd, boring

He used BANAL phrases like "have a nice day" and "another day, another dollar."

Related words:

BANALITY: the quality of being banal

Words with similar meanings:

BLAND	BROMIDIC	CLICHÉD
COMMONPLACE	FATUOUS	HACKNEYED
INNOCUOUS	INSIPID	JEJUNE
MUSTY	PLATITUDINOUS	PROSAIC
QUOTIDIAN	SHOPWORN	STALE
STEREOTYPIC	THREADBARE	TIMEWORN
TIRED	TRITE	VAPID
WORN-OUT		

BOLSTER: to support; to prop up

The presence of giant footprints BOLSTERED the argument that Sasquatch was in the area.

Words with similar meanings:

BRACE	BUTTRESS	PROP
SUPPORT	SUSTAIN	UNDERPIN
UPHOLD		

BOMBASTIC: pompous in speech and manner

Mussolini's speeches were mostly BOMBASTIC; his boasting and outrageous claims had no basis in fact.

Related words:

BOMBAST: pompous speech or writing

Words with similar meanings:

BLOATED	DECLAMATORY	FUSTIAN
GRANDILOQUENT	GRANDIOSE	HIGH-FLOWN
MAGNILOQUENT	OROTUND	PRETENTIOUS
RHETORICAL	SELF-IMPORTANT	

CACOPHONY: harsh, jarring noise

The junior high orchestra created an almost unbearable CACOPHONY as they tried to tune their instruments.

Words with similar meanings:

CHAOS	CLAMOR	DIN
DISCORD	DISHARMONY	NOISE

CANDID: impartial and honest in speech

The observations of a child can be charming since they are CANDID and unpretentious.

Words with similar meanings:

DIRECT	FORTHRIGHT	FRANK
HONEST	OPEN	SINCERE
STRAIGHT	STRAIGHTFORWARD	UNDISGUISED

CAPRICIOUS: changing one's mind quickly and often

Queen Elizabeth I was quite CAPRICIOUS; her courtiers could never be sure which of their number would catch her fancy.

Related words:

CAPRICE: whim, sudden fancy

Words with similar meanings:

ARBITRARY	CHANCE	CHANGEABLE
ERRATIC	FICKLE	INCONSTANT
MERCURIAL	RANDOM	WHIMSICAL
WILLFUL		

CASTIGATE: to punish or criticize harshly

Many Americans are amazed at how harshly the authorities in Singapore CASTIGATE perpetrators of what would be considered minor crimes in the United States.

Words with similar meanings:

ADMONISH	CHASTISE	CHIDE
REBUKE	REPRIMAND	REPROACH
REPROVE	SCOLD	TAX
UPBRAID		

CATALYST: something that brings about a change in something else

The imposition of harsh taxes was the CATALYST that finally brought on the revolution.

Related words:

CATALYZE: to bring about a change in something else

CAUSTIC: biting in wit

Dorothy Parker gained her reputation for CAUSTIC wit from her cutting, yet clever, insults.

Words with similar meanings:

ACERBIC	BITING	MORDANT
TRENCHANT		

CHAOS: great disorder or confusion

In most religious traditions, God created an ordered universe from CHAOS.

Related words:

CHAOTIC: jumbled, confused

Words with similar meanings:

CLUTTER	CONFUSION	DISARRANGEMENT
DISARRAY	DISORDER	DISORDERLINESS
DISORGANIZATION	JUMBLE	MESS
MUDDLE	SCRAMBLE	SNARL
TOPSY-TURVINESS	TURMOIL	

CHAUVINIST: someone prejudiced in favor of a group to which he or she belongs

The attitude that men are inherently superior to women and therefore must be obeyed is common among male CHAUVINISTS.

Words with similar meanings:

PARTISAN

CHICANERY: deception by means of craft or guile

Dishonest used car salespeople often use CHICANERY to sell their beat-up old cars.

Words with similar meanings:

ARTIFICE	CONNIVING	CRAFTINESS
DECEPTION	DEVIOUSNESS	MISREPRESENTATION
PETTIFOGGERY	SHADINESS	SNEAKINESS
SOPHISTRY	SUBTERFUGE	UNDERHANDEDNESS

COGENT: convincing and well-reasoned

Swayed by the COGENT argument of the defense, the jury had no choice but to acquit the defendant.

Related words:

COGITATE: to think deeply

Words with similar meanings:

CONVINCING	PERSUASIVE	SOLID
SOUND	TELLING	VALID

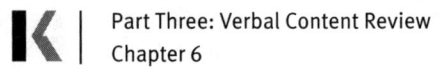

CONDONE: to overlook, pardon, or disregard

Some theorists believe that failing to prosecute minor crimes is the same as CONDONING an air of lawlessness.

Words with similar meanings:

EXCULPATE	EXCUSE	PARDON
REMIT		

CONVOLUTED: intricate and complicated

Although many people bought *A Brief History of Time*, few could follow its CONVOLUTED ideas and theories.

Words with similar meanings:

BYZANTINE	COMPLEX	ELABORATE
INTRICATE	KNOTTY	LABYRINTHINE
PERPLEXING	TANGLED	

CORROBORATE: to provide supporting evidence

Fingerprints CORROBORATED the witness's testimony that he saw the defendant in the victim's apartment.

Words with similar meanings:

AUTHENTICATE	BACK	BEAR OUT
BUTTRESS	CONFIRM	SUBSTANTIATE
VALIDATE	VERIFY	

CREDULOUS: too trusting; gullible

Although some four-year-olds believe in the Easter Bunny, only the most CREDULOUS nine-year-olds still believe in him.

Related words:

CREDULITY: the quality of being credulous

Words with similar meanings:

NAIVE	SUSCEPTIBLE	TRUSTING

CRESCENDO: steadily increasing in volume or force

The CRESCENDO of tension became unbearable as Evel Knievel prepared to jump his motorcycle over the school buses.

Words with similar meanings:

ESCALATION	INCREASE	INTENSIFICATION

DECORUM: appropriateness of behavior or conduct; propriety

The countess complained that the vulgar peasants lacked the DECORUM appropriate for a visit to the palace.

Related words:

DECOROUS: conforming to acceptable standards

Words with similar meanings:

CORRECTNESS	DECENCY	ETIQUETTE
MANNERS	MORES	PROPRIETY
SEEMLINESS		

DEFERENCE: respect, courtesy

The respectful young law clerk treated the Supreme Court justice with the utmost DEFERENCE.

Related words:

DEFER: to delay; to show someone deference

DEFERENTIAL: courteous and respectful

Words with similar meanings:

COURTESY	HOMAGE	HONOR
OBEISANCE	RESPECT	REVERENCE
VENERATION		

DERIDE: to speak of or treat with contempt; to mock

The awkward child was often DERIDED by his “cooler” peers.

Related words:

DERISION: mockery and taunts

DERISIVE: in a mocking manner

Words with similar meanings:

GIBE	JEER	MOCK
RIDICULE	SCOFF	SNEER
TAUNT		

DESICCATE: to dry out thoroughly

After a few weeks of lying on the desert’s baking sands, the cow’s carcass became completely DESICCATED.

Related words:

DESICCANT: something that removes water from another substance

Words with similar meanings:

DEHYDRATE	DRY	PARCH

DESULTORY: jumping from one thing to another; disconnected

Diane had a DESULTORY academic record; she had changed majors twelve times in three years.

Words with similar meanings:

AIMLESS	DISCONNECTED	ERRATIC
HAPHAZARD	INDISCRIMINATE	OBJECTLESS
PURPOSELESS	RANDOM	STRAY
UNCONSIDERED	UNPLANNED	

DIATRIBE: an abusive, condemnatory speech

The trucker bellowed a DIATRIBE at the driver who had cut him off.

Words with similar meanings:

FULMINATION	HARANGUE	INVECTIVE
JEREMIAD	MALEDICTION	OBLOQUY
TIRADE		

DIFFIDENT: lacking self-confidence

Steve's DIFFIDENT manner during the job interview stemmed from his nervous nature and lack of experience in the field.

Words with similar meanings:

BACKWARD	BASHFUL	COY
DEMURE	MODEST	RETIRING
SELF-EFFACING	SHY	TIMID

DILATE: to make larger; to expand

When you enter a darkened room, the pupils of your eyes DILATE to let in more light.

Words with similar meanings:

AMPLIFY	DEVELOP	ELABORATE
ENLARGE	EXPAND	EXPATIATE

DILATORY: intended to delay

The congressman used DILATORY measures to delay the passage of the bill.

Words with similar meanings:

DRAGGING	FLAGGING	LAGGARD
LAGGING	SLOW	SLOW-FOOTED
SLOW-GOING	SLOW-PACED	TARDY

DILETTANTE: someone with an amateurish and superficial interest in a topic

Jerry's friends were such DILETTANTES that they seemed to have new jobs and hobbies every week.

Words with similar meanings:

AMATEUR	DABBLER	SUPERFICIAL
TYRO		

DIRGE: a funeral hymn or mournful speech

Melville wrote the poem "A DIRGE for James McPherson" for the funeral of a Union general who was killed in 1864.

Words with similar meanings:

ELEGY	LAMENT

DISABUSE: to set right; to free from error

Galileo's observations DISABUSED scholars of the notion that the sun revolved around the Earth.

Words with similar meanings:

CORRECT	UNDECEIVE

DISCERN: to perceive; to recognize

It is easy to DISCERN the difference between butter and butter-flavored topping.

Related words:

DISCERNMENT: taste and cultivation

Words with similar meanings:

CATCH	DESCRY	DETECT
DIFFERENTIATE	DISCRIMINATE	DISTINGUISH
ESPY	GLIMPSE	KNOW
SEPARATE	SPOT	SPY
TELL		

DISPARATE: fundamentally different; entirely unlike

Although the twins appear to be identical physically, their personalities are DISPARATE.

Words with similar meanings:

DIFFERENT	DISSIMILAR	DIVERGENT
DIVERSE	VARIANT	VARIOUS

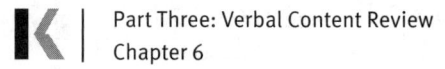

DISSEMBLE: to present a false appearance; to disguise one's real intentions or character

The villain could DISSEMBLE to the police no longer—he admitted the deed and tore up the floor to reveal the body of the old man.

Words with similar meanings:

ACT	AFFECT	ASSUME
CLOAK	COUNTERFEIT	CAMOUFLAGE
COVER UP	DISGUISE	DISSIMULATE
FAKE	FEIGN	MASK
MASQUERADE	POSE	PRETEND
PUT ON	SHAM	SIMULATE

DISSONANCE: a harsh and disagreeable combination, often of sounds

Cognitive DISSONANCE is the inner conflict produced when long-standing beliefs are contradicted by new evidence.

Words with similar meanings:

CLASH	CONTENTION	DISCORD
DISSENSION	DISSENT	DISSIDENCE
FRICTION	STRIFE	VARIANCE

DOGMA: a firmly held opinion, often a religious belief

Linus's central DOGMA was that children who believed in the Great Pumpkin would be rewarded.

Words with similar meanings:

CREED	CREDO	DOCTRINE
TEACHING	TENET	

DOGMATIC: dictatorial in one's opinions

The dictator was DOGMATIC—he, and only he, was right.

Words with similar meanings:

AUTHORITARIAN	BOSSY	DICTATORIAL
DOCTRINAIRE	DOMINEERING	IMPERIOUS
MAGISTERIAL	MASTERFUL	OVERBEARING
PEREMPTORY		

DUPE: to deceive; a person who is easily deceived

Bugs Bunny was able to DUPE Elmer Fudd by dressing up as a lady rabbit.

Words with similar meanings:

BEGUILE	BETRAY	BLUFF
COZEN	DECEIVE	DELUDE
FOOL	HOODWINK	HUMBUG
MISLEAD	TAKE IN	TRICK

ECLECTIC: selecting from or made up from a variety of sources

Budapest's architecture is an ECLECTIC mix of Eastern and Western styles.

Words with similar meanings:

BROAD	CATHOLIC	DIVERSE

EFFICACY: effectiveness

The EFFICACY of penicillin was unsurpassed when it was first introduced; the drug completely eliminated almost all bacterial infections for which it was administered.

Related words:
EFFICACIOUS: effective; productive

Words with similar meanings:

DYNAMISM	EFFECTIVENESS	EFFICIENCY
FORCE	POWER	PRODUCTIVENESS
PROFICIENCY	STRENGTH	VIGOR

ELEGY: a sorrowful poem or speech

Although Thomas Gray's "ELEGY Written in a Country Churchyard" is about death and loss, it urges its readers to endure this life and to trust in spirituality.

Related words:
ELEGIAC: like an elegy; mournful

Words with similar meanings:

DIRGE	LAMENT

ELOQUENT: persuasive and moving, especially in speech

The Gettysburg Address is moving not only because of its lofty sentiments but also because of its ELOQUENT words.

Words with similar meanings:

ARTICULATE	EXPRESSIVE	FLUENT
MEANINGFUL	SIGNIFICANT	SMOOTH-SPOKEN

EMULATE: to copy; to try to equal or excel

The graduate student sought to EMULATE his professor in every way, copying not only how she taught, but also how she conducted herself outside of class.

Words with similar meanings:

APE	IMITATE	SIMULATE

ENERVATE: to reduce in strength

The guerrillas hoped that a series of surprise attacks would ENERVATE the regular army.

Related words:

UNNERVE: to deprive of strength or courage

Words with similar meanings:

DEBILITATE	ENFEEBLE	SAP
WEAKEN		

ENGENDER: to produce, cause, or bring about

His fear and hatred of clowns was ENGENDERED when he witnessed the death of his father at the hands of a clown.

Words with similar meanings:

BEGET	GENERATE	PROCREATE
PROLIFERATE	REPRODUCE	SPAWN

ENIGMA: a puzzle; a mystery

Speaking in riddles and dressed in old robes, the artist gained a reputation as something of an ENIGMA.

Words with similar meanings:

CONUNDRUM	PERPLEXITY

ENUMERATE: to count, list, or itemize

Moses returned from the mountain with tablets on which the commandments were ENUMERATED.

Words with similar meanings:

CATALOG	INDEX	TABULATE

EPHEMERAL: lasting a short time

The lives of mayflies seem EPHEMERAL to us, since the flies' average life span is a matter of hours.

Words with similar meanings:

EVANESCENT	FLEETING	MOMENTARY
TRANSIENT		

EQUIVOCATE: to use expressions of double meaning in order to mislead

When faced with criticism of his policies, the politician EQUIVOCATED and left all parties thinking he agreed with them.

Related words:

EQUIVOCAL: undecided; trying to deceive

EQUIVOCATION: the act or state of equivocating

Words with similar meanings:

AMBIGUOUS EVASIVE WAFFLING

ERRATIC: wandering and unpredictable

The plot seemed predictable until it suddenly took a series of ERRATIC turns that surprised the audience.

Related words:

Errant: straying, mistaken, roving

Words with similar meanings:

CAPRICIOUS INCONSTANT IRRESOLUTE
WHIMSICAL

ERUDITE: learned, scholarly, bookish

The annual meeting of philosophy professors was a gathering of the most ERUDITE, well-published individuals in the field.

Related words:

ERUDITION: extensive knowledge or learning

Words with similar meanings:

SCHOLASTIC LEARNED WISE

ESOTERIC: known or understood by only a few

Only a handful of experts are knowledgeable about the ESOTERIC world of particle physics.

Words with similar meanings:

ABSTRUSE ARCANE OBSCURE

ESTIMABLE: admirable

Most people consider it ESTIMABLE that Mother Teresa spent her life helping the poor of India.

Related words:

ESTEEM: high regard

Words with similar meanings:

ADMIRABLE COMMENDABLE CREDITABLE
HONORABLE LAUDABLE MERITORIOUS
PRAISEWORTHY RESPECTABLE VENERABLE
WORTHY

EULOGY: speech in praise of someone

His best friend gave the EULOGY, outlining his many achievements and talents.

Words with similar meanings:

COMMEND EXTOL LAUD

EUPHEMISM: use of an inoffensive word or phrase in place of a more distasteful one

The funeral director preferred to use the EUPHEMISM "sleeping" instead of the word "dead."

Words with similar meanings:

CIRCUMLOCUTION WHITEWASH

EXACERBATE: to make worse

It is unwise to take aspirin to try to relieve heartburn; instead of providing relief, the drug will only EXACERBATE the problem.

Words with similar meanings:

ANNOY AGGRAVATE INTENSIFY
IRRITATE PROVOKE

EXCULPATE: to clear from blame; prove innocent

The adversarial legal system is intended to convict those who are guilty and to EXCULPATE those who are innocent.

Words with similar meanings:

ABSOLVE ACQUIT CLEAR
EXONERATE VINDICATE

EXIGENT: urgent; requiring immediate action

The patient was losing blood so rapidly that it was EXIGENT to stop the source of the bleeding.

Words with similar meanings:

CRITICAL IMPERATIVE NEEDED
URGENT

EXONERATE: to clear of blame

The fugitive was EXONERATED when another criminal confessed to committing the crime.

Words with similar meanings:

ABSOLVE ACQUIT CLEAR
EXCULPATE VINDICATE

EXPLICIT: clearly stated or shown; forthright in expression

The owners of the house left a list of EXPLICIT instructions detailing their house sitter's duties, including a schedule for watering the house plants.

Related words:

EXPLICABLE: capable of being explained

EXPLICATE: to give a detailed explanation

Words with similar meanings:

CLEAR-CUT	DEFINITIVE	PRECISE
STRAIGHTFORWARD	UNEQUIVOCAL	

FANATICAL: acting excessively enthusiastic; filled with extreme, unquestioned devotion

The stormtroopers were FANATICAL in their devotion to the Emperor, readily sacrificing their lives for him.

Words with similar meanings:

EXTREMIST	FIERY	FRENZIED
ZEALOUS		

FAWN: to grovel

The understudy FAWNED over the director in hopes of being cast in the part on a permanent basis.

Words with similar meanings:

BOOTLICK	GROVEL	PANDER
TOADY		

FERVID: intensely emotional; feverish

The fans of Maria Callas were particularly FERVID, doing anything to catch a glimpse of the great opera singer.

Related words:

FERVENT: enthusiastic

FERVOR: passion

Words with similar meanings:

BURNING	IMPASSIONED	PASSIONATE
VEHEMENT	ZEALOUS	

FLORID: excessively decorated or embellished

The palace had been decorated in a FLORID style; every surface had been carved and gilded.

Words with similar meanings:

BAROQUE	ELABORATE	FLAMBOYANT
ORNATE	OSTENTATIOUS	ROCOCO

FOMENT: to arouse or incite

The protesters tried to FOMENT feeling against the war through their speeches and demonstrations.

Words with similar meanings:

AGITATE	IMPASSION	INFLAME
INSTIGATE	KINDLE	

FRUGALITY: a tendency to be thrifty or cheap

Scrooge McDuck's FRUGALITY was so great that he accumulated enough wealth to fill a giant storehouse with money.

Words with similar meanings:

ECONOMICAL	PARSIMONY	PRUDENCE
SPARING	SCRIMPING	THRIFT

GARRULOUS: tending to talk a lot

The GARRULOUS parakeet distracted its owner with its continuous talking.

Words with similar meanings:

EFFUSIVE	LOQUACIOUS

GREGARIOUS: outgoing, sociable

She was so GREGARIOUS that when she found herself alone she felt quite sad.

Words with similar meanings:

AFFABLE	COMMUNICATIVE	CONGENIAL
SOCIABLE		

GUILE: deceit or trickery

Since he was not fast enough to catch the roadrunner on foot, the coyote resorted to GUILE in an effort to trap his enemy.

Related words:

GUILELESS: innocent, without trickery

Words with similar meanings:

ARTIFICE	CHICANERY	CONNIVERY
DUPLICITY		

GULLIBLE: easily deceived

The con man pretended to be a bank officer so as to fool GULLIBLE bank customers into giving him their account information.

Related words:

GULL: a person who is easily tricked

Words with similar meanings:

CREDULOUS EXPLOITABLE NAIVE

HOMOGENEOUS (or HOMOGENOUS): of a similar kind

The class was fairly HOMOGENEOUS, since almost all of the students were senior journalism majors.

Related words:

HOMOGENIZED: thoroughly mixed together

Words with similar meanings:

CONSISTENT STANDARDIZED UNIFORM
UNVARYING

ICONOCLAST: one who opposes established beliefs, customs, and institutions

His lack of regard for traditional beliefs soon established him as an ICONOCLAST.

Words with similar meanings:

MAVERICK NONCONFORMIST REBEL
REVOLUTIONARY

IMPERTURBABLE: not capable of being disturbed

The counselor had so much experience dealing with distraught children that she seemed IMPERTURBABLE, even when faced with the wildest tantrums.

Related words:

PERTURB: to disturb greatly

Words with similar meanings:

COMPOSED DISPASSIONATE IMPASSIVE
SERENE STOICAL

IMPERVIOUS: impossible to penetrate; incapable of being affected

A good raincoat is IMPERVIOUS to moisture.

Words with similar meanings:

RESISTANT IMPREGNABLE

IMPETUOUS: quick to act without thinking

It is not good for an investment broker to be IMPETUOUS, because much thought should be given to all the possible options.

Related words:

IMPETUS: impulse

Words with similar meanings:

IMPULSIVE	PRECIPITATE	RASH
RECKLESS	SPONTANEOUS	

IMPLACABLE: unable to be calmed down or made peaceful

His rage at the betrayal was so great that he remained IMPLACABLE for weeks.

Related words:

PLACATE: to make peaceful

Words with similar meanings:

INEXORABLE	INTRANSIGENT	IRRECONCILABLE
RELENTLESS	REMORSELESS	UNFORGIVING
UNRELENTING		

INCHOATE: not fully formed; disorganized

The ideas expressed in Nietzsche's mature work also appear in an INCHOATE form in his earliest writing.

Words with similar meanings:

AMORPHOUS	INCOHERENT	INCOMPLETE
UNORGANIZED		

INGENUOUS: showing innocence or childlike simplicity

She was so INGENUOUS that her friends feared that her innocence and trustfulness would be exploited when she visited the big city.

Related words:

INGÉNUE: a naive girl or young woman

DISINGENUOUS: giving a false impression of innocence

Words with similar meanings:

ARTLESS	GUILELESS	INNOCENT
NAIVE	SIMPLE	UNAFFECTED

INIMICAL: hostile, unfriendly

Even though a cease-fire had been in place for months, the two sides were still INIMICAL to each other.

Words with similar meanings:

ADVERSE ANTAGONISTIC DISSIDENT
RECALCITRANT

INNOCUOUS: harmless

Some snakes are poisonous, but most species are INNOCUOUS and pose no danger to humans.

Words with similar meanings:

BENIGN HARMLESS INOFFENSIVE

INSIPID: lacking interest or flavor

The critic claimed that the painting was INSIPID, containing no interesting qualities at all.

Words with similar meanings:

BANAL BLAND DULL
STALE VAPID

INTRANSIGENT: uncompromising; refusing to be reconciled

The professor was INTRANSIGENT on the deadline, insisting that everyone turn the assignment in at the same time.

Words with similar meanings:

IMPLACABLE INEXORABLE IRRECONCILABLE
OBDURATE OBSTINATE REMORSELESS
RIGID UNBENDING UNRELENTING
UNYIELDING

INUNDATE: to overwhelm; to cover with water

The tidal wave INUNDATED Atlantis, which was lost beneath the water.

Words with similar meanings:

DELUGE DROWN ENGULF
FLOOD SUBMERGE

IRASCIBLE: easily made angry

Attila the Hun's IRASCIBLE and violent nature made all who dealt with him fear for their lives.

Related words:

IRATE: angry

Words with similar meanings:

CANTANKEROUS IRRITABLE ORNERY
TESTY

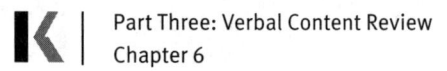

LACONIC: using few words

She was a LACONIC poet who built her reputation on using words as sparingly as possible.

Words with similar meanings:

CONCISE	CURT	PITHY
TACITURN	TERSE	

LAMENT: to express sorrow; to grieve

The children continued to LAMENT the death of the goldfish weeks after its demise.

Words with similar meanings:

BEWAIL	DEPLORE	GRIEVE
MOURN		

LAUD: to give praise; to glorify

Parades and fireworks were staged to LAUD the success of the rebels.

Related words:

LAUDABLE: worthy of praise

LAUDATORY: expressing praise

Words with similar meanings:

ACCLAIM	APPLAUD	COMMEND
COMPLIMENT	EXALT	EXTOL
HAIL	PRAISE	

LAVISH: to give unsparingly (v.); extremely generous or extravagant (adj.)

She LAVISHED the puppy with so many treats that it soon became overweight and spoiled.

Words with similar meanings:

BESTOW	CONFER	EXTRAVAGANT
EXUBERANT	LUXURIANT	OPULENT
PRODIGAL	PROFUSE	SUPERABUNDANT

LETHARGIC: acting in an indifferent or slow, sluggish manner

The clerk was so LETHARGIC that, even when the store was not busy, he always had a long line in front of him.

Words with similar meanings:

APATHETIC	LACKADAISICAL	LANGUID
LISTLESS	TORPID	

LOQUACIOUS: talkative

She was naturally LOQUACIOUS, which was a problem in situations in which listening was more important than talking.

Related words:

ELOQUENCE: powerful, convincing speaking

LOQUACITY: the quality of being loquacious

Words with similar meanings:

EFFUSIVE	GARRULOUS	VERBOSE

LUCID: clear and easily understood

The explanations were written in a simple and LUCID manner so that students were immediately able to apply what they learned.

Related words:

LUCIDITY: clarity

LUCENT: glowing with light

Words with similar meanings:

CLEAR	COHERENT	EXPLICIT
INTELLIGIBLE	LIMPID	

LUMINOUS: bright, brilliant, glowing

The park was bathed in LUMINOUS sunshine, which warmed the bodies and the souls of the visitors.

Related words:

ILLUMINATE: to shine light on

LUMINARY: an inspiring person

Words with similar meanings:

INCANDESCENT	LUCENT	LUSTROUS
RADIANT	RESPLENDENT	

MALINGER: to evade responsibility by pretending to be ill

A common way to avoid the draft was by MALINGERING—pretending to be mentally or physically ill so as to avoid being taken by the Army.

Related words:

LINGER: to be slow in leaving

Words with similar meanings:

SHIRK	SLACK

MALLEABLE: capable of being shaped

Gold is the most MALLEABLE of precious metals; it can easily be formed into almost any shape.

Words with similar meanings:

ADAPTABLE	DUCTILE	PLASTIC
PLIABLE	PLIANT	

METAPHOR: a figure of speech comparing two different things; a symbol

The METAPHOR "a sea of troubles" suggests a lot of troubles by comparing their number to the vastness of the sea.

Related words:

METAPHORICAL: standing as a symbol for something else

Words with similar meanings:

ANALOGY	COMPARISON

METICULOUS: extremely careful about details

To find all the clues at the crime scene, the investigators METICULOUSLY examined every inch of the area.

Words with similar meanings:

CONSCIENTIOUS	PRECISE	SCRUPULOUS

MISANTHROPE: a person who dislikes others

The character Scrooge in *A Christmas Carol* is such a MISANTHROPE that even the sight of children singing makes him angry.

Words with similar meanings:

CURMUDGEON	RECLUSE

MITIGATE: to soften; to lessen

A judge may MITIGATE a sentence if she decides that a person committed a crime out of need.

Words with similar meanings:

ALLAY	ALLEVIATE	ASSUAGE
EASE	LIGHTEN	MODERATE
MOLLIFY	PALLIATE	TEMPER

MOLLIFY: to calm or make less severe

Their argument was so intense that it was difficult to believe any compromise would MOLLIFY them.

Words with similar meanings:

APPEASE	ASSUAGE	CONCILIATE
PACIFY		

MONOTONY: lack of variation

The MONOTONY of the sound of the dripping faucet almost drove the research assistant crazy.

Related words:

MONOTONE: a sound that is made at the same tone or pitch

Words with similar meanings:

DRONE	TEDIUM

NAIVE: lacking sophistication or experience

Having never traveled before, the hillbillies were more NAIVE than the people they met in Beverly Hills.

Related words:

NAIVETÉ: the state of being naive

Words with similar meanings:

ARTLESS	CREDULOUS	GUILELESS
INGENUOUS	SIMPLE	UNAFFECTED

OBDURATE: hardened in feeling; resistant to persuasion

The president was completely OBDURATE on the issue, and no amount of persuasion would change his mind.

Words with similar meanings:

INFLEXIBLE	INTRANSIGENT	RECALCITRANT
TENACIOUS	UNYIELDING	

OBSEQUIOUS: overly submissive and eager to please

The OBSEQUIOUS new associate made sure to compliment her supervisor's tie and agree with him on every issue.

Related words:

OBEISANCE: a physical show of respect or submission, such as a bow

Words with similar meanings:

COMPLIANT	DEFERENTIAL	SERVILE
SUBSERVIENT		

OBSTINATE: stubborn, unyielding

The OBSTINATE child could not be made to eat any food that he disliked.

Words with similar meanings:

INTRANSIGENT MULISH PERSISTENT
PERTINACIOUS STUBBORN TENACIOUS

OBVIATE: to prevent; to make unnecessary

The river was shallow enough to wade across at many points, which OBVIATED the need for a bridge.

Words with similar meanings:

FORESTALL PRECLUDE PROHIBIT

OCCLUDE: to stop up; to prevent the passage of

A shadow is thrown across the Earth's surface during a solar eclipse, when the light from the sun is OCCLUDED by the moon.

Words with similar meanings:

BARRICADE BLOCK CLOSE
OBSTRUCT

ONEROUS: troublesome and oppressive; burdensome

The assignment was so extensive and difficult to manage that it proved ONEROUS to the team in charge of it.

Words with similar meanings:

ARDUOUS BACKBREAKING BURDENSOME
CUMBERSOME DIFFICULT EXACTING
FORMIDABLE HARD LABORIOUS
OPPRESSIVE RIGOROUS TAXING
TRYING

OPAQUE: impossible to see through; preventing the passage of light

The heavy buildup of dirt and grime on the windows almost made them OPAQUE.

Related words:

OPACITY: the quality of being obscure and indecipherable

Words with similar meanings:

OBSCURE

OPPROBRIUM: public disgrace

After the scheme to embezzle from the elderly was made public, the treasurer resigned in utter OPPROBRIUM.

Words with similar meanings:

DISCREDIT	DISGRACE	DISHONOR
DISREPUTE	IGNOMINY	INFAMY
OBLOQUY	SHAME	

OSTENTATION: excessive showiness

The OSTENTATION of the Sun King's court is evident in the lavish decoration and luxuriousness of his palace at Versailles.

Related words:

OSTENSIBLE: apparent

Words with similar meanings:

CONSPICUOUSNESS	FLASHINESS	PRETENTIOUSNESS
SHOWINESS		

PARADOX: a contradiction or dilemma

It is a PARADOX that those most in need of medical attention are often those least able to obtain it.

Words with similar meanings:

ANOMALY	IRONY	CONTRADICTION

PARAGON: model of excellence or perfection

She is the PARAGON of what a judge should be: honest, intelligent, hardworking, and just.

Words with similar meanings:

APOTHEOSIS	IDEAL	QUINTESSENCE
STANDARD		

PEDANT: someone who shows off learning

The graduate instructor's tedious and excessive commentary on the subject soon gained her a reputation as a PEDANT.

Related words:

PEDANTIC: making an excessive display of learning

PERFIDIOUS: willing to betray one's trust

The actress's PERFIDIOUS companion revealed all of her intimate secrets to the gossip columnist.

Related words:

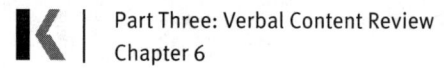

PERFIDY: deceit, treachery

Words with similar meanings:

DISLOYAL FAITHLESS TRAITOROUS
TREACHEROUS

PERFUNCTORY: done in a routine way; indifferent

The machinelike bank teller processed the transaction and gave the waiting customer a PERFUNCTORY smile.

Words with similar meanings:

APATHETIC AUTOMATIC MECHANICAL

PERMEATE: to penetrate

This miraculous new cleaning fluid is able to PERMEATE stains and dissolve them in minutes!

Related words:

IMPERMEABLE: unable to be permeated

Words with similar meanings:

IMBUE INFUSE SUFFUSE

PHILANTHROPY: charity; a desire or effort to promote goodness

New York's Metropolitan Museum of Art owes much of its collection to the PHILANTHROPY of private collectors who willed their estates to the museum.

Related words:

PHILANTHROPIST: someone who is generous and desires to promote goodness

Words with similar meanings:

ALTRUISM HUMANITARIANISM

PLACATE: to soothe or pacify

The burglar tried to PLACATE the snarling dog by saying, "Nice doggy," and offering it a treat.

Related words:

PLACID: tolerant; calm

IMPLACABLE: unable to be made peaceful

Words with similar meanings:

APPEASE CONCILIATE MOLLIFY

PLASTIC: able to be molded, altered, or bent

The new material was very PLASTIC and could be formed into products of vastly different shapes.

Words with similar meanings:

ADAPTABLE	DUCTILE	MALLEABLE
PLIANT		

PLETHORA: excess

Assuming that more was better, the defendant offered the judge a PLETHORA of excuses.

Words with similar meanings:

GLUT	OVERABUNDANCE	SUPERFLUITY
SURFEIT		

PRAGMATIC: practical as opposed to idealistic

While daydreaming gamblers think they can get rich by frequenting casinos, PRAGMATIC gamblers realize that the odds are heavily stacked against them.

Related words:

PRAGMATISM: a practical approach to problem solving

Words with similar meanings:

RATIONAL	REALISTIC

PRECIPITATE: to throw violently or bring about abruptly; lacking deliberation

Upon learning that the couple married after knowing each other only two months, friends and family members expected such a PRECIPITATE marriage to end in divorce.

Related words:

PRECIPICE: a steep cliff

PRECIPITATION: weather phenomena, like rain or snow, that falls from the sky

PRECIPITOUS: very steep

Words with similar meanings:

ABRUPT	HASTY	HEADLONG
HURRIED	ILL-CONSIDERED	IMPETUOUS
IMPULSIVE	PROMPT	RASH
RECKLESS	SUDDEN	

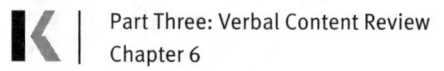

PREVARICATE: to lie or deviate from the truth

Rather than admit that he had overslept again, the employee PREVARICATED and claimed that heavy traffic had prevented him from arriving at work on time.

Words with similar meanings:

EQUIVOCATE	LIE	PERJURE

PRISTINE: fresh and clean; uncorrupted

Since concerted measures had been taken to prevent looting, the archeological site was still PRISTINE when researchers arrived.

Words with similar meanings:

INNOCENT	UNDAMAGED

PRODIGAL: lavish; wasteful

The PRODIGAL son quickly wasted all of his inheritance on a lavish lifestyle devoted to pleasure.

Related words:

PRODIGALITY: excessive or reckless spending

Words with similar meanings:

EXTRAVAGANT	LAVISH	PROFLIGATE
SPENDTHRIFT	WASTEFUL	

PROLIFERATE: to increase in number quickly

Although he only kept two guinea pigs initially, they PROLIFERATED to such an extent that he soon had dozens.

Related words:

PROLIFIC: very productive or highly able to reproduce rapidly

Words with similar meanings:

BREED	MULTIPLY	PROCREATE
PROPAGATE	REPRODUCE	SPAWN

PROPITIATE: to conciliate; to appease

The management PROPITIATED the irate union by agreeing to raise wages for its members.

Related words:

PROPITIOUS: advantageous, favorable

Words with similar meanings:

APPEASE	CONCILIATE	MOLLIFY
PACIFY	PLACATE	

PROPRIETY: correct behavior; obedience to rules and customs

The aristocracy maintained a high level of PROPRIETY, adhering to even the most minor social rules.

Related words:

APPROPRIATE: suitable for a particular occasion or place

Words with similar meanings:

DECENCY	DECORUM	MODESTY
SEEMLINESS		

PRUDENCE: wisdom, caution, or restraint

The college student exhibited PRUDENCE by obtaining practical experience along with her studies, which greatly strengthened her résumé.

Related words:

PRUDE: someone who is excessively concerned with propriety

PRUDISH: prissy and puritanical

Words with similar meanings:

ASTUTENESS	CIRCUMSPECTION	DISCRETION
FRUGALITY	JUDICIOUSNESS	PROVIDENCE
THRIFT		

PUNGENT: sharp and irritating to the senses

The smoke from the burning tires was extremely PUNGENT.

Words with similar meanings:

ACRID	CAUSTIC	PIQUANT
POIGNANT	STINGING	

QUIESCENT: motionless

Many animals are QUIESCENT over the winter months, minimizing activity in order to conserve energy.

Related words:

QUIESCENCE: state of rest or inactivity

Words with similar meanings:

DORMANT LATENT

RAREFY: to make thinner or sparser

Since the atmosphere RAREFIES as altitudes increase, the air at the top of very tall mountains is too thin to breathe.

Related words:

RAREFACTION: the process of making something less dense

Words with similar meanings:

ATTENUATE THIN

REPUDIATE: to reject the validity of

The old woman's claim that she was Russian royalty was REPUDIATED when DNA tests showed she was of no relation to them.

Words with similar meanings:

DENY DISAVOW DISCLAIM
DISOWN RENOUNCE

RETICENT: silent, reserved

Physically small and RETICENT in her speech, Joan Didion often went unnoticed by those upon whom she was reporting.

Words with similar meanings:

COOL INTROVERTED LACONIC
STANDOFFISH TACITURN UNDEMONSTRATIVE

RHETORIC: effective writing or speaking

Lincoln's talent for RHETORIC was evident in his beautifully expressed Gettysburg Address.

Words with similar meanings:

ELOQUENCE ORATORY

SATIATE: to satisfy fully or overindulge

His desire for power was so great that nothing less than complete control of the country could SATIATE it.

Related words:

SATE: to fully satisfy or overindulge

INSATIABLE: incapable of being satisfied

Words with similar meanings:

CLOY	GLUT	GORGE
SURFEIT		

SOPORIFIC: causing sleep or lethargy

The movie proved to be so SOPORIFIC that soon loud snores were heard throughout the theater.

Related words:

SOPOR: deep sleep

Words with similar meanings:

HYPNOTIC	NARCOTIC	SLUMBEROUS
SOMNOLENT		

SPECIOUS: deceptively attractive; seemingly plausible but fallacious

The student's SPECIOUS excuse for being late sounded legitimate, but was proved otherwise when his teacher called his home.

Words with similar meanings:

ILLUSORY	OSTENSIBLE	PLAUSIBLE
SPURIOUS	SOPHISTICAL	

STIGMA: a mark of shame or discredit

In *The Scarlet Letter*, Hester Prynne was required to wear the letter "A" on her clothes as a public STIGMA for her adultery.

Related words:

STIGMATIZE: to disgrace; to label with negative terms or reputation

Words with similar meanings:

BLEMISH	BLOT	OPPROBRIUM
STAIN	TAINT	

STOLID: unemotional; lacking sensitivity

The prisoner appeared STOLID and unaffected by the judge's harsh sentence.

Words with similar meanings:

APATHETIC	IMPASSIVE	INDIFFERENT
PHLEGMATIC	STOICAL	UNCONCERNED

SUBLIME: lofty or grand

The music was so SUBLIME that it transformed the rude surroundings into a special place.

Related words:

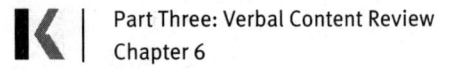

SUBLIMATE: to elevate or convert into something of higher worth

SUBLIMINAL: existing outside conscious awareness

Words with similar meanings:

AUGUST	EXALTED	GLORIOUS
GRAND	MAGNIFICENT	MAJESTIC
NOBLE	REGAL	RESPLENDENT
SUPERB		

TACIT: done without using words

Although not a word had been said, everyone in the room knew that a TACIT agreement had been made about which course of action to take.

Related words:

TACITURN: silent, not talkative

Words with similar meanings:

IMPLICIT	IMPLIED	UNDECLARED
UNSAID	UNUTTERED	

TACITURN: silent, not talkative

The clerk's TACITURN nature earned him the nickname "Silent Bob."

Related words:

TACIT: done without using words

Words with similar meanings:

LACONIC	RETICENT

TIRADE: long, harsh speech or verbal attack

Observers were shocked at the manager's TIRADE over such a minor mistake.

Words with similar meanings:

DIATRIBE	FULMINATION	HARANGUE
OBLOQUY	REVILEMENT	VILIFICATION

TORPOR: extreme mental and physical sluggishness

After surgery, the patient experienced TORPOR until the anesthesia wore off.

Related words:

TORPID: sluggish, lacking movement

Words with similar meanings:

APATHY	LANGUOR

TRANSITORY: temporary, lasting a brief time

The reporter lived a TRANSITORY life, staying in one place only long enough to cover the current story.

Related words:

TRANSIT: to pass through; to change or make a transition

TRANSIENT: passing quickly in and out of existence; one who stays a short time

Words with similar meanings:

EPHEMERAL	EVANESCENT	FLEETING
IMPERMANENT	MOMENTARY	

VACILLATE: to sway physically; to be indecisive

The customer held up the line as he VACILLATED between ordering chocolate chip or rocky road ice cream.

Words with similar meanings:

DITHER	FALTER	FLUCTUATE
OSCILLATE	WAVER	

VENERATE: to respect deeply

In a traditional Confucian society, the young VENERATE their elders, deferring to the elders' wisdom and experience.

Related words:

VENERABLE: old, worthy of respect

Words with similar meanings:

ADORE	HONOR	IDOLIZE
REVERE		

VERACITY: truthfulness; accuracy

She had a reputation for VERACITY, so everyone trusted her description of events.

Related words:

VERITY: truth

VERACIOUS: filled with truth and accuracy

Words with similar meanings:

CANDOR	EXACTITUDE	FIDELITY
PROBITY		

VERBOSE: wordy

The professor's answer was so VERBOSE that his student forgot what the original question had been.

Related words:

VERBALIZE: to put into words

VERBATIM: using the exact words; word for word

VERBIAGE: lots of words that are usually superfluous

Words with similar meanings:

LONG-WINDED	LOQUACIOUS	PROLIX
SUPERFLUOUS		

VEX: to annoy

The old man who loved his peace and quiet was VEXED by his neighbor's loud music.

Related words:

VEXATION: a feeling of irritation

Words with similar meanings:

ANNOY	BOTHER	CHAFE
EXASPERATE	IRK	NETTLE
PEEVE	PROVOKE	

VOLATILE: easily aroused or changeable; lively or explosive

His VOLATILE personality made it difficult to predict his reaction to anything.

Words with similar meanings:

CAPRICIOUS	ERRATIC	FICKLE
INCONSISTENT	INCONSTANT	MERCURIAL
TEMPERAMENTAL		

WAVER: to fluctuate between choices

If you WAVER too long before making a decision about which testing site to register for, you may not get your first choice.

Words with similar meanings:

DITHER	FALTER	FLUCTUATE
OSCILLATE	VACILLATE	

WHIMSICAL: acting in a fanciful or capricious manner; unpredictable

The ballet was WHIMSICAL, delighting the children with its imaginative characters and unpredictable sets.

Related words:

WHIM: a fancy or sudden notion

Words with similar meanings:

CAPRICIOUS	ERRATIC	FLIPPANT
FRIVOLOUS		

ZEAL: passion, excitement

She brought her typical ZEAL to the project, sparking enthusiasm in the other team members.

Related words:

ZEALOT: a fanatic

Words with similar meanings:

ARDENCY	FERVOR	FIRE
PASSION		

WORDS IN CONTEXT EXERCISE

1. Which sentence uses the word **capricious** correctly, in meaning and form?

   (A) When it rained during the picnic, the party shivered under a tree until John's fiancée laughed, lifting the party's *capricious* mood.

   (B) Senators debated several *capricious* economic issues until the budget had been balanced.

   (C) Jane's mother speculated that her daughter's failing grades were due to her carefree, *capricious* nature.

2. Which sentence uses the word **misanthrope** correctly, in meaning and form?

   (A) Intelligent students are usually *misanthropes* because they tend to study hard in school.

   (B) The *misanthrope* liked to go deer hunting with his friends each summer to add to his collection.

   (C) Although he did well in graduate school, Gary is too much of a *misanthrope* to succeed as a professor.

3. Which sentence uses the word **paragon** correctly, in meaning and form?

   (A) Firefighters are often the biggest *paragons* of smoke detectors, fire extinguishers, and other forms of fire safety.
   (B) The decorated army commander was a *paragon* of team leadership, discipline, and professionalism.
   (C) The chief of police did not support his *paragon* views on crime reduction.

4. Which sentence uses the word **venerate** correctly, in meaning and form?

   (A) In ancient times, kings and great warriors were *venerated* by being buried with many riches.
   (B) To regain control of his soccer team, the coach *venerated* players who were not taking the sport seriously.
   (C) When the retailer *venerated* the brass bed frame, the antique piece looked like new.

5. Which sentence uses the word **cacophony** correctly, in meaning and form?

   (A) The discordant music was a dreadful *cacophony* of synthesizer, accordion, and bells.
   (B) Due to hip surgery, her *cacophony* was off-balance and clumsy.
   (C) The novel's premise was so weak that the very *cacophony* of the motivation was questionable.

6. Which sentence uses the word **chicanery** correctly, in meaning and form?

   (A) The cashmere sweater was light as *chicanery*, as if knit of the softest goose feathers.
   (B) The smells of oregano and *chicanery* wafted from the kitchen into the living room.
   (C) Though he is usually good at detecting *chicanery*, that swindler cheated him out of a month's pay.

7. Which sentence uses the word **impetuous(ly)** correctly, in meaning and form?

   (A) She maintained a fiercely *impetuous* hold on her job title and never let anyone else perform the office duties.
   (B) Because she'd experienced his rage before, she approached her boss *impetuously* with the updated meeting outline.
   (C) She answered the questions on the form *impetuously*, filling them in randomly and without consideration.

8. Which sentence uses the word **vacillating** correctly, in meaning and form?

   (A) The music stopped suddenly and the *vacillating* silence was deafening.
   (B) After *vacillating* for days over whether to go to the doctor, she finally made an appointment when the swelling worsened dramatically.
   (C) The *vacillating* foundation held the monument steady in the high winds.

9. Which sentence uses the word **obstinate** correctly, in meaning and form?

   (A) Old maps and charts are too imprecise to give *obstinate* locations of geographic landmarks.
   (B) The new features added to the cell phone, including Internet access and photography, make it an *obstinate* piece of equipment.
   (C) Her *obstinate* political philosophy allowed her to see her own conditioned, inherited beliefs only.

10. Which sentence uses the word **apathy** correctly, in meaning and form?

   (A) The abhorrent criminal sneered maliciously, while the uninterested detective looked on with *apathy*.
   (B) Even wearing a heavy cape and tight corset, the opera singer carried herself across the stage with great *apathy*.
   (C) When the delicate gardenia blossoms opened, a scented *apathy* filtered through the air.

11. Which sentence uses the word **banal** correctly, in meaning and form?

    (A) The protesting crowd quickly formed a *banal* and crossed it to reach the locked offices of the politicians.
    (B) Thoughtful as her overtures were, his sister's insistence on traditions as *banal* as birthday cards and candles on the cake irritated him.
    (C) Her effervescent light-heartedness made a *banal* impression on him.

12. Which sentence uses the word **castigate** correctly, in meaning and form?

    (A) They stayed a long time by the shore, to watch the boats *castigate* in the setting sun.
    (B) She wrote the paper the night before it was due, so she was fully prepared for her professor to *castigate* her weak efforts.
    (C) She insisted on chewing vigorously to *castigate* her food before swallowing.

13. Which sentence uses the word **cogent** correctly, in meaning and form?

    (A) The doctor presented *cogent* reasons for continuing the treatment.
    (B) The doctor prepared a *cogent* supply of medical resources for the patient.
    (C) Not all forms of cancer have symptoms *cogent* to only one prescribed type.

14. Which sentence uses the word **lavish** correctly, in meaning and form?

    (A) Her efforts to create a *lavish* party to entertain her new in-laws included a four-course dinner and live musicians.
    (B) Her *lavish* stinginess eventually drew the attention of all her acquaintances.
    (C) He kept his skin disorder *lavish* by concealing it discreetly beneath long sleeves.

15. Which sentence uses the word **garrulous** correctly, in meaning and form?

    (A) The *garrulous* guest regaled the party with songs and stories all evening.
    (B) The police set out to apprehend the *garrulous* thief who stole the vehicle.
    (C) The student developed a *garrulous* model to illustrate her geography assignment.

16. Which sentence uses the word **pungent** correctly, in meaning and form?

    (A) The scent of mold assaulted her senses with its *pungent* odor.
    (B) The babysitter developed a *pungent* fondness for the children she cared for.
    (C) Nobody associated with the *pungent* student who lost his temper so easily.

17. Which sentence uses the word **onerous** correctly, in meaning and form?

    (A) Her *onerous* view of the world became apparent during the debate when she mistook libertarianism for liberalism.
    (B) In the fall, the responsibility of driving her brother to practice became more *onerous* because he played twice as many fall sports as summer sports.
    (C) Chad grew concerned that chemicals were being used for a more *onerous* purpose than to study medicine.

18. Which sentence uses the word **plethora** correctly, in meaning and form?

    (A) The new student's hilarious stories brought a lot of *plethora* to the strait-laced campus.
    (B) The newlyweds' home was filled with a *plethora* of gifts, flowers, and letters wishing them good fortune.
    (C) Elephants *plethora* before they begin a long journey.

19. Which sentence uses the word **taciturn** correctly, in meaning and form?

    (A) After his wife died, the widower grew isolated and became *taciturn* in public.
    (B) Her *taciturn* fear of public speaking caused her palms to sweat and her heart to flutter.
    (C) *Taciturn* by nature, she spoke to anyone who would listen about any subject on her mind.

20. Which sentence uses the word **efficacy** correctly, in meaning and form?

    (A) The man fought with fierce *efficacy*, but ultimately lost the boxing match.
    (B) The car owner decided that a damaged fender was too negligible to warrant making an *efficacy*.
    (C) Due to the *efficacy* of his business, a store owner was able to open another branch.

21. Which sentence uses the word **repudiate** correctly, in meaning and form?

    (A) The leftover crumbs, dirty plates, and chocolate-smudged faces helped them *repudiate* what they had for dessert.
    (B) The investor *repudiated* the business plan once she demonstrated that it was nothing more than a pyramid scheme.
    (C) Gamblers work hard to conceal tics and behaviors that might *repudiate* their strategies.

22. Which sentence uses the word **deferential** correctly, in meaning and form?

    (A) The courts make it clear that *deferential* behaviors will not be tolerated during jury selection.
    (B) The miscreant kicked rocks into the yard next door with a *deferential* attitude toward the homeowners.
    (C) The young man guided his grandmother with *deferential* patience to her car.

23. Which sentence uses the word **dupe** correctly, in meaning and form?

    (A) When the boy's cousin revealed a well-known secret, the boy had to *dupe* surprise.
    (B) No one would ever *dupe* to interrupt the patriarch of the family during mealtimes.
    (C) She *duped* her boyfriend into believing she lived in a better neighborhood.

24. Which sentence uses the word **stolid** correctly, in meaning and form?

Ⓐ She painted the landscape with *stolid* and acrylic paints.
Ⓑ Mother complained about the *stolid* couple who stayed so much later than all the other guests.
Ⓒ The *stolid* professor remained unmoved by the students' story of how they had missed the exam because of the blizzard.

25. Which sentence uses the word **zealous** correctly, in meaning and form?

Ⓐ He had a *zealous* crush on her that he was much too shy to make known.
Ⓑ The candidate's *zealous* campaign impressed his supporters with his enthusiasm.
Ⓒ He had a *zealous* feeling for his boss and always made snide comments right to his face.

26. Which sentence uses the word **implacable** correctly, in meaning and form?

Ⓐ Observing a young couple, the older woman briefly felt an *implacable* grief for her lost youth.
Ⓑ She could never convince her *implacable* son to eat anything but his favorite foods.
Ⓒ The violinist in the subway station played with an *implacable* skill that no one even recognized.

27. Which sentence uses the word **insipid** correctly, in meaning and form?

Ⓐ Despite its enormous popularity, the book struck Tom as *insipid*, lacking creativity and inspiration.
Ⓑ With *insipid* legal maneuvering, the lawyer connected the witness to the crime.
Ⓒ Homeless shelters handle the poverty of those on the streets by providing *insipid* food and comfort.

28. Which sentence uses the word **transient** correctly, in meaning and form?

- (A) The thin girl pulled a shawl over her chilled, *transient* shoulders.
- (B) The sophomore regretted socializing with such *transient* abandon during his freshman year.
- (C) For a sudden, *transient* moment, the actor seemed to forget his lines completely.

29. Which sentence uses the word **naive** correctly, in meaning and form?

- (A) The film critic's *naive* comment about the classic film illustrated his lack of experience.
- (B) The shape of the yew bushes grew more *naive* when she stopped trimming them.
- (C) The pain in her side grew so intensely *naive* that she doubled over.

30. Which sentence uses the word **audacity** correctly, in meaning and form?

- (A) The *audacity* with which she voiced her complaints startled everyone in the room.
- (B) She left her parents' home in *audacity* to their wishes that she stay.
- (C) Finally leaving her parents' home, she was able to embrace her autonomy and make choices of her own *audacity*.

ANSWER KEY FOR WORDS IN CONTEXT EXERCISE

1. C
2. C
3. B
4. A
5. A
6. C
7. C
8. B
9. C
10. A
11. B
12. B
13. A
14. A
15. A
16. A
17. B
18. B
19. A
20. C
21. B
22. C
23. C
24. C
25. B
26. B
27. A
28. C
29. A
30. A

PART FOUR

Analytical Writing

CHAPTER 7

The Issue Essay

THE ISSUE ESSAY

The first of the Analytical Writing essay tasks is the Issue essay. On the Issue essay, you are given a point of view about which you'll have to form an opinion and then provide a well-supported and justifiable case for that opinion. The Issue essay requires you to construct your own argument by making claims and providing evidence to support your position on a given issue. The directions will ask you to take a position on the issue and instruct you to explain your position convincingly, using evidence and/or examples to support your assertions.

For the assignment topic, expect a one- to two-sentence prompt that discusses a broad, general issue, sometimes presenting only one point of view, sometimes presenting two conflicting points. Either way, the test will present a statement that can reasonably be either supported or opposed. Your job is to form an opinion on the topic and make a case for that opinion.

The directions for the Issue essay will look like this:

> **Directions**: You will be given a brief quotation that states or implies a topic of general interest, along with explicit instructions on how to respond to that topic. Your response will be evaluated according to how well you:

- respond to the specific directions the task gives you.
- reflect on the complexities of the issue.
- organize and develop your thoughts.
- support your reasoning with relevant examples.
- express yourself in standard written English.

The following is a list of the types of possible Issue essay tasks you might encounter on the GRE Analytical Writing section:

- Write a response in which you examine your own position on the statement. Explore the extent to which you either agree or disagree with it, and support your reasoning with evidence and/or examples. Be sure to reflect on ways in which the statement might or might not be true, and how this informs your thinking on the subject.
- Write your own response to the recommendation in which you discuss why you either agree or disagree with it. Support your response with evidence and/or examples. Use a hypothetical set of circumstances to illustrate the consequences of accepting or rejecting the recommendation, and explain how this informs your thinking.
- Develop a response to the claim in which you discuss whether or not you agree with it. Focus specifically on the most powerful or compelling examples that could be used to refute your position.
- Write a response in which you determine which view bears the closest resemblance to your own. In justifying your reasoning and supporting your position, be sure to include your reaction to both of the views presented.
- Develop a response to the claim in which you discuss whether or not you agree with it. Focus specifically on whether or not you agree with the reason upon which the claim is based.
- Write a response discussing your reaction to the stated policy. Justify your reasoning for the position you take. Explain the potential consequences or implications for implementing such a policy and how this informs your position.

THE KAPLAN METHOD FOR ANALYTICAL WRITING

STEP 1 Take the issue/argument apart.

STEP 2 Select the points you will make.

STEP 3 Organize, using Kaplan's essay templates.

STEP 4 Type your essay.

STEP 5 Proofread your work.

How the Kaplan Method for Analytical Writing Works

Here's how the Kaplan Method for Analytical Writing works for the Issue essay:

STEP 1

Take the issue apart.

Read the assignment and consider both sides of the issue. Use your scratch paper throughout Steps 1–3. Restate the issue in your own words. Consider the other side of the issue, and put that into your own words as well.

STEP 2

Select the points you will make.

After you consider what both sides of the issue mean, think of reasons and examples for both sides and decide which side you will support or the extent to which you agree with the stated position.

STEP 3

Organize, using Kaplan's essay templates.

Organize your thoughts by outlining what you want to say, so that you'll be able to approach the actual writing process confidently and focus on expressing your ideas clearly. In the introduction, restate the prompt in your own words, state whether you agree or disagree, and give a preview of the supporting points you plan to make. In the middle paragraphs, give your points of agreement (or disagreement) and provide support. Determine the evidence you'll use to support each point. Be sure to lead with your best argument. Think about how the essay as a whole will flow. Conclude by summing up your position on the issue. See the Strategy Sheet at the back of this book for concise templates describing what should go in each paragraph.

STEP 4

Type your essay.

You shouldn't proceed with this step until you've completed the three preceding ones. Graders have a limited amount of time in which to read your essay, so start out and conclude with strong statements. Be emphatic and concise with your prose, and link related ideas with transitions. This will help your writing flow and make things easier on the grader. Furthermore, you'll save time and energy by preparing your essay before you start typing it.

STEP 5

Proofread your work.

Save enough time to read quickly through the entire essay. Look for errors you can address quickly: capitalization, paragraph divisions, double-typed words, general typos, and small grammatical errors.

Apply the Kaplan Method for Analytical Writing to the Issue Essay

Now, apply the Kaplan Method for Analytical Writing to a sample Issue prompt:

Claim: High-school students should be graded on a pass/fail basis, rather than a scaled system of letter grades (A–F).

Reason: It is more important to assess whether or not students have a basic command of the subjects they take than how they fare against their peers.

Develop a response to the claim in which you discuss whether or not you agree with it. Focus specifically on whether or not you agree with the reason upon which the claim is based.

STEP 1

Take the issue apart.

Your first step is to dissect the issue. Take notes on your scratch paper. Start by restating the issue, and the claim it is based on, in your own words: "We should grade high-school students as either pass or fail because we only need to know if they understand the material, while ranking them against their peers is less important." Now, consider the other side of the issue—in your own words: "We need a scaled grading system to be able to measure students against one another, as this is important for college admissions."

STEP 2

Select the points you will make.

Your job, as stated in the directions, is to decide whether or not you agree with the statement and then to explain your decision. Some would argue that the use of scaled grades is useless, as well as demoralizing for students who test poorly. Others would say that it's imperative that we use them, as their use allows colleges and universities to distinguish between applicants. Which side do you take? Remember, this isn't about showing the essay graders your deep-seated beliefs about education—it's about demonstrating that you can formulate an argument and communicate it clearly. The position you choose for the Issue essay doesn't have to be one you actually believe in. Quickly jot down on your scratch paper the pros and cons of each side, and choose the side for which you have the most relevant support. For this topic, that process might go something like this:

Arguments *for* the use of scaled grades:

- It helps colleges differentiate between applicants.
- It will help schools determine how far behind their peers poorly performing students are.

- Grades are useful as long as they are consistently applied, and steps can be taken to make sure they aren't subjective.

Arguments *against* the use of scaled grades:

- They are subjectively determined and therefore useless as an assessment.
- They are damaging to students' self-esteem.
- Pass/fail allows schools to determine if students understand the material at a high enough level to graduate them.

Again, it doesn't matter which side you take. Strictly speaking, there is no *right* answer, as far the testmaker is concerned. Let's say that in this case you decide to argue against the claim. Remember, the prompt asks you to argue for or against the use of a scaled grading system for high-school students, and also to focus specifically on the reason upon which the claim is based.

STEP 3

Organize, using Kaplan's essay templates.

You should already have begun to think out your arguments—that's how you picked the side you support in the first place. Now is the time to write your arguments, including those that weaken the opposing side. You're writing these notes for yourself, so feel free to use abbreviations.

Paragraph 1: We should not dispense with a grading scale in favor of a pass/fail rubric.

Paragraph 2: Scaled grades are important in college admissions.

Paragraph 3: Accurate grades can help identify students who are either in need of specialized help or advanced placement.

Paragraph 4: Grades are useful as long as they are applied consistently.

Paragraph 5: The grading scale serves an important function both pedagogically and within society.

STEP 4

Type your essay.

Remember, open up with a general statement indicating that you understand the issue and then assert your position. From there, make your main points.

Sample Issue Essay 1

Proponents of a "pass/fail" grading rubric have made a case over the years that a scaled grading rubric, such as the traditional "A to F" method, should be dispensed with in favor of a system in which students would either pass or fail their classes. However, a close examination of the issue reveals that doing so would be detrimental to student welfare, as well as to society at large. The reason upon which the claim is based, that ensuring students have a basic command of the material is more important than comparing them to their peers, is misplaced as a justification for changing the grading scale that schools use.

First, we must consider the effect that such a change in assessment would have on society. Colleges and universities depend on a grading system that allows them to assess the relative academic skills of their applicant pool. One of the most expedient ways to provide that comparative scaffolding is a scaled grading system in the secondary school system. This allows institutions of higher learning to meaningfully distinguish between applicants, as a homogeneous mass of "passes" would be difficult to choose from in a nonarbitrary way. Our higher education system works because it can determine, on the basis of empirical data, what students are most academically gifted at and best suited for. Grading helps to filter the right people into the right vocations (or, at a minimum, vocations to which they are well suited).

Second, the more precise and accurate a grading system is, the more accurately the school system can determine the specific needs of individual children. Different children learn in different ways and at different rates. For example, there are children who are very proficient in mathematics but less so in language arts and reading. Scaled grades allow schools to assess how far along students are compared to their peers, and to then place them in the appropriate class with appropriate instruction, be it advanced or remedial. A student who is precociously gifted in foreign languages will not be as encouraged to pursue it if her evaluation does not go beyond the knowledge that her command of the subject is sufficient to pass the course.

A final consideration is that the reason upon which the claim is based does not necessarily lead to the claim as a conclusion. A scaled grading rubric does allow the system to determine whether or not students have reached the minimum threshold of academic ability to graduate high school. It provides for the additional benefit of being a more precise indicator of a student's grasp of the material. Some have contended that grading from A to F is detrimental to students' self-esteem. Logically, however, this is far outweighed by the disservice done to our youth by allowing them to leave high school without the best possible education.

STEP 5

Proofread your work.

Be sure to allot a few minutes after you have finished writing to review your essay. Although you don't have to write a grammatically flawless essay to score well, you should review it to correct some of the obvious mistakes. You can practice your writing skills in Chapter 9: Writing Foundations.

Assessment of Sample Issue Essay 1: "Outstanding," Score of 6

Now we'll look at how this essay would have been scored on the actual GRE Analytical Writing section:

This essay is carefully constructed throughout, enabling the reader to move effortlessly from point to point as the writer examines the multifaceted implications of the issue. The writer begins by acknowledging arguments for the opposing side, and then uses her thesis statement ("However, a close examination of the issue reveals that doing so would be detrimental to student welfare, as well as to society at large") to explain her own position on the issue. She proceeds to provide compelling reasons and examples to support the premise, and then takes the argument to an effective conclusion. The writing is clean and concise, and the grammar and usage errors minor enough not to lower the score. Sentence structure is varied, and diction and vocabulary are strong and expressive.

PACING STRATEGY

You'll have a limited amount of time to show the graders that you can think logically, analyze critically, and express yourself in clearly written English. Consequently, you'll need to know ahead of time how you're going to approach the Issue essay. The Kaplan Method for Analytical Writing will help you plan and execute a clear, organized essay in the amount of time allotted. Note that the following timing guidelines are suggestions for how you should most effectively divide the 30 minutes you'll have for the Issue essay. Different writers go through different steps at their own pace, so don't feel chained to the breakdown of time described here. As you practice, you'll get a better sense of the amount of time you need to spend on each step to produce the best essay possible.

Analyze an Issue

Number of Questions: 1

Time per Question: 30 minutes

Keep these estimates in mind as you prepare for the test. If you use them as you work on the practice items, you will be comfortable keeping to the same amounts of time on Test Day.

- **STEP 1 TAKE THE ISSUE APART: 2 MINUTES**
- **STEP 2 SELECT THE POINTS YOU WILL MAKE: 4 MINUTES**
- **STEP 3 ORGANIZE, USING KAPLAN'S ESSAY TEMPLATES: 2 MINUTES**
- **STEP 4 TYPE YOUR ESSAY: 20 MINUTES**
- **STEP 5 PROOFREAD YOUR WORK: 2 MINUTES**

Scoring

The essay scoring for the Analytical Writing section is *holistic*, which means that the graders base your score on their overall impression of your essay, rather than deducting specific point values for errors. A holistic score emphasizes the interrelationship of content, organization, and syntax, and denotes the unified effect of these combined elements. The scoring scale is from 0–6, with 6 being the highest score. One human grader and one computer program will score each essay. If their scores differ by a certain margin, a second human grader will also score the essay, and the two human scores will be averaged.

Although the Analytical Writing section comprises two separate essays, ETS reports a single score that represents the average of your scores for the two essays, rounded to the nearest half-point. You will receive your essay score, along with your official score report, within 10–15 days of your test date.

The Scoring Rubric

The following rubric will give you a general idea of the guidelines graders have in mind when they score Issue essays.

6: "Outstanding" Essay

- Insightfully presents and convincingly supports an opinion on the issue
- Communicates ideas clearly and is generally well organized; connections are logical
- Demonstrates superior control of language: grammar, stylistic variety, and accepted conventions of writing; minor flaws may occur

5: "Strong" Essay

- Presents well-chosen examples and strongly supports an opinion on the issue
- Communicates ideas clearly and is generally well organized; connections are logical
- Demonstrates solid control of language: grammar, stylistic variety, and accepted conventions of writing; minor flaws may occur

4: "Adequate" Essay

- Presents and adequately supports an opinion on the issue
- Communicates ideas fairly clearly and is adequately organized; logical connections are satisfactory
- Demonstrates satisfactory control of language: grammar, stylistic variety, and accepted conventions of writing; some flaws may occur

3: "Limited" Essay

- Succeeds only partially in presenting and supporting an opinion on the issue
- Communicates ideas unclearly and is poorly organized
- Demonstrates less than satisfactory control of language: contains significant mistakes in grammar, usage, and sentence structure

2: "Weak" Essay

- Shows little success in presenting and supporting an opinion on the issue
- Struggles to communicate ideas; essay shows a lack of clarity and organization
- Meaning is impeded by many serious mistakes in grammar, usage, and sentence structure

1: "Fundamentally Deficient" Essay

- Fails to present a coherent opinion and/or evidence on the issue
- Fails to communicate ideas; essay is seriously unclear and disorganized
- Lacks meaning due to widespread and severe mistakes in grammar, usage, and sentence structure

0: "Unscorable" Essay

- Completely ignores topic
- Attempts to copy the task
- Written in a language other than English or contains indecipherable text

ISSUE ESSAY PRACTICE PROMPTS

The following is a list of sample Issue essay prompts similar to those you might encounter on the GRE Analytical Writing section. Those preceded by an asterisk (*) have a sample essay response in the subsequent section of this chapter.

Issue 1:

Some people believe that strong relationships can only develop after conflict and resolution have enabled the partners to speak openly and trust deeply. Others believe that each conflict creates rifts in a relationship that can never be repaired, weakening its foundation.

Write a response in which you determine which view bears the closest resemblance to your own. In justifying your reasoning and supporting your position, be sure to include your reaction to both of the views presented.

Issue 2:

Claim: Military training strategies, such as unit cohesion and drilling, are powerful techniques to use in a classroom.

Reason: These strategies allow students to focus on a task and think like a team, supporting one another to reach a goal.

Develop a response to the claim in which you discuss whether or not you agree with it. Focus specifically on whether or not you agree with the reason upon which the claim is based.

Issue 3:

A nation should ultimately be responsible for the health, welfare, and prosperity of its own citizens.

Write a response discussing your reaction to the stated policy. Justify your reasoning for the position you take. Explain the potential consequences or implications of implementing such a policy and how this informs your position.

***Issue 4:**

People who work in the arts and humanities should earn less than those who work in the sciences and economics because the benefit of the arts and humanities to the population is less important than that of scientific or economic endeavors.

Write your own response to the recommendation in which you discuss why you either agree or disagree with it. Support your response with evidence and/or examples. Use a hypothetical set of circumstances to illustrate the consequences of accepting or rejecting the recommendation, and explain how this informs your thinking.

***Issue 5:**

Some people argue that confidence and optimism are critical to achieving a dream, while others believe that selfless hard work is the only way to reach a goal.

Write a response in which you determine which view bears the closest resemblance to your own. In justifying your reasoning and supporting your position, be sure to include your reaction to both of the views presented.

***Issue 6:**

Claim: The study of a nation's prominent historical leaders and figures is a poor way to study its history.

Reason: The clearest lens through which to view a nation's history is the welfare of its entire population.

Develop a response to the claim in which you discuss whether or not you agree with it. Focus specifically on whether or not you agree with the reason upon which the claim is based.

***Issue 7:**

Educational institutions have a responsibility to dissuade students from pursuing fields of study in which they are unlikely to succeed.

Develop a response to the claim in which you discuss whether or not you agree with it. Focus specifically on the most powerful or compelling examples that could be used to refute your position.

***Issue 8:**

The main reason we should study history is to ensure that we do not repeat the mistakes of the past.

Write a response in which you examine your own position on the statement. Explore the extent to which you either agree or disagree with it, and support your reasoning with evidence and/or examples. Be sure to reflect on ways in which the statement might or might not be true, and how this informs your thinking on the subject.

Issue 9:

Governments in democratic societies should not restrict the public's access to information, even if it is of a sensitive or classified nature.

Write a response in which you examine your own position on the statement. Explore the extent to which you either agree or disagree with it, and support your reasoning with evidence and/or examples. Be sure to reflect on ways in which the statement might or might not be true, and how this informs your thinking on the subject.

Issue 10:

Professors who work at public universities should not automatically be entitled to periodic sabbaticals, because sabbaticals are expensive and do not necessarily yield anything of value in return.

Write your own response to the recommendation in which you discuss why you either agree or disagree with it. Support your response with evidence and/or examples. Use a hypothetical set of circumstances to illustrate the consequences of accepting or rejecting the recommendation, and explain how this informs your thinking.

Issue 11:

The United States should dispense with regulated speed limits on interstate highways, since drivers rarely abide by them.

Write a response discussing your reaction to the stated policy. Justify your reasoning for the position you take. Explain the potential consequences or implications for implementing such a policy and how this informs your position.

Issue 12:

Claim: The educational curriculum for young children should emphasize social skills and the arts over math and reading skills.

Reason: Such a curriculum would foster important moral and social development in children and lead to them becoming well-adjusted adults.

Develop a response to the claim in which you discuss whether or not you agree with it. Focus specifically on whether or not you agree with the reason upon which the claim is based.

Issue 13:

Some economists use the measure of the total value of goods and services that a country produces annually, called the "gross domestic product," or GDP, as the measure of a nation's economic health. Others contend that the GDP is an inadequate measure, because it fails to take into account many important factors, such as unequal distribution of wealth and the health of the environment, that affect people's quality of life.

Write a response in which you determine which view bears the closest resemblance to your own. In justifying your reasoning and supporting your position, be sure to include your reaction to both of the views presented.

Issue 14:

Claim: It is in the best interest of the U.S. government to cease funding the National Aeronautics and Space Administration (NASA).

Reason: The cost of a federal agency like NASA is gargantuan, and the returns on the investment are limited. Funding could be better allocated to dealing with pressing social problems, such as homelessness and poverty.

Develop a response to the claim in which you discuss whether or not you agree with it. Focus specifically on the most powerful or compelling examples that could be used to refute your position.

Issue 15:

The only way to have a meaningful interaction with a foreign culture is not simply to learn the language, but to live within that culture for an extended period of time.

Write a response in which you examine your own position on the statement. Explore the extent to which you either agree or disagree with it, and support your reasoning with evidence and/or examples. Be sure to reflect on ways in which the statement might or might not be true, and how this informs your thinking on the subject.

ISSUE ESSAY PRACTICE PROMPTS SAMPLE ESSAYS AND EXPLANATIONS

Here are sample top-scoring essays for five of the sample Issue prompts found in the previous section. Remember that an essay does not have to be perfect to receive a top score. Review these essays and note the qualities that earned them a score of 6.

Issue 4:

People who work in the arts and humanities should earn less than those who work in the sciences and economics because the benefit of the arts and humanities to the population is less important than that of scientific or economic endeavors.

Write your own response to the recommendation in which you discuss why you either agree or disagree with it. Support your response with evidence and/or examples. Use a hypothetical set of circumstances to illustrate the consequences of accepting or rejecting the recommendation, and explain how this informs your thinking.

Sample Response

The average American, when asked whether people who work in the sciences or economics should be paid more than people who work in the arts or humanities, would probably say yes. Scientific progress benefits society by making life easier and more enjoyable for the population. The study and regulation of economics enables society to develop and interact with people around the world. These two fields surely generate substantial, quantifiable benefit to the population. At first blush it seems logical to infer that people working in these fields should be compensated more generously. However, we do not determine payment for a group purely by measuring the benefit they create for society. It is difficult to quantify, purely in dollars, how much a professional golfer or a middle school math teacher actually contributes to the population. Furthermore, one cannot categorically assert that the fields of science and economics generate more benefit than arts and humanities. Deciding how much one person or field of study is responsible for the generation of a discrete amount of wealth is difficult. For these reasons, among others, such a recommendation should not be followed.

First, a method for measuring financial reimbursement for different types of occupations must be determined. In an ideal world, wages would be based on merit and contribution to the benefit of society. Things are not that simple in the "real" world. Consider the following two professions: a custodian at a hospital, and a researcher working on theoretical physics in an advanced technology laboratory. The two are working concurrently: the custodian disinfects a hospital bed so a new patient can be admitted, and the physicist calculates the results of a test to prove String Theory. Determining which of the two is contributing more to the benefit of society is difficult. The two workers most likely make substantially different wages. The usual justification for the discrepancy in the wages is that many people can do the custodian's job, while very few can do the researcher's job. Thus, the difference in wage is not based on merit or benefit to society at large, but upon basic supply and demand (limited supply of advanced intelligence and high demand for that skill). Justifying earnings in this way does not attend to the fact that the custodian's duties are still quite necessary. An antiseptic environment such as a hospital could not possibly function without the contributions of the custodial staff.

Secondly, in addition to determining fair compensation, determining the benefit to the population as a whole is problematic. Not all people necessarily agree that scientists and economists benefit society more than artists and those who work the humanities. Imagine that the recommendation was actually put into effect. If society were to provide reduced incentives for teachers, the education of the population as a whole would suffer. Future generations of scientists and economists would be less well equipped to make important scientific or economic contributions. Education is holistic, and draws upon a broad range of disciplines, from the Arts and Humanities to Economics and the Sciences. Even though teachers' contributions to such benefits are indirect and less easily quantified, they are still unassailably real. A scientist can never publish a groundbreaking, economically lucrative discovery if she is never taught to write in grammar school.

In the final analysis, it is difficult to assert that science offers a greater benefit to the population than art. Firstly, it is an inherently subjective value judgment and is not empirically determined. Secondly, even if we try to determine quantitatively how much "work" has been put into such profitable endeavors in the sciences and economics.

Analysis

This essay is particularly well constructed; the author begins by acknowledging the argument for compensating at a higher rate people who work in the sciences or economics than people who work in the humanities. While admitting that the argument seems to make sense, he asserts that this is not necessarily the case. He takes the contrary point of view, and his position is nuanced. He cites two basic assumptions upon which the recommendation depends, neither of which are necessarily founded. The first is that we reward people fairly according to the work they do. The second is that it is difficult to determine, quantitatively, how much someone has contributed to a job or endeavor. The author cites the example of teachers. Without teachers, scientists and economists would never be able to develop intellectually to the point where they can make their contributions. There are a few grammatical errors, as would occur under normal test conditions, but they will not detract from the score. Essays with some small errors or imperfections can still earn a score of 6. For these reasons, this essay receives a score of 6.

Issue 5:

Some people argue that confidence and optimism are critical to achieving a dream, while others believe that selfless hard work is the only way to reach a goal.

Write a response in which you determine which view bears the closest resemblance to your own. In justifying your reasoning and supporting your position, be sure to include your reaction to both of the views presented.

Sample Response

Rather than relying solely on self-assurance and a positive outlook, sustained levels of effort and industry must be maintained in order to reach a goal. While some claim that a positive outlook alone can bring about good things, and others say only a nose-to-the-grindstone attitude will get you where you want to be, it seems to me that the former flows from the latter. Most truly successful people are positive and confident hard workers who derive confidence from their work ethic. Goal-seeking people put in so much time and energy because they actually believe that those goals are achievable and probable results of their efforts. This in itself is characteristic of a positive outlook and leads me to believe that these two attitudes can exist independently, but, hard work is the key ingredient to successfully achieving a goal.

Personally, while my constant optimism certainly helps me to maintain my strong work ethic, my ability to achieve a goal is grounded in hard work. When obstacles and set-backs occur, I am able to convince myself that a goal is still attainable and that a particular situation will improve if I put in the necessary work. I can offer, as anecdotal evidence, an instance in which I had three papers due on the same day for three different classes. I felt overwhelmed, as I had gotten a late start on all of them, but what motivated me was the knowledge that working hard would ultimately lead me to success. A positive attitude could not write my papers, but I was positive as a result of my drive to work hard. What pushes me to stay focused and determined is the conviction that hard work will lead directly to accomplishing a goal. While I do believe that they work best in union, there are certainly benefits to each goal-seeking approach mentioned earlier.

Hard work often results in measurable progress, a gain of experience, and skill development, to name a few. This, in and of itself, will inculcate a positive attitude that will reinforce that strong work ethic. Maintaining a positive outlook and remaining self-confident can help goal-seekers stay persistent and focused despite the inevitable setbacks that occur on the road to reaching any goal. Although these goal-seeking approaches both do have positive outcomes and can individually result in the achievement of goals, goals can only be successfully attained if the goal-seeker is driven by an indefatigable work ethic.

Analysis

This essay is a solid 6. The author adopts a personal, first-person tone, which is acceptable in this case, as that is what the prompt calls for. She tackles the issue head-on, offering her position that hard work is the key factor in achieving a dream. She goes one step further and points out that optimism can be a byproduct of such a work ethic. The personal anecdote cited in the second paragraph is perfectly suited to reinforcing the author's point. The structure of the essay is taut, and the writing is without superfluous fluff. Although the essay is in the first person, the author avoids needless self-reference. There are a few grammatical errors, as would occur under normal test conditions, and they will not detract from the score. Essays with some small errors or imperfections can still earn a score of 6. For these reasons, this essay receives a score of 6.

Issue 6:

Claim: The study of a nation's prominent historical leaders and figures is a poor way to study its history.

Reason: The clearest lens through which to view a nation's history is the welfare of its entire population.

Develop a response to the claim in which you discuss whether or not you agree with it. Focus specifically on whether or not you agree with the reason upon which the claim is based.

Sample Response

This claim is poorly supported because if a nation has had poor leaders, the people will, in turn, suffer. On a much smaller scale, how a child is raised is a reflection of how their parents raised them. If parents are attentive and loving, the children will, most likely, display similar attributes. Similarly, with regards to leaders and nations, if a leader actually cares about his country and its people, the standard of living in that country will reflect that care. People will be happier and have fewer worries. Studying historical figures, therefore, provides as much of a bellwether as studying the welfare of the people they lead.

If one were to examine the situation of a crumbling country, such as 1980s Zimbabwe, for example, one would see a prime example that backs up the above statement. The leader was corrupt and did not know how to properly run a country and, as a result, people fled the country and many who stayed starved and had very little money. In fact, the currency itself was practically worthless. With a leader who knows what he's doing, and actually cares about his citizens, Zimbabwe has the potential to thrive, and its people would have full pockets and full bellies.

Ancient Egypt can be cited as a counterexample to the claim. We know a great deal about Egypt's culture and achievements, and our knowledge comes from studying Egypt's leaders and rulers, not the welfare of its common people. The fact that Egypt's leaders were autocratic despots is beside the point; we know a great deal about Egypt's achievements and what life was like there through the study of the Pharaohs (even if the conditions for the average person were morally indefensible).

As John Donne once said, "no man is an island." This theme reflects throughout our history, for if a leader feels as though he or she is all that matters, the people under such a leader are going to suffer the consequences of his or her self-serving leadership decisions. No leader will ever be perfect, but if he or she has the right focus—that is, his people's welfare—then the decisions will be a reflection of his caring heart. A country's history will have its up and downs, but if it is able to learn from its mistakes, that can make all the difference.

A nation's history is certainly not solely about the leaders of countries and what each of them as individuals are able to accomplish, but how a leader conducts him or herself will reflect on how his or her citizens are living. If a leader becomes too power-hungry, the citizens are going to struggle as a result. Consider the situation with Hitler and Nazi Germany. He wanted ultimate control, and at whose cost? That's right, the people's. History is never one-sided, of course, and a bad leader does not necessarily mean that the country's citizens are also bad. However, a leader should be aware that how he or she behaves will affect other countries' views of his or her country. After all, if citizens are happy and content, then there will be less trouble to be recorded in the history books.

Analysis

This essay is emphatically and passionately argued. The author begins by immediately providing a justification for arguing the contrary of the claim. He insists that without great leaders, the people will suffer. He supports his position with compelling evidence, drawing on notable periods of history, such as ancient Egypt, which he uses as a counterexample to refute the claim. He uses this example to support a second counterargument, which is that the study of the pharaohs and their achievements has taught us a great deal about ancient Egypt. There are a few grammatical errors, as would occur under normal test conditions, and they will not detract from the score. Essays with some small errors or imperfections can still earn a score of 6. The diction is straightforward, but effective, which is what counts when it comes to grading. For these reasons, this essay receives a score of 6.

Issue 7:

Educational institutions have a responsibility to dissuade students from pursuing fields of study in which they are unlikely to succeed.

Develop a response to the claim in which you discuss whether or not you agree with it. Focus specifically on the most powerful or compelling examples that could be used to refute your position.

Sample Response

Educational institutions have a great many responsibilities on their shoulders; apart from giving future generations an idea of what the real world is like and how it functions, they also allows students to build on and develop their own personal beliefs and abilities. Any skills that you possess today are partially the result of your own hard work, but also of the institutions and people who taught you the meaning of hard work. There can be no question that all students need some form of guidance when learning who they are, how the world works, and their role in it. There are limits as to what educational institutions should do. If another person takes it upon themselves to dissuade a student against a certain career (solely for the reason that they might not succeed), what does that say about belief in the student's ability? There can be no hope for the world or for future generations if students are told by the very people teaching them that there are fields of study in which they will never succeed.

There is little question that educators should be honest about certain fields; there are inescapable realities about each of them. Politics is complex; medical professions require a strong stomach. What must be addressed, however, is that if a particular student feels a heightened interest towards the practice of any profession, should somebody else be the one to speak negatively about it? Imagine somebody telling Martin Luther King, Jr. all those years ago that his dreams would never succeed. What kind of society would we be living in if somebody had tried to dissuade him from the advancement of civil liberties? Consider Thomas Edison. He tried to produce the light bulb (or incandescent lamp) hundreds of times before it actually worked. Suppose somebody told him to give up after the first three or four attempts —how would that have worked out?

Eleanor Roosevelt is quoted as saying that "the future belongs to those who believe in the beauty of their dreams." It is a direct contradiction to everything the educational institutions stand for if they take upon themselves a responsibility to dissuade students from going into a particular field. If it is unlikely they will succeed, why is the field being taught? Why bother teaching it if there is no future for it?

All of the arguments aside, the responsibilities of educational institutions should not be second-guessed. The incredible knowledge and fortitude of all who take part in student education ought to be applauded (especially if you can read this). However, it is overstepping the boundaries of teaching to say that all educators have a responsibility to dissuade students from going into an unsuccessful career. Based on the education each student has been given, they have each earned the right to make that decision on their own, not because the institution told them so.

Analysis

This essay tackles a socially sensitive issue in a respectful and candid way. The author begins by acknowledging a powerful argument in support of the position. She does concede that schools should be honest about a student's chances of success in a difficult field (i.e., medicine or politics). While acknowledging this, she constructs an argument that asserts that institutions inculcate not only a specific set of skills, but also a reverence for learning and passion for dreams and ideas. She underscores this by citing examples such as Martin Luther King and Thomas Edison. There are a few grammatical errors, as would occur under normal test conditions, and they will not detract from the score. Essays with some small errors or imperfections can still earn a score of 6. The author uses rhetorical questions only sparingly and for good effect. For these reasons, this essay receives a score of 6.

Issue 8:

The main reason we should study history is to ensure that we do not repeat the mistakes of the past.

Write a response in which you examine your own position on the statement. Explore the extent to which you either agree or disagree with it, and support your reasoning with evidence and/or examples. Be sure to reflect on ways in which the statement might or might not be true, and how this informs your thinking on the subject.

Sample Response

While civilization has made several noted strides, other events throughout time have been denied and swept under the carpet. Although these situations are preferred to be forgotten, they often serve as warning signals that help prevent us from causing the same faults again. This is why the study of our past is crucial to the success of our present and future.

A prime example of a moment in history that is important to study in order to prevent a reoccurrence is the Holocaust. Around the 1930s through the mid 1940s, Hitler and Nazi supporters took the lives of over six million Jews, Gypsies, homosexuals, and other groups of people across Europe that were deemed threats to the Aryan race. While Hitler continued carrying out his plans for the genocide, authoritative figures and religious sects, such as President Roosevelt and the Catholic Church, were accused of neglecting to save victims. Nazi attempts to cover up the horrific events of the Holocaust were generally unsuccessful. However, despite war crime trials, records, and survivor accounts, some still deny the genocide ever occurred. Personal accounts, artifacts, and historical texts have helped open the eyes of several citizens to what really happened. This has helped prevent many populations from becoming clouded by feelings of uncertainty over the differences of others and allowing hatred to escalate to events similar to the Holocaust.

It can be argued that history should be taught in schools for other reasons. It helps students develop critical reading and analytical writing skills that will be useful in most career paths, as well as in college. It also provides a meaningful context in which to interpret contemporary political and social events. For example, it is difficult to understand the nuances and complexities of the precarious situation in the Middle East without a solid understanding of the history of the region. However, while this is certainly true, properly understood it is also part and parcel of the reason cited in the argument. Providing a proper context for interpreting contemporary events will only help in avoiding the mistakes of the past. Therefore, this reason can be subsumed into the overarching one presented by the argument.

In several instances, history has proved to repeat itself. People who ignore events like the Holocaust follow the saying that "Ignorance is bliss." Past warning signs left unaddressed have allowed citizens in some African countries to become genocide victims today. Despite the pain of reality, shedding light on yesterday's mistakes will help us prevent the same ones tomorrow.

Analysis

This essay is well constructed. The author agrees with the statement, and cites a specific set of examples (i.e., atrocities being "swept under the rug") as the best proof of the statement. The author moves on to specifically offer Nazi Germany as a prominent example. He also attends to possible alternative reasons for studying history, but deftly points out that those can all be ultimately "subsumed" into the reason for studying history that is advocated by the Issue statement. The writing is largely clear and direct. The use of diction is skillful and varied, but at the same time not bombastic or excessive. Pretentious word choice can sometimes be used to camouflage weak writing, but in this case diction supports content. For all these reasons, this essay receives a score of 6.

The Argument Essay

THE ARGUMENT ESSAY

The second type of Analytical Writing essay you have to contend with is the Argument essay. Here, you're given an argument that contains a conclusion and supporting evidence. The writer tries to persuade you of something (her conclusion) by citing facts or premises (her evidence). You should read the argument with a critical eye. Be on the lookout for unstated *assumptions* in the way the writer moves from evidence to conclusion. You aren't asked to agree or disagree with the author's *position* or *conclusion*; instead, the directions ask you to express how convincing you find the argument to be. You must analyze the reasoning used in the argument. Every argument presented for this GRE essay is flawed. To make your case, first analyze the argument itself and evaluate its use of evidence; then, explain how a different approach or more information would make the argument better (or possibly worse).

The directions for the Argument essay will look like this:

Directions: You will be presented with a short passage that asserts an argument or position, along with explicit instructions on how to respond to the passage. Your response will be evaluated according to how well you:

- respond to the specific directions the task gives you.
- analyze and interpret important elements of the passage.
- organize and develop your analysis.
- support your reasoning with relevant examples.
- express yourself in standard written English.

The following is a list of the types of Argument essay tasks you might encounter on the GRE Analytical Writing section:

- Write a response in which you describe specific examples or evidence needed to evaluate the argument and how those examples or evidence would weaken or strengthen the argument.

- Write a response in which you explain what information would be necessary in order to decide whether the recommendation and the argument on which it is based are reasonable. Be sure to explain how the answers to these questions or pieces of information would help to evaluate the recommendation.
- Write a response in which you discuss what questions would need to be answered to decide how likely the stated recommendation is to yield the predicted result. Be sure to explain how the answers to these questions would help to evaluate the recommendation.
- Write a response in which you discuss what questions would need to be answered in order to assess the reasonableness of both the prediction and the argument upon which it is based. Be sure to explain how the answers to these questions would help to evaluate the prediction.
- Write a response in which you discuss one or more viable alternatives to the proposed explanation. Justify, with support, why your explanation could rival the proposed explanation and explain how your explanation(s) can plausibly account for the facts presented in the argument.

THE KAPLAN METHOD FOR ANALYTICAL WRITING

STEP 1 Take the issue/argument apart.

STEP 2 Select the points you will make.

STEP 3 Organize, using Kaplan's essay templates.

STEP 4 Type your essay.

STEP 5 Proofread your work.

How the Kaplan Method for Analytical Writing Works

Here's how the Kaplan Method for Analytical Writing works for the Argument essay:

STEP 1

Take the argument apart.

The first step in deconstructing an argument is to identify the conclusion—that is, the main point the author is trying to make. After you've nailed down the conclusion, your next step is to locate the evidence used to support the conclusion. Finally, identify the unstated assumptions (pieces of evidence that are not explicitly stated but that are necessary for the evidence to lead validly to the conclusion). Note any terms that are ambiguous and need definition.

STEP 2

Select the points you will make.

If you have identified several assumptions in Step 1, select what you feel are the two or three most important ones to use in your essay.

STEP 3

Organize, using Kaplan's essay templates.

Organize your thoughts by outlining how the essay, as a whole, will flow. In the introduction, show that you understand the argument by putting it into your own words. Point out the author's conclusion and the evidence she uses to support that conclusion. In each of the middle paragraphs, identify assumptions or overlooked alternatives, depending on the specific instructions given in the prompt, in the author's reasoning. Detail the unstated assumption(s) and explain why the argument is logically invalid if the assumptions prove unfounded, or if the prompt requires you to consider alternatives, discuss the possibilities the author of the argument has overlooked. Conclude by summarizing your main points; be sure to directly address the task given in the specific instructions. See the Strategy Sheet at the back of this book for concise templates describing what should go in each paragraph.

STEP 4

Type your essay.

You shouldn't proceed with this step until you've completed the three preceding ones. Essay graders have a limited amount of time to work with, so start out and conclude with strong statements. Be emphatic and concise with your prose, and use transitions to link related or contrasting ideas. This will help your writing flow and make your essay easier for the grader to follow.

STEP 5

Proofread your work.

Save enough time to read through your response in its entirety. As you do so, have a sense of the errors you are likely to make.

Apply the Kaplan Method for Analytical Writing to the Argument Essay

Now, apply the Kaplan Method for Analytical Writing to a sample Argument prompt:

The following memorandum is from the Edwintown City Council:

"This year, in view of our pledge to be more environmentally conscious, we will be requiring all homeowners within the city limits to recycle their glass, plastic, and paper waste. According to a recent study by Edwintown University, the volume of trash in Edwintown and its surrounding environs has increased by 20 percent over the past 15 years. The only way to combat this burden is for our citizens to actively make an effort to recycle their trash. By enforcing recycling laws for all houses within the city limits, we will improve the aesthetic and public health conditions of our area."

Write a response in which you discuss what questions would need to be answered to decide how likely the stated recommendation is to yield the predicted result. Be sure to explain how the answers to these questions would help to evaluate the recommendation.

STEP 1

Take the argument apart.

Conclusion (the point the author is trying to make): The only way to combat this burden is for our citizens to actively make an effort to recycle their trash. Enforcing recycling laws will improve town conditions.

Evidence (premises or facts offered to support the conclusion): According to a recent study by Edwintown University, the volume of trash in Edwintown and its surrounding environs has increased by 20 percent over the past 15 years.

Assumptions (unspoken conditions or beliefs necessary for the conclusion to make sense in light of the evidence):

- Homeowners are not currently recycling at effective levels; citizens will become more aware of the environment if they are legally obligated to recycle.
- Current trash levels constitute a "burden."
- Enforcement of the recycling program will improve the "aesthetic and public health conditions" in the area.

STEP 2

Select the points you will make.

Analyze the use of evidence in the argument. Determine whether there's anything relevant that's not discussed:

- Whether or not there was any form of environmental regulation in the past that succeeded or failed
- Whether or not Edwintown residents were recycling voluntarily even without enforcement
- How much of the type of trash produced in Edwintown can be recycled
- Whether the growth in the actual amount of trash is unreasonable and places an undue burden on the community
- Whether Edwintown's trash is disposed of in a way that is aesthetically displeasing or that results in health risks

Also determine what types of evidence would make the argument stronger or more logically sound. In this case, we need more information to support the government's decision to implement recycling regulations and increase citizen awareness:

- Evidence that there will be incentives for citizen cooperation and participation
- Evidence that the government will support members of the community to help them meet the new requirements
- Evidence that the guidelines will be effective: have they already been applied to another community and produced effective improvements?

STEP 3

Organize, using Kaplan's essay templates.

Paragraph 1: The argument is that recycling regulations will help improve the overall environment of the surrounding area.

Paragraph 2: The Edwintown University study needs to release additional details and findings to determine whether the plan will be effective.

Paragraph 3: What will citizen participation in the recycling program entail? For community support, the city council needs to release more information to the public.

Paragraph 4: What is the enforcement strategy for the program?

Paragraph 5: More information is needed to evaluate the argument.

Use your notes as a working outline. In Argument essays, you'll primarily address the ways in which the assumptions are unsupported. You will also recommend new evidence you'd like to see and explain why. Remember to lead with your strongest points.

STEP 4

Type your essay.

Begin writing your essay now. Your essay for this assignment might look like the following sample.

Sample Argument Essay 1

There has been a recent push for greater environmental awareness. This often includes governmental regulations designed to increase community participation, such as recycling laws. The memorandum from the Edwintown City Council exemplifies a positive strategy for impacting the local environment, but without more concrete evidence, the results predicted by the city council are speculative at best.

To win support for their anticipated recycling program, the Edwintown City Council should release more extensive information from Edwintown University's study. According to the city council, the study found that trash increased in the urban area over the past 15 years by 20 percent. We don't, however, know what the makeup of this trash was and whether the items responsible for the increase are recyclable. We also do not know whether the increase in trash is unreasonable compared to the increase in population over the same time period. Further, we have no information about how and whether there has been any change over the past 15 years in the manner and cost of waste management in Edwintown. If, for instance, the city has changed from using landfills to a state-of-the-art garbage-to-energy plant, the positive environmental impact of increased recycling may be minimal.

Along with providing a more thorough examination of the university's study, the city council should also outline citizen participation. If Edwintonians have already been recycling, even without a requirement to do so, the new plan is unlikely to have much of an effect. To assess the potential efficacy of the plan, we'd need to know the current levels of recycling in the city. Other specifics of the plan are missing, too. Are there particular products, for example, that the city is or is not prepared to recycle? How can citizens decrease the amount of non-recyclable waste they produce? Would other household actions, such as developing a compost pile, also help the environment? Giving citizens this kind of information would add to the advantages of the proposal and increase their willingness to embrace new regulations.

Additionally, the city council should detail their methods for enforcing the recycling regulations. At this point, we can only speculate on the effect that various enforcement mechanisms—fines, public service, and so on—would have on citizen participation. Related to this question is the issue of how easy it will be to participate. If citizens can simply put the recycling out for pickup, participation levels should be high. If, on the other hand, they have to travel a distance and deliver recycling to a collection center, enforcement will be much more difficult. Possible disciplinary actions and incentives alike will stimulate citizen awareness and participation.

The city council's desire to improve environmental conditions is admirable. However, more information is needed before we can determine whether their proposal is likely to be effective. In any case, it is likely that informing citizens directly as to how and why these recycling regulations would be beneficial will help ensure the community's cooperation.

STEP 5

Proofread your work.

Be sure to allot some time after you have finished writing to review your essay. While a few grammatical errors here and there won't harm your score, having enough of them will, as will having a few so severe that the meaning of the essay is lost. Make sure the graders are as favorably disposed to you as possible; a well-written essay makes their job a bit less tedious.

Assessment of Sample Argument Essay 1: "Outstanding," Score of 6

Now we'll look at how this essay would have been scored on the actual GRE Analytical Writing section:

This outstanding response demonstrates the writer's insightful analytical skills. The introduction notes the prompt's specious reasoning occasioned by unsupported assumptions and a lack of definition and evidence. The writer follows this up with a one-paragraph examination of each of the root flaws in the argument. Specifically, the author exposes these points undermining the argument:

- A city-wide required program for glass, paper, and plastic recycling will help citizens become more aware of the environment.
- The recycling program will improve upon the "aesthetic and public health conditions" in the area.

Each point receives thorough and cogent development (given the time constraints) in a smooth and logically organized discourse. There are a few grammatical flaws, but minor issues of grammar and mechanics will not prevent an outstanding essay from scoring a 6. This essay is succinct, economical, and generally error-free, with sentences that vary in length and complexity, while the diction and vocabulary are precise and expressive.

PACING STRATEGY

You'll have a limited amount of time to show the graders that you can think logically, analyze critically, and express yourself in clearly written English. Consequently, you'll need to know ahead of time how you're going to approach the Argument essay. The Kaplan Method for Analytical Writing will help you plan and execute a clear, organized essay in the allotted time. Note that the following timing guidelines are suggestions for how you should most effectively divide the 30 minutes you'll have for the Argument essay. Different writers go through different steps at their own pace, so don't feel chained to the breakdown of time described here. As you practice, you'll get a better sense of the amount of time you need to spend on each step to produce the best essay possible.

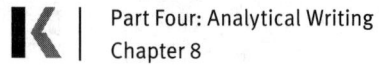

Analyze an Argument

Number of Questions: 1

Time per Question: 30 minutes

Keep these estimates in mind as you prepare for the test. Use them as you work on the practice items so you'll be comfortable keeping to the same amounts of time on test day.

STEP 1

Take the argument apart: 2 minutes

STEP 2

Select the points you will make: 4 minutes

STEP 3

Organize, using Kaplan's essay templates: 2 minutes

STEP 4

Type your essay: 20 minutes

STEP 5

Proofread your work: 2 minutes

Scoring

The essay scoring for the Analytical Writing sections is *holistic*, which means that the graders base your score on their overall impression of your essay, rather than deducting specific point values for errors. A holistic score emphasizes the interrelationship of content, organization, and syntax, and denotes the unified effect of these combined elements. The scoring scale is from 0–6, with 6 being the highest score. One human grader and one computer program will score each essay. If their scores differ by a certain margin, a second human grader will also score the essay, and the two human scores will be averaged.

Although the Analytical Writing section comprises two separate essays, ETS reports a single score that represents the average of your scores for the two essays, rounded to the nearest half-point. You will receive your essay score, along with your official score report, within 10–15 days of your test date.

The Scoring Rubric

The following rubric will give you a general idea of the guidelines graders have in mind when they score Argument essays.

6: "Outstanding" Essay

- Insightfully presents and convincingly supports a critique of the argument
- Communicates ideas clearly and is generally well organized; connections are logical
- Demonstrates superior control of language: grammar, stylistic variety, and accepted conventions of writing; minor flaws may occur

5: "Strong" Essay

- Presents well-chosen examples and strongly supports a critique of the argument
- Communicates ideas clearly and is generally well organized; connections are logical
- Demonstrates solid control of language: grammar, stylistic variety, and accepted conventions of writing; minor flaws may occur

4: "Adequate" Essay

- Presents and adequately supports a critique of the argument
- Communicates ideas fairly clearly and is adequately organized; logical connections are satisfactory
- Demonstrates satisfactory control of language: grammar, stylistic variety, and accepted conventions of writing; some flaws may occur

3: "Limited" Essay

- Succeeds only partially in presenting and supporting a critique of the argument
- Communicates ideas unclearly and is poorly organized
- Demonstrates less than satisfactory control of language: contains significant mistakes in grammar, usage, and sentence structure

2: "Weak" Essay

- Shows little success in presenting and supporting a critique of the argument
- Struggles to communicate ideas; essay shows a lack of clarity and organization
- Meaning is impeded by many serious mistakes in grammar, usage, and sentence structure

1: "Fundamentally Deficient" Essay

- Fails to present a coherent critique of the argument
- Fails to communicate ideas; essay is seriously unclear and disorganized
- Lacks meaning due to widespread and severe mistakes in grammar, usage, and sentence structure

0: "Unscorable" Essay

- Completely ignores topic
- Attempts to copy the task
- Written in a language other than English or contains undecipherable text

ARGUMENT ESSAY PRACTICE PROMPTS

The following is a list of sample Argument essay prompts similar to those you might encounter on the GRE Analytical Writing section. Those preceded by an asterisk (*) have a sample essay response in the subsequent section of the chapter.

Argument 1:

The following memorandum is from the production manager of SingSong radio:

"This year, in deference to our many listeners who do not celebrate any of the winter holidays, we will not play holiday music related to any religion on our station. According to an online survey of our listeners, fewer than 20 percent indicated that they enjoy listening to religious songs. Eighty percent noted in the survey that if SingSong began broadcasting religious music (of any faith or denomination), they would 'dramatically' reduce their listening hours.

"Therefore, to retain our listeners during the holidays, we will respectfully decline any requests for holiday music this year."

Write a response in which you discuss what questions would need to be answered to decide how likely the stated recommendation is to yield the predicted result. Be sure to explain how the answers to these questions would help to evaluate the recommendation.

Argument 2:

Fifty years ago, an entomologist in Ballaland identified a new species of beetle: the scalawag. This beetle is nearly identical to the Andover mop beetle, but is slightly larger. A recent comparison of a colony of Ballaland beetles and Andover mop beetles demonstrates that the two beetles may be more similar than previously thought. The range of size between the largest beetle and the smallest beetle was identical in both colonies, and, as the beetles were physically identical in every other way, it was concluded that the two species were actually the same and that the differences in behavior and diet could be attributed to differences in habitat. Some biologists suggest that before a proposed interbreeding experiment is conducted, more research on behavior and diet of the two beetle species should be conducted.

Write a response in which you discuss what questions would need to be answered in order to assess the reasonableness of both the recommendation and the argument upon which it is based. Be sure to explain how the answers to these questions would help to evaluate the recommendation.

Argument 3:

The following is a letter to the editor of a psychology journal:

"The data collected from a variety of studies now suggest a relationship between the medicine Hypathia and heightened risk of anxiety in patients afflicted with bipolar disorder. In 1950, before Hypathia was widely used to treat bipolar disorder, relatively few patients were diagnosed as anxious or had symptoms that suggested anxiety. However, in five studies published between 2005 and 2010, more than 60 percent of the subjects with bipolar disorder who took Hypathia demonstrated symptoms of anxiety or reported having episodes of heightened anxiety."

Write a response in which you discuss one or more viable alternatives to the proposed explanation. Justify, with support, why your explanation could rival the proposed explanation and explain how your explanation(s) can plausibly account for the facts presented in the argument.

***Argument 4:**

A recently issued five-year study on the common cold investigated the possible therapeutic effect of a raw food diet. Raw foods contain antioxidants that boost the immune system. While many foods are naturally rich in antioxidants, food-processing companies also sell isolated antioxidants. The five-year study found a strong correlation between a raw food diet and a steep decline in the average number of colds reported by study participants. A control group that increased their antioxidant intake using supplements did not have a decrease in the number of colds. Based on these study results, some health experts recommend a raw food diet over the use of packaged antioxidants.

Write a response in which you discuss what questions would need to be answered in order to assess the reasonableness of both the recommendation and the argument upon which it is based. Be sure to explain how the answers to these questions would help to evaluate the recommendation.

***Argument 5:**

The following was written as part of an application for a permit to congregate by a religious group in the city of Gustav:

"We plan to meet at the Hunter Pavilion on the north side of the park. We expect about 200 attendees. Although we do plan to celebrate our message in words and song, we will be mindful of others who are sharing the park on that day. We have found that in the past, when our group meets in a public space, we run the risk of harassment by those who do not agree with our message. Therefore, we would like to hire five security officers to protect our congregants from religious intolerance. We would like to post one guard at the entrance to the park and others, who will dress in plain clothes, at the perimeter of our gathering. We hope you understand and will endorse this request."

Write a response in which you describe what specific examples or evidence is needed to evaluate the argument and how those examples or evidence would weaken or strengthen the argument.

***Argument 6:**

The following memo appeared in the newsletter of the Happy Sun Happy Moon daycare center:

"Since the road construction on I-72 has begun, we've noticed that parents are picking up their children after the center is officially closed. Effective immediately, parents who pick up their children more than five minutes after closing will have to pay a $10 fee. Parents who pick up their children more than one hour after closing will be subject to an additional $30 fee. We predict this will encourage parents to leave earlier from work to pick up their children on time each day."

Write a response in which you discuss what questions would need to be answered to decide how likely the stated recommendation is to yield the predicted result. Be sure to explain how these answers would help to evaluate the recommendation.

***Argument 7:**

In 1992, many farmers in Jalikistan began using a hormone designed to produce larger cows that would produce more milk. Since then, childhood obesity in Jalikistan has grown by 200 percent. The amount of milk and dairy consumed by children in this area has not increased or decreased. Children in the same area who are lactose intolerant, and who drink almond milk or soy milk, have not had the same increase in childhood obesity. The only clear explanation is that the introduction of the hormone is responsible for the increase in childhood obesity in that area.

Write a response in which you discuss one or more viable alternatives to the proposed explanation. Justify, with support, why the alternatives could rival the proposed explanation and explain how those explanation(s) plausibly account for the facts presented in the argument.

***Argument 8:**

The following appeared in a memo from an advertisement by Pest Protection, Inc.:

"Gardens along the coast are already being infested by the mill bug, a slimy purple pest that can decimate a vegetable garden in seconds flat. If you live within 100 miles of the coast, you need the Pest Protection cure today. Thousands of satisfied customers who have used our chemical-free treatments have never had mill bug problems. One treatment per year will ensure that you never have to lose your valuable crops to this pest."

Write a response in which you examine the underlying assumptions of the argument. Be sure to explain how the argument hinges on these assumptions and what the implications are for the argument if the assumptions prove unfounded.

Argument 9:

The following appeared in a letter to the Director of the Department of Motor Vehicles:

"The use of cell phones while driving is a source of great concern to the community, particularly to parents with young children. Teenage drivers, who are the most likely to text or talk on the phone while driving, are among the most dangerous. In our county alone there were 75 fatalities from traffic collisions. If we raise the legal driving age from 16 to 20, the problem would largely be solved because the most dangerous drivers would no longer be on the road."

Write a response in which you discuss what questions would need to be answered in order to assess the reasonableness of both the prediction and the argument upon which it is based. Be sure to explain how the answers to these questions would help to evaluate the prediction.

Argument 10:

The following memorandum is from the Media Director of the Athletic Department at Burtsdale University:

"We have decided to recommend that the school no longer offer free student access to University athletic events, regardless of level, sport, or gender of the participants. Our policy in the past has been to sell tickets only to events with significant popularity, such as men's Division I football and basketball games, and other nationally televised events. Although other sports do not typically sell out, or generate the same level of interest outside the student body, we feel it is unfair to Division II sports and the women's teams not to charge admission to their events as well. Charging admission to all events is the only way to treat all athletic teams equitably."

Write a response in which you describe what specific examples or evidence is needed to evaluate the argument and how those examples or evidence would weaken or strengthen the argument.

Argument 11:

The following is from an editorial in a legal journal:

"It is now apparent, based on data that has been collated from several independent studies, that asbestos is the cause of lung cancer, emphysema, and other respiratory illnesses in the miners of Coal Valley. The studies show a high incidence of such ailments among the miners, far higher than that of the general population. In 1920, before the mine opened, relatively few miners were known to have had such conditions. Studies published in 1960, 1980, and 2000 show that the incidence of such ailments has risen dramatically among the miners of Coal Valley."

Write a response in which you discuss one or more viable alternatives to the proposed explanation. Justify, with support, why your explanation could rival the proposed explanation and explain how your explanation(s) can plausibly account for the facts presented in the argument.

Argument 12:

The following is an excerpt from a letter to the editor of the *Billington Bugle*:

"There is no possible downside to the community in bringing the Grand Prix to Billington. Though it has not proved financially successful in other cities that have hosted the race, this will not be the case for Billington. The race's course will run through the economic center of downtown, and the organizers of the event have offered to pay to repave the downtown streets through which the race will run. Those streets are in such disrepair that having them repaired will be a tremendous boon to the city. Furthermore, though most downtown businesses (aside from restaurants and food vendors) will likely be shut down for three days, the influx of tourist dollars will be immense. Finally, the international prestige of hosting such a race will raise the city's profile significantly, generating new interest in doing business here."

Write a response in which you describe what specific examples or evidence is needed to evaluate the argument and how those examples or evidence would weaken or strengthen the argument.

Argument 13:

The following is a recommendation from the Board of Directors of the Cheshire College Preparatory Academy:

"We recommend that Cheshire College Preparatory Academy dispense with the use of standardized tests as an entrance requirement. Cheshire has been an elite school for more than 100 years, but we have recently seen a decline in enrollments. We have had particular difficulty in attracting students from non-legacy families (those who have never had a member attend Cheshire). We do not require entrance exams for legacy applicants, and those enrollments have not declined. Cutting the standardized entrance requirement will allow us to better compete with Surrey Academy, which recently dropped its exam requirements and concurrently overtook Cheshire in enrollments."

Write a response in which you discuss what questions would need to be answered to decide how likely the stated recommendation is to yield the predicted result. Be sure to explain how the answers to these questions would help to evaluate the recommendation.

Argument 14:

The Supreme Court of the United States must be composed in such a way that it accurately reflects the demographics of the country. As the highest court in the land, it functions as the final arbiter of justice. In a multicultural and multiethnic society, with a variety of races, creeds, and beliefs, it is imperative that the backgrounds of the justices on the court reflect that diversity. Since our society is not homogeneous, our judicial system must follow suit. Otherwise, it will be impossible to fairly represent the views, beliefs, and cultural norms of the entire country.

Write a response in which you describe what specific examples or evidence is needed to evaluate the argument and how those examples or evidence would weaken or strengthen the argument.

Argument 15:

The problem of poorly trained teachers that has plagued the state public school system is bound to become a good deal less serious in the future. The state has initiated comprehensive guidelines that oblige state teachers to complete a number of required credits in education and educational psychology at the graduate level before being certified.

Write a response in which you discuss how well reasoned you find the argument. In your response, describe specific examples or evidence needed to evaluate the argument and how those examples or evidence would weaken or strengthen the argument.

ARGUMENT ESSAY PRACTICE PROMPTS SAMPLE ESSAYS AND EXPLANATIONS

Here are sample top-scoring essays to five of the sample Argument prompts found in the previous section. Remember that an essay does not have to be perfect to receive a top score. Review these essays and note the qualities that earned them each a score of 6.

Argument 4:

A recently issued five-year study on the common cold investigated the possible therapeutic effect of a raw food diet. Raw foods contain antioxidants that boost the immune system. While many foods are naturally rich in antioxidants, food-processing companies also sell isolated antioxidants. The five-year study found a strong correlation between a raw food diet and a steep decline in the average number of colds reported by study participants. A control group that increased their antioxidant intake using supplements did not have a decrease in the number of colds. Based on these study results, some health experts recommend a raw food diet over the use of packaged antioxidants.

Write a response in which you discuss what questions would need to be answered in order to assess the reasonableness of both the recommendation and the argument upon which it is based. Be sure to explain how the answers to these questions would help to evaluate the recommendation.

Sample Response

The fields of health and medicine offer constant breakthroughs and varying viewpoints to today's society. Popular nutritional foods and eating habits supported for several years are now up for debate. With that said, new recommendations, such as the inclusion of raw foods in a balanced diet that boosts the immune system, should be proven before they're practiced.

One question that is important to address over claims that a study proved the successful use of raw food to fight against the common cold is which foods were included in the study. If the foods discussed in the study are fruits and vegetables, which are already commonly consumed raw, people would be more apt to accept the study results. However, if the study used raw meats, the population may be hesitant to embrace a diet change due to previous claims of diseases. These elements should be addressed before a public claim is made.

Along with addressing the type of raw food that was used in the study, scientists should also discuss the control group that was used. Oftentimes, the immune system of a younger person will differ from that of an older person. Was the control group composed of healthier, younger citizens, or older ones who are more prone to catching the common cold? The representativeness of the samples would affect the validity of the study results.

In addition to supplying information with regard to the demographics of the control group, the designers of the study should also disclose the environmental factors that may have influenced the control group. Were members of the control group, which used supplements, also parents who were exposed to school children who attend school and are more susceptible to catching colds? Were the parties who consumed raw foods also exercising more frequently than the control group? These factors may dissuade society, or reinforce the importance of other elements of a healthy immune system.

With new studies presented to the population each day, it becomes difficult to distinguish reputable ones from those that may need more evidence. The addition of raw foods in the average healthy diet may bring controversy. Nonetheless, society will continue to adapt to lifestyle suggestions when adequate proof is provided.

Analysis

The author successfully identifies and analyzes this argument's recommendation: raw food diets should take the place of packaged antioxidants. In the opening paragraph, the author states his position: the safety of new diets should be proved before being implemented. The essay then points out an unanswered question on which the argument depends. Namely, is it raw vegetables or meats that are being advocated in this diet? In the subsequent paragraphs, the author identifies flaws, particularly those involving the study's methodology, in the assumptions and perceptively suggests what needs to be known to make the recommendation stronger, and how knowing this information would help in evaluating this recommendation.

The author also cites these points undermining the argument:

1. The assumption that the control group was diverse in terms of age and health
2. Environmental factors that affect populations

Throughout the essay, the author uses well-organized paragraphs—each starts with a broad statement followed by supporting statements—and his ideas logically flow from one sentence to the next. He uses succinct, economical diction and alternates between complicated and more straightforward sentences. The essay remains focused and clear throughout, earning a score of 6.

Argument 5:

The following was written as part of an application for a permit to congregate by a religious group in the city of Gustav:

"We plan to meet at the Hunter Pavilion on the north side of the park. We expect about 200 attendees. Although we do plan to celebrate our message in words and song, we will be mindful of others who are sharing the park on that day. We have found that in the past, when our group meets in a public space, we run the risk of harassment by those who do not agree with our message. Therefore, we would like to hire five security officers to protect our congregants from religious intolerance. We would like to post one guard at the entrance to the park and others, who will dress in plain clothes, at the perimeter of our gathering. We hope you understand and will endorse this request."

Write a response in which you describe what specific examples or evidence is needed to evaluate the argument and how those examples or evidence would weaken or strengthen the argument.

Sample Response

The Bill of Rights was designed to protect the rights of the American People in the best way possible without infringing on the rights of others. Assuming that this situation takes place in the United States, this group should have the right to carry out all the requests written in this application. The main issues in question seem to be covered under freedom of religion, freedom of speech, and freedom to congregate, all of which are protected by the U.S. Constitution.

We can assume, by the request for security guards, that this group is not looked upon with favor by the community. Unfortunately for their opponents, if they go through the proper channels (such as applying for permits like this one seems to be), they are within their legal rights to gather and practice their religious ceremony nonviolently. Thus, one important question that needs to be answered in order to evaluate this argument is whether this is the proper permit and whether their request is within the laws and regulations of the city. It is one of the foundational ideals in the creation of this country that practicing an unpopular religion is entirely protected. Some of the founders of the early colonies came here to be safe from religious persecution. It would be hypocritical to cast aside a group because their views are unpopular.

The hiring of private security officers could potentially pose problems for this group. The county police force should be in charge of, and capable of, maintaining the peace in the area. It is the job of the police force to protect citizens from being harassed by intolerant fellow citizens. If the harassment gets to the point where it becomes dangerous or criminal in some way, the police should step in. The fact that this group has been harassed before, and now feel the need for additional undercover security officers, is cause for concern. To properly evaluate this argument, we would need to know what kind of harassment is going on (i.e., physical or verbal), and whether or not the police themselves are capable of handling the situation. This would obviate the need to resort to armed guards, who may or may not actually be necessary. It would help to determine whether or not the group's civil rights are being violated and whether the city would be within its legal obligations to grant such a request.

It is within the rights of private groups and citizens to hire private security officers. Celebrities, concert venues, and even high-powered business people hire security agents to maintain order when trouble is expected. Assuming there is some legal paperwork that must be filed, and this group completes it all correctly, there is no reason why they should not be allowed to hire outside help. But the outstanding factual and legal questions need to be cleared up before that conclusion is unequivocal. The group may feel it has been let down by the official police force and that they will not be safe without additional security measures.

Analysis

The author successfully identifies and analyzes this argument's contention: that the group in question should be allowed to have armed security guards at their event. In the opening paragraph, the author acknowledges that the group has the right to freedom of expression, and that this should not be infringed upon. However, she draws attention to the questions that need to be answered in order to hire private security guards at a public venue.

The author also cites these points, which must be determined before assessing the argument:

1. The nature of the harassment/threats being made against the group
2. Whether or not the police are capable of handling the situation
3. The legal considerations surrounding the hiring of private security

The author makes judicious use of well-structured paragraphs—each starts with a strong assertion followed by supporting statements. Her ideas logically flow from one sentence to the next. She uses succinct, economical diction and intersperses complex and simpler sentences. The essay concludes strongly by summarizing the conditions necessary for allowing the group to hire their guards, and, if these conditions are met, stating that they should be allowed to do so. The essay remains focused and clear throughout, earning a score of 6.

Argument 6:

The following memo appeared in the newsletter of the Happy Sun Happy Moon daycare center.

"Since the road construction on I-72 has begun, we've noticed that parents are picking up their children after the center is officially closed. Effective immediately, parents who pick up their children more than five minutes after closing will have to pay a $10 fee. Parents who pick up their children more than one hour after closing will be subject to an additional $30 fee. We predict this will encourage parents to leave earlier from work to pick up their children on time each day."

Write a response in which you discuss what questions would need to be answered to decide how likely the stated recommendation is to yield the predicted result. Be sure to explain how these answers would help to evaluate the recommendation.

Sample Response

If I were to put myself in the place of one of these parents, the first question I would have is, "How can you charge us, as parents, more if we are only a few minutes late? Traffic is always present, whether construction projects are taking place or not, so it does not seem fair to charge us extra for something that is out of our control." Six minutes late would, technically, mean a charge, and that seems a bit extreme. As such, I do not think that this recommendation would have the anticipated result. I think that some parents may leave work a bit earlier to try to get to their children earlier, but heavy traffic can begin before the standard five or six o'clock traffic, so to assume that if a parent leaves earlier they will arrive on time is false. I would imagine that some parents would arrive on time more frequently, as they would not want to be charged, but it could not be guaranteed. Without more information, the best one could say is that there's a chance that parents will always be on time. In fact, how could the daycare presume that parents could leave earlier, when some companies are quite stringent and do not allow their employees to leave before the very end of the day?

In the past, for example, I have had jobs where I could not leave early, unless I had a previously scheduled appointment. Certain tasks had to be completed by certain times, which tied me to my desk until the end of the day. Consequently, depending on traffic, sometimes I would have been late to pick up my child, and sometimes I would have been on time. I think that an hour late would warrant a fee, as the people who work at the daycare also have families to go home to, but merely a few minutes late, even up to 15 or 20 minutes late, should not be an issue.

To charge parents for being slightly late is unwarranted. Being too late is, of course, a problem, but slightly late should not be. The daycare should be more understanding and try to put themselves in the parents' shoes. Consequently, the final question that I would ask the daycare would be, "Could you only charge a fee at the end of the month to those parents who were consistently late, say, more than three times that month?" That, I think, would be a reasonable alternative. After all, if parents are dedicated to arriving on time, they will do their best to pick up their children at the appropriate hour. Naturally, they may get caught in traffic and arrive late sometimes, but if they are generally on time, I do not think that they should be penalized.

Analysis

The author begins with a provocative rhetorical question that grabs the reader's attention. He emphatically denies that the recommendation will have the predicted result. He notes that simply installing this policy will not make parents show up on time. The primary reason is that there are a number of circumstances beyond parents' control that affect their ability to arrive promptly. These include traffic and work restrictions, both of which cannot be solved simply by fining parents for being late.

Throughout the essay, the author uses well-organized paragraphs—each starts with a broad statement followed by supporting statements. He uses strong, emotional language to convey his point. The essay remains focused and clear throughout, earning a score of 6.

Argument 7:

In 1992, many farmers in Jalikistan began using a hormone designed to produce larger cows that would produce more milk. Since then, childhood obesity in Jalikistan has grown by 200 percent. The amount of milk and dairy consumed by children in this area has not increased or decreased. Children in the same area who are lactose intolerant, and who drink almond milk or soy milk, have not had the same increase in childhood obesity. The only clear explanation is that the introduction of the hormone is responsible for the increase in childhood obesity in that area.

Write a response in which you discuss one or more viable alternatives to the proposed explanation. Justify, with support, why the alternatives could rival the proposed explanation and explain how those explanation(s) can plausibly account for the facts presented in the argument.

Sample Response

While the hormone may well contribute to an increase in childhood obesity, it does not have to be the only problem. A 200 percent rise in obesity over a given period of time begs the question of whether other factors are at work. Obesity in all ages can be linked to many different factors: physical activity, increased consumption of solid food, or the type of food being ingested. A milk hormone—while being a potential source—is not the "only clear explanation." Other factors, from diet to physical activity, could be at work.

The argument concludes that the hormone is causing obesity in children. This is an assumption that is not necessarily true. This scenario says nothing about the activity level of the children; this is a large gap in the reasoning that could help the reader further understand the role that the hormone played in the children's obesity. If the hormone usage in 1992 converged with a decline in physical activity, then either factor, or both, could have caused the uptick in obesity rates. The fact that the use of the hormone coincided with the start of a period in which, due to the availability of automotive transportation, people are more sedentary, is worth investigating.

During the time in question, television and video games may have become more prevalent, furthering a sedentary lifestyle. Nothing is mentioned about the levels of physical activity among these two groups of children.

The argument states that the children's dairy consumption hasn't changed, but says nothing else about their dietary habits. It is possible that the children who eat dairy products also have, since 1992, taken to eating richer foods, fewer vegetables, or more carbohydrates. Such a change in diet could account for the obesity rates within the population. It is also possible that, during the time in question, lactose-tolerant children have been eating more fattening food products that, while not dairy products themselves, employ milk, cheese, or butter in their preparation. This could cause the increase in obesity rates, and the lactose-intolerant children would be unaffected.

Given that we do not know the answers to these questions, the argument goes beyond the available data in asserting that it must be the hormone that is to blame for the obesity rates among the children who are lactose tolerant.

Analysis

The author of this essay recognizes that the argument depends on two unqualified assumptions and that simply stopping the use of the hormone may or may not have the desired effect. The author argues throughout the essay that the only difference between the two groups of children that we are made aware of is the type of milk they drink (or do not drink). We do not know:

1. The effect of diet (aside from dairy products)
2. Level of physical activity

Because we don't know the facts pertinent to environmental and behavioral factors affecting the two groups of children, both diet and exercise can be considered as potential alternative explanations. The argument in the prompt simply assumes that both groups are otherwise identical, and that assumption stretches beyond the known information.

Throughout the essay, the author uses well-organized paragraphs—each starts with a broad statement followed by supporting statements—and her ideas logically flow from one sentence to the next. She uses succinct, economical diction and rotates complicated and straightforward sentences. The essay remains focused and clear throughout, earning a score of 6.

Argument 8:

The following appeared in a memo from an advertisement by Pest Protection, Inc.:

"Gardens along the coast are already being infested by the mill bug, a slimy purple pest that can decimate a vegetable garden in seconds flat. If you live within 100 miles of the coast, you need the Pest Protection cure today. Thousands of satisfied customers who have used our chemical-free treatments have never had mill bug problems. One treatment per year will ensure that you never have to lose your valuable crops to this pest."

Write a response in which you examine the underlying assumptions of the argument. Be sure to explain how the argument hinges on these assumptions and what the implications are for the argument if the assumptions prove unfounded.

Sample Response

At first glance, the argument proffered by the advertisement seems to make sense. Those who use Pest Protection will not suffer an infestation of mill bugs. The author makes claims that seem to meet the needs of someone living in the region. However, the author relies on several unproven assumptions. First, the argument mistakenly assumes that because the mill bug "can" decimate a garden, that it will in fact do so. There's no way to assess the extent of the current infestation. Nor is there anything that states which types of vegetables or flowers the bug devours. In order to assess the validity of the advertisement, it would valuable to know the true extent of the threat that the bug poses. If it's the case that the mill bug eats only root vegetables or only flowering plants, it's unlikely that everyone within 100 miles of the coast needs Pest Protection. If "thousands of satisfied customers have never had mill bug problems," how can we even be sure that the bugs do in fact pose a serious threat?

The biggest flaw in the author's reasoning is that the author assumes, without providing proof, that there is a direct, causal relationship between using the Pest Protection cure and being free of mill bug problems. Even if both are true, that someone is using the Pest Protection cure and they do not have a mill bug problem, there is no proof that the former has caused the latter. There could be other factors at work, such as climate, migration patterns, lack of food supply, or other such extrinsic concerns.

Many who used the Pest Protection treatment may have done so unnecessarily. There is no information to suggest what the level of infestation would have been without the treatment. The advertisement's reasoning amounts to arguing that since a town began sending police officers on "Bear Patrol," no one in the town has been attacked by a bear. Depending on where the town is, there may never have been a bear attack to begin with.

Finally, the company's claim that a single, yearly treatment will ensure that customers will "never have to lose . . . valuable crops" is broad. In order to assess the argument, we need to know the price and process for this treatment. It may be price prohibitive to have annual treatments. Alternately, the treatments may have side effects. The advertisement does qualify its claim: you never have to lose crops to this pest. But, if the treatment makes it impossible to grow certain crops or depletes the soil over time, the user would lose crops in another way. Pest Protection offers no support for the claim that the treatment will last for such a long time. Many things, such as climate change and inclement weather, could mitigate or dilute the effect of such a treatment over the course of a year. Thus, from a sales and customer standpoint, this argument is persuasive but has too many gaps in its logic to be convincing without further evidence.

Analysis

The author successfully identifies and analyzes this argument's underlying assumptions. The author of this essay recognizes that the argument depends on assuming that the use of the product will result in getting rid of the mill bugs. Additionally, we do not know:

1. Whether one yearly treatment will be enough
2. Whether the treatment is effective or not
3. Whether there is a causal relationship between Pest Protection treatments and prevention of the mill bug

The advertisement also does not indicate whether mill bugs have been killed in the past by inclement weather or environmental factors, as opposed to the product. Because we do not know these pertinent environmental factors, it is impossible to predict whether using the product will have the desired result.

Throughout the essay, the author uses well-organized paragraphs—each is taut and incisive, and the main point is quickly followed by supporting statements—and his ideas logically flow from one sentence to the next. He uses succinct, economical diction and rotates complex and simpler sentences. The essay remains focused and clear throughout, earning a score of 6.

PART FIVE

Analytical Writing Content Review

CHAPTER 9

Writing Foundations

OVERVIEW

The focus of the GRE writing sample is on not only how well you write, but also the thought processes you employ to formulate and articulate a position. There are two GRE Analytical Writing sections, each 30 minutes long.

You'll write essays on two different types of prompts:

- The Issue essay task provides a brief quotation on an issue of general interest and instructions on how to respond to the issue. You can discuss the issue from any perspective, making use of your own educational and personal background, examples from current or historical events, things you've read, or even relevant hypothetical situations. In this task, you will develop your own argument.
- The Argument essay task contains a short argument that may or may not be complete, and specific instructions on how to evaluate the argument's strength. You will assess the argument's cogency, analyze the author's reasoning, and evaluate her use (or lack) of evidence. In this task, you critique the argument presented in the prompt.

The Analytical Writing section allows schools to evaluate your ability to plan and compose a logical, well-reasoned essay under timed conditions. You'll write the essays on the computer, using a simple word processing program.

This section of the book will review Kaplan's 22 principles for effective writing. Numbers 1–10 relate to writing style, 11–17 to grammar, and 18–22 to mechanics. Study these principles to refine your writing skills and score well on the GRE Analytical Writing essays.

WRITING STYLE

Remember, each GRE essay is a formal writing assignment. Here are a few elements of style to keep in mind while you're writing:

Concision

- Omit words, phrases, and sentences that do not add to your argument or support your position. An experienced GRE essay grader can spot such padding a mile away. Make every word count.
- Avoid redundant phrases such as *refer back*, *serious crisis*, and *general consensus*, which weaken your writing.

Structure

- Use transition words and phrases to show the relationship between your ideas.
- Start a new paragraph for every new topic or example.

Formal and Forceful

- Don't use slang or text-message abbreviations, and don't use an ampersand (&) in place of the word *and*. This is a formal assignment—treat it as such.
- Avoid weak sentence openings, such as *There is* or *There are*.
- Avoid the passive voice: *I finished my essay* is stronger and more concise than *The essay was finished by me*.
- Avoid clichés and overused terms or phrases. Remember, the graders are reading a lot of these; try to make your essays memorable.
- Use precise wording and avoid generalizations ("many people") and abstractions. Make your meaning clear.
- Avoid referring to your own opinion with constructions like "I think," "I feel," or "I believe." Also avoid retelling personal anecdotes or sharing your own philosophy.
- Vary sentence length and style.

In all of the exercises that follow, read the sentences given and revise them to correct any errors. The headings will give you an idea of what errors to look for.

WRITING STYLE EXERCISES

1st Principle of Effective Writing: Streamlining Wordy Phrases

1. An essential element of our consideration of the problem was finding the means to identify the more dubious aspects of the plan.

   ____

2. Foremost in their thinking was the capacity of the vehicle to traverse various kinds of terrain.

   ____

3. Anthony engaged a professional interior decorator to undertake the refurbishment of his apartment.

____

2nd Principle of Effective Writing: Eliminating Redundancy

4. At this point in time the scout experienced a serious setback.

____

5. None of her fellow classmates were at the party.

____

6. The leader had a special reputation for being calm in a crisis situation.

____

3rd Principle of Effective Writing: Avoiding Excessive Qualification

7. In a fairly rare moment of frustration, Toni pretty much lost her temper.

____

8. Lee's actions at Gettysburg seemed relatively uncharacteristic for someone whose qualities as a commander were usually sound for the most part.

____

9. I have to say that, as an employer, Helen showed a certain amount of boldness in providing what most would regard as generous benefits to her workers.

____

4th Principle of Effective Writing: Removing Unnecessary Sentences

10. This city's transportation system is a model for urban infrastructure elsewhere. Our bus and light-rail lines are second to none.

____

11. Where would this company be without the vision of someone like Carlo? Our success as a company owes everything to his belief in the future.

____

12. The builders of medieval cathedrals were not primitive laborers who had little idea of what they were doing. They were often highly skilled masons, carpenters, and workers in stained glass who were guided by a detailed plan drawn up by a master builder.

___

5th Principle of Effective Writing: Avoiding Needless Self-Reference

13. I am of the opinion that we can design cars that are much more fuel-efficient.

___

14. From my point of view, the pottery could increase its output simply by using a different glaze.

___

15. I feel it would be a mistake to take part in such a demonstration without a clear sense of purpose.

___

6th Principle of Effective Writing: Using Active Rather than Passive Voice

16. As the prisoner was brought into court by the guards, he glared at his accuser.

___

17. The question of who is to inherit the estate has never been asked.

___

18. When do you think the problem will have been solved by them?

___

7th Principle of Effective Writing: Including Strong Openings

19. There is every possibility that the police have found your lost dog.

___

20. It is to be hoped that officials can resolve this crisis before it gets out of hand.

___

21. There is a proverb that says, "Half a loaf is better than none."

____

8th Principle of Effective Writing: Avoiding Needlessly Vague Language

22. To really demonstrate our obligation to some valued customer, we will forego the standard admission fee.

____

23. All our employees are content here.

____

24. Both kind of indigent and without much accommodation, she is indeed a sad spectacle.

____

9th Principle of Effective Writing: Rewording Clichés

25. That man sleeping on the bench looks a bit over the hill.

____

26. She always seemed to me to have ice water in her veins.

____

27. With this win, the team looks like it might finally be on a roll.

____

10th Principle of Effective Writing: Avoiding Jargon

28. The consultant said that, if a company is going to downsize, it should go for the low-hanging fruit first.

____

29. Let's connect ear-to-ear on this one.

____

30. Just give me a ballpark figure so I can consider the offer.

____

WRITING STYLE EXERCISES ANSWERS AND EXPLANATIONS

1. Finding the plan's weaknesses was essential to evaluating it.

2. Their main interest was the vehicle's cross-country capability.

3. Anthony hired a professional interior decorator to redecorate his apartment.

4. The scout experienced a setback.

5. None of her classmates were at the party.

6. The leader was known to be calm in a crisis.

7. In a rare moment of frustration, Toni lost her temper.

8. Lee's actions at Gettysburg were uncharacteristic of a generally sound commander.

9. Helen showed boldness by providing generous benefits to her workers.

10. The city's transportation system, with bus and light-rail lines that are second to none, is a model for other cities.

11. The success of our company owes everything to Carlo's belief in the future.

12. The builders of medieval cathedrals were not primitive laborers, but often highly skilled masons, carpenters, and workers in stained glass, guided by a detailed plan drawn up by a master builder.

13. We can design cars that are much more fuel-efficient.

14. The pottery could increase its output simply by using a different glaze.

15. It would be a mistake to take part in such a demonstration without a clear sense of purpose.

16. As the guards brought the prisoner into court, he glared at his accuser.

17. No one has ever asked who will inherit the estate.

18. When do you think they will have solved the problem?

19. The police have quite possibly found your lost dog.

20. Hopefully, officials can resolve this crisis before it gets out of hand.

21. "Half a loaf is better than none," as the proverb says.

22. We forego the standard admission fee for a valued customer.

23. All our employees have said they are satisfied with working conditions and benefits here.

24. Poor and homeless, she is sad to see.

25. That man sleeping on the bench looks old.

26. She always seemed unemotional to me.

27. With this win, the team looks like it might finally be gaining momentum.

28. The consultant said that, if a company is going to lay off workers, it should go for the easy targets first.

29. Let's discuss the details of this on the phone.

30. Just give me a cost estimate so I can consider the offer.

GRAMMAR

On the GRE, your control of language is important. Writing that is grammatical, concise, direct, and persuasive displays the "superior facility with the conventions of standard written English" (as the testmakers term it) that earns top GRE essay scores. If your writing style isn't clear, your ideas won't come across, no matter how brilliant they are. Good GRE English is not only grammatical but also clear and concise, and by using some basic principles, you'll be able to express your ideas clearly and effectively in both of your essays. To display effective writing style in your essays, your writing must follow the rules of standard written English. If you're not confident of your mastery of grammar, brush up before the test using the exercises below.

GRAMMAR EXERCISES

11th Principle of Effective Writing: Ensuring Subject-Verb Agreement

31. If you or a member of your family have this problem, contact a doctor right away.

____

32. The training given to car mechanics, particularly those who work in modern dealerships on cars with the latest electronic gadgets, are more complicated than ever.

____

33. Each of the times you spoke about overcoming troubles were inspirational to me.

____

34. Our staff are discussing this proposal in our monthly meeting on Friday.

____

35. A range of options are open to businesses hoping to expand.

____

12th Principle of Effective Writing: Avoiding Faulty Modification

36. Pleading innocent to all the charges, the jury was very sympathetic to the accused.

____

37. A portrait artist would probably not be successful painting sitters without a deep appreciation of personal character.

____

38. Lost when the ship sank, the rescued passengers had no possessions when they reached shore.

____

39. Cynthia found the credit card she had misplaced when she looked under the bed.

____

40. Usually never at a loss for words, the unresponsive audience left the comedian speechless.

____

13th Principle of Effective Writing: Avoiding Unclear Pronoun Reference

41. Marie told her mother that it was time for her to leave home.

____

42. Because of heavy snow on the roads, car drivers moved at a snail's pace until they were salted.

____

43. Bob was generous in his praise of Gil because of his pleasant nature.

____

44. Whenever the sergeant and the captain met, he saluted smartly.

____

14th Principle of Effective Writing: Including Parallelism

45. The food you buy at the Wonder King Supermarket is less expensive than the Bislet Hypermarket.

____

46. Helicopter pilots use one hand to control up-and-down motion, the other hand to control motion forward, backward, and sideways, while the feet control the turns.

____

47. A good teacher knows her subject, her students, and has a good sense of humor.

____

48. Students commonly preferred the teaching of Dr. Wolf to Professor Smith.

____

15th Principle of Effective Writing: Using a Consistent Narrative Voice

49. If one is genuinely serious about helping the homeless, you must become familiar with their living conditions.

____

50. From my perspective, you have to be truthful all the time. I don't see how we can claim to have integrity if we do anything less.

____

51. When we vote, we take part in an extraordinary process. One chooses not a ruler but a representative for all of us.

____

52. Each of you has a special responsibility to yourself and to others. We all have our own talents that we should develop for our own benefit and for the good of our families, our friends, and everyone we meet.

____

16th Principle of Effective Writing: Avoiding Slang and Colloquialisms

53. It was agreed that, if James wanted to get to the theater on time, he had better get on the stick.

____

54. When the city councilwoman tried to cover up her mistakes with lies, she just jumped from the frying pan into the fire.

____

55. The city high-school football team creamed their opponents, 35 to nothing.

56. According to fund-raising gurus, you should concentrate on people with deep pockets.

17th Principle of Effective Writing: Avoiding Sentence Fragments and Run-Ons

57. Bad drivers seem to be on the road in large numbers, many never signal what they intend to do.

58. High-speed trains are once again a popular topic. Especially among businesspeople.

59. Ever since our earliest ancestors discovered fire. We have needed to live near reasonable sources of fuel.

60. In England, lawyers are usually either solicitors or barristers, in the past, solicitors gave advice to clients and practiced in lower courts, while barristers practiced before the "bar" in the higher courts.

GRAMMAR EXERCISES ANSWERS AND EXPLANATIONS

31. If you or a member of your family has this problem, contact a doctor right away.

32. The training given to car mechanics, particularly those who work in modern dealerships on cars with the latest electronic gadgets, is more complicated than ever.

33. Each of the times you spoke about overcoming troubles was inspirational to me.

34. Our staff is discussing this proposal in our monthly meeting on Friday.

35. A range of options is open to businesses hoping to expand.

36. The jury was very sympathetic to the accused, who pled innocent to all the charges.

37. A portrait artist without a deep appreciation of personal character would probably not be successful painting sitters.

38. Lost when the ship sank, the rescued passengers' possessions were gone when the passengers reached shore.

39. When she looked under the bed, Cynthia found the credit card she had misplaced.

40. Usually never at a loss for words, the comedian was speechless before the unresponsive audience.

41. Marie decided it was time for her to leave home, and she told her mother so.

42. Because of heavy snow, car drivers moved at a snail's pace until the roads were salted.

43. Bob was generous in his praise of Gil's pleasant nature.

44. The sergeant saluted the captain smartly whenever they met.

45. The food you buy at the Wonder King Supermarket is less expensive than the food at the Bislet Hypermarket.

46. Helicopter pilots use one hand to control up-and-down motion; the other hand to control forward, backward, and sideways motion; and the feet to control turns.

47. A good teacher knows her subject and her students, and has a good sense of humor.

48. Students commonly preferred the teaching of Dr. Wolf to that of Professor Smith.

49. If you are genuinely serious about helping the homeless, you must become familiar with their living conditions.

50. We must be truthful all the time. We cannot claim to have integrity if we do anything less.

51. When we vote, we take part in an extraordinary process. We choose not a ruler but a representative for all of us.

52. Each of you has a special responsibility to yourself and to others. You all have your own talents that you should develop for your own benefit and for the good of your families, your friends, and everyone you meet.

53. It was agreed that, if James wanted to get to the theater on time, he would have to hurry.

54. When the city councilwoman tried to cover up her mistakes with lies, she went from a bad situation to a worse one.

55. The city high-school football team overwhelmed their opponents by a score of 35 to 0.

56. According to fund-raising experts, you should concentrate on people with plenty of money.

57. Bad drivers seem to be on the road in large numbers. Many never signal what they intend to do.

58. High-speed trains are once again a popular topic, especially among businesspeople.

59. Ever since our earliest ancestors discovered fire, we have needed to live near reasonable sources of fuel.

60. In England, lawyers are usually either solicitors or barristers. In the past, solicitors gave advice to clients and practiced in lower courts, while barristers practiced before the "bar" in the higher courts.

MECHANICS

Mechanics are more technical in nature than grammatical issues. They are the established conventions of punctuation, capitalization, pronouns, and so on. Remember, minor grammatical errors will not ruin your score. Many test takers mistakenly believe that they'll lose points because of a few mechanical missteps such as misplaced commas, spelling errors, or other minor mistakes. In fact, the testmakers' description of a top-scoring essay acknowledges that there may be minor grammatical flaws. The graders understand that you are writing first-draft essays under timed conditions. However, if your errors obscure your meaning or make your essay difficult to follow, this will most likely be reflected in your scores.

To write an effective essay, you must be concise, forceful, and correct. An effective essay wastes no words, makes its point in a clear, direct way, and conforms to the generally accepted rules of grammar and form.

MECHANICS EXERCISES

18th Principle of Effective Writing: Correctly Using Commas

61. By federal law, interstate drivers of heavy trucks may be on duty for 14 straight hours, but must then take a 10-hour break.

____

62. Monica, who was normally a conscientious agreeable colleague shocked her coworkers with her angry outburst.

____

63. Spectators argued that the motorcycle stunt was an example of, sheer bravado, enormous courage, or arrant stupidity.

____

64. Historically mounting a horse from the left side, dates back to the time when knights wore their swords on their left hip and could swing their right leg onto the horse's back without the sword getting in the way.

____

65. Seeing the opportunity to make a quick breakthrough against her chess opponent she risked her queen by moving her remaining bishop well ahead of her pawns.

____

66. During the American Civil War, doctors regularly treated ill soldiers with "blue mass," a concoction made up of ingredients such as mercury, honey, glycerol and, licorice.

____

19th Principle of Effective Writing: Correctly Using Semicolons

67. We try to watch as little television as possible in our house, moreover we encourage reading by buying each other books as presents.

____

68. We did not know what to do, we could either run, stay, or hide.

____

69. Bringing a book to publication has often taken years, today, however, a book can appear on the Internet in a matter of weeks or even less.

____

70. The success of the operation was particularly due to the efforts of Dr. Williams, a heart specialist with an innovative approach to surgery, Dr. Mallory, the anesthesiologist, who first noted the patient's breathing problems, and Dr. Thurman, the blood specialist, who overcame dangerous clotting that could have traveled to the patient's lungs.

____

71. In recent weeks, Jake skimped on his training, therefore, his weak performance kept him from entering the tennis finals.

____

72. The 19th-century scholar Thomas Malthus wrote that limited food supplies would ultimately halt world population growth through starvation, this observation, highly influential at the time, may have prompted the historian Thomas Carlyle to describe economics as "the dismal science."

____

20th Principle of Effective Writing: Correctly Using Colons

73. A tragic hero may be: a powerful individual, a monarch, or, in modern tragedy, an ordinary person.

____

74. In recent years, Canada has produced a large number of world-class artists: including the following, the author Margaret Atwood, comedian Jim Carrey, singer Celine Dion, musician Neil Young, and actor Donald Sutherland.

____

75. The Navajo code talkers of World War II created special terms for wartime topics such as the following, submarine (iron fish), Britain (between waters), Germany (iron hat), dive bomber (chicken hawk), and August (big harvest).

____

76. I have one goal I really want to accomplish in my life, and that is: to scuba dive off the Great Barrier Reef.

____

77. The Empire State Building's special lighting system has been used: to honor only two non-Americans, Queen Elizabeth II of England and South Africa's Nelson Mandela.

____

78. Among the most sought-after qualities in a leader are the following character, enthusiasm, determination, confidence, cool-headedness, and decisiveness.

____

21st Principle of Effective Writing: Correctly Using Hyphens and Dashes

79. The company upgraded its technology system to what it called "a 21st century standard."

____

80. In a soon to be released statement, the chairman of the local soccer club reveals details of the club's new strip.

____

81. Only a few of the original members signed up for the forty seventh reunion of the class.

____

82. My objection—insignificant as it may seem, is the product of a lot of careful thought.

____

83. Almost certain ruin, the collapse of everything we have striven for, awaits us, such is the inevitable result of this change of policy.

____

84. It is to this extraordinary woman, and to her alone—that the credit for the reversal of this unjust law must go.

____

22nd Principle of Effective Writing: Correctly Using Apostrophes

85. You do know, I trust, that youre no longer just the assistant manager.

____

86. The dealership was selling tire's and rim's at less than list price.

____

87. The passengers confidence faded every time their bus broke down.

____

88. Youd be surprised how many childrens books are now collectors items.

____

89. Its easy for some people to say, "Go out and get a job," but they dont know how few jobs are open to you if you dont have a car.

____

90. The veterinarian has no idea why the cat has lost most of it's fur.

____

MECHANICS EXERCISES
ANSWERS AND EXPLANATIONS

61. By federal law, interstate drivers of heavy trucks may be on duty for 14 straight hours but must then take a 10-hour break.

62. Monica, who was normally a conscientious, agreeable colleague, shocked her coworkers with her angry outburst.

63. Spectators argued that the motorcycle stunt was an example of sheer bravado, enormous courage, or arrant stupidity.

64. Historically, mounting a horse from the left side dates back to the time when knights wore their swords on their left hip and could swing their right leg onto the horse's back without the sword getting in the way.

65. Seeing the opportunity to make a quick breakthrough against her chess opponent, she risked her queen by moving her remaining bishop well ahead of her pawns.

66. During the American Civil War, doctors regularly treated ill soldiers with "blue mass," a concoction made up of ingredients such as mercury, honey, glycerol, and licorice.

67. We try to watch as little television as possible in our house; moreover, we encourage reading by buying each other books as presents.

68. We did not know what to do; we could either run, stay, or hide.

69. Bringing a book to publication has often taken years; today, however, a book can appear on the Internet in a matter of weeks or even less.

70. The success of the operation was particularly due to the efforts of Dr. Williams, a heart specialist with an innovative approach to surgery; Dr. Mallory, the anesthesiologist, who first noted the patient's breathing problems; and Dr. Thurman, the blood specialist, who overcame dangerous clotting that could have traveled to the patient's lungs.

71. In recent weeks, Jake skimped on his training; therefore, his weak performance kept him from entering the tennis finals.

72. The 19th-century scholar Thomas Malthus wrote that limited food supplies would ultimately halt world population growth through starvation; this observation, highly influential at the time, may have prompted the historian Thomas Carlyle to describe economics as "the dismal science."

73. A tragic hero may be a powerful individual, a monarch, or—in modern tragedy—an ordinary person.

74. In recent years, Canada has produced a large number of world-class artists, including the following: author Margaret Atwood, comedian Jim Carrey, singer Celine Dion, musician Neil Young, and actor Donald Sutherland.

75. The Navajo code talkers of World War II created special terms for wartime topics such as the following: submarine (iron fish), Britain (between waters), Germany (iron hat), dive bomber (chicken hawk), and August (big harvest).

76. I have one goal I really want to accomplish in my life, and that is to scuba dive off the Great Barrier Reef.

77. The Empire State Building's special lighting system has been used to honor only two non-Americans: Queen Elizabeth II of England and Nelson Mandela of South Africa.

78. Among the most sought-after qualities in a leader are the following: character, enthusiasm, determination, confidence, cool-headedness, and decisiveness.

79. The company upgraded its technology system to what it called "a 21st-century standard."

80. In a soon-to-be-released statement, the chairman of the local soccer club will reveal details of the club's new strip.

81. Only a few of the original members signed up for the forty-seventh reunion of the class.

82. My objection—insignificant as it may seem—is the product of a lot of careful thought.

83. Almost certain ruin, the collapse of everything we have striven for, awaits us—such is the inevitable result of this change of policy.

84. It is to this extraordinary woman—and to her alone—that the credit for the reversal of this unjust law must go.

85. You do know, I trust, that you're no longer just the assistant manager.

86. The dealership was selling tires and rims at less than list price.

87. The passengers' confidence faded every time their bus broke down.

88. You'd be surprised how many children's books are now collectors' items.

89. It's easy for some people to say, "Go out and get a job," but they don't know how few jobs are open to you if you don't have a car.

90. The veterinarian has no idea why the cat has lost most of its fur.

PART SIX

GRE Resources

Kaplan's Word Groups

The following lists contain a lot of common GRE words grouped together by meaning. Make flashcards from these lists and look over your cards a few times a week from now until the day of the test. Look over the word group lists once or twice a week every week until the test. If you don't have much time until the exam date, look over your lists more frequently. Then, by the day of the test, you should have a rough idea of what most of the words on your lists mean.

Note: The categories in which these words are listed are *general* and should *not* be interpreted as the exact definitions of the words.

A

Abbreviated Communication
- abridge
- compendium
- cursory
- curtail
- syllabus
- synopsis
- terse

Act Quickly
- abrupt
- apace
- headlong
- impetuous
- precipitate

Assist
- abet
- advocate
- ancillary
- bolster
- corroborate
- countenance
- espouse
- mainstay
- munificent
- proponent
- stalwart
- sustenance

B

Bad Mood
- bilious
- dudgeon
- irascible
- pettish
- petulant
- pique
- querulous
- umbrage
- waspish

Beginner/Amateur
- dilettante
- fledgling
- neophyte
- novitiate
- proselyte
- tyro

Beginning/Young
- burgeoning
- callow
- engender
- inchoate
- incipient
- nascent

Biting (as in wit or temperament)
- acerbic
- acidulous
- acrimonious
- asperity
- caustic
- mordacious
- mordant
- trenchant

Bold
- audacious
- courageous
- dauntless

Boring
- banal
- fatuous
- hackneyed
- insipid
- mundane
- pedestrian
- platitude
- prosaic
- quotidian
- trite

C

Carousal
- bacchanalian
- debauchery
- depraved
- dissipated
- iniquity
- libertine
- libidinous

licentious
reprobate
ribald
salacious
sordid
turpitude

Changing Quickly
capricious
mercurial
volatile

Copy
counterpart
emulate
facsimile
factitious
paradigm
precursor
simulate
vicarious

Criticize/Criticism
aspersion
belittle
berate
calumny
castigate
decry
defame/defamation
denounce
deride/derisive
diatribe
disparage
excoriate
gainsay
harangue
impugn
inveigh
lambaste
objurgate
obloquy
opprobrium
pillory
rebuke
remonstrate
reprehend
reprove
revile
tirade
vituperate

D

Death/Mourning
bereave
cadaver
defunct
demise
dolorous
elegy
knell
lament
macabre
moribund
obsequies
sepulchral
wraith

Denying of Self
abnegate
abstain
ascetic
spartan
stoic
temperate

Dictatorial
authoritarian
despotic
dogmatic
hegemonic/
hegemony
imperious
peremptory
tyrannical

Difficult to Understand
abstruse
ambiguous
arcane
bemusing
cryptic
enigmatic
esoteric
inscrutable
obscure
opaque
paradoxical
perplexing
recondite
turbid

Disgusting/Offensive
defile
fetid
invidious
noisome
odious
putrid
rebarbative

E

Easy to Understand
articulate
cogent
eloquent
evident
limpid
lucid
pellucid

Eccentric/Dissimilar
aberrant
anachronism
anomalous
discrete
eclectic
esoteric
iconoclast

Embarrass
abash
chagrin
compunction
contrition
diffidence
expiate
foible
gaucherie
rue

Equal
equitable
equity
tantamount

F

Falsehood
apocryphal
canard
chicanery
dissemble
duplicity
equivocate
erroneous
ersatz
fallacious
feigned
guile
mendacious/
mendacity
perfidy
prevaricate
specious
spurious

Family
conjugal
consanguine
distaff
endogamous
filial
fratricide
progenitor
scion

Favoring/Not Impartial
ardent/ardor
doctrinaire
fervid
partisan
tendentious
zealot

Forgive/Make Amends
absolve
acquit
exculpate
exonerate
expiate
palliate
redress
vindicate

Funny
chortle
droll
facetious
flippant
gibe
jocular
levity
ludicrous
raillery
riposte
simper

G

Gaps/Openings

abatement
aperture
fissure
hiatus
interregnum
interstice
lull
orifice
rent
respite
rift

Generous/Kind

altruistic
beneficent
clement
largess
magnanimous
munificent
philanthropic
unstinting

Greedy

avaricious
covetous
mercenary
miserly
penurious
rapacious
venal

H

Hard-Hearted

asperity
baleful
dour
fell
malevolent
mordant
sardonic
scathing
truculent
vitriolic
vituperation

Harmful

baleful
baneful
deleterious
inimical
injurious
insidious
minatory
perfidious
pernicious

Harsh-Sounding

cacophony
din
dissonant
raucous
strident

Hatred

abhorrence
anathema
antagonism
antipathy
detestation
enmity
loathing
malice
odium
rancor

Healthy

beneficial
salubrious
salutary

Hesitate

dither
oscillate
teeter
vacillate
waver

Hostile

antithetic
churlish
curmudgeon
irascible
malevolent
misanthropic
truculent
vindictive

I

Innocent/Inexperienced

credulous
gullible
ingenuous
naive
novitiate
tyro

Insincere

disingenuous
dissemble
fulsome
ostensible
unctuous

Investigate

appraise
ascertain
assay
descry
peruse

L

Lazy/Sluggish

indolent
inert
lackadaisical
languid
lassitude
lethargic
phlegmatic
quiescent
slothful
torpid

Luck

adventitious
amulet
auspicious
fortuitous
kismet
optimum
portentous
propitiate
propitious
providential
serendipity
talisman

N

Nag

admonish
belabor
cavil
enjoin
exhort
harangue
hector
martinet
remonstrate
reproof

Nasty

fetid
noisome
noxious

Not a Straight Line

askance
awry
careen
carom
circuitous
circumvent
gyrate
labyrinth
meander
oblique
serrated
sidle
sinuous
undulating
vortex

O

Overblown/Wordy

bombastic
circumlocution
garrulous
grandiloquent
loquacious
periphrastic
prolix
rhetoric
turgid
verbose

P

Pacify/Satisfy

ameliorate
appease
assuage
defer
mitigate
mollify
placate

propitiate
satiate
slake
soothe

Pleasant-Sounding
euphonious
harmonious
melodious
sonorous

Poor
destitute
esurient
impecunious
indigent

Praise
acclaim
accolade
aggrandize
encomium
eulogize
extol
fawn
laud/laudatory
venerate/veneration

Predict
augur
auspice
fey
harbinger
portentous
precursor
presage
prescient
prognosticate

Prevent/Obstruct
discomfit
encumber
fetter
forfend
hinder
impede
inhibit
occlude

S

Smart/Learned
astute
canny
erudite
perspicacious

Sorrow
disconsolate
doleful
dolor
elegiac
forlorn
lament
lugubrious
melancholy
morose
plaintive
threnody

Stubborn
implacable
inexorable
intractable
intransigent
obdurate
obstinate
recalcitrant
refractory
renitent
untoward
vexing

T

Terse
compendious
curt
laconic
pithy
succinct
taciturn

Time/Order/Duration
anachronism
antecede
antedate
anterior
archaic
diurnal
eon
ephemeral
epoch
fortnight
millennium
penultimate
synchronous
temporal

Timid/Timidity
craven
diffident
pusillanimous
recreant
timorous
trepidation

Truth
candor/candid
fealty
frankness
indisputable
indubitable
legitimate
probity
sincere
veracious
verity

U

Unusual
aberration
anomaly
iconoclast
idiosyncrasy

W

Walking About
ambulatory
itinerant
meander
peripatetic

Wandering
discursive
expatiate
forage
itinerant
peregrination
peripatetic
sojourn

Weaken
adulterate
enervate
exacerbate
inhibit
obviate
stultify
undermine
vitiate

Wisdom
adage
aphorism
apothegm
axiom
bromide
dictum
epigram
platitude
sententious
truism

Withdrawal/Retreat
abeyance
abjure
abnegation
abortive
abrogate
decamp
demur
recant
recidivism
remission
renege
rescind
retrograde

APPENDIX B

Kaplan's Root List

Kaplan's Root List can boost your knowledge of GRE-level words, and that can help you get more questions right. No one can predict exactly which words will show up on your test, but the testmakers favor certain words. The Root List gives you the component parts of many typical GRE words. Knowing these words can help you because you may run across them on your GRE. Also, becoming comfortable with the types of words that pop up will reduce your anxiety about the test.

Knowing roots can help you in two more ways. First, instead of learning one word at a time, you can learn a whole group of words that contain a certain root. They'll be related in meaning, so if you remember one, it will be easier for you to remember others. Second, roots can often help you decode an unknown GRE word. If you recognize a familiar root, you could get a good enough grasp of the word to answer the question.

This list is a starting point and a quick review, not an exhaustive guide. Roots are given in their most common forms, with their most common or broadest definitions; often, other forms and meanings exist. Similarly, the definitions for the words given as examples may be incomplete, and other senses of those words may exist. Get into the habit of looking up unfamiliar words in a good, current dictionary—whether on paper or on the Internet—and be sure to check their etymologies while you're there.

A

A/AN: not, without

agnostic: one who believes the existence of God is not provable

amoral: neither moral nor immoral; having no relation to morality

anomaly: an irregularity

anonymous: of unknown authorship or origin

apathy: lack of interest or emotion

atheist: one who does not believe in God

atrophy: the wasting away of body tissue

atypical: not typical

AB: off, away from, apart, down

abdicate: to renounce or relinquish a throne

abduct: to take away by force

abhor: to hate, detest

abject: cast down; degraded

abnormal: deviating from a standard

abolish: to do away with, make void

abstinence: forbearance from any indulgence of appetite

abstract: conceived apart from concrete realities, specific objects, or actual instances

abstruse: hard to understand; secret, hidden

ABLE/IBLE: capable of, worthy of

changeable: able to be changed

combustible: capable of being burned; easily inflamed

inevitable: impossible to be avoided; certain to happen

presentable: suitable for being presented

AC/ACR: sharp, bitter, sour

acerbic: sour or astringent in taste; harsh in temper

acid: something that is sharp, sour, or ill-natured

acrimonious: caustic, stinging, or bitter in nature

acumen: mental sharpness; quickness of wit

acute: sharp at the end; ending in a point

exacerbate: to increase bitterness or violence; aggravate

ACT/AG: to do, to drive, to force, to lead

agile: quick and well-coordinated in movement; active, lively

agitate: to move or force into violent, irregular action

litigate: to make the subject of a lawsuit

pedagogue: a teacher

prodigal: wastefully or recklessly extravagant

synagogue: a gathering or congregation of Jews for the purpose of religious worship

ACOU: hearing

acoustic: pertaining to hearing; sound made through mechanical, not electronic, means

AD: to, toward, near

(Often the *d* is dropped and the first letter to which *a* is prefixed is doubled.)

accede: to yield to a demand; to enter office

adapt: adjust or modify fittingly

addict: to give oneself over, as to a habit or pursuit

address: to direct a speech or written statement to

adhere: to stick fast; cleave; cling

adjacent: near, close, or contiguous; adjoining

adjoin: to be close or in contact with

admire: to regard with wonder, pleasure, and approval

advocate: to plead in favor of

attract: to draw either by physical force or by an appeal to emotions or senses

AL/ALI/ALTER: other, another

alias: an assumed name; another name

alibi: the defense by an accused person that he was verifiably elsewhere at the time of the crime with which he is charged

alien: one born in another country; a foreigner

allegory: figurative treatment of one subject under the guise of another

alter ego: the second self; a substitute or deputy

alternative: a possible choice

altruist: a person unselfishly concerned for the welfare of others

AM: love

amateur: a person who engages in an activity for pleasure rather than financial or professional gain

amatory: of or pertaining to lovers or lovemaking

amiable: having or showing agreeable personal qualities

amicable: characterized by exhibiting good will

amity: friendship; peaceful harmony

amorous: inclined to love, esp. sexual love

enamored: inflamed with love; charmed; captivated

inamorata: a female lover

AMBI/AMPHI: both, on both sides, around

ambidextrous: able to use both hands equally well

ambient: moving around freely; circulating

ambiguous: open to various interpretations

amphibian: any cold-blooded vertebrate, the larva of which is aquatic and the adult of which is terrestrial; a person or thing having a twofold nature

AMBL/AMBUL: to go, to walk

ambulance: a vehicle equipped for carrying sick people (from a phrase meaning "walking hospital")

ambulatory: of, pertaining to, or capable of walking

perambulator: one who makes a tour of inspection on foot

preamble: an introductory statement (originally: to walk in front)

ANIM: of the life, mind, soul, breath

animal: a living being

animosity: a feeling of ill will or enmity

equanimity: mental or emotional stability, especially under tension

magnanimous: generous in forgiving an insult or injury

unanimous: of one mind; in complete accord

ANNUI/ENNI: year

annals: a record of events, esp. a yearly record

anniversary: the yearly recurrence of the date of a past event

annual: of, for, or pertaining to a year; yearly

annuity: a specified income payable at stated intervals

perennial: lasting for an indefinite amount of time

ANT/ANTE: before

antebellum: before the war (especially the American Civil War)

antecedent: existing, being, or going before

antedate: precede in time

antediluvian: belonging to the period before the biblical flood; very old or old-fashioned

anterior: placed before

ANTHRO/ANDR: man, human

androgen: any substance that promotes masculine characteristics

androgynous: being both male and female

android: a robot; a mechanical man

anthropocentric: regarding humanity as the central fact of the universe

anthropology: the science that deals with the origins of humankind

misanthrope: one who hates humans or humanity

philanderer: one who carries on flirtations

ANTI: against, opposite

antibody: a protein naturally existing in blood serum that reacts to overcome the toxic effects of an antigen

antidote: a remedy for counteracting the effects of poison, disease, etc.

antipathy: aversion

antipodal: on the opposite side of the globe

antiseptic: free from germs; particularly clean or neat

APO: away

apocalypse: revelation; discovery; disclosure

apocryphal: of doubtful authorship or authenticity

apogee: the highest or most distant point

apology: an expression of one's regret or sorrow for having wronged another

apostasy: a total desertion of one's religion, principles, party, cause, etc.

apostle: one of the 12 disciples sent forth by Jesus to preach the Gospel

AQUA/AQUE: water

aquamarine: a bluish-green color

aquarium: a tank for keeping fish and other underwater creatures

aquatic: having to do with water

aqueduct: a channel for transporting water

subaqueous: underwater

ARCH/ARCHI/ARCHY: chief, principal, ruler

anarchy: a state or society without government or law

archenemy: chief enemy

architect: the devisor, maker, or planner of anything

monarchy: a government in which the supreme power is lodged in a sovereign

oligarchy: a state or society ruled by a select group

ARD: to burn

ardent: burning; fierce; passionate

ardor: flame; passion

arson: the crime of setting property on fire

AUTO: self

autocrat: an absolute ruler

automatic: self-moving or self-acting

autonomy: independence or freedom

B

BE: about, to make, to surround, to affect (often used to transform words into transitive verbs)

belie: to misrepresent; to contradict

belittle: to make small; to make something appear smaller

bemoan: to moan for; to lament

bewilder: to confuse completely (that is, to make one mentally wander)

BEL/BELL: beautiful

belle: a beautiful woman

embellish: to make beautiful; to ornament

BELL: war

antebellum: before the war (especially the American Civil War)

belligerent: warlike, given to waging war

rebel: a person who resists authority, control, or tradition

BEN/BENE: good

benediction: act of uttering a blessing

benefit: anything advantageous to a person or thing

benevolent: desiring to do good to others

benign: having a kindly disposition

BI/BIN: two

biennial: happening every two years

bilateral: pertaining to or affecting two or both sides

bilingual: able to speak one's native language and another with equal facility

binocular: involving two eyes

bipartisan: representing two parties

combination: the joining of two or more things into a whole

BON/BOUN: good, generous

bona fide: in good faith; without fraud

bonus: something given over and above what is due

bountiful: generous

BREV/BRID: short, small

abbreviate: to shorten

abridge: to shorten

brevet: an honorary promotion with no additional pay

breviloquent: laconic; concise in one's speech

brevity: shortness

brief: short

BURS: purse, money

bursar: treasurer

bursary: treasury

disburse: to pay

reimburse: to pay back

C

CAD/CID: to fall, to happen by chance

accident: happening by chance; unexpected

cascade: a waterfall descending over a steep surface

coincidence: a striking occurrence of two or more events at one time, apparently by chance

decadent: decaying; deteriorating

recidivist: one who repeatedly relapses, as into crime

CANT/CENT/CHANT: to sing

accent: prominence of a syllable in terms of pronunciation

chant: a song; singing

enchant: to subject to magical influence; bewitch

incantation: the chanting of words purporting to have magical power

incentive: that which incites action

recant: to withdraw or disavow a statement

CAP/CIP/CEPT: to take, to get

anticipate: to realize beforehand; foretaste or foresee

capture: to take by force or stratagem

emancipate: to free from restraint

percipient: having perception; discerning; discriminating

precept: a commandment or direction given as a rule of conduct

susceptible: capable of receiving, admitting, undergoing, or being affected by something

CAP/CAPIT/CIPIT: head, headlong

capital: the city or town that is the official seat of government

capitulate: to surrender unconditionally or on stipulated terms

caption: a heading or title

disciple: one who is a pupil of the doctrines of another

precipice: a cliff with a vertical face

precipitate: to hasten the occurrence of; to bring about prematurely

CARD/CORD/COUR: heart

cardiac: pertaining to the heart

concord: agreement; peace, amity

concordance: agreement, concord, harmony

discord: lack of harmony between persons or things

encourage: to inspire with spirit or confidence

CARN: flesh

carnage: the slaughter of a great number of people

carnival: a traveling amusement show

carnivorous: eating flesh

incarnation: a being invested with a bodily form

reincarnation: rebirth of a soul in a new body

CAST/CHAST: to cut

cast: to throw or hurl; fling

caste: a hereditary social group, limited to people of the same rank

castigate: to punish in order to correct

chaste: free from obscenity; decent

chastise: to discipline, esp. by corporal punishment

CAUS/CAUT: to burn

caustic: burning or corrosive

cauterize: to burn or deaden

cautery: an instrument used for branding; branding

holocaust: a burnt offering; complete destruction by fire or other means

CED/CEED/CESS: to go, to yield, to stop

accede: to yield to a demand; to enter office

antecedent: existing, being, or going before

cessation: a temporary or complete discontinuance

concede: to acknowledge as true, just, or proper; admit

incessant: without stop

predecessor: one who comes before another in an office, position, etc.

CELER: speed

accelerant: something used to speed up a process

accelerate: to increase in speed

celerity: speed; quickness

decelerate: to decrease in speed

CENT: hundred, hundredth

bicentennial: two-hundredth anniversary

cent: a hundredth of a dollar

centigrade: a temperature system with one hundred degrees between the freezing and boiling points of water

centimeter: one-hundredth of a meter

centipede: a creature with many legs

century: one hundred years

percent: in every hundred

CENTR: center

centrifuge: an apparatus that rotates at high speed and separates substances of different densities using centrifugal force

centrist: of or pertaining to moderate political or social ideas

concentrate: to bring to a common center; to converge, to direct toward one point

concentric: having a common center, as in circles or spheres

eccentric: off-center

CERN/CERT/CRET/CRIM/CRIT: to separate, to judge, to distinguish, to decide

ascertain: to make sure of; to determine

certitude: freedom from doubt

criterion: a standard of judgment or criticism

discreet: judicious in one's conduct of speech, esp. with regard to maintaining silence about something of a delicate nature

discrete: detached from others, separate

hypocrite: a person who pretends to have beliefs that she does not

CHROM: color

chromatic: having to do with color

chrome: a metallic element (chromium) used to make vivid colors or something plated with chromium

chromosome: genetic material that can be studied by coloring it with dyes

monochromatic: having only one color

CHRON: time

anachronism: something that is out-of-date or belonging to the wrong time

chronic: constant, habitual

chronology: the sequential order in which past events occurred

chronometer: a highly accurate clock or watch

synchronize: to occur at the same time or agree in time

CIRCU/CIRCUM: around

circuit: a line around an area; a racecourse; the path traveled by electrical current

circuitous: roundabout, indirect

circumference: the outer boundary of a circular area

circumspect: cautious; watching all sides

circumstances: the existing conditions or state of affairs surrounding and affecting an agent

CIS: to cut

exorcise: to seek to expel an evil spirit by ceremony

incision: a cut, gash, or notch

incisive: penetrating, cutting

precise: definitely stated or defined

scissors: cutting instrument for paper

CLA/CLO/CLU: to shut, to close

claustrophobia: an abnormal fear of enclosed places

cloister: a courtyard bordered with covered walks, esp. in a religious institution

conclude: to bring to an end; finish; to terminate

disclose: to make known, reveal, or uncover

exclusive: not admitting of something else; shutting out others

preclude: to prevent the presence, existence, or occurrence of

CLAIM/CLAM: to shout, to cry out

clamor: a loud uproar

disclaim: to deny interest in or connection with

exclaim: to cry out or speak suddenly and vehemently

proclaim: to announce or declare in an official way

reclaim: to claim or demand the return of a right or possession

CLI: to lean toward

climax: the most intense point in the development of something

decline: to cause to slope or incline downward

disinclination: aversion, distaste

proclivity: inclination, bias

recline: to lean back

CO/COL/COM/CON: with, together

coerce: to compel by force, intimidation, or authority

collaborate: to work with another, cooperate

collide: to strike one another with a forceful impact

commensurate: suitable in measure, proportionate

compatible: capable of existing together in harmony

conciliate: to placate, win over

connect: to bind or fasten together

COGN/CONN: to know

cognition: the process of knowing

incognito: with one's name or identity concealed

recognize: to identify as already known

CONTRA/CONTRO/COUNTER: against

contradict: to oppose; to speak against

contrary: opposed to; opposite

controversy: a disputation; a quarrel

counterfeit: fake; a false imitation

countermand: to retract an order

encounter: a meeting, often with an opponent

CORP/CORS: body

corporation: a company legally treated as an individual

corps: a body (an organized group) of troops

corpse: a dead body

corpulent: obese; having a lot of flesh

corset: a garment used to give shape and support to the body

incorporation: combining into a single body

COSM: order, universe, world

cosmetic: improving the appearance (making it look better ordered)

cosmic: relating to the universe

cosmology: a theory of the universe as a whole

cosmonaut: an astronaut; an explorer of outer space

cosmopolitan: worldly

cosmos: the universe; an orderly system; order

microcosm: a small system that reflects a larger whole

COUR/CUR: running, a course

concur: to accord in opinion; agree

courier: a messenger traveling in haste who bears news

curriculum: the regular course of study

cursive: handwriting in flowing strokes with the letters joined together

cursory: going rapidly over something; hasty; superficial

excursion: a short journey or trip

incursion: a hostile entrance into a place, esp. suddenly

recur: to happen again

CRE/CRESC/CRET: to grow

accretion: an increase by natural growth

accrue: to be added as a matter of periodic gain

creation: the act of producing or causing to exist

excrescence: an outgrowth

increase: to make greater in any respect

increment: something added or gained; an addition or increase

CRED: to believe, to trust

credentials: anything that provides the basis for belief

credit: trustworthiness

credo: any formula of belief

credulity: willingness to believe or trust too readily

incredible: unbelievable

CRYPT: hidden

apocryphal: of doubtful authorship or authenticity

crypt: a subterranean chamber or vault

cryptography: procedures of making and using secret writing

cryptology: the science of interpreting secret writings, codes, ciphers, and the like

CUB/CUMB: to lie down

cubicle: any small space or compartment that is partitioned off

incubate: to sit upon for the purpose of hatching

incumbent: holding an indicated position

recumbent: lying down; reclining; leaning

succumb: to give away to superior force; yield

CULP: fault, blame

culpable: deserving blame or censure

culprit: a person guilty of an offense

inculpate: to charge with fault

mea culpa: through my fault; my fault

D

DAC/DOC: to teach

didactic: intended for instruction

docile: easily managed or handled; tractable

doctor: someone licensed to practice medicine; a learned person

doctrine: a particular principle advocated, as of a government or religion

indoctrinate: to imbue a person with learning

DE: away, off, down, completely, reversal

decipher: to make out the meaning; to interpret

defame: to attack the good name or reputation of

deferential: respectful; to yield to judgment

defile: to make foul, dirty, or unclean

delineate: to trace the outline of; sketch or trace in outline

descend: to move from a higher to a lower place

DELE: to erase

delete: erase; blot out; remove

indelible: impossible to erase; lasting

DEM: people

democracy: government by the people

demographics: vital and social statistics of populations

endemic: peculiar to a particular people or locality

epidemic: affecting a large number of people at the same time and spreading from person to person

pandemic: general, universal

DEXT: right hand, right side, deft
ambidextrous: equally able to use both hands
dexter: on the right
dexterity: deftness; adroitness

DI: day
dial: a device for seeing the hour of the day; a clock face; rotatable discs or knobs used as a control input
diary: a record of one's days
dismal: gloomy (from "bad days")
diurnal: daily
meridian: a direct line from the North Pole to the South Pole; the highest point reached by the sun; noon
quotidian: everyday; ordinary

DI/DIA: in two, through, across
diagnose: to identify disease or fault from symptoms
dialogue: a conversation between two or more persons
diameter: a line going through a circle, dividing it in two
dichotomy: division into two parts, kinds, etc.

DI/DIF/DIS: away from, apart, reversal, not
diffuse: to pour out and spread, as in a fluid
dilate: to make wider or larger; to cause to expand
dilatory: inclined to delay or procrastinate
disperse: to drive or send off in various directions
disseminate: to scatter or spread widely; promulgate
dissipate: to scatter wastefully
dissuade: to deter by advice or persuasion

DIC/DICT/DIT: to say, to tell, to use words
dictionary: a book containing a selection of the words of a language
interdict: to forbid; prohibit
predict: to tell in advance
verdict: a judgment or decision

DIGN: worth
condign: well deserved; fitting; adequate
deign: to think fit or in accordance with one's dignity
dignitary: a person who holds a high rank or office
dignity: nobility or elevation of character; worthiness
disdain: to look upon or treat with contempt

DOG/DOX: opinion
dogma: a system of tenets, as of a church
orthodox: sound or correct in opinion or doctrine
paradox: an opinion or statement contrary to accepted opinion

DOL: to suffer, to pain, to grieve
condolence: expression of sympathy with one who is suffering
doleful: sorrowful, mournful
dolorous: full of pain or sorrow, grievous
indolence: a state of being lazy or slothful

DON/DOT/DOW: to give
anecdote: a short narrative about an interesting event
antidote: something that prevents or counteracts ill effects
donate: to present as a gift or contribution
endow: to provide with a permanent fund
pardon: kind indulgence, forgiveness

DORM: sleep
dormant: sleeping; inactive
dormitory: a place for sleeping; a residence hall

DORS: back
dorsal: having to do with the back
endorse: to sign on the back; to vouch for

DUB: doubt
dubiety: doubtfulness
dubious: doubtful
indubitable: unquestionable

DUC/DUCT: to lead
abduct: to carry off or lead away
conducive: contributive, helpful
conduct: personal behavior, way of acting
induce: to lead or move by influence
induct: to install in a position with formal ceremonies
produce: to bring into existence; give cause to

DULC: sweet
dulcet: sweet; pleasing
dulcified: sweetened; softened
dulcimer: a musical instrument

DUR: hard, lasting
dour: sullen, gloomy (originally: hard, obstinate)

durable: able to resist decay
duration: the length of time something exists
duress: compulsion by threat, coercion
endure: to hold out against; to sustain without yielding
obdurate: stubborn, resistant to persuasion

DYS: faulty, abnormal
dysfunctional: poorly functioning
dyslexia: an impairment of the ability to read due to a brain defect
dyspepsia: impaired digestion
dystrophy: faulty or inadequate nutrition or development

E

E/EX: out, out of, from, former, completely
efface: to rub or wipe out; surpass, eclipse
evade: to escape from, avoid
exclude: to shut out; to leave out
exonerate: to free or declare free from blame
expire: to breathe out; to breathe one's last; to end
extricate: to disentangle, release

EGO: self
ego: oneself; the part of oneself that is self-aware
egocentric: focused on oneself
egoism/egotism: selfishness; self-absorption

EM/EN: in, into
embrace: to clasp in the arms; to include or contain
enclose: to close in on all sides

EPI: upon
epidemic: affecting a large number of people at the same time and spreading from person to person
epidermis: the outer layer of the skin
epigram: a witty or pointed saying tersely expressed
epilogue: a concluding part added to a literary work
epithet: a word or phrase, used invectively as a term of abuse

EQU: equal, even
adequate: equal to the requirement or occasion
equation: the act of making equal
equidistant: equally distant
iniquity: gross injustice; wickedness

ERR: to wander
arrant: notorious; downright (originally: wandering)
err: to go astray in thought or belief, to be mistaken
erratic: deviating from the proper or usual course in conduct
error: a deviation from accuracy or correctness

ESCE: becoming
adolescent: between childhood and adulthood
convalescent: recovering from illness
incandescent: glowing with heat, shining
obsolescent: becoming obsolete
reminiscent: reminding or suggestive of

EU: good, well
eugenics: improvement of qualities of race by control of inherited characteristics
eulogy: speech or writing in praise or commendation
euphemism: pleasant-sounding term for something unpleasant
euphony: pleasantness of sound
euthanasia: killing a person painlessly, usually one who has an incurable, painful disease

EXTRA: outside, beyond
extract: to take out, obtain against a person's will
extradite: to hand over (person accused of crime) to state where crime was committed
extraordinary: beyond the ordinary
extrapolate: to estimate (unknown facts or values) from known data
extrasensory: derived by means other than known senses

F

FAB/FAM: to speak
affable: friendly, courteous
defame: to attack the good name of
fable: fictional tale, esp. legendary
famous: well known, celebrated
ineffable: too great for description in words; that which must not be uttered

FAC/FIC/FIG/FAIT/FEIT/FY: to do, to make
configuration: manner of arrangement, shape
counterfeit: imitation, forgery

deficient: incomplete or insufficient
effigy: sculpture or model of person
faction: small dissenting group within larger one, esp. in politics
factory: building for manufacture of goods
prolific: producing many offspring or much output
ratify: to confirm or accept by formal consent

FAL: to err, to deceive
default: to fail
fail: to be insufficient; to be unsuccessful; to die out
fallacy: a flawed argument
false: not true; erroneous; lying
faux pas: a false step; a social gaffe
infallible: incapable of being wrong or being deceived

FATU: foolish
fatuity: foolishness; stupidity
fatuous: foolish; stupid
infatuated: swept up in a fit of passion, impairing one's reason

FER: to bring, to carry, to bear
confer: to grant, bestow
offer: to present for acceptance, refusal, or consideration
proffer: to offer
proliferate: to reproduce; produce rapidly
referendum: a vote on a political question open to the entire electorate

FERV: to boil, to bubble
effervescent: with the quality of giving off bubbles of gas
fervid: ardent, intense
fervor: passion, zeal

FI/FID: faith, trust
affidavit: a written statement on oath
confide: to entrust with a secret
fidelity: faithfulness, loyalty
fiduciary: of a trust; held or given in trust
infidel: disbeliever in the supposed true religion

FIN: end
confine: to keep or restrict within certain limits; imprison
definitive: decisive, unconditional, final
final: at the end; coming last
infinite: boundless; endless
infinitesimal: infinitely or very small

FLAGR/FLAM: to burn
conflagration: a large, destructive fire
flagrant: blatant, scandalous
flambeau: a lighted torch
inflame: to set on fire

FLECT/FLEX: to bend, to turn
deflect: to bend or turn aside from a purpose
flexible: able to bend without breaking
genuflect: to bend knee, esp. in worship
inflect: to change or vary pitch of
reflect: to throw back

FLU/FLUX: to flow
confluence: merging into one
effluence: flowing out of (light, electricity, etc.)
fluctuation: something that varies, rising and falling
fluid: a substance, esp. gas or liquid, capable of flowing freely
mellifluous: pleasing, musical

FORE: before
foreshadow: be warning or indication of (future event)
foresight: care or provision for future
forestall: to prevent by advance action
forthright: straightforward, outspoken, decisive

FORT: chance
fortuitous: happening by luck
fortunate: lucky, auspicious
fortune: chance or luck in human affairs

FORT: strength
forte: strong point; something a person does well
fortify: to provide with fortifications; strengthen
fortissimo: very loud

FRA/FRAC/FRAG/FRING: to break
fractious: irritable, peevish
fracture: breakage, esp. of a bone
fragment: a part broken off
infringe: to break or violate (a law, etc.)
refractory: stubborn, unmanageable, rebellious

FUG: to flee, to fly
centrifugal: flying off from the center

fugitive: on the run; someone who flees

fugue: a musical composition in which subsequent parts imitate or pursue the first part; a psychological state in which one flies from one's own identity

refuge: a haven for those fleeing

refugee: a fleeing person who seeks refuge

subterfuge: a deception used to avoid a confrontation

FULG: to shine

effulgent: shining forth

refulgent: radiant; shining

FUM: smoke

fume: smoke; scented vapor; to emit smoke or vapors

fumigate: to treat with smoke or vapors

perfume: scents, from burning incense or other sources of fragrance

FUS: to pour

diffuse: to spread widely or thinly

fusillade: continuous discharge of firearms or outburst of criticism

infusion: the act of permeating or steeping; liquid extract so obtained

profuse: lavish, extravagant, copious

suffuse: to spread throughout or over from within

G

GEN: birth, creation, race, kind

carcinogenic: producing cancer

congenital: existing or as such from birth

gender: classification roughly corresponding to the two sexes and sexlessness

generous: giving or given freely

genetics: the study of heredity and variation among animals and plants

progeny: offspring, descendants

GNI/GNO: to know

agnostic: one who believes that the existence of God is not provable

diagnose: to identify disease or fault from symptoms

ignoramus: a person lacking knowledge, uninformed

ignore: to refuse to take notice of

prognosis: to forecast, especially of disease

GRAD/GRESS: to step

aggressive: given to hostile acts or feelings

degrade: to humiliate, dishonor, reduce to lower rank

digress: to depart from the main subject

egress: going out; way out

progress: forward movement

regress: to move backward, revert to an earlier state

GRAM/GRAPH: to write, to draw

diagram: a figure made by drawing lines; an illustration

epigram: a short poem; a pointed statement

grammar: a system of language and its rules

graph: a diagram used to convey mathematical information

graphite: mineral used for writing, as the "lead" in pencils

photograph: a picture, originally made by exposing chemically treated film to light

GRAT: pleasing

gracious: kindly, esp. to inferiors; merciful

grateful: thankful

gratuity: money given for good service

ingratiate: to bring oneself into favor

GREG: flock

aggregate: a number of things considered as a collective whole

congregate: to come together in a group

egregious: remarkably bad; standing out from the crowd

gregarious: sociable; enjoying spending time with others

segregate: to separate from the crowd

H

HAP: by chance

haphazard: at random

hapless: without luck

happen: occur (originally: to occur by chance)

happily: through good fortune

happy: pleased, as by good fortune

mishap: an unlucky accident

perhaps: a qualifier suggesting something might (or might not) take place

HEMI: half

hemisphere: half a sphere; half of the Earth

hemistich: half a line of poetry

HER/HES: to stick

adherent: able to adhere; believer or advocate of a particular thing

adhesive: tending to remain in memory; sticky; an adhesive substance

coherent: logically consistent; having waves in phase and of one wavelength

inherent: involved in the constitution or essential character of something

(H)ETERO: different, other

heterodox: different from acknowledged standard; holding unorthodox opinions or doctrines

heterogeneous: of other origin; not originating in the body

heterosexual: of or pertaining to sexual orientation toward members of the opposite sex; relating to different sexes

HOL: whole

catholic: universal

holocaust: a burnt offering; complete destruction by fire or other means

hologram: a sort of three-dimensional image

holograph: a document written entirely by the person whose name it's in

holistic: considering something as a unified whole

(H)OM: same

anomaly: deviation from the common rule

homeostasis: a relatively stable state of equilibrium

homogeneous: of the same or a similar kind of nature; of uniform structure of composition throughout

homonym: one of two or more words spelled and pronounced alike but different in meaning

homosexual: of, relating to, or exhibiting sexual desire toward a member of one's own sex

HUM: earth

exhume: unearth

humble: down-to-earth

humility: the state of being humble

HYPER: over, excessive

hyperactive: excessively active

hyperbole: purposeful exaggeration for effect

hyperglycemia: an abnormally high concentration of sugar in the blood

HYPO: under, beneath, less than

hypochondriac: one affected by extreme depression of mind or spirits, often centered on imaginary physical ailments

hypocritical: pretending to have beliefs one does not

hypodermic: relating to the parts beneath the skin

hypothesis: assumption subject to proof

I

ICON: image, idol

icon: a symbolic picture; a statue; something seen as representative of a culture or movement

iconic: being representative of a culture or movement

iconoclast: one who attacks established beliefs; one who tears down images

iconology: symbolism

IDIO: one's own

idiom: a language, dialect, or style of speaking particular to a people

idiosyncrasy: peculiarity of temperament; eccentricity

idiot: an utterly stupid person

IN/IM: not, without

(Often the *m* is dropped and the first letter to which *i* is prefixed is doubled.)

immoral: not moral; evil

impartial: not partial or biased; just

inactive: not active

indigent: deficient in what is requisite

indolence: showing a disposition to avoid exertion; slothful

innocuous: not harmful or injurious

IN/IM: in, into

(Often the *m* is dropped and the first letter to which *i* is prefixed is doubled.)

implicit: not expressly stated; implied

incarnate: given a bodily, esp. a human, form

indigenous: native; innate, natural

influx: the act of flowing in; inflow

intrinsic: belonging to a thing by its very nature

INTER: between, among

interim: a temporary or provisional arrangement; meantime

interloper: one who intrudes in the domain of others

intermittent: stopping or ceasing for a time

intersperse: to scatter here and there

interstate: connecting or jointly involving states

INTRA: inside, within

intramural: within a school; inside a city

intrastate: within a state

intravenous: inside the veins

IT/ITER: way, journey

ambition: strong desire to achieve (from "going around" for votes)

circuit: a line around an area; a racecourse; the path traveled by electrical current

itinerant: traveling

itinerary: travel plans

reiterate: to repeat

transit: traveling; means of transportation

J

JECT: to throw, to throw down

abject: utterly hopeless, humiliating, or wretched

conjecture: formation of opinion on incomplete information

dejected: sad, depressed

eject: to throw out, expel

inject: to place (quality, etc.) where needed in something

JOC: joke

jocose: given to joking; playful

jocular: in a joking manner; funny

jocund: merry; cheerful

joke: a witticism; a humorous anecdote; something funny

JOIN/JUG/JUNCT: to meet, to join

adjoin: to be next to and joined with

conjugal: related to marriage

conjunction: joining; occurring together; a connecting word

injunction: a command; an act of enjoining

junction: the act of joining; combining; a place where multiple paths join

junta: a group of military officers who join together to run a country; a council

rejoinder: to reply, retort

subjugate: to make subservient; to place under a yoke

JOUR: day

adjourn: to close a meeting; to put off further proceedings for another day

journal: a record of one's days

journey: a trip (originally: a day's travel)

JUD: to judge

adjudicate: to act as a judge

judiciary: a system of courts; members of a court system

judicious: having good judgment

prejudice: a previous or premature judgment; bias

JUR: law, to swear

abjure: to renounce on oath

adjure: to beg or command

jurisprudence: a system of law; knowledge of law

perjury: willful lying while on oath

JUV: young

juvenile: young; immature

juvenilia: writings or art produced in one's youth

rejuvenate: to refresh; to make young again

L

LANG/LING: tongue

bilingual: speaking two languages

language: a system of (usually spoken) communication

linguistics: the study of language

LAUD: praise, honor

cum laude: with honors

laudable: praiseworthy

laudatory: expressing praise

LAV/LAU/LU: to wash

ablution: act of cleansing

antediluvian: before the biblical flood; extremely old

deluge: a great flood of water

dilute: to make thinner or weaker by the addition of water

laundry: items to be, or that have been, washed

lavatory: a room with equipment for washing hands and face

LAX/LEAS/LES: loose

lax: loose; undisciplined

laxative: medicine or food that loosens the bowels

lease: to rent out (that is, to let something loose for others' use)

leash: a cord used to hold an animal while giving it some freedom to run loose

relax: loosen; be less strict; calm down

release: let go; set free

LEC/LEG/LEX: to read, to speak

dialect: a manner of speaking; a regional variety of a language

lectern: a reading desk

lecture: an instructional speech

legend: a story; a written explanation of a map or illustration

legible: readable

lesson: instruction (originally: part of a book or oral instruction to be studied and repeated to a teacher)

lexicographer: a writer of dictionaries

lexicon: a dictionary

LECT/LEG: to select, to choose

collect: to gather together or assemble

eclectic: selecting ideas, etc. from various sources

elect: to choose; to decide

predilection: preference, liking

select: to choose with care

LEV: to lift, to rise, light (weight)

alleviate: to make easier to endure, lessen

levee: an embankment against river flooding

levitate: to rise in the air or cause to rise

levity: humor, frivolity, gaiety

relevant: bearing on or pertinent to information at hand

relieve: to mitigate; to free from a burden

LI/LIG: to tie, to bind

ally: to unite; one in an alliance

league: an association; a group of nations, teams, etc. that have agreed to work for a common cause

liable: legally responsible; bound by law

liaison: a connection; one who serves to connect

lien: the right to hold a property due to an outstanding debt

ligament: a band holding bones together; a bond

ligature: a connection between two letters; a bond

oblige: to obligate; to make indebted or form personal bonds by doing a favor

rely: to depend upon (originally: to come together; to rally)

LIBER: free

deliver: to set free; to save; to hand over

liberal: generous; giving away freely

liberality: generosity

liberate: set free

libertine: one who follows one's own path, without regard for morals or other restrictions

liberty: freedom

livery: a uniform; an emblem indicating an owner or manufacturer (originally: an allowance of food or other provisions given to servants)

LITH: stone

acrolith: a statue with a stone head and limbs (but a wooden body)

lithography: a printing process that originally involved writing on a flat stone

lithology: the study of rocks and stones

lithotomy: an operation to remove stones from the body

megalith: a very big stone

monolith: a single block of stone, often shaped into a monument

LOC/LOG/LOQU: word, speech, thought

colloquial: of ordinary or familiar conversation

dialogue: a conversation, esp. in a literary work

elocution: art of clear and expressive speaking

eulogy: a speech or writing in praise of someone

grandiloquent: pompous or inflated in language

loquacious: talkative

prologue: introduction to a poem, play, etc.

LUC/LUM/LUS: light (brightness)

illuminate: to supply or brighten with light

illustrate: to make intelligible with examples or analogies
illustrious: highly distinguished
lackluster: lacking brilliance or radiance
lucid: easily understood, intelligible
luminous: bright, brilliant, glowing
translucent: permitting light to pass through

LUD/LUS: to play
allude: to refer casually or indirectly
delude: to mislead the mind or judgment of, deceive
elude: to avoid capture or escape defection by
illusion: something that deceives by producing a false impression of reality
ludicrous: ridiculous, laughable
prelude: a preliminary to an action, event, etc.

M

MACRO: great, long
macro: broad; large; a single computer command that executes a longer set of commands
macrobiotics: a system intended to prolong life
macrocephalous: having a large head
macrocosm: the universe; a large system that is reflected in at least one of its subsets
macroscopic: large enough to be visible to the naked eye

MAG/MAJ/MAX: big, great
magnanimous: generous in forgiving an insult or injury
magnate: a powerful or influential person
magnify: to increase the apparent size of
magnitude: greatness of size, extent, or dimensions
maxim: an expression of general truth or principle
maximum: the highest amount, value, or degree attained

MAL/MALE: bad, ill, evil, wrong
maladroit: clumsy; tactless
malady: a disorder or disease of the body
malapropism: humorous misuse of a word
malediction: a curse
malfeasance: misconduct or wrongdoing often committed by a public official
malfunction: failure to function properly
malicious: full of or showing malice
malign: to speak harmful untruths about, to slander

MAN/MANU: hand
emancipate: to free from bondage
manifest: readily perceived by the eye or the understanding
manual: operated by hand
manufacture: to make by hand or machinery

MAND/MEND: to command, to order, to entrust
command: to order; an order; control
commend: to give something over to the care of another; to praise
countermand: to retract an order
demand: to strongly ask for; to claim; to require
mandatory: commanded; required
recommend: to praise and suggest the use of; to advise
remand: to send back

MEDI: middle
immediate: nearest; having nothing in between
intermediate: in the middle
mean: average; in the middle
mediate: to serve as a go-between; to try to settle an argument
medieval: related to the Middle Ages
mediocre: neither good nor bad; so-so
medium: size between small and large; a substance or agency that things travel through (as, for example, light travels through air, and news is conveyed by television and newspapers)

MEGA: large, great
megalith: a very big stone
megalomania: a mental condition involving delusions of greatness; an obsession with doing great things
megalopolis: a very large city
megaphone: a device for magnifying the sound of one's voice
megaton: explosive power equal to 1,000 tons of T.N.T.

MICRO: very small
microbe: a very small organism
microcosm: a small system that reflects a larger whole

micron: a millionth of a meter

microorganism: a very small organism

microscope: a device that magnifies very small things for viewing

MIN: small

diminish: to lessen

diminution: the act or process of diminishing

miniature: a copy or model that represents something in greatly reduced size

minute: a unit of time equal to one-sixtieth of an hour

minutiae: small or trivial details

MIN: to project, to hang over

eminent: towering above others; projecting

imminent: about to occur; impending

preeminent: superior to or notable above all others

prominent: projecting outward

MIS: bad, wrong, to hate

misadventure: bad luck; an unlucky accident

misanthrope: one who hates people or humanity

misapply: to use something incorrectly

mischance: bad luck; an unlucky accident

mischief: bad or annoying behavior

misconstrue: to take something in a way that wasn't intended; to understand something incorrectly

misfit: somebody or something that doesn't fit in

MIS/MIT: to send

emissary: a messenger or agent sent to represent the interests of another

intermittent: stopping and starting at intervals

remission: a lessening of intensity or degree

remit: to send money

transmit: to send from one person, thing, or place to another

MISC: mixed

miscellaneous: made up of a variety of parts or ingredients

promiscuous: consisting of diverse and unrelated parts or individuals; indiscriminate

MOB/MOM/MOT/MOV: to move

automobile: a vehicle that moves under its own power; a motorized car

demote: to move downward in an organization

immovable: incapable of being moved; unyielding

locomotion: moving from place to place; the ability to do so

mob: the rabble; a disorderly group of people (from the Latin *mobile vulgus*, meaning "the fickle crowd")

mobile: movable

mobilize: to make ready for movement; to assemble

moment: an instant; importance

momentous: of great importance (originally: having the power to move)

momentum: the force driving a moving object to keep moving; a growing force

motion: movement

motive: a reason for action; what moves a person to do something

motor: a device that makes something move

mutiny: rebellion against authority, esp. by sailors

promote: to move to a higher rank in an organization

remove: to take away; to move away

MOLL: soft

emollient: something that softens or soothes (e.g., a lotion)

mild: gentle; kind

mollify: soothe; soften; calm

mollusk: a phylum of invertebrate animals—including octopuses, squids, oysters, clams, and slugs—with soft bodies

MON/MONO: one

monarchy: rule by a single person

monk: a man in a religious order living apart from society (originally: a religious hermit)

monochord: a musical instrument with a single string

monogram: a design combining multiple letters into one

monograph: a scholarly study of a single subject

monologue: a speech or other dramatic composition recited by one person

monomania: an obsession with a single subject

monotonous: boring; spoken using only one tone

MON/MONIT: to remind, to warn

admonish: to counsel against something; caution

monitor: one that admonishes, cautions, or reminds

monument: a structure, such as a building, tower, or sculpture, erected as a memorial

premonition: forewarning, presentiment

remonstrate: to say or plead in protect, objection, or reproof

summon: to call together; convene

MOR/MORT: death

immortal: not subject to death

morbid: susceptible to preoccupation with unwholesome matters

moribund: dying, decaying

MORPH: shape

amorphous: without definite form; lacking a specific shape

anthropomorphism: attribution of human characteristics to inanimate objects, animals, or natural phenomena

metamorphosis: a transformation, as by magic or sorcery

MULT: many

multiple: many, having many parts; a number containing some quantity of a smaller number without remainder

multiplex: having many parts; a movie theater or other building with many separate units

multiply: to increase; to become many

multitudinous: very many; containing very many; having very many forms

MUT: to change

commute: to substitute; exchange; interchange

immutable: unchangeable, invariable

mutation: the process of being changed

permutation: a complete change; transformation

transmute: to change from one form into another

N

NAT/NAS/NAI/GNA: birth

cognate: related by blood; having a common ancestor

naive: lacking worldliness and sophistication; artless

nascent: starting to develop

native: belonging to one by nature; inborn; innate

natural: present due to nature, not to artificial or man-made means

renaissance: rebirth, esp. referring to culture

NAU/NAV: ship, sailor

astronaut: one who travels in outer space

circumnavigate: to sail all the way around

cosmonaut: one who travels in outer space

nauseous: causing a squeamish feeling (originally: seasickness)

nautical: related to sailing or sailors

naval: related to the navy

nave: the central portion of a church (which resembles the shape of a ship)

navy: a military force consisting of ships and sailors

NIHIL: nothing, none

annihilate: wipe out; reduce to nothing

nihilism: denial of all moral beliefs; denial that existence has any meaning

NOC/NOX: harm

innocent: uncorrupted by evil, malice, or wrongdoing

innocuous: not harmful or injurious

noxious: injurious or harmful to health or morals

obnoxious: highly disagreeable or offensive

NOCT/NOX: night

equinox: one of two times in a year when day and night are equal in length

noctambulant: walking at night; sleepwalking

nocturnal: related to the night; active at night

nocturne: a dreamlike piece of music; a painting set at night

NOM: rule, order

astronomy: the scientific study of the universe beyond the Earth

autonomy: independence, self-governance

economy: the careful or thrifty use of resources, as of income, materials, or labor

gastronomy: the art or science of good eating

taxonomy: the science, laws, or principles of classification

NOM/NYM/NOUN/NOWN: name

acronym: a word formed from the initial letters of a name

anonymous: having an unknown or unacknowledged name

nomenclature: a system of names; systematic naming

nominal: existing in name only; negligible

nominate: to propose by name as a candidate

noun: a word that names a person, place, or thing

renown: fame; reputation

synonym: a word having a meaning similar to that of another word of the same language

NON: not

nonconformist: one who does not conform to a church or other societal institution

nonentity: something that doesn't exist; something that is unimportant

nonpareil: something with no equal

nonpartisan: not affiliated with a political party

NOUNC/NUNC: to announce

announce: to proclaim

pronounce: to articulate

renounce: to give up, especially by formal announcement

NOV/NEO/NOU: new

innovate: to begin or introduce something new

neologism: a newly coined word, phrase, or expression

neophyte: a beginner; a new convert; a new worker

neoplasm: a new growth in the body; a tumor

nouveau riche: one who has lately become rich

novice: a person new to any field or activity

renovate: to restore to an earlier condition

NULL: nothing

annul: to cancel; to make into nothing

nullify: to cancel; to make into nothing

nullity: the condition of being nothing

O

OB: toward, to, against, over

obese: extremely fat, corpulent

obfuscate: to render indistinct or dim; darken

oblique: having a slanting or sloping direction

obsequious: overly submissive

obstinate: stubbornly adhering to an idea, inflexible

obstreperous: noisily defiant, unruly

obstruct: to block or fill with obstacles

obtuse: not sharp, pointed, or acute in any form

OMNI: all

omnibus: an anthology of the works of one author or of writings on related subjects

omnipotent: all powerful

omnipresent: everywhere at one time

omniscient: having infinite knowledge

ONER: burden

exonerate: to free from blame (originally: to relieve of a burden)

onerous: burdensome; difficult

onus: a burden; a responsibility

OSS/OSTE: bone

ossify: to become bone; to harden; to become callous

ossuary: a place where bones are kept; a charnel house

osteopathy: a medical system based on the belief that many illnesses can be traced to issues in the skeletal system

P

PAC/PEAC: peace

appease: to bring peace to

pacifier: something or someone that eases the anger or agitation of

pacify: to ease the anger or agitation of

pact: a formal agreement, as between nations

PALP: to feel

palpable: capable of being felt; tangible

palpate: to feel; to examine by feeling

palpitate: to beat quickly, as the heart; to throb

PAN/PANT: all, everyone

pandemic: widespread, general, universal

panegyric: formal or elaborate praise at an assembly

panoply: a wide-ranging and impressive array or display

panorama: an unobstructed and wide view of an extensive area

pantheon: a public building containing tombs or memorials of the illustrious dead of a nation

PAR: equal

apartheid: any system or caste that separates people according to race, etc.

disparage: to belittle, speak disrespectfully about

disparate: essentially different

par: an equality in value or standing

parity: equally, as in amount, status, or character

PARA: next to, beside

parable: a short, allegorical story designed to illustrate a moral lesson or religious principle

paragon: a model of excellence

parallel: extending in the same direction

paranoid: suffering from a baseless distrust of others

parasite: an organism that lives on or within a plant or animal of another species, from which it obtains nutrients

parody: to imitate for purposes of satire

PAS/PAT/PATH: feeling, suffering, disease

compassion: a feeling of deep sympathy for someone struck by misfortune, accompanied by a desire to alleviate suffering

dispassionate: devoid of personal feeling or bias

empathy: the identification with the feelings or thoughts of others

impassive: showing or feeling no emotion

pathogenic: causing disease

sociopath: a person whose behavior is antisocial and who lacks a sense of moral responsibility

sympathy: harmony or agreement in feeling

PAU/PO/POV/PU: few, little, poor

impoverish: to deplete

paucity: smallness of quantity; scarcity; scantiness

pauper: a person without any personal means of support

poverty: the condition of being poor

puerile: childish, immature

pusillanimous: lacking courage or resolution

PEC: money

impecunious: having no money; penniless

peculation: embezzlement

pecuniary: relating to money

PED: child, education

encyclopedia: book or set of books containing articles on various topics, covering all branches of knowledge or of one particular subject

pedagogue: a teacher

pedant: one who displays learning ostentatiously

pediatrician: a doctor who primarily has children as patients

PED/POD: foot

antipodes: places that are diametrically opposite each other on the globe

expedite: to speed up the progress of

impede: to retard progress by means of obstacles or hindrances

pedal: a foot-operated lever or part used to control

pedestrian: a person who travels on foot

podium: a small platform for an orchestra conductor, speaker, etc.

PEL: to drive, to push

compel: to force; to command

dispel: to drive away; to disperse

expel: to drive out; to banish; to eject

impel: to force; to drive forward

propel: to drive forward

PEN/PUN: to pay, to compensate

penal: of or pertaining to punishment, as for crimes

penalty: a punishment imposed for a violation of law or rule

penance: a punishment undergone to express regret for a sin

penitent: contrite

punitive: serving for, concerned with, or inflicting punishment

PEN/PENE: almost

peninsula: a landmass that is mostly surrounded by water, making it almost an island

penultimate: second-to-last

penumbra: a shaded area between pure shadow and pure light

PEND/PENS: to hang, to weight, to pay

appendage: a limb or other subsidiary part that diverges from the central structure

appendix: supplementary material at the end of a text

compensate: to counterbalance, offset

depend: to rely; to place trust in

indispensable: absolutely necessary, essential, or requisite

stipend: a periodic payment; fixed or regular pay

PER: completely

perforate: to make a way through or into something

perfunctory: performed merely as routine duty

perplex: to cause to be puzzled or bewildered over what is not understood

persistent: lasting or enduring tenaciously

perspicacious: shrewd, astute

pertinacious: resolute, persistent

peruse: to read with thoroughness or care

PERI: around

perimeter: the border or outer boundary of a two-dimensional figure

peripatetic: walking or traveling about; itinerant

periscope: an optical instrument for seeing objects in an obstructed field of vision

PET/PIT: to go, to seek, to strive

appetite: a desire for food or drink

centripetal: moving toward the center

compete: to strive to outdo another

impetuous: characterized by sudden or rash action or emotion

petition: a formally drawn request soliciting some benefit

petulant: showing sudden irritation, esp. over some annoyance

PHIL: love

bibliophile: one who loves or collects books

philatelist: one who loves or collects postage stamps

philology: the study of literary texts to establish their authenticity and determine their meaning

philosopher: one who investigates the truths and principles of being, knowledge, or conduct (originally: lover of wisdom)

PHOB: fear

claustrophobia: fear of enclosed places

hydrophobia: fear of water, which is a symptom of rabies; rabies

phobia: fear; an irrational fear

xenophobia: fear of foreigners; hatred of foreigners

PHON: sound

euphony: the quality of sounding good

megaphone: a device for magnifying the sound of one's voice

phonetics: the study of the sounds used in speech

polyphony: the use of simultaneous melodic lines to produce harmonies in musical compositions

telephone: a device for transmitting sound at a distance

PHOTO: light

photograph: a picture, originally made by exposing chemically treated film to light

photon: a packet of light or other electromagnetic radiation

photosynthesis: a process by which plants create carbohydrates when under light

PLAC: to please

complacent: self-satisfied, unconcerned

complaisant: inclined or disposed to please

implacable: unable to be pleased

placebo: a substance with no pharmacological effect that acts to placate a patient who believes it to be a medicine

placid: pleasantly calm or peaceful

PLE/PLEN: to fill, full

complete: having all parts or elements

deplete: to decrease seriously or exhaust the supply of

implement: an instrument, tool, or utensil for accomplishing work

plenitude: fullness

plethora: excess, overabundance

replete: abundantly supplied

supplement: something added to supply a deficiency

PLEX/PLIC/PLY: to fold, twist, tangle, or bend

complex: composed of many interconnected parts

duplicity: deceitfulness in speech or conduct, double-dealing

implicate: to show to be involved, usually in an incriminating manner

implicit: not expressly stated, implied

replica: any close copy or reproduction

supplicate: to make humble and earnest entreaty

POLY: many

polyandry: the practice of having multiple husbands

polygamy: the practice of having multiple wives

polyglot: someone who speaks many languages

polygon: a figure with many sides

polytheism: belief in many gods

PON/POS/POUND: to put, to place

component: a constituent part, elemental ingredient

expose: to lay open to danger, attack, or harm

expound: to set forth in detail

juxtapose: to place close together or side by side

repository: a receptacle or place where things are deposited

PORT: to carry

deportment: conduct, behavior

disport: to divert or amuse oneself

export: to transmit abroad

import: to bring in from a foreign country

importune: to urge or press with excessive persistence

portable: easily carried

POST: behind, after

post facto: after the fact

posterior: situated at the rear

posterity: future generations

posthumous: after death

POT: to drink

potable: drinkable; safe to drink; a drink

potation: drinking; a drink

potion: a drinkable medicine, poison, or other concoction

PRE: before, in front

precarious: dependent on circumstances beyond one's control

precedent: an act that serves as an example for subsequent situations

precept: a commandment given as a rule of action or conduct

precocious: unusually advanced or mature in mental development or talent

premonition: a feeling of anticipation over a future event

presentiment: foreboding

PREHEND/PRISE: to take, to get, to seize

apprehend: to take into custody

comprise: to include or contain

enterprise: a project undertaken

reprehensible: deserving rebuke or censure

reprisals: retaliation against an enemy

surprise: to strike with an unexpected feeling of wonder or astonishment

PRI/PRIM: first

primary: first; most important

primal: original; most important

prime: first in quality; best

primeval: ancient; going back to the first age of the world

pristine: original; like new; unspoiled; pure

PRO: in front, before, much, for

problem: a difficult question (originally: one put before another for solution)

proceed: to go forward

profuse: spending or giving freely

prolific: highly fruitful

propound: to set forth for consideration

proselytize: to convert or attempt to recruit

provident: having or showing foresight

PROB: to prove, to test

approbation: praise, consideration

opprobrium: the disgrace incurred by shameful conduct

probe: to search or examine thoroughly

probity: honesty, high-mindedness

reprobate: a depraved or wicked person

PROP/PROX: near

approximate: very near; close to being accurate

proximate: nearby; coming just before or just after

proximity: nearness; distance

PROT/PROTO: first

protagonist: the main character in a play or story

protocol: diplomatic etiquette; a system of proper conduct; the original record of a treaty or other negotiation
prototype: the first version of an invention, on which later models are based
protozoan: belonging to a group of single-celled animals, which came before more complex animals

PSEUD/PSEUDO: false
pseudonym: a false name; a pen name
pseudopod: part of a single-celled organism that can be stuck out (like a foot) and used to move around
pseudoscience: false science; something believed to be based on the scientific method but that actually is not

PUG: to fight
impugn: to challenge as false
pugilist: a fighter or boxer
pugnacious: to quarrel or fight readily
repugnant: objectionable or offensive

PUNC/PUNG/POIGN: to point, to prick, to pierce
compunction: a feeling of uneasiness for doing wrong
expunge: to erase, eliminate completely
point: a sharp or tapering end
punctilious: strict or exact in the observance of formalities
puncture: the act of piercing
pungent: caustic or sharply expressive

PYR: fire
pyre: a bonfire, usually for burning a dead body
pyromania: an urge to start fires
pyrosis: heartburn
pyrotechnics: fireworks

Q

QUAD/QUAR/QUAT: four
quadrant: a quarter of a circle; a 90-degree arc
quadrille: a square dance involving four couples
quadruple: four times as many
quadruplets: four children born in one birth
quart: one fourth of a gallon
quaternary: the number four; the fourth in a series

QUE/QUIS: to seek
acquire: to come into possession of
conquest: the act gaining control by force
exquisite: of special beauty or charm
inquisitive: given to research, eager for knowledge
perquisite: a gratuity, tip
querulous: full of complaints
query: a question, inquiry

QUIE/QUIT: quiet, rest
acquiesce: to comply, give in
disquiet: lack of calm or peace
quiescence: the condition of being at rest, still, inactive
quiet: making little or no sound
tranquil: free from commotion or tumult

QUIN/QUINT: five
quinquennial: a five-year period; a fifth anniversary
quintessence: the essential part of something (originally: the "fifth essence," which was believed to permeate everything and be what stars and planets were made of)
quintuple: five times as many

R

RACI/RADI: root
deracinate: to uproot
eradicate: to uproot; to wipe out
radical: pertaining to roots; questioning everything, even basic beliefs; going to root causes; thorough
radish: a root vegetable

RAMI: branch
ramification: a branch; an offshoot; a collection of branches; a consequence
ramiform: branchlike

RE: back, again
recline: to lean back; to lie down
regain: to gain again; to take back
remain: to stay behind; to be left; to continue to be
reorganize: to organize again
request: to ask (originally: to seek again)

RECT: straight, right
correct: to set right
direct: to guide; to put straight
erect: upright; starting up straight

SEN: old

senate: the highest legislative body (from "council of elders")

senescent: getting old

senile: relating to old age; experiencing memory loss or other age-related mental impairments

sire: a title for a king; a father (originally: an important person, an old man)

SENS/SENT: to feel, to be aware

dissent: to differ in opinion, esp. from the majority

insensate: without feeling or sensitivity

presentiment: a feeling that something is about to happen

resent: to feel or show displeasure

sense: any of the faculties by which humans and animals perceive stimuli originating outside the body

sensory: of or pertaining to the senses or sensation

sentiment: an attitude or feeling toward something

sentinel: a person or thing that stands watch

SIN/SINU: bend, fold, curve

insinuate: to introduce in sneaky or winding ways

sinuous: moving in a bending or wavy manner

sinus: a curved or irregularly shaped cavity in the body, such as those related to the nostrils

SOL: alone

desolate: deserted; laid waste; left alone

isolate: to set apart from others

soliloquize: talk to oneself; talk onstage as if to oneself

solipsism: the belief that the only thing that really exists, or can really be known, is oneself

solitude: the state of being alone

SOL: to loosen, to free

absolution: forgiveness for wrongdoing

dissolute: indifferent to moral restraints

dissolution: the act or process of dissolving into parts or elements

dissolve: to make a solution of, as by mixing in a liquid

resolution: a formal expression of opinion or intention made

soluble: capable of being dissolved or liquefied

SOL: sun

parasol: an umbrella that protects from the sun

solar: related to the sun

solarium: a sunroom; a room with windows for taking in the sun

solstice: one of two days when the sun reaches its highest point at noon and seems to stand still

SOMN: sleep

insomnia: inability to sleep

somnambulist: a sleepwalker

somniferous: sleep-inducing

somniloquist: one who talks while asleep

somnolent: sleep-inducing; sleepy; drowsy

SOPH: wisdom

philosopher: one who studies logic, beauty, truth, etc.; one who seeks wisdom

sophism: a superficially appealing but fallacious argument

sophisticated: complex; worldly; experienced

SOURC/SURG/SURRECT: to rise

insurgent: rising up in revolution; rushing in

insurrection: rising up in armed rebellion

resurrection: coming back to life; rising again

source: where something comes from (such as spring water rising out of the ground)

surge: to rise up forcefully, as ocean waves

SPEC/SPIC: to look, to see

circumspect: watchful and discreet, cautious

conspicuous: easily seen or noticed; readily observable

perspective: one's mental view of facts, ideas, and their interrelationships

perspicacious: having keen mental perception and understanding

retrospective: contemplative of past situations

specious: deceptively attractive

spectrum: a broad range of related things that form a continuous series

speculation: the contemplation or consideration of some subject

SPIR: breath

aspire: to desire; to pant for (originally: to breathe on)

expire: to breathe out; to breathe one's last; to come to an end

spirit: the breath of life; the soul; an incorporeal supernatural being; an outlook; a lively quality

STA/STI: to stand, to be in place

apostasy: renunciation of an object of one's previous loyalty

constitute: to make up

destitute: without means of subsistence

obstinate: stubbornly adhering to a purpose, opinion, or course of action

stasis: the state of equilibrium or inactivity caused by opposing equal forces

static: of bodies or forces at rest or in equilibrium

STRICT/STRING/STRAN: to tighten, to bind

astringent: causing to tighten

constrain: to confine; to bind within certain limits

restriction: a limitation

strangle: to kill by suffocation, usually by tightening a cord or one's hand around the throat

SUA: sweet, pleasing, to urge

assuage: to make less severe, ease, relieve

dissuade: to deter; to advise against

persuade: to encourage; to convince

suave: smoothly agreeable or polite; sweet

SUB/SUP: below, under

subliminal: existing or operating below the threshold of consciousness

submissive: inclined or ready to submit

subsidiary: serving to assist or supplement

subterfuge: an artifice or expedient used to evade a rule

subtle: thin, tenuous, or rarefied

suppose: to put down as a hypothesis; to use as the underlying basis of an argument; to assume

SUMM: highest, total

consummate: highly qualified; complete; perfect

sum: total; amount of money

summary: concise statement of the total findings on a subject; comprehensive

summit: highest point

SUPER/SUR: over, above

supercilious: arrogant, haughty, condescending

superfluous: extra, more than necessary

superlative: the highest kind or order

supersede: to replace in power, as by another person or thing

surmount: to get over or across, to prevail

surpass: to go beyond in amount, extent, or degree

surveillance: a watch kept over someone or something

SYM/SYN: together

symbiosis: living together in a mutually beneficial relationship

symmetry: balanced proportions; having opposite parts that mirror one another

sympathy: affinity; feeling affected by what happens to another

symposium: a meeting at which ideas are discussed (originally: a party at which people drink together)

synonym: a word that means the same thing as another

synthesis: combining things to create a new whole

T

TAC/TIC: to be silent

reticent: disposed to be silent or not to speak freely

tacit: unspoken understanding

taciturn: uncommunicative

TACT/TAG/TAM/TANG: to touch

contact: to touch; to get in touch

contagious: able to spread by contact, as disease

contaminate: to corrupt, taint, or otherwise damage the integrity of something by contact or mixture

contiguous: directly touching; sharing a boundary

intact: untouched; whole

intangible: unable to be touched

tactile: pertaining to touch; touchable

TAIN/TEN/TENT/TIN: to hold

abstention: the act of refraining voluntarily

detain: to keep from proceeding

pertain: to have reference or relation

pertinacious: persistent, stubborn

sustenance: nourishment, means of livelihood

tenable: capable of being held, maintained, or defended

tenacious: holding fast

tenure: the holding or possessing of anything

TEND/TENS/TENT/TENU: to stretch, to thin

attenuate: to weaken or reduce in force

contentious: quarrelsome, disagreeable, belligerent

distend: to expand by stretching

extenuating: making less serious by offering excuses

tendentious: having a predisposition toward a point of view

tension: the act of stretching or straining

tentative: of the nature of, or done as a trial, attempt

TEST: to bear witness

attest: bear witness

contest: to dispute (from bringing a lawsuit by calling witnesses)

detest: to despise; to hate (originally: to curse something by calling upon God to witness it)

protest: a dissent; a declaration, esp. of disagreement

testament: a statement of a person's wishes for the disposal of his or her property after death; a will

testify: bear witness

THEO: god

apotheosis: glorification, glorified ideal

atheist: one who does not believe in a deity or divine system

theocracy: a form of government in which a deity is recognized as the supreme ruler

theology: the study of divine things and the divine faith

THERM: heat

thermal: relating to heat; retaining heat

thermometer: a device for measuring heat

thermonuclear: relating to a nuclear reaction that takes place at high temperatures

thermostat: a device for regulating heat

TIM: fear

intimidate: to strike fear into; to make fearful

timid: fearful; shy

TOR/TORQ/TORT: to twist

contort: to twist; to distort

distort: to pull out of shape, often by twisting; to twist or misrepresent facts

extort: to wring money, property, or services out of somebody using threats or force

torch: a portable flame used for light (perhaps derived from hemp twisted around sticks, then dipped in pitch)

torque: twisting force; a force that creates rotation

tort: a wrongful act (other than breach of contract) that legally entitles one to damages

torture: to inflict pain (including by twisting instruments like the rack or wheel)

TORP: stiff, numb

torpedo: a explosive weapon used to sink ships (originally: a fish—the electric ray—that could shock victims to numbness)

torpid: numbed; sluggish

torpor: numbness; listlessness; apathy

TOX: poison

antitoxin: an antibody that counteracts a given poison

intoxication: being poisoned; drunkenness

toxic: poisonous

TRACT: to drag, to pull, to draw

abstract: to draw or pull away, remove

attract: to draw either by physical force or by an appeal to emotions or senses

contract: a legally binding document

detract: to take away from, esp. a positive thing

protract: to prolong, draw out, extend

tractable: easily managed or controlled

tractor: a powerful vehicle used to pull farm machinery

TRANS: across, beyond

intransigent: refusing to agree or compromise

transaction: the act of carrying on or conduct to a conclusion or settlement

transcendent: going beyond ordinary limits

transgress: to violate a law, command, or moral code

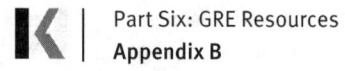

transition: a change from one way of being to another

transparent: easily seen through, recognized, or detected

U

ULT: last, beyond

penultimate: second-to-last

ulterior: beyond what is immediately present; future; beyond what is stated; hidden

ultimate: last; final

ultimatum: final offer; final terms

ultraviolet: beyond the violet end of the spectrum

UMBR: shadow

adumbrate: to foreshadow; to sketch; to overshadow

penumbra: a shaded area between pure shadow and pure light

somber: gloomy; darkened

umbrage: shade; shadow; displeasure; resentment

umbrella: a device providing shade from the sun or protection from rain

UN: not

unseen: not seen

unusual: not usual; exceptional; strange

UND: wave

abound: to be plentiful; to overflow (from water flowing in waves)

inundate: to flood

undulate: to move in a wavelike way

UNI/UN: one

reunion: a meeting that brings people back together

unanimous: of one mind; in complete accord

unicorn: a mythical animal with a single horn

uniform: of one kind; consistent

universe: all things considered as one whole

URB: city

suburb: a residential area just outside a city; an outlying area of a city

urban: relating to a city

urbane: polite; refined; polished (considered characteristic of those in cities)

urbanization: the process of an area becoming more like a city

US/UT: to use

abuse: to use wrongly or improperly

usage: a customary way of doing something

usurp: to seize and hold

utilitarian: efficient, functional, useful

V

VAIL/VAL: strength, use, worth

ambivalent: being caught between contradictory feelings of equal power or worth

avail: to have force; to be useful; to be of value

convalescent: recovering strength; healing

equivalent: of equal worth, strength, or use

evaluate: to determine the worth of

invalid: having no force or strength; void

valediction: a farewell (from wishing that someone be well; i.e., that someone have strength)

valid: having force; legally binding; effective; useful

value: worth

VEN/VENT: to come or to move toward

adventitious: accidental

contravene: to come into conflict with

convene: to assemble for some public purpose

intervene: to come between disputing factions, mediate

venturesome: showing a disposition to undertake risks

VER: truth

aver: to affirm, to declare to be true

veracious: habitually truthful

verdict: a judgment or decision

verisimilitude: the appearance or semblance of truth

verity: truthfulness

VERB: word

proverb: an adage; a byword; a short, commonly known saying

verbatim: exactly as stated; word-for-word

verbose: wordy

verbiage: excessive use of words; diction

VERD: green

verdant: green with vegetation; inexperienced

verdure: fresh, rich vegetation

VERS/VERT: to turn

aversion: dislike

avert: to turn away from

controversy: a public dispute involving a matter of opinion

diverse: of a different kind, form, character

extrovert: an outgoing person

inadvertent: unintentional

introvert: a person concerned primarily with inner thoughts and feelings

revert: to return to a former habit

VI: life

convivial: sociable

joie de vivre: joy of life (French expression)

viable: capable of living

vivacity: the quality of being lively, animated, spirited

vivid: strikingly bright or intense

VID/VIS: to see

adviser: one who gives counsel

evident: plain or clear to the sight or understanding

survey: to view in a general or comprehensive way

video: elements pertaining to the transmission or reception of an image

vista: a view or prospect

VIL: base, mean

revile: to criticize with harsh language

vile: loathsome, unpleasant

vilify: to slander, to defame

VIRU: poison

virulent: acrimonious; very bitter; very poisonous

viruliferous: containing a virus

virus: a submicroscopic agent that infects an organism and causes disease

VOC/VOK: call, word

advocate: to support or urge by argument

avocation: something one does in addition to a principle occupation

convoke: to call together

equivocate: to use ambiguous or unclear expressions

invoke: to call on a deity

vocabulary: the stock of words used by or known to a particular person or group

vocation: a particular occupation

vociferous: crying out noisily

VOL: wish

benevolent: characterized by or expressing goodwill

malevolent: characterized by or expressing bad will

volition: free choice, free will; act of choosing

voluntary: undertaken of one's own accord or by free choice

VOLU/VOLV: to roll, to turn

convolution: a twisting or folding

evolve: to develop naturally; literally, to unfold or unroll

revolt: to rebel; to turn against those in authority

revolve: to rotate; to turn around

voluble: easily turning; fluent; changeable

volume: a book (originally: a scroll); size or dimensions (originally: of a book)

VOR: to eat

carnivorous: meat-eating

omnivorous: eating or absorbing everything

voracious: having a great appetite

Common GRE Words in Context

The GRE tests the same kinds of words over and over again. Here you will find some common GRE words with their definitions in context to help you to remember them. If you see a word that's unfamiliar to you, take a moment to study the definition and, most importantly, reread the sentence with the word's definition in mind.

Remember: Learning vocabulary words in context is one of the best ways for your brain to retain the words' meanings. A broader vocabulary will serve you well on all four GRE Verbal question types and will also be extremely helpful in the Analytical Writing section.

A

ABATE: to reduce in amount, degree, or severity
As the hurricane's force ABATED, the winds dropped and the sea became calm.

ABSCOND: to leave secretly
The patron ABSCONDED from the restaurant without paying his bill by sneaking out the back door.

ABSTAIN: to choose not to do something
She ABSTAINED from choosing a mouthwatering dessert from the tray.

ABYSS: an extremely deep hole
The submarine dove into the ABYSS to chart the previously unseen depths.

ADULTERATE: to make impure
The chef made his ketchup last longer by ADULTERATING it with water.

ADVOCATE: to speak in favor of
The vegetarian ADVOCATED a diet containing no meat.

AESTHETIC: concerning the appreciation of beauty
Followers of the AESTHETIC Movement regarded the pursuit of beauty as the only true purpose of art.

AGGRANDIZE: to increase in power, influence, and reputation
The supervisor sought to AGGRANDIZE herself by claiming that the achievements of her staff were actually her own.

ALLEVIATE: to make more bearable
Taking aspirin helps to ALLEVIATE a headache.

AMALGAMATE: to combine; to mix together
Giant Industries AMALGAMATED with Mega Products to form Giant-Mega Products Incorporated.

AMBIGUOUS: doubtful or uncertain; able to be interpreted several ways
The directions she gave were so AMBIGUOUS that we disagreed on which way to turn.

AMELIORATE: to make better; to improve
The doctor was able to AMELIORATE the patient's suffering using painkillers.

ANACHRONISM: something out of place in time
The aged hippie used ANACHRONISTIC phrases, like "groovy" and "far out," that had not been popular for years.

ANALOGOUS: similar or alike in some way; equivalent to
In the Newtonian construct for explaining the existence of God, the universe is ANALOGOUS to a mechanical timepiece, the creation of a divinely intelligent "clockmaker."

ANOMALY: deviation from what is normal
Albino animals may display too great an ANOMALY in their coloring to attract normally colored mates.

ANTAGONIZE: to annoy or provoke to anger
The child discovered that he could ANTAGONIZE the cat by pulling its tail.

ANTIPATHY: extreme dislike
The ANTIPATHY between the French and the English regularly erupted into open warfare.

APATHY: lack of interest or emotion
The APATHY of voters is so great that less than half the people who are eligible to vote actually bother to do so.

ARBITRATE: to judge a dispute between two opposing parties
Since the couple could not come to an agreement, a judge was forced to ARBITRATE their divorce proceedings.

ARCHAIC: ancient, old-fashioned
Her ARCHAIC Commodore computer could not run the latest software.

ARDOR: intense and passionate feeling
Bishop's ARDOR for the landscape was evident when he passionately described the beauty of the scenic Hudson Valley.

ARTICULATE: able to speak clearly and expressively
She is such an ARTICULATE defender of labor that unions are among her strongest supporters.

ASSUAGE: to make something unpleasant less severe
Serena used aspirin to ASSUAGE her pounding headache.

ATTENUATE: to reduce in force or degree; to weaken
The Bill of Rights ATTENUATED the traditional power of governments to change laws at will.

AUDACIOUS: fearless and daring
Her AUDACIOUS nature allowed her to fulfill her dream of skydiving.

AUSTERE: severe or stern in appearance; undecorated
The lack of decoration makes military barracks seem AUSTERE to the civilian eye.

B

BANAL: predictable, clichéd, boring
He used BANAL phrases like "have a nice day" and "another day, another dollar."

BOLSTER: to support; to prop up
The presence of giant footprints BOLSTERED the argument that Sasquatch was in the area.

BOMBASTIC: pompous in speech and manner
The ranting of the radio talk-show host was mostly BOMBASTIC; his boasting and outrageous claims had no basis in fact.

C

CACOPHONY: harsh, jarring noise
The junior high orchestra created an almost unbearable CACOPHONY as they tried to tune their instruments.

CANDID: impartial and honest in speech
The observations of a child can be charming since they are CANDID and unpretentious.

CAPRICIOUS: changing one's mind quickly and often
Queen Elizabeth I was quite CAPRICIOUS; her courtiers could never be sure which of their number would catch her fancy.

CASTIGATE: to punish or criticize harshly
Many Americans are amazed at how harshly the authorities in Singapore CASTIGATE perpetrators of what would be considered minor crimes in the United States.

CATALYST: something that brings about a change in something else
The imposition of harsh taxes was the CATALYST that finally brought on the revolution.

CAUSTIC: biting in wit
Dorothy Parker gained her reputation for CAUSTIC wit from her cutting, yet clever, insults.

CHAOS: great disorder or confusion
In many religious traditions, God created an ordered universe from CHAOS.

CHAUVINIST: someone prejudiced in favor of a group to which he or she belongs
The attitude that men are inherently superior to women and therefore must be obeyed is common among male CHAUVINISTS.

CHICANERY: deception by means of craft or guile
Dishonest used car salespeople often use CHICANERY to sell their beat-up old cars.

COGENT: convincing and well reasoned
Swayed by the COGENT argument of the defense, the jury had no choice but to acquit the defendant.

CONDONE: to overlook, pardon, or disregard
Some theorists believe that failing to prosecute minor crimes is the same as CONDONING an air of lawlessness.

CONVOLUTED: intricate and complicated
Although many people bought *A Brief History of Time,* few could follow its CONVOLUTED ideas and theories.

CORROBORATE: to provide supporting evidence
Fingerprints CORROBORATED the witness's testimony that he saw the defendant in the victim's apartment.

CREDULOUS: too trusting; gullible
Although some four-year-olds believe in the Easter Bunny, only the most CREDULOUS nine-year-olds still believe in him.

CRESCENDO: steadily increasing volume or force
The CRESCENDO of tension became unbearable as Evel Knievel prepared to jump his motorcycle over the school buses.

D

DECORUM: appropriateness of behavior or conduct; propriety
The countess complained that the vulgar peasants lacked the DECORUM appropriate for a visit to the palace.

DEFERENCE: respect, courtesy
The respectful young law clerk treated the Supreme Court justice with the utmost DEFERENCE.

DERIDE: to speak of or treat with contempt; to mock
The awkward child was often DERIDED by his "cooler" peers.

DESICCATE: to dry out thoroughly
After a few weeks of lying on the desert's baking sands, the cow's carcass became completely DESICCATED.

DESULTORY: jumping from one thing to another; disconnected
Diane had a DESULTORY academic record; she had changed majors 12 times in three years.

DIATRIBE: an abusive, condemnatory speech
The trucker bellowed a DIATRIBE at the driver who had cut him off.

DIFFIDENT: lacking self-confidence
Steve's DIFFIDENT manner during the job interview stemmed from his nervous nature and lack of experience in the field.

DILATE: to make larger; to expand
When you enter a darkened room, the pupils of your eyes DILATE to let in more light.

DILATORY: intended to delay
The congressman used DILATORY measures to delay the passage of the bill.

DILETTANTE: someone with an amateurish and superficial interest in a topic
Jerry's friends were such DILETTANTES that they seemed to have new jobs and hobbies every week.

DIRGE: a funeral hymn or mournful speech
Melville wrote the poem "A DIRGE for James McPherson" for the funeral of a Union general who was killed in 1864.

DISABUSE: to set right; to free from error
Galileo's observations DISABUSED scholars of the notion that the Sun revolved around the Earth.

DISCERN: to perceive; to recognize
It is easy to DISCERN the difference between butter and butter-flavored topping.

DISPARATE: fundamentally different; entirely unlike
Although the twins appear to be identical physically, their personalities are DISPARATE.

DISSEMBLE: to present a false appearance; to disguise one's real intentions or character
The villain could DISSEMBLE to the police no longer—he admitted the deed and tore up the floor to reveal the body of the old man.

DISSONANCE: a harsh and disagreeable combination, often of sounds
Cognitive DISSONANCE is the inner conflict produced when long-standing beliefs are contradicted by new evidence.

DOGMA: a firmly held opinion, often a religious belief
Linus's central DOGMA was that children who believed in the Great Pumpkin would be rewarded.

DOGMATIC: dictatorial in one's opinions
The dictator was DOGMATIC—he, and only he, was right.

DUPE: to deceive; a person who is easily deceived
Bugs Bunny was able to DUPE Elmer Fudd by dressing up as a lady rabbit.

E

ECLECTIC: selecting from or made up from a variety of sources
Budapest's architecture is an ECLECTIC mix of Eastern and Western styles.

EFFICACY: effectiveness
The EFFICACY of penicillin was unsurpassed when it was first introduced; the drug completely eliminated almost all bacterial infections for which it was administered.

ELEGY: a sorrowful poem or speech
Although Thomas Gray's "ELEGY Written in a Country Churchyard" is about death and loss, it urges its readers to endure this life and to trust in spirituality.

ELOQUENT: persuasive and moving, especially in speech
The Gettysburg Address is moving not only because of its lofty sentiments but also because of its ELOQUENT words.

EMULATE: to copy; to try to equal or excel
The graduate student sought to EMULATE his professor in every way, copying not only how she taught but also how she conducted herself outside of class.

ENERVATE: to reduce in strength
The guerrillas hoped that a series of surprise attacks would ENERVATE the regular army.

ENGENDER: to produce, cause, or bring about
His fear and hatred of clowns was ENGENDERED when he witnessed the death of his father at the hands of a clown.

ENIGMA: a puzzle; a mystery
Speaking in riddles and dressed in old robes, the artist gained a reputation as something of an ENIGMA.

ENUMERATE: to count, list, or itemize
Moses returned from the mountain with tablets on which the commandments were ENUMERATED.

EPHEMERAL: lasting a short time
The lives of mayflies seem EPHEMERAL to us, since the flies' average life span is a matter of hours.

EQUIVOCATE: to use expressions of double meaning in order to mislead
When faced with criticism of her policies, the politician EQUIVOCATED and left all parties thinking she agreed with them.

ERRATIC: wandering and unpredictable
The plot seemed predictable until it suddenly took a series of ERRATIC turns that surprised the audience.

ERUDITE: learned, scholarly, bookish
The annual meeting of philosophy professors was a gathering of the most ERUDITE, well-published individuals in the field.

ESOTERIC: known or understood by only a few
Only a handful of experts are knowledgeable about the ESOTERIC world of particle physics.

ESTIMABLE: admirable
Most people consider it ESTIMABLE that Mother Teresa spent her life helping the poor of India.

EULOGY: speech in praise of someone
His best friend gave the EULOGY, outlining his many achievements and talents.

EUPHEMISM: use of an inoffensive word or phrase in place of a more distasteful one
The funeral director preferred to use the EUPHEMISM "sleeping" instead of the word "dead."

EXACERBATE: to make worse
It is unwise to take aspirin to try to relieve heartburn; instead of providing relief, the drug will only EXACERBATE the problem.

EXCULPATE: to clear from blame; prove innocent
The adversarial legal system is intended to convict those who are guilty and to EXCULPATE those who are innocent.

EXIGENT: urgent; requiring immediate action
The patient was losing blood so rapidly that it was EXIGENT to stop the source of the bleeding.

EXONERATE: to clear of blame
The fugitive was EXONERATED when another criminal confessed to committing the crime.

EXPLICIT: clearly stated or shown; forthright in expression
The owners of the house left a list of EXPLICIT instructions detailing their house sitter's duties, including a schedule for watering the house plants.

F

FANATICAL: acting excessively enthusiastic; filled with extreme, unquestioned devotion
The stormtroopers were FANATICAL in their devotion to the emperor, readily sacrificing their lives for him.

FAWN: to grovel
The understudy FAWNED over the director in hopes of being cast in the part on a permanent basis.

FERVID: intensely emotional; feverish
The fans of Maria Callas were unusually FERVID, doing anything to catch a glimpse of the great opera singer.

FLORID: excessively decorated or embellished
The palace had been decorated in a FLORID style; every surface had been carved and gilded.

FOMENT: to arouse or incite
The protesters tried to FOMENT feeling against the war through their speeches and demonstrations.

FRUGALITY: a tendency to be thrifty or cheap
Scrooge McDuck's FRUGALITY was so great that he accumulated enough wealth to fill a giant storehouse with money.

G

GARRULOUS: tending to talk a lot
The GARRULOUS parakeet distracted its owner with its continuous talking.

GREGARIOUS: outgoing, sociable
She was so GREGARIOUS that when she found herself alone, she felt quite sad.

GUILE: deceit or trickery

Since he was not fast enough to catch the roadrunner on foot, the coyote resorted to GUILE in an effort to trap his enemy.

GULLIBLE: easily deceived

The con man pretended to be a bank officer so as to fool GULLIBLE bank customers into giving him their account information.

H

HOMOGENEOUS (or HOMOGENOUS): of a similar kind

The class was fairly HOMOGENEOUS, since almost all of the students were senior journalism majors.

I

ICONOCLAST: one who opposes established beliefs, customs, and institutions

His lack of regard for traditional beliefs soon established him as an ICONOCLAST.

IMPERTURBABLE: not capable of being disturbed

The counselor had so much experience dealing with distraught children that she seemed IMPERTURBABLE, even when faced with the wildest tantrums.

IMPERVIOUS: impossible to penetrate; incapable of being affected

A good raincoat will be IMPERVIOUS to moisture.

IMPETUOUS: quick to act without thinking

It is not good for an investment broker to be IMPETUOUS, since much thought should be given to all the possible options.

IMPLACABLE: unable to be calmed down or made peaceful

His rage at the betrayal was so great that he remained IMPLACABLE for weeks.

INCHOATE: not fully formed; disorganized

The ideas expressed in Nietzsche's mature work also appear in an INCHOATE form in his earliest writing.

INGENUOUS: showing innocence or childlike simplicity

She was so INGENUOUS that her friends feared that her innocence and trustfulness would be exploited when she visited the big city.

INIMICAL: hostile, unfriendly

Even though the children had grown up together, they were INIMICAL to each other at school.

INNOCUOUS: harmless

Some snakes are poisonous, but most species are INNOCUOUS and pose no danger to humans.

INSIPID: lacking interest or flavor

The critic claimed that the painting was INSIPID, containing no interesting qualities at all.

INTRANSIGENT: uncompromising; refusing to be reconciled

The professor was INTRANSIGENT on the deadline, insisting that everyone turn the assignment in at the same time.

INUNDATE: to overwhelm; to cover with water

The tidal wave INUNDATED Atlantis, which was lost beneath the water.

IRASCIBLE: easily made angry

Attila the Hun's IRASCIBLE and violent nature made all who dealt with him fear for their lives.

L

LACONIC: using few words

She was a LACONIC poet who built her reputation on using words as sparingly as possible.

LAMENT: to express sorrow; to grieve

The children continued to LAMENT the death of the goldfish weeks after its demise.

LAUD: to give praise; to glorify

Parades and fireworks were staged to LAUD the success of the rebels.

LAVISH: to give unsparingly (v.); extremely generous or extravagant (adj.)

She LAVISHED the puppy with so many treats that it soon became overweight and spoiled.

LETHARGIC: acting in an indifferent or slow, sluggish manner

The clerk was so LETHARGIC that, even when the store was slow, he always had a long line in front of him.

LOQUACIOUS: talkative

She was naturally LOQUACIOUS, which was a problem in situations in which listening was more important than talking.

LUCID: clear and easily understood
The explanations were written in a simple and LUCID manner so that students were immediately able to apply what they learned.

LUMINOUS: bright, brilliant, glowing
The park was bathed in LUMINOUS sunshine, which warmed the bodies and the souls of the visitors.

M

MALINGER: to evade responsibility by pretending to be ill
A common way to avoid the draft was by MALINGERING—pretending to be mentally or physically ill so as to avoid being taken by the Army.

MALLEABLE: capable of being shaped
Gold is the most MALLEABLE of precious metals; it can easily be formed into almost any shape.

METAPHOR: a figure of speech comparing two different things; a symbol
The METAPHOR "a sea of troubles" suggests a lot of troubles by comparing their number to the vastness of the sea.

METICULOUS: extremely careful about details
To find all the clues at the crime scene, the investigators METICULOUSLY examined every inch of the area.

MISANTHROPE: a person who dislikes others
The character Scrooge in *A Christmas Carol* is such a MISANTHROPE that even the sight of children singing makes him angry.

MITIGATE: to soften; to lessen
A judge may MITIGATE a sentence if she decides that a person committed a crime out of need.

MOLLIFY: to calm or make less severe
Their argument was so intense that it was difficult to believe any compromise would MOLLIFY them.

MONOTONY: lack of variation
The MONOTONY of the sound of the dripping faucet almost drove the research assistant crazy.

N

NAIVE: lacking sophistication or experience
Having never traveled before, the elementary school students were more NAIVE than their high school counterparts on the field trip.

O

OBDURATE: hardened in feeling; resistant to persuasion
The president was completely OBDURATE on the issue, and no amount of persuasion would change his mind.

OBSEQUIOUS: overly submissive and eager to please
The OBSEQUIOUS new associate made sure to compliment her supervisor's tie and agree with him on every issue.

OBSTINATE: stubborn, unyielding
The OBSTINATE child could not be made to eat any food that he disliked.

OBVIATE: to prevent; to make unnecessary
The river was shallow enough to wade across at many points, which OBVIATED the need for a bridge.

OCCLUDE: to stop up; to prevent the passage of
A shadow is thrown across the earth's surface during a solar eclipse, when the light from the sun is OCCLUDED by the moon.

ONEROUS: troublesome and oppressive; burdensome
The assignment was so extensive and difficult to manage that it proved ONEROUS to the team in charge of it.

OPAQUE: impossible to see through; preventing the passage of light
The heavy buildup of dirt and grime on the windows almost made them OPAQUE.

OPPROBRIUM: public disgrace
After the scheme to embezzle the elderly was made public, the treasurer resigned in utter OPPROBRIUM.

OSTENTATION: excessive showiness
The OSTENTATION of the Sun King's court is evident in the lavish decoration and luxuriousness of his palace at Versailles.

P

PARADOX: a contradiction or dilemma
It is a PARADOX that those most in need of medical attention are often those least able to obtain it.

PARAGON: model of excellence or perfection
She is the PARAGON of what a judge should be: honest, intelligent, hardworking, and just.

PEDANT: someone who shows off learning
The graduate instructor's tedious and excessive commentary on the subject soon gained her a reputation as a PEDANT.

PERFIDIOUS: willing to betray one's trust
The actress's PERFIDIOUS companion revealed all of her intimate secrets to the gossip columnist.

PERFUNCTORY: done in a routine way; indifferent
The machinelike bank teller processed the transaction and gave the waiting customer a PERFUNCTORY smile.

PERMEATE: to penetrate
This miraculous new cleaning fluid is able to PERMEATE stains and dissolve them in minutes!

PHILANTHROPY: charity; a desire or effort to promote goodness
New York's Metropolitan Museum of Art owes much of its collection to the PHILANTHROPY of private collectors who willed their estates to the museum.

PLACATE: to soothe or pacify
The burglar tried to PLACATE the snarling dog by saying "Nice doggy," and offering it a treat.

PLASTIC: able to be molded, altered, or bent
The new material was very PLASTIC and could be formed into products of vastly different shapes.

PLETHORA: excess
Assuming that more was better, the defendant offered the judge a PLETHORA of excuses.

PRAGMATIC: practical as opposed to idealistic
While daydreaming gamblers think they can get rich by frequenting casinos, PRAGMATIC gamblers realize that the odds are heavily stacked against them.

PRECIPITATE: to throw violently or bring about abruptly; lacking deliberation
Upon learning that the couple married after knowing each other only two months, friends and family members expected such a PRECIPITATE marriage to end in divorce.

PREVARICATE: to lie or deviate from the truth
Rather than admit that he had overslept again, the employee PREVARICATED and claimed that heavy traffic had prevented him from arriving at work on time.

PRISTINE: fresh and clean; uncorrupted
Since concerted measures had been taken to prevent looting, the archeological site was still PRISTINE when researchers arrived.

PRODIGAL: lavish, wasteful
The PRODIGAL son quickly wasted all of his inheritance on a lavish lifestyle devoted to pleasure.

PROLIFERATE: to increase in number quickly
Although she only kept two guinea pigs initially, they PROLIFERATED to such an extent that she soon had dozens.

PROPITIATE: to conciliate; to appease
The management PROPITIATED the irate union by agreeing to raise wages for its members.

PROPRIETY: correct behavior; obedience to rules and customs
The aristocracy maintained a high level of PROPRIETY, adhering to even the most minor social rules.

PRUDENCE: wisdom, caution, or restraint
The college student exhibited PRUDENCE by obtaining practical experience along with her studies, which greatly strengthened her résumé.

PUNGENT: sharp and irritating to the senses
The smoke from the burning tires was extremely PUNGENT.

Q

QUIESCENT: motionless
Many animals are QUIESCENT over the winter months, minimizing activity in order to conserve energy.

R

RAREFY: to make thinner or sparser
Since the atmosphere RAREFIES as altitudes increase, the air at the top of very tall mountains is too thin to breathe.

REPUDIATE: to reject the validity of
The old woman's claim that she was Russian royalty was REPUDIATED when DNA tests showed she was of no relation to them.

RETICENT: silent, reserved
Physically small and RETICENT in her speech, Joan Didion often went unnoticed by those upon whom she was reporting.

RHETORIC: effective writing or speaking
Lincoln's talent for RHETORIC was evident in his beautifully expressed Gettysburg Address.

S

SATIATE: to satisfy fully or overindulge
His desire for power was so great that nothing less than complete control of the country could SATIATE it.

SOPORIFIC: causing sleep or lethargy
The movie proved to be so SOPORIFIC that soon loud snores were heard throughout the theater.

SPECIOUS: deceptively attractive; seemingly plausible but fallacious
The student's SPECIOUS excuse for being late sounded legitimate but was proved otherwise when her teacher called her home.

STIGMA: a mark of shame or discredit
In *The Scarlet Letter*, Hester Prynne was required to wear the letter *A* on her clothes as a public STIGMA for her adultery.

STOLID: unemotional; lacking sensitivity
The prisoner appeared STOLID and unaffected by the judge's harsh sentence.

SUBLIME: lofty or grand
The music was so SUBLIME that it transformed the rude surroundings into a special place.

T

TACIT: done without using words
Although not a word had been said, everyone in the room knew that a TACIT agreement had been made about which course of action to take.

TACITURN: silent, not talkative
The clerk's TACITURN nature earned him the nickname "Silent Bob."

TIRADE: long, harsh speech or verbal attack
Observers were shocked at the manager's TIRADE over such a minor mistake.

TORPOR: extreme mental and physical sluggishness
After surgery, the patient experienced TORPOR until the anesthesia wore off.

TRANSITORY: temporary, lasting a brief time
The reporter lived a TRANSITORY life, staying in one place only long enough to cover the current story.

V

VACILLATE: to sway physically; to be indecisive
The customer held up the line as he VACILLATED between ordering chocolate chip or rocky road ice cream.

VENERATE: to respect deeply
In a traditional Confucian society, the young VENERATE their elders, deferring to the elders' wisdom and experience.

VERACITY: truthfulness; accuracy
She had a reputation for VERACITY, so everyone trusted her description of events.

VERBOSE: wordy
The professor's answer was so VERBOSE that his student forgot what the original question had been.

VEX: to annoy
The old man who loved his peace and quiet was VEXED by his neighbor's loud music.

VOLATILE: easily aroused or changeable; lively or explosive
His VOLATILE personality made it difficult to predict his reaction to anything.

W

WAVER: to fluctuate between choices
If you WAVER too long before making a decision about which testing site to register for, you may not get your first choice.

WHIMSICAL: acting in a fanciful or capricious manner; unpredictable
The ballet was WHIMSICAL, delighting the children with its imaginative characters and unpredictable sets.

Z

ZEAL: passion, excitement
She brought her typical ZEAL to the project, sparking enthusiasm in the other team members.

COMMONLY CONFUSED WORDS

ALREADY: by this or that time, previously
He already completed his work.

ALL READY: completely prepared
The students were all ready to take their exam.

ALTOGETHER: entirely, completely
I am altogether certain that I turned in my homework.

ALL TOGETHER: in the same place
She kept the figurines all together on her mantle.

CAPITAL: a city containing the seat of government; the wealth or funds owned by a business or individual; resources
Atlanta is the capital of Georgia.
The company's capital gains have diminished in recent years.

CAPITOL: the building in which a legislative body meets
Our trip included a visit to the Capitol building in Washington, D.C.

COARSE: rough, not smooth; lacking refinement
The truck's large wheels enabled it to navigate the coarse, rough terrain.
His coarse language prevented him from getting hired for the job.

COURSE: path, series of classes or studies
James's favorite course is biology.
The doctor suggested that Amy rest and let the disease run its course.

HERE: in this location
George Washington used to live here.

HEAR: to listen to or to perceive by the ear
Did you hear the question?

ITS: a personal pronoun that shows possession
Please put the book back in its place.

IT'S: the contraction of "it is" or "it has"
It's snowing outside.
It's been too long.

LEAD: to act as a leader, to go first, or to take a superior position
The guide will lead us through the forest.

LED: past tense of "lead"
The guide led us through the forest.

LEAD: a metal
It is dangerous to inhale fumes from paint containing lead.

LOOSE: free, to set free, not tight
She always wears loose clothing when she does yoga.

LOSE: to become without
Use a bookmark so you don't lose your place in your book.

PASSED: the past tense of pass; a euphemism for someone dying
We passed by her house on Sunday.

PAST: that which has gone by or elapsed in time
In the past, Abby never used to study.
We drove past her house.

PRINCIPAL: the head of a school; main or important
The quarterback's injury is the principal reason the team lost.
The principal of the school meets with parents regularly.

PRINCIPLE: a fundamental law or truth
The laws of motion are among the most important principles in physics.

STATIONARY: fixed, not moving
Thomas rode a stationary bicycle at the gym.

STATIONERY: paper used for letter writing
The principal's stationery has the school's logo on the top.

THEIR: possessive of "they"
Paul and Ben studied for their test together.

THERE: a place; in that matter or respect
There are several question types on the GRE.
Please hang up your jacket over there.

THEY'RE: contraction of "they are"
Be careful of the bushes, as they're filled with thorns.